Honoring America

For Americans, the flag has always had a special meaning. It is a symbol of our nation's freedom and democracy.

Flag Etiquette

Over the years, Americans have developed rules and customs concerning the use and display of the flag. One of the most important things every American should remember is to treat the flag with respect.

- The flag should be raised and lowered by hand and displayed only from sunrise to sunset. On special occasions, the flag may be displayed at night, but it should be illuminated.
- The flag may be displayed on all days, weather permitting, particularly on national and state holidays and on historic and special occasions.
- No flag may be flown above the American flag or to the right of it at the same height.
- The flag should never touch the ground or floor beneath it.
- The flag may be flown at half-staff by order of the president, usually to mourn the death of a public official.
- The flag may be flown upside down only to signal distress.
- The flag should never be carried flat or horizontally, but always carried aloft and free.
- When the flag becomes old and tattered, it should be destroyed by burning. According to an approved custom, the Union (stars on blue field) is first cut from the flag; then the two pieces, which no longer form a flag, are burned.

The American's Creed

I believe in the United States of America as a Government of the people, by the people, for the people, whose just powers are derived from the consent of the governed; a democracy in a republic; a sovereign Nation of many sovereign States; a perfect union, one and inseparable; established upon those principles of freedom, equality, justice, and humanity for which American patriots sacrificed their lives and fortunes.

I therefore believe it is my duty to my Country to love it; to support its Constitution; to obey its laws; to respect its flag, and to defend it against all enemies.

The Pledge of Allegiance

I pledge allegiance to the Flag of the United States of America and to the Republic for which it stands, one Nation under God, indivisible, with liberty and justice for all.

Honoring America

The Star-Spangled Banner

O! say, can you see, by the dawn's early light,
What so proudly we hail'd at the twilight's last gleaming?
Whose broad stripes and bright stars, thro' the perilous fight,
O'er the ramparts we watched were so gallantly streaming?
And the rockets' red glare, the bombs bursting in air,
Gave proof thro' the night, that our flag was still there.
O! say, does that Star-Spangled Banner yet wave
O'er the land of the free and the home of the brave?

On the shore, dimly seen thro' the mist of the deep,
Where the foe's haughty host in dread silence reposes,
What is that which the breeze, o'er the towering steep,
As it fitfully blows, half conceals, half discloses?
Now it catches the gleam of the morning's first beam,
In full glory reflected now shines on the stream.
'Tis the Star-Spangled Banner. O long may it wave
O'er the land of the free and the home of the brave.

And where is that band who so vauntingly swore,
That the havoc of war and the battle's confusion
A home and a country should leave us no more?
Their blood has wash'd out their foul footstep's pollution.
No refuge could save the hireling and slave
From the terror of flight or the gloom of the grave,
And the Star-Spangled Banner in triumph doth wave
O'er the land of the free and the home of the brave.

O thus be it e'er when free men shall stand
Between their lov'd home and war's desolation,
Blest with vict'ry and peace, may the Heav'n-rescued land
Praise the pow'r that hath made and preserv'd us a nation.
Then conquer we must, when our cause it is just,
And this be our motto, "In God is our Trust."
And the Star-Spangled Banner in triumph shall wave
O'er the land of the free and the home of the brave.

Teacher's Wraparound Edition

Sociology and You

Jon M. Shepard
Virginia Polytechnic Institute and State University

Robert W. Greene
*Greenfield High School
Greenfield, Wisconsin*

Glencoe McGraw-Hill

New York, New York   Columbus, Ohio   Chicago, Illinois   Peoria, Illinois   Woodland Hills, California

About the Authors

Jon M. Shepard

Jon M. Shepard earned a Ph.D. in sociology at Michigan State University before assuming a teaching position at the University of Kentucky. The eighth edition of his popular college sociology textbook has recently been published. He has also has written extensively for academic journals and professional sociology associations. Dr. Shepard has received teaching awards at both the University of Kentucky and Virginia Polytechnic Institute adn State University where he currently teaches. His love of sociology and extensive experience with introductory sociology students have motivated and guided him in the creation of this unique text for high school students.

Robert W. Greene

Robert W. Greene has taught high school sociology for fifteen years. In that time, he has served as Secretary of the Wisconsin Sociological Association and is currently its President-elect. He has also served on the American Sociological Association's "Teaching Sociology in K-12 Committee," and chaired that committee in 1998. Mr. Greene was just recently nominated to the American Sociological Association's Task Force for the creation of an Advanced Placement Sociology course and exam. Over the last four years, he has chaired the Sociology Special Interest Group of the National Council for the Social Studies. In addition to his high school teaching responsibilities, Mr. Greene teaches sociology part-time at Alverno College in Milwaukee and extension courses for Marian College of Wisconsin.

Glencoe/McGraw-Hill

*A Division of The **McGraw-Hill** Companies*

Send all inquiries to:
Glencoe/McGraw-Hill
8787 Orion Place
Columbus, OH 43240

ISBN 0-07-828576-3 (Student Edition) 0-07-828577-1 (Teacher's Wraparound Edition)
ISBN 0-07-828579-8 (Texas)
Printed in the United States of America.

8 7 6 5 4 3 2 1 0 QB 10 09 08 07 06 05 04 03

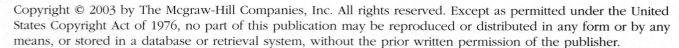

Reviewers/Contributors

Carolyn Andrews
Eisenhower High School
Houston, TX

Sandy Eichhorst
Centennial High School
Champaign, IL

Sally Raskoff
University of Southern California
Los Angeles, CA

Nancy Browning
Land O'Lakes High School
Land O'Lakes, FL

Dianne Brunt
Canyon Springs High School
Moreno Valley, CA

John D. Bush
Bedford No. Law High School
Bedford, IN

Candee Collins
Pine Tree High School
Longview, TX

Barb Damon
Merrimack High School
Merrimack, NH

Patricia Darnell
Killeen High School
Killeen, TX

Diane G. Dowler
Buena High School
Ventura, CA

Tom Dubay
Trinity High School
Louisville, KY

Frances D. Duncan
Hudson's Bay High School
Vancouver, WA

Richard B. DuRall
Evergreen High School
Seattle, WA

Beth Duron
Santa Clarita Christian School
Canyon Country, CA

Debbie Stuart Everett
Park Tudor High School
Indianapolis, IN

Matthew Ferren
Seminole High School
Sanford, FL

James E. Flora
New Holstein High School
New Holstein, WI

Glenn Gritzon
Preble High School
Green Bay, WI

Robin Heisig
South Grand Prairie High School
Grand Prairie, TX

Mark R. Henthorn
Shadyside High School
Shadyside, OH

Kim Ibach
Kelly Walsh High School
Casper, WY

Debra Ann Jones
Bloomington High School North
Bloomington, IN

Donna Juren
Denton High School
Denton, TX

B. Dale Kinney
Ralston High School
Omaha, NE

Kathleen M. Knoll
South Milwaukee High School
Milwaukee, WI

Jim Kraft
Wausau West High School
Wausau, WI

Kimberly Landers-George
McNeil High School
Austin, TX

Kathrine Leonard
Southern High School
Louisville, KY

Linda McDanal
Machebeaf High School
Denver, CO

Susan Mirra
West Genesee High School
Camillus, NY

Jeff Morgenstein
Land O'Lakes High School
Land O'Lakes, FL

Catherine Morris
Grapevine High School
Grapevine, TX

Ed Pottenger
Lakota West High School
West Chester, OH

Tom Ramos
Bay High School
Panama City, FL

Alison Record
A&M Consolidated High School
College Station, TX

Rebecca Reeves
Cullman High School
Cullman, AL

Tom Robertson
Carlsbad High School
Carlsbad, CA

Lianne K. Schneider
Msgr. Kelly Catholic High School
Beaumont, TX

Sandra Setter
Eagan High School
Eagan, MN

Dan Sheesley
North Platte High School
North Platte, NE

Toni C. Tropiak
Parkland High School
El Paso, TX

Bob Walls
Lakeview High School
Cortland, OH

Mary Beth Wilson
Gallatin County High School
Warsaw, KY

Table of Contents

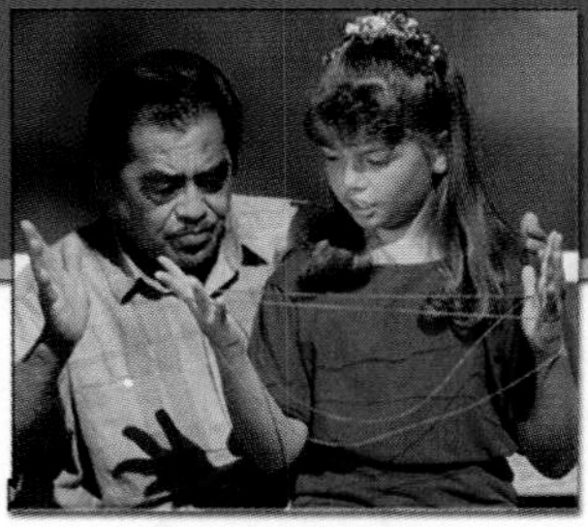

Unit 4
Social Institutions 344

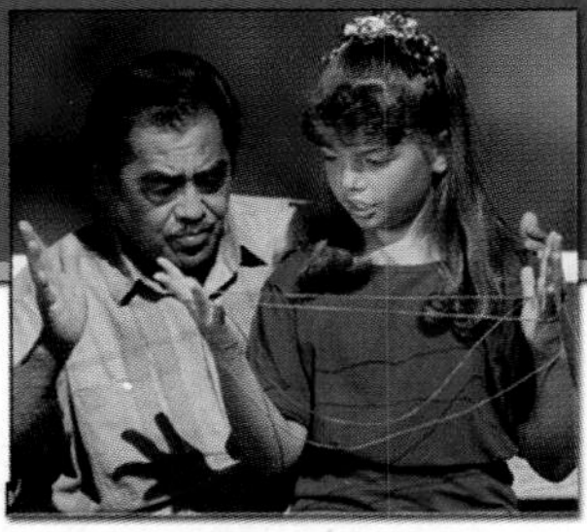

Unit 5
Social Change

Features

Another Place Another Time

Focus on Research

Sociology Today

Tech Trends

Enrichment Reading

World View

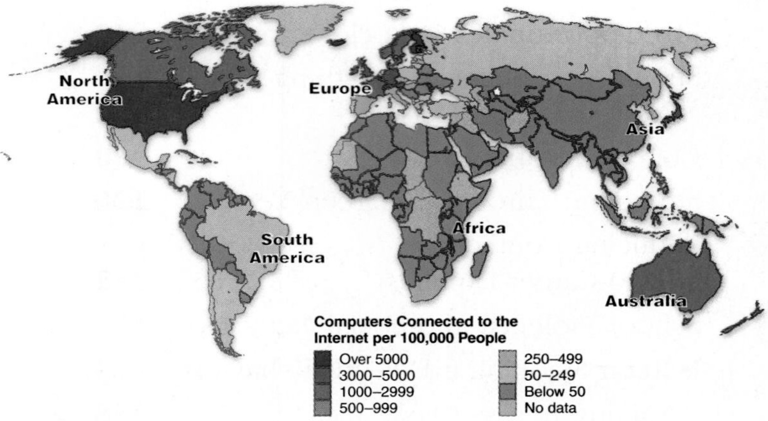

Snapshot of America

Focus on Theoretical Perspectives

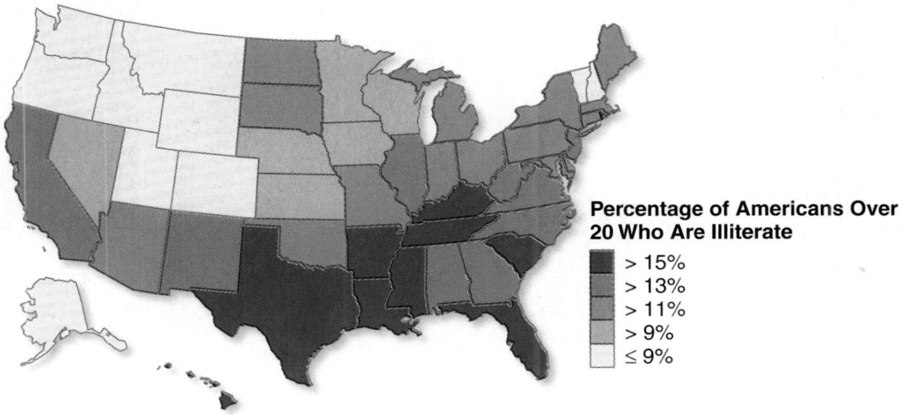

Charts & Graphs

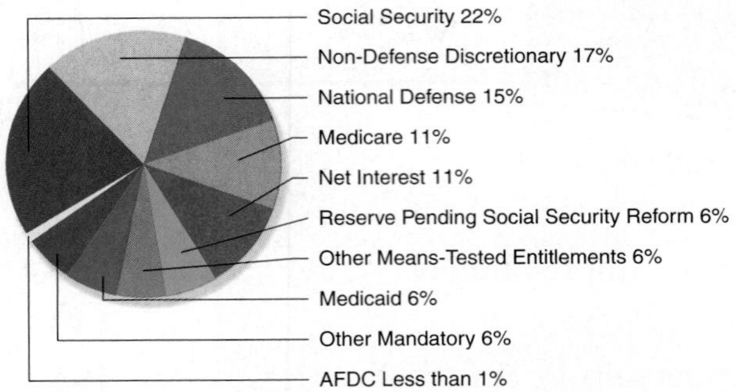

Social Security 22%
Non-Defense Discretionary 17%
National Defense 15%
Medicare 11%
Net Interest 11%
Reserve Pending Social Security Reform 6%
Other Means-Tested Entitlements 6%
Medicaid 6%
Other Mandatory 6%
AFDC Less than 1%

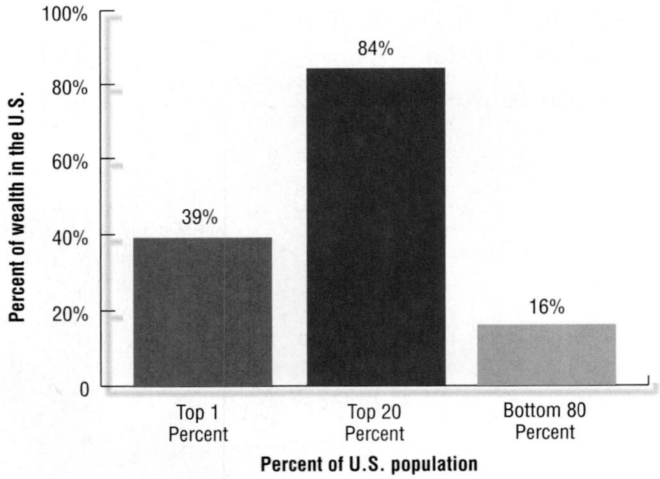

100%
80%
60%
40%
20%
0
Percent of wealth in the U.S.
39%
84%
16%
Top 1 Percent
Top 20 Percent
Bottom 80 Percent
Percent of U.S. population

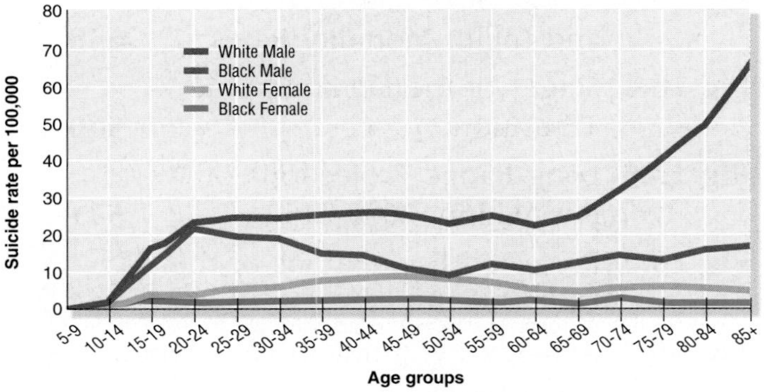

80
70
60
50
40
30
20
10
0
Suicide rate per 100,000
White Male
Black Male
White Female
Black Female
5-9
10-14
15-19
20-24
25-29
30-34
35-39
40-44
45-49
50-54
55-59
60-64
65-69
70-74
75-79
80-84
85+
Age groups

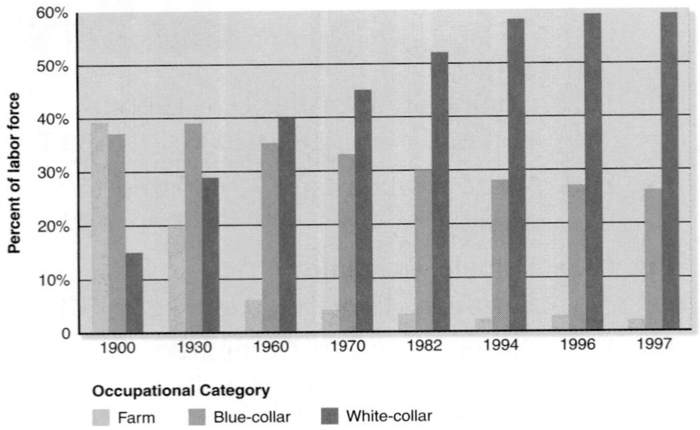
60%
50%
40%
30%
20%
10%
0
Percent of labor force
1900
1930
1960
1970
1982
1994
1996
1997
Occupational Category
Farm
Blue-collar
White-collar

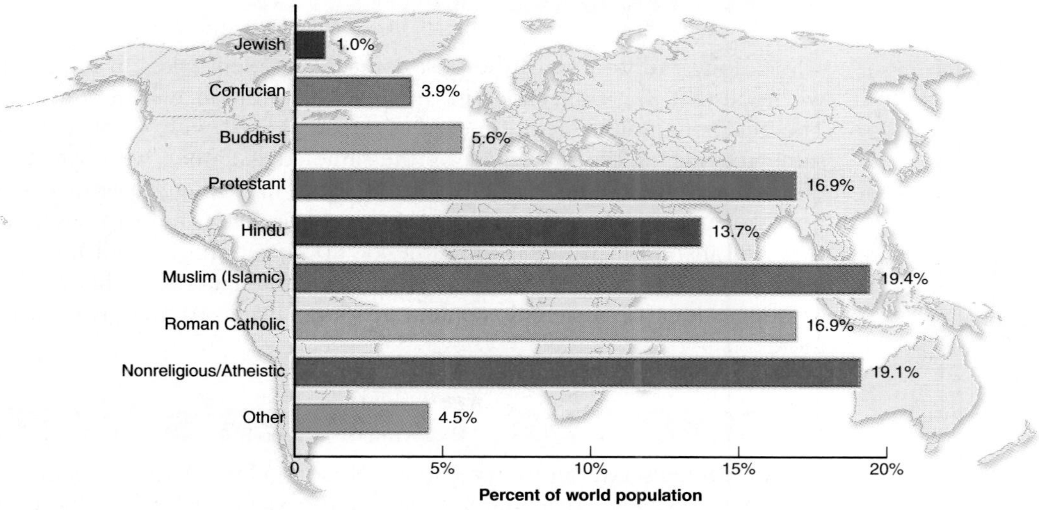

Jewish 1.0%
Confucian 3.9%
Buddhist 5.6%
Protestant 16.9%
Hindu 13.7%
Muslim (Islamic) 19.4%
Roman Catholic 16.9%
Nonreligious/Atheistic 19.1%
Other 4.5%
0
5%
10%
15%
20%
Percent of world population

Trade
Tools
Technology
Goods
Services
Jobs
Business
Transportation
Communications
Food, Shelter,
Clothing
Family
Government
Education
Religion
Economy
Art
Literature
Dance
Theater
Music
Crafts
Folk tales
Words
Expressions
Pronunciations
Alphabet
Symbols
Communities
Geography
Geology
Habitat
Wildlife
Climates
Resources
Games
Toys
Arts
Media
Holidays
Festivals
Values
Traditions
Ethnicity
Customs
Religions
Morals
ECONOMY
INSTITUTIONS
ARTS
LANGUAGE
ENVIRONMENT
RECREATION
BELIEFS
CULTURAL UNIVERSALS

TEACHING AN INTRODUCTORY SOCIOLOGY COURSE

Sociology can be one of the best courses a student takes in high school, and we hope that the suggestions in the Teacher's Edition will help to ensure this. The Teacher's Edition is not meant to create clones, with all of us teaching the same activities in the same way on the same day. Rather, we invite you to veer off, add, delete and, most of all, have fun with these suggestions. Regardless of how you use the ideas, we trust that you will find that they are original and that they will inspire in students an authentic appreciation of sociology.

What follows are some ideas on how to use the material in this edition as well as suggestions on teaching content reading, using cooperative learning, and more.

USING THE TEACHER'S EDITION

The Teacher's Edition to accompany Sociology and You is organized by side and bottom panels. Teaching stratagies and pedagogical information needed by the teacher to carry out daily lesson plans is located along the side of the reduced student pages. Special activity boxes have been placed below the student pages for quick and easy reference. A description of the kind of information in each area follows.

Teaching Strategies

Using Your Sociological Imagination Find suggestions here for demonstrating for students a basic premise of sociology–the ongoing need to examine and question assumptions.

Using the Section Preview Start students thinking about the section content with these anticipatory questions or mini-activities.

Points to Stress, Teaching Strategies, Open-Response Questions, Reinforcing Vocabulary, Reteaching Quick question prompts, suggestions for reteaching, and key points have been gathered under these headings to help you move students through the chapter.

Controversy and Debate Students love controversy and these items will provide you with some background information to help students debate from a point of knowledge.

Making Connections to Other Cultures These suggestions will help the students make comparisons and connections with other countries and cultures.

Net Worthy This feature highlights some of the best web sites for students of sociology–and for you. These web sites have been previewed, but as always, we recommend you review these sites for yourself since content is continually added or deleted. While we have tried to include only those sites that are reliable and affliliated with well respected organizations, we cannot guarantee that these sites will always remain accessible. As anyone familiar with the Internet knows, URLs can and do change.

Addressing Current Social Issues Additional information about topical areas of interest, such as cloning, overpopulation, pollution, and so forth are addressed here.

Working with the Quote Question prompts and background information will help students get the most from the famous (and not so famous) quotations sprinkled throughout the student text.

More About . . . These items provide additional information about topics the students (and teachers) may want to know "more about" than is found in the student text.

Feature Support The Another Time, Another Place, Tech Trends, Sociology Today, and Focus on Research features that appear in every chapter are supported with a teaching strategy and answers to the thinking questions that appear at the end of these features.

Working with the Data, Using the Illustration, and Answers to the Section Assessments Answers to questions in the student text about the graphs and photographs, as well as complete answers to all Section Assessments and Chapter Assessments, are provided under these headings.

Activity Boxes

Lead-Off Activity Grab students attention with these minimum preparation, kick-start activities that help students anticipate main chapter themes.

Demonstration These high-impact teacher-directed strategies illustrate basic concepts in a visual and memorable manner.

Observation and Survey In keeping with importance in sociology for conducting research, teachers are provided with ideas for observations or simple surveys that students can conduct, both individually and in groups, to practice application of critical thinking skills.

Careers in Sociology Every chapter has two or three information or activity boxes that provide teachers with background on sociology-related careers. Internet sites are provided as sources for additional information.

Cooperative Learning Activity Every chapter contains multiple suggestions for projects and activities that will have students developing group skills and taking responsibility for planning and supervising their own work.

Paired Learning Activity Designed to let students teach students, these activities allow you to pair students who have dissimilar strengths and skills so that each one can help another.

Role Play Take advantage of students' natural love of acting to reinforce concepts and themes using these suggestions for skits and role playing.

On-Demand Writing Help students develop their writing skills with these high interest prompts, and provide them with practice in organizing and expressing their thoughts while you assess their understanding of basic concepts.

Using Problem Solving Skills, Using Decision Making Skills, and Using Conflict Resolution Skills These activities require students to use various types of interpersonal skills. Typically, a scenario is established and students work in groups to solve or recommend a course of action, keeping in mind sociological concepts to guide their thinking processes.

Learning Styles Activities under this heading are designed to appeal to or strengthen various multiple intelligences as described by Howard Gardner. The activities use film, music, art, or bodily movements to reinforce or teach basic concepts.

Encouraging Citizenship Activity Many high schools require students to perform some hours of community service as a requirement for graduation. The study of sociology in high school is an ideal venue to generate service projects. Suggestions for these projects, most of which have been successfully completed by their students, have been provided by teachers around the country. Even if not required by the school, these projects are excellent learning tools that provide students with opportunities to apply sociological concepts to the real world.

Interdisciplinary Activity Connect student learning to other disciplines, including history, biology, music, and art.

Note: In Sociology and You, focus questions in the student text help the students look for key points as they read. Examples include:

- How does your looking glass process work?
- Can your looking glass be distorted?
- Do we use some people more than others as mirrors?

TEACHING CONTENT READING

DON'T ASSUME THAT YOUR STUDENTS KNOW HOW TO READ THEIR TEXTS!

The following material has been developed by Gloria Moeller of El Cajon, California; Martha Berner of San Diego, California; and Pete Pitard, Director of Colonial Williamsburg's Department of School and Group Services. It contains strategies for teachers to use to help their students become independent readers of nonfiction content materials.

IT IS UNFORTUNATE BUT TRUE, that too often students do not know that there are different techniques used when reading "for content" and reading "for pleasure"—not that content reading can't be pleasurable! Two common misconceptions held by secondary school teachers are that (1) reading is a skill mastered in the early grades and (2) that it is best taught as a separate subject. We have come to believe that once "learning to read" is mastered, it is automatically replaced by "reading to learn."

There are many reasons why students can't or don't read their texts:

- Students don't read their texts because they don't need to read them.
- Students have not had experiences with successfully reading content texts and don't know how to read them.
- Reading strategies students have developed and used to comprehend fiction do not necessarily help them understand texts.
- Proficient readers of fiction assume they can read anything. Then, when they encounter difficulties with their texts, they question their ability and give up trying to read it.

RESEARCH TELLS US however that instruction in how to read for content need not take time away from the actual learning of content. Each new text demands some new learning about reading to be fully utilized. You may ask why you should take the time to teach reading "in the content classes". (You probably already have more content than you can cover!) There are at least three good reasons:

1. The best way to learn to read a textbook is to do so with the support from someone experienced in reading this type of material—in other words, a content-area teacher like yourself.
2. Techniques used to improve reading proficiency also help students' understanding and comprehension of the material.
3. Students become independent learners—the ultimate goal of any teacher!

Let's look now at some basic strategies for teaching content reading.

BEFORE THE READING

1. HELP STUDENTS FIND A FOCUS. Before making a reading assignment, develop a purpose for their reading. This will help students focus on what you want them to learn from the text. Students need to know you do not intend that they memorize every single idea in the text. This will help reduce their anxiety level. Let them know you expect them to read all the material, but you will always let them know what they should focus on in each lesson. This means you, as the teacher, must be familiar with the assignment and have already decided where you want your students to go.

Students may need assistance in deciding what is important and what is not important in a reading selection. Establishing a focus will give them practice in determining what the author of the piece regards as the most important information, so they can become independent readers.

2. ACCESS PRIOR KNOWLEDGE. Current brain and learning research shows that people more readily store information in long-term memory when they can attach new concepts to information they have already stored in their brains. The following suggestions provide opportunities for you to support your students in accessing or initiating prior knowledge before they begin to read. Pick and choose from the following activities to use with each unit of instruction:

- Brainstorming is a method to find out what your students already know about a topic. Have small groups discuss what they already know. Record all ideas on a chart. Use this chart later during reading to correct any misconceptions.
- Rather than saving your films, videos, storytelling, CD-ROMs, etc. for the end of the unit, use them before reading. This strategy activates prior knowledge in some students and provides a basis of knowledge for the students who have no prior knowledge of the topic. This gives a framework on which students can "hang" the new knowledge they encounter in the chapter.
- When possible, relate the content to events in the students' lives or in the news. For example, before assigning the chapter on groups and organizations, you might ask students about their own experiences with bureaucracies such as school or work. Or, you may want to discuss any upcoming

Students can use the Learning Goals worksheets in the Mastering Basic Concept booklets to focus their reading. In addition, unit booklets contain graphic organizers for students to that help identify main concepts.

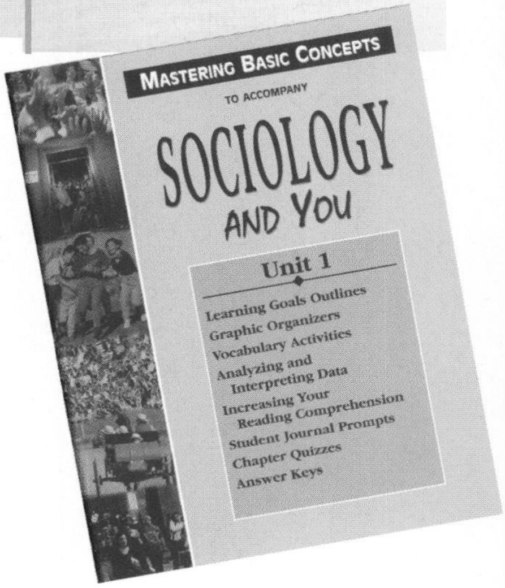

elections prior to beginning the chapter on the political institution.

3. DO A WALK THROUGH OF THE READING ASSIGNMENT. The three main components of the reading cycle are predicting, gathering data, and confirming or disconfirming what you predicted. Previewing and predicting help students establish their own purpose for reading. Students will need to be directed to take notice of the Focus Questions, bolded section headings, captions under the photos, artwork, graphics, charts, timelines, maps, etc. Point out that the authors use these elements to make the material more understandable. The benefits of pointing these things out include:

- Students are more aware of the organization of the text content
- It provides teachers with information to guide instruction, including areas of misconceptions.

4. A TREASURE HUNT. An alternative to the walk through is the "treasure hunt." This is an introductory activity for facilitating reading and enhancing understanding of content area text. This form of previewing and predicting will set the stage for the actual reading and will help the students connect prior knowledge and process the new information they will encounter.

- Organization: students can be working alone, in pairs, in groups, or any variation thereof.
- Procedure: Ask the class to go on a treasure hunt in search of any vocabulary term, artwork, photo, caption, graphic, that is included in the text. You will already have identified these items. The students will note the pages on which the items were found, working within a time limit. In pairs or small groups, students can discuss their predictions on how each item will relate to the topic of the text. You may wish to record some of the students' predictions, adding questions the students may have. For closure at the end of the unit, revisit this log, checking predictions and clarifying any misconceptions.

Possible starters for experience based questions include

- How would you . . . ?
- What would you . . . ?
- If you . . . ?
- Do you think . . . ? Explain why.
- Why do you think . . . ?
- Could you . . . ? Explain why.
- Where would you . . . ?
- What would it be like . . . ?
- If someone . . . ?

DURING THE READING

In order to become thoughtful, reflective readers, students need to know how to organize information into meaningful segments.

1. HOW TO DETERMINE THE MAIN IDEAS. Main ideas are ideas that are relevant to your learning objectives for the students. If you provide the students with notetaking skills, study guides, graphic organizers, and/or purpose for reading, they will have some support in narrowing the focus for their reading.

- Use overheads of the reading asignment when you first teach this concept to let students see how you and others determine the main ideas. Model

Cornell Notetaking Method

Main Ideas Concept	Details	Discussion Questions
• Sapir-Whorf hypothesis	• Cultural perspectives depend on language • Language influences the development of norms • Exposure to other languages can extend our world view	• Can you imagine an idea or thing if you don't have a word for it?

your thinking aloud as you decide what you believe to be the main idea and why. Express confusion when something you read is unclear to you. This modeling of metacognitive skills promotes better learning for the student.

- Ask your more proficient readers to verbalize how they decide what the main ideas are. It may seem painfully slow at first, but taking the time now helps your students develop the skills that will allow them to work more independently later. Using this modeling format helps your less proficient readers become aware of the way proficient readers find meaning in a difficult text.

2. USE THE ADAPTED CORNELL NOTETAKING METHOD. Have students divide their paper into three columns.

Main Idea Concept Column

- Select a section of material you want students to read. They decide what they think the main idea(s) is and why.
- Call on individual students, asking them for their opinion of what the main idea is and why. Do not validate at this point, just keep asking students until you hear a consensus forming.
- Write the main idea in the first column on your overhead and have students copy it on their papers.

Details Column

- Establish with your students that the criteria for including information in this column is (1) ideas connected to the main idea concept in the left column, (2) ideas related to the previously stated purpose for reading, (3) ideas important enough to be on the test, and (4) ideas the students find especially interesting.
- Call on individual students, asking them their opinion of what details should be included and why.
- When consensus is reached, list the details on the overhead and have students copy them on their paper.

Discussion Questions Column

- Teach your students effective questioning techniques. Research shows that when students write their own questions for discussion, they engage in the text more completely and become more involved during small group discussion time (Simpson, 1996).
- Teach students to recognize and use explicit, implicit, and experience-based questions.

  Text explicit questions are "right there." Readers can point to the answer in the text.

  Text implicit questions are "think and search." Readers must take the information from several places in the text and infer from what the text implicit states. Experience-based questions will be the most helpful for initiating discussions in small groups.

  Experience-based questions are "on my own." The answers will be based on the reader's prior experience and will vary. For example, students might be asked "Do you think men and women will always have different styles of communication?"

Teachers using Sociology and You will find the Doing Sociology: Focus on Research booklet and the Ethics, Values, and Technology booklet helpful for developing cooperative group projects.

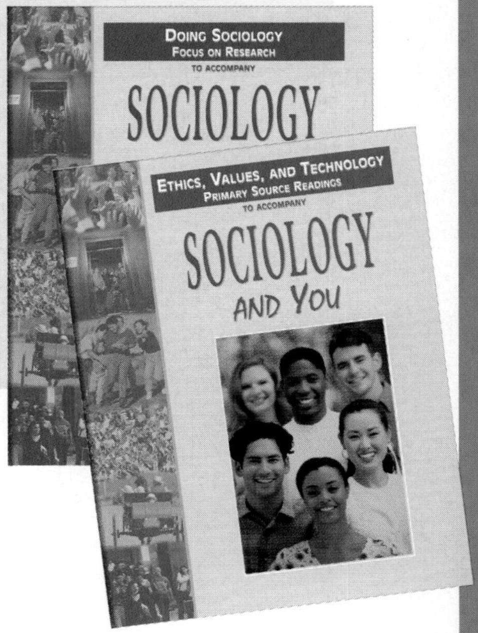

3. PROVIDE CLASS TIME FOR STUDENTS TO SILENTLY READ their text assignment. Research has shown (Armbruster, 1991) that most students will learn and retain the material more effectively if they read it silently. While your capable readers are silently reading, use partner reading or work with small groups of English learners or limited English proficient readers. Additional strategies for students who have difficulty reading include:

- Have a proficient student (or tutor) read the entire lesson selection to the student who has difficulty prior to lesson time.
- Pair a proficient reader with a less able reader for partner reading. Both will read aloud, although the proficient reader will read most of the selection.
- Arrange (for extra credit) for a good reader to record text selections on tape and have the student listen to taped lessons ahead of time and after the lesson time.
- Supplement the text with easier to read books on related subjects.
- Monitor and reduce the amount of required reading in the text.

AFTER THE READING

After a reading assignment there are several strategies that can be followed to reinforce comprehension.

1. HAVE SMALL GROUPS DISCUSS THEIR NOTES, answering each others' questions and/or sharing interesting quotes from the text. This part is critical because it provides the students the opportunity to revisit the text to "prove" their answers. Verbalizing will also help them gain more meaning from the text. Allow students to add more ideas to their notes (using a different color pen or pencil). This also provides another purpose for taking the notes in the first place! Be an observer, not a participant during this time. Take note of misconceptions you want to clarify and concepts you feel the students missed in their reading to bring back up during whole class discussions.

2. CONDUCT A WHOLE-GROUP DISCUSSION to answer outstanding questions or clear up misconceptions you heard. Allow students to be in charge. They ask the questions and call on other students to answer. Try to maintain a facilitator role and only interject when students are "off base" and other students don't dispute the misconception. At the end, bring up any important points you feel the students have not discussed. This is your time to use a lecture format to cover any important points you feel the students missed while reading. Students modify and add to their notes at this time. Have students make all additional notes with a different color.

3. COOPERATIVE GROUPS provide students with the opportunity to further their learning, debate opposing viewpoints, learn to reach consensus, be in charge of their own learning, practice cooperation skills, acquire respect for each other's differences. Each group becomes an expert on one section of the text and presents their knowledge in some graphic format for the class.

4. EXAMINE THE SUPPLEMENTAL MATERIALS provided in the Teacher's Resource Box for additional activities and worksheets that strengthen basic reading skills.

COOPERATIVE LEARNING

If you are interested in cooperative learning, taking a class on the topic is an excellent way to experience the benefits of working together. Being a student in a cooperative-learning class also gives you valuable insight into your own students' reactions to this format of learning. The cooperative-learning ideas in the Teacher's Edition, however, are designed to work effectively even if you don't have this kind of training.

Here are some of the main principles and techniques of cooperative learning:

1. Small groups sit in a circle with desks touching. This helps the group members focus on each other and the task at hand. It also means that they don't have to shout to be heard by other group members, and consequently other groups will not be disturbed by loud voices.

2. Each group is given a specific task on which to work. The goals of the task are well defined. For students with practice in working independently, tasks and goals can be estabished by the group members themselves.

3. Each member of the group is assigned or elects to perform a specific task, such as recorder, facilitator, artist, or timer.

4. If one member does not complete his or her task, it becomes difficult or impossible for the group to complete the group task. Knowing this creates a feeling of interdependency in the group.

If cooperative learning is new to you, you will probably want to gradually incorporate it into your lesson plans until you feel comfortable with it. Also, be prepared for a few objections from your students. Your better students may complain that group grades are unfair or that other students do not contribute their share. You can avoid this problem by making each student individually accountable in some way. If your "A" students are not satisfied with this, give them a chance to hand in extra credit. Also, you might stress that sometimes the process of reaching consensus is as important as the actual conclusion.

Once you become comfortable using cooperative learning and learn a few general strategies, you can apply these strategies in a variety of situations, regardless of content. For instance, Spencer Kagan recommends a method he calls "numbered heads together." A useful reteaching strategy, the method works particularly well for review or as a comprehension check. Divide the class into groups of four, for example. Each group member picks a number from one to four. If one group has fewer members than everyone else, one member picks two numbers. The teacher asks a question and allows about 30 seconds for each student to write down an answer. Group members then put their heads together to formulate a single answer. At this point the teacher may want to rephrase the question. Rather than asking, "What is the definition of psychology?" the teacher says, "Make sure everyone in your group knows the definition of psychology." The teacher then calls on a number to answer the question. If the teacher calls "3," only 3s can answer. If only a few 3s raise their hands, the teacher might allow more time. This is an excellent strategy for keeping everyone involved in what could otherwise be a boring review.

You can create some friendly competition by using what Kagan calls "simultaneous numbered heads together." In this case, all number 3s write down their answers on a group answer sheet. They then pass the answer sheet to the person whose number is called for the next question. You can use a spinner to make the number-calling seem more game-like. To motivate students, you might offer extra credit to the group with the most correct answers.

ON-DEMAND/JOURNAL WRITING

The Teacher's Edition contains several ideas for on-demand writing, and the Unit booklets suggest prompts for journal writing. Don't be afraid to make students write. They may complain from time to time, but they're just trying to condition you; condition them instead! The papers don't have to be lengthy, you don't need to take out your red pen, and you need not grade every page. In fact, much of the writing can be done in class, five or ten minutes here and there to allow students to process an activity or discussion (on-demand writing). The very act of writing often helps us discover how we feel about a particular issue. Many of the journal entries suggested in the Unit Booklets are designed just for this processing purpose.

If you decide that you want students to keep journals in class, here are some general tips:

1. Limit journal-writing to about five to ten minutes.
2. Ask students to bring in a notebook that is exclusively for journal entries.
3. Encourage students to free-write—that is, they need not worry about-spelling, grammar, or punctuation.
4. Use journals often. Once students realize that journals are part of the routine, they'll soon comply. After a few weeks, many will realize the power of putting thoughts on paper.
5. Don't collect the journals until the end of the term. If students feel that you are checking up on them every week, they may not feel that they own their journals. You may, however, want to look around while students write to make sure that everyone is participating.

At the end of each term, students can process the journal as a whole. You may want students to dupilcate one of the options below to help them evaluate their work.

Option A

Pretend that you have lost your journal. Someone finds it and decides to write an introduction to the journal, summarizing what he or she thinks about the author of the journal. Write that introduction! Remember, you're writing from the point of view of the person who finds it.

Option B

Again, assume that you have lost your journal. An editor finds it and decides to publish it. Pretend you are that editor and think of a title for the book. Then write an essay that will appear on the inside jacket of the book.

Option C

No gimmicks this time. Simply review your journal and analyze the content. What surprised you? What discoveries did you make in the process of writing the entries? Which topics were difficult to write about? Which were easy? Why?

Option D

Pick any one entry that you especially like for revision and development reason. Briefly explain why you selected this entry and not others. The final product should be clear, organized, and considerably more extensive than the original entry. Even though this essay will be more polished than the original entry, allow your voice to come through—be yourself.

CONTENT STANDARDS FOR THE HIGH SCHOOL COURSE IN SOCIOLOGY

One of the purposes of drafting high school content standards is to help secondary school social studies department heads who wish to adopt national, standardized curriculum guidelines for their existing sociology courses. Another goal is to provide content guidelines for teachers who are interested in establishing new sociology courses in their schools. The standards specify areas of content investigation and mastery. (A task force of the ASA developed these draft standards. Please contact Carla Howery at that organization for more information. As of September 2000, these standards had not yet been officially submitted to the ASA for formal approval or adoption.)

1 SOCIOLOGICAL PERSPECTIVES. The learner will be able to	**PAGE NUMBERS**
A. define sociology.	**6**
B. explain why sociology is a social science.	**7**
C. explain and illustrate the "sociological imagination" as introduced by C. Wright Mills.	**11**
D. recognize how sociology's focus differs from and is similar to the focus of each of the other social sciences.	**6-8**
E. differentiate micro and macro approaches to the study of society.	**23TE**
F. define "theory" and explain its role in science.	**58-59**
G. explain the basic principles of the functional perspective (i.e. ideas and perspectives of Auguste Comte and Emile Durkheim).	**14-15, 16-17, 23-27**
H. explain the basic principles of the conflict perspective (i.e. ideas and perspectives of Karl Marx, Max Weber, and W.E.B. DuBois.	**16-17, 22, 27-29,**
I. explain the basic principles of the symbolic interaction perspective (i.e. perspectives of Charles Cooley and George Herbert Mead).	**29-31**

2 SOCIOLOGICAL METHODS OF INQUIRY The learner will be able to	**PAGE NUMBERS**
A. explain the concept of empirical research.	**38**
B. explain why a particular way of knowing (empiricism) is the defining characteristic of any science.	**58-59**
C. list the seven steps of the scientific method of investigation.	**58-59**
D. differentiate between qualitative and quantitative methods of research.	**38-40, 45**
E. define hypothesis, independent variable, dependent variable and intervening variable.	**51-52**
F. evaluate scientific evidence and describe its applications and limitations.	**38-50***
G. calculate the measures of central tendency: the mean, median and mode.	**46-47**
H. explain the relationship between two variables (such as positive and negative correlations) and distinguish causal relationships from correlations.	**51-55**
I. distinguish between an experiment, participant observation, survey and a field study.	**38-45**
J. identify the ethical dilemmas of conducting research to human beings.	**59-61**

**** See the Focus on Research features thoughout the text.***

3 CULTURE The learner will be able to		PAGE NUMBERS
A.	define culture and explain some of the universal functions of culture.	**72-73, 100-102**
B.	differentiate between material and non-material culture.	**92-93**
C.	recognize how sociologists distinguish between the terms "culture" and "society."	**72-73**
D.	give examples of ideal culture and real culture.	**94**
E.	explain and illustrate the role language plays in creating and perpetuating culture (Sapir-Whorf hypothesis).	**77-79**
F.	identify the characteristics and functions of symbols in society.	**77**
G.	explain ways in which cultures are unified.	**98-102**
H.	explain the factors which lead to increased cultural diversity or multiculturalism in American society and describe costs and benefits of this diversity.	**98**
I.	define and illustrate ethnocentrism.	**98-99**
J.	differentiate and recognize examples of "subculture," "microculture," and "counterculture."	**98-99**
K.	define values and norms and explain the relationships between them.	**81-87, 90-91**
L.	contrast and illustrate the concepts of folkway, more and law.	
M.	recognize the difference between conflict, functional, and symbolic interaction approaches to the study of culture.	**83-87** **96-97**
N.	identify three effects of globalization on national or local cultures.	**95**

4 SOCIAL STRUCTURE The learner will be able to		PAGE NUMBERS
A.	define and provide examples of the major components of social: status, role, social institution, and group.	**140-147, 172-175, 347**
B.	explain and illustrate role strain and role conflict.	**149-151**
C.	define social networks.	**178-179**
D.	explain the functions of each of the primary institutions in the American society.	**Ch. 11-15**
E.	illustrate how social institutions are linked and interdependent within a social system.	**Ch. 11-15**
F.	identify changes occurring in American social institutions.	**Ch. 11-15**
G.	define and give examples of the major types of social groups: primary, secondary, in-group, out-group, peer group, and reference group.	**173-178**
H.	discuss how these groups shape the learner's life and how individuals influence the groups.	**173-178**
I.	recognize the difference between conflict, functional, and symbolic interaction approaches to the study of social structure.	**181-186**

5 SOCIALIZATION. The learner will be able to		PAGE NUMBERS
A.	evaluate the influences of heredity and environment on the development of personality.	73-75, 110-114
B.	define and illustrate socialization, resocialization, and anticipatory socialization.	128-132
C.	define and provide an example of a total institution.	128
D.	describe how our sense of self emerges.	116-119
E.	describe the importance and function of role-taking in the development of "self."	118
F.	describe the various stages of cognitive and moral development.	116-119
G.	identify the most important agents of socialization in the United States.	121-127
H.	explain the difference between conflict, functional, and symbolic interaction approaches to socialization.	117
I.	explain how the socialization process changes throughout the life course	129-131

6 SELF AND SOCIAL INTERACTION The learner will be able to		PAGE NUMBERS
A.	identify in writing the lessons from isolation studies for development of the self.	109, 113-114
B.	explain the key points of the nature-nurture debate.	73-75
C.	describe Charles Cooley's "looking glass self" process.	116-117
D.	discuss George H. Mead's development of the self, including the "I", "me", and "taking the role of the other."	117-119
E.	compare the importance of the significant other and the generalized other.	119
F.	list the developmental stages of the self as laid out by George Herbert Mead.	117-118
G.	illustrate the meaning of status and role, and show how they are related.	140-148
H.	describe the importance of verbal and non-verbal language in social interaction.	78-79, 79TE
I.	explain Erving Goffman's ideas of "presentation self."	31
J.	analyze the importance of the symbolic interaction theory in understanding the development of self.	116-119
K.	describe how emotions are socially constructed—shaped by social norms and interactions.	121

7 DEVIANCE, CRIME, AND SOCIAL CONTROL The learner will be able to		PAGE NUMBERS
A.	define social control and distinguish between formal and informal methods of social control.	**206-207**
B.	differentiate between deviance and crime.	**204-205**
C.	give examples that demonstrate that deviance is universal to all groups and individuals.	**204-205, 208**
D.	give examples that demonstrate how the definition of deviance is relative to time, place, situation and social status, that is, how social deviance is socially constructed.	**214-217, 222-223**
E.	give examples that demonstrate how deviance can be both functional and dysfunctional.	**209-210**
F.	differentiate between individual (biological, psychological) explanations of deviance and structural, sociological theories of deviance and crime.	**210-212**
G.	summarize the sociological theories of crime and deviance.	**210-217**
H.	state the various type of crime and assess their effects on society.	**220-221, 224-227**
I.	interpret differences in crime and arrest rates by social categories of people (ethnicity, gender, socioeconomic status, age, etc.).	**218-220**
J.	compare crime rates in terms of race, class and gender differences.	**224-227**
K.	explain the effects of the value conflict that exists between the individual desire for freedom and the group need for social order and social control.	**211, 213, 218**
L.	assess the effects of various policies and laws relating to social control, such as the question of the deterrent effect of capital punishment	**227-232**

8 GROUPS AND ORGANIZATIONS The learner will be able to		PAGE NUMBERS
A.	define and illustrate "primary group" and "secondary group."	**173-175**
B.	distinguish a peer group from a reference group.	**177-178**
C.	define and identify examples of task functions in a small group.	**173-174**
D.	define and identify examples of "expressive" or "maintenance" functions in a small group.	**173-174**
E.	define and illustrate a "complex organization."	**190**
F.	recognize the key characteristics of rationalization of society.	**191-194**
G.	explain why rationalization is a defining characteristic of the modern world.	**191-194, 200-202**
H.	evaluate the consequences of rationalization in the modern world.	**191-194, 200-202**
I.	distinguish between a formal and informal structure in an organization.	**190-195**
J.	distinguish between a conflict and a structural functional analysis of complex organizations.	**186TE**
K.	explain dysfunctions in complex organizations.	**17, 26, 194-5**
L.	explain the characteristics of bureaucracies identified by Max Weber.	**191-192**
M.	identify aspects of the learner's life that are influenced by bureaucracies.	**191-194, 200-204**
N.	discuss how the characteristics of bureaucracy influence the learner's relationships with others.	**194-195**
O.	illustrate rationalization of society in the learner's own everyday life.	**200-202, 388-399**

9 SOCIAL INSTITUTIONS The learner will be able to		PAGE NUMBERS
A.	define social institutions and identify the primary institutions in a society.	344-345TE, 347
B.	identify secondary institutions which are significant in the functioning of complex industrial and postindustrial societies (science, medicine, sport, etc.)	495
C.	identify which basic societal needs are satisfied by the family institution.	357-359
D.	analyze ways in which family life can be disrupted.	364-369
E.	identify the major changes that have taken place in the American family in this century.	371-380
F.	explain how preindustrial and industrial societies view the individual and groups.	153-162, 371
G.	analyze the functions of at least one major institution other than the family.	Chapters 12, 13, 14
H.	explain the relationship of institutions to stability, to explicate the change-resistant characteristic of institutions.	388-90, 425-29, 440-42
I.	delineate the relationship of at least one institution to reproduction of social inequality (racial, sexual, or socioeconomic).	284-301, 322-328, 433-439
J.	compare and contrast the functionalism perspective and conflict perspective on institutions.	363, 411, 437, 473

10 STRATIFICATION The learner will be able to		PAGE NUMBERS
A.	define social stratification and social inequality and explain why stratification is such a powerful variable in human experience.	242-247
B.	explain intersections of race, class, and gender in social systems of inequality.	254-257
C.	distinguish between systems of class stratification: slavery, castes and social classes.	254-257, 265-266
D.	explain the components of social class: wealth, power, prestige, occupation and status.	242-247
E.	identify the social classes of American society: capitalist, upper middle, lower middle, working, underclass.	254-257
F.	define socio-economic status (SES) and explain how ascribed status differs from achieved status.	140-143, 265-268
G.	define social mobility and differentiate between the types of social mobility: structural, horizontal, vertical and inter/intra-generational.	265-268
H.	evaluate the impact of social institutions on social mobility.	265-268
I.	distinguish between the functionalist, conflict and interactionist perspectives of stratification.	252
J.	examine class consciousness utilizing the three sociological perspectives.	254
K.	compare and contrast individual vs. structural perspectives on poverty, especially as they apply to the feminization of poverty.	260-261
L.	differentiate between relative and absolute poverty and explain how the poverty line is determined.	259
M.	discuss the controversies regarding culture of poverty theory.	259, 261TE
N.	compare and contrast modernization and world systems (dependency) theories of global inequality.	259, 447-49, 450-56

11 RACIAL AND ETHNIC RELATIONS The learner will be able to		PAGE NUMBERS
A.	define "race" and "ethnic group."	277-279
B.	explain the social construction of race, including global and historical variations in conceptualizations of the notion of "race."	74-75, 277, 281
C.	distinguish between prejudice and discrimination and provide an example of symbolic racism.	284-285
D.	distinguish between racism and ethnocentrism.	97-99, 277
E.	identify the defining characteristics of a minority group.	276-277
F.	explain the consequences of xenophobia and other forms of social distancing.	281-285, 289, 298-299
G.	explain the difference between assimilation and multiculturalism.	280-281
H.	explain the sources of prejudice and discrimination, and especially the resource-conflict theory.	280-283
I.	describe the five most common patterns of minority group treatment by majority groups (assimilation, pluralism, subjugation, population transfer, genocide).	280-283
J.	explain how institutional racism works in American society.	290-291
K.	explain the difference between conflict and functional approaches to racial and ethnic inequality.	286, 288
L.	compare and contrast the experiences of at least two ethnic groups in American society.	291-301
M.	evaluate the impact of various social policies designed to redress institutional discrimination.	262-263, 291-301

12 GENDER, AND AGE INEQUALITY The learner will be able to		PAGE NUMBERS
A.	differentiate between sex and gender as social constructs.	310-314
B.	compare and contrast gender identity and gender roles.	316-319
C.	define gender-role socialization and illustrate the ways in which family, media, and schools contribute to it.	310-319
D.	explain the relationships among the following concepts: pink-collar jobs, glass ceiling, and feminization of poverty.	321-324
E.	identify the major effects of traditional gender-role socialization on the health of men and women.	313TE
F.	evaluate gender inequality from the structural functional, conflict, and interactionist perspectives.	318-320
G.	explain and evaluate political programs that reduce gender inequality.	319, 323, 325-6, 495, 517-18
H.	list three major changes in the age distribution of the U.S. population during the twentieth century.	331, 336
I.	recognize the difference between biological and sociological approaches to the study of aging.	330-332
J.	define and illustrate the life course perspective.	113-114, 126-27, 336-338, 544TE, 564
K.	explain adolescence as a socially constructed stage in the life course within industrial and postindustrial societies.	126-7, 132
L.	explain what is meant by the expression "graying of America" and identify the major social changes caused by this trend.	337, 330-332, 535
M.	describe and evaluate disengagement theory and activity theory.	334TE
N.	compare and contrast the structural functional, conflict, and interactionist perspectives on aging.	330-332

13 DEMOGRAPHY & URBANIZATION The learner will be able to		PAGE NUMBERS
A.	describe the study of demography and define the basic demographic concepts of fertility, mortality, and migration and explain their effects on population change.	530-535
B.	differentiate between population growth and population density.	536
C.	explain the causes and consequences of population growth.	536-541
D.	analyze population composition using age-sex population pyramids.	545-546
E.	delineate the push-pull factors that affect immigration and emigration.	551-2, 534
F.	explain why people in poor nations have so many children and discuss the implications of rapid population growth.	531-532, 541
G.	explain and critique various theories of population growth.	539-541
H.	evaluate the merits of the Demographic Transition Theory and explain why this theory may not apply to population growth in all societies.	539-540
I.	explain the social forces in modern societies around the globe toward suburbanization and toward the creation of the metropolis and the megalopolis.	552-554
J.	explain issues of social cohesion and disorganization in an urban setting.	548-551
K.	trace the historical development of cities and identify the major characteristics of preindustrial, industrial, and postindustrial cities.	549-551
L.	discuss the major reasons for the decline of the city and the impact of this decline.	551-554
M.	compare and contrast pressures on urban, suburban, and rural residents in the modern world.	548-554

14 SOCIAL CHANGE The learner will be able to		PAGE NUMBERS
A.	discuss the theories that have been developed to explain collective behavior.	581, 587-589
B.	compare and contrast the various types of collective behavior.	582-587
C.	identify the preconditions that guide the outcome of collective behavior.	582-589
D.	discuss the theories that have been developed to explain social movements.	591-596
E.	compare and contrast the various types of social movements.	592-593
F.	apply one or more theories of social change to a social movement in the United States.	593-596
G.	explain how population shifts can cause social change.	572
H.	evaluate the positive and negative consequences of modernization on social life.	159-166, 569, 571
I.	list some key features of postindustrial society.	162-163
J.	identify the major population shifts that have taken place in the United States.	552-554
K.	explain how globalization influences change.	569-572
L.	compare how modernization theory and world systems theory differ in their analysis of globalization.	572TE
M.	explain the difference between conflict, functional, and symbolic interaction approaches to social change.	578-580
N.	compare and contrast cyclical and evolutionary theories of social change.	592-596

Teaching Strategy

Discuss with students that the perspectives used by sociologists differ from those used in other social sciences, and most likely, from the perspectives to which the students are accustomed. The material presented in this Handbook will help students understand the sociological perspective, and thus learn about sociology—a field that will likely be very new and different to most students.

Sociology Handbook

Contents

Thinking Like a Sociologist

Why Should You Study Sociology?

If someone in the United States is asked why he or she acted in a certain way, most of us would expect the person to provide an explanation that described the causes of the behavior in terms of his or her *individual* choices. Americans are generally taught to think that they totally determine their own thoughts, feelings, and actions. However, sociologists recognize that the groups, or social structures, that one belongs to have a profound influence over the way individuals think, feel, and act. Sociology provides tools to understand what these social structures are, how they affect our beliefs and behaviors, and how individuals relate to each other. Developing a sociological imagination—the mindset that enables individuals to see the relationship between events in their personal lives and events in their society—will help you to see how social forces affect your life in a way that a more individualistic perspective does not.

Sociologists recognize the influence that groups have on individuals.

What Should You Expect?

As you begin your study of sociology, you will probably find that it is very different from other classes you have taken. This is because sociology looks at groups rather than at individuals. It is this focus on groups, rather than on individuals, that distinguishes sociology from psychology, the study of individual behavior. Although sociology employs a distinct perspective, it does share some common features with other social sciences, including anthropology, psychology, economics, political science, and history. You will find elements of all of these disciplines in this sociology textbook. You will also find that you will begin to look at your life and your interactions with other people and with social institutions in a different way as you proceed through this course.

Sociologists as Scientists

In your study of sociology, you will learn to think like a social scientist. Scientists constantly question their own assumptions and look for alternative evidence and conclusions. All scientists—including sociologists—use the scientific method as a problem-solving tool. It teaches them to think critically by encouraging open-mindedness, intellectual curiosity, and evaluation of reasons. Using the scientific method will help you think critically and be objective when applying sociological principles to everyday events, issues, and problems.

Teaching Strategy

One of the first things that the study of sociology requires is the adoption of the sociological perspective—a way of looking at events and behaviors that focuses on groups, not individuals. Because the students have been conditioned to think in terms of individual causes of behavior, it will be necessary to stress the importance of looking for patterns of behavior among members of a group or society. Consciously taking the perspective of a sociologist will help the students recognize the influences that groups have on how we all think, feel, and act. One way to begin this process of adopting the sociological perspective is to ask the students to think about the different ways they and their friends act when they are alone and when they are with different groups (e.g., their family, religious group, sports team, music ensemble, etc.).

Reinforcing Vocabulary

Remind the students that every field of study has its own vocabulary—words that have a special meaning within that particular field. Some of these vocabularies are easily identified as belonging to a specific topic, like the names of elements in chemistry's periodic table, or the names of specific bones and muscles in anatomy. Sociology is no different in that it, too, has its own vocabulary with meanings specific to this field. However, many of the words used by sociologists are often encountered in everyday language as well. Explain to the students that they will need to be sure that they understand and use sociological terms with precision, to avoid confusing the words with their more common counterparts. To illustrate this, have the students look through the glossary in the back of the textbook and give examples of words whose sociological meaning differ from their everyday usage.

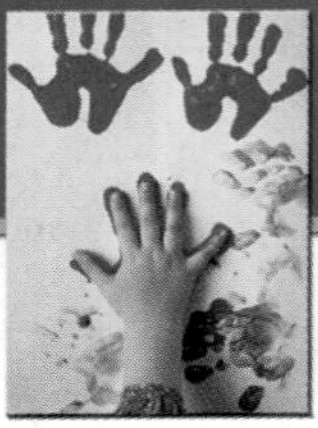

Study and Writing Skills

Study Skills

To get the most out of any course you take, you must be active in learning the material. All fields of study have their own terminology, and sociology is no different in that respect. However, in sociology, understanding the central concepts is confounded by the fact that many of the terms used by sociologists are often also used in everyday language with different meanings. Because it is important for you to understand such definitional differences, sociological concepts are carefully defined throughout the textbook.

Studying sociology can open doors for you.

Learning the Skill

To understand the central concepts used in sociology:

- Identify the terms that sociologists use to represent specific scientific concepts. You must be careful at this point, because many of the words that sociologists use are also used in everyday language. You may mistakenly think that you already understand a word, when, in fact, its scientific meaning is different.
- Be sure that you understand the words that are used to define a sociological term.
- Try to put the definition in your own words. If you cannot do this at first, keep working at it until you can. But be careful not to lapse back into everyday usage of the term.
- Understand the context in which the term is used, not just its specific definition.
- Practice using sociological terms with their scientific meanings.

Practicing the Skill

Read the following paragraph and then answer the questions below.

Prejudice is a widely held preconception of a group and its individual members. These preconceptions are often based on strong emotions and unchallenged ideas. Consequently, they are difficult to change, even in the face of overwhelming evidence to the contrary. Prejudice involves an either/or type of logic: A group is either good or bad, and it is assumed that each of the members of that group possesses the characteristics attributed to the group. Prejudice, then, involves an overgeneralization based on biased or insufficient information. While prejudice refers to an attitude, discrimi-

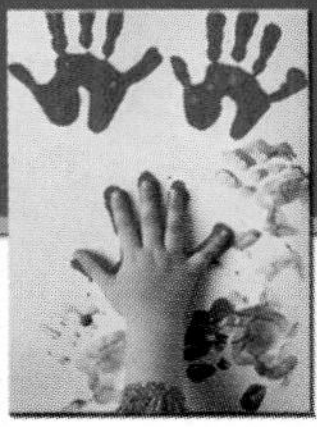

nation describes unequal treatment of others. Prejudice does not always result in discrimination, but it often does.

1. Define *prejudice* in its sociological meaning. Do the same for *discrimination*.
2. Based on their sociological meanings, are prejudice and discrimination always negative?
3. Based on their sociological meanings, can discrimination occur without prejudice?

Applying the Skill

1. Look up the sociological definitions of culture and society. How are these meanings different from everyday usage?
2. How are these terms similar to each other?
3. How are they different?

The Writing Process

Researching and writing allow you to organize your ideas in a logical manner. Actually, writing a paper is only the final step in a process that involves using other skills you have already learned, such as identifying central issues, distinguishing fact from opinion, and making generalizations.

Learning the Skill

Use the following guidelines in the writing process:

- Select an interesting topic. As you identify possible topics, focus on resources that are available. Do preliminary research to determine whether your topic is too broad or too narrow.
- Write a thesis statement that defines what you want to prove, discover, or illustrate in your writing. This will be the focus of your entire paper.
- Research your topic. First, formulate a list of central questions. Prepare note cards on each question, listing the information sources.
- Organize your information by building an outline. Then follow your outline in writing a rough draft of your report.

The Internet has made certain kinds of research much quicker and easier. But, the researcher must still use critical thinking skills to evaluate the information obtained from the Internet.

Teaching Strategy

Students should realize the importance of written communication. Writers must be able to convey the meaning of their ideas without ever seeing or talking with their audience. This means that the writer has only one chance to communicate his or her thoughts, with no opportunity to clarify the meaning of the written word. As a result of this solitary opportunity, all writers must strive to do two things in their communiqués—capture the readers' interest and make the ideas clear to the readers. To do this well, the writer must first fully understand his or her topic and then have a clear plan for conveying that information to the reader. Writing well takes a great deal of practice, and should be one of the students' primary educational goals.

Answers to Practicing the Skill

1. Prejudice is a widely held preconception of a group and its individual members. Discrimination is unequal treatment of others. Students should distinguish between an attitude and actual behavior.
2. No. Prejudice can be based on favorable preconceptions and discrimination can provide favorable treatment of others. Of course, this implies that individuals of other groups are not viewed or treated as favorably as the esteemed group members.
3. This question will generate a good discussion.

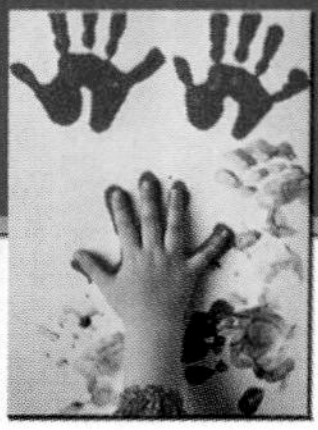

Teaching Strategy

Students will probably not be enthused about writing a report for their sociology class. Let the students know that writing reports is not solely a school activity. As employees of almost any type of organization, they will be writing reports on a regular basis as part of their work. Although writing sociological reports can be very useful to their understanding of the subject, remind them that they are also getting much-needed practice in the more general field of written communication, which will serve them well for their futures.

Answers to Practicing the Skill

1. The student could focus on a single racial or sex category.
2. Family income is a key factor in determining the educational level of the children in the family.
3. The main ideas would include the role higher incomes play in allowing children in the family to pursue educational opportunities; to pay for higher quality education; and to live in middle and upper class neighborhoods that have better quality schools.
4. U.S. Census Bureau, State Departments of Education, Children's Defense Fund.

- A report should have three main parts: the introduction, the body, and the conclusion. The introduction briefly presents the topic and gives your topic statement. In the body, follow your outline to develop the important ideas in your argument. The conclusion summarizes and restates your findings.
- Each paragraph should express one main idea in a topic sentence. Additional sentences support or explain the main idea by using details and facts.
- Revise the draft into a final report. Wait for a day, then reread and revise it.

Practicing the Skill

Suppose you are writing a report on the role family income plays in the children's educational attainment. Answer the following questions about the writing process.

1. How could you narrow the topic?
2. Write a thesis statement.
3. What are the main ideas?
4. What are three possible sources of information?

Applying the Skill

Use research resources in your library to find information on the role of the family in society. Narrow the topic and write a short report on it.

Critical Thinking Skills

Identifying Central Issues

Identifying central issues will help you organize information and assess the most important concepts to remember.

Good debaters must identify the central issues in a topic and in their opponents' arguments. Do you think political candidates do this well?

Learning the Skill

To identify a central issue, follow these steps:

1. Understand the context in which the reading was written.
2. Skim the material to identify its general subject. Look at headings and subheadings.
3. Read the information carefully to pinpoint the ideas that the details support.
4. Identify the central issue. Ask what part of the reading conveys the main idea?

Read the following excerpt from a paper entitled "The Crisis of the Young African American Male and the Criminal Justice System."

> *In recent years policy attention regarding the crisis of the African American male has focused on a variety of areas in which African American males have suffered disproportionately from social ills. These have included education, housing, employment, and health care, among others. Perhaps in no other area, though, have these problems been displayed as prominently as in the rate of crime and*

Teaching Strategy

Students may not realize that being able to identify the central issue in a written document or in a conversation is relevant to a wide range of activities. This skill is not simply for studying sociology, or just for studying in general. Finding the central issue is important in virtually any endeavor, from reading the sports page of your local newspaper, to listening to a news broadcast, or watching a political debate. Ask your students to name some of the movies that are popular at the present time. Pick one or two of these movies and ask the students to explain the central issue involved in them. Encourage discussion among the students—they may find that identifying central issues is more difficult than they originally thought.

Teaching Strategy

As your students will be happy to verify, parents tend to lecture teenagers about many things. Ask your students to think back to their most recent "discussion" with their parent(s) or guardian(s). What was the central idea that the adult was trying to convey? What was the student's central issue? Ask the students if either or both parties made the central issue clear to the other party. Do they feel like their parent(s) or guardian(s) understood them? Were they able to figure out what the adult's central idea was? If difficulties were encountered in either direction, ask the students to discuss the reasons for the problems.

Answers to Practicing the Skill

1. No, it is not clear. Mauer says that there is mixed research evidence. Astute students will also note that the 4.3 times greater chance of receiving the death penalty is related to the race of the victim, not the offender.
2. The race of both victim and offender has a significant impact on the determination of a sentence of death as opposed to life in prison.

the criminal justice system. African Americans have been affected in this area in two significant regards. First, African Americans are more likely to be victimized by crime than are other groups.... Second, the dramatic rates at which African American males have come under some form of criminal justice supervision has created a complex set of consequences which affect not only individual victims and offenders, but families and communities as well (Mauer, 1999).

A first step in identifying the central issue is to find out who wrote the piece and understand the author's purposes in writing it. Marc Mauer is the Assistant Director of The Sentencing Project, a non-profit organization engaged in research on criminal justice issues. In this paper, Mr. Mauer wanted to explore the current status of African American males in America's criminal justice system and recommend policies that would help change the system's destructive impacts on public safety.

Practicing the Skill

Read another paragraph from Mr. Mauer's paper and answer the questions that follow.

In assessing the extent to which racial bias within the criminal justice system has contributed to these disparities, there is mixed research evidence. Imposition of the death penalty provides the most compelling evidence for ongoing racial disparity. A series of studies has demonstrated that . . . the race of both victim and offender has a significant impact on the determination of a sentence of death as opposed to life in prison. [M]urder defendants charged with killing whites faced a 4.3 times greater chance of receiving death than those charged with killing blacks (Mauer, 1999).

1. According to Mauer, is it clear that African Americans receive harsher treatment from the courts?
2. Summarize the central issue of this paragraph in one sentence.

Applying the Skill

1. Bring to class three editorials from your local newspaper, national newspaper, or a newsmagazine. Try to find examples written by the publications' readers ("Letters to the Editor" are a good source for these) and professional writers.
2. Identify the central issue in each editorial.
3. Discuss how clearly each writer made his or her main point(s).

Determining Cause and Effect

Understanding cause and effect involves determining *why* an event occurred. A *cause* is the action or situation that produces an event. What happens as a result of a cause is an *effect*. Despite the seeming simplicity of this relationship, determining the true cause of an event is often very difficult. This is the case because there is seldom a single cause of any effect. Like other scientists, sociologists realize that almost all events occur as a result of several factors operating in combination. This viewpoint is known as the principle of multiple causation.

Calvin has obviously discovered the difficulties of determining cause-and-effect relationships.

Learning the Skill

Just because two things happen at nearly the same time, or they seem to occur regularly together, does not mean that they have a causal relationship. To identify cause-and-effect relationships, follow these steps:

- Identify two or more events.
- Decide whether one event caused the other. Look for clue words such as *because, led to, brought about, produced, as a result of, so that, since,* and *therefore.*
- Look for logical relationships between events, such as "She overslept, and then she missed her bus."
- Identify the outcomes of events. Remember that some effects have more than one cause, and some causes lead to more than one effect. Also, an effect can become the cause of yet another effect.

Practicing the Skill

Sociologists have studied the relationship between violence on television and violent behavior for many years. For decades, no one was willing to conclude that there was a cause-and-effect relationship between the two, but in 1999 The Milton S. Eisenhower Foundation issued a report that established a causal link between viewing violence on television and increased levels of violent behavior among viewers.

1. Why do you think that earlier researchers were reluctant to say that watching violence on television caused violent behavior?
2. Why did The Milton S. Eisenhower Foundation (see page 126 of the text) conclude that a cause-and-effect relationship does exist?

Sociology Handbook

Teaching Strategy

The scientific method is used by sociologists and other scientists to formulate and test hypotheses, in order to better understand the world around them. It seems reasonable to think that scientists are trying to determine cause-and-effect relationships among the events they are studying. However, as scientists would be quick to point out, it is very rare to be able to conclude a direct causal relationship between two or more events. The more common conclusion is that the events are correlated, meaning that the variables are related in some ways, but causality may not be indicated. As the scientists' work indicates, identifying cause-and-effect relationships is extremely difficult in the social sciences. One way to illustrate this difficulty would be to ask your students to determine whether the chicken or the egg came first, i.e., which one caused the other?

Answers to Practicing the Skill

1. Students' answers will vary, but may include insufficient evidence, the need for further research, and the possibility of causes of violent behavior other than television viewing.
2. The cumulative weight of the findings from previous studies, and the recognition that every exposure to violence increases the chances that a child will behave violently.

Teaching Strategy

People tend to mix facts and opinions when discussing social issues about which they feel strongly. Ask your students to identify a controversial topic they would like to discuss (obviously, you must be careful while doing this—some of the issues may be very sensitive or offensive to some students). Have the students list the key points that different sides of the topic use in their arguments. Ask them to distinguish between facts and opinions in these key points. How do they decide which is fact and which is opinion? After sorting out the facts and opinions, ask the students to evaluate the arguments that the various sides to the issue use to support their positions.

Applying the Skill

1. Do some research on the causes of criminal behavior. Prepare a short report that summarizes your findings.
2. Discuss how the principle of multiple causation applies to criminal behavior.
3. What other questions does your research raise?

Separating Fact from Opinion

Separating fact from opinion can be very important to you in everyday life.

Being able to distinguish fact from opinion can help you make reasonable judgments about what others say and write. Unfortunately, fact and opinion are often confused with each other, and separating them can be difficult. Facts must be verified by evidence. Opinions are simply based on people's differing values and beliefs.

Learning the Skill

The following steps will help you distinguish facts from opinions:

- Read or listen to the information carefully. Identify the facts by asking: Can these statements be proved? Where would I find information to verify them?
- If a statement can be verified, it is factual. Check the sources for the facts. Often statistics sound impressive, but they may come from an unreliable source.
- Identify opinions by looking for statements of feelings or beliefs. If the statement refers to situations that are desirable or undesirable, important or unimportant, or likely or unlikely, then the statement is an opinion. Opinions may also contain words like *should, would, could, best, greatest, all, every,* or *always.*

Practicing the Skill

Read the following paragraph, then answer the questions below it.

According to data collected by the Census Bureau, African Americans who have received a high school diploma earned a median income in 1999 of $23,990, and their white counterparts earned $29,261, nearly 22 percent more. The gap between blacks and whites with

lor's degrees is even greater—median earnings of $36,930 for African Americans and $45,737 for whites, or 24 percent more (U.S. Bureau of the Census, 2000e). Does this discrepancy between blacks and whites extend to other areas of life as well? Almost seven out of ten whites say that blacks are treated the same as whites in their communities, but only 41 percent of African Americans agree with that statement. Less than half of African Americans believe they receive equal housing opportunities, while 83 percent of whites responded that their communities provide equal housing opportunities for everyone (Ludwig, 2001).

1. Which of the statements in the preceding paragraph are facts? How did you identify the facts?
2. Which of the statements in the preceding paragraph are opinions? How did you identify them?

Applying the Skill

1. Watch a television interview. List three facts and three opinions that were stated.
2. Can you verify the facts?
3. How did you identify the opinions?
4. What statements, if any, seemed to contain both fact and opinion?

Making Generalizations

Generalizations are statements assumed to represent the truth by those who make them. If you say, "People who work hard make more money," you are making a generalization. If you also say that every hard working person you know makes more money, you are attempting to support your generalization. Keep in mind that making a generalization from a small number of observations does not provide strong evidence that your generalization is actually true.

Sociologists study processes of socialization and make generalizations about how these processes shape individuals' ways of thinking, feeling, and acting.

Learning the Skill

To make a valid generalization, you must first collect factual information relevant to the topic. Follow these steps:

- Identify the subject matter.
- Gather related facts and examples.
- Identify similarities among these facts.
- Use these similarities to form some general conclusions about the subject.

Teaching Strategy

Accounts of historical events often get distorted over time. Some possible reasons for this include poor memories, lack of accurate documentation, or deliberate attempts to revise history. Ask the students to identify some historical events that seem implausible to them. Some examples might be the existence of extraterrestrial beings held at Roswell, New Mexico, staged videos of astronauts landing on the moon, or any number of conspiracy theories. Once a topic has been selected, have the students discuss how they might go about separating the facts from opinions.

Answers to Practicing the Skill

1. The median income figures and percentage differences are facts. They can be verified by consulting the Census Bureau figures.
2. The answers of blacks and whites who responded to the questions about equal treatment and equal housing opportunities were opinion, because they were stating their beliefs about the subject. It should be noted, though, that the percentages of the races that answered a certain way are facts. They are facts about differences in opinions, but they do not verify that any of the opinions reflect reality. The percentages can be verified by referring to Gallup's surveys.

Teaching Strategy

Suggest to your students that people often make generalizations about other, unfamiliar, categories of people. These generalizations are usually based on little or no factual evidence. Ask the students to think about some of the generalizations they and their friends make about others. (You may want to use adults or teachers as examples of "others" to start the discussion.) Once the conversation begins, these generalizations should flow rather easily. However, you must be careful that the discussion does not get insulting or belittling to members of the class. Try to steer the conversation toward examples that are obviously false, then ask the students how such generalizations could have initially been made. This discussion should point out to the students how easy it is to make generalizations without sufficient evidence to support them.

Answers to Practicing the Skill

1. The poor are lazy and deserve to be poor.
2. No. Surveys show that the poor subscribe to the same work ethic as Americans in the middle and upper classes.
3. No. Answers will vary, but may include prejudice, lack of knowledge about the poor, and other similar thoughts.

Practicing the Skill

Read this paragraph, and then answer the questions below:

Many people in America believe that people at the bottom of the economic scale belong there because they don't have the motivation to succeed in a competitive marketplace. In a series of surveys, Americans were asked to account for poverty in the U.S. The most popular reasons blamed the poverty on the poor themselves. However, in studies of the poor and those receiving welfare, researchers have consistently found that a majority want to work, to support themselves, and to get off the welfare rolls.

1. Based on the preceding paragraph, what generalizations are made about the poor?
2. Is the generalization about the poor based on facts?
3. Is the generalization accurate? If so, how does that influence our policies regarding the poor? If not, why does the generalization persist?

Applying the Skill

Read the editorials in your local or a national newspaper for one week. Then write a list of generalizations about the newspaper's position on issues such as political ideology, economic policy, or the environment.

Analyzing Graphics

Line and Bar Graphs

A graph, like a picture, may present information in a more concise way than words. Line graphs and bar graphs are drawings that compare numerical values. They often are used to compare changes over time or differences between places, groups of items, or other related events. Both types of graphs can be used to display the same information, and the choice between the two is often at the discretion of the author. In general, however, line graphs are used to show trends over time related to one type of data (e.g. percentage of the population that believes in God, average age at first marriage, or number of households headed by a single woman). Bar graphs may be used to show trends over time or to compare different types of information, such as median income for men and women, or age groups of a population.

Learning the Skill

Follow these steps to learn how to understand and use line and bar graphs.

- Read the title of the graph. This should tell you what to expect or look for.
- Note the information on the left side of the graph—the vertical axis. The information being compared usually appears on this axis.
- Note the information along the bottom of the graph—the horizontal axis. Time often appears along this axis.
- Determine what the line(s) or bar(s) symbolizes.
- Select a point on the line or bar, then note the date below this point on the horizontal axis and the quantity measured on the vertical axis.
- Analyze the movement of the line (whether increasing or decreasing over time), or compare bars to determine the point being made.

Practicing the Skill

Review the graphs then answer the questions. Note that both graphs present the same information.

1. About what percentage of families with children under 18 were headed by single parents in 1985? In 1996?
2. How would you describe the general trend shown by these graphs?
3. Based on the data for the last four years shown, can you state what the current trend is for families headed by single parents?
4. Which graph represents this data in a more meaningful way?

Sociology Handbook

Teaching Strategy

Emphasize to the students that graphs present data in a way that readers can grasp easily and quickly. Inform them that graphs come in many forms—line graphs, bar graphs, and circle graphs are the most common. Each type of graph has a difference way of displaying information. Line graphs show how data change over time, which helps to show trends and patterns. Remind the students to study the labels on the axes of the graph to determine what is being measured, and over what time periods. Asking the students to prepare a line graph, using data that is of interest to them (e.g., the number of victories their favorite sports team has won over the past five years) is a good way to foster understanding.

Answers to Practicing the Skill

1. 24 percent
2. The general trend is up. The percentage of children living with a single parent in 2000 (29%) is nearly double that of 1975 (17%).
3. There does not appear to be a general trend over the last four years presented. The percentages go up and down, between 29% and 30%. Some may interpret this as a "flat" trend.
4. Students will differ in their choices, based on personal preferences. However, most should prefer the line graph because the data represents a single type of data over time.

Teaching Strategy

Unlike line graphs, which usually show how data change over time, bar graphs show data in relation to a fixed scale. This is a good way to compare items to each other. Have students sit in rows, and direct each row of students to count the amount of money they have in their possession. Note the totals on the board. Then have the students present the information on the board in the form of a bar graph.

Percent of Families with Children Under 18 Headed by a Single Parent, 1975-2000

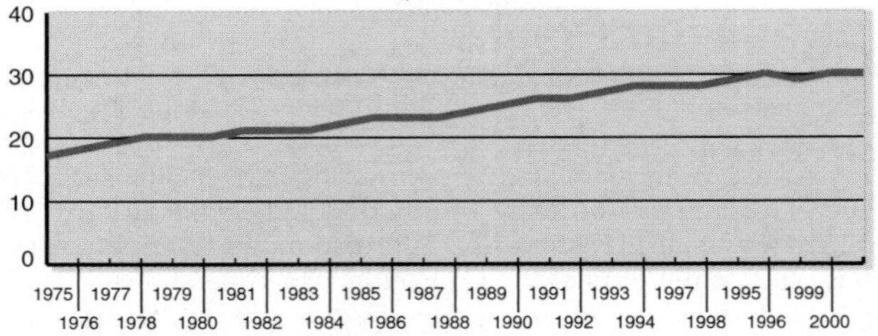

Source: *2001 Kids Count Data Sheet.* Baltimore, MD: The Annie E. Casey Foundation, 2001.

Percent of Families with Children Under 18 Headed by a Single Parent, 1975–2000

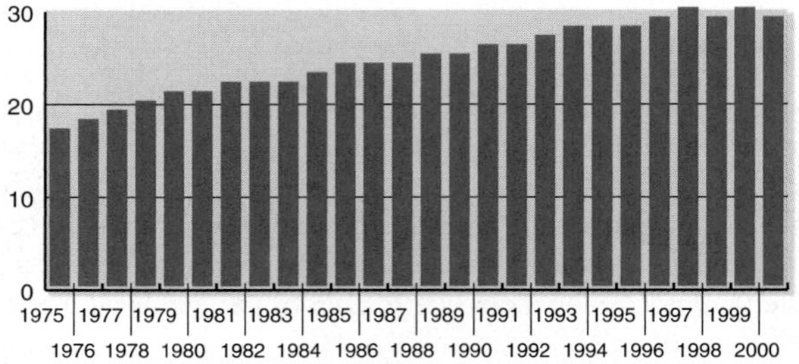

Source: *2001 Kids Count Data Sheet.* Baltimore, MD: The Annie E. Casey Foundation, 2001.

Applying the Skill

1. Create line and bar graphs that show the number and percent of children living in poverty in the United States from 1975 through 2000.
2. Pose two questions that the graphs you created raise in your mind.
3. Answer the questions you pose.
4. Which graph do you think is easier to understand and presents the information more meaningfully?

Circle Graphs and Tables

Circle graphs (also called pie charts) are often used to present information that shows the proportions of a whole. The particular data being presented can vary widely, but the common element in circle graphs is to show how

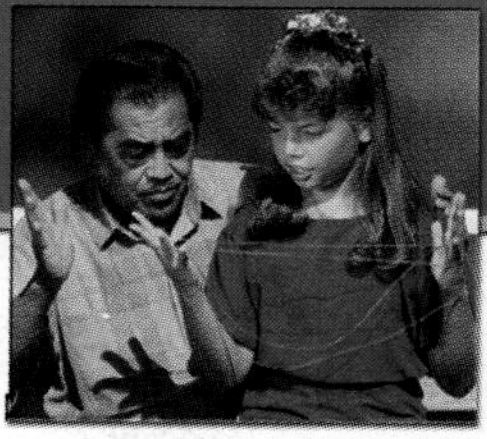

the entire population is divided into subgroups. The same information can be presented in tables, but in numerical, rather than graphic, form. Tables have the advantage of being able to present multiple categories of data in one location, whereas circle graphs are limited to one type of data.

Learning the Skill

Follow these steps to learn how to understand and use circle graphs and tables.

- Read the graph or table title to determine the content being presented.
- Read the labels (on circle graphs) or row headings (in tables). These will tell you what information is to be compared.
- For tables, examine the labels in the left-hand column. They describe ranges or subgroups, and are often organized chronologically or alphabetically.
- Note the source of the data. It may tell you about the reliability of the data, or where to go for further information.
- Compare the data presented to discover the relationships among categories.

Percentage of World Population by Continent, 2001

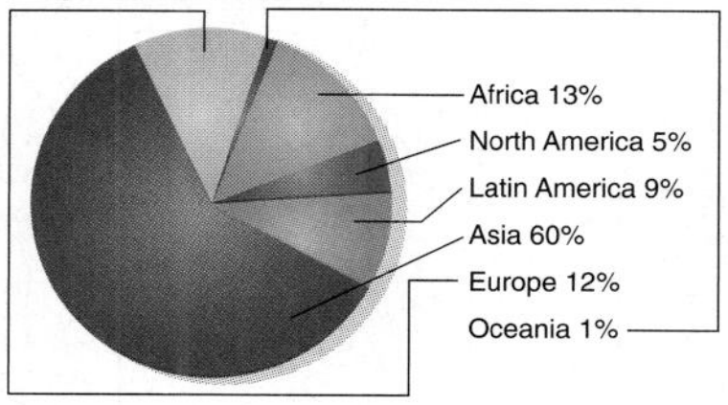

Source: *2001 World Population Data Sheet.* Washington, DC: Population Reference Bureau, 2001.

Practicing the Skill

Study the following table and circle graph and then answer the questions following them.

1. Which medium presents more information to the reader?
2. If you were concerned solely with the world's population, which graph/table would you prefer? Why?

Demographic Data for Regions of the World

Location	Population 2001 (in millions)	Crude Birth Rate	Crude Death Rate	Life Expectancy
World	6,137	22	9	67
Africa	818	38	14	54
North America	316	14	9	77
Latin America	525	24	6	71
Oceania	31	18	7	74
Asia	3,720	22	8	67
Europe	727	10	11	74

Source: *2001 World Population Data Sheet.* Washington, D.C.: Population Reference Bureau, 2001.

Applying the Skill

1. Gather information on the demographics (for example, age, sex, parental income) of high school students in your state.
2. Present selected information in a table and in circle graphs.

Maps

Maps are visual tools that show the relative size and location of specific geographic areas. There are political maps, which show human-made

Teaching Strategy

Explain to the students that a circle graph is like a sliced pie—in fact, it is even called a pie chart. Circle graphs show proportions rather than absolute amounts. They are often used when the information being compared totals one hundred percent. Ask the students to think of different ways in which their sociology class can be categorized (some examples are by sex, race, age, or horoscope sign). Have each student develop a circle graph based on a category they choose.

Ask your students how many of them have after-school jobs. How many play on a sports team? Then tell them that statistics like these could be presented in a text format, but a table or chart would display the information in a more concise and easily interpreted format. Have students analyze the data in the table on this page. Ask them "What information is being compared?" (demographic data for regions of the world) "How is the information grouped into categories?" (by location).

Answers to Practicing the Skill

1. The table provides more information.
2. The table would still probably be more useful. It presents actual population figures, from which the percentages can be calculated. The circle graph does not allow the reader to extract the population figures.

Teaching Strategy

Discuss with students their use of maps. Most have probably used a map to locate a particular geographic region or land feature. In addition, most have probably used a map to help them navigate from one place to another. Find some interesting maps that show various elements of culture, such as regional tastes in food, music, or sports. Have students study the maps and determine what information is being provided to them. What can they learn from the maps? What questions do the students have that are not answered by the maps?

Answers to Practicing the Skill

1. It shows the number of teen deaths per 100,000 teens, by state.
2. There does not appear to be a pattern based on geography, but there may be patterns based on other possible causes, such as access to firearms, violent crimes rates, etc. This should lead to the next question.
3. Students answers will vary, but could include relations with gun control laws, general or violent crime rates, population density, as well as general questions about why the rates vary so widely. Another good question would be why Washington, DC's teen death rate is so much higher than anywhere else in the country.
4. Foundations and non-profit organizations that support children's welfare (such as the Children's Defense Fund or the Annie E. Casey Foundation) have information on their websites.

boundaries; physical maps, which show physical features of an area; and special purpose maps that can show historical change, cultural features, population, climate, land use, resources, or any other information of interest. Regardless of type, all maps use symbols to convey information.

Learning the Skill

Follow these steps to learn how to understand and use maps.

- Read the title to determine the map's content.
- Examine the map's scale, which indicates the ratio between the map's size and the actual area being represented. However, for many special purpose maps, this information will not be provided, and is not relevant to the information being presented.
- Read the legend, or key, to interpret any shapes, colors, boundary lines, or symbols. This step is, in many ways, the most important for maps of interest to sociologists.
- Interpret the information being presented. Determine patterns or other interesting points of interest. What questions does the map raise in your mind?

Practicing the Skill

Study the map and answer the questions that follow.

1. What information does this map present to the reader?
2. Do you see any patterns in the information?
3. What questions does the map raise for you?
4. Where could you find the answers to the questions you posed?

Rate of Teen Deaths by Accident, Homicide, and Suicide*

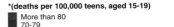

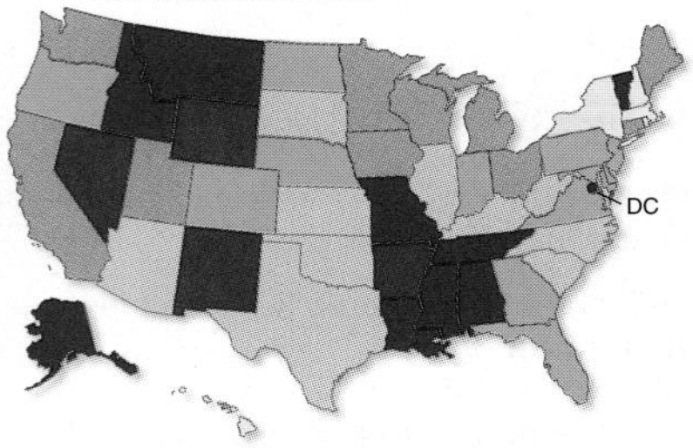

***(deaths per 100,000 teens, aged 15-19)**

- More than 80
- 70-79
- 60-69
- 50-59
- 40-49
- > 40

Source: *2001 Kids Count Data Sheet.* Baltimore, MD: The Annie E. Casey Foundation, 2001.

Applying the Skill

1. Do research on participation of high school students in school-sponsored music programs, by state.
2. Summarize your findings by preparing a map of the United States that depicts the information you found.

Interpreting Data

Percentages

Sociologists use the concept of percentages quite often in their work on groups and social structures. Percent means "parts per hundred." So when a sociologist notes that, say, 18 percent of a group has a certain trait, she means that 18 out of 100 members of that group possess the trait in question. Changes in the size or number of a particular item (usually over time) can be expressed in percentages also. Stating the amount of change as a percentage allows you to analyze the relative size of the change. For example, if you knew that the populations of two states each increased by 250,000 people, you would have some information. But knowing that the percentage change in one state was 1 percent, while in the other state it was 15 percent, would provide you with substantially more information about the relative size of the increase, and would allow you to infer some of the possible consequences for the states.

The individuals in this group can be categorized in many different ways. What percentage of the group is male? Female? African American? Redheaded?

Learning the Skill

Follow these steps to learn how to calculate and use percentages.

- Calculate the percent by dividing the number of the sub-group or change by the number of the original group population. Multiply your answer by 100 to express it as a percentage.
- Compare the percentage you calculated with other relevant measures.
- Remember that numbers or percentages by themselves tell you very little. This type of information is most useful when compared to other, similar types of information, so that you can put it into its proper context.

Practicing the Skill

Complete the table on page HB-16 by calculating the missing percentages. Then answer the questions below the table.

1. Look at the percentages of students studying sociology at each school. Do you see a pattern? Does sociology seem to be more popular at some schools than others?
2. Now look at the differences between the percentages studying sociology in 1990 and 2000 at each school. Do you see a pattern of change during the ten-year period?
3. What might account for the changes you noticed?

Teaching Strategy

To reinforce the concept of percentages, you might want to try this activity. Place one hundred pennies into a jar. Remove five pennies and ask the students what percentage of the total number of pennies the five represent. Tell students that percent means parts per hundred, just as cents are a portion or percentage of a dollar. Call on a student to determine the sales tax on an item that sells for $10.00 if the tax rate is four percent. Have the student write the calculation on the board.

Answers to Practicing the Skill

1. There doesn't appear to be any strong pattern in the data. Sociology may be more consistently popular at Glenvar and Wm. Fleming.
2. There doesn't appear to be any strong pattern in the data. Four of the six schools have an increase in the percentage of students taking sociology, and two show a decline. There has been a significant increase at Cave Spring.
3. The students can use their imagination here. Possible answers could range from gaining or losing a popular teacher, increased or decreased emphasis on the course, or college entrance requirements, among others.

Teaching Strategy

Mean, median, and mode are statistics that are often used to summarize information about large groups of data. They are particularly useful for comparing data over time or among different categories, such as showing an increase or a decrease in household income over a five-year period. Students should understand the differences among mean, median, and mode. Have them follow the steps and calculations several times to be certain that they know how to determine each measure.

School	1990 # Student Body	1990 # Studying Sociology	1990 % Studying Sociology	2000 # Student Body	2000 # Studying Sociology	2000 % Studying Sociology
Cave Spring	928	83	8.9%	1008	164	
Glenvar	316	40		421	44	10.5%
Northside	745	52		763	79	
Patrick Henry	866	54	6.2%	940	30	
William Byrd	643	37		715	55	
Wm. Fleming	872	91		948	116	

Applying the Skill

1. Survey 50 students at your high school to determine their favorite style of music. Based on the results of your survey, determine the percentages of your sample that listed each kind of music as their favorite.
2. Do the results of your survey surprise you? Why or why not?
3. How did you categorize students who named more than one style of music as their favorite?

Mean, Median, and Mode

Suppose a group of your friends wanted to compare scores on a college entrance exam. How would you calculate the groups mean score? Its median score? Its mode score? Which measure would be most meaningful?

The most commonly used summary statistic is the average. Generally speaking, an average is a measure of central tendency, indicating where the middle of a series of number lies. There are three ways to compute the average: the mean, median, and mode. The mean is the arithmetic average of a series of items. However, using the mean to represent the average can sometimes be misleading. This generally occurs when a few of the numbers in the series are much higher or lower than the others, resulting in a skewed or biased mean. When this happens, using the median or mode to represent the average may be more meaningful. The median is the midpoint in a series of numbers when they are arranged in order from low to high. The mode is the number that appears most frequently in the series.

Learning the Skill

Follow the steps below to learn how to determine and use measures of central tendency.

- To find the mean, add all of the numbers in the series. Then divide the sum by the number of observations in the series.

- Locate the median by arranging all of the numbers in the series from low to high. Then find the number that is the midpoint in the series. When an even number of figures is in the series, the median is the mean of the two middle numbers.
- The mode is the number in the series that appears most frequently. Simply look at the series and count which number appears the most.
- Compare the mean, median, and mode. Determine which one or combination is the most accurate in a particular case.

Practicing the Skill

Read the paragraph below and answer the questions.

An academic department at a major university conducts a survey each year of its recent graduates. One of the questions on the survey asks the respondents to report their annual income. Suppose this question drew the following responses from some graduates:

$23,500	$18,760	$43,000	$32,400
$26,750	$28,410	$1,466,980	$27,600
$26,750	$34,500	$24,580	

1. Determine the mean, median, and mode for these earnings figures.
2. Which measure of central tendency would you recommend using for this series? Why?

Applying the Skill

1. What are some of the data that you would want to know?
2. Which of the three measures of central tendency would you use for each type of data?
3. Explain your choices.

Sociology Handbook

Teaching Strategy

Albert Einstein was quoted as saying, "Not everything that can be counted counts, and not everything that counts can be counted." Ask students what they think Einstein meant by that statement. Do they agree with his assessment? If they do, what are some things that they can think of that are important, but cannot be counted (e.g., love, friendship, courage, etc.). Toward the end of the discussion, bring the conversation back to the benefits of numbers. Why are numbers, and measure such as the mean, median, and mode used so often by social scientists?

Answers to Practicing the Skill

1. Mean = $159,385; Median = $27,600; Mode = $26,750
2. The median or mode would be the most useful in this case. The mean would not be useful because of the one salary that is so far above the others.

NOTES to the Teacher

Students often confuse sociology with psychology and anthropology. While all of these disciplines are social sciences, they each focus on different aspects of what it means to be human. Psychology delves into the individual and anthropology looks primarily at culture while sociology deals with interactions between people and the phenomena that those interactions create: social structure, institutions, stratification, and collective behavior.

Looking at society with a sociological imagination focuses on the history and biographies of people in a given space and time. C. Wright Mills told us in 1959 that personal troubles are really public issues, highlighting the connection between our individual lived experience and large scale social phenomena. For example, while divorce is a personal event occurring between two people, it is also a public issue since high divorce rates exert influence on the status of women in society, governmental funding of aid programs for families with children, and housing patterns. Since most women are awarded custody of children and over half of all awarded child support goes uncollected, many women with small children must rely on governmental aid to survive.

As sociology is a social science, understanding the scientific method as applied to social groups is paramount. The scientific method, consisting of logical systematic inquiry, asks the researcher to be as objective as possible, clearly define theoretical concepts and statements, derive testable hypotheses from those theories, collect data through surveys, interviews, observations, and documentary analysis, and analyze that data with respect to the theoretical ideas guiding the inquiry, refining the theoretical ideas as needed. Since human life is so complex, the scientific method applied to people is not as "clean" as it is in the natural and physical sciences. Most sociologists agree that while we can never "prove" our theories, through replication we may be able to "support" theories, especially those that are situational, contextual, and partial in nature. Historically speaking, early sociologists and philosophers sought to develop abstract "grand" theories that would explain the totality of society while recent work

UNIT 1

SOCIOLOGICAL PERSPECTIVES

Chapter 1

An Invitation to Sociology

Chapter 2

Sociologists Doing Research

Enrichment Readings

Chapter 1 – Peter L. Berger
"Invitation to Sociology,"
page 35

Chapter 2 – Donna Eder
"School Talk,"
page 66

3

seeks to explain and better understand smaller pieces of society, such as community development, criminal behavior, and the impact of sports on society. Robert Merton was one of the first proponents of this "middle range" theory, statements about the world that are neither abstract grand theory nor overly empirical and lacking in generalizability. Merton's call for theories of the middle range—not overly abstract and ungrounded nor overly empirical and atheoretical—has been answered as most work done in sociology today does strive for a balance: empirical work linked to and guided by various theoretical perspectives.

Your students may be quite familiar with surveys and short interviews as marketing research has proliferated in recent years. You may be invited to participate in survey research while shopping in a mall, answering your phone at dinner time, opening your mail, reading a magazine or newspaper, or watching television. Whether or not these studies are done in a scientific manner is an open question; television phone-in polls may mention a number relating to their accuracy in sampling that has to do with how representative their respondents are of the overall population, yet most viewers are unaware of the relevance of this figure. Learning about the scientific method as applied to human society tells us that most of the information gathered in the aforementioned situations may not be accurate. It also explains why so many people, including politicians, are so vocal about the census.

The sociological perspective can help us to understand what we see in the news and in the world as well as in our own lives. What we take for granted as common sense is not always accurate information about how the world works. For example, Durkheim's study on suicide (Chapter 2) tells us that suicide does not always occur because people are despondent; different groups of people experience suicide at different rates. Thus, there are larger forces at work of which we must be aware if we intend on addressing the situation through policy and education. Sociologists, and other social scientists, believe that using the scientific method can help us to better understand the world around us and, subsequently, more effectively deal with social problems.

UNIT 1 Sociological Perspectives

Chapters

Pacing Chart*

1 AN INVITATION TO SOCIOLOGY

1. The Sociological Perspective
2. Origins of Sociology
3. Theoretical Perspectives

Pages 3-16; and 23-31. Assigning these pages will provide students with an introduction to the discipline, explain the concept of the sociological imagination, and cover basic terminology. Also included is the explanation of the three major theoretical perspectives.

Not included in this accelerated plan are the historical roots of sociology in the European Industrial Revolutions and biographical data on some of the early founders.

2 SOCIOLOGISTS DOING RESEARCH

1. Research Methods
2. Causation in Science
3. Procedures and Ethics in Research

Pages 40-43, 45, 50-55, 59-61. These pages contain figures and tables that summarize and compare the methods of research explained in detail in the text material. If you are pressed for time, spending a day discussing these figures will give students the information needed to move forward. These pages also include a discussion on multiple causation and ethics of sociological research.

Not included in this accelerated plan are a discussion of the scientific method; a review of basic skills for figuring mean, median, and mode; reading tables and graphs; and evaluating Internet web sites.

Lesson Planning

You will find detailed daily lesson plans for both traditional class scheduling and block scheduling in your Teacher's Resource Box.

***Note: While the authors of *Sociology and You* do not recommend skipping chapters or sections of the textbook, they are teachers like yourselves and know you must sometimes make scheduling compromises. If your schedule demands that you move more quickly through this book, you may want to focus on the pages listed above.**

Key to Ability Levels

Activities in the teacher's material have been coded for varying learning styles and abilities.

- L1 **BASIC** activities for all students
- L2 **AVERAGE** activities for average to above-average students
- L3 **CHALLENGING** activities for above-average students
- **ELL** **ENGLISH LANGUAGE LEARNER** activities

Teacher Resource Manager

Teacher Classroom Resources

Unit 1 Mastering Basic Concepts
- Learning Goals Outlines
- Graphic Organizers
- Vocabulary Activities
- Analyzing and Interpreting Data
- Increasing Your Reading Comprehension
- Guided Readings
- Student Journal Prompts
- Vocabulary and Chapter Review Quizzes

Spanish Supplements
- Learning Goals Outlines
- Bilingual Chapter Summaries
- Vocabulary and Chapter Review Quizzes

Chapter & Unit Tests w/ Final Exam and Answer Key
- Chapter 1 Tests A and B
- Chapter 2 Tests A and B
- Unit 1 Test

Alternative Assessments
- Performance Assessments
- Portfolio Assessments
- Chapter Essay Tests

Culture Studies: The Sociological Perspective
- Reading 1: Such As We
- Reading 2: Modern Wisdom: Urban Legends
- Reading 3: Fieldwork Among the Irish Travelers

Doing Sociology: Focus on Research
- Research Project 1: May I Take Your Order, Please?

Ethics, Values, and Technology: Real-Life Issues in Society
- Reading 1: Will We Have Any Privacy Left?
- Reading 2: Statistics: Cheating in American Schools

Transparency Binder

Chapter 1
- 1: Comparing Theoretical Perspectives
- 2: Mixed-Up Calendar

Chapter 2
- 3: Wheel of Science
- 4: How Variables Are Related
- 5: Mode, Mean, and Median of Salaries

Multimedia

TeacherWorks™
All-In-One Planner and Resource Center
- **Interactive Teacher Edition** Access your Teacher Wraparound Edition and your classroom resources with a few easy clicks.
- **Interactive Lesson Planner** Planning has never been easier! Organize your week, month, semester, or year with all the lesson helps you need to make teaching creative, timely, and relevant.

Interactive Student Edition CD-ROM

This CD-ROM contains the complete Student Edition with, simple navigation and search functions and links to Web activities and resources.

ExamView® Pro Testmaker CD-ROM

Easy-to-use software includes an extensive question bank and allows you to create fully customized tests that can be administered in print or online.

Vocabulary PuzzleMaker CD-ROM

This software lets you create crossword puzzles, word search puzzles, and jumbo puzzles using chapter vocabulary.

Presentations for the Classroom on CD-ROM

This PowerPoint presentation provides a step-by-step outline and supporting visuals for classroom lectures.

SOCIOLOGY Online

Use our Web site for additional resources. All essential content is covered in the Student Edition.

You and your students can visit soc.glencoe.com, the Web site companion to *Sociology and You*. The student text directs students to the Web site for **Chapter Overviews, Student Web Activities, Self-Check Quizzes,** and **Textbook Updates**.

Answers are provided for you in the **Web Activity Lesson Plan**.

Chapter Preview

Section 1 (pages 6–13)

Sociology studies human social behavior. It assumes a group, rather than an individual perspective. Sociologists look for the patterns in social relationships. Individuals can benefit by using their sociological imaginations to look at events in their personal lives.

Section 2 (pages 14–22)

Sociology is a young science. It started with the writings of European scholars like Auguste Comte, Harriet Martineau, Herbert Spencer, Karl Marx, Emile Durkheim, and Max Weber. Jane Addams and W.E.B. DuBois helped to focus American's attention on social issues. After World War II, America took the lead in developing the field.

Section 3 (pages 23–31)

Sociology includes three major theoretical perspectives. Functionalism views society as an integrated whole. Conflict theory looks at class, race, and gender struggles. Symbolic interactionism examines how group members use shared symbols as they interact.

CHAPTER 1

An Invitation to Sociology

Please see the correlation to the American Sociology Association standards located in the front of this text.

Lead-Off Activity

One effective strategy for teaching about perspective while generating a lively discussion is to dress outrageously the first day of class. One teacher has worn boxer shorts on the outside of his slacks, but you may want to think of something less extreme! Before starting any discussion, have students take five minutes to write down their reactions to what they saw. When time is up, ask students to share their perspectives on it.

During the discussion introduce the term *norms* and what it means to violate them. Students will start to become aware of behaviors that are shaped by custom and cultures. You may want to encourage them to keep a notebook listing various norms they observe over the next few weeks.

Here are some other ideas you might want to try to get their attention:

U S I N G
Your Sociological Imagination

"Study shows juvenile delinquency increases as church attendance decreases"

If you saw this headline in your local paper, you might be tempted to think "Well, duh . . . ." After all, applying a little common sense to this topic would probably lead you to draw exactly the same conclusion. If you assumed, however, that lower church attendance *causes* delinquency, you would be making a common mistake. Research shows that delinquency increases as church attendance decreases because of a third factor—age. Older adolescents go to church less often *and* they are also more likely than younger teens to be delinquents. What may seem to be a relationship between church attendance and delinquency is actually caused by a third factor—age—that affects both of the other two factors.

Questioning and researching assumptions is an important aspect of sociology. By learning to question *conventional wisdom* (what most people believe to be true) you will be in a better position to make decisions or judgments. Your decisions will be based on reality rather than on socially accepted false beliefs. (This does not mean that all conventional wisdom is false, of course. But it is important to know that the facts are accurate when policies affecting people's lives are being made.)

Sociological research is relatively new. In fact, sociology is the "infant of the social sciences." You will see this as you become acquainted with the founders of sociology. Before turning to these pioneers, however, you need an introduction to the unique perspective of sociology.

Sections

1. **The Sociological Perspective**
2. **The Origins of Sociology**
3. **Theoretical Perspectives**

Learning Objectives

After reading this chapter, you will be able to

- define *sociology.*
- describe two uses of the sociological perspective.
- distinguish sociology from other social sciences.
- outline the contributions of the major pioneers of sociology.
- summarize the development of sociology in the United States.
- identify the three major theoretical perspectives in sociology today.

SOCIOLOGY Online

Chapter Overview

Visit the *Sociology and You* Web site at soc.glencoe.com and click on **Chapter 1—Chapter Overviews** to preview chapter information.

U S I N G
Your Sociological Imagination

This feature points out that almost always, when examining human behavior, things are not as simple as they might appear. It also helps to lay the groundwork for Chapter 2, which discusses cause and effect, variables, and spurious correlations. You may want to ask students some of the following questions: (1) Do you agree with the findings that older adolescents go to church less often than younger children? If so, why do you think this is so? (2) Can you think of a similar example where age might be a hidden factor in behavior?

1. Stop class, and announce that it is time to sing Happy Birthday to some celebrity.
2. Ask students how many would like a low grade and if they would like it announced over the public address system.
3. Tell them to memorize all the J names in the phone book for tomorrow's class (act serious). Convince them it is a valid technique to improve memorization skills.
4. Walk into class, and say absolutely nothing for the first five minutes. As students become uncomfortable say, "What's going on here?"

L1

Using the Section Preview

Read aloud the section preview with the students. Ask students what they think "patterns in social relationships" means. Review the meaning of a pattern in behavior. Can they identify any behavior patterns from their own lives? *(Students might suggest common forms of greeting, ways to ask for dates, manners of addressing those in authority, etc.).* Remind students that things are rarely, if ever, the way they are because of "accident."

Section 1 The Sociological Perspective

Key Terms

- perspective
- sociology
- sociological perspective
- social structure
- sociological imagination

Section Preview

Sociology studies human social behavior. It assumes a group, rather than an individual, perspective. Sociologists look for the patterns in social relationships. Individuals can benefit by using their sociological imaginations to look at events in their personal lives.

The Nature of Sociology

A **perspective** is a particular point of view. Babies are usually brighter and better looking to their parents than they are to others. Newlyweds nearly always find their spouses much more attractive than do their friends. We all see what is happening around us through our own perspectives—our own points of view.

We normally do not realize how much of our attitudes and beliefs are determined by our perspectives. Sometimes, though, when our outlook is challenged, we may be jarred into realizing how much we take it for granted. As you will see, sociology has its own perspective. To understand it, you must have an idea of just what sociology is.

What is sociology? As a newcomer to the field, you may at first view sociology as the study of human social behavior. As you go along, however, you will acquire a more precise understanding of **sociology** as the scientific study of *social structure*. (Social structure is discussed later in this section.)

What is unique about sociology? Sociology, as stated earlier, has its own perspective. The **sociological perspective** never focuses on the individual. Psychologists may study the individual, but not sociologists. The view through the lens of sociology always remains at the social, or group, level.

perspective
a particular point of view

sociology
the scientific study of social structure (human social behavior)

sociological perspective
a view that looks at behavior of groups, not individuals

These elephant tusks were burned to discourage trade in ivory. Whether you support this action depends upon your beliefs about conservation and national sovereignty.

Integrating the Teacher Resources

Look for the Chapter 1 Vocabulary Activity worksheet in the Unit 1 Mastering Basic Concepts booklet in your Teacher's Resource Box. It provides reinforcement for vocabulary in this chapter.

Demonstration

Societal vs. Individual Responsibilities Students are probably familiar with television talk shows that emphasize people's individual problems without exploring societal explanations for personal difficulties. To reinforce student understanding of how social forces contribute to molding human behavior, write the following phrases on the board or on an overhead transparency:

1. *Someone who can't find a job is ___.*
2. *Homelessness is the result of ___.*
3. *Immigrants come here because of ____.*

After students have completed the sentences individually, ask them to share their sentences with the class. List their responses in two columns you have drawn on the board labeled "Personal" and "Societal." Some examples of personal (or individual) causes that students might use

The Social Sciences

Social science is a branch of learning that deals with human society. It includes a number of disciplines, which we generally refer to as the social sciences. These disciplines differ, but they share enough in common to overlap. Descriptions of the major social sciences are presented in this table.

Social Science	Description	Example
Sociology	Sociology investigates human social behavior from a group rather than an individual perspective. It concentrates on patterns of social relationships, primarily in modern societies.	Relationship between the employment of women and family size
Anthropology	 Anthropology investigates culture, the customary beliefs and material traits of groups. It is the social science most closely related to sociology. Anthropologists, however, concentrate on the study of preliterate societies (societies that do not use writing.) Sociologists focus on modern, industrial societies.	Nature of the family in preliterate societies
Psychology	Psychology investigates human mental and emotional processes. While sociologists concentrate on the group, psychologists also study the development and functioning of the individual. 	Effects of birth order on emotional development
Economics	Economics is the study of the production, distribution, and consumption of goods and services.	Annual income levels of American families
Political science	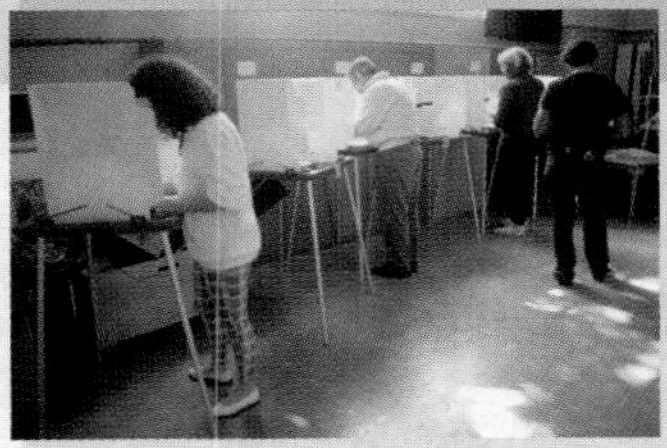 Political science investigates the organization, administration, history, and theory of government. Political scientists are concerned, for example, with voting patterns and participation in political parties.	Relationship between a family's social class and voting behavior
History	History examines past events in human societies. Historians generally rely on newspapers, historical documents, and oral histories as sources of information. 	Nature of family life in colonial society

to complete their sentences are: lifestyle choices, ability, talent, morals, drunkenness and substance abuse, or lack of effort. On the other hand, themes that focus on wages, exploitation, lack of jobs, poor schools, or lack of opportunities are societal causes and students completing the above sentences using these words have taken a sociological perspective. Explain that though sociologists as caring professionals are interested in individual causes and explanations, they are more concerned with explaining behaviors in terms of societal causes.
L2

Teaching Strategy

It is helpful to students to understand that sociology is only one of several disciplines that deal with the human condition. Most of your students probably will have taken history, a few may even have had a beginning psychology or economics course. Discuss the focus of each of these fields of study and emphasize that there is a significant amount of overlap in these subjects. You may wish to discuss the difference between the "hard" sciences that are empirical in focus (such as biology, chemistry, and physics) and the "soft" sciences that are less exact. Ask students if any of their parents are employed in these fields and would consider talking to the class about their careers or experiences.

Teaching Strategy

Ask students if they can think of a discipline or subject they studied in school that is not on the table. They might realize that geography is not listed. This is because geography is what is known as a *bridge discipline.* Physical geographers are earth scientists, comparable to geologists or botanists (and more of the hard science school). Human geographers are either social scientists (economic geography) or humanists (comparable to historians) and thus, belong more to the social sciences category.

Using the Illustration

Students should benefit from being able to place some of the early sociologists in the context of events and people they studied in American history. You may want to ask them what events on the time line could have had a direct influence on the writings of these famous sociologists.

This may also be a good time to reinforce the concept of cause-and-effect, which is the focus of Chapter 2. Finally, ask them to identify the events that they believe sociologists today would have a special interest in researching. What were the effects of these events on society?

In addition to cause and effect, many relationships are more "chicken and egg." Some events foster developments in other areas, and these developments work to strengthen the affects of the original event, creating a circular kind of effect. For example, the invention of the car spurred the building of roads, which led to the increased demand for cars, which strengthened the automobile industry and led to the increased production of cars, which led to . . . well, they should get the idea.

Integrating the Transparencies

A transparency of the Mixed-Up Calendar for the Demonstration activity on page 9 is provided in the *Sociology and You* Transparency Binder.

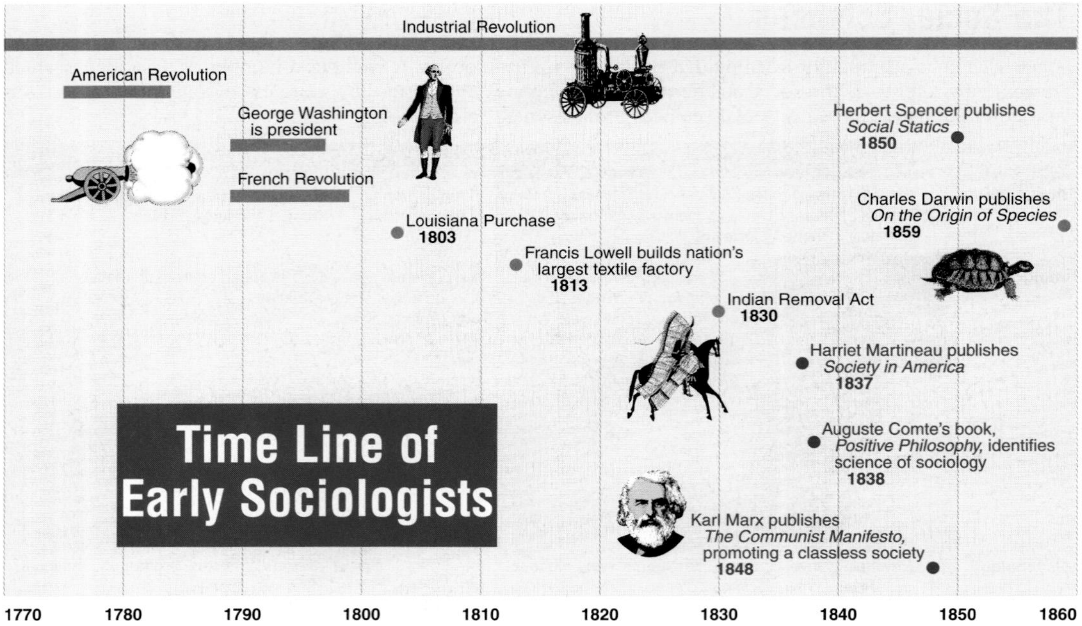

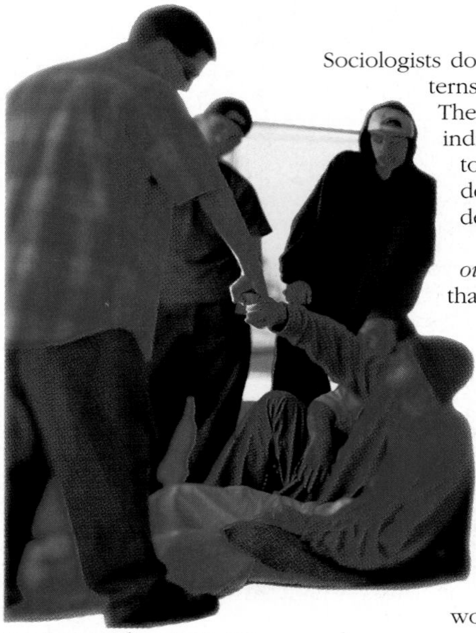

Joining a gang provides some young men—and women— with a sense of security and belonging they haven't found elsewhere.

Sociologists do not focus on the behavior of individuals but on the patterns of behavior shared by members of a group or society. The person on the street might explain human behavior in individualistic or personal terms—a young man joins a gang to prove his toughness; a woman divorces her husband to develop her potential; a teen commits suicide to escape depression.

Sociologists attempt to explain these same events *without* relying on personal factors. They look for social rather than personal explanations when they examine delinquency, divorce, or suicide. Sociologists might explain the events in the following ways:

- Young men join gangs because they have been taught by their society to be "masculine."
- More women divorce because of the social trend toward sexual equality.
- Teens commit suicide because of peer group expectations of performance, material possessions, and physical appearance.

Sociologists do not speak of *a* young man, *a* married woman, or *a* teenager. They concentrate on *categories* of people—young men, married women, and teenagers.

Demonstration

Perspectives To reinforce student understanding of the concept of perspective, direct students to draw road maps to a destination in your building or close to your school. Choose a destination that a person could get to via several different routes. Instruct students that their maps should start right from where they are sitting. When students are done, ask them to share their maps with the class. There will likely be several different maps, with several different ways of getting to the same point. Ask them to discuss reasons they chose the routes they did. (Some may go past favorite food stops or hang-out haunts.) Encourage them to defend their routes as being "the best." This exercise illustrates that, as social beings, our perspectives (or social maps) are not always the same as those of other people and therefore, our reality is not the same, either. **L2**

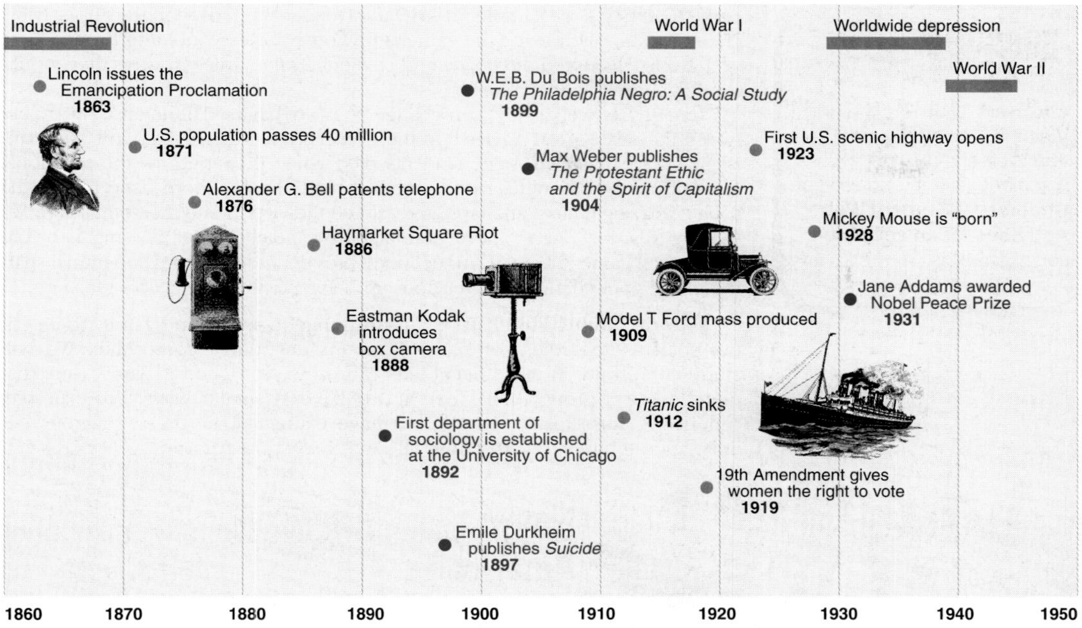

This time line shows when important developments in sociology occurred in relation to well known events in American history. Entries marked with a blue dot indicate important sociology landmarks (The sociologists on this time line are discussed in the next sections of this chapter.) How might the development of the box camera in 1888 have influenced the growth of sociology as a field of study?

The Importance of Patterns

As you well know, high school students in a classroom behave in different ways. Some students listen to everything their teacher says. Some tune in and out, and others spend much of the time daydreaming. Yet, if you visit almost any high school, you will find *patterned* relationships. Teachers walk around the room, work with students, lecture, and give tests. Students follow the teacher's lesson plan, make notes, and take tests. Although the personal characteristics of students and teachers may vary from school to school, students and teachers relate in similar patterned ways. It is the patterned interaction of people in social relationships—what sociologists call **social structure**—that captures the attention of sociologists.

social structure
the patterned interaction of people in social relationships

How do group behavior and individual behavior differ? Sociologists assume that social relationships are not determined by the particular characteristics of the individuals involved. Emile Durkheim, a pioneering nineteenth-century sociologist, helped develop the sociological perspective. He argued, for example, that we do not attempt to explain bronze in terms of its separate parts (lead, copper, and tin). Instead, we consider bronze a totally new metal created by the combination of several other metals. We cannot even predict the characteristics of bronze from the traits of its parts. For example, bronze is hard, while lead, copper, and tin are soft and pliable. The mixing of the individual parts creates a new whole with new characteristics. Durkheim reasoned that a similar process happens with groups of people.

Indeed, people's behavior within a group setting cannot be predicted from their personal characteristics. Something new is created when individuals

Reteaching

Read the following story to your students.

A man is walking down the street late at night. A mugger, with a dog, approaches the man and says, "Give me all your money or I'll have my dog attack you." The man turns away and begins to run when he hears the dog growl, but realizing he will not be able to outrun the dog, he jumps on top of a car. The dog continues to bark and tries to jump up on the car. The commotion attracts the attention of the clerk of a 24-hour market across the street, who runs out of the store and subdues the animal with pepper spray. The police arrive twenty minutes later, handcuff the mugger, and take the dog off to the pound. The police warn the man who was attacked against walking alone in that neighborhood late at night.

Ask the students, "How might a sociologist view this incident?" Students might say a sociologist would be interested in the background of the mugger, the type of neighborhood the man was walking in, whether or not muggings are typical of the neighborhood, and whether police perceptions of the neighborhood might have affected their response time. Then, ask students what a psychologist's viewpoint might be.

Teaching Strategy

You might want to explain group violence, such as the Denver Bronco celebration, in terms of the power of the situation. Ask students to consider what they would do if a fight broke out in the school cafeteria. Would they stand and watch, cheer, or try to break it up? Research suggests that students would do whatever most members of the group did and that certain situations create certain behaviors.

Another Time

Students should already be somewhat familiar with the general pattern of discounting Native American traditions that the colonists and early settlers exhibited. Explain that sociologists call this attitude *ethnocentrism* and that they will learn more about this in Chapter 3. It might be worthwhile to ask ahead of time for a good reader to practice reading this letter aloud and to give it as an "address" to the class.

Answers to Thinking It Over

1. Student answers will vary.
2. Have students share those perspectives with the class. They might find that some of their scenarios are similar.
3. Students often complain that what they learn is irrelevant. Could that be because the perspectives of the adults at school—teachers, principal, staff—are not compatible with their own?

SOCIOLOGY Online

Student Web Activity
Visit the *Sociology and You* Web site at soc.glencoe.com and click on **Chapter 1—Student Web Activities** for an activity on social patterns.

come together. For example, in 1999 the Denver Broncos won the Super Bowl championship. Following the game, a few otherwise law-abiding Bronco fans, as a group, disrupted the peace and challenged the police in ways they would not have done as individuals.

Tragedy, as well as joy, can change group behavior. The intense rivalry between the Texas A&M Aggies and the University of Texas Longhorns was banished the year twelve Aggie students died while preparing for the traditional football pregame bonfire. During the half time, the Longhorn band played the song "Amazing Grace" and taps, and saluted the victims and their families by removing their hats. At a joint Aggie-Longhorn candlelight vigil two nights before the football game, the A&M student body president said that the communal sharing of the grief changed the relationship between the two schools forever.

Why do people conform? Groups range in size from a family to an entire society. Regardless of size, all groups encourage conformity. We will study conformity in more detail later. For now, you need to know only that members of a group think, feel, and behave in similar ways. For example, Americans, Russians, and Nigerians have eating habits, dress, religious beliefs, and attitudes toward family life that reflect their group.

Another Time: Native American's Speech

Virginia colonists had offered to "properly educate" some young Indian boys at the College of William and Mary in Williamsburg. To the surprise of the colonists, the benefits of a white gentleman's education were not highly valued by the tribal elders. Below is a Native American's reply to the white men's offer.

We know that you highly esteem the kind of learning taught in . . . [your] colleges. . . . But you, who are wise, must know that different nations have different conceptions of things; and you will not therefore take it amiss, if our ideas of this kind of education happen not to be the same with yours. We have had some experience of it; several of our young people were formerly brought up at the colleges of the northern provinces; they were instructed in all your sciences; but, when they came back to us, they were bad runners, ignorant of every means of living in the woods, unable to bear either cold or hunger, knew neither how to build a cabin, take a deer, nor kill an enemy, spoke our language imperfectly, were therefore neither fit for hunters, warriors, nor councellors; they were totally good for nothing.

We are however not the less obligated by your kind offer, though we decline accepting it; and, to show our grateful sense of it, if the gentlemen of Virginia will send us a dozen of their sons, we will take care of their education, instruct them in all we know, and make men of them.

Thinking It Over

1. Describe your reaction to this passage. What does it tell you about the importance of perspective in interpreting the social world?
2. Describe a social encounter where you personally experienced a "clash of perspectives" with someone from another culture.
3. Do you think your education is preparing you to succeed in the world outside school?

Demonstration

Social Patterns So students may better understand how social patterns can be generalized, ask them to write down their schedules and plans for the day in hourly increments. Tell them to be sure to include time they'll spend at home, school, work, or involved in extracurricular activities. Ask for volunteers to read their schedules aloud or arrange to have some schedules made into overheads. Class members will begin to recognize that schedules do not vary much from student to student. They should be able to see that patterns are emerging. Ask students what kinds of school-day schedules their friends who go to other schools have. Students will see how social structure exists in schools. Though they won't fully understand this concept until Chapter 4, doing this activity will help them anticipate the coming lessons. **L1**

Conformity within a group occurs, in part, because members have been taught to value the group's ways. Members generally tend to conform even when their personal preferences are not the same as the group's. Some teens, for example, start smoking only to gain group acceptance.

Behavior within a group cannot be predicted simply from knowledge about its individual members. This could be because members truly value their group's ways or because they give in to social pressures. Like bronze, the group is more than the sum of its parts.

To the outsider, these teenagers seem to be dressed alike. How does this photo show that a group is more than the sum of its parts?

Acquiring the Sociological Imagination

The sociological perspective enables us to develop a sociological imagination. That is, knowing how social forces affect our lives can prevent us from being prisoners of those forces. C. Wright Mills (1959), an American sociologist, called this personal use of sociology the **sociological imagination**—the ability of individuals to see the relationship between events in their personal lives and events in their society.

What is gained by using our sociological imagination? People do not make decisions, big or small, in isolation. Historically, for example, American society has shown a strong bias against childless and one-child marriages. Couples without children have been considered selfish, and an only child has often been labeled "spoiled" (Benokraitis, 1999). These values date back to a time when large families were needed for survival. Most people lived on family farms, where children were needed to help with the work. Furthermore, many children died at birth or in infancy. People responded to society's needs by having large families. Now, as the need for large families is disappearing, we are beginning to read about benefits of one-child families—to the child, to the family, and to society. This change in attitude is reflected in the decrease in family size.

sociological imagination the ability to see the link between society and self

The sociological imagination helps us understand the effects of events, such as the social pressures just discussed, on our daily lives. With this understanding, we are in a better position to make our own decisions rather than merely conform (Erikson, 1997; Game and Metcalfe, 1996).

This social awareness permits us to read the newspaper with a fuller understanding of the events. Instead of interpreting a letter opposing welfare as an expression of someone with no compassion, we might instead see the writer as a person who places great importance on independence and self-help. The sociological imagination questions common interpretations of human social behavior. It challenges *conventional social wisdom*—ideas people assume are true.

Teaching Strategy

For more information on the topic of group violence, view *Quiet Rage: The Stanford Prison Experiment,* available from Insight Media, 2162 Broadway, New York, NY 10024-0621. This video is also appropriate for Chapter 7—Deviance and Social Control— in regard to issues of conformity and deviance.

More About . . . C. Wright Mills

Sociologist C. Wright Mills is sometimes referred to as the father of the student movement of the 1960s. He is known for several classic works in sociology besides *Sociological Imagination,* published in 1959. In *White Collar* (1951), Mills first describes the emergence of a new middle class made up of bureaucratized office workers and salesmen who work for a corporate entity. Mills hypothesized in *The Power Elite* (1956) that power in modern America was becoming more concentrated in the hands of three groups: businessmen, politicians, and the military. Comprised overwhelmingly of white males, these groups, he hypothesized, would begin to morally direct society. Mills died at age 45, in 1962.

Using Problem-Solving Skills

Tell students the following story and have students discuss what they would do and how this relates to the dilemma faced by students of sociology. A group of people is walking down a trail, looking for a town where people always tell the truth. They come to a fork in the road and one sign says "Town of Truth," the other sign says "Town of Lies." It's hard to tell if the signs are pointing in the right direction. The group meets two men walking down the road, having come from one of the towns. People in the group want to ask them for directions, but it occurs to them that they might be from different towns. They aren't sure that one of them won't lie about which town is which. What should these people do? This situation is a variation of a classic logic problem but, it can be used to demonstrate perspective again. Tell students in real life we would believe more readily people who are the closest to ourselves in behavior and appearances.

L2

Sociology Today: Job Opportunities in Sociology

In general, all employers are interested in four types of skills regardless of what specific career path you choose. These skills are:

- the ability to work with others
- the ability to write and speak well
- the ability to solve problems
- the ability to analyze information

Because computers have revolutionized the office, for example, information analysis skills are becoming much more important to managers in all types of organizations. The increasing complexity of work demands greater critical thinking and problem-solving skills. Knowledge is of limited use if you can't convey what you know to others.

The study of sociology helps students to develop these general skills, so it is a solid base for many career paths. For sociology majors, the following list of possibilities is only the beginning—many other paths are open to you.

- **Social services**—in rehabilitation, case management, group work with youth or the elderly, recreation, or administration
- **Community work**—in fund-raising for social service organizations, nonprofits, child-care or community development agencies, or environmental groups
- **Corrections**—in probation, parole, or other criminal justice work
- **Business**—in advertising, marketing and consumer research, insurance, real estate, personnel work, training, or sales
- **College settings**—in admissions, alumni relations, or placement offices
- **Health services**—in family planning, substance abuse, rehabilitation counseling, health planning, hospital admissions, and insurance companies
- **Publishing, journalism, and public relations**—in writing, research, and editing
- **Government services**—in federal, state, and local government jobs in such areas as transportation, housing, agriculture, and labor
- **Teaching**—in elementary and secondary schools, in conjunction with appropriate teacher certification; also in universities, with research opportunities.

Doing Sociology

1. Which of the above career paths is most interesting to you? What is it about this area that you find interesting?
2. Evaluate your current strengths and weaknesses in the four primary skill areas.
3. Look at the employment opportunities in the Sunday edition of your local paper. Clip out ads for jobs that you might qualify for with a sociology degree.

Adapted from *Careers in Sociology,* 4th ed., American Sociological Association, 1995.

Sociology Today

To find out more about careers, students with Internet access can find the ASA at **http://www. asanet.org** or do a key-word search for **Career Visions,** an interactive site that asks students a series of questions, then interprets the results and suggests possible career options.

Answers to Doing Sociology

1. Suggest students contact the American Sociological Association and ask for the brochures, *Careers in Sociology* and *Majoring in Sociology.*
2. You might want to bring in an expert such as someone who works in a human resources department to help students analyze their interests, as well as their strengths and weaknesses in the four primary skill areas.
3. Remind students that many professions hire people who have sociology degrees because of the wide range of skills these job applicants possess.

Working with the Quote

(See page 13.) Simone de Beauvoir (1908–1986) was known primarily for her treatise *The Second Sex* (1949), a scholarly and passionate plea for the abolition of what she called the myth of the "eternal feminine." It became a classic of feminist literature.

Demonstration

Sociological Imagination To show students how the sociological imagination works, put two objects on your desk or podium in front of the room—for example, you might use a sneaker and a baseball glove. Ask students to focus on the object that has the most personal meaning to them. Instruct the students to describe the object by writing a few brief sentences. Don't give them any specific guidance at this point. When they have finished, ask them who manufactures the object, who sells the object, who buys the object, and when it originated. Does everyone use it? Are there other uses for this object? Who, if anyone, suffers from this object? Students should begin to see that besides holding personal meaning, most objects have a wider social and economic significance. Other lives are connected to it. The sociological imagination asks us to see our lives in terms of the larger picture. **L1**

Snapshot of America

Illiteracy Rates

One of the assumptions of conventional wisdom is that nearly all American adults know how to read and write. Research has shown, however, that a large percentage of adults are illiterate. Literacy is defined as the ability to read at a fourth-grade level. This map shows, by state, the percentage of Americans over twenty years old who are illiterate.

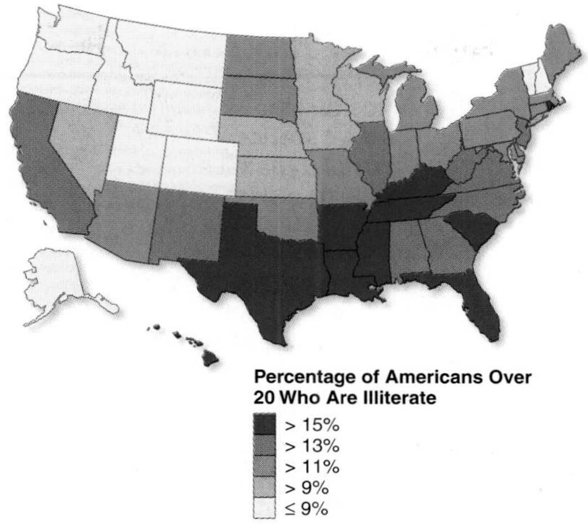

Interpreting the Map

1. List the states with highest and lowest literacy rates.
2. How does your state rate on literacy?
3. What might be some reasons for adult illiteracy?

Adapted from Doug Henwood. *The State of the U.S.A. Atlas.*

Snapshot of America

Answers to Interpreting the Map

1. The highest illiteracy rates are found primarily in the South; the lowest in the Northwest.
2. Answers will vary.
3. Reasons include a lack of opportunity to attend school, learning English as a second language, and a failure of the public school system to identify these functional illiterates.

Section 1 Assessment

1. Define sociology.
2. Explain the significance of patterns for sociologists.
3. Give an example from your life that illustrates conformity within a group.
4. How does the sociological imagination help people to understand the effects of society on their personal lives?

Critical Thinking

5. **Making Comparisons** Examine the idea of perspectives by identifying an issue that you look at in one way and your parent(s) or other adults look at in a different way. Write about the issue from both perspectives.

> "It is doubtless impossible to approach any human problem with a mind free of bias."
>
> **Simone de Beauvoir**
> **feminist author**

Answers to Section 1 Assessment

1. Sociology is the scientific study of social structure.
2. People interact in similar, predictable ways. Sociologists are interested in the patterned interaction of people in social relationships.
3. Answers will vary.
4. Answers will vary.

Critical Thinking

5. Answers will vary.

Using Problem-Solving Skills

Illiteracy Let students hypothesize why illiteracy rates vary from state to state. Some of their answers may be far-fetched, which is okay. The U.S. Department of Education estimates that functional illiteracy, (incompetence in such basic functions as reading, writing, and mathematics), plagues twenty-four million Americans. Thirteen percent of seventeen-year olds are illiterate, according to *Time;* the estimate for minority youth is 40 percent.

The National Assessment of Educational Progress cites that just 5 percent of 17–year–old high school students can read well enough to understand technical materials, literary essays, or historical documents. Ninety years ago, in 1910, only 2.2 percent of American children between the ages of ten and fourteen could neither read nor write—and this figure represents mostly children who never had the opportunity to attend school. **L1**

Using the Section Preview

This section introduces students to key figures in the development of sociology. By studying these scholars, students will understand the history and foundation of the field of sociology and be able to identify the contributions each pioneer made to the discipline. You might want to write some of the names of these individuals on the board before assigning this reading and see what previous knowledge the students have about these figures. Ask students what the context was when they first learned about the figures (e.g. history class, English, etc.) and then ask students if they realized these men and women were early sociologists.

More About . . . August Comte

Although quite brilliant, Comte—like many remarkable figures from history—was also extremely eccentric. One of his phobias involved germs and contamination. Students may remember Comte long after they complete this study of great sociologists if you tell them he formulated a principle called "cerebral hygiene." To prevent others from "polluting" his thoughts, Comte stopped reading! (Then again, you may not want to give students any more reasons to resist reading.)

Section 2

The Origins of Sociology

Key Terms

- positivism
- social statics
- social dynamics
- bourgeoisie
- capitalist
- proletariat
- class conflict
- mechanical solidarity
- organic solidarity
- verstehen
- rationalization

Section Preview

Sociology is a young science. It started with the writings of European scholars like Auguste Comte, Harriet Martineau, Herbert Spencer, Karl Marx, Emile Durkheim, and Max Weber. Jane Addams and W.E.B. DuBois helped to focus America's attention on social issues. After World War II, America took the lead in developing the field of sociology.

positivism
the belief that knowledge should be derived from scientific observation

social statics
the study of social stability and order

social dynamics
the study of social change

European Origins

Sociology is a relatively new science. It began in late nineteenth-century Europe during a time of great social upheaval. The social and economic effects of the Industrial Revolution and the French Revolution were touching all aspects of life. People were moving from farms to factory life, losing a sense of community.

Some intellectuals were fascinated and troubled by the sudden changes. Auguste Comte, Harriet Martineau, and others began to grapple with ideas for bringing back a sense of community and for restoring order. These ideas led to the rise of the science of sociology. Examining the central ideas of the major pioneers of sociology will help you better understand what sociology is today.

Auguste Comte is considered to be the founder of sociology. He was the first to advocate the scientific study of society.

What were Auguste Comte's major ideas?

Auguste Comte (1798–1857), a Frenchman, is recognized as the father of sociology. As a child he was often ill, but he proved early to be an excellent student. He had difficulty balancing his genuine interest in school and his rebellious and stubborn nature. In fact, he was expelled for protesting against the examination procedures at the elite *Ecole Polytechnique.*

As an adult, Comte's main concern was the improvement of society. If societies were to advance, Comte believed, social behavior had to be studied scientifically. Because no science of society existed, Comte attempted to create one himself. He coined the term *sociology* to describe this science.

Comte wanted to use scientific observation in the study of social behavior. He called this **positivism.** He meant that sociology should be a science based on knowledge of which we can be "positive," or sure. Comte also distinguished between **social statics,** the study of social stability and order, and **social dynamics,** the study of social change. This distinction between social stability and social change remains at the center of modern sociology.

Interdisciplinary Activity

Current Events To help students understand that sociology was an attempt to view society in an analytical or rational way for the first time (and prepare the groundwork for the study of research methods in Chapter 2) emphasize the need for accurate data in making predictions or analyses. Ask them to begin looking through newspapers for coverage of social issues and include any supporting statistics used to explain trends in social behavior. Have students clip these articles and collect them on poster board or some other means of display. They should identify the sources of statistics they find. Explain that statistics are used by sociologists to measure what they are researching and that valid research requires that sources be identified. You might want to begin to have students form opinions about the fairness of the reporting of the research. **L1**

Comte published his theories in a book titled *Positive Philosophy,* but he died before people generally came to appreciate his work. His belief that sociology could use scientific procedures and promote social progress, however, was widely adopted by other European scholars.

What were Harriet Martineau's contributions? Harriet Martineau (1802–1876), an Englishwoman, is another important figure in the founding of sociology. She was born into a solidly middle-class home. Never in good health, Martineau lost her sense of taste, smell, and hearing at an early age. Her writing career, which included fiction as well as sociological work, began in 1825 after the Martineau's family textile mill was lost to a business depression. Without the family income, and following a broken engagement, Martineau was forced to seek a dependable source of income to support herself. She became a popular writer of celebrity status, whose work initially outsold Charles Dickens's.

Harriet Martineau emphasized sociology as a science and introduced feminism. Her profound deafness prevented her earning a living as a teacher so she became an author.

Martineau is best known today for her translation of Comte's great book. Her English translation remains even today the most readable one. Despite being severely hearing impaired, she also made original contributions in the areas of research methods, political economy, and feminist theory.

In *Society in America,* Martineau established herself as a pioneering feminist theorist. Because she saw a link between slavery and the oppression of women, she was a strong and outspoken supporter of the emancipation of both women and slaves. Martineau believed women's lack of economic power helped keep them dependent. By writing about the inferior position of women in society, she helped inspire future feminist theorists.

Why did Herbert Spencer oppose social reform? Herbert Spencer (1820–1903), the sole survivor of nine children, was born to an English schoolteacher. Because of continual ill health, Spencer was taught exclusively by his father and uncle, mostly in mathematics and the natural sciences. With his poor background in Latin, Greek, English, and history, Spencer did not feel qualified to enter Cambridge University, his father's alma mater. His career became a mixture of engineering, drafting, inventing, journalism, and writing.

Herbert Spencer was an early proponent of Social Darwinism and evolutionary social change.

To explain social stability, Herbert Spencer compared society to the human body. He explained that, like a body, a society is composed of parts working together to promote its well-being and survival. People have brains, stomachs, nervous systems, limbs. Societies have economies, religions, governments, families. Just as the eyes and the heart make essential contributions to the functioning of the human body, religious and educational institutions are crucial for a society's functioning.

> An unexamined idea, to paraphrase Socrates, is not worth having.
>
> **Mark Van Doren**
> **American poet**

More About . . . Sociology in America

America is still taking the lead in the field of sociology. An on-line academic journal was initiated in March of 2000 containing studies that shed light on how everyday life is socially constructed. The title is the *Journal of Mundane Behavior.* Its mission is to "elevate the dull" and fill a void in social science research with scholarly analyses of the ordinary, earthy, and just plain normal. Some examples of studies include the mysterious silence of passengers in office elevators, the political significance of a morning shave and the cultural impact of plain talk among friends. The journal's managing editor says, "We are trying to make it so that we look at everyday life as something that is valuable and to understand how it gets constructed." The focus on the ordinary is their answer to what they believe has been too much emphasis on the field on deviancy.

Demonstration

To help students grasp how previous experience can contribute to understanding and perspective, have them turn their chairs so that students are paired back-to-back, with one desk facing the front of the room and the other facing the back (assuming the chalkboard is in the front). The students facing away from the board should have blank pieces of paper in front of them. On the board draw an abstract shape or shapes. The task of the students facing the board is to describe the shape so that their partners can reproduce it *without looking at the original.* Have students share with the rest of the class what they drew. This will literally and figuratively illustrate the concept of perspective. Though each student heard basically the same thing, there were numerous interpretations of that picture. As members of society we are always interpreting what we hear and see based on our own perspectives. **L1**

Net Worthy

Another excellent web site to help students to explore more career options in the field of sociology is **http://www.uncwil.edu/stuaff/career/sociology.htm** Students can click on a variety of career options in sociology from a career services counselor to systems and programming specialist and get detailed information on the career of their choice. Interested students might want to write a paper outlining the steps necessary for them find a job in the field.

More About . . . Emile Durkheim

Emile Durkheim originally studied to be a rabbi, but became a sociologist instead. Durkheim believed that science and religion are compatible. Both disciplines are directed toward the universal, and both seek truth. Ask students if they agree or disagree with Durkheim about the compatibility of science and religion.

Spencer also introduced a theory of social change called *Social Darwinism,* based on Charles Darwin's theory of evolution. Spencer thought that evolutionary social change led to progress—provided people did not interfere. If left alone, natural social selection would ensure the survival of the fittest society. On these grounds, Spencer opposed social reform because it interfered with the selection process. The poor, he wrote, deserve to be poor and the rich to be rich. Society profits from allowing individuals to find their own social-class level without outside help or hindrance. To interfere with the existence of poverty—or the result of any other natural process—is harmful to society.

When Spencer visited America in 1882, he was warmly greeted, particularly by corporate leaders. After all, his ideas provided moral justification for their cutthroat competitive actions. Later, public support for government intervention increased, and Spencer's ideas began to slip out of fashion. He reportedly died with a sense of having failed. His contribution in sociology was a discussion of how societies should be structured.

Karl Marx was the social scientist who underscored the importance of conflict in social change. Parts of his writings were later used as a basis for communism.

What is the legacy of Karl Marx? Karl Marx (1818–1883), a German scholar, did not consider himself a sociologist, but his ideas have had a major effect on the field. Marx felt great concern for the poverty and inequality suffered by the working class of the capitalist system of his day. His life was guided by the principle that social scientists should try to *change* the world rather than merely study it.

bourgeoisie
class owning the means for producing wealth

capitalist
person who owns or controls the means for producing wealth

proletariat
working class; those who labor for the bourgeoisie

class conflict
the ongoing struggle between the bourgeoisie (owners) and the proletariat (working) classes

Marx identified several social classes in nineteenth-century industrial society. Among them were farmers, servants, factory workers, craftspeople, owners of small businesses, and moneyed capitalists. He predicted that at some point all industrial societies would contain only two social classes: the *bourgeoisie* and the *proletariat.* The **bourgeoisie** (burzh-wa-zee) are those who own the means for producing wealth in industrial society (for example, factories and equipment). The means for producing wealth are called *capital.* Thus, those who own them are also called **capitalists.** The **proletariat** work for the bourgeoisie and are paid just enough to stay alive.

For Marx, the key to the unfolding of history was **class conflict**—a clash between the bourgeoisie, who controlled the means for producing wealth, and the proletariat, who labored for them. Just as slaves overthrew slave owners, wage workers would overtake capitalists. Out of this conflict would come a classless *(communistic)* society—one in which there would be no powerless proletariat.

Planned revolution, Marx was convinced, could speed up the change from capitalism to communism. His political objective was to explain the workings of capitalism in order to hasten its fall through revolution. He believed, though, that capitalism would eventually self-destruct anyway.

What were Emile Durkheim's greatest contributions? Emile Durkheim (1858–1917) was the son of a French rabbi. Durkheim was a brilliant student even during his early school years. In college, he was so intensely studious that his schoolmates nicknamed him "the metaphysician."

Learning Styles

Auditory, Visual, and Kinesthetic Learners Students who have difficulty interpreting the written word may require special consideration when instruction revolves around the textbook content. Some students are auditory learners who learn best through hearing. Others are visual learners—their preferred method of taking in information is by reading or sight. All of us are kinesthetic learners (learn by doing), but some students learn primarily in this manner. These active learners need lessons broken down into more concrete steps to facilitate learning. It is also important that kinesthetic learners successfully complete one step in the lesson before progressing to the next.

According to Durkheim, society exists because of broad *consensus,* or agreement, among members of a society. In preindustrial times, societies were based on what sociologists call **mechanical solidarity.** With these societies, there was widespread consensus of values and beliefs, strong social pressures for conformity, and dependence on tradition and family. In contrast, industrial societies are based on **organic solidarity**—social interdependency based on a web of highly specialized roles. These specialized roles make members of a society dependent on one another for goods and services. For example, instead of being self-sufficient, people need bankers and bankers need customers.

Emile Durkheim was the first sociologist to use statistical methods in the study of human groups. He was also the first to teach a university sociology course.

Although early sociologists emphasized the need to make sociology scientific, they did not have the research tools that are available today. Later sociologists developed the methods to replace speculation with observation, to collect and classify data, and to use data for testing social theories.

Durkheim was the most prominent of these later sociologists. He first introduced the use of statistical techniques in his groundbreaking research on suicide, which we will discuss in Chapter 2. In that study, Durkheim demonstrated that suicide involves more than individuals acting alone and that suicide rates vary according to group characteristics. Durkheim showed that human social behavior must be explained by social factors rather than psychological ones.

mechanical solidarity
social dependency based on a widespread consensus of values and beliefs, enforced conformity, and dependence on tradition and family

organic solidarity
social interdependency based on a high degree of specialization in roles

Max Weber's model of a bureaucracy reflected greatly increased efficiency in business and government. Today, however, bureaucratic *is often used as a synonym for unimaginative, plodding, or despotic.*

Who was Max Weber?

Max Weber (1864–1920) was the eldest son of a father who was a well-to-do German lawyer and politician. His mother, in stark contrast, was a strongly devout Calvinist who rejected the wordly lifestyle of her husband. Weber was affected psychologically by the conflicting values of his parents. Weber eventually suffered a complete mental breakdown from which he recovered to do some of his best work. As a university professor trained in law and economics, Weber wrote on a wide variety of topics, including the nature of power, the religions of the world, the nature of social classes, and the development and nature of bureaucracy. We will look more closely at all these topics in later chapters.

Through the quality of his work and the diversity of his interests, Weber has had the single most important influence on the development of sociological theory. Human beings act on the basis of their own understanding of a situation, Weber said. Thus, sociologists must discover the personal meanings, values, beliefs, and attitudes underlying human social behavior. Weber believed that an understanding of the personal intentions of people in groups can be best accomplished through the method of **verstehen**—understanding the social behavior of others by putting yourself mentally in their places. Putting yourself in someone else's "shoes" allows you to temporarily shed your values and see things from a different point of view.

Weber also identified *rationalization* as a key influence in the change from a preindustrial to an industrial society. **Rationalization** is the mind-set

verstehen
understanding social behavior by putting yourself in the place of others

rationalization
the mind-set emphasizing knowledge, reason, and planning

Points to Stress

When the students are reading about Durkheim, it may be a good time to reinforce that sociology is based on the gathering of scientific data and evidence. Students at this level are just beginning to think in terms of abstract statistical data as opposed to anecdotal evidence. Remind students that anecdotal evidence is based on reports or observations of individuals, usually by unscientific observers. Ask them to think of examples of anecdotal evidence that flatly contradict statistical evidence. For example, several years ago in Florida a man was admitted to a hospital where the doctors amputated the wrong leg. Is this considered evidence that Florida is a dangerous place to have an operation? Wouldn't many students naturally conclude that one should never seek medical care while vacationing there? Remind them that many people actually base their perceptions of reality on events they hear about from family and friends that are really just examples of anecdotal evidence.

Seven Intelligences Overview We all use all of these intelligences to some varying degree, but students are often more comfortable with one or two and tend to understand more if the material is presented using their favored method. It would also benefit students who are not particularly comfortable with a style of teaching to be exposed to that, as well. The seven major intelligences are linguistic; musical; logical-mathematical; spatial; bodily-kinesthetic; interpersonal; and intrapersonal. In the chapters to come, activities directed at students who strongly favor various learning styles have been included.

that emphasizes the use of knowledge, reason, and planning. It marked a change from the tradition, emotion, and superstition of preindustrial society. For example, agriculture became grounded in science rather than belief in luck, fate, or magic. In stressing rationality and objectivity, Weber pioneered research techniques that helped prevent personal biases from unduly affecting the results of sociological investigations.

Sociology in America

Although the early development of sociology occurred in Europe, the greatest development of sociology has taken place in the United States. Because sociology has become a science largely through the efforts of American sociologists, it is not surprising that the majority of all sociologists are from the United States. Sociological writings in English are used by sociologists throughout the world, reflecting the global influence of American sociologists.

In 1892, the first department of sociology was established at the University of Chicago. From its founding up to World War II, the sociology department at the University of Chicago stood at the forefront of American sociology. After World War II, sociology departments at eastern universities such as Harvard and Columbia, midwestern universities such as Wisconsin and Michigan, and western universities such as Stanford and the University of California at Berkeley emerged as leaders.

In later chapters we will be studying the works of major American sociologists. Two early contributors, however, who are often left out of the history of American sociology are Jane Addams and W.E.B. DuBois. Although

> What is not good for the hive is not good for the bee.
>
> **Marcus Aurelius**
> **Roman emperor**

Everyone manages his or her behavior to create a desired impression. What face have you put on today?

Working with the Quote

Marcus Aurelius Antonius (121–180) was a Roman Emperor who was known for following the Stoic philosophy. Ask students what they think he meant by this quote. Do they agree? Why would this quote be of special interest to sociologists? What is this quote saying about the value of the individual compared to the value of society?

Net Worthy

Dead Sociologists' Society **http:// www.runet.edu/ ~lridener/DSS/ DEADSOC.HTML**

This is an excellent site and is well maintained. Its purpose is to provide students with general biographical information on well-known sociologists. Select Dead Sociologists' Index and sixteen photos of sociologists will appear. Students may click on any picture to obtain background information and a list of the sociologists' works. Ask students to identify major sociologists and explain their contributions to the field of sociology.

In addition, biographical material can be found at: **http://staff.uwsuper.edu/ hps/mball/dead_soc.htm**.

On-Demand Writing

Allow students ten to fifteen minutes to respond to the following writing prompt: *Why is Weber's concept of verstehen the very essence of modern sociology?*

Students should understand that without a value-free basis, sociology is not scientific nor objective. Sociologists do not judge; they report.

L3

Jane Addams was a social reformer who spent her life working on the social problems created by the imbalance of power among social classes.

neither of these remarkable people were researchers or scientists, both were greatly concerned with social problems in America.

Why should we remember Jane Addams? The best known of the early women social reformers in the United States was Jane Addams (1860–1935). Although her mother died when she was two years old, Addams's wealthy father provided a loving and comfortable home for her and her eight brothers and sisters. Addams was an excellent student. Her early education emphasized practical knowledge and the improvement of "the organizations of human society." She attended the Women's Medical College of Philadelphia, but was compelled to drop out of the school because of illness.

When she was a child, Addams saw many examples of government corruption and business practices that harmed workers. She never forgot their suffering. While on one of her European trips, she saw the work being done to help the poor in London. With this example of social action, Addams began her life's work seeking social justice. She co-founded Hull House in Chicago's slums. Here, people who needed refuge—immigrants, the sick, the poor, the aged—could find help.

Addams focused on the problems caused by the imbalance of power among the social classes. She invited sociologists from the University of Chicago to Hull House to witness firsthand the effects of the exploitation of the lower class. In addition to her work with the underclass, Addams was active in the women's suffrage and peace movements. As a result of her tireless work for social reform, Addams was awarded the Nobel Peace Prize in 1931—the only sociologist to receive this honor. The irony is that Addams herself suffered a sort of class discrimination. She was not considered a sociologist during her life, in part because she did not teach at a university. She was considered a social worker (a less prestigious career) because she was a woman and because she worked directly with the poor.

More About . . . Jane Addams

Most students will have heard of Jane Addams and W.E.B. DuBois from their American history classes, so you might want to ask your students what they remember. Addams was a reformer and social worker who established Hull House in Chicago in 1889. Her work with the poor was part of the progressive spirit of the times and was called the social gospel. She believed it was a service to society to help less fortunate people. Her work was an inspiration for Eleanor Roosevelt, who was involved in many reform causes as first lady in the 1930s and 40s.

Integrating the Teacher Resources

To reinforce key ideas, use the Chapter 1 Graphic Organizer, a reproducible student worksheet available in the Unit 1 Mastering Basic Concepts booklet in your Teacher's Resource Box.

Careers in Sociology

A multitude of different career prospects are available to the BA graduate in Sociology. The following is only a partial list—many other doors may open for you: social services—in rehabilitation, case management, group work with youth or the elderly, recreation, or administration; community work—in fund-raising for community development agencies or environmental groups; corrections; probation, parole, or other criminal justice work; business—in advertising, marketing and consumer research; college settings—in admissions, alumni relations, or placement offices; health services—in family planning, substance abuse, rehabilitation counseling and hospital admissions; journalism; public relations—in writing, research, and editing; government services—in such areas as transportation, housing, agriculture, and labor relations; and teaching—in elementary and secondary schools, in conjunction with appropriate teacher certification.

Focus on Research

Point out to students that selecting the right college is like making a major purchase in one's life—it needs to be carefully researched so that you make the best decision within the constraints of your options. Like any major purchase, your choices are limited by available resources. Ask students to write down the steps in the college selection process after consulting their school guidance counselors or the Internet. Publications that categorize colleges around the country by their size, location, degrees offered, availability of financial aid, and so on are also good resources. Have students share their lists with the class.

Focus on Research

Secondary Analysis: The McDonaldization of Higher Education

Research is to sociology what lab experiments are to chemists. Through the research process sociologists gather information, or data, to help them understand how people behave in social settings. (In the next chapter, you will learn more about how sociologists do research.) The research project described below will give you some idea of how sociologists use already-collected data to study human social behavior.

In this study, George Ritzer investigated how Max Weber's process of *rationalization* (see pages 17–18) is being used by a popular fast-food company. Like Weber, Ritzer was interested in the movement of organizations toward ever-increasing efficiency, predictability, calculability, and control. After explaining each of these characteristics, Ritzer applies rationalization to the field of education in what he calls the "McDonaldization" of higher education.

According to George Ritzer, universities share some of the organizational characteristics of popular fast-food restaurants.

Efficiency refers to the relationship between effort and result. An organization is most efficient when the maximum results are achieved with minimum effort. For example, fast-food restaurants are efficient in part because they transfer work usually done by employees to customers. For example, self-service drink centers allow customers to get refills on drinks while disguising the fact they are waiting on themselves. *Calculability* involves estimation based on probabilities. High calculability exists when the output, cost, and effort associated with products can be predicted. A McDonald's manager trains employees to make *each* Big Mac within a rigid time limit. *Predictabilty* pertains to consistency of results. Predictability exists when products turn out as planned. Big Macs are the same everywhere. *Control* is increased by re-

Using Decision-Making Skills

Tell students that your local newspaper ran the following item:

> Sociology has nothing to do with reading, writing, or mathematics, believes school board member Mrs. Janet Learner. She has commented that there is no reason to study human interaction. Students should be taught the basic core courses plus how to follow rules and regulations. "That's what school is for; it's not a breeding ground for socializing."
>
> She proposes dropping Sociology from the curriculum
>
> The next school board meeting will be held in two weeks at the Central Administration Office.

Ask students to use the decision-making process to determine a plan of action for mobilizing the community to urge the school board to keep sociology in the curriculum as an elective.

L2

placing human activity with technology. McDonald's drink machines stop after a cup has been filled to its prescribed limit.

Because Ritzer believes that McDonald's restaurants reflect the rationalization process, he refers to the "McDonaldization" of society (1998). His sources of information include newspapers, books, magazines, and industry publications. Since many of you are now thinking about attending college, Ritzer's findings on the "McUniversity" should be of interest.

Increasingly, students and parents view a college degree as a necessity to compete successfully in the job market. "Shopping" for the right college requires many of the consumer skills used in making any major purchase. This consumer orientation, Ritzer asserts, can be seen on most college campuses in the United States. For example, students want education to be conveniently located and they want it open as long as possible each day. They seek inexpensive parking, efficient service, and short waiting lines. Students want high-quality service at the lowest cost. A "best buy" label in national academic rankings catches the attention of parents and students.

Public colleges and universities, Ritzer contends, are responding to this consumer orientation. They are doing so in part because government funding for higher education is becoming more scarce. To meet reduced funding, colleges and universities are cutting costs and paying more attention to "customers." For example, Ritzer points to student unions. Many of them are being transformed into mini-malls with fast-food restaurants, video games, and ATMs.

Ritzer predicts that a far-reaching customer-oriented tactic will be to "McDonaldize" through new technology. The "McUniversity" will still have a central campus, but it will also have convenient satellite locations in community colleges, high schools, businesses, and malls. "Students will 'drop by' for a course or two. Parking lots will be adjacent to McUniversity's satellites (as they are to fast-food restaurants) to make access easy" (Ritzer, 1998: 156).

McDonaldization, Ritzer contends, will dehumanize the process of education. Most instructors at satellites will be part-timers hired to teach one or more courses. They will come and go quickly, so students will not have the opportunity to form relationships as with more permanent faculty members. In order to make the courses alike from satellite to satellite, course content, requirements, and materials will be highly standardized, losing the flavor individual professors bring to their classes. Students will not be able to choose a particular instructor for a course because there will be only one per satellite. Often, there may be no teacher physically present at all. More courses will be delivered by professors televised from distant places.

In spite of these predictions, colleges and universities will not be a chain of fast-food restaurants or a shopping mall, Ritzer concludes. Institutions of higher education will retain many traditional aspects, but there will undoubtedly be a significant degree of McDonaldization.

Working with the Research

1. Do you think the benefits of the "McUniversity" outweigh the disadvantages? Why or why not?
2. What other industries or professions are being affected by McDonaldization? Give examples.

Observation

To help students understand and apply the McDonaldization thesis, have students work in pairs or small groups to complete an observation at a local business such as a fast-food restaurant, bank, school, or a car wash. Instruct students to identify and record as many examples of four criteria for McDonaldization as they can: efficiency, predictability, calculability, and control. This will be good preparation for Chapter 2's discussion of how sociologists use observations to gather data about human behavior. Ask students to share their observations with the class. **L2**

Answers to Working with the Research

1. The advantages of McUniversity are: (1) students who are not in close proximity to a college or university may take college courses; and (2) as Weber said, it guarantees efficiency and calculability.
2. Answers will vary. Students might mention the clothing or music industries. All fast-food businesses are McDonaldized; they resemble McDonald's except for the menu. The clothing industry tries to give customers the most for the least; the music industry offers CDs that are portable and can be stored easily.

Integrating the Teacher Resources

A lesson plan for a student research project related to the content of this chapter can be found in Doing Sociology: Focus on Research, available in your Teacher's Resource Box.

DuBois used science and sociology to disprove racist assumptions about African Americans.

W.E.B. DuBois focused on the question of race inside and outside the United States.

What were the contributions of W.E.B. DuBois? W.E.B. DuBois (1868–1963), an African American educator and social activist, also influenced the early development of sociology in the United States. DuBois attended an integrated high school in Great Barrington, Massachusetts, and was the first black to receive a diploma there. He earned a doctorate degree from Harvard University in 1895 and taught at a number of predominantly black universities during his career.

DuBois learned firsthand about racial discrimination and segregation when he attended Fisk University in Nashville, Tennessee as an undergraduate student. Partly from this experience, and from teaching in rural, all-black schools around Nashville, DuBois decided to attack the "Negro problem." This racist policy was based on the assumption that blacks were an inferior race. DuBois analyzed the sophisticated social structure of black communities, first in Philadelphia and later in many other places.

DuBois's concern for his race did not stop at the borders of the United States—he was also active in the *Pan African* movement, which was concerned with the rights of all African descendants, no matter where they lived. While documenting the experience and contributions of African people throughout the world, DuBois died in the African country of Ghana, at the age of ninety-five.

Section 2 Assessment

1. Define the term *positivism*.
2. Name and explain the theory of social change proposed by Herbert Spencer.
3. Give an example to illustrate Emile Durkheim's idea of organic solidarity.

Critical Thinking

4. **Evaluating Information** Max Weber introduced the concept of *verstehen*. How would you use this approach to social research if you wanted to investigate the importance of money to your peers? Explain.

Pulling it All Together

This section looked at the giants who laid the foundation for the discipline of sociology. In subsequent chapters students will see how these contributions are utilized to heighten our understanding of the social forces that affect human behavior. (They will be returning most frequently to Max Weber, Emile Durkheim, and Karl Marx.) If students are looking for extra credit projects, a report with a class presentation on any one of the key sociologists would be a good suggestion.

Answers to Section 2 Assessment

1. Positivism is the use of scientific observation and experimentation in the study of social behavior. Sociology, according to Comte, should be a science based on empirical or observable knowledge that can be measured.
2. Herbert's theory of social change, called Social Darwinism, was based on Darwin's theory of evolution. Herbert thought evolutionary social change would ultimately lead to progress if people did not interfere. His ideas were later discredited by key sociologists and others.
3. Answers will vary.

Critical Thinking

4. Answers should be based on student understanding of *verstehen*—understanding the social behaviors of others by putting yourself mentally in their place. This is also known as "perspective taking."

Interdisciplinary Activity

Biography W.E.B. DuBois, born during Reconstruction, was the founder of the NAACP and wrote the first sociological study of American blacks, *The Philadelphia Negro* in 1899. In this work, DuBois explored the reasons blacks migrated to Philadelphia, as opposed to other cities. His research revealed that job opportunities were available there that did not exist elsewhere and consequently, blacks encountered less racial discrimination than in other cities. Students might be interested to know that DuBois died at age 95 on Aug. 28, 1963, the same day that Martin Luther King Jr. delivered his famous "I Have a Dream" speech in Washington D.C. Assign a student or group of students the task of researching some aspect of this remarkable person and presenting their findings to the class in the form of an oral report, a skit, or a display. **L1**

Section 3

Theoretical Perspectives

Key Terms

- theoretical perspective
- functionalism
- manifest functions
- latent functions
- dysfunction
- conflict perspective
- power
- symbol
- symbolic interactionism
- dramaturgy

The Role of Theoretical Perspectives

Perception is the way the brain interprets an image or event. Similarly, perspective is the way you interpret the *meaning* of an image or event. Your perspective is influenced by beliefs or values you hold. It draws your attention to some things and blinds you to others. This is demonstrated in two drawings psychologists often use to illustrate the concept of perception. (See Figure 1.1.) If you stare at the old woman long enough, she becomes a beautiful young woman with a feather boa around her neck. If you stare at Figure 1.1b, it alternates between two facing profiles and a vase. You cannot, however, see the old woman and the young woman or the faces and the vase at the same time.

Which image is real depends on your focus—your perspective influences what you see. One perspective emphasizes certain aspects of an event, while another perspective accents different aspects of the same event. When a perspective highlights certain parts of something, it must place other parts in the background.

What is a theoretical perspective? A **theoretical perspective** is a set of assumptions about an area of study—in this case, about the workings

a. b.

Fig. 1.1 *These two famous images are used by psychologists to illustrate perception and perspective. What did you see first in Figure 1.1a—an old woman or a beautiful young lady? What did you see first in Figure 1.1b—a vase or two human faces?*

Section Preview

Sociology includes three major theoretical perspectives. Functionalism views society as an integrated whole. Conflict theory looks at class, race, and gender struggles. Symbolic interactionism examines how group members use shared symbols as they interact.

theoretical perspective a set of assumptions accepted as true

Using the Section Preview

One of the greatest challenges for many teachers is to help students understand these three perspectives. *Functionalism* can be simply explained as a viewpoint that emphasizes the smooth functioning of society. *Conflict theory* looks at the problems caused by groups who oppose each other. *Symbolic interactionism* looks at the interactions based on shared symbols. Understandings of these three perspectives are explored throughout the text as social phenomena are discussed. Explain to students that sociologists use three major perspectives. The functionalist and conflict perspectives take a "macro" approach, examining whole societies, large scale social structures, and social systems. The symbolic interactionist perspective takes a "micro" approach, focusing on small groups.

Using the Illustration

These classic images appear often in psychology texts to help illustrate the concept of perception. Perception and perspective are closely related. You might make an analogy for students who have taken psychology, that perception is to psychology as perspective is to sociology.

Using Problem-Solving Skills

To help students begin to gain an appreciation and understanding of these different perspectives, ask students to identify any problem or condition in their own lives and decide which of the perspectives they believe would be most helpful in analyzing the situation. For example, if they find they seem to have too many demands on their time, they might look at the symbolic interactionist approach and wonder if they were trying to please too many people by filling too many roles. Or they might think that looking at the need to balance the social, educational, and economic needs is better explained by the functionalist approach. After they have decided upon an approach, have each student share his or her response with a classmate and see if the classmate agrees with the assessment.
L2

World View

A World Turned Upside Down

Without turning this book upside down, try to locate the United States. If you find this view of the world disorienting because you are used to conventional maps, you may reject this new worldview. So it is with any perspective. In this book you will be asked to abandon the conventional or psychological perspective in favor of the sociological perspective.

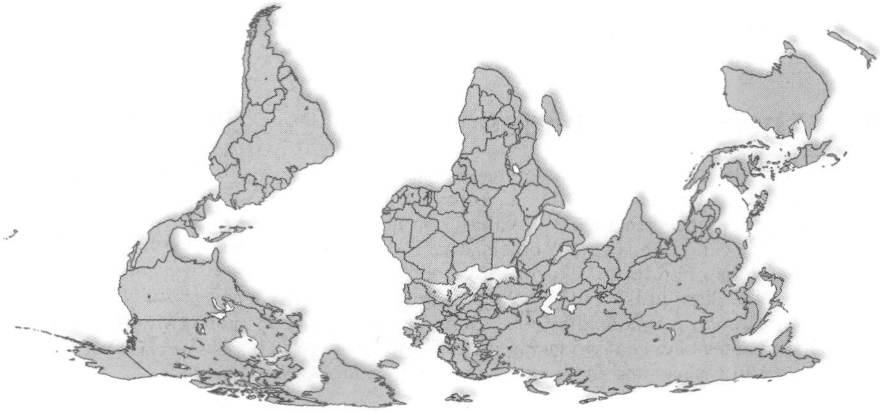

Interpreting the Map

1. What does your reaction to this map tell you about the power of the perspective you bring to a situation?
2. Look at world maps in your various social studies classes as you progress through the day. Where are North America and Europe located on these maps? What does that tell you about the perspective of these map publishers and their customers?

of society. A theoretical perspective is viewed as true by its supporters and it helps them organize their research.

Competing, even conflicting, theories in science usually exist at the same time. Perhaps not enough evidence exists to determine which theory is accurate, or different theories may explain different aspects of the problem. This is even true in the so-called "hard" sciences like modern physics. Einstein's theory of general relativity, for example, contradicts the widely accepted Big Bang theory of the origin of the physical universe. Einstein himself never accepted the quantum theory. Nonetheless, this theory has become the foundation of modern developments in such fields as chemistry and molecular biology (Hawking, 1998). Today theories are being put forth that hold promise for combining relativity and quantum theory. If theories still compete in physics, it should not be surprising that several major theoretical perspectives exist in sociology.

World View

It will be hard for some students to resist turning the book upside down to locate the United States or any other countries you might ask them to look for. You may want to tell students that there is no geographic or scientific reason for why north shows up at the top of maps—only conventionality. The first maps of the known world put the Mediterranean Sea in the center and were rectangular to honor the biblical reference to the four corners of the Earth. In medieval times, map makers placed Jerusalem in the center of the world—early Christianity was more concerned with "the perfection of God's work than with physical reality." Ask students if they can suggest why maps in the Arab countries were drawn with East at the top. (This was to honor the birthplace of the prophet Mohammed.) If your school has not bought pull-down maps for some time, you may be able to find world maps that put the United States and Europe in the center, splitting Asia into two that were on the outer edges, an outdated Eurocentric approach. Today, more world maps show the Western Hemisphere at the far left and the Eastern Hemisphere at the far right. This study of maps is very useful for explaining the importance and the subtleties of how cultural perspectives create "knowledge."

See page 25 for Answers to Interpreting the Map.

Demonstration

To help students better understand the concepts of the functionalist, conflict, and interactionist perspectives, play the Chairs Game. You will need music and chairs for this version of the child's game, Musical Chairs. First, introduce the activity by telling students that you are going to play the familiar game, musical chairs. (Remember to remove a chair after each round.) After the first few rounds, tell students that anyone left without a place to sit at the end of future rounds may share a chair with someone. (This relaxing of the typical rules of the game will emphasize cooperation instead of the usual competition, but don't verbalize this, yet.) Sharing chairs is going to get interesting as the rounds continue. It is probably not advisable to let students sit on laps, so have them problem solve what to do. Someone will probably suggest that

Sociology has three overarching theoretical perspectives: *functionalism, conflict theory,* and *symbolic interactionism*. Each of these perspectives provides a different slant on human social behavior. The exclusive use of any one of them prevents our seeing other aspects of social behavior, just as one cannot see the old woman and the young woman at the same time. All three perspectives together, however, allow us to see most of the important dimensions of human social behavior.

Functionalism

Functionalism emphasizes the contributions (functions) of each part of a society. For example, family, economy, and religion are "parts" of a society. The family contributes to society by providing for the reproduction and care of its new members. The economy contributes by dealing with production, distribution, and consumption of goods and services. Religion contributes by emphasizing beliefs and practices related to sacred things.

functionalism
approach that emphasizes the contributions made by each part of society

How does functionalism explain social change? Functionalists see the parts of a society as an integrated whole. A change in one part of a society leads to changes in other parts. A major change in the economy, for example, may change the family—which is precisely what happened as a result of the Industrial Revolution. Before the Industrial Revolution, when most people made their living by farming, a large farm labor force was needed. Families fulfilled this need by having many children. The need disappeared as industrialization proceeded, and smaller families became the norm.

Functionalism assumes that societies tend to return to a state of stability after some upheaval has occurred. A society may change over time, but functionalists believe that it will return to a stable state. It will do this by changing in such a way that society will be similar to what it was before. Student unrest on college and university campuses during the late 1960s illustrates this. The activities of student protesters created some changes:

- The American public no longer accepts involvement in all wars as legitimate.
- Schools and universities are now more responsive to students' needs and goals.
- The public is more aware of the importance of environmental protection.

These changes, however, have not revolutionized American society. They have been absorbed into it. As a result, our society is only somewhat different from the way it was before the student unrest. In fact, most of the student radicals are now part of the middle-class society they once rejected.

Because of social and economic changes, norms that dictate women's roles have changed greatly over the years. Functionalists study how a change in one part of a society affects other parts.

Answers to Interpreting the Map

1. Students might say that having to look at the map upside down caused them a moment or two of discomfort, maybe even stress. Changing one's perspective can be a slow process, as witnessed by how long it took Americans to begin to change their perspectives on issues related to race and gender.
2. If maps were not standardized, our perspective would constantly be subject to one's whims. Luckily map makers have developed sophisticated methods to guarantee that we always use and see maps the same way.

Using the Illustration

Many students are familiar with old television programs that portrayed men as the breadwinner and women in the traditional homemaker role. Interestingly, although the women in these shows were supposed to be subservient to the husbands, it was almost always the father/husband figure who was the one who showed poor judgement and caused the problem that was resolved by the wife. Tell students that they can look forward to examining gender relationships in a later chapter.

students without chairs could sit on the floor. Ask the class how they think this game is representative of the functionalist and conflict perspectives. When resources (chairs) become limited, cooperation becomes necessary (functionalist). In the first round, as resources (chairs) became limited, competition developed—the conflict perspective. Students sitting on the floor eliminated the need for competition or conflict and the cooperation made the situation functional for everyone. You can also ask students how this exercise exemplifies manifest and latent functions. What is the intended function of musical chairs? What is the latent function? Students will probably respond with phrases such as to have fun, to win, to have something to do, or to compete.
L2

Reteaching

To help students understand manifest and latent functions, ask students why their parents think they are going to school. *(Answers may include: to learn, to get a good job, to become good citizens.)* Then ask students why they go to school *(to get a boyfriend, girlfriend, to have fun, to socialize).* **ELL**

Teaching Strategy

To see if students understand the concept of manifest and latent functions, as well as the major perspectives, refer them back to the Focus on Research for this chapter (pages 20–21) and ask the following questions:

- What are the manifest functions of college?
- What are the latent functions?
- From a conflict perspective, how is the McDonaldization of higher education problematic?
- How would the interactionist perspective view this new process?

(The obvious manifest function of education is to get a job related to a person's field of study. There seems to be a shift from learning for the sake of knowledge to learning to perform in a chosen career. Conflict theory would view college as a resource that elitists would control so would probably not approve of the trend toward McDonalidization. From the interactionist perspective, McDonaldization will create less social interaction, and symbolically the interaction will be with inanimate objects, like a satellite or the Internet.)

Do all functions have a positive effect? Most aspects of a society exist to promote a society's survival and welfare. It is for this reason that all complex societies have economies, families, governments, and religions. If these elements did not contribute to a society's well-being and survival, they would disappear.

Recall that a function is a contribution made by some part of a society. According to Robert Merton (1996), there are two kinds of functions. **Manifest functions** are intended and recognized. **Latent functions** are unintended and unrecognized. One of the manifest functions of school, for example, is to teach math skills. A latent (and positive) function of schools is the development of close friendships.

manifest functions intended and recognized consequences of an aspect of society

latent functions unintended and unrecognized consequences of an aspect of society

dysfunction negative consequence of an aspect of society

Not all elements of a society make a positive contribution. Elements that have negative consequences result in **dysfunction.** Dysfunctions of bureaucracies, for example, include rigidity, inefficiency, and impersonality. When you go to the division of motor vehicles to register your car or get your driver's license, the clerk may treat you like a "number" rather than as an individual. You don't like his bureaucratic inflexibility and impersonality.

How does functionalism view values? Finally, according to functionalism, there is a consensus on values. Most Americans, for example, agree on the desirability of democracy, success, and equal opportunity. This consensus of values, say the functionalists, accounts for the high degree of cooperation found in any society.

How does this photo emphasize the approach to studying society that is taken by the conflict perspective?

Figure 1.2 Focus on Theoretical Perspectives

Assumptions of the Major Theoretical Perspectives. This table compares the most important assumptions of the functionalist, conflict, and symbolic interactionist perspectives. Do you believe, as the functionalists do, that society is relatively well integrated? Or do you support the conflict theorists' assumption that society experiences conflict on all levels?

Functionalism

1. A society is a relatively integrated whole.
2. A society tends to seek relative stability.
3. Most aspects of a society contribute to the society's well-being and survival.
4. A society rests on the consensus of its members.

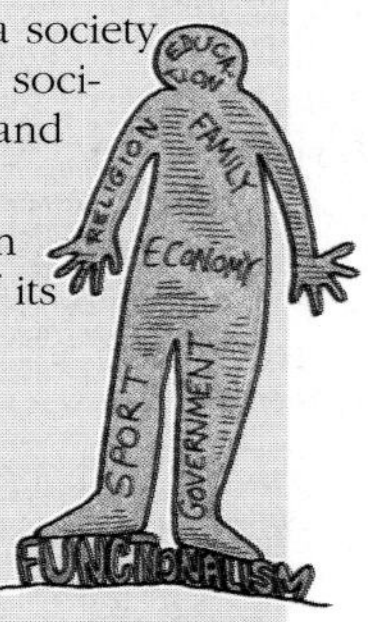

Conflict Perspective

1. A society experiences inconsistency and conflict everywhere.
2. A society is continually subjected to change.
3. A society involves the constraint and coercion of some members by others.

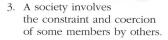

Symbolic Interactionism

1. People's interpretations of symbols are based on the meanings they learn from others.
2. People base their interaction on their interpretations of symbols.
3. Symbols permit people to have internal conversations. Thus, they can gear their interaction to the behavior that they think others expect of them and the behavior they expect of others.

Conflict Perspective

The **conflict perspective** emphasizes conflict, competition, change, and constraint within a society (Giddens, 1987, 1997). Understanding the conflict perspective is easier when you understand functionalism, because the assumptions behind these two perspectives are the reverse of each other. This is shown in Figure 1.2 above.

conflict perspective approach emphasizing the role of conflict, competition, and constraint within a society

What is the role of conflict and constraint? Functionalists see a basic agreement on values within a society. This leads them to emphasize the ways people cooperate to reach common goals. The conflict perspective, in contrast, focuses on the disagreements among various groups in a society or between societies. Groups and societies compete as they attempt to preserve and promote their own special values and interests.

Supporters of the conflict perspective, then, see social living as a contest. Their central question is "Who gets what?" It is those with the most **power**—the ability to control the behavior of others—who get the largest share of

power the ability to control the behavior of others

Working with the Data

Figure 1.2 Every chapter in the text includes a table like this one that compares approaches to a social issue taken by the three major theoretical perspectives. The purpose of the tables is to help students remember the assumptions of each perspective. As always, remind students that no one perspective can explain adequately all social relationships. Some perspectives just seem to have a better "take" than others.

Integrating the Teacher Resources

Look for the Chapter 1 Analyzing and Interpreting Data worksheet in the Unit 1 Mastering Basic Concepts **booklet in your Teacher's Resource Box. It provides skill-building exercises based on the graphs, charts, and maps in this chapter.**

Using Problem-Solving Skills

Another way to help students to better understand the concept of conflict perspective, is to lay down two strips of masking tape several feet apart. Have students stand in front of the room on opposite sides of the strips, facing a partner of their choice. Ask students to persuade their partners, without speaking, to come across to their side. Tell them that one person in each pair will be a winner. Some students may resort to force to get their partners to move. After allowing five minutes or so for the activity, ask students if any of them can come up with a way to accomplish the same thing without exerting physical power. Students may suggest compromising or trading places. Explain that the conflict perspective emphasizes competition and the use of power over one group by another. Students will see that when one group feels powerless in relation to another, conflict exists. **L1**

Tech Trends: Sociology Looks at the Internet

The number of Americans paying for an on-line Internet service is skyrocketing. The Internet began as a way for military and scientific users to share information after a nuclear war. ARPAnet (the Internet's forerunner) was formed in 1969 with only four connected computers. By 2000, an estimated 55 percent of Americans had access to the Internet. According to some estimates, there will be more than 500 million users worldwide by the year 2003.

Because of its rapid spread through American society, cyberspace technology is a timely example for showcasing the usefulness of the three theoretical perspectives. The viewpoints of functionalism, conflict theory, and symbolic interactionism contribute to an understanding of the social implications of this new technology in very different ways.

Functionalism. Functionalists see cyberspace technology as having both positive and negative consequences. On the one hand, computer links bring advantages. Parents can work at home and spend more time with their children. Individuals with disabilities can do jobs at home that would be denied them otherwise, thus becoming more fully integrated into society. On the other hand, there are dysfunctions. Young people may have easy access to pornographic material, which can distort their view of the opposite sex. Hate groups can be formed by strangers who live hundreds or thousands of miles apart. Their anonymity may encourage them to engage in antisocial or violent behavior that they would otherwise avoid.

Conflict Theory. The Internet is clearly changing American society. The Internet, conflict theorists point out, is contributing to the increasing speed of technological change. An advocate of conflict theory might investigate the social instability created by this rapid change. Workers may be let go by corporations in increasing numbers as more tasks are performed by computers.

Conflict theory could guide an investigation comparing the numbers of computers used in school districts of varying socioeconomic levels. Computer literacy is becoming an essential skill for obtaining a well-paying job. Thus, students who attend wealthy schools with

whatever is considered valuable in a society. Those with the most power have the most wealth, prestige, and privileges. Because some groups have more power than others, they are able to constrain, or limit, the less powerful.

How does the conflict perspective explain social change? Many conflicting groups exist in a society. As the balance of power among these groups shifts, change occurs. For example, the women's movement is attempting to change the balance of power between men and women. As this movement progresses, we see larger numbers of women in occupations once limited to men. More women are either making or influencing decisions in business, politics, medicine, and law. Gender relations are changing in other ways as well. More women are choosing to remain single, to marry later in life, to have fewer children, and to divide household tasks with their husbands. According to the conflict perspective, these changes are the result of increasing power among women.

Tech Trends

The overriding importance of technological developments to American and global societies in this century is obvious even to students lacking background in the social sciences. Because students are almost always interested in new technology, this feature is in every chapter. It will examine some aspect of technological developments in many fields that directly impact social research and developments, including biology, the media, and communications.

To apply this feature, you might ask students to generate a list, "How the Internet and Computers Have Affected My Life." Some student lists will be entirely positive, emphasizing how they love the technology and can't imagine life without it. Some may have formed e-mail groups and interact with people they would never have met otherwise. Others will write lists that reflect their dislike for the technology and that they want nothing to do with it. As students generate these lists, have them categorize them into the functionalist, conflict, or interactionist perspectives.

Careers in Sociology

Now that students are a little familiar with what sociology is, ask them to work in groups to brainstorm answers to the following question:

What career benefits are to be gained from studying sociology? (More answers to this question can be found in the Careers box on page 19.)

A complete answer might include: jobs require workers to have social skills, and to relate well to people—customers, co-workers, and superiors. Sociology provides a strong base in behavioral science, to understand why and how people behave as they do. Following is a partial list of skills to be gained from the study of sociology that will serve you well no matter what your ultimate career choice.

- Ability to read, write, and speak articulately, analytically, and effectively
- Proficiency in interpersonal communication

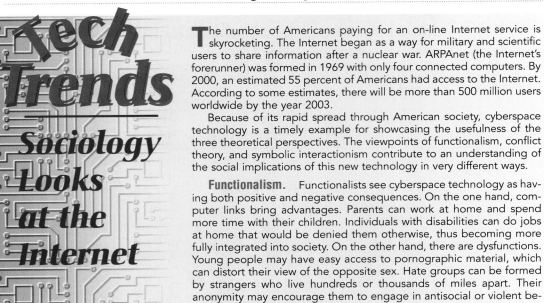

access to computers have an advantage over students in poorer schools.

Symbolic Interactionism. Symbolic interactionists are interested in how the Internet can affect a child's social development. The popularity of cartoon characters on television is reinforced by web pages that allow children to join fan clubs, interact with other fans, and view video clips of their favorite cartoon characters whenever they want. The popular cartoons *The Simpsons* and *South Park* feature children behaving in ways unacceptable in nearly all American homes. Television provides limited exposure to these characters, but the Internet allows them to become an important part of a child's daily life. What children come to accept as desirable behavior is being based increasingly on their interpretations of the symbols and behaviors represented by these characters. Symbolic interactionists might conclude that to the extent this occurs, the Internet lessens adult influence on children.

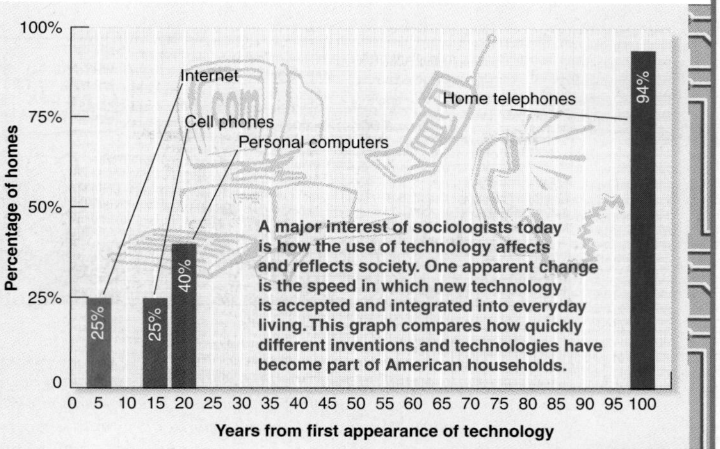

A major interest of sociologists today is how the use of technology affects and reflects society. One apparent change is the speed in which new technology is accepted and integrated into everyday living. This graph compares how quickly different inventions and technologies have become part of American households.

Analyzing the Trends

1. Which perspective would you choose to conduct an in-depth study of the Internet's effect on society? Explain why you chose this perspective.
2. Do you think that the Internet has some dysfunctions that Americans should consider? Consider the advantages and disadvantages of the Internet on society.

Which perspective is better? There is no "better" theoretical perspective. Each perspective highlights certain areas of social life. The advantages of one perspective are the disadvantages of the other. Functionalism explains much of the consensus, stability, and cooperation within a society. The conflict perspective explains much of the constraint, conflict, and change. Each chapter, throughout the text, will illustrate both perspectives, as well as the perspective discussed next—*symbolic interactionism.*

Symbolic Interactionism

Both functionalism and conflict theory deal with large social units, such as the economy, and broad social processes, such as conflict among social classes. At the close of the nineteenth century, some sociologists began to

Answers to Analyzing the Trends

1. You may want students to answer these individually, or you might turn this into a group activity. Separate students into three teams and ask them to prepare to debate the merits of their assigned perspective. Afterwards, so that students begin to consider other perspectives besides their own, ask them to verbalize one of the other perspectives. For example, if a student feels strongly that computers create more harm than benefits for society, have him or her say why a computer might improve the quality of life.
2. Some dysfunctions students might mention could include (1) our reliance on the Internet (if a computer crashes, everything could shut down); and that (2) some people seem to interact with a computer more than their own family members. The day may come when each room will have a computer and family members will send e-mails to one another at home.

- Effective interaction with people of different backgrounds in various situations
- Developing team work skills among work group members
- Ability to work well under pressure
- Ability to maintain composure in stressful situations
- Ability to conduct and clearly explain sociological research
- Ability to analyze relationships between factors
- Ability to clearly conceptualize problems
- Competence in setting goals/objectives
- Ability to use various problem solving techniques (how to achieve goals)
- Ability to plan organizational projects
- Designing new projects/programs

L1

More About . . . Symbols

To further explain the meanings of objects as symbols, tell students about Durkheim's descriptions of the sacred and the profane. (This subject will be introduced in Chapter 14 on religion, but it won't hurt to give them a preview.) A simple object, like a flag, is profane, but when it represents a nation, it takes on great meaning and becomes sacred. Humans will perform great rituals in front of a sacred object. Students, for example, might parade around the school mascot because it has become "sacred." The object by itself had no meaning; people gave it meaning.

Reteaching

To represent the symbolic interactionist perspective, take the American flag off your classroom wall if you can, or borrow one. Ask the students what the flag means to them. Students will say, it represents freedom, it's a symbol of our country, or Americans died for it; some students will say it's nothing, it's just a flag, just a piece of cloth on a stick. Similarly, ask students about the meaning the school mascot has for them. Some students will say it gets them excited at a game to see it and it encourages them to wear their school colors with pride. Others will say it means nothing to them. This illustrates how some people attach deep meaning to some symbols, while others do not.

According to conflict theory, the interests of groups will clash at times. If questioned, the men around the water cooler may offer a functionalist interpretation of their pastime—talking sports brings them together. Women who are not "sports savvy" may see their exclusion from such office talk more from a conflict perspective.

change their approach to the study of society. Instead of concentrating on large social structures, they began to recognize the importance of the ways people interact. Two sociologists, Charles Horton Cooley and George Herbert Mead, developed the insight that groups exist only because their members influence each other's behavior. These early American sociologists, in short, created symbolic interactionism, a perspective that focuses on the actual *interaction* among people.

symbol
anything that stands for something else and has an agreed upon meaning attached to it

What is the significance of symbols in symbolic interactionism? To understand social interactionism, we need to talk first about symbols. A **symbol** is something chosen to represent something else. It may be an object, a word, a gesture, a facial expression, a sound. A symbol is something observable that often represents something not observable, something that is abstract. For example, your school's team mascot is often used as a symbol of school loyalty. The American flag is used as a symbol of the United States.

The meaning of a symbol is not determined by its own physical characteristics. Those who create and use the symbols assign the meanings to them. If people in a group do not share the same meanings for a given symbol, confusion results. For example, if some people interpreted the red light of a traffic signal to mean go, while others interpreted it to mean stop, chaos would result.

symbolic interactionism
approach that focuses on the interactions among people based on mutually understood symbols

The importance of shared symbols is reflected in the formal definition of **symbolic interactionism.** It is the theoretical perspective that focuses on interaction among people—interaction based on mutually understood symbols.

What are the basic assumptions of symbolic interactionism? Herbert Blumer (1969a, 1969b), who coined the term *symbolic interactionism,* outlined three assumptions central to this perspective. (Refer to Figure 1.2 on page 27.)

First, according to symbolic interactionism, we learn the meaning of a symbol from the way we see others reacting to it. For example, American musicians in Latin America soon learn that when audience members whistle at the end of a performance, they are expressing disapproval. In other words, their whistling is a symbol of disapproval, as booing is in the United States.

Demonstration

With the help of your students, rename ten objects in your classroom. For example, call the chalkboard a detention room and identify chalk with the word *mascot.* (Or, assign nonsense words to these objects.) Have everyone use these new words for about one-half the class period to illustrate that words are just symbols for objects. We have to learn which words represent particular objects. Ask students to imagine how they would feel if they didn't know the language, or had never learned the correct symbols. Students will understand that when they were socialized as children and learned what their noses and ears were, they were actually learning the correct symbols so they could function in their culture. (Socialization is discussed in Chapter 4.) **L1**

Second, once we learn the meanings of symbols, we base our behavior (interaction) on them. Now that the musicians have learned that whistling symbolizes a negative response, they will definitely avoid an encore if the crowd begins whistling. (They would likely have the opposite response in the United States, where the symbol of whistling has a very different meaning.)

Finally, we use the meanings of symbols to imagine how others will respond to our behavior. Through this capability, we can have "internal conversations" with ourselves. These conversations enable us to visualize how others will respond to us *before* we act. This is crucial because we guide our interactions with people according to the behavior we think others expect of us and we expect of others. Meanwhile, these others are also having internal conversations. The interaction (acting on each other) that follows is therefore *symbolic* interaction.

In an attempt to better understand human interaction, Erving Goffman introduced **dramaturgy,** which depicts human interaction as theatrical performance (Goffman, 1961a, 1963, 1974, 1979, 1983; Lemert and Branaman, 1997). Like actors on a stage, people present themselves through dress, gestures, tone of voice. Teenagers sometimes act in a particular way in order to attract the attention of someone they want to like them. Goffman calls this *presentation of self* or *impression management*.

dramaturgy
approach that depicts human interaction as theatrical performances

According to symbolic interactionism, social life can be likened to a theatrical performance. Don't we convey as much about ourselves in the way we dress as do the actors above?

Section 3 Assessment

1. What is a theoretical perspective?
2. Indicate whether the following statements represent functionalism (F), the conflict perspective (C), or symbolic interactionism (S).
   a. Societies are in relative balance.
   b. Power is one of the most important elements in social life.
   c. Religion helps hold a society together morally.
   d. Symbols are crucial to social life.
   e. Many elements of a society exist to benefit the powerful.
   f. Different segments of a society compete to achieve their own self-interest rather than cooperate to benefit others.
   g. Social life should be understood from the viewpoint of the individuals involved.
   h. Social change is constantly occurring.
   i. Conflict is harmful and disruptive to society.
3. Does dramaturgy explain human interaction in a way that is meaningful to you? Why or why not?

Critical Thinking

4. **Analyzing Information** Think of an aspect of human social behavior (for example, dating or team sports) that you would like to know more about. Which of the three theoretical perspectives would you use to help you understand this aspect of behavior? Explain your choice.

> "A person gets from a symbol the meaning he puts into it, and what is one man's comfort and inspiration is another's jest and scorn."
>
> **William Shakespeare**
> **English playwright**

Pulling It All Together

The three sociological perspectives, functionalist, conflict, and interactionist, are essential to understanding sociology. Sociologists have used these perspectives to interpret human society. The ability to do that is also part of the sociological imagination.

Answers to Section 3 Assessment

1. A theoretical perspective is a set of assumptions accepted as true by its advocates. Each of the three perspectives provides a different slant on human social behavior.
2. (Students may successfully argue that there is more than one answer for a–i.)
   a. F
   b. C
   c. F
   d. S
   e. C
   f. C
   g. S
   h. C
   i. F

Cooperative Learning Activity

After students finish reading about the three perspectives, divide the class into three groups. Have one group write down all the elements of the functionalist perspective; have the second group do the same for the conflict perspective. Ask the third group for the symbolic interactionist perspective. When students have collected the information, have two students from each group go to another group and teach what they learned about their assigned perspectives. When everyone is done, have representatives from the three groups share what they were taught by the other groups. **L1**

ANSWERS CHAPTER 1 ASSESSMENT

Reviewing Vocabulary

1. j	6. e
2. h	7. b
3. g	8. f
4. i	9. a
5. c	10. d

Reviewing the Facts

1. The sociological imagination allows people to see relationships between events in their personal life and their society.
2. Sociology is the scientific study of social structure.
3. Herbert Spencer believed that social change would lead to progress provided that people did not interfere.
4. The three sociological perspectives are: Functionalism—emphasizes the contribution of each part of society. Conflict Perspective—emphasizes conflict, competition, change as constraints within a society Symbolic Interaction—emphasizes the interaction among people based on mutually understood symbols.
5. Manifest functions are intended and recognized contributions made by some part of a society. Latent functions are unintended and unrecognized contributions.

CHAPTER 1 ASSESSMENT

Summary

Section 1: The Sociological Perspective

Main Idea: Sociology studies human social behavior. It assumes a group, rather than an individual perspective. Sociologists look for the patterns in social relationships. Individuals can benefit by using their sociological imaginations to look at events in their personal lives.

Section 2: The Origins of Sociology

Main Idea: Sociology is a young science. It started with the writings of European scholars like Auguste Comte, Harriet Martineau, Herbert Spencer, Karl Marx, Emile Durkheim, and Max Weber. Jane Addams and W.E.B. DuBois helped to focus America's attention on social issues. After World War II, America took the lead in developing the field of sociology.

Section 3: Theoretical Perspectives

Main Idea: Sociology includes three major theoretical perspectives. Functionalism views society as an integrated whole. Conflict theory looks at class, race, and gender struggles. Symbolic interactionism examines how group members use shared symbols as they interact.

SOCIOLOGY Online

Self-Check Quiz
Visit the *Sociology and You* Web site at soc.glencoe.com and click on **Chapter 1—Self-Check Quizzes** to prepare for the chapter test.

Reviewing Vocabulary

Complete each sentence using each term once.

a. mechanical solidarity
b. positivism
c. social structure
d. bourgeoisie
e. sociology
f. symbol
g. latent function
h. conflict perspective
i. presentation of self
j. theoretical perspective

1. ______________ is a set of assumptions accepted as true by supporters.
2. The perspective that emphasizes conflict is called ______________.
3. ______________ is an unintended and unrecognized consequence of some element of a society.
4. ______________ is the way that people attempt to make a favorable impression of themselves in the minds of others.
5. The patterned interaction of people in social relationships is called ______________.
6. ______________ is the study of social structure from a scientific perspective.
7. The use of observation, experimentation and other methods to study social life is known as ______________.
8. A ______________ is something that stands for or represents something else.
9. ______________ is social unity based on a consensus of values and norms, strong social pressure to conform and a dependence on family and tradition.
10. The ______________ are members of an industrial society who own the means for producing wealth.

Reviewing the Facts

1. According to C. Wright Mills, what is the sociological imagination?
2. Explain "sociology" as defined in this chapter.

6.

Sociologist	Major Idea	Brief Explanation
Karl Marx	Class Conflict	Struggle between bourgeoisie class (owners) and the proletariat class (workers)
Max Weber	Verstehen	Understanding social behavior by mentally putting yourself in the place of others
Auguste Comte	Positivism	Belief that sociology should be based on knowledge of which we can be "positive" or sure.
Emile Durkheim	mechanical solidarity organic solidarity	Societies exist because of broad consensus among members of a society.

3. What did Herbert Spencer belief about the relationship between people, progress and social change.
4. List and explain the three sociological perspectives.
5. What are manifest functions and latent functions? Provide an example of each.
6. Using the chart below, give a major idea expressed by each of the sociologists listed. Briefly explain each idea. The first one has been completed. Use this as your model and complete the chart.

Sociologist	Major Idea	Brief Explanation
Karl Marx	class conflict	Struggle between bourgeoisie class (owners) and the proletariat class (workers)
Max Weber		
Auguste Comte		
Emile Durkheim		

Thinking Critically

1. **Applying Concepts** Give three examples of how the sociological perspective can be applied to your life.
2. **Analyzing Information** Using your own words, define the term sociology imagination. What is the relationship to the sociological perspective?
3. **Making Inferences** Select two early sociologists discussed in your text and construct a dialogue between them about the current social issue of homelessness.
4. **Summarizing Information** You have been selected to be on a panel to discuss illiteracy in your community. The panel also includes an economist, a psychologist, and an anthropologist. As a sociologist, what areas of this topic would be of most interest to you? Consider what aspects would be of interest to each of the other panel members. Complete the chart below to summarize the aspects of interest to you and the other panel members.

Panel Member	Aspects of Interest
Sociologist (you)	
Economist	
Psychologist	
Anthropologist	

5. **Making Comparisons** Both a sociologist and a psychologist would be interested in the ACT (achievement) and SAT (assessment) test scores of high school students. Consider how the scientific interest of the sociologist would differ from that of the psychologist. Compare the similarities and contrast the differences.
6. **Categorizing Information** Merton's theory of manifest and latent functions (see page 26) could be easily applied to high schools. Using your particular school as a model, identify three manifest functions of high schools and three latent functions of high schools.
7. **Evaluating Information** You must select one of the job opportunities in sociology listed on page 12 for your career. Which one would you choose? Suggest ways in which the job fits your personality, abilities, interests, and ambitions.
8. **Analyzing Information** Spitting in public is not an appropriate behavior, but people "spit" all the time. When we drink soda we usually leave a little spit in the can. When we kiss someone, we are transmitting spit. We don't think of it in these terms, because in some cases we call spit by a more scientific term—saliva. How would the sociologist perspective help to understand and explain why we flip back and forth between the two terms?

Sociology Projects

1. **Theoretical Perspectives** Based on what you read about the Internet from the functionalist, conflict, and symbolic interactionist perspectives, how is each perspective useful in understanding the popularity of the Internet? Write a brief statement describing how each perspective would approach this issue. You might see

Thinking Critically

1. Answers will vary.
2. Answers will vary
3. Students may need some information about homelessness from a sociological perspective. You might provide them with the following information: (a) less than 6% of all homeless people are that way by choice; (b) many homeless people are among the working poor; (c) most homeless people are not mentally ill or heavy drug users; (d) one out of four homeless people is a child.
4. Answers will vary
5. Again, students should approach this question from the perspective that the psychologist would focus on individual consequences and the sociologist on the group or societal implications.
6. In general students should understand that the manifest function of school is basically to educate in preparation for the job market. The latent functions include fun, social interactions, sports and some activities not necessarily sanctioned by the school.
7. Answers will vary.
8. Suggest to students that kissing and spitting are not really physiologically that different. The transmission of saliva is still evident. Students seem to love this extreme example and of course will argue. That is the point, our perception of something is based on the words that we choose for it, and how society defines it.

Sociology Projects

1. Students should use the Tech Trends article to argue their point from one of the three perspectives. You might want to ask students as they pose their arguments, how important computers are in their personal lives. A personal attachment to something can have a great influence on a person's perspective toward that article or issue.

Chapter 1 Assessment

positive or negative effects, depending upon your interpretation. (For instance, the conflict perspective may focus on the fact that the underprivileged classes would not have full access because of the cost of the hardware and therefore decreased power.)

2. **Developing a Commercial** Develop a commercial for sociology using a video camera. Think of the field of sociology as a product to sell. Market it as "a way to improve your understanding of the world around you."
3. **Observations** Go to a public place (such as a mass, school cafeteria, or restaurant) and discreetly observe people there for 15 minutes. It is important that you do not appear to be spying on individuals, both because it may be interpreted as being rude and also because it would probably affect their normal behaviors. Write down your observations, noting such details as the type of dress, general interactions, and level of activity. Do not assume any value judgments about your subjects, just make factual observations.

   When you return home, rewrite your observations applying the sociological concepts in this chapter. Consider and list the ways your second analysis is different from the first? Compare and contrast them. How does sociology help to describe what you observed? What might you want to study from your observation?
4. **Sociology and Careers** Research one of the career options for sociology majors that interest you. Look for such important information as the education requirements, income expectations, and management opportunities. Write a short report on the advantages and disadvantages of that particular career in sociology.

Technology Activities

1. In this chapter, you learned about several of the founders of sociology and their contributions to the field. To learn more about these sociologists and others, go to the Dead Sociologists web page at http://raven.jmu.edu/~ridenelr/DSS. Select three sociologists named on the web site who were not included in the textbook and create a database including their year of birth, place of birth, and primary contributions they made to sociology.
2. Use the Internet to do further research on the pioneers of sociology. Design a poster representing the pioneers in sociology. Describe each one's basic ideas, including their theories and information attained through research. You may want to start your research at the Dead Sociologists web page listed above.
3. Write or use the Internet to contact the American Sociological Association and request the booklet "Majoring in Sociology." Using standard grammar, spelling, sentence structure, and punctuation prepare a report for your class from the information. (The address is American Sociological Association, 1722 N. Street NW, Washington, DC 20036. For Internet access, the URL is www.asanet.org.)

ANSWERS
Chapter 1 Assessment

2. Students could shoot "pretend research scenes" that would be of interest to sociologists, such as computer use by adolescent or teacher-student interactions. Encourage students to follow good marketing strategies. They could, for example, include positive reasons for studying sociology and some of the benefits to society from this field of study to "sell" sociology to an audience of high school students.
3. Before assigning this activity, you may want to explain to students that we observe behavior all the time; we are all budding sociologists. For the first observation, they should simply watch. But as they watch, advise them to think about the functionalist, conflict and interactionist perspective as well as the manifest and latent functions of that observation. How might one or all of the major theorists interpret their observations? (For example if they observed a teen at the mall dressed in Goth attire, might their behavior reflect the conflict perspective? Does their dress symbolize the interactions they have with their peers? Is the function of their dress to "make a statement" or are they just being themselves?) Remind them that this is practice in being good observers—one of the requirements of a research sociologist.
4. Students can refer to the Sociology Today feature on page 12 to check out the various web sites. You might also want to provide them with additional URLs listed in the careers boxes in this teacher's edition.

Technology Activities

1. You may want students to refer to the feature on pp. 47–48 in Chapter 2 about how to evaluate a good web site. This site has already been evaluated, however, and comes highly recommended.
2. If students do this activity, they might want to display the concepts with pictures. Display the posters around the class; they can become reference materials later.
3. These brochures are available from the American Sociological Association and are free. You can easily order a classroom set.

Chapter 1

Enrichment Reading

Invitation to Sociology by *Peter L. Berger*

The sociologist . . . is a person intensively, endlessly, shamelessly interested in the doings of men. His natural habitat is all the human gathering places of the world, wherever men come together. The sociologist may be interested in many other things. But his consuming interest remains in the world of men, their institutions, their history, their passions. And since he is interested in men, nothing that men do can be altogether tedious for him. He will naturally be interested in the events that engage men's ultimate beliefs, their moments of tragedy and grandeur and ecstasy. But he will also be fascinated by the commonplace, the everyday. He will know reverence, but this reverence will not prevent him from wanting to see and to understand. He may sometimes feel revulsion or contempt. But this also will not deter him from wanting to have his questions answered. The sociologist, in his quest for understanding, moves through the world of men without respect for the usual lines of **demarcation.** Nobility and **degradation,** power and obscurity, intelligence and folly—these are equally interesting to him, however unequal they may be in his personal values or tastes. Thus his questions may lead him to all possible levels of society, the best and the least known places, the most respected and the most despised. And, if he is a good sociologist, he will find himself in all these places because his own questions have so taken possession of him that he has little choice but to seek for answers. . . .

The sociologist moves in the common world of men, close to what most of them would call real. As a result, there is a deceptive simplicity and obviousness about some sociological investigations. One reads them, nods at the familiar scene, remarks that one has heard all this before and concludes that people have better things to do than to waste their time on truisms—until one is suddenly brought up against an insight that radically questions everything one had previously assumed about this familiar scene. This is the point at which one begins to sense the excitement of sociology.

It can be said that the first wisdom of sociology is this—things are not what they seem. This . . . is a deceptively simple statement. It ceases to be simple after a while. Social reality turns out to have many layers of meaning. The discovery of each new layer changes the perception of the whole.

People who feel no temptation before closed doors, who have no curiosity about human beings, who are content to admire scenery without wondering about the people who live in those houses on the other side of that river, should probably . . . stay away from sociology. And people whose interest is mainly in their own **conceptual constructions** will do just as well to turn to the study of little white mice. Sociology will be satisfying, in the long run, only to those who can think of nothing more entrancing than to watch men and to understand things human.

Source: Excerpted from *Invitation to Sociology*. New York: Doubleday & Company, Inc., 1963.

What Does it Mean?

conceptual construction
personal idea of reality

degradation
low esteem, corruption

demarcation
setting apart, separation

Read and React

How is this excerpt different in style from most articles by scientists? Why do you think the author chose this style to describe his field of study?

Enrichment Reading

Some of your female students might have difficulty with, or note the use of, sexist language used in this article. Many students will notice this article uses the male pronoun *he* and the word *men* to stand for human society. This is a great example of perspective because when this article was written people were not as sensitivie to gender issues as they are today. Point out to students that the source line indicates this article was written in 1963, almost forty years ago.

The point to emphasize here is that sociologists are observers of society, constantly looking, analyzing, and drawing conclusions. Sociologists are acutely aware that a theory thought to be valid today might not be embraced in the future. Sociology is constantly redefining itself as people and events change.

Students can begin understanding the discipline by observing people in all settings without making judgments on what they see. As they develop some sociological insights, students may begin to define what their observations might mean.

Answer to Read and React

This article was intended to appeal to people's emotions and affective processes, rather than the cognitive or scientific aspects. The author is trying to persuade, enlighten, and encourage, rather than make observations or describe.

Chapter Preview

Section 1 (pages 38–49)

When sociologists do quantitative research, they generally use either surveys or precollected data. Each has its own advantages and disadvantages. Field studies are best used when interaction needs to be observed in a natural setting, and when in-depth analysis is needed. The case study is the most popular approach to field research.

Section 2 (pages 50–57)

Causation in science is the idea that one event leads to another event. Scientists assume that all events have causes, or determinants. Sociologists work to discover these causes. Three standards must be met before causation can be proved.

Section 3 (pages 58–62)

The research process is made up of several distinct steps. These steps represent an ideal for scientific research. It is not always necessary or even possible that they always be strictly followed. Researchers have an ethical obligation to protect participants' privacy and to avoid deceiving or harming them. Preserving the rights of subjects is sometimes weighed against the value of the knowledge to be gained.

Please see the correlation to the American Sociology Association standards located in the front of this text.

CHAPTER 2

Sociologists Doing Research

Lead-Off Activity

One of the benefits of sociological research is that we have statistics to let us compare how things have changed over time. To help students become accustomed to dealing with statistics, ask them to predict how they think conditions have changed from the year 1900 to the year 2000 by completing these statements. *(Answers are given in italics following each statement.)* (1) _____ times as many adults are getting high school degrees. *Four.* (2) _____ percent of all American homes have telephones, electricity, and a flush toilet. *98 percent.* (3) Accidental deaths have decreased by _____. *61percent- in spite of car and plane travel.* (4) Wages in the manufacturing sector are _____times greater. *Four.* (5) Average household assets are ____ times greater. *Seven.* (6) The average work-

USING Your Sociological Imagination

Two headlines appear on the front page of two different papers in the newsstand. The first reads "Cure for Alzheimer's disease just around the corner." The second, while more accurate, is less exciting. It reads "Scientists cautiously declare that a promising—but as yet unduplicated—test result may lead to some small progress in the long-term effort to prevent Alzheimer's disease."

Which paper do you think would sell more copies? Like savvy news editors, you probably know that both fear and hope are emotions that sell papers. For this reason, research results, especially on social and health studies, are often exaggerated by the media.

We routinely read that tomato sauce can prevent prostate cancer, that tea prevents heart disease, and that eating blueberries can reduce the effects of aging and improve short-term memory. On the other hand, milk, eggs, anger, too-strict parenting, too-lax parenting, and marrying before age thirty have all been blamed for various deadly diseases and social disorders. To further complicate matters, stories often contradict each other from week to week. Caffeine, fish, milk, and butter are only some of the products that can heal or harm, depending on the date.

People who know what questions to ask about research reports can better protect themselves from acting on inaccurate information. Chapter 2 will look at some of the basic research methods used by sociologists and explore the area of ethics in social research.

Sections

1. **Research Methods**
2. **Causation in Science**
3. **Procedures and Ethics in Research**

Learning Objectives

After reading this chapter, you will be able to

- describe the basic quantitative and qualitative research methods used by sociologists.
- discuss basic research concepts, including variables and correlations.
- list the standards for proving cause-and-effect relationships.
- explain the steps sociologists use to guide their research.
- discuss ethics in sociological research.

SOCIOLOGY Online

Chapter Overview
Visit the *Sociology and You* Web site at soc.glencoe.com and click on **Chapter 2—Chapter Overviews** to preview chapter information.

USING Your Sociological Imagination

This feature highlights the tendency of the news media to exaggerate research findings to make them more newsworthy. Students might be able to identify with this tendency because all of us exaggerate sometimes for emphasis or to get more attention. Being able to think critically and analytically is essential for sociologists, however, since most events and processes being researched in this field have multiple causes. Ask students if they can remember any reports they heard on TV or read in the newspapers that turned out to be false, misleading, or just premature. Ask students what skills might be the most valuable in today's world of "information overkill."

week is _____percent shorter. *30 percent.* (7) The air we breathe is ____percent cleaner/dirtier. *97 percent cleaner.* (8) More than _____of Americans have at least one automotible, VCR, microwave oven, air conditioner, cable television, washer and dryer. *70 percent.* (You might ask students to get into groups and discuss the likely answers to these questions).

Based on this activity, students should realize that by almost every indicator of health, welfare, and safety, analysis shows that the United States has made great progress. (Statistics compiled by the Cato Institute in Washington, D.C.)
L1

Using the Section Preview

Most students have probably had exposure to a survey. Have students recall the surveys they have seen and answered. Ask students what they did and did not like about the surveys. Explain that designing effective research tools is sometimes the most difficult and sophisticated part of an experiment or project.

Reinforcing Vocabulary

To help students remember the difference between quantitative and qualitative, share the following mnemonic with them: *Quantitative* has an "n" that stands for "number," as in how much of something. *Qualitative* has an "l" that stands for "like," as in whether or not you agree with something. **ELL**

Using the Illustration

Students should answer that the important advantages of the survey method include its low cost, ease of comparison of answers, and that responses can be gathered from large numbers of people.

Section 1

Research Methods

Key Terms

- survey
- population
- sample
- representative sample
- questionnaire
- interview
- closed-ended questions
- open-ended questions
- secondary analysis
- field research
- case study
- participant observation

Section Preview

When sociologists do quantitative research, they generally use either surveys or precollected data. Each has its own advantages and disadvantages. Qualitative research uses descriptive rather than numerical data. Field studies are best used when interaction needs to be observed in a natural setting, and when in-depth analysis is needed. The case study is the most popular approach to field research.

survey
research method in which people respond to questions

Doing Research in the Social Sciences

Like all scientists, sociologists gain their knowledge by doing research. The goal of sociological research is to test common sense assumptions and replace false ideas with facts and evidence. Part of the sociological perspective is to ask "why" and "how" questions and then to form hypotheses to arrive at accurate understandings.

Social scientists differ from other scientists, however, in how they conduct much of their research. Unlike chemists, biologists, or physicists, sociologists (and often psychologists) are very limited in their ability to set up laboratory experiments to replicate real-life conditions. Even if they reproduce conditions as they are in the outside world, the ethical issues involved in manipulating people and controlling events would prevent most sociologists from pursuing this kind of research. For sociologists, the world is their laboratory.

How then do sociologists do research? The methods that sociologists rely on are described below. These methods are classified as either *quantitative* or *qualitative*. Quantitative research uses numerical data, while qualitative research rests on narrative and descriptive data. Quantitative research tools include *surveys* and *precollected data*. About 90 percent of the research published in major sociological journals is based on surveys, so this approach is discussed first.

Survey Research

The **survey,** in which people are asked to answer a series of questions, is the most widely used research method among sociologists. It is ideal for studying large numbers of people.

The survey is the most widely used research method for collecting data in sociology.

Demonstration

Quantitative Research Bring in a box of Lego blocks with enough pieces so they can be distributed to class members. (You will need to know exactly how many Legos are in the box because they represent your population.) Hand out several Legos, perhaps five, to each student. Ask students to count the connectors on each Lego they have. After they have counted the connectors on each Lego, ask each student to determine the mean (average) of all their connectors. Write each student's mean on the board. The numbers will be very close. There will probably be Legos left over that have not been counted. Ask students whether this constitutes a random sample. *(No, because leaving some Legos uncounted means that if they were counted it would have skewed the mean, even if slightly.)* This should impress upon them why it is so important to randomly sample. Otherwise, your findings might not be truly representative of the whole population. **L2**

Integrating the Transparencies

A transparency, Wheel of Science, is provided in the *Sociology and You* Transparency Binder.

Survey researchers must guard against affecting a respondent's answer.

How are effective surveys conducted? In survey research, care must be taken that surveys are sent to the right number and type of people (Black, 1998). Researchers describe the people surveyed in terms of *populations* and *samples*.

A **population** is all those people with the characteristics a researcher wants to study. A population could be all high school seniors in the United States, all retired postal workers living in Connecticut, or the number of freshmen who buy school yearbooks.

Sociologists would like to collect information on all members of a population, but most populations are too large. Surveys including the entire population would cost too much and take too long for most research projects. Instead, a sample is drawn. A **sample** is a limited number of cases drawn from the larger population. A sample must be selected carefully if it is to have the same basic characteristics as the general population—that is, if it is to be a **representative sample.** If a sample is not representative of the population from which it is drawn, the survey findings cannot be used to make generalizations about the entire population. For example, if you were to conduct a survey using ten students from an advanced biology class, this sample would not be representative of your school. On the other hand, if you randomly selected ten students who walked into the school cafeteria for your survey, these students would probably be more representative of the student body. The sample would probably be too small, however, to give accurate results. The United States Census Bureau regularly uses sample surveys in its highly accurate work. The Gallup Poll and Harris Poll are recognized all over the country as reliable indicators of national trends and public opinion because they use representative samples in their surveys.

How are representative samples selected? The standard way of getting a representative sample is by random, or chance, selection. A random sample can be selected by assigning each member of the population a number and then drawing numbers from a container after they have been thoroughly scrambled. An easier and more practical method uses a table of random numbers. After each member of the population has been assigned a number, the researcher begins with any number in the table and goes down the list until enough subjects have been selected.

population
a group of people with certain specified characteristics

sample
a group of people that represent a larger population

representative sample
a sample that accurately reflects the characteristics of the population as a whole

SOCIOLOGY Online

Student Web Activity
Visit the *Sociology and You* Web site at soc.glencoe.com and click on **Chapter 2—Student Web Activities** for an activity on survey research.

Open-Response Question

Ask students if any of them have ever had any experience with surveys, either taking them or giving them. If so, ask them to discuss as many aspects of the experience as they can remember. If anyone has ever been an interviewer, ask them to talk about how people responded to them.

Teaching Strategy

To help students understand the idea of a sample population, pose this problem: You are responsible for the purchase of a large number of widgets for a major corporation. You can't possibly check the whole shipment, but you must ensure that the shipment is not damaged because you have to pay in cash and will not be able to get a refund on your money. You can check as many widgets as you want, but each check takes several hours and will cost $100 in labor. How many checks would you make on a shipment of 1,000 widgets before you felt comfortable making the deal? *(Obviously there is no exact answer to this question. It will, however, get students thinking about the opportunity costs of sampling too few or too many of a population.)*
L1

Demonstration

Qualitative Research Place some ordinary items, such as paper clips, coffee cups, and computer disks in a box. Pass the box around the room and have each student choose an item from the box and describe it. Stop them if they begin to express an assumption about the function of the item as they are describing it. Students will begin to see that researchers doing qualitative research must be objective in their observations. They cannot assume anything about function or draw conclusions until they have asked appropriate questions and made sure they have gathered all the relevant data.
L1

Points to Stress

Point out ways surveys can influence research by how the questions are phrased. Write the following two statements on the board and ask students if they would respond differently to these statements:

(1) I believe that minors (individuals under the age of 18) should not be allowed to purchase handguns.

(2) I support gun control measures.

Discuss how, in spite of the differences between these two statements, it might be possible to interpret them as being the same question.

Working with the Data

Figure 2.1 and **Figure 2.2** Before embarking on class research projects, have students review these tables. If students are going to collect their data with a survey, their most difficult task will be creating survey questions that will yield measurable results. (Note: Always check and approve survey questions your students write before surveys are distributed.) If you aren't sure the survey will be a good research tool, have students hand out a few to see if they get the desired results. They might find that they have asked questions that don't lead them to prove or disprove their hypotheses. If students ask open-ended questions, remind them that responses might vary so much as to not be measurable. Yet, sometimes those questions get at a variety of attitudes, which is exactly what the researcher wants.

questionnaire
a written set of questions to be answered by a research participant

interview
a survey method in which a trained researcher asks questions and records the answers

closed-ended questions
questions a person must answer by choosing from a limited, predetermined set of responses

How is survey information gathered? In surveys, information is obtained through either a questionnaire or an interview. A **questionnaire** is a written set of questions that survey participants answer by themselves. In an **interview,** a trained interviewer asks questions and records the answers. Questionnaires and interviews may contain *closed-ended* or *open-ended* questions.

 Closed-ended questions are those that a person answers by choosing from a limited, predetermined set of responses. Multiple choice questions are closed ended, for example. Because participants are limited to certain responses, closed-ended questions sometimes fail to uncover underlying attitudes and opinions. On the positive side, closed-ended questions make answers easier to tabulate and compare.

Figure 2.1 Closed-ended and Open-ended Questions

Examples of Closed-Ended Questions

PLEASE INDICATE WHETHER YOU STRONGLY AGREE, AGREE, DISAGREE, OR STRONGLY DISAGREE WITH EACH OF THE FOLLOWING STATEMENTS:

	Strongly Agree	Agree	Disagree	Strongly Disagree
a. Most schoolteachers really don't know what they are talking about.	1	2	3	4
b. To get ahead in life, you have to get a good education.	1	2	3	4
c. My parents encouraged me to get a good education.	1	2	3	4
d. School is a lonely place.	1	2	3	4
e. Too much emphasis is put on education these days.	1	2	3	4
f. Most students cheat on tests.	1	2	3	4

QUANTITATIVE BRITTANY

IN YOUR OWN WORDS, PLEASE DESCRIBE THE IMPORTANCE OF EDUCATION TO YOU.

QUALITATIVE ERIC

Examples of Open-Ended Questions

1. In your own words, please describe your views on the education you have received so far.

2. Do you think school adequately prepares you for employment? Why or why not?

Demonstration

Surveys Explain to students that a survey must be measurable or have close-ended statements, so that the large number of results can be tabulated accurately. You can demonstrate the importance of this by asking students to name their favorite flavors of ice cream. List them on the board. Their answers will likely be varied and there may not be consensus on any one flavor. This demonstrates how an open-ended survey question asks for a lot of information that is difficult to quantify. Now ask students to select their favorites from a list of five flavors: vanilla, strawberry, chocolate, mint, and bubble gum. What is their least favorite from this list of choices? You have now turned your survey of ice cream preferences into something that is measurable.

L1

Figure 2.2 Closed-ended Survey Research

Advantages	Disadvantages
❖ Closed-ended answers can be more precisely measured.	❖ Surveys are expensive to produce and distribute.
❖ Responses can be easily compared.	❖ Responses are limited to preset answers.
❖ Statistical techniques can be used to make sense of the data.	❖ Many people don't respond to surveys, resulting in low cost effectiveness.
❖ A large number of responses can be collected.	❖ The way a question is stated may influence the answer given. (Negatively phrased questions are more likely to get a negative answer.)

Open-ended questions ask the person to answer in his or her own words. Answers to open-ended questions can reveal many attitudes. However, these answers are not easy to quantify or compare. Another problem may arise if an interviewer changes the meaning of questions by rephrasing them. The same question phrased in different ways can place the emphasis on different issues and evoke different responses.

open-ended questions
questions a person is to answer in his or her own words

Secondary Analysis

Using precollected information—that is, information someone else has already gathered—is known as **secondary analysis.** It is a well-respected method of collecting data in sociology. In fact, the first sociologist to use statistics in a sociological study—Emile Durkheim—relied on precollected data. (See Focus on Research on page 56.)

secondary analysis
using precollected information for data collection and research purposes

What are some sources for secondary analysis? Types of precollected data include government reports, company records, voting lists, prison records, and reports of research done by other social scientists.

The United States Census Bureau is one of the most important sources of precollected data for American sociologists. The Census Bureau collects information on the total population every ten years and conducts countless specific surveys every year. The census contains detailed information on such topics as income, education, race, sex, age, marital status, occupation, and death and birth rates.

Other government agencies also collect information that is of great value to sociologists. The U.S. Department of Labor regularly collects information on the nation's income and unemployment levels across a variety of jobs. The U.S. Department of Commerce issues monthly reports on various aspects of the economy.

"Science is the refusal to believe on the basis of hope."

C.P. Snow
English physicist

Working with the Quote

C.P. Snow (1905–1980) was a British novelist, scientist, and government administrator. Snow argued that literature (the arts) and science know little, if anything, about the other and that communication is difficult, if not impossible, between them. Snow thus called attention to a breach in two of the major branches of Western culture. Snow acknowledged the emergence of a third "culture" as well, the social sciences and arts concerned with "how human beings are living or have lived."

Integrating the Teacher Resources

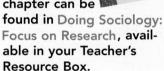

A lesson plan for a student research project related to the content of this chapter can be found in Doing Sociology: Focus on Research, available in your Teacher's Resource Box.

Working with the Data

Figure 2.3 The Internet has opened up all types of research possibilities for sociologists. Most rely on precollected data and can find it quickly there. Advise students to avoid using old data, anything more than seven or eight years old. Most research is updated or revised after five to ten years.

Net Worthy

U.S. Census Students in your class who are curious about census statistics can look up the Census Bureau on the Internet at **www.census.gov/**. This site has literally hundreds of interesting byways and links concerning demographic studies.

Addressing Current Social Issues

The Bureau of the Census made a "significant error" in surveying undocumented aliens in its 1990 report. Discuss the validity of census results by asking: How does the Census Bureau survey undocumented workers? Is the survey process effective? Why or why not? Can the Census Bureau get accurate results in surveying undocumented workers? Why or why not? How did the bureau improve the survey process for the 2000 Census? Have students research the effects of the 1990 census on their state and city. What changes resulted from the census figures? Why?

Figure 2.3 Secondary Analysis

Advantages	Disadvantages
❖ Precollected data provide sociologists with inexpensive, high-quality information.	❖ The existing information may not exactly suit the researcher's needs because it was gathered for a different reason.
❖ Existing sources of information permit the study of a topic over a long period of time. (With census data, for example, we can trace the changes in the relative income levels of African Americans and whites.)	❖ Sometimes precollected data are outdated.
❖ The researcher cannot influence answers because the data have been collected by others.	❖ Little may be known about collection methods. The people who first collected the data or the collection methods may have been biased.

Field Research

field research
research that takes place in a natural (nonlaboratory) setting

case study
intensive study of a single group, incident, or community

participant observation
a case study where the researcher becomes a member of the group being studied

Qualitative research uses narrative or descriptive data rather than quantitative, numerical data. Some aspects of society can best be revealed by qualitative methods. Most of these methods fall under the heading of *field research*. **Field research** looks closely at aspects of social life that cannot be measured quantitatively and that are best understood within a natural setting. High school cliques and "jock" culture are examples of topics best studied by field research.

When do sociologists use case studies? The most often used approach to field research is the **case study**—a thorough investigation of a single group, incident, or community. This method assumes that the findings in one case can be generalized to similar situations. The conclusions of a study on drug use in Chicago, for example, should apply to other large cities as well. It is the researcher's responsibility to point out the factors in the study that are unique and that would not apply to other situations.

When do case studies involve participant observation? In **participant observation,** a researcher becomes a member of the group being studied. A researcher may join a group with or without informing its members that he or she is a sociologist.

A compelling account of undercover participant observation appears in *Black Like Me,* a book written by John Howard Griffin (1961). Griffin, a white journalist, dyed his skin to study the life of African Americans in the South. Although he had previously visited the South as a white man, his experiences while posing as an African American were quite different.

Participant researchers sometimes do not keep their identities secret. Elliot Liebow studied disadvantaged African American males. Even though he was a white outsider, Liebow was allowed to participate in the daily activities of the men. He said, "The people I was observing knew that I was observing them, yet they allowed me to participate in their activities and take part in their lives to a degree that continues to surprise me" (Liebow, 1967:253).

Cooperative Learning Activity

School Census Survey Have your students meet in small groups to write questions for a survey designed to obtain information on their school's vital statistics. Use the Census Bureau questions for the year 2000 as models. (See More About . . . the Census on page 46.) Reconvene the whole class to review all the questions, then select ten for the survey. (You may want to consult with the school's administration before distributing questionnaires to other students or asking students to interview other classes.)

Discuss with students the size needed for a sample population and the best way to obtain it. Or, you may decide to try to get

Every ten years the Constitution of the United States requires a count of the nation's population. The Census Bureau uses survey research techniques to create this statistical picture. Why do you think the Census Bureau asked Congress to authorize the use of sampling techniques?

Figure 2.4 Focus on Theoretical Perspectives

Investigating School Violence and School Funding. This table illustrates the research method a sociologist of a particular theoretical persuasion would most likely choose to investigate school violence and school funding. Any of the three sociologists, of course, could use any of the three research methods.

Theoretical Perspective	Research Method	Approach to the Research Question
Functionalism	Survey	A questionnaire on violence in high schools is sent to a national, random sample of principals. The survey examines a possible relationship between incidence of school violence and level of school funding.
Conflict Theory	Case Study	A particular high school with low funding is studied with respect to a relationship between school violence and school funding. Researchers interview administrators, teachers, and students.
Symbolic Interactionism	Participant Observation	Concealing her identity, a researcher takes a temporary job at a high school with low funding. She attempts to observe covertly a possible link between school violence and school funding.

Working with the Data

Figure 2.4 The Focus on Theoretical Perspectives table appears in every chapter and is designed to help students understand differences in the emphasis that these perspectives place on sociological issues and how they approach research topics. Stress with students that the chart is not meant to suggest that the example provided is the only approach taken by each perspective.
The more you refer to these perspectives, the more likely that, by the end of the semester, students will have internalized them. Have the students hypothesize whether or not a lack of school funding might explain higher incidences of school violence.

all of the school's students to complete the questionnaire.

After taking the survey, ask your students to meet again in their small groups to analyze results, note patterns, create data bases or charts, and draw conclusions about their school's population. Ask students if they were surprised about the results. Were they able to keep themselves from forming assumptions or drawing conclusions until after the results of the survey were in? Ask students to assess what, if anything, they could do to improve the survey process. Encourage interested students to write news articles on the school census results and submit them for publication to the school newspaper, newsletter, or yearbook. **L3**

Pulling It All Together

Students should understand after completing this section that sociological knowledge is gained by conducting research. Methods employed to gather data are classified as quantitative or qualitative. Quantitative research uses numerical data, often in the form of a survey. Qualitative research uses descriptive data, called field research. Finally, sociologists always ask if the population being studied is representative of the population at large, or specific to that group or location.

Answers to Section 1 Assessment

1. c
2. a
3. d
4. b
5. e
6. Answers will vary.
7. Participant observation will result in qualitative research. Surveys more often yield quantitative data.

Critical Thinking

8. Yes, if it's a representative sample (the sample has the same basic characteristics as the population). Even though the sample is small in comparison with the entire population, it is large enough to provide statistically significant results.
9. Answers will vary, but students should explain what type of data they are hoping to gather, and then the best method to obtain that data.
10. Answers will vary.

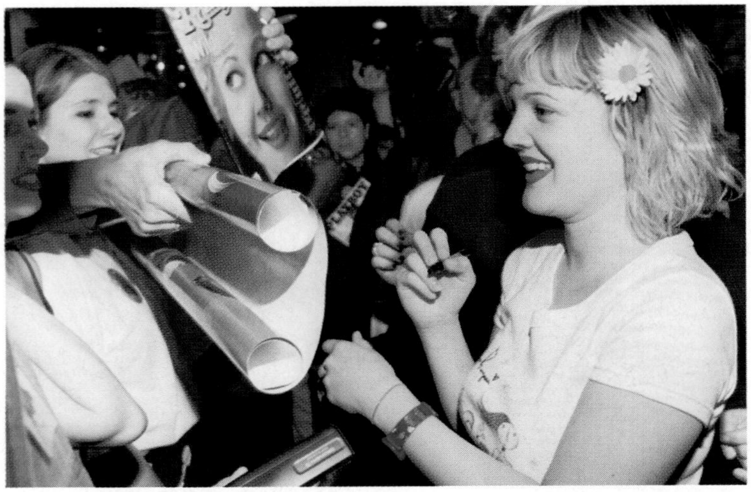

Sometimes field research requires going undercover, something that occurred in the movie Never Been Kissed (starring Drew Barrymore pictured here with fans of the movie). When this happens in real life, however, sociologists have a responsibility to make sure they meet the standards of the Code of Ethics.

Section 1 Assessment

Match terms a–e with the numbered statements.

1. selected on the basis of chance, so that each member of a population has an equal opportunity of being selected
2. all those people with the characteristics the researcher wants to study within the context of a particular research question
3. a limited number of cases drawn from the larger population
4. a sample that has basically the same relevant characteristics as the population
5. the research method in which people are asked to answer a series of questions

a. population
b. representative sample
c. random sample
d. sample
e. survey

6. Provide an example of using precollected data.
7. For what reasons would you use participant observation instead of a survey?

Critical Thinking

8. **Analyzing Information** Do you think that selecting a sample of three thousand individuals could yield an accurate picture of the eating habits of Americans? Why or why not?
9. **Drawing Conclusions** You are a sociologist who wants to see if receiving welfare benefits affects long-term job commitment. Describe the research method you would use. Why is the method you chose the best for this topic?
10. **Synthesizing Information** Suggest several areas in your own school or community where field research could be used for a research project.

On-Demand Writing

The long form sent out by the Census Bureau in 2000 was 38 pages. Many recipients of this form were not only disgruntled about the length, but were unhappy at the questions that were asked. They believed that it crossed the line from information gathering to invasion of privacy.

Ask students to write a paragraph or two on whether or not they think the Census Bureau invades Americans' privacy when it asks questions about who they are, how they live, and what they believe. Have students support their answers.
L2

Figure 2.5 Summary of Research Methods

Research Method	Definition	Advantages	Disadvantages
Quantitative Methods			
Survey Research	People answer a series of questions, usually predetermined	❖ Precision and comparability of answers ❖ Use of statistical techniques ❖ Information on large numbers of people ❖ Detailed analysis	❖ Expensive due to large numbers ❖ Low response rate ❖ Phrasing of questions introduces bias in favor of certain answers ❖ Researchers' behavior can affect answers given
Secondary Analysis	Information gathered by one researcher is used by another researcher for a different purpose.	❖ Inexpensive ❖ Can study a topic over a long period of time ❖ Researcher's influence on subjects avoided	❖ Information collected for a different reason may not suit another researcher's needs ❖ Original researcher may have already introduced biases ❖ Information may be outdated
Experiment	Research occurs in a laboratory setting with a minimum of contaminating influences (Not often used in social research.)	❖ Can be replicated with precision ❖ Variables can be manipulated ❖ Can be relatively inexpensive ❖ Permits the establishment of causation (rather than just correlation)	❖ Laboratory environment is artificial ❖ Not suited to most sociological research ❖ Number of variables studied is limited
Qualitative Methods			
Case Study	Thorough investigation is done of a small group, incident, or community	❖ Provides depth of understanding from group members' viewpoint ❖ Unexpected discoveries and new insights can be incorporated into the research ❖ Permits the study of social behavior not feasible with quantitative methods	❖ Difficult to generalize findings from one group to another group ❖ Presence of researcher can influence results ❖ Hard to duplicate ❖ Takes lots of time ❖ Difficult to be accepted as a group member (in case of participant observation)

More About . . . Field Research

Excellent qualitative field research studies were conducted by avant-garde sociologist, Donna Gaines. With its emphasis on field research and participant observation, her work, *Teenage Wasteland,* won an award from the American Sociological Association. Gaines was interested in a series of teen suicides that took place in an East Coast suburb, so she researched the behavior of a group of teens for one year. The result is a classic study of teenage life in suburbia in the early 1990s.

Careers in Sociology

Tell students who may be interested in doing sociological research professionally that research is done in universities; public agencies at the federal, state, or local level; businesses or industrial firms; and at research institutes in the non-profit or advocacy sector. Some researchers are self-employed, and head their own consulting firms. Sociologists study people in natural and in controlled settings. Some work closely with people, others with data and computers. Link to **http://www.soc.umn.edu/~edwards/soclinks.htm** for a contact list of research organizations.

Skills at a Glance

Using Basic Statistical Measures

Statistics are methods used for tabulating, analyzing, and presenting quantitative data. Sociologists, like all scientists, use statistical measures. You will encounter certain statistical measures in this textbook and in periodicals such as *Time, Newsweek,* or *The Economist.* Among the basic statistical measures are averages—including modes, means, and medians.

An *average* is a single number representing the distribution of several figures. For example, suppose the following figures are the salaries of the nine highest-paid major league baseball players:

$3,300,000 (catcher)	$4,200,000 (center field)
$4,900,000 (starting pitcher)	
$3,600,000 (second base)	$4,300,000 (shortstop)
$5,300,000 (left field)	
$3,600,000 (third base)	$4,500,000 (first base)
$6,100,000 (right field)	

There are three kinds of averages that will make these numerical values more meaningful. Each gives a slightly different picture.

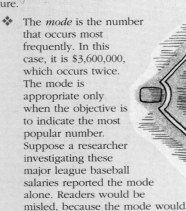

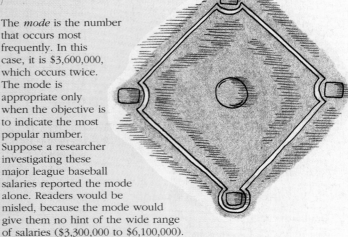

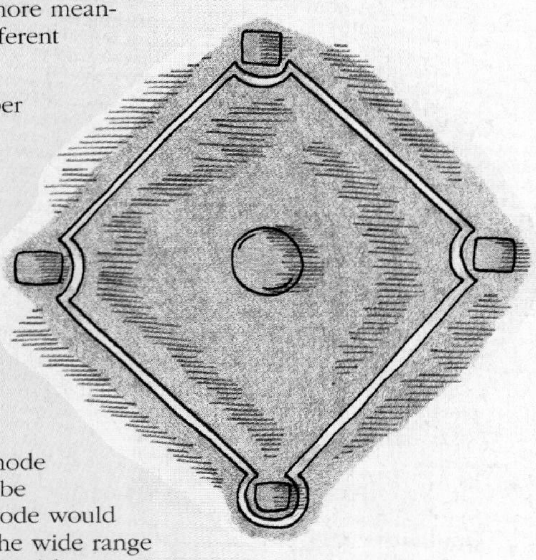

- The *mode* is the number that occurs most frequently. In this case, it is $3,600,000, which occurs twice. The mode is appropriate only when the objective is to indicate the most popular number. Suppose a researcher investigating these major league baseball salaries reported the mode alone. Readers would be misled, because the mode would give them no hint of the wide range of salaries ($3,300,000 to $6,100,000).
- The *mean* is the measure closest to the everyday meaning of the term *average.* It lies somewhere in the middle of a range. The mean of the salary figures above—$4,422,222—is calculated by adding all of the salaries together ($39,800,000) and dividing by the number of salaries (9). The mean, unlike the mode, takes all of the figures into account. It is distorted, however, by the highest figure, $6,100,000. Although one player earns $6,100,000, most players make considerably less—the

Working with the Data

The next four pages constitute a mini-handbook that will help students review basic statistical techniques such as calculating measures of central tendency and interpreting graphs. This first activity deals with the concepts of average: mean, mode, and median.

More About . . . the Census

The U.S. Constitution, in Article I, Section 2, requires that the federal government take an "enumeration," or census, every ten years. The census is required because the number of representatives each state can elect to the House of Representatives depends on the state's population. The census results are also used to determine where to build highways, schools, restaurants, and banks, as well as how much money in federal grants should be given to local government institutions such as hospitals.

Here are some of the questions asked in the 2000 census:

How many people were living or staying in this house, apartment, or mobile home on April 1, 2000?

What is the name of one of the people living here who owns, is buying or rents this house, apartment, or mobile home?

For each person living or staying in the house, what is the person's telephone number? What is the person's date of birth? What is the person's race?

Cooperative Learning Activity

Statistics Review Assign each student a country and have them locate and bring to class: (1) the size of the country in square miles, and (2) the country's population.

Put the students into groups of five or six and have them rank order their assigned countries by each category. Have them calculate the population per square mile of each country and use that to rank the countries as well. Have each group explain to the class how the rankings of their assigned countries changed depending upon which criteria they use.

Provide the students with the same three

highest-paid player earns nearly twice as much as the lowest-paid player. The mean is distorted when there are extreme values at either the high or the low end of a scale. The mean is more accurate when the high and low values are not widely separated.

❖ The *median* is the number that divides a series of values in half. Half of the values lie above the median, half below. In this example, the median is $4,300,000. Half of the salaries are above $4,300,000, and half are below it. The advantage here is that the median is not distorted by extremes at either end. If the median falls between two numbers, the average of those two numbers becomes the median.

The World Champion New York Yankees celebrate after winning the World Series in 1999. This win might result in salary increases for next year.

Working with Statistics

1. Cassie collected newspapers for a recycling plant at the rate of $2.30 per pound of paper. On consecutive days she turned in the following weights: 12 lbs., 13 lbs., 8 lbs., 22 lbs., 8.5 lbs., 13 lbs., and 19 lbs. What was her average pay per day? What was the median pay?
2. The grades on a student's sociology quizzes for a six-week period were 99 percent, 99 percent, 68 percent, 99 percent, 75 percent, and 80 percent. Determine the mean score, the mode, and the median score for that student.

Evaluating Internet Resources

The Internet is one of the most exciting research tools developed in the last century. It can put a library of the most current information at your fingertips. Like every tool, however, it is only as good as its operator. Reading the "instruction manual" and following a few basic "safely rules" will ensure that you get the best results from your online research efforts.

To determine if the site is a valid one, consider the source material. The questions on the following page will help you evaluate the reliability of the information. They will also let you deselect those sources (or articles) that are not particularly relevant to your needs.

Answers to Working with Statistics

1. The average pay is $31.38. ($27.70 + 29.90 + 18.40 + 50.60 + 19.55 + 29.90 + 43.70 / 7 days). The median pay is $29.90.
2. The mean score is 87% (86.666). The mode is 99% because it appears three times. The median is 89.5% [(80 + 99)/2].

More About . . . Classic Studies

Students might enjoy looking at some of these classic works in field research, some of which have been mentioned in this text.

1. Elliot Leibow: *Talley's Corner.*
   The study concerns unemployed workers in Washington, D.C.
2. Steven Vanderstaay: *Street Lives: An Oral History of Homelessness.*
3. *Donna Gaines: Teenage Wasteland: Suburbia's Dead End Kids.*
   These works will help students appreciate the richness that field research contributes to the sociological body of knowledge.

sets of data (size, population, and population per square mile) on the state that they live in or are most familiar with. Use the activity to discuss the need to anchor statistics in some base that allows for understandable comparisons; and how one can use comparisons to make facts look different. If they want to make a nation look heavily populated or lightly populated, what countries might they select for comparison? What other characteristics might need to be known about a country to really understand the significance of its population per square mile?
L2

Making Connections to Other Cultures

Using Precollected Data
Have teams of students use encyclopedias, world almanacs, and Internet resources such as the CIA World Factbook to gather what they consider to be the five crucial pieces of statistical data about specific countries or cultures. In order to link students to context beyond your classroom, you might select countries or cultures based upon the foreign languages taught in your school, or the core ethnic backgrounds represented in your community. In addition, since this text periodically uses Chinese, Japanese, and Native American examples, you might consider including those cultures even if they are not a part of your local community. Have students present the data that they have gathered in a way that it can be seen and understood by all students in the class. Some ideas might include models, charts, graphs, or data bases. Have students write and answer questions about cultural patterns. They should also provide and justify the reasons for selecting the categories of data. Use the variety that you will find in their efforts and results in a discussion of the difficulties of defining what constitutes crucial statistical data when doing sociological research.
L2

WHO

- ❖ Who maintains the site? An established authority? An organization? A government?
- ❖ Who produced the information? Is he or she qualified, a noted authority? Are you sure?
- ❖ Has the site been reviewed, recommended, or given an award? By whom?
- ❖ Are there standards or selection criteria that must be met for information to be on this site?
- ❖ Can the webmaster be contacted by e-mail?

WHAT

- ❖ Is the information reliable?
- ❖ Is the information original?
- ❖ Is the information scholarly, professional, popular? Is there documentation?
- ❖ Is the site comprehensive? Are other sites more comprehensive?
- ❖ Does the site contain information, links to other sites, or both?

WHEN

- ❖ Is the information up-to-date? Are other sites more current?
- ❖ When was the site last updated? How often is the site updated?
- ❖ Do the links work?

WHERE

- ❖ From where was the information derived?
- ❖ Is the information based on personal opinion, experience, interviews, library research, questionnaires or laboratory experiments?
- ❖ How did you access the information on the Internet (for example, web, ftp, telnet, listserv, newsgroup, e-mail)?

HOW

- ❖ How is the information presented? Is it presented clearly, accurately, and objectively?
- ❖ Is there distortion or bias in meaning?
- ❖ Is more than one viewpoint represented?
- ❖ Is the information modified in any way?

WHY

- ❖ Why is the information being presented?
- ❖ What is the purpose/motive? Is it easy to determine the purpose?
- ❖ Who is the intended audience?
- ❖ Does a sponsoring organization influence what is published here? Is there an e-mail or "snail mail" address to contact the organization?
- ❖ Does the information suit your purpose?

Applying Skills
Select a sociology-related Internet site. Evaluate it based on the criteria above.

Reading Tables and Graphs

Tables and graphs present information concisely. Figures 2.6 and 2.7 on the following page show the same information in two different formats. Use these figures to complete these steps for decoding tables and graphs.

1. Begin by reading the title of the table or graph carefully. It will tell you what information is being presented. What information is being presented in Figure 2.6?
2. Find out the source of information. You will want to know whether the source is reliable and whether its techniques for gathering and presenting data are sound. What is the source of the information in these figures? Is it a reliable source?

Careers in Sociology

Students might consider careers as marketing research analysts, who are concerned with sales of a product or service. Tell students that these researchers analyze data on past sales to predict future sales. They use data to analyze prices, sales, and methods of marketing and distribution, and they devise methods and procedures for obtaining data they need. Analysts may conduct opinion research to determine public attitudes on various issues. This can help political or business leaders and others assess public support for their electoral prospects or advertising policies.

For careers as a marketing research analyst, students need the ability to pay attention to details. Patience and persistence are necessary since they'll spend long hours on

3. Read any notes accompanying the table or graph. Not all tables and graphs have notes, but if notes are present, they offer further information about the data. The notes in Figure 2.6 and in Figure 2.7 explain that the data refer to the total money income of full-time and part-time workers, aged 18 and over, in a March 2000 survey. Why is the note in this table important?
4. Examine any footnotes (marked with asterisks). Footnotes in Figure 2.6 and Figure 2.7 indicate that the data are categorized by the highest grade actually completed. What other interpretation could be made from the term *years of schooling?*
5. Look at the headings across the top and down the left-hand side of the table or graph. To observe any pattern in the data, it is usually necessary to keep both types of headings in mind. Figure 2.6 and Figure 2.7 show the median annual income of African American and white males and females for several levels of education.
6. Find out what units are being used. Data can be expressed in percentages, hundreds, thousands, millions, billions, means, and so forth. Figure 2.6 and Figure 2.7 use two different units. What are they? When making comparison, it is important that you compare like units.
7. Check for trends in the data. For tables, look down the columns (vertically) and across the rows (horizontally) for the highest figures, lowest figures, repeat numbers, irregularities, and sudden shifts. If you read Figure 2.6 vertically, you can see how income varies by race and sex within each level of education. If you read the table horizontally, you can see how income varies with educational attainment for white males, African American males, white females, and African American females. What is the advantage of presenting this information as a graph, as in Figure 2.7? What is the disadvantage of using a graph?
8. Draw conclusions from your own observations. Looking carefully at these figures, write a narrative paragraph that summarizes your conclusions based on the data presented in these figures.

Demographic group	Overall median income in dollars	Median income in dollars as compared with years of schooling[a]				
		Less than 9	9–11	12	13–15	16 or more
White males	30,409	13,995	18,403	28,843	36,474	51,985
African American males	21,531	11,791	16,323	22,124	26,912	39,441
White females	17,784	9,338	9,883	16,426	22,983	32,102
African American females	16,754	9,730	9,416	15,293	23,759	32,595

Note: These figures include the total money income of full-time and part-time workers, ages 18 and over, surveyed as of March 2000.

[a] In terms of highest grade completed.

Figure 2.6 Median Income in Dollars

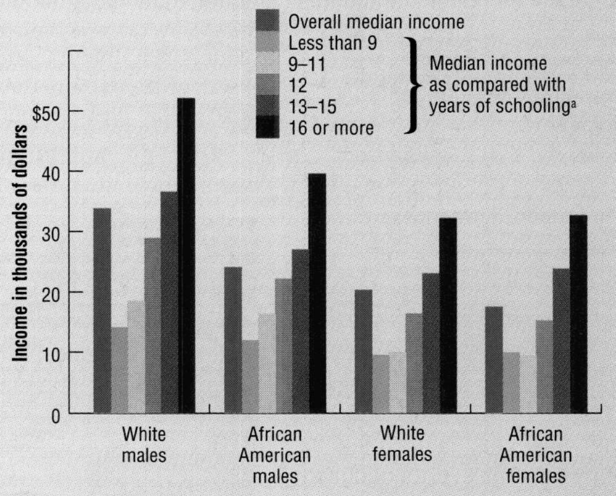

Note: These figures include the total money income of full-time and part-time workers, ages 18 and over, surveyed as of March 2000.

[a] In terms of highest grade completed.

Figure 2.7 Median Annual Income by Gender, Race, and Education

Source: U.S. Bureau of the Census.

Answers to Applying Skills, p. 48

Students should select an Internet site to evaluate. It would be a good idea for students to have this checklist with them when they begin researching on the Internet.

Answers to Reading Tables and Graphs

1. Figure 2.6 is a table that shows the median income in dollars earned by white and African American men and women according to the number of years of schooling.
2. The source of information in these figures is the U.S. Census Bureau, a reliable source.
3. The note clarifies that all workers, full-time and part-time have been included. It defines the population of the study.
4. The terms make it clear that the school year had to have been completed to count. Thus, one semester of college would not be credited as a school year.
5. No answer required.
6. Figure 2.6 uses actual dollar amounts. Figure 2.7 uses thousands of dollars. Both figures use years of schooling as the unit.
7. The advantage to the graph is that you can see patterns immediately. The disadvantage of the graph is that while trends are easier to spot, accuracy is lost. Ask students if they have any questions about cultural patterns shown on the graph.
8. Answers will vary.

independent study and problem solving. Because marketing research analysts often oversee interviews for a wide variety of individuals, the ability to work well with others is important. Marketing research analysts are able to present their findings, both orally and in writing, clearly.

For information about careers in marketing research, contact: Marketing Research Association, **http://www. mra-net.org**, or Council of American Survey Research Organizations, **http://www.casro.org/ index.htm**.

Using the Section Preview

Before students begin reading the chapter, ask them what they think causes crime. Answers may include neglectful parents, drugs, violence on TV, and so on. Once students have shared their responses in small groups or with the whole class, emphasize that the variety of answers they gave shows that no one knows of one single cause for crime. Sociologists and criminologists suggest that there are multiple causes of crime and other events, though the media often tends to oversimplify and focus on single causes, and then sensationalize events. Ask students if they can think of specific examples to illustrate this.

Points to Stress

To help students understand multiple causation, ask them to think of events in their own lives and analyze them for causation. For example, have they lost a girlfriend or a boyfriend? Did they do poorly on an important exam? Can they really isolate the reasons for these events to one all encompassing cause?

Using the Illustration

Reinforce to the students that while causes in social interactions may not be as easy to identify as in some of the "hard" sciences, the consequences or results can be just as unavoidable as what will happen when this receiver is tackled.

Section 2 Causation in Science

Key Terms

- causation
- multiple causation
- variable
- quantitative variable
- qualitative variable
- independent variable
- dependent variable
- intervening variable
- correlation
- spurious correlation

Section Preview

Causation in science is the idea that one event leads to another event. Scientists assume that all events have causes, or determinants. Social events are so complex, however, that many factors may be identified as causes. Three standards must be met before causation can be proved.

causation
the belief that events occur in predictable ways and that one event leads to another

multiple causation
the belief that an event occurs as a result of several factors working in combination

The Nature of Causation

Scientists assume that an event occurs for a reason. According to the concept of **causation,** events occur in predictable, nonrandom ways. One event leads to another. Why does this book remain sitting on your desk rather than rising slowly, going past your eyes, and resting against the ceiling? Why does a ball thrown into the air return to the ground? Why do the planets stay in orbit around the sun? Today, the main goal of scientists is to discover the factors that cause events to happen. Social scientists look for the factors that cause social events to happen.

Why do sociologists look for multiple causes? Leo Rosten, a twentieth-century novelist, once wrote "If an explanation relies on a single cause, it is surely wrong." Social events are generally too complex to be explained by any single factor. The concept of **multiple causation** states that an event occurs as a result of several factors working in combination. What, for example, causes crime? Cesare Lombroso, a nineteenth-century Italian criminologist, mistakenly believed that the tendency to commit crimes was inherited. Criminals, he thought, could be identified by certain physical traits such as large jaws or receding foreheads. Modern criminologists have shown that many factors contribute to crime, including peer pressure, the use of drugs, hopeless poverty, and poor parenting. Each of these single factors is called a *variable.*

What is the cause and effect in this interaction?

World View

The Wired World

This world map shows the number of telephone mainlines per one hundred people for the year 2000. It illustrates the creation of a quantitative variable that could be used in social research.

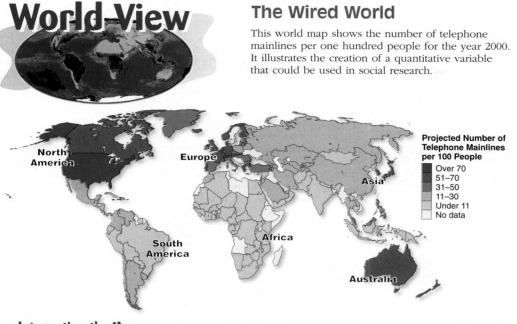

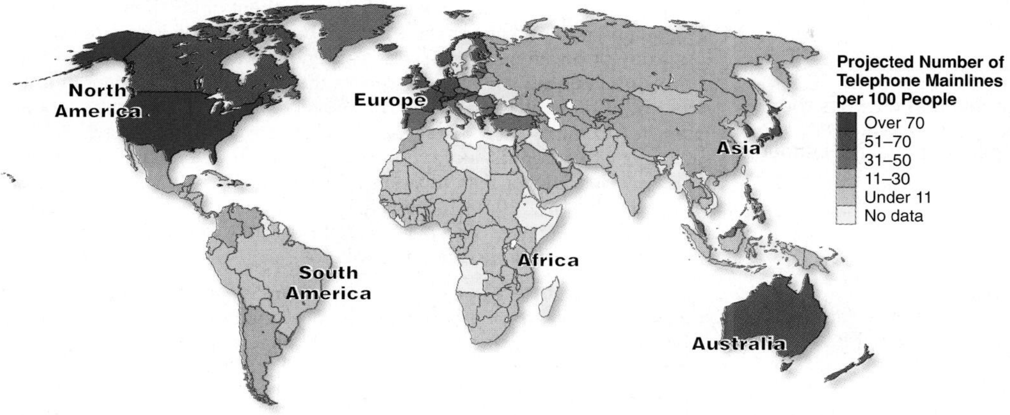

Interpreting the Map

1. Explain why the data in this map constitutes a quantitative variable.
2. What would need to be done with the data to make it a qualitative variable?
3. If you were to use the number of telephone mainlines per 100 people as a research variable, to which sociological variable would you most like to relate it? Would it be a dependent or independent variable? Explain.

Adapted from *Atlas of the Future*. New York: MacMillan, 1998.

World View

Answers to Interpreting the Map

1. The data is quantitative because it can be given a specific numerical value (number of telephone mainlines per 100 people).
2. To make it qualitative, the data would have to be classified as "Countries with more than 50 mainlines per 100 people" or some other either/or or yes/no classifaction.
3. Answers will vary, but it might be used as a dependent variable for national income levels (as income level rises the number of telephone mainlines also rise).

Variables and Correlations

A **variable** is a characteristic—such as age, education, or occupation—that is subject to change.Variables can be *quantitative* or *qualitative, independent* or *dependent*.

variable
a characteristic that is subject to change

How do variables differ? Some materials have greater density than others. Some people have higher incomes than others. The literacy rate is higher in developed countries than in developing countries. Each of these characteristics is a **quantitative variable,** a variable that can be measured and given a numerical value.

quantitative variable
a characteristic that can be measured numerically

In contrast, a **qualitative variable** is identified by membership in a category. It is an "either/or" or a "yes/no" variable. Sex, marital status, and group membership are three qualitative variables often used by sociologists. People are either male or female; they are married or unmarried; they are band members, football players, sophomores—or they are not.

qualitative variable
a characteristic that is defined by its presence or absence in a category

Demonstration

Variables To reinforce the concept of dependent and independent variables, conduct the following demonstration. Propose a simple hypothesis: "In a game of catch, the way a ball is thrown will affect whether the ball will get caught." Lob a tennis ball around the room, making erratic throws, and note which throws are caught. Now that you've got students' attention, explain about independent and dependent variables. The way you threw the ball was *independent* of any other factors: you could have thrown fast, slow, high, low. Whether the ball was caught was *dependent* on the type of throw (or the independent variable). **L1**

Teaching Strategy

To show students how the existence of a correlation does not imply that a cause-and-effect relationship exists, write on the board: "Ice cream consumption is directly related to higher crime." Students will laugh, but point out that crime rates do rise in the summer and people probably do consume more ice cream in the summer. Ask students if this correlation isn't really a multiple causation. What factors contribute to high crime rates during the summer months? It is definitely not ice cream consumption. Ask students what the hidden variables are in this example. **L1**

Reteaching

In order to help students to see how a correlation works, ask them to simply consider whether the dependent variable showed an increase or decrease. For example, if students are food servers, do they get better tips if they offer better service? If they do, then we could say that better service is positively correlated with better tips. If they have not noticed that the tips go up if they offer better service, then there would be no correlation established.

Working with the Data

Figure 2.8 Remind students that in statistics, the term *positive* does not always mean good or beneficial. Negative does not always mean bad. Rather, positive means an increase and negative means a decrease. These definitions are similar to how the terms are used in mathematics.

independent variable
a characteristic that causes something to occur

dependent variable
a characteristic that reflects a change

intervening variable
a variable that changes the relationship between an independent and a dependent variable

correlation
a measure of the relationship between two variables

When they conduct studies, sociologists and other scientists identify the qualitative and quantitative variables to investigate. They then define these variables as either independent or dependent. The **independent variable** in a study is the variable that causes something to occur. The researcher changes, or looks for changes, in this variable. The **dependent variable** is what results from the change in the independent variable. For example, you might look at the time spent studying for a test as an independent variable that could cause a change in a grade—a dependent variable. The independent variable of poverty is one of several independent variables that can produce a change in the dependent variable of hunger. Whether a variable is dependent or independent can change depending on the situation. The extent of hunger may be a dependent variable in a study of poverty; it may be an independent variable in a study of crime.

An **intervening variable** influences the relationship between an independent and a dependent variable. The existence of a government support program, for example, may intervene between poverty and hunger. If a strong safety net exists, for instance, very poor parents and their children may experience no more hunger than those in the working class. Poverty is the cause of hunger but does not have to be if government intervention in the form of income and food exists. The poor *without* a safety net will experience more hunger. The poor *with* a safety net will not.

What is a correlation? A **correlation** is simply a measure of how things are related to one another. When a change in a trait, behavior, or an event (independent variable) is tied to a change in another trait, behavior, or event (dependent variable), a correlation exists. The correlation may be positive or negative.

A *positive correlation* exists if both the independent variable and the dependent variable change in the same direction. A positive correlation exists if we find that grades (dependent variable) improve as study time increases (independent variable). (See Figure 2.8.)

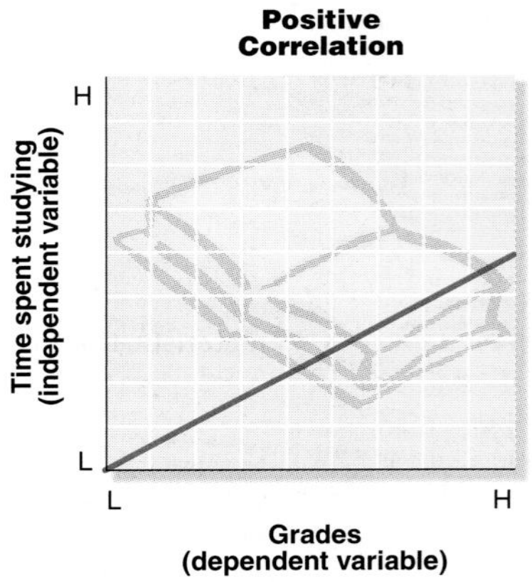

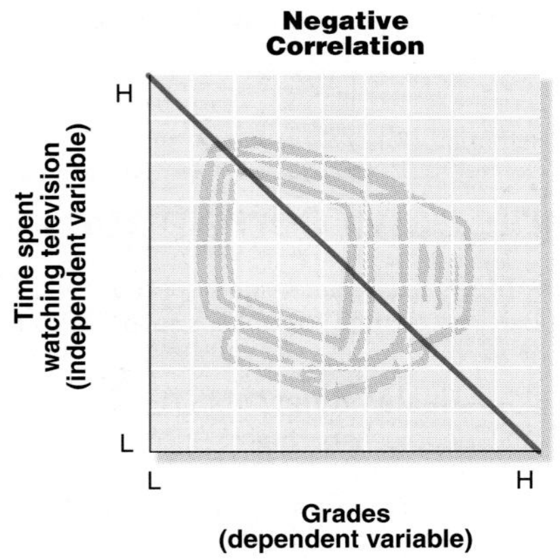

Figure 2.8 Positive and Negative Correlations
In a positive correlation, increases in the independent variable are associated with increases in the dependent variable. Grades improve with time spent studying.

In a negative correlation, increases in the independent variable are associated with decreases in the dependent variable. Grades decrease as time spent watching television increases.

Paired Learning Activity

An easy way to help students grasp the concepts of independent and dependent variables is to have them see it in terms of "if/then" statements, where If = independent and Then = dependent. For example, if people use drugs, then crime rates increase. Or, if students study, then their grades are higher. Ask students to work in pairs to come up with as many of these if/then statements as possible. You may also want to inform students that although most social events do have multiple causes, for the sake of this activity they can think in terms of one cause and effect. Debrief the activity by asking the pairs to read two or three of their statements and letting the rest of the class see if they agree with the independent and dependent labels. **L2**

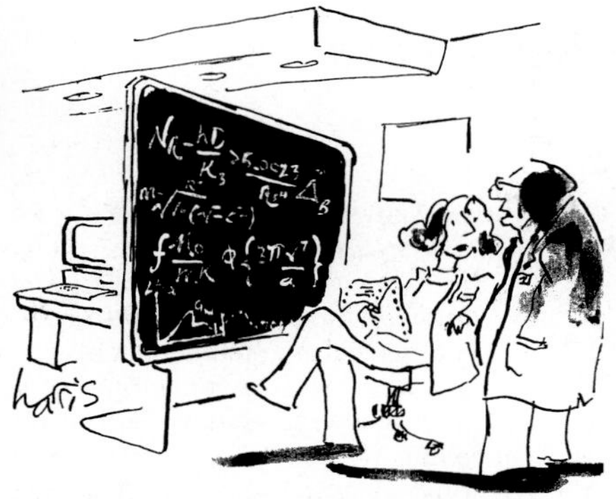

"In the social sciences we hardly use numbers, but we can write long, complicated sentences."

The man in this cartoon believes social science research is not very scientific. What do you think?

In a *negative correlation,* the variables change in opposite directions. An *increase* in the independent variable is linked to a *decrease* in the dependent variable. A negative correlation exists if we find that grades (dependent variable) go down as time spent watching television (independent variable) increases.

It is very important to remember that the existence of a correlation does not necessarily mean a cause-and-effect relationship exists. People with long arms often have long legs. However, the length of a person's arms does not cause the legs to grow longer. Both of these variables are controlled by other factors. It is much easier to show a correlation between two variables than it is to show causation.

> "It is the sample that we observe, but it is the population which we seek to know."
>
> **William G. Cochran**
> **statistician**

Standards for Showing Causation

In a causal relationship, one variable actually causes the other to occur. Three standards are commonly used to determine causal relationships. Let's look at the example of church attendance and juvenile delinquency discussed on page 5 to illustrate these standards.

- **Standard 1:** *Two variables must be correlated.* Some researchers found that juvenile delinquency increases as church attendance declines—a negative correlation. Does this negative correlation mean that not attending church causes higher delinquency? To answer this question, the second standard of causality must be met.
- **Standard 2:** *All other possible factors must be taken into account.* The fact that two events are correlated does not mean that one causes the other. The negative correlation between church attendance and delinquency occurs because age is related to both church attendance (older adolescents attend church less frequently) and delinquency (older adolescents are more likely to be delinquents). In fact, the correlation

Points to Stress

The standards for showing causation are key to students understanding the difference between correlations and cause-and-effect relationships—especially the third standard that covers the time element. Often the inability to say which occurred first is the most definitive and clearest way for students to understand the difference between correlation and cause-and-effect.

Reteaching

One way to help students to understand the concept of a spurious relationship is to have them visualize it. Use two variables previously mentioned and draw an arrow between them. If students think that a third variable might explain what is really happening, draw an arrow to it, placing the word above the two original variables. The three arrows now represent a triangle, thus the original two-variable correlation might be spurious.

Cooperative Learning Activity

Variables and Correlations Ask students to think of two variables that they think are correlated: height and shoe size; GPA and the number of hours spent studying each night; GPA and hours spent at work each week. One variable does not cause the other; the two are simply related. Working in small groups, have everyone walk around the room collecting data on their variables. You may want to give everyone a name tag and assign a number to each student to make the collecting of data more manageable. Afterward, students can create scatter plots, which are visual representations of correlation. Finally, have them review the text discussion on correlation. Did they find a strong or weak positive correlation, a strong or weak negative correlation, or zero correlation?
L3

Another Time: Reason and Science

Seventeenth-century Europe was an exciting place for those interested in using scientific methods in the search for truth. Copernicus was an astronomer who held that the sun was at the center of the solar system. Traditional belief at the time placed the earth at the center. Galileo sought to replace traditional myths with new knowledge based on reason and observation. This is one essential aspect of the scientific method.

In 1609, . . . Galileo turned his recently constructed telescope to the heavens, and through his startling observations made available to astronomy the first *qualitatively* new evidence it had known since the ancients. And each of his observations—the craters and mountains on the surface of the Moon, the moving spots on the Sun, the four moons revolving around Jupiter, the phases of Venus, the "unbelievably" numerous individual stars of the Milky Way—was interpreted by Galileo as powerful evidence in favor of the Copernican heliocentric [sun-centered] theory.

. . . Many individuals not previously involved in scientific studies now took up the telescope and saw for themselves the nature of the new Copernican universe. Astronomy, by virtue of the telescope and Galileo's compelling writings, became of vital interest to more than specialists. Successive generations of late Renaissance and post-Renaissance Europeans, increasingly willing to doubt the absolute authority of traditional doctrines both ancient and ecclesiastical, were finding the Copernican theory not only plausible but liberating. A new celestial world was opening up to the Western mind, just as a new terrestrial world was being opened by the global explorers.

Source: Excerpted from *The Passion of the Western Mind.* Copyright, © 1991 by Richard Tarnas. Reprinted by permission of Ballantine Books, a Division of Random House, Inc.

Thinking It Over

1. Can you analyze two important effects that the scientific revolution fueled by Galileo has had on individual behavior in the West?
2. How did Galileo employ the sociological imagination in his work?

between lower church attendance and delinquency is known as a **spurious correlation**—an apparent relationship between two variables that is actually caused by a third variable affecting both of the other variables. Thus, before we can predict that a causal relationship exists between church attendance and delinquency, we need to take other factors into consideration. In this instance, the age variable reveals that the relationship between church attendance and delinquency is not a *causal* one. Finding hidden causes and exposing spurious correlations is one of the greatest challenges in scientific research.

spurious correlation
a relationship between two variables that is actually caused by a third factor

❖ **Standard 3:** *A change in the independent variable must occur before a change in the dependent variable can occur.* This means that the cause must occur before the effect. Do people stop attending church before they become delinquents? Or does delinquent behavior occur before people stop attending church? Or do these variables appear at the same time? Even if age was not a factor in this correlation and no other factor could be found, causality between these two variables still could not be established. Why? Because it cannot be determined which occurs first.

Another Time

Review the concept of a theory by asking students to explain the prevailing theory of the nature of the universe at the time Galileo began making his observations. How did Galileo's discoveries change perceptions of the universe? Students should see that an existing belief was challenged by scientific evidence to the contrary. You may also point out that there is even today some debate about when a theory passes into the realm of fact, or scientific law. Sociologists are scientists who are always looking to validate existing theories or discover new ones to explain human behavior.

Answers to Thinking It Over

1. First, the introduction to these paragraphs indicates that Galileo's scientific discoveries encouraged people to search for new knowledge through the use of reason and observation. Second, his scientific discoveries caused people to doubt traditional doctrines, including long-held religious doctrines.
2. Galileo's study of the universe is sociologically symbolic. Sociologists are always trying to understand how the "big picture" is related to the details of individual lives. Galileo saw the stars individually, but he also saw them in the context of the entire universe, thus bringing people a new scientific understanding of the universe.

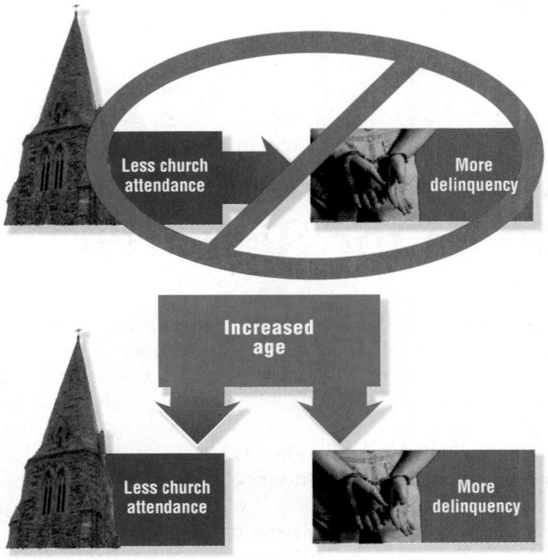

Figure 2.9 A Spurious Correlation *As you read on page 54, the correlation between juvenile delinquency and not attending church is a spurious correlation.*

Section 2 Assessment

Match terms a–i with the numbered statements below.

1. something that occurs in varying degrees
2. the variable in which a change or effect is observed
3. a change in one variable associated with a change in another variable
4. the idea that an event occurs as a result of several factors operating in combination
5. a factor that causes something to happen
6. the idea that the occurrence of one event leads to the occurrence of another event
7. a factor consisting of categories
8. when a relationship between two variables is actually the result of a third variable
9. a variable measured in numerical units

a. causation
b. multiple causation
c. variable
d. quantitative variable
e. qualitative variable
f. independent variable
g. dependent variable
h. correlation
i. spurious correlation

Critical Thinking

10. **Making Comparisons** In your own words, explain the difference between correlations and causation. Illustrate each with an example not found in the text.

Answers to Section 2 Assessment

1. c
2. g
3. h
4. b
5. f
6. a
7. e
8. i
9. d

Critical Thinking

10. Answers should include that correlations measure how things are related to one another and may be positive or negative; and causation means events occur in predictable, nonrandom ways where one event leads to another.

Integrating the Teacher Resources

For Spanish-speaking students, you may wish to use the reproducible worksheets available in the Spanish Supplements booklet in your Teacher's Resource Box. In addition to providing Spanish translations of selected Mastering Basic Concepts worksheets, the booklet contains English and Spanish summaries of the chapter's key points.

Paired Learning Activity

This is a fun activity to give students some idea of how complex society is and to help them understand the difficulty of doing sociological research. Ask students to work in pairs to write five questions about society that they would like to see answered. They could include any approach or subject, as long as it could be measured and involves social dynamics. Examples might include "Do men work harder than women?" or "What are the major differences in the ways teens communicate compared to adults?" After they have written their questions, ask them to look at each question and begin to write down all the variables they would have to examine to begin to research the answer to that question. Probably they will realize that their questions were very broad and they will wish to narrow them down. Let them rephrase the questions and repeat the process of generating a variables list. **L2**

Focus on Research

Students will be fascinated with Durkheim's understanding of suicide. Emphasize that Durkheim saw suicide as the loss of social networks. Draw a circle on the board and lines that emanate from that circle. Tell students that the circle represents the individual and the lines represent all that person's social networks such as parents, friends, coworkers, teachers, team members, and so on. When that person becomes depressed, he or she will begin to close off from those social networks. To illustrate this, erase the lines on the chalkboard one at a time. Explain that when teens become depressed and begin to close themselves off from their social networks, the risk of suicide increases.

Teaching Strategy

Make this statement: "Girls are more likely than boys to attempt suicide. True or false?" *(The correct answer is true, girls are more likely.)* Next, ask students which gender is more likely to complete the suicide. *(The answer is boys.)* Have students research suicide and gender, and gender-peer relationships. Suggest they focus on a specific issue such as whether or not the friendships that boys and girls form influence the likelihood that they will commit suicide. **L1**

Focus on Research

Secondary Analysis: A Model for Research

Emile Durkheim was the first person to be formally recognized as a sociologist. (See pp. 16–17 for more on this pioneer.) He was also the most scientific of the pioneers. Durkheim conducted a study that stands as a classic research model for sociologists today. His investigation of suicide was, in fact, the first sociological study to use statistics. In *Suicide* (1964, originally published in 1897), Durkheim argued that some aspects of human behavior—even something as personal as suicide—can be explained on the societal level, without reference to individuals.

To carry out his secondary analysis, Durkheim used precollected data from the government population reports of several countries. Much of it was from the French government statistical office. He collected data for approximately 26,000 suicides and classified them by age, sex, marital status, whether there were children in the family, religion, location, time of year, method of suicide, and other factors. (And all this before there were computers!) As he gathered his data, he continually refined and adjusted his hypotheses.

Durkheim wanted to see if suicide rates were related to how socially involved individuals felt. He identified three suicide types in his study: egoistic, altruistic, and anomic.

He hypothesized that *egoistic* suicide increases when individuals do not have sufficient social ties. For example, he proposed that adults who never married and were not heavily involved with family life were more likely to commit suicide than married adults.

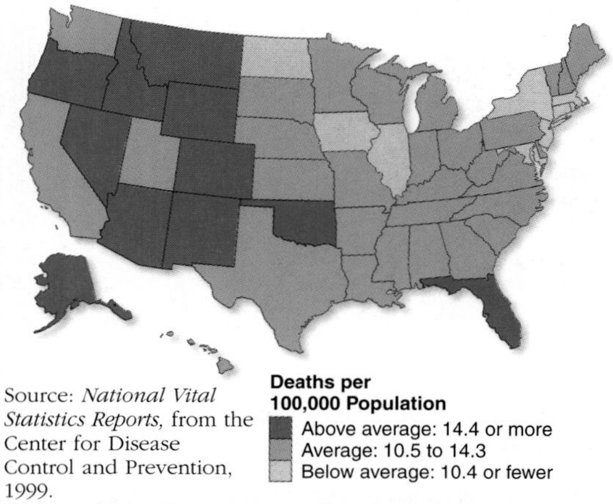

Map A—Suicide Rates for the Year 1997

Source: *National Vital Statistics Reports*, from the Center for Disease Control and Prevention, 1999.

Map B—People Per Square Mile

Source: Lisa Thomas, *Student Atlas,* New York: DK Publishing, 1998, p. 39.

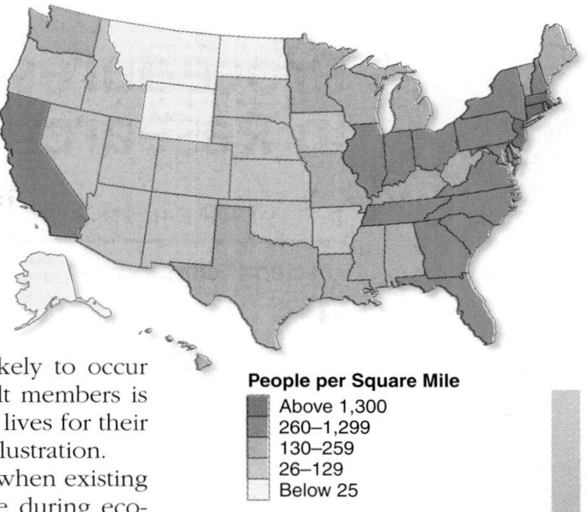

He also predicted that *altruistic* suicide was more likely to occur when social ties are too strong. The mass suicides of cult members is one example. Military personnel trained to lay down their lives for their countries (such as Japanese kamikaze pilots) is another illustration.

Durkheim also thought that *anomic* suicide increased when existing social ties were broken. For example, suicide rates spike during economic depressions. People suddenly without jobs are more prone to kill themselves. Suicide may also increase during periods of prosperity. People may loosen their social ties by taking new jobs, moving to new communities, or finding new mates.

Durkheim found strong support for his predictions. Suicide rates were higher among unmarried than married people and among military personnel than civilians. They were also higher among people involved in nationwide economic crises.

As a result of his study, Durkheim drew several important conclusions. First, social behavior can be explained by social rather than psychological factors. Second, suicide is affected by the closeness of social ties. Finally, society can be studied scientifically, and sociology is worthy of academic recognition (Ritzer, 1996).

Working with the Research

1. Emile Durkheim's study of suicide suggested that one factor in the suicide rate is the degree to which the individual has group ties. One indication of social ties is population density. Based on Map B, where would you expect to find the highest suicide rates in the United States? Does Map A agree with your predictions?
2. Durkheim noted that "psychological explanations are insufficient when analyzing social behavior." In your own words, tell what this statement means.
3. Which perspective do you think Durkheim followed in his study of suicide: the functionalist, the conflict, or the symbolic interactionist? Give reasons for your answer.
4. Using what you have learned from Durkheim's research, formulate a hypothesis about mass suicide.

Answers to Working with the Research

1. Students may answer that they would expect the suicide rate to be higher in the more populated areas, but in fact there is more chance of a person's social network falling apart in the less densely populated areas. The maps support the idea that suicide rates are higher in the less populated states.
2. Students should understand that the group itself has an influence on behavior that is out of the control of the individual in many cases.
3. Students will probably make a stronger case for symbolic interactionist or possibly the functionalist approaches. The important point is that they support their arguments with good reasoning.
4. Student answers will vary but might reflect a theory presented after the student murders at Columbine High School that the killers were disconnected from the social network.

Encouraging Citizenship Activity

Although a sociologist's interest in suicide is on a different level than that of a psychologist, it might be very beneficial to take a class period to discuss the issue of teen suicide. Invite a psychologist to talk to the class about suicide and related mental health. Explain to students that they may be given the information they need to recognize signs of depression in their friends or relatives should it occur. Ask the guest speaker if he or she could relate suicide or mental health to a withdrawal or lack of an individual's social network.

Using the Section Preview

A research project at this time will encourage students and also reinforce learning across all the disciplines. Remind students that in order to be accepted by the scientific community, all research must be reproducible. That is, if other researchers cannot reproduce your experiment or study and get the same results then it may not be considered valid. That is one reason why it is so important to follow a standardized and accepted methodology for conducting research.

Integrating the Teacher Resources

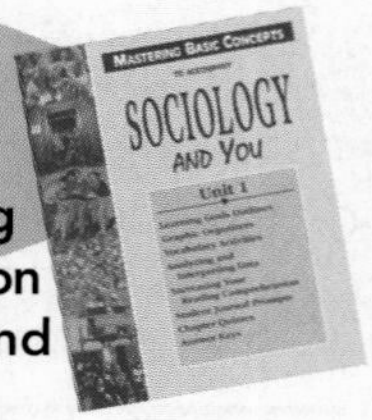

Look for the Chapter 2 Increasing Your Reading Comprehension worksheet and the Guided Reading worksheet in the Unit 1 Mastering Basic Concepts booklet in your Teacher's Resource Box. Both will strengthen student reading comprehension skills.

Section 3 Procedures and Ethics in Research

Key Terms

- scientific method
- hypothesis

Section Preview

The research process is made up of several distinct steps. These steps represent an ideal for scientific research. It is not always necessary or even possible that they always be strictly followed. Researchers have an ethical obligation to protect participants' privacy and to avoid deceiving or harming them. Preserving the rights of subjects must sometimes be weighed against the value of the knowledge to be gained.

scientific method the recognition and formulation of a problem, the collection of data through observation and experiment, and the formulation and testing of hypotheses

hypothesis testable statement of relationships among variables

Steps for Doing Research

Scientists use a research model known as the **scientific method.** It involves the pursuit of knowledge in a systematic way. As shown in Figure 2.10 on the following page, the steps in the scientific method include identifying a problem, reviewing the literature, formulating hypotheses, developing a research design, collecting data, analyzing data, and stating findings and conclusions.

1. **Identify the Problem.** Researchers begin by choosing an object or topic for study. Most topics are chosen because they interest the researcher, address a social problem, test a major theory, or respond to a government agency's or organization's needs.
2. **Review the Literature.** Once the object or topic of study has been identified, the researcher must find out all he or she can about any earlier research. This process is called a *literature search.* For example, a sociologist investigating suicide will probably develop an approach related to the classic study of suicide by Emile Durkheim, as well as to the work of other sociologists who have since researched the topic.
3. **Formulate Hypotheses.** The next step is for a sociologist to develop a *hypothesis* based on what is known about the issue so far. A **hypothesis** is a testable statement of relationships among well-defined variables. One hypothesis might be "The longer couples are married, the less likely they are to divorce." The independent variable is length of marriage, and the dependent variable is divorce.
4. **Develop a Research Design.** A research design states the procedures the researcher will follow for collecting and analyzing data. Will the study be a survey or a case study? If it is a survey, will data be collected from a cross-section of an entire population, such as the Harris and Gallup polls, or will a sample be selected from only one city? Will simple percentages or more sophisticated statistical methods be used? These and many other questions must be answered so the researcher will have a sound plan to follow.
5. **Collect Data.** There are three basic ways of gathering data in sociological research—asking people questions, observing behavior, and analyzing existing materials and records. Sociologists studying interracial marriages could question couples about ways they communicate. They could locate an organization with a large number of interracially married couples and observe couples' behavior. Or they could compare the divorce rate among interracially married couples with the divorce rate of the population as a whole.

Encouraging Citizenship Activity

Ask students, in small groups, to identify a problem or possible need in your school. For example, is the school changing its calendar or is there an expressed or unexpressed need for bilingual classes?

Students should devise a questionnaire or survey that can be used to gauge opinions on the selected issues. Caution students to be objective and refrain from allowing their own biases to color the way the questions are worded. Encourage students to look at some sample surveys before they begin. Ask students to keep careful records as they distribute and collect the surveys. If they need assistance in statistically analyzing the data, bring in a numbers expert or one of the school's math teachers to help them. Students should next draw conclu-

6. **Analyze Data.** Once the data have been collected and classified, they can be analyzed to determine whether the hypotheses are supported. It is not unlike putting together pieces of a jigsaw puzzle. This is not as easy or automatic as it sounds, because results are not always obvious. Because the same data can be interpreted in several ways, judgments have to be made. Guarding against personal preferences for particular outcomes is especially important in this phase of research.
7. **State Findings and Conclusions.** After analyzing the data, a researcher is ready to state the conclusions of the study. It is during this phase that the methods are described (for example, survey, case study) and hypotheses are formally accepted, rejected, or modified. By making the research procedures public, scientists make it possible for others to duplicate the research, conduct a slightly modified study, or go in a very different direction.

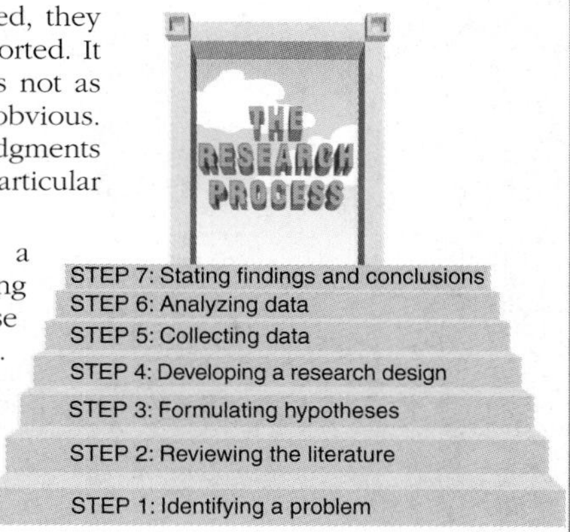

Figure 2.10 Steps in the Research Process

Realistically, do sociologists follow these steps? Some sociologists believe that this research model is too rigid to be used in studying human society. Even though most sociologists do follow the model, they do not necessarily follow it mechanically. They may conduct exploratory studies prior to stating hypotheses and developing research designs. Or they may change their hypotheses and research designs as their investigations proceed.

Ethics in Social Research

Research is a distinctly human activity. Although there are principles for conducting research, such as objectivity and verifiability, scientists sometimes fail to live up to these principles. At times, even the ethics of research is not honored by researchers.

Unfortunately, there is a long list of examples of ethical lapses in medical research. During the Nuremberg trials, twenty Nazi doctors were convicted of conducting sadistic experiments on concentration camp inmates. From 1932 to 1972, the Public Health Service of the U.S. government deliberately did not treat four hundred syphilitic African American agricultural workers and day laborers so that biomedical researchers could study the full evolution of the disease (Jones, 1993). For twenty years, researchers at Germany's University of Heidelberg used human corpses, those of adults and children, in high-speed automobile crash tests (Fedarko, 1993). Federal investigators in the United States have documented over ten years of fraud in some of the most important breast cancer research ever done (Crewdson, 1994).

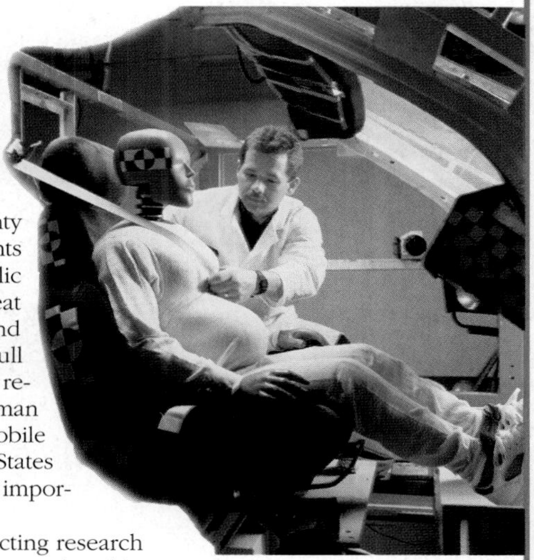

It is generally thought that using human corpses in automobile crash tests is unethical. Do you agree?

Several social scientists, also, have been criticized for conducting research that many scientists consider unethical. In each case, subjects were placed in stressful situations without being informed of the true nature of the experiments (See pages 144 and 188 for a discussion of two of these studies).

More often, however, sociologists routinely protect the rights of research subjects and avoid deceiving or harming them. For example, Mario Brajuha, a graduate student at a major American university, kept detailed field notes while doing a participant observation study of restaurant work (Brajuha and Hallowell, 1986).

Teaching Strategy

Ask students which ethical standard is being violated in each of the following scenarios:

1. After a field study of deviant behavior during a riot, law enforcement officials demand that the researcher identify those people who were observed looting. Rather than risk arrest as an accomplice after the fact, the researcher complies. *(protecting the subjects' rights to privacy)*
2. A research questionnaire is circulated among students as part of the university registration packet. Although students are not told they must complete the questionnaire, the hope is that they will believe they must—thus ensuring a higher completion rate. *(not being truthful in reporting and disclosing methods)*
3. Researchers obtain a list of right-wing radicals they wish to study. They contact the radicals with the explanation that each has been selected "at random" from among the general population to take a sampling of "public opinion." *(protecting the freedom and privacy of research subjects; not being truthful)*

L2

sions, based on their findings, and write recommendations for action. Have students arrange to present their research to the faculty, the student council, or the board of education. Be sure they practice their presentations in advance.

This exercise can be planned together with another teacher to emphasize its interdisciplinary nature. An English class may help with the writing and editing of the survey; a math class may do the statistics. Besides teaching data collection and analysis, the activity also teaches presentation skills and group cooperation. Additionally, students develop a sense of ownership in their school, which may lead to solving campus problems.

L2

Tech Trends

Tell students about a sociologist who was interested in researching so-called "ecoterrorists." While observing the terrorists, she saw them put spikes in trees. Their actions could result in the serious injury or death of loggers who use chain saws to cut through trees. Though local police wanted to arrest the ecoterrorists, the sociologist was committed to maintaining the terrorists' confidentiality. What Code of Ethics issues do students see in this situation? Do they think the sociologist should turn over her research notes, which could identify the ecoterrorists? Is the use of the term *ecoterrorist* just another example of the media trying to label people to create a story? Divide the class into three groups that will act as members of ethical review boards, and have students decide if they should ask the sociologist to turn her research over to local authorities.

Answer to Analyzing the Trends

Pro and con arguments should be based on students' familiarity with the Code of Ethics. Students may write their arguments as a homework assignment, or present the arguments, for and against, to the whole class. To extend the exercise, students could write mock research proposals in which video cameras would be used.

Tech Trends

Has Technology Made Privacy Obsolete?

A recent episode of NBC's *Today* show featured a segment about a Louisiana woman whose male neighbor had secretly installed video cameras in her bedroom and bathroom. Because of the cameras, the neighbor was able to secretly observe this woman in her most private moments. While researchers have been observing subjects for many years, it is alarming that this immoral and extremely illegal use of technology is now within the financial range and technical ability of many people.

Some sociologists and psychologists are concerned about the ethics of videotaping research subjects.

One of the requirements of the Code of Ethics of the American Sociological Association found in the Appendix is to protect the privacy of research subjects. Imagine, then, that a sociologist came to your school to conduct research and asked permission to place video cameras in the hallways, classrooms, and cafeteria. Do you think that permission from school administrators would be enough to meet this requirement? How would you respond to this request? What if every student in the school gave permission for the cameras? How would you feel if you gave your permission, but then did something really silly or wrong in front of one of the cameras?

Lawsuits have been filed in some states by workers after discovering that their employers had installed hidden cameras in rest rooms or changing rooms to help reduce high levels of employee theft. Managers claim that dishonest employees often use these areas to hide company products in their purses or bags. Workers argue that they are entitled to expect a minimum level of privacy and that hidden cameras violate that expectation. But, objects management, if workers know the cameras are there, they won't be caught. Similarly, if researchers begin videotaping with the consent of their subjects, will they get a true record of behavior? If they do not advise their subjects of the taping, what happens if a criminal act is recorded? Do the researchers have an obligation to release the tape to the authorities? Ethical issues will continue to arise as technology allows investigators to invade areas where custom and culture had prevented them from going.

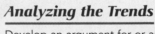

Analyzing the Trends

Develop an argument for or against the use of video equipment in a sociological research project. Be sure to use logical arguments and evaluate the issues of maximizing benefits to society while minimizing the harms sociological work might create.

Using Decision-Making Skills

Read the following paragraph to the class or post it up on the board or on an overhead projector.

Dr. Peter Publish, a well-known sociologist at Potato University, is interested in researching the effects of low grades on student perceptions of teacher competence. He believes that students who receive lower grades will give their teachers lower evaluations than students who receive higher grades. He plans to give out grades before the semester is over. One group of his students will get higher grades than they have earned, another will get lower grades than they deserve, and a third group will get the grades they actually at-

Because of suspected arson at a restaurant where he was employed as a waiter, his field notes became an object of interest to the police, the district attorney, the courts, and some suspects. For two years, Brajuha refused to reveal the contents of his field notes to the police. He did so in the face of a subpoena, the threat of imprisonment, and possible harm to himself, his wife, and his children. Brajuha was protecting the privacy rights of those individuals described in his notes.

What is sociology's code of ethics? Conducting ethical research means showing objectivity; using superior research standards; reporting findings and methods truthfully; and protecting the rights, privacy, integrity, dignity, and freedom of research subjects. The American Sociological Association has published guidelines for conducting research. (This code has been reproduced in full in the Appendix of this text.) Briefly put, the Code of Ethics is concerned with getting the greatest possible benefit with the least possible harm.

Can researchers act ethically and still get the information they need? Sometimes acting ethically is difficult. The researcher must sometimes make hard decisions about morally questionable issues, such as the situation in which Mario Brajuha found himself. Moreover, the researcher must balance the interests of those being studied against the need for accurate, timely data. Balance is the key to the issue of ethics. At the least, the people involved in sociological research should be protected from social, financial, or psychological damage or legal prosecution.

"The world has achieved brilliance without conscience. Ours is a world of nuclear giants and ethical infants."

Omar Bradley
American general

Section 3 Assessment

1. The steps below describe a research project on children without brothers or sisters ("only" children). Put steps a–g in order of how they would occur according to the steps in the research process.
   - **a.** A researcher reads many articles about theory and research on the intelligence level of only children.
   - **b.** From previous research and existing theory, a researcher states that only children appear to be more intelligent than children with siblings.
   - **c.** A researcher collects data on only children from a high school in a large city.
   - **d.** A researcher writes a report giving evidence that only children are more intelligent than children with brothers or sisters.
   - **e.** A researcher decides to study the intelligence level of only children.
   - **f.** A researcher classifies and processes the data collected in order to test a hypothesis.
   - **g.** A researcher decides on the data needed to test a hypothesis, the methods for data collection, and the techniques for data analysis.

Critical Thinking

2. **Drawing Conclusions** What issues in studying society might interfere with following the scientific method precisely?
3. **Analyzing Information** Can secret observation of people ever be considered ethical? Why or why not?

Answers to Section 3 Assessment

1. The steps in order are e, a, b, g, c, f, and d.

Critical Thinking

2. Answers will vary, but might include a lack of time, a shortage of funds, and pressure to arrive at preconceived results.
3. Answers will vary. Students should include examples of morally questionable issues where an individual's safety or health is at risk, as in the case of a child molester or suspected rapist.

Integrating the Teacher Resources

For review or enrichment, use the Student Journal Prompts for this chapter available in the Unit 1 Mastering Basic Concepts **booklet in your Teacher's Resource Box.**

tained. Dr. Publish believes that his research method is acceptable since the study is being done for scientific purposes.

Ask students to review the American Sociological Association's Code of Ethics on pages 602–607 of the text, and decide what part, if any, of the Code of Ethics is being violated. What issues does the Potato University research project raise in students' minds? Have the class act as if they were members of Potato University's ethical review board. What is the future for Dr. Publish and sociological research at Potato University? Have the class write an "Ethics in Research" policy statement for Potato University.
L2

Sociology Today

Have students ever heard or read about public figures whom they know or suspect have been misquoted in an interview? Have students try to recall specific instances. What issues are raised when people or sources are misquoted in print or quoted out of context? Have students also identify and discuss potential problems concerning taped interviews that are edited before being shown on television. For extra credit, students might be asked to bring in newspaper or magazine articles to support the discussion.

Answer to
Doing Sociology

Answers will vary. Students will assess the articles they bring in, using the consumer steps outlined in the feature.

Integrating the
Teacher Resources

Look for the Alternative Assessments **booklet in your Teacher's Resource Box for essay tests and performance assessment activities based on this chapter.**

Sociology Today

Should You Believe Everything You Read?

It is sometimes said that we are living in the "age of instant information." One unfortunate side effect is the tendency for studies and research results to be reported in the media without background or explanation. There are, however, some easy steps you can follow that will make you a savvy consumer in the information marketplace.

Be Skeptical. Be suspicious of what you read. The media soundbite treatment tends to sensationalize and distort information. For example, the media may report that $500,000 was spent to find out that love keeps families together. In fact, this may have been only one small part of a larger research project. Moreover, chances are the media have oversimplified even this part of the researcher's conclusions.

Consider the Source of Information. The credibility of a study may be affected by who paid for the results. For example, you should know whether a study on the relationship between cancer and tobacco has been sponsored by the tobacco industry or by the American Cancer Society. Suppose that representatives of tobacco companies denied the existence of any research linking throat and mouth cancer with snuff dipping. Further suppose that an independent medical researcher concluded that putting a "pinch between your cheek and gum" has, in the long run, led to cancer in humans. The self-interest of the tobacco companies taints their objectivity and requires further investigation on your part.

At the very least, you want to know the source of information before making a judgment about scientific conclusions. This caution is especially relevant to the Internet. Because this information varies widely in its accuracy and reliability, sources must be evaluated with particular care.

Do Not Mistake Correlation for Causation. Remember that a correlation between two variables does not mean that one caused the other. At one time, the percentage of Americans who smoked was increasing at the same time that life expectancy was increasing. Did this mean that smoking caused people to live longer? Actually, a third factor—improved health care—accounted for the increased life expectancy. Do not assume that two events are related causally just because they occur together.

Doing Sociology

Bring to class an article reporting on a study. These can be found in periodicals or weekly news magazines. Be prepared to share with your classmates how these three safeguards can be applied to the reported study.

Cooperative Learning Activity

Interview Ask students to work in cooperative groups to interview a willing authority figure, such as an outspoken teacher or administrator, on a controversial or sensitive issue. Then ask students to write up the interview as a newspaper article and ask the interviewee to evaluate their articles on the basis of how accurately they interpreted and conveyed his or her words.
L2

CHAPTER 2 ASSESSMENT

Summary

Section 1: Research Methods

Main Idea: When sociologists do quantitative research, they generally use either surveys or precollected data. Each has its own advantages and disadvantages. Qualitative research uses descriptive rather than numerical data. Field studies are best used when interaction needs to be observed in a natural setting, and when in-depth analysis is needed. The case study is the most popular approach to field research.

Section 2: Causation In Science

Main Idea: Causation in science is the idea that one event leads to another event. Scientists assume that all events have causes, or determinants. Sociologists work to discover these causes. Three standards must be met before causation can be proved.

Section 3: Procedures and Ethics In Research

Main Idea: The research process is made up of several distinct steps. These steps represent an ideal for scientific research. It is not always necessary or even possible that they always be strictly followed. Researchers have an ethical obligation to protect participants' privacy and to avoid deceiving or harming them. Preserving the rights of subjects must sometimes be weighed against the value of the knowledge to be gained.

SOCIOLOGY Online

Self-Check Quiz
Visit the *Sociology and You* Web site at soc.glencoe.com and click on **Chapter 2—Self-Check Quizzes** to prepare for the chapter test.

Reviewing Vocabulary

Complete each sentence using each term once.

a. causation
b. code of ethics
c. correlation
d. dependent variable
e. field research
f. independent variable
g. multiple causation
h. qualitative variable
i. quantitative variable
j. representative sample
k. scientific method
l. secondary analysis

1. A variable that can be measured and given a numerical value is called a ______________.
2. ______________ states that an event occurs as a result of several factors working in combination.
3. The use of existing information as a method of collecting data best describes ______________.
4. A random sample that accurately reflects the whole population is called ______________.
5. The ______________ is a research principle that is concerned with achieving the greatest possible benefit with the last possible harm.
6. The idea that events occur in predictable ways, with one event leading to another is called ______________.
7. ______________ is a measure of how things are related to one another.
8. ______________ is a variable identified by membership in a category.
9. The steps that include identifying a problem reviewing the literature, and collecting data are part of the ______________.
10. ______________ is used to investigate aspects of social life that cannot be measured quantitatively and are best understood in a natural setting.
11. ______________ are variables in which change has occurred.
12. Variables that cause something to occur are called ______________.

ANSWERS CHAPTER 2 ASSESSMENT

Reviewing Vocabulary

1. i	**5.** b	**9.** k
2. g	**6.** a	**10.** e
3. l	**7.** c	**11.** d
4. j	**8.** h	**12.** f

Reviewing the Facts

1. Field research
2. secondary analysis
3. altruistic suicide
4. participant observation
5. Identify the problem, review the literature, formulate hypotheses, develop a research design, collect data, analyze data, state finding and conclusions.
6. Advantages: the person answers in his or her own words, reveals many attitudes. Disadvantages: Not easy to quantify or compare. Meaning of questions can change.

Thinking Critically

1. Answers will vary.
2. This is quite challenging. Students will most likely suggest just asking people. However, if you conducted a survey, would employees lie to protect themselves? Would it be possible to interview employers and ask for instances when alcoholism has entered the workplace? Could you ask employers to assess the impact these instances had on worker performance, company productivity, and employee relations? After students have suggested research methods, you might want them to consider some of the ethical issues involved in doing this research.
3. Students should answer that males rarely find it possible to leave the workforce because of pregnancies. In some professions women were not compensated for time off, but if a woman takes a year more off to have and raise a child, it is not likely that she will be compensated for that

ANSWERS CHAPTER 2 ASSESSMENT

length of time, lowering her earnings over time. Even a few years away from the workforce to raise children will seriously affect a woman's income levels over the course of her career.

4. The high suicide rates in Cobain's home state were due in part to an economic downturn that had devastating implications for job opportunities. The state that he grew up in did not cause him to commit suicide, of course.
5. Numerous examples are given in the text, such as in the Enrichment Reading on pages 66–67. The sociologist's dilemma with conducting research in a school is common, since many research projects are focused on education. If your students embark on a research project that is school-based, they should read and understand the Code of Ethics in its entirety.
Steps to Ensure Privacy of Participants:
Ask permission to use voice recorders
Distort voices
Use fictitious names of students
Use fictitious locations
Do not reveal sources
Report honestly

CHAPTER 2 ASSESSMENT

Reviewing the Facts

1. If a sociologist wanted to study high school cliques, what would be the best method for collecting data? Support your choice by giving two benefits of using this method.
2. Examine Figures 2.6 and 2.7 on page 49 showing median annual income by sex, race and education. What is the scientific name given for this type of information?
3. Donna Gaines, a sociologist, studied teen suicides and reported her findings in a book, *Teenage Wasteland: Suburbia's Dead End Kids.* She found several suicides that were committed by teens in a group. How might Emile Durkeim classify or describe this type of suicide?
4. Sociologist Elijah Anderson studied gangs in Philadelphia. In order to do that, he had to take off his shirt and tie and dress like the young men he was going to study. What is the name of the method of research that Anderson used here?
5. What are the seven steps in the scientific method?
6. Survey research is obtained through the use of questionnaires and interviews containing closed-ended questions and/or open-ended questions. Using a table like the one below, list the advantages and disadvantages of open-ended survey research.

Advantages	Disadvantages

Thinking Critically

1. **Applying Concepts** In this chapter you read about positive and negative correlations. Give two examples each of relationships that you suspect may be positive and negative correlations. For example, you may propose that an increase in income is positively correlated to increased dining out.
2. **Identifying Alternatives** Identify the methods of research you would use if you wanted to study the effects of alcoholism on the work force. Explain why you would use this method. Briefly describe how you might conduct the research.
3. **Drawing Conclusions** Figure 2.6 on page 49 indicates that males make more money on average than females. Some sociologists would tell you that pregnancy contributes to the variations in male's vs. female's income earnings. What variables might explain this conclusion?
4. **Synthesizing Information** Rock musician Kurt Cobain, of the band Nirvana, committed suicide in 1994. In the years that Cobain was growing up in the state of Washington, the suicide rate there was higher than that of many other states. (It has since decreased.) What variables would you look at to examine a state's suicide rate?
5. **Drawing Conclusions** You have been assigned a research project in a high school. Using the American Sociological Association's Code of Ethics (found at the back of the book), what considerations would first have to be made? Using a diagram similar to the one below, list and discuss the steps that you believe would be necessary to ensure the privacy of the student participants.

Sociology Projects

1. **Qualitative Research** In order to strengthen your skills in qualitative research, perform the following activity. Look around your classroom and select an object that you see in the room, such as a blackboard eraser. Imagine that you have never seen this object before and have no

Sociology Projects

1. The intent of this activity is to give students experience with qualitative research. By excluding function from the description, students are forced to be observant.
2. This is ultimately the purpose of this chapter, to give students the knowledge they need to conduct "mini" research projects. They need to follow all the procedures of research. Students will probably need about one week outside of class to be able to get their ideas down on paper.
3. This is a simple way to quantify data. Be sure that students agree on the definition of what constitutes violent behavior. (Is bumping up against someone considered violent? That's okay as long as the entire class specifies that behavior as one of their variables). Students are usually astonished when they begin recording the number of acts of violence. They are

idea what it is or what it is used for. Write a brief description of the object in terms of its physical nature but do not try to determine its function. In this exercise, you are simply making an observation. Compare your description with those of your classmates.

2. **Conducting a Research Study** Write a proposal for a study that you would like to see conducted at your school. You must decide how you will conduct the research. Will it be a survey, interview, or observation? Follow the standards set out in the textbook on pages 58–59, indicating variables, research design, hypothesis, and a review of the literature if possible. Include information on how you will identify your sample population. Also include sample questions (open or closed). Be prepared to present this study to your class "ethics board" for approval.
3. **Quantitative Research** Try this quantitative research project at home. Over the next few days or nights, watch three television shows, each at least thirty minutes long. For the purpose of this activity, the programs you select should be prime time dramas for mature audiences. Record the number of times a person or animal is subjected to physical violence. Remember that physical violence is everything from shoving to shooting. When you have finished collecting your data, create a graph that illustrates the number of violent acts for the shows that you watched. You have just done quantitative research and you will probably be amazed at the results.
4. **Observation** Find a place in your town or neighborhood that has a four-way stop sign. Find a place to observe that is not immediately noticeable from the street. Observe how many people come to a full stop, how long people stop, and how people yield for each other. You might want to see if women yield more for men than other women and if older people yield more than younger people. Record your observations and share it with classmates. See if you can determine any patterns from what may apparently be random behaviors.
5. **Analyzing Information** Collect newspaper articles that announce medical or health breakthroughs or that publicize results of social studies. Analyze them by asking the following questions:
   - **a.** What claims or promises were made in the article?
   - **b.** What actual quotes by the researchers were included, if any?
   - **c.** Was the article well documented? Did it provide source information?
   - **d.** Were there any "disclaimers," or warnings about the results not being proven, or more testing needing to be done? If so, where were these cautionary words placed in the article?
   - **e.** What is your opinion about the actions of the reporter? Do you think he or she was journalistically responsible or do you think the article was an attempt to grab headlines?
6. **Filtering** Some high schools are concerned about Internet use by high school students and are considering *filtering,* a process that blocks access to web sites that have certain words or phrases in their text. Some teachers are concerned that this imposed censorship will hamper student research, since the filtering process looks for words only, and generally does not evaluate the context in which the word is used. Choose a partner to debate the issue of Internet filtering in high schools. Develop arguments that support your position of being in favor or being against high school Internet filtering. Support your arguments with research.

Technology Activity

1. Visit an Internet site on a current events topic that interests you. Using the criteria for determining a valid web resource found on pages 47–48, determine if your site qualifies. If not, keep searching for a related site until you find one that meets the criteria. Bring your recommended URL to class to create a database of great current events sites.

65

so desensitized to televised violence that they don't even "see" it unless they record it.

4. This is another opportunity for students to practice gathering quantitative research. If students pick a busy intersection, advise students to position themselves so they can discreetly observe. They will be fascinated with what they see. They also might want to include an estimate of the ages of the drivers.
5. You may wish to have students begin to collect articles throughout the year that discuss topics that you will be covering in your curriculum. Students will begin to be amazed at the number of articles appearing in daily newspapers that directly touch upon sociological issues. Or, as this activity suggests, you may want students to restrict their "portfolios" or scrapbooks to articles that report the results of sociological or health studies.
6. Students will probably think filtering is unnecessary, but it might be useful for them to interview teachers to find out what they think about it. Tell them that in one school a teacher had a student research homeless teens and the student pulled up numerous pornographic teen web sites. Under some circumstances, the teacher could lose his or her job. Have students debate filtering from that perspective, as well.

Technology Activity

1. Students might become frustrated as they visit some of their favorite sites and realize that very few of these sites meet the criteria described in the skills feature. This could be a real eye-opener for them. Tell students that major on-line universities and government libraries are always reliable sources of credible information and all the necessary information is provided in the abstract.

Enrichment Reading

This article is an opportunity for students to identify the key concepts of this chapter. Students should be able to identify the hypothesis, research methods, and ethical considerations. Opinions will vary as to what the research team's hypothesis might have been, since it is not specifically stated. The article brings up several issues from the text, including interviews, participant observation, ethics of privacy, and the role of the researcher as interventionist. This is a classic example of good field research. As a follow-up, have students discuss whether or not a similar study could be replicated at your high school.

Chapter 2

Enrichment Reading

School Talk

by Donna Eder

This excerpt describes research methods and ethical issues in a well-known study of middle-school culture.

Collecting data on students' experiences. We used a variety of means to collect data on students' experiences with peers in school. All four researchers observed lunchtime interaction at least twice weekly for periods of time ranging from five months to twelve months. We never took notes openly during the lunch period, but sometimes recorded brief notes in the bathroom or hallway between lunch sessions. These notes were expanded upon and all notes were recorded fully immediately after leaving the setting.

Donna Eder and Steve Parker also attended male and female **extracurricular** activities twice weekly for an entire academic year. Given the importance of athletic activities and cheerleading, we focused primarily on them, going to athletic games and practices, pep rallies, and cheerleading practices and tryouts. In addition, we observed choir and band practices and concerts, talent shows, and the one school play that was performed during the three-year period of the study. We were able to take some notes during these events, since our roles were more those of observers than participants. Afterward, we expanded on these notes and recorded them fully.

Once we had been in the setting for several months, we began doing informal interviews with individuals or groups of students on issues that arose from our observations. They included questions about the meaning of popularity, attitudes toward other students in the school, and views on male-female relationships. While some were so informal they were simply recorded as *field notes,* ten of the more extensive interviews were tape-recorded and **transcribed** in full.

Finally, we tape-recorded conversations in most of the lunch groups which we observed. Typically, we sat with the group members for three to seven months prior to taping them, so they were already used to our presence. We got written permission from both the students and their parents before we made a recording. On the permission forms we assured them that no one who knew them would be able to listen to or watch the tapes. We also told them that their real names would not be used in any written report. To further insure the participants' privacy, we have also changed all names of identifying locations and modified discussions about particular people or events. Only one parent requested that her daughter not participate in the study. Since she could not be asked to separate from her group, we decided to omit the entire group from the study. . . .

More About . . . Donna Eder

The following information is contained on Dr. Eder's web site at Indiana State University. This site was last updated in 1995.

DONNA EDER's interests fall primarily in the areas of gender, culture and education. She has completed an in-depth study of adolescent peer culture, showing how the common speech activities of adolescents—insulting, teasing, gossip and story-telling—are used to further traditional gender roles as well as to provide opportunities to mock and challenge these roles. She has also worked with others, on a study of the cultural side of the women's movement by focusing on the National Women's Music Festival, in examining the processes by which such festivals promote social change as well as provide arenas for conflict between different groups of women. Currently she is implementing and studying a peer culture approach to conflict intervention in elementary schools.

If you are interested in reading more about Donna Eder's research, there is a position paper published by the National Council of Social Studies at the following URL: **http://www.ncss.org/standards/positions/ability.html** The title is *Ability Grouping in Social Studies* and it is prepared by the Ad Hoc Committee on Ability Grouping, approved by NCSS Board of Directors, 1992.

Ethical issues. When we first began the study, we openly informed all of the students that we were from Indiana University and were doing a study of middle school students. We assured students of our concern with protecting their privacy by not using their actual names or revealing private information to others who might know them. The only concern expressed by a few students was that they not get in trouble for swearing. Since we were not aware of a no-swearing rule and had not been asked to enforce it, they soon lost this concern. Several students again expressed a similar concern when they were first tape-recorded, asking us who would be allowed to hear the tapes. We assured them that the tapes would not be seen or heard by anyone who could identify them and that we would not use their names in papers or books about the study.

We were prepared in advance for these particular ethical issues and had ready responses that relieved people's concerns. Other ethical dilemmas arose during the course of the study for which we did not have clear solutions. [Two of the researchers] . . . witnessed several incidents of verbal harassment, and Steve witnessed one incident that included physical harassment. Since we had tried from the start to minimize our roles as authority figures in the school, neither of them intervened as adults to stop these incidents. Instead they relied on **non-intrusive** strategies such as not participating themselves, or drawing the attention of others away from the target of ridicule to some other activity.

These incidents raise challenging questions about the role of researchers as observers of naturally occurring behavior, as opposed to **interventionists** who try to change the behavior of others, especially if it appears to be cruel or abusive. Had we decided to intervene more directly, we would have been seen as authority figures, and it is likely that students would no longer have acted as naturally in our presence, thus limiting the extent to which we could gain information about peer interactions. On the other hand, it was deeply disturbing to the researchers to witness these events without intervening. We struggled with the question of whether nonintervention might convey an implicit message that such behavior is acceptable to adults.

Source: Donna Eder, *School Talk*, New Brunswick, N.J.: Rutgers University Press, 1995, pp. 172–175.

What Does it Mean?

extracurricular
after school; beyond the normal school courses

interventionist
someone who gets involved to make a change

non-intrusive
not obviously noticeable; non-threatening

transcribed
made a written copy; put into written form

Read and React

1. In the first paragraph, the author writes that the observers did not openly take notes. Wouldn't it make more sense to take notes while the events were happening? Why would the observers wait to record their observations?
2. What do you think the author means by the term *field notes* in the third paragraph?
3. What steps did the research team take to ensure that the students' privacy rights were not abused?
4. What ethical problems did the researchers face in the course of their observations? Would you have taken the same steps as the researchers? What other action could have been taken?

Answers to Read and React

1. The rationale for not taking notes from a theoretical perspective is to maintain the integrity of the participant-observation. Taking notes makes the interaction appear clinical in nature and might cause students to hesitate. Not taking notes is simply more natural.
2. Field notes are scribbles based on informal conversation. They lack the thoroughness of an intensive interview, but still can be rich with relevant information for the researcher.
3. The researchers guaranteed the students that there would be no consequences for any swearing. Students were told of the nature of the tape-recordings and assured that no one but the researchers would hear them. In these ways, student anonymity was maintained.
4. Ethical problems included deciding what to do if one group member refused to be involved in the study and notifying parents. *(Parental permission had to be obtained because all the participants were minors.)* Students whom researchers had observed participating in incidents were not reported, since that was not the role of the researchers. They were not interventionists, only observers.

NOTES to the Teacher

UNIT 2

This unit begins with the sociological perspective on culture—one of the main components and conduits of social structure. The article on the Nacirema highlights not only how we can study culture—seeing it from an outsider's point of view—but also how much we take our culture for granted. The norms and values surrounding us are not always obvious or explicit; it is when cultural norms are violated or broken that they become known. Harold Garfinkel, a sociologist at UCLA, introduced the idea of norm-breaking experiments: taking a small taken-for-granted cultural norm, breaking it in a public setting, and observing the reactions of people. Garfinkel's classic example is standing in an elevator facing the back wall. For a sociologist, the fascinating part of these experiments is the reactions of people in or near the situation: what do they do when norms are violated? The reaction of those near the norm-breaking event will highlight what norms exist, how important a norm is, and how that norm is reinforced by society. In Garfinkel's elevator experiment, people often fidget, avoid looking at the person, and sometimes get off the elevator before their floor arrives. In few cases will someone say something directly to the norm-breaking person. This simple experiment highlights the unwritten and often tacit rules guiding our behavior: when entering an elevator, one is expected to face forward and not speak to those one does not know. If these rules are followed, we can all be comfortable in the presence of strangers in a confining physical space; if these rules are not followed, we become uncomfortable, even threatened, that the strangers are unstable people to be feared and shunned or, if they are younger or otherwise of a lower status than ourselves, taught the correct behavior.

In this public space, strangers become agents of socialization. Parents, teachers, and peers are not the only source of information and guidance as media is exerting an increasingly powerful influence over our lives. Our socialization process does not end when reaching adulthood, as we continue to learn and reinforce our previous lessons through our experiences and perceptions.

Status and roles are two of the more confusing concepts to many sociology students.

CULTURE AND SOCIAL STRUCTURES

Enrichment Readings

69

"Role" is a concept that is directly analogous to the role of an actor. We have a collection of tasks depending on the particular identity we will enact, e.g., student, sibling, teacher, friend. Erving Goffman, a Canadian sociologist, offers a dramaturgical theory of behavior. We all perform, taking on different roles in different acts in our lives, complete with scripts of appropriate dialogue, front stages where the action takes place, and back stages where we prepare or rest from these performances.

"Status" rests with one's position, usually tied to a particular role, and is what gives us varying amounts of social prestige. Identifying roles is much easier than identifying status. For this reason, sociologists often measure status through one's occupation, specifically as occupational prestige.

Group dynamics and organizations are also part of social structure. We live our lives within groups of varying sizes and functions that are interlaced together through social networks. Primary groups (and primary relationships within those groups) are important for forming our identity, while secondary groups (and secondary relationships) are more impersonal, segmented structures in which we perform various functions such as productive work (paid labor) and consuming behavior (shopping). Secondary group activities are segmented in the sense that they are partial and specific, focusing on a particular goal or event, rather than all encompassing as are primary group activities. Increasingly, and especially in urban areas, we find that our membership in secondary groups and our secondary relationships are more numerous than our primary group membership and primary relationships.

Social structure is also evident through deviance and control. Much like the norm breaking experiments mentioned above, there will always be some violations of society's norms, a phenomenon called deviance. While conformity to norms and values is expected, it may not always be possible or even preferable to do so. Rosa Parks, in refusing to sit in the back of the bus, engaged in a form of deviance which many feel was justified. Deviance helps to define and reinforce society's norms, but it also helps to change those norms and challenge those norms that are outdated or otherwise unjust.

UNIT 2 Culture and Social Structures

Chapters	Pacing Chart
3 CULTURE 1. The Basis of Culture 2. Language and Culture 3. Norms and Values 4. Beliefs and Material Culture 5. Cultural Diversity and Similarity	**Pages 74-75, 81-91, and 99-102.** Basic concepts of culture including: folkways, mores and laws; sanctions; values; material, real and ideal culture, diversity, ethnocentrism, and cultural universals. *Not included in this accelerated plan are sociobiology, language and culture, and social change (dealt with in greater detail in Chapter 17).*
4 SOCIALIZATION 1. The Importance of Socialization 2. Socialization and the Self 3. Agents of Socialization 4. Processes of Socialization	**Pages 113-114, 116-117, 121-125, and 128-127.** Includes stories of children raised in isolation and a summary table of how the major theoretical perspectives view socialization. The socializing roles of the family and reference groups are presented. *Not included are discussions of Harlow's experiment on rhesus monkeys and how the role-taking process develops.*
5 SOCIAL STRUCTURE AND SOCIETY 1. Social Structure and Status 2. Social Structure and Roles 3. Preindustrial Societies 4. Industrial and Postindustrial Societies	**Pages 140-152 and 159-163.** Topics include the various forms of status and different types of roles, ending the chapter with a look at the characteristics of industrial and post industrial societies. *Not included is a discussion of preliterate and agricultural societies.*
6 GROUPS AND FORMAL ORGANIZATIONS 1. Primary and Secondary Groups 2. Other Groups and Networks 3. Types of Social Interaction 4. Formal Organizations	All sections of this chapter are necessary for building on concepts developed in the unit on social institutions. Covered are types of groups, types of social interactions, and the nature of bureaucracies.
7 DEVIANCE AND SOCIAL CONTROL 1. Deviance and Social Control 2. Functionalism and Deviance 3. Symbolic Interactionism and Deviance 4. Conflict Theory and Deviance 5. Crime and Punishment	**Pages 204-207, 210-221, and 227-232.** The nature of deviance and social control; strain, control, and labeling theories; the relationship of race, ethnicity, and crime, and white collar crime. Chapter-end with modern approaches to controlling crime.

Key to Ability Levels

Activities in the teacher's material have been coded for varying learning styles and abilities.

L1 **BASIC** activities for all students

L2 **AVERAGE** activities for average to above-average students

L3 **CHALLENGING** activities for above-average students

ELL **ENGLISH LANGUAGE LEARNER** activities

Teacher Resource Manager

Teacher Classroom Resources

Unit 2 Mastering Basic Concepts
- Learning Goals Outlines
- Graphic Organizers
- Vocabulary Activities
- Analyzing and Interpreting Data
- Increasing Your Reading Comprehension
- Guided Readings
- Student Journal Prompts
- Vocabulary and Chapter Review Quizzes

Spanish Supplements
- Learning Goals Outlines
- Bilingual Chapter Summaries
- Vocabulary and Chapter Review Quizzes

Chapter & Unit Tests w/ Final Exam and Answer Key
- Chapters 3–7 Tests A and B
- Unit 2 Test

Alternative Assessments
- Performance Assessments
- Portfolio Assessments
- Chapter Essay Tests

Culture Studies: The Sociological Perspective
- Readings 4–13

Including:
- Reading 6: One Hundred Percent American
- Reading 13: Spare the Rod?

Doing Sociology: Focus on Research
- Research Projects 2–6

Ethics, Values, and Technology: Real-Life Issues in Society
- Readings 3–11

Including:
- Reading 7: The Curse of Cliques
- Reading 9: Kids in the Klan

Transparency Binder

Chapter 3
- 6: Top Ten Languages by Population
- 7: Top Languages by Distribution
- 8: Secondary Schools Teaching Foreign Languages

Chapter 5
- 9: Social Structures

Chapter 6
- 10: Characteristics of a Bureaucracy
- 11: Classic Groupthink Scenario by Janis

Chapter 7
- 12: Distribution of Deviance Curve
- 13: Major Assumptions of Labeling Theory
- 14: Control Theory
- 15: Strain Theory
- 16: Juvenile & Adult Crime Labels
- 17: Violence and Guns
- 18: Who's On Death Row?
- 19: Annual Application of Capital Punishment

Multimedia

TeacherWorks™
All-In-One Planner and Resource Center
- **Interactive Teacher Edition** Access your Teacher Wraparound Edition and your classroom resources with a few easy clicks.
- **Interactive Lesson Planner** Planning has never been easier! Organize your week, month, semester, or year with all the lesson helps you need to make teaching creative, timely, and relevant.

Interactive Student Edition CD-ROM
This CD-ROM contains the complete Student Edition with, simple navigation and search functions and links to Web activities and resources.

ExamView® Pro Testmaker CD-ROM
Easy-to-use software includes an extensive question bank and allows you to create fully customized tests that can be administered in print or online.

Vocabulary PuzzleMaker CD-ROM
This software lets you create crossword puzzles, word search puzzles, and jumbo puzzles using chapter vocabulary.

Presentations for the Classroom on CD-ROM
This PowerPoint presentation provides a step-by-step outline and supporting visuals for classroom lectures.

SOCIOLOGY Online

Use our Web site for additional resources. All essential content is covered in the Student Edition.

You and your students can visit soc.glencoe.com, the Web site companion to *Sociology and You.* The student text directs students to the Web site for **Chapter Overviews, Student Web Activities, Self-Check Quizzes,** and **Textbook Updates**.

Answers are provided for you in the **Web Activity Lesson Plan**.

Chapter Preview

Section 1 (pages 72–76)

Culture defines how people in a society behave in relation to others and to physical objects. Although most behavior among animals is instinctual, human behavior is learned. Even reflexes and drives do not completely determine how humans will behave, because people are heavily influenced by culture.

Section 2 (pages 77–80)

Humans can create and transmit culture. The symbols of language play a role in determining people's views of reality.

Section 3 (pages 81–91)

The essential components of culture are norms, values, beliefs, and material objects. Sanctions are used to encourage conformity to norms. Values, the broadest cultural ideas, form the basis for norms.

Section 4 (pages 92–94)

Besides norms and values, beliefs and physical objects make up culture. Ideal culture includes the guidelines we claim to accept, while real culture describes how we actually behave.

Section 5 (pages 95–102)

Cultures change according to three major processes. Cultures contain groups within them called subcultures and countercultures that differ in important ways from the main culture. People tend to make judgments based on the values of their own cultures. While apparently very different on the surface, all cultures have common traits or elements that sociologists call cultural universals.

CHAPTER 3

Culture

Lead-Off Activity

To help students understand what sociologists mean by the term *culture,* ask students to brainstorm a list of the elements of culture. Most students will call out aspects of "pop culture," such as fashions, music, or art. Or, they might suggest elements of foreign cultures, such as French food or Spanish dancing. Let the list grow for a while and then suggest (if no students do) some elements of "deep culture," such as

USING Your Sociological Imagination

The crowing rooster wakes Jabu very early. Her mother has already carried a bucket of water from the community tap and put it on the fire to heat. Bread wrapped in newspaper and lying on the ground is ready to cut and spread with jam. Jabu wraps her crying baby brother in a blanket and ties him on her back, soothing him with a melody as she begins her chores. The goats must be milked and the cattle need to be watered and let loose to graze. After her chores, Jabu quickly washes up and dons her school uniform. Her friends are waiting for her on the dirt path. She gossips and laughs with the girls as they half-walk, half-run the two miles to school. Jabu stops to greet a village elder who inquires after her father who is working in the distant diamond mines. By now she is worried because the time is late. As she approaches the school, Jabu sees that the daily school assembly has already begun. Unluckily, the headmistress decides to set an example and calls Jabu up front to slap her hand with a ruler. After singing hymns and the national anthem, Jabu moves quickly to her first class under a large acacia tree in the courtyard.

At first glance, Jabu's life appears very different from yours. If you use your sociological imagination to look beyond the surface differences, though, you will see that both you and Jabu attend school and church; obey authority figures; and have strong family bonds, supportive friends, parents who work, and ties to the larger community. When sociologists look at societies around the world they discover similar patterns in all cultures. This chapter will look at the common elements that make up culture.

Sections

1. **The Basis of Culture**
2. **Language and Culture**
3. **Norms and Values**
4. **Beliefs and Material Culture**
5. **Cultural Diversity and Similarity**

Learning Objectives

After reading this chapter, you will be able to

- explain how culture and heredity affect social behavior.
- describe how language and culture are related.
- name the essential components of culture.
- discuss how cultural diversity is promoted within a society.
- understand the role of ethnocentrism in society.
- identify similarities in cultures around the world.

SOCIOLOGY Online

Chapter Overview
Visit the *Sociology and You* Web site at soc.glencoe.com and click on **Chapter 3—Chapter Overviews** to preview chapter information.

USING Your Sociological Imagination

The purpose of the story about Jabu is to help students recognize that life in different cultures may seem to be very different. From the sociological perspective, however, cultures actually have more common elements than elements that make them different. Lead students to this conclusion by asking them to identify specific examples of culture illustrated in the story. For example, ask, "What specific example is provided for the strong family bond in Jabu's life? What example is given of friendship? What example is provided of authority figures?"

After students have identified family, friends, school, religion, and teachers as parts of the culture, ask them to create a story based on their daily lives, similar to the Jabu story, that includes these sociological concepts. Tell students that the sociological imagination is the ability to translate our knowledge of public life to our private lives; to see the connection between ourselves and the "big picture."

language, common inventions, or common norms and values. Explain to students that while they were certainly correct, to sociologists culture consists of the sum total of human intellectual, technical, physical, and moral creations. Explain that they will be learning about society (structures) and cultures (knowledge and physical objects) in this chapter.
L1

Using the Section Preview

Have students make lists of how they resemble their parents, brothers, and sisters. To prompt them ask if they have ever been told, "You laugh just like your mother" or if they share a physical trait, such as being double-jointed, with a family member. The students should next consider how the culture influences them. Do their parents dislike the music that they prefer? Do students like a style of dress because it is popular with their friends? Students will begin to see that they are the products of both heredity and culture.

Using the Illustration

This photo brings up the question of whether or not having fun is relative to cultural concepts. What are your students' concepts of fun? Can they identify how their ideas of fun are relative to their cultures? What does it mean to have fun in "your own way"?

Section 1

The Basis Of Culture

Key Terms

- culture
- society
- instincts
- reflexes
- drives
- sociobiology

Section Preview

Culture defines how people in a society behave in relation to others and to physical objects. Although most behavior among animals is instinctual, human behavior is learned. Even reflexes and drives do not completely determine how humans will behave, because people are heavily influenced by culture.

culture
knowledge, values, customs, and physical objects that are shared by members of a society

Culture and Society

Culture consists of the knowledge, language, values, customs, and physical objects that are passed from generation to generation among members of a group. On the *material* side, the culture of the United States includes such physical objects as skyscrapers, fast-food restaurants, cell phones, and cars. On the *nonmaterial* side, American culture includes beliefs, rules, customs, family systems, and a capitalist economy.

Culture helps to explain human social behavior. What people do and don't do, what they like and dislike, what they believe and don't believe, and what they value and discount are all based on culture. Culture provides the blueprint that people in a society use to guide their relationships with others. It is because of culture that teenage girls are encouraged to compete for a position on the women's basketball team. It is from culture that teenage boys come to believe that "pumping iron" is a gateway to masculinity.

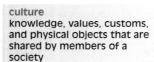

Coming from a different culture than that of the other sunbathers doesn't prevent this Amish family from enjoying a day at the beach.

Using Conflict Resolution Skills

This activity is most effective in classes with culturally diverse students. To develop an appreciation of cultural diversity, we often emphasize differences instead of similarities. For this lesson, however, we want students to see cultural differences as mostly superficial compared to underlying deep cultural and social structures. One basic element of conflict resolution is being able to see similarities or shared interests in what might appear to be widely different customs or habits. Assign students to groups, ensuring that there are at least two cultural backgrounds represented in any one group. Ask students to analyze the different cultures by looking for similar customs, habits, holidays, family arrangements, and so forth, rather than emphasizing differences. They will soon see that all cultures have more elements in common than they do elements that separate them. **L1**

Culture and society are tightly interwoven. One cannot exist without the other, but they are not identical. A **society** is a group of people who live in a defined territory and participate in a common culture. Culture is that society's total way of life.

Human behavior, then, is based on culture. Since people are not born knowing their culture, human cultural behavior must be learned. In this section we will examine the relative importance of biology in influencing behavior.

society
a specific territory inhabited by people who share a common culture

Culture and Heredity

Instincts are genetically inherited patterns of behavior. Nonhuman animals, especially insects, are highly dependent on instincts for survival. Human infants, in contrast, cannot go very far on instincts alone. Instincts are not enough to solve the problems that humans face.

instincts
innate (unlearned) patterns of behavior

Why is culture more important than instinct in determining human behavior? If humans were controlled by instincts alone, they would all behave in the same way with respect to those instincts. If, for example, women had an instinct for mothering, then *all* women would want children, and all women would love and protect their children. In fact, some women do not want to have children, and some women who give birth abuse or abandon their children.

Without instincts to dictate the type of shelter to build, the kind of food to eat, the time of year to have children, or when to mate, humans are forced to create and learn their own ways of thinking, feeling, and behaving. Even for meeting basic needs such as those involving reproduction, food, and survival, humans rely on the culture they have created.

How does heredity affect behavior? Of course, culture is not the only influence on human behavior. Genetic inheritance plays a role. For example, you may have heard people argue about how much of personality is a result of heredity and how much is the product of the environment. (This is sometimes called the "nature versus nurture" argument.) Using studies of identical twins, researchers have determined that about half of your personality traits are determined by your genetic makeup and about half by environmental factors (Tellegen et al., 1993).

In addition, humans have **reflexes**—simple, biologically inherited, automatic reactions to physical stimuli. A human baby, for example, cries when pinched; the pupils of the eyes contract in bright light. We also have biologically inherited **drives,** or impulses, to reduce discomfort. We want to eat, drink, sleep, and associate with others.

You should realize, however, that genetically inherited personality traits, reflexes, and drives do not control human social behavior. Culture *channels* the expression of these biological characteristics. Boys in some Native American cultures, for example, are taught not to cry in response to pain. This is very different from boys in Jewish and Italian cultures, who are taught to pay more attention to physical discomfort and express it more openly (Zborowski, 1952, 1969).

reflex
automatic reaction to physical stimulus

drive
impulse to reduce discomfort

Net Worthy

Some years ago, the University of Minnesota did substantial research on twins. The findings are quite interesting, particularly the similarities of identical twins who had been separated at birth. Some students may wish to do an investigation into this research. Direct them to the web site **www.chiroman.com/twins.htm** for more information. Then, ask them to share their findings with the class.

There are also numerous web sites that consider the nature versus nurture argument. Keywords for web searches include *nature vs. nurture* in any search engine.

Integrating the Teacher Resources

Look for the Vocabulary Activity worksheet in the Unit 2 Mastering Basic Concepts booklet in your Teacher's Resource Box. It provides reinforcement for vocabulary in this chapter.

Using Problem-Solving Skills

After students read about reflexes, drives, and instincts, divide them into two camps (or let them choose for themselves). One group should argue that humans are mostly the products of genetics (nature), and the other should argue that people are primarily the products of the environment (nurture). Allow them some time to research from the text or bring additional materials for them to examine. This is an exercise in learning how to present evidence, so explain that it is not necessary in this activity for them to actually believe the ideas of the camp they are in.

L2

Sociobiology

sociobiology
the study of the biological basis of human behavior

Sociobiology is the study of the biological basis of human behavior. It combines Darwin's theory of natural selection with modern genetics.

How do sociobiologists view human behavior? According to Darwin's theory of evolution, organisms evolve through natural selection. The plants and animals best suited to an environment survive and reproduce, while the rest perish. Sociobiologists assume that the behaviors that best help people are biologically based and transmitted in the genetic code (Degler, 1991; Wright, 1996). Behaviors that would contribute to the survival of the human species include parental affection and care, friendship, sexual reproduction, and the education of children.

Folds of skin around the eyelids of this Inuit fisherman protect his eyes from the sun's glare off the ice and snow.

Sociobiologists do not draw a sharp line between human and nonhuman animals. They claim that nonhuman animals also act on knowledge—as when baboons use long sticks to pull ants from an anthill for a meal. Many nonhuman animals, claim sociobiologists, show intelligence of a kind formerly thought to be unique to humans, such as the ability to use language (Begley, 1993; Linden, 1993a).

What are some criticisms of sociobiology? The major criticism of sociobiology is that the importance placed on genetics could be used as a justification to label specific races as superior or inferior. Critics of sociobiology also point out that there is too much variation in societies around the world for human behavior to be explained on strictly biological grounds. They believe that the capacity for using language is uniquely human and that humans have created a social life that goes far beyond what heredity alone could accomplish.

Is there a middle ground? Some common ground has emerged in this debate. A growing body of sociologists believe that genes work with culture in a complex way to shape and limit human nature and social life. They would like this relationship to be further examined (Lopreato, 1990; Weingart, 1997; Konner, 1999).

A 1998 study found that women look for one set of characteristics in men they marry while men value different characteristics in women (Buss,

Controversy and Debate

Sociobiology is the academic branch that emphasizes the role of innate biological urges, some genetically based in human behavior. It has always been a controversial topic, but is especially so today. (When the debate first broke out in the 1970s, its proponent, Harvard's E.O. Wilson, was actually doused with a pitcher of water and knocked to the floor when he appeared at an academic forum.)

Sociobiology is especially reviled in some communities because of its association with *eugenics*, the genetic-purity movement powerful early in the twentieth century. It was a basis for many racist philosophies, including Nazism, and some historians believe it was used to justify the forced sterilization of thousands of institutionalized people and prison inmates. Today most of the arguments against sociobiology focus on the overriding importance of economic, environmental, and political influences on human behavior. One present-day conflict over sociobiology is reflected in the work of Napoleon Chagnon, famous for his seminal work with the Yanomamö people of Venezuela. His work has been interpreted by many as incorporating many of the elements of sociobiology. Currently, he has been denied entry into the jungle to conclude his work. (For more about this conflict see the *Los Angeles Times Magazine*, January 30, 2000.)

Using Decision-Making Skills

Ask students to use what they have learned in biology and history to predict what environments would favor (a) a darker skin, (b) blonde hair color, and (c) a stocky body size. (*A hot, dry climate favors the development of a dark skin to protect the body from the effects of sunburn; blonde, straight hair typical of Scandinavia is more likely to develop in a climate with less sun to stimulate the development of color pigment and curl in the hair; and a stocky body size is favored in a climate where conserving heat and building up layers of fat provides an edge for survival.*) This activity will help students see that who we are physically is partially the result of nature's need to prepare us for the elements.
L3

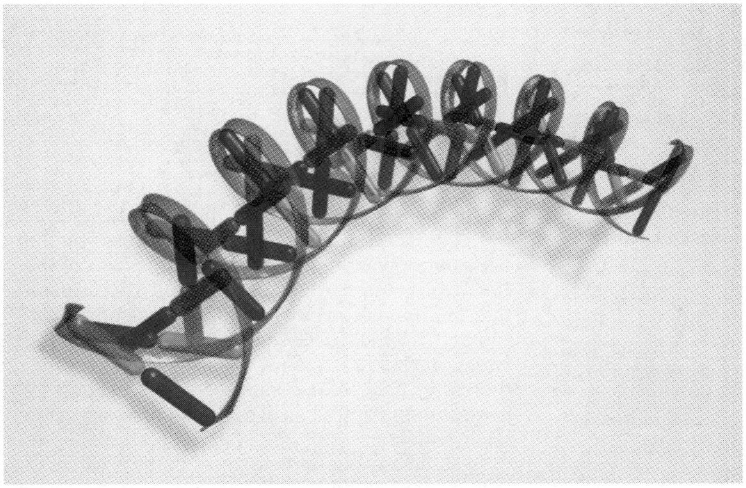

DNA, the genetic material in all cells, is the molecular basis of heredity. Sociobiology focuses on the relationship between heredity and human behavior.

Malamuth, and Windstad, 1998). The researchers believe this behavior is programmed into the genetic code. Studies have also determined that stepfathers are more likely than biological fathers to abuse their children (Daly and Wilson, 1997). Is this because men are more protective of their own biological offspring? Because of the speed of discoveries in the field of biology, the relationships between heredity, culture, and behavior are of growing interest to sociobiologists.

"Men's natures are alike; it is their habits that carry them apart."

Confucius
Chinese philosopher

Section 1 Assessment

1. How is society different from culture?
2. About what percentage of personality is determined by genetics?
3. What are two arguments against the theory of sociobiology?
4. Predict which of the following are drives (D), which are reflexes (R), which are instincts (I), and which are creations of culture (C).
   - **a.** eye blinking in dust storm
   - **b.** need for sleep
   - **c.** reaction to a loud noise
   - **d.** socialism
   - **e.** reproduction
   - **f.** racial inequality

Critical Thinking

5. **Synthesizing Information** Name three nonmaterial and three material elements that represent American culture to you.
6. **Making Generalizations** Do you think human behavior is more a result of culture or of heredity? Give reasons to support your answer.

Answers to Section 1 Assessment

1. A society is defined by geographical territory, whereas culture is not restricted to location.
2. Studies on identical twins have determined that about one-half of personality is determined by genetic make-up.
3. Key arguments against sociobiology include: the amount of diversity in the world cannot be accounted for by genetics alone; and genetic explanations for behavior would and could lead to justify certain races as inferior or superior.
4. **a**=R, **b**=D, **c**=I or R, **d**=C, **e**=D, **f**=C

Critical Thinking

5. Answers will vary.
6. Students may take the middle road and provide examples of when behavior is genetic and when it is cultural. Answers should be well defended with examples or support material.

Role Play

Marshall McLuhan was a Canadian communications theorist and educator, whose aphorism "the medium is the message" summarized his views about the strong influence of television, computers, and other electronic disseminators of information in shaping ideas and styles of thinking. McLuhan claimed that we cannot really perceive our own culture any more than a fish can perceive the water that it swims in. However, unlike fish, who cannot see other lakes, humans can see other cultures. That perception allows us to gain an outside perspective from which to see our own culture. Ask students who have traveled to other countries what they learned about those countries, and how they could use their experiences to note what they learned about their own culture. Ask for volunteers to present a skit to the class that would tell the audience what they learned about their own culture as a result of their travels.
L2

Another Time

Ask students if any of them picked up on what culture the feature is actually about before they had finished reading the article. Was it difficult for them to recognize that Nacirema is our own culture?

Students might want to explore further the author's prediction of the self-destruction of the American culture. What environmental concerns are triggered by our dependence on cars? What global and atmospheric considerations have to be addressed? If you have students from other countries, ask them to describe some of their experiences with what they thought were strange American customs.

Answers to Thinking It Over

1. Answers will vary. Most students will admit that they were more accepting once they realized the culture under discussion was their own.
2. Answers will vary. Students should describe why they think these items would be misinterpreted.

Integrating the Teacher Resources

To reinforce key concepts, use the Chapter 3 Graphic Organizer, a reproducible student worksheet available in the Unit 2 Mastering Basic Concepts booklet in your Teacher's Resource Box.

Another Time: The Mysterious Fall of Nacirema

The following reading is excerpted from a review on a little-known North American culture.

Although the Nacirema left a large number of documents, our linguists have been unable to decipher any more than a few scattered fragments of the Nacirema language. Eventually, with the complete translation of these documents, we will undoubtedly learn a great deal about the reasons for the sudden disappearance of what . . . must have been an explosive and expansive culture . . . .

When we examine the area occupied by these people . . . it is immediately apparent that the Nacirema considered it of primary importance to completely remake the environment. . . . Trees . . . were removed. . . . Most of the land . . . was sowed each year with a limited variety of plants . . . .

For a period of about 300 solar cycles . . . the Nacirema devoted a major part of their effort to the special environmental problem of changing the appearance of air and water. Until the last fifty solar cycles of the culture's existence, they seemed to have had only indifferent success. But during the short period before the fall of the culture, they mastered their art magnificently. They changed the color of the waters from the cool end of the spectrum (blues and greens) toward the warm ends (reds and browns). . . .

Early research has disclosed the importance of . . . the presence of the . . . Elibomotua [RAC] Cult, which sought to create an intense sense of individual involvement in the community effort to completely control the environment . . . .

There seems to be little doubt that the Cult of the Elibomotua was so fervently embraced by the general population, and that the daily rituals of the RAC's care and use were so faithfully performed, that the minute quantities of [chemicals] thus distributed may have had a decisive effect on the chemical characteristics of the air. The elibomotua, therefore, may have contributed in a major way toward the prized objective of a totally man-made environment.

In summary, our evaluation of . . . the Nacirema's man-made environmental alterations . . . lead us to advance the hypothesis that they may have been responsible for their own extinction. The Nacirema culture may have been so successful in achieving its objectives that . . . its people were unable to cope with its manufactured environment.

If the Nacirema seem vaguely familiar, it's because *Nacirema* is *American* spelled backward. Neil Thompson's description strikes us as strange. This is because Americans are not used to looking at their culture as others from the outside might see it. Like fish in water, Americans are so close to their own customs and rituals that we are in a sense unaware of them. Looking at culture from the sociological perspective will heighten your awareness of your own culture as well as the cultures of others.

Source: Neil B. Thompson, "The Mysterious Fall of Nacirema." *Natural History* (December, 1972). Copyright the American Museum of Natural History (1972). Reprinted with permission.

Thinking It Over

1. Describe how your feeling toward the Nacirema changed when you knew their true identity.
2. What other items in today's American culture might be misinterpreted by future anthropologists?

On-Demand Writing

Poet T.S. Eliot noted, "We shall not cease from exploration/ And the end of all our exploring/ Will be to arrive where we started/ And know the place for the first time." After the students have read and discussed "The Mysterious Fall of Nacirema," have them write a page or two describing some aspect of everyday American life from the Nacirema perspective. You might want to try your own hand at the activity and share the results with the students.
L2

Section 2 Language and Culture

Key Terms

- symbols
- hypothesis of linguistic relativity

Symbols, Language, and Culture

If culture is to be transmitted, it must be learned anew by each generation. Both the creation and the transmission of culture depend heavily on the use of symbols. The most powerful symbols are those that make up language.

What are symbols? In Lewis Carroll's *Through the Looking Glass,* Humpty Dumpty says to Alice, "When I use a word, it means just what I choose it to mean—neither more nor less." So it is with **symbols**—things that stand for or represent something else.

Symbols range from physical objects to sounds, smells, and tastes. As you read in Chapter 1, the meaning of a symbol is not based on physical characteristics. For example, there is nothing naturally pleasing about the sound created by hands loudly clapping together. Applause warms the heart of an entertainer, a politician, or a high school athlete in the United States, but in Latin America the same sound means disapproval. The ball Mark McGwire hit for his 70th home run in 1998 is a symbol. The Confederate flag that represents oppression for many African Americans and a proud cultural heritage for many white Southerners is a symbol with different meanings attached.

How are language and culture related? Language frees humans from the limits of time and place. It allows us to create culture. The Wright brothers' successful flight did not come just from their own personal efforts. They built their airplane according to principles of flight already existing in American culture. Through language they could read, discuss, and recombine existing ideas and technology.

Equipped with language, humans can pass their experiences, ideas, and knowledge to others. Although it may take time and repetition, children can be taught the dangers of fire and heights without being burned or toppling down stairs. This process of social learning, of course, applies to other cultural patterns as well, such as eating, showing patriotism, or staying awake in class.

Section Preview

Humans can create and transmit culture. The symbols of language play a role in determining people's views of reality.

symbol
a thing that stands for or represents something else

Some symbols are recognized and understood by people all over the world.

Using the Section Preview

A great way to start this section is to bring in two easily identifiable objects. One of them should have significant symbolic meaning, such as a wedding ring; and the other one should carry very little symbolism, such as a stapler. Ask students to describe the objects in terms of their functions. They will be able to tell you very easily what the stapler does, but when it comes to the ring there may be some differences of opinion. Ask them to consider each object's social meaning. Why does the ring have so much more meaning than the stapler does? Answers will vary, but students will understand that a wedding ring is socially identifiable. Our culture places great meaning in that symbol. When a person stops wearing one, people notice. Students will see that some symbols have great meaning, while others do not.

Next, have the students rename the objects. Say, "As of today, we will call the stapler ______." What problems would be encountered by changing the name of an object? Make the point that cultures give names and meanings to objects, which by themselves mean nothing.

Demonstration

Knowing Your Culture As they study this chapter, students will become familiar with various elements of culture. One fun way to start them off is to tell them about proverbs—brief, but pithy sayings that express commonly held ideas and beliefs. To see if students are familiar with some of the more familiar proverbs in traditional Anglo American culture, try writing the first half of the following proverbs on the board and see if they can correctly complete them:

1. The pen is mightier than ___
2. Better safe than ___
3. It's always darkest before ___
4. Don't bite the hand that ____
5. No news is _____
6. If you lie down with dogs, you'll ___
7. A penny saved is a ___
8. None are so blind as ___
9. Children should be seen and not ___
10. Better late than ___.

L1

Working with the Data

Figure 3.1 Some students today are familiar with sign language since districts have begun mainstreaming many hearing-impaired children. If you have a teacher of sign language in your district, invite her to visit your class to talk about and demonstrate sign language.

Some hand signals are not part of a formal language, but are well understood in this culture. Ask students to consider symbolic hand movements that are part of our culture. For example, signaling a friend to come, or warning someone to be quiet. Students might want to try to invent some hand signs just for your class. You will have created your own signing subculture.

Working with the Quote

Ask students why they think Shaw emphasized the differences in the language between America and England. Many sources, some of them humorous, are available for finding words and phrases that are unique to British and American English. Suggest interested students do some research on this topic.

Alternatively, the class might enjoy brainstorming to identify words they know have different meanings in the United States and England. In a related activity, you may suggest that students work in small groups to think of words used in American culture that have been borrowed from other cultures.

How to Speak with Your Hands

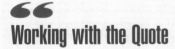

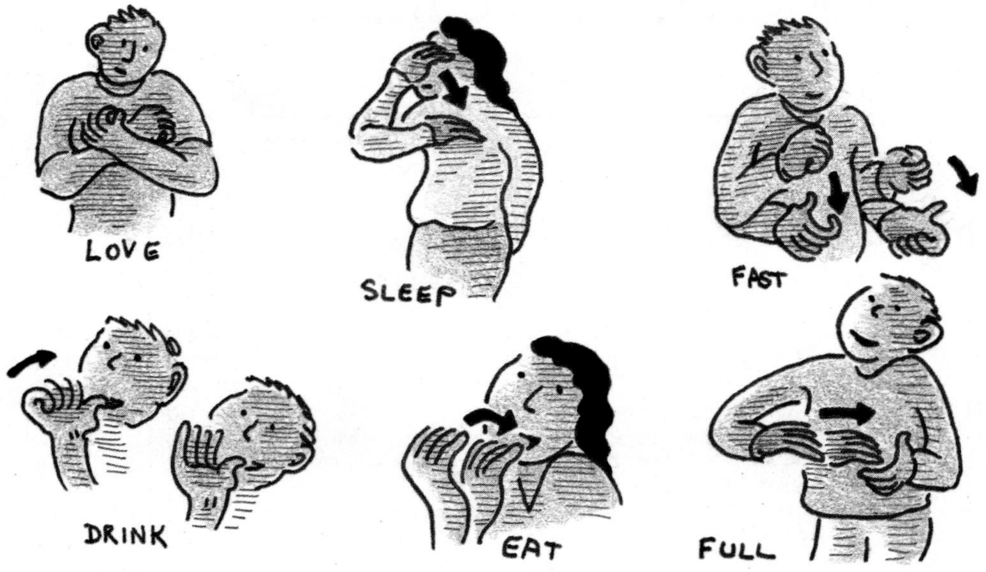

Figure 3.1 Sign Language. *Hand movements in sign language are symbols.*

The Sapir-Whorf Hypothesis

hypothesis of linguistic relativity
theory stating that our idea of reality depends largely upon language

According to Edward Sapir (1929) and Benjamin Whorf (1956), language is our guide to reality. How we think about a thing relates to the number and complexity of words available to describe that thing. In effect, our perceptions of the world depend in part on the particular language we have learned. Since languages differ, perceptions differ as well. This theory is known as the Sapir-Whorf Hypothesis, or the **hypothesis of linguistic relativity.**

What can vocabulary tell you about a culture? When something is important to a society, its language will have many words to describe it. The importance of time in American culture is reflected in the many words that describe time intervals—*nanosecond, millisecond, moment, minute, hour, era, interim, recurrent, century, light-year, afternoon, eternal, annual, meanwhile*, and *regularly*, just to name a few. When something is unimportant to people, they may not have even one word for it. When Christian missionaries first went to Asia, they were dismayed because the Chinese language contained no word for sin. Other missionaries were no less distressed to learn that Africans and Polynesians had no word to express the idea of a single, all-powerful God. While English has only a few words that describe snow, the Inuit (Eskimo) language has over twenty.

> England and America are two countries separated by the same language.
>
> G. B. Shaw
> British playwright

Demonstration

Keeping the Time To illustrate the American obsession with time, remove or cover up the clocks in your room and ask students with watches to put them out of sight. You will be the only person in the room who knows the correct time. This will probably drive students crazy, giving you an opportunity to discuss how Americans are so dependent on time to do everything. Share with students that because Native Americans had a different concept of time than Anglos, they sometimes missed the appointed times for treaty negotiations. Ask students how they think United States government representatives would have interpreted this. (Later, students should be able to explain how this is an example of cultural relativism.) Under what value other than punctuality might the Native Americans have been operating?
L1

Does the hypothesis of linguistic relativity mean we are prisoners of our language? Even if our view of the world is shaped largely by language, we are not forever trapped by our own language. Exposure to another language or to new words can alter a person's perception of the world. (This is one reason why it is important to avoid using racist slurs and stereotypical labels.) People can begin to view the world differently as they learn a new language or vocabulary. However, most people do confine themselves to the language and vocabulary they learned from birth. They tend not to change their views of the world. You can either expand or limit your outlook, depending upon how you use language.

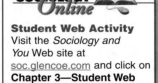

In Japanese culture an emphasis on politeness has helped people learn to live harmoniously in close quarters.

What other factors help to shape our perception of reality? How we perceive the world around us is influenced by more than vocabulary. Cultures may differ in many ways, and these differences influence how their members experience the world. The Japanese use paper walls as sound barriers and are not bothered by noise in adjacent rooms. Americans staying at hotels in Japan complain they are being bombarded with noise because Westerners have not been *conditioned* (mentally trained) to screen out sound.

Privacy is so important to most Germans that German executives generally have a "closed-door policy." Problems arise, as you might imagine, in American firms located in Germany because American executives leave their doors open.

Section 2 Assessment

1. What are symbols?
2. How does language affect culture?

Critical Thinking

3. **Understanding Cause and Effect** Describe some specific ways you see language affecting social behavior among students in your school.
4. **Drawing Conclusions** Some experts believe that without language there is no thought. Do you agree? Why or why not?

SOCIOLOGY Online

Student Web Activity
Visit the *Sociology and You* Web site at soc.glencoe.com and click on **Chapter 3—Student Web Activities** for an activity on language.

Teaching Strategy

Reinforce with students that all communication is not verbal—most, in fact, is nonverbal and deals with body language and symbolic gestures. The Japanese bowing is a nonverbal form of expressing harmony, politeness, and respect. The German businessman with the closed door is expressing the importance of privacy. Ask students to suggest examples of nonverbal communication in their own culture. **L1**

Answers to Section 2 Assessment

1. Symbols are things that stand for or represent something else.
2. Language affects culture in different ways. It helps define reality by restricting thought to available words. It shapes behavior in the same manner.

Critical Thinking

3. Answers will vary.
4. Answers will vary. You may want to refer students to language pioneer Noam Chomsky.

Demonstration

The Importance of Language To reinforce how we rely on language, ask students to form a line at the front of the room according to their birthdays (month and date). Tell the students their task will be to arrange themselves in order, but without talking. Give them a few minutes at their desks to think to themselves about how they could nonverbally communicate their birthdays to one another. They might decide they could hold up fingers to represent dates, for example. This exercise will show students how hard it can be when people who want to communicate do not share the same language. It also shows, however, that people are able to communicate very basic concepts even without a common language. (At the least, this activity will provide you with a few minutes of deserved quiet time!) **L1**

Sociology Today: Cultural Relativism

Different behaviors, traditions, and expectations can often result in misunderstandings between people of different cultures. Learning to look at things from a point of view different from your own, and not making value judgments based on your beliefs and norms, is called *cultural relativism*. Having mutual respect and understanding for other cultures is sometimes more effective than modern technology and money in producing change and goodwill between nations.

Cultural relativism is illustrated in the true story of a young Peace Corps volunteer who was sent to a remote village to help build a well. The stream that was near the village was used for everything from watering goats to bathing to washing clothes to cooking and drinking. It was obvious that clean drinking water would benefit the village and improve health. Armed with plans, equipment, and budget and schedule, the hopeful volunteer arrived ready to begin.

At first, the village people were not very willing to help. After several weeks of lonely effort the volunteer met with the council to ask why nobody was helping her with this urgent project. "A well would be nice," the people agreed, "but what we really need is a good soccer field where we can play without getting hurt on the stones and uneven ground." So the volunteer agreed that some of the money and equipment could be used to build a good soccer field first.

After several weeks of effort, the soccer field was complete and a village soccer team was formed. Now work was able to start on the well, but once again the villagers seemed reluctant to help. Another council meeting was held, and the volunteer was told, "Ah yes, the well would be nice, but what we really need is a bridge across the stream so other villages can easily come to play soccer on our field." Since she couldn't dig the well alone, the volunteer agreed that some more time and money would be used to build a bridge. Unfortunately, the bridge proved to be more difficult than expected, and by the time it was complete, the budget and schedule were both used up.

The volunteer went back to the capital, disappointed and resentful that she had not been able to improve the village. Some weeks later, she was invited back by the villagers for a festival to celebrate the success of the soccer tournament they had arranged. When she arrived she was astonished to find a new well in the very center of the village. She asked the village elders for an explanation.

"The soccer tournament is important to us," she was told, "because it gives us pride and importance and gives us a reason to meet with the people of the other villages. We really never wanted a well."

"Then why did you build it?" she asked.

"We didn't build it because we wanted it," was the answer. "We built it because YOU wanted it."

Doing Sociology

1. What assumptions did the volunteer make about the needs of the villagers? What were the actual needs? Who was more right about what the villagers needed? Why?
2. Describe a time when you made assumptions that turned out to be culturally based.

Careers in Sociology

Students may be interested in knowing how a career in policy making and administration would allow them to use what they learn from sociology. The application of sociological knowledge is key to careers in policy making and administration, government, business, social services, and industry. Career opportunities have broadened recently for sociologists who can use basic training to help others make informed policy decisions and administer programs effectively and imaginatively. These sociologists may not officially teach, but often explain the critical elements of research design, methods, and data analysis to nonsocial scientists. A skilled policy administra-

Sociology Today: Answers to Doing Sociology

1. The volunteer assumed that the people would feel that they would benefit from having a well. The village people knew that a soccer field could become a symbol of a force that would unite the villages in the area. The villagers knew what they needed. They had assessed what was important to them.
2. Students should think of how they reacted to times when they were confronted with a different custom, value, or situation. Most likely their perceptions of these situations were based on their own culturally based values.

Making Connections to Other Cultures

Tell students they are dinner guests of people who put steaming bowls of soup in front of the five-year old daughter. She is asked to blow on the soup to cool it, then the soup is served. What do students think of this? If they are "grossed out" by this image, remind them that at every birthday party, that very thing happens. Brainstorm with students a list of additional habits and traditions that might appear to be "gross" to other cultures when examined from a different perspective.
L1

Section 3 Norms and Values

Key Terms

- norms
- folkways
- mores
- taboo
- law
- sanctions
- formal sanctions
- informal sanctions
- values

Norms: The Rules We Live By

If you wanted to describe your culture, what would you look for? How could you begin to classify the elements of the American way of life? Sociologists begin with the defining components of a culture: its norms, its values and beliefs, and its use of material objects.

Norms are rules defining appropriate and inappropriate behavior. A Hindu peasant in India can be found lying dead of starvation beside perfectly healthy cattle. In order to strengthen bonds between clans, a young Basarwa girl in Africa might become engaged to a man she has not met. Roman emperors routinely exiled relatives to small isolated islands for "disgracing" the family. Each of these instances reflects cultural norms—ways of behaving in specific situations. Norms help to explain why people in a society or group behave similarly in similar circumstances.

William Graham Sumner (1906) was an early sociologist who wrote about norms. Anything, he stated, can be considered appropriate when norms approve of it. This is because once norms are learned, members of a society

Section Preview

Two essential components of culture are norms and values. There are several types of norms—folkways, mores, and laws. Sanctions are used to encourage conformity to norms. Values, the broadest cultural ideas, form the basis for norms.

norms
rules defining appropriate and inappropriate behavior

All cultures have norms relating to marriage and family life; weddings are always important occasions. This Hindu couple is celebrating their marriage with a garland ritual.

Using the Section Preview

An effective way to illustrate the power of norms is by doing something that is unexpected, breaching a norm. One way to illustrate this is to come into class about thirty seconds after the bell has rung, go to the front of the room, and say nothing for five minutes. Students will begin to get agitated; some will become restless, others will be concerned. When time has elapsed, ask students what they think is going on. What is the expected behavior of the teacher to the students? They can be led to the conclusion that your silence was inappropriate behavior because it was not predictable or customary, and that it caused them great discomfort. The experiment also allows them to explore the idea of how easily a norm can be changed.

tor might not conduct research, but would be expected to read the research literature, design useful projects that others conduct, cooperate with full-time researchers or outside consultants, and apply the developing knowledge of sociology and the social sciences. As with most occupations, younger persons typically work their way up from lower-level staff positions. It is not uncommon for recent sociology graduates to be hired as staff members and then follow a career involving increased policy influence and administrative responsibility. For social sciences career information, go to **http://osiris.colorado.edu/POLSCI/RES/job.html**.

Working with the Data

Figure 3.2 Discussion of this table will give foreign-born students in your class the opportunity to share some of their cultural heritage. Ask them if they can offer any additional "etiquette" lessons. Students who have traveled abroad may also have valuable contributions to make. Have students discuss the cultural relativism of each of these behaviors. Are students aware of why cultures value these etiquettes? For example, ask students to suggest possible explanations for why the British do not appreciate early arrivals or unannounced guests.

Teaching Strategy

This might be a good time to preview the video *The Gods Must Be Crazy* to see if it is appropriate for viewing in your class. Supposedly produced in Botswana, the film is the story of a Khoi/San (Bushman) headman who finds a mysterious artifact that begins to disrupt the cultural patterns of his clan. To protect his family, he sets off on a journey to the "ends of the earth." It illustrates in a humorous and fanciful way (poking gentle fun at all cultures and societies in the area) what might happen when one culture comes into contact with an artifact of a different culture.

Figure 3.2 Cultural Etiquette

It might prevent some embarrassing moments if you were aware of norms and customs before traveling to foreign places.

Country	Custom
England, Scotland, and Wales	Appointments are essential. You may be ten minutes late but not ten minutes early.
Greece	Be careful not to praise a specific object too enthusiastically or the host may insist on giving it to you.
Libya	If you are invited to a Libyan home for dinner, only men will be present. Take a gift for the host but not for his wife.
Senegal	Never eat food with the left hand, as this is considered offensive.
Zambia	Avoid direct eye contact with members of the opposite sex—it may suggest romantic overtures.
Saudi Arabia	It is an insult to sit in such a way as to face your host with the soles of your shoes showing. Do not place your feet on a desk, table, or chair.
Oman	If an Arab businessman takes your hand and holds it as you walk, do not be alarmed. He means it only as a sign of friendship.
China	A visit to a Chinese home is rare—unless the government has given prior approval.
Japan	If you are offered a gift, thank the person and wait for one or two more offers before accepting it. Receive the gift with both hands.
South Korea	Men go through doors first. Women help men with their coats.

Source: Roger E. Axtell, *Do's and Taboos Around the World*, 3rd ed. (New York: John Wiley & Sons, 1993).

Interdisciplinary Activity

(You may want to complete the Demonstration on page 77 of this teacher's edition prior to doing this activity.) Comparisons of proverbs found in various parts of the world show that the same kernel of wisdom may be gleaned under different cultural conditions and languages. The biblical proverb "An eye for an eye, a tooth for a tooth," for example, has an equivalent among the Nandi of East Africa: "A goat's hide buys a goat's hide, and a gourd, a gourd." Both form part of codes of behavior and exemplify the proverb's use for the transmission of tribal wisdom and rules of conduct. Many biblical proverbs have parallels in ancient Greece. "A soft answer turneth away wrath" was known to Aeschylus as well as to Solomon, and "Physician, heal thyself" was also known to the Greeks.

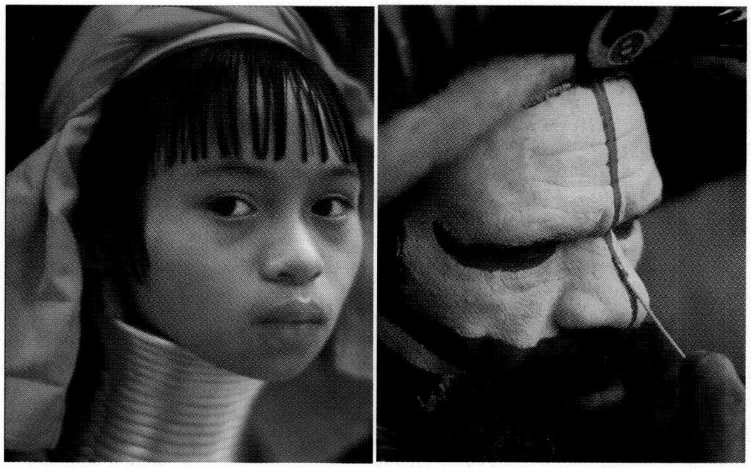

Norms help define a culture's perception of beauty for both males and females. What are some norms that shape the American ideal of beauty?

use them to guide their social behavior. Norms are so ingrained they guide behavior without our awareness. In fact, we may not be consciously aware of a norm until it has been broken. For instance, you may not think about standing in line for concert tickets as a norm until someone attempts to step in front of you. Then it immediately registers that waiting your turn in line is expected behavior. Cutting in front of someone violates that norm. Norms range from relatively minor rules, such as the idea that we should applaud after a performance, to extremely important ones, such as laws against stealing.

> "A knowledge of one other culture should sharpen our ability to scrutinize more steadily, to appreciate more lovingly, our own."
>
> **Margaret Mead**
> **U.S. anthropologist**

Folkways, Mores, and Laws

Sumner identified three basic types of norms: *folkways, mores*, and *laws*. These three types of norms vary in their importance within a society. Accordingly, their violation is tolerated to different degrees.

What are folkways? Rules that cover customary ways of thinking, feeling, and behaving but lack moral overtones are called **folkways.** For example, sleeping in a bed versus sleeping on the floor is not a moral issue; it qualifies as a folkway. Folkways in the United States include supporting school activities, speaking to other students in the hall, and, if you are male, removing your hat in church.

folkways norms that lack moral significance

Because folkways are not considered vital to group welfare, disapproval of those who break them is not very great. Those who consistently violate folkways—say, by talking loudly in quiet places, wearing shorts with a suit coat and tie, or wearing a different-colored sock on each foot—may appear odd. We may avoid these people, but we do not consider them wicked or immoral.

Some folkways are more important than others, and the social reaction to their violation is more intense. Failure to offer a woman a seat on a crowded bus draws little notice today. In contrast, obnoxious behavior at a party after excessive drinking may bring a strong negative reaction from others.

Using the Illustration

These photos illustrate the concept of relative standards of beauty, a subject that students are usually very eager to talk about. Students sometimes have experience within their own families about what they and their parents think is beautiful. Ask students who they think set the standards for what Americans think is beautiful. (*advertisers, the media, and so on*) Have the girls answer for the boys and vice versa. Then ask students if they believe that being good looking is advantageous in society. You might want to tell students that research confirms that people who are perceived to be physically attractive do seem to get more promotions and opportunities. What does that research seem to say about our culture?

Paired Learning Activity

Emphasize to students that folkways are so ingrained into everyday behavior, so taken-for-granted, that they may be hard to distinguish as folkways. They may seen to be "just the way we do things." People also may fail to realize that some folkways eventually disappear. Men used to always take off their hats when they entered a home or building, but today many men keep their baseball caps on, never thinking to remove them. Ask students to work in pairs to identify common folkways. Then ask the class whether they agree that the behavior described was, in fact, a folkway.
L1

mores
norms that have moral dimensions and that should be followed by members of the society

taboo
a rule of behavior, the violation of which calls for strong punishment

What are mores? The term **mores** (pronounced "MOR-ays") is based on the word *moral*. Morality deals with conduct related to right and wrong. Mores are norms of great moral significance. They are vital to the well-being of a society. Conformity to mores draws strong social approval; violation of this type of norm brings strong disapproval. For example, Americans believe that able-bodied men should work for a living. Able-bodied men who do not work are scorned.

Although following folkways is generally a matter of personal choice, conformity to mores is a social requirement. Still, some mores are more vital to a society than others. Failure to stand at attention while the national anthem is being played is not as serious a violation of American mores as using loud profanity during a religious service.

The most serious mores are taboos. A **taboo** is a norm so strong that its violation demands punishment by the group (or, some people think even the supernatural). In India, followers of Hinduism have a taboo forbidding the killing of cows. Other taboos are related to sexual behaviors. Although definitions of incest vary from society to society, the incest taboo (forbidding sexual contact with close relatives) is generally regarded as the only taboo that is present in all societies. The "mother-in-law" taboo existing in some societies prohibits or severely restricts social contact between a husband and his wife's mother.

What folkways, mores, or laws are being demonstrated (or broken) in these scenes?

Open-Response Questions

It is important that students understand the connection between mores and morality; that there is a sense of right and wrong connected to mores. Do students agree with the text example about unemployed, able-bodied men being scorned for not working? Ask them to describe how men who choose not to work are treated. This class discussion will form a basis for the eventual introduction of the ideas of formal and informal sanctions later in this section.

Ask students how they feel about able-bodied women without children to care for who do not work outside the home. Are their attitudes about unemployed women the same as their attitudes about unemployed men? Why or why not? What cultural traditions are at work here? Are some of these traditions changing?

Using the Illustration

Students will notice that the woman is smoking a cigar, not an acceptable folkway for women. The overturned car represents violation of a law, especially if the driver was speeding or under the influence of alcohol. Everyone in the church is standing, the appropriate behavior (folkway) in the church. They are dressed in their "Sunday best," a folkway that is disappearing in some churches and regions of the country.

Learning Styles

Bodily-Kinesthetic Students may have difficulty distinguishing between types of norms: folkways, mores, and laws. To provide an opportunity to practice these terms in a physical way, ask students to act out scenarios depicting different cultural behaviors, both acceptable and unacceptable. You may want to have them work in three small groups to create the situations to be acted out, with one group assigned to show folkways, another to show mores, and the third to demonstrate laws. Then, after each scenario is shown, have students act as judges and juries to determine what type of norm was enacted, whether or not it was acceptable, and if a consequence is needed. Another option would be to provide scenarios to be enacted and then ask students to identify what type of norm is being depicted. **L1**

World View

Patterns of Tourism

Although people often want to observe and experience cultures different from their own, exposure to cultural diversity can be uncomfortable. Most international tourist travel occurs among countries sharing common cultural traditions and languages.

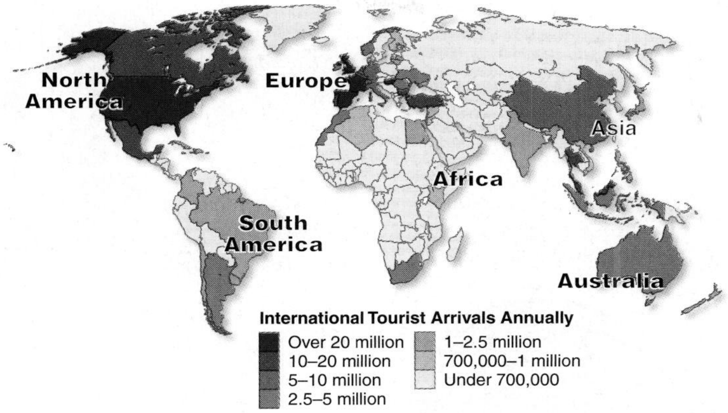

Interpreting the Map

1. Identify the world regions that receive the highest and lowest number of tourists.
2. Are there any reasons to believe that these travel patterns might change in the near future? If so, what factors might bring about this change?

Adapted from the *Student Atlas:* DK Publishing, Inc.

How do laws differ from mores? The third type of norm is **law.** Laws are norms that are formally defined and enforced by officials. Folkways and mores emerge slowly and are often unconsciously created, while laws are consciously created and enforced.

law
a norm that is formally defined and enforced by officials

Mores are an important source for laws. At one time, the norm against murder was not written down. But as civilization advanced, the norm against murder became formally defined and enforced by public officials.

Folkways can become mores or laws. Smoking, for example, was an acceptable behavior to most Americans until the late 1970s, when mounting health concerns convinced many that smoking should be limited or banned in public places. Today, many states have laws against smoking in airports, government buildings, restaurants, and other places open to the general public.

Not all mores become laws. For example, it is not against the law to cheat on an exam (although you may be suspended or punished by the teacher). Furthermore, not all laws started out as mores. Fines for overtime parking and laws against littering have never been mores.

World View

Discuss with students the idea that, as the map indicates, people are more likely to travel to destinations that have cultural and societal norms similar to their own. Ask students to identify areas of the world where they would most like to travel.

Answers to Interpreting the Map

1. The areas of the world that receive the highest number of tourists are the United States and Western Europe. The lowest number of tourists seem to visit Russia, Africa, Southwest Asia, and the Middle East.
2. Have students speculate about what might contribute to a change in travel patterns. (*climate, political turmoil, and so on*)

Learning Styles

Interpersonal/Linguistic Ask students to create a pamphlet that could be distributed to teenage visitors from other cultures who will be spending a week with an American family. First, have students brainstorm to determine what types of information they think would be necessary to help a guest feel more comfortable during their visit. Topics may include material concepts such as places to visit, typical foods, technology, and transportation and nonmaterial concepts of society such as rules, family systems, and traditions. Ask each student to write a short article that could be included in a welcome pamphlet. If possible, you may want students to use a computer to actually design a pamphlet that could be printed and given to visitors at local teen centers, churches, and clubs.
L1

Working with the Data

Figure 3.3 Have students research laws for their own state. A good resource on this subject is the book *Crazy Laws* by Dick Hyman, first published in 1976 by Scholastic, Inc. Share with the students how very recently (1999) a little-known law that had been on the books since 1845 was used by the state of New York to force members of the KKK to take off their masks at a planned rally. This law prohibited concealing one's face at public events. What other gender-related sanctions can students recall?

Figure 3.3 Silly Laws Still on the Books

There are many laws throughout the country whose purposes and existence have long been forgotten. At the time, they may have been perfectly logical. As society changed, the need for them disappeared.

State	Law
Alabama	It is illegal for a driver to be blindfolded while operating a vehicle.
Arizona	Hunting camels is prohibited.
Florida	If an elephant is left tied to a parking meter, the fee has to be paid just as it would be for a vehicle.
Illinois	You must contact the police before entering the city in an automobile.
Iowa	Kisses may last for as much as, but no more than, five minutes.
Maine	You must not step out of a plane in flight.
Massachusetts	No gorilla is allowed in the back seat of any car.
Minnesota	A person may not cross state lines with a duck atop his or her head.
Vermont	Whistling underwater is illegal.
Washington	It is illegal to pretend that one's parents are rich.

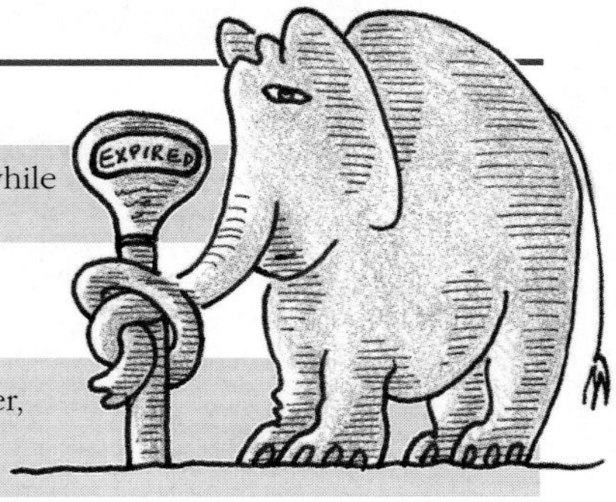

Integrating the Teacher Resources

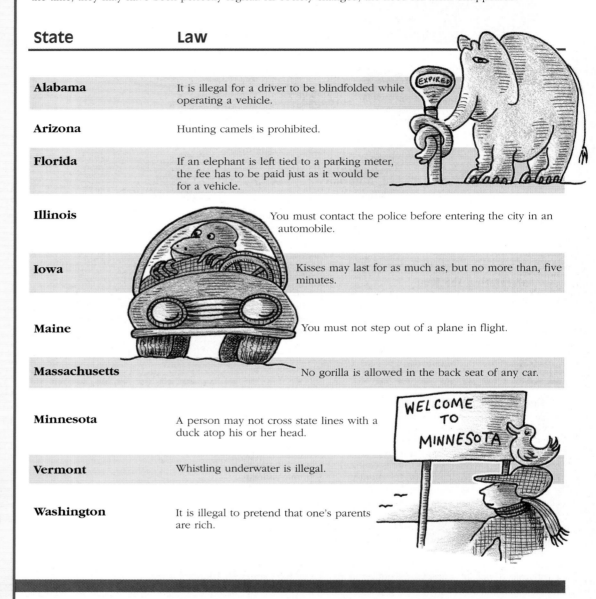

For Spanish-speaking students, you may wish to use the reproducible worksheets available in the Spanish Supplements booklet in your Teacher's Resource Box. In addition to providing Spanish translations of selected Mastering Basic Concepts worksheets, the booklet contains English and Spanish summaries of the chapter's key points.

Cooperative Learning Activity

Divide the class into small groups and assign the following problem or question for them to answer: How is cultural relativism part of the sociological imagination? They may choose to present the answer in any format, including a skit, debate, oral reading, etc. Encourage students to use their imaginations—sociological and otherwise.

The answer involves the fact that researchers must be able to imagine themselves as part of another culture to do unbiased work. Researchers need to be aware of the customs and norms of the society they are studying and be able to examine their own background assumptions against the norms of the culture. For exam-

Laws often remain on the books for a long time after the mores of a society have changed. It is illegal in Minnesota to hang male and female undergarments on the same clothesline. New York prohibits card playing on trains; elephants in Natchez, Mississippi, cannot legally drink beer; and it is against the law to wear roller skates in public bathrooms in Portland, Oregon. (For additional laws that seem strange to us today, see Figure 3.3.)

Enforcing the Rules

People do not automatically conform to norms. Norms must be learned and accepted. Groups teach norms, in part, through the use of *sanctions*. **Sanctions** are rewards and punishments used to encourage conformity to norms. They can be formal or informal.

sanctions rewards and punishments used to encourage people to follow norms

What are formal sanctions? **Formal sanctions** are sanctions that may be applied only by officially designated persons, such as judges and teachers. Formal sanctions can take the form of positive as well as negative rewards. A soldier earns a Congressional Medal of Honor as a positive sanction for heroism. Teachers reward outstanding students with A's. Of course, formal sanctions can also take the form of punishments.

formal sanctions sanctions imposed by persons given special authority

Formal punishments range widely in their severity. From the Middle Ages to the Protestant Reformation, it was an unpardonable sin for lenders to charge interest on money. (This practice was called *usury* and was condemned in the Bible.) This crime was punishable on the third offense by public humiliation and social and economic ruin. More recently, a few courts across the United States have handed down sentences involving public shaming. For example, some courts have required child molesters to display, in front of their homes, signs describing their crimes (El Nasser, 1996). In

> "A law's final justification is in the good it does or fails to do to the society of a given place and time."
>
> **Albert Camus**
> **French philosopher**

Formal sanctions often involve action in the criminal or civil judicial systems.

Working with the Quote

Albert Camus was a French moralist and political theorist. His writings addressed the isolation of man in an alien universe, the estrangement of the individual from himself, the problem of evil, and the pressing finality of death. In his last works, Camus wrote from a liberal humanist outlook that rejected the dogmatic aspects of both Christianity and Marxism.

Ask students what they think Camus was saying in the quote. Was he implying that some laws, while appearing to be just, cannot be evaluated without looking at the effects on society? Ask students if they can think of any laws that are "bad" laws. (*They will probably mention curfews, restrictive driving laws and other laws that hamper individual and personal freedoms.*) You might want to discuss how laws change with the times. Many states have changed the drinking age, driving age, and the voting age over the years.

ple, Americans might believe that Hindus do not kill and eat cows in India because of their religious beliefs. However, a noted sociologist, Marvin Harris, points out that there are very good economic reasons for the taboo against killing cows. Cows are of more value alive as milk producers, and oxen are more needed for pulling plows than they are for meat. Meat does not go very far in feeding people—it is an expensive source of protein. To assume that the restrictions on killing these animals are solely based on religion and are causing needless suffering reflects a lack of sociological imagination.
L3

Reinforcing Vocabulary

A sanction is a mechanism of social control for enforcing a society's standards. The students might be confused because you can sanction both positively (to reward) or negatively (to punish). Without an understanding of the overriding definition above, students might interpret *to sanction* to mean both to reward and to punish. (There are a few words in English that can mean opposite things, such as *to cleave*.)

Using the Illustration

Many informal sanctions are imposed that are gender-related. The man in the cartoon should not be crossing his legs, according to the "code of the West." What might women be sanctioned for in a similar situation? What other gender-related sanctions can students recall?

Integrating the Teacher Resources

Look for the Chapter 3 Vocabulary Activity in the Unit 2 Mastering Basic Concepts booklet in your Teacher's Resource Box. It provides reinforcement for vocabulary in this chapter.

1997, Latrell Sprewell, star basketball player for the Golden State Warriors, physically attacked his coach, P. J. Carlesimo. The NBA revoked his $32 million, four-year contract and suspended him for one year before he joined the New York Knicks.

informal sanctions rewards or punishments that can be applied by most members of a group

What are informal sanctions? **Informal sanctions** are sanctions that can be applied by most members of a group. They, too, can be positive or negative. Informal sanctions include thanking someone for pushing a car out of a snowbank (positive) or staring at someone who is talking loudly during a movie (negative).

Sanctions are not used randomly or without reason. Specific sanctions are associated with specific norms. A high school student who violates his parents' curfew is not supposed to be locked in a closet, for example.

After we reach a certain age, most of us conform without the threat of sanctions. We may conform to norms because we believe that the behavior expected of us is appropriate, because we wish to avoid guilt feelings, or because we fear social disapproval. In other words, we sanction ourselves mentally.

THE FAR SIDE By GARY LARSON

"Frank. ... Don't do that."

Frank seems to have forgotten that "real men" don't cross their legs. This informal sanction will probably bring him into line.

Values—The Basis for Norms

Norms and sanctions are relatively specific. The next major component of culture—*values*—is much more general.

What are values? **Values** are broad ideas about what most people in a society consider to be desirable. Values are so general that they do not dictate precise ways of thinking, feeling, and behaving. Thus, different societies or different groups within the same society can have quite different norms based on the same value.

values
broad ideas about what is good or desirable shared by people in a society

For instance, consider the norms used to express the value of freedom in America and in the former Soviet Union. In the Soviet Union, freedom was expressed as the right to such things as employment, medical care, and education. Americans have different norms based on the value of freedom. These norms include the right to free speech and assembly, the right to engage in private enterprise, and the right to a representative government. Identical values do not result in identical norms.

Why are values important? Values have a tremendous influence on human social behavior because they form the basis for norms. A society that values democracy will have norms ensuring personal freedom. A society that values human welfare will have norms providing for its most unfortunate members. A society that values hard work will have norms against laziness.

Values are also important because they are so general that they are involved in most aspects of daily life. In America, for example, the influence of the value of freedom goes beyond political life. The value of freedom affects how family relationships are conducted, how people are treated within the legal system, how organizations are run, and how people worship.

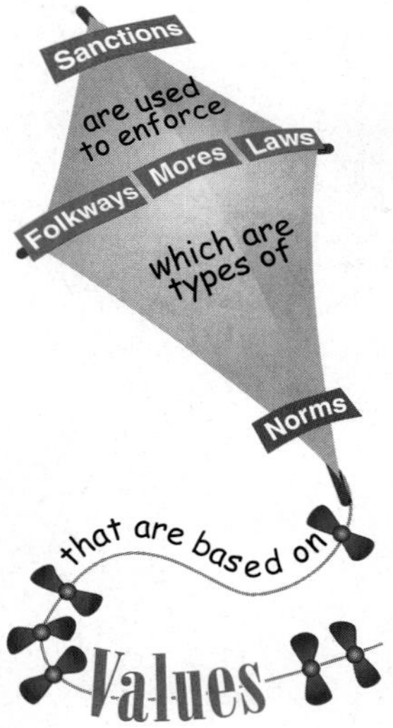

Figure 3.4 The Norm Kite. *If a society is to fly, it must have these basic elements of social structure. Sanctions (rewards and punishments) are needed to enforce norms (folkways, mores, laws). Guiding the Norm Kite are a society's values, the basis for norms.*

After winning the World Cup, members of the U.S. women's soccer team became role models for many girls. What strong cultural values do these young women demonstrate?

Teaching Strategy

Using four pieces of construction paper or tagboard, make four signs with the following labels: *Agree, Somewhat Agree, Disagree, Unsure*. Put each one of the signs in a different location around the room so students can see them. Read the list of five subjective value statements below.

1. Although we should not be unnecessarily cruel to animals, they were put on earth to serve the needs of human beings.
2. The death penalty should be abolished because it is inherently racist in its application.
3. Men and women are not politically or intellectually equal because they are biologically different.
4. There is too much violence and sex in the media, especially on television.
5. There is too much freedom given to young, unmarried boys and girls today.

As you read each statement, have the students go to the sign that reflects how they feel about the statement. Tell them to shake hands with the other students in their group—they now share a value in common. At the end, have students review whether or not their friends were the people they most encountered in each group. Ask any students if they are surprised about the number of students with whom they share common values.
L1

Using Decision-Making Skills

Values Clarification This activity, if done honestly, will help students discover what they really value. Students should make a list of fifteen things, both material and nonmaterial, that they value. Lists might include family, health, friends, honesty, and money. Once students have finished their lists, have them rank the items by the value they place on them. The most important would be number one, the least important would be last, number fifteen. Then tell students that you are giving them $1000.00 to spend on these values. They must decide how much they would be willing to spend on each item, based on how important they are to students. They can put all their money on one item, or spread the money out. You might want to list their number one values on the board and see how many are similar.
L1

Basic Values in the United States

What cultural values are represented in these photos?

The United States is home to many different groups. No single set of values is likely to hold across the entire country. Despite this problem, sociologist Robin Williams (1970) identified important values that guide the daily lives of most people in the U.S. A partial list includes:

- *Achievement and success.* People emphasize achievement, especially in the world of work. Success is supposed to be based on effort and competition and is viewed as a reward for performance. Wealth is viewed as a symbol of success and personal worth.
- *Activity and work.* People tend to prefer action over inaction in almost every case. For most Americans, continuous and regular work is a goal in itself. Promotion should be for merit rather than favoritism. Finally, all citizens should have the opportunity to perform at their best.
- *Efficiency and practicality.* People pride themselves on getting things done by the most rational means. We search for better (faster) ways of doing things, praise good workmanship, and judge performance by the results. We love to rely on science and technology.
- *Equality.* From the very beginning of our history as a nation, we have declared a belief in equality for all citizens. As minority groups and women achieved citizenship, our concept of equality grew. We tend to treat one another as equals, defend everyone's legal rights, and favor equal opportunity—if not equal results—for everyone.
- *Democracy.* People emphasize that all citizens are entitled to equal rights and equal opportunity under the law. In a democracy, the people elect their government officials. Power is not in the hands of an elite few.
- *Group superiority.* Despite their concern for equality of opportunity, people in the U.S. tend to place a greater value on people of their own race, ethnic group, social class, or religious group.

These values are clearly interrelated. Achievement and success affect and are affected by efficiency and practicality, for example. But we can also see conflicts among some values. For instance, people in the U.S. value group superiority while at the same time stressing equality and democracy.

Do these values still prevail in the United States today? Williams identified these major values approximately thirty years ago—about the time many of your parents were teenagers. Although these values have remained remarkably stable over the years, some have changed. Today there is less emphasis on group superiority in America than in the past. This can be seen in the decline of openly racist attitudes and behaviors (Farley, 1996; Rochen, 1998). In reality, however, it is usually norms and behavior rather than underlying values that change radically. It is probably because of the passage of civil rights laws that many Americans are now less likely to make overt racist statements. Racism (group superiority) remains part of the fabric of American culture.

The norms related to hard work and activity have also changed in recent years. Many Americans now work as hard at their leisure activities (for example, long-distance running and mountain climbing) as they do at their

Open-Response Question

When Robin Williams identified American values in the 1970s, he was looking at the predominant social class: white middle class males. Do students think that if Williams were researching today, he would come to the same conclusions? Are these values multicultural? Do they cross racial and ethnic boundaries?

Working with the Quote

(See page 91.) Explain to students that Carrie Chapman Catt was a U.S. feminist leader who led the women's rights movement for more than twenty-five years. Her efforts culminated with the adoption of the Nineteenth Amendment (suffrage) to the U.S. Constitution in 1920. After the adoption of the amendment, Mrs. Catt reorganized her suffrage association—2,000,000 strong—into the League of Women Voters in order to work for continuing progressive legislation throughout the nation.

Ask students what Catt is saying in this quote. Why is this quote included at this point in the chapter?

Cooperative Learning Activity

Some sociologists have identified what is known as changing American values. They say that self-fulfillment and narcissism have now become *enculturated.* Discuss these terms with the students so that they understand what they mean. Ask students to identify where one aspect of self-fulfillment is seen in contemporary society (*i.e., the development of the self-help industry*). Narcissism suggests that Americans have become increasingly self-centered, thinking only of themselves. What can students point to in the culture of the United States that would support this value? Alternately, students might want to challenge these assumptions. Set up a class debate on this topic: Are self-fulfillment and narcissism basic values in the United States today? **L2**

Calvin's father is trying to transmit the cultural value of competition. As usual, Calvin has his own view. What is yours?

Although Williams's analysis of major American values remains basically sound today, some sociologists believe that his list is incomplete. They would add, for example, optimism, honesty, and friendliness to the list of major values in the United States.

> No written law has ever been more binding than unwritten custom supported by popular opinion.
>
> **Carrie Chapman Catt**
> **American reformer**

Section 3 Assessment

1. Indicate whether these statements best reflect a folkway (F), a more (M), a law (L), or a value (V).
   - **a.** norm against cursing aloud in church
   - **b.** norm encouraging eating three meals daily
   - **c.** idea of progress
   - **d.** norm against burning a national flag
   - **e.** norm encouraging sleeping in a bed
   - **f.** norm prohibiting murder
   - **g.** norm against overtime parking
   - **h.** idea of freedom
2. Sociologists make a distinction between norms and values. How are these concepts different? Support your answer with examples.

Critical Thinking

3. **Analyzing Information** Review the partial list of values identified by Robin Williams on the previous page. Is there a value not listed that you think should be included? What is it? Why would you include it?

Pulling It All Together

Ask students to write a paragraph summarizing the key points of this chapter. Their writing should include the following points.

1. Norms are rules that determine appropriate and inappropriate behavior in a culture or society. These norms are identified by three basic types: folkways, mores, and laws.
2. Sanctions are imposed for violating these norms, some are informal, some formal.
3. Norms are largely the result of values that a culture or society has; their influence on society is great.
4. Basic American values have remained constant with some degree of change. Norms and values reflect the people in their specific place in time.

Answers to Section 3 Assessment

1. There could be some variation in these answers depending upon the region and particular culture.
   - **a.** M
   - **b.** F
   - **c.** V
   - **d.** M or L
   - **e.** F
   - **f.** L
   - **g.** L
   - **h.** V
2. Students should understand that values are the root source of norms; that values determine norms.

Critical Thinking

3. Answers will vary.

Encouraging Citizenship Activity

Ask students to plan and implement a Culture Day for your school. Better yet, plan and implement a subculture day, or even a sub-sub-culture day. The first step is to get permission from your principal and to set a date. Next, you need to get the rest of the school on board. Have students in each department or club learn all they can about a particular culture.

Have them assemble as many symbols of material culture as they can. Have them draw conclusions about the nonmaterial culture, based on the material culture they have amassed. On Culture Day have each department/club set up a booth displaying their results. The rest of the school can move from booth to booth.

If you do a subculture day, have students concentrate on the subcultures in your area. If you do a sub-sub culture day, concentrate on the subcultures in your school.

L2

Using the Section Preview

Have students brainstorm a list of things that our society used to believe to be true, but are not true today. One example might be that women did not have the intelligence to make valid political choices. Students should be able to explain why the beliefs they list are no longer held to be generally true.

Open-Response Question

Ask students what the word *belief* means. At first they will think this is a no-brainer question. As students volunteer their answers, however, it should become apparent that there are a lot of different understandings about this concept.

Section 4

Beliefs and Material Culture

Key Terms

- nonmaterial culture
- beliefs
- material culture
- ideal culture
- real culture

Section Preview

Besides norms and values, beliefs and physical objects make up culture. Ideal culture includes the guidelines we claim to accept, while real culture describes how we actually behave.

nonmaterial culture
ideas, knowledge and beliefs that influence people's behavior

beliefs
ideas about the nature of reality

material culture
the concrete, tangible objects of a culture

Beliefs and Physical Objects

The **nonmaterial culture** involves beliefs, ideas, and knowledge. The *material culture* is about how we relate to physical objects. Values, norms, knowledge, ideas (nonmaterial), and physical objects (material) make up a culture.

Why do beliefs matter? **Beliefs** are ideas about the nature of reality. Beliefs can be true or false. The Romans believed Caesar Augustus to be a god; the Tanala, a hill tribe of Madagascar, believed that the souls of their kings passed into snakes; and many Germans believed that pictures of Hitler on their walls would prevent the walls from crumbling during bombing raids. We would certainly consider these beliefs to be false. In contrast, other beliefs—such as the belief that the human eye can distinguish over seven million colors and the belief that no intelligent life exists on Mars—are supported by factual evidence. We consider these to be true. Beliefs are important because people base their behavior on what they believe, regardless of how true or false the beliefs are.

What is material culture? **Material culture** consists of the concrete, tangible objects within a culture—automobiles, basketballs, chairs, highways, art. These physical objects have no meaning or use apart from the meanings people give them.

Acres of discarded cars in a junkyard plainly show that the automobile is one of the most common objects of America's material culture.

Paired Learning Activity

Ask student pairs to select an activity that they enjoy, such as a sport or a hobby. They should analyze this activity in terms of its material and nonmaterial aspects, and its cultural components. If they select a sport, the material culture would include all the paraphernalia and locations needed to play it. The nonmaterial aspects would include team spirit, competitiveness, skill, and submission to the coach's authority. Have the pairs share their results with the class. Class members may want to add other nonmaterial aspects to the lists of other pairs. **L2**

Consider newspaper and pepper as physical objects. Each has some meaning for you, but can you think of a use for them in combination? Some Americans have used pepper and newspaper in a process known as "nettling." An elderly medical doctor tells the story of his first encounter with nettling:

The ink of my medical license was hardly dry, and as I was soon to find out, my ears would not be dry for some time. I had never delivered a baby on my own and faced my maiden voyage with some fear.

Upon entering Mrs. Williamson's house, I found a local midwife and several neighbors busily at work preparing for the delivery. My fear caused me to move rather slowly and my happiness over my reprieve prompted me to tell the women that they were doing just fine and to proceed without my services.

Having gotten myself off the hook, I watched the ladies with a fascination that soon turned to horror.

At the height of Mrs. Williamson's labor pains, one of the neighbors rolled a piece of newspaper into a funnel shape. Holding the bottom end of the cone she poured a liberal amount of pepper into it. Her next move was to insert the sharp end of the cone into Mrs. Williamson's nose. With the cone in its "proper" place, the neighbor inhaled deeply and blew the pepper from the cone into the inner recesses of Mrs. Williamson's nose—if not her mind.

Suddenly alert, Mrs. Williamson's eyes widened as her senses rebelled against the pepper. With a mighty sneeze, I was introduced to nettling. The violence of that sneeze reverberated through her body to force the baby from her womb in a skittering flight across the bed. An appropriately positioned assistant fielded the baby in midflight and only minor details of Orville's rite of birth remained.

For this country doctor, the physical objects of newspaper and pepper took on new meaning.

Before this doctor was introduced to nettling, this particular combination of newspaper and pepper had no meaning for him. And until nettling was devised, the combination was without meaning for anyone, even though the separate physical objects existed as part of the culture.

How is material culture related to nonmaterial culture? The uses and meanings of physical objects can vary among societies. Although it is conventional to use a 747 jet for traveling, it is possible that a 747 downed in a remote jungle region of the world could be used as a place of worship, a storage bin, or a home. In the United States, out-of-service buses, trains, and trolley cars have been converted to restaurants.

Clearly, the cultural meaning of physical objects is not determined by the physical characteristics of the objects. The meanings of physical objects are based on the beliefs, norms, and values people hold with regard to them. This is obvious when new meanings of a physical object are considered. At one time, only pianos and organs were used in church services. Guitars, drums, and trumpets were not "holy" enough to accompany a choir. Yet many churches today use these "worldly" instruments regularly in their worship activities. The instruments have not changed, but the cultural meanings placed on them have.

Open-Response Question

The concept of nettling can be used to help students understand how objects alone may have no meaning. Ask students to consider objects that have meaning when used in conjunction with something else, like a hot dog and bun. Even though a hot dog and bun do not have to go together, serving one without the other is not as common. In fact, many young children become quite upset if they are asked to eat a hot dog wrapped in a piece of bread. Have students share similar ideas.

Teaching Strategy

Have students identify objects and explain their cultural meanings. It might seem obvious, but ask them to consider if each object's cultural meaning has changed. For example, the phone was originally a way of communicating important messages. Later, it became a means for keeping in touch. Today it is also a device for connecting to the Internet. The cultural meaning of the object has broadened and also changed. **L1**

Careers in Sociology

A young person used to ask, "What will I be when I grow up?" Today, there may be more than just one answer. Our increasingly complex technological and global economy often requires people to pursue a series of careers rather than keeping the same job for a lifetime. Most young adults will explore more than one option before settling on a clear path, and older adults may find themselves retooling with sociology after a successful career in another field. Solid training in sociology forms a foundation for flexible career development. Sociology offers a source for conceptual organization of the most pressing issues of our times, and a powerful set of tools with which to study them. Students can find some ideas for different sociology-related careers at **http://www.utexas.edu/student/careercenter/career ideas/soc.html**.

Pulling It All Together

Distinguishing between the nonmaterial and material culture allows us to see how objects have meaning only because cultures determine that these objects should have meaning. A country's flag is just a material object, but the symbolic meaning behind the flag (patriotism, country, honor) clearly shows how elements of the nonmaterial culture relate to the object.

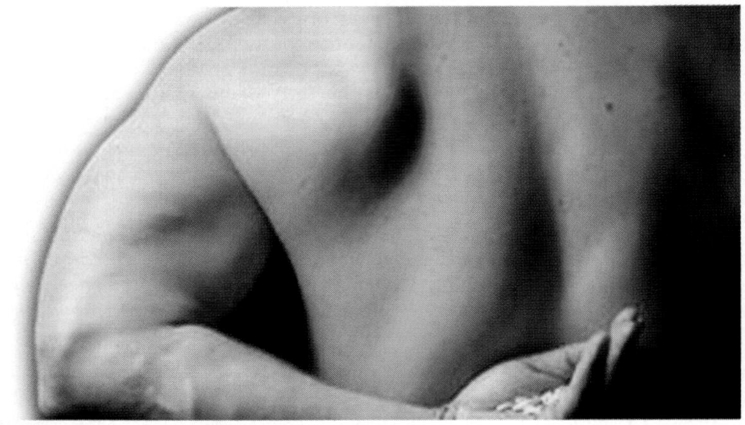

Though American ideal culture values natural athletic ability, in reality, some professional and amateur athletes use drugs or steroids to improve their performances.

Ideal and Real Culture

ideal culture
cultural guidelines that group members claim to accept

real culture
actual behavior patterns of members of a group

A gap sometimes exists between cultural guidelines and actual behavior. This gap is captured in the concepts of ideal and real culture. **Ideal culture** refers to cultural guidelines publicly embraced by members of a society. **Real culture** refers to actual behavior patterns, which often conflict with these guidelines.

One value of America's ideal culture is honesty. Yet in real culture, honesty is not always practiced. Some taxpayers annually violate both the letter and spirit of existing tax laws. Some businesspeople engage in dishonest business practices. Some students cheat on exams. Some college athletes do the "high $500" handshake, during which a team booster leaves illegal money in their palms. These are not isolated instances. They are real cultural patterns passed on from generation to generation.

It is important to remember that we are not referring here to individuals whose violations of norms include murder, rape, and robbery. These types of antisocial behavior violate even real culture.

Does the fact that we sometimes ignore cultural guidelines make ideal culture meaningless? Absolutely not. In an imperfect world, ideal culture provides high standards. These ideals are targets that most people attempt to reach most of the time. Ideal culture also permits the detection of deviant behavior. Individuals who deviate too far from the ideal pattern are sanctioned. This helps to preserve the ideal culture.

Section 4 Assessment

1. How is the material culture influenced by the nonmaterial culture?
2. How is real culture different from ideal culture?

Critical Thinking

3. **Drawing Conclusions** Think of an example of real and ideal culture in your school. Should the aspect of ideal culture be abandoned? Why or why not?

Answers to Section 4 Assessment

1. How objects are used is a function of ideas about the objects and the values and needs of the society.
2. Real culture is how people actually respond in most cases. Ideal culture is a standard against which real culture is measured.

Critical Thinking

3. Answers will vary.

Observation

Ideal and Real Culture Cheating on exams is something students can relate to as they try to understand the concepts of ideal and real culture. Ask students if they have ever cheated on an exam, no matter how long ago. If truthful, most students should reply, "yes." Ask them why they cheated. Answers will vary and might include: I needed the grade; Everyone else does; I didn't study; It was too easy not to. Next, ask students why, if everyone knows cheating is wrong, so many people do it anyway. Follow up by asking students to spend a few days noting behaviors of people that represent examples of the gap between real and ideal culture.

L1

Section 5

Cultural Diversity and Similarity

Key Terms

- **social categories**
- **subculture**
- **counterculture**
- **ethnocentrism**
- **cultural universals**
- **cultural particulars**

Cultural Change

So far we have talked about culture as if it did not change. Actually the processes that govern cultural change are so important they are discussed in Chapter 17 on social movements and collective behavior. Briefly, however, you should realize that all cultures experience change. Norms, values, and beliefs are relatively stable, but they do change over time. For example, many of your grandparents never went to college; as teenagers, your parents never e-mailed friends or made last-minute dates on their cell phones. It was not that long ago that middle-class women with young children were discouraged from working outside the home. Interracial dating, while still relatively uncommon, is becoming more acceptable in the United States. These are aspects of culture that are changing in response to certain processes.

Why does culture change? Culture changes for three reasons. One cause is *discovery*, the process of finding something that already exists. The United States is currently discovering the generally unrecognized athletic abilities of females. This is changing the perception of women and the relationship between males and females.

Culture is also changed through *invention*, the creation of something new. Science has led to inventions that have changed the world since the fifteenth century, from the creation of the steam engine to the cellular phone. Such inventions have greatly altered our way of life.

A third cause of cultural change is *diffusion*, the borrowing of aspects of culture from other cultures. One aspect of culture that diffuses rapidly is food. Tacos, pizza, and hamburgers can be found on menus all over the world. Christmas trees and piñatas are part of celebrations in many countries. Ideas are also diffused. Japanese society has been fundamentally transformed as a result of the adoption of democracy and capitalism after World War II. As stated earlier, these three processes will be examined more closely in a later chapter.

The Scottish kilt is an essential part of this South African traditional dance that tells the story of a historic battle with the British in the 1800s.

Section Preview

Cultures change according to three major processes. Cultures contain groups within them called *subcultures* and *countercultures* that differ in important ways from the main culture. People tend to make judgments based on the values of their own cultures. While apparently very different on the surface, all cultures have common traits or elements that sociologists call *cultural universals*.

Using the Section Preview

To help students see where they are heading in this section, tell them that computers are slowly changing the face of all cultures. Terms such as mouse, CD-ROM, PC, and digital are quickly becoming cultural universals for people in the United States. This cultural change has not been embraced by all, but no one can ignore that it is happening.

Integrating the Teacher Resources

Look for the Chapter 3 Learning Goals Outline, a reproducible student worksheet in the Unit 2 Mastering Basic Concepts booklet in your Teacher's Resource Box. It can be used to review chapter content.

Using Problem-Solving Skills

Propose the following scenario to the class: Early this morning your best friend calls you on the phone, crying heartily and mumbling choked words between sobs. You eventually understand why she's upset. Her parents have told her that she is expected to follow the Philippino tradition of marrying a boy who was chosen for her at birth; a marriage to her current boyfriend is strictly forbidden. It would be considered taboo for her to continue thinking about him. As soon as she turns twenty-one, she is expected to marry Manuel, a young man she has never met.

Using the problem-solving process, determine the extent of loyalty to tradition as well as following one's heart. Should Philippino traditions rule behavior when living in America? Whose values should be taken into consideration? Fashion a solution to this difficulty, and evaluate its effectiveness in keeping peace in the family. L2

Focus on Research

Emphasis should be placed on how sociological research identified the problems found in this study. Students might want to create a survey that asks similar questions about their school and home lives. You can refer to Chapter 2 for tips on how to conduct such a survey.

Focus on Research

Survey Research: How Do Schools and Parents Fail Teens?

Adolescence is often marked with drama and difficulty. Jacquelynne Eccles (1993) investigated the experience of American teenagers entering a midwestern junior high school and discovered that some teenage troubles are more than hormonal—they are cultural as well.

Eccles studied 1,500 early adolescents moving from sixth-grade elementary schools to seventh-grade junior high schools. The junior high schools were located in twelve school districts in middle-class Michigan communities. Students filled out questionnaires at school for two consecutive years—the sixth and seventh grades. This procedure permitted Eccles to document changes the teenagers experienced after the first year of their transition.

The findings were not encouraging. The relationships between students and teachers tended to worsen over the year. At the very time when the young adolescents especially needed supportive relationships outside of their homes, personal and positive relationships with teachers were strained by cultural and organizational changes in junior high school.

There was more grouping based on academic achievement and more comparing of students with one another. This increased emphasis on student ranking comes just when young adolescents are most insecure about their status relative to their peers. In addition, in the junior high culture, the students experienced less opportunity to participate in classroom decision making.

As a result, student motivation and self-confidence declined. Eccles concluded that junior high school culture denies adolescents the emotionally supportive environment they need for proper social development.

Junior high students who are in supportive environments are more likely to have higher motivation and self-esteem than students in less supportive schools and families.

Survey

Have your students identify some of the problems mentioned in this study, such as a lack of decision-making power, teacher-student relationships, and so on. Once they have identified all these problems, have students create survey questions. Remind students that the questions need to have measurable responses. Therefore, whether they ask a qualitative or quantitative question, the question should be able to be easily interpreted. Students might want to set up closed-ended responses such as *strongly agree, agree somewhat, unsure, disagree somewhat,* and *strongly disagree.* Students should be reminded also that they can write statements rather than questions.

Eccles's news was no better on the home front. Changes in family paralleled those of the school system. Parental control over teenagers went up during the year, often to excessive levels. At the same time, school motivation and self-esteem of the junior high students went down.

As a check on these general findings, Eccles compared students in more supportive schools and families with those in less supportive ones. In both the school and the family settings, she found more positive results in supportive environments. Students who were able to participate in school and family decision making showed higher levels of academic motivation and self-esteem than their peers with less opportunity to participate.

The solution to this problem, Eccles concludes, lies in a change in the norms and values of the schools and families. Schools and families need to develop balanced cultural expectations of young adolescents based on their developmental needs. Adolescents, Eccles points out, have a growing need for independence that is rarely encouraged in the culture of the public school system. Neither cracking down on them nor giving up control strikes the proper balance. The task is for the family and school to provide "an environment that changes in the right way and at the right pace" (Eccles, 1993:99).

Working with the Research

1. Do you recall your junior high experience? Was your situation similar to the one described by Eccles? Did you feel the same pressures?
2. Which of the three theoretical perspectives do you think is most helpful in understanding the social relationships Eccles describes? Apply this perspective to explain her findings.

Answers to Working with the Research

1. Answers will vary. Students will most likely identify with this article. You might want to tell the students that sociologists are able to generalize about groups of people because so often the behaviors and experiences are similar. Group behavior is predictable.
2. Students should easily see the conflict perspective in this approach. Groups are competing and one group is using its power over another. Not so obvious is the interactionist perspective, specifically the interactions that exist between parents and teachers and the symbolic meanings of those interactions.

Integrating the Teacher Resources

A lesson plan for a student research project related to the content of this chapter can be found in Doing Sociology: Focus on Research, available in your Teacher's Resource Box.

Examples might be, "My parents are supportive of my efforts to complete my schoolwork," or, "My teachers involve me in decision-making, such as homework assignments, tests, and projects." It is probably best to have students confine their surveys to ten good questions. Surveys that get too long decrease the likelihood that respondents will consider each question carefully. Students will then need to quantify their results, draw conclusions, and follow the research guidelines from Chapter 2. You might want to post the survey results on the class bulletin board or share the results with a school administrator to see if any positive change can result from your findings.
L2

Cultural Diversity

social categories
groupings of persons who share a social characteristic

subculture
a group that is part of the dominant culture but that differs from it in some important respects

counterculture
a subculture deliberately and consciously opposed to certain central beliefs or attitudes of the dominant culture

ethnocentrism
judging others in terms of one's own cultural standards

Cultural diversity exists in all societies. Some diversity is a result of **social categories**—groups that share a social characteristic such as age, gender, or religion. Certain behaviors are associated with particular ages, genders, or religions. For example, devout Catholics are expected to attend Mass regularly.

What are subcultures and countercultures? Cultural diversity also comes from groups that differ in particular ways from the larger culture. These groups participate in the larger culture. They may speak the language, work regular jobs, eat and dress like most others, and attend recognized houses of worship. But despite sharing in the broader culture, these groups have some ways of thinking, feeling, and behaving that set them apart. Such groups—known as *subcultures* and *countercultures*—are usually found in large, complex societies.

Subculture is part of the dominant culture but differs from it in some important respects. The subculture of San Francisco's Chinatown is a good example. Early Chinese immigrants brought much of their native culture with them to America and have attempted to retain it by passing it from generation to generation. Although Chinese residents of Chinatown have been greatly affected by American culture, they have kept many cultural patterns of their own, such as language, diet, and family structure. Other examples of subcultures are those formed by circus people, musicians, and mental patients (Fine, 1996; Redhead, 1997; Kephart and Zellner, 1998).

Counterculture is a subculture deliberately and consciously opposed to certain central beliefs or attitudes of the dominant culture. A counterculture can be understood only within the context of this opposition.

The punk movement began in Britain and quickly developed into an American counterculture.

Examples of primarily teenage countercultures include the "goth" and the "punk" scenes. Goth is a shortening of the term *gothic*, meaning dark, strangely mysterious, and remote. Punk is a philosophy of rebellion and sexual revolution popularized by the lyrics and music of punk-rock bands.

Prison counterculture surfaced at the trial of John King, a man convicted of the gruesome truck-dragging murder of James Byrd, Jr. During an earlier prison stretch, King had become a member of a white supremacist gang that promoted many forms of violence. The gang's motto was "blood in, blood out," meaning that entry into the gang demanded a violent act, and leaving the gang would result in violence as well (Galloway, 1999). Delinquent gangs, motorcycle gangs, certain types of drug groups, and revolutionary or religious groups may also form countercultures (Zellner, 1999).

Ethnocentrism

Once people learn their culture, they tend to become strongly committed to it. In fact, they often cannot imagine any other way of life. They may judge others in terms of their own cultural standards—a practice referred to as **ethnocentrism.**

Using the Illustration

What would students in your community call the two teens in this photo? Go around the class and ask students if they would avoid classmates who dressed in the manner shown in the photo or be perfectly comfortable with them. Perhaps students believe the punk movement has been around so long that these counterculture members are fairly common and accepted. Do people who dress this way still have an ability to shock? Then, transition into a discussion of labeling. Tell students they will learn more about how people are labeled and how deviance is defined in Chapter 7.

Integrating the Teacher Resources

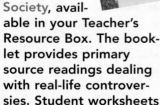

Look for Ethics, Values, and Technology: Real-Life Issues in Society, available in your Teacher's Resource Box. The booklet provides primary source readings dealing with real-life controversies. Student worksheets are included.

Survey

Students whose parents were teens or young adults in the 1960s might want to interview their parents to find out how involved they were in the counterculture movement. How did their parents view the movement at the time? What do they think the permanent results, if any, of the sixties counterculture have been? Students could either present their findings as a skit, oral report, or a videotape presentation.
L1

Tech Trends

Star Wars and the Internet

When *Star Wars* first appeared in theaters in the late 1970s, director George Lucas probably did not realize that he had almost single-handedly created a full-fledged cultural phenomenon. Virtually everyone in the United States now recognizes Luke Skywalker, Darth Vader, and Yoda. Most Americans know what "May the Force be with you" means.

The movies in the *Star Wars* series have certainly been extremely popular in their own right, but the Internet has also been important in their penetration into popular culture. In 1999, *Star Wars* fans kept in touch over the Internet as they eagerly awaited *The Phantom Menace*, the first new *Star Wars* film in sixteen years. Anticipation of the first "prequel" was incredibly intense, and pirated footage spread to more than sixty web sites within hours of first being posted. In response, Lucasfilm's official web site posted the film's trailer and was promptly overwhelmed with 340 "hits" per second. The impact of the Internet on this bit of American culture is undeniable.

"Everyone said this was the most top-secret movie ever made, that it was tighter than Fort Knox, no leaks whatsoever," says Scott Chitwood, aged twenty-five, who's the emperor of TheForce.net. "Well, most web site operators knew the plot a year ago. That's all because of the Internet."

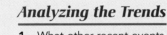

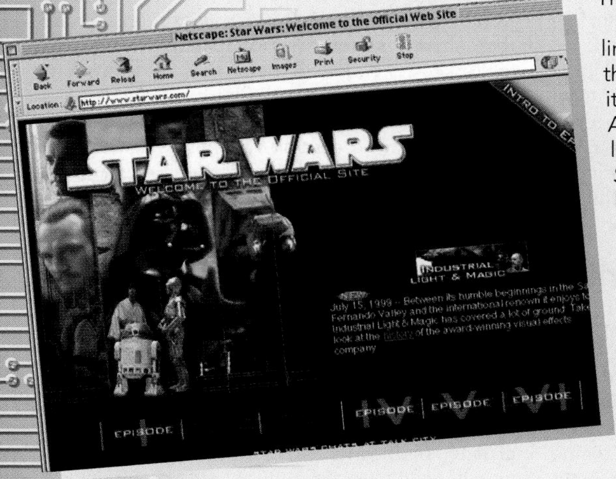

Of course, the cultural effects of *Star Wars* are not limited to the box office. *Star Wars* is much more than a movie. It is a mini-culture, or subculture, unto itself. It has its own icons, symbols, and language. And elements of this subculture have entered the larger culture. Merchandise related to the first three *Star Wars* movies totaled over $4.5 billion in sales between 1977 and 1999. That alone amounts to more than four times the revenues generated from the films themselves. These items include toys, soundtracks, costumes, and licensing fees. With the increased popularity of e-commerce, the Internet has become a cultural force to be reckoned with.

Analyzing the Trends

1. What other recent events are now part of popular culture in the United States? Tell what aspects of these events have made their way into our thinking, feeling, and behaving.
2. Predict ways in which the increasing popularity of the Internet may alter our understanding of culture.

Tech Trends

There will probably be several students in the class who can demonstrate the huge impact of *Star Wars* on our culture. Ask them to suggest words, phrases, characters, and scenarios that have become cultural icons to a segment of the population. Can students suggest other movies that have had a similar, though perhaps smaller, impact on our cultural identity? Many science fiction genre movies seem to generate a cult-like following, including *Star Trek* and *Alien*. Products for young children, based on Pokémon and Disney movies, for example, can also generate this kind of culture effect.

Answers to Analyzing the Trends

1. Students might mention Pokéman and Disney movies like *The Lion King* and *Tarzan*. Pokéman cards created competitions across the country; many fast food restaurants base sales around recent movies and fads.
2. Concerns about the Internet include the loss of cultural traditions. Many people today are looking for advice, information, and relationships on-line. The Internet has allowed us to access information about our own culture and other cultures with alarming speed. Whether the Internet will severely alter our concept of culture or simply modify it, remains to be seen.

Reinforcing Vocabulary

A similar term to ethnocentrism is *xenocentrism.* Xenocentrism is when someone loves another culture more than their own. This might be a little more challenging for students, but you might want to look for examples of people who appear to be xenocentric. (For example, some Americans who think the British manners and moves are superior to those of the U.S. and who adopt British mannerisms are called Anglophiles.)

Reteaching

To check whether or not students understand the concepts of cultural universals and particulars, ask them to consider the effects of global communication and computer technology. Do they think global diversity would increase or decrease with this global technology? Ask them to explain their answers. *(Arguments could be made for either side. Diversity could increase as Americans are exposed to cultural particulars from other cultures. Likewise, diversity could decrease as a dominant culture's particulars are adapted by other cultures.)*

What are some examples of ethnocentrism? Examples of ethnocentrism are plentiful. The Olympic Games are much more than an arena of competition for young men and women. In addition to competition, the games are an expression of ethnocentrism. Political and nationalistic undercurrents run through the Olympics. A country's final ranking in this athletic competition for gold, silver, and bronze medals is frequently taken as a reflection of the country's worth and status on the world stage.

Ethnocentrism also exists within societies. Regional rivalries in the United States are a source of many humorous stories, but these jokes reflect an underlying ethnocentrism. Boston is said by some (mostly Bostonians) to be the hub of the universe. Texans often claim to have the biggest and best of everything. New Yorkers bemoan the lack of culture in Los Angeles. Finally, members of churches, schools, and country clubs all over America feel that their particular ways of living should be adopted by others.

Ethnocentrism is still a divisive force in Germany. A riot erupts when members of the ultraright National Democratic Party march in support of their racist policies.

Does ethnocentrism help or hurt society? Ethnocentrism has two faces—it offers both advantages and disadvantages. People feel good about themselves and about others in their group when they believe that what they are doing is right and superior to what other groups do. Stability is promoted because traditions and behaviors are highly valued. If a society is too rigid, however, it becomes inflexible. Extreme ethnocentrism can prevent change for the better. Societies whose members are firmly convinced of their superiority tend not to create anything new. The ancient Chinese built a wall to keep both invaders and new ideas out. The civil rights movement was born to combat racial ethnocentrism. Hitler's Final Solution was ethnocentrism at its worst. Today many states are passing laws that increase the penalties against people who commit violent acts against others based on their race, origin, or religion. (Civil rights and hate crimes are discussed in more detail in Chapter 9.)

Cultural Universals

cultural universals general cultural traits that exist in all cultures

Although it may seem that different cultures have little in common, researchers have identified more than seventy common cultural traits. These **cultural universals** are traits that exist in all cultures. They include such things as sports, cooking, courtship, division of labor, education, etiquette, funeral rites, family, government, hospitality, housing, inheritance rules, joking, language, medicine, marriage, mourning, music, property rights, religious rituals, sexual restrictions, status differences, and tool making (Murdock, 1945). Because all societies have these cultural universals, they are more similar than you think. (See Figure 3.5 on page 102 for a more detailed list of cultural universals.)

cultural particulars the ways in which a culture expresses universal traits

How are cultural universals expressed? Cultural universals are not always carried out in the same way. In fact, different cultures have developed quite different ways to express universals. These are called **cultural particulars.** One cultural universal is caring for children. In the United States, women have traditionally worked within the home caring for children, and men have worked outside the home. (Although this is changing, women in this country are still largely responsible for child care.) Among the

Cooperative Learning Activity

Ask students to search their daily newspapers for examples of ethnocentrism. (It would be an unusual—but wonderful—day that there was nothing in the news about culturally-based hostilities.) Students should bring in the articles for analysis in groups. The groups should define precisely the areas of conflict, the basis for this conflict (historical, economic, etc.) and try to identify cultural values that might be in the way of attempting a solution to the problem. **L2**

Snapshot of America

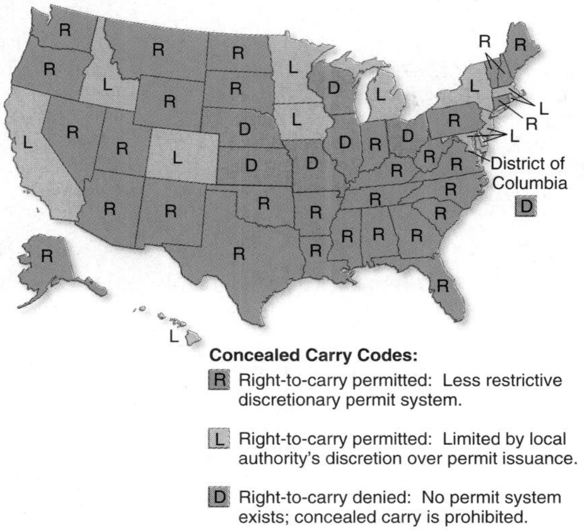

Gun Control

Some observers believe groups that promote gun ownership form a subculture. For example, the National Rifle Association (NRA) brings together people who share an interest in guns and the right to own them. The map displays the states that permit citizens to carry concealed guns.

Interpreting the Map

1. What code marks the states with the most liberal gun control laws?
2. Can you find a pattern between gun control and regions in the U.S.?
3. How might regional differences in gun control laws reflect variations in socialization patterns?

Manus of New Guinea, in contrast, the man is completely in charge of child rearing. Among the Mbuti pygmies, the Lovedu of Africa, and the Navajo and Iroquois Indians, men and women share equally in domestic and economic tasks (Little, 1975).

Why do cultural universals exist? The biological similarity shared by all human beings helps to account for many cultural universals. If a society is to survive, children must be born and cared for, and some type of family structure must exist. (Groups that deliberately eliminate the family—such as the Shakers religious sect of New England—disappear.) Because people become ill, there must be some sort of medical care. Because people die, there must be funeral rites, mourning, and inheritance rules. Because food is necessary, cooking must be done.

The physical environment provides another reason why cultural universals exist. Because humans cannot survive without protection from the environment, some form of shelter must be created. Armies were formed to settle disputes over boundaries and important waterways.

Finally, cultural universals exist because societies face many of the same social problems. If a society is to survive, new members must be taught the

Snapshot of America

The subject of gun control can be controversial because it is value laden, yet students are very interested in this topic. You may want students to debate the merits of the issues for and against, and thus practice using the cultural norm of showing respect for different opinions. Have students emphasize the contention that NRA membership constitutes belonging to a subculture.

Answers to Interpreting the Map

1. The states with the most liberal gun control laws are marked in green.
2. The states with large urban populations, such as California and New York, are in the middle on gun control. The most liberal states are those of the South and the West. Generally, the most restrictive are in the Midwest.
3. Answers should reflect attempts to understand the effects of socialization in the South and West that might make citizens more opposed to gun control laws.

ECONOMY	INSTITUTIONS	ARTS	LANGUAGE	ENVIRONMENT	RECREATION	BELIEFS
Trade Tools Technology Goods Services Jobs Business Transportation Communications Food, Shelter, Clothing	Family Government Education Religion Economy	Art Literature Dance Theater Music Crafts Folk tales	Words Expressions Pronunciations Alphabet Symbols	Communities Geography Geology Habitat Wildlife Climates Resources	Games Toys Arts Media Holidays Festivals	Values Traditions Ethnicity Customs Religions Morals

CULTURAL UNIVERSALS

Figure 3.5 Cultural Universals. *Researchers have identified more than seventy traits that appear to one degree or another in all cultures.*

culture. Goods and services must be produced and distributed. Tasks must be assigned, and work must be accomplished. Cultures develop similar methods of solving these problems.

> If we cannot end now our differences, at least we can help make the world safe for diversity.
>
> **John F. Kennedy**
> **U.S. president**

Section 5 Assessment

1. Identify each of the following as a social category (SC), subculture (S), or counterculture (C).
   a. Chinatown in New York City
   b. motorcycle gang
   c. Catholics
   d. females
   e. revolutionary political group
   f. the super rich
2. Define ethnocentrism.
3. What are cultural universals? Why do they exist?

Critical Thinking

4. **Analyzing Information** Are you and your friends members of a subculture? If so, describe some specific elements of that subculture.
5. **Making Comparisons** From the chart above, choose a cultural universal. Compare or contrast how this cultural universal is addressed by two different cultures. For example, how do the United States and Mexico differ in recreational activities?

Working With the Data

Figure 3.5 Ask students to study the chart carefully to see if there are any universals that they think are out of place or questionable. For example, media is listed under recreation. Where else might media, as an institution, have an important effect? Looking at the social institutions, you might want to tell students that sports is considered an institution by some sociologists. Let students discuss how our culture seems to have institutionalized sports.

Answers to Section 5 Assessment

1. **a**=S, **b**=C, **c**=SC, **d**=SC, **e**=C, **f**=S or SC
2. Ethnocentrism is the perspective that judges all other cultures and behaviors against the standards of one's own culture.
3. Cultural universals are behaviors or social institutions that appear in all cultures. They exist because humans have certain common needs that are dictated by their physical biology and by their environment.

Critical Thinking

4. Answers will vary.
5. Answers will vary.

Integrating the Teacher Resources

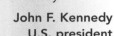

For review, use the Chapter 3 Vocabulary Quiz and Chapter Quiz available in the Unit 2 Mastering Basic Concepts booklet in your Teacher's Resource Box.

Chapter 3 Assessment

Summary

Section 1: The Basis Of Culture

Main Idea: Culture defines how people in a society behave in relation to others and to physical objects. Although most behavior among animals is instinctual, human behavior is learned. Even reflexes and drives do not completely determine how humans will behave, because people are heavily influenced by culture.

Section 2: Language and Culture

Main Idea: Humans can create and transmit culture. The symbols of language play a role in determining people's view of reality.

Section 3: Norms and Values

Main Idea: Two essential components of culture are norms and values. There are several types of norms—folkways, mores, and laws. Sanctions are used to encourage conformity to norms. Values, the broadest cultural ideas, form the basis for norms.

Section 4: Beliefs and Material Culture

Main Idea: Besides norms and values, beliefs and physical objects make up culture. Ideal culture includes the guidelines we claim to accept, while real culture describes how we actually behave.

Section 5: Cultural Diversity and Similarity

Main Idea: Cultures change according to three major processes. Cultures contain groups within them called subcultures and countercultures.

SOCIOLOGY Online

Self-Check Quiz
Visit the *Sociology and You* Web site at soc.glencoe.com and click on **Chapter 3—Self-Check Quizzes** to prepare for the chapter test.

Reviewing Vocabulary

Complete each sentence using each term once.

a. sociobiology
b. sanctions
c. real culture
d. beliefs
e. society
f. laws
g. mores
h. subculture
i. ethnocentrism
j. informal sanctions

1. ____________ are the ideas about the nature of reality.
2. A group that belongs to the larger culture but differs from it in some significant way is called ____________.
3. ____________ is the study of the biological basis of human behavior.
4. Formally defined norms enforced by officials are called ____________.
5. ____________ are rewards and punishments that can be applied by most members of a group.
6. Actual behavior patterns of the members of a group are called ____________.
7. ____________ are rewards and punishments used to encourage desired behaviors.
8. Norms with moral dimensions are called ____________.
9. A specific territory composed of people who share a common culture are called ____________.
10. Judging others in terms of one's own cultural standards is called ____________.

Reviewing the Facts

1. According to sociobiology, how is human behavior influenced?
2. What are the differences between reflexes and drives?

Answers Chapter 3 Assessment

Reviewing Vocabulary

1. d
2. h
3. a
4. f
5. j
6. c
7. b
8. g
9. e
10. i

Reviewing the Facts

1. Influenced more by genetics than by culture.
2. Reflexes are simple, biologically inherited, automatic reactions to physical stimuli. Drives are biologically inherited impulses to reduce discomfort.
3. Folkways are rules that cover customary ways of thinking, feeling, and behaving but lack moral overtones.
4. The Spair-Whort hypothesis holds that our view of the world depends on the particular language we have learned.
5. Folkways, mores and laws.
6. Formal sanctions are sanctions that may only be applied by persons who are officially chosen and who have special authority, such as judges and teachers.
7. Sanctions are used to enforce norms.
8. A social category is a grouping of people of the dominant culture who share a social characteristic. A subculture is a group that is part of the dominant culture but differs from it in some important aspect.
9. Ethnocentrism plays a positive role when it helps people to feel good about themselves and believe what they are doing is superior to what other groups do. Example: Participants in the Olympics use competition as an expression of ethnocentrism. Ethnocentrism plays a negative role when it is too rigid and based on feelings of superiority

Chapter 3 Assessment

3. What are folkways? Give three examples of folkways in the United States.
4. Explain the Sapir-Whorf hypothesis.
5. What are the three basic types of norms?
6. Define formal and informal sanctions.
7. Describe the relationship between norms and sanctions.
8. How does a social category differ from a subculture?
9. Ethnocentrism offers both advantages and disadvantages. Give an example of a positive role that ethnocentrism can play in a society. When is ethnocentrism a negative force in a society?
10. What are cultural universals?

Thinking Critically

1. **Making Inferences** More than any other symbol of our country, the American flag provokes emotional responses. Some people are willing to give their lives for it, while others have burned it in protest. In groups, discuss why this symbol is so powerful.
2. **Applying Concepts** All societies have cultural universals, as discussed in this chapter. Why, then, are so many groups in conflict? Think of examples of groups in this country that seem to be in conflict (such as animal rights activists and fur shop owners), and examine the reasons for these conflicts.
3. **Making Comparisons** Discuss how you think a functionalist would look at the topic of culture. How do you think a conflict theorist would view it?
4. **Evaluating Information** Some Amish parents have gone to jail rather than enroll their children in public schools. Even though you might wish that your parents had taken this stand on your behalf, what does it say about Amish cultural values?
5. **Categorizing Information** We have created a whole new language as a result of computers. A mouse is no longer necessarily an animal; another definition would be a device for navigating through electronic files. Make a list of the words in your school that are unique to your community (or school group) and that would take an "outsider" awhile to learn.
6. **Understanding Cause and Effect** Use the diagram below to illustrate three causes of cultural change.

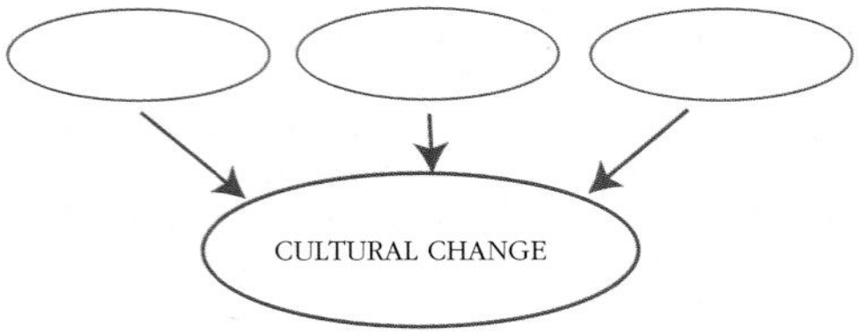

Sociology Projects

1. **Cultural Universals** Using the cultural universals diagram in your text (Figure 3.5 on page 102), create your own culture. Your culture must include all the components of the second level: an economy, institutions, arts, language, environment, recreation, and beliefs. Make sure that elements of the third level on the cultural universal diagram are part of your culture. For example, how will your culture entertain itself? What types of music will you listen to? How old are the members of your culture? You must also name this culture and locate it on a world map. Present your culture to the class with a detailed poster.
2. **Culture** You are an archaeologist and you have just uncovered a civilization called "America." Find at least one item from each of these aspects of culture: economy, religion, sports, science/technology, education, families, and politics/ government. For example, you might uncover a checkbook, a small cross, a baseball card, a mouse (not the animal), a piece of chalk, pictures, and campaign buttons. As you find these items around your house or school, try to imagine what they might mean to this American culture by answering the following questions.

ANSWERS CHAPTER 3 ASSESSMENT

that act as a wall to keep others out or to suppress them. Example: Racial hate groups.

10. Cultural universals are general traits thought to exist in all cultures.

Thinking Critically

1. The Supreme Court considers burning the American flag an act that is protected by the First Amendment right to free speech. In 1989, the U.S. Supreme Court decided in favor of Gregory Johnson, who had been convicted of violating a Texas law by burning a U.S. flag. In 1990, Congress attempted to pass an amendment to the U.S. Constitution, granting states the right to pass such laws. Different versions of these bills were defeated in both the House and the Senate.
2. Students will probably have several examples and members of the class will take both sides of these issues. This would be a good time to do informal debates by appointing a spokesperson for each side. Let the supporters and opponents meet with their spokespeople for five or ten minutes to prepare their arguments.
3. The functionalist would look at how culture reflects order and stability and the interdependence of all the related aspects of the culture. A conflict theorist would look at how culture creates competition for limited resources and how certain members of a culture try to maintain their power over other groups.
4. As an introduction, ask students what they feel strongly about. What do they value so much that they would go to jail for it? If they can identify one thing, they might understand how the Amish feel about their right to control the content and belief system of the education for their children.
5. Some school policies also have created words unique to your school. If students know of other schools, maybe they could share some words unique to those schools, as well.
6. Causes: Discovery, Invention, Diffusion

a. Is this item culturally universal? Can it be found in other cultures?

b. What uses might someone from another culture find for this item? Be creative.

c. What does this item tell us about this culture?

3. **Popular Culture** T-shirts are a great example of popular culture. Everyone wears them, and they are very symbolic; they say a lot about our culture and about the people that wear them. Find a public place where you can discreetly observe people. Look for individuals wearing T-shirts, and jot down your observations of those shirts. Do the shirts make a statement about the people wearing them? Do they carry messages related to any different aspects of culture such as family, politics, or religion? Do they reflect social values? Are any of them inappropriate? If so, what does it say about the wearer's values compared to yours? Did you see similarities in T-shirts, such as a lot of black T-shirts or sports T-shirts? Use standard grammar, spelling, sentence structure and punctuation to write a brief report on your observations.

4. **Handshakes in U.S. Culture** Handshakes are also symbolic representations of cultures. List some situations in which people shake hands in U.S. culture. For example, do boyfriends and girlfriends shake hands in the hallway when they meet? Do some students use special handshakes when they greet other students? As a class, determine all the ways in which handshakes are used in U.S. culture, and explain how the social situation can change the meaning of a handshake.

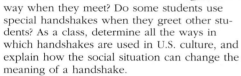

5. **American Values** Based on the section on American values in your text (see pages 89–91), find ads in several magazines that reflect aspects of American values. For example, many ads for fast-food restaurants emphasize efficiency. These businesses pride themselves on their ability to get your meal out fast. The value of efficiency is seen as very American. Look for ads that reflect each one of the American values listed in your text. Put the ads together in a booklet with a title page and conclusions drawn from what you discovered.

6. **Cultural Lag** Material tools of a culture, such as computers, change faster than nonmaterial tools, such as norms and values. This difference creates what has been called *cultural lag*. (You will learn more about this topic in Chapter 17.) Computers have been around for some time. Still, many Americans lag behind in their proficiency with the technology. Interview people you know of varying ages: someone under age twelve, some fellow teens, some young adults, and some elderly adults. Ask them how computer literate they are. Do they know how to use Windows? The Internet? Does cultural lag exist in your sample? If so, try to find reasons or explanations for the lag. Does everyone have equal access to computers? Do certain populations tend to avoid computers? Is fear of technology or change involved?

7. **Cultural Norms** Create a chart comparing cultural norms among U.S. subculture groups such as ethnic, socioeconomic strata, and gender groups.

Technology Activity

1. Compare the use of language between two social categories within your culture (e.g., teenagers and parents). Make a list of ten examples of words or phrases that differ in meaning between the members of each social category. Using the Internet and your school or local library, find the original derivation of the word or phrase. Record your information in a database.

ANSWERS CHAPTER 3 ASSESSMENT

Sociology Projects

1. The key here is to allow students lots of creativity to name and define their culture. They will come up with some creative stuff. Be sure they include as many of the cultural universals as possible.

2. This can be an educational activity if students put enough thought into it. They should spend some time writing up their reports; you want students to really think about the object.

a. If they think that it can be found in other cultures, is it safe to assume that? Do they have some proof that it does exist elsewhere?

b. Students usually can get very creative with the object and find several other uses for the object.

c. Here, students should determine what the object means to culture, and how this culture is dependent or not dependent on its existence.

3. This activity could turn into a little research project as students observe others in their T-shirts. Warn students about the dangers of making assumptions based solely on what a person is wearing. (This is not really a good example of sociological research. Still, students can have a lot of fun with it.)

4. Answers will vary.

5. Students might want to focus on these ads and who is in them. Do they reflect middle-class Americans or are all the best-looking, upper-class people portrayed? Also, do these values truly speak for all Americans?

6. The Tech Trend feature in subsequent chapters will deal with various aspects of computer technology on various populations.

7. Answers will vary.

Technology Activity

1. Answers will vary.

Enrichment Reading

If each student in the class wrote down one explanation for what happened at Columbine High School in 1999, there would be numerous explanations. After reading the article, what new insights could help students understand this tragedy? Students might also want to brainstorm what they could do to prevent such events from occurring at their high school.

Chapter 3

Enrichment Reading

Cultural Explanations for Teen Violence

from an article by James Gilbert

Every social crisis generates its share of easy explanations, but adolescent crime wins the contest for pat answers. Not only is everyone an expert, but out-of-control children are often already the focus of uneasiness about social change, general anxiety, and just plain undisguised dislike. The tragic shootings at Columbine High School in Littleton, Colorado, have generated more than the usual number of theories. Few of these are original, and, in fact, many of them repeat a formula tried out almost 45 years ago, during the national panic over juvenile delinquency. True, the supposed cultural influences have changed, with blame pointed now at the dark lyrics of Marilyn Manson or virtual-reality, murder-and-mayhem computer games, but the ultimate message is pretty much the same: our children's behavior is out of control because our culture is out of control. The only solution is to find a form of censorship that can block adolescents' access to the violent images that impel them to behave violently.

One problem with the cultural explanation for teen violence is that, notwithstanding numerous scientific attempts to do so, it is impossible to prove—there are simply too many other possible causes to factor into the equation. Not that this should necessarily deter critics of our current teen culture. But it is one thing to regard what young people listen to, play, or consume as strange or vulgar or even mildly threatening, and another to argue that it incites specific behavior. Teenagers might be persuaded by advertising to buy a Big Mac or smoke a Camel, but that doesn't mean that song lyrics can make them commit mass murder.

Another problem with the cultural explanation is that we have been there before and ought to recognize from our experience some of the outcomes and implications of the argument. In the mid-'50s, especially between 1954 and 1956, Americans worried as deeply about juvenile delinquency as they did about the cold war, atomic **annihilation,** unemployment, and other social ills. The reason for this is not hard to figure out. Government commissions, the FBI . . . , and a number of leading psychologists and social critics were all warning of a terrible **scourge** of juvenile crime. Cities and towns rushed to pass new ordinances . . . . The favorites of these were local curfews, naming the hour when children under 18 had to be home. Quite naturally, this led to some increased incidence of lawbreaking by youths. But, overall, during the '50s juvenile crime was no higher than the decade that preceded it. Yet fears of juvenile delinquency continued to soar.

While there were many explanations offered for delinquency, the one most printed in the pages of popular magazines and voiced during congressional hearings convened to examine the problem was the **malevolent** influence of crime and horror comic books. No one could accuse "Howdy Doody" or "I Love Lucy" of inciting teen violence, although there were cop-and-gangster TV shows and scores of films that might have been blamed. . . . Comic books, on the other hand, particularly violent and horror comics, . . . became the focus of a **concerted** effort to censor youth culture. The effort was led by liberal Senator Estes Kefauver of Tennessee and was founded on the psychological theories of Fredric Wertham, whose 1954 best-seller, *Seduction of the Innocent*, inspired a vast outcry against the comics. Wertham's theory was based on asking teenage criminals if they read comic books—not much different from the logic behind today's blaming of computer games or music. Kefauver and Wertham's movement ultimately persuaded the publishing industry to impose self-censorship. Juvenile crime didn't fall, but the comics changed; and some of the most violent ones disappeared altogether.

If the anti–comic-book agitation did nothing much to end juvenile crime . . . what explains this panic? Clearly, something was happening in the '50s, just as it appears to be happening in our own time. The postwar era was a revolutionary time, the first generation in American history wherein children had substantial amounts of spending money. The result was the explosion of a youth culture designed to appeal specifically and exclusively to young people. The teenage market expanded rapidly, from clothing to automobiles to movies and fast food. . . . Children were growing up faster; they acted more like adults or at least demanded adult privileges. All of this looked immensely threatening to parents and parenting experts in the '50s. Parents and parenting experts in our age are also confronting a major new development. In this case, it's the advent of the Internet—which has exponentially increased the amount and scope of influences to which American kids are exposed.

So what can we learn from the experience of the '50s . . . ? First, we should be wary of the attempt to link behavior directly and precisely to culture. There is no clear evidence to support this, and, besides, we can probably never develop a form of acceptable censorship anyway. It is also important to separate things that we don't like (or understand) from those social problems that might, in fact, cause teenage alienation and criminal behavior. Banning Marilyn Manson, hip-hop clothes, and rap music will certainly have an effect, but not the desired one. And, finally, we need to remind ourselves that youth culture is something that modern society has invented and celebrated. By extending affluence to children, by giving them computers and spending money, by making them consumers and therefore members of the marketplace, we have given them access to an adult world and an adult culture. We will have to learn to live with the consequences of that.

Source: Excerpted from James Gilbert, "Juvenilia," *The New Republic* (June 14, 1999), 54. Reprinted by permission of *The New Republic*, © 1999, The New Republic, Inc.

What Does it Mean?

annihilation
total destruction

concerted
organized; mutually arranged

malevolent
vicious or harmful

scourge
a cause of widespread distress

Read and React

1. What common assumption about juvenile crime is the author questioning?
2. Why does Gilbert think it is not possible to scientifically prove how culture affects a particular behavior?
3. What does Gilbert say about the power of advertising to affect teenage behavior?
4. What modern day invention does Gilbert compare to the influence of comic books in the 1950s?
5. In two or three sentences, state the main point that the author makes in this article. Do you agree or disagree with his assessment? Why or why not?

Answers to Read and React

1. The author questions whether one can realistically blame teen violence on one cause; it is better understood as multicausational factors.
2. The suggestion is that blaming teenage behavior on lyrics negates a variety of other factors that need to be considered.
3. There is no question that advertising effects teen choices, but it can't be said with authority that it dictates teen behavior.
4. Television and computers have given teens access to the adult world at the same time that these mediums have liberalized what we are exposed to.
5. Single causes are not sufficient to explain this phenomenon, multicausational variables and the proliferation of consumerism made available to teens. Social changes, such as the number of families with dual-labor earners, have had a profound impact on teens.

Integrating the Teacher Resources

Additional primary source readings for this chapter can be found in Culture Studies: The Sociological Perspective, **available in your Teacher's Resource Box. Questions for students are included.**

Chapter Preview

Section 1 (pages 110–114)

Socialization is the cultural process of learning to participate in group life. Studies have shown that animals and human infants who are deprived of intensive and prolonged social contact with others are stunted in their emotional and social growth.

Section 2 (pages 115–120)

Symbolic interactionism offers the most fully developed perspective for studying socialization. In this approach, the self-concept is developed by using other people as mirrors for learning about ourselves.

Section 3 (pages 121–127)

During childhood and adolescence, the major agents of socialization are the family, school, peer group, and mass media. The family's role is critical in forming basic values. Schools introduce children to life beyond the family. In peer groups young people learn to relate as equals. The mass media provide role models for full integration into society.

Section 4 (pages 128–132)

Desocialization is the process of having to give up old norms. Resocialization begins as people adopt new norms and values. Anticipatory socialization and reference groups are concerned with voluntary change as when moving from one life stage to another.

CHAPTER 4

Socialization

108

Lead-Off Activity

To show students how socialization also reflects cultural norms of the times, read several of these statements to them.

Proper Manners for Dating:

1. A man should not sit down at the table in a restaurant until the woman is seated.
2. A man should always pull out a woman's chair for her and see that she is served first.
3. A man should never let a woman carry anything heavy, she should only carry a small package and her coat.
4. A man should help a woman put on and take off her coat.
5. A man always leads when dancing.
6. A man should always open a door for a woman and let her pass in front of him.

Using Your Sociological Imagination

All of us have feelings of love. We assume that such an emotion is innate, that we are born with it. Actually, we learn our feelings from those close to us, our parents and others who take care of us.

One story that illustrates that we need to learn how to express love is the story of Genie. Genie had been kept isolated in a locked room by her father from the time she was nearly two. When she was found at the age of thirteen, much of her behavior was subhuman. Because Genie's father severely punished her for making any sounds whatever, she was completely silent. She never sobbed when she cried or spoke when angry. Never having been given solid food, she could not chew. Because she had spent her entire life strapped in a potty chair, Genie could not stand erect, straighten her arms or legs, or run. Her social behavior was primitive. She blew her nose on whatever was handy or into the air when nothing was available. Without asking, she would take from people things that attracted her attention.

Attempts to socialize Genie were not successful. At the end of the four-year period, she could not read, could speak only in short phrases, and had just begun to control some of her feelings and behavior. Genie paid a high price—her full development as a human being—for the isolation, abuse, and lack of human warmth she experienced.

As you will see in this chapter on socialization, infants denied close and continuous human care have no chance to learn all the feelings we mistakenly assume to be inborn.

Sections

Learning Objectives

After reading this chapter, you will be able to

- define the term *socialization.*
- discuss the role socialization plays in human development.
- describe the effects of extreme isolation on children.
- explain key concepts of socialization from the symbolic interactionist perspective.
- analyze the role of the family, school, peer group, and media in socializing young people.
- discuss processes for socialization in adulthood.

SOCIOLOGY Online

Chapter Overview
Visit the *Sociology and You* Web site at soc.glencoe.com and click on **Chapter 4—Chapter Overviews** to preview chapter information.

Using Your Sociological Imagination

It is almost impossible to ethically conduct studies with new-born babies. Much of what is known about socialization is learned through careful observation and by the tragic examples of neglected or abused children. If you have class time you might want to give students more background information about Genie. NOVA has published a video, *Genie: The Wild Child,* which you might want to show. Also, a book about Genie entitled *Genie: A Scientific Tragedy* by Russ Rymer, (1993) was published by Harper Perennial. Students will want to know what happened to Genie. You might share with them the following information. Since the time that she was rescued in 1971 at age 13, her life has taken some tragic turns. She failed in six foster homes, largely due to the abuse she suffered at them. Genie currently lives in an adult foster home.

Students will probably find these statements quaint and they might want to ask some veteran teachers or their parents or grandparents if they remember following these dating guidelines. Ask students to describe the proper dating socialization habits of today. Are they similar to those listed here? In what ways are they similar? In what ways are they different? Why do these habits change? Is the change good or bad? **L1**

Using the Section Preview

Here is a simple demonstration of the power of socialization. Ask the students to touch the following (their own, of course): nose, eye, writing hand, big toe. Ask, How did you know to do that? They will say, "Silly—we learned." And that's right. Ask if they know when they learned it and they will only remember it was long before they went to school. Explain that the family is the primary socializer and one of the family's most important tasks is to teach language. Without language—a means to communicate—a person could not function in society.

Teaching Strategy

To help students understand the concept of socialization, ask students to come up with new names for some of the objects in your class. What would happen if they began to do this in other classes? You might tell students that the famous Orwell classic, *1984*, devotes a whole passage to convincing a man that 2+2=5. By the end of the book, he has been resocialized to believe it himself. (Some people might say "brainwashed.") Is socialization a form of brainwashing?

Please see the correlation to the American Sociology Association standards located in the front of this text.

Section 1 The Importance of Socialization

Key Term

- socialization

Section Preview

Socialization is the cultural process of learning to participate in group life. Without it, we would not develop many of the characteristics we associate with being human. Studies have shown that animals and human infants who are deprived of intensive and prolonged social contact with others are stunted in their emotional and social growth.

Socialization and Personality

Nearly all the human social behavior we consider natural and normal is learned. It is natural to us in the United States for husbands and wives to walk along side-by-side. In many places in India, however, it seems natural for wives to walk slightly behind their husbands. In fact, nearly all aspects of social life (including walking patterns) are not natural but learned through the process of socialization. Human beings at birth are helpless and without knowledge of their society's ways of thinking, feeling, and behaving. If a human infant is to participate in cultural life, much learning has to take place. **Socialization** is the cultural process of learning to participate in group life.

Socialization begins at birth and continues throughout life. Successful socialization enables people to fit into all kinds of social groups. Socialization must occur if high school freshmen are to adjust to their new situation, if graduating seniors are to look for employment, and if presidents of the United States are to govern successfully.

socialization
the process of learning to participate in a group

Monkeys fail to develop psychologically and socially when deprived of their mothers. Can we generalize from monkeys to human children?

Encouraging Citizenship Activity

You may have some students who are interested in volunteering time at a day care center. Even in a day care center children often do not get the individual time needed to become fully socialized. This chapter will help students understand the importance of socialization to child development. They may wish to research these developmental stages. What, for instance, should three year olds, as opposed to two year olds, be learning in order to become socialized? What kinds of skills do toddlers have, or lack?

Ask students who interact regularly with children outside of a family setting to comment on the childrens' behaviors.
L1

Orphanages, such as this one in Russia, are of interest to sociologists. They worry what effect growing up without prolonged social contact with parents will have on children.

The most important learning occurs early in life. Psychological case studies reveal that without prolonged and intensive social contact, children do not learn such basics as walking, talking, and loving. Without socialization, a human infant cannot develop the set of attitudes, beliefs, values, and behaviors associated with being an individual.

How do we know socialization is important? Suppose you wanted to design an experiment to see how socialization affects infants. You would have to set up an experiment that compared a group of normally socialized infants (the *control* group) with a group of isolated infants—infants with little or no human contact (the *experimental* group). For obvious reasons, such experiments are not conducted with human infants. We do, however, have some nonexperimental evidence from studies of socially isolated children. Experiments have been done with monkeys.

How do monkeys react to social isolation? A psychologist, Harry Harlow, devised a famous experiment that showed the negative effects of social isolation on rhesus monkeys (Harlow and Zimmerman, 1959; Harlow and Harlow, 1962; Harlow, 1967). In one experiment, infant monkeys, separated from their mothers at birth, were exposed to two artificial mothers—wire dummies of the same approximate size and shape as real adult monkeys. One of the substitute mothers had an exposed wire body. The other was covered with soft terry cloth. Free to choose between them, the infant monkeys consistently spent more time with the soft, warm mother. Even when the exposed wire dummy became the only source of food, the terry cloth mother remained the favorite. Apparently, closeness and comfort were more important to these monkeys than food. When frightened by a mechanical toy bear or a rubber snake, these infant monkeys consistently ran to their cloth mothers for security and protection.

Harlow showed that infant monkeys need intimacy, warmth, physical contact, and comfort. Infant monkeys raised in isolation became distressed, apathetic, withdrawn, hostile adult animals. They never exhibited normal sexual patterns. As mothers, they either rejected or ignored their babies. Sometimes, they even physically abused them.

> "Man is the only one that knows nothing, that can learn nothing without being taught. He can neither speak nor walk nor eat, and in short he can do nothing at the prompting of nature only, but weep."
>
> **Pliny the Elder**
> **Roman scholar**

Controversy and Debate

The Harlow experiment results may seem painfully obvious to students today, and many will question the need for such research. Suggest that perhaps the reason these findings seem so obvious and full of common sense is because of experiments such as Harlow's. Also, the practical implications of this research should point out how worthwhile the studies have been.

More About . . . Contact Comfort

Students who are interested in the applications of Harlow's experiment may be interested in the following story about a study conducted during World War II. Infants reared in an institution where there was almost no personal attention in the form of touching or holding were compared with infants who were reared in a prison nursery where they had contact with their mothers. The results were frightening: 37 percent of the institution-reared children died within a year, despite being fed and kept clean (Spitz, 1946).

Interdisciplinary Activity

There are numerous studies that show how animal socialization has implications for human socialization. Tell students that the Code of Ethics for psychology and sociology both are very clear about the ethical restraints of using human subjects for research.

Ask students to debate the appropriateness of animal research, remembering to consider both the effects on the animals, as well as the benefits gained by the research. For a specific example, you might tell them that psychologist Martin Seligman conducted extensive research involving electrical shocks given to dogs that resulted in some extremely important knowledge about how the brain functions. He writes, "New therapies and new ways of preventing depression were developed as a result of this work . . . But I also maintained that as soon as we had documented the basic facts . . . we should stop our experiments."
L2

Tech Trends

Ask students if they think using the Internet interferes with social development. Remind them that although anecdotal evidence is not scientific, if enough people have the same reaction or opinion, it is certainly worth investigating. You might have students research the pros and cons of Internet use on social growth, then present their findings to the rest of the class. Students should provide quantitative data (statistics) to defend their positions.

Answer to Analyzing the Trends

One argument students might discuss is that the Internet socially isolates teens who spend all their time alone at a computer. Another argument is that teens often sit together by the computer, so they are actually sitting in more intimate circles. Some students will argue that there are cases of kids who ran away to find someone through a chat room discussion. Others will argue that kids are no less likely to be involved in community groups as a result of the Internet age.

Integrating the Teacher Resources

Ethics, Values, and Technology: Real-Life Issues in Society, in your Teacher's Resource Box, provides primary source readings dealing with real-life controversies. Student worksheets are included.

Tech Trends

Can the Internet Stunt Your Social Growth?

You will read in this section about the effects of extreme social isolation in Anna, Isabelle, and Genie. Although no one expects the results to be nearly as harmful, many sociologists today are concerned about how the increased use of computers and the Internet might affect young people. They wonder if this will be the first generation of children to grow up lacking adequate social skills.

Traditional games—sandlot ball games, for example—are socially oriented. These games require interaction and negotiation with other people, encourage sensitivity to others' viewpoints, help establish mutual understanding, and increase cooperative behavior (Casbergue and Kieff, 1998). These social skills are not developed by children who spend a great deal of time in isolated computer activities.

One researcher, Sherry Turkle, claims that the social isolation brought about by heavy use of the Internet leads to the destruction of meaningful social contact (Katz and Aspden, 1997). Similarly, Cliff Stoll (1995) says that excessive Internet activity lowers people's commitment to real friendships.

Perhaps you have read stories in the news about children who arranged to meet adults through the Internet. These stories often suggest that it was possible to lure these children to these meetings because they did not have the social skills and experience needed to make sound judgments about their actions.

According to an important nationwide study, the Internet is promoting social isolation (Nie and Erbring, 2000). As people spend more time on the Internet (55 percent of Americans have access), they experience less meaningful social contact. Impersonal electronic relationships are replacing face-to-face interaction with family and friends. According to the author of this study, political scientist Norman Nie, "When you spend time on the Internet, you don't hear a human voice and you never get a hug."

Another concern is that extensive video game use will shorten the natural attention span of children. This could cause them to grow up requiring a continuous flow of outside stimulation which interferes with normal social interaction ("Lego: Fighting the Video Monsters," 1999).

Defenders of computers and the Internet point to a survey (based on 2,500 Americans) that showed Internet users were just as likely as non–Internet users to join religious, leisure, or community groups (Katz and Aspden, 1997). The survey results, according to these observers, indicate that Internet users are just as socially active as other people.

Critics of this survey point out that the researchers failed to ask some important questions. They did not distinguish between heavy users of the Internet and more moderate users. Also, those surveyed were adults who had already gone through the early years of socialization. There will have to be more research before we understand the effects of new technologies on children's social growth.

Analyzing the Trends

What is your position in the debate about whether heavy Internet use stunts social skills? Give reasons for your answers.

Learning Styles

Logical-mathematical Read and discuss the Tech Trends feature, "Can the Internet Stunt Your Social Growth?" Surveys can be structured with closed- or open-ended questions. (It will be easier to compare results if you use the closed-ended type.) Work with students to develop the survey questions dealing with Internet use, then have each student collect a specified number of responses. You may want to have students work in small groups to tabulate the results of their surveys and then compare the findings from the different groups. To conclude this activity, you might discuss the students' own answers to the survey questions. How do they see the Internet affecting their lives? Do they socialize less? Would they agree with the findings of the research that is shared in the Tech Trends article? Refer students back to the Harry Harlow study and the case studies on isolated children. What relationship do they see? **L2**

Can we generalize from monkeys to humans?

It is risky to assume that knowledge gained about nonhumans also applies to humans. Nevertheless, many experts on human development believe that for human infants—as for Harlow's monkeys—emotional needs for affection, intimacy, and warmth are as important as physiological needs for food, water, and protection. Human babies denied close contact usually have difficulty forming emotional ties with others. Touching, holding, stroking, and communicating appear to be essential to normal human development. According to a classic study by Lawrence Casler (1965), the developmental growth rate of institutionalized children—who receive less physical contact than normal—can be improved with only twenty minutes of extra touching a day.

Studies have shown that children raised under extremely isolated conditions have little or no chance of ever being socialized.

Case Studies on Isolated Children: Anna and Isabelle

To understand more about how socialization affects development, we will look at the case histories of two children—Anna and Isabelle—who were socially and emotionally abused. You already know the story of Genie from the Sociological Imagination on page 109. Anna and Isabelle also had traumatic childhoods. Although these three children were born many years ago, similar situations still occur today, unfortunately.

Who was Anna? Anna was the second child born to her unmarried mother. At first, Anna's strict grandfather had forced her mother to take Anna and leave home, but desperation drove them back again. Anna's mother so feared that the sight of the child would anger her father that she kept Anna confined to a small room on the second floor of their farmhouse. For five years, Anna received only milk to drink. When finally found, she was barely alive. Her legs were skeleton-like and her stomach bloated from malnutrition. Apparently, Anna had seldom been moved from one position to another, and her clothes and bedding were filthy. She did not know what it was like to be held or comforted. At the time of her discovery, Anna could not walk or talk and showed few signs of intelligence.

During the first year and a half after being found, Anna lived in a county home for children. Here, she learned to walk, to understand simple commands, and to feed herself. She could recall people she had seen. But her speech was that of a one-year-old.

Anna was then transferred to a school for learning disabled children, where she made some further progress. Still, at the age of seven, her mental age was only nineteen months, and her social maturity was that of a two-year-old. A year later, she could bounce and catch a ball, participate as a follower in group activities, eat normally (although with a spoon only), attend

Addressing Current Social Problems

Anna, Isabelle, and Genie (Using Your Sociological Imagination) are the most fully documented cases of socially isolated children. Betty Topper's case has yet to be examined. Six-year-old Betty was discovered by officials in Los Angeles, California in 1999. She had been kept chained to a bedpost by a two-foot-long chain and a harness normally used on horses from the time she was a year old, in a home littered with trash and debris. Early reports state that, when found, 30-pound Betty was covered with her own waste and could only make moaning sounds (McNary, 1999). Reports of her social development should be available in the future.

Integrating the Teacher Resources

Look for the Chapter 4 Learning Goals Outline, a reproducible student worksheet in the Unit 2 Mastering Basic Concepts **booklet in your Teacher's Resource Box. It can be used to preview or review chapter content.**

Interdisciplinary Activity

Literature Many books have been written about individuals who are discovered living alone or being raised by wild animals (for example, Tarzan, Lord of the Apes by Edgar Rice Burroughs and the Jungle Boy adventures by Rudyard Kipling.) Unfortunately, these fantasies have little, if any, scientific basis. The romanticism of these authors is not borne out by reality. The social isolation case studies of Anna and Isabelle are classics in social science research. Several videos exist about these and similar cases. (See Using Your Sociological Imagination for this chapter for a reference for Genie.) A similar story is told in the movie Nell, starring Jodie Foster, which should be available in video stores. In this case, social isolation is aggravated by a lack of language skills.

Have students who are avid readers list all the characters they can think of who were supposedly raised by animals, or isolated from the humans. Why do they think writers romanticized this kind of upbringing? **L3**

Pulling it All Together

This section discussed socialization as the process that allows us to participate in group life. Examples of socially isolated individuals and the difficulties that isolation creates speaks to the power of socialization.

Answers to Section 1 Assessment

1. Socialization is the cultural process of learning to participate in group life.

2. Harlow's research showed that infant monkeys need intimacy, warmth, physical contact, and comfort. Monkeys raised in isolation became apathetic, withdrawn, hostile adult animals (even rejecting or abusing their offspring).

3. Answers should include some of the following concepts: The severe lack of development of these children during the time they were abused and neglected proves that close contact (touching, holding, stroking, and communicating) is as essential to normal development as physiological needs (food, water, protection). The ability to "catch up" was affected even after environments were improved. Isabelle was the only one who managed to attain normal function and, besides intensive instruction, this may have been due to the fact that she was the only one confined with her mother for company and comforting; this also supports Harlow's conclusions.

Critical Thinking

4. Answers will vary.

to her toilet needs, and dress herself (except for handling buttons and snaps). At this point, she had acquired the speech level of a two-year-old. By the time of her death at age ten, she had made some additional progress. She could carry out instructions, identify a few colors, build with blocks, wash her hands, brush her teeth, and try to help other children. Her developing capacity for emotional attachment was reflected in the love she had developed for a doll.

Who was Isabelle? Nine months after Anna was found, Isabelle was discovered. She, too, had been hidden away because her mother was unmarried. Isabelle's mother had been deaf since the age of two and did not speak. She stayed with her child in a dark room, secluded from the rest of the family. When found at the age of six and a half, Isabelle was physically ill from an inadequate diet and lack of sunshine. Her legs were so bowed that when she stood the soles of her shoes rested against each other, and her walk was a skittering movement. Some of her actions were like those of a six-month-old infant. Unable to talk except for a strange croaking sound, Isabelle communicated with her mother by means of gestures. Like an animal in the wild, she reacted with fear and hostility to strangers, especially men.

At first, Isabelle was thought to be severely learning disabled. (Her initial IQ score was near the zero point.) Nevertheless, an intensive program of rehabilitation was begun. After a slow start, Isabelle progressed through the usual stages of learning and development at a faster pace than normal. It took her only two years to acquire the skills mastered by a normal six-year-old. By the time she was eight and a half, Isabelle was on an educational par with children her age. By outward appearances, she was an intelligent, happy, energetic child. At age fourteen, she participated in all the school activities normal for other children in her grade.

To Isabelle's good fortune, she, unlike Anna, benefited from intensive instruction at the hands of trained professionals. Her ability to progress may also have been because she was confined with her mother for company and comforting.

What can we learn from these case studies? The implication of the cases of Anna, Isabelle, and Genie is unmistakable. The personal and social development associated with being human is acquired through intensive and prolonged social contact with others.

Section 1 Assessment

1. Define the term *socialization*.
2. What did Harlow's research on rhesus monkeys reveal?
3. Did the case studies on Anna, Isabelle and Genie support Harlow's conclusions? Why or why not?

Critical Thinking

4. **Analyzing Information** Do you think sociologists have overemphasized the importance of social contact in learning? What are some legal and moral implications for the government in this kind of child abuse? Should the state protect children from their parents?

Using Conflict Resolution Skills

Read this scenario to your students:

In the newspaper recently, there was a headline that read: "Parents charged with denying food, medical care to 7-year-old." Reading through the article, you realize that this little girl weighed 38 pounds, was skin and bones, had a protruding stomach from starvation, and was covered with sores and scratches on her body. Her father, who makes over $75,000 a year, and her stepmother will be charged with injuring and endangering this child, a felony if convicted. Literally starving to death, the little girl was often seen rummaging in garbage cans at school and begging food from other students. She apparently endured over six months of abuse before authorities acted on her behalf.

Section 2 Socialization and the Self

Key Terms

- self-concept
- looking-glass self
- significant others
- role taking
- imitation stage
- play stage
- game stage
- generalized other
- "me"
- "I"

The Functionalist and Conflict Perspectives on Socialization

Each of the three major theoretical perspectives provides insights into socialization. However, the symbolic interactionist perspective allows a more complete understanding than the other two.

How does the functionalist perspective explain socialization? Functionalism stresses the ways in which groups work together to create a stable society. Schools and families, for example, socialize children by teaching the same basic norms, beliefs, and values. If it were otherwise, society could not exist as a whole. It would be fragmented and chaotic.

How does the conflict perspective explain socialization? The conflict perspective views socialization as a way of perpetuating the status quo. When people are socialized to accept their family's social class, for example,

Section Preview

All three theoretical perspectives agree that socialization is needed if cultural and societal values are to be learned. Symbolic interactionism offers the most fully developed perspective for studying socialization. In this approach, the self-concept is developed by using other people as mirrors for learning about ourselves.

According to the conflict theory, these young boys are being socialized to accept their social class.

Using the Section Preview

Write the following question on the board or an overhead: How has my family socialized me? Have students jot down several examples. *(Possible answers might include: they taught me right from wrong; they raised me with religious values; they taught me the meaning of work; and so on.)* It needs to be emphasized that socialization occurs because of internalization. One must internalize what they are being socialized to. They must accept it.

Integrating the Teacher Resources

Look for the Chapter 4 Vocabulary Activity in the Unit 2 Mastering Basic Concepts booklet in your Teacher's Resource Box. It provides reinforcement for vocabulary in this chapter.

Ask students to decide if and how this little girl will be able to overcome her early abuse. Break the class into: 2 parents, 2 lawyers, 1 judge, the little girl, 2 friends of the family, 2 teachers, 1 principal, 1 social worker, 1 doctor, and 1 police officer. Each student will role-play his/her assigned part with the end result being a judgment for or against the parents. Tell students that the verdict of guilty or not guilty will set the precedent in their state for handling child abuse cases; therefore, it is important that statements be prepared in advance by the prosecutor and defending attorney. Use the prescribed conflict resolution skills to enact and judge this case.
L2

Points to Stress

Write on the board this quote from Eleanor Roosevelt: "No one can make you feel inferior without your consent." Ask students to explain how this statement is an example of the looking-glass self.

Reteaching

Another way to explain the idea of the looking-glass self is to ask students the following: When you wake up in the morning, look in the mirror, are you dressing for yourself or for how others see you? This should get them thinking about how powerful the social influence is.

Open-Response Question

Ask students to be honest in response to this prompt: If not for rules and expectations, would you dress differently than you do? How and why?

Integrating the Teacher Resources

To reinforce key concepts, use the Chapter 4 Graphic Organizer, a reproducible student worksheet available in the Unit 2 Mastering Basic Concepts **booklet in your Teacher's Resource Box.**

they help preserve the current class system. People learn to accept their social status before they have enough self-awareness to realize what is happening. Because they do not challenge their position in life, they do not upset the existing class structure. Consequently, socialization maintains the social, political, and economic advantages of the higher social classes.

Symbolic Interactionism and Socialization

self-concept
an image of yourself as having an identity separate from other people

looking-glass self
an image of yourself based on what you believe others think of you

In the early part of the twentieth century, Charles Horton Cooley and George Herbert Mead developed the symbolic interactionist perspective. They challenged the once widely held belief that human nature is biologically determined (that you are a certain way because you were born that way). For them, human nature is a product of society.

How does symbolic interactionism help us understand socialization? Symbolic interactionism uses a number of key concepts to explain socialization. These concepts include

- the self-concept
- the looking-glass self
- significant others
- role taking (the imitation stage, the play stage, the game stage)
- the generalized other.

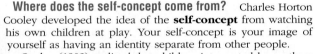

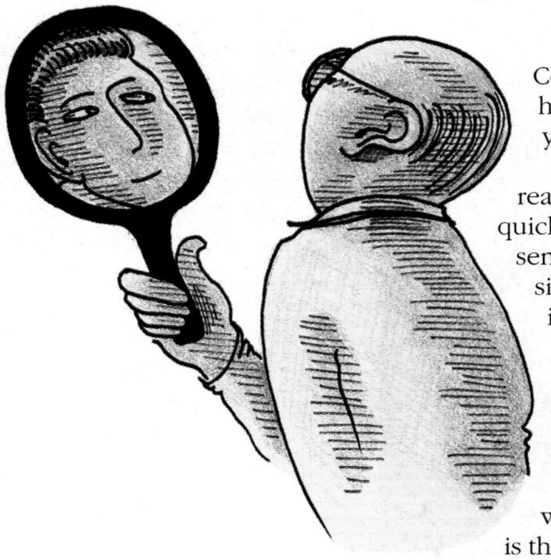

Where does the self-concept come from? Charles Horton Cooley developed the idea of the **self-concept** from watching his own children at play. Your self-concept is your image of yourself as having an identity separate from other people.

Cooley (1902) realized that children interpreted how others reacted to them in many ways. For example, young children learn quickly that causing some disturbance when adult visitors are present turns attention from the guests to themselves. From such insights, children learn to judge themselves in terms of how they imagine others *will* react to them. Thus, other people serve as mirrors for the development of the self. Cooley called this way of learning the **looking-glass self**—a self-concept based on our idea of others' judgments of us.

How does the looking-glass process work? According to Cooley, we use other people as mirrors to reflect back what we imagine they think of us. In this view, the looking-glass self is the product of a three-stage process that is constantly taking place.

1. First, we imagine how we appear to others. (What is our perception of how others see us?)
2. Next, we imagine the reaction of others to our (imagined) appearance.
3. Finally, we evaluate ourselves according to how we imagine others have judged us.

This is not a conscious process, and the three stages can occur in very rapid succession. The result of the process is a positive or negative self-evaluation.

Consider this example of the looking-glass process. Suppose you have a new teacher you want to impress. You prepare hard for the next day's class.

On-Demand Writing

Students learn in the chapter that the self concept is the image of yourself as having an identity separate from others. Teens are in the developmental stage where being separate or different from others can be a very scary proposition. To help them clarify their own sense of self concept, ask them to describe themselves in one paragraph without referring to physical features, but rather focusing on values, attitudes, beliefs, and personality. You may then want to read some of them (with permission, of course) to see if their classmates would recognize the writer as seen through his or her own eyes.
L1

Figure 4.1 Focus on Theoretical Perspectives

Socialization and Mass Media. Each theoretical perspective has a unique view of the socialization process. This table identifies these views and illustrates the unique interpretation of each view with respect to the influence of the mass media on the socialization process.

Theoretical Perspective	View of Socialization	How the Media Influence Socialization
Functionalism	Stresses how socialization contributes to a stable society	Network television programs encourage social integration by exposing the entire society to shared beliefs, values, and norms.
Conflict Theory	Views socialization as a way for the powerful to keep things the same	Newspaper owners and editors exercise power by setting the political agenda for a community.
Symbolic Interactionism	Holds that socialization is the major determinant of human nature	Through words and pictures, children's books expose the young to the meaning of love, manners, and motherhood.

In class, as you are making a comment on the assignment, you have an image of your performance (stage 1). After finishing your comments, you think your teacher is disappointed (stage 2). Because you wanted your teacher to be impressed, you feel bad about yourself (stage 3).

Can the looking glass be distorted? Because the looking glass we use comes from our imaginations, it may be distorted. The mirror may not accurately reflect others' opinions of us. The teacher in the above example may not have been disappointed at all.

Unfortunately, the looking-glass process works even if we are mistaken about others' perceptions of us. If we incorrectly believe that a teacher, or a date, or our parents dislike us, the consequences to us are just as real as if it were true.

Do we use some people as mirrors more than others? George Herbert Mead pointed out that some people are more important to us than others (Mead, 1934). The people whose judgments are most important to our self-concepts are called **significant others.** For a child, significant others are likely to include mother, father, grandparent, teachers, and playmates. Teenagers place heavy reliance on their peers. The variety of significant others is greater for adults, ranging from spouses, parents, and friends to ministers and employers.

significant others
those people whose reactions are most important to your self-concept

Working with the Table

Figure 4.1 Have students evaluate how the three sociological perspectives might be used to understand Internet usage. (*From the functionalist perspective, the Internet allows information to be transmitted rapidly, e-mail is sent in seconds, a highly functional process. From the perspective of the conflict theorists, entrepreneurs like Bill Gates have become extremely powerful as a result of the technology, and Internet use is related to income level, thus perpetuating inequality. From an interactionist perspective, young children are exposed to more and more information and have the ability to communicate with larger circles of people.*)

On-Demand Writing

After you feel students understand the concept of significant others, ask them to write a few paragraphs describing who their significant others are. They should include information about why these individuals are so important to them and how they have helped to shape their self-concept. They may want to focus on significant others from their past or from the current perspective. They should use standard grammar, spelling, sentence structure, and punctuation. **L1**

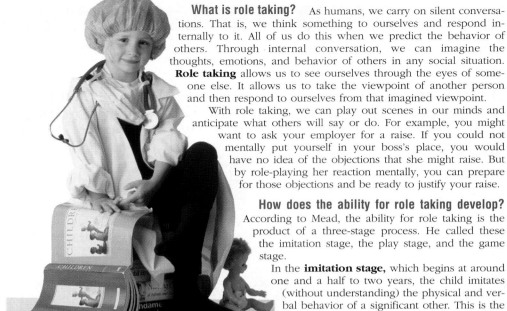

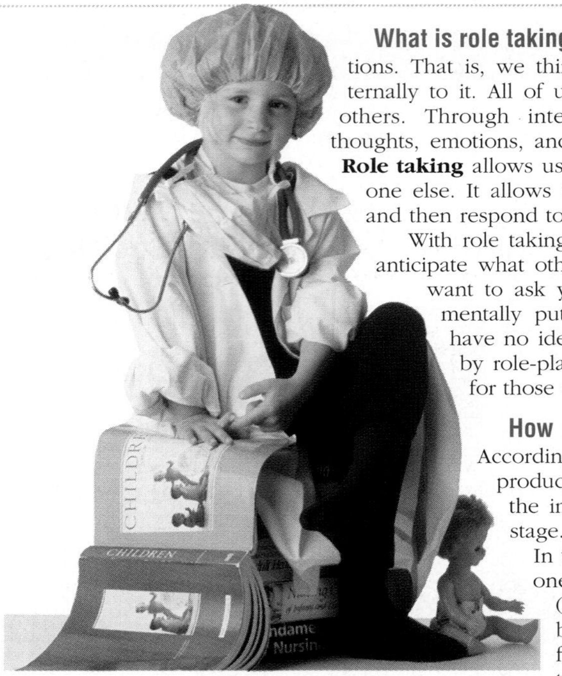

What is role taking? As humans, we carry on silent conversations. That is, we think something to ourselves and respond internally to it. All of us do this when we predict the behavior of others. Through internal conversation, we can imagine the thoughts, emotions, and behavior of others in any social situation. **Role taking** allows us to see ourselves through the eyes of someone else. It allows us to take the viewpoint of another person and then respond to ourselves from that imagined viewpoint.

With role taking, we can play out scenes in our minds and anticipate what others will say or do. For example, you might want to ask your employer for a raise. If you could not mentally put yourself in your boss's place, you would have no idea of the objections that she might raise. But by role-playing her reaction mentally, you can prepare for those objections and be ready to justify your raise.

How does the ability for role taking develop? According to Mead, the ability for role taking is the product of a three-stage process. He called these the imitation stage, the play stage, and the game stage.

In the **imitation stage,** which begins at around one and a half to two years, the child imitates (without understanding) the physical and verbal behavior of a significant other. This is the first step in developing the capacity for role taking.

At the age of three or four, a young child can be seen playing at being mother, father, police officer, teacher, or astronaut. This play involves acting and thinking as a child imagines another person would. This is what Mead called the **play stage**—the stage during which children take on roles of others one at a time.

The third phase in the development of role taking Mead labeled the **game stage.** In this stage, children learn to engage in more sophisticated role taking as they become able to consider the roles of several people simultaneously. Games they play involve several participants, and there are specific rules designed to ensure that the behaviors of the participants fit together. All participants in a game must know what they are supposed to do and what is expected of others in the game. Imagine the confusion in a baseball game if young first-base players have not yet mastered the idea that the ball hit to a teammate will usually be thrown to them. In the second stage of role taking (the play stage) a child may pretend to be a first-base player one moment and pretend to be a base runner the next. In the game stage, however, first-base players who drop their gloves and run to second base when the other team hits the ball will not remain in the game for very long. It is during the game stage that children learn to gear their behavior to the norms of the group.

When do we start acting out of principle? During the game stage, a child's self-concept, attitudes, beliefs, and values gradually come to depend less on individuals and more on general concepts. For example, being an honest person is no longer merely a matter of pleasing significant others such

role taking
assuming the viewpoint of another person and using that viewpoint to shape the self-concept

imitation stage
Mead's first stage in the development of role taking; children begin to imitate behaviors without understanding why

play stage
Mead's second stage in the development of role taking; children act in ways they imagine other people would

game stage
Mead's third stage in the development of role taking; children anticipate the actions of others based on social rules

Points to Stress

Mead emphasized that we are able to take on the role of the other because we have an idea of what an experience might be like for the other since we might have had the same experience ourselves. Empathy comes through understanding another human being, even when we have not experienced something ourselves. No one could imagine what Genie's life was like, but we can have empathy for her.

Reteaching

Here is another way for students to interpret and understand Mead's concept of I and me. Tell them simply that "I" is myself as I am. "Me" is myself as others see me.

You might also use Genie as an analogy. Genie didn't have a concept of "Me" because she had never been socialized to understand how others might see her or how she might understand others. She only had a concept of "I." She was like a little baby, egocentric, with no concept beyond her own needs.

Another way to look at the concept of "I" and "Me" is to consider the usage of the terms *I* and *me* in English grammar. *I* is used when speaking of ourselves as we complete an action (I went to the store.). *Me* is used as the object of another's actions (He threw the ball to me.).

Finally, be sure to explain that students should not confuse Mead's concepts with Freud's psychological concepts of the id and the superego, sometimes also referred to as the "me and I."

Learning Styles

Musical/Intrapersonal In every era, songs are written to convey nearly every emotion conceivable. Ask students to think of a song they are familiar with that deals with the topic of a personal relationship. Either a positive or negative message may be conveyed. Screen the music for appropriateness, then listen in class with the students to the songs they have found. Discuss the emotions being expressed, and ask the students to imagine what it would feel like to have a relationship like the people in the song. Ask what the effect on the personal and social development of the people involved might be. Focus on the positive aspects of the relationship, and ask students what changes they would make to make it a more positive relationship. Then focus on the negative aspects of the relationship. Again ask students what changes they would make to make the relationship more positive. **L1**

as one's mother, father, or minister. Rather, it begins to seem wrong *in principle* to be dishonest. As this change takes place, a **generalized other**—an integrated conception of the norms, values, and beliefs of one's community or society—emerges.

What is the self?

According to Mead, we can think of the self as being composed of two parts: the *"me"* and the *"I."* The **"me"** is the part of the self created through socialization. The "me" accounts for predictability and conformity. Yet much human behavior is spontaneous and unpredictable. An angry child may, for example, suddenly and unexpectedly yell hurtful words at the parent whom he loves. To account for this spontaneous, unpredictable, often creative part of the self, Mead proposed the **"I."**

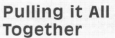

What do you think is the developmental level of the "generalized other" in each of these two shoplifters?

generalized other
integrated conception of the norms, values, and beliefs of one's community or society

"me"
the part of the self formed through socialization

"I"
the part of the self that accounts for unlearned, spontaneous acts

The "I" does not operate only in extreme situations of rage or excitement. It interacts constantly with the "me" as we conduct ourselves in social situations. According to Mead, the first reaction of the self comes from the "I." Before we act, however, this reaction is directed into socially acceptable channels by the socialized "me." When the "I" wants a piece of a friend's candy bar, the "me" reflects on the consequences of taking the candy without permission. Thus, the "I" normally takes the "me" into account before acting. However, the unpredictability of much human behavior demonstrates that the "me" is not always in control!

> Man can be defined as the animal that can say I, that can be aware of himself as a separate entity.
>
> Erich Fromm
> American psychiatrist

Section 2 Assessment

1. What is the looking-glass self?
2. What are the consequences of having a distorted looking glass?
3. Which "self" is the first to react to a situation, the "me" or the "I"?

Critical Thinking

4. **Applying Concepts** Describe an experience you have had with the looking-glass process. How did this experience touch or change your self-concept?

Pulling it All Together

This section shows students how the three sociological perspectives can be used to understand socialization. Emphasis was placed on the interactionist perspective because this perspective combines the individual as well as social process of socialization.

Answers to Section 2 Assessment

1. The "looking-glass self" is a self-concept based on our idea of others' judgments of us.
2. Having a distorted looking glass (incorrectly imagining others' opinions of us) can cause bad feelings, or a negative self-image.
3. According to George Herbert Mead, the first reaction of the self comes from "I."

Critical Thinking

4. Answers will vary.

Working with the Quote

Erich Fromm (1900–1980) was a German-born U.S. psychoanalyst and social philosopher who explored the interaction between psychology and society. By applying psychoanalytic principles to the remedy of cultural ills, Fromm believed mankind could develop a psychologically balanced "sane society."

Ask students if they agree with Fromm's assessment that animals lack the ability to form a self concept.

Another Time

Surviving a Prisoner-of-War Camp

By learning the culture around them—whatever that culture is—human beings can and do adapt to almost any situation. This learning process is a type of socialization. The following description of adaptation in a German prison camp during World War II was written by Bruno Bettelheim, a noted American scholar who survived imprisonment.

When a prisoner had reached the final stage of adjustment to the camp situation, he had changed his personality so as to accept various values of the SS [Hitler's elite troops] as his own. A few examples may illustrate how this acceptance expressed itself.

Slowly prisoners accepted, as the expression of their verbal aggressions, terms which definitely did not originate in their previous vocabularies, but were taken over from the very different vocabulary of the SS. From copying the verbal aggressions of the SS to copying its form of bodily aggressions was one more step, but it took several years to make this step. It was not unusual to find old prisoners, when in charge of others, behaving worse than the SS.

Old prisoners who identified themselves with the SS did so not only in respect to aggressive behavior. They would try to acquire old pieces of SS uniforms. If that was not possible, they tried to sew and mend their uniforms so that they would resemble those of the guards. The length to which prisoners would go in these efforts seemed unbelievable, particularly since the SS punished them for their efforts to copy SS uniforms. When asked why they did it, the old prisoners admitted that they loved to look like the guards.

The old prisoners' identification with the SS did not stop with the copying of their outer appearance and behavior. Old prisoners accepted Nazi goals and values, too, even when these seemed opposed to their own interests. It was appalling to see how far even politically well-educated prisoners would go with this identification. At one time American and English newspapers were full of stories about the cruelties committed in these camps. The SS punished prisoners for the appearance of these stories, true to its policy of punishing the group for whatever a member or a former member did, since the stories must have originated in reports from former prisoners. In discussions of this event, old prisoners would insist that it was not the business of foreign correspondents or newspapers to bother with German institutions, expressing their hatred of the journalists who tried to help them.

After so much has been said about the old prisoners' tendency to conform and to identify with the SS, it ought to be stressed that this was only part of the picture. The author has tried to concentrate on interesting psychological mechanisms in group behavior rather than on reporting types of behavior which are either well known or could reasonably be expected. These same old prisoners who identified with the SS defied it at other moments, demonstrating extraordinary courage in doing so.

Source: From *Surviving and Other Essays*, by Bruno Bettelheim. © 1979 by Bruno Bettelheim and Trude Bettelheim as Trustees.

Thinking It Over

1. Describe an experience you have had in which you or someone you know, as a new member of a group, imitated the ways of the group.
2. How does gang affiliation (such as wearing gang colors or using their slogans) demonstrate the tendency to conform?

Interdisciplinary Activity

Literature William Golding (1911–1993) was awarded the Nobel Prize for Literature for his novels *Lord of the Flies, Pincher Martin, The Inheritors,* and *Spire*. Many of your students should be familiar with *Lord of the Flies,* a classic study of the depths of human nature that follows the marooning of a group of British schoolboys on a desert isle. The boys abandon social norms and revert to barbarism and murder as the trappings of civilization (or the socialization process of civilization) fall away.

Ask a student who read this book to identify a few pages describing the resocialization process of the boys.

L3

Another Time

This article illustrates how easily people can be resocialized and desocialized from their previous cultures. Ask the students if they believe the prisoners' behavior reflected that they were simply trying to survive the camp? Or did they really come to believe that the SS were superior? Do students think it would have been hard to get desocialized and resocialized back into the mainstream?

Answers to Thinking It Over

1. You might ask students to focus on some aspect of school life such as students who are new to the school or from another country.
2. Students will probably point out that the failure to conform in a gang situation has severe consequences, which was the case for the prisoners faced with SS reprisals. These are extreme cases, however. Suggest students think about which school behaviors illustrate the power of conformity.

Integrating the Teacher Resources

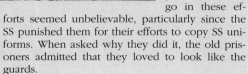

Look for the Chapter 4 Increasing Your Reading Comprehension worksheet and the Guided Reading worksheet in the Unit 2 Mastering Basic Concepts booklet in your Teacher's Resource Box. Both will strengthen student reading comprehension skills.

Section 3

Agents of Socialization

Key Terms

- **hidden curriculum**
- **peer group**
- **mass media**

The Family and Socialization

The child's first exposure to the world occurs within the family. Some essential developments occur through close interaction with a small number of people—none of whom the child has selected. Within the family the child learns to

- think and speak
- internalize norms, beliefs, and values
- form some basic attitudes
- develop a capacity for intimate and personal relationships
- acquire a self-image (Handel, 1990).

The impact of the family reaches far beyond its direct effects on the child. Our family's social class shapes what we think of ourselves and how others treat us, even far into adulthood. Author Jean Evans offers an illustration of this in the case of Johnny Rocco, a twenty-year-old living in a city slum.

> Johnny hadn't been running the streets long when the knowledge was borne in on him that being a Rocco made him "something special"; the reputation of the notorious Roccos, known to neighbors, schools, police, and welfare agencies as "chiselers, thieves, and trouble-makers" preceded him. The cop on the beat, Johnny says, always had some cynical smart crack to make. . . . Certain children were not permitted to play with him. Wherever he went—on the streets, in the neighborhood, settlement house, at the welfare agency's penny milk station, at school, where other Roccos had been before him—he recognized himself by a gesture, an oblique remark, a wrong laugh. (Evans, 1954:11)

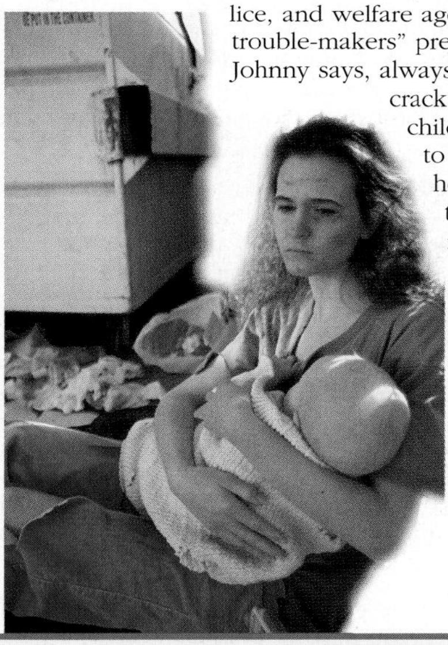

The infant in the photo on the left is likely to be socialized in a very different way from the two children above. What are some differences in attitudes that will probably be formed by these children because of their different family life?

Section Preview

During childhood and adolescence, the major agents of socialization are the family, school, peer group, and mass media. The family's role is critical in forming basic values. Schools introduce children to life beyond the family. In peer groups, young people learn to relate as equals. The mass media provide role models for full integration into society.

Using the Section Preview

As an introduction to socialization in the family, play a section from a popular children's TV program such as *Sesame Street* or *Barney.* Ask students to identify as best they can how these shows act as agents of socialization. They might point to specific directions the characters give viewers to act in certain ways or say particular things.

Integrating the Teacher Resources

For Spanish-speaking students, you may wish to use the reproducible worksheets available in the Spanish Supplements booklet in your Teacher's Resource Box. In addition to providing Spanish translations of selected Mastering Basic Concepts worksheets, the booklet contains English and Spanish summaries of the chapter's key points.

Cooperative Learning Activity

Have students brainstorm a list of proverbs from the United States and post the results of their efforts. Follow up by assigning groups of students to work together to search the Internet for proverbs from specific cultures. Post the results of their findings, and use the entire posting as the basis for discussions of the role that proverbs play in the teaching of values to the young. Discussion questions might include: Do proverbs really teach values? How accurately do the U.S. proverbs reflect current values? Should they be updated? If so, what can students suggest? If some U.S. proverbs are outdated, what kinds of cautions does that suggest for interpreting proverbs from other cultures?
L2

Using the Illustration

This cartoon illustrates the growing power of the mass media in children's lives. Ask students why they think many parents let their children watch television if they don't like the effects the media has on their offspring.

More About . . . School Socialization

Currently, more than 50 percent of all U.S. preschool children are in day care (private homes or institutions) and this number is increasing. Silverstein (1991) has found that generally these preschool programs have a positive socializing influence on children, especially for children from less advantaged backgrounds. For these children, they are provided with valuable learning experiences not available at home.

Teaching Strategy

Ask students to list specific actions that support the hidden curriculum. (*Being to school on time, sitting quietly, respecting your teacher, being neat, completing assignments, etc.*) Ask them what these types of activities will best prepare a student for—a position that requires obedience and following orders or a leadership position? What are the implications for the workplace of the hidden curriculum? *(Students might wonder if following the hidden curriculum at the expense of innovation would produce the most capable leaders.)* **L2**

Parents are no longer the only significant socializing force.

Socialization in Schools

In school, children are under the care and supervision of adults who are not relatives. For the first time, many of the child's relationships with other people are impersonal. Rewards and punishments are based on performance rather than affection. Although a mother may cherish any picture that her child creates, a teacher evaluates her students by more objective standards. Slowly, children are taught to be less dependent emotionally on their parents. The school also creates feelings of loyalty and allegiance to something beyond the family.

hidden curriculum the informal and unofficial aspects of culture that children are taught in school

How do schools socialize students? The socialization process in school involves more than reading, writing, and arithmetic. Underlying the formal goals of the school is the **hidden curriculum**—the informal and unofficial aspects of culture that children are taught in preparation for life. The hidden curriculum teaches children discipline, order, cooperation, and conformity—characteristics required for success in the adult world of work. (You will learn more about the hidden curriculum in Chapter 12.)

School also teaches children the reality of how we experience time in the real world. According to education critic John Holt (1967), life in schools is run by the clock, as it is in the working world. A bell signals when children must move to the next scheduled event, whether or not they understand what they have been working on and whether or not they are ready to switch to a different subject. Getting through a preset number of activities within a given time period often becomes more important than learning.

Learning Styles

Visual Have students prewrite about the ways in which they've changed since they began high school. They should describe physical and personal challenges they have faced. Be sure to tell them they won't have to share personal answers. Now have the class use their lists to brainstorm the various tasks of adolescence. Write this list on the board. It is helpful for students to understand that many of the joys or traumas they experience are societally-determined and "normal."

You might want to follow up this activity by putting a long piece of butcher paper along one wall of the classroom. This will become a "graffiti wall." Have students

Schools have rules and regulations to cover almost all activities—how to dress, how to wear one's hair, which side of the hall to walk on, when to speak in class. Teachers reward children with praise and acceptance when they recite the "right" answers, behave "properly," or exhibit "desirable" attitudes.

Children are isolated from the working adult society by being set apart in school for most of their preadult lives. Because they are separated from the adult world for such a long time, young people must depend on one another for much of their social life.

peer group
set of individuals of roughly the same age and interests

Peer Group Socialization

The family and the school are both agencies of socialization organized and operated by adults. The child's **peer group**—composed of individuals of roughly the same age and interests—is the only agency of socialization that is not controlled primarily by adults. Children usually belong to several peer groups. A child may belong to a play group in the neighborhood, a clique at school, an after-school club or sports team.

How do peer groups contribute to socialization? In the family and at school, children are subordinated to adults. In the peer group, young people have an opportunity to engage in give-and-take relationships. Children experience conflict, competition, and cooperation in such groups. The peer group also gives children experience in self-direction. They can begin to make their own decisions; experiment with new ways of thinking, feeling, and behaving; and engage in activities that involve self-expression.

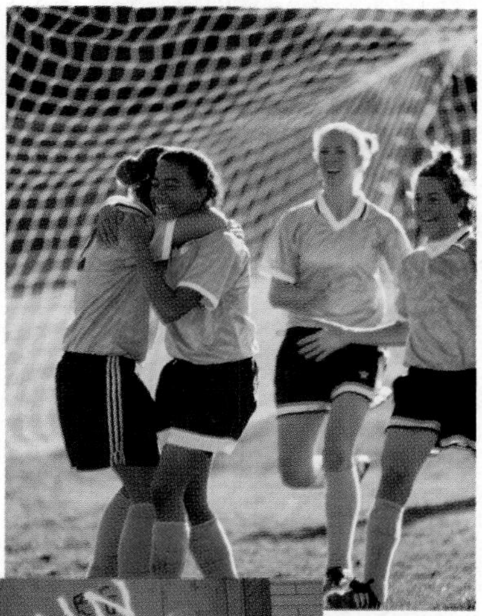

Socialization is occurring in each of the peer groups pictured here, perhaps with far different consequences for the larger society.

Points to Stress

Students should understand that peer groups are important because they provide a sense of belonging that is free from authority figures. You might also want to throw the discussion open to the idea of peer group pressure. Is this a negative or a positive force?

Making Connections to Other Cultures

The basic intent of the socialization process is the passing on of the culture from one generation to the next. Core values that cultures hold and wish to pass on to their children may sometimes be found in their proverbs. For example, Henry David Thoreau's "If a man does not keep pace with his companions, perhaps it is because he hears a different drummer," tends to personify American individualism. By way of contrast, a Japanese proverb states that "The nail that stands up gets pounded down." It should be noted that the very interpretation of a proverb might be culturally based. That is, an American may view the proverb stated here as a call for conformity, while the Japanese may see it as pointing out the need for each individual to do his or her share for the common good.

brainstorm a theme for the paper. After consensus is reached, have someone write the theme on the butcher paper. Examples of themes might include: Adolescence is . . . or Who am I? Tell students that as they enter the classroom each day, they can add a line or two of graffiti to the butcher paper. Their writing must relate to the theme, however. Students can use lines from songs and poems, or a line mentioned in class. (You might want to set some ground rules about the use of profanity or other offensive language.) Students will probably begin to look forward to "writing on the wall" in your classroom. **L1**

Teaching Strategy

Much is written about the negative effects of the mass media. For a change of pace, have students brainstorm some of the positive effects of the mass media that they can see from personal experience. (*Among other effects, they inform us about events; they introduce us to a wide variety of people; they produce a range of viewpoints on important issues; they make people aware of new products and processes; and they entertain us.*)
L1

Controversy and Debate

A recent (2000) AP news article covered a protest by child advocates who were critical of a marketing campaign by fast food companies that advertised with characters from a popular television program for very young children. The McDonald's corporation and Burger King both had agreements with Teletubbies to promote their products. The critics claim that (1) children younger than two shouldn't be watching television anyway; (2) they shouldn't be encouraged to prefer "junk" food at that age. PBS, the station carrying the program, defended both the content of the show—which has won several awards—as well as the sponsors.

Ask your students if they believe that companies should have the right to market to any age group over television. What societal norms and issues are involved in this debate?

Independence from adults is also promoted by the peer group, because often the norms of the peer group conflict with those of the adult world. Children learn to be different from their parents in ways that help to develop self-sufficiency.

The peer group also provides an opportunity for children to develop close ties with friends outside the family, including members of the opposite sex. At the same time, they are learning to get along with large numbers of people, many of whom are quite different from themselves. This helps develop the social flexibility needed in a mobile, rapidly changing society.

mass media
means of communication designed to reach the general population

Do friends or family have more influence on young people? The majority of Americans now live in either urban or suburban areas. In both two-income families and single-parent families, parents may commute many miles to work and spend much of their time away from home. Consequently, once children reach the upper levels of grade school, they may spend more time with their peers than they do with their parents.

According to psychologist Judith Harris (1998), peers are more important than parents in socializing children. Even though most sociologists do not agree with this extreme conclusion, many do believe that the peer group is having a growing effect on social development.

The mass media are a relatively new source of socialization. How does television advertising influence the dating behavior of teenagers?

The Mass Media and Socialization

Mass media are means of communication designed to reach the general population. They include such things as television, radio, newspapers, magazines, movies, books, the Internet, tapes, and discs. Many popular images presented in the mass media are highly distorted. For example, detective and police work are not as exciting and glamorous as depicted in books, in movies, and on television. Nevertheless, it is often through the mass media that children are first introduced to numerous aspects of their culture (Fishman and Cavender, 1998).

What role do the mass media play in socialization? The mass media display role models for children to imitate. Learning these role models helps to integrate the young into society.

> *The mass media, by their content alone, teach many of the ways of the society. This is evident in the behavior we take for granted—the duties of the detective, waitress, or sheriff; the functions of the hospital, advertising agency, and police court; behavior in hotel, airplane, or cruise ship; the language of the prison, army, or courtroom; the relationship between nurses and doctors or secretaries and their bosses. Such settings and relationships are portrayed time and again in films, television*

Interdisciplinary Activity

Culture Studies To relate the elements of culture studied in Chapter 3 with socialization concepts, you might want to have students do some research to develop a chart of cultural practices in other countries and the correlating practice in the United States. The chart would have three columns: Country, Cultural Practice, Correlating U.S. Practice. Using the example given above you would put *India* in the Country column; *wives walk behind husbands* in the Cultural Practice column; and *wives walk beside husband* in the Correlating U.S. Practice column. Topics

World View

Availability of Television

The mass media play a key role in the socialization process. Since nearly every U.S. home has at least one television (the majority have more), this medium is one of the most influential in the United States. This map shows that ownership of televisions varies widely around the world.

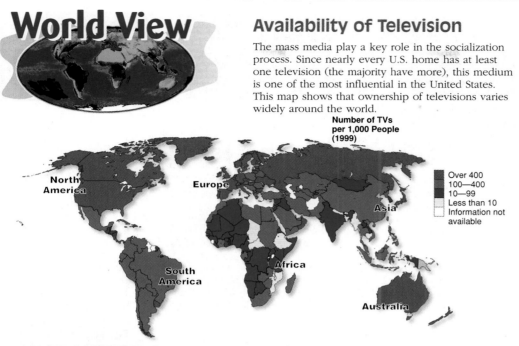

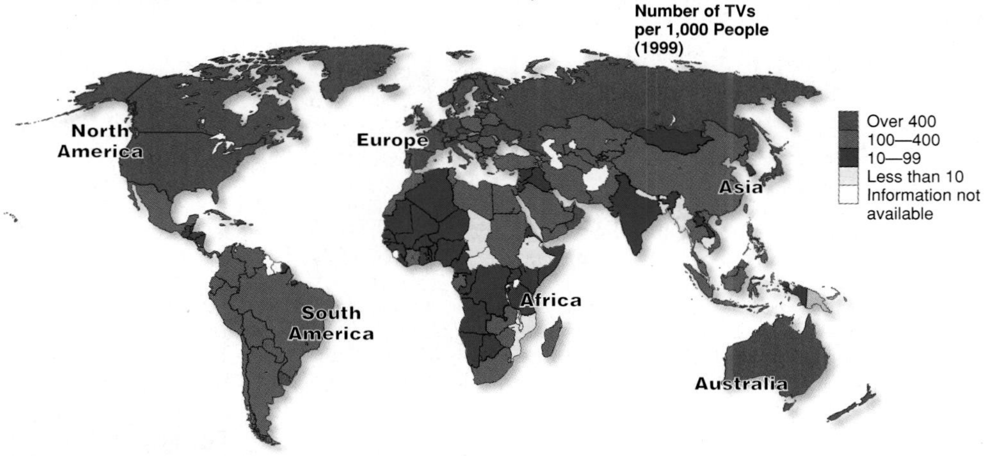

Interpreting the Map

1. What geographical factor(s) might contribute to the density of TV households in South America?
2. Do you think the attitudes of members of societies with more televisions are influenced more by government advertising than members of societies with fewer televisions? Why or why not?

Adapted from the *Atlas of the Future*. New York: MacMillan Books, 1998.

shows, and comic strips; and all "teach"—however misleadingly— norms, status positions, and institutional functions (Elkin and Handel, 1991:189).

The mass media also offer children ideas about the values in their society. They provide children with images of achievement and success, activity and work, equality and democracy.

What about violence in the mass media? On the negative side, consider the relationship between violence on television and real-life violence. By age sixteen, the average American child will have seen twenty thousand homicides on television (Leonard, 1998). Social scientists have been reluctant in the past to recognize a causal connection between television violence and real-life violence. However, based on hundreds of studies involving over ten thousand children, most now conclude that watching aggressive behavior on television significantly increases aggression (Hepburn, 1993; Strasburger, 1995; Dudley, 1999).

SOCIOLOGY Online

Student Web Activity
Visit the *Sociology and You* Web site at soc.glencoe.com and click on **Chapter 4—Student Web Activities** for an activity on mass media and socialization.

Answers to Interpreting the Map

1. Students might recognize that not only wealth, but geographical factors such as mountain ranges, sparse population, and rainforest topography would slow the spread of television.
2. Answers will vary. Some students will legitimately argue that government advertising is more influential in societies with more televisions. Other students can legitimately argue that the greater the number of televisions the harder it is for government to monopolize public attention and opinion.

that might be of interest to students include:

- Dating Norms
- Marriage Traditions
- Child Rearing Practices
- School Activities
- Religious Practices
- Family Life
- Gender Roles

Discuss students' findings with the entire class, relating the customs to the socialization process. Be sure to ask students' opinions about the practices they discovered. **L2**

Sociology Today

Psychologists explain that adolescents go through a period known as *adolescent moratorium* as they mourn the loss of childhood and prepare for the rigors of adulthood. Have students each create a list of what they believe adults don't understand about adolescents. Then ask them to find time at home to discuss with their parents what adults generally find hard to understand about teens. Encourage them to share and compare their lists with the parents' to see if open discussion might diffuse some trouble areas.

Answer to Doing Sociology

Answers will vary. Students might suggest that adults should understand the emotional and physiological changes teens go through or that adults should understand the "imaginary audience" that teens create. Hopefully, some students will respond that teens should also make a similar effort.

Sociology Today

Struggling Through the Teen Years

Adolescents do not get good press. They are often portrayed by the media as awkward, unreasonable, strong-willed, and overconfident. Some parents, taking their cue from comedian Bill Cosby, jokingly attribute teen behavior to temporary "brain damage." Researcher David Elkind (1981) offers another explanation for much troublesome adolescent behavior. Teens' problem, he concludes, is not brain damage. They are simply struggling through the emotional and physiological changes of the teen years as best they can.

Teenagers may appear to behave irrationally (by adult standards) because of new thinking capabilities not yet under their control. Contrary to the long-accepted belief that the human brain is fully developed by the age of 8 or 12, startling new research reveals that the brain remains a construction site even into the 20s (Begley, 2000). And the part of the brain that undergoes the greatest change between puberty and young adulthood is responsible for such activities as judgment, emotional control, and organization and planning.

Whereas adults are accustomed to looking at situations from several different viewpoints, teens are not. Confusion can result when inexperienced young people attempt to move from making simple, one-factor decisions to consideration of several factors simultaneously. For example, a teen who wants to join friends in a ride from a night football game may consider that the driver has a license, but may fail to consider the driver's experience, driving habits, or drinking behavior.

Teens assume that other people have as much interest in them as they have in themselves. Consequently, they surround themselves with an

Consider a few examples. A two-year-old girl died when her older brother, age five, set the house on fire with matches while imitating behavior he had seen on the cartoon program *Beavis and Butt-Head*. Just on the basis of televised *reports* of violence, a rash of would-be copycat crimes followed the shooting massacre of thirteen students and one teacher at Columbine High School by two students who then shot themselves. Television's effects, of course, are usually more hidden, subtle, and long term:

> *. . . [N]ot every child who watched a lot of violence or plays a lot of violent games will grow up to be violent. Other forces must converge, as they did [at Columbine]. . . . But just as every cigarette increases the chance that someday you will get lung cancer, every exposure to violence increases the chances that some day a child will behave more violently than they would otherwise (To Establish Justice, 1999:vi).*

Survey

Have your students conduct a survey of television programs. Some students should watch programs on commercial stations and others should watch public broadcast stations. Students should make a chart on which they list the title of the program they watch and the time it is shown. They should keep track of the subtle or overt messages about race, gender, or disabilities. Students should watch a variety of programs: children's programs, primetime programs, etc.

The findings should be compared and contrasted by commercial and public broadcast stations. Students should also compare different children's programs. Tally results and ask students to reach some conclusions based on the data they collected. **L1**

"imaginary audience." Since teenagers believe that everyone is watching and evaluating them, they are extremely self-conscious. In groups, adolescents often play to this imaginary audience by engaging in loud and provocative behavior. Yet they fail to understand why adults become annoyed with them. Gradually, they begin to realize that others have their own preoccupations, and the imaginary-audience behavior lessens.

Teenagers frequently have the feeling of invulnerability. For example, they may think that drug addiction, cancer from smoking, pregnancy, and death happen only to others. Their reckless behavior must be seen within this context.

Young people tend to assume that fairly common adolescent experiences are unique. Common complaints include "Mom, you just don't know how much it hurt for Carlos to take out Maria," and "Dad, you don't know what it's like not to have my own bike." At the other extreme, adolescents may feel that their own perceptions are shared by everyone. A young boy, for example, may believe that others find him unattractive because of what he thinks is a large nose. No amount of talking can convince him that he is exaggerating the size of his nose or that others pay little attention to it. This self-centered view of reality begins to decrease as teens discover that others are having similar feelings and experiences.

Doing Sociology

Identify three ways in which adults and adolescents could use this developmental awareness to ease the struggle of the teen years.

Section 3 Assessment

1. Why does the family have such strong influence on a child's socialization?
2. What aspect of socialization does the child first encounter in school that he or she does not meet in the family?
3. What is the hidden curriculum?
4. Besides family and school, identify two other socializing agents.

Critical Thinking

5. **Evaluating Information** Some pyschologists believe that peer groups have more influence on later socialization than the family group. Give reasons why you agree or disagree with that premise.

Answers to Section 3 Assessment

1. Being in a family provides a child's first exposure to the world, where he learns to think and speak; internalize norms, beliefs, and values; form basic attitudes; develop a capacity for intimate and personal relationships; and acquire a self-image.
2. For the first time, relationships are impersonal, and rewards and punishments are based on performance rather than affection, thereby teaching the child to be less dependent emotionally. School also creates feelings of loyalty and allegiance to something beyond the family.
3. The hidden curriculum is the teaching of the informal and unofficial aspects of culture such as discipline, order, cooperation, and conformity to prepare children for life.
4. Answers will vary but could include any of the following: Peer groups and types of mass media including television, radio, newspapers, magazines, movies, books, the Internet, tapes, and discs.

Critical Thinking

5. Answers will vary.

Interdisciplinary Activity

Political Science For many years, television broadcasting in South Africa was restricted (even delayed) because the apartheid regime was concerned about the socialization effects of the media. How can you keep strict separateness between races if you allowed a "window" into private lives via television? Censors could never figure out how to restrict reception of "white" television shows to only white households. They were also concerned about the imported content from the U.S. and Europe conflicting with norms and values of the established racist government.

Assign students to groups to discuss whether they think television is a force that contributes more toward maintaining the status quo or toward change and disruption. (This is another way to point out the different ways functionalist and a conflict perspective sociologists might approach media study.) **L2**

Using the Section Preview

Before reading this section, ask students to discuss whether they believe that prisons rehabilitate or punish. This will be a good way to evaluate what real information students possess about the efficacy of the judicial system and about the process of desocialization and resocialization.

Reinforcing Vocabulary

Stress to students that while it may, at times, seem as though their high school is a *total institution*, in fact, as long as they wear their own clothes, choose their own friends, bring their own lunch, etc., their school does not fit under that category of organization.

Points to Stress

You may want to emphasize with students the fact that while socialization is a gradual process, resocialization usually occurs in the setting of a total institution where complete control over the individual can be maintained.

More About . . Total Institutions

The concept of total institutions was introduced by sociologist Erving Goffman in his seminal work, Asylums: Essays on the Social Situation of Mental Patients and Other Inmates, Chicago: Aldine, (1961). In order to study the inside of a mental institution, Goffman took a job as a janitor. His field study uncovered the relationship between the patients and the staff and the institutionalized nature of that relationship.

Section 4 Processes of Socialization

Key Terms

- total institutions
- desocialization
- resocialization
- anticipatory socialization
- reference group

Section Preview

Symbolic interactionism views socialization as a lifelong process. Desocialization is the process of having to give up old norms. Resocialization begins as people adopt new norms and values. Anticipatory socialization and reference groups are concerned with voluntary change as when moving from one life stage to another.

total institutions places in which people are separated from the rest of society and controlled by officials in charge

desocialization the process of giving up old norms, values, attitudes, and behaviors

resocialization the process of adopting new norms, values, attitudes, and behaviors

Desocialization and Resocialization

Whenever change occurs over the course of your life, you will learn new behaviors and skills. This learning is important to socialization. Symbolic interactionism describes four processes associated with socialization after childhood: *desocialization, resocialization, anticipatory socialization,* and *reference groups.*

How does desocialization prepare people for new learning? Mental hospitals, cults, and prisons are **total institutions**—places where residents are separated from the rest of society. These residents are not free to manage their own lives, but are controlled and manipulated by those in charge. The end purpose of this control and manipulation is to permanently change the residents. The first step is **desocialization**—the process by which people give up old norms, values, attitudes, and behaviors. For those in total institutions, desocialization often means the destruction of old self-concepts of personal identity.

Desocialization in institutions is accomplished in many ways. Replacing personal possessions with standard-issue items promotes sameness among the residents. It deprives them of the personal items (long hair, hair brushes, ball caps, T-shirts) they have used to present themselves as unique individuals. The use of serial numbers to identify people and the loss of privacy also contribute to the breakdown of past identity. Cult members, for example, may even be denied use of their given names.

How does resocialization begin? Once the self-concept has been broken down, **resocialization**—the process in which people adopt new norms, values, attitudes, and behaviors—can begin. Those in control of total institutions, using an elaborate system of rewards and punishments, attempt to give residents new self-

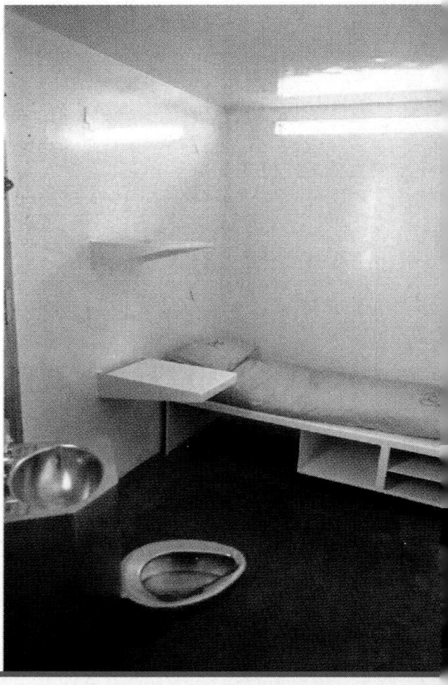

The starkness of this prison cell with its lack of individual possessions aids in the desocialization process.

Careers in Sociology

Public Relations People who choose public relations as a career need an outgoing personality, self-confidence, an understanding of others, and an enthusiasm for motivating people. Creativity, initiative, good judgment, and the ability to express thoughts persuasively, clearly, and simply, both orally and in writing, are essential. Decision-making, problem-solving, and research skills are also important. Public relations managers assist in drafting speeches, arranging interviews, and other forms of public contact. Some handle special events such as sponsorship of races, parties introducing new products, or other activities to gain public attention. Public relations spe-

Rates of Imprisonment

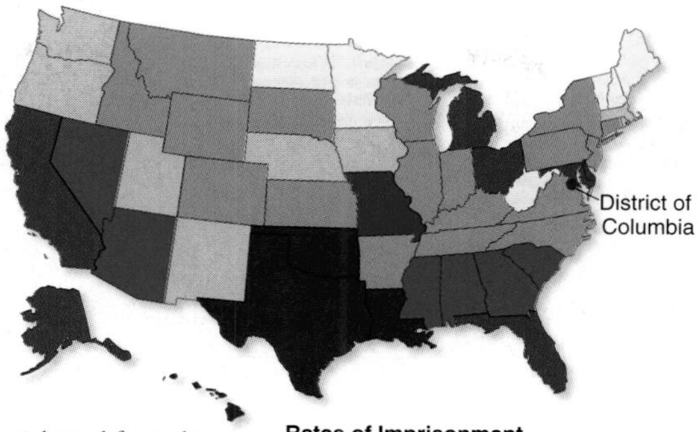

The U.S. has one of the highest rates of imprisonment in the industrialized world—over four times that of any Western European country. Justice officials worry that some prisons function as "schools for crime." If prisons do first desocialize and then resocialize inmates toward a criminal identity, then the U.S. prison system is unintentionally increasing the criminal portion of the population. This map shows the number of prisoners with sentences of more than one year per 100,000 U.S. residents.

Source: Adapted from the *Bureau of Justice Statistics Bulletin*. Washington, D.C.: U.S. Department of Justice, 1999.

Interpreting the Map

1. Where does your state rank in terms of imprisonment rate? Can you relate the extent of imprisonment in your state to the nature of the socialization that occurs in your state?
2. Do the states adjoining your state have imprisonment rates that are similar or dissimilar to your state?

Online UPDATE Visit soc.glencoe.com and click on **Textbook Updates–Chapter 4** for an update of the data.

concepts. Rewards for taking on a new "identity" can include extra food, special responsibilities, or periods of privacy. Punishments for nonconformity involve shaming, loss of special privileges, physical punishment, and physical isolation.

The concepts of desocialization and resocialization were developed to analyze social processes in extreme situations. They still apply to other social settings, including basic training in the U.S. Marine Corps and plebe (freshman) year at the United States Military Academy. In much less extreme form, these concepts illuminate changes in our normal life course. Desocialization and resocialization occur as a child becomes a teenager, when young adults begin careers, and as the elderly move into retirement or widowhood.

Anticipatory Socialization

Anticipatory socialization is the process of preparing (in advance) for new norms, values, attitudes, and behaviors. It does not generally occur in prisons or mental hospitals because it involves *voluntary change*.

anticipatory socialization the voluntary process of preparing to accept new norms, values, attitudes, and behaviors

The argument about whether prisons rehabilitate or reinforce criminal behavior is a very old one. Many sociologists spend their whole careers addressing this issue. Students may be interested in learning if there is a direct concern in their own community with prisons. Is there a prison located nearby? Are there plans to build a prison? Unfortunately, funding requests for new prisons pass more often than educational millages.

Answers to Interpreting the Map

1. Answers will vary.
2. Answers will vary.

Reteaching

A fun way to get students to understand anticipatory socialization is to ask them what dating is all about. They will say that it is to meet people, to find someone special, and to learn to become intimate with someone else. But it is also preparation for longer relationships that will most likely lead to marriage. This is a form of anticipatory socialization.

cialists create favorable attitudes through effective communication.

For entry into public relations jobs, many employers prefer a broad liberal arts background. A bachelor's degree in sociology, among other subjects, is acceptable. Requirements vary depending upon the particular job. Other workers with similar jobs include fund raisers; lobbyists; advertising, marketing, and promotion managers; and police officers involved in community relations. Students can find additional information at Public Relations Society of America, Inc.: **http://www.prsa.org**.

Focus on Research

Few, if any, of the students will have had any "up close" experience with a total institution. Some may have seen or heard of *Scared Straight,* an award-winning documentary produced in 1978 that took adolescents into a New Jersey prison to be shocked away from a life of crime. This film has highly graphic content and has been very controversial, but parts of it might be suitable for class viewing (with careful editing). While the Juvenile Awareness Project Help claimed huge reductions in recidivism rates of juveniles as a result of this program, these claims were later investigated in a highly interesting sociological study. An overview of the study makes for interesting reading and can be reviewed at **www.ncianet.organization/ncia/scared.html**

Focus on Research

Case Study: High School Reunions

Socialization occurs throughout life. Even high school reunions play a part. If you asked most Americans to talk about their experiences at a recent high school reunion, what would they say?

"It was great seeing old friends."

"I was curious about how things turned out for people I loved and hated as a teenager."

"I plan to get together with some old friends in the near future."

High school reunions are generally thought to be a time to recapture fond memories of youth.

One researcher wished to investigate the meaning of high school reunions. Keiko Ikeda (1998) studied eight reunions in the American Midwest. He observed these reunions armed with a camera, a tape recorder, and a notebook. After each reunion, he also conducted in-depth, life-story interviews with samples of participants.

Ikeda's results are too complex and varied to easily summarize. (This is typical of in-depth observational studies.) One aspect of the study, however, reveals the socializing aspect of high school reunions. Ikeda compared several reunions of one high school—tenth, fifteenth, twentieth, thirtieth, fortieth, and fiftieth. He focused on the relative emphasis on the past and the present. As you can see from the passage below, the past becomes more important as age increases.

> *In the earlier reunions (the tenth and fifteenth years), a concern with relative status and a sense of competitiveness is expressed, often blatantly, through award-giving ceremonies. . . . The hall was decorated in the school colors, and images of the high school mascot were present, but beyond this no high school memorabilia were displayed. The music, too, was current, and not the rock 'n' roll of the late sixties and early seventies.*
>
> *The twentieth-year reunion of the Class of '62 is typical of a transitional phase in which elements from the past begin to assume an important role. The past is expressed in high school memorabilia . . . in . . . films and slides taken during high school, and in . . . high school anecdotes that are playfully interwoven throughout the ceremonial events.*

"It is thus with most of us; we are what other people say we are. We are ourselves chiefly by hearsay."

Eric Hoffer
American author

On-Demand Writing

Have students choose one of the photos from the chapter and build a story around it using as many key terms from the chapter as possible. Tell them they won't have to read their story aloud, so they should not be afraid to be creative. Ask them to save the stories. After a few days, direct students to re-read their stories silently to themselves. They will probably find that they have put much of their own personality and experiences into the story.
L1

Cathy, © 1990, Cathy Guisewite, Universal Press Syndicate. (Reprinted with permission.)

In the thirtieth-year reunion of the Class of '52, the past firmly occupied center stage. A carefully crafted, chronological narrative of the senior year, entitled "The Way We Were," was read, in which major class activities were recalled month by month. . . .

In the fiftieth-year reunion, we find a dramatic disappearance of all ritual activities. According to the president of the Class of '32, his class had held reunions every ten years since graduation, and in earlier ceremonies they had given awards, but this time, "none of the folks in the reunion committee felt like doing that kind of thing." It seemed that attendees at the fiftieth-year reunion, for the most part, had risen above concerns of past and present and were content to celebrate together the simple fact that they all still had the vigor to attend a reunion.

Source: Keiko Ikeda, *A Room Full of Mirrors*. Stanford, CA: Stanford University Press, 1998, pp. 143–145.

Working with the Research

1. Ask an adult to describe the activities at one or more high school reunions that he or she has attended. Compare the description with Ikeda's findings.
2. Suppose you had a class assignment to study an upcoming reunion at your school. Select a research question you would want to ask. Identify the research methods you would use.

Answers to Working with the Research

1. Students should ask open-ended questions during the interview, so they should not go in expecting certain answers. Emphasis should be on asking what was done at the reunion. Did you give out awards? Did people just visit? etc. As the article states, this will involve extensive writing but will really get at the heart of people's perceptions and what was important.

2. Students might ask (if this is not the first reunion): How was this one different than the first? Students could conduct a survey with closed-ended and open-ended questions, they could conduct interviews, or if they could get invited to a reunion, they could simply observe and take notes.

Role Play

As an adjunct to this research study, students might want to contact the coordinators of the ten-year, twenty-year, or thirty-year reunions at their high school. They could interview the coordinators to see what plans are in the works for a particular reunion. Another project would be to have students simulate a class reunion, the one they will have in ten years or so. Consulting someone who has already planned a reunion might be helpful. Students could make up hypothetical roles for each other. One student might want to imagine that he or she owns a multinational corporation and another student is out of work with two kids. Let students ham it up.

L1

Pulling It All Together

This section discussed the three processes associated with socialization after childhood. The first is desocialization—the process in which people give up old norms, values, attitudes, and behaviors. Next, is resocialization—the process in which people adopt new norms, values, attitudes, and behaviors. The third process is anticipatory socialization—preparing (in advance) for new norms, values, attitudes, and behaviors. This process involves use of the reference group to evaluate oneself and from which attitudes, values, beliefs, and norms are acquired. Ask students if they think all people experience all these types of socialization, or if some people avoid one.

Using the Illustration

Individuals compare their own values, norms, and goals to see if they are consistent and compatible with those of the new reference group.

Answers to Section 4 Assessment

1. a. R
b. D
c. A
2. d
Critical Thinking
3. Answers will vary. Many students will probably feel that their peer group is the most influential, although parents should still rank fairly high on the list.

The dress on these young people indicates they are preparing for entry into the adult world of work or higher education. How does a peer group act as a tool for anticipatory socialization?

reference group
group whose norms and values are used to guide behavior; group with whom you identify

Anticipatory socialization may occur in people who are moving from one stage in their lives to another. Consider teenagers, for example. Because they want to resemble those their own age, they may willingly abandon many of the norms, values, attitudes, and behaviors learned previously. This process generally begins in the preteen years. Preteens begin early to observe the ways of teenagers. Teens become their new **reference group**—the group they use to evaluate themselves and from which they acquire attitudes, values, beliefs, and norms. In this situation, the new reference group is a tool for anticipatory socialization.

Seniors in college, normally seen on campus only in jeans and oversized sweatshirts, suddenly, as graduation nears, are wearing tailored suits and much more serious expressions. In preparing for entry into the business world, they are talking with friends who have graduated as well as company recruiters. In effect, they are preparing themselves for the resocialization they know awaits them (Atchley, 1997).

Section 4 Assessment

1. Identify the following actions as desocialization (D), resocialization (R), or anticipatory socialization (A).
   - **a.** First-year students acquire a new identity during their freshman year at a military academy.
   - **b.** Prison personnel deliberately attempt to destroy the self-concepts of inmates.
   - **c.** High school students identify with college students.
2. Which of the following is *not* an example of a reference group?
   - **a.** Rock-star subculture
   - **b.** United States Military Academy
   - **c.** Terrorists
   - **d.** Mass media

Critical Thinking

3. **Applying Concepts** Which group do you feel is the most influential in the present stage of your socialization—family, peers, school, or the media? Why?

Chapter 4 Assessment

Summary

Section 1: The Importance of Socialization

Main Idea: Socialization is the cultural process of learning to participate in group life. Without it, we would not develop many of the characteristics we associate with being human. Studies have shown that animals and human infants who are deprived of intensive and prolonged social contact with others are stunted in their emotional and social growth.

Section 2: Socialization and the Self

Main Idea: All three theoretical perspectives agree that socialization is needed if cultural and societal values are to be learned. Symbolic interactionism offers the most fully developed perspective for studying socialization. In this approach, the self-concept is developed by using other people as mirrors for learning about ourselves.

Section 3: Agents of Socialization

Main Idea: During childhood and adolescence, the major agents of socialization are the family, school, peer group, and mass media. The family's role is critical in forming basic values. Schools introduce children to life beyond the family. In peer groups, young people learn to relate as equals. The mass media provide role models for full integration into society.

Section 4: Processes of Socialization

Main Idea: Symbolic interactionism views socialization as a lifelong process. Desocialization is the process of having to give up old norms. Resocialization begins as people adopt new norms and values. Anticipatory socialization and reference groups are concerned with voluntary change as when moving from one life stage to another.

SOCIOLOGY Online

Self-Check Quiz
Visit the *Sociology and You* Web site at soc.glencoe.com and click on **Chapter 4—Self-Check Quizzes** to prepare for the chapter test.

Reviewing Vocabulary

Complete each sentence using each term once.

a. socialization
b. personality
c. anticipatory socialization
d. looking-glass self
e. role taking
f. generalized other
g. total institutions
h. resocialization

1. ____________ is the attitudes, beliefs, values, and behaviors associated with an individual.
2. The cultural process of learning to participate in group life is called ____________.
3. ____________ allows us to assume the viewpoint of another person and use that viewpoint to shape our self-concept.
4. ____________ are places in which people are separated from the rest of society and controlled by officials in charge.
5. The process of adopting new norms, values, attitudes, and behaviors is known as ____________.
6. An image of yourself based on what you believe others think of you is called ____________.
7. ____________ is the voluntary process of preparing to accept new norms, values, attitudes, and behaviors.
8. The integrated conception of the norms, values, and beliefs of one's society is called the ____________.

Reviewing the Facts

1. What does the study involving rhesus monkeys suggest about the choices that human infants would make in the same situation?
2. What is socialization from the viewpoint of symbolic interactionism?
3. What are the three major theoretical perspectives of sociology?
4. What concept discussed in this chapter relates to the song lyric: "Walk a Mile in My Shoes"?

133

ANSWERS Chapter 4 Assessment

Reviewing Vocabulary

1. b
2. a
3. e
4. g
5. h
6. d
7. c
8. f

Reviewing the Facts

1. Would choose emotional needs over physiological needs.
2. Socialization is a major determinant of human nature.
3. Functionalism, conflict, and symbolic interactionism
4. Role taking
5. Family, schools, peers, media
6. Strict control over inmates' behavior
7. Resocialization is the adopting of new norms, values, attitudes, and behaviors. Anticipatory socialization is the process of preparing in advance to accept new norms, values, attitudes, and behaviors.

Thinking Critically

1. If people can't learn or don't have the opportunity to work on their computer skills, they will be disadvantaged in finding adequate jobs and will miss out on relevant information. The U.S. government is working to see that no one loses out to the information age.
2. Many young women are extremely aware of how the media portrays them. Many times they complain that no one they know looks like the super models. Young men should also realize that the media drive for high ratings also encourages programmers to hire male role models that are physically appealing to viewers.
3. You might want to encourage students to create "webs" (concept maps) that contain all the networks that make up their daily lives. All of these agents are socializers.
4. The sociologists' numbers are statistical means so that the highs and lows are reported. Some people watch as much TV as a normal work week and some watch virtually none. Students

ANSWERS CHAPTER 4 ASSESSMENT

might want to analyze how these figures are obtained and whether studies that alarming results are used to attract reader attention and sell newspapers (as discussed in Chapter 2).

5. The idea that a prison is for rehabilitation thus resocialization and desocialization is negated by the influence of the prison subculture. In a related issue, you might ask students how much personal choice has to do with resocialization. Can a person be resocialized against his or her will? Is that what brainwashing really is?

Sociology Projects

1. Students might find it fun to re-read some of their favorite childhood story books and look to see the socializing influence these books had. Now they can look for sociological factors like gender roles, values, and racial and ethnic considerations. Have them read a story book to the class with their new-found realization of its socializing influence.

2. Students seem to appreciate the opportunity to share songs that are meaningful to them. You can have the student present the tape to the class, however, some may not want to do this since teens can be very judgmental about something as personal as taste in music. You might want to listen to the tapes yourself; students will appreciate it even if your own ears don't.

3. This activity is a comparison of TV and real life. This can help students distinguish between TV's portrayal of life and what is really out there. Students' perceptions of this subject can be very enlightening.

4. Answers will vary.

5. Answers will vary.

CHAPTER 4 ASSESSMENT

5. What are the four major agents of socialization? Use a ladder as your diagram and list the agents on the steps of the ladder.

1.
2.
3.
4.

6. What is a distinguishing characteristic of total institutions?

7. How does resocialization differ from anticipatory socialization?

Thinking Critically

1. Making Predictions You read in this chapter about the concern that extensive computer use stunts social development. Another growing concern is that some people (and groups of people) are being "left behind" because they don't have equal access to technology. How might this become a problem for your generation?

2. Evaluating Information This chapter discusses the socializing influences of mass media. Our perceptions of the ideal body types seem to be largely a product of media socialization. In a later chapter, you will have an opportunity to look at how the media idealizes body types. Girls feel the need to be thin and boys tend to measure how muscular they are. Discuss how television, magazines, CDs, and video games reinforce these images. Give examples from your experience of how the media has socialized Americans to admire certain figure and body types.

3. Analyzing Information Your daily life includes many social networks, or groups that regularly contribute to your socialization. They include family, friends, teachers, people at work, teammates, and so forth. Identify one of these groups, and imagine your day if you suddenly lost contact with those people. What support would you be missing? What key elements are provided by this particular social network?

4. Interpreting Information Sociologists claim the average American watches television seven hours a day, yet some students say they never watch TV. How could you account for this fact? Remember to refer to what you learned from the chapter in discussing this question.

5. Making Generalizations Total institutions, such as prisons, presume that desocialization and resocialization occur, since one of their goals is to make prisoners law abiding. Yet nearly half of the inmates released in the United States return to prison. If desocialization and resocialization really do take place, why is the recidivism rate (the number of prisoners who return to prison) so high? Propose a theory for what might be happening, using the concept of resocialization.

Sociology Projects

1. Socialization As you read in the chapter, children are socialized in many ways. Some books that you read when you were a child probably had a lasting impact on you. Your task is to analyze children's books armed with your new-found sociological knowledge. Read three children's books or re-read three of your favorites. Use the following questions to help you in your analysis.

a. What was the socializing message of the book? (In other words, what lesson did it teach?)

b. How are females/males portrayed in the book?

c. Are any values dealt with? Do you agree or disagree with those values?

d. What ethnic groups are portrayed in the book? How are they portrayed?

e. Are any other concepts from the chapter presented in the books (resocialization, anticipatory socialization, looking-glass self, and so forth)?

2. **Socialization and Music** Create the "Song of Your Life." From several different songs, select the lyrics that best describe your life. Try to create a flow, as your life represents a continuous flow of events and circumstances. Prepare a written summary of each song's significance to you, using the socialization concepts presented in the text. Do you think music is a socializing agent?
3. **TV and Real Life** The text mentioned the impact of TV on our daily lives. This activity asks you to assess how "real" TV is compared with what we see and do every day. You are to watch two hours of TV. Watch shows that fictionally portray real life (sporting events, the news, and documentaries are not appropriate for this activity). Take detailed notes on the characters, commenting on their clothing, body types, occupations, social class, race, ethnic group, age, and so forth. Then venture out into the real world, to a public place such as a park, laundromat, mall, bus terminal, or airport, and observe for two hours. (It might be easier to do this one hour at a time.) Concentrate on several people, and note the same features that you did for the TV characters. You might want to focus on shows that portray teens or the elderly and then observe members of that group. (Remember the ethics of doing research, and do not invade a subject's privacy without permission.) Write a paragraph comparing the characters on television with those you observed in real life.
4. **Violence on TV and in Film** Select a classmate to debate the issue of violence on TV and in film. Take the position that violence on TV and in film promotes real life violence and propose a solution to this problem. Your classmate should try to persuade the audience that violence on TV does not encourage people to become more violent in real life. Base your arguments on research.
5. **Major Agents of Socialization** Some children, without parents or close family, find themselves being moved from one foster home to another for the greater part of their childhood. Write an essay of at least one page in length using standard grammar, proper spelling and sentence structure which examines the role of each major agent of socialization in the development of an individual growing up in this environment.

   HINT: Family is a major agent of socialization. Family exists in the traditional sense and in variations of all kinds.

Technology Activities

1. As indicated in this chapter, the process of socialization occurs throughout a person's life. The Internet has assumed a significant role in the socialization of Americans. It actually aids television in the process.
   1. What are the most popular television shows among your friends?
   2. Use a search engine to see if these shows have a web site on the Internet.
   3. Describe the kinds of information available on the web sites.
   4. What benefits do the web sites provide to the viewers? To the television show?
2. Using the Internet and your school or local library, research the role the following technological inventions of their time played in the socialization of Americans: the popularity of the radio during 1940–1950; the growing popularity of color television from 1960 to the present; and the popularity of the Internet over the last five years. Consider the positive and negative effects, analyzing how norms and behaviors were changed by the available programming and/or advertising.

Integrating the Teacher Resources

To further assess student comprehension of this chapter, use Chapter Test A or B available in the Chapter and Unit Tests booklet in your Teacher's Resource Box.

Technology Activities

1. You might take a survey among your students to see how much television they watch—and what kind of programs. Do students who watch a lot of TV also surf the Net? or is the Internet replacing TV as an activity?
2. Answers will vary.

Enrichment Reading

The real challenge for students would be to find a TV show that has absolutely no violence. Cartoons would not count because in theory they are very violent. Present this challenge to students: The television show they watch can have absolutely no violence, not even a clip of something violent. Have students report back on how many shows were completely nonviolent.

Chapter 4

Enrichment Reading

National Television Violence

Key Findings

Today, violence is not only seen on the streets but also in the schools. During the last five years of the twentieth century, there were just over 150 school shootings. We now hear stories in the news about young people participating in violent shootings on school grounds and killing innocent bystanders. In a Michigan school in 2000, one six-year-old shot and killed a classmate at school. These violent acts raise questions: Why is there an increase in violence, especially among today's youth? Does television have a negative effect on individuals? Does television encourage violent behaviors?

In 1994, the National Television Violence Study initiated the first part of its three-year project to assess violence on television. This study, which is the largest study of media content ever undertaken, was funded by the National Cable Television Association. The project examined approximately 2,500 hours of television programming that included 2,693 programs.

The first of the three studies analyzes violent content in television programming. The second study examines children's reactions to ratings and viewer advisories. The final study analyzes the content of antiviolence public service announcements (PSAs).

Following is a summary of the first study conducted in 1994–1995. Collectively, these findings establish the norms that exist in the overall television environment. Many of the patterns observed cause some concern.

Overall Conclusions about Violence on Television

❖ **Violence predominates on television, often including large numbers of violent interactions per program.**

The majority (57 percent) of programs on television contain violence, and roughly one third of violent programs contain nine or more violent interactions. The frequency of violence on television can contribute to **desensitization** and fear, as well as provide ample opportunities to learn violent attitudes and behaviors.

This man is holding up the V-chip used to control television viewing by children.

❖ **In the majority of the episodes of violence, the perpetrator engages in repeated violent acts.**
The perpetrator engages in repeated acts of violence in more than half (58 percent) of all violent interactions. This increases the amount of violence to which viewers are exposed.

❖ **In one-quarter of the violent interactions, a gun is used.**
Certain visual cues, such as weapons, tend to activate aggressive thoughts in viewers. Later, these thoughts cause individuals to interpret neutral events as possibly threatening or aggressive.

❖ **In about three-quarters of all violent scenes, perpetrators go unpunished.**
The portrayal of rewards and punishments is probably the most important of all **contextual** factors for viewers as they interpret the meaning of what they see on television. Viewers who would otherwise think of a class of behaviors such as violence as bad may eventually learn that those behaviors are good (useful, successful, or desirable) if they are repeatedly and consistently portrayed as rewarded or unpunished. Across all channel types, this study discovered a common pattern that the majority of violent scenes lack any form of punishment for the perpetrators.

❖ **In a high proportion of violent episodes, the consequences are not realistically portrayed.**
Less than half of violent interactions show the victims experiencing any signs of pain. Furthermore, only about one in six programs depict any long-term negative consequences, such as physical suffering, or financial or emotional harm. All of these patterns increase the risk that viewers will believe that violence is not a particularly painful or harmful behavior.

❖ **Violence is often presented as humorous.**
More than one third of all violent scenes involve a humorous context. Humor tends to **trivialize** or undermine the seriousness with which violence is regarded. Humorous violence can serve to desensitize viewers to the serious or harmful effects of violence.

❖ **Violent programs rarely employ a strong antiviolence theme.**
Only 4 percent of all television programs emphasize a strong anti-violence theme. *Touched by an Angel, Little House on the Prairie,* and *Mr. Rogers,* are among the exceptions.

Source: Adapted from "National Television Violence Study: Executive Summary." Studio City, CA: Mediascope, Inc., 1998.

What Does it Mean?

contextual
meaning that is derived from the setting or the environment; not stated, but implied

desensitization
the process of preventing an emotional response; make less sensitive

perpetrator
someone who carries out or brings about an action; in law, one who commits a crime

predominate
to exert control over; to hold an advantage in numbers

trivialize
to make something less important or serious than it is

Read and React

1. What was the stated purpose of the first study?
2. Why does the report state that the contextual factors for viewing violence are the most important?
3. Do you think the report reaches its stated purpose (see Question #1)? Why or why not?

Answers to Read and React

1. The purpose of the first part of the research was to analyze the type and patterns of violence in television programming.
2. If violence is rewarded or goes unpunished, viewers may eventually learn that violent behavior is the best approach.
3. Answers will vary.

Integrating the Teacher Resources

Additional primary source readings for this chapter can be found in Culture Studies: The Sociological Perspective, **available in your Teacher's Resource Box. Questions for students are included.**

Chapter Preview

Section 1 (pages 140–145)

The underlying pattern of social relationships in a group is called social structure. Status is one very important element of social structure. Ascribed statuses are assigned at birth; achieved statuses are earned or chosen.

Section 2 (pages 146–152)

People interact according to prescribed roles. These roles carry certain rights and obligations. Sometimes conflict or strain occurs when an individual has too many roles to play.

Section 3 (pages 153–158)

The way a society provides for basic needs greatly affects its culture and social structure. Preindustrial, industrial, and postindustrial societies meet basic needs in different ways. Preindustrial societies include hunting and gathering, horticultural, pastoral, and agricultural societies.

Section 4 (pages 159–164)

The Industrial Revolution created a new type of society called industrial society. Characteristics that distinguish this society from all earlier ones include the growth of large cities and a widespread dependence on machines and technology. Postindustrial society has a predominately white-collar labor force that is concentrated in service industries. Social instability has been linked to the transition from an industrial to a postindustrial society.

CHAPTER 5

Social Structure and Society

Lead-Off Activity

To introduce students to some of the concepts they will be studying in this chapter, you might want to have them list the different "roles" they play in their lives today. Start them off with a few roles such as son/daughter, student, sibling, etc. Then have them list the expectations that go along with each role. Finally, have them explain how the different roles are connected. Ask volunteers to share their lists with the rest of the class.
L1

USING Your Sociological Imagination

Because we are deeply involved in our own social world, we forget that our ability to participate in daily life is based on years of socialization. In the play, *As You Like It,* William Shakespeare wrote a line reminding us of the place of social learning in our lives: "All the world's a stage. And all the men and women merely players; They have their exits and their entrances; And one man in his time plays many parts."

All members of a group (including you) have parts they are expected to play. Students are expected to attend class, listen to the instructor, and participate in class activities. Teachers are expected to be in the classroom when students arrive, hold class, teach and guide the class, and make assignments. In any American high school, you will find similar relationships between students and staff. Interactions are orderly and predictable. In most cases, the teacher knows what the student expects of her and the student knows what the teacher expects of him.

If, however, you suddenly found yourself in a class where the teacher raised his hand to talk and brought his dog to class; where students played frisbee and took naps on the floor, you might wonder what planet you had beamed down to. Missing the order and predictability you expected, you would wonder how you should act in this unfamiliar setting. To fit in, what you would need is some awareness of the underlying *social structure.* This chapter will discuss concepts that underlie social structure.

Sections

1. **Social Structure and Status**
2. **Social Structure and Roles**
3. **Preindustrial Societies**
4. **Industrial and Postindustrial Societies**

Learning Objectives

After reading this chapter, you will be able to

- explain what sociologists mean by *social structure.*
- discuss how statuses and roles are related to social structure.
- identify and illustrate the concepts of social structure.
- explain how culture and social structures are related.
- describe the means of subsistence in preindustrial societies.
- discuss the characteristics of industrial society.
- compare and contrast preindustrial, industrial, and postindustrial societies.

SOCIOLOGY Online

Chapter Overview
Visit the *Sociology and You* Web site at soc.glencoe.com and click on **Chapter 5—Chapter Overviews** to preview chapter information.

USING Your Sociological Imagination

Here is an opportunity to have students look at all the roles they take on and how the other actors change throughout the course of a day. For example, a student might be a son or a daughter at home but probably won't have that role in school. However, a student might be a sibling at home as well as at school. Have students create diagrams of these various roles, share them in groups, and look for similarities and differences among classmates.

Since the Using Your Sociological Imagination scenario implies that behavior is predictable during class, you might use some of the ideas suggested. Discuss with students why we have this great need for patterned social structure.

Using the Section Preview

Ask students what status they have. Is someone the captain of the football team or the forensics team, or a leader in ROTC? If they are, they have a certain status. Follow up on the role activity in the Using Your Sociological Imagination box on page 139 by having students add their statuses to their diagrams. Do students have more roles than they have statuses? Why might that be?

Teaching Strategy

Activity #5 on page 167 in the Chapter 5 Assessment is appropriate to complete at this time. You might want to have students bring in some of their representations of status, or social badges to post around the classroom. These status symbols will help students relate to the concept of status. It would also be interesting to see if students from different racial, ethnic, and socioeconomic classes choose the same type of status symbols.
L1

Integrating the Transparencies

A Social Structures transparency is provided in the *Sociology and You* Transparency Binder.

Section 1

Social Structure and Status

Key Terms

- **social structure**
- **status**
- **ascribed status**
- **achieved status**
- **status set**
- **master status**

Section Preview

The underlying pattern of social relationships in a group is called social structure. Status is one very important element of social structure. Ascribed statuses are assigned at birth; achieved statuses are earned or chosen.

social structure
the underlying patterns of relationships in a group

status
a position a person occupies within a social structure

Social Structure Is All Around You

You learned in Chapter 4 that culture shapes human social behavior. In the absence of biological pre-programming, culture guides us in our thinking, feeling, and behaving. Without culture, humans would have no blueprint for social living. This chapter helps explain the relationship between culture and social structure.

So, what is social structure? The chapter opening described a situation in which unexpected classroom behavior resulted in confusion for a newcomer. We are usually spared such confusion when entering a new group because we bring some knowledge of how people will normally relate to one another. In our minds, we carry a "social map" for various group situations. We have mental images of the new group with its patterns of social relationships. This underlying pattern is called **social structure.**

Everyone Has Status

We are not born with mental maps of social structure; we must learn them from others. In the process, we learn about *statuses* and *roles*—major elements of social structure.

What do sociologists mean by status? People may refer to themselves as students, doctors, welders, secretaries, mothers, or sons. Each of these labels refers to a **status**—a position a person occupies within a social structure. Status helps us define who and what we are in relation to others within the same social structure. Some social statuses are acquired at birth. For example, a newborn female instantly becomes a child and a daughter. From then on, she assumes an increasingly larger number and variety of statuses.

Sociologists are interested in the relationships among social statuses. A sociologist investigating delinquency, for example, may focus on the status of social worker in relation to the statuses of the police officer, judge, and teacher. Figure 5.1 illustrates the status of a high

The two different status people in this photograph are behaving exactly as most people would expect.

Demonstration

Bring in a deck of playing cards without the jokers. Hand each student a card. As you pass out the cards, say, "This is the card that you have been dealt." Now write the following on the board: King, Queen, or Jack = privileged people; 10, 9, 8, or 7 = semi-privileged people; 6, 5, and 4 = not privileged people; 3, 2, and ace are the inferior people. Tell students that the cards they were dealt indicate their current status in the class. (Of course, you should reinforce throughout the activity that this is just a simulation.) This activity should help students understand ascribed status, status that was assigned to them. An achieved status is earned.
L1

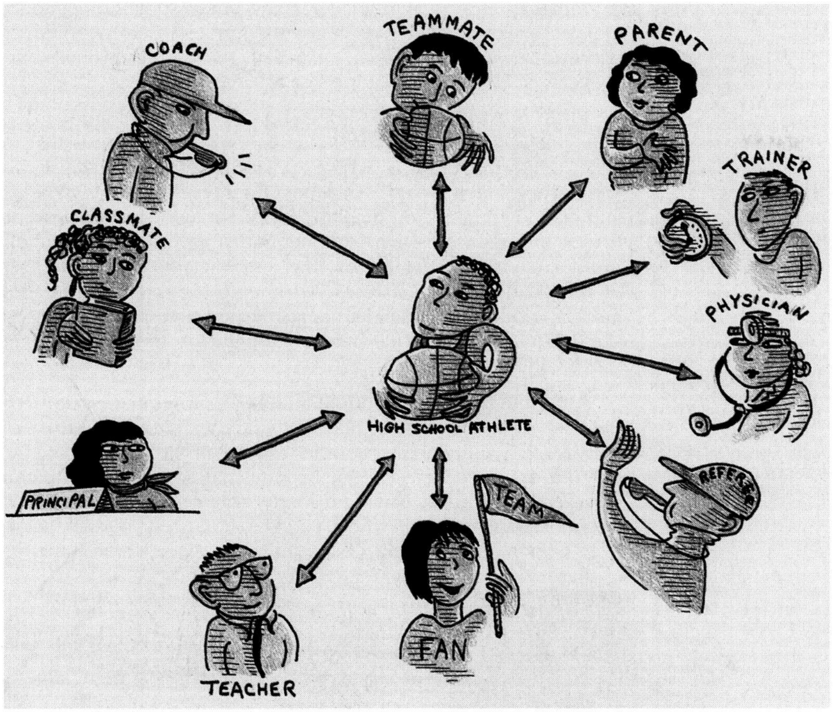

Figure 5.1 The Interrelationships of Social Statuses. *Social statuses do not exist in isolation. All statuses are interrelated with other statuses.*

school athlete related to various other statuses. There are two basic types of social statuses—*ascribed* and *achieved*.

What is an ascribed status? An **ascribed status** is neither earned nor chosen; it is assigned to us. At birth, an infant is either a male or a female. We do not choose our gender. Age is another example of an ascribed social status. In some societies, religion and social class are ascribed by the family of birth. If you were born into a lower-class home in India, for example, you would not be permitted to rise to a higher social class.

How is status achieved? An **achieved status** is earned or chosen. Achieving statuses is possible where people have some degree of control and choice. In most modern societies, for

Pictured above is an African Masai tribesman in tribal clothes. Do you think that his clothing reflects an ascribed or an achieved status?

ascribed status
a position that is neither earned nor chosen but assigned

achieved status
a position that is earned or chosen

Using the Illustration

Students might enjoy diagramming their own social status, similar to the illustration in the text, or, they may be more comfortable predicting a social status in their future. It might be the status of parent or it might be a career-oriented status. For example, a student might be working toward the career of television newscaster. What social statuses would he or she relate to in this career? Answers might include such statuses as fellow reporters, news writers, directors, producers, camera operators, sound people, people being interviewed, and so on. You might have students work in pairs or groups to develop this activity. They might even use drawings similar to those in the text to illustrate their web of relationships.

Integrating the Teacher Resources

Look for the Chapter 5 Learning Goals Outline, a reproducible student worksheet in the Unit 2 Mastering Basic Concepts booklet in your Teacher's Resources Box. It can be used to preview or review chapter content.

Role Play

To help students understand the distinction between status and role, the following activity is useful. Begin by asking for six volunteers. One student will represent status. That student should hold a sign that says "Student," an obvious status they can all relate to. Ask the class to brainstorm a list of expectations and responsibilities of being a student.

As they make suggestions, make a sign for the first five mentioned. Give the signs to the remaining volunteers. Now have the volunteers, one by one, take the sign given and act out the role they are playing. Roles will probably include such things as studying, hanging out, doing homework, etc. If the original volunteer, the "Student," is kept separate from the volunteers who took on roles, the class will see how a status and a role differ.

L1

Reteaching

In addition to the webs students created on roles and status (see the activity for Using Your Sociological Imagination), have them create a web called "status set." On this web they will include interactions they have with others. This web will center around the students' different statuses. For example, a musician interacts with other musicians, a sound person, the janitor, the bus driver who takes them to practice, etc. This musician may also be a mother who interacts with her child's teacher, babysitter, and pediatrician.

This intricate web should show students how social we are and how we take for granted the magnitude of our daily interactions based on various roles and status.

Please see the correlation to the American Sociology Association standards located in the front of this text.

example, an individual can decide to become a spouse or a parent. Occupations are also achieved statuses in modern societies where people have freedom to choose their work. Plumber, electrician, sales representative, nurse, executive, lawyer, and doctor are examples of achieved statuses.

status set
all of the statuses that a person occupies at any particular time

What is a status set? A person who is a social worker does not occupy only one status. This person holds various other statuses that may be totally unrelated to that of social worker. A **status set** is all of the statuses that a person occupies at any particular time. One social worker may be a wife, mother, author, and church choir director. Another may be a single parent, service club leader, and jazz musician. Another status set might be that of a student, a brother, a tennis player, a tutor, and a store clerk. Each of these statuses is part of another network of statuses. Assume, for example, that in addition to being a social worker, an individual is also a part-time jazz musician. In this status, she might interact with the statuses of nightclub owner, dancer, and fellow musician, among others.

master status
a position that strongly affects most other aspects of a person's life

Are all of a person's statuses equal? Among the statuses held by an individual, some are more important than others. **Master statuses** are important because they influence most other aspects of the person's life. Master statuses may be achieved or ascribed. In industrial societies, occupations—achieved statuses for the most part—are master statuses. Your occupation strongly influences such matters as where you live, how well you live, and how long you live. "Criminal" is an achieved master status, since it affects the rest of your life.

"I hunt and she gathers—otherwise, we couldn't make ends meet."

Expected behavior is often based on master statuses such as gender.

Paired Learning Activity

Have students work together in pairs to help each other develop a better understanding of the vocabulary terms for Section 1. (Terms include: social structure, status, ascribed status, achieved status, status set, and master status.) You'll need to give each pair of students twelve index cards. On six of the cards they will write the vocabulary terms, one per card. On the other six cards they will write the definitions for the terms, again, one per card. After the cards have been completed, they can be used in various ways. Students can use them in a matching game. Or they can divide the cards and hold them up one at a time for their partners to read. Each partner would then give the corresponding word or definition to go with the card.
L1

Explain why the status of a lawyer is a master status.

Age, gender, race, and ethnicity are examples of ascribed master statuses. These statuses are master statuses because they significantly affect the likelihood of achieving other social statuses. When will the United States have a female president? Would you let a nineteen-year-old or a ninety-year-old handle your case in court? Or remove your appendix?

Section 1 Assessment

1. Briefly define the term *social structure*.

Match the definition with the type of status (a–d) it best describes.

2. wife, mother, author, church choir director
3. electrician, spouse
4. the presidency of the United States, professional athlete
5. sex, gender, race
6. daughter, son
7. quarterback, coach, fan, trainer

a. ascribed status
b. achieved status
c. master status
d. status set

Critical Thinking

8. **Categorizing Information** On a separate piece of paper, make a diagram of your life—the statuses you possess and the responsibilities or role expectations for each. Examples of statuses include son/daughter, student, band member, etc.
9. **Applying Concepts** What is the most important master status you have held? Has the master status helped or hindered you? What master status would you like to achieve? Why?

SOCIOLOGY Online

Student Web Activity
Visit the *Sociology and You* Web site at soc.glencoe.com and click on **Chapter 5—Student Web Activities** for an activity on social status.

Our individual lives cannot generally be works of art unless the social order is also.

Charles Horton Cooley
American sociologist

Pulling it All Together

Social structure is the underlying pattern of social relationships. It is based on various roles and statuses. These roles and statuses can be multiple and form a complex web of human interaction.

Answers to Section 1 Assessment

1. Social structures are the underlying patterns of relationships in a group.
2. d
3. b
4. c
5. a
6. a
7. d

Critical Thinking

8. Answers will vary.
9. Answers will vary.

Interdisciplinary Activity

History To reinforce the concept of master status, have students generate a list of historical figures, or use the list provided below. Students should write the person's name and why they are known in history. Next, they should tell whether they think the reason the person is known in history is the person's master status and explain why they think this. For example, for Abraham Lincoln students would list him as the sixteenth president of the United States. They should say this was a master status because it influenced all other aspects of his life (including costing him his life). Here's a list of historical figures you might want to use: Benedict Arnold, Eric the Red, Genghis Khan, Henry the VIII, Galileo, Susan B. Anthony, Joan of Arc, Florence Nightingale, Anne Frank, Evita (Eva Peron). For an additional level, ask students to identify whether the status of the figure was achieved or ascribed.
L3

Focus on Research

Experiment: Adopting Statuses in a Simulated Prison

Social psychologist Philip Zimbardo and his colleagues designed an experiment to observe the behavior of people without criminal records in a mock "prison." They were amazed at the rapidity with which statuses were adopted and roles fulfilled by the college students playing "prisoners" and "guards." This experiment reveals the ease with which people can be socialized to statuses and roles. Zimbardo's own words describe the design and results of this experiment.

In an attempt to understand just what it means . . . to be a prisoner or a prison guard, Craig Haney, Curt Banks, Dave Jaffe and I created our own prison. We carefully screened over 70 volunteers who answered an ad in a Palo Alto city newspaper and ended up with about two dozen young men who were selected to be part of this study. They were mature, emotionally stable, normal, intelligent college students from middle-class homes. . . . They appeared to represent the cream of the crop of this generation. None had any criminal record. . . .

Students on the right in Zimbardo's mock prison experiment held very low statuses.

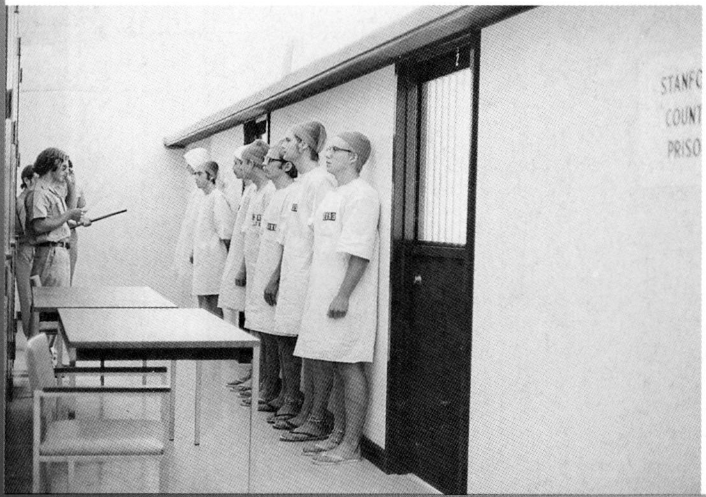

Half were arbitrarily designated as prisoners by a flip of a coin, the others as guards. These were the roles they were to play in our simulated prison. The guards . . . made up their own formal rules for maintaining law, order and respect, and were generally free to improvise new ones during their eight-hour, three-man shifts. The prisoners were unexpectedly picked up at their homes by a city policeman in a squad car, searched, handcuffed, fingerprinted, booked at the Palo Alto station house and taken

Focus on Research

This is one of the most famous and controversial studies ever conducted in the field of social science. Philip Zimbardo would not have passed an ethical review board today with his proposal to create a mock prison. The irony is that Zimbardo's study is a classic example of the power of the situation and how easily an individual can slip into a role and have it become real. (The video, *Quiet Rage: The Stanford Prison Experiment,* which documents the Zimbardo experiment, is available through Insight Media: 2162 Broadway, NYC, New York.)

Remind students that in the Another Time feature on page 120 they read how some prisoners in the German prisoner-of-war camp became resocialized and identified with the guards while they were still prisoners. Ask students to point out the similarities and differences between these two situations.

Integrating the Teacher Resources

A lesson plan for a student research project related to the content of this chapter can be found in Doing Sociology: Focus on Research, available in your Teacher's Resource Box.

Learning Styles

Visual Our understanding of total institutions is due largely to the work of sociologist Erving Goffman. Goffman applied for a job as a janitor at a mental institution, which enabled him to write *Asylums* (1961). It is still one of the most definitive works in understanding the complexity of the relationships between staff and patients/prisoners in institutions. Goffman observed that each group perceived the other based on narrow, hostile stereotypes. The staff saw themselves as superior while patients/prisoners felt weak, inferior, and guilty. A large degree of social distancing is maintained between staff and patients to reduce episodes of hostility. Arrange to show the video *Quiet Rage* (referenced above). You might want to share Goffman's observations with students. He wrote over thirty-nine years ago. Ask students whether they think these observations still seem true today.

blindfolded to our jail. There they were stripped, deloused, put into a uniform, given a number and put into a cell with two other prisoners where they expected to live for the next two weeks. . . .

At the end of only six days we had to close down our mock prison because what we saw was frightening. It was no longer apparent to most of the subjects (or to us) where reality ended and their roles began. The majority had indeed become prisoners or guards, no longer able to clearly differentiate between role playing and self. There were dramatic changes in virtually every aspect of their behavior, thinking and feeling. . . . We were horrified because we saw some boys (guards) treat others as if they were despicable animals, taking pleasure in cruelty, while other boys (prisoners) became servile, dehumanized robots who thought only of escape, of their own individual survival and of their mounting hatred for the guards. We had to release three prisoners in the first four days because they had such acute situational traumatic reactions as hysterical crying, confusion in thinking, and severe depression. Others begged to be paroled, and all but three were willing to forfeit all the money they had earned [$15 per day] if they could be paroled. By then (the fifth day) they had been so programmed to think of themselves as prisoners that when their request for parole was denied they returned docilely to their cells. . . .

About a third of the guards became tyrannical in their arbitrary use of power, in enjoying their control over other people. They were corrupted by the power of their roles and became quite inventive in their techniques of breaking the spirit of the prisoners and making them feel they were worthless. . . . By the end of the week the experiment had become a reality. . . .

Working with the Research

1. If you were asked to discuss Zimbardo's experiment in light of one of the three major theoretical perspectives, which would you choose? Why?
2. One of Zimbardo's conclusions, not stated in the above account, is that the brutal behavior found in real-life prisons is not due to the antisocial characteristics or personality defects of guards and prisoners. Can you argue, sociologically, that he is right in this conclusion? How?
3. There was some controversy over the ethics of this experiment. Do you think this experiment could be carried out today under the ASA Code of Ethics? Why or why not?

Answers to Working with the Research

1. Students might interpret the question several ways. Are we asking about the mock prison or the entire experiment? From a functionalist perspective, prisons are necessary because criminals threaten the order and stability of a functioning society. The conflict perspective would see the conflict as the power relationship and the guards' need to maintain that power. The interactionists would focus on the symbols; status symbols that are part of the relationships of guards to prisoners. The assigning of numbers to prisoners is part of the depersonalization.
2. Emphasize the power of the situation. Guards are given power by virtue of their position in the prison and prisoners are delegated to the opposite, powerless role. You could argue that it is the conflict of two opposing forces that creates the social reality of the prison. The situation creates the climate.
3. Answers will vary.

On-Demand Writing

After students have read the Focus on Research "Experiment: Adopting Statuses in a Simulated Prison," ask them to choose to be either a guard or a prisoner. They should try to imagine what the guards and prisoners in the experiment were feeling and then write several paragraphs about those feelings from the perspective of either a guard or prisoner. Students might want to explore why they feel the things they feel and how they will deal with those feelings. Ask if they can understand why the guards and prisoners in the experiment acted the way they did. Do they think they would have acted similarly?

L2

Using the Section Preview

Even if students are not familiar with the terms *role conflict* and *role strain,* they are probably very familiar with stress resulting from those pressures. Ask students to describe times when they have felt role conflict or role strain. Many times adults complain that they are stretched too thin trying to be a parent, teacher, spouse, etc.

If students have completed the web they created earlier in the chapter, have them analyze times when these roles and statuses have been strained or conflicted.

Section 2 Social Structure and Roles

Key Terms

- role
- rights
- obligations
- role performance
- social interaction
- role conflict
- role strain

Section Preview

People interact according to prescribed roles. These roles carry certain rights and obligations. Sometimes conflict or strain occurs when an individual has too many roles to play.

Rights and Obligations

An expected behavior associated with a particular status is a **role.** Any status carries with it a variety of roles. The roles of a modern doctor, for example, include keeping informed about new medical developments, scheduling office appointments, diagnosing illnesses, and prescribing treatments.

Roles can be thought of as statuses "in action." Whereas statuses describe positions, roles describe behaviors. These behaviors are based on the rights and obligations attached to various statuses. **Rights** are behaviors that individuals expect from others. **Obligations** are behaviors that individuals are expected to perform toward others. The rights of one status correspond to the obligations of another. Doctors, for example, are obligated to diagnose

role
an expected behavior associated with a particular status

right
a behavior that individuals can expect from others

obligation
a behavior that individuals are expected to perform toward others

"No, Hoskins, you're not going to do it just because I'm telling you to do it. You're going to do it because you believe in it."

Hoskins is being forced to follow roles whether he wants to or not. Are such cues ever sent your way?

Integrating the Teacher Resources

For Spanish-speaking students, you may wish to use the reproducible worksheets available in the Spanish Supplements booklet in your Teacher's Resource Box. In addition to providing Spanish translations of selected Mastering Basic Concepts worksheets, the booklet contains English and Spanish summaries of the chapter's key points.

Demonstration

Have students write a paragraph on the topic "My Most Embarrassing Moment." Tell them not to write down names of anyone that others might know. Have them change names, if possible. Students should not put their own names on the papers. Collect the papers, shuffle them, and hand them out to other students. Ask a few volunteers to read the paragraphs they have in front of them. As students read these aloud, ask the other students to consider some of these questions: What role performance occurred? Was the embarrassment caused by having to change roles without preparation? At the least, this activity should get them thinking about how we expect to perform a certain way in a particular role.
L1

their patients' illnesses. Correspondingly, patients have the right to expect their doctors to diagnose to the best of their ability. Teachers have an obligation to be prepared to teach the daily lesson. Students have a right to expect that teachers will be adequately prepared to explain the material. Correspondingly, teachers have a right to expect that students will make the attempt to learn. Students have the obligation to make that effort.

Recall that this chapter began with a quotation from Shakespeare's play *As You Like It.* In terms of a play, roles are the part of the script that tells the actors (status holders) what beliefs, feelings, and actions are expected of them. A playwright or screenwriter specifies the content of a performer's part. In the same way, culture underlies the parts played in real life. Mothers, for instance, have different maternal "scripts" in different cultures. Most American mothers emphasize independence more than most Iranian mothers.

> It is never too late to be what you might have been.
>
> George Eliot
> English author

Role Performance and Social Interaction

Statuses and roles provide the basis for group life. It is primarily when people interact with each other socially that they "perform" in the roles attached to their statuses.

Role performance is the actual conduct, or behavior, involved in carrying out (or performing) a role. Role performance can occur without an audience (as when a student studies alone for a test). Most role performance, though, involves social interaction.

role performance the actual behavior of an individual in a role

Social interaction is the process of influencing each other as people relate. For example, before two boys begin to fight, they have probably gone through a process of insulting and challenging each other. Fortunately, most social interaction is not as negative and violent, but the same process of influence and reaction to others is involved.

social interaction the process of influencing each other as people relate

Think again of the analogy of the play. If statuses are like the parts in a play and roles are like the script, then social interaction represents the way actors respond

These students each have particular roles and statuses within their group.

Working with the Quote

Tell students that George Eliot, author of *Middlemarch,* was the pseudonym of Marian Evans, an Englishwoman who lived from 1819 to 1880. She was one of a small group of women writers who broke with tradition during a time in Victorian England when women were extremely constrained in their lifestyles. She was friends with Herbert Spencer and was critical of many established institutions of the time.

After reading the quote with the class, have volunteers explain what they think the quote means. Ask students whether they believe the quote is true for themselves or other teenagers. Why or why not? Do they believe it is true for someone in their 30s, 40s, 50s, 60s, 70s? Is there ever a time when they believe the quote would not be true? When would that time be? How does this quote relate to one's roles in life?

Learning Styles

Linguistic/Spatial To help clarify the definitions of the key terms, especially in Sections 1 and 2, you may want to give students the opportunity to visualize the definitions of the following terms: *status, ascribed status, achieved status, status set, master status, role, rights, obligations, role performance, social interaction, role conflict,* and *role strain.* Discuss definitions, then ask students to work in pairs to create a visual or graphic representation of the terms. They should focus on the relationship between the words and provide personal, real-life examples that will help to differentiate between the words. Example: Students may draw a flowchart with connecting branches to link their status as a son or daughter with their role of taking out the trash each week. Then they would include other links to depict other terms applicable in their lives.
L2

Working with the Data

Figure 5.2 As you discuss this figure with students, you might want to have them take turns giving concrete examples of each concept from culture to social structure. You might get them started with their thinking by giving an example of your own.

Reteaching

To reinforce how much real life can be like a scripted scene, ask students how many times they have been in an emotional situation and left it feeling they did not "come off" as well as they would have liked. The natural inclination is to replay the scene over again, this time reading your "lines" the way you meant to the first time. They will also realize, however, that in real life, you don't get "second takes."

Using the Illustration

The answers to the question posed will vary but should involve some specific ways in which community culture affects teacher-student role behavior. For example, bilingual education is more likely to occur in schools in heavily ethnic communities.

to cues given by other actors. Role performance is the performance itself.

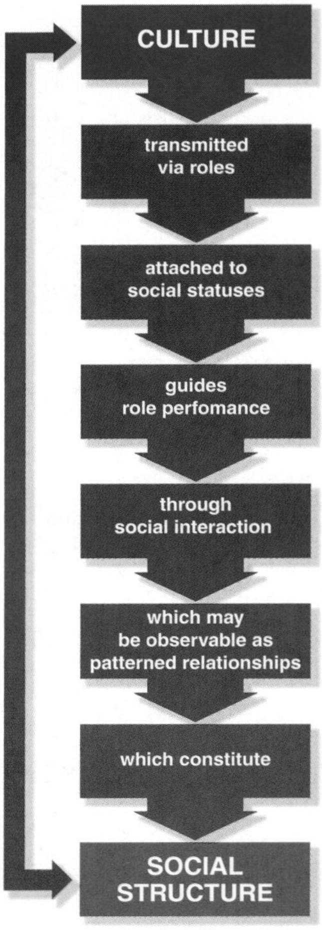

Figure 5.2 The Links Between Culture and Social Structure. *Sociologists concentrate on the study of social structure. They have developed a set of concepts and an understanding of their relationships in order to examine the basic nature of social structure.*

How does play-acting differ from social interactions? The play analogy is a valid one, but it is dangerous to take it too far. For one thing, "delivery of the lines" in real life is not the conscious process used by actors. Unlike stage performances, most real-life role performance occurs without planning.

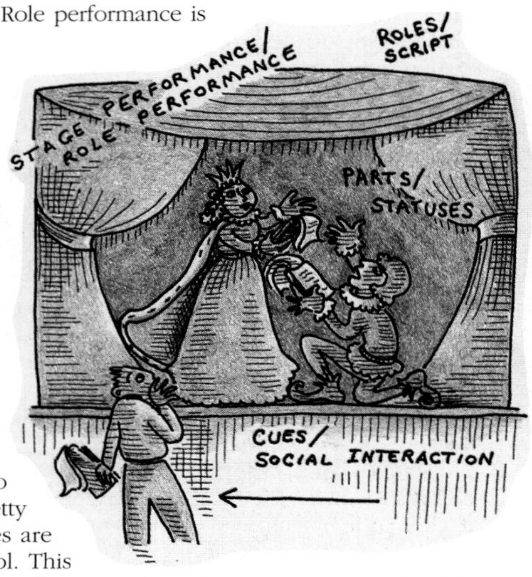

This illustration draws an analogy between rehearsed behavior on the stage and real social behavior. How do community cultural standards affect the role behavior of students and teachers?

Second, although actors may sometimes ad-lib, change lines to suit themselves, and so forth, overall they stick pretty closely to the script. Departures are fairly easy to detect and control. This is not the case with differences between a role and a role performance.

Third, on the stage, there is a programmed and predictable relationship between cues and responses. One performer's line is a cue for a specific response from another actor. In life, we can choose our own cues and responses. A student may decide to tell a teacher that her tests are the worst he has ever encountered. On hearing this, the teacher may tell the student that it is not his place to judge, or the teacher may ask for further explanation so that improvement may be made. In effect, the teacher can choose from several roles to play at that time. Likewise, the student can choose from a variety of responses to the teacher's behavior. If the teacher tells the student he is out of line, the student may report the matter to a counselor, or he may decide to forget it altogether. The process of choosing the role and then acting it out occurs in nearly all instances of social interaction.

Keep in mind, however, that the range of responses is not limitless. Only certain responses are culturally acceptable. It is not an appropriate response for the teacher to bodily eject the student from her classroom, and the student would be very foolish to pound the teacher's desk in protest.

Figure 5.2 outlines the connection between culture and social structure. As you can see at the top of the figure, the first link between culture and social structure is the concept of role (behavior associated with a status). Roles are in turn attached to statuses (a position a person occupies within a group). Yet people do not always follow roles exactly. The manner in which roles are actually carried out is role performance, the third link in the conceptual chain. Role performance occurs through social interaction. This is the fourth link between culture and social structure. Social interaction based on roles is observable as patterned relationships, which make up social structure. In turn, existing social structure affects the creation of and changes in culture.

Careers in Sociology

Sociological practice is a broad category of career activities involving "applied" or "clinical" sociology. Applied sociology is knowledge directed to understanding immediate problems and their solutions. Clinical sociology extends into involvement in the world by intervening in social settings. Sociologists may carry out interventions at the individual, group, organizational, community and/or societal levels. They are experts in counseling, evaluation, facilitation, and mediation and techniques of conflict resolution (between couples, ethnic groups, communities, even nation-states). These approaches all help citizens, groups, organizations, or governments to identify problems and their deeper causes and to suggest possible strategies for solutions. Students can get additional information about careers in sociology from the American Sociological Association at **http://www.asanet.org**

Snapshot of America

Guns in School

Bringing firearms to school is a major violation of the student role. Teachers have a right to expect students to come to school unarmed. Students are obligated not to bring weapons to school. This map gives us some idea of the relative extent to which this role is being violated and punished in various states. In total, 3,523 students were expelled during the 1998–99 school year for carrying guns to school. The good news—this number represents a substantial drop over the two previous survey years.

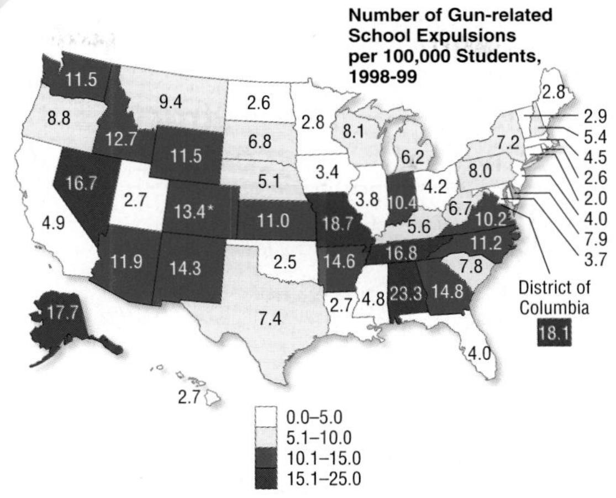

Source: U.S. Dept. of Education, 2000.

*Includes all weapons, not just firearms.

Interpreting the Map

1. Which states reported the most expulsions per 100,000 students in the 1998–1999 school year? (Which states fall in the over 15.0 range?)
2. Explain why violation of a law can also be a role violation.

Online UPDATE
Visit soc.glencoe.com and click on **Textbook Updates–Chapter 5** for an update of the data.

Source: U.S. Dept. of Education

Role Conflict and Role Strain

The existence of statuses and roles permits social life to be predictable and orderly. At the same time, each status involves many roles, and each individual holds many statuses. This diversity invites conflict and strain.

What are role conflict and role strain? **Role conflict** exists when the performance of a role in one status clashes with the performance of a role in another. Many teenagers, for example, hold the statuses of student and employee. Those who do often find it difficult to balance study and work demands.

role conflict
condition in which the performance of a role in one status interferes with the performance of a role in another status

Snapshot of America

The state of Colorado reported no gun-related expulsions for the 1997-1998 school year. You might remind students of the Columbine High School incident in Littleton, Colorado, which occurred during the 1998-1999 school year. Do students see quite a jump from no gun-related expulsions to a mass murder in one school year? To what would they attribute this jump?

Answers to Interpreting the Map

1. South Dakota and Oregon reported expulsions over 20.1.
2. Using the example given, bringing firearms to school violates the student role because a teacher has the right to expect students to be unarmed; students are expected not to bring weapons to school.

Role Play

Give students the following scenario: Mr. Jones is a member of a high school board and his daughter is a sophomore at the same high school. The board recently considered a proposal to drastically cut spending in the art department. Mr. Jones' daughter is an aspiring artist with dreams of opening her own studio someday. Mr. Jones' vote could be crucial. What should Mr. Jones do? Should he hope to work out a compromise, avoid the issue, say this is a conflict of interest? Have students relate any examples of role conflict in their own lives, or have them create their own scenarios. Allow students time to make their scenarios into role plays and to perform the role plays for classmates.
L1

Working with the Data

Figure 5.3 Ask students to explain roles, ascribed master status, and social interaction from the three theoretical perspectives. For example, explanations for *role* include: the functionalist perspective, which states that social integration is promoted by culturally defined rights and obligations honored by group members; the conflict perspective, in which roles are sometimes used to empower some and subjugate others; and the interactionist perspective that sees role as based on the symbolic meanings of these roles. Have students repeat the process with the terms *ascribed master status* and *social interaction.*

Points to Stress

Role strain can appear to be hypocritical at times. Take, for example, the star athlete who is a role model, but is repeatedly busted for drug use. Students might want to explore various issues of role strain. Should a priest maintain the confidentiality of someone who just confessed to a crime? Are these roles in conflict, or are they necessary parts of the role and status of the person?

Figure 5.3 Focus on Theoretical Perspectives

Illustrating Social Structure Concepts. This table illustrates how each theoretical perspective might approach the study of social structures. The concepts could be switched to any other theoretical perspective and illustrated from that perspective. Associate each concept with a different theoretical perspective and provide your own example.

Theoretical Perspective	Social Structure Concept	Example
Functionalism	Role	Social integration is promoted by culturally defined rights and obligations honored by group members.
Conflict Theory	Ascribed Master Status	Ascribed master statuses such as gender and race empower some to subjugate others.
Symbolic Interactionism	Social Interaction	Roles are carried out by individuals on the basis of the symbols and meanings they share.

role strain
condition in which the roles of a single status are inconsistent or conflicting

Role strain occurs when a person has trouble meeting the many roles connected with a single status. College basketball coaches, for example, have to recruit for next year's season while trying to win games in the current season. Besides preparing daily lessons, high school teachers often are required to sponsor social clubs. Each of these roles (coach and recruiter or teacher and advisor) is time consuming, and the fulfillment of one role may interfere with the performance of the others. If your expectations as a high school student require you to perform well academically, join a social organization, pursue a sport, date, and participate in other school activities, you will probably experience some degree of role strain as a result of these expectations.

How do we manage role conflict and strain? Role conflict and strain may lead to discomfort and confusion. To feel better and to have smoother relationships with others, we often solve role dilemmas by setting priorities. When roles clash, we decide which role is most important to us and act accordingly. For example, a student who frequently misses school-related activities because of work demands will have to assess her priorities. She can eliminate the role conflict completely by quitting work and putting a priority on school activities. If she remains in both statuses, she can reduce work hours or cut down on extracurricular school activities.

We also segregate roles. That is, we separate our behavior in one role from our behavior in another. This is especially effective for reducing the negative

Survey

Have students develop a survey for their fellow students to determine how many feel they are suffering from role strain. The survey could contain only one question, depending on what kinds of information students decide they want to gather. If they only want to know about fellow students feeling role strain, they could ask students to rate their day from 1–5, with 1 being "I have too much time on my hands, I'm bored" and 5 being "I never have enough time to do everything I need/want to do in a day." After analyzing the results, students might want to publish their findings in the school newspaper.
L1

effects of conflicting roles. A college coach experiencing the role strain associated with coaching and recruiting simultaneously can decide to give priority to one over the other. He may, for example, let his assistant coach do most of the recruiting until the season ends. Ranking incompatible roles in terms of their importance is a good way to reduce role conflict and strain. An organized crime member may reduce role conflict by segregating his criminal activities from his role as a loving father.

Because of role conflict and role strain, meeting the goals and expectations of all our roles is impossible. This poses no problem as long as role performance occurs within accepted limits. Professors at research-oriented universities may be permitted to emphasize teaching over research. Coaches may accent fair play, character building, and scholarship rather than a winning record. Professors at research universities who do too little publishing or coaches who win too few games, however, usually will not be rewarded for very long. At some point they will be judged as failing to meet expected role performance. (For more on handling role conflict, see Sociology Today on the next page.)

Do you think this young man is suffering from role conflict or role strain?

Section 2 Assessment

Match each situation below with the key term (a–e) it illustrates.

1. A husband and wife discuss the disciplining of one of their children.
2. A mother is expected to take care of her children.
3. A businessman has no time for his children.
4. A school principal hands out diplomas at a graduation ceremony.
5. A corporate chief executive officer is economically forced to terminate employees who are his friends.

a. role
b. role conflict
c. role performance
d. role strain
e. social interaction

6. Which of the following is *not* one of the differences between a play and social life?
   a. There is considerably more difference between roles and role performance in social life than between a script and a stage performance.
   b. Unlike the stage, there are no cues and responses in real life.
   c. Role performance in real life is not the conscious process that actors go through on the stage.
   d. In social life, the cues and responses are not as programmed and predictable as on the stage.

Critical Thinking

7. **Applying Concepts** Are you presently experiencing role conflict or role strain? If you are, analyze the source. If not, explain why at this time you are free from role conflict and role strain, making clear the meaning of the concepts.

Pulling it All Together

This section examined social structure related to roles. These roles can sometimes be strained or in conflict, and sometimes there is a need to segregate these roles.

Answers to Section 2 Assessment

1. e
2. a
3. d
4. c
5. b
6. b

Critical Thinking

7. Answers will vary.

Integrating the Teacher Resources

To reinforce key concepts, use the Chapter 5 Graphic Organizer, a reproducible student worksheet available in the Unit 2 Mastering Basic Concepts booklet in your Teacher's Resource Box.

Cooperative Learning Activity

Give students the following scenario (or a similar scenario) and have them work together in groups to develop resolutions to the conflict.

Dave is the manager of a team of computer engineers. Dave's good friend Ted is assigned to Dave's team. Dave has to play the roles of both supervisor and friend. Ted has to play the roles of both employee and friend. Each role contains a variety of expectations. As a friend, Dave is expected to support Ted (and vice versa) when difficulties arise. But as a supervisor Dave is expected to treat employees without partiality. What is Dave to do if Ted messes up on the job? How is Ted to react if Dave has to discipline him? What other potential problems do students see in this relationship? How would they handle them?

This activity could also be used to spark a lively classroom debate.

L1

Sociology Today: Reducing Conflict in Two-Career Families

Families with two working adults have special strains. While in 1960, less than 20 percent of married women with young children worked outside of the home, by 2000, the figure was about 65 percent (U.S. Bureau of the Census). This increase has resulted in added role conflict for women. In a two-career family, the woman is more likely to suffer from conflict because she is still generally expected to balance her traditional homemaker roles with her career roles. The women are not the only ones who suffer, however. The effects of this conflict are felt by husbands and children, as well. Since you will likely be faced with the stress associated with dual-career families, you would be wise to learn now some techniques for reducing role conflict.

1. Focus on the Positive

Conflict can be reduced when couples define their situation positively. If both partners are working from choice rather than necessity, it can be helpful to remember some of the reasons why they first made the choice for both to work. These reasons might include additional income or personal satisfaction.

2. Put Family Needs First

Role conflict can be most effectively managed when family roles are placed ahead of working roles. When a baby-sitter fails to show up, when a child is sick, or when a parent-teacher conference is called, one of the parents can place these demands above work-related demands. Placing a higher priority on family needs will help keep the family support structure intact.

3. Assume One Role at a Time

Conflict can be reduced if a person focuses on only one role at a time. Leaving job-related problems at work and family issues at home is often difficult but is very effective in reducing role conflict.

4. Find the Compromise Balance

Although many men take active roles in child care today in order to meet family obligations, women still make the most compromises in their careers. With the increasing number of women in better-paying professional careers, we should expect more equality in career compromises between husbands and wives.

Doing Sociology

Identify three ways that you believe would help reduce role conflict in dual-career families. Provide specific examples not given in the text.

Sociology Today

Here is a great example of role conflict and strain. After reading the feature, you might want to open this up to a debate to see if students would really want to implement these ideas in their own homes. There will probably be a lot of negativity about this, but some students might see the benefit in it. The practical goal of sociology has always been to bring about positive social change.

Answer to Doing Sociology

Answers will obviously vary, but students might say that they could help relieve some of the transportation duties by giving rides to younger siblings. They might help pick up someone or car pool with friends. They might also suggest helping with some of the chores. Family meetings can help reduce strain and conflict because they help everyone know that they have the same goals.

Integrating the Teacher Resources

For review or enrichment, use the Student Journal Prompts for this chapter available in the Unit 2 Mastering Basic Concepts booklet in your Teacher's Resource Box.

On-Demand Writing

Encourage students to think about their family's current work arrangements and compare them to the ideal family lifestyle they dream of. Have them write about personal goals for having their own families and careers, and how they plan to balance them, using ideas offered in the Sociology Today feature on this page or ideas of their own. Ask for volunteers to read their papers aloud. It is a good idea to limit, or better yet, prohibit, comments from class members—these are personal goals. Close with a class discussion that emphasizes the work and sacrifice involved in balancing family and career.
L1

Section 3

Preindustrial Societies

Key Terms

- society
- hunting and gathering society
- horticultural society
- pastoral societies
- agricultural society

Through mostly grunts and exaggerated gestures, two fishermen/gatherers attempt to communicate.

Even the earliest societies had patterned and predictable social relationships.

Types of Society

The culture and social structure of a society are greatly affected by the way the society provides for basic needs. A **society,** as you may remember from Chapter 3, is composed of people living within defined territorial borders who share a common culture. Societies meet their members' basic needs, such as the needs for food and shelter, in diffferent ways. These differences form the basis of a system anthropologists often use to classify societies. In this system, societies are classified as preindustrial, industrial, or postindustrial. We will look at preindustrial societies in this section and examine industrial and postindustrial societies in the following sections.

In theory, a society is independent of outsiders. It contains enough smaller social structures—family, economy, and so forth—to meet the needs of its members. As you will see, preindustrial societies actually could be independent and self-sufficient. Modern societies, although capable of caring for most members' needs, must have political, military, economic, cultural, and technological ties with other societies. In fact, modern societies are rapidly moving toward the creation of a global society.

In the next few pages, several basic types of societies will be distinguished. Each type of society is unique in important ways. All societies, however, are comprised of social structures. Members in each type of society know what is expected of them and what they can expect from others. Members of a particular type of society engage in the same basic social patterns time after time because they share patterned and predictable social relationships that are passed from generation to generation.

Section Preview

The way a society provides for basic needs greatly affects its culture and social structure. Preindustrial, industrial, and postindustrial societies meet basic needs in different ways. Preindustrial societies include hunting and gathering, horticultural, pastoral, and agricultural societies.

society
people living within defined territorial borders and sharing a common culture

Using the Section Preview

For some students this will appear to be dry material, but if you can find a video that shows life in a hunting and gathering society, it can highlight the patterned social relationships, the organic solidarity, and modernization. A classic video is *Nari: The Story of a Kung Woman,* a John Marshall film, available through PBS. This ninety-minute video poignantly shows how modernization destroyed hunting and gathering societies with laws that made hunting illegal. It is a great example of the clash of cultures. *Dances with Wolves,* which is available at any video store, is another such video.

Integrating the Teacher Resources

Look for the Chapter 5 Vocabulary Activity in the Unit 2 Mastering Basic Concepts booklet in your Teacher's Resource Box. It provides reinforcement for vocabulary in this chapter.

Demonstration

Anthropologists predict that in the next fifty years all hunting and gathering societies will cease to exist. Over 90 percent of all human existence has based its survival on this way of living. To have students grasp the magnitude of this, ask them to work in pairs or groups over the weekend to visit a wooded area or area that has lots of foragers (squirrels, birds, etc.). Ask the students to look for items that might be edible, medicinal, or for use as a weapon. (Remind them never to eat vegetation or food that is unknown to them, especially fungi or molds, or to use the "weapons" they have found to threaten or harm another.) They should bring back to class what they found, ready to describe how they would use what they found to survive. **L1**

Making Connections to Other Cultures

Option 1: If you have teams of students who are responsible for particular cultures as suggested in the Connections to Other Cultures feature on page 48 in Chapter 2, have the teams research and explain the social structure in the cultures they have been assigned.

Option 2: Assign groups of students to the specific types of societies: hunting and gathering, horticultural, pastoral, agricultural, and industrial. Have groups use a "hub and spokes" type of graphic organizer to create a visual display of what they believe would be the component qualities that might measure status in their assigned society. Have the groups explain their choices.

Option 3: The criteria used in this book to examine social structure is economic in its primary focus. Brainstorm with students non-economic criteria that might influence social structure, status, and roles. Discuss the results of their efforts in light of their understanding of the social structure of the United States.
L2

Hunting and Gathering Societies

hunting and gathering society a society that survives by hunting animals and gathering edible plants

The **hunting and gathering society** survives by hunting animals and gathering edible foods such as wild fruits and vegetables. This is the oldest solution to the problem of providing for the basic need for food, or subsistence. In fact, it was only about nine thousand years ago that other methods of solving the subsistence problem emerged.

Hunting and gathering societies are usually nomadic—they move from place to place as the food supply and seasons change. Because nomads must carry all their possessions with them, they have few material goods. Hunting and gathering societies also tend to be very small—usually fewer than fifty people—with members scattered over a wide area. Because the family is the only institution in hunting and gathering societies, it tends to all the needs of its members. Most members are related by blood or marriage, although marriage is usually limited to those outside the family or band.

Judging from this photograph, to what type of society do these Navajo women belong?

Economic relationships within hunting and gathering societies are based on cooperation—members share what they have with other members. Members of hunting and gathering societies seem simply to give things to one another without worrying about how "payment" will be made. In fact, the more scarce something is, the more freely it is shared. Generosity and hospitality are valued. Thrift is considered a reflection of selfishness. Because the obligation to share goods is one of the most binding aspects of their culture, members of hunting and gathering societies have little or no conception of private property or ownership.

Without a sense of private ownership and with few possessions for anyone to own, hunting and gathering societies have no social classes, no rich or poor. These societies lack status differences based on political authority because they have no political institutions; there is no one to organize and control activities. When the traditional Inuit in Canada and Alaska, for example, want to settle disputes, they use dueling songs. The people involved in the dispute prepare and sing songs to express their sides of the issue. Their families, as choruses, accompany them. Those listening to the duel applaud their choice for the victor (Hoebel, 1983).

Interdisciplinary Activity

Film Arts You might want to show the video *Dances with Wolves* as an example of a hunting and gathering society, and bring in a history teacher to help students relate the sociological to the historical. Since most students will have had a history class, they might be able to relate historical facts themselves.

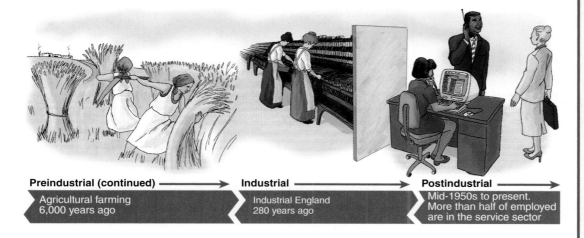

Preindustrial (continued) → Agricultural farming 6,000 years ago

Industrial → Industrial England 280 years ago

Postindustrial → Mid-1950s to present. More than half of employed are in the service sector

The division of labor in hunting and gathering societies is limited to the sex and age distinctions found in most families, since the family is the only institution. Men and women are assigned separate tasks, and certain tasks are given to the old, the young, and young adults. There is more leisure time in hunting and gathering societies than in any other. Today, few true hunting and gathering societies remain other than the Khoi-San (Bushmen) in Southern Africa, the Kaska Indians in Canada, and the Yanomamö of Brazil. (See Another Place on page 158.)

Horticultural Societies

A **horticultural society** solves the subsistence problem primarily through the growing of plants. This type of society came into being about ten to twelve thousand years ago, when people learned they could grow and harvest certain plants instead of simply gathering them. The gradual change from hunting and gathering to horticultural societies occurred over several centuries (Nolan and Lenski, 1999).

horticultural society
a society that survives primarily through the growing of plants

The shift from hunting and gathering to horticulture, or gardening, led to more permanent settlements. People no longer needed to move frequently to find food. Even without plows and animals to pull them, they could work a piece of land for extended periods of time before moving on to more fertile soil. This relative stability permitted the growth of multicommunity societies averaging one thousand to two thousand people each.

The family is even more basic to social life in horticultural societies than in hunting and gathering societies. In hunting and gathering societies, the survival of the group usually has top priority. In horticultural societies, primary emphasis is on providing for household members. This is because producing food in horticultural societies can be handled through the labor of family members. With the labor necessary for survival, households depend more on themselves and less on others outside the family unit for their subsistence.

Net Worthy

To enhance your students' study of this chapter, you may want to have them visit the URL cited below. As with all web sites, you should check this out first to be sure the information found there is appropriate for your students.

http//www.cs.ius.indiana.edu/AK/GSLOSS/WEB_DOCS/tth&g.HTM. This site lists several hunting and gathering societies where students can learn about the social institutions that made up those societies. They can also link to more information on types of societies, modern and prehistorical.

Using the Illustration

Remind students that this time line is a visual aid to help them remember the linear progression and development of societies. While it is chronological, the dates are not exact because even the experts disagree. Also, social science is not an exact science, as students should be understanding by now. The transition between these different types of societies often takes place very gradually, and a society may well show characteristics of more than one type.

Learning Styles

Artistic Some of your students may have artistic talents and would be interested in doing some research (see Net Worthy on this page). From this data they could create wall murals that would illustrate these major types of societies. Suggest that students look closely at social relationships, as well as agricultural and economic functions of the society.
L3

Teaching Strategy

One teacher in an urban community makes an annual field trip to a small farming community (through the connections and help of a local teacher). It is quite an experience for her students to be shown the inner workings of a tractor or combine. Later in the semester, the favor is returned and the teacher and students from the farming community visit the urban area. This experience helps students understand how a way of life shapes the community. Consider locating a willing sociology teacher near you so you can arrange a similar activity.

Pulling It All Together

In this section students are shown how the nature of societies has changed or remained the same over time. Almost all preindustrial societies will die out in the next century as modernization takes over. For some closure to this section, you might ask students to write an essay on what they believe life will be like for high school students in the U.S. in 100 years.

Pastoral Societies

pastoral society
a society in which food is obtained primarily by raising and taking care of animals

Most horticultural societies keep domesticated animals such as pigs and chickens. They do not, however, depend economically on the products of these animals the way *pastoralists*, or herders, do. In **pastoral societies,** food is obtained primarily by raising and taking care of animals. For the most part, these are herd animals such as cattle, camels, goats, and sheep, all of which provide both milk and meat. Since grains are needed to feed the animals, pastoralists must also either farm or trade with people who do (Nanda and Warms, 1998; Peoples and Bailey, 2000).

There is more migration in pastoral societies than in those based more fully on cultivation of land. However, permanent (or at least long-term) villages can be maintained if, as seasons change, herd animals are simply moved to different pastures within a given area. In such societies, the women remain at home while the men take the herds to different pastures. With men being responsible for providing food, the status of women in pastoral societies is low. These societies are male dominated.

Because both horticultural and pastoral societies can produce a surplus of food, they usher in important social changes unknown in hunting and gathering societies. With a surplus food supply, some members of the community are free to create a more complex division of labor. People can become political and religious leaders or make goods such as pottery, spears, and clothing. Because nonedible goods are produced, an incentive to trade with other peoples emerges.

The creation of a surplus also permits the development of social inequality (class or caste), although it is limited. Even a relatively small surplus, however, means that some families, villages, or clans have more wealth than others.

agricultural society
a society that uses plows and draft animals in growing food

This Bali farmer lives in an agricultural society. How does his society differ technologically from a horticultural society?

Agricultural Societies

An **agricultural society,** like a horticultural society, subsists by growing food. The difference is that agricultural societies use plows and animals. In fact, the transition from horticultural to agricultural society was made possible largely through the invention of the plow (Nolan and Lenski, 1999).

The plow not only allows the farmer to control weeds but also turns the weeds into fertilizer by burying them under the soil. By digging more deeply into the ground than was possible with sticks, hoes, and spades, the plow is able to reach nutrient-rich dirt that had sunk below root level. The result is more productivity—more food per unit of land.

Paired Learning Activity

For this activity, students should work together in pairs to develop a chart that compares and contrasts hunting and gathering societies, horticultural societies, pastoral societies, and agricultural societies. They should list the types of societies down the left-hand side of the chart. Across the top of the chart they should have the following heads (other heads can be added, of course): use of tools, importance of animals, leisure time, government, living conditions. After pairs of students have completed their charts, you might want to develop a class chart, which consolidates all of the different information pairs have listed.
L2

This medieval manuscript shows a noble instructing villeins on crop harvesting. Why would this type of superior-subordinate behavior first appear in an agricultural society?

Using animals also increases productivity, because larger areas can be cultivated with fewer people. As a result, more people are free to engage in noneconomic activities such as formal education, concerts, and political rallies. Cities can be built, and occupations appear that are not directly tied to farming, such as politician, blacksmith, and hat maker. New political, economic, and religious institutions emerge. Although family ties remain important, government replaces the family group as the guiding force for agricultural societies.

In the past, agricultural societies were headed by a king or an emperor. Distinct social classes appeared for the first time. Wealth and power were based on land ownership, which was controlled by the governing upper class. These elites enjoyed the benefits of the work done by the peasants. Urban merchants were better off than peasants, but they, too, worked hard for their livings. An economy based on trade began to emerge as an identifiable institution during this time. Monetary systems, which use money rather than goods for payment, began to be used as well. Increasingly, religion and government became separate as institutions. Rulers were believed to be divinely chosen, but few of them were also religious leaders.

Section 3 Assessment

1. Briefly restate the chief traits of each type of society: hunting and gathering, horticultural, pastoral, and agricultural.
2. In which type of society did a marked class system first appear? Explain why.

Critical Thinking

3. **Synthesizing Information** Using information from this section, develop a theory that would explain why conflict increases as society becomes more complex.

> Money is the most egalitarian force in society. It confers power on whoever holds it.
>
> **Roger Starr**
> **American economist**

On-Demand Writing

After students have carefully read the section on Agricultural Societies, review the quote on this page together. Be sure students understand the meaning of the words *egalitarian* (believing that all people are equal with respect to economic, social, and political rights) and *confers* (bestows or gives). Have students write a page-long essay in which they discuss the changes that occurred in agricultural societies with regard to economic, social, and political rights and privileges. They should discuss the message in the quote as part of their essays. You might want to have a class discussion before the writing assignment so students have some ideas to work with. Or, you might want to have a discussion after students have had a chance to put their thoughts down on paper.

L3

Answers to Section 3 Assessment

1. *Hunting and gathering society:* Nomadic—hunts and gathers food, moving from place to place with seasons; few material goods; societies are small; families are the only institution; economic relationships based on cooperation and sharing; little or no private ownership. *Horticultural society:* Grows plants; more permanent settlements; family is basic to social life; frequently fight. *Pastoral society:* depends economically on the products of domestic animals; more migration than in societies based on cultivation of land; women tend the home and men tend the pasturing of animals; *Agricultural society:* Increased food productivity frees more people for noneconomic activities and the building of cities; appearance of occupations not directly tied to farming; emergence of new political, economic, and religious institutions; government replacing family group as guiding force; distinct social classes, emergence of trade economy.
2. Distinct social stratification first appeared in agricultural societies because the governing class was able to control the source of wealth (land) and accumulate wealth in the form of money.

Critical Thinking

3. Answers will vary.

Another Place

To help students better understand the ritualistic behavior that characterizes social structure, have them describe the events leading up to a sporting event: the pre-game hype, the timed ritual that the team engages in while warming up, as well as the role that cheerleaders and fans exhibit. Have students watch a game or recall the last game they participated in or observed. Students should then record their observations. Ask the following questions: Why do these patterns of social relationships and social structure exist? What would happen if the team just walked on the field or court and started playing?

Answer to Thinking It Over

Sporting events, a classroom setting, and going to church or a movie all have specific patterns of behavior.

Another Place: The Chest-Pounding Duel

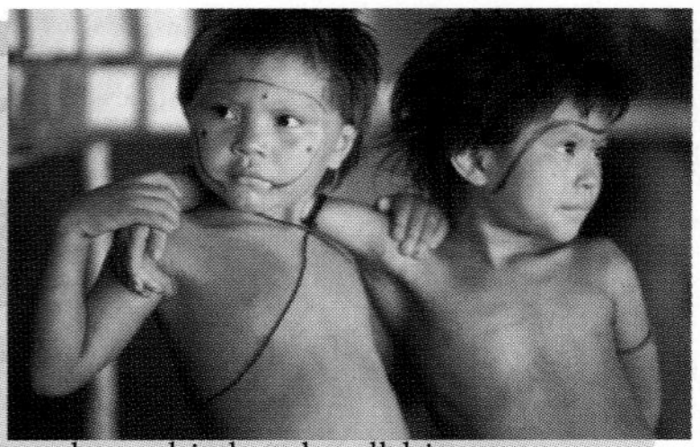

A description of the "chest-pounding" ritual that takes place among the Yanomamö tribe in Southern Venezuela was recorded by anthropologist Napoleon Chagnon. It provides a good example of social structure in a preindustrial society. All of the participants in this activity—even those merely observing—know exactly what is expected of them and what to expect of the others. This is what sociologists mean by *social structure*.

. . . There were about sixty adult men on each side in the fight divided into two arenas, each comprised of hosts and guests. Two men, one from each side, would step into the center of the milling, belligerent crowd of weapon-wielding partisans, urged on by their comrades. One would step up, spread his legs apart, bare his chest, and hold his arms behind his back, daring the other to hit him. The opponent would size him up, adjust the man's chest or arms so as to give himself the greatest advantage when he struck and then step back to deliver his close-fisted blow. The striker would painstakingly adjust his own distance from his victim by measuring his arm length to the man's chest, taking several dry runs before delivering his blow. He would then wind up like a baseball pitcher, but keeping both feet on the ground, and deliver a tremendous wallop with his fist to the man's left pectoral muscle, putting all of his weight into the blow. The victim's knees would often buckle and he would stagger around a few moments, shaking his head to clear the stars, but remain silent. The blow invariably raised a "frog" on the recipient's pectoral muscle where the striker's knuckles bit into his flesh. After each blow, the comrades of the deliverer would cheer and bounce up and down from the knees, waving and clacking their weapons over their heads. The victim's supporters, meanwhile, would urge their champion on frantically, insisting that he take another blow. If the delivery were made with sufficient force to knock the recipient to the ground, the man who delivered it would throw his arms above his head, roll his eyes back, and prance victoriously in a circle around his victim, growling and screaming, his feet almost a blur from his excited dance. The recipient would stand poised and take as many as four blows before demanding to hit his adversary. He would be permitted to strike his opponent as many times as the latter struck him, provided that the opponent could take it. If not, he would be forced to retire, much to the dismay of his comrades and the delirious joy of their opponents. No fighter could retire after delivering a blow. If he attempted to do so, his adversary would plunge into the crowd and roughly haul him back out, sometimes being aided by the man's own supporters. Only after having received his just dues could he retire. If he had delivered three blows, he had to receive three or else be proven a poor fighter. He could retire with less than three only if he were injured. Then, one of his comrades would replace him and demand to hit the victorious opponent. The injured man's two remaining blows would be canceled and the man who delivered the victorious blow would have to receive more blows than he delivered. Thus, good fighters are at a disadvantage, since they receive disproportionately more punishment than they deliver. Their only reward is . . . [prestige]: they earn the reputation of being fierce.

Source: Excerpted from Napoleon A. Chagnon, *Yanomamö: The Fierce People* (New York: Holt, Rinehart and Winston, 1977), pp. 113–115.

Thinking It Over

Describe an activity in your culture that illustrates patterned social relationships. Explain the statuses and roles involved.

Careers in Sociology

President Dwight D. Eisenhower said, "Whatever America hopes to bring to pass in the world must first come to pass in the heart of America." A career in writing (with a background in sociology) gives the opportunity to share with others.

Writers communicate by developing original fiction and nonfiction for books, magazines and trade journals, newspapers, technical reports, online distribution, company newsletters, radio and television broadcasts, movies, and advertisements.

Writers select a topic or are assigned one by an editor. Then they gather information through personal observation, library and Internet research, and interviews. Next, they select material they want to use, organize it into a meaningful format, and use the written word to express ideas and convey information to readers.

For information on professions in media, go to **http://www.mediabistro.com/**.

Section 4 Industrial and Postindustrial Societies

Key Terms

- industrial society
- mechanization
- urbanization
- Gemeinschaft
- Gesellschaft
- social solidarity
- mechanical solidarity
- organic solidarity
- postindustrial society

Basic Features of Industrial Societies

The Industrial Revolution created a society that is dependent upon science and technology to produce its basic goods and services. Sociologists call this an **industrial society.**

What happens when agricultural societies become industrial societies? Neil Smelser (1976) has identified some basic structural changes that occur in societies shifting from an agricultural to an industrial base. Industrialism brings with it a change—*away* from simple, traditional technology (plows, hammers, harnesses) *toward* the application of scientific knowledge to create more complex technological devices. Early examples of

Section Preview

The Industrial Revolution created a new type of society, called industrial society. Characteristics that distinguish this society from all earlier ones include the growth of large cities and a wide-spread dependence on machines and technology. Postindustrial society has a predominately white-collar labor force that is concentrated in service industries. Social instability has been linked to the transition from an industrial to a postindustrial society.

industrial society
a society that depends on science and technology to produce its basic goods and services

Ford Motor Company employees work on the Model T assembly line. What technology underlies industrial society?

Using the Section Preview

The transition to an industrial society is the basis of much of the social thought of the early sociologists like Marx, Weber, Durkheim, and so on. If necessary, have students review Chapter 1 and find the concepts outlined by these theorists that show that their writings took place during the industrial revolution. Sociologist William Julius Wilson's book, *When Work Disappears: The World of the New Urban Poor,* has won awards for its depiction of the profound effects that the postindustrial age has had on the urban poor. The growth of suburbs, coupled with the relocation of jobs out of the city and abroad and the decline of manufacturing jobs, once the staple of urban centers, has contributed to the emergence of the inner city poor. Wilson explains that crime, drugs, and teen pregnancy in the inner city are the result of the structural changes brought about by this social transformation. This book is a "must" read for teachers of beginning sociology.

Learning Styles

Bodily-Kinesthetic Comparing and contrasting preindustrial, industrial, and postindustrial societies is one of the learning objectives of this chapter. To aid students in mastering this objective, it may help to give them an opportunity to physically put themselves into the information to be learned. As a class, decide on one or more situations that teens deal with regularly (curfew, dating, grades, getting a job or a car, etc.). Then divide students into groups representing the following societies: preindustrial (hunting and gathering, horticultural, pastoral, and /or agricultural), industrial, and postindustrial. Ask them to develop and then act out skits depicting how teens in that society might deal with the situation. Conclude with a discussion of the similarities and differences they discover during role play.
L1

More About . . . Durkheim and Tönnies

Sociologist Emile Durkheim coined the term *anomie,* which is a state of normlessness. The changes brought on by social transformations such as the industrial and postindustrial revolutions have contributed to this normlessness. Durkheim believed that this contributed to the increase in suicide rates. Ask students if Durkheim's hypothesis still seems true today, 100 years later.

Tönnies was somewhat mystical in his approach to society. Although he disavowed totalitarianism (including Nazism in his country) and found some degree of voluntarism in all social relationships, he believed that every social organization has a collective will, presenting aspects of both an absolute and a pragmatic "will." To him, the "public opinion" of a total society expresses the communal will that certain social and political actions be performed or abstained from and implies the use of sanctions against dissidents.

mechanization
the process of replacing animal and human power with machine power

urbanization
the shifting of population from farms and villages to large cities

industrial technology include the steam engine and the use of electrical power in manufacturing. More recent technological developments include nuclear energy, aerospace-related inventions, and the computer.

In industrial societies, intensive animal and human labor is replaced by power-driven machines, a process known as **mechanization.** These machines are operated by wage earners who produce goods for sale on the market. With the help of machinery, farmers are able to produce enough food to support themselves and many others. This surplus allows people to move away from farms and villages, adding to the growing population in large cities. **Urbanization,** then, is also a basic feature of industrial societies.

How does the role of the family change? With industrialization, family functions change in many ways. Economic activities, once carried out in the home, move to the factory. Similarly, the education of the young, which in agricultural societies centered on teaching farming, moves from the home to the formal school. An industrial society requires a more broadly educated and trained labor force, so young people can no longer be prepared for the work force by their families. Blood relationships decline in importance as families begin to separate socially and physically due to urbanization and the necessity of taking jobs in distant locations where factories have been built. Personal choice and love replace arranged marriages. Women, through their entrance into the work force, become less subordinate to their husbands. Individual mobility increases dramatically, and social class is based more on occupational achievement than the social class of one's parents. Because the United States has been an industrial society for so long, its characteristics are taken as a given. The effects of industrialization are easier to observe in societies currently moving from an agricultural to an industrial economic base. For example, Vietnam and Malaysia are experiencing mechanization and urbanization at the beginning of the twenty-first century (Singh, 1998; Phu, 1998).

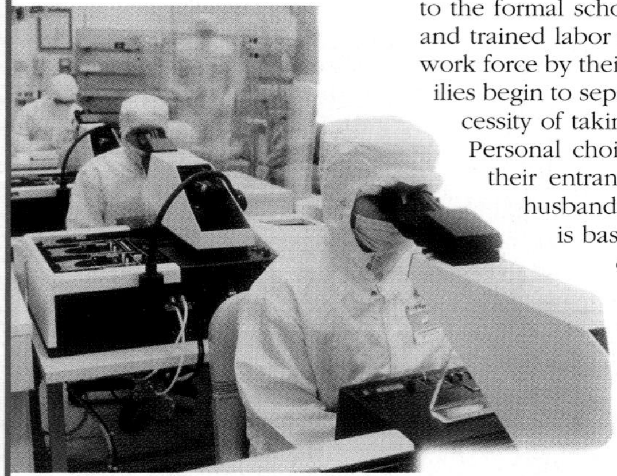

Job skills in an industrial society, like those needed here, cannot be learned in the home. What does this mean for education in an industrial society?

Gemeinschaft
preindustrial society based on tradition, kinship, and close social ties

Gesellschaft
industrial society characterized by weak family ties, competition, and impersonal social relationships

social solidarity
the degree to which a society is unified

A Conversation with Two Sociologists

Ferdinand Tönnies and Emile Durkheim were two early sociologists who wrote about preindustrial and industrial societies. Sociologists today still study their writings.

What did Tönnies write? Ferdinand Tönnies (1957, originally published in 1887), was an early German sociologist. In his writing, he distinguished between *gemeinschaft* (ga MINE shoft) and *gesellschaft* (ga ZELL shoft). **Gemeinschaft** is German for "community." It describes a society based on tradition, kinship, and intimate social relationships. These are the types of communities found in preindustrial societies. **Gesellschaft** is the German word for "society." This concept represents industrial society and is characterized by weak family ties, competition, and less personal social relationships.

What were Durkheim's views? Shortly after Tönnies published his theory, Emile Durkheim (1964a, originally published in 1893) made a similar observation. He distinguished the two types of societies by the nature of their social *solidarity.* **Social solidarity** is the degree to which a society is unified or can hold itself together in the face of obstacles.

Role Play

Before assigning this activity, you might bring an elderly person into class to talk with students about the changes to the family he or she has seen in his or her lifetime.

Students should reread the text section that answers the question: How does the role of the family change? Afterwards, have students work in pairs or groups to write scenarios that illustrate one or more of the changes illustrated in this paragraph. For example, they could script a scene about a young man telling his parents he was moving from the farm to a city miles away that had job opportunities in the factories. When finished, ask for volunteers to, perform their "mini-plays" for the class.
L1

World View

Agricultural Employment

As societies move from the preindustrial to the postindustrial stage, fewer people are required to raise food to feed the population. This map shows the percentage of each country's population involved in the production of agricultural products.

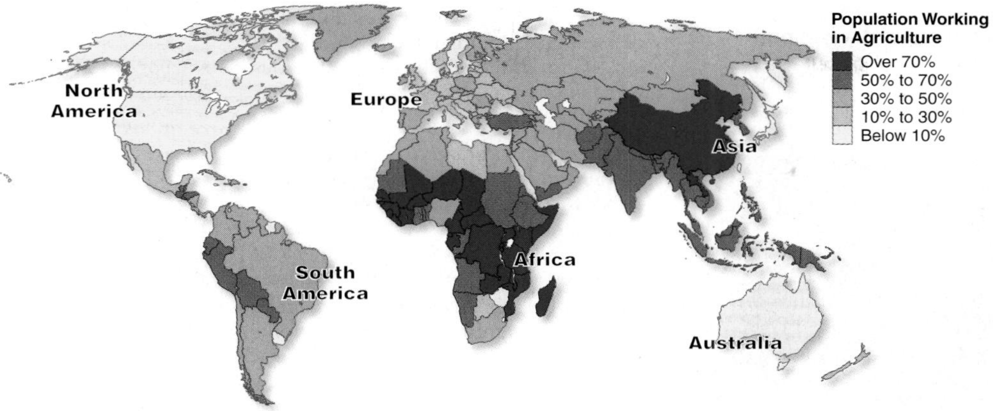

Interpreting the Map

1. After examining this map, what generalizations about types of societies around the world would you make? Explain.
2. Which countries do you think could be ready to move from one type of society to another? Be specific about countries and types of societies.
3. What parts of the world are least likely to change in the near future? Explain your answer.

Adapted from *Compact Peters Atlas of the World*. Essex, England: Longman Group UK Limited.

World View

Answers to Interpreting the Map

1. Students should see that those countries with 50 percent or more of their population in agricultural work are in the area of the world commonly referred to as "developing nations."
2. Countries in the 10 percent to 30 percent range could be ready to move toward industrialization. Note, however, that countries that were formerly part of the USSR may be seeing an increase in the percentage of people in agriculture.
3. It will be very hard for countries with politically unstable governments and single crop economies to move forward in development.

Social solidarity, Durkheim contended, is a result of society's division of labor. In societies in which the division of labor is simple—in which most people are doing the same type of work—**mechanical solidarity** is the foundation for social unity. A society based on mechanical solidarity achieves social unity through a consensus of beliefs, values, and norms; strong social pressures for conformity; and dependence on tradition and family. In this type of society, which is best observed in small, nonliterate societies, people tend to behave, think, and feel in much the same ways, to place the group above the individual, and to emphasize tradition and family.

In contrast, in an industrial society, members depend on a variety of people to fulfill their needs—barbers, bakers, manufacturers, and other suppliers of services. This modern industrial society is based on **organic solidarity.** It achieves social unity through a complex of specialized statuses that make members of the society interdependent.

mechanical solidarity
a type of social unity achieved by people doing the same type of work and holding similar values

organic solidarity
a type of social unity in which members' interdependence is based on specialized functions and statuses

Survey

Have students develop a survey that will answer the question: How has computer use changed your life? Questions for the survey should be developed so that they can be answered by people of all ages. The survey should be given to children, teens, young adults, and students' parents and grandparents (or other people in those age groups). As students analyze the results of their survey, they should look at answers that are not age-specific and answers that are age-specific. Before you have students begin work on the survey, you might have them predict the ways they think the different age groups will answer the questions.
L1

Points to Stress

Tell students that a country doesn't have to meet all of the criteria (features) to be considered a postindustrial society. In fact, the U.S. is the only country that meets the first criteria.

Reteaching

Using the five major features of the postindustrial society, have students come up with five new examples of each.

The term *organic solidarity* is based on an analogy with biological organisms. If a biological organism composed of highly specialized parts is to survive, its parts must work together. Similarly, the parts of a society based on organic solidarity must cooperate if the society is to survive.

Major Features of Postindustrial Society

postindustrial society
a society in which the economic emphasis is on providing services and information

Some societies, such as the United States, have passed beyond industrial society into **postindustrial society.** In this type of society, the economic emphasis is on providing services and information rather than on producing goods through basic manufacturing.

Sociologist Daniel Bell (1999) identifies five major features of a postindustrial society, a society based on a service economy.

1. *For the first time, the majority of the labor force are employed in services rather than in agriculture or manufacturing.* These industries emphasize services (banking, medical care, fast food, entertainment) rather than producing tangible goods, such as oil or steel. They include organizations in the areas of trade, finance, transportation, health, recreation, research, and government. In 2000, about 75 percent of all employed workers in the United States were in service jobs.
2. *White-collar employment replaces much blue-collar work.* White-collar workers outnumbered blue-collar workers in the United States for the first time in 1956, and the gap is still increasing. The most rapid growth has been in professional and technical employment.
3. *Technical knowledge is the key organizing feature in postindustrial society.* Knowledge is used for the creation of innovations as well as for making government policy. As technical knowledge becomes more important, so do educational and research institutions.
4. *Technological change is planned and assessed.* In an industrial society, the effects of a technology are not assessed before its introduction. When the automobile engine was invented, no one asked whether it would have an effect on the environment. In postindustrial societies, the effects—good and bad—of an innovation can be considered before it is introduced.
5. *Reliance on computer modeling in all areas.* With modern computers, it is possible to consider a large number of interacting variables simultaneously. This "intellectual technology" allows us to manage complex organizations—including government at national, state, and local levels.

The New York Stock Exchange symbolizes the shift from production-based work to knowledge-based work in postindustrial society.

Social Instability in Postindustrial Society

Historian Francis Fukuyama (1990) believes that the transition to a service economy has increased social instability in nations undergoing this change. He writes the following about deteriorating social conditions that began in the mid-1960s.

> *Crime and social disorder began to rise, making inner-city areas of the wealthiest societies on earth almost uninhabitable. The decline of kinship*

Using Decision-Making Skills

Give students this scenario: The postindustrial United States has been left in ruins after a war with Country XYZ. Most technology has been destroyed; computer systems are ineffective because there are no generators. The resulting chaos has cut off food supply systems, transportation, medical care, education, and banking. People are reduced to foraging for fruits and vegetables, killing animals, and moving from place to place to follow the food supply. People without these skills are left to the mercies of those who can provide. All social classes have been eliminated; there are no rich or poor. Private ownership is a distant dream. Small communities form for the sake of cooperation, and a division of labor is necessary to complete required tasks.

Ask students to use the decision-making process (identify the situation requiring a decision, gather information, identify options, predict consequences, and take action to implement a decision) to determine how they would provide for their families.

as a social institution, which has been going on for more than 200 years, accelerated sharply in the second half of the twentieth century. Marriages and births declined and divorce soared; and one out of every three children in the United States and more than half of all children in Scandinavia were born out of wedlock. Finally, trust and confidence in institutions went into a forty-year decline (Fukuyama, 1999:55).

Will social instability continue? According to Fukuyama, this social instability is now lessening. He sees current indications of a return to social stability. The establishment of new social norms, he believes, is reflected in the slowing down of increases in divorce, crime, distrust, and illegitimacy. In the 1990s, Fukuyama notes, many societies have even seen a reversal of these rates—crime, divorce, illegitimacy, and distrust have actually declined.

This is particularly true in the United States, where levels of crime are down a good 15 percent from their peaks in the early 1990s. Divorce rates peaked in the early 1980s, and births to single mothers appear to have stopped increasing. Welfare rolls have diminished almost as dramatically as crime rates, in response both to the 1996 welfare-reform measures and to opportunities provided by a nearly full-employment economy in the 1990s. Levels of trust in both institutions and individuals have also recovered significantly since the early 1990s (Fukuyama, 1999:80).

What has caused the return to social stability? Fukuyama believes that humans find it difficult to live without values and norms:

The situation of normlessness . . . is intensely uncomfortable for us, and we will seek to create new rules to replace the old ones that have been undercut (Fukuyama, 1999:76).

Because culture can be changed, it can be used to create new social structures better adapted to changing social and economic circumstances.

Section 4 Assessment

1. Explain why blood relationships are less important in an industrial society than in a preindustrial society.
2. State whether each of the following is or is not a major feature of a postindustrial society.
   a. emphasis on technical knowledge
   b. employment of the majority of the labor force in service industries
   c. reliance on advanced technology
   d. increased dependence on skilled blue-collar workers
   e. shift toward the employment of white-collar workers

Critical Thinking

3. **Analyzing Information** Explain from your own observation why family relationships would probably weaken in an industrial society.
4. **Making Predictions** As the United States becomes a more complete information society, how may life for you change?

> "We live in a moment of history where change is so speeded up that we begin to see the present only when it is disappearing."
>
> **R.D. Laing**
> **Scottish psychiatrist**

Pulling It All Together

The Industrial Revolution had a profound effect on the nature of work, the location of jobs and the role of the family. Urbanization and mechanization were part of the push and pull that characterized this social transformation.

Answers to Section 4 Assessment

1. Blood relationships became less important because families began to separate socially and physically due to urbanization and the necessity of taking jobs in distant locations. Personal choice and love replaced arranged marriages. Women became less subordinate, individual mobility increased, and social class became based on occupational achievement rather than social class of one's parents.
2. **a.** is
   b. is
   c. is
   d. is not
   e. is

Critical Thinking

4. Answers should be based on students' personal experiences (see Question #1 above for reference).
5. Answers will vary.

Encouraging Citizenship Activity

People in many inner city areas (and even some older suburban areas) are organizing clean-up projects to help restore the areas to their original beauty. It might be a real eye-opening experience for some of your students to be involved in such a project. You might want to contact your local chamber of commerce or city hall to find out about clean-up projects in your area. Be sure to get administrative and parental permission and help if you decide to undertake such an activity.
L1

Tech Trends

A good follow-up activity for this feature is to ask students to interview people they know who work in virtual organizations, such as a parent or friend of a parent, and ask them how they feel based on some of the concepts outlined in the article. Remind students that they can refer back to Chapter 2 for review in how to use close-ended or open-ended questions.

Answers to Analyzing the Trends

1. From a functionalist perspective, virtual organizations guarantee that the order and stability of the corporation will be maintained. From a conflict perspective, workers might feel that those in power create this situation to maintain their power over workers. The interactionist perspective would look at the symbolic meaning attached to these interactions.
2. Answers will vary, but the issue of the value of privacy will certainly be mentioned.

Integrating the Teacher Resources

Look for Ethics, Values, and Technology: Real-Life Issues in Society, **available in your Teacher's Resource Box for additional primary source readings dealing with real-life controversies. Student worksheets are included.**

Tech Trends

The Dark Side of Workplace Technology

According to a business visionary, one of the most important changes that will occur in the postindustrial workplace is the "virtual organization." The virtual organization is a workplace of digital technologies, wireless transfer of information, computer networks, and telecommuting. In this picture, the worker has more freedom, independence, and job satisfaction than ever before (Barner, 1996).

If this optimistic view of new technology is correct, workers in high-tech jobs should be much happier than employees doing low-tech work. However, in a survey of 1,509 workers in California's Silicon Valley (an area where high-tech industry is concentrated), researchers found no differences in job satisfaction between employees in high-tech companies and those in more traditional manufacturing firms. They also found that there are still large social class differences within the workplace. These findings challenge the belief that work in high-tech society will be more satisfying and economically fair (Gamst and Otten, 1992).

Other researchers found that job security decreases in high-tech positions. Employees are forced to learn new skills and upgrade present skills throughout their careers; lifelong learning is the key to economic survival. Management positions are also at risk. Functions that managers have been performing for centuries, such as decision making and training, will be done by technology rather than humans.

Another feature of the high-tech workplace is the use of technology to monitor employee performance. This practice can make employees feel helpless, manipulated, and exploited. Many workers feel that their managers are spying on them, constantly looking over their shoulders (Barner, 1996). In fact, there has been a dramatic rise in employer workplace surveillance. Over two-thirds of U.S. companies now engage in electronic cybersnooping of employees: reviewing e-mail, examining computer files, documenting web sites visited each day (Naughton, 1999). How would you feel if all of your actions at work were being monitored by a computer, creating a record of your behavior that can be replayed and reexamined? (Remember the discussion in Chapter 2 about the ethics of researchers' use of video cameras.)

Digitally based technology offers many benefits. It has boosted productivity and created many new employment opportunities. Like any technology that has wide-ranging effects on society, there are some undesirable consequences. Postindustrial societies are just beginning to deal with the dark side of a very bright technology.

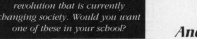

A video camera has been implanted inside the smoke detector above. These tiny cameras are part of the technological revolution that is currently changing society. Would you want one of these in your school?

Analyzing the Trends

1. Which theoretical perspective do you think underlies this research and speculation? Indicate specific features of the research to support your conclusions.
2. Does the use of technology to monitor employees clash with any values in American society? Explain.

Cooperative Learning Activity

Group students by fours or fives to discuss the question raised in the Tech Trends feature: How would you feel if all of your actions at work (or school) were being monitored by a computer, creating a record of your behavior that can be replayed and reexamined? Each group should choose a recorder and then brainstorm thoughts and feelings they believe they would have if they were in the situation described above. The recorder should write down as much of the brainstorming session as possible. Next, students should go over the list they generated and discard or combine similar answers. Then have each group reach consensus on the five strongest thoughts or feelings on the list. Each group should choose a representative to share their group's answers with the rest of the class. **L1**

Chapter 5 Assessment

Summary

Section 1: Social Structure and Status

Main Idea: The underlying pattern of social relationships in a group is called social structure. Status is one very important element of social structure. Ascribed statuses are assigned at birth; achieved statuses are earned or chosen.

Section 2: Social Structures and Roles

Main Idea: People interact according to prescribed roles. These roles carry certain rights and obligations. Sometimes conflict or strain occurs when an individual has too many roles to play.

Section 3: Preindustrial Societies

Main Idea: The way a society provides for basic needs greatly affects its cultural and social structure. Preindustrial, industrial, and postindustrial societies meet basic needs in different ways. Preindustrial societies include hunting and gathering, horticultural, pastoral, and agricultural societies.

Section 4: Industrial and Postindustrial Societies

Main Idea: The Industrial Revolution created a new type of society, called industrial society. Characteristics that distinguish this society from all earlier ones included the growth of large cities and a wide-spread dependence on machines and technology. Postindustrial society has a predominantly white-collar labor force that is concentrated in service industries. Social instability has been linked to the transition from an industrial to a postindustrial society.

Sociology Online

Self-Check Quiz
Visit the *Sociology and You* Web site at soc.glencoe.com and click on **Chapter 5—Self-Check Quizzes** to prepare for the chapter test.

Reviewing Vocabulary

Complete each sentence using each term once.

a. social structure
b. achieved status
c. ascribed status
d. roles
e. role conflict
f. society
g. horticulture society
h. hunting and gathering society
i. agricultural society
j. industrial society
k. organic solidarity
l. mechanical solidarity

1. The underlying pattern of social relationships is called ______.
2. ______ is the social unity achieved through interdependence based on specialized functions.
3. ______ is status that is assigned.
4. ______ is a society that solves the subsistence problem by learning to grow and harvest plants.
5. ______ is a nomadic society characterized by economic cooperation.
6. Status that can be earned is called ______.
7. People living within defined territorial borders and sharing a common culture are called a ______.
8. Culturally defined rights and obligations attached to statuses are known as ______.
9. The society that releases some people from the land to engage in noneconomic activities is called ______.
10. ______ occurs when the roles of a single status are inconsistent or conflicting.
11. Social unity accomplished through a consensus of values, beliefs, and norms is known as ______.
12. ______ is a society characterized by the replacement of human labor with mechanical labor.

Answers Chapter 5 Assessment

Reviewing Vocabulary

1. a	**5.** j	**9.** k
2. n	**6.** c	**10.** f
3. d	**7.** h	**11.** o
4. i	**8.** e	**12.** l

Reviewing the Facts

1. Role strain
2. The underlying pattern of social relationship.
3. Role strain is a condition in which roles of a single status are inconsistent or conflicting. Involves a single status. Role conflict exists when performance of a role in one status clashes with performance of a role in another status. Involves more than one status.
4. DIFFERENCES: low-tech position provides more social interaction with coworkers—it is built into the job; high-tech job isolates worker from coworkers; SIMILARITIES: they experience the same social class differences; no differences in job satisfaction
5. Durkheim referred to the shift as the change from mechanical solidarity to organic solidarity.
   DIAGRAM OVALS: Weak Family Ties; Competition; Decrease in Personal Social Relationships

Thinking Critically

1. This is known as breaching a norm, a concept that will be reviewed in Chapter 7. In this chapter, the implication is that the underlying pattern of social structure has been violated; we don't walk up to strangers and just hand out money.
2. Answers will vary but the athlete might also be the captain, thus he has the right to lead the team with the consent of the team. A performer in the play might be in the lead role and their status is higher than the stage hand, although no less important.
3. This might provoke an interesting debate. Students may not have sympathy for those who don't eat since they may not know of any situations personally. Some might feel that it is wrong for Americans to overeat while some don't eat at all.

Chapter 5 Assessment

Reviewing the Facts

1. What is the sociological term for the dilemma of women who have careers and who also must run households?
2. What do sociologists mean by social structure?
3. What is the difference between role strain and role conflict?
4. In what ways do workers in the "virtual organization" differ from low-tech workers? In what ways are the workers the same?
5. As people move away from agricultural societies to industrial societies, they also move from the personal to the impersonal. What sociological terminology did Emil Durkeim give to such a shift? Use the diagram below to illustrate the cause and effect relationship of the shift from personal to impersonal.

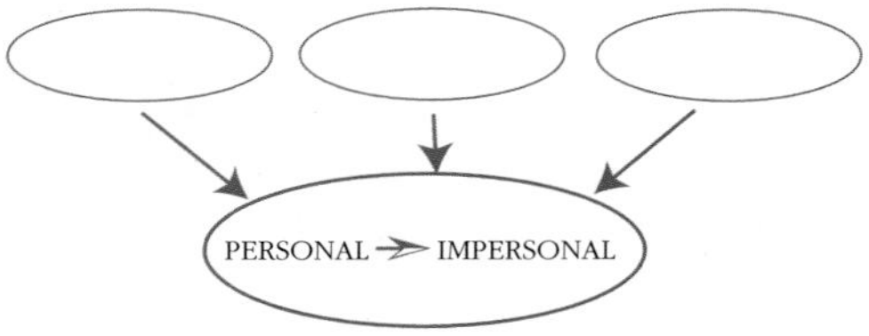

Thinking Critically

1. **Making Inferences** The chapter suggests that society functions because social patterns are usually predictable. History records that John D. Rockefeller, the founder of Standard Oil Company, was so rich he would walk down the street and pass out dimes to children. Allegedly, he gave out three million dollars worth of dimes before he died. Let's say you decided to go to the mall and hand out a dollar to all the children who passed by. How do you think people would react? Would they be suspicious? Do you think mall security would be concerned by your behavior? What has changed since the days of Rockefeller that would make your behavior suspect?
2. **Applying Concepts** What are some of the roles and statuses that you fill in the course of your day? List them, and describe the basic rights connected to each status.
3. **Analyzing Information** In hunting and gathering societies, resources are distributed equally. If one person eats, everyone eats. Is that the case in industrial and postindustrial societies? Should Americans be concerned whether everyone eats every day? Why might they *not* be concerned?
4. **Drawing Conclusions** Modern societies have been given the role of providing an education for all of their members. This education is conducted in schools. Some people, however, are returning to the ways of older societies and teaching their children at home rather than sending them to school. What are some of the role conflicts and strains that might exist for those who choose to home-school their children? What do you think some of the advantages and disadvantages of home schooling might be?

Sociology Projects

1. **Role Performance** George Herbert Mead said that humans are social beings because they can "take on the role of another person." Your task here is to create a one-minute improvisational skit in which you react to a basic statement through the "persona" of another individual. This person might be the school principal, a favorite teacher, a school liaison police officer, or a parent. If you are not confident that you can improvise, take the time to write out the lines of the statement you are reacting to: *Teenagers today need to assume more responsibility.*
2. **Social Cues** You have probably watched so much television over the course of your lifetime that you can watch it without really paying attention. Here's a twist on TV watching. Watch television tonight for ten minutes without turning the set on—that's right, sit in front of it without turning it on. Concentrate on everything that is happening as you focus on the TV. Next, actually turn on the TV, but turn the vol-

ANSWERS Chapter 5 Assessment

4. To advocates of home schooling, children in those situations are free of the problems that infest schools, i.e. drugs, violence, etc. Those opposed to home schooling believe that a parent can't possibly teach all the subject areas and teach them well. Some say that home schooled kids don't do school work every day but they get more individual attention. This could turn into a full debate.

Sociology Projects

1. As an example, students could create a skit in which the class valedictorian gets suspended for being arrested at a party. One student could be the parent, another the principal, another the class advisor, and others could play some friends. Have students try to consider all sides of this argument.
2. This is a fun way for students to concentrate on how predictable the patterned social structure of TV is. They will probably know what's going on without the sound because they have seen so much TV. Most enlightening for them might be watching the TV without turning it on. What sounds do they hear that they normally block out?
3. This collage should really help bring home the various roles and statuses they have. It will also allow them to see that others play the same roles and statuses. If they use pictures from magazines, they must show common patterns of social relationships.
4. A great place to do this is in the school cafeteria. Since most students tend to segregate themselves at lunch, the groups will most likely be distinct and easily identifiable. Students should remember to concentrate on the patterns of behavior.
5. Students might want to bring a picture of their car, an award, or something that allowed them to feel that they made a name for themselves. Have students share these and the feelings they evoke with the class.
6. Answers will vary. Examples: picture of a baby boy or baby girl = ascribed status (i.e., male, female) or a young person or old person (i.e., age is an ascribed social status; social structure = picture of a family or a group of friends; status = person in a uniform or business suit; achieved status = criminal, doctor; judge; master

ume all the way down. Try to figure out what is going on by reading faces and nonverbal expressions. Try this for ten minutes. This activity might give you an idea of how good human beings are at grasping certain ideas without words. Next, try watching the news for ten minutes without the sound on. Then spend another ten minutes watching the news with the sound on but concentrating on the technical aspects of the program: camera changes, graphics, sound, music, voices, changes in color, and so forth. Identify and describe in a brief paragraph two or three cues or expressions that allowed you to correctly interpret a situation.

3. **Individuals as Players On a Stage** Create a collage entitled "Society" using pictures from magazines or old photographs. In this collage, depict yourself in various statuses. For example, if you are in a club at school or in a band, include that. If you are a sister or daughter, that is another status you hold. Then show how your statuses are related to society, family, education, religion, the economy (your job), and so forth. This collage should help you understand how individuals are players on a stage.
4. **Observation** As you learned in Chapter 2, observation is one method that sociologists use to accumulate data. In this activity, you will observe the structure and interactions of three groups (without drawing attention to your project!). Look for general patterns in the group that you observe, such as style of dress, language, status positions, values, routines, and social boundaries. You might want to try observing your family or a group at the mall, in the school cafeteria, or any other place that groups meet. Write down your observations, concentrating on patterns of behavior.
5. **Status Symbols** Roles are behaviors associated with certain statuses. Status symbols are products or items that represent a status, or position. For example, a luxury automobile or a vacation home are status symbols for wealth. High school status symbols might involve a letter sweater, a trendy article of clothing, or a video game player. Search newspaper and magazine advertisements for examples of products that you believe are status symbols for a particular status or occupation. (It is not only wealthy and powerful people that possess status symbols.) Make a montage of these images.
6. **Status** Use newspapers and magazines to find pictures that can be used to make a visual explanation of the following terms: status, ascribed status, status set, master statuses and social structure. Create a pictorial chart using the terms and pictures.

Technology Activity

1. This chapter describes rights as the behaviors individuals can expect from others and obligations as the behaviors others expect from them. Different societies place emphasis on different rights and obligations, but there is a common understanding of some basic human rights. One organization that provides a list of these basic rights is the European Commission of Human Rights. Visit its web site at http://194.250.50.201/. From its home page, select the section entitled "organization, procedure and activities." Then go to the document called "Convention for the Protection of Human Rights and Fundamental Freedoms." Scroll down to Section I Article 2 of this document.
   - **a.** What are the basic human rights listed there?
   - **b.** Are any of these rights built into some of the roles you are expected to perform? Explain.
   - **c.** Do you believe that these rights should be a part of the role prescriptions in any society? Why or why not?

statuses = may be achieved or ascribed; status set = picture of a person in various interactions (a mother who is a teacher who is an athlete.)

Technology Activity

1. The basic human rights listed at this site include:
   a. Everyone's right to life shall be protected by law. No one shall be deprived of his life intentionally save in the execution of a sentence of a court following his conviction of a crime for which this penalty is provided by law.
   b. Deprivation of life shall not be regarded as inflicted in contravention of this article when it results from the use of force which is no more than absolutely necessary
      (1) in defence of any person from unlawful violence
      (2) in order to effect a lawful arrest or to prevent the escape of a person lawfully detained;
      (3) in action lawfully taken for the purpose of quelling a riot or insurrection.

   Students answers to parts b and c of this question will vary.

Integrating the Teacher Resources

Look for the Alternative Assessments booklet in your Teacher's Resource Box for essay tests and performance assessment activities based on this chapter.

Enrichment Reading

Have students visit a local mall and observe teen patterns of interaction and the existing social structure. Have them concentrate on the groups, their dress, interactions, what stores they frequent, gender distribution, etc. Hypothesize what you expect to find and compare it with what you actually find. If observing teens is not possible, have students observe other groups that frequent malls. Many older people walk the malls; students might want to observe those interactions.

Chapter 5

Enrichment Reading

Social Functions of Malls

by Wayne S. Wooden

In *The Mall: An Attempted Escape from Everyday Life,* Jerry Jacobs presents an ethnographic account of a midsize, enclosed suburban shopping center. Karen Lansky's article, "Mall Rats," for *Los Angeles* magazine discusses what it means for teenagers when they "just hang out" at these "indoor shopping palaces."

In recent years several excellent books and magazine articles have been published on the **social phenomenon** of teenagers and suburban shopping malls.

The modern mall, Jacobs argues, provides three things for its participants. First, it offers people entertainment or just plain diversion. Second, it provides the public with convenient shopping. And, third, the mall offers public, social space—a place to meet and interact with others. In other words, the modern shopping center has become an "indoor street corner society."

Karen Lansky contends that kids spend so much time in the mall partly because parents encourage it, assuming it is safe and that there is adult supervision. The structured and controlling environment of the mall is ideal for them. According to Lansky

> *True mall rats lack structure in their home lives, and adolescents about to make the big leap into growing up crave more structure than our modern society cares to acknowledge.*

Lansky also believes that the mall has become the focus of these young people's lives.

> *Malls are easy. Food, drink, bathrooms, shops, movie theaters—every part of the life-support system a modern kid needs is in the mall.* ***Instant gratification*** *for body and senses—and all of it close at hand, since malls are designed to make life more comfortable by eliminating parking problems, long walks, heavy doors, hot sun, depressing clouds. It is ironic, in fact, that the mall is becoming all that many kids know of the outside world, since the mall is a placeless space whose primary virtue is that it's all inside. Kids come in from the cold (or heat) for a variety of reasons, of course. But the main reason kids seek the mall, especially in the summer when school's out, seems to be because they can't think of anything better to do.*

Lansky sees mall rats as kids with nowhere else to go.

> *Their parents may drink or take drugs, be violent or just gone. Whatever, the mall becomes the home they don't have. For them, the mall is a rich, stimulating, warm, clean, organized, comfortable [social] structure—the only [social] structure in some of their lives.*

In gathering research for her article, Lansky interviewed several adolescents. Although teenagers in several high schools would be approached as well, the vast majority of the interviews and surveys gathered for the Youth Survey portion of this study were completed by over four hundred youths contacted in Southern California malls. The initial focus of this study, therefore, began with my meeting and talking with these so-called teenage mall rats.

One male expressed the belief that the mall "belongs to the mall rats." Arguing that the mall is *his* property, his mission in life, he said, is to become "top mall rat," adding, "Without the mall, we'd be street people."

Another female mall **habitué** interviewed by Lansky complained that the only place in the mall that is "theirs" is the arcade. She and her friends get kicked out of the other places. Security warns them to keep moving if they are not buying anything. It is these kids, according to Lansky, that the mall owners do not like. The managers resent having to set limits for these kids—limits that should be the responsibility of the community or the family. The owners discourage these kids because they often do not have much money to spend, yet drain the resources of the mall.

One of the first young men so contacted was Bob Bogan, or "Skidd Marx," as he preferred to be called, who allowed me to spend several afternoons with him as he wandered through the Brea Mall. Seventeen and 5′10″ tall, Skidd struck a mean pose. With his black hair spiked all over with three separate 1-foot tails in back, Skidd also sported eye makeup, a leather jacket studded with spikes, a white T-shirt with a punk band logo on it, black Levis rolled up high, and black Converse high tops. Skidd also sported four hanging earrings in each ear and a loop pierced into his right nostril. Skidd, decked out in full punk regalia, cut the swaggering image of the "young man about the mall."

Skidd, like all of the teenagers studied in this book, resided in suburbia. He came from a middle-class background. Both of his parents worked. He defined himself as "a suburban punk bordering on the punk funk." Skidd, in true mall-rat fashion, spent much of his free time and social life in the Brea Mall.

Q: *When did you first define yourself as being into punk or punk funk? How did the process occur?*

A: *It was in my third year of high school. I really wasn't feeling that good about myself at the time. I felt very self-conscious at school. I always kind of dressed differently. Being tall, people usually looked at me physically, and I used to be very insecure about that. So I kind of had the attitude, if I do something a little bit different, then that would be the reason why they're staring at me. I can't do anything about the fact that I'm tall.*

Q: *So it gave you a rationalization?*

A: *Right. The punk thing is when I just didn't care what I looked like. My parents were always saying, "You're such a nice looking young man. Why do you want to do that?" That really used to bother me.*

What Does it Mean?

ethnographic
the descriptive study of human cultures

habitué
one who regularly visits a place

instant gratification
the immediate satisfaction of wishes or wants

social phenomenon
a fact or event of social interest subject to scientific interpretation or explanation

Source: Adapted from an article by Wayne S. Wooden, *Renegade Kids, Suburban Outlaws: From Youth Culture to Delinquency,* Belmont: Wadsworth Publishing Company, 1994.

Read and React

1. According to this reading, what effect do malls have upon teenage values?
2. Given what you have learned in this chapter, what does it mean to say that people have no social structure in their lives except in the malls? Could this really be true? Explain.
3. Do you agree with the claims in this writing? Why or why not?

Answers to Read and React

1. Teenagers are large consumers; in that sense the mall is a manifestation of this phenomenon. They're exposed to the latest trends and all their needs are met in one place.
2. Social structure exists everywhere, in school, in families and in the workplace; the social structure of the mall provides teens with an outlet to the other social structures of their lives.
3. Answers will vary. Some teens will say that they frequent the mall and this study is accurate; others will believe that teens are so diverse that this represents a small population of teens for study.

Integrating the Teacher Resources

Additional primary source readings for this chapter can be found in Culture Studies: The Sociological Perspective, **available in your Teacher's Resource Box. Questions for students are included.**

Chapter Preview

Section 1 (pages 172–176)

Groups are classified by how they develop and function. Primary groups meet emotional and support needs, while secondary groups are task focused.

Section 2 (pages 177–180)

Reference groups help us evaluate ourselves and form identities. In-groups and out-groups divide people into "we" and "they." Social networks extend our contacts and let us form links to many other people.

Section 3 (pages 181–189)

Five types of social interaction are basic to group life: cooperation, conflict, social exchange, coercion, and conformity.

Section 4 (pages 190–196)

A formal organization is created to achieve some goal. Most are bureaucratic. The existence of primary groups and relationships within formal organizations can either help or hinder the achievement of goals.

Please see the correlation to the American Sociology Association standards located in the front of this text.

CHAPTER 6

Groups and Formal Organizations

Lead-Off Activity

Bring in several pounds of spaghetti noodles. (Three pounds should be sufficient for a class of twenty-five.) Also, bring in three to four bags of marshmallows. The task for student groups will be to construct a functional object. Have students assemble in groups of four or five. Have one person from each group collect noodles and marshmallows for their group. You might want to divide the students so they are not with their friends, thus forming secondary groups that will be more task-focused. (As a control, you could also maintain one primary group of friends.) See how students cooperate, make decisions, assume leadership or submissive roles in the group. Students can write about the experience or discuss it. Ask students if the process was more important than the product. Did it matter what they made as long as the group reached consensus on decisions related to the object?

L1

USING Your Sociological Imagination

Most people assume that conflict should be avoided because it is disruptive and interferes with group effectiveness. While this can be true, there are also social benefits associated with conflict and disagreement. Willingness to tolerate (and even encourage) disagreement can prevent what sociologists call *groupthink.*

The *Challenger* space shuttle disaster is an excellent example of a group making a catastrophic decision because it conformed to the larger group commitment. The *Challenger* was launched from Kennedy Space Center on January 28, 1986. Just over a minute after the launch, the *Challenger* exploded, taking the lives of all seven astronauts on board.

Like the teams of all space missions, the *Challenger* team was composed of a number of specialists. Its engineers had earlier recommended against takeoff because crucial parts had never been tested at a temperature as low as the temperature was on the morning of the takeoff. As victims of groupthink do, NASA leaders screened out this opposition by discounting the engineers' ability to make the "right" decision. Except for the engineers, the decision "to go" was unanimous. By avoiding consideration of a dissenting view, the majority lost the shuttle passengers and harmed NASA's long-term objectives. This chapter will look closely at behaviors of groups and organizations.

Sections

1. **Primary and Secondary Groups**
2. **Other Groups and Networks**
3. **Types of Social Interaction**
4. **Formal Organizations**

Learning Objectives

After reading this chapter, you will be able to

- define the concepts of group, social category, and social aggregate.
- list the major characteristics of primary and secondary groups.
- describe five types of social interaction.
- discuss the advantages and disadvantages of bureaucracy.
- distinguish between formal and informal organizations.
- discuss the use of power within an organization and demonstrate its importance with examples.

SOCIOLOGY Online

Chapter Overview
Visit the *Sociology and You* Web site at soc.glencoe.com and click on **Chapter 6—Chapter Overviews** to preview chapter information.

USING Your Sociological Imagination

This feature provides an excellent opportunity for you to discuss times throughout history when intragroup conflict turned out to be beneficial, times when groups were in obvious opposition but the resulting conflict had long-term benefits. Any discussion centered around the civil rights movement or some of the famous union/labor strikes will help students see how group conflict can be beneficial. Unfortunately, when group conflict was nonexistent, the consequences have been grave, as in the space shuttle disaster and the Bay of Pigs invasion.

Using the Section Preview

Here you can have students write a list of their primary groups; those groups that they are emotionally and socially close to. Students should preview the characteristics of primary groups found on page 173 and create a web of primary group relationships.

Using the Illustration

Ask students the following questions: Do the people in these photos meet the criteria for a group?

Students should realize that the choir is a secondary group, while the shoppers at the mall form a social aggregate because they fail to meet the four criteria listed on this page.

Integrating the Teacher Resources

Look for Chapter 6 Learning Goals Outline, a reproducible student worksheet in the Unit 2 Mastering Basic Concepts **booklet in your Teacher's Resource Box. It can be used to preview or review chapter content.**

Section 1 Primary and Secondary Groups

Key Terms

- group
- social category
- social aggregate
- primary group
- primary relationships
- secondary group
- secondary relationships

Section Preview

Groups are classified by how they develop and function. Primary groups meet emotional and support needs, while secondary groups are task focused.

group at least two people who have one or more goals in common and share common ways of thinking and behaving

Groups, Categories, and Aggregates

A **group** is composed of people who share several features, including the following.

- They are in regular contact with one another.
- They share some ways of thinking, feeling, and behaving.
- They take one another's behavior into account.
- They have one or more interests or goals in common.

Groups play important roles in the lives of their members, as well as influence society around them. Groups range from the small and informal to the large and formal. They tend to draw lines around themselves, creating insiders and outsiders. Some groups have tighter, more definite boundaries than others. Boundaries between African Americans and whites in the South of the early 1960s were rigid. Members of the minority were unable to drink from the same water fountains, use the same rest rooms, or eat at the same restaurants as whites. Group boundaries may change over time, however. Since the 1960s, boundaries between African Americans and whites in the United States are much looser.

Compare these Korean choir members with the Denver concert goers. Explain why one is a group and the other is not.

On-Demand Writing

After students have completed the Using the Section Preview activity above, have them write about the boundaries of each group they listed. They should name each group and write at least a paragraph about each group. In the paragraphs they should describe the boundaries of the groups as they see them. Are the boundaries tight? Are others allowed in? How does one become part of the group? After students have written the paragraphs, they should compare what they wrote about the primary groups and about the secondary groups. Are the boundaries different for primary and secondary groups? Which groups are more difficult to gain entrance to? Is it possible to become a member of all of the groups? If not, why not? Ask volunteers to share their thoughts on groups with the rest of the class.

L2

A group is not the same as a **social category**—people who share a social characteristic. High school seniors are a social category, for example. Women belong to another social category. A group is also sometimes confused with a **social aggregate**—people who happen to be in the same place at the same time, such as students waiting in line for concert tickets.

social category
people who share a social characteristic

Although neither categories nor aggregates are groups, some of their members may form groups. Witnesses of a disaster (an aggregate) may work together to cope with an emergency. Citizens of a state (a social category) may band together in an organized tax revolt. These people may form a group if they begin to interact regularly; share ways of thinking, feeling, and behaving; take one another's behavior into account; and have some common goals.

social aggregate
people temporarily in the same place at the same time

Primary Groups

primary group
people who are emotionally close, know one another well, and seek one another's company

Two principal types of groups are *primary* and *secondary*. At the extremes, the characteristics of these two types of groups—and the relationships that occur within them—are opposites. But most groups sit at different points along a continuum from primary to secondary.

What is a primary group? Charles Horton Cooley, one of the founders of symbolic interactionism, was the first to use the term *primary group*. A **primary group** is composed of people who are emotionally close, know one another well, and seek one another's company. The members of a primary group have a "we" feeling and enjoy being together. These groups are characterized by **primary relationships** that are intimate, personal, caring, and fulfilling.

Primary groups are the most important setting for socialization. Family and childhood play groups are the first primary groups a child experiences. People, of course, participate in primary groups throughout life. Close friends in high school and college, neighbors who keep an eye on one another's children, and friends who meet weekly for golf are all examples of primary groups.

How do primary groups develop? A number of conditions favor the development of primary groups and primary relationships.

What type of group do you think is pictured above?

- **Small size.** It is hard for members of large groups to develop close emotional ties. The chances of knowing everyone fairly well are far greater in small groups. The boys or girls who play for the school basketball team are more likely to develop primary relationships than the multitude of student spectators who cheer them on.
- **Face-to-face contact.** Primary relationships occur more easily when interaction is face to face. People who can see each other and who can experience nonverbal communication such as facial expressions, tone of voice, and touch are much more likely to develop close ties.
- **Continuous contact.** Closeness rarely develops in a short period of time. In spite of reported love at first sight, most of us require repeated social contact for the development of a primary relationship.
- **Proper social environment.** Just seeing someone every day in a close setting is not enough to form a primary relationship. You may visit your local video store every day and never form a relationship with the video

primary relationships
interactions that are intimate, personal, caring, and fulfilling

More About . . . Gender Interaction

Studies on boys and girls show distinct differences in how the two groups interact. Girls' groups are smaller and more intimate; boys' groups are larger and less intimate. Boys tend to be more willing to allow other boys into their circles. Girls, due to the level of intimacy, are not. Ask students if they think that these differences may be the result of socibiological as well as socializational factors.

Reinforcing Vocabulary

The term *aggregate* is from a Latin root that means a collection of animals such as a flock or herd. It might help students to remember the meaning of social aggregate if they get a mental image of shoppers at a mall milling around like a herd of cattle or sheep. Or, they might be familiar with the meaning of aggregate as a paving material where the particles stay separate and individual, bound together only by the mortar.
ELL

Careers in Sociology

Social professionals assist members of society in areas of personal need and concern. Working with people is more important to them than working with information, instruments, tools, or machines. Speaking, teaching, empathizing, listening, and conciliating are developed to the level of career skills. If you have several of these characteristics, you should explore occupations in this career area.

The social professions involve providing society with services rather than goods. The service sector is growing faster than the goods-producing sector. Services can't be seen or touched, but they are in great demand. Personal services are paid for by the individual consumer, and public services are provided by government agencies and are paid for with taxes.

For links to some great job search resources, connect to **http://www.career.pdx.edu/linkgreatsites.htm**

Making Connections to Other Cultures

You might want to read to students the final verse of Rudyard Kipling's poem "We and They." This verse reminds us of the crucial roles that perspective and location play in the we/they mentality often used in our attempts to understand others. One way for students to explore this issue is to have them list five groups they belong to and five categories they fit into. Once they have their lists, they should attempt to examine them from the perspective of someone their own age from another culture. They should mark the groups and categories that they think that person would also claim. Use a discussion of how much the two lists overlap as the basis for an exploration of the extent to which human and group similarities exist in spite of what may be dramatic cultural differences. Ask students the following questions. Don't all cultures have family systems? Don't all people form friendship groups? Don't all cultures have ways of classifying and categorizing people? Why is that? **L2**

clerk. The social setting does not encourage personal relationships, and the statuses are unequal. This is why primary relationships do not usually develop between students and teachers, bosses and employees, or judges and lawyers.

What are the functions of primary groups? Primary groups provide three important functions in society.

- **Emotional support.** During World War II, the German army refused to crumble despite years of being outnumbered, undersupplied, and outfought. These conditions should have led to desertion and surrender, but they did not. Strong emotional support ties within German combat units kept them fighting against overwhelming odds.
- **Socialization.** For children, the family is the primary group that teaches them how to participate in social life. In like manner, primary groups promote adult socialization—as adults enter college, take new jobs, change social classes, marry, and retire.
- **Encourage conformity.** Primary groups not only teach new members the appropriate norms and values, these groups provide pressure to conform. William F. Whyte's (1993) study of an Italian slum gang illustrates encouragement to conform within primary groups. Whyte reported that bowling scores corresponded with status in the gang—the higher the rank, the higher the score. If a lower-ranked member began to bowl better than those above him, verbal remarks—"You're bowling over your head" or "How lucky can you get?"—were used to remind him that he was stepping out of line.

Secondary Groups

secondary group
people who share only part of their lives while focusing on a goal or task

secondary relationships
impersonal interactions involving limited parts of personalities

Unlike a primary group, a **secondary group** is impersonal and goal oriented. It involves only a segment of its members' lives. Secondary groups exist to accomplish a specific purpose. Work groups, volunteers during disasters, and environmentalist organizations are examples of secondary groups. Members of secondary groups interact impersonally, in ways involving only limited parts of their personalities. These interactions are called **secondary relationships.** Interactions between clerks and customers, employers and workers, and dentists and patients are secondary relationships.

What are secondary relationships like? Members of secondary groups may be friends and identify with one another, but the purpose of the group is to accomplish a task, not to enrich friendships. In fact, if friendship becomes more important than the task, a secondary group may become ineffective. If the members of a basketball team become more interested in the emotional relationships among themselves or with their coach than in playing their best basketball, their play on the court could suffer.

Do secondary groups ever include primary relationships? Although primary relationships are more likely to occur in primary groups and secondary relationships in secondary groups, there are a number of exceptions. Many secondary groups include some primary relationships. Members of work groups may relate in personal terms, demonstrate genuine concern for one another, and have

Observation

If you did the Using the Section Preview activity, students have already created a web of primary groups. Have students build on that information to create a web of secondary groups. Ask students if they noticed if there was cross-over from the primary to the secondary groups. For instance, do their best friends also work with them? Students might want to look at their secondary group affiliations to see if any primary interaction exists in their secondary groups.
L2

Why are these young people probably not a primary group?

"Love thy neighbor as thyself, but choose your neighborhood."

Louise Beal
American author

relationships that are fulfilling in themselves. Similarly, members of a primary group sometimes engage in secondary interaction. One family member may, for example, lend money to another member of the family with a set interest rate and repayment schedule.

Section 1 Assessment

1. Listed below are some examples of primary and secondary relationships. Indicate which examples are most likely to be primary relationships (P) and which are most likely to be secondary relationships (S).
   - **a.** a marine recruit and his drill instructor at boot camp
   - **b.** a married couple
   - **c.** a coach and her soccer team
   - **d.** a teacher and his students
   - **e.** a car salesperson and her potential customer
2. Which of the following is not a condition that promotes the development of primary groups?
   - **a.** small group size
   - **b.** face-to-face contact
   - **c.** continuous contact
   - **d.** interaction on the basis of status or role
3. What are the three main functions of primary groups?

Critical Thinking

4. **Making Comparisons** Identify a primary group and a secondary group to which you belong. Describe three functions of each of these groups based on your personal experiences. Then compare and contrast your relationships in each group. (Note: It may help if you create a diagram.)

Using the Illustration

These young people are probably not a primary group because they seem to be focused upon a specific task, more like a secondary group would be.

Pulling it All Together

The concept of groups, primary and secondary, is the focus of this first section. Primary groups are characterized by close, emotional ties, while secondary groups exist to achieve specific goals. Some crossing over of primary and secondary group behavior does exist.

Answers to Section 1 Assessment

1. a. S
b. P
c. S
d. S
e. S
2. d
3. emotional support, socialization, encourage conformity

Critical Thinking

4. Answers will vary.

Survey

Primary and Secondary groups Conducting a survey regarding primary and secondary groups will give students an opportunity to gain a working understanding of most of the vocabulary terms in this chapter as well as an opportunity to practice research and math skills. After reading and discussing Sections 1 and 2, students can begin collecting data by interviewing an assigned number of people of different genders and ages. Students should ask people to list the groups they belong to, both formal and informal, without giving any hints to the kinds of groups that should be included. When data has been gathered, you may want to have students work in small groups to identify the types of groups that were listed, and then to tabulate the results of their survey, comparing the findings from the different groups. **L2**

Another Place

Refer students back to Chapter 3 and some of the concepts that help us understand culture. The work unit in China is an example of cultural relativism. The Chinese workers situation is unique to them and should be understood in relation to the larger cultural context.

Answer to Thinking it Over

Answers will variously express the ways in which work units are integrated with other social groups off the job.

Another Place: Work Life in China

Generally, Americans separate their work and nonwork life. When they don't, we say that they are "married" to their jobs. This means that most American work relationships are secondary relationships. They are impersonal and goal oriented. In China, however, work relationships are mostly primary because they are intimate, personal, caring, and fulfilling in themselves. This excerpt from *Streetlife China* describes a typical work situation in present-day China.

Everyone exists in China in terms of a work unit. When meeting for the first time, they will usually ask each other what work unit they are from. When ringing someone, the first question likely to be asked is "what is your work unit?", which usually precedes the question of one's own name. When registering in a hotel, the registrar will list the guest in terms of "guest from such and such a work unit." . . .

The contemporary Chinese work unit, then is really quite extraordinary. Apart from functioning as a department or organization, the work unit is also in charge of the management of the household register, the staple and non-staple food supply, all medical services, and all housing. It is also in charge of ideological remolding, political study, policing and security matters, marriages and divorce, entry into the Chinese Communist Youth League and into the Party, awarding merit and carrying out disciplinary action. If one wants to run for election as a deputy for either the National People's Congress or the Chinese People's Consultative Congress, one must firstly get the permission of one's work unit. When administrative sanctions are deployed to detain somebody, or they are to be sent for labor reform, then the authorities must consult with the work unit. "I am a person working in a work unit" is worn as a badge of pride in China; conversely, the expression "I don't have a work unit" basically identifies the speaker as little short of a swindler. . . .

Chinese have a love-hate relationship with the work unit. On the one hand, they cannot stand it, but on the other, they are unable to live without it. The work unit is like their family: they must love their commune as they love their family, love their factory as they love their home, and love their shop as they would their kin. In work units with a very rigid system, one's rank within the unit is a symbol of one's status; the individual's worth is realized in the rank attributed to them. Whether one's name is first or last, the order of arrival at the unit, their address, their living conditions, what transport is available to them, their access to documents of varying levels of classification are all things of great concern and are fought over at great length.

Source: Excerpted from Michael Dutton, *Streetlife China,* Cambridge: Cambridge University Press, 1998, pp. 43–44, 46–47.

Thinking It Over

Can you analyze the effects of the work unit in China in terms of its relationship to other groups to which workers belong?

Integrating the Teacher Resources

To reinforce key ideas, use the Chapter 6 Graphic Organizer, a reproducible student worksheet available in the Unit 2 Mastering Basic Concepts booklet in your Teacher's Resource Box.

Survey

The people of the United States may not put as much social emphasis on their places of employment as the Chinese put on their work units; but students might be surprised at the importance most people do give to their jobs. Students can put together a simple oral or written survey to illustrate this point. On the survey, students should ask only one question: Tell me five things about yourself. Participants would either list five things (if the survey is written) or verbally tell the interviewer five things (if the survey is oral). Participants should be people who are currently working or who have retired. As students analyze the results, they may be surprised at how many people will list what they do (or did) for a living not only in the five things they tell about themselves, but list it as the first or second piece of information. (Men may define themselves more by their jobs than women do.) Students may want to rank how many listed their job first, second, and so on.
L1

Section 2

Other Groups and Networks

Key Terms

- reference group
- in-group
- out-group
- social network

Reference Groups

We use certain groups to evaluate ourselves and to acquire attitudes, values, beliefs, and norms. Groups used in this way are called **reference groups.**

Reference groups may include our families, teachers, classmates, student government leaders, social organizations, rock groups, or professional football teams. We may consider a group to be a reference group without being a member; we may only aspire to be a member. For example, junior high school girls may imitate high school girls' leadership style or athletic interests. Junior high school boys may copy high school boys' taste in clothing and music. Similarly, you need not be a member of a rock band to view musicians as a reference group. You need only evaluate yourself in terms of their standards and subscribe to their beliefs, values, and norms.

Reference groups do not have to be positive. Observing the behavior of some group you dislike may reinforce a preference for other ways of acting, feeling, and behaving. For example, a violent gang should provide a blueprint of behavior for people to avoid.

Section Preview

Reference groups help us evaluate ourselves and form identities. In-groups and out-groups divide people into "we" and "they." Social networks extend our contacts and let us form links to many other people.

reference group group used for self-evaluation and the formation of attitudes, values, beliefs, and norms

This choir commemorating the Emancipation Proclamation constitutes a positive reference group. Gangs are a negative reference group for neighborhood children.

Using the Section Preview

Have students brainstorm some specific reference groups. The list will be extensive once you establish the groups they all have in common, such as family and school. Ask students why they identify with these reference groups. How do these reference groups lead to an entire social network beyond their primary groups?

Integrating the Teacher Resources

Look for the Chapter 6 Vocabulary Activity worksheet in the Unit 2 Mastering Basic Concepts booklet in your Teacher's Resource Box. It provides reinforcement for vocabulary in this chapter.

Cooperative Learning Activity

Have students form groups based on their reference groups. Each student should identify his or her own reference groups and then you should write them on the board. Move the desks and have students form a human web based on their similar reference groups. Since some students will share reference groups, those students should stand as close to both as possible. This web will become very intricate. Emphasize that the intricacy of the web shows how many similarities classmates have. Even though they see themselves as being different, they really have much in common.
L1

Points to Stress

Sociologists talk about boundaries. This is particularly true for in-groups and out-groups. Boundaries might include style of dress, uniforms, or hairstyle. These boundaries serve to identify the members and set the boundary for those on the outside.

Teaching Strategy

Sociologist Emile Durkheim's research on suicide addressed the need for social networks. Durkeim hypothesized that when those social networks disappeared, individuals were at risk for suicide. You might want to invite an expert on suicide to talk to the class and address the importance of maintaining social networks, particularly when a person is feeling depressed or isolated.

Using the Illustration

Students may not have ever seen this old-fashioned telephone switchboard before, unless they are fans of old movies. Explain that "in the old days" operators had to route calls manually and that this process required great skill to keep up with hundreds of incoming calls. Many people balancing busy social and work lives also demonstrate great interpersonal skills.

In-Groups and Out-Groups

in-group
exclusive group demanding intense loyalty

out-group
group targeted by an in-group for opposition, antagonism, or competition

In-groups and out-groups are like two sides of a coin—you can't have one without the other. An **in-group** requires extreme loyalty from its members. Its norms compel members to exclude others. The in-group competes with and is opposed to the **out-group.** An out-group is a group toward which in-group members feel opposition, antagonism, or competition. Based on membership in these groups, people divide into "we" and "they."

Where are these groups found? In-groups and out-groups may form around schools, athletic teams, cheerleading squads, racially or ethnically divided neighborhoods, or countries at war. High school students can easily identify the many "in" and "out" groups in their schools. Jocks, cheerleaders, geeks, and nerds are in-groups for some and out-groups for others.

What are group boundaries? In-groups must have ways of telling who is and is not "in." If nothing distinguishes "us" from "them," then there can be no "ins" and "outs." A boundary is often a symbol (badges, clothes, or a particular slang); it may be an action (handshake, high five); or it may be an actual place. New in-group members are often taught the boundaries at initiation ceremonies. To outsiders, group boundaries form an entrance barrier.

How are group boundaries maintained? Maintaining group boundaries requires intense loyalty and commitment from the group members. Unfortunately, this may involve clashes with outsiders. Urban gang members may injure or kill an enemy gang member who has entered their "territory."

Social Networks

social network
a web of social relationships that join a person to other people and groups

As individuals and as members of primary and secondary groups, we interact with many people. All of a person's social relationships make up his or her **social network**—the web of social relationships that join a person to other people and groups. This social network includes family members, work colleagues, classmates, church members, close friends, car mechanics, and store clerks. Social networks tie us to hundreds of people within our communities, throughout the country, and even around the world (Doreian and Stokman, 1997).

Busy people have social networks that interconnect like this old telephone switchboard.

Your broader social network can be thought of as containing smaller webs within the larger web of social relationships, depending on how finely you wish to break it down. All of your friends are only one part of your total social network. Another part might be composed of all the people at your school with whom you have social relationships of various kinds.

The Internet is expanding the amount of interaction and the flow of information within networks. Before the Internet, for example, environmental

Observation

As the text states, your students probably know the in-groups and out-groups in your high school. Begin this activity by brainstorming with students the in-groups and out-groups represented in your school. Then assign students to observe these different groups. The observations can be made during breaks between classes or during lunch break. Students should look for the boundaries that distinguish the groups. Do they have different clothing? Handshakes? Language? Can the boundaries be overcome by outsiders, or are others allowed into the groups? Ask students to share their findings with the rest of the class. Be sure to tell students that their observations should be objective, not critical. Ask for volunteers to share what they learned about groups from their observations.
L1

activists across the United States had to depend on slower, more cumbersome means of communication, such as the print media, the telephone, and letter writing. With the Internet, members of environmental organizations can supply almost unlimited information to as many people as they can reach. Volunteers, for example, can recruit others to write to political leaders protesting the Chesapeake Bay environmental problems. Protests in various regions of the country can be organized very quickly. Feedback among network members can be instantaneous.

This increased ease, speed, and frequency of social contact can promote a sense of membership in a particular network. Whereas in the past, opponents to gun control were largely unaware of each other, they may now feel part of a nationwide social network.

Are social networks groups? Although a person's social network includes groups, it is not a group itself. A social network lacks the boundaries of a group and it does not involve close or continuous interaction among all members. Thus, all members of a social network do not necessarily experience a feeling of membership because many of the relationships are too temporary for a sense of belonging to develop.

How strong are the ties in a social network? Social networks include both primary and secondary groups. Thus, the social relationships within a network involve both strong and weak ties (Granovetter, 1973; Freeman, 1992). Strong ties exist in primary relationships. Weak ties are most often found in secondary relationships.

What are the functions of social networks? Social networks can serve several important functions. They can provide a sense of belonging and purpose. They can furnish support in the form of help and advice. Finally, networks can be a useful tool for those entering the labor market. Getting to know people who can help you in your career is very important.

Section 2 Assessment

1. Provide an example, not given in the text, of each of the following:
   - **a.** out-group
   - **b.** in-group
   - **c.** social aggregate
   - **d.** social category
   - **e.** reference group
2. How are social networks different from social aggregates?

Critical Thinking

3. **Making Comparisons** Your high school has in-groups and out-groups. Concentrate on two of these groups and analyze sociologically the differences in the roles of group membership in one in-group and one out-group.

"Organization has been made by man; it can be changed by man."

William H. Whyte
American sociologist

Working with the Quote

Ask for volunteers to restate the quote in their own words. Then ask how many believe the quote is true. Can most formal organizations be changed? If so, how? What kind of effort would be needed to make the changes necessary?

Pulling it All Together

In this section students learned that reference groups help us form identities and evaluate ourselves. Social networks extend our contacts and allow us to form links to other people.

Answers to Section 2 Assessment

1. **a-e.** Answers will vary according to students' particular examples.
2. A social network is made up of an individual's primary and secondary relationships. A social aggregate is merely a gathering of people in close physical proximity.

Critical Thinking

3. Answers will vary.

Using Problem-Solving Skills

You may want to "anticipate" the next section by asking students to problem-solve a group/conformity issue.

You have a chance for a great job in the medical field at a terrific salary. This job is part of a cooperative group dedicated to providing needed body replacement parts to those who have money to pay for these services. Body parts are harvested from healthy inmates on death row. Inmates have the option to sell their body parts for profit for their families or donate needed organs.

In four days you must sign the contract for employment or give up the opportunity. As you ponder the position, you begin to think about this cooperative effort to reach a goal through the best use of limited means. Your thoughts conflict, however, as you realize the social inequities inherent in this type of work. Will you cooperate with and conform to group work expectations? Using problem-solving skills, determine your course of action and evaluate the effectiveness of your choice. **L2**

Sociology Today: School Violence and Social Networks

The 1999 murders of twelve students and one teacher at Columbine High in Littleton, Colorado, captured the attention of the American public. There had been many earlier incidents of violence in schools, but the Columbine tragedy forced Americans to finally recognize that violence was not confined to troubled inner-city schools.

Explanations for the attack, which was carried out by two students, came rapidly. Some blamed the lack of gun control. Others looked to violent video games and movies. For others, it was the parents' fault. A fourth reason, suggested by many sociologists, involved failure of the community's social networks.

Social networks reduce violence in at least three ways.

1. Strong social bonds reinforce acceptable and unacceptable behavior.
2. Social networks allow community or neighborhood members to share information about other members.
3. Social networks provide help and social support.

According to Laub and Lauritsen (1998), when many people are involved in their community networks, "social capital" is amassed. Social capital is the degree to which a person can depend on others in the community for help and support. For young people, community support can help compensate for a lack of closeness in families.

> *The social capital of the community can to a considerable extent offset its absence in particular families in the community. For example, children from single-parent families are more like their two-parent counterparts in both achievement and in continuation in school when the schools are in communities with extensive social capital (Coleman, 1987:10).*

In the Littleton case, social capital seemed in short supply. The parents of Eric Harris, one of the students who carried out the attack, were out of touch with the bomb-making activity occurring in their own home. More important, the rest of the community seemed unaware of any problem with these students. The only exception was a family that alerted authorities to threats Harris had posted on the Internet. But upon receiving this information, the sheriff's office apparently did not seek additional information from other members of the community (Gegax and Bai, 1999).

School violence can be diminished through the building of community networks. Both parents and young people must be willing to build social ties with other people in their neighborhoods and communities.

Doing Sociology

Examine some of the social networks in your neighborhood and community. How strong are they? What could be done to strengthen them?

Careers in Sociology

Human resources, training, and labor relations specialists often have backgrounds in sociology. These individuals recruit and interview employees, and advise on hiring decisions. In an effort to improve morale and productivity and limit job turnover, they also help firms effectively use employee skills, provide training opportunities to enhance skills, and boost satisfaction with jobs and working conditions. Although some jobs in these fields require only limited contact with people outside the office, dealing with people is an essential part of the job.

Directors of human resources may oversee several departments, each headed by an experienced manager, who specializes in one personnel activity (employment, compensation, benefits, training and development, or employee relations).

For information on careers dealing with people, link to **http://clem.mscd.edu/~career/sociolog.htm**

Sociology Today

Students might want to go back and research all the possible explanations given in the media at the time of the Columbine High School incident. One newspaper blamed it on the boys' brains, saying it was due to a chemical imbalance. See if students can find any purely sociological explanation, such as the one offered in this article. Another sociological explanation might be the "culture of violence" that many believe we have created. Put all the articles together on a wall entitled, What happened at Columbine HS? The display could be very powerful.

Answer to Doing Sociology

Student interpretations of this question will vary. They should concentrate on whether the community offers resources, health services, teen centers, and community activities that foster social networks or whether people feel fairly isolated. Each student's perspective on this will be different. See if there is a consensus on the relative strengths or weaknesses of these networks.

Section 3

Types of Social Interaction

Key Terms

- cooperation
- conflict
- social exchange
- coercion
- conformity
- groupthink

Five Types of Group Social Interaction

Social interaction is crucial to groups. In group settings, people take on roles and adopt appropriate norms and behaviors. These may be very different from the norms and behaviors that the individual holds in other settings. For example, you may behave one way as a member of a choir or a basketball team, but act quite differently when you are at home or out with your friends. In this section, we will look closely at those processes or forces that determine how individuals behave in a group setting. Robert Nisbert (1970) describes five types of social interaction basic to group life: *cooperation, conflict, social exchange, coercion,* and *conformity.* Some of these interactions keep the group stable and ongoing, while others encourage change.

Section Preview

Five types of social interaction are basic to group life: cooperation, conflict, social exchange, coercion, and conformity.

cooperation interaction in which individuals or groups combine their efforts to reach a goal

conflict interaction aimed at defeating an opponent

Cooperation

Cooperation is a form of interaction in which individuals or groups combine their efforts to reach some goal. Cooperation usually occurs when reaching a goal demands the best use of limited resources and efforts. The survivors of a plane crash in a snow-covered mountain range must cooperate to survive. Victims of floods, mudslides, tornadoes, droughts, or famines must help one another to get through their crisis.

Cooperation exists outside of emergencies as well: Children agree to a set of rules for a game, couples agree to share household duties, and students organize to march in support of a community project. Indeed, without some degree of cooperation, social life could not exist.

These Habitat for Humanity volunteers are cooperating in an effort to provide shelter for a family in need.

Conflict

Groups or individuals that work together to obtain certain benefits are cooperating. Groups or individuals that work against one another for a larger share of the rewards are in **conflict.** In conflict, defeating the opponent is considered essential. In fact, defeating the opponent may become more important than achieving the goal and may bring more satisfaction than winning the prize.

What are the societal benefits of conflict? As you read in Using Your Sociological Imagination on page 171, conflict is usually considered a

Using the Section Preview

To demonstrate types of social interaction, rearrange the desks or tables in your room every day for one week. Don't tell the students that you plan to do this. As they enter the room, there will be a sense of tremendous uneasiness. Each day, ascertain the level of social interaction. At the end of the week, determine which desk or table rearrangement lent itself to the best social interaction. Ask students why this was. Consider rearranging desks or tables facing each other in pairs, for example, to force positive social interactions.

Using the Illustration

You may have students in your class who have had experience working with a volunteer organization such as Habit for Humanity. Ask them to share their recollections of how people related. Was it different working with a cooperative group as opposed to working in a salaried or paid position?

Cooperative Learning Activity

This activity will investigate whether increasing social interactions will increase creativity. First, have students spend five minutes brainstorming individually the topic, "What changes would occur if, from now on, all people were born with an extra thumb on each hand?" Remind students that brainstorming does not involve evaluation. They should write down whatever idea comes to mind, regardless of the practicality. When time is up, have students total the number of responses they wrote.

Now, have students work in groups of four to brainstorm responses to this topic: "What would you do if you had one million pipe cleaners?" Have students count the number of responses generated by each member of the group on this topic.

Students should compare the totals of all the responses generated. Do students think brainstorming alone or in a group was more creative? Why? L1

More About . . . Conflict Resolution

Many schools have conflict management or conflict resolution groups. If your school doesn't have a conflict resolution group, you might want to consider creating one. In several high schools these groups have been instrumental in preventing violence; students are asked to consider sitting down with a mediator to resolve potential conflicts. Educators for Social Responsibility can provide you with information on how to start a group in your school. You can contact them at: **www.esrnational.org**

Controversy and Debate

Tell students that even an organization such as the Ku Klux Klan can have a functional purpose. Naturally, some of your students will disagree. Remind students that people will go out of their way to protest every time the KKK shows up in a town. Some students may suggest that there are less hurtful ways to achieve social unity and many people would agree.

A group of demonstrators, their hands painted in white to symbolize their opposition to violence, march through downtown Genoa, Italy, to protest against the 2001 Group of Eight summit. What was one possible societal benefit of this demonstration?

SOCIOLOGY Online

Student Web Activity
Visit the *Sociology and You* Web site at soc.glencoe.com and click on **Chapter 6—Student Web Activities** for an activity on conflict resolution.

disruptive form of interaction. A cooperative, peaceful society is assumed to be better than one in conflict. Conflict can be socially beneficial, however.

According to sociologist Georg Simmel (1858–1918), one of the major benefits of conflict is the promotion of cooperation and unity *within* opposing groups. The Revolutionary War drew the American colonists together, even though it brought them into conflict with the British. Similarly, a labor union becomes more united during the process of collective bargaining. A neighborhood bully can unite (at least temporarily) even the most argumentative of brothers.

Another positive effect of conflict is the attention it draws to social inequities. Norms and values are reexamined when crises and conflicts erupt. Civil rights activists in the early 1960s, for instance, jarred the American Congress into passing laws that ensure basic rights and freedoms to all people.

Conflict may also be beneficial when it changes norms, beliefs, and values. Student protests in the late 1960s and early 70s (many of which were violent) resulted in changes to previously accepted norms and behaviors within universities. University administrations became more sensitive to diverse student needs and more emphasis was placed on teaching.

Interdisciplinary Activity

World History You might ask one of your school's history teachers to talk to your class about conflict in history. Several examples are given in the text (Revolutionary War, civil rights protests in the 60s, student protests in the 60s and 70s). Even though the examples in the book are from U.S. history, it might be interesting for students to hear some examples from other parts of the world. Ask the world history teacher to describe an event and then ask students whether they know the outcome. Was it positive or negative, or both? What changes, if any, resulted from the conflict? What can be learned from these conflicts in history? For example, the League of Nations was a positive outgrowth (international cooperation) of a very serious conflict.

Social Exchange

All men, or most men, wish what is noble but choose what is profitable; and while it is noble to render a service not with an eye to receiving one in return, it is profitable to receive one. One ought, therefore, if one can, to return the equivalent of services received, and to do so willingly.

In this passage from *The Nicomachean Ethics,* Aristotle touches on **social exchange,** a type of social interaction in which one person voluntarily does something for another, expecting a reward in return. If you help a friend wash her car, expecting that she will help you study for a test, the relationship is one of exchange.

social exchange
a voluntary action performed in the expectation of getting a reward in return

In an exchange relationship, it is the benefit to be earned rather than the relationship itself that is key. When you do something for someone else, he or she becomes obligated to return the favor. Thus, the basis of an exchange relationship is *reciprocity,* the idea that you should do for others as they have done for you.

What is the difference between cooperation and social exchange? While both cooperation and social exchange involve working together, there is a significant difference between these two types of interaction. In cooperation, individuals or groups work together to achieve a shared goal. Reaching this goal, however, may or may not benefit those who are cooperating. And although individuals or groups may profit from cooperating, that is not their main objective.

For example, group members may work to build and maintain an adequate supply of blood for a local blood bank without thought of benefit to themselves. This is an example of cooperation. Suppose, though, that the group is working to ensure availability of blood for its own members. In this case, it has an exchange relationship with the blood bank. In cooperation, the question is, "How can we reach our goal?" In exchange relationships, the implied question is, "What is in it for me?"

These high school students are working together in a computer lab. Explain why this could be a social exchange relationship.

Reteaching

Have students observe interactions between people for several days at school or at work. They should pay particular attention to eye contact, who initiates conversation, body language, and group dynamics. Do certain situations elicit changes in behavior? Do students act differently around adults? Do adults act differently around other adults?

Points to Stress

Write this sentence on the board: Social interaction takes place at all times; humans can't help but interact. Students will say that it's not true, because people (strangers) can sit in a room and not interact. Ask students if nonverbal communication is a form of interaction. Is remaining silent, in itself a form of interaction? Each person is showing his or her uneasiness with the others and is thus, interacting. This should help students see the broader interaction concept.

Encouraging Citizenship Activity

After discussing with students the concept of social exchange, ask them if they ever do things for others "just because," with no thought of reciprocity. Why or why not?

If your school doesn't already have a Random Acts of Kindness Day, you might talk with the administration about instituting one. Your class could help with the details of getting it off the ground (advertising posters, etc.). If this isn't possible, have a Random Acts of Kindness Day just for your class. Ask your students to make a conscious effort to do something kind for someone else without any thought of reciprocity. Have students share what they did and how it made them feel. (Some philosophers and psychologists would argue that even altruism is self-serving, since the doer expects to receive "good feelings" about him or herself in return for the random act of kindness.)

L1

Using the Illustration

Students might suggest that coercion is the type of social interaction involved in curfews. Others might suggest that conformity is a better answer, since most people conform to the law.

Looking Ahead

Before students read the section on conformity, ask them the following question: Beyond adolescence and into adulthood, is there a lessening or increasing need to conform? Those who believe conformity needs remain the same may offer these kinds of examples: adults must conform to the workplace, dressing and behaving as expected; adults conform at home, by mowing their lawns and raking leaves. Other students may argue that adults conform less; adults have established identities, choose their own careers, and are independent of home-adult supervision.

Working with the Data

Figure 6.1 Some students may find it very hard to believe that anyone could actually be convinced to give the wrong answer on purpose. They would have to imagine the type of pressure in the experiment, where the designers of the experiment were expert at creating peer-pressure situations. The "test" was given under very psuedo-scientific conditions and the participants were sure that the other test-takers were given honest responses.

Coercion

coercion
interaction in which individuals or groups are forced to behave in a particular way

Coercion is social interaction in which individuals or groups are forced to give in to the will of other individuals or groups. Prisoners of war can be forced to reveal information to enemies, governments can enforce laws through legalized punishment, and parents can control the behavior of young children by threatening to withdraw privileges.

Coercion is the opposite of social exchange. Whereas social exchange involves voluntary conformity for mutual benefit, coercion is a one-way street. The central element in coercion, then, is domination. This domination may occur through physical force, such as imprisonment, torture, or death. More often, however, coercion is expressed more subtly through social pressure—ridicule, rejection, withdrawal of affection, or denial of recognition.

Conflict theory best describes this type of social interaction. When parents coerce children with a curfew, guards coerce prisoners with force, and governments coerce drivers with fines, obvious power differentials are at work.

What type of social interaction is involved in city curfews?

Conformity

conformity
behavior that matches group expectations

Conformity is behavior that matches group expectations. When we conform, we adapt our behavior to fit the behavior of those around us. Social life—with all its uniformity, predictability, and orderliness—simply could not exist without this type of social interaction. Without conformity, there could be no churches, families, universities, or governments. Without conformity, there could be no culture or social structure.

Do most people conform to group pressures? The tendency to conform to group pressure has been dramatically illustrated in a classic experiment by Solomon Asch (1955). In this experiment, many participants publicly denied their own senses because they wanted to avoid disagreeing with majority opinion.

Asch asked groups of male college students to compare lines printed on two cards. (See Figure 6.1.) The students were asked to identify the line on the second card that matched, in length, one of the lines on the first card. In each group, all but one of the subjects had been instructed by Asch to choose a line that obviously did not match. The *naive* subject—the only member of each group unaware of the real nature of the experiment—was forced either to select the line he actually thought matched the standard line or to yield to the unanimous opinion of the group.

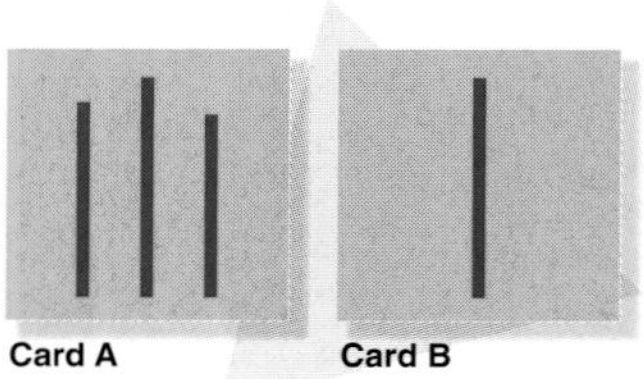

Figure 6.1 Cards for Asch's Experiments. *Which of the lines on Card A matches the line on Card B? You may be surprised to learn that in a group setting many people associated the first and the third lines with the longer line on Card B. Read about Asch's experiment in the text.*

In earlier tests of individuals in isolation, Asch had found that the error rate in matching the lines was only 1 percent. Under group pressure, however, the naive subjects went along with the majority's wrong opinion over one-third of the time. If this large a proportion of naive subjects yielded to group pressure in a group of strangers, it is not difficult to imagine the conformity rate in groups where people are emotionally committed to the welfare of the group (Myers, 1999).

Demonstration

Find a part of the building that will allow enough space for students in your class to form a large circle. Have students face the back of the person in front of them. Once they have formed the circle in that fashion, have them march in the circle to a cadence, left, right, left, right. After thirty seconds, stop them. Have them march to a different cadence, right, left, right, left, etc. Now have them march anyway they want in the circle, they are free to do as they please. This illustrates how easy it is to get people to conform. As an authority figure (the teacher) you can get students to conform to your expectation of marching. Once you allow them to do their own thing, however, some students will be able to, but some will not, because they prefer the conformity. Ask students what you could have told them to do. Would they have hopped on one leg? Crawled on the floor?
L1

What is groupthink? Because of the difficulty of going against decisions made by the group, Irving Janis (1982) has argued that many decisions are likely to be the product of *groupthink*. **Groupthink** exists when thinking in a group is self-deceptive, based on conformity to group beliefs, and created by group pressure. In groupthink, pressures toward uniformity discourage members from expressing their concerns about group decisions.

groupthink
self-deceptive thinking that is based on conformity to group beliefs, and created by group pressure to conform

During the administration of President John F. Kennedy in the early 1960s, for example, the president and his advisers decided to launch an invasion of Cuba at the Bay of Pigs. The invasion failed. Analysis by Janis revealed that during the decision process, because of group pressure, several top advisers failed to admit that they thought the plan would probably not succeed.

Research indicates that groupthink can be avoided when leaders or group members make a conscious effort to see that all group members participate actively in a multisided discussion. In addition, members must know that points of disagreement and conflict will be tolerated (Moorhead, Neck, and West, 1998; Myers, 1999).

How is groupthink promoted?

Using the Illustration

The cartoon, obviously, illustrates the concept of groupthink. Ask students if they think this happens often. Why or why not? Do students enjoy participating in some groups more than others because there is less pressure to conform? Have they ever been in a situation when they have not given their opinion on a matter because of actual or perceived group pressure? Ask volunteers to share their experiences and the outcome of the decisions made.

In a related vein, you might also ask students if they think groupthink is more or less likely to occur in bureaucratic, vertical organizations than in more open and democratic groups.

Integrating the Transparencies

A Classic Groupthink Scenario on the Bay of Pigs invasion is provided in the *Sociology and You* Transparency Binder.

Interdisciplinary Activity

History The planning of the Bay of Pigs Invasion is a good example of groupthink. Historian Arthur Schlesinger attended the meeting when the final decision was made to proceed with the mission that ended in disaster. President John Kennedy asked everyone in the room whether or not the invasion should proceed. Schlesinger wrote in his book, *A Thousand Days,* that not one man in the room dared to say that the invasion was doomed to fail, even though many felt it would. Schlesinger stated years later that they were all afraid that they would be accused of being "soft on communism." Students might want to discuss the ramifications of not speaking up when one believes something is wrong. What is lost to society when only the dominant opinion is publicized? Discuss the power of the group and how we conform to the group.

Figure 6.2 Focus on Theoretical Perspectives

Illustrating Types of Social Interaction. A type of social interaction is illustrated below from the viewpoint of a particular theoretical perspective. Each concept can be viewed from either of the other two perspectives. Associate a type of social interaction with a different theoretical perspective and make up your own example.

Theoretical Perspective	Type of Social Interaction	Example
Functionalism	Conformity	Team integration is promoted when basketball players accept their roles on the floor.
Conflict Theory	Coercion	Conflict in prisons is kept in check by the superior power of the guards.
Symbolic Interactionism	Social Exchange	Two neighbors share recipes and ideas so each benefits.

Section 3 Assessment

Match terms a–e with the appropriate numbered example.

1. Blood donors expect payment.
2. Students read what a teacher assigns.
3. Saddam Hussein invades Kuwait.
4. Flood victims help each other.
5. Employees are forced to work overtime or be fired.

a. cooperation
b. conflict
c. social exchange
d. coercion
e. conformity

6. Solomon Asch's experiment demonstrates the positive consequences of group pressure. *T* or *F*?
7. Why is conformity essential for the development of social structures?

Critical Thinking

8. **Analyzing Information** Describe an example of groupthink in your school. Analyze this situation in terms of its positive or negative consequences.

Working with the Data

Figure 6.2 Functionalism underlies Max Weber's theory of bureaucracy. The assumption is that organizations based on the characteristics of bureaucracy—division of labor, hierarchy of authority, rules and procedures, written records, merit-based promotion—will be more efficient. Weber saw bureaucracy as generally superior to earlier, nonbureaucratic forms of organization. Along with some dysfunctions, bureaucracy makes positive contributions to society. Conflict theory is reflected in the iron law of bureaucracy. Its formulator, Robert Michels, contended that a few individuals eventually gain control in organizations, leaving most organization members powerless. This happens, he believed, even in organizations founded on a democratic basis.

Pulling it All Together

Remind students that five types of social interactions exist: cooperation, conflict, social exchange, coercion, and conformity.

Answers to Section 3 Assessment

1. c
2. e
3. b
4. a
5. d
6. F (Incorrect answers were selected because naïve subjects yielded to group pressure.)
7. Without conformity we could not predict how others would behave. Order would not exist.

Critical Thinking

8. Answers will vary.

Learning Styles

Intrapersonal/Linguistic Understanding the importance and types of social interaction within groups may help students to deal more effectively with peer pressure and other difficult situations in their lives. After discussing the information in Section 3, ask students to keep a journal for a week. In it, they should record situations in which they were interacting in a group. Ask them to reflect on the types of interactions—cooperative, conflict, social exchange, coercion, and conformity. At the end of the week, ask students to review the journal entries and write a summary identifying what they have learned about themselves and their social interactions as a result of being more aware of their own behaviors and those of others. You may want to suggest that they brainstorm to create a list of ideas for making social interactions more positive and beneficial, if needed. (If students have difficulty writing, you may consider allowing them to tape record their observations for this activity.) **L1**

Tech Trends

Working in the Virtual Office

Vanishing are the traditional offices [in formal organizations] that occupy a common, fixed space, and employ a totally permanent workforce. Numerous companies are now utilizing what have come to be called "virtual offices." For the most part, these offices are staffed by at-home employees who telecommute, use Internet resources, and are frequently temporary employees.

Virtual offices offer many benefits in today's climate of global competition. For those workers who previously found it difficult to work outside the home (the elderly, [disabled], or parents with child-care responsibilities), telecommuting can be a vehicle into the workforce. What's more, corporate executives and managers enjoy advantages of the Internet: It provides rich resources of both people and information; it improves operations; it markets products. In fact, telecommuting has been shown to result in productivity gains of between 15–20%. Finally, virtual offices afford companies dramatic savings in the costs of employees and facilities.

But what of the problems associated with telecommuting? Notable is the telecommuters' sense of alienation. They may feel isolated from fellow workers and the larger organization. This alienation can be minimized by bringing telecommuters together for periodic meetings. Ostensibly established to allow telecommuters to report to their supervisors, such get-togethers serve to reinforce the telecommuters' membership in, and loyalty to, the organization for which they work.

Two other difficulties confront the telecommuter. The first is low wages. In most instances, wages paid for work done by home telecommuters lag noticeably behind wages paid to office workers. This is unlikely to change given the difficulties that trade unions face in unionizing such workers. The second difficulty is the family tension stemming from the home/office merger. Until traditional views about appropriate work locations become more enlightened, home telecommuters are likely to be perceived by other family members as "not really working."

Source: William E. Snizek, "Virtual Offices: Some Neglected Considerations," *Communications of the ACM*, 38 (September 1995):15, 16. Reprinted by permission of the author.

Analyzing the Trends

Do you think the trend toward the virtual office is a good thing? Defend your answer from a functionalist viewpoint.

Careers in Sociology

Sociology is also a good background for people interested in careers in training. Planning and program development is an important part of the training specialist's job. In order to identify and assess training needs, trainers may confer with managers and supervisors or conduct surveys. They also evaluate training effectiveness.

Training specialists and managers must speak and write effectively. The growing diversity of the workforce requires that they work with or supervise people with various cultural backgrounds, levels of education, and experience. They must be able to cope with conflicting points of view, function under pressure, and demonstrate discretion, integrity, fair-mindedness, and a persuasive, congenial personality.

For information about careers in employee training and development, contact the American Society for Training and Development, **http://www.astd.org**

Tech Trends

Ask students if they think this article describes the future. How will the virtual office transform other parts of society? Students might want to locate someone they know and interview them about the pluses and minuses of virtual offices.

Answer to Analyzing the Trends

Answers will include the benefits for parents with children; they won't need to travel each day to work, they will have time to work at their own leisure, and they won't have the stresses of an eight-hour day. The functionalist would say that as long as it maintains the order and stability of the social system, it is good. If work is being transformed in this manner, it is just another way that change can occur without upsetting the status quo.

Integrating the Teacher Resources

Look for Ethics, Values, and Technology: Real-Life Issues in Society, available in your Teacher's Resource Box. The booklet provides primary source readings dealing with real-life controversies. Student worksheets are included.

Focus on Research

Stanley Milgram's experiment is available on video from Insight Media. Even though the tape is very dated now, it will really help students see how the experiment was conducted and how easy it was for the experimenters to convince the participants to increase the voltage without much persuasion.

Focus on Research

Experiment: Group Pressure and Obedience

Can a group cause a person to physically punish a victim with increasing severity despite the victim's pleas for mercy? Researcher Stanley Milgram (1964) has shown that this could happen.

As noted in the text, Solomon Asch demonstrated that group pressure can influence people to make false claims about what they see. Specifically, experimental subjects can be pressured to claim that two lines (drawn on a card) match in length even though they originally perceived these same two lines as different in length. Milgram wanted to know if group pressure can have the same effect on behavior. Can group pressure cause people to treat others in ways they otherwise would not?

To test this question, Milgram could have chosen a desired behavior relatively easy to induce, such as sharing food with a stranger or damaging someone else's property. Choosing a much harder case, Milgram asked research participants to administer increasingly stronger electric shocks to people who appeared to be in pain. And these research participants were people just like you and me!

Milgram placed eighty males in an experimental situation in which a team of three individuals (two "confederates" who knew the nature of the experiment and one "subject" who did not) tested a fourth person (who was also in on the experiment) on a learning task. Each mistake by the fourth party brought an apparent electric shock from the subject. The two confederates (participants cooperating with Milgram) on each team suggested increasingly higher shock levels for successive mistakes made by the "learner" (the third confederate in the electric chair). The researcher recorded the degree to which the "operator" (the subject of the experiment) resisted or went along with group pressure to increase the voltage levels.

After explaining to the subject that the purpose of the experiment was to determine the effects of punishment (electric shocks) on memory, the learner was strapped into an electric-chair apparatus in full view of the other three team members. These three were seated in front of a large shock generator whose switches were labeled from 15 to 450 volts in 15-volt increments. The lowest-level group of switches was labeled "Slight Shock"; the highest-level group of switches read "Danger: Severe Shock."

The "operator" controled the maximum shock that could be administered. He could keep the shock level at 15 volts throughout or

Demonstration

Ask a shop teacher to rig up a panel of authentic-looking voltage meters so you can recreate Milgram's experiment in class. (Remember, according to the social exchange principle, however, that the shop teacher will probably want something back in the future.) Are you *shocked*? You should be. Although Milgram's subjects were not harmed, they were put under a fair amount of stress. This is NOT an experiment to recreate in class. Pretend, however, that you intend to conduct the experiment at school. Many students will get excited and begin offering ideas on how to make it work. Encourage this for a while to see if anyone objects. If no one does, halt the discussion, and, as if it suddenly dawned on you, discuss the ethics of conducting such an experiment. Explain that such an experiment would likely not be approved today—even at a university.

increase the shock level in line with the group's recommendation. It was his decision. (Remember—he was the only one not in on the real purpose.)

The learner was primed to not only answer questions incorrectly. As the shocks become stronger, he grunted, protested, and finally demanded that the experiment stop. Each of these complaints was actually prerecorded and played in coordination with a given shock level. No discomfort was indicated until a 75-volt shock was administered. At 120 volts, the learner shouted that the shocks were becoming painful. Groans followed a 135-volt shock, and at 150 volts the learner cried out to be released from the experiment, complaining of a heart condition. At 180 volts, the learner cried out, "I can't stand the pain," and 285 volts was followed by an agonized scream. From 300 to 450 volts, the learner continuously shouted desperately that he would no longer answer questions.

Milgram first needed to know how far the operator would go in administering shocks *without* group influence. To accomplish this, an identical experiment was run minus the two confederates in the punishing group. Response to group pressure was measured by the difference in the operator's behavior in the two situations.

Group pressure heavily affected the level of shock administered by the operator. That is, the average shock level in the three-person situation was significantly higher than in the one-person situation. Perhaps most interesting are the results on *maximum* shock levels. When alone, only two operators went beyond the point where the learner first vehemently protested. Under group pressure, twenty-seven of the operators went beyond this point. Nineteen of the operators went above 255 volts ("Intense Shock") and ten went into the group of voltages labeled "Danger: Severe Shock." Seven even reached 450 volts (the highest shock level possible).

The research by Milgrim and Asch reveal the power of group pressure to create conformity in thought and behavior. Clearly, conformity must occur for social structure and society to exist. What worries many scholars is the extent to which social pressure can determine how humans think and act.

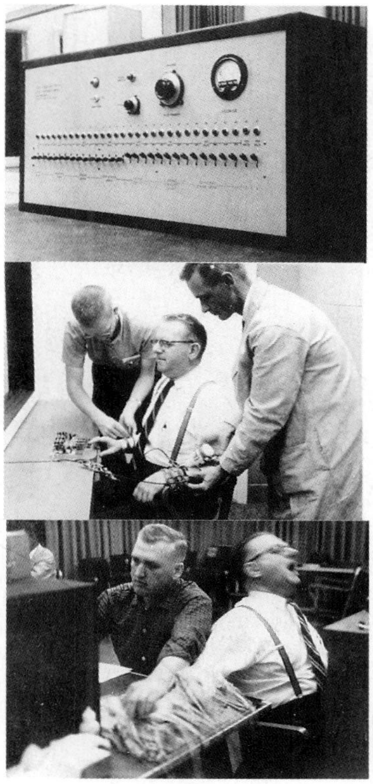

Photographs from Stanley Milgram's experiment show participants ordering higher and higher level shocks for the actor pretending to be shocked.

Working with the Research

1. Discuss the ethical implications of Milgram's experiment. (You may want to refer to Chapter 2, pp. 59–61 for a discussion about ethics in social research.)
2. If the researcher had not been present as an authority figure during the experiment to approve the use of all shock levels, do you think group pressure would have been as effective? Explain.
3. Discuss some implications of this experiment for democratic government. Can you relate it to George Orwell's novel, *1984*?
4. Do you think society would be possible without this tendency to conform? Explain your position.

Answers to Working with the Research

1. Student answers will vary, but should focus on the harm to the subjects and those who administered the shocks. Also, when participants emphasized that they no longer wanted to continue increasing the voltage for incorrect answers, they were encouraged to continue. That was unethical. The subjects were debriefed after the experiment, but still they were deceived for the sake of the research.
2. Students might want to discuss how the group is capable of influencing one's behavior. Ask students if they have ever done anything just because the crowd, "egged them on." Would an authority figure have had the same ability to make them do something they might not have done otherwise?
3. Answers will vary.
4. Answers will vary.

Integrating the Teacher Resources

A lesson plan for a student research project related to the content of this chapter can be found in Doing Sociology: Focus on Research, available in your Teacher's Resource Box.

Section 4 Formal Organizations

Key Terms

- formal organization
- bureaucracy
- power
- authority
- rationalization
- informal organization
- iron law of oligarchy

Section Preview

A formal organization is created to achieve some goal. Most are bureaucratic. The existence of primary groups and primary relationships within formal organizations can either help or hinder the achievement of goals.

The Nature of Formal Organizations

Until the 1930s, the majority of Americans lived on farms or in small towns and villages. Nearly all of their daily lives were spent in primary groups such as families, neighborhoods, and churches. As industrialization and urbanization have advanced, however, Americans have become more involved in secondary groups. Born in hospitals, educated in large schools, employed by huge corporations, regulated by government agencies, cared for in nursing homes, and buried by funeral establishments, Americans, like members of other industrialized societies, now often find themselves within *formal organizations* (Pfeffer, 1997).

Both these Japanese workers and these bank customers in the U.S. feel the affects of the formal organization structure. Do you think most organizations are bureaucratic in nature?

How are formal organizations and bureaucracies related? A **formal organization** is deliberately created to achieve one or more long-term goals. Examples of formal organizations are high schools, colleges, corporations, government agencies, and hospitals.

formal organization
a group deliberately created to achieve one or more long-term goals

bureaucracy
a formal organization based on rationality and efficiency

Most formal organizations today are also **bureaucracies**—formal organizations based on rationality and efficiency. Although bureaucracies are popularly thought of as "monuments to inefficiency," they have proven to be effective in industrial societies.

Using the Section Preview

In order for students to understand formal organizations, have them take the characteristics of bureaucracies and find one or two examples in your school. Have them report back to the class with their findings. If they create an organizational chart, it will help them see how the bureaucratic structure of their school works. They might be able to obtain an organizational chart from an administrator.

Using the Illustration

The bureaucratic nature of these organizations should be apparent to students. It is illustrated by the high level of conformity, the red-tape delays, and the frustration levels of the customers.

Integrating the Teacher Resources

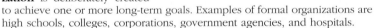

For Spanish-speaking students, you may wish to use the reproducible worksheets available in your Spanish Supplements booklet in your Teacher's Resource Box. In addition to providing Spanish translations of selected Mastering Basic Concepts worksheets, the booklet contains English and Spanish summaries of the chapter's key points.

Observation

Have students think about a large organization with which they frequently interact (your high school, their work, etc.). If students don't feel they interact with a large organization frequently, they might think about someone they know who does (a parent, friend, etc.). Ask students the following questions. Answers should be based on their interactions or those of someone they know. Do the organization's bureaucratic characteristics make it more effective or efficient? Why or why not? Have you ever been upset (angry, frustrated, etc.) when dealing with this organization? Do you think

Major Characteristics of Bureaucracies

All bureaucracies possess certain characteristics. The most important of these are listed below.

- **A division of labor based on the principle of specialization.** Each person in a bureaucracy is responsible for certain functions or tasks. (See Figure 6.3 for an organizational chart outlining the division of labor in a public school district.) This specialization allows an individual to become an expert in a limited area.
- **A hierarchy of authority.** Before discussing authority, it is necessary to define power. **Power** refers to the ability to control the behavior of others, even against their will. **Authority** is the exercise of legitimate power—power that derives from a recognized or approved source.

power
the ability to control the behavior of others

authority
the legitimate or socially approved use of power

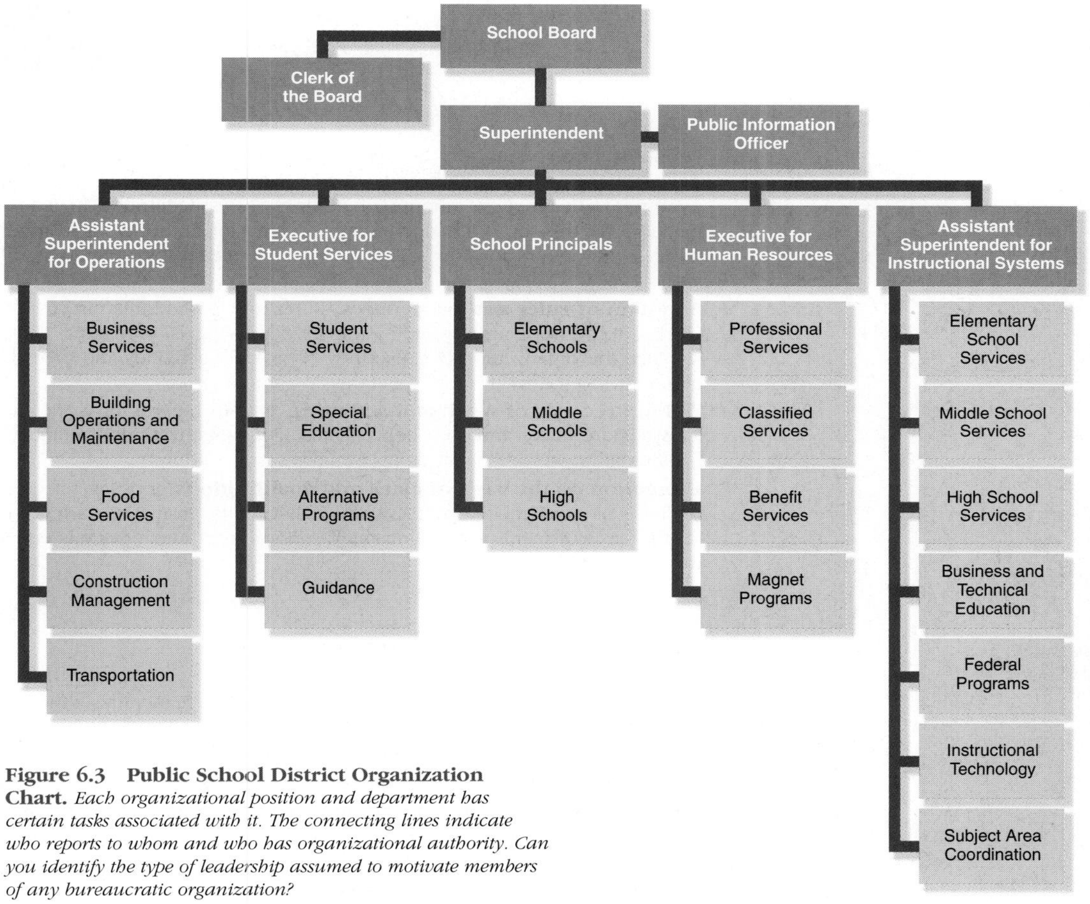

Figure 6.3 Public School District Organization Chart. *Each organizational position and department has certain tasks associated with it. The connecting lines indicate who reports to whom and who has organizational authority. Can you identify the type of leadership assumed to motivate members of any bureaucratic organization?*

Working with the Data

Figure 6.3 Some students may not have seen an organization chart before. You might make sure they understand that the level of power is illustrated in a vertical fashion. However, they need to realize that the departments or tasks listed in the gold boxes are not listed hierarchically. For example, under School Principals, the middle school principals and high school principals do not answer to the elementary school principals. All of the principals are equal in their power. Still, the first three basic characteristics of bureaucracy should lead students to conclude that authoritarian leadership tends to motivate people in bureaucracies.

Integrating the Transparencies

A Characteristics of a Bureaucracy transparency is provided in the *Sociology and You* Transparency Binder.

the upsetting situation was related to or caused by problems in the bureaucracy of the organization? Do you think the problems of the organization are related to the attempts to be effective and efficient? Describe the organizational structure of the organization. What are the positions of power? How has this organization changed you since your involvement with it? Have the changes been positive or negative? Discuss with students whether they think bureaucracies could operate on a more human level and still retain their effectiveness and efficiency.
L2

Calvin doesn't think that bureaucratic rules should apply to him if they interfere with his wishes.

People submit to authority because they believe it is the right thing to do. With respect to authority, bureaucratic organizations are like pyramids. The greatest amount of authority is concentrated in a few positions at the top, with decreasing amounts of authority in a larger number of lower positions. This is what is meant by "hierarchy of authority."

- **A system of rules and procedures.** Rules and procedures direct how work is to be done and provide a framework for decision making. They stabilize the organization because they coordinate activities and provide guidelines to follow in most situations.
- **Written records of work and activities.** Written records of work and activities are made and then kept in files. This organizational "memory" is essential to smooth functioning, stability, and continuity.
- **Promotion on the basis of merit and qualifications.** Jobs are filled on the basis of technical and professional qualifications. Promotions are given on the basis of merit, not favoritism. The norm in a bureaucracy is equal treatment for all.

Max Weber and Bureaucracy

Max Weber was the first to analyze the nature of bureaucracy. Although he recognized there were problems with this type of organization, overall he believed that bureaucracies were very efficient in dealing with the needs of industrial societies.

What are the advantages of bureaucracy? In Chapter 1, you read how Weber feared the dehumanizing effects of bureaucracies. As the values of preindustrial societies began to weaken, however, Weber also saw advantages to bureaucracy. On these advantages, he wrote the following:

Using the Illustration

If students are familiar with *Calvin and Hobbes* cartoons, they will know that Calvin seldom thinks of anyone other than himself. He is, in fact, the ultimate individualist. Ask students if they think a bureaucracy will work if everyone thinks the way Calvin does. Have them explain their answers.

More About . . . Bureaucracies

Another characteristic of bureaucracies, which you might want to reinforce with students, is that bureaucracies are impersonal. Rules rather than personal feelings are set up to guide interactions. Application of rules and regulations helps to eliminate favoritism. Bureaucracies are set up so that no one is irreplaceable. Employees must keep documentation and records to leave a "paper trail" that can be followed by others. While this may seem heartless to students, they should appreciate that Weber worked in a time and culture where the incompetence and whimsy of unqualified individuals often brought vital processes to a complete halt.

Using Problem-Solving Skills

Ask students to think about the organizations to which they belong. Do they consider the organizations to be democratic? Why or why not? Is the effectiveness of an organization related to how democratic the students perceive the organization to be? Have students use their knowledge of groups and interaction among people to analyze the groups to which they belong. Can they apply this knowledge to the organizations to find ways to help them become more effective and more democratic? How would they go about implementing their plans?
L2

The decisive reason for the advance of bureaucratic organization has always been its purely technical superiority over any other form of organization. The fully developed bureaucratic mechanism compares with other organizations exactly as does the machine with the nonmechanical modes of production (Gerth and Mills, 1958:214).

Earlier kinds of organizations, where the decision makers were chosen on the basis of family or wealth, were just not capable of dealing with an industrial economy. The fast-moving industrial economy required steadiness, precision, continuity, speed, efficiency, and minimum cost—advantages bureaucracy could offer. **Rationalization**—the mindset emphasizing knowledge, reason, and planning rather than tradition and superstition—was on the rise. (See pages 17–18 for a review of this concept.)

rationalization
the mind-set emphasizing knowledge, reason, and planning

Snapshot of America

Membership in Fraternal Orders

You may not realize it, but fraternal orders, such as Moose, Elk, Eagles, and Shriners, are bureaucracies. They have a division of labor, hierarchy of authority, system of rules and procedures, written records, and promotion based on merit within the organization. This map shows fraternal organization membership by region in relation to the national average.

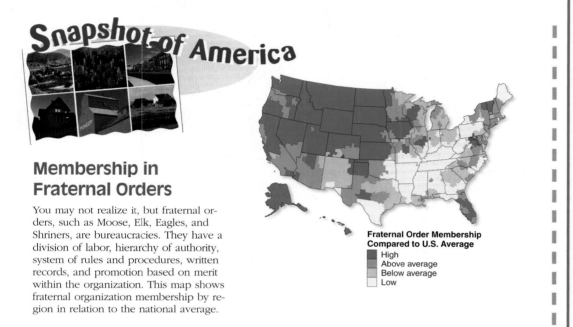

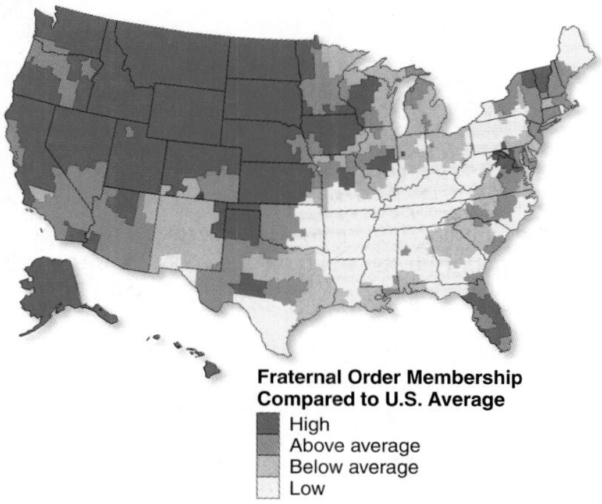

Interpreting the Map

Look back at the map of population densities in the United States on page 57. Do you see any patterns common to that map and this one? Explain.

Adapted from *Latitudes and Attitudes: An Atlas of American Tastes, Trends, Politics, and Passions.* Boston: Little Brown.

Demonstration

On the board or an overhead transparency, develop with students an organization chart that locates your position as teacher in the structure of your high school. (You may need to think about this in advance.) Ask students how they feel the structure affects this sociology class. You might share with students how you feel the structure affects your class.
L1

Snapshot of America

More about . . . Fraternal Organizations

The history of fraternal orders is a fascinating subject, but cannot be adequately addressed here. Today, the general term *fraternal organization* describes not-for-profit associations set up to provide companionship or economic benefits for its members and, in many cases, to perform community service. There are three common types of fraternal organizations: college fraternities/sororities, social fraternal societies, and fraternal benefit societies.

College fraternities and sororities operate to offer social and educational opportunities to college students. Examples: Lambda Chi Alpha, Delta Tau Delta and Delta Zeta.

Social fraternal societies are usually open to adults to provide a social opportunity and, in some cases, the chance to preserve and celebrate American ideals. Examples: Benevolent and Protective Order of Elks and the American Legion.

Fraternal benefit societies are open to men, women, and children to provide social, educational, and community service opportunities. By law each must: be not for profit, have a representative form of government, have a system of local lodges, and provide insurance and other benefits to members.

Answers to Interpreting the Map

Answers will vary.

World View

Answer to Interpreting the Map

Some students might think this an unfair question, since it is designed to check their ability to see patterns—and to not see patterns where none exist. At first, students may be tempted to conclude that citizens in more communistic societies participate in the military to a greater extent because of the data on Russia (and its former member states) and Cuba. A look at China, for example, negates such a relationship.

World View

Military Might

In preindustrial societies, military groups are loosely organized and informal in nature. They are composed of group members who live nonmilitary lives except during defense emergencies. In industrial societies, bureaucratic principles are applied to military organizations.

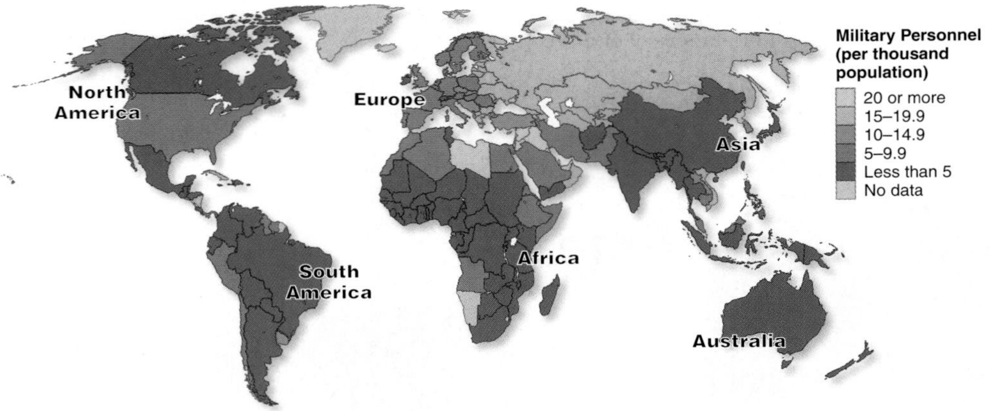

Interpreting the Map

Does this map show a relationship between the type of political leadership and the extent of citizen participation in the military? If so, describe this relationship.

Adapted from *Atlas of the World Today*. New York: Harper & Row.

Do bureaucracies undervalue people? As strange as it might sound, bureaucracy is designed to protect individuals. People often complain about the rules, procedures, and impersonal treatment that characterize bureaucracy. Without them, though, decision making would be arbitrary and without reason. It might sound great, for example, to abolish final exams, but then grading would not be objective. For example, a teacher might give higher grades to males. This is not to say that favoritism never occurs in bureaucratic organizations. Nevertheless, the presence of rules guarantees at least a measure of equal treatment.

informal organization groups within a formal organization in which personal relationships are guided by norms, rituals, and sentiments that are not part of the formal organization

Informal Structure within Organizations

Bureaucracies are designed to act as secondary groups. As anyone who has worked in a bureaucratic organization knows, though, there are primary relationships as well. Primary relationships emerge as part of the **informal organization**—groups within a formal organization in which personal rela-

Integrating the Teacher Resources

Look for the Chapter 6 Analyzing and Interpreting Data worksheet in the Unit 2 Mastering Basic Concepts booklet in your Teacher's Resource Box for skill-building exercises based on the graphs, charts, and maps in this chapter.

Careers in Sociology

Applied sociology is an important part of management. Management analysts, or consultants, analyze and propose ways to improve an organization's structure, efficiency, or profits. Some analysts and consultants specialize in a specific industry, while others specialize by type of business function, such as human resources or information systems.

After obtaining an assignment, management analysts define the nature and extent of the problem. They then develop solutions. In the course of preparing recommendations, they take into account the tionships are guided by norms, rituals, and sentiments that are not part of the formal organization. Based on common interests and personal relationships, informal groups are usually formed spontaneously.

When were informal organizations first studied? The existence of informal organizations within bureaucracies was first documented in the mid-1920s, when a group of Harvard researchers were studying the Hawthorne plant of the Western Electric Company in Chicago. In a study of fourteen male machine operators in the Bank Wiring Observation Room, F. J. Roethlisberger and William Dickson (1964, originally published in 1939) observed that work activities and job relationships were based on norms and social sanctions of that particular group of male operators. Group norms prohibited "rate busting" (doing too much work), "chiseling" (doing too little work), and "squealing" (telling group secrets to supervisors). Conformity to these norms was maintained through ridicule, sarcasm, criticism, and hostility.

Why do informal organizations develop? Informal groups exist to meet needs ignored by the formal organization. Modern organizations tend to be impersonal, and informal groups offer personal affection, support, humor, and protection. The study mentioned above pointed out that informal organizations encourage conformity, but the resulting solidarity protects group members from mistreatment by those outside the group.

Despite working in a bureaucratic organization, these construction workers seem to be on very personal terms. How do sociologists explain this?

Teaching Strategy

Add to the earlier observation of the formal organization of your school (see Using the Section Preview for Section 4) by having students look for evidence that an informal organization exists. Be careful that students don't name people. They should observe and objectively report their findings.

Using the Illustration

Informal groups (in this case, a primary group) often spring up within the larger context of formal, bureaucratic work organizations. In fact, many large corporations work hard to encourage the development of these types of informal groups within their larger organizations. Literally hundreds of books have been written on informal processes within formal organizations, especially aspects such as the "information grapevine."

nature of the organization, the relationship it has with others, and internal organization and culture. Once they have decided on a course of action, consultants report their findings and recommendations to the client. These suggestions are usually submitted in writing, but oral presentations are also common.

Information about career opportunities in management consulting is available from The Association of Management Consulting Firms, **http://www.amcf.org**

Information on obtaining a management analyst position with the federal government is available from their Internet site: **http://www.usajobs.opm.gov**

Teaching Strategy

You might want students to ascertain to what extent an oligarchy exists at your school. Do some individuals wield more power than others?

Pulling it All Together

Section 4 covered the nature of formal organizations, characteristics of bureaucracies, Max Weber's ideas on bureaucracy, informal structure within organizations, and the iron law of oligarchy.

Answers to Section 4 Assessment

1. A formal organization is one that is deliberately created to achieve one or more long-term goals. (Most formal organizations are also bureaucracies.)
2. Max Weber believed that bureaucracies were characterized by steadiness, precision, continuity, speed, efficiency, and minimum cost; and knowledge, reason, and planning, rather than tradition and superstition.
3. **a.** A
   b. A
   c. D
   d. A
4. Democratic leadership theoretically combats the iron law of oligarchy most effectively. Michels, however, contended that even democratic organizations cannot stop the iron law of oligarchy.

Critical Thinking

5. Answers will vary.

Iron Law of Oligarchy

If an organization's goals are to be achieved, power must be exercised. Sometimes this power may be grabbed by individuals for their own purposes. This process is described by the *iron law of oligarchy* (Michels, 1949; originally published in 1911).

iron law of oligarchy theory that power increasingly becomes concentrated in the hands of a few members of any organization

What is the iron law of oligarchy? According to the **iron law of oligarchy,** formulated by German sociologist Robert Michels, power increasingly tends to become more and more concentrated in the hands of fewer members of any organization. Michels observed that, even in organizations intended to be democratic, a few leaders eventually gain control, and other members become virtually powerless. He concluded that this increased concentration of power occurs because those in power want to remain in power.

The government in communist China is a prime example of Michels's principle. Not subject to popular election, the aging individuals at the top have been able to consolidate, or strengthen, their power over a long period of time. Each of the leaders is able to build a loyal staff, control money, offer jobs, and give favors.

Why does organization lead to oligarchy? According to Michels, three organizational factors encourage oligarchy. First, organizations need a hierarchy of authority to delegate decision making. Second, the advantages held by those at the top allow them to consolidate their powers. They can create a staff that is loyal to them, control the channels of communication, and use organizational resources to increase their power. Finally, other members of the organization tend to defer to leaders—to give in to those who take charge.

> "Guidelines for Bureaucrats:
> (1) When in charge—ponder.
> (2) When in trouble—delegate.
> (3) When in doubt—mumble."
>
> **James H. Boren**
> **business author**

Section 4 Assessment

1. Define the term *formal organization*.
2. List the major characteristics of bureaucracy, according to Max Weber.
3. Identify whether the following are advantages (A) or disadvantages (D) of a bureaucracy:
   a. its use of appropriate criteria in hiring employees
   b. its use of rules to provide definite guidelines for behavior within the organization
   c. its ability to hide the true nature of authority relationships
   d. its encouragement of administrative competence in managers
4. Can you describe the form of leadership most suited to the operation of the iron law of oligarchy? Explain your answer.

Critical Thinking

5. **Synthesizing Information** Analyze your school as a bureaucracy. Give an example of the following characteristics of bureaucracy: (1) system of rules and procedures; (2) impersonality and impartiality (lack of favoritism). Discuss a positive and negative consequence of each characteristic.

On-Demand Writing

Have students write one-page essays using standard grammar, spelling, sentence structure, and punctuation, on the informal organizations that exist within the formal organizations they are part of. In their essays they should address such things as the norms, rituals, and sentiments that guide the personal relationships in the informal organizations. They should also answer such questions as the following. Do the informal organizations supply support that the formal organizations do not supply? What kinds of support are supplied? Would the formal organizations be tolerable without the support offered by the informal organizations? Why or why not?
L2

Chapter 6 Assessment

Summary

Section 1: Primary and Secondary Groups

Main Idea: Groups are classified by how they develop and function. Primary groups meet emotional and support needs, while secondary groups are task focused.

Section 2: Other Groups and Networks

Main Idea: Reference groups help us evaluate ourselves and form identities. In-groups and out-groups divide people into "we" and "they." Social networks extend our contacts and let us form links to many other people.

Section 3: Types of Social Interaction

Main Idea: Five types of social interaction are basic to group life: cooperation, conflict, social exchange, coercion, and conformity.

Section 4: Formal Organizations

Main Idea: A formal organization is created to achieve some goal. Most are bureaucratic. The existence of primary groups and primary relationships within formal organizations can either help or hinder the achievement of goals.

SOCIOLOGY Online

Self-Check Quiz
Visit the *Sociology and You* Web site at soc.glencoe.com and click on **Chapter 6—Self-Check Quizzes** to prepare for the chapter test.

Reviewing Vocabulary

Complete each sentence using each term once.

a. social category
b. social aggregate
c. primary group
d. secondary group
e. reference group
f. social network
g. social exchange
h. conformity
i. groupthink
j. formal organization
k. bureaucracy
l. rationalism

1. A ____________ is an impersonal and goal oriented group that involves only a segment of one's life.
2. A group of people who are in the same place at the same time is called ____________.
3. A ____________ is a web of social relationships that join a person to other people and groups.
4. A ____________ is composed of people who are emotionally close, know one another well, and seek one another's company.
5. A situation in which pressures toward uniformity discourage members from expressing their reservations about group decisions is called ____________.
6. A type of social interaction in which one person voluntarily does something for another, expecting a reward in return is called ____________.
7. ____________ is behavior that goes according to group expectations.
8. A ____________ is a group used for self-evaluation.
9. ____________ are deliberately created to achieve one or more long-term goals.
10. A ____________ is a formal organization based on efficiency and rationality.
11. The solution of problems on the basis of logic, data, and planning is called ____________.
12. People who share a social characteristic are called a ____________.

ANSWERS Chapter 6 Assessment

Reviewing Vocabulary

1. d	4. c	7. h	10. k
2. b	5. i	8. e	11. l
3. f	6. g	9. j	12. a

Reviewing the Facts

1. Emotional Support; Socialization; Encourage Conformity
2. Primary groups are composed of people who are emotionally close, know one another well and seek one another's company. Secondary groups are impersonal and goal oriented.
3. A reference group is a group used for self-evaluation and the formation of attitudes, values, beliefs, and norms. A social network is a web of social relationships that join a person to other people and groups. It is not a group itself. It lacks the boundaries of a group and does not involve close or continuous interactions among its members.
4. In cooperation the people bind together to achieve a goal without expectation of benefit or reward. Social exchange is interaction with the expectation of a reward or benefit.
5. In-groups are the flip side of out-groups.

Thinking Critically

1. If students have identified their primary groups, they will see the connection to their in-groups. Here they want to look for commonality among all the in-groups, they all take certain classes and share similar activities. Discuss further how highly functional the school environment is despite the diversity of all these groups.
2. Here students should focus on the strength of the ties within these groups. Some students might feel close to a sibling or parent but not to another. They might want to discuss how these dynamics develop.
3. This is an opportunity for a class debate. Divide students into their primary/in-groups and have them identify areas where the potential for

Chapter 6 Assessment

Reviewing the Facts

1. Use the diagram below to list the basic societal functions of primary groups.

BASIC SOCIETAL FUNCTION OF PRIMARY GROUPS

2. List the major characteristics of primary and secondary groups.
3. What is the difference between a reference group and a social network?
4. What is the main difference between cooperation and social exchange?
5. Explain the relationship between in-groups and out-groups.

Thinking Critically

1. **Applying Concepts** Your high school is probably made up of many diverse in-groups. Identify some of these groups with their own labels, and then list common links joining all of the groups. Look for characteristics that the groups share, not for what separates them. For example, all members of the various groups might need to take two math classes in order to graduate. See how many items you can list that all the different groups share.
2. **Making Generalizations** Social networks are an important component of group interactions. Are there any people in your sociology class you would consider part of your social network? Are there any classmates that are part of your family, work, church, team, or neighborhood groups? Are the people that you sit next to closely related to your social network? Do these people have strong or weak ties to you? Are any of them among your best friends?
3. **Evaluating Information** Some high school administrators and educators have expressed concern that school violence is an indication that many high school groups are in conflict. Do you believe conflicts exist between the in-groups in your school? Have these conflicts ever erupted or are they just below the surface? How could your school work to lessen any potential group conflicts?
4. **Analyzing Information** You read about social exchange, the type of interaction in which someone does something for another person and expects a reward in return. This might also be described as the "I'll scratch your back if you'll scratch mine" expectation. Do you think that this expectation is always present? Is it possible to perform truly random acts of kindness? If you have ever done volunteer work, haven't you done something with no reward expected?
5. **Making Inferences** The text discusses the issue of groupthink in the Kennedy administration. Have you ever been in a situation in which you disagreed with the majority opinion or felt that something that was about to happen was wrong? Did you speak up? If not, did the power of the group influence you? When might failing to speak up lead to harm?
6. **Making Comparisons** You are a member of a variety of informal groups—church, school clubs, work, sports, band, and so forth. Compare and contrast the roles of group membership in two of these groups.

Sociology Projects

1. **Formal and Informal Groups** Places such as teen centers, homeless shelters, food pantries, and crisis centers are all formal organizations established to help people. Sometimes these organizations are less bureaucratic than more official government aid agencies. Informal groups are often more apparent. Create a brochure that describes such social agencies in your neighborhood, city, or town. Identify as many agencies as you can, and list an address, phone number, and contact person for each. Then select one agency to call. Ask if you can interview someone who works there to get an idea of what the agency does. Ask him or her to describe the organization in terms of formality or informality. Ask about regulations, rules, and procedures. Does he or she think the procedures are gener-

ANSWERS
Chapter 6 Assessment

conflict exists. Have students try to devise methods that might eliminate or reduce potential conflicts by instituting a conflict resolution program. For details on how to start one, refer back to the More About . . . Conflict Resolution activity on page 182.

4. Have students try to recollect times when they have done something and expected nothing in return.
5. Students should discuss how the group will influence a person's willingness to dissent. Would you be willing to be the sole objector if you thought the group's decision was harmful?
6. Answers will vary.

Sociology Projects

1. If students create this brochure, have them distribute the brochures locally. One teacher offered it to several social service agencies and they were delighted to have the free advertising.
2. You may want to suggest that students divide a piece of paper into these sections: 20 Something, 30 Something, 40 Something, 50 Something, 60 Something, 70 Something. These are the ages of the people that they will interview. Questions students should ask include: What things define your generation? You might need to provide an example of what you mean. Teens today might include the following in their list of things that define their generation: Sega, Nintendo, Pokéman, and Magic Cards.
3. Answers will vary.
4. You might want to collect several newspaper or magazine articles about school students involved in sexual harassment cases. Read the articles to your class and discuss whether the students being charged were truly at fault or whether their actions were misinterpreted.
5. As a class activity, list all reference groups students have identified on the board. How many distinct reference groups are there? More or less than students would have thought? You also might have students determine the average number of reference groups schoolmates have. What is the largest number of reference groups listed by one person? What is the smallest number of references groups listed? You might want to have students create a graph to represent the information they have gathered.
6. Answers will vary.

ally helpful or a barrier to providing service? Create a special brochure on this organization alone. Share the results of your work with the social agency.

2. **Social Categories** In this activity, you will look at generations as social categories. Write down some of the things that you believe define your generation—for example, skateboarding, extreme sports, rap music, Gap clothes. Then find adults in their forties or early fifties and ask them to define their own generation. What were the things that identified their generation? What are the things that define them now? Each list should include about ten cultural items of that generation. Share your findings with the class. If possible, bring in some items that represent the two generations.
3. **Promotions According to Merit** The text discusses the major characteristics of a bureaucracy. One of these involves the principle of promoting people according to merit. Another principle, however, is that people are treated equally and not given special consideration or shown favoritism. In many organizations, merit is sometimes synonymous for seniority so that the length of time on the job becomes just as important or more important than the skill exercised in the job. Do an informal interview of six people who work for relatively large corporations or businesses to determine what role they think seniority should play in promotion decisions. Should a mediocre—but satisfactory—employee who has been with a company for many years be skipped over for a position in favor of an employee with much less time on the job, but who has demonstrated superior skill? Summarize the results of your interviews and be prepared to share your feelings with the class.
4. **Sexual Harassment in Schools** As you know, individual actions are linked to group and organizational norms. One of the emerging norms in all grades of school involves behaviors that could be interpreted as sexual harassment. Even very young children are being cautioned about comments and actions that could be interpreted as being sexist or being intimidating to one gender. Check with your school administration or guidance office to find out about the formal policy about sexual harassment in schools. What constitutes harassing behavior? Do you think your school has an effective policy to help prevent sexual harassment? Or do you think that sometimes the bureaucracy misinterprets behavior and assigns motivations that may not be intended?
5. **Reference Groups** Re-read the section on reference groups. Then take a quick survey of ten or fifteen of your schoolmates. Ask them to identify their three most important reference groups. Compare the lists to see what groups show up most frequently. What are the norms and objectives of these most commonly cited groups?
6. **Groupthink** Using articles from the newspaper and magazines, find an article that is an example of groupthink. Using the article as a starting point, write a brief report that describes a model of group system in which the interactive roles of the individuals would have brought about a better outcome.

Technology Activity

1. *Dilbert* is a popular cartoon strip that makes fun of the bureaucratic structures in American corporations. Go to the *Dilbert* web site at http://www.unitedmedia.com/comics/ dilbert and read several of the comic strips.
    1. Find a few cartoons that illustrate some important ideas presented in this chapter. Explain the cartoons in terms of knowledge gained in this chapter.
    2. Discuss some of the strips with an adult who works in a corporation. What does that person think about the accuracy of the situations portrayed in *Dilbert?*
    3. Prepare a brief report describing what you learned about formal organizations and bureaucracies from your review of *Dilbert*.

ANSWERS CHAPTER 6 ASSESSMENT

Integrating the Teacher Resources

To further assess student comprehension of this chapter, use Chapter Test A or B available in the Chapter and Unit Tests booklet in your Teacher's Resource Box. Also, you may wish to look for the Alternative Assessments booklet for essay tests and performance assessment activities based on this chapter.

Technology Activity

1. If students are interested, you might have them work in pairs or groups to develop Dilbert-like cartoons about school. They should be sure to focus on the group and organizational structure of the school.

Enrichment Reading

Have students observe a fast food restaurant other than McDonald's and look for Weber's concepts of efficiency, calculability, predictability, and use of technology for humans. They should look for two good examples of each concept. This will help them also understand the concept of the McDonaldization of society.

Chapter 6

Enrichment Reading

The McDonaldization of Society

by George Ritzer

George Ritzer defines McDonaldization as "the process by which the principles of the fast-food restaurant are coming to dominate more and more sectors of American society as well as of the rest of the world" (Ritzer, 1996:1). Ritzer sees McDonaldization as an extension of Max Weber's theory of rationalization. (See p. 17 in Chapter 1.) For Weber, the industrial West was becoming increasingly rational—dominated by efficiency, predictability, calculability, and nonhuman technology. These features, in his view, were beginning to control human social behaviors.

Why has the McDonald's model proven so irresistible? Four **alluring** dimensions lie at the heart of the success of this model and, more generally, of McDonaldization. In short, McDonald's has succeeded because it offers consumers, workers, and managers efficiency, **calculability,** predictability, and control.

Efficiency First, McDonald's offers *efficiency,* or the optimum method for getting from one point to another. For consumers, this means that McDonald's offers the best available way to get from being hungry to being satisfied. . . . Other institutions, fashioned on the McDonald's model, offer similar efficiency in losing weight, lubricating cars, getting new glasses or contacts, or completing income-tax forms. In a society where both parents are likely to work, or where there may be only a single parent, efficiently satisfying the hunger and many other needs of people is very attractive. In a society where people rush, usually by car, from one spot to another, the efficiency of a fast-food meal, perhaps even without leaving their cars by **wending** their way along the drive-through lane, often proves impossible to resist. The fast-food model offers people, or at least appears to offer them, an efficient method for satisfying many needs.

Calculability Second, McDonald's offers *calculability,* or an emphasis on the quantitative aspects of products sold (portion size, cost) and service offered (the time it takes to get the product). Quantity has become equivalent to quality; a lot of something, or the quick delivery of it, means it must be good. As two observers of contemporary American culture put it, "As a culture, we tend to believe deeply that in general 'bigger is better.'"

Predictability Third, McDonald's offers *predictability,* the assurance that their products and services will be the same over time and in all locales. The Egg McMuffin in New York will be, for all intents and purposes, identical to those in Chicago and Los Angeles. Also, those eaten next week or next year will be identical to those eaten today. There is great comfort in knowing that McDonald's offers no surprises. People know that the next Egg McMuffin they eat will taste about the same as the others they have eaten; it will not be awful, but it will not be exceptionally delicious, either. The success of the McDonald's

Explain why you would expect service at this McDonald's restaurant in Guang Zhou, China, except for language, to be the same as the one in your neighborhood. Use sociological terms in your response.

What Does it Mean?

albeit
even though; although

alluring
attractive or fascinating

calculability
bring about by deliberate intent by controlling quantities

wending
traveling; proceeding on your way

model suggests that many people have come to prefer a world in which there are few surprises.

Control Fourth, *control,* especially through the *substitution of nonhuman for human technology,* is exerted over the people who enter the world of McDonald's. A *human technology* (a screwdriver, for example) is controlled by people; a *nonhuman technology* (the assembly line, for instance) controls people. The people who eat in fast-food restaurants are controlled, **albeit** (usually) subtly. Lines, limited menus, few options, and uncomfortable seats all lead diners to do what management wishes them to do—eat quickly and leave. Further, the drive-through (in some cases walk-through) window leads diners to leave before they eat.

Source: Adapted from George Ritzer, *McDonaldization of Society,* rev. ed., Thousand Oaks, CA: Pine Forge Press, 1996.

Read and React

1. State what Ritzer means by *McDonaldization.*
2. Since Ritzer contends that McDonaldization is spreading throughout modern society, he thinks you are affected by it. Describe a part of your social life, aside from eating at fast-food restaurants, that has been McDonaldized.
3. Describe your feelings about the McDonaldization you are experiencing.
4. Do you think McDonaldization is a rational or an irrational process? That is, does McDonaldization produce results that work for or against an organization's goal? Defend your answer.

Answers to Read and React

1. If students read the introduction to this article (which many don't!) they will find the definition clearly stated. If not, they should suggest something about applying the methods of selling fast food to organizations that provide service to other sectors of society.
2. Answers will vary. Students might think of the entertainment industry, where a lot of animation is being jobbed out overseas in piece-meal fashion.
3. Answers will vary.
4. Answers will vary but examples would include McDonald's emphasis on preparing good food, when in fact the food is salty, high in cholesterol and fatty. Kids are growing up on food that is not nutritional. McDonalds and other establishments are creating a generation hooked on fast food. It is also possible that this rational system will eventually control us and be controlled by a few individuals who will exercise this control in other ways.

Integrating the Teacher Resources

Additional primary source readings for this chapter can be found in Culture Studies: The Sociological Perspective, **available in your Teacher's Resource Box. Questions for students are included.**

Chapter Preview

Section 1 (pages 204–208)

Deviance is the violation of social norms. It is difficult to define because not everyone agrees on what should be considered deviant behavior.

Section 2 (pages 209–213)

According to functionalists, deviance has both negative and positive consequences for society. Functionalism also forms the basis for two important theories of deviance: strain theory and control theory.

Section 3 (pages 214–217)

The symbolic interactionist perspective yields two theories of deviance. We learned in Chapter 3 that culture is learned. Sociologists believe that deviance is also culturally transmitted. Labeling theory holds that an act is deviant only if other people deem it so.

Section 4 (pages 218–223)

The conflict perspective looks at deviance in terms of social inequality and power. The most powerful members of a society determine who is regarded as deviant. Conflict theorists point out the relationship between minorities and crime.

Section 5 (pages 224–232)

Crime statistics in the U.S. come from two major sources: the FBI and the Census Bureau. Four approaches to crime control are deterrence, retribution, incarceration, and rehabilitation.

CHAPTER 7

Deviance and Social Control

Lead-Off Activity

A similar activity appears in Chapter 6, but is also useful here to introduce the idea of deviance. Take your students to an open area of the building or to the gym or soccer field. Instruct them to form a circle, lined up one behind the other. Then, have them march for thirty to forty-five seconds to your command of left, right, left, right before you tell them to halt. Repeat the marching. Finally, tell students that they now may do anything they want as long as they continue to move around in the circle. They may deviate from the prescribed norm of marching. Some students will relish the opportunity;

Using Your Sociological Imagination

What would a Martian, after watching an evening of prime time television, think about American culture? If the impression of our culture were formed solely from these programs, the Martian likely would conclude that the inhabitants of earth are an exceptionally violent people. If the Martian then began to display violent behavior, could we conclude that he or she had been watching too much television?

Before answering this question, think for a moment about these statistics: Children aged two to eleven spend an average of twenty-eight hours per week watching television (compared to thirty hours in school). Fifty-seven percent of television programming contains violence. In one-quarter of the violent interactions, a gun is used. Finally, in about three-quarters of all violent scenes, the persons committing the violent acts go unpunished (National Television Violence Study, 1998).

In the past sociologists have hesitated to link violent behavior with exposure to television violence. But after hundreds of studies, researchers now confirm a link between televised aggression and personal aggressiveness. This link between imagined and actual violence is an example of culturally transmitted social behavior.

As humans learn the culture around them, they adopt certain patterns of behavior. In this chapter we will examine the learned behavior called *deviance.*

Sections

1. **Deviance and Social Control**
2. **Functionalism and Deviance**
3. **Symbolic Interactionism and Deviance**
4. **Conflict Theory and Deviance**
5. **Crime and Punishment**

Learning Objectives

After reading this chapter, you will be able to

- define deviance.
- define social control and identify the major types of social control.
- discuss the positive and negative consequences of deviance.
- differentiate the major functional theories of deviance.
- discuss the conflict theory view of deviance.
- describe four approaches to crime control.

SOCIOLOGY Online

Chapter Overview
Visit the *Sociology and You* Web site at soc.glencoe.com and click on **Chapter 7—Chapter Overviews** to preview chapter information.

Using Your Sociological Imagination

One of the most famous studies conducted on deviance is a longitudinal study that assessed subjects who had watched large amounts of television by age eight. Researchers compared the behavior of these individuals with that of a control group. Members of the control group had watched little TV at an early age. Subjects that watched more television displayed more violent behavior by age nineteen; several were incarcerated by the age of thirty. This study is regarded as the most conclusive evidence that exposure to television violence at an early age can have long-term behavioral effects.

others will not be as willing.

This demonstration illustrates how easily an authority figure like a teacher can demand conformity, or social control. The marching keeps everyone in line and guarantees the stability of the circle. Once students are allowed to deviate, some do, but others find it difficult. Of course, this deviation is minor. What would happen if one student started pushing nearby people? Depending upon the maturity level of the students, they may or may not develop some sanction for that person's actions. **L1**

Section 1

Deviance and Social Control

Key Terms

- deviance
- negative deviance
- positive deviance
- deviant
- social control
- social sanctions

Section Preview

Deviance is the violation of social norms. It is difficult to define because not everyone agrees on what should be considered deviant behavior.

deviance
behavior that departs from societal or group norms

The Nature of Deviance

Deviance refers to behavior that departs from societal or group norms. It can range from criminal behavior (recognized by almost all members of a society as deviant) to wearing heavy makeup (considered deviant by some religious groups). Some people violate norms by robbing banks or committing assault or murder. Incidents of deviance sometimes receive a great deal of attention because they involve prominent figures whose behavior is captured on national television. Former heavyweight boxing champion Mike Tyson, in a bout with the current champion, Evander Holyfield, actually bit off the tip of Holyfield's right ear and spat it onto the ring mat. Figure 7.1 illustrates the frequency of two types of juvenile deviance.

These examples appear clear-cut, but deviance is not always so easy to identify. Because deviance is a matter of social definition, it can vary from group to group and society to society. In a diverse society like that of the United States, it is often difficult to agree on what is or is not deviant behavior. In a groundbreaking study, Simmons (1969) polled people on this issue:

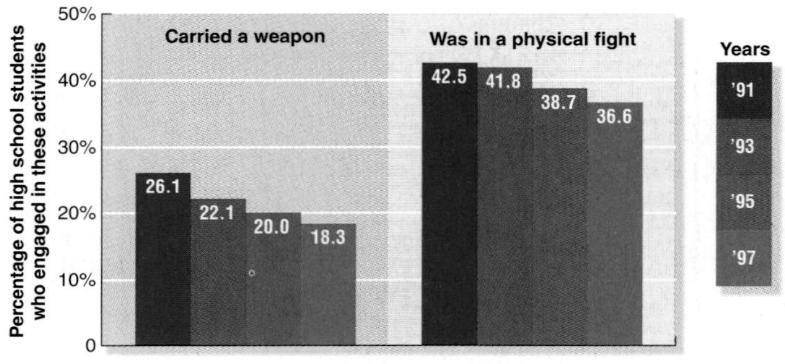

Figure 7.1 Two Types of Youth Deviance. *What does the graph say about the trend in youth violence?*

Source: *Journal of the American Medical Association* 282 (August, 1999): 440–446.

> *The sheer range of responses [to the question "What constitutes deviant behavior?"] predictably included homosexuals, prostitutes, drug addicts, radicals, and criminals. But it also included liars, career women, Democrats, reckless drivers, atheists, Christians, suburbanites, the retired, young folks, card players, bearded men, artists, pacifists, priests, prudes, hippies, straights, girls who wear makeup, the President of the United States, conservatives, integrationists, executives, divorcees, perverts, motorcycle gangs, smart-alec students, know-it-all professors, modern people, and Americans.*

To this list, one researcher would add obese people. For a week, she wore a "fat suit," adding 150 pounds to her normal body weight, in order to experience firsthand what it feels like to be

Using the Section Preview

Although tattoos and body piercings are now relatively common, this was not always the case. Inform students that twenty years ago, only bikers and other "so-called deviants" wore tattoos. Certainly, no man would have pierced his ears without facing social stigma. With this in mind, ask students who they think decides what and who is deviant. *(Explain to students that what is defined as deviant is agreed upon by consensus. When a society deems a behavior is no longer deviant, the behavior usually works its way into the mainstream, as evidenced by the current proliferation of tattoos and ear-pierced men of all ages.)*

Open-Response Question

Ask students what behavior, which was considered deviant when your parents were in high school, is no longer thought to be a departure from societal norms?

Working with the Data

Figure 7.1 Students should be able to interpret the graph to see that the number of juvenile violent acts has been decreasing since 1991. Ask students if they think that 36 percent is a high percentage of youths to be involved in fights? (You might also listen to hear if they assume that this graph is referring to males. The data actually refers to *youths,* without specifying the sex. This would be an interesting way to test their gender assumptions.)

Using Conflict Resolution Skills

Give students the following information.

If deviance is defined as behavior that departs from societal or group norms, then social control is needed to decrease crime and reduce acts of violence and deviance. The criminal justice system has been designed to maintain order, stability, and predictability in social life. When deviance continues to occur, crime escalates. One such control factor is a registration system where a database would include information on every person residing in and visiting the United States. Computer technology would link all governmental systems, which could effectively reduce welfare fraud, eliminate crime, and monitor movement of criminals from coast to coast and border to border.

The national registration system would include a retinal scan, a digital voice recording, a DNA sample, and fingerprints joined together by a social security number. This system would issue one card to be used for an overweight woman in American society. She concluded that American "society not only hates fat people, it feels entitled to participate in a prejudice that at many levels parallels racism and religious bigotry" (Lampert, 1993:154).

Deviance may be either *positive* or *negative*. **Negative deviance** involves behavior that fails to meet accepted norms. People expressing negative deviance either reject the norms, misinterpret the norms, or are unaware of the norms. This is the kind of behavior popularly associated with the idea of deviance. There is, however, another type of deviance. **Positive deviance** involves overconformity to norms—leading to imbalance and extremes of perfectionism. Positive deviants idealize group norms. In its own way, positive deviance can be as disruptive and hard to manage as negative deviance. Think about the norms related to personal appearance in American society. The mass media are constantly telling young people that "lean is mean." Negative deviants will miss the mark on the obese side. Positive deviants may push themselves to the point of anorexia. Most young people will weigh somewhere between these two extremes.

Singapore political opposition leader Chee Soon Juan is selling his book without a license, an example of negative deviance in that culture.

Minor instances of behavior that some might consider deviant occur frequently in modern societies. For that reason, sociologists generally reserve the term *deviance* for violations of significant social norms. Significant norms are those that are highly important either to most members of a society or to the members with the most power. For a sociologist, a **deviant** is a person who has violated one or more of society's most highly valued norms. Reactions to deviants are usually negative and involve attempts to change or control the deviant behavior.

negative deviance
involves behavior that underconforms to accepted norms

positive deviance
involves behavior that overconforms to social expectations

deviant
a person who breaks significant societal or group norms

This anorexic teenager in a made-for-television movie is displaying positive deviance. How would you explain to her mother that her child's behavior is "positive"?

Addressing Current Social Issues

Help students understand the association between deviance and addictions such as eating disorders and other addictive/ obsessive disorders. Ask students to name things that people become obsessed with or addicted to. *(drugs, cigarettes, food, gambling, sex, thinness, money)* List their answers on the board.

Ask students if they would consider people with these addictions to be deviant in their behavior. Have them explain why they feel the way they do. You will probably have students who feel passionately that people with addictions are deviant in their behavior and students who feel just as passionately that they are not deviant. Ask students if they think our society accepts some addictive/obsessive behaviors and not others. Why do they think this is?

Using the Illustration

The purpose of the question in the photo caption is to make sure that students understand that the term *positive deviance* does not mean it is a good thing, but rather that the deviance is in the direction of overachieving the goal rather than not attempting the desired goal.

a driver's license, for voter registration, for a concealed carry license, and for any governmental benefits. The beauty of the system is, for example, that crime could be thwarted early. If a kidnapper demanded ransom on the phone for the child of the President of the United States, the voice could be identified and the perpetrator identified quickly.

Separate the class into two groups, those for such a system and those opposed. After lengthy preparation, conduct a debate and urge both sides to reach an agreement prior to the end of the class period. Through persuasion, compromise, and negotiation, students should build a case for their point of view and participate energetically. Will this proposed solution to deviance create an invasion of privacy, or is the cost worthwhile? Would this system truly benefit our society?
L2

Snapshot of America

Answers to Interpreting the Map

1. Answers will vary.
2. Answers will vary. In addition to creating a graph, have students write a question about the geographic distribution shown in the graph.
3. Students should note the regional or geographic pattern to reported violent crimes and wonder what influence that has on behavior. They should also note the exceptions, such as the unusually low rates for Maine, Vermont, and New Hampshire. They might conclude that these states and Montana and North and South Dakota have low rates because there are few people and thus not as much "crowding." Students might note that these states are in cold climates and hypothesize that the long winters keep people indoors and thus present less opportunity to would-be muggers. (This can lead to a review of the concept of spurious correlations discussed in Chapter 2. Encourage students to hypothesize additional reasons for the low rates in those states.

Snapshot of America

Violent Crime

Although experiencing a recent decline, the U.S. has one of the highest violent crime rates of the major industrialized countries. In fact, the U.S. has the highest murder, rape, and robbery rates, and keeps pace in burglaries and auto thefts. This map indicates the number of violent crimes by state per 100,000 residents.

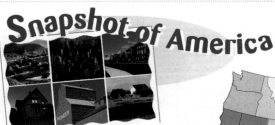

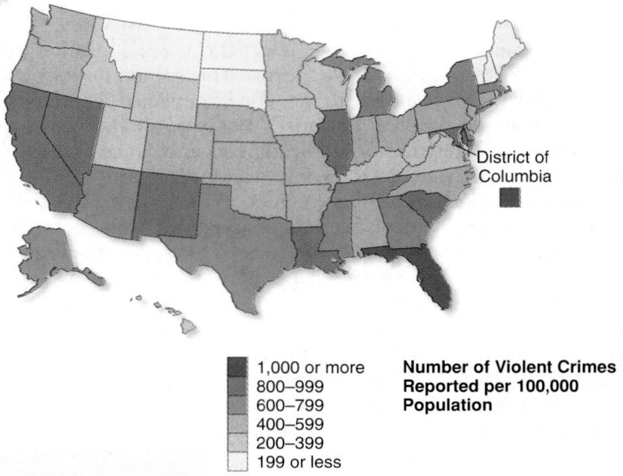

Interpreting the Map

1. Create a graph showing how the violent crime rate in your state compares with the rates in other states?
2. Pose a question which relates to the relative ranking of your state with other states.
3. What sociological conclusion can you draw from this map?

Adapted from *The World Almanac of the U.S.A.*, Mahwah, NJ, 1998.

Online UPDATE
Visit soc.glencoe.com and click on **Textbook Updates–Chapter 7** for an update of the data.

Social Control

social control
ways to encourage conformity to society's norms

All societies have ways to promote order, stability, and predictability in social life. We feel confident that drivers will stop for red lights, that waiters will not pour soup in our laps, and that store clerks will give us the correct change. Without **social control**—ways to promote conformity to norms—social life would be unpredictable, even chaotic. There are two broad types of social control: internal and external.

What is internal social control? Internal social control lies within the individual. It is developed during the socialization process. You are practicing internal social control when you do something because you know it is the right thing to do or when you don't do something because you know it would be wrong. For example, most people most of the time do not steal. They act this way not just because they fear arrest or lack the opportunity to steal but because they consider theft to be wrong. The norm against stealing has become a part of them. This is known as the *internalization* of social norms.

On-Demand Writing

Ask students to think of an activity they do habitually, such as brushing their teeth, combing their hair, taking a shower, etc. Have them write a few paragraphs explaining why they do these things. (It may seem silly at first for them to analyze why they do something that so obviously needs doing, but here is another good opportunity to remind them that people who don't understand the importance of challenging "the obvious" often miss the point of sociological pursuits.) How would they feel if they didn't do these things? How do they think their peers or society would view them if they didn't do these things? After students have finished writing, ask for volunteers to share their essays with the rest of the class. Do students see any similarities in the reasons people do these things?
L1

What is external social control? Unfortunately for society, the process of socialization does not ensure that all people will conform all of the time. For this reason, external social control must also be present. External social control is based on **social sanctions**—rewards and punishments designed to encourage desired behavior. Positive sanctions, such as awards, increases in allowances, promotions, and smiles of approval, are used to encourage conformity. Negative sanctions, such as criticism, fines, and imprisonment, are intended to stop socially unacceptable behavior.

Sanctions may be formal or informal. Ridicule, gossip and smiles are examples of informal sanctions. Imprisonment, low grades, and official awards are formal sanctions.

social sanctions
rewards or punishments that encourage conformity to social norms

Because of its hurtful nature, gossip can be a very effective informal sanction.

Section 1 Assessment

1. What is the term sociologists use for behavior that significantly violates societal or group norms?
2. State a major problem sociologists have in defining deviance.
3. What is the purpose of a social sanction?

Critical Thinking

4. **Applying Concepts** At some point in growing up, nearly everyone displays some minor deviant behaviors, such as cutting class or telling a lie. Getting "caught" in such behaviors generally results in attempts at social control. Recall such an instance for yourself. How successful were these controls in changing your behavior? (Be specific as to the types of social control and their precise application to you.)

> "No crime is rational."
>
> Livy
> Roman historian

Pulling it All Together

This section explains the nature of deviance, how it is defined, and the difficulties of defining it. Social control is the method used by cultures and societies to guarantee compliance with the social norms. Violation of norms is sanctioned accordingly.

Answers to Section 1 Assessment

1. Deviance is the term that sociologists use for behavior that significantly violates societal or group norms.
2. Deviance is a matter of social definition and can vary from group to group and society to society.
3. A social sanction is a reward or punishment designed to encourage desired behavior.

Critical Thinking

4. Answers will vary.

Integrating the Teacher Resources

To reinforce key ideas, use the Chapter 7 Graphic Organizer, a reproducible student worksheet available in the Unit 2 Mastering Basic Concepts booklet in your Teacher's Resource Box.

Observation

Discuss with students the problems many stores have with shoplifting. Then have students spend some time in a retail store. While there they should consider the following questions. What internal means of control are being relied upon to prevent theft in the store? What external means of control are being relied upon? At the next class meeting after the observation, have students work together to compile a list of the internal methods of social control that stores must rely on to prevent theft. Then have them compile a list of external means of social control that stores use. Ask which method(s) they think are more effective, internal or external. Why do they think this? **L1**

Another Time

This story is a powerful example of one culture's view of homicide. After students have read this story, ask them if they think that our society actually glorifies homicide. What examples show that this is true? Are there any examples in our society of similar banishments based on an individual's deviant behavior? *(Early in our nation's history, religious "deviants," such as Anne Hutchinson, were often banished to keep them from "polluting" the rest of the community.)*

Answer to Thinking it Over

Answers will vary. Several social scientists have suggested that because of the responsibility involved in parenting, we should require people to have a license to be parents, similar to how we require people to have driver's licenses to drive a car. These social scientists believe that all parents would have to do is show competency and attend parenting classes prior to the birth of a child. Students might want to research this topic and set up a debate format.

Another Time: Murder among the Cheyenne

Historically, the Cheyenne believed that when a member of the tribe committed murder, the whole tribe suffered the consequences. The punishment for this terrible crime was banishment from the tribe. The Cheyenne way of dealing with murders illustrates both deviance and social control.

[The Cheyenne have] specific concepts related to the killing of a fellow tribesman and specific mechanisms for dealing with homicide when it does occur.

The first of these is purely mystical and relates to the major tribal fetish, the Four Sacred Arrows. A murderer becomes personally polluted, and specks of blood contaminate the feathers of the Arrows. The very word for murder is *he'joxones,* "putrid." A Cheyenne who kills a fellow Cheyenne rots internally. His body gives off a fetid odor, a symbolic stigma of personal disintegration, which contrition may stay, but for which there is no cure. The smell is offensive to other Cheyennes, who will never again take food from a bowl used by the killer. Nor will they smoke a pipe that has touched his lips. They fear personal contamination with his "leprous" affliction. This means that the person who has become so un-Cheyenne as to fly in the face of the greatest of Cheyenne injunctions is cut off from participation in the symbolic acts of mutuality—eating from a common bowl and smoking the ritual pipe. With this alienation goes the loss of many civil privileges and the cooperative assistance of one's fellows outside of one's own family. The basic penalty for murder is therefore a lifetime of partial social ostracism [forced isolation from society].

On the legal level, the ostracism takes the form of immediate exile imposed by the Tribal Council sitting as a judicial body. The sentence of exile is enforced, if need be, by the military societies. The rationalization of the banishment is that the murderer's stink is noisome to the buffalo. As long as an unatoned murderer is with the tribe, "game shuns the territory; it makes the tribe lonesome." Therefore, the murderer must leave.

Banishment is not in itself enough, however. His act has disrupted the fabric of tribal life. Symbolically, this is expressed in the soiling of the Arrows, the allegorical identity of the tribe itself. As long as the Arrows remain polluted, bad luck is believed to dog the tribe. Not only does the spectre of starvation threaten, but there can be no success in war or any other enterprise. The earth is disjointed and the tribe out of harmony with it. The Arrow Renewal is the means of righting the situation. The oneness of the tribe is reasserted in the required presence at the ceremony of every family—save those of murderers. The renewed earth, effected by the rites in the Lone Tipi, is fresh and unsullied, once again free of the stain of killing.

Source: Excerpted from E. Adamson Hoebel, *The Cheyennes: Indians of the Great Plains* (New York: Holt, Rinehart and Winston, 1960), pp. 50–52. © 1960 by Holt, Rinehart and Winston, Inc. Reprinted by permission.

Thinking It Over

Many societies, both in the past and today, placed responsibility for the behavior of an individual on the family or tribe. Would you favor similar laws in the U.S., such as those making parents accountable for their children's actions? Why or why not?

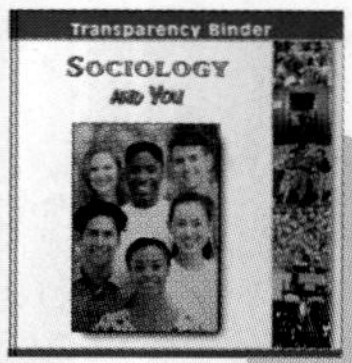

Integrating the Transparencies

Numerous transparencies for this chapter are provided in the *Sociology and You* Transparency Binder.

Learning Styles

Logical-Mathematical To provide an opportunity to practice research/math skills, ask students to conduct a survey regarding deviance. After reading and discussing the chapter, students can begin collecting data by interviewing an assigned number of people of different genders and ages. Students should ask people to list the ten most deviant behaviors they can think of.

You might also want students to collect data regarding opinions concerning the death penalty or alternatives to the death penalty. When data has been gathered, you might want to have students work in small groups to analyze the data, and then to tabulate the results of the survey, comparing the findings from the different groups. **L1**

Section 2

Functionalism and Deviance

Key Terms

- **anomie**
- **strain theory**
- **control theory**

Costs and Benefits of Deviance

As you probably remember from earlier chapters, the functionalist perspective emphasizes social stability and the way the different parts of society contribute to the whole. It may surprise you to know that functionalists believe that some deviance can contribute to the smooth operation of society. Deviance, therefore, has both positive and negative consequences for society.

What are some of the negative effects of deviance? Deviance erodes trust. If bus drivers do not follow planned routes, if television stations constantly change their schedules, if parents are not consistent in their discipline, trust will be undermined. A society with widespread suspicion and distrust cannot function smoothly.

If not punished or corrected, deviance can also cause nonconforming behavior in others. If bus drivers regularly pass students waiting for the bus, the students may begin to heave rocks at the bus. If television stations offer random programming, customers may picket the stations in protest. If parents neglect their children, more teenagers may turn to delinquency. Deviance stimulates more deviance in others.

Deviant behavior is also expensive. It diverts resources, both human and monetary. Police may have to spend their time dealing with wayward bus drivers and angry students rather than performing more serious duties.

How does deviance benefit society? Society can sometimes benefit from deviance in spite of its negative effects. Emile Durkheim observed that deviance clarifies norms by exercising social control to defend its values; society defines, adjusts, and reaffirms norms. When parents are taken to court or lose their children because of neglect, for example, society shows other parents and children how it expects parents to act.

Deviance can be a temporary safety valve. Teens listen to music, watch television programs, and wear clothes that adults may view as deviating from expected behavior. This relatively minor deviance may act to relieve some of the pressure teens feel from the many authority figures in their lives, including parents, relatives, teachers, and clergy.

Deviance increases unity within a society or group. When deviance reminds people of something they value, it strengthens their commitment to that value. Consider

How did the Reverend King's use of nonviolent deviance benefit American society?

Section Preview

According to functionalists, deviance has both negative and positive consequences for society. Functionalism also forms the basis for two important theories of deviance: strain theory and control theory.

Using the Section Preview

A functional aspect of deviance is that it creates jobs. (It also creates huge dysfunctions, of course.) For example, a result of increased efforts by lawmakers to wage war on drugs is the proliferation of new prisons across the country. New prisons mean jobs for communities and a boost to local economies—although many communities decide the drawbacks outweigh any benefits. If a prison has been built in your area lately, have students assess the impact it has had on the community. Students could informally survey local merchants to ask if they have noticed a difference in their businesses. Have they noticed an increase or decrease in profits? Has the employment rate improved?

Integrating the Teacher Resources

Look for the Chapter 7 Vocabulary Activity worksheet in the Unit 2 Mastering Basic Concepts booklet in your Teacher's Resource Box. It provides reinforcement for vocabulary in this chapter.

Role Play

Divide the class into groups of four or five students. Each group is to write a brief skit that illustrates deviant behavior in which they have participated or considered participating. Deviant behaviors should not be criminal, but might include wearing clothes, hairstyle, or jewelry that others consider deviant, listening to music or watching television programs or movies that others consider to be deviant, and so on. In the role plays, students should portray not only the deviant behavior, but also the persons (parents, teachers, etc.) who consider the behavior to be deviant. Have groups perform the role plays for the rest of the class. This could lead to a lively discussion about parents and the things they will and won't let their children do. During the discussion, help students to understand their parents' (teachers', society's) points of view on the behaviors considered deviant.

L1

spies who sell government secrets to an enemy, for example. When they are discovered, citizens who read or hear about them experience stronger feelings of patriotism.

Deviance promotes needed social change. Suffragettes who took to the streets in the early 1900s scandalized the nation but helped bring women the right to vote. Prison riots in the past have led to the reform of inhuman conditions.

anomie
a social condition in which norms are weak, conflicting, or absent

strain theory
theory that deviance is more likely to occur when a gap exists between cultural goals and the ability to achieve these goals by legitimate means

Strain Theory

According to Emile Durkheim, **anomie** (*AN-uh-me*) is a social condition in which norms are weak, conflicting, or absent. Without shared norms, individuals are uncertain about how they should think and act. Societies become disorganized. In 1968, sociologist Robert Merton adapted Durkheim's concept of anomie to deviant behavior and called his hypothesis the **strain theory.** Deviance, said Merton, is most likely to occur when there is a gap between culturally desirable goals, such as money and prestige, and a legitimate way of obtaining them. Every society establishes some goals and socially approved ways of reaching them. In the United States, an important goal is success and the material possessions that go with it. Education and hard work are two of the approved means for being successful. This is when people accept the goal and the means to achieve it; Merton calls this *conformity*. Wealthy people conform, but so do poor people who continue to work hard in low-paying jobs in the hope of improving life for themselves or their children.

How do people respond to strain? By definition, conformity is not deviant behavior. Each of the remaining four responses to strain are considered deviant, however. (See Figure 7.2.)

- In *innovation,* the individual accepts the goal of success but uses illegal means to achieve it. People engaging in this response may use robbery, drug dealing, or other lucrative criminal behavior to be successful. Innovation is the most widespread and obvious type of deviant response.
- In *ritualism,* the individual rejects the goal (success) but continues to use the legitimate means. Here people go through the motions without really believing in the process. An example is the teacher who goes about the daily routines of work without any concern for students or the quality of his or her teaching.
- *Retreatism* is a deviant response in which both the legitimate means and the approved goals are rejected. Skid-row alcoholics, drug addicts, and bag ladies are retreatists; they have dropped out. They are not successful by either legitimate or illegitimate means and they do not seek success.
- In *rebellion,* people reject both success and the approved means for achieving it. At the same time, they substitute a new set of goals and means. Some militia group members in the United States illustrate this response. They may live in near isolation as they pursue the goal of changing society through deviant means: creating their own currency, deliberately violating gun laws, and threatening (or engaging in) violent behavior against law enforcement officers.

According to strain theory, what kind of deviance is homelessness?

More About . . . Strain Theory

For a greater understanding of the real life application of Merton's structural strain theory, you might enjoy reading *Crime and the American Dream* by Steven F. Messner and Richard Rosenfeld (Wadsworth Publishing Company, 1994). This book examines how the pursuit of the American Dream, which involves making money and obtaining wealth, pushes people to commit criminal acts. The structure of modern society forces people to obtain money by any means necessary. You might want to posit this thesis with your students.

Controversy and Debate

In one U.S. city, marijuana can be purchased simply by walking into a store with a medical prescription. Merton would call this innovation because the goal of success is achieved using illegal means (assuming the marijuana buyer doesn't actually need it for medical reasons). Have students debate the issue of the legalization of marijuana for medicinal purposes. Does legalization serve as a deterrent to crime?

Using the Illustration

According to strain theory, homelessness is an example of retreatism.

On-Demand Writing

The American culture puts great emphasis on material success as a goal of society, which can be achieved through education and careers and is available to all who are willing to work for it.

Merton, however, points out that American culture is not structured in such a way as to allow all segments of society equal opportunity or access to the education, careers, etc. necessary to achieve material success. He asserts that this inconsistency in the structure of American society puts an added strain on those unable to achieve success through approved means and so contributes to much of the deviance seen among the poorer classes.

People's responses to this strain vary from conformity to deviance. Deviant responses

Figure 7.2 Merton's Strain Theory

Culturally Approved Goal: Success	Socially Accepted Way to Succeed: Hard Work	Conformity Response	Deviant Responses	Examples
Accepts goal of success	Accepts hard work as the appropriate way to succeed	**Conformity**—works hard to succeed		Business executive
Accepts goal of success	Rejects hard work as the appropriate way to succeed	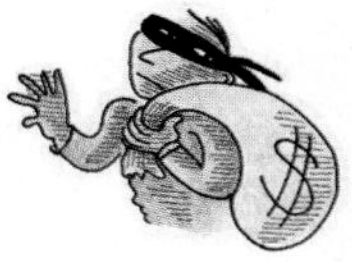	**Innovation**—finds illegal ways to succeed	Criminal
Rejects goal of success	Accepts hard work as the appropriate way to succeed		**Ritualism**—acts as if he wants to succeed but does not exert much effort	Unmotivated teacher
Rejects goal of success	Rejects hard work as the appropriate way to succeed		**Retreatism**—drops out of the race for success	Skid row alcoholic
Rejects goal of success	Rejects hard work as the appropriate way to succeed		**Rebellion**—substitutes new way to achieve new goal	Militia group member 

Adapted from Robert K. Merton, *Social Theory and Social Structure,* rev. ed. New York: Free Press.

Control Theory

Travis Hirschi's control theory (1972) is also based on Durkheim's views. According to **control theory,** conformity to social norms depends on the presence of strong bonds between individuals and society. If those bonds are weak—if anomie is present—deviance occurs.

In this theory, social bonds *control* the behavior of people, thus preventing deviant acts. People conform because they don't want to "lose face" with family members, friends, or classmates.

control theory
theory that compliance with social norms requires strong bonds between individuals and society

Working with the Data

Figure 7.2 Many texts help students understand Merton's typology by giving a + to represent the positive means and the positive goal. If the conformist accepts the means to the goal, they get a + for the means and a + for the goal. The socially accepted means is to work hard, resulting in the culturally approved goal. This should help students understand how society views the means and the goals.

Looking Ahead

There is a body of evidence that suggests religious people are less inclined to commit deviant acts. The strong social bonds of religious affiliation serve to control behavior. This subject will be revisited in Chapter 14, but students might want to research the links between religiousness and pro- and anti-social behaviors.

to strain include innovation, ritualism, retreatism, and rebellion.

Have students write mini-essays that cover the points mentioned here. They should discuss Merton's ideas about society's inconsistencies and people's responses to the inconsistencies. After students have written their papers, divide the class into two teams to debate the issues presented here. You might want to read students' papers first and put students with similar ideas on the same team, or you might intentionally mix the teams so students will have to reach agreement within their teams before the debate begins.
L2

Using the Illustration

Students might note that this person is smiling and seems to be enjoying her job as a cashier. Her appearance would lead you to think she is highly conforming and thus there is little anomie present in her life.

Pulling it All Together

This section reviewed the two major functionalist theories of deviance: structural strain theory and control theory. It also considered the benefits and negative consequences of deviance. Another sociological perspective on deviance will be covered in Section 3.

Answers to Section 2 Assessment

1. a.
2. Merton's theory states that deviance is most likely to occur when there is a gap between culturally desirable goals such as money and material goods, and a legitimate way of obtaining them.
3. ritualism
4. The four basic elements needed to create strong social bonds are: attachment, commitment, involvement, and belief.

Critical Thinking

5. Answers will vary.

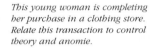

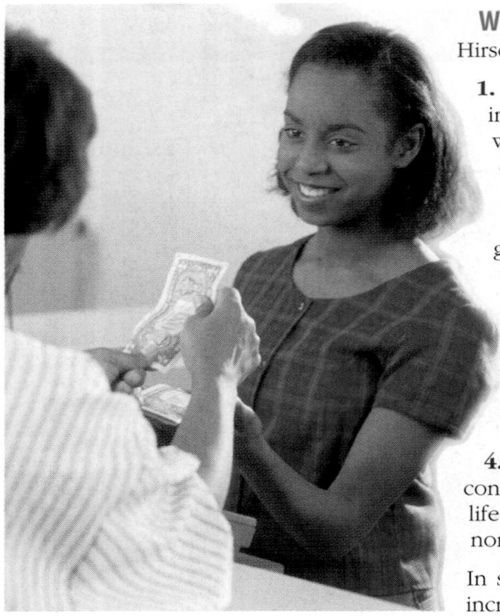

This young woman is completing her purchase in a clothing store. Relate this transaction to control theory and anomie.

What are the basic elements of social bonds? According to Hirschi, the social bond has four basic components:

1. *Attachment.* The stronger your attachment to groups or individuals, the more likely you are to conform. In other words, the likelihood of conformity varies with the strength of ties with parents, friends, and institutions such as schools and churches.
2. *Commitment.* The greater your commitment to social goals, the more likely you are to conform. The commitment of individuals who believe their hard work will be rewarded is greater than the commitment of people who do not believe they can compete within the system.
3. *Involvement.* Participation in approved social activities increases the probability of conformity. Besides positively focusing your time and energy, participation puts you in contact with people whose opinions you value.
4. *Belief.* Belief in the norms and values of society promotes conformity. A belief in the appropriateness of the rules of social life strengthens people's resolve not to deviate from those norms.

In short, when social bonds are weak, the chances for deviance increase. Individuals who lack attachment, commitment, involvement, and belief have little incentive to follow the rules of society.

> A loving person lives in a loving world. A hostile person lives in a hostile world. Everyone you meet is your mirror.
>
> **Ken Keys**
> **U.S. author**

Section 2 Assessment

1. Which of the following is *NOT* one of the benefits of deviance for society?
   - **a.** It decreases suspicion and mistrust among members of a society.
   - **b.** It promotes social change.
   - **c.** It increases social unity.
   - **d.** It provides a safety valve.
   - **e.** It promotes clarification of norms.
2. Briefly describe the main idea of Merton's strain theory.
3. A high school teacher who simply goes through the motions of teaching classes without any thought of success is an example of which response in strain theory?
4. What are the four basic elements needed to create strong social bonds?

Critical Thinking

5. **Applying Concepts** Describe someone you know (anonymously, of course) who falls into one of the four deviant response categories identified by strain theory. Use specific characteristics of this person to show the influence of different aspirations on economic decisions.

Careers in Sociology

Q. How do protective service careers utilize sociological theory?

A. Service careers involve interaction with other humans, so information gained from liberal arts, specifically sociology, will be in some measure used daily. For example, police work deals with human beings in life and death situations. The police officers and the people they serve must be as close as possible. Such closeness can generate police-citizen cooperation necessary for the involvement of the community in their own protection.

The basic mission for the police is to prevent crime and disorder. When the police fail to prevent crime, it becomes important to apprehend the person responsible for the crime and gather evidence that might be used in a subsequent trial.

Sociology Today: Is Teen Smoking a Deviant Behavior?

Sociologist Philip Hilts believes that tobacco companies target young people in their advertisements and that the strategy has a sociological basis.

> *[C]hildren are just beginning to shape their image of themselves, elbowing out a niche in the world, and must somehow differentiate themselves from parents and other adults, and get out from under what the authorities in life want from them. They dress differently, sometimes shockingly. They listen to different, sometimes shocking, music. In this quest, the children are worried, insecure, seeking to make choices and have them supported by their friends or others they respect. Most obviously, their choices are supported by each other. They have learned to lean on each other for aid and assent. Sometimes older siblings lend support. But because the insecurity is great, as many supports as possible are needed (Hilts, 1997:33).*

Cigarette advertising, claims Hilts, portrays smoking as another ally in teenagers' attempts to find their own identities. Smoking is portrayed as a pleasurable, cool way for them to declare their successful transition into adulthood. In other words, tobacco corporations assume correctly that teenagers are at a time in their lives when deviant behavior can serve a developmental need. To teens, smoking (like their choice of clothing, music, and slang) begins as simply a form of deviance.

Doing Sociology

Do you agree with Hilts's analysis? State your arguments for or against it. Search magazines and newspapers for examples of advertising that emphasizes "young adult smokers" moving into adult activities. Or, see if you can find any advertisements that picture middle-aged or older people smoking. Why do you think these ads are virtually unknown?

This mural advertising a brand of cigarettes is designed to attract the attention and admiration of teenagers.

Sociology Today

If you can find a television commercial from the 1960s or early 1970s that advertises tobacco, show it to the class and ask students who they think is the target audience. Many adults still remember the Marlboro man and the Virginia Slims woman. Why has the marketing strategy changed? Students might want to research how attitudes toward and tolerance of cigarette smoking have changed. How do these changes reflect on society?

Answer to Doing Sociology

If students research this topic, have them look at the content of magazines that carry tobacco advertisements. Do the magazines lend credibility to the argument that tobacco companies are targeting teens?

The ability of the police to perform their duties depends upon public approval of police existence, actions, behavior, and ability to secure and maintain public respect. The police seek and preserve public favor by readily offering individual service and friendship to all members of society without regard to race or social standing.

You can find law enforcement links at: **http://www.criminology.fsu.edu/cj.html** and **http://www.policechief.com/links.cfm** and **http://www.unl.edu/crimjust/html/AGENCIES.html** and **http://www.statesnews.org/other_resources/law_and_justice.htm**

Using the Section Preview

Before students begin reading the chapter, ask them if they think deviance is a learned behavior, or if they believe a person can be born with a biological predisposition to deviance. In the 1970s, some social scientists believed that a particular chromosome was linked to criminal behavior. It is now known that this is not true, and that environment, not heredity, determines deviance. People are taught behaviors that are deviant.

Reinforcing Vocabulary

Although the vocabulary terms for this section appear daunting, upon close examination they are longer versions of words and terms already familiar to the students. Ask students to try to figure out what the terms mean before reading the text as practice in breaking down words to root meanings. For example, *differential association theory:* differential has the root word different, meaning varying. Association obviously refers to relations with other people. Students might figure out that this term has something to do with how much time people spend together—and they would be right.

Section 3 Symbolic Interactionism and Deviance

Key Terms

- differential association theory
- labeling theory
- primary deviance
- secondary deviance
- stigma

Section Preview

The symbolic interactionist perspective yields two theories of deviance. We read in Chapter 3 that culture is learned. Sociologists believe that deviance is a learned behavior that is culturally transmitted. Labeling theory holds that an act is deviant only if other people name it so.

differential association theory theory that individuals learn deviance in proportion to number of deviant acts they are exposed to

labeling theory theory that society creates deviance by identifying particular members as deviant

Differential Association Theory

According to symbolic interactionism, deviance is transmitted through socialization in the same way that nondeviant behavior is learned. For example, an early study revealed that delinquent behavior can be transmitted through play groups and gangs. Even when new ethnic groups enter neighborhoods, they learn delinquent behavior from the current residents. *Differential association* and *labeling theory* are both based on symbolic interactionism.

How is deviance learned? **Differential association theory** emphasizes the role of primary groups in transmitting deviance. Just as we learn preferences in religion and politics from others we associate with closely, people can learn deviance by association, as well. The more that individuals are exposed to people who break the law, the more apt they are to become criminals. Three characteristics affect differential association:

- *the ratio of deviant to nondeviant individuals.* A person who knows mostly deviants is more likely to learn deviant behavior.
- *whether the deviant behavior is practiced by significant others.* A person is more likely to copy deviant behavior from a significant other than from people less important to him or her.
- *the age of exposure.* Younger children learn deviant behavior more quickly than older children.

Labeling Theory

Strain theory, control theory, and differential association theory help us understand why deviance occurs. **Labeling theory** explains why deviance is *relative*—that is, sometimes of two people breaking the norm only one may be labeled a deviant.

Is deviance defined by the act or by the individual? According to labeling theory, deviant behaviors are always a matter of social definition. In this view, deviance exists when some members of a group or society label others as deviants. Howard Becker, a pioneer of labeling theory, writes:

Encouraging Citizenship Activity

Read the following to students.

Deviance is relative. What one person calls deviant, another might call normal. Labeling some people as deviant, and then ostracizing them as a result of the label has caused some fearsome problems in high schools; the Columbine massacre may be an extreme example.

All social change begins with one person. In this service exercise, the one person is you.

First, identify a particular individual at your school that you, personally, have labeled or secretly considered as deviant. Make a list of the traits that led you to this conclusion. Then make a list of the traits that you possess that this person might label as deviant. Think of new, non-pejorative terms to describe the person. (Be sure not to substitute a pejorative term with a condescending

Deviance is relative. Some members of a society, such as athletes and celebrities, are often treated more tolerantly.

Social groups create deviance by making the rules whose infraction constitutes deviance, and by applying these rules to particular people and labeling them as outsiders. From this point of view, deviance is not a quality of the act the person commits, but rather a consequence of the application by others of rules and sanctions to an "offender." The deviant is one to whom that label has successfully been applied; deviant behavior is behavior that people so label (Becker, 1991:9).

Labeling theory allows us to understand the relativity of deviance. It explains, for example, why unmarried pregnant teenage girls are more negatively sanctioned than the teenage biological fathers. An unsanctioned pregnancy requires two people, but usually only one of the pair is labeled deviant. Traditionally, society expects females to set the boundaries—to be the ones to say "no." When females become pregnant outside of marriage, they have violated this norm and are considered deviant. Even today, males are not considered as deviant, not because they do not literally bear the child, but because our ideas about their sexual responsibility are still different than for females. And, of course, it is easier to stigmatize women because advanced pregnancy is so visible. Labeling theory also explains why a middle-class youth who steals a car may go unpunished for "borrowing" the vehicle whereas a lower-class youth goes to court for stealing. Too often, lower-class youths are "expected" to be criminals while middle-class youths are not.

Are there degrees of deviance? Edwin Lemert's (1972) distinction between primary and secondary deviance helps clarify the labeling process. In cases of **primary deviance,** a person engages only in isolated acts of deviance. For example, when college students are asked to respond to a checklist of unlawful activities, most admit to having violated one or more norms. Yet the vast majority of college students have never been arrested, convicted, or labeled as criminals. Certainly, those who break the law for the first time do not consider themselves criminals. If their deviance stops at this point, they have engaged in primary deviance; deviance is not a part of their lifestyles or

primary deviance
deviance involving occasional breaking of norms that is not a part of a person's lifestyle or self-concept

Student pranksters decorated the Massachusetts Institute of Technology dome to look like the Star Wars character, R2D2. Was this an example of primary or secondary deviance?

More About . . . Deviance and Labeling Theory

To illustrate the effect of labeling, write three derogatory (but not too offensive) words on the board and ask students how they would feel if they were given these undesirable labels. Do they think these are some of the worst labels a person could have? Labels typically evoke one of two responses. The label may become a self-fulfilling prophecy where a person begins to see himself or herself solely in that role and acts in accordance with it. On the other hand, a person might go out of his or her way to live down the label. In either case, labeling can have very negative consequences.

Integrating the Teacher Resources

For review or enrichment, use the Student Journal Prompts for this chapter, available in the Unit 2 Mastering Basic Concepts booklet in your Teacher's Resource Box.

term). If you realize that the new terms are value or morality-free, you should be able to start thinking of the person in the new terms. (Stress to students that there may be very valid and justifiable reasons for considering a person deviant and avoiding contact. The point is to examine these reasons and make sure they are not based on stereotypes or assumptions.)

Finally, make contact with the person. Talk to him or her; eat lunch with him or her; spend some quality, out-of-school time with him or her. In other words, get to know the person. Build a bridge. Your actions might well be contagious, and you might make a new friend.

L1

Teaching Strategy

This exercise is called the Labeling Game. As students read in the chapter, labels can be powerful tools that help or hurt people. Have students brainstorm a list of ten common labels students have for one another at your school (for example, jocks, burnouts, losers, preppies, etc.). Divide the class into two groups, the Labeled and the Reactors. Ask the Labeled to leave the room to prepare. As they leave, give each of them an index card with a label written on it. The Labeled will hang the index cards around their necks with string so that the labels are on their backs. This will make it difficult for the Reactors to immediately know what label each Labeled has received. When the Labeled return to the room, have them act out their labels for the Reactors. The Reactors should then treat the Labeled accordingly. After about fifteen minutes, have everyone return to their seats and reflect, either orally or on paper, about how it felt to be a Labeled or a Reactor. Students should also recognize how labels begin to cause generalizations about other behaviors. Did the Labelers feel the need to defend their labels? Did the Reactors immediately stereotype behavior? How did students feel about taking on the role of another person?
L1

self-concepts. Juveniles, likewise, may commit a few delinquent acts without becoming committed to a delinquent career or regarding themselves as delinquents.

secondary deviance
deviance in which an individual's life and identity are organized around breaking society's norms

Secondary deviance, on the other hand, refers to deviance as a lifestyle and as a personal identity. A secondary deviant is a person whose life and identity are organized around deviance. In this case, the deviant status overshadows all other statuses. Individuals identify themselves primarily as deviants and organize their behavior largely in terms of deviant roles. Other people label them as deviant as well and respond to them accordingly. When this occurs, these individuals usually begin to spend most of their time committing acts of deviance. Deviance becomes a way of life, a career (Kelly, 1996).

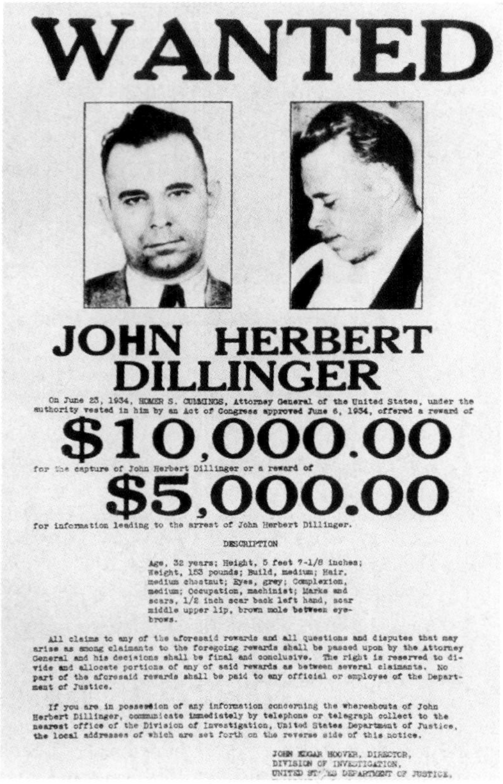
WANTED

JOHN HERBERT DILLINGER

On June 23, 1934, HOMER S. CUMMINGS, Attorney General of the United States, under the authority vested in him by an Act of Congress approved June 6, 1934, offered a reward of

$10,000.00

for the capture of John Herbert Dillinger or a reward of

$5,000.00

for information leading to the arrest of John Herbert Dillinger.

DESCRIPTION

Age, 32 years; Height, 5 feet 7-1/8 inches; Weight, 153 pounds; Build, medium; Hair, medium chestnut; Eyes, grey; Complexion, medium; Occupation, machinist; Marks and scars, 1/2 inch scar back left hand, scar middle upper lip, brown mole between eyebrows.

All claims to any of the aforesaid rewards and all questions and disputes that may arise as among claimants to the foregoing rewards shall be passed upon by the Attorney General and his decisions shall be final and conclusive. The right is reserved to divide and allocate portions of any of said rewards as between several claimants. No part of the aforesaid rewards shall be paid to any official or employee of the Department of Justice.

If you are in possession of any information concerning the whereabouts of John Herbert Dillinger, communicate immediately by telephone or telegraph collect to the nearest office of the Division of Investigation, United States Department of Justice, the local addresses of which are set forth on the reverse side of this notice.

JOHN EDGAR HOOVER, DIRECTOR,
DIVISION OF INVESTIGATION,
UNITED STATES DEPARTMENT OF JUSTICE.

John Dillinger was at one time the FBI's "public enemy number 1." Explain why Dillinger is considered a secondary deviant.

Secondary deviance is reflected in the words of Carolyn Hamilton-Ballard—known as "Bubbles" to her fellow gang members in Los Angeles:

> *Because of my size, I was automatically labeled a bully-type person. . . . I mean, people saw that Bloods jacket and since everybody thought I was crazy, I started acting crazy. At first it was an act, but then it became me. After being the target for drive-bys and going through different things, that became my life-style. I started retaliating back and I got more involved (Johnson, 1994:209).*

What are the consequences of labeling? Labeling people as deviants can cause them pain and suffering, as well as determine the direction of their lives. Erving Goffman examined some of the negative effects of labeling when he wrote about **stigma**—an undesirable characteristic or label used by others to deny the deviant full social acceptance. For example, an ex-convict is not accepted by many members of society. Why? Because a stigmatic label—*jailbird*—spoils the individual's entire social identity. One stigma, a prison record, is used to discredit the individual's entire worth. The same

stigma
an undesirable trait or label that is used to characterize an individual

Demonstration

Another way to demonstrate labeling theory and primary/secondary deviance is to tell the class that they are either your worst class ever or your best class ever. Repeat the label several times during each class period, and make a point of saying it for an entire week. At the end of the week, ask students if they began to believe what you told them. If they did, they accepted the label and their primary deviance might begin to move to secondary deviance.

may be true for a person with a disability or an unemployed person.

The words of a forty-three-year-old bricklayer, who was unemployed during the Depression, illustrate this point.

> *How hard and humiliating it is to bear the name of an unemployed man. When I go out, I cast down my eyes because I feel myself wholly inferior. When I go along the street, it seems to me that I can't be compared with an average citizen, that everybody is pointing at me with his finger. I instinctively avoid meeting anyone. Former acquaintances and friends of better times are no longer so cordial. They greet me indifferently when we meet. They no longer offer me a cigarette and their eyes seem to say, "You are not worth it, you don't work."*

This young man in New York City in the 1940s probably felt the stigma of being unemployed. How does this stigma relate to the labeling of deviants?

Section 3 Assessment

1. Which of the following describes what is meant by differential association?
   - **a.** Crime is more likely to occur among individuals who have been treated differently.
   - **b.** People may become criminals through close association with criminals.
   - **c.** Crime is not transmitted culturally.
   - **d.** Crime comes from conflict between two cultures.
2. Name the sociological theory that takes into account the relativity of deviance.
3. What is secondary deviance?
4. What are the social consequences of labeling?

Critical Thinking

5. **Analyzing Information** Think of someone you know or know of who has been labeled as deviant by some members of society. Analyze the consequences of this labeling for the person identified as a deviant.
6. **Drawing Conclusions** What actions could be taken against students who are viewed as secondary deviants?

More About . . . Stigma

Erving Goffman's book *Stigma* is a classic in sociology. Written in 1963, it tells of the stigma of having a disability at a time before Americans were socially conscious of the disabled. Students interested in understanding the stigma of disability and what the disabled experience, might want to read this book.

Answers to Section 3 Assessment

1. b.
2. The labeling theory takes into account the relativity of deviance.
3. Secondary deviance refers to deviance as a lifestyle and as a personal identity.
4. Labeling people can cause pain and suffering to the persons labeled, as well as influence their behavior and thereby determine the direction of their lives. Stigma is an undesirable characteristic or label used by others to deny the deviant full social acceptance.

Critical Thinking

5. Answers will vary.
6. Answers will vary.

Interdisciplinary Activity

Creative Writing After students have read and have a good understanding of labeling theory and primary and secondary deviance, have them write a creative story about a child who engages in primary deviance and grows into a secondary deviant. They should trace the childhood—how the child was treated by parents, teachers, and others—after an act of deviance. The story should show a correlation between how the child is perceived and treated and his or her behavior. How will this child turn out? Will he or she end up with a prison record? Allow students to use their creativity, but they should also be sure to use the information presented in this section. Ask volunteers to share their compositions with the rest of the class.
L3

Using the Section Preview

Tell the class about a study conducted by a major television network that investigated whether race was a factor in how police dealt with young males. Four black male college students were sent to a suburban neighborhood and were told to drive around the neighborhood all night. Four white male college students did the same thing in the same neighborhood. The black men were stopped four times by the local police, while the white men were not stopped even once. Ask students why the police would have made it a point to stop the black males and not the white males.

Points to Stress

Ask students if they have ever stolen anything, even something as small as a candy bar. Most likely, almost all students have stolen something at one time or another. Then ask the students if they consider themselves criminals. If the stealing was only an isolated incident, chances are they do not consider themselves criminals. They have engaged in primary deviance. However, if a student began to steal regularly, was arrested, or gained a reputation as a thief, then he or she would be engaging in secondary deviance, confirming the criminal label.

Section 4 Conflict Theory and Deviance

Key Terms

- victim discounting
- white-collar crime

Section Preview

The conflict perspective looks at deviance in terms of social inequality and power. The most powerful members of a society determine who will be regarded as deviant. Conflict theorists point to some disproportional statistical relationships between minorities and crime.

Deviance in Industrial Society

From the conflict perspective, deviance in an industrial society is behavior that those in control see as threatening to their interests. Consequently, the rich and powerful use their positions to determine which acts are deviant and how deviants should be punished.

Sociologist Steven Spitzer (1980) proposed some basic ways in which the culture of an industrial society defends itself against deviants.

1. Critics of industrial society are considered deviants because their beliefs challenge its economic, political, and social basis.
2. Because industrial society requires a willing workforce, those who will not work are considered deviants.
3. Those who threaten private property, especially that belonging to the rich, are prime targets for punishment.
4. Because of society's need for respect of authority, people who show a lack of respect for authority—agitators on the job, people who stage nonviolent demonstrations against established practices—are treated as deviants.
5. Certain activities are encouraged depending on how well they fit within industrial society. For example, violent behavior in sports is accepted because it fosters competition, achievement, teamwork, and winning (Eder, 1995; Adler and Adler, 1999).

Conflict theorists predict that this suspect's race is likely to have a negative impact on his treatment in the criminal justice system.

Race, Ethnicity, and Crime

The relationship between minorities and the judicial system is another way to view deviance from the conflict perspective.

What is the relationship between race, ethnicity, and crime? Supporters of the conflict perspective believe that minorities receive unequal treatment in the American criminal justice system. They cite statistics showing that African Americans and Latinos are dealt with more harshly than whites. This is true throughout the criminal justice process—from arrest

Cooperative Learning Activity

Read the following quote to students.

> Since I cannot remain sane without the sense of "I", I am driven to do almost anything to acquire this sense. Behind the intense passion for status and conformity is this very need . . . people are willing to risk their lives, to give up their love, to surrender their freedom, to sacrifice their own thoughts for the sake of being one of the herd, of conforming, and thus of acquiring a sense of identity, even though it is an illusory one. (Erich Fromm, *The Sane Society*)

Have students work together in groups to discuss what the author meant by this statement. How does it relate to conflict theory and deviance? Do students see a connection? Have a representative from each group share the group's ideas with the rest of the class.

L2

Even when they have committed the same crimes, African Americans and Latinos are more severely punished than whites.

through indictment, conviction, sentencing, and parole (Schaefer, 1993; Sknolnick, 1998).

Even when the criminal offense is the same, African Americans and Latinos are more likely than whites to be convicted, and they serve more time in prison than whites. Although African Americans account for only 12 percent of the total population in the United States, more than 43 percent of inmates under the death penalty are African American. In interracial murders, an African American is thirteen times as likely to be sentenced to death for the murder of a white person as a white person is for murdering an African American.

Nearly one-half of all homicide victims in the United States are African American. Nevertheless, the overwhelming majority of prisoners on death row are there for murdering whites (U.S. Bureau of the Census, 1998a). Prosecutors are less likely to seek the death penalty when an African American has been killed, and juries and judges are less likely to impose the death penalty in cases involving African American victims.

Why are minorities and whites treated so differently? The conflict theory suggests several reasons for differences in the way minorities and whites are treated in the criminal justice system. For one thing, conflict theorists point to the fact that minorities generally do not have the economic resources to buy good legal services. Thus, the outcomes of their trials are not likely to be as favorable to them.

Another source of difference involves the fact that crimes against whites tend to be punished more severely than crimes against minorities. Sociologists who follow the conflict perspective believe that this happens because society sees minority interests as less important than the interests of whites. **Victim discounting** reduces the seriousness of crimes directed at members of lower social classes (Gibbons, 1985). According to the logic behind victim discounting, if the victim is less valuable, the crime is less serious, and the penalty is less severe.

victim discounting
process of reducing the seriousness of the crimes that injure people of lower status

Controversy and Debate

Students may have heard about racial profiling, which is the practice of using race as a factor in how police handle certain procedures, such as stopping "suspicious" late night travellers for questioning. Have students check newspapers or the Internet and report back to the class about this topic.

Points to Stress

Discuss with students the meaning of the term *victim discounting.* What are students' impressions of the concept? Do they think this actually happens? What are their personal feelings about this concept? Does the concept have any validity?

Cooperative Learning Activity

Share with students the following statistics from the U.S. Bureau of Justice.

In 1998, according to the FBI's *Uniform Crime Reports* of murder victims: about 47 percent were black, 49 percent were white, and 2 percent were Asians, Pacific Islanders, and Native Americans. Most victims were likely to be male and relatively young: 75 percent were male and 63 percent were under the age of 35. About 11 percent were under the age of 18.

Have students work together in groups to arrive at some conclusions based on this information. For example, they might conclude that there is more crime in neighborhoods that have high concentrations of blacks, probably inner city areas. After arriving at some conclusions, students should find statistics that support or refute their conclusions. A good starting point is the Bureau of Justice web site at **www.ojp.usdoj.gov/bjs/**
L1

Figure 7.3 Focus on Theoretical Perspectives

Deviance. This figure illustrates approaches to understanding deviance using concepts associated with a particular theoretical perspective. Construct some examples of your own.

Theoretical Perspective	Sociological Concept	Example of Deviance
Functionalism	Anomie	Delinquent gangs sell drugs because they want success without holding conventional jobs.
Conflict Theory	White-Collar Crime	A convicted Wall Street stock broker (a more powerful member of society) may spend less time in prison than a factory worker (a less powerful member of society) found guilty of a less serious crime.
Symbolic Interactionism	Labeling	Some high school students reject dating because they have been consistently treated and described as "not cool."

White-Collar Crime

white-collar crime job-related crimes committed by high-status people

White-collar crime is yet another way to view deviance. According to Edwin Sutherland (1940, 1983), **white-collar crime** is any crime committed by respectable and high-status people in the course of their occupations. As one researcher put it, lower-status people commit crimes of the streets; higher-status people engage in "crimes of the suites." Officially, the term *white-collar crime* is used for economic crimes such as price fixing, insider trading, illegal rebates, embezzlement, bribery of a corporate customer, manufacture of hazardous products, toxic pollution, and tax evasion.

What are the costs of white-collar crime? According to the U.S. Department of Justice, the costs of white-collar crime are eighteen times higher than the costs of street crime. Illegal working environments (for example, factories that expose workers to toxic chemicals) account for about one-third of all work-related deaths in the United States. Five times more Americans are killed each year from illegal job conditions than are murdered on the streets.

Reinforcing Vocabulary

Assign students to find definitions for the white-collar crimes listed here: price fixing, insider trading, illegal rebates, embezzlement, bribery of a corporate customer, manufacture of hazardous products, toxic pollution, and tax evasion. Discuss the meaning of the terms with students.
ELL

Net Worthy

A fact-filled web site for students interested in more information white collar crime is **http://www.nw3c.org** or **http://www.iir.com/nwccc/**

The Institute for Intergovernmental IIR provides research and analysis activities in the areas of:

1. Management performance research and analysis related to NW3C organization, management, and information on service delivery;
2. Technical training and policy research, including NW3C activities and services used by its member agencies; and
3. Activity data collection, analysis, and reporting of information presented in progress reports and other documents.

Paired Learning Activity

Students should work in pairs to discuss the seeming inequalities in the justice system. They should discuss answers to questions such as these: Why do you think there are fewer convictions and less time served for white-collar criminals than for lower status criminals (those who commit "crimes of the streets")? Why are white-collar criminals often incarcerated in prisons with tennis courts or private rooms? Why do white-collar criminals often make money from their experience by writing books, giving lectures, or appearing on television talk shows? Should the justice system be changed so that punishments are more equal? How would you go about implementing a change? Do you think society will ever do anything to change the system? Why or why not? What rationale is used to explain the difference in the levels of punishment between white-collar criminals and street criminals?
L2

What kinds of punishment do the majority of white-collar criminals receive? Despite the fact that white-collar crime costs taxpayers hundreds of billions of dollars every year, the people that commit these crimes are treated more leniently than other criminals. In federal court, where most white-collar cases are tried, probation is granted to 40 percent of antitrust-law violators, 61 percent of fraud defendants, and 70 percent of embezzlers. In general, convicted white-collar criminals are less likely to be imprisoned. If they are imprisoned, they receive shorter average sentences and are more likely to be placed in prisons with extra amenities, such as tennis courts or private rooms. Both Charles Colson and G. Gordon Liddy, convicted conspirators in the Watergate cover-up in the early 1970s, served their sentences in minimum-security federal facilities.

White-collar criminals often receive milder punishments than other criminals. G. Gordon Liddy, shown here outside the radio station that broadcasts his national radio show, spent four years in prison for Watergate-related crimes during the Nixon administration.

Section 4 Assessment

1. Which of the following IS NOT one of the basic ways in which the culture of an industrial society defends itself in the face of deviance?
   - **a.** People whose beliefs clash with those of industrial society are labeled deviants.
   - **b.** Industrial society requires a willing work force.
   - **c.** Innovation is rewarded.
   - **d.** People who fail to show respect for authority are likely to be considered deviant.
2. What is the term that describes reducing the seriousness of crimes against victims from lower social classes?
3. What is white-collar crime?

Critical Thinking

4. **Evaluating Information** How could the conflict theory be misused to rationalize deviant behavior?
5. **Summarizing Information** Using the concept of victim discounting, explain why lower-class criminals are usually punished more severely than white-collar criminals for the same crime.

> "The reason that crime doesn't pay is that when it does it is called something else."
>
> **Dr. Lawrence Peter**
> **American author**

Pulling it All Together

The conflict perspective looks at how powerful interests determine deviance and the extent to which racial and ethnic minorities receive unequal treatment as a result. Part of the conflict stems from the fact that white collar criminals, who are typically powerful, high-status people, are punished and treated less severely than street criminals.

Answers to Section 4 Assessment

1. b
2. Victim discounting is the term that refers to reducing the seriousness of crimes committed against members of lower social classes.
3. White-collar crime is any crime committed by socially advantaged and high-status people in the course of their occupations.

Critical Thinking
4. Answers will vary.
5. Answers will vary.

Integrating the Teacher Resources

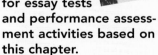

Look for the Alternative Assessments booklet in your Teacher's Resource Box for essay tests and performance assessment activities based on this chapter.

Survey

Students of sociology are especially interested in the way crime is perceived and reported by the media. Studies have shown that the media favors reports of criminal actions and criminals themselves or reasons why crimes are committed. Read these facts to students: more than $100 million per year is laundered through banks by white collar criminals; the cost of corporate crime in America is over ten times greater than the combined larcenies, robberies, burglaries, and auto thefts committed by individuals; and for every murder committed in the United States, two people die as a result of unsafe working conditions. Have students design a simple survey that tests what people's perception of the extent of white-collar corporate crime is compared to property crimes committed by individuals. (Facts from Lee and Solomon, *Unreliable Sources: A Guide to Detecting Bias in News Media,* New York: Carol Publishing Group.)
L1

Focus on Research

This article is a classic in sociology. You should refer to it again in Chapter 8, Social Stratification, to show the relationship between social class and perceptions of deviance.

Focus on Research

Case Study: Saints and Roughnecks

In this classic study, William Chambliss (1973) observed the behavior of two white teenage gangs at "Hanibal High School" over a two-year period. In addition to gang activity, Chambliss documented the responses of parents, teachers, and police to the delinquent behavior.

The Saints On weekends the automobile was even more critical than during the week, for on weekends the Saints [a delinquent high school gang] went to Big Town—a large city with a population of over a million. . . . Every Friday and Saturday night most of the Saints would meet between 8:00 and 8:30 and would go into Big Town. Big Town activities included drinking heavily in taverns or nightclubs, driving drunkenly through the streets, and committing acts of vandalism and playing pranks. . . .

Searching for "fair game" for a prank was the boys' principal activity after they left the tavern. The boys would drive alongside a foot patrolman and ask directions to some street. If the policeman leaned on the car in the course of answering the question, the driver would speed away, causing him to lose his balance. The Saints were careful to play this prank only in an area where they were not going to spend much time and where they could quickly disappear around a corner to avoid having their license plate number taken.

Construction sites and road repair areas were the special province of the Saints' mischief. A soon-to-be-repaired hole in the road inevitably invited the Saints to remove lanterns and wooden barricades and put them in the car, leaving the hole unprotected. The boys would find a safe vantage point and wait for an unsuspecting motorist to drive into the hole. Often, though not always, the boys would go up to the motorist and commiserate [sympathize] with him about the dreadful way the city protected its citizenry.

Leaving the scene of the open hole and the motorist, the boys would then go searching for an appropriate place to erect the stolen barricade. An "appropriate place" was often a spot on a highway near a curve in the road where the barricade would not be seen by an oncoming motorist. The boys would wait to watch an unsuspecting motorist attempt to stop and (usually) crash into the wooden barricade.

A stolen lantern might well find its way onto the back of a police car or hang from a street lamp. Once a lantern served as a prop for a reenactment of the "midnight ride of Paul Revere" until the "play," which was taking place at 2:00 A.M. in the center of a main street of Big Town, was interrupted by a police car several blocks away. The boys ran, leaving the lanterns on the street . . . .

Careers in Sociology

Q. Can sociology help *now* to make my neighborhood safer?

A. Crime prevention cannot be accomplished by the police alone. This requires the cooperation of police and public working together. When people work with others in their neighborhood, they can reduce crime.

It must be recognized, though, that the police and the people alone cannot successfully resolve the problems of crime. The criminal justice system must operate as a total system with all of its elements working together. The close cooperation of the police with prosecutors, courts, and correctional officers is necessary to ensure a safer community.

The American Society of Criminology is an international organization concerned with criminology: the etiology, prevention, con-

The Roughnecks [T]ownspeople never perceived the Saints' . . . delinquency. The Saints were good boys who just went in for an occasional prank. After all, they were well dressed, well mannered and had nice cars. The Roughnecks [a delinquent gang at the same high school] were a different story. Although the two gangs of boys were the same age, and both groups engaged in an equal amount of wild-oat sowing, everyone agreed that the not-so-well-dressed, not-so-well-mannered, not-so-rich boys were heading for trouble. . . .

From the community's viewpoint, the real indication that these kids were in for trouble was that they were constantly involved with the police. Some of them had been picked up for stealing, mostly small stuff, of course, "but still it's stealing small stuff that leads to big time crimes." "Too bad," people said. "Too bad that these boys couldn't behave like the other kids in town; stay out of trouble, be polite to adults, and look to their future." . . .

The fighting activities of the group were fairly readily and accurately perceived by almost everyone. At least once a month, the boys would get into some sort of fight, although most fights were scraps between members of the group or involved only one member of the group and some peripheral hanger-on. Only three times in the period of observation did the group fight together: once against a gang from across town, once against two blacks and once against a group of boys from another school. For the first two fights the group went out "looking for trouble"—and they found it both times. The third fight followed a football game and began spontaneously with an argument on the football field between one of the Roughnecks and a member of the opposition's football team.

More serious than fighting, had the community been aware of it, was theft. Although almost everyone was aware that the boys occasionally stole things, they did not realize the extent of the activity. Petty stealing was a frequent event for the Roughnecks. Sometimes they stole as a group and coordinated their efforts; other times they stole in pairs. Rarely did they steal alone. . . . Types of thievery varied with the whim of the gang. Some forms of thievery were more profitable than others, but all thefts were for profit, not for thrills.

Roughnecks siphoned gasoline from cars as often as they had access to an automobile, which was not very often. Unlike the Saints, who owned their own cars, the Roughnecks would have to borrow their parents' cars, an event which occurred only eight or nine times a year. The boys claimed to have stolen cars for joy rides from time to time.

Source: Excerpted from William J. Chambliss, "The Saints and the Roughnecks," *Society* 11 (November/December, 1973):24–31.

Working with the Research

1. From your understanding of Chambliss's study, is deviance socially created? Explain.
2. Which of the three major theoretical perspectives best explains Chambliss's findings? Support your choice.

Answers to Working with the Research

1. The study lends credence to the perception that deviance is socially created and subjective. The police had targeted the Roughnecks and ignored the behavior of the Saints. The Roughnecks were considered deviant because the police perception that anyone from the Roughneck part of town must be deviant. The police created the social reality.
2. The conflict theory perspective best explains Chambliss' findings. Those in power (the police) determined that the boys of the lower class were deviant. The upper class boys enjoyed the privileges of their social class standing and status. From a functionalist point of view, deviant behavior helped maintain jobs and social control. The interactionist perspective might cite differential association. The deviant behavior was culturally transmitted, as the boys learned to be deviant from one another.

trol, and treatment of crime and delinquency. This includes the measurement and detection of crime, legislation and practice of criminal law, and the law enforcement, judicial and correctional systems.

For information about the American Society of Criminology, check out **http://www.asc41.com/**

For information about law enforcement, try **http://www.lawenforcementjob.com/**

Using the Section Preview

Use the web site listed in the Net Worthy activity below and other sources to collect crime statistics to share with students. Be sure to find statistics on the same information, for example, crimes committed with guns. Have students compare the statistics to see whether there are any differences and if there are differences whether they are significant.

Net Worthy

To enhance your students' study of this chapter, you may want to have them visit the URL cited below. As with all web sites, you should check this out first to be sure the information found there is appropriate for your students.

Students can visit the FBI and Uniform Crime Reports (UCR) statistics web site at **www.fbi.gov** Users can link to the Uniform Crime Reports page as well as numerous other links. Once they have browsed the site, students might want to research specific topics related to crime statistics such as domestic violence, juvenile crime, etc.

Section 5

Crime and Punishment

Key Terms

- **crime**
- **criminal justice system**
- **deterrence**
- **retribution**
- **incarceration**
- **rehabilitation**
- **recidivism**

Section Preview

Crime statistics in the U.S. come from two major sources: the FBI and the Census Bureau. Differences in statistics between the two agencies are due to differences in methods of collecting data. Four approaches to crime control are deterrence, retribution, incarceration, and rehabilitation.

Measurement of Crime

Most Americans think of **crime**—acts in violation of statute law—as including a narrow range of behavior. On the contrary, more than 2,800 acts are classified as federal crimes. Many more acts violate state and local statutes.

How much crime is there in the United States today? Crime increased sharply between the 1960s and the 1990s. For example, the FBI Index of violent crime has increased from a big city offense rate per 100,000 of 860 in 1969 to 1207 in 1999. Violent crime rates are considerably higher in the U.S. than in most other industrialized countries.

> *Today the rate of homicide death for a young man is 23 times higher in the U.S. than in England. In 1995, handguns were used to kill 2 people in New Zealand, 15 in Japan, 30 in Great Britain, 106 in Canada, 213 in Germany, and 9,390 in the United States (To Establish Justice, 1999:iv).*

crime
acts committed in violation of the law

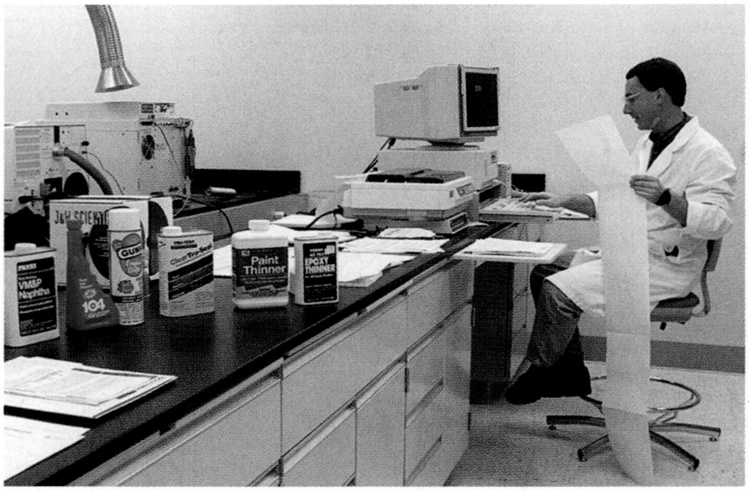

The job of this forensic scientist is to examine evidence—fingerprints, DNA, handwriting, firearms—for indications that a crime has occurred.

Demonstration

Here is a memorable (if deafening) way to show students the prevalence of crime. Bring in some noise making devices such as whistles, horns, drums, etc. You will need eight devices and eight volunteers, and a clock with a second hand. Have students sound their devices at the following intervals: the first device should go off every three seconds; the second, every twenty-one seconds; the third, every sixty seconds; the fourth, every thirty-two seconds; the fifth, every fourteen seconds; the sixth, every four seconds; the seventh, every twenty-five seconds; and the eighth, every three seconds. Inform the volunteers of the intervals, but don't tell the entire class.

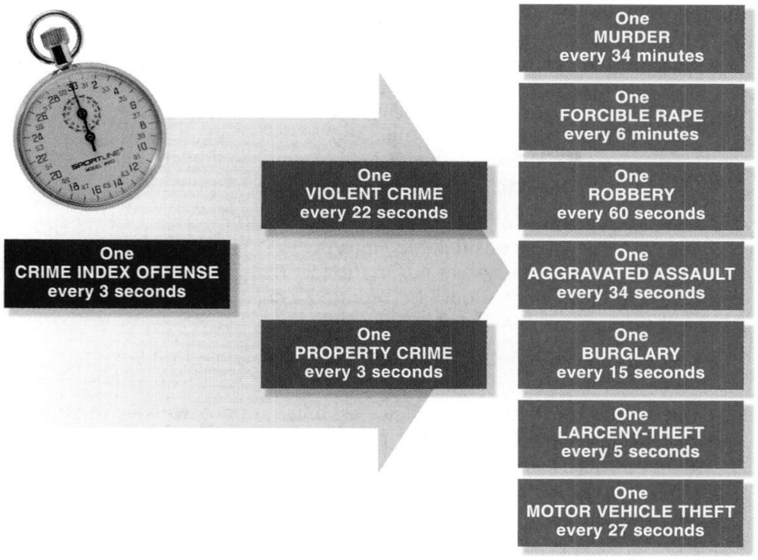

Figure 7.4 FBI's Crime Clock: 1999. How often do Americans commit crimes? *The number to the far left, of course, does not mean that one Crime Index offense actually occurs every three seconds. It does mean that when all Crime Index offenses for 1999 are divided by the total number of seconds in a year there are enough of them to be spaced out every three seconds.*

Source: Federal Bureau of Investigation, *Uniform Crime Reports,* 1999.

Online UPDATE
Visit soc.glencoe.com and click on **Textbook Updates–Chapter 7** for an update of the data.

How are crime statistics collected? The major source of American crime statistics is the Federal Bureau of Investigation's *Uniform Crime Reports* (UCR). These official statistics are gathered from police departments across the country. Reports are submitted voluntarily by law enforcement agencies.

What do UCR statistics cover? Nine types of crimes (called crime index offenses) are tracked: murder, forcible rape, robbery, aggravated assault, burglary, larceny–theft, motor vehicle theft, arson, and hate crimes.

Figure 7.4 shows UCR statistics on the frequency of seven of these crimes in the United States in 1999. Figure 7.5 presents another view of the 1998 statistics. Crimes known to the police totaled 11,635,900 (total violent crime plus total property crime). As the table shows, both violent crime and property crime have declined since 1990. Since murder receives the most publicity, it can be used to highlight this general, across-the-board reduction in

Types of crime	Number of crimes	Crime rate per 100,000 residents	1990–1999 Percent change in crime rate	1990–1999 Percent change in number of crimes
Violent crime	**1,430,690**	**524.7**	**-28.3**	**-21.4**
Murder	15,530	5.7	-39.4	-33.7
Forcible rape	89,110	32.7	-20.6	-13.1
Robbery	409,670	150.2	-41.6	-35.9
Aggravated assault	916,380	336.1	-20.7	-13.1
Property crime	**10,284,500**	**3,742.1**	**-26.5**	**-19.4**
Burglary	2,099,700	770.0	-37.7	-31.7
Larceny-theft	6,957,400	2,551.4	-20.1	-12.4
Motor vehicle theft	1,147,300	420.7	-36.0	-29.9

Figure 7.5 Crimes in the United States, 1999. *If you were a law enforcement officer, would you be encouraged or discouraged by this data? Why?*

Source: Federal Bureau of Investigation, *Uniform Crime Reports,* 1999.

Addressing Current Social Issues

One way to have students understand the societal costs of crime is to have them research how much it costs to run a facility or agency that handles crime. What are the costs of running a police station, a prison, or a detention center? Students can obtain this information by contacting local facilities. Next have them calculate the costs of upkeep for prisoners, costs of repairing property crimes, etc. Again, local agencies should be able to help with those numbers. Another group might want to explore the costs of preventative measures. Would society be better off if we could keep people out of jail or is it better (from a financial standpoint) for society to have crime and prisons?

Working with the Data

Figure 7.5 Explain the categories in this table to make sure students understand what the table headings refer to. Ask students if it would be possible for the number of crimes to increase if the rate of crimes were to decrease. (This would happen if the population growth was greater than the decrease in the crime rate—fewer crimes per person were committed, but there were more people in the total "victim pool.")

Here is what each noise represents: every three seconds one crime index offense is committed; every twenty-one seconds a violent crime is committed, every sixty seconds a robbery is committed; every thirty-two seconds an aggravated assault is committed; every fourteen seconds a burglary is committed; every four seconds a larceny/theft is committed; every twenty-five seconds a motor vehicle theft is committed; every three seconds a property crime is committed. This is a powerful demonstration.

Working with the Data

Figure 7.6 Students might comment that they are surprised the numbers for murder and forcible rape are so low. They will probably say that those are the crimes they hear about more than others. Ask how much they think the media has to do with they way they think about crimes. At this point, you might have an in-depth discussion on the media's influence on society as a whole.

Integrating the Teacher Resources

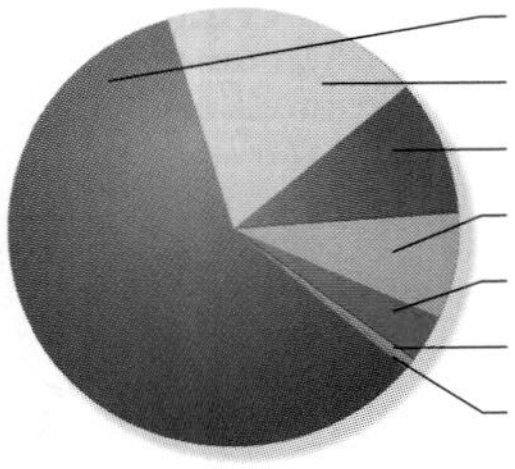

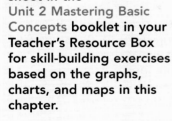

Look for the Chapter 7 Analyzing and Interpreting Data worksheet in the Unit 2 Mastering Basic Concepts **booklet in your Teacher's Resource Box for skill-building exercises based on the graphs, charts, and maps in this chapter.**

- Larceny-theft 59.8%
- Burglary 18.0%
- Motor vehicle theft 9.9%
- Aggravated assault 7.9%
- Robbery 3.5%
- Forcible rape 0.8%
- Murder 0.1%

Figure 7.6 Types of Crimes Americans Commit. *This figure shows the contribution each major type of crime makes to the total of U.S. crime.*

Source: Federal Bureau of Investigation, *Uniform Crime Reports,* 1999.

SOCIOLOGY *Online*

Student Web Activity
Visit the *Sociology and You* Web site at soc.glencoe.com for an activity on juvenile crime.

crime. The murder rate in the United States has declined more than 39 percent since the late 1980s. This decline has gained momentum since the mid-1990s. One major reason for this new downward crime trend is a recent reduction in juvenile crime.

Figure 7.6 indicates that violent crime—murder, forcible rape, aggravated assault, and robbery—made up 12.3 percent of the known crimes. Property crime—burglary, larceny-theft, motor vehicle theft—accounted for 87.7 percent.

How reliable are UCR statistics? The UCR statistics provide considerable information about crime. A major strength of this reporting system lies in the fact that experienced police officers decide if an incident should be reported as a crime. The UCR statistics also have serious limitations, however:

- ❖ The UCR tends to overrepresent the lower classes and undercount the middle and upper classes.
- ❖ Some crimes (amateur thefts, minor assaults) are not as likely to be reported to the police as murder and auto thefts.
- ❖ Prostitutes and intoxicated persons are subject to arrest in public places, but are fairly safe in private settings where the police cannot enter without a warrant.
- ❖ About two-thirds of U.S. crimes are not reported at all.
- ❖ Crime reporting varies from place to place and crime to crime and white-collar offenders are seldom included.

Are any other crime statistics available? In response to these criticisms, the *National Crime Victimization Survey* (NCVS) was launched in the early 1970s. This survey is conducted semiannually for the Bureau of Justice Statistics by the U.S. Census Bureau.

The NCVS has two advantages. First, it helps make up for the underreporting of crime. Second, its surveys are more scientifically sound than methods used in the UCR. At the very least, the NCVS is an increasingly important supplement to the FBI's official statistics. Together they provide a more complete account of the extent and nature of crime in the United States (Wright, 1987; U.S. Department of Justice, 1999).

Juvenile Crime

Juvenile crime refers to legal violations among those under 18 years of age. Juvenile offenders are the third largest category of criminals in the United States. Teenage criminal activity includes theft, murder, rape, robbery, assault, and the sale of illegal substances. Juvenile delinquent behavior includes deviance that only the young can commit, such as failing to attend school, fighting in school, and underage drinking and smoking.

What is the trend in juvenile crime? Violent juvenile crime reached its lowest level in a decade in 1999, a fall of 36 percent since 1994 (Office of Justice Programs, 2000). During the 1990s

- ❖ the juvenile murder arrest rate dropped by 68 percent
- ❖ juvenile arrests for weapons violations declined by a third
- ❖ the juvenile rape arrest rate went down by 31 percent

Cooperative Learning Activity ——————

Identify the different types of crimes (homicide, rape, robbery, aggravated assault) and then have students list specific kinds of crimes (for example, killing a child, incest, grand theft, auto theft). Ask students to classify the severity of each. What type of punishment would they assign for each

crime? To try something different, have students classify the severity of the crimes using movie ratings, such as X-rated crimes, R-rated crimes, etc. This list could be fairly extensive and might help students understand the complexity of understanding deviance agreed upon by consensus.

L1

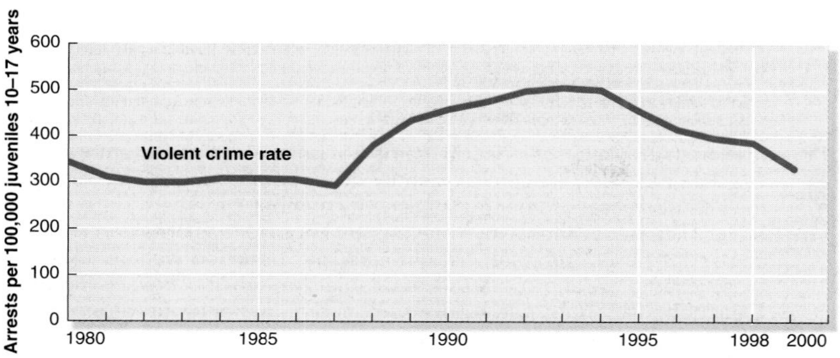

Figure 7.7 Juvenile Violent Crime Declines. *Why is the juvenile violent crime rate in the U.S. dropping?*

Source: U.S. Bureau of the Census, *Juvenile Offenders and Victims,* 1999, and Office of Justice Programs, 2000.

Online UPDATE
Visit soc.glencoe.com and click on **Textbook Updates–Chapter 7** for an update of the data.

There were also fewer juvenile victims of murder—down from almost 3,000 to about 2,000. Juvenile crime, in short, returned to the rates typical of the years prior to the crack epidemic of the late 1980s.

Why has juvenile crime gone down? Several factors are said to account for this decline in juvenile crime. For one, there has been a decline in the demand for crack cocaine. Remaining crack gangs that provided guns to juveniles have reached truces. Repeat violent juvenile offenders have been given stiffer sentences. Finally, police are cracking down on illegal guns on the street.

Approaches to Crime Control

The **criminal justice system** is made up of the institutions and processes responsible for enforcing criminal statutes. It includes the police, courts, and correctional system. A criminal justice system may draw on four approaches to control and punish lawbreakers—*deterrence, retribution, incarceration,* and *rehabilitation.*

criminal justice system
system comprising institutions and processes responsible for enforcing criminal statutes

Does punishment discourage crime? The **deterrence** approach uses the threat of punishment to discourage criminal actions. A basic idea of this approach is that punishment of convicted criminals will serve as an example to keep other people from committing crimes. There is considerable debate on the effectiveness of deterrence (DiIulio and Piehl, 1991). Research indicates that the threat of punishment *does* deter crime if potential lawbreakers know two things: that they are likely to get caught and that the punishment will be severe. In the U.S., however, the punishment for crime is usually not certain, swift, or severe. Consequently, punishment does not have the deterrent effect that it could have (Pontell, 1984).

deterrence
discouraging criminal acts by threatening punishment

Capital punishment (the death penalty) is a special case. Over four thousand people have been executed in the United States since 1930, the year the federal government began gathering statistics on capital punishment. Unless

Working with the Data

Figure 7.7 As students read the text they will see that some of the reasons the juvenile crime rate is dropping include the declining demand for crack cocaine and the police crackdown on illegal guns on the streets. Students may be able to research other possible reasons.

Making Connections to Other Cultures

According to the Sentencing Project, only Russia locks up more of its own citizens at a higher rate than does the U.S. In addition, Amnesty International, lists the U.S. with other countries that regularly violate basic human rights because it has and uses the death penalty. Have each student write a hypothetical letter to someone in another country, outlining the contradictions in U.S. human rights policies. Though we proclaim ourselves to be the land of the free and a champion of human rights, we have a high rate of incarceration and use the death penalty. Get students' permission to publish their letters for the class. Use them, along with information about the work of Amnesty International and its definition of the death penalty as the ultimate human rights abuse, as a basis for class discussion.
L3

On-Demand Writing

Share the following with students and then have them write about their reactions.

Between the years 1985 and 1997, the number of prison inmates under the age of eighteen more than doubled. More states are now allowing people under the age of eighteen to be tried as adults, depending on the type of crime committed. The thinking behind this trend is that if states take away a youth's minor status, and they are tried as adults, they will be more accountable for the crime committed.

Gang and drug-related violence, along with an increase in school shootings over the past ten years has caused state lawmakers to favor adult prison terms for violent juvenile offenders.

Currently, there are approximately 7,500 juveniles in adult prisons. The adult prison population is around two million.
L1

Tech Trends

Computer technology might be part of the explanation for identity theft. Information about anyone can be found easily on the Internet. Have students discuss how technology creates a new set of problems not previously encountered. What limits should be placed on the availability of personal information on the Internet?

Answer to Analyzing the Trends

Answers will vary. Any of the theoretical perspectives could be used to study the issue of identity theft.

Teaching Strategy

Contact a local agency that helps ex-convicts reenter society. Ask if a speaker might visit your school to talk about his or her experiences. Students are usually fascinated by prison life and want to discuss it. (You may want to check with a school administrator before proceeding with this idea.)

Integrating the Teacher Resources

Look for Ethics, Values, and Technology: Real-Life Issues in Society, available in your Teacher's Resource Box. The booklet provides primary source readings dealing with real-life controversies. Student worksheets are included.

Tech Trends

Look Out for Identity Thieves!

One of the newest forms of deviance is "identity theft." An identity thief "steals" credit information belonging to another person, then commits fraud with it. The results for victims can be devastating.

In testimony before the Maryland legislature, one couple reported that a thief used their credit cards to purchase five automobiles. Graciela has been a victim of identity theft for more than ten years. A thief gained access to her Social Security number, birth certificate, and driver's license. With this information, the imposter has obtained credit cards, purchased furniture, bought cars, and obtained welfare. (All of these examples, and more, are available through the Privacy Rights Clearinghouse, http://www.privacyrights.org, a nonprofit group for consumers' privacy rights.)

Beth Givens of the Privacy Rights Clearinghouse explains that identity theft can occur in many ways. A thief can steal a wallet or purse, get copies of credit card slips from trash, or steal someone's mail. There are also high-tech methods of identity theft. The most common method is to illegally gain access to credit rating company computers. These companies maintain credit reports that provide valuable information about a consumer—Social Security number, birth date, credit card numbers, and address. Although credit rating companies try to prevent high-tech identity theft, the very nature of their service makes this information accessible through computer terminals. This access is an open invitation to criminals.

The victims of identity theft obviously suffer great damage. Unless the thief is caught in the act, there seems to be little the police can do to stop this kind of crime. Many victims also have to deal with abusive collection agencies. It has taken some people ten years or more to clean up the mess the thieves have created. Victims are often scarred emotionally and report feelings of violation, hopelessness, and great anger.

The goal of today's identity thieves is to get items at no cost, not to take over the victims' identities. But what if identity theft also involved losing one's identity? What would happen if a person's identity were actually "stolen"? This was the topic of a film called *The Net*. In this movie, a woman's entire identity is erased. The villains in the movie steal the documents that would prove her identity and destroy all of her existing computer records. Using her photograph and Social Security number, they create a whole new identity for her, including a new name, a bad credit report, and a criminal record. As the woman in the movie says, "They knew everything about me. It was all on the Internet."

Analyzing the Trends

Which theoretical perspective would be most useful in analyzing identity theft? Explain your choice, and apply that perspective to the issue of identity theft.

Learning Styles

Interpersonal/Linguistic This chapter includes descriptions and information regarding several different theories. To help students clarify the similarities and differences between these theories, give them the opportunity to explain the following theories to each other: 1) functionalists—strain theory and control theory; 2) symbolic interactionists—differential association theory and labeling theory; 3) conflict theorists—victim-discounting and white-collar crime. You can divide students into three or six groups, depending on how much time you have to spend. Ask the students to use different examples than those found in the text to explain the theories. Each group will study the information in the appropriate section of the text, develop a multimedia presentation, and present their assigned theory or theories to the rest of the class. L2 it is premeditated, a murder is an extremely emotional and irrational act. Under such circumstances, you would not expect the threat of capital punishment to be a deterrent, and research shows that it is not. If the death penalty were a deterrent to murder, a decline in its use should be followed by an increase in the murder rate. Research indicates, however, that the murder rate remains constant, or even drops, following a decline in the use of the death penalty (Sellin, 1991; Lester, 1998; Sarat, 1998).

Do Americans believe capital punishment deters criminals? Despite those findings, about three-fourths of Americans believe that the death penalty acts as a deterrent to murder. Actually, attitudes regarding the ability of the death penalty to prevent crime do not seem to affect attitudes toward the death penalty itself. Of those Americans who favor the death penalty, over three-fourths indicate they would continue to favor it even if confronted with conclusive evidence that the death penalty does not act as a deterrent to murder and that it does not lower the murder rate. Feelings of revenge and a desire for retribution, then, appear to contribute more to the support of capital punishment than do its deterrent effects. When asked to choose, a significantly higher proportion of the American population support the death penalty for murder (66 percent) than oppose it (26 percent; Gallup, 2001).

Why does the attitude toward the death penalty vary? Attitudes toward the death penalty in the United States vary according to race and ethnicity. Over three-fourths of whites favor the death penalty compared with 40 percent of African Americans and 52 percent of Latinos. This racial and ethnic variation in attitude toward the death penalty is not surprising. The less favorable African American and Latino attitude is due, in part, to the fact that, when convicted, they are more likely than whites to receive the death penalty (Spohn, 1995). While African Americans comprise only about 13 percent of the U.S. population, they make up 43 percent of death row inmates. Racial minorities constitute half of all inmates in U.S. prisons.

Demostrators protest in support of and in opposition to the death penalty. Based on the evidence, do you think support for the death penalty is motivated by deterrence or retribution?

What is retribution? **Retribution** is a type of punishment intended to make criminals pay compensation for their acts. It comes from the idea of "an eye for an eye and a tooth for a tooth." The law allows designated officials to exact retribution. However, it does not allow individuals to take personal vengeance. If a mother "takes the law into her own hands" by shooting her son's killer, she must also answer to society for her action.

retribution
punishment intended to make criminals pay compensation for their acts

Why does society keep criminals in prisons? The basic idea behind **incarceration**—keeping criminals in prisons—is that criminals who are not on the street cannot commit crimes. Recently, the United States has taken a tougher stance in favor of the incarceration approach with such bills as the *three strikes law*. As a result, the number of local, state, and federal prisoners increased by almost 700,000 between 1990 and 2000, and is expected to exceed 2 million very shortly. In more repressive societies, such as the former Soviet Union and present-day Nationalist China, people may spend their entire lives in prison camps for crimes ranging from political opposition to murder.

incarceration
a method of protecting society from criminals by keeping them in prisons

More About . . . the Death Penalty

There is an organization called the Innocence Project at the Benjamin N. Cardozo Law School in New York that works to establish the guilt or innocence of prisoners on death row. The organization runs tests and examines evidence with procedures that were not available when the original investigations occurred. According to this group, in the last decade DNA tests have provided "stone-cold proof" that sixty-four people were sent to prison and death row in North America for crimes they did not commit. The number has been rising at a rate of more than one a month.

It is facts like these that caused Illinois Governnor George Ryan to declare a moratorium on executions in early 2000. Although the state had executed twelve people since 1976, they had also released thirteen from death row due to evidence that showed their innocence. There have also been cases of police frame-ups (as in Los Angeles) where judges have thrown out convictions of a number of prisoners due to tainted evidence.

Careers in Sociology

This chapter is an opportunity for you to bring people with experience in the criminal justice system into your classroom. If your school has a police liaison, have him or her come to your class to talk about juvenile crime, or ask him or her for a recommendation of someone who would. You might want to contact a local agency that serves as a transitional program for criminals and see if the agency would have some rehabilitated people come in as guest speakers. You can also see if it would be feasible for your class to visit a minimum security prison.

World View

Answers to Interpreting the Map

1. Students should note that the United States is the only country indicated on the map where death penalty varies with the state. Explain to students that the appeal process through the federal courts helps to level this seemingly unfair policy. They may also note that many of the countries in Western Europe have abolished capital punishment. In fact, Europeans are very active in protesting capital punishment around the world, as are some of the larger European-based corporations such as the clothing company, Benetton.
2. No one has been able to prove that capital punishment is an effective deterrent to crime, regardless of the political regime or the location. Government may not always be concerned with the deterrence factor, however. They may be more concerned with maintaining immediate social control.

World View

Death Penalty Policy

Countries vary in their approach to the control of crime. The most extreme form of social control, the death penalty, is utilized in many countries, while some countries have abolished capital punishment completely. This map shows variations in national policy regarding the death penalty.

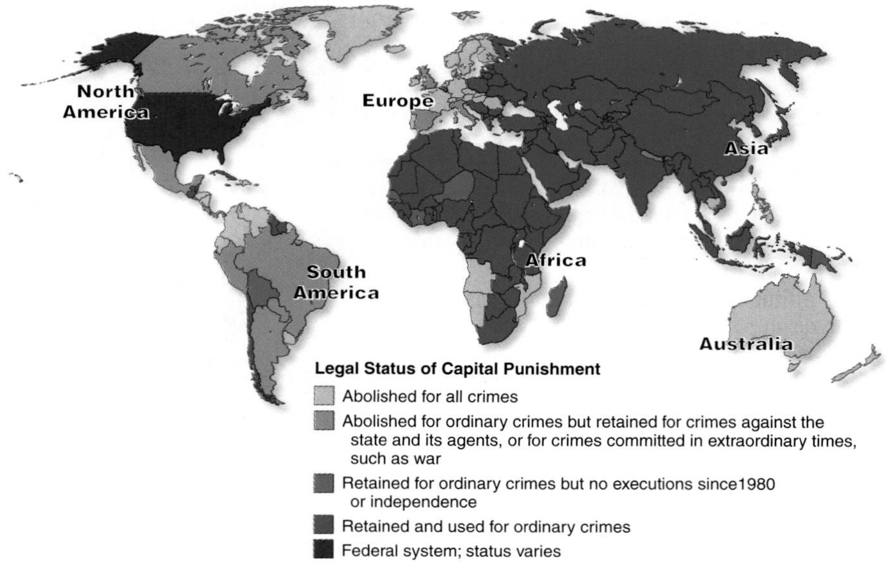

Interpreting the Map

1. Do you notice any pattern in the use of the death penalty? Describe it.
2. What additional information would you need to determine if capital punishment is an effective deterrent to crime? Explain.

Adapted from *The State of the World Atlas,* 5th ed. New York: Penguin Books.

rehabilitation process of changing or reforming a criminal through socialization

Do prisons rehabilitate criminals? **Rehabilitation** is an approach to crime control that attempts to resocialize criminals. Most prisons have programs aimed at giving prisoners both social and work skills that will help them adjust to normal society after their release. Unfortunately, 30 to 60 percent of those released from penal institutions are sent back to prison in two

Survey

The text states that in the United States, more than 75 percent of whites, 52 percent of Latinos, and 40 percent of African Americans favor the death penalty. Ask students to devise a closed-ended survey that will allow them to sample their school population to see if their school reflects the national average. Ask them to discuss factors that might affect the school's results, such as the younger age of the respondents and the socioeconomic strata of the school. You may want students to do this activity as a cooperative project, with one team designing the survey, another team deciding the method and procedure for sampling, and a third team tallying and interpreting the results.
L1

to five years. This return to criminal behavior is called **recidivism.** The relatively high rate of recidivism makes it seem unlikely that prison rehabilitation programs are working (Elikann, 1996; Zamble and Quinsey, 1997). Reasons for the high rate of recidivism include

- the basic nature of the offenders
- influences of more hardened criminals
- the stigma of being an ex-convict.

recidivism
a repetition of or return to criminal behavior

It is difficult to change attitudes and behavior within the prison subculture. Conformity with the "inmate code" stresses loyalty among inmates as well as opposition to correctional authorities. Also, a released prisoner is likely to bring the toughness reinforced in prison life to the workplace. This transfer of prison norms does not work because most jobs in the service economy require interpersonal skills (Hagan, 1994b).

What are some alternatives to prisons? If prisons do not rehabilitate, what are some alternatives? Several are being considered.

1. *A combination of prison and probation.* A mixed or split sentence, known as *shock probation,* is designed to shock offenders into recognizing the realities of prison life. Prisoners serve part of their sentences in an institution and the rest on probation.
2. *Community-based programs.* These programs are designed to reintroduce criminals into society. By getting convicts out of prison for at least part of the day, community-based programs help break the inmate code. At the same time, prisoners have a chance to become part of society—participating in the community but under professional guidance and supervision.
3. *Diversion strategy.* Diversion is aimed at preventing, or greatly reducing, the offender's involvement in the criminal justice system. Diversion involves a referral to a community-based treatment program rather than a prison or a probationary program. Because offenders are handled outside the formal system of criminal law, authorities believe the offenders will not acquire stigmatizing labels and other liabilities (Morris and Tonry, 1990; Lanier and Henry, 1997).

These juveniles are in the Texas-based Del Valle Correctional Boot Camp. What is the reasoning behind this alternative to imprisonment?

Will any of these alternatives work? Most of the alternative programs have not been sufficiently evaluated to determine how well they work. Continued use of these alternatives will depend on what American voters believe are the appropriate functions of prisons. These programs can exist only so long as rehabilitation has a high priority. Recently, Americans have taken a harsher view toward criminals, so support for alternatives may be eroding.

Controversy and Debate

In 1978 the film *Scared Straight* was shown for the first time on television. In the film, which was produced by the Juvenile Awareness Project Help, offenders and at-risk youth are shown inside the Rahway maximum security prison in New Jersey. While there they learn first-hand from inmate volunteers what prison life is really like. For two hours the prisoners rant, berate, and menace the youths in the hope that their behavior will change the behavior of the youths.

After the film aired on national television, many states instituted the same or similar programs in an attempt to turn young offenders away from crime and probable imprisonment.

The effectiveness of the program has been questioned, but proponents argue that if only one youth stays out of prison because he or she has been "scared straight," then the program is effective and worth the time and effort.

You might lead a class discussion at this point. Ask for students' reactions to the idea behind the program. Do they think it would be effective? Why or why not?

Role Play

Divide the class into groups of four or five. Each group is to develop a role play that illustrates the stigma of being an ex-convict. They should include society's reaction to ex-convicts and the difficulty they have in getting jobs because they bring the toughness of the prison to the workplace. The skit should also include the realistic concerns of employers and property owners about the high recidivism rate and responsibilities to other employees.

After groups have shared their role plays with the rest of the class, involve the entire class in a discussion of ways ex-convicts might be better integrated into society. What ideas do students have? How practical (viable) are the ideas?
L1

Working with the Data

Figure 7.8 This chart will emphasize again for students that there does not seem to be a direct correlation between level of economic development and crime. Although the type of crime will depend to some extent on the level of development, the incarceration rate for prisoners is high in some developed countries, such as the United States, and low in others, such as Japan. (Point out to students that although the U.S. has more prisoners than Russia, the rate of incarceration is greater in Russia.)

Answers to Section 5 Assessment

1.
   - **a.** I
   - **b.** I or D
   - **c.** Rb or D
   - **d.** R
   - **e.** D
2. Crime has decreased since 1989.
3. A government controlled by Americans who subscribe strongly to the value of an eye for an eye is likely to formulate policies emphasizing the use of retribution in crime control. If a government's leaders are more heavily committed to the value of forgiveness, its policies are likely to emphasize rehabilitation in attempting to control crime.
4. No, research has not supported the position that the threat of capital punishment deters crime.

Critical Thinking

5. Answers will vary.
6. Answers will vary.

Rank	Country	Prisoners*	Population (in millions)	Incarceration rate per 1,000
1	United States	1,630,940	272.5	5.99
2	Russia	1,051,515	146.5	7.18
3	Germany	71,047	82.0	0.87
4	Poland	57,320	38.7	1.48
5	England and Wales	55,537	59.4	0.93
6	France	54,014	59.1	0.91
7	Italy	48,747	57.7	0.84
8	Spain	42,105	39.4	1.07
9	Japan	40,389	126.7	0.32
10	Canada	33,785	30.6	1.10

*In latest year for which figures are available.

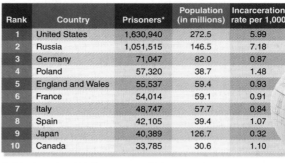

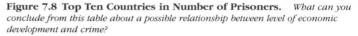

Figure 7.8 Top Ten Countries in Number of Prisoners. *What can you conclude from this table about a possible relationship between level of economic development and crime?*

Sources: Russell Ash. *The Top 10 of Everything 1999.* New York and the Population Reference Bureau, 1999.

> "Violence is the last refuge of the incompetent."
>
> Isaac Asimov
> author

Section 5 Assessment

1. Indicate whether the approaches to punishment listed below are rehabilitation (R), deterrence (D), retribution (Rb), or incarceration (I).
   - **a.** imprisonment without parole
   - **b.** longer prison sentences
   - **c.** extremely harsh prison conditions
   - **d.** psychological counseling in prison
   - **e.** swift justice
2. According to the FBI's *Uniform Crime Reports,* has crime in the United States increased or decreased since 1989?
3. Do you believe that the cultural values of American society affect the policies of government regarding approaches to crime control? Why or why not?
4. Has research supported the position that the death penalty deters crime?

Critical Thinking

5. **Synthesizing Information** The text outlines several distinct approaches to crime control. Choose one approach, and explain why you believe it is or is not successful. Use functionalism, conflict theory, or symbolic interactionism as a reference point.
6. **Evaluating Information** What are your beliefs on capital punishment? Defend your viewpoint.

Interdisciplinary Activity

Cultural Studies Assign students to study the justice and penal systems in the countries represented in Figure 7.8 at the top of the page. Students might work in groups, with each group studying one country, or you might have several students study the same country and then compare and contrast the information they found. After information on each country has been collected, have the class compare and contrast the justice and penal systems of the different countries. Do students see similarities among the countries with high incarceration rates? What are the main differences between the countries with high rates of incarceration and those with low rates of incarceration? To what do students attribute those differences?
L2

Chapter 7 Assessment

Summary

Section 1: Deviance and Social Control

Main Idea: Deviance is the violation of social norms. It is difficult to define because not everyone agrees on what should be considered deviant behavior.

Section 2: Functionalism and Deviance

Main Idea: According to functionalists, deviance has both negative and positive consequences for society. Functionalism also forms the basis for two important theories of deviance: strain theory and control theory.

Section 3: Symbolic Interactionism and Deviance

Main Idea: The symbolic interactionist perspective yields two theories of deviance. We read in Chapter 3 that culture is learned. Sociologists believe that deviance is a learned behavior that is culturally transmitted. Labeling theory holds that an act is deviant only if other people name it so.

Section 4: Conflict Theory and Deviance

Main Idea: The conflict perspective looks at deviance in terms of social inequality and power. The most powerful members of a society determine who will be regarded as deviant. Conflict theorists point to some disproportional statistical relationships between minorities and crime.

Section 5: Crime and Punishment

Main Idea: Crime statistics in the U.S. come from two major sources: the FBI and the Census Bureau.

SOCIOLOGY Online

Self-Check Quiz
Visit the *Sociology and You* Web site at soc.glencoe.com and click on **Chapter 7—Self-Check Quizzes** to prepare for the chapter test.

Reviewing Vocabulary

Complete each sentence using each term once.

a. deviance
b. stigma
c. social control
d. white-collar crimes
e. social sanctions
f. anomie
g. Uniform Crime Reports
h. strain theory
i. deterrence
j. control theory
k. recidivism
l. rehabilitation
m. differential association theory
n. retribution
o. labeling theory

1. The tactic that uses intimidation to prevent crime is called ____________.
2. ____________ is the approach to crime control that attempts to resocialize criminals.
3. ____________ is an undesirable characteristic or label used to deny the deviant acceptance.
4. A violation of social norms is called ____________.
5. ____________ are crimes committed by high-status people in the course of their occupation.
6. ____________ is a theory that states that people are defined by those in power as deviant.
7. The theory that states that deviance exists when there is a gap between culturally desirable goals and means is called ____________.
8. The theory that conformity to social norms depends on a strong bond between individuals and society is known as the ____________.
9. ____________ are rewards or punishments designed to encourage desired behavior.
10. ____________ is a theory that states that deviance is learned in proportion to exposure to deviant acts.
11. When past offenders return to prison, such an occurrence is called ____________.
12. ____________ are ways for promoting conformity to norms.

Answers Chapter 7 Assessment

Reviewing Vocabulary

1. i	**5.** d	**9.** e	**13.** f
2. l	**6.** o	**10.** m	**14.** g
3. b	**7.** h	**11.** k	**15.** n
4. a	**8.** j	**12.** c	

Reviewing the Facts

1. Deterrence theory
2. Labeling theory
3. Because it was an isolated act of deviance; it was not part of the person's life style or self-concept
4. The Uniform Crime Reports (UCR) largely represent offenders in the lower classes and undercounts those in the middle and upper classes. Some crimes like auto thefts and minor assaults are never reported and therefore undercounted. White- collar offenders are seldom included in the UCR statistics so crime reporting is arbitrary. The National Crime Victimization Survey (NCVS) helps to make up for the underreporting of crimes by using surveys with sound scientific methods. NCVS statistics are used to supplement the FBI's official statistics. NCVS seem more reliable because of scientific methods used to gather and report statistics. The FBI uses the information gathered by the NCVS which gives credibility to the data.
5. Deviance is more likely to occur when there is a gap between cultural goals and the ability to achieve the goals by legitimate means.
6. **Ritualism** - Individual rejects success as a goal, but uses legitimate means (i.e., goes through the motions). Ex. Retail clerk who comes to work but puts little effort into customer service (does the bare minimum)

   Retreatism - Individual rejects the legitimate goal and the legitimate means. Ex. People who "drop out o fsociety"—a street person

   Rebellion - Individual rejects the legitimate goal and the legitimate means and

ANSWERS CHAPTER 7 ASSESSMENT

substitutes them with new set of goals and means. Ex. Militia group members who ive in isolation with the goal of changing society through deviant means.

Thinking Critically

1. This is the interpretation that deviance is subjective and defined by the culture that one lives in. It can also reflect the time that people live in. What was deviant yesterday, may not be today.
2. People enjoy the outrageous behavior. It is positively sanctioned—otherwise, people wouldn't visit the restaurant. The conduct of the servers is not deviant since the patrons don't see it that way.
3. People who occasionally commit deviant acts are unpredictable. We prefer people whose behavior is predictable, whether they are never or rarely deviant, or whether they are often deviant. Unpredictability of behavior might be alarming or disturbing because others are unprepared for what to expect from that person, and with how to respond to them.
4. Answers will vary. Students might want to research whether their state has given this proposal consideration. Thirty-eight states have the death penalty but some want to change the death penalty to life in prison without any chance of parole. Have students report back on their findings.
5. White collar crimes and the excessive amount of mall theft are indications of American materialistic values. Theft from stores costs shop owners millions of dollars per year. Ask students if they think people would stop stealing if they no longer felt the pressure or need to have the latest or trendiest material goods.
6. This question is a good springboard for class discussion. Have students discuss the following about your school: Are some students treated differently from others? Are the actions of some students considered deviant while similar actions performed by other students are not? If these situations don't occur at your school, why do you think that is?

CHAPTER 7 ASSESSMENT

13. ______________ is the social condition in which norms are weak, conflicting or absent.
14. The major source of American statistics on crime gathered from police departments is known as ______________.
15. ______________ is the practice in which criminals pay compensation equal to their offenses.

Reviewing the Facts

1. In a famous study known as the Minneapolis Domestic Violence Study, sociologists discovered that arresting someone for hitting his wife did not necessarily stop him from hitting her again. What is the name of the theory upon which they based their hypothesis that arrest would stop the behavior?
2. A group of lower-class youths are accused of a crime for behavior that higher-status teens have engaged in without punishment. What sociological term describes this process?
3. When a high school student admits to cheating on a test, this behavior is labeled as primary deviance. Explain why.
4. Give two reasons why the crime statistics reported by the Uniform Crime Reports differ from those statistics reported by the National Crime Victimization Survey. Which report would you consider more reliable and why?
5. What is the strain theory?
6. Robert Merton's strain theory of deviance is based on four types of responses. Using the chart below, list each response. Then, from the perspective of means and goals explain each response and give an example.

MERTON'S DEVIANT RESPONSES TO STRAIN

Response	Explanation	Example
Innovation	Individual accepts success as a goal but uses illegal means to achieve it.	Shoplifter

Thinking Critically

1. **Interpreting Information** Use the information in this chapter to explain the following statement: "Deviance, like beauty, is in the eye of the beholder."
2. **Applying Concepts** There is a chain of restaurants in this country known for the outrageous behavior of its servers. At these restaurants, servers might purposely spill drinks and food on the patrons. Despite this apparently deviant behavior, patrons seem to love the restaurants and recommend them to friends. How do these restaurants, which clearly violate concepts of social control, continue to attract customers?
3. **Making Inferences** If a person is rarely deviant, people come to expect that behavior. If a person is often deviant, people expect *that* behavior. What do you think happens when people are deviant occasionally? How might unpredictability of behavior be more alarming or disturbing?
4. **Drawing Conclusions** Some states are considering life imprisonment with no chance of parole as an alternative to the death penalty. The states argue that the capital punishment process is more costly than imprisonment over time. Proponents also claim that offenders given lifetime sentences are more likely to develop remorse for their crimes. Do you think this argument has merit? Why or why not?
5. **Evaluating Information** The conflict perspective says that the capitalistic society of the United States—with its emphasis on gaining wealth—is really responsible for crime. Find examples to support or to refute the hypothesis that crime is the result of society's materialistic values.
6. **Analyzing Information** The chapter case study "Saints and Roughnecks" describes how social class contributed to people's perceptions of the level of deviance of two groups of boys. Some students complain that there are special groups in their schools (athletes, honor students, and so forth) that never seem to be held responsible for their actions. Is this true of your school? If so, why? If not, what do you credit for the even-handed discipline?

Sociology Projects

1. **Random Acts of Kindness and Positive Deviance** Go out of your way to help a stranger (not a friend or family member). You might give someone directions, help someone to carry parcels, or even smile and say a friendly hello. (*Important note:* Remember to keep safety and sensitivity to others' feelings in mind when you approach people you don't know.) Write answers to the following questions to help you evaluate the stranger's reactions to your act.
   - **a.** How do you think the traits of the individual you helped (race, age, gender) affected the situation?
   - **b.** Why did you choose your particular act of kindness?
   - **c.** How did you feel while performing the random act of kindness?
   - **d.** What surprised or impressed you the most about the individual's reaction?
2. **Categorizing Deviance** As you read in the quotation on page 204, in a diverse society such as that of the United States, many groups of people may be categorized as deviant by someone. List the groups named in the quotation on a piece of paper. For each group, assign a number from 1 to 7, with 1 being the most deviant and 7 the least deviant. Afterward, compare your list with those of two or three of your classmates to see if there was any agreement. Discuss possible reasons for major differences.
3. **Deviant Crimes** What crimes today do people consider the most severe? Working individually, make a list of the five crimes you consider the most deviant, with the first item on the list the most deviant, the second item the next most deviant, and so forth. Next, assign a punishment for each crime. Does the crime warrant the death penalty? Life imprisonment? After you have completed your list, work with two or three classmates until you agree on a new list. You must reach consensus on the crimes included on the list, their rankings, and the punishment assigned to each. Finally, compare your group's results with the results of other groups in your class. What have you learned about the difficulty of reaching agreement on this sensitive topic?
4. **The Role of the Media** The text discussed how race is an important factor in understanding deviance. Another factor you might wish to consider is the role of the media in shaping our perceptions of crime and criminals. Your task is to collect one crime-related newspaper article per day for one week. Analyze the article for information such as the race, age, gender, and status, of the accused. Also consider the geographic location of the crime. How does the newspaper describe the area where the crime took place? Do you detect any bias in the type of words used to report these incidents?
5. **Preparing a News Broadcast** As an extension of the project above (i.e., number 4), imagine yourself as a news anchor on the local news. Choose one of the stories that you have collected. Limiting yourself to one paragraph, prepare your news broadcast using the facts as reported in the newspaper. Now, evaluate your broadcast and write another version that is neutral (i.e., gives no indication of race, gender or age). Which version do you feel the program producer would choose to put on the air? Why?

Technology Activity

1. Using the Internet, your school or local library, find a murder case from the year 1900. Find a similar type of murder case from the year 2000. Consider how each murder was reported and punished (i.e., the type of approach to crime control that was used). Design a database to illustrate similarities and differences between the two deviant acts. What can you conclude about society's view of deviance at the time the crime was committed?

ANSWERS
Chapter 7 Assessment

Sociology Projects

1. Students can have a lot of fun with this as long as they are aware that some of the people they try to help might be put off by it. You might want to hold a debate about trust in our society. Have people become so distrustful that no one can perform a kind act without falling under suspicion or appearing to have ulterior motives?
2. You might want to explain to students that a label of deviance might also reflect the degree of social distancing they feel regarding a group. In other words, a student might feel a desire to stay as far away as possible from a group he or she labels as being most deviant.
3. The answers could vary. Let the groups put their five top crimes on the board and try to have the students come to a class consensus. Do groups agree on the methods of punishment?
4. Have students analyze the words that describe the crime as well as how issues of race, gender and geographic location are treated. Could students rewrite the article in another way so that it would sound totally objective?
5. Answers will vary. The idea is that society responds with negative interest to information that reinforces preconceptions that are strengthened by the labeling theory. A neutrally presented story will hold little interest and will probably not be chosen as the on-air story.

Technology Activity

1. Answers will vary.

Enrichment Reading

This is a great example of a field study. Elijah Anderson left his classroom at the University of Pittsburgh and began hanging out in Philadelphia with African American males. The subsequent research project became the basis for his book, *Streetwise.* A variety of topics could be researched here: police and the social construction of reality, racial profiling, race, ethnicity and crime, black manhood, etc. Invite students to explore these topics. A good book on black manhood is called *Cool Pose: The Dilemmas of Black Manhood in America* by Richard Rogers and Janet Mancini Billson (Touchstone Books, 1992).

Chapter 7

Enrichment Reading

The Police and the Black Male

by Elijah Anderson

The police, in the Village-Northton [neighborhood] as elsewhere, represent society's formal, legitimate means of social control. Their role includes protecting law-abiding citizens from those who are not law-abiding by preventing crime and by apprehending likely criminals. Precisely how the police fulfill the public's expectations is strongly related to how they view the neighborhood and the people who live there. On the streets, color-coding often works to confuse race, age, class, gender, incivility, and criminality, and it expresses itself most concretely in the person of the **anonymous** black male. In doing their job, the police often become willing parties to this general color-coding of the public environment, and related distinctions, particularly those of skin color and gender, come to convey definite meanings. Although such coding may make the work of the police more manageable, it may also fit well with their own **presuppositions** regarding race and class relations, thus shaping officers' perceptions of crime "in the city." Moreover, the anonymous black male is usually an **ambiguous** figure who arouses the utmost caution and is generally considered dangerous until he proves he is not. . . .

To be white is to be seen by the police—at least superficially—as an ally, eligible for consideration and for much more deferential treatment than that accorded to blacks in general. This attitude may be grounded in the backgrounds of the police themselves. Many have grown up in . . . "ethnic" neighborhoods. They may serve what they perceive as their own class and neighborhood interests, which often translates as keeping blacks "in their place"—away from neighborhoods that are socially defined as "white." In trying to do their job, the police appear to engage in an informal policy of monitoring young black men as a means of controlling crime, and often they seem to go beyond the bounds of duty. . . .

On the streets late at night, the average young black man is suspicious of others he encounters, and he is particularly wary of the police. If he is dressed in the uniform of the "gangster," such as a black leather jacket, sneakers, and a "gangster cap," if he is carrying a radio or a suspicious bag (which may be confiscated), or if he is moving too fast or too slow, the police may stop him. As part of the routine, they search him and make him sit in the police car while they run a check to see whether there is a "detainer" on him. If there is nothing, he is allowed to go on his way. After this ordeal the youth is often left afraid, sometimes shaking, and uncertain about the area he had previously taken for granted. He is upset in part because he is painfully aware of how close he has come to being in "big trouble." He knows of other youths who have gotten into a "world of trouble" simply by being on the streets at the wrong time or when the police were pursuing a criminal. In these circumstances, particularly at night, it is relatively easy for one black man to be mistaken for another. Over the years, while walking through the neighborhood I have on occasion been stopped and questioned by police chasing a mugger, but after explaining myself I was released.

Many youths, however, have reason to fear such mistaken identity or harassment, since they might be jailed, if only for a short time, and would have to post bail money and pay legal fees to **extricate** themselves from the mess. . . . When law-abiding blacks are ensnared by the criminal justice system, the scenario may proceed as follows. A young man is **arbitrarily** stopped by the police and questioned. If he cannot effectively negotiate with the officer(s), he may be accused of a crime and arrested. To resolve this situation he needs financial resources, which for him are in short supply. If he does not have money for any attorney, which often happens, he is left to a public defender who may be more interested in going along with the court system than in fighting for a poor black person. Without legal support, he may well wind up "doing time" even if he is innocent of the charges brought against him. The next time he is stopped for questioning he will have a record, which will make detention all the more likely.

Because the young black man is aware of many cases when an "innocent" black person was wrongly accused and detained, he develops an "attitude" toward the police. The street word for police is "the man," signifying a certain machismo, power, and authority. He becomes concerned when he notices "the man" in the community or when the police focus on him because he is outside his own neighborhood. The youth knows, or soon finds out, that he exists in a legally precarious state. Hence he is motivated to avoid the police, and his public life becomes severely **circumscribed**. . . .

To avoid encounters with the man, some streetwise young men camouflage themselves, giving up the urban uniform and emblems that identify them as "legitimate" objects of police attention. They may adopt a more conventional presentation of self, wearing chinos, sweat suits, and generally more conservative dress. Some youths have been known to "ditch" a favorite jacket if they see others wearing one like it, because wearing it increases their chances of being mistaken for someone else who may have committed a crime.

But such strategies do not always work over the long run and must be constantly modified. For instance, because so many young ghetto blacks have begun to wear Fila and Adidas sweat suits as status symbols, such dress has become incorporated into the public image generally associated with young black males. These athletic suits, particularly the more expensive and colorful ones, along with high-priced sneakers, have become the leisure dress of successful drug dealers. . . .

What Does it Mean?

ambiguous
capable of being understood in two or more ways

anonymous
lacking individuality, distinction, or recognition

arbitrarily
without meaning; resulting from the unrestrained exercise of power

circumscribe
reduce the range or scope of action

extricate
to remove from an entanglement

presuppositions
assumed knowledge

Ed. note: This article is based on the author's field research on two city neighborhoods he calls Village-Northton.

From: Elijah Anderson, *Streetwise* (Chicago: University of Chicago Press, 1990), pp. 190–206. © 1990 University of Chicago Press. Reprinted by permission of the publisher and author.

Read and React

1. According to the article, what are some consequences to black youth of being arresteπd, innocent or not?
2. What presuppositions regarding race and class exist in your neighborhood?
3. Do you think color-coding exists in your town or city? Why or why not?

Answers to Read and React

1. If a black youth is arrested, he then has a police record, has to post bail and pay legal costs involved in the procedures.
2. Answers will depend completely on where the students live. In some cities, students of color openly discuss the situation in their sociology classes. This kind of discussion, if carefully led, tends to enlighten white students to the dilemmas of black males.
3. If one uses the current analogy to racial profiling which has been in the news, then the situation still exists. Again, it will depend on where your school is located. Some students might be able to share stories that they have heard from students at other schools. (Remind them that stories are enlightening but remain in the category of anecdotal evidence.)

Integrating the Teacher Resources

Additional primary source readings for this chapter can be found in Culture Studies: The Sociological Perspective, **available in your Teacher's Resource Box. Questions for students are included.**

UNIT 3

NOTES to the Teacher

While we think of the United States as the land of opportunity and one without a strict class system, research on social class and stratification show these assumptions to be mythic. Poverty rates show a population direly affected by discrimination of race, ethnicity, gender, and age. If all things were equal, we would expect the rates of those in poverty to match the same proportion in the general population.

The phrase *feminization of poverty* underscores the fact that women and their children are over-represented among those living below the poverty line. Also over-represented are people of color, particularly African Americans and Latinos. The reasons for these figures lie partly with prejudicial attitudes and discriminatory behaviors, both direct and institutional. Prejudicial attitudes are formed by socialization processes and scapegoating among different groups of people. For example, we often judge people differently based on skin color or other perceived group characteristics because we are taught to do so, sometimes because those "other" people are seen to limit our own group's opportunities.

Discrimination, on the other hand, rests with behaviors that are sometimes guided by prejudicial attitudes, yet not always. Discrimination can occur without a bigot in the situation! Institutional discrimination is the term for policy-based discrimination, which non-prejudiced people may enforce unwittingly. One example is red-lining, a policy of financial institutions in which they will omit certain low income areas from loan program opportunities because of potential high default rates.

That gender is not identical to sex is a surprise—and quite disturbing—to many people. While most of us are born with the sexually identifiable genitalia of male or female, we are labeled and socialized into the appropriate gender identity and role based on that initial sex category. If we do not know someone's sex/gender, we usually do what we can to discover their "correct" identity. The character Pat on *Saturday Night Live* is a humorous example of this phenomenon. S/he never makes it clear, yet all the skits with this character revolve around how to find out what his or her gender is. The movie, *Boys Don't Cry,* for which actress Hilary Swank won an Academy Award, is an

SOCIAL INEQUALITY

Chapter 8

Social Stratification

Chapter 9

Inequalities of Race and Ethnicity

Chapter 10

Inequalities of Gender and Age

Enrichment Readings

239

excellent example of the social construction of gender as well as issues of class, discrimination, and prejudice. (While this is an R-rated movie based on a true story, Hilary Swank appeared on the popular television show *Beverly Hills 90210,* thus many students have probably seen or at least heard of the movie.)

Our society is deeply structured by our definitions of gender and what it means to be a man or a woman. Even with more women working, we still design the workday and careers for people with stay-at-home spouses who can tend children and the home while the worker leaves the home for more than forty hours a week. Women as a group get paid less than men, whether we look at women and men in the same jobs or in comparable jobs that may have different titles. The "equal pay" movement has been redefined as the "comparable worth" movement since most women and men do work in different occupations although they often do similar types of work. The gendered wage gap and gendered occupational segregation is not easily dealt with since these differences stem from socialized patterns of occupational aspirations and family obligations. That women are primarily responsible for domestic work (children and home) leaves women with a "second shift" to perform once home from their paid jobs (Hochschild, 1989). Women are more likely than men to take time off from their careers to care for family members, thus interrupting or derailing their career paths. The infamous "Mommy track" refers to women who are perceived to have chosen their families over their work, thus limiting their promotional opportunities.

Ageism is another issue of social inequality that will be increasingly apparent due to the growing size of our aging population. While those in the retirement years are doing much better than those of the same age did forty years ago, inequalities based on age still occur. Many have been forcibly retired from jobs due to financial reasons (they're more expensive than newly hired workers) or perceived disabilities (they're "too old" to work). However, with an increased life span and other improvements in health and our understanding of aging, many people over sixty are not retired nor are they thinking of doing so. Many assumptions that people have made about the elderly have been challenged as we have more examples of physically and intellectually active senior citizens.

UNIT 3 Social Inequality

Chapters	Pacing Chart*
8 SOCIAL STRATIFICATION 1. Dimensions of Stratification 2. Explanations of Stratification 3. Social Classes in America 4. Poverty in America 5. Social Mobility	**Pages 242-244, 252, 254-254-257, 260-261, 265-268.** These pages introduce concepts of social class. Use Figure 8.1 to explain the inequity of wealth in the U.S. Also included is a table summarizing the approaches of the major perspectives; describes the social classes and discusses poverty in the U.S. and ends with social mobility. *This plan does not cover the power and prestige dimensions; the text specific approaches of the major theoretical perspectives; or welfare reform.*
9 INEQUALITIES OF RACE AND ETHNICITY 1. Minority, Race, and Ethnicity 2. Racial and Ethnic Relations 3. Theories of Prejudice and Discrimination 4. Minority Groups in the United States	All sections of this chapter build on concepts and terms that are needed for a complete understanding of the unit of social institutions.
10 INEQUALITIES OF GENDER AND AGE 1. Sex and Gender Identity 2. Theoretical Perspectives on Gender 3. Gender Inequality 4. Ageism 5. Inequality in America's Elderly Population	**Pages 310-311, 316-320, 322-238.** These pages cover the definitions of sex and gender; the approaches of the major theoretical perspectives to gender equality, and the effects of gender on politics and economics for women. *Not included in this accelerated plan are the biological basis of behavior and the sections on ageism.*

*Note: While the authors of *Sociology and You* do not recommend skipping chapters or sections of the textbook, they are teachers like yourselves and know you must sometimes make scheduling compromises. If your schedule demands that you move more quickly through this book, you may want to focus on the pages listed above.

Key to Ability Levels

Activities in the teacher's material have been coded for varying learning styles and abilities.

L1 **BASIC** activities for all students

L2 **AVERAGE** activities for average to above-average students

L3 **CHALLENGING** activities for above-average students

ELL **ENGLISH LANGUAGE LEARNER** activities

Teacher Resource Manager

Teacher Classroom Resources

Unit 3 Mastering Basic Concepts
- Learning Goals Outlines
- Graphic Organizers
- Vocabulary Activities
- Analyzing and Interpreting Data
- Increasing Your Reading Comprehension
- Guided Readings
- Student Journal Prompts
- Vocabulary and Chapter Review Quizzes

Spanish Supplements
- Learning Goals Outlines
- Bilingual Chapter Summaries
- Vocabulary and Chapter Review Quizzes

Chapter & Unit Tests w/ Final Exam and Answer Key
- Chapters 8–10 Tests A and B
- Unit 3 Test

Alternative Assessments
- Performance Assessments
- Portfolio Assessments
- Chapter Essay Tests

Culture Studies: The Sociological Perspective
- Readings 14–18

Including:
- Reading 18: Behind the Veil

Doing Sociology: Focus on Research
- Research Projects 7–9

Ethics, Values, and Technology: Real-Life Issues in Society
- Readings 12–16

Including:
- Reading 15: Lucy Stone on Marriage

Transparency Binder

Chapter 8
- 20: Concentration of Wealth
- 21: Income Distribution
- 22: Portrait of a Typical Millionaire
- 23: Unemployment Rate as of January 2000

Chapter 9
- 24: Hate Crimes in the United States
- 25: Projected Changes in U.S. Racial/Ethnic Composition
- 26: Who's on the Net—by Income Level
- 27: Who's on the Net—Race & Education

Chapter 10
- 28: What Women Earn compared to Men by Age and Race
- 29: U.S. Labor Force Participation Rates, by Sex: 1890–1997

Multimedia

TeacherWorks™
All-In-One Planner and Resource Center
- **Interactive Teacher Edition** Access your Teacher Wraparound Edition and your classroom resources with a few easy clicks.
- **Interactive Lesson Planner** Planning has never been easier! Organize your week, month, semester, or year with all the lesson helps you need to make teaching creative, timely, and relevant.

Interactive Student Edition CD-ROM

This CD-ROM contains the complete Student Edition with, simple navigation and search functions and links to Web activities and resources.

ExamView® Pro Testmaker CD-ROM

Easy-to-use software includes an extensive question bank and allows you to create fully customized tests that can be administered in print or online.

Vocabulary PuzzleMaker CD-ROM

This software lets you create crossword puzzles, word search puzzles, and jumbo puzzles using chapter vocabulary.

Presentations for the Classroom on CD-ROM

This PowerPoint presentation provides a step-by-step outline and supporting visuals for classroom lectures.

SOCIOLOGY Online

Use our Web site for additional resources. All essential content is covered in the Student Edition.

You and your students can visit soc.glencoe.com, the Web site companion to *Sociology and You.* The student text directs students to the Web site for **Chapter Overviews, Student Web Activities, Self-Check Quizzes,** and **Textbook Updates**.

Answers are provided for you in the **Web Activity Lesson Plan**.

Chapter Preview

Section 1 (pages 242–249)

Stratification is the division of society into classes that have unequal amounts of wealth, power, and prestige. Karl Marx and Max Weber studied these dimensions of stratification in great detail.

Section 2 (page 250–253)

Each of the three perspectives—functionalism, conflict theory, and symbolic interactionism—explains stratification in society in a different way.

Section 3 (pages 254–258)

Sociologists have identified several social classes in the United States. They include the upper, middle, working, and lower classes.

Section 4 (pages 259–264)

Poverty can be measured in absolute or relative terms. The poor in the U.S. are disproportionately represented by African Americans, Latinos, women, and children.

Section 5 (pages 265–268)

Social mobility, the movement of individuals or groups within the stratification structure, is usually measured by changes in occupational status. Sociologists are most interested in upward or downward (vertical) mobility. Closed-class systems permit little vertical mobility; open-class systems, such as those in industrialized countries, allow considerable vertical mobility.

CHAPTER 8

Social Stratification

Lead-Off Activity

Bring in a cake and a cupcake. Hide the cake, and show students the cupcake. Ask: How will we distribute this? Should we have an essay contest and give the winner the cupcake? Students probably will decide that one student can get the cupcake, but they might have to earn it. Then bring out the big cake. Tell students that if they can come up with an equitable way to distribute the cake, they earn a piece. Should students conduct a lottery? Should the athletes or National Honor Society members get first

USING Your Sociological Imagination

Jane Smith, aged forty and reeling from a bitter divorce, was discouraged. A serious back injury meant she could no longer work at her nursing aide job. Without a high school diploma, she found that no one was willing to hire her. Reluctantly, she applied for welfare and was enrolled in a program designed to develop job skills. She completed an eighteen-month course and was hired by an engineering firm. After two years, Jane has moved up in the company and now thinks of herself as an intelligent, capable person.

A different type of welfare story involves Mary, the "welfare queen." Many politicians have used her as a typical example of how the social welfare system is abused. Mary managed to register for government aid under dozens of assumed names and collected thousands of dollars from food stamps and other federally subsidized programs. With this money, she supported her drug and alcohol habits while her children were left cold and underfed.

Which welfare case do you believe is typical? Your answer depends a lot on your social class and such characteristics as age, education, politics, and income. Sociologists know that most Americans seriously overestimate both the amount of welfare fraud and the amount of money spent on welfare. At the same time, negative attitudes about welfare recipients have become part of the American culture. This chapter will look at attitudes and behaviors of different social classes.

Sections

1. **Dimensions of Stratification**
2. **Explanations of Stratification**
3. **Social Classes in America**
4. **Poverty in America**
5. **Social Mobility**

Learning Objectives

After reading this chapter, you will be able to

- explain the relationship between stratification and social class.
- compare and contrast the three dimensions of stratification.
- state the differences among the three major perspectives on social stratification.
- identify the distinguishing characteristics of the major social classes in America.
- describe the measurement and extent of poverty in the United States.
- discuss social mobility in the United States.

SOCIOLOGY Online

Chapter Overview
Visit the *Sociology and You* Web site at soc.glencoe.com and click on **Chapter 8—Chapter Overviews** to preview chapter information.

USING Your Sociological Imagination

Remind students the first rule of sociology is that things are not always what they seem. This feature shows students that the perception of Mary, the welfare queen, is largely media created. The reality is much closer to the first lady, Jane Smith, depicted in the story. Ask students to think about where they have gotten their information about welfare. *(parents, newspapers, friends, neighbors, etc.)* Students who know people on welfare or who have received some government assistance themselves might be able to shed light on how different the reality is from what the media often presents.

choice? Students will probably decide that this cake can easily be cut into pieces that all can enjoy. Ask students if you should save a piece for the absent students. As students argue, some will decide it's not worth the piece of cake to argue. You can now discuss how the conflict perspective looks at competition for limited resources. Suppose this was money instead of cake. Would we feel that the solution was to get an even amount? If everyone doesn't feel this way, then a stratified system is created.
L1

Using the Section Preview

Students should be familiar with Karl Marx from history class and from Chapter 1. They should also be familiar with *The Communist Manifesto.* The opening line of the treatise is, "The history of the world hitherto is the history of class struggles." Marx has been called the father of the conflict perspective. Ask students why this title fits him well.

More About . . . the Industrial Revolution

Emile Durkheim, Karl Marx, and Max Weber wrote during the Industrial Revolution, one of the great social transformations in history. All were acutely aware of how changes brought about by mechanization and industrialization stratified society. Have students review the basic concepts developed by these three men as outlined in previous chapters and then relate these concepts to the Industrial Revolution.

Integrating the Teacher Resources

Look for the Chapter 8 Vocabulary Activity worksheet in the Unit 3 Mastering Basic Concepts booklet in your Teacher's Resource Box. It provides reinforcement for vocabulary in this chapter.

Section 1

Dimensions of Stratification

Key Terms

- **social stratification**
- **social class**
- **bourgeoisie**
- **proletariat**
- **income**
- **wealth**
- **power**
- **prestige**

Section Preview

Stratification is the division of society into classes that have unequal amounts of wealth, power, and prestige. Karl Marx and Max Weber studied these dimensions of stratification in great detail.

social stratification
ranking of people or groups according to their unequal access to scarce resources

social class
segment of society whose members hold similar amounts of resources and share values, norms, and an identifiable lifestyle

Social Stratification and Social Class

In George Orwell's Animal Farm, *the animals overthrew their human master to form their own soon-to-be stratified society.*

In one of his best-known children's books, Dr. Seuss writes of the Sneetches, birds whose rank depends on whether or not they have a large star on their stomachs. Star-bellied Sneetches have high status, and plain-bellied Sneetches have low status. In the classic novel *Animal Farm,* George Orwell creates a barnyard society where the pigs ultimately take over the previously classless animal society. The animals' motto changes from "All animals are equal" to "All animals are equal—but some animals are more equal than others." Although these books are very different, both mock the tendency of humans to form ranks. **Social stratification** is the creation of layers (or strata) of people who possess unequal shares of scarce resources. The most important of these resources are income, wealth, power, and prestige (Levine, 1998).

How is social stratification related to social class? Each of the layers in a stratification system is a **social class**—a segment of a population whose members hold similar amounts of scarce resources and share values, norms, and an identifiable lifestyle. The number of social classes in a society varies. Technologically developed countries generally have three broad classes—upper, middle, and lower—subdivided into smaller categories. In some developing countries, there might only be an upper class and a lower class.

Karl Marx and Max Weber made the most significant early contributions to the study of social stratification. (See Chapter 1, pages 16–18 for an introduction to these two pioneers of sociology.) Marx explained the importance of the economic foundations of social classes, while Weber emphasized the prestige and power aspects of stratification.

Learning Styles

Bodily-Kinesthetic/Interpersonal Dr. Seuss' *Sneetches* and George Orwell's *Animal Farm* were used to introduce the concepts of social stratification and social class. To assist students in personalizing the content of this chapter, bring in copies of Dr. Seuss' book. Read it to students, and then have them act it out, with students taking the parts of the characters in the story. Afterwards, give students a chance to talk about how they felt. What was it like to be a star-bellied Sneetch? How was it different to be a plain-bellied Sneetch? To conclude this activity, you may want to arrange for students to visit a local elementary school to read stories to younger children, to help foster good relations between students of all social classes.
L1

World View

Poverty and Death

Receiving basic nutrition and medical care is critical to survival in the early years of human life. Because wealth and income have a significant impact on a family's ability to provide these necessities of life, extreme poverty matters a great deal. This map shows the number of deaths of children less than five years old per 1,000 live births in each country.

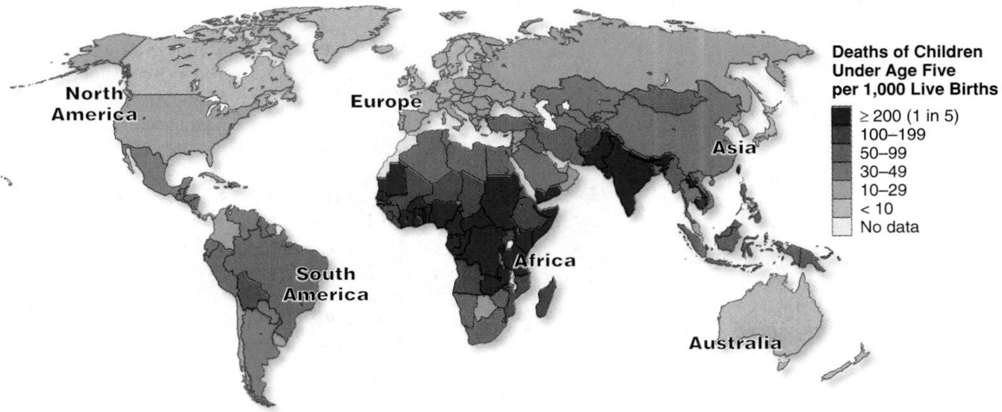

Interpreting the Map

1. Do you see a pattern in the death rates for children under five years old? Explain.
2. Why do you think the U.S. ranks higher than some countries in Europe?
3. Imagine you have the job of reducing the world's death rate among children under age five. What programs would you introduce?

Adapted from *The State of the World Atlas,* 5th ed.

The Economic Dimension

Marx identified several social classes in nineteenth-century industrial society, including laborers, servants, factory workers, craftspeople, proprietors of small businesses, and moneyed capitalists. He predicted, however, that capitalist societies would ultimately be reduced to two social classes. He thought that those who owned the means of production—the **bourgeoisie**—would be the rulers. Those who worked for wages—the **proletariat**—would be the ruled. Marx predicted that because the capitalists owned the means of production (factories, land, and so forth), they would both rule and exploit the working class. The working class would have nothing to sell but its labor.

bourgeoisie
class that owns the means of production

proletariat
class that labors without owning the means of production

World View

As far as preventative medicine goes, the U.S. lags behind most other developed nations. Some critics believe this is because providing emergency care is more profitable than providing preventative care. Critics also point to the inequity between social classes and the fact that poverty has a great bearing on health, especially for infants. The U.S. has tried to combat this problem by offering universal prenatal and postnatal health care, much like Europe does. But the U.S. is fighting against a head wind because it has levels of poverty that Europe does not. Again, a person's health is affected by more factors outside the formal health care system than within it.

Answers to Interpreting the Map

1. Obviously, deaths to children under age five are higher in the developed nations where adequate health care is not readily available.
2. There is a large, but hidden, population of poor in this country who cannot avail themselves of health care.
3. Answers will vary.

Interdisciplinary Activity

History Discuss with students the following information about the bourgeoisie and proletariat. Marx considered the bourgeoisie—the middle class—to be the oppressor. Members of the proletariat—the working class—were the oppressed. The upper class disappears in this theory. Why do students think this is?

Marx predicted that the struggle between the bourgeoisie and proletariat would finally break into open revolution with the violent overthrow of the bourgeoisie by the proletariat. For a while the proletariat would form a dictatorship in order to organize the means of production. However, because social classes themselves arose from the economic differences that had been abolished, a classless society would be the end result. Ask students to explain why they think this did not happen.
L2

Points to Stress

In Melvin Oliver's and Thomas Shapiro's book, *Black Wealth, White Wealth: A New Perspective on Racial Inequality,* they give a simple example for understanding the difference between wealth and income: Income is money that one spends and wealth is what prepares one for the future (i.e. your savings, etc.). This usually helps students understand that making a paycheck doesn't translate into accumulating wealth. Wealth allows people to get ahead.

Working with the Data

Figure 8.1 The lowest fifth, middle fifth, and top fifth refer to the lowest 20 percent, middle 20 percent, and top 20 percent of American families.

Integrating the Teacher Resources

To reinforce key ideas, use the Chapter 8 Graphic Organizer, a reproducible student worksheet available in the Unit 3 Mastering Basic Concepts **booklet in your Teacher's Resource Box.**

income
amount of money received by an individual or group over a specific time period

wealth
total economic resources held by a person or group

Marx believed that control of the economy gave the capitalists control over the legal, educational, and government systems as well. For Karl Marx, the economy determined the nature of society.

Are there extremes of income and poverty in the United States? In his writings, Marx emphasized the unequal distribution of economic resources. How unequally are these resources distributed in the United States? When discussing this issue, economists often make a distinction between income and wealth. **Income** is the amount of money received within a given time period by an individual or group. **Wealth** refers to all the economic resources possessed by an individual or group. In brief, your income is your paycheck, and your wealth is what you own.

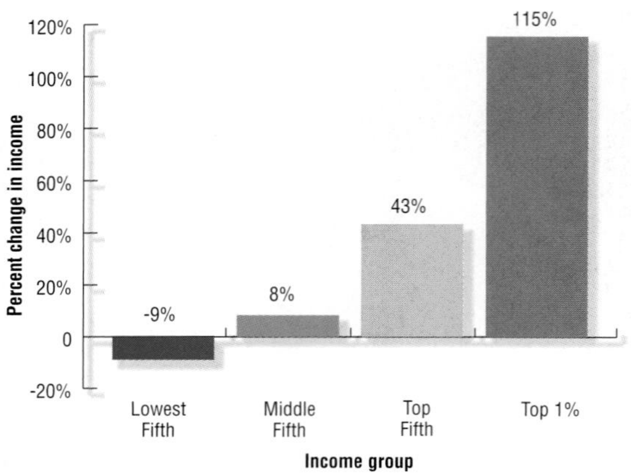

Figure 8.1 Percentage Change in After-Tax Income 1977 to 1999. *To what percentages do the labels Lowest, Middle, and Top Fifth refer?*

Sources: Washington, DC: Center on Budget and Policy Priorities, 1999.

Online UPDATE
Visit soc.glencoe.com and click on **Textbook Updates–Chapter 8** for an update of the data.

In 1999, over thirty-two million Americans were living in poverty. (In 2000, the poverty level was set at $17,761 for a family of four.) At the other extreme, there were over ten million millionaire households and some fifty billionaires in the United States. The economist Paul Samuelson described income inequality in America in these words: "If we made an income pyramid out of a child's blocks, with each layer portraying $500 of income, the peak would be far higher than Mt. Everest, but most people would be within a few feet of the ground" (Samuelson and Nordhaus, 1995). The truth in Samuelson's statement is supported by government figures on the distribution of income. In 1999, the richest 20 percent of American families received over 49 percent of the nation's income. The poorest 20 percent controlled under 4 percent (U.S. Bureau of the Census, 2000a).

Income inequality exists and is growing. Figure 8.1 charts percentage changes in after-tax income in the United States over a twenty-two year period. During this period, the income

"Actually, Lou, I think it was more than just my being in the right place at the right time. I think it was my being the right race, the right religion, the right sex, the right socioeconomic group, having the right accent, the right clothes, going to the right schools..."

This cartoon is illustrating what sociologists have confirmed—usually, those who have, get.

On-Demand Writing

In the United States during the 1870s the gap between the rich and poor widened and came under criticism. The professional and business classes became wealthier because of industrialization. At the same time, the working class became poorer. Henry George, a newspaper reporter, observed, "It is as though an immense wedge were being forced, not underneath society, but through society. Those who are above the point of separation are elevated, but those who are below are crushed down . . .. This

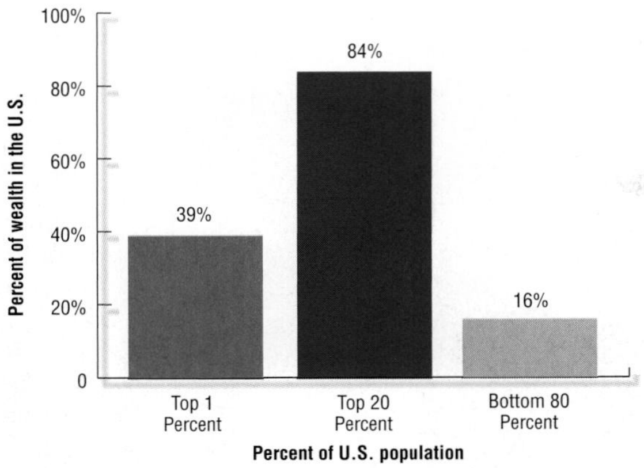

Figure 8.2 Shares of Wealth. *Is this picture of the distribution of wealth different from what you would expect? Explain.*

Source: Washington, DC: Center on Budget and Policy Priorities, 1999.

of the top 1 percent of the population increased by 115 percent. Compare this to a 9 percent decline for the lowest fifth of the population. How much inequality in wealth exists in the United States?

Income distribution figures reveal economic inequality, but they do not show the full extent of inequality. For that, inequality in wealth (what you own) must be considered. In the United States, there is a high concentration of wealth. The richest 20 percent of the population holds 84 percent of the wealth. The top 1 percent alone has 39 percent of the total wealth in the United States. (See Figure 8.2)

The Power Dimension

You will recall from Chapter 1 that **power** is the ability to control the behavior of others, even against their will. Individuals or groups who possess power are able to use it to enhance their own interests, often—but not necessarily—at the expense of society.

power
the ability to control the behavior of others, even against their will

Can you exercise power without being wealthy? According to Marx, those who own and control capital have the power in a society. Weber, on the other hand, argued that while having money certainly helps, economic success and power are not the same. Money and ownership of the means of production are not the only resources that can be used as a basis for power. Expert knowledge can be used to expand power, too. For example, many lawyers convert their expertise into substantial amounts of political power. Fame is another basis for power. In 1952, for example, Albert Einstein was offered the presidency of Israel. (He refused, saying, "I know a little about nature, and hardly anything about men.")

Power is also attached to the social positions we hold. Elected officers in organizations have more power than rank-and-file members. People in top executive positions in the mass media are powerful, even if they themselves do not have great wealth. People who are wealthy and powerful also are assumed to have characteristics they may not have. Not all of these people are as intelligent and wise as is usually assumed. Still, these attributed characteristics help them gain prestige.

Working with the Data

Figure 8.2 Students may point out that the three percentages given on the graph add up to more than 100 percent. Be sure students understand that the "Top 1 Percent" figure is included in the "Top 20 Percent" figure. The "Top 20 Percent" plus the "Bottom 80 Percent" figures do add up to 100 percent.

Open-Response Questions

Ask students the following questions: How would you explain the power dimension at your school? Which groups seem to have the most power? Do any student groups have power?

Integrating the Transparencies

Transparencies related to the context of this section are provided in the *Sociology and You* Transparency Binder.

association of poverty with progress is the great enigma of our times."

After reading the above paragraph to students, discuss whether students think this is still true today. If so, to what extent? How is society the same now? How is it different?

Have students write compositions expressing their opinions on this matter. They should include answers to the above questions in their compositions. Ask volunteers to share their compositions with the rest of the class.
L2

Reinforcing Vocabulary

After reviewing the definition of *prestige* with students, ask them to list people in their own lives who have prestige in their social circles. Ask them to explain why certain people seem to have prestige and others do not. What part do recognition, respect, and admiration play in an individual's prestige factor? In other words, how do they decide who does and does not possess prestige?

Using the Illustration

Ask students whether all celebrities (actors, singers, musicians, athletes, etc.) have prestige. Why do some have prestige while others do not? How much does popularity and money earned have to do with prestige? How do these relate to recognition, respect, and admiration? Is there a discrepancy in the way prestige is gained?

Jesse Jackson has channeled his intense interest in civil rights into the exercise of power on behalf of the poor and disadvantaged.

Finally, we can overcome a lack of wealth if we have large numbers of people on our side or if we are skillful at organizing our resources. Hitler, for example, was able to turn the problem of limited resources into a mass political movement. He gained absolute power by promising to deliver Germany from economic hardship following World War I.

The Prestige Dimension

prestige
recognition, respect, and admiration attached to social positions

A third dimension of social stratification is **prestige**—recognition, respect, and admiration attached to social positions. Prestige is defined by your culture and society. Honor, admiration, respect, and deference are extended to dons within the Mafia, for example; but outside their own circles Mafia chiefs do not have high prestige.

Popular actors such as Julia Roberts and Will Smith have considerable wealth. Their prestige rating is stronger in some circles than others, however.

Cooperative Learning Activity

As stated in the text, most people achieve prestige because of their occupations. White-collar occupations have higher prestige rankings than blue-collar occupations. Max Weber suggested that a person's prestige is generally based on wealth, political power, and occupation. However, even though wealth and power usually determine prestige, that is not always the case. For example, basketball superstar Shaquille O'Neal attains much greater wealth than the office of the President of the United States, but very little of the political power achieved by the status of President.

After giving students this information, divide the class into groups to discuss

Occupations	Prestige Score	Occupations	Prestige Score	Occupations	Prestige Score
Surgeon	87	Police officer	61	Automobile dealer	43
Astronaut	80	Actor	60	Deep-sea diver	43
Lawyer	75	Journalist	60	Landlord	41
College professor	74	TV anchorman	60	Prison guard	40
Airline pilot	73	Businessperson	60	Auto mechanic	40
Dentist	72	Actress	59	Roofer	37
Priest	71	Nursery school teacher	55	Barber	36
Engineer	71	Fashion designer	55	Sales clerk in a store	36
TV anchorwoman	70	Firefighter	53	Bus driver	32
Secret Service agent	70	Airplane mechanic	53	Dry cleaner	32
School principal	69	Commercial artist	52	Waitress	29
Medical technician	68	Housewife	51	Taxicab driver	28
Optometrist	67	Funeral director	49	Used car salesperson	25
Registered nurse	66	Jazz musician	48	Bill collector	24
High school teacher	66	Mail carrier	47	Janitor	22
Air traffic controller	65	Insurance agent	46	Grocery bagger	18
Professional athlete	65	Mechanic	46	Street-corner drug dealer	13
Paramedic	64	Disc jockey	45	Fortune teller	13
Public grade school teacher	64	Photographer	45	Panhandler	11
Advertising executive	63	Plumber	45		
Veterinarian	62	Bank teller	43		

Figure 8.3 Prestige Rankings of Selected Occupations in the United States. *Why do you think the highest listed prestige score is 87? What occupations might rate a higher score?*

Prestige must be voluntarily given, not claimed. Scientists cannot proclaim themselves Nobel Prize winners; journalists cannot award themselves Pulitzer Prizes; and corporate executives cannot grant themselves honorary doctorates. Recognition must come from others.

People with similar levels of prestige share identifiable lifestyles. The offspring of upper-class families are more likely to attend private universities and Episcopalian churches. Children from lower-class homes are less likely to attend college at all and tend to belong to fundamentalist religious groups. In fact, some sociologists view social classes as subcultures because their members participate in distinctive ways of life.

How is prestige distributed? The social positions that are considered the most important, or are valued the most highly, have the most prestige. Because Americans value the acquisition of wealth and power, they tend to assign higher prestige to persons in positions of wealth and power.

In America, most people achieve prestige because of their occupations. (See Figure 8.3.) White-collar occupations (doctors, ministers, schoolteachers) have higher prestige than blue-collar jobs (carpenters, plumbers, mechanics). Even though wealth and power usually determine prestige, that is not always the case. You may find it somewhat surprising, for example, that priests and college professors have more prestige than bankers.

“All wealth is power, so power must infallibly draw wealth to itself by some means or other.”

Edmund Burke
British statesman

Working with the Data

Figure 8.3 The occupations missing from chart include positions that are only filled by one or a few persons, such as president or chief justice or the Supreme Court. The more exclusive the occupation, the higher the prestige ranking. Ask students if they agree with the rankings of the occupations shown here. If not, how would they change the rankings? If time allows, have students re-rank the occupations listed here according to their own standards. Ask for volunteers to explain why they changed the rankings. What criteria did they use to re-rank the occupations?

Integrating the Teacher Resources

Look for the Chapter 8 Analyzing and Interpreting Data worksheet in the Unit 3 Mastering Basic Concepts booklet in your Teacher's Resource Box for skill-building exercises based on the graphs, charts, and maps in this chapter.

whether they think O'Neal (or an equally popular sports figure) or the current president has more prestige. Hopefully, students will realize that prestige is also a function of the age group involved and the norms of the group. Students should determine which age groups would look at O'Neal and the president differently and why. At this point, you might want students to discuss other aspects of prestige. Finally, have each group appoint one person to relate the group's answers and decisions to the rest of the class. A class discussion might follow, depending on time and interest. **L1**

Pulling it All Together

Section 1 defines social stratification and social class. It also explains Marx's emphasis on the economic dimension of stratification and Weber's emphasis on prestige and power related to stratification.

Using the Illustration

Ask students to look at this photo and rank the individuals according to prestige. Have students compare lists and work in groups to come up with one list. Put the final lists on the board. Ask students to explain how they ranked the individuals. What criteria did they use? How did they justify the criteria? Is the criteria fair? Why or why not? How does this relate to the way society ranks individuals? Is society's ranking fair? Why or why not?

Answers to Section 1 Assessment

1. Social stratification is the creation of layers (or strata) of people who possess unequal shares of scarce resources.
2. a. Pr
b. Po
c. Pr
d. W
e. Po
f. W
3. 49
4. wealth, power, occupation

Critical Thinking

5. Answers will vary.

Associate each of these people with a prestige level. If an occupation is not obvious, choose a likely one for that person. Can the young girl even be ranked?

Section 1 Assessment

1. What is social stratification?
2. Match the dimensions of stratifications with the examples below. Use (W) for wealth, (Po) for power, and (Pr) for prestige.
   - **a.** the respect accorded doctors
   - **b.** a politician considering the interests of a lobby
   - **c.** the Nobel Peace Prize
   - **d.** stock market holdings
   - **e.** a Supreme Court ruling
   - **f.** real estate assets
3. The top 20 percent of U.S. households receive approximately what percent of the total income?
4. What are the most common sources of prestige in U.S. society?

Critical Thinking

5. **Analyzing Information** Social class level influences the likelihood of gaining political power. Can you analyze the relationship between social class level and political power?

Careers in Sociology

After students have offered some answers to the following questions, share this information with them. What opportunities are available for sociologists in business and industry?

Sociologists with B. A. degrees go into a variety of industries, predominantly in sales, human resources, and management. Those with advanced degrees are employed by (or consult with) many corporations, concentrating in the fields of marketing, advertising, telecommunications, and insurance. Their specialties tend to be in demography—the study of population and its changes—and in market research—the study of the needs, wants, and lifestyles of

Another Time: You Are What You Wear

Social rank in Europe in the Middle Ages was reflected, as it is today, in clothing and accessories. The following excerpt describes some of the norms associated with dress and status.

Clothing [in medieval Europe] served as a kind of uniform, designating status. Lepers were required to wear gray coats and red hats, the skirts of prostitutes had to be scarlet, released heretics carried crosses sewn on both sides of their chests—you were expected to pray as you passed them—and the breast of every Jew, as [required] by law, bore a huge yellow circle.

The rest of society belonged to one of the three great classes: the nobility, the clergy, and the commons. Establishing one's social identity was important. Each man knew his place, believed it had been [determined] in heaven, and was aware that what he wore must reflect it.

Clothing in medieval society was strictly regulated.

To be sure, certain fashions were shared by all. Styles had changed since Greece and Rome shimmered in their glory; then garments had been wrapped on; now all classes put them on and fastened them. Most clothing—except the leather gauntlets and leggings of hunters, and the crude animal skins worn by the very poor—was now woven of wool. (Since few Europeans possessed a change of clothes, the same [dress] was worn daily; as a consequence, skin diseases were astonishingly prevalent.) But there was no mistaking the distinctions between the parson in his vestments; the toiler in his dirty cloth tunic, loose trousers, and heavy boots; and the aristocrat with his jewelry, his hairdress, and his extravagant finery. Every knight wore a signet ring, and wearing fur was as much a sign of knighthood as wearing a sword or carrying a falcon. Indeed, in some European states it was illegal for anyone not nobly born to adorn himself with fur. "Many a petty noble," wrote historian W. S. Davis, "will cling to his frayed tippet of black lambskin, even in the hottest weather, merely to prove that he is not a villein [a type of serf]."

Source: Excerpted from *A World Lit Only by Fire,* © 1992 by William Manchester. By permission of Little, Brown and Company. Reprinted by permission of Don Congdon Associates, Inc. © 1993 by William Manchester.

Thinking It Over

Think about how you and your classmates dress. Identify some ways in which differences in dress reflect social status in your school.

Another Time

This selection is of great interest to students because they often forget about the little things we take for granted, such as washable clothing and dry cleaning. Paved sidewalks and streets also make modern dressing a lot more healthy and convenient. Remind them that children and young people did not have special clothes designed for them or for activities such as playing, swimming, or sports. The history of clothing is a fascinating topic; some of your students may want to research the relationship between clothes, fashion, and status in more detail.

Students might want to identify all the types of clothing that make up your particular high school and what the clothing means. Do athletes enjoy a lofty status with their jackets? Are the students dressed in black seen as goths and assigned lower status? Do students think that this reflects one's social class, or does this cross social class boundaries?

Answer to Thinking It Over

Answers will vary.

various populations who may be potential clients or customers. Many sociologists are also prominent in public opinion research, which is of interest to those in politics, communications, and advertising.

In industry, they often are employed as industrial sociologists—experts on productivity, work relations, minorities and women in the work force, linking technology to the organization, corporate cultures, and organizational development.

For access to employment ads from major U.S. newspapers that can be searched by industry and location, have students try **http://www.careerpath.com**

Section 2

Explanations of Stratification

Key Term

- false consciousness

Section Preview

Each of the three perspectives—functionalism, conflict theory, and symbolic interactionism—explains stratification in society in a different way.

Functionalist Theory of Stratification

According to the functionalists, stratification assures that the most qualified people fill the most important positions, that these qualified people perform their tasks competently, and that they are rewarded for their efforts. The functionalist theory recognizes that inequality exists because certain jobs are more important than others and that these jobs often involve special talent and training. To encourage people to make the sacrifices necessary to fill these jobs (such as acquiring the necessary education), society attaches special monetary rewards and prestige to the positions. That is why, for example, doctors make more money and have more prestige than bus drivers. A higher level of skill is required in the medical profession, and our society's need for highly qualified doctors is great.

Conflict Theory of Stratification

According to the conflict theory of stratification, inequality exists because some people are willing to exploit others. Stratification, from this perspective, is based on force rather than on people voluntarily agreeing to it.

The conflict theory of stratification is based on Marx's ideas regarding class conflict. For Marx, all of history has been a class struggle between the powerful and the powerless, the exploiters and the exploited. Capitalist society is the final stage of the class struggle. Although the capitalists are outnumbered, they are able to control the workers. This is because the capitalists use a belief system that legitimizes the way things are. For example, the powerful contend that income and wealth are based on ability, hard work, and individual effort. Those who own the means of production are able to spread their ideas, beliefs, and values through the schools, the media, the churches, and the government. (More will be said about how this might happen in the next section.) Marx used the term **false consciousness** to refer to working-class acceptance of capitalist ideas and values.

false consciousness adoption of the ideas of the dominant class by the less powerful class

How would functionalists explain the different places of these people on the stratification structure?

Using the Section Preview

You might want to use Bill Gates, founder of Microsoft, as an analogy to help students understand the three perspectives: functionalism, conflict theory, and symbolic interactionism. The functionalist would say that Gates worked hard and used his genius to recreate the computer industry, therefore he deserves the fruits of his labor. The conflict theorist would say that Gates' wealth exemplifies the inequality inherent in society. The interactionist theorist would look at how people accept Gates' right to enjoy his status with the wealthiest people in the world.

Using the Illustration

A functionalist would probably say that the business couple in the right-hand photo are higher skilled and have more education than the restaurant owners in the left-hand photo. As such, the businesspeople are entitled to be in a higher social class.

Role Play

Divide the class into groups to work together to develop role plays. The role plays should illustrate one or more aspects of the concept of exploitation according to Marx's conflict theory of stratification. Students might want to focus on schools, the media, the churches, or the government. They might want to look at employers and employees. After groups have developed their role plays, ask them to perform them for the rest of the class. You might want to have a class discussion after each role play or have one after each group has finished presenting.

L1

Later conflict sociologists have proposed that stratification is based more on power than on property ownership. America's legal system, for example, is used by the wealthy for their benefit, and the political system is skewed toward the interests of the powerful. For followers of the conflict perspective, stratification occurs through the struggle for scarce resources.

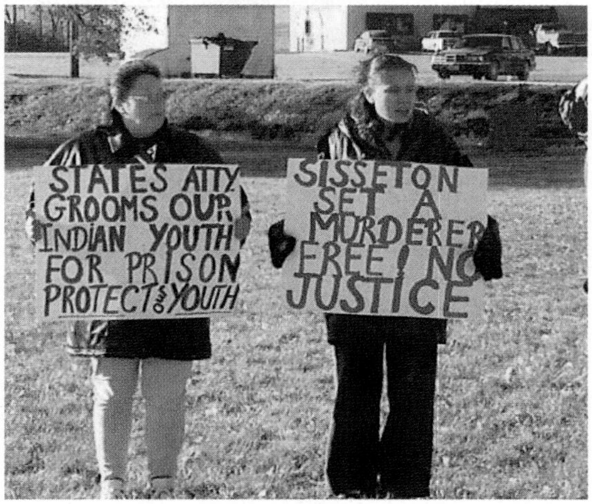

These South Dakotans are protesting the unequal treatment of Native Americans in the criminal justice system. How could the protestors use conflict theory to support their viewpoint?

Symbolic Interactionism and Stratification

Symbolic interactionism helps us understand how people are socialized to accept the existing stratification structure. According to this perspective, American children are taught that a person's social class is the result of talent and effort. Those "on top" have worked hard and used their abilities, whereas those "on the bottom" lack the talent or the motivation to succeed. Hence, it is not fair to challenge the system. In this way, people come to accept the existing system.

Understandably, people in the lower social classes or social strata tend to suffer from lower self-esteem. How could it be otherwise when messages from all sides tell them they are inferior? Remember that, in the symbolic interactionist view, self-esteem is based on how we think others see us. In other words, the looking-glass process is at work. Those at the top blame the victims; the victims blame themselves. (See pages 114–115 for an explanation of the looking-glass self.)

The reverse is true for the higher classes. Those profiting most from the stratification structure tend to have higher self-esteem. This, in turn, fuels their conviction that the present arrangement is just. In short, people's self-concepts also help preserve the status quo.

It isn't always easy being out of the "in-group."

Observation

Research indicates that there is a direct relationship between control over decisions and goals and level of self-concept. Individuals who believe they are in control of their lives have a higher level of self-concept than individuals who do not perceive themselves as being in control. Those with a high self-concept feel freer to make decisions and plan for the future. From a teaching viewpoint, this means that helping students take control of their lives should have a positive impact on self-concept development and, potentially, on the development of their futures.

Encourage students to choose their own goals for part of this course. Allow them to choose a specific number of the activities to complete at the end of the chapters. Ownership of the learning process is one way to aid improved self-concept in teens.

Using the Illustration

Students by now should be able to easily identify conflict theory with the idea of groups fighting over limited resources—which is what this protest is about.

Teaching Strategy

Reread the first sentence on this page with students: "Later conflict sociologists have proposed that stratification is based more on power than on property ownership." Ask students whether they think power and property ownership are distinct. Can a person own a large amount of property and not be powerful? Can a person be powerful and not own a large amount of property? Ask students to explain their answers.
L2

Controversy and Debate

Symbolic interactionism proposes that a person is socialized to accept that social class is a result of talent and effort. People are taught to believe that those in the highest social classes have worked hard for what they have, and those on the bottom haven't. Ask students whether they agree with this statement. Is this socialization a conscious or unconscious process? You might want to divide the class into two teams to debate this issue.

Figure 8.4 Focus on Theoretical Perspectives

Social Stratification. This table summarizes what issues of social stratification might be of interest to each of the major perspectives and predictions that they would make. Why would the symbolic interactionists be more likely than the functionalists to look at issues of self-esteem?

Theoretical Perspective	Research Topic	Expected Result
Functionalism	Relationship between job performance and pay	Pay levels increase with job performance. 
Conflict Theory	Relationship between social class and the likelihood of punishment for a crime	 The chances for prosecution decrease as the level of social class increases.
Symbolic Interactionism	Link between social class and self-esteem	Self-esteem is higher among the upper class than the lower class. 

Section 2 Assessment

1. Identify which of the major perspectives describes the examples below.
   - **a.** Corporate executives make more money because they decide who gets what in their organizations.
   - **b.** Engineers make more money than butlers because of their education.
   - **c.** Poor children tend to have low self-esteem.
2. How did Marx explain the stratification of society?
3. According to the symbolic interactionists, people are socialized to accept the existing stratification structure through ______.
   - **a.** the "I"
   - **b.** evolution
   - **c.** conflict
   - **d.** the self-concept

Critical Thinking

4. **Making Comparisons** Compare and contrast the explanations given by functionalism, conflict theory, and symbolic interactionism for the existence of poor people in the United States.

Working with the Data

Figure 8.4 Functionalists are concerned with how a social phenomenon like stratification maintains order and stability. They would not be as interested in self-esteem. Symbolic interactionists would be concerned about self-esteem because it is related to class consciousness.

Pulling it All Together

The three sociological perspectives, functionalist, conflict, and interactionist, help students understand why stratification exists. Ask students, "Are you a functionalist, conflict theorist, or interactionist theorist when it comes to understanding stratification?"

Answers to Section 2 Assessment

1. a. conflict theory of stratification
   b. functionalist theory of stratification
   c. symbolic interactionism and stratification
2. Marx believed that all of history has been a class struggle between the powerful and the powerless, the exploiters and the exploited, and capitalist society is the final stage. He used the term *false consciousness* to refer to working class acceptance of capitalist ideas.
3. d (the self-concept)

Critical Thinking

4. Answers will vary.

Careers in Sociology

Although areas of expertise vary, sociologists command skills, knowledge, and experience that can be put to good use at all levels of government service. They are employed in a wide variety of agencies, including, at the federal level, Bureau of the Census, the Department of Agriculture, the General Accounting Office, the National Institutes of Health, or the Centers for Disease Control, for example. At the state level, many are engaged in urban planning, health planning, and in criminal justice systems.

Have students check out the web sites for these agencies: Bureau of the Census - **http://www.census.gov/**, Department of Agriculture - **http://www.usda.gov/**, General Accounting Office - **http://www.gao.gov/**, the National Institutes of Health - **http://www.nih.gov/**, or the Centers for Disease Control - **http://www.cdc.gov/**

Focus on Research

Field Research: Who's Popular, Who's Not?

For adolescent males, playing sports is a way to become popular.

In 1995, sociologist Donna Eder and her research team studied popularity among middle-schoolers. They observed lunchtime interactions and attended extracurricular activities. After several months of observation, informal interviews were conducted with individuals and groups. To capture interaction for closer study, the researchers received student and parental permission for audio and video recordings.

Eder and her colleagues found that in the sixth grade, there were no elite groups. Seventh and eighth graders, however, did not see each other as equals; popular seventh graders were divided along gender lines. By the eighth grade, the two groups intermingled. In both grades, popularity was based on how many others knew who you were and wanted to talk with you.

Status differences could arise in the seventh and eighth grades because cheerleading and team sports existed as a way to become highly visible. Realizing the source of their prestige, male athletes took every opportunity to display symbols of their team affiliation. Team uniforms, jerseys, and athletic shoes were among the most important items of dress. Bandages, casts, and crutches were worn with pride.

Girls could not use sports to gain visibility because female athletics were not as valued by faculty, administrators, or students. Girls, therefore, used cheerleading to make themselves widely known. In addition to performing at basketball and football games, cheerleaders appeared in front of the entire student body at pep rallies and other school events.

Boys made fun of this high-status female activity by mockingly imitating cheers. One male coach joined the mockery by telling football players that either they must practice harder or he would get them cheerleading skirts. He then pretended to cheer in a falsetto voice.

Girls, in contrast, regarded cheerleaders highly. Popular girls in the seventh and eighth grades were either cheerleaders or friends of cheerleaders. Flaunting their status (just as the male athletes did), cheerleaders put on their uniforms as far ahead of games as possible and wore their cheerleading skirts for extracurricular school activities.

Working with the Research

Which of the three major theoretical perspectives best explains the stratification structure described in this feature? Give reasons for your choice.

Focus on Research

Have students examine the stratification system at their school. You might have different groups of students present their analyses. Remind students that as sociologists their job is not to judge, but to observe and record.

Answer to Working with the Research

The conflict perspective would best explain the stratification issues presented in this feature. The groups began to see each other in opposition and competition. This was gender stratified, a topic discussed in Chapter 10. Boy athletes and girl cheerleaders enjoyed status within their own gender but between genders, the boys possessed superior status.

Integrating the Teacher Resources

A lesson plan for a student research project related to the content of this chapter can be found in Doing Sociology: Focus on Research available in your Teacher's Resource Box.

Using Problem-Solving Skills

Use students' answers to the questions presented in the Focus on Research activity in the side panel above to begin a discussion about stratification in your school. Why do students think there is stratification? Where does it start? With students? With teachers? With administration? How could students go about developing a plan to abolish stratification in your school? Where would they have to start? With administration? With teachers? With students? Do parents have any influence on the stratification system? If so, what influence do they have? Help students develop a realistic plan to rid your school of stratification. Do students think it will really work? Why or why not?

L2

Using the Section Preview

Bring in 100 pieces of candy. Put up signs around the room, one sign for each of the following: upper class, upper middle class, middle class, working class, and underclass. Using the percentages given in Figure 8.5, divide students accordingly. One percent of the class population becomes upper class. (In a class of 25, that would not be quite one student, but for now one will have to do.) Then put 14 percent of the class in upper middle, 30 percent in middle class, etc. Pretend that the candy is really income. (If you have a chart that calculates wealth too, use that, it is even more powerful.) The one student in upper class would get approximately sixty-seven pieces of candy. Distribute the rest according to the income figures. The 12 percent at the bottom would get 1 piece of candy for all in that social class. Then ask students if they would consider sharing this candy (money) so that all could have an equal share. Which students would be most and least likely to redistribute the candy?

Section 3 Social Classes in America

Key Terms

- class consciousness
- working poor
- underclass

Section Preview

Sociologists have identified several social classes in the United States. They include the upper class, the middle class, the working class and the working poor, and the underclass.

class consciousness identification with the goals and interests of a social class

Class Consciousness

Americans have always been aware of inequality, but they have never developed a sense of **class consciousness**—a sense of identification with the goals and interests of the members of a particular social class. In part because the American public has shown relatively little interest in class differences, sociologists began to investigate inequality rather late. It was not until the 1920s that sociologists in the United States began systematically to identify social classes. Since that time, however, research on this subject has been plentiful. Early efforts to study stratification were mostly case studies of specific communities. Only in relatively recent times have attempts been made to describe the stratification structure of America as a whole.

Since social classes are changeable and full of exceptions, any attempt to identify the social-class structure of American society is hazardous. Nevertheless, sociologists have described some of the major classifications. (See Figure 8.5.)

Figure 8.5 American Class Structure. *What does this chart of the American class structure indicate about stratification in the U.S.?*

Source: Adapted from Dennis Gilbert, *The American Class Structure,* 1998.

Class	Typical Occupations	%	Typical Incomes
Upper Class	Investors, heirs, chief executive officers	1%	$1.5 million
Upper Middle Class	Upper-level managers, professionals, owners of medium-sized businesses	14%	$80,000+
Middle Class	Lower-level managers, semiprofessionals, craftspeople, foremen, non-retail salespeople, clerical	30%	$45,000
Working Class	Low-skill manual, clerical, and retail sales workers	30%	$30,000
Working Poor	Lowest-paid manual, retail, and service workers	13%	$20,000
Underclass	Unemployed people, people in part-time menial jobs, people receiving public assistance	12%	$10,000

Survey

Have students conduct a survey of their peers, parents, and other adults. The survey could consist of only one question, "Which social class do you believe you belong to?" (An additional question might be, "Why do you think this?") Students should give people the following choices: underclass, working poor, working class, middle class, upper middle class, upper class. Students should not provide typical incomes for the different classes. After students have collected their data, they should determine what percentage of people think they are middle class. Do most, as stated in the text, think they are middle class? Or, are the numbers more realistic, 40–50 percent of the population? **L1**

The Upper Class

The upper class includes only 1 percent of the population (Gilbert, 1998) and may be divided into the upper-upper class and the lower-upper class. At the top is the "aristocracy." Its members represent the old-money families whose names appear in high society—Ford, Rockefeller, Vanderbilt, and du Pont, among others. The basis for membership in this most elite of clubs is blood rather than sweat and tears. Parents in this class send their children to the best private schools and universities. People in this group seldom marry outside their class.

People are in the lower-upper class more often because of achievement and earned income than because of birth and inherited wealth. Some have made fortunes running large corporations or investing in the stock market. Members of this class may actually be better off financially than members of the upper-upper class. However, they often are not accepted into the most exclusive social circles.

Upper class people tend to shop at upscale stores such as Saks and Company.

The Middle Classes

Most Americans think of themselves as middle class. In reality, though, only about 40 to 50 percent of Americans fit this description. And most of these people are not in the upper-middle class.

The upper-middle class (14 percent of the population) is composed of those who have been successful in business, the professions, politics, and the military. Basically, this class is made up of individuals and families who benefited

SOCIOLOGY Online

Student Web Activity
Visit the *Sociology and You Web* site at soc.glencoe.com and click on **Chapter 8—Student Web Activities** for an activity on social class.

This family fulfills the American image of comfortable middle-class living.

More About . . . Social Mobility

Henry Ford, part of the corporate rich, was never accepted into the upper class. In fact, Ford himself had no interest in the upper class; he disliked their flamboyant lifestyle. His son, Edsel, on the other hand, had a great desire to become part of the upper class. To help achieve his end, he married into an upper class family in Detroit. He also built a summer lodge where many of the upper class spent their summers. He sent his children to the best private schools and universities. These devices allowed Edsel to build social networks that finally achieved his end, acceptance into the upper class.

Integrating the Teacher Resources

Look for the Chapter 8 Increasing Your Reading Comprehension worksheet and the Guided Reading worksheet in the Unit 3 Mastering Basic Concepts booklet in your Teacher's Resource Box. Both will strengthen student reading comprehension skills.

Points to Stress

The working poor are sometimes referred to as the forgotten Americans. They work but have no ability to get ahead. They destroy the stereotype that the poor don't work. Only recently have sociologists begun to consider their stories.

Teaching Strategy

A great book on the homeless is Steven Vanderstaay's *Street Lives: An Oral History of Homeless Americans,* New Society Publishers, 1992. It is a collection of eighty stories of the homeless.

If you can, have students visit a homeless shelter. They might be allowed to distribute food. Some teachers have been permitted to have their students conduct interviews with former homeless people. You could turn this into a collection of oral histories of the homeless similar to *Street Lives.* Remember to have students follow the Code of Ethics; you can't use someone's name without their permission.
L2

from the tremendous corporate and professional expansion following World War II. Members of this class earn enough to live well and to save money. They are typically college educated and have high educational and career goals for their children. They do not have national or international power, but they tend to be active in voluntary and political organizations in their communities.

The middle-middle class (30 percent of the population) is a very mixed bag. Its members include owners of small businesses and farms; independent professionals (small-town doctors and lawyers); other professionals (clergy, teachers, nurses, firefighters, social workers, police officers); lower-level managers; and some sales and clerical workers. Their income level, which is at about the national average ($21,181 in 1999), does not permit them to live as well as the upper-middle class. Many have only a high school education, although many have some college, and some have college degrees. Members of this class are interested in civic affairs. They participate in political activities less than the classes above them but more than either the working class or the lower class.

> The upper class is a nation's past; the middle class is its future.
>
> **Ayn Rand**
> **novelist**

The Working Class

The working class (often referred to as the lower-middle class) comprises almost one-third of the population. Working class people include roofers, delivery truck drivers, machine operators, and salespeople and clerical workers (Rubin, 1994). Although some of these workers may earn more than some middle-class people, in general the economic resources of the working class are lower than those of the middle class.

Members of the working class have below-average income and unstable employment. They generally lack hospital insurance and retirement benefits. The threat of unemployment or illness is real and haunting. Outside of union activities, members of the working class have little opportunity to exercise power or participate in organizations. Members of the working class—even those with higher incomes—are not likely to enter the middle class.

The Working Poor

working poor
people employed in low-skill jobs with the lowest pay who do not earn enough to rise out of poverty

The **working poor** (13 percent of the population) consists of people employed in low-skill jobs with the lowest pay. Its members are typically the lowest-level clerical workers, manual workers (laborers), and service workers (fast-food servers). Lacking steady employment, the working poor do not earn enough to rise above the poverty line ($17,761 in 2000). The working poor tend not to belong to organizations or to participate in the political process. (See also Enrichment Reading: No Shame in My Game on page 460 in Chapter 13.)

The Underclass

underclass
people typically unemployed who came from families that have been poor for generations

The **underclass** (12 percent of the population) is composed of people who are usually unemployed and who come from families with a history of unemployment for generations. They either work in part-time menial jobs (unloading trucks, picking up litter) or are on public assistance. In addition

Interdisciplinary Activity

Psychology Obtain a copy of Maslow's hierarchy from any psychology book. This hierarchy is based on needs. Ask students to consider whether they think that their basic needs of food, shelter, and safety are met on a daily basis. Most will say yes. Then ask them to consider if they were homeless, whether they would be thinking about higher needs such as self-actualization when they would be trying to fulfill their basic needs.
L1

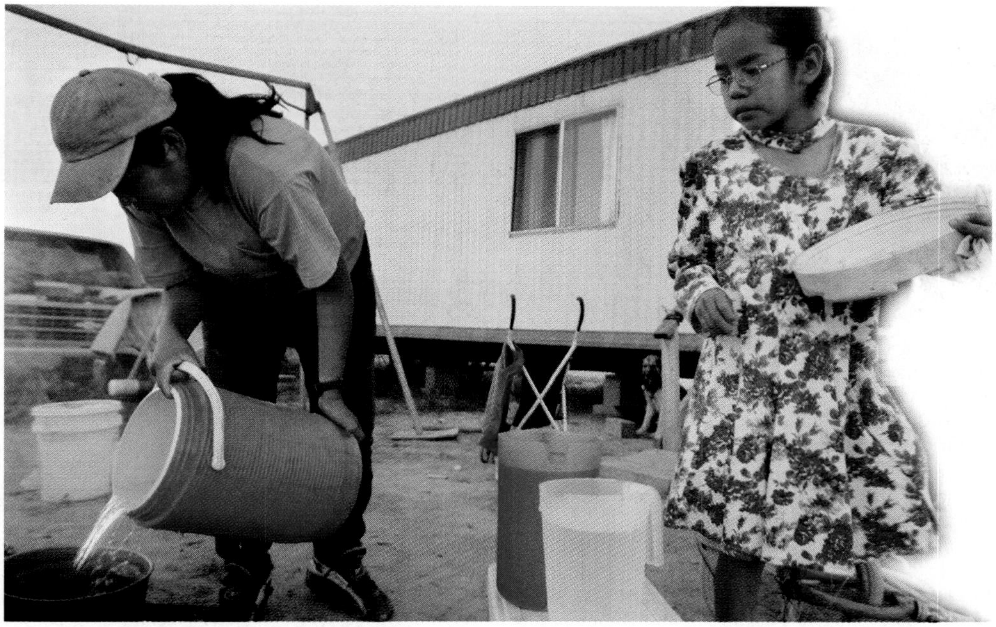

This Navajo single mother belongs to the underclass, America's poorest.

to a lack of education and skills, many members of the underclass have other problems. Physical or mental disabilities are common and many are single mothers with little or no income.

The most common shared characteristic of the working poor and the underclass is a lack of skills to obtain jobs that pay enough to meet basic needs. There are many routes into these classes—birth, old age, loss of a marriage partner, lack of education or training, alcoholism, physical or mental disability. There are, however, very few paths out. Poverty in the United States, another way to discuss the working poor and the underclass, is the topic of the next section.

Section 3 Assessment

1. Statistically, out of 500 people, how many would belong to the upper class?
2. What is a major distinction between members of the upper-middle and the middle-middle classes?
3. Which class is the largest segment of society?

Critical Thinking

4. **Summarizing Information** Chapter 5 discussed the concept of status. How does ascribed status relate to social class? How does achieved status relate to social class?

Answers to Section 3 Assessment

1. Five
2. The major distinction between the upper-middle and the middle classes is in percentage of population. While the middle class accounts for about 30 percent of the population, the upper-middle class includes only 14 percent of the population. Another distinction is amount of money.
3. The working class is the largest segment of society (comprising 1/3 of the population).

Critical Thinking

4. Answers will vary. An example would be, in reference to the upper classes, being born into the "aristocracy" (old-money families); the upper-upper class would be an ascribed status; members of the lower-upper class are those who have that status through achievement and earned income.

On-Demand Writing

Ask students to write a composition in which they locate themselves in the stratification system. They should explain why they believe they fit into the category they have decided upon. In the composition they should include answers to the following questions. Are there some stratification categories where most of your friends and family fall? Which categories do they fall into? What does this tell you about your social network? In what ways could this information affect your career plans? You might want to ask for volunteers to read their compositions to the rest of the class. L2

Sociology Today

The rationale for parenting according to social class is that historically it has always been important for people in the lower social classes to know their place. If children were taught to be mindful of authority, they would fare better in a stratified society. Upper class families then taught their children how privilege could be utilized. You might want to refer students to the movie *Titanic.* How was Rose raised?

Answer to Doing Sociology

This might be a touchy subject for some parents, so students should gauge whether they think that their parents would be willing to discuss this.

Integrating the Teacher Resources

For Spanish-speaking students, you may wish to use the reproducible worksheets available in the Spanish Supplements booklet in your Teacher's Resource Box. In addition to providing Spanish translations of selected Mastering Basic Concepts worksheets, the booklet contains English and Spanish summaries of the chapter's key points.

Sociology Today: Parenting Across Class Lines

Most marriages occur among people of the same social class. Because people from the same class are likely to share similar values, they will likely agree on how to raise their children. Among couples who do marry across social-class lines, however, there is tremendous potential for conflict over parenting practices.

Research reveals many class differences in child-rearing practices. Parents in the middle and higher social classes generally work hardest to develop happiness, curiosity, responsibility, dependability, and self-control in their children. These are characteristics associated with independence. Parents in the lower classes tend to emphasize obedience, neatness, cleanliness, self-defense, good manners, and honesty. These parents stress characteristics that respect authority and help children conform, or "get along."

Once people in any class have been successfully socialized to accept certain values, beliefs, and norms, they tend to feel very strongly that these are the correct ways of thinking, feeling, and behaving. They often feel defensive in the presence of any threat to their values. Just imagine what might happen when parents from different social classes have very different ideas about the "right" way to raise their child! Knowing what problems are likely to develop and discussing them thoroughly before marriage may help such couples avoid future unhappiness.

Doing Sociology

Find time to sit down with one or both of your parents to discuss their approach to child rearing. Give some examples from your own family that support or refute the ideas presented in this feature.

The movie Sabrina *might not have had such a happy ending if this couple from different social classes had children to raise.*

Using Decision-Making Skills

Divide the class into five groups: upper class, middle class, working class, working poor, and the underclass. Because the middle class comprises about 40 percent of the population, the number of members for this group should be higher than the other groups. For example, if there are twenty students in class, one represents the upper class, eight represent the middle class, seven are part of the working class, two are the working poor, and two are the underclass.

Each group will write dialog for a soap opera that factually represents American life in the class they represent. As they write the scripts, students should pay special attention to details such as language, dress, norms, goals, aspirations, education, work skills, income, and family trees. They should create a neighborhood where the dialog will take place, a title for the show, and they should choose occupations appropriate to the social class they represent. **L1**

Section 4

Poverty in America

Key Terms

- absolute poverty
- relative poverty
- feminization of poverty

Measuring Poverty

Absolute poverty is the absence of enough money to secure life's necessities—enough food, a safe place to live, and so forth. It is possible, however, to have the things required to remain alive and still be poor. We measure **relative poverty** by comparing the economic condition of those at the bottom of a society with the economic conditions of other members of that society. According to this measure, the definition of poverty can vary. It would not, for example, be the same in India as in the United States.

How is poverty measured in the United States? Historically, the United States government has measured poverty by setting an annual income level and considering people poor if their income is below that level. As noted earlier, in 2000 that figure was $17,761 for a family of four.

How many Americans are poor? Poverty is widespread throughout the United States. According to 2000 U.S. Census Bureau reports, the poor comprise 11.8 percent of the American population, or more than 32.2 million people. Great poverty existed when it became a national political and social issue in the 1960s. Forty years later, poverty in America is still a problem (Newman, 1999). (See Figure 8.6 on page 260.)

Section Preview

Poverty can be measured in absolute or relative terms. The poor in the U.S. are disproportionately represented by African Americans, Latinos, women, and children.

absolute poverty
the absence of enough money to secure life's necessities

relative poverty
a measure of poverty based on the economic disparity between those at the bottom of a society and the rest of the society

From the slums of Calcutta to a project in the United States, what do these photos say about the relativity of poverty?

Paired Learning Activity

Divide the class into pairs and then read the following scenario to students.

There are those in America who live at the poverty level, or very close to it. They may have a roof over their heads and food to eat, but they might be eating too much pasta and their car might need servicing and new brakes. They might be facing eviction and their television might be broken, and they don't have enough money to take family members to the doctor or dentist.

Have pairs discuss whether this scenario describes absolute poverty or relative poverty and why they decided on their answer. Have them make a list of differences between absolute and relative poverty. Have pairs share their answers with the rest of the class. Be sure to correct any misconceptions students might have.
L1

Using the Section Preview

Have students visit the web site for the Institute for Poverty Research, located on the campus of the University of Wisconsin-Madison. The URL is: **www.ssc.wisc.edu/irp/** Students will get an objective view of poverty and related issues.

More About . . . Poverty in the United States

Students may be interested to know that the poverty figure of $17,050 is for the continental states only. In Alaska the figure is $21,320 and in Hawaii the figure is $19,610. Ask students why they think the poverty figure in those states is higher than in the rest of the U.S.

Points to Stress

Ask students which measure of poverty, absolute or relative, they think of when they hear the word poverty. Most probably think of relative poverty. Some from upper or middle classes will think of themselves as "poor" if they can't afford a pair of one-hundred dollar athletic shoes. Help students understand how relative poverty changes from one society to another.

Working with the Data

Figure 8.6 Double line graphs are useful when you want to show the same data in two different formats—in this case as absolute numbers and as percentages of the total population.

Controversy and Debate

Following are some media myths about welfare. Discuss with your students whether these statements are true or false. See how many they believe to be true.

1. Poor women have more children as a result of the financial benefits. *(False. Studies show no correlation between benefit levels and number of children. Also, welfare benefits are far too low to serve as an incentive to have additional children.)*
2. We don't subsidize middle class families. (*False. Families receive a premium for additional children in the form of a $2,450 tax deduction. Tax credits to partially pay for childcare are also available.)*
3. The public is fed up with spending money on the poor. *(False. A 1994 poll by the Center for the Study of Policy Attitudes indicated that 80 percent of respondents said that the government has "a responsibility to try to do away with poverty." In addition, only 21 percent said spending should be cut for unemployed single mothers with children and 29 percent said it should be increased.)*

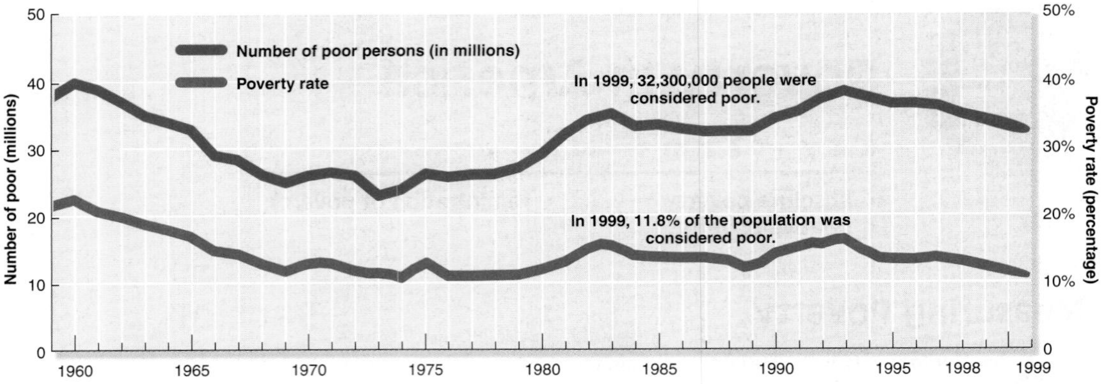

Source: U.S. Bureau of the Census, *Poverty in the United States: 1999,* 2000.

Figure 8.6 Number of Poor and Poverty Rate: 1959–1999. *This graph shows two types of information: (1) the number of poor in the total population and (2) the poverty rate as a percentage of the total population. Why is it often helpful to have related information plotted on the same graph?*

Source: U.S. Bureau of the Census, *Poverty in the United States: 1999,* 2000.

Identifying the Poor

Minorities, female-headed households, children under eighteen years of age, elderly people, people with disabilities, and people who live alone or with nonrelatives make up the most disadvantaged groups in the United States.

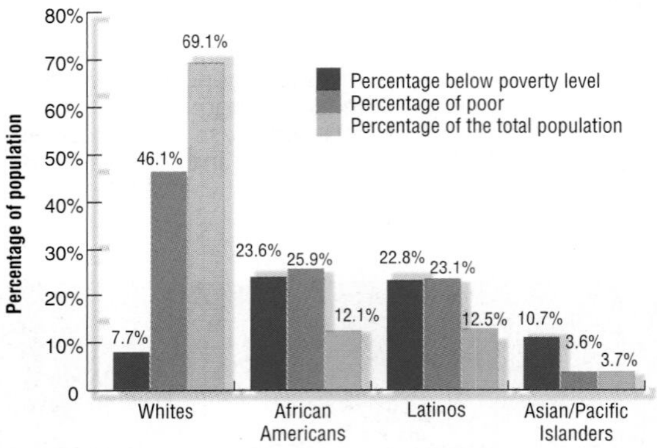

Figure 8.7 The Distribution of Poverty in the U.S. *What are the most important conclusions you would reach from this figure?*

Source: U.S. Bureau of the Census, 2000.

How are race and ethnicity related to poverty? About 46 percent of the poor in America today are white. The poverty rate for African Americans and Latinos is much higher than that for whites, however. The poverty rate for whites is 7.7 percent; for African Americans and Latinos about 23 percent. African Americans and Latinos together account for only about one-fourth of the total population, but they make up nearly half of the poor population. (See Figure 8.7.)

How are gender and age related to poverty? Another large segment of the poor population is made up of female-headed households. We can look at this issue in two different ways. We can look at all poor households as a group and determine what proportion of them are headed by females. When we do this, we find that over one-half of poor households are female headed. In contrast, when we look at nonpoor households, we find that only about 14 percent are headed by females. Another approach would be to look at all female-headed households as a group and determine what proportion of them are poor. We find that the poverty rate for these households is about 30 percent, compared with just over 10 percent for all families.

Using Problem-Solving Skills

Despite all the information in the chapter about poverty, most middle class high school students (and their parents) have little real understanding of the plight of the poor. To remedy that situation, make up an imaginary poor person—preferably female, preferably undereducated, preferably a parent. Part of the class will scan the want ads and find out what kind of jobs are available to such a person. Another part of the class will read the classified ads to find out the availability and cost of decent housing for such a person and her family. Another part of the class will find out the costs of day care, as well as the rules and regulations about after hour care, baby care, sick child

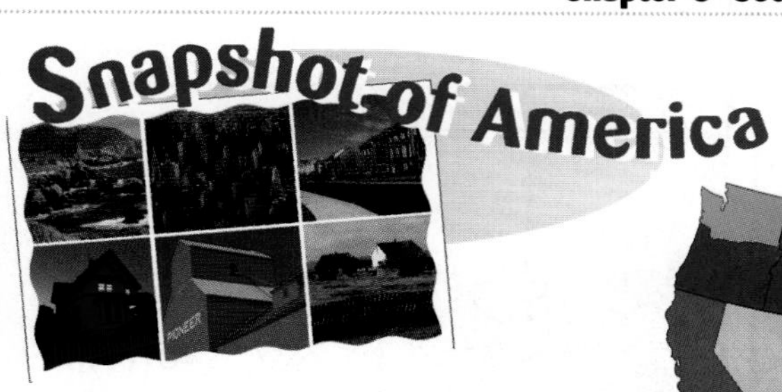

Percentage of Population in Poverty

Although the U.S. economy is booming, some people are concerned that many have not benefited from this prosperity. In fact, many people still live in povery. This map shows the percentage of the poor by state.

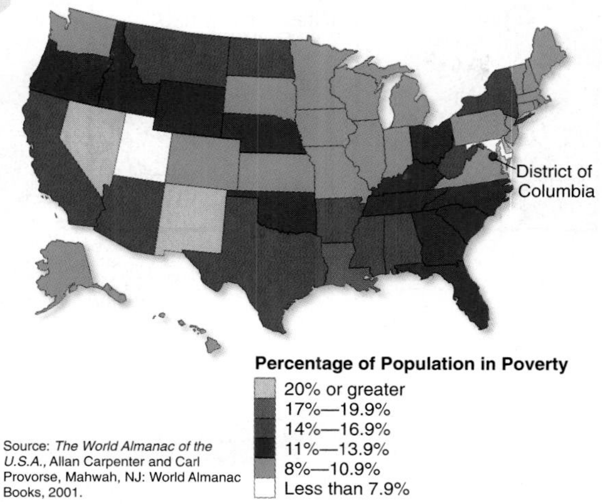

Source: *The World Almanac of the U.S.A.*, Allan Carpenter and Carl Provorse, Mahwah, NJ: World Almanac Books, 2001.

Interpreting the Map

1. Can you make any generalization about poverty from this map?
2. If you were the governor of your state, what would your platform on poverty be? Be specific.

Adapted from *The World Almanac of the U.S.A.*, 1998.

Answers to Interpreting the Map

1. The pattern of poverty predicts large populations of disadvantaged minority groups, such as Native Americans in Oklahoma, New Mexico, and Arizona. Ask students to pose questions about the cultural patterns shown on this map.
2. Answers will vary.

By either measure, then, households headed by females are poorer than those headed by males. A related factor is the poverty rate for children under six years of age. The current rate for this group is about 22 percent—the highest rate for any age group in the United States (U.S. Bureau of the Census, 1999a). The high poverty rates for women and children reflect a trend in U.S. society. Between 1960 and today, women and children make up a larger proportion of the poor. Sociologists refer to this trend as the **feminization of poverty** (*The State of America's Children,* 1998).

feminization of poverty a trend in U.S. society in which women and children make up an increasing proportion of the poor

There are several reasons why women have a higher risk of being poor. As we discuss in more detail in Chapter 10 (see pages 323–324), women earn only about $.72 for every dollar earned by men. Women with children find it more difficult to find and keep regular, long-term employment. A lack of good child-care facilities adds to the likelihood that they will not be able to continue working.

Older Americans account for another large segment of the poor. About 9 percent of people aged sixty-five or older live in poverty (U.S. Bureau of the Census, 2000b). Another large segment of the poor are people with disabilities—those who are blind, deaf, or otherwise disabled. This group accounts for some 12 percent of America's poor. Finally, more than one out of every four poor persons lives either alone or with nonrelatives.

care, etc. Another part will make up a balanced diet for the person and her family. Then, they will go to the grocery store and find out how much that diet would actually cost. Another part of the class will find out the costs of clothing, transportation, utilities, household goods, etc. When each of the groups has finished collecting their data, have the class come together and compare how much the person could earn in each month (less taxes) to how much her monthly expenses would be. It's unlikely that the income will be sufficient to meet expenses. The final step is to have the class devise a solution to the problem.
L2

Working with the Illustration

This cartoon uses humor to point out the double standard many of us use when judging people. When it happens to "them," unemployment is a matter of choice. When it happens to "me" it is out of my control.

More About . . . the Poor

One of the perceptions of the poor is that their values differ from those of Americans who are not poor. In Julius Wilson's book, *When Work Disappears: The New Urban Poverty,* he describes a study he conducted that proved the poor want the same things as other Americans: good education, good health care, good jobs. It is the lack of opportunity that prevents the poor from attaining their dreams.

Net Worthy

To enhance your students' study of this chapter, you may want to have them visit the URL cited below. As with all web sites, you should check this out first to be sure the information found there is appropriate for your students.

If you or your students are interested in poverty rates worldwide, a good resource is **www.worldbank.org/poverty/data/povmon.htm** There are over thirty-two indicators from population to the environment, income, and more.

Blaming the victim is easy. Accepting blame is harder.

> Wealth is conspicuous, but poverty hides.
>
> James Reston
> American journalist

Responses to the Problem of Poverty

Before the mid-1960s, fighting poverty was not a major goal of the federal government. Some programs, such as Social Security and Aid to Dependent Children, had been enacted during the Great Depression. These measures did not usually reach the lowest levels of needy citizens, however. Finally in 1964, President Lyndon Johnson marshalled the forces of the federal government to begin a War on Poverty.

What were the goals of the War on Poverty? The philosophy behind the War on Poverty was to help poor people help themselves (Patterson, 1986; Jacoby, 1997; Barry, 1999). President Johnson's predecessor, President John F. Kennedy, believed that if the chains of poverty were to be broken, it had to be through self-improvement, not temporary relief. Accordingly, almost 60 percent of the first poverty budget was earmarked for youth opportunity programs and the work experience program (work and job training designed primarily for welfare recipients and unemployed fathers).

Hopes for positive results from the War on Poverty were high. However, not all of the programs were as successful as predicted. Indeed, some have come under severe criticism. These criticisms center around supposed widespread abuses and the fear that the system encourages people to become dependent upon the government longer than is necessary. "Fixing" the way social welfare should be provided and payments should be distributed has been the focus of many hot political debates.

Welfare Reform

In 1999, actual spending for education, training, employment, and social services was $56 billion, or 3 percent of total U.S. government expenditures. Payments for Aid to Families with Dependent Children (AFDC) and food stamps was less than 1 percent of the federal budget. (See Figure 8.8 on page 263.)

Interdisciplinary Activity

History Have students research President Lyndon Johnson's War on Poverty. Students might be interested to see what impact having two "wars" at the same time (Vietnam War and War on Poverty) had on the people and economy of the United States. **L2**

What is the nature of welfare reform?

The most recent legislation on welfare reform, enacted in 1996, limits the amount of time those able to work can receive welfare payments. The bill has three major elements: it reduces welfare spending, it increases state and local power to oversee welfare rules, and it adds new restrictions on welfare eligibility. For example, benefits to children of unwed teenage mothers are denied unless the mothers remain in school and live with an adult. Cash aid to able-bodied adults will be terminated if they fail to get a job after two years.

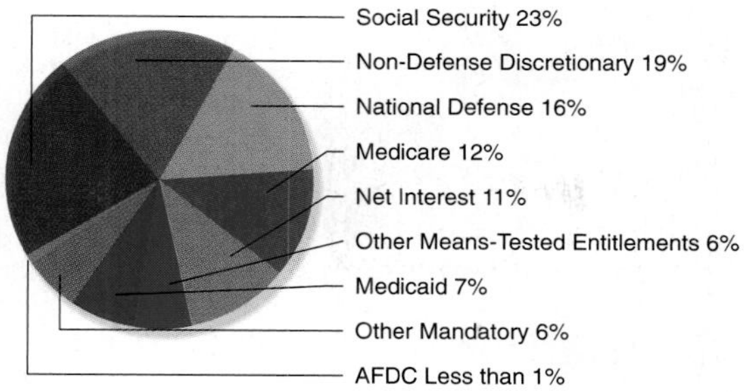

Figure 8.8 The Federal Government Dollar—Where It Goes. *Where is the largest share of the federal dollar spent?*

Source: "A Citizen's Guide to the Federal Budget," Washington, D.C., 2001.

Has welfare reform worked? It is too early to give a final evaluation of this latest attempt at welfare reform. But a recent major study indicates that the welfare rolls have decreased more dramatically than most predicted (Loprest, 1999). Just over seven million people are on welfare, down from over twelve million in 1996 when the welfare bill was signed. Well over half of those leaving the welfare rolls report finding jobs. Only a small percentage of recipients have been removed from the rolls because of the new time limits on benefits.

There is a darker side, however. Most of those leaving the rolls since 1996 hold entry-level jobs—in restaurants, cleaning services, and retail stores—earning less than $7 per hour. Despite extraordinary national economic prosperity, most of those leaving public assistance are at the bottom of the economy with little hope of advancing. One-fourth work at night, and over half report child-care problems. Most have jobs without health insurance. A substantial minority report a food shortage and difficulty paying rent. In short, many of those leaving welfare still live in poverty. The true test of the success of welfare reform will come in a few years when the economy weakens, when we get down to the harder cases still on the rolls, and when the last time limits take effect for the more difficult cases (Rosin and Harris, 1999).

Learning Check–Section 4

1. Discuss the difference between absolute and relative measures of poverty.
2. Which of the following is *not* one of the major categories of poor people in the United States?
   - **a.** children under age eighteen
   - **b.** able-bodied men who refuse to work
   - **c.** elderly people
   - **d.** people with disabilities
   - **e.** people who live alone or with nonrelatives
3. Do government welfare programs affect the poor's decision to work? Explain?

Critical Thinking

4. **Understanding Cause and Effect** Describe the feminization of poverty. How does this trend affect the motivation to have children?

Working with the Data

Figure 8.8 The largest one-item portion of the federal government dollar is spent on Social Security.

Answers to Section 4 Assessment

1. Absolute poverty is the absence of enough money to secure life's necessities (food, housing, etc.). However, a person having the things required to stay alive may still be considered poor if his or her status is measured by relative poverty, which is a comparison of the economic conditions of those at the bottom of a society with other members of that society.
2. b
3. Early results of recent welfare reform indicate that government programs do affect employment of the poor. One important study showed that over half of those removed from the welfare rolls found jobs.

Critical Thinking

4. The feminization of poverty refers to the trend of women and children making up a larger portion of the poor since 1960.

Encouraging Citizenship Activity

There are many ways to serve the poor. The most popular service projects are volunteering in a soup kitchen and staging canned food drives, toy drives, or book drives. These service projects are popular ideas and with the exception of the soup kitchen project, they are fairly impersonal.

Brainstorm with your students to identify a project that will meet a specific need in your community—something more one-on-one. For example, students may save aluminum cans and instead of recycling them, which *everybody* does, find an urban or suburban alley populated by "dumpster divers" and give the cans to them. Or, volunteer baby-sitting time at an institution that houses poor mothers. Collect books, canned goods, clothes, and toys for a specific family and donate them anonymously.

Tech Trends

Street-Smart Technology

During the last century, when mass production changed the way goods were produced, a favorite adage of businesspeople was "Time is money." In today's service economy (where most people are not producing a tangible product), information is money. Children from disadvantaged families have far less access (both at school and at home) to information technology, such as computers and the Internet, than children in wealthier families. This puts them at a disadvantage in competition for grades and in the job market.

Because of this situation, educators are designing special school-based programs to provide computers in low-income schools and to train teachers in those schools to use them. Harlem-based "Playing to Win" is one of these programs. This computer center offers classes and workshops to nearly four hundred people per week. It also provides assistance to other community groups that want to set up their own computer centers (George et al., 1993).

Another successful program is "Street-Level Youth Media" in Chicago's inner city. Street-Level's mission is to educate disadvantaged young people about new technologies. Street-Level began by asking inner-city youths to make videos about their everyday lives on the streets of Chicago. These videos helped residents to see the youths as real human beings trapped in desperate, life-threatening situations. Street-Level continues to work with youths who have been rejected by mainstream society, helping them find solutions to their problems, strengthen their communities, and achieve economic success. With revenue earned from providing technical support to local businesses, Street-Level pays over $70,000 in salaries to young people (*Street-Level*, 1999).

Analyzing the Trends

Do you think the rise of computer technology is affecting the social stratification structure in America? Do you think these computer-training programs can seriously affect the cultural values and subsequent economic behavior of those who participate in them? Why or why not?

Computer training is the gateway to success in the information-based economy. Students in these classrooms will have an advantage in the job market because of their computer-based skills.

Tech Trends

This feature could foster an interesting conversation about computer use. Ignoring social class for the moment, do students think that computer literacy will create another class-based distinction of technocrat haves and have nots? Will those with the best computer skills be the most marketable?

Answer to Analyzing the Trends

You might want to allow students to make up a stratification model based on computer use. Those with the most skills would be of the highest class (Bill Gates is, after all, the founder of Microsoft). They might also list technology-based "status symbols" and collect a list of lingo and slang terms that would identify high-status technocrats. Ask students to develop questions and answers based on the stratification model.

Integrating the Teacher Resources

Look for Ethics, Values, and Technology: Real-Life Issues in Society, available in your Teacher's Resource Box. The booklet provides primary source readings dealing with real-life controversies. Student worksheets are included.

Section 5

Social Mobility

Key Terms

- social mobility
- horizontal mobility
- vertical mobility
- intergenerational mobility
- caste (closed-class system)
- open class system

Types of Social Mobility

Mobility is the ability to move; **social mobility** is the movement of people between social classes.

What are the types of social mobility? Social mobility can be horizontal or vertical. **Horizontal mobility** involves changing from one occupation to another at the same social class level, as when an Army captain becomes a public school teacher, a minister becomes a psychologist, or a restaurant server becomes a taxi driver. Because horizontal mobility involves no real change in occupational status or social class, sociologists are not generally interested in investigating it. Vertical mobility, however, is another story.

With **vertical mobility,** a person's occupational status or social class moves upward or downward. When the change takes place over a generation, it is called **intergenerational mobility.** If a plumber's daughter becomes a physician, upward intergenerational mobility has occurred. If a lawyer's son becomes a carpenter, downward intergenerational mobility has occurred.

Night school is a popular way for adults to improve skills needed for upward social mobility.

Section Preview

Social mobility, the movement of individuals or groups within the stratification structure, is usually measured by changes in occupational status. Sociologists are most interested in upward or downward (vertical) mobility. Closed-class systems permit little vertical mobility; open-class systems, such as those in industrialized countries, allow considerable vertical mobility.

social mobility
the movement of individuals or groups between social classes

horizontal mobility
a change in occupation within the same social class

vertical mobility
a change upward or downward in occupational status or social class

intergenerational mobility
a change in status or class from one generation to the next

Using the Section Preview

To really drive home the point about mobility, bring a ladder to class. Since mobility is sometimes referred to as a socioeconomic ladder, you can label the steps of the ladder with these labels: upper class, upper middle class, middle class, working class, working poor, and underclass. If you walk up and down the steps, you are demonstrating upward and downward mobility. If you step out on the ladder (be careful!) you are demonstrating horizontal mobility. Like physical phenomena, it is easier to fall down (the ladder) than it is to climb up. Students will get the point that mobility can change one's position on the ladder. Ask students what sociological explanations might be given to help us better understand the concept of mobility. *(A person gets a better job [upward mobility], a person loses a job [downward mobility], a person takes another job that has higher status but not necessarily more pay [horizontal mobility])* These are sociological reasons why mobility changes.

Learning Styles

Intra-personal/Spatial To give students an opportunity to acquaint themselves with their own backgrounds, ask them to interview relatives (parents, aunts and uncles, grandparents, siblings) regarding employment histories. Have them create a graphic illustrating the types and categories of jobs held by family members. The graphic must include a method indicating any social mobility that may have taken place. (A genealogy-type "tree" can be suggested if students need a place to get started.) What kinds of trends, if any, are evident? Then ask students to think about their own goals for the future. Where would they like their children to be in the social strata? Can they do anything now to make those goals more likely to be reached?
L2

Using the Illustration

The caste system prohibits extensive interaction between the various castes. With computer technology, especially that of the Internet, it is not always possible to know who your correspondent really is. It is possible for members from different castes to develop relationships. Only their language and cultural experiences would allow them to be identified by caste.

More About . . . India's Caste System

The East Indian caste system is greatly influenced by the Hindu principle of *karma.* This principle states that a person's soul follows a destiny governed by the person's actions in a previous life. If a person fulfills his or her duties of the caste they are born into, they will be born into a higher caste in their next life (reincarnation). If the duties are not fulfilled, they are born into a lower caste in their next life. The system justifies the inherent inequality by rationalizing that the person himself (or herself) has earned his or her treatment.

Points to Stress

Remind them that it has not been all that long, historically speaking, that the Western world has left its own caste system. Students should remember studying about the French Revolution, a protest against the strict stratification of the nobility, the clergy, and the peasant classes.

These Indian women learning about computers belong to one of the upper castes, as indicated by their clothes and body ornamentation.

Caste and Open-Class Systems

The extent of vertical mobility varies from society to society. Some societies have considerable mobility; others have little or none. This is the major difference between *caste* (or closed-class) system and *open-class systems.*

caste system
a stratification structure that does not allow for social mobility

What is a caste system? In a **caste system,** there is no social mobility because social status is inherited and cannot be changed. In a caste system, statuses (including occupations) are ascribed or assigned at birth. Individuals cannot change their statuses through any efforts of their own. By reason of religious, biological, superstitious, or legal justification, those in one caste are allowed to marry only within their own caste and must limit relationships of all types with those below and above them in the stratification structure. Apartheid, as practiced in South Africa before the election of Nelson Mandela, was a caste system based on race.

The caste system in India is one based on occupation and the Hindu religion. It is as complex as it is rigid. In it are four primary caste categories, ranked according to their degree of religious purity. The Brahmin, the top caste, is composed of priests and scholars. Next comes the Kshatriyas, including professional, governing, and military occupations. Merchants and businessmen form the third caste, called the Vaisyas. Finally, there is the Sudra caste, containing farmers, menial workers, and craftsmen. Actually, there is a fifth category called the "untouchables." This group of Indians are thought to be so impure that any physical contact contaminates the religious purity of all other caste members. They are so low on the scale that they are not even considered to be part of the caste system. They are given the dirty, degrading tasks, such as collecting trash and handling dead bodies.

How is the caste system kept intact? Traditional rules exist in India to prevent movement into a higher caste. Members of different castes are not permitted to eat together, and higher-caste people will hardly accept anything to eat or drink from lower-caste persons. Untouchables, who must live

Interdisciplinary Activity

History Have students do research on the caste system in India, apartheid in South Africa, and the caste system brought about by the slavery system in the United States. They should make a chart, create a model, or use some other form of illustration to show the differences and similarities among the different systems.

apart from everyone else, cannot even drink water from the wells used by higher castes. Although the long-standing legal prohibition against dating or marrying someone in a higher caste no longer exists, such crossings are still extremely rare. Most important, the caste system is maintained as a result of the power of the higher castes, who use their political clout, wealth, and prestige to prevent change.

What is an open-class system? In an **open-class system,** an individual's social class is based on merit and individual effort. Individuals move up and down the stratification structure as their abilities, education, and resources permit. Most people in the United States believe they live in an open-class system. In reality, the opportunity for upward mobility is sometimes denied individuals or groups in America today. For example, because of race or ethnicity, some members of minority groups, such as African Americans, Native Americans, and Latinos, have been denied opportunities for social mobility. Therefore, because it imposes some limitations on upward mobility, U.S. society cannot be considered truly and completely open. It is, however, a relatively open-class system.

open-class system
a system in which social class is based on merit and individual effort; movement is allowed between classes

Upward and Downward Mobility

Few places in the world provide the opportunities for advancement that are available in the United States. Nevertheless, countless Americans fail to be upwardly mobile, despite their talents and dedication to work. This is hard for many people to accept because American tradition—both historical and fictional—is filled with examples of upward mobility. Earlier generations have been raised on the "rags to riches" Horatio Alger stories. In these books, a young, down-on-his-luck boy "makes good" through honesty, pluck, and diligence. The lesson to be learned is that the only thing standing between any American citizen and success is talent, a willingness to work, and perseverance. Teachers point to political leaders such as Abraham Lincoln and to early business leaders such as Cornelius Vanderbilt, John D. Rockefeller, and Henry Ford to support the idea of unlimited mobility in American society. These men, in reality, are exceptions to the rule. While considerable upward mobility has occurred, great leaps in social-class level are rare (Gilbert, 1998). Upward mobility typically involves only a small improvement over the social class situation of one's parents.

Why is Microsoft founder Bill Gates the exception to the rule in terms of social mobility?

Is upward mobility increasing? After World War II, an explosion in the availability of high-paying manufacturing jobs made it relatively easy for people to move upward. Americans came to expect that their children would have more than they had, but this may not be the case for future generations. This change is the result of new technology and the globalization of business. With computer-driven production, improved means of communication, and better transportation, it is possible for U.S. companies seeking to lower their costs to move their manufacturing operations overseas. And they are doing so often. As a result, high-paying U.S. manufacturing jobs are being transferred to lower-paid foreign workers. U.S. workers, then, who lack the

Points to Stress

Ask students if they think that someone can go from rags to riches. They will probably point out people like Michael Jordan and other athletes or celebrities who have gone from having little money to being very wealthy. Ask students if they think that most people will become rich in their lifetimes. Most will not think so, perhaps saying that is a myth of Horatio Alger. Although Americans like to believe that we can become rich, in reality we tend to improve our social standing by only one social class above the one that we were born into.

Using the Illustration

Although it may be easier in a booming economy, it is still difficult to make an upwardly social move of the kind Bill Gates made. His leap in net worth was accomplished without family money or an ivy league education.

Interdisciplinary Activity

Psychology If students are interested in psychology and want to study social mobility and schizophrenia or any other mental illness, have them look for theories that explain how social mobility can change with the onset of mental illness. This will help them also understand the homeless problem. One-third of the homeless are believed to be suffering from mental illness. **L3**

Pulling it All Together

In this section the types of social mobility were discussed, as well as the open-class and caste systems of social classes. Consideration was given to the likelihood of upward mobility and social mobility for the future.

Answers to Section 5 Assessment

1. Social mobility is the movement of people between social classes.
2. a. HM
   b. VM
   c. IM
3. Answers will vary. Answers should be tied to definitions of a caste and an open-class system and should reflect the idea that in a caste system cultural values discourage economic competitiveness and that in an open-class system cultural values encourage economic competitiveness.
4. U.S. society cannot be considered truly and completely an open-class system because it imposes some limitations on upward mobility for some individuals or groups, such as minorities.

Critical Thinking

5. Answers will vary.

The costs of downward mobility are already etched on this corporate executive's face.

> Inequity of property will exist as long as liberty exists.
>
> **Alexander Hamilton**
> **American statesman**

education needed to perform the more technologically sophisticated jobs are being forced to take lower-paying jobs. Compared to their parents, more U.S. workers are experiencing downward mobility (Newman, 1999).

What are the social and psychological costs of downward mobility? In *Falling from Grace,* sociologist Katherine Newman (1999) describes America's enduring belief in the rewards of hard work. This belief, she fears, prevents recognition of a major problem: downward mobility for many middle-class people. And, she argues, the consequences are enormous for people in a society that measures self-worth by occupational status. Downwardly mobile people experience lowered self-esteem, despair, depression, feelings of powerlessness, and a loss of a sense of honor.

Section 5 Assessment

1. What is social mobility?
2. Match the major types of social mobility with the examples. Use (IM) for intergenerational mobility, (VM) for vertical mobility, and (HM) for horizontal mobility.
   a. a restaurant waiter becomes a taxi driver
   b. an auto worker becomes a manager
   c. the daughter of a hairdresser becomes a college professor
3. How do you think that the cultural values associated with a caste and an open-class system differently affect economic behavior?
4. Why is the United States not a completely open-class system?

Critical Thinking

5. **Analyzing Information** Analyze the social mobility that has occurred in your family for the last two generations (or more, if you prefer). Use sociological concepts in your analysis.

Cooperative Learning Activity

Have students work in groups to answer the following questions: Do you think society looks at downwardly mobile people differently than they look at upwardly mobile people? Why or why not? What if a downwardly mobile person is an executive who has lost his job because of a corporate buyout? Does that make the situation different? Why or why not? Does the difference in the way we look at people have to do with the fact that some don't try (drop out of school, move from job to job), while others try but circumstances work against them (such as the fired executive)?

After groups have discussed their answers to these questions, open the discussion to the entire class. It might be interesting to learn whether personal experience or knowing someone who is or has been downwardly mobile affects students' perspectives on these questions. **L1**

CHAPTER 8 ASSESSMENT

Summary

Section 1: Dimensions of Stratification

Main Idea: Stratification is the division of society into classes that have unequal amounts of wealth, power, and prestige. Karl Marx and Max Weber studied these dimensions of stratification in great detail.

Section 2: Explanations of Stratification

Main Idea: Each of the three perspectives—functionalism, conflict theory, and symbolic interactionism—explains stratification in society in a different way.

Section 3: Social Classes in America

Main Idea: Sociologists have identified several social classes in the United States. They include the upper class, the middle class, the working class and the working poor, and the underclass.

Section 4: Poverty in America

Main Idea: Poverty can be measured in absolute or relative terms. The poor in the U.S. are disproportionately represented by African Americans, Latinos, women, and children.

Section 5: Social Mobility

Main Idea: Social mobility, the movement of individuals or groups within the stratification structure, is usually measured by changes in occupational status. Sociologists are most interested in upward or downward (vertical) mobility. Closed-class systems permit little vertical mobility; open-class systems, such as those in industrialized countries, allow considerable vertical mobility.

SOCIOLOGY Online

Self-Check Quiz
Visit the *Sociology and You* Web site at soc.glencoe.com and click on **Chapter 8—Self-Check Quizzes** to prepare for the chapter test.

Reviewing Vocabulary

Complete each sentence using each term once.

- **a.** social stratification
- **b.** feminization of povery
- **c.** social class
- **d.** social mobility
- **e.** bourgeoisie
- **f.** vertical mobility
- **g.** proletariat
- **h.** intergenerational mobility
- **i.** wealth
- **j.** horizontal mobility
- **k.** income
- **l.** open-class system
- **m.** prestige
- **n.** absolute poverty
- **o.** relative poverty
- **p.** caste system

1. A class system with no social mobility is called ______________.
2. ______________ is movement among social classes based on merit and individual effort.
3. ______________ is upward or downward mobility based on occupational status.
4. The changing from one occupation to another at the same general status level is known as ______________.
5. ______________ is the movement of individuals or groups within social classes.
6. The trend involving an increase in the number of women and children living in poverty is called ______________.
7. The recognition, respect, and admiration attached to social positions are known as ______________.
8. ______________ is the amount of money received by an individual or group.
9. The economic resources possessed by an individual or group is called ______________.
10. ______________ is the name given to those who are ruled; the worker class.
11. ______________ is the name given to rulers; or those who own the means of production.
12. The measure that compares the economic condition of those at the bottom of society with

ANSWERS CHAPTER 8 ASSESSMENT

Reviewing Vocabulary

1. p
2. l
3. f
4. j
5. d
6. b
7. m
8. k
9. i
10. g
11. e
12. o
13. a
14. n
15. c
16. h

Reviewing the Facts

1. White people are underrepresented as a group among poor people.
2. Social Security
3. False consciousness is the poor's acceptance of the ideas of the dominant class.
4. The sociologist determines relative poverty by comparing the poor with those above them in the stratification system; measures poverty based on the economic disparity between those on the bottom of society and the rest of the society.
5. Vertical mobility
6. Upper-upperclass

Thinking Critically

1. This might be explained best by a concept known as "blaming the victim." It is easier for Americans to see welfare as an individual problem rather than a problem of the system. Since our perceptions of society are media driven, most accept that as the truth.
2. Running for political office is time consuming and expensive. Launching a campaign requires resources. The poor are the least likely to participate in the political system, because many feel that their vote doesn't count, an attitude pervasive among all Americans.
3. Students will have different opinions, many students will say that teachers are important,

CHAPTER 8 ASSESSMENT

the economic conditions of others is called ____________.

13. The creation of layers, or strata, of people who possess unequal shares of scarce resources is called ____________.
14. ____________ is the absence of enough money to secure life's necessities.
15. A segment of the population whose members hold similar amount of resources and share values, norms, and an identifiable lifestyle is called ____________.
16. The mobility that occurs from one generation to the next is known as ____________.

Reviewing the Facts

1. Examine the graph in Figure 8.7 on page 260 of your text. The graph illustrates that nearly 46 percent of all poor people in the United States are white, while only 12% of the population is poor. What can you conclude from the graph about the representation of white people in terms of the total population of poor people?
2. According to Figure 8.8 on page 263, where does the Federal Government spend the largest share of the federal budget?
3. Describe false consciousness.
4. Explain how a sociologist determines relative poverty.
5. A man who has worked at a factory for twenty years loses his job because of layoffs. After several months, he ends up homeless. What type of social mobility is illustrated in this scenario?
6. Bill Gates has an estimated net worth of $90 billion. How would sociologists label Gates in terms of social class?

Thinking Critically

1. **Analyzing Information** As implied in the *Sociological Imagination* on page 241, attitudes about welfare spending are partially shaped by politicians and the media. Why do you think the media portray welfare spending as such a serious problem when it represents such a small portion of federal spending? Why do Americans seem to complain less about the money spent on military or science projects?
2. **Applying Concepts** At least a hundred members of Congress are millionaires, which suggests that power and wealth do go hand in hand. Why is it unlikely that a poor person would become a member of Congress? Why do many poor people not participate in voting and political parties? What implications does this have for democratic government?
3. **Interpreting Graphs** In Figure 8.3, "Prestige Rankings of Selected Occupations in the United States," surgeons are rated as having the most prestigious job. In your view, what jobs on this list are essential? What jobs could society do without? Are there high-prestige jobs that are really not essential? What does this say about prestige rankings?

   Create a diagram similar to the one below to record your answer.

   JOBS—ESSENTIAL AND NOT ESSENTIAL TO SOCIETY

Essential	Prestige Rank	Not Essential	Prestige Rank
Surgeon	87	Disc Jockey	45

4. **Analyzing Information** Herbert Gans (1971), a noted sociologist, has written about the functions of poverty. He says that poverty serves many useful purposes in society. For example, the poor act as dishwashers, maids, and parking attendants. What are some other ways in which poverty might benefit society? What are some conflicts that poverty causes?
5. **Summarizing Information** Can you describe the cultural values underlying the federal government's philosophy in the War on Poverty in the 1960s?
6. **Making Inferences** The sinking of the luxury liner *Titanic* offers some insights into social class. Among first-class passengers, only 3 percent of the women died, and none of the children died. Among third-class passengers, 45 percent of the women died, and 33 percent of

ANSWERS CHAPTER 8 ASSESSMENT

so ask them why they think teachers aren't paid more. Why should professional athletes get paid millions? Why are there discrepancies between education and pay?

4. Having a group at the bottom of the stratification system motivates people to work harder, or so the thinking goes. The poor take the jobs that others wouldn't take unless they were just starting out in the job market. The conflict is that poverty ultimately poses a burden to society since resources are needed to help the poor. Eradicating poverty would allow resources to be focused in other areas.
5. Cultural values involved in the War on Poverty in the 1960s include independence, hard work, merit, and self-sufficiency.
6. This is such a poignant example of social class. Even after death, social class was a factor. The dead from third class were thrown out to sea when the *Carpathia* arrived to collect the bodies. The dead from first class were all returned to port and given "proper" burials.

Sociology Projects

1. As students remove one of the pieces of paper (for example, "car maintenance") they must now figure out how they will deal without that particular necessity. This should help them understand the dilemma of having to do without, and what that means for a family.
2. Ask students if they feel that most jobs are highly skilled, semi-skilled, or require no skills. Are the higher-skilled jobs not necessarily listed in the paper? Where would students go to find a higher-skilled job? You might want to tell them that most teachers don't find their jobs in the newspaper. Where do teachers look for jobs?
3. Students might write that the poor are lazy, the rich are snobs, the middle class drive their kids to exercise classes. What is the danger of perpetuating these myths?
4. This could present some interesting scenarios. For example if students find a picture of a rapper, would they label that person according to their actual

the children died. In all, 76 percent of the third-class passengers died, compared with 40 percent of the first-class passengers. What implications would you draw from these numbers? Is it important to know that the third-class passengers were restricted to the lower decks and thus farther away from the lifeboats?

Sociology Projects

1. **Understanding Disadvantaged Families** This activity may provide some insight into the difficulties faced by disadvantaged families every day. Work on the task with three or four of your classmates. Tear a sheet of paper into six pieces. On each piece, write one of the following: health care, education for my children, car maintenance, food, and housing. Now, imagine that because of an unexpected financial setback, you do not have enough money to take care of all these necessities and will need to eliminate one. Reach consensus to decide which category to eliminate.
2. **Researching Employment** Using the employment section from your local newspaper, look for job ads in the following categories: jobs that require postgraduate degrees (highly skilled), jobs that require college or special training, and unskilled jobs. Which category has the most jobs available? What assumptions could you make about the job market based on analyzing these ads? What factors might influence how and where employers advertise certain kinds of jobs?
3. **Perception and Reality** One of the themes of sociology is the difference between perception and reality. Write down five perceptions that you have heard people say about others based on their social class. Next to each, describe the reality based on information in this text or additional research. If not sure, write "unknown–needs further research." For example, a common perception of wealthy people is that they consider themselves superior to other people (snobbery). The reality is that no one has ever found a correlation between how much money you have and how nice you are.
4. **Social Class** From magazines and newspapers, cut out as many pictures as you can find of different classes to make a montage. Label or circle traits that led you to determine that a person was in a particular class. (For example, the person may be driving a luxury car or working with hand tools.)

Technology Activity

1. The National Center for Children in Poverty measures poverty rates for children in the United States. Visit its web site at http://cpmcnet.columbia.edu/dept/nccp/.
   a. What is the Young Child Poverty Rate (YCPR) in the United States?
   b. How does the YCPR in the United States compare to that of other industrialized Western nations?
   c. Now click on "Child Poverty Facts" and select "Young Child Poverty in the States—Wide Variation and Significant Change." Scroll down to the map of the United States. How does your state compare to the other states?
   d. Now scroll further down the page to the table entitled "Change in the percentage and number of children under age six in poverty, by state, 1979–1983 to 1992–1996." What is your state's most recent YCPR? Has the percentage increased or decreased from the earlier YCPR?
   e. Go back to the "Child Poverty Facts" page and select "Poverty and Brain Development in Early Childhood." According to this page, when is the period for a child's optimal brain development? What are some of the pathways through which a child in poverty is put at risk for poor brain development? How do you think poverty

Integrating the Teacher Resources

To further assess student comprehension of this chapter, use Chapter Test A or B available in the Chapter and Unit Tests booklet in your Teacher's Resource Box.

social class or what they think the picture is portraying? Aren't our perceptions based on what we think is real?

Technology Activity

1. *(Answers to this question are based on material in the web site as of publication. The content may have changed since that time.)* (a) The YCPR was 20.6 percent. (b) The U.S. rate is significantly higher than the rate in other industrialized countries. (c) Student answers will vary. (d) Student answers will vary. (e) This window of optimal brain development is from the prenatal period to the first years of a child's life. Pathways include inadequate nutrition, substance abuse, maternal depression, exposure to environmental toxins, trauma and abuse, and the quality of day care.

Chapter 8

Enrichment Reading

The Lives of Homeless Women

by Elliot Liebow

On the street or in a shelter, homelessness is hard living. . . . How do they manage to slog through day after day, with no end in sight? How, in a world of **unremitting** grimness, do they manage to laugh, love, enjoy friends, even dance and play the fool? How, in short, do they stay fully human while body and soul are under continuous and grievous assault?

Simple physical survival is within the grasp of almost everyone willing and able to reach out for it. As the women thrash about, awash in a sea of need, emergency shelters, along with public assistance in the form of cash, food stamps, and medical assistance, make it just possible for many of the women to keep their heads above water. Through the use of shelters, soup kitchens, and hospital emergency rooms, it is even possible for most homeless people who do not get public assistance to survive at some minimal level without benefit of a structured assistance program.

At their very best, however, these bare-boned elements of a life-support system merely make life possible, not necessarily tolerable or livable. Serious problems remain. Homelessness can transform what for others are little things into **insurmountable hurdles.** Indeed, homelessness in general puts a premium on "little things." Just as some homeless women seem to have learned (more than most of us, perhaps) to value a small gesture of friendship, a nice day, a bus token, or a little courtesy that others might take for granted or not notice at all, so too can events or circumstances that would be trivial irritants to others approach **catastrophic proportions** for the homeless person.

For homeless women on the street, the struggle for **subsistence** begins at the animal level—for food, water, shelter, security, and safe sleep. In contrast, homeless women in shelters usually have these things; their struggle begins at the level of human rather than animal needs—protection of one's property, health care, and avoidance of boredom. The struggle then moves rapidly to the search for companionship, modest measures of independence, dignity, and self-respect, and some hope and faith in the future. . . .

For some of the women, day-by-day hardships begin with the problem of getting enough sleep. A few women complained they could never get any sleep in a shelter. Grace was one of them. "There's no getting sleep in a shelter," she said. "Only rest. . . ."

There was indeed much night noise and movement. There was snoring, coughing, sneezing, wheezing, retching, . . . cries from bad dreams, occasional weeping or seizures, talking aloud to oneself or to someone else who may or may not have been present, and always movement to and from the bathroom. Grace was complaining about noise, and she found a partial remedy in ear plugs. But ear plugs could not help those women like Kathleen who were kept awake not by noise but by questions: Is this for me? How did I end up here? How will I get out? But eventually, as the night wore on, there was a lot of snoring, and that meant that, Grace and Kathleen notwithstanding, there was a lot of sleeping, too.

Having to get up at 5:30 A.M., and be out of the shelter by 7:00 was a major hardship of shelter life. It was not simply the fact of having to get up

Enrichment Reading

The feminization of poverty has created a phenomenon known as the "new poverty," women and children on the streets. Another great resource is Jonathan Kozel's *Rachel and Her Children: Homeless Families in America,* Crown Publishers, 1988.

The feminization of poverty is not a phenomenon that is confined to the United States. Recent statistics confirm the existence of growing numbers of "female heads of household" worldwide and link this family structure to an increase in the poverty of women.

The percentage of households headed by women increased world-wide in the 1980s. In Western Europe, for example, it grew from 24 percent in 1980 to 31 percent in 1990. In the developing world, it varies from less than 20 percent in certain Southern and South-eastern Asian countries to almost 50 percent in certain African countries and the Caribbean.

The factors associated with this growth vary from one region to another according to social, demographic and economic conditions. The most important factors are migrations, divorce, abandonment, civil strife, widowhood, unpartnered adolescent parenthood and, more generally, the notion that children are women's responsibility.

and out, but rather that the women had to do this every day of the week, every day of the year (Thanksgiving and Christmas Day excepted), no matter what the weather or how they felt. On any given morning, as the women drifted onto the street, one might see two or three ailing women—this one with a fever or cough or a headache, that one with a limp or stomach ache or other ailment—pick up their bags and walk silently into the weather. . . .

Along with **perennial** fatigue, boredom was one of the great trials of homelessness. Killing time was not a major problem for everyone but it was high on most women's lists of hardships. Betty could have been speaking for most of them when she talked about the problem. On a social visit to the state psychiatric hospital where, four years earlier, she had been an inpatient in an alcoholic program, Betty sought out a nurse named Lou. They embraced and Lou asked Betty what she was doing these days. Betty said she was living in a shelter. Lou said that was a shame, and asked Betty how she spent her time.

"I walk the streets," said Betty. "Twelve hours and 15 minutes a day, every day, I walk the streets. Is that what I got sober for? To walk the streets?" Betty went on to say that she sits on a lot of park benches looking for someone to talk to. Many times there is no one, so she talks to the birds. She and the birds have done a lot of talking in her day, she said. . . .

Some of the women with jobs also had trouble killing time. Like the others, Grace had to leave the shelter by 7:00 A.M. but she couldn't report to work much before 9:00, and her job was less than a 10-minute drive away. "Have you ever tried to kill two hours in the morning, every morning, with nowhere to go and nothing to do?" she asked. "I have some tapes I can listen to in the car—some Christmas carols and some Bible readings. But two hours? Every day?"

. . . It is all too easy to think of homeless people as having few or no possessions . . . , but one of the major and most talked-about problems was storage—how to keep one's clothing, essential documents, and other belongings secure and **accessible.** . . . Stealing was believed to be common: "You've got to expect these things in shelters" was heard from staff and women alike. The end result was that many homeless women who would have left their belongings behind had they had a safe place to store them were forced to take most of their belongings with them. Some wore them in layers. Others carried them. They had become, in short, bag ladies.

During a discussion of Luther Place, one of the best-run shelters in downtown Washington, one of the women said Luther Place was OK but she didn't like the women there—they were all bag ladies. One of the other women objected that the women at Luther Place were no different from women in other shelters. They were bag ladies, she said, because Luther Place had no storage space. . . .

Past and future . . . and even one's self were **embedded** in one's belongings. When Louise could no longer pay for storage and lost her belongings to auction, she was surprised at her own reaction to the loss. Her belongings had been so much a part of her, she said, that now that she's lost them, she's not sure who she is.

Source: Excerpted from Elliot Liebow, *Tell Them Who I Am: The Lives of Homeless Women*. New York: Penguin Books, 1995.

What Does it Mean?

accessible
available; easy to reach

catastrophic proportions
a size approaching disaster; too large to deal with individually

embedded
made a part of; surrounded by

insurmountable hurdles
obstacles or barriers that cannot be overcome

perennial
regularly repeated; enduring and persistent

subsistence
meeting basic needs

unremitting
constant; never ending

Read and React

1. What are the two major problems related to homelessness discussed in this writing?
2. What attitude or belief about the homeless that you had before reading this article has been changed? If none, what did you learn that you didn't know before?

Answers to Read and React

1. Struggling for subsistence and alleviating the boredom are discussed. Students will probably say that homeless women should get jobs. Remind them that it is not easy to get a job without a permanent residence.
2. This article might not change attitudes about homelessness. You might want to have students read excerpts from the books mentioned before or obtain a copy of the video: *Down and Out in America,* available through Insight Media. It shows urban homelessness as well as rural poverty.

Integrating the Teacher Resources

Additional primary source readings for this chapter can be found in Culture Studies: The Sociological Perspective, **available in your Teacher's Resource Box. Questions for students are included.**

Chapter Preview

Section 1 (pages 276–279)

Sociologists have specific definitions for minority, race, and ethnicity. Ethnic minorities have often been subjected to prejudice and discrimination.

Section 2 (pages 280–283)

Patterns of racial and ethnic relations take two forms: assimilation and conflict. Patterns of assimilation include Anglo-conformity, melting pot, and cultural pluralism. Conflict patterns include genocide, population transfer, and subjugation.

Section 3 (pages 284–289)

Prejudice refers to attitudes, while discrimination is about behavior. Prejudice usually leads to discrimination, but in some instances discrimination creates prejudiced attitudes due to stereotyping. Each of the three major perspectives looks at different aspects of prejudice.

Section 4 (pages 290–301)

Discrimination has caused some ethnic and racial groups to lag behind the white majority in jobs, income, and education. Progress is being made, but the gains of all minorities remain fragile. African American, Latino, Asian American, Native American and white ethnics are the largest minorities in this country.

Please see the correlation to the American Sociology Association standards located in the front of this text.

CHAPTER 9

Inequalities of Race and Ethnicity

Lead-Off Activity

Before beginning this chapter, identify several prime-time television programs that are popular with high school aged youth. Ask them to watch these programs over the course of the week. Have students note when and how often members of minority groups appear. (Since students will look closely at gender in Chapter 10 you might ask them to consider primarily racial, ethnic, and religious minorities for this activity.) The students' task is to assess how the various members of the minority groups are portrayed by the television media. Ask them to note when stereotypical characterizations or events occur. (This aspect of the activity is especially interesting if you have a significant number of minority students in your classroom, because they are usually more

USING Your Sociological Imagination

"The Four Americas" is a report published by a major think tank, a national newspaper, and a prestigious university (Brodie, 1995). These organizations used an extensive national survey to investigate race in the United States. The survey asked people to respond to such questions as "Do you think the average African American is better off, worse off, or as well off as the average white person in terms of jobs, education, housing, and health care?"

Most Asians and Latinos answered that African Americans are doing less well than whites. But most whites thought blacks were doing about equally well.

In reality, the evidence shows that the average income of African American households is considerably less than that of white households. Moreover, at each level of education—the gateway to good jobs—African American males earn less than white males. On average, for example, white high school graduates can expect to earn annually nearly as much as African American college graduates. The report concluded that while most minorities understand each other's real-life difficulties, "whites stand alone in their misperceptions of the problems facing minorities in America today."

Whites, of course, are not the only group of people who would benefit from a better understanding of the issues facing all Americans. This chapter will take a close look at how race and ethnicity have affected the ability of people to achieve the American dream.

Sections

1. **Minority, Race, and Ethnicity**
2. **Racial and Ethnic Relations**
3. **Theories of Prejudice and Discrimination**
4. **Minority Groups in the United States**

Learning Objectives

After reading this chapter, you will be able to

- describe what sociologists mean by the terms *minority, race,* and *ethnicity*.
- discuss patterns of racial and ethnic relations.
- discuss the difference between prejudice and discrimination.
- explain how functionalists, conflict theorists, and symbolic interactionists view racial inequalities.
- compare the condition of American minorities with that of the white majority.

SOCIOLOGY Online

Chapter Overview
Visit the *Sociology and You* Web site at soc.glencoe.com and click on **Chapter 9—Chapter Overviews** to preview chapter information.

USING Your Sociological Imagination

Ask students if they agree that many white Americans have misconceptions about the relative status and economic condition of minorities. What reasons might explain these attitudes? *(Students might answer lack of familiarity with minorities, television stereotyping, considering anecdotal rather than statistical evidence, etc.)* Tell students that you will ask them to note three misconceptions that they held before studying the chapter.

Using the Illustration

In 1995 the Ramapough Mountain Indians protested so the government would recognize their tribe. Ask students why they would protest outside the Department of the Interior. *(They handle Indian affairs.)*

sensitive to what constitutes a stereotype than the members of the predominant race or class.) Ask them also to look at the portrayals in terms of how equitably power and wealth are distributed among the various races, classes, or ethnicities. Then let them meet in groups to compare their notes and see if they all recorded similar kinds of comments and evaluations. Ask them as a group to evaluate how realistically the television portrays how resources are shared in society. Then tell them that after they study the chapter they will be asked to make the same evaluation to see if their ideas have changed.
L2

Using the Section Preview

Before reading from the text, ask students to write a definition of each of the following terms: *minority, race, ethnicity.* After they have done that, have them read the first section and compare their definitions to the definitions that sociologists have developed.

Teaching Strategy

This chapter can be both stimulating and/or upsetting for students, depending upon how the issues of race and ethnicity are approached. You may find that it is necessary to remind students on a fairly regular basis of the importance of being sensitive to the feelings of others. It is also important that students are reminded that sociology deals with general trends and groups—not personalities and individuals. For every statement that explains a trend and for every generalization, there will be exceptions.

Since it will probably be very hard for them to leave specific cases and anecdotal experiences behind, it might be helpful to let them share at the beginning of the chapter any personal experiences with issues of discrimination or prejudice. This might "clear the air" and help all students get past individual experiences and move to the level of society in general.

Section 1 Minority, Race, and Ethnicity

Key Terms

- minority
- race
- ethnic minority

Section Preview

Sociologists have specific definitions particular to their field of study for *minority, race,* and *ethnicity.* Ethnic minorities have historically been subjected to prejudice and discrimination.

minority
a group of people with physical or cultural traits different from those of the dominant group in the society

Minorities

Imagine that one evening, you and eight friends are unable to decide whether to go bowling or to the movies. Being a democratic group, you decide to put the question to a vote. If only three of you vote for the show, the movie fans—being fewer in number—will make up a minority.

But numbers alone are not the basis of the sociological definition of minority. Women in the United States outnumber males, and yet they are still referred to as a minority. Blacks in South Africa and in many large cities in the United States are minority populations even though they outnumber the white population. For sociologists, then, a minority population is defined by something more than size or number.

What are the characteristics of a minority? In 1945, sociologist Louis Wirth offered the following definition of **minority:**

> *We may define a minority as a group of people who, because of their physical or cultural characteristics, are singled out from the others in the society in which they live for differential and unequal treatment, and who therefore regard themselves as objects of collective discrimination. The existence of a minority in a society implies the existence of a corresponding dominant group with higher social status and greater privileges. Minority carries with it the exclusion from full participation in the life of the society.*

A minority, then, has several key features.

Which of these teens are members of a minority group? Explain why.

1. *A minority has distinctive physical or cultural characteristics which can be used to separate it from the majority.* Physical characteristics may include such things as skin color, facial features, and disabilities. Cultural characteristics may include accent, religion, language, and parentage. In the past, some people have been forced to carry papers or wear badges that marked them as members of a minority. For example, during the Nazi regime, Jews in German-occupied countries were forced to wear yellow stars to separate them from non-Jewish Germans.
2. *The minority is dominated by the majority.* Because the majority is the dominating group, it holds an unequal share of the desired goods, services, and privileges. Further, minority members have fewer opportunities to get these goods and services. The best jobs are hard for minorities to get because of a lack of education or unfair hiring practices.

Survey

Students might find it interesting to begin this chapter with a survey to determine their school's racial and ethnic composition. They should meet in groups and decide the best way to conduct the poll. For instance, will they try to poll each and every student? Will they get a random sampling? Or, will they go to the office to try to get precollected data? If they collect their own data, what categories will they use? Will they follow the U.S. Census categories?

Once they have decided on the methodology, students should prepare the questionnaire or survey and bring it back to you for approval. (You may want to enlarge the survey to include more than just race/ethnicity.) Tell students to tabulate their results and that they will use this data in upcoming activities. You may also have more than one survey taken to see if the students get similar results.
L1

3. *Minority traits are often believed by the dominant majority to be inferior.* This presumed inferiority can be used to justify unequal treatment. For example, a majority may justify job discrimination by depicting a minority as shiftless or lazy.
4. *Members of the minority have a common sense of identity, with strong group loyalty.* Efforts to keep the minority isolated create empathy among those suffering discrimination. Within the minority, there is a "consciousness of kind." Because of this sense of common identity, members of the minority accept a "we" and "they" vocabulary.
5. *The majority determines who belongs to the minority through ascribed status.* People become members of the minority at birth. Thus, membership is an ascribed status and is not easily changed. This is especially true when physical characteristics such as *race* are involved.

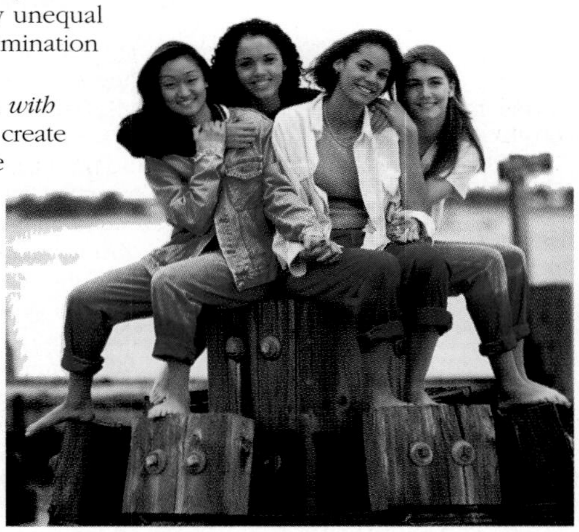

How many races are represented in this photo? On what basis did you make that determination?

Defining Race

Members of a **race** share certain biologically inherited physical characteristics that are considered equally important within a society. Biologists use characteristics such as skin color, hair color, hair texture, facial features, head form, eye color, and height to determine race. The most common system classifies races into three major divisions—Negroid, Mongoloid, and Caucasian.

race
people sharing certain inherited physical characteristics that are considered important within a society

Is there a scientific basis for race? Although certain physical features have been associated with particular races, scientists have known for a long time that there is no such thing as a "pure" race. Features, or markers, typical of one race show up in other races quite frequently. For example, some people born into African American families are assumed to be white because of their facial features and light skin color. Most scientists consider racial classifications arbitrary and misleading. For students of sociology, social attitudes and characteristics that relate to race are more important than physical differences.

But aren't some physical characteristics superior? It has sometimes been argued that certain physical characteristics often associated with race are superior and others are inferior. In fact, physical characteristics are superior only in the sense that they provide advantages for living in particular environments. For example, a narrow opening between eyelids protects against bright light and driving cold such as found in Siberia or Alaska. A darker skin is better able to withstand a hot sun. But these physical differences are controlled by a very few genes. In fact, geneticists claim that there may be more genetic difference between a tall person and a short person than between two people of different races who are the same height. Only about six genes in the human cell control skin color, while a person's height is affected by dozens of genes. Thus a six-foot white male may be closer genetically to a black male of the same height than to a five-foot white male. What is important to remember is that there is no scientific evidence that connects any racial characteristic with innate superiority or inferiority (Hurley, 1998). There is, for example, no evidence of *innate* differences in athleticism or intelligence among the various races.

Open-Response Question

The problem with defining race by skin color should be obvious to all the students. One of the problems with this approach is that many Latinos, for example, do not think of themselves as either white or nonwhite. Today, the government uses classifications of "race" for census purposes that scientists would not recognize, such as Japanese, Chinese, Korean, or Filipino. Ask students why they think the government wants this kind of racial information. Do they think people are generally willing or unwilling to provide it? *(Government census takers confirm that minorities are generally very unwilling to divulge personal information on the census, even if they are told it will benefit their population in some way. Many minority groups harbor a sense of suspicion towards the government for different reasons.)*

Learning Styles

Artistic Students with artistic talents should take the tabulated results from the racial/ethnic survey from page 276 and create attractive posters that display the results of the school survey. If they are really creative, they might learn a little bit about each racial/ethnic category to illustrate the poster with some of the achievements of individuals that represent each group. They could also present the information in as many formats as they can, for instance, pie graphs, bar graphs, line graphs, and so forth.
L3

Ethnicity

ethnic minority
group identified by cultural, religious, or national characteristics

The term *ethnicity* comes from the Greek word *ethnos*, originally meaning "people" or "nation." Thus, the Greek word referred to cultural and national identity. Today, an **ethnic minority** is socially identified by unique characteristics related to culture or nationality. Just as physical characteristics define racial minorities, cultural differences define ethnic minorities.

An ethnic minority is a subculture defined by its own language, religion, values, beliefs, norms, and customs. (See page 98 in Chapter 3 for an introduction to subcultures.) Like any subculture, it is part of the larger culture—its members work in the majority, or host, economy, send their children through the host educational system, and are subject to the laws of the land. Ethnic minorities are also separate from the larger culture. The separation may continue because the ethnic minority wishes to maintain its cultural and national origins or because the majority erects barriers that prevent the ethnic group from blending in with the larger culture. For example, Michael Novak (1996) makes a case that members of white ethnic minorities from southern and eastern Europe—Poles, Slavs, Italians, Greeks—have not been able to blend completely into American society. Compared with other white European immigrant groups, such as German immigrants, groups from southern and eastern Europe were more culturally different from the white Anglo-Saxon Protestant (WASP) majority and thus mixed less easily with the majority culture.

Why are ethnic minorities seen as inferior? Negative attitudes toward ethnic minorities exist in part because of *ethnocentrism*. As you read in Chapter 3, ethnocentrism involves judging others in terms of one's own cultural standards. Ethnocentrism creates the feeling of "us," the group one belongs to, versus "them," the other groups that are out there.

People in the majority, out of loyalty to and preference for their own values, beliefs, and norms, may consider other views to be inferior. Because members of ethnic minorities do not measure up to the majority's conception of appropriate ways of behaving, it may be assumed that something is wrong with them. Ethnocentric judgments are often expressed as prejudice and discrimination. Figure 9.1 shows American attitudes toward specific immigrant groups. In general, European immigrants are viewed more positively than non-European immigrants.

Figure 9.1. Attitudes of Americans Toward Immigrant Minorities. *The results of a Gallup poll are displayed in this graph of attitudes toward various immigrant groups in the United States. What pattern is reflected in this graph among the groups that are most favored as helping the country?*

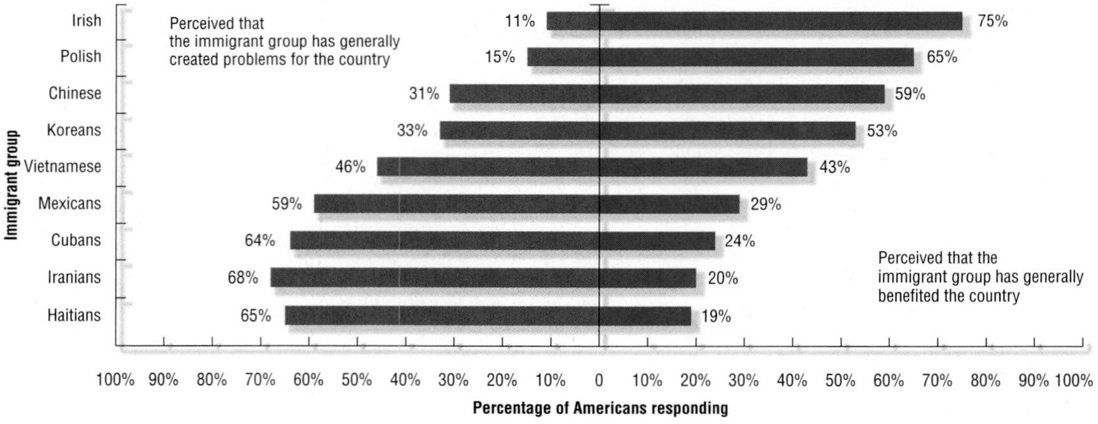

Making Connections to Other Cultures

Remind students that ethnocentrism is not limited to the white majority or just to Americans, or even Western Europeans. Many other cultures have displayed ethnocentric or racist behaviors toward minorities in their societies. For example, the Chinese and the Japanese have historically been very isolationist based on feelings of their own cultural superiority. Recent examples include the Hutus and Tutsis, the Serbs and the Kosovars, and the Armenians and the Turks.

Working with the Data

Figure 9.1 shows how surveyed Americans responded to a question about how they perceived the relative contributions of various ethnic groups to the culture and society of the U.S. Discuss with students the subjectivity of such a question and reinforce the fact that the perception is not the same as the reality. The intent of the survey was to judge American perceptions, not to judge minority or ethnic contributions. Ask students if any of the survey results surprised them, and if so, why. Then ask students if they notice a pattern or trend in the data. *(Students should respond that the group that physically looks the most like mainstream Anglos is also the group that got the highest "positive" rating.)*

Careers in Sociology

Students should be aware that federal legislation exists to regulate discriminatory practices in the workplace. Employment and placement managers oversee the hiring and separation of employees and supervise various workers, including equal employment opportunity specialists and recruitment specialists. Recruiters maintain contacts within the community and may travel extensively to search for promising job applicants. Recruiters screen, interview, and in some cases, test applicants. They may also check references and extend job offers. These workers must be thoroughly familiar with the organization and its personnel policies to discuss wages, working conditions, and promotional opportunities with prospective employees. They must

Another Place: The Travelling People

The following excerpt describes the Irish "Travelling People," who are viewed by mainstream Irish as inferior.

They are Ireland's unrecognized minority—homeless and ostracized. Despite public disapproval, their family groups wander the Irish countryside. Other than a limited number of official halting sites they have no place to stop. Most live by the side of the road. They bathe, eat, and sleep in public. They live without electricity or permanent running water, bathing facilities, or toilets. Their child-mortality rate is similar to those in Third World countries, and there is a 98 percent illiteracy rate among adults. According to the Economic and Social Research Institute's 1985 report, "The circumstances of the Irish Travelling People are intolerable. No humane and decent society once made aware of such circumstances could permit them to persist."

But although local political groups and organizations have expressed the need to create permanent housing for the Travellers (most commonly described as "gypsies" or "tinkers"), the settled community prefers what Traveller Nell McDonaugh calls an "unspoken segregation." Travellers are evicted from areas not designated as official halting sites, and grassy lanes that Traveller groups have frequented for years are blocked and barred. Most official halting sites are located in undesirable, often industrial, areas.

Most settled people want nothing to do with Travellers. Popular belief has it that Travellers draw the dole [welfare] in more than one county at a time, are troublemakers, and leave piles of garbage in their wake. Many local people are opposed to having halting sites in their vicinity. Why should "respectable" people support itinerants?

But these "homeless" outcasts have filled a social niche in Ireland for centuries. Theirs may be a distinct lifestyle, and their traditions are unlike those of other Irish, but they are, nonetheless, Irish. In a traditionally rural society, Travellers served acceptable social purposes as itinerant farm workers, metal craftsmen, lace makers, and storytellers. But in today's settled urban society, this integrated group of nomads are a people displaced by and at odds with contemporary expectations. They are a community without a place in its own homeland and a cultural group in danger of losing its identity.

Source: Excerpted and reprinted with permission from *The World & I*, Amy Seidman, June 1993, *The Washington Times Corporation*, © 1993, pp. 250, 252.

Thinking It Over

Use either functionalism or conflict theory to explain this attitude toward the Travellers.

Section 1 Assessment

1. Which of the following is NOT always a characteristic of a minority?
   - **a.** distinctive physical or cultural characteristics
   - **b.** smaller in number than the majority
   - **c.** dominated by the majority
   - **d.** denied equal treatment
   - **e.** a sense of collective identity
2. What is the difference between race and ethnicity? Between race and nationality?

Critical Thinking

3. **Summarizing Information** Identify the main racial or ethnic minorities in your area. Are you a member of any minority groups? What are they?

> "I know of no rights of race superior to the rights of man."
>
> **Frederick Douglas**
> **American abolitionist**

also keep informed about equal employment opportunity (EEO) and affirmative action guidelines and laws, such as the Americans With Disabilities Act.

EEO officers, representatives or affirmative action coordinators handle this area in large organizations. They investigate and resolve EEO grievances, examine corporate practices for possible violations, and compile and submit EEO statistical reports. Students would probably benefit from having an EEO representative address your class on issues of race and ethnic discrimination in the workplace. To contact the Equal Employment Opportunity Commission, link to **http://www.eeoc.gov/**.

Another Place

This article should remind students of things they have probably heard people say about the homeless. Tell them that some communities, especially those with tourist attractions that attract a lot of visitors, now fine the homeless for loitering. Since they can't pay the tickets, they eventually are arrested and end up with a police record.

Answer to Thinking It Over

Students will either defend the property-owning interests and argue that people should contribute in "constructive" ways or argue from the conflict perspective that the Travellers are the victims of an elitist class structure.

Answers to Section 1 Assessment

1. b
2. A difference between race and ethnicity is that shared physical characteristics are usually associated with race, and culture and nationality are associated with ethnicity. Again, race involves physical characteristics but nationality describes one's origin.

Critical Thinking

3. Answers will vary.

Using the Section Preview

The analogies of the melting pot and the tossed salad tend to remain with students a long time, and so they are good ones to use. Emphasize that the *melting pot* implies a desire to have everyone assimilated according to the dominant culture's standards; the *tossed salad* metaphor would seem to allow for more diversity within a larger unity (cultural pluralism). Discuss with students why they think this change in thinking might have developed.

Open-Response Questions

Ask students to discuss how the meaning of race is changing in the United States today. Do they have the same racial attitudes as their parents? As their grandparents? How do they imagine their own children might view the concept of race? What trends do they see developing in racial attitudes?

Integrating the Teacher Resources

Look for the Chapter 9 Learning Goals Outline, a reproducible student worksheet in the Unit 3 Mastering Basic Concepts booklet in your Teacher's Resource Box. It can be used to preview or review chapter content.

Section 2 Racial and Ethnic Relations

Key Terms

- assimilation
- cultural pluralism
- genocide
- subjugation
- de jure segregation
- de facto segregation

Section Preview

Patterns of racial and ethnic relations take two forms: assimilation and conflict. Patterns of assimilation include Anglo-conformity, melting pot, cultural pluralism, and accommodation. Conflict patterns include genocide, population transfer, and subjugation.

assimilation
the blending or fusing of minority groups into the dominant society

Patterns of Assimilation

Generally, minority groups are either accepted—which leads to *assimilation*—or rejected—which leads to *conflict*. Within these two broad approaches, however, is a wide range of outcomes.

Assimilation refers to the blending or fusing of minority groups into the dominant society. When a racial or ethnic minority is integrated into a society, its members are given full participation in all aspects of the society. Assimilation has taken several forms in the United States: *Anglo-conformity, melting pot, cultural pluralism,* and *accommodation.*

Anglo-conformity has been the most common form of assimilation in U.S. society.

What is the most common pattern of assimilation? Anglo-conformity has been the most prevalent pattern of assimilation in America. *Anglo* is a prefix used to indicate an American of English descent. In Anglo-conformity, traditional American institutions are maintained. Immigrants are accepted as long as they conform to the "accepted standards" of the society. Anglo-conformity is the least egalitarian pattern of assimilation because the immigrant minority is required to conform. By implication, it must either give up or suppress its own values.

Is America more like a melting pot or a tossed salad? A second pattern of assimilation is the *melting pot*, in which all ethnic and racial minorities voluntarily blend together. Older history textbooks, in describing the immigrant experience in the United States, often referred to a melting pot of cultures. However, there is some question about how much fusing of cultures has really taken place. Instead of a melting pot, many sociologists are now using the idea of a "tossed salad," in which traditions and cultures exist side by side. The cultures of the Tejanos in Texas and the Creoles of New

Using Problem-Solving Skills

Break students into groups to problem solve the following scenario: Rumor has it that one of five assistants at your school unfairly punishes members of a certain race and gender when dealing with discipline referrals. You and your best friend (who is also a member of this unfavored group) are sent to this assistant because of tardiness. You receive a counseling session and your parents are called; your friend gets five days of lunch detention, a parent conference, and one Saturday morning study period.

During your sociology class discussion you mention what you think is an inequitable re-

How does this drawing show accommodation?

Orleans are examples. This pattern of assimilation is called **cultural pluralism.** It recognizes immigrants' desire to maintain at least a remnant of their "old" ways.

Accommodation is an extreme form of cultural pluralism. It occurs when a minority maintains its own culturally unique way of life. The minority learns to deal with, or accommodate, the dominant culture when necessary but remains independent in language and culture. The Cubans in Miami and the Amish in Pennsylvania are examples of distinct groups within larger communities that have kept separate identities.

cultural pluralism
desire of a group to maintain some sense of identity separate from the dominant group

Patterns of Conflict

In looking for broad patterns of conflict, sociologists examine historical records and analyze current events. Three basic patterns have emerged that describe approaches that dominant cultures take in their rejection of minority groups. These are *genocide, population transfer,* and *subjugation* (Mason, 1970).

What is the most extreme pattern of conflict? At the extreme, conflict takes the form of **genocide,** the systematic effort to destroy an entire population. One of the best-known examples is the Holocaust, Adolph Hitler's attempt to destroy all European Jews during the 1930s and 1940s. (See Figure 9.2 below.) Less well known is the "Rape of Nanking," begun in

genocide
the systematic effort to destroy an entire population

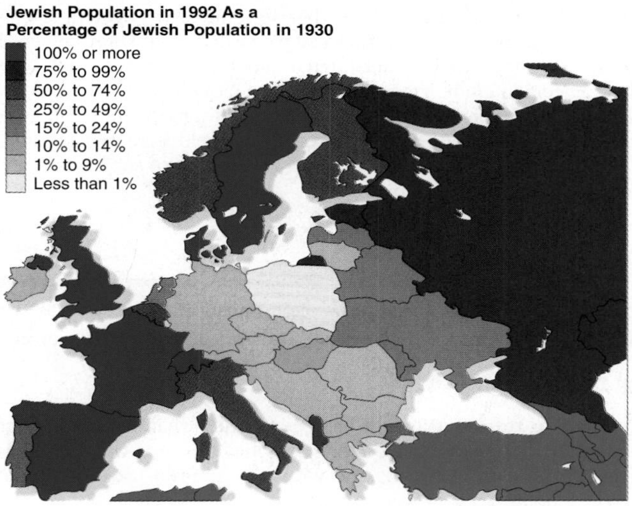

Figure 9.2. Impact of the Holocaust. *One of the worst examples of genocide was the Nazis' attempt, in the 1930s and 1940s, to exterminate the European Jewish population. This map shows the decline in Jewish population in European countries as a result of the Holocaust.*

Reinforcing Vocabulary

The terms describing patterns of assimilation can be difficult for native English speakers, much less ESL students. For native Spanish speakers, these terms might not be as difficult as for other students, since the Spanish equivalents have the same Latin roots as the English terms. Ask your Spanish ESL students to translate *assimilation, accommodation, culture,* and *pluralism.* Then ask them to explain their understanding of the meanings of these terms. They should be able to make a connection between the Spanish and English meanings.
ELL

Working with the Data

Figure 9.2 Students should note how the Jewish population in Poland, the center of the Holocaust, is less than 1 percent of the pre-World War II population. Tell students that anti-Semitic incidents are again on the rise in many of these European countries.

sponse from the administration. Your teacher suggests you formulate a plan of action to remedy the situation. Decide whether you would proceed at all, or whether it would be wiser to assume that life is not fair and sometimes you just have to grin and bear it. If you decide to take action, brainstorm the steps you would take to (1) ascertain that there really was an inequity and (2) come up with a remedy for the situation.

Compare the responses of the different groups to see if a concensus was reached.
L1

The Cherokees were not the only Native American population transferred from their homes. The Creeks and the Seminoles were also forcibly removed by U.S. troops.

1937, during which the Japanese massacred an estimated 260,000 to 350,000 Chinese men, women, and children (Chang, 1998).

Tragically, genocide campaigns are more common in world history than might be supposed. Recently, the Serbians have been accused of conducting campaigns of "ethnic cleansing" against the Muslims in Bosnia and Kosovo. In 1994, the Tutsi tribe of Rwanda slaughtered 500,000 to 1 million of the minority Hutu tribe.

What is population transfer? In *population transfer*, a minority is forced either to move to a remote location or to leave entirely the territory controlled by the majority. This was the policy most often used against Native Americans. For example, in 1838, sixteen thousand Cherokees from the southeastern United States were set on a forced march along the "Trail of Tears" to Oklahoma reservations, where they became dependent on the U.S. government. Four to eight thousand Cherokees (nearly a fourth of the tribes) died because of harsh conditions along the Trail of Tears.

subjugation
process by which a minority group is denied equal access to the benefits of a society

de jure segregation
denial of equal access based on the law

de facto segregation
denial of equal access based on everyday practice

What conflict pattern appears most often? **Subjugation** is the most common pattern of conflict. A subjugated minority is denied equal access to the culture and lifestyle of the larger society. Subjugation may be based on the law, or *de jure*. An example was the **de jure segregation** of public schools in the United States during the latter part of the nineteenth century and the first half of the twentieth century. In *Brown vs. Board of Education of Topeka* (1954) the Supreme Court overturned previous case law that had made racial segregation legal in the U.S.

Subjugation may also arise from the everyday practices of people, even when specific laws do not exist to deny opportunities to minority groups. *De facto* is a term used in case law that describes the actual, or real, situation regardless of what the law is. **De facto segregation** is operating when, for example, neighboring homeowners agree among themselves not to sell to members of certain ethnic groups or races. De facto discrimination exists when people of certain backgrounds are not promoted to important positions in local government or in businesses because of widely held stereotypes. Although illegal, the difficulty of proving bias can make this type of subjugation a very effective tool for controlling a minority.

> "We're not where we want to be. And we're not where we're going to be. But we are sure a long way from where we were."
>
> **Rev. M. L. King, Jr. civil rights leader**

Section 2 Assessment

1. Identify and define four patterns of assimilation.
2. What is the difference between de jure and de facto segregation?

Critical Thinking

3. **Evaluating Information** It has been argued that both the pattern of immigrant assimilation accurately describes the state of race relations between African Americans and whites in America today. Do you agree? Explain your position.

Pulling it All Together

Check student understanding of patterns of assimilation by asking them to rank these terms by degree of hostility or control each term indicates is exerted against a minority group by a majority culture: *subjugation, assimilation, de jure segregation, de facto segregation, genocide, cultural pluralism, accommodation,* and *population transfer.* There are no absolute right and wrong answers, but the ranking activity should force students to examine their understandings.

Answers to Section 2 Assessment

1. *Anglo-conformity:* An American of English descent; traditional American institutions are maintained, and immigrants are accepted as long as they conform to society's "accepted standards." *Melting pot:* All ethnic and racial minorities voluntarily blend together. *Cultural pluralism ("tossed salad"):* Traditions and cultures exist side by side. *Accommodation:* An extreme form of cultural pluralism—when a minority maintains its own culturally unique way of life.
2. *De jure* means "based on law." *De jure* segregation was legal separation of races (a form of subjugation), which was abolished with the *Brown vs. Board of Education of Topeka* decision in 1954. *De facto* is a term for an actual, or real, situation regardless of the law.

Critical Thinking

3. Answers will vary.

Interdisciplinary Activity

History Have students research other examples of genocide in history, for example the Turkish genocide of Armenia in 1915 or ethnic cleansing in the former Yugoslavia. Students should look at how the prejudicial attitudes of the people are formulated and make comparisons to our society. Or, ask them to investigate and report on the civil rights cases mentioned in this chapter. There are hundreds of excellent sites for students to visit to find out more about *Brown vs. Board of Education of Topeka,*

Sociology Today: Bridging the Digital Divide

In 2000, Delta Airlines and Ford Motor Company both publicly announced their multimillion dollar (hundreds of millions, in fact) bet they are placing on their employees (Miller and Silverstein, 2000). Each intends to provide home computers and Internet access to all of their 442,000 workers. It is a new company benefit costing each employee as little as $5 per month.

The bet is that employees become more efficient and effective when they are proficient with computers. Expected payoffs for the companies is improved communication with their workforces, heightened employee morale, and increased employee loyalty. Employees at Ford and Delta enthusiastically welcomed the new benefit.

There is a possible downside for employees. When workers can be reached instantaneously at home day or night, the traditional boundaries between the home and the work place could erode. And Ford and Delta do have plans to communicate with workers at home. According to sociologist Arlie Hochschild, this apparent gift could be a Trojan horse by extending the "long arm of the workplace." Even worse, some workers fear that companies might intrude on their private lives by monitoring their Internet activities.

There could also be a social upside to wide scale on-line access. Sociologists have recognized computer literacy as a key to social mobility in the twenty-first century. (See the *Enrichment Reading* entitled "Falling Through the Net" in Chapter 17.) Since those nearer the bottom of the social class structure lack the resources necessary to be computer literate, sociologists fear they will be hopelessly left behind.

Given this situation, widespread exposure of less-skilled workers to computer technology could have benefits Ford and Delta employees may not have considered. Since both companies are encouraging workers' families to use the technology, the spouses and children of a significant number of individuals will have access to an indispensable tool for occupational advancement. While Ford and Delta may be concerned only about keeping their employees out of the digital divide, their action may unintentionally enable many more Americans to cross this divide. Company-provided computer technology at home may become a staple in most future corporate benefit packages.

Doing Sociology

1. Do you believe that computer literacy is a key element in today's job market? Tomorrow's?
2. Evaluate your own capabilities regarding computer technology.
3. Go to your library and examine the employment page of the Sunday edition of a major newspaper. Write a brief report on the extent to which computer literacy appears to be an important qualification in today's urban marketplace.

Sociology Today

Besides the costs involved in getting on the Internet, some minority groups face another disadvantage in technology parity. A study released in April 2000 conducted by Children's Partnership ("Online Content for Low-Income and Underserved Americans: The Digital Divide's New Frontier") found that at least fifty million Americans are poorly served by the Internet because of a lack of web sites targeting the needs of people with low incomes and those who don't read or speak English well. The report found limited information about jobs, housing, or the educational needs of low-income Americans. What they found missing was practical, local information about poorer and minority neighborhoods. Yet, it is estimated that these fifty million Americans possess more than $300 billion in purchasing power.

Answers to Doing Sociology

1. Students should realize that computer literacy is a basic necessity in almost every field of endeavor, and that the need will only continue to increase.
2. Answers will vary.
3. Students should compare the results of their "literature" searches.

Kansas. One recommended site follows:
http://www.mecca.org/ ~crights/

Remind students that the *Brown* case was a landmark case. And even though it was a unanimous decision, 100 members of Congress signed a document protesting the Court's decision as an abuse of judicial power.
L2

Using the Section Preview

Ask students the following question to introduce this section: *Do you believe most people are prejudiced or do you believe that most people are free from prejudice?* Let them debate this question for a while. As you listen to their comments, make notes of some of the misconceptions they hold about both the meanings of terms and the "facts" they use to support their statements. Tell them that you would like to ask them this same question at the end of the chapter to see if they hold the same opinions.

Open-Response Question

Students are used to thinking about prejudice in terms of race and ethnicity, which is certainly the most usual way. But ask them to suggest ways in which people are prejudiced that don't involve race or ethnicity. (*For example, they might know people who are prejudiced against a certain type of music, a certain sport, a style of dress, a type of book, people who are overweight, too loud, or too old.*) This activity should help students understand how subtle prejudice is and how everyone prejudges at times.

Section 3 Theories of Prejudice and Discrimination

Key Terms

- prejudice
- racism
- discrimination
- hate crime
- stereotype
- self-fulfilling prophecy

Section Preview

Prejudice involves attitudes, while discrimination is about behavior. Prejudice usually leads to discrimination. Conversely, in some instances, discrimination creates prejudiced attitudes through stereotyping. Each of the three major perspectives looks at different aspects of prejudice.

prejudice
widely held negative attitudes toward a group (minority or majority) and its individual members

racism
an extreme form of prejudice that assumes superiority of one group over others

Prejudice, Racism, and Discrimination

Individuals hold prejudices of many types. To a sociologist, though, **prejudice** has a very particular meaning. It refers to widely held preconceptions of a group (minority or majority) and its individual members. Prejudice involves a generalization based on biased or insufficient information. Prejudiced attitudes are based on strong emotions, so they are often difficult to change, even in the face of overwhelming evidence. It is easier to explain individuals who don't fit the stereotype as exceptions than it is to reexamine a whole set of established beliefs. For example, many people believe that Asian students have a particular "gift" for mathematics. Suppose that Susie is one of these people. In algebra class, she sits next to an Asian student who is not doing well. Will Susie change her idea about the mathematical abilities of Asian people as a result of this? Probably not. It will be less trouble for her to think that this one Asian student is the exception to the rule.

Racism is an extreme form of prejudice, because it not only involves judging people unfairly, but it assumes that a person's own race or ethnic group is superior. Racists believe that discrimination or exclusion is morally justified because of their own natural superiority.

When prejudice is used as a basis for making decisions—as in denying minorities advancement—then it becomes discrimination.

Survey

This is an opportunity for students to design a survey for their own use to help them become aware of how diverse (or how limited) their exposure to other races and/or ethnicities is. Ask students to design a questionnaire that would measure people's exposure to other races and cultures. Examples of questions might be: How many people do you associate with daily (or weekly) who are not a member of your own race? How many times in the past week (or month) have you had a conflict with someone of a different race or culture? When they have formulated some good questions, ask them to answer the questions for themselves. You may want to explain that being relatively prejudice-free may be a function of lack of opportunity. That is, if they have limited association with people who are different there are limited opportunities for either cooperation or conflict. **L2**

How is discrimination different from prejudice? While prejudice involves holding biased opinions, **discrimination** involves acting upon those opinions by treating people unfairly. Prejudice does not always result in discrimination, but it often does.

discrimination
treating people differently based on ethnicity, race, religion, or culture

Discrimination takes many forms, including avoiding social contact with members of minority groups, denying them positions that carry authority, and blocking their access to the more exclusive neighborhoods. It can also involve such extremes as attacking or killing minority members.

Hate Crimes

In 1999, James Byrd, Jr., an African American from Texas, was chained to a pickup truck, then dragged to death. That same year saw Matthew Shepard, a gay college student, tied to a fence and beaten to death. Both incidents fell under a special kind of crime called *hate crimes.*

These federal agency employees are searching through the ashes of an African American church in Mississippi. What would make this case of arson a hate crime?

How are hate crimes different? A **hate crime** is a criminal act that is motivated by extreme prejudice (Lawrence, 1999). Hate crimes involve bias related to race, religion, sexual orientation, national origin, or ancestry (Levin and McDevitt, 1993). Victims include, but are not limited to, African Americans, Native Americans, Latinos, Asian Americans, Jews, gay men, lesbian women, and people with disabilities. While the term *hate crime* is relatively new, the behavior is not. The federal government has kept statistics since 1900. Hate crimes still occur in relatively small numbers, but the frequency is increasing. Just under 8,000 cases were reported to the FBI in 1999. By 1999, thirty-seven states had passed hate-crime laws.

How does sociology interpret hate crimes? Each of the theoretical perspectives discussed below can help us understand hate crimes. The functionalist might notice that members of a group are bolstering their sense of unity against a common enemy. Some hate crimes, consistent with conflict theory, are based on the belief that the victim is somehow threatening the person's livelihood or self-interest. This is the case when immigrants are attacked out of fear that they will take the jobs of the white majority. Finally, hate crimes always involve labeling. People who commit hate crimes have vocabularies filled with demeaning stereotypes that attempt to justify violence directed against the victims.

hate crime
a criminal act motivated by prejudice

Stereotypes

A **stereotype** is a set of ideas—based on distortion, exaggeration, and oversimplification—that is applied to all members of a group. Stereotypes appear throughout any society. In the United States, examples of stereotypes include that athletes are "all brawn and no brain" and that politicians are corrupt.

Stereotypes are sometimes created to justify unethical behavior against minority groups. For example, very early relationships between the colonists and

stereotype
a distorted, exaggerated, or oversimplified image applied to a category of people

Open-Response Question

Ask students to what extent they think change is brought about by government mandate as compared to the actions of individuals who challenge the status quo.

To stimulate discussion on this question, you might tell them that as late as two years after the 1954 Supreme Court *Brown vs. Board of Education* decision, six southern states had still not integrated their public schools. Many historians believe that the civil rights movement succeeded not because of traditional or mainstream institutional forces, but because of the strength, persistence, and vitality of grassroots African American institutions and participation.

Finally, inform students that they will learn more about the processes of social change and social movements in Chapter 17.

Integrating the Transparencies

A transparency, Hate Crimes in the U.S., as well as other transparencies related to this chapter, are provided in the *Sociology and You* Transparency Binder.

Encouraging Citizenship Activity

Give students this true or false mini-quiz to check their prior knowledge of hate crime activity. (1) Most hate crimes are extremely brutal and involve violence done to a person. *True. Research shows that more force than necessary is often used against the victims than to just render them helpless.* (2) The U.S. Constitution has identified English as the official language of the country. *False.* (3) The frequency of hate crimes in the U.S. has finally begun to decrease. *False. In 1999, hate crimes were still on the rise.* (4) Most school-related hate crimes are committed by students who belonged to organized hate groups. *False. Students arrested for hate crimes are more likely to be acting alone or with one or two friends.* (5) Some kinds of hatred toward certain groups of people are instinctive and biologically-based. *False. Racism is a culturally transmitted or learned behavior.*

Teaching Strategy

Students are usually very happy to describe all the different negative stereotypes they are aware of, but this can be an unproductive use of class time. Instead, to check student comprehension of the idea of stereotypes, ask students to come up with positive examples that would not be hurtful to any students in the class. Examples include the belief that boys are better at math than girls, or that people who wear glasses are smart, or that Italians are sexy!
L1

Teaching Strategy

Have students look in their own community for examples of the conflict perspective, that is, groups that see themselves in competition for limited resources. An example of this might be the Korean shop owners and African Americans in South Central Los Angeles.
L2

Integrating the Teacher Resources

To reinforce key ideas, use the Chapter 9 Graphic Organizer, a reproducible student worksheet available in the Unit 3 Mastering Basic Concepts **booklet in your Teacher's Resource Box.**

Native Americans in early colonial times were relatively peaceful and cooperative. As the population of the colonies grew, however, conflicts over land and resources became more frequent and intense. To justify expansion onto Indian territory, the colonists began perceiving Native Americans as "lying, thieving, un-Christian savages" who did not deserve the rights accorded to white settlers. This image helped the colonists defend their otherwise unjustifiable treatment of the Native American population.

Even marching band members suffer from stereotyping.

SOCIOLOGY Online

Student Web Activity
Visit the *Sociology and You* Web site at soc.glencoe.com and click on **Chapter 9—Student Web Activities** for an activity on examples of stereotypes.

The Functionalist Perspective

In studying prejudice and discrimination, functionalists focus on the dysfunctions caused by these practices. (We will look at this topic in greater detail in Section 4.) When minorities are exploited or oppressed, the social, political, educational, and economic costs to society are extremely high. Furthermore, the safety and stability of the larger society are at risk, because violence periodically erupts between the groups.

Functionalists recognize, however, that by fostering prejudice, a dominant group can create a feeling of superiority over minority groups. This feeling can strengthen its members' own self-concepts. Strangely, then, for the majority culture, functionalists can see a positive aspect to discrimination.

The Conflict Perspective

According to conflict theory, a majority uses prejudice and discrimination as weapons of power to control a minority. The majority does this to increase its control over property, goods, and other resources. The example about stereotypes used by colonists to portray Native Americans is based on the conflict perspective.

In the conflict perspective, despite being common targets, different minorities tend to view one another as competitors rather than as allies in their struggle against the majority (Olzak and Nagel, 1986). Conflict among minorities, particularly African Americans and Latinos, is increasing in the United States as whites leave cities and African Americans assume political power. To many urban blacks, Latinos appear to be benefiting from the civil rights movement waged by African Americans. Many Latinos, on the other hand, believe that African Americans are using their political clout to push an agenda that favors their own community at the expense of others. It remains to be seen if urban African Americans and Latinos will become allies for their mutual welfare or if they will engage in fierce conflict over the scarce resources available to them.

> "Prejudice is what fools use for reason."
>
> **Voltaire**
> **French philosopher**

Learning Styles

Visual/Spatial This is a game that may help students understand the difference between prejudice and discrimination. Sociologist Robert K. Merton categorized Americans according to whether or not they hold prejudices or discriminate. Draw a large square on the board and divide it in quarters. Along one axis and even with the boxes write *prejudiced* and *non-prejudiced.* Along the other axis write *discriminates* and *does not discriminate.* Students can now see that by using these two characteristics, four types of people emerge: (1) the unprejudiced non-discriminator—a person who is committed to American values involving equality; (2) the unprejudiced discriminator—a person who holds no racist attitudes, but may discriminate for practical/business

Snapshot of America

Minority Populations and Hate Groups

Race in the United States is no longer a "black and white" issue. Our population is becoming more complex, with many different races and ethnicities represented in increasingly large numbers. This map shows the percentage of the largest minorities in each state, as well as the location of hate groups in America.

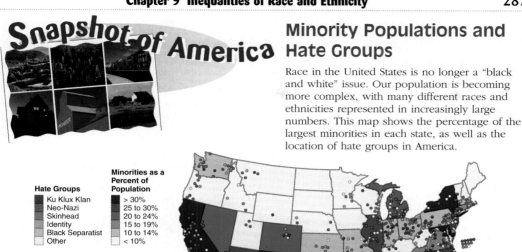

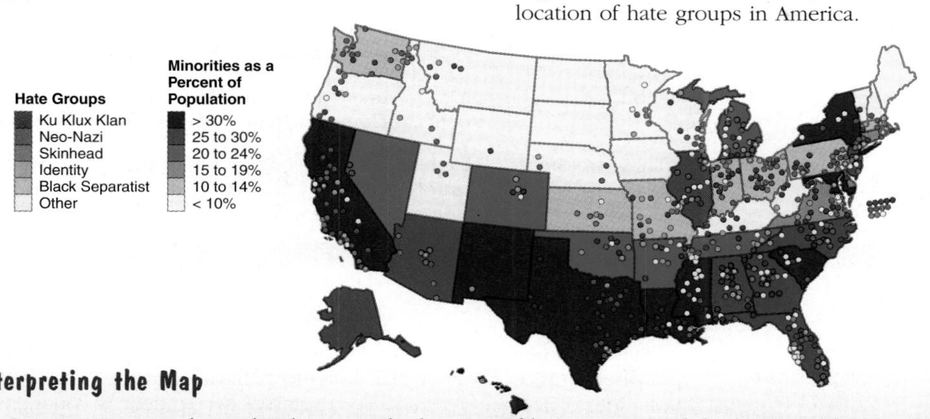

Interpreting the Map

1. Do you see any relationship between the location of hate groups and the location of minority populations? Explain.
2. Do you see a pattern in the location of U.S. minority populations? Why might U.S. minority populations be distributed as they are?
3. Create a question for your classmates to answer regarding the geographic distribution of U.S. minority populations.

Adapted from the *The State of the U.S.A. Atlas,* New York and Southern Poverty Law Center.

The Symbolic Interactionist Perspective

According to the symbolic interactionist perspective, members of a society learn to be prejudiced in much the same way they learn to be patriotic. Sociologist Gordon Allport (1958) described two stages in the learning of prejudice. In the *pregeneralized learning period,* children may overhear parents make racist or prejudiced statements, but they have not yet learned to separate people by race or ethnic group. By the time children reach the *total rejection stage,* however, they are able to use physical clues to sort people into groups. If children repeatedly hear parents malign a minority, they will reject all members of the group, on all counts and in all situations.

Symbolic interactionists also point out that language itself can reflect prejudices. For example, in Anglo culture, many terms that include *black* are negative. Such terms as *blackball, blacklist, black mark,* and *black eye* illustrate the negative slant associated with the word *black.*

Snapshot of America

Answers to Interpreting the Map

1. Hate groups are more common in areas with the heaviest minority concentrations. Exceptions to this pattern are the location of groups in the Northwestern U.S.
2. Students should be able to reason that Hispanic groups would be concentrated in areas along the southern border and in California and Texas where Mexico was the original landholder; other Hispanic groups migrated to industrial cities in the North where work was available. African Americans spread out from the southern states after industrialization opened job opportunities in the North and the Midwest.
3. Answers will vary.

reasons; (3) the prejudiced non-discriminator —a person who feels some level of hostility toward a minority group but does not show it; and (4) the prejudiced discriminator —a person who holds strongly prejudiced or even racist attitudes and actively discriminates.

Have students come up with general examples of people who might fit each of these categories. For example, a high-rent district landlord might belong to category 2. Then ask them to assess what percentages of the population they think might fit into each of these categories. Which category do they think Merton felt most people belonged to? *(Merton believed most people fell into category 3, the prejudiced non-discriminator.)*

Working with the Data

Figure 9.3 From the conflict perspective, ethnocentrism could be used to justify the position of those in power as being superior to minorities. Differential power could be functional as it causes one group to work harder to maintain its status. A self-fulfilling prophecy would be functional if others were elevated as a result of higher expectations and conflict ridden if others exploited minorities because they perceived them as inferior.

Answers to Section 3 Assessment

1. Yes; a biased opinion towards a group does not necessarily lead to action.
2. Stereotypes are often negative because they can then be used to defend or justify unethical behavior against other groups. Stereotypes can be positive.
3. Prejudice and discrimination are used as weapons of power by a majority to control a minority.

Critical Thinking

4. Answers will vary.

Figure 9.3 Focus on Theoretical Perspectives

Prejudice and Discrimination. This table illustrates how a particular theoretical perspective views a central sociological concept. Switch the concepts around and illustrate how each theoretical perspective would view a different concept. For example, discuss some functions and dysfunctions of the self-fulfilling prophecy.

Theoretical Perspective	Concept	Example
Functionalism	Ethnocentrism	White colonists used negative sterotypes as a justification for taking Native American land.
Conflict Theory	Competition for power	African Americans accuse Latinos of using their political clout to win advantages for themselves.
Symbolic Interactionism	Self-fulfilling prophecy	Members of a minority fail because of the low expectations they have for their own success.

self-fulfilling prophecy an expectation that leads to behavior that causes the expectation to become reality

Symbolic interactionism underlies the concept of the **self-fulfilling prophecy**—an expectation that leads to behavior that then causes the expectation to become a reality. For example, if a student is continually encouraged and told that she is capable of succeeding at a task, she will likely act as if she can succeed. If, however, she is discouraged from trying and told she will probably fail, that same student will likely act in a manner that will cause her to fail. Similarly, if members of any minority are continually treated as if they are less intelligent or less competent than the majority, they may eventually accept this limitation. This acceptance, in turn, may lead them to place less emphasis on education as a way of succeeding. Given this negative interaction, and the lack of opportunity to develop their abilities, members of minorities may become locked in low-level jobs.

Section 3 Assessment

1. Can you hold a prejudice about a group without discriminating against that group? Why or why not?
2. Why do you think most stereotypes are negative? Can you think of any positive stereotypes?
3. Why does conflict exist between African Americans and Latinos?

Critical Thinking

4. **Evaluating Information** Discuss specific ways in which African Americans and Latinos have attempted to resolve their role conflicts.

Careers in Sociology

Have students work in groups to get information on *affirmative action* and *equal employment opportunity* laws in your state.

Affirmative Action/Equal Employment Opportunity (AA/EEO) representatives research, analyze, and monitor staffing policies in order to achieve affirmative action goals. They conduct outreach activities in order to identify and attract qualified women and minority applicants for company openings.

Positions requiring specialists in affirmative action and equal employment opportunity are rapidly emerging among corporations, secondary and higher education, social service institutions, and government agencies. Federal and state legislation and executive laws and regula-

Tech Trends

Spinning a Web of Hate

White supremacists, neo-Nazis, and other hate groups have discovered the Internet as a channel to spread hatred of Jews, African Americans, homosexuals, and fundamentalist Christians, among others (Sandberg, 1999). From one hate site in 1995, the Anti-Defamation League estimates that there are now 2,000 web sites advocating racism, anti-Semitism, and violence. Aryan Nation identifies Jews as the natural enemy of whites; White Pride Network offers a racist joke center; Posse Comitatus defends alleged abortion-clinic bomber Eric Robert Rudolph; World Church of the Creator is violently anti-Christian.

Organized racists use high technology to deliver their message to a mass audience. While members of hate groups used to be recognized by their white hoods or neo-Nazi swastikas, they can now just as easily be wearing business suits instead of brown shirts. The Southern Poverty Law Center is especially concerned about the repackaging of hate-based ideologies to make them appear more respectable to mainstream America. To reach the young, hate web sites offer such child-friendly attractions as crossword puzzles, jokes, cartoons, coloring books, contests, games, and interactive comic strips.

Not all hate-group activity comes from white supremacists who target African Americans. The Southern Poverty Law Center also tracks the activities of Black Separatists and documents several recent hate crimes committed by blacks against whites. In addition, the continued immigration of Asians and Central and South Americans is drawing the angry attention of hate groups of all types. More information on hate group activities can be found at the Southern Poverty Law Center web site, http://www.splcenter.org.

Analyzing the Trends

When the economy is not performing well, membership in hate groups rises, and membership declines when the economy is doing well. Relate this fluctuating membership pattern to scapegoating and conflict theory.

How is propaganda used by hate groups to deliver their message?

Young people today may grow up to be "Internet policemen." This software company CEO designs and markets programs that prevent children from accessing web sites their parents think unsuitable.

Tech Trends

Many of your students may have inadvertently stumbled upon hate group sites as they surfed the Net. Ask students to discuss their reactions to these groups. What do they think the government should do, if anything, about the accessibility of these sites?

Answer to Analyzing the Trends

Students should note that frustration levels rise when people cannot get work and bills come due. Rather than blaming forces they have no control over and cannot even conceptualize, it is easier to blame a visible target such as a minority group. The conflict perspective would emphasize the struggle between the elites and the underclass or working classes over the control of resources.

tions have led to an increasing demand for trained professionals with responsibility to implement affirmative action and equal employment opportunity policies.

AA/EEO professionals need a comprehensive understanding of the impact of federal and state regulations in the workplace, employment discrimination, equal pay issues, lawful termination, employment of aliens, affirmative action workforce analysis goals and timetables, and other program facets that affect today's employers.

For information on job requirements students can connect to **http://www.affirmativeaction.org/**

Using the Section Preview

To give students some idea of the issues involved in one response to insitutionalized discrimination—affirmative action—make up a task that involves sending four students out of the room for a few minutes. While they are out, teach two concepts to the class they have not already learned, such as institutionalized discrimination and affirmative action. When they come back, give the whole class a pop quiz on the new material. The absent students should object on the grounds they are being discriminated against. Ask the class if they agree, and if so, what policy should be instituted that would make it fair and yet not delay the quiz. This should provoke an interesting debate on affirmative action, reverse discrimination, etc.

Integrating the Teacher Resources

For review or enrichment, use the Student Journal Prompts for this chapter, available in the Unit 3 Mastering Basic Concepts **booklet in your Teacher's Resource Box.**

Section 4 Minority Groups in the United States

Key Terms

- **institutionalized discrimination**
- **hidden unemployment**
- **underclass**

Section Preview

Discrimination in the United States has caused some ethnic and racial groups to lag behind the white majority in jobs, income, and education. Progress is being made, but gains remain fragile. African American, Latino, Asian American, Native American, and white ethnics are the largest minority groups in this country.

institutionalized discrimination unfair practices that grow out of common behaviors and attitudes and that are a part of the structure of a society

Institutionalized Discrimination

Many people believe that discrimination in the United States ended when civil rights legislation was passed in the 1960s. These laws did stop many discriminatory practices. Nevertheless, minorities in this country still suffer from what sociologists call **institutionalized discrimination.** This type of discrimination results from unfair practices that are part of the structure of society and that have grown out of traditional, accepted behaviors.

Seniority systems, in which promotion and pay increase with years of service, for example, can discriminate against minority workers. Because they were shut out of jobs in the past, members of minorities are just now beginning to enter seniority systems. Having fewer years of service than majority members who have been in the system for years, minority members' chances for quick promotion are slight, even though the seniority systems may not have been intentionally designed to obstruct their progress.

Another example of institutionalized discrimination exists in public education. Schools with large numbers of minority students are more likely to be located in large urban areas than in wealthier suburbs. This is the case in part

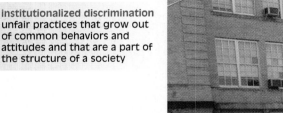

Institutionalized discrimination has contributed to the deterioration of some inner-city public schools.

Demonstration

One way to illustrate the idea of institutionalized discrimination is to bring in a chess or checkers board and set it up in front of the classroom. Have two students that are similar in ability agree to play. *After they choose colors* tell the student with the red or white pieces that he or she will get two moves, for every one move the student with the dark pieces gets. For the sake of time, have students move the game along as quickly as possible. The player using the red or white pieces has an unfair advantage so the other player will lose regardless of the student's talent. If these rules or laws persist, they have become institutionalized.

because of white flight to the suburbs. As a result, minority children in many states are more concentrated in school districts with a tax base too low to provide resources equal to those in the suburbs. This lack of funding means that teachers in minority schools receive fewer opportunities for training. Textbooks, when students have them, are outdated. Parental and community support is generally not as strong. There is little, if any, money for new technology, and buildings are badly in need of repair.

Institutionalized discrimination in the United States is reflected in the experiences of minorities—African Americans, Latinos, Native Americans, Asian Americans, white ethnics, and Jewish Americans. For each minority, the social and economic costs of discrimination have been enormous.

African Americans

African Americans make up the largest racial minority group in the United States, numbering almost 34 million, or about 12 percent of the total population. (See Figure 9.4.) They are also one of the oldest minorities, first brought to America as indentured servants and slaves in the early 1600s.

What are the barriers to African American assimilation? There are many reasons for the lack of acceptance of African Americans into the mainstream of U.S. society. Skin color and physical features make it possible to identify at a glance people of African American lineage. This makes it easy for the dominant white ethnic group to create negative stereotypes based on physical characteristics.

A second reason for the continuing minority status of African Americans has its roots in early American history. Brought into the country to labor on plantations, African Americans were immediately assigned to the lowest class status. Even when freed, ex-slaves and their descendants in the United States

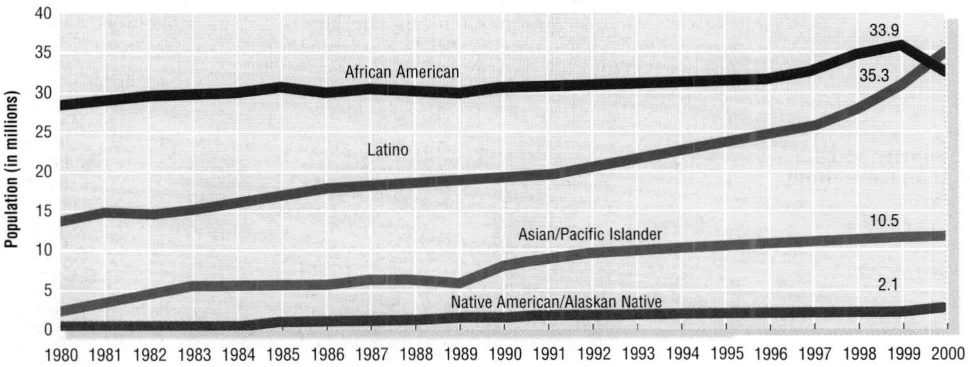

Figure 9.4 U.S. Resident Minority Populations, 1980–1999. *This graph shows the increase in the larger minority populations in the United States since 1980. Are you surprised by the growth of any group?*

Source: U.S. Bureau of the Census, 2000.

Teaching Strategy

Barnga, a commercial simulation, is a fun and educational card game that teaches some basic concepts of prejudice and discrimination. It is available from Intercultural Press, Inc. P.O. Box 700, Yarmouth, ME 04096, Phone: 207-846-5168

Teaching Strategy

Massey and Denton's book, *American Apartheid: The Black Underclass,* discusses institutionalized discrimination and its impact on racial segregation. Some college sociology texts have excerpts based on the book that you may want to share with the more advanced students.

Working with the Data

Figure 9.4 Ask students to summarize in a sentence the meaning of the data provided on the graph. Students should respond that the fastest growing minority is the Latino minority group, the next fastest is the Asian group; African Americans and Native Americans are maintaining a steady population.

Ask students what factors might be contributing to the rapid growth of the Latino population. *(immigration and higher birth rates)*

Cooperative Learning Activity

Have students work in cooperative groups to design projects that will look at some of the most important events from the civil rights movement of the 1950s and 60s. These events were results of de jure and de facto segregation. Suggestions include the Montgomery bus strike, the freedom rides, or the March on Birmingham.
L1

Could institutionalized discrimination help to account for the near absence of African Americans in this corporate merger meeting?

were rarely accepted as equal to free whites. Upward social mobility for freed slaves (or any African Americans) was virtually impossible.

Slavery was legally abolished by the Thirteenth Amendment (1865), but the legacy of prejudice and discrimination that grew out of slavery affects African Americans to this day. Practices and laws that segregated the races became institutionalized, especially in the South, but also throughout the country. Such practices continued until the late 1960s, when they were made illegal by the passage of civil rights legislation and by key Supreme Court decisions. In a very real sense, then, African Americans have experienced barely forty years of constitutional equality. The gap between African Americans and whites in education, income, and employment represents the legacy of centuries of prejudice and discrimination.

What are average income levels for African Americans? As noted in the Sociological Imagination feature opening this chapter, average African American income in the United States is far from equal to the average income for whites. Specifically, African American income is approximately 64 percent that of whites. This means that for every $100 an average white family earns, an average African American family earns $64. Figure 9.5 shows differences in household income for various minority groups.

Not surprisingly, African Americans and whites also differ in wealth (home and car, business assets, and the like). The average African American family holds less than one-quarter of the wealth of the average white family (U.S. Bureau of the Census, 1999e).

How do African Americans fare in the job market? Part of the reason for the economic differences can be traced to employment patterns. Compared with white men and women, a lower percentage of African American men and women are employed in professional, managerial, technical, and administrative occupations. African Americans are almost twice as likely as whites to work in low-level service jobs (U.S. Department of Labor, 1997).

Figure 9.5 Majority and Minority Median Household Incomes. *Explain why sociologists consider Asian Americans a minority group despite their relatively high annual income.*

Source: U.S. Bureau of the Census, 2000.

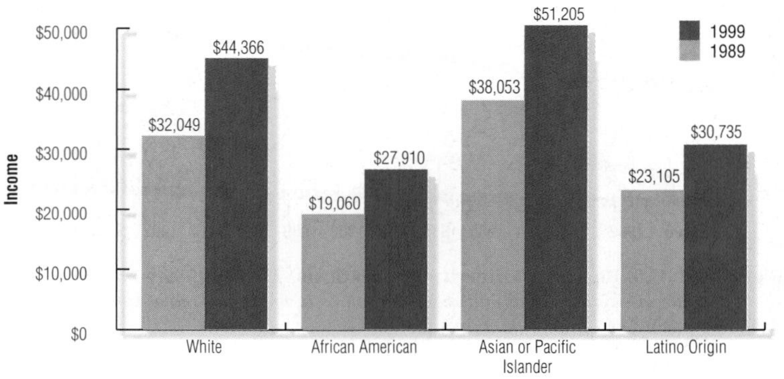

Using the Illustration

Students may or may not have noticed that there are very few minorities represented in this photo. Since this is a photo of a real business meeting and not staged by a stock photo agency, it illustrates the general underrepresentation of minorities and women in the business community.

Working with the Data

Figure 9.5 Asian Americans are considered a minority because they meet all the criteria for a minority explained on pages 276–277. These include distinctive physical or cultural characteristics; being dominated by a majority; having characteristics believed to be inferior; having a common sense of identity; and belonging to the minority by virtue of birth (ascribed status). Students should understand that wealth, or lack of wealth by itself, is not a criteria for minority status.

Integrating the Teacher Resources

Look for the Chapter 9 Analyzing and Interpreting Data worksheet in the Unit 3 Mastering Basic Concepts booklet in your Teacher's Resource Box for skill-building exercises based on the graphs, charts, and maps in this chapter.

Learning Styles

Interpersonal Inequalities of race and ethnicity stir up strong emotions in most people for better or worse. You may want to give students who have not had the experience the opportunity to feel what it is like to be singled out because of physical differences. At the same time, you will be giving them an opportunity to bond as a class. Ask students to wear, for at least a 24-hour period something striking that identifies them as members of a distinct group. (You may want to get administrative clearance for this activity first.) Examples might be paper hats made out of newspapers or

New long-term economic trends threaten to make matters even worse. These trends include a shift from higher-paying manufacturing jobs to lower-paying service jobs and replacement of workers because of the transfer of high-wage jobs to low-wage countries.

Patterns of unemployment also affect the economic status of African Americans. Jobless rates among African Americans are double those of whites, and these rates do not account for all unemployed persons. Traditional unemployment rates are based on the number of unemployed people who are looking for jobs. They do not include so-called **hidden unemployment**—discouraged workers who have stopped looking or part-time workers who would prefer to have full-time jobs. When hidden unemployment is considered, the jobless rate for African Americans exceeds one in four workers, the national unemployment rate during the Great Depression of the 1930s (Swinton, 1989; Wilson, 1997).

hidden unemployment
unemployment that includes people not counted in the traditional unemployment categories

The greatest unemployment problem exists among African American teenagers. According to official statistics, about one out of every three African American teenagers is unsuccessfully looking for work. With hidden unemployment taken into account, it is estimated that over 40 percent of all African American teenagers are unemployed. Consequently, thousands of African American youths are becoming adults without the job experience vital to securing good employment in the future (*World Without Work,* 1999).

Have African Americans made advances? Education is the traditional American path to economic gain and occupational prestige. The educational story for African Americans is mixed. As of 1999, 84 percent of whites had finished high school, compared with 77 percent of African Americans. Similarly, where 25 percent of whites had completed college, only 15 percent of African Americans had done so.

This African American congressman has made providing quality education a top priority.

Moreover, higher educational attainment doesn't pay off for African Americans as it does for whites. Although income tends to rise with educational level for both African Americans and whites, it increases much less for African American men (and for women of both races) than for white men. White male high school graduates, on the average, earn nearly as much each year as African American men with college degrees. At each level of schooling, black men tend to gain less than their white peers.

While these figures may seem discouraging, real gains have been made. Since the 1960s, the number of African Americans in professional and technical occupations—doctors, engineers, lawyers, teachers, writers—has increased by 128 percent. The number of African American managers or officials is more than twice as high as in 1960. As a result of the recent upward mobility of educated African Americans, some sociologists predict the emergence of two black Americas—a growing black middle class and a black **underclass** composed of unemployed people who come from families that have been poor for generations (Wilson, 1984; Landry, 1988; Kilson, 1998).

underclass
people typically unemployed who come from families that have been poor for generations

African Americans have seen their political power grow since 1970. More than 4,800 African Americans are serving as city and county officials, up from 715 in 1970. There are nearly 9,000 African American elected officials in the United States, a sixfold increase since 1970 (Yorke, 2000). The emergence of "biracial politics"—election of African Americans in predominantly

Open Response Questions

The text refers briefly to the business practice of using foreign labor to produce goods that are then sold in the United States. While the ethics of this practice are debatable on many levels, for sociologists a question of norms arises. Many editorial writers assume that there is a broad "societal consensus that sweatshop labor violates some civilized norm, just as it did a century ago." Ask students if they agree there is a norm against using cheap foreign labor in this country, or whether there is a stronger norm that says it is OK to make a profit as long as no one is being directly harmed and the norms of that country are not being violated? What are the societal implications of not using business strategies that maximize profits? Isn't competition also a competing value? Students will gain by exploring the complexities of these issues.

necklaces made of large colored-paper chains. The items should be easily distinguished at a distance and readily available to all students in the class. At the end of the allocated time period, discuss the reactions that the students received from students outside the class, and share feelings about whether they developed any special feelings of closeness due to being labelled differently by "society at large." Ask students if they have any suggestions for how they could have reacted to their schoolmates and made the experiment a more positive experience.
L1

Points to Stress

Students will notice that this author uses the terms *Latino* or *Latina* instead of *Hispanic* in this text to refer to people who speak Spanish as their primary language and who originate in North, Central, or South America. While both forms are acceptable, some groups favor one over the other. At this particular time, sociologists seem to use the term *Latino/Latina* more commonly. This could change, and probably will. The point to stress, of course, is that all peoples are proud of their heritage and deserve to be addressed with respect and according to their preference when possible.

Open-Response Questions

Ask students why it is important to know the history and reasons for a particular group immigrating to the United States. What difference would it make to know that Mexicans often immigrate for economic reasons while Cubans (at least in the 1960s) more often entered the country as political exiles?

Working with the Data

Figure 9.6 Ask students if the information presented in Figure 9.6 is consistent with the interpretation of the data made for Figure 9.4 on page 291. *(If students correctly concluded that Latinos are the fastest growing minority group, then they will see that that growth is being projected for future years, as well.)*

white areas—is a hopeful sign. African Americans, though still vastly underrepresented, have entered the "power elite" of America:

> *Although the power elite is still composed primarily of Christian white men, there are now . . . blacks . . . on the boards of the country's largest corporations; presidential cabinets are far more diverse than was the case forty years ago; and the highest ranks of the military are no longer filled solely by white men (Zweigenhaft and Dumhoff, 1998:176).*

Latinos

Latino is a term that refers to ethnic minorities from Latin America, a region that includes Mexico, Central America, South America, and the islands of the Caribbean. High birth rates and immigration rates make Latinos (along with Asian Americans) one of the fastest-growing minorities in the United States. In fact, early in the twenty-first century, Latinos overtook African Americans as America's largest minority group (U.S. Bureau of the Census, 2000). By the time you retire—about the year 2050—it is predicted that nearly one out of every four Americans will be Latino. (See Figure 9.6.)

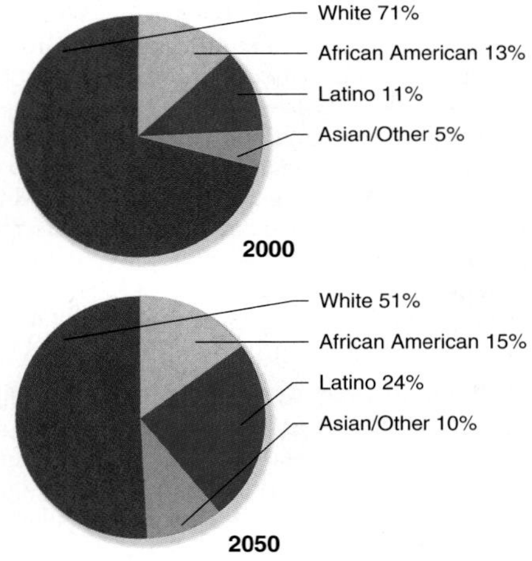

Percentages do not total 100% due to rounding.
Note: The White, African American, and Asian/Other categories exclude Latinos, who may be of any race.

Figure 9.6 The U.S. Population by Race and Ethnicity, 2000 and 2050. *The racial and ethnic composition in the U.S. is expected to look very different by 2050. Discuss some social consequences of this changing composition.*

Source: U.S. Bureau of the Census, 2000.

What are the largest Latino groups in the United States? Over 60 percent of Latinos today are of Mexican descent. Puerto Ricans make up a little less than one-eighth of the total Latino population. Most Puerto Ricans are concentrated in or near New York City, although the population is beginning to shift to the outlying areas. Cubans make up the third most populous group of Latinos, with about one million people. Most Cuban Americans are located in the Miami, Florida, area (U.S. Bureau of the Census, 1998a).

Like Anglos, Native Americans, and African Americans, Latino peoples are diverse. Each group came to the United States under different circumstances and retains a sense of its own identity and separateness. In addition, there are significant internal differences within individual Latino minorities. For example, the first large group of Cuban immigrants to enter the United States were successful middle- and upper-class people who fled from Cuba when Fidel

Encouraging Citizenship Activity

Break students into cooperative groups to research the arrival of major ethnic and racial groups in your community. Each group should represent one ethnicity and create a visual aid that will tell people about the "who, what, when, where, why, and how" of that group's arrival in the country. The aim of the project is to teach students about the special circumstances, achievements, and hardships of the various peoples that make up our nation and contribute to our national identity. **L1**

Castro instituted a communist government there in the late 1950s. These Cuban Americans differ substantially from later Cuban immigrants, who were relatively uneducated members of the lower class.

What is the general level of education among Latinos? Latinos fall behind white Americans in formal education. Just over half of adult Latinos have completed high school, compared with 84 percent of non-Latinos. Mexican Americans have the lowest levels of educational attainment. Cubans have the highest, owing to the fact that many Cuban immigrants to the United States were middle- and upper-class people, as explained earlier (Stefancic and Delgado, 1998).

The meager wages earned by migrant farm laborers still keep many Latino children in the fields and out of schools where they could receive an education.

How much money do Latinos earn? Average income for Latinos ($30,735) is higher than that of African Americans but significantly lower than that of non-Latino whites ($44,366). Cubans are the most affluent Latinos, but their median income is only about 75 percent that of whites. The poorest among the large Latino groups are the Puerto Ricans, whose income is only half that of whites. Almost one-fourth of Latino families live below the poverty level, compared with about one-tenth of white non-Latinos (U.S. Bureau of the Census, 1999).

From the data above, it should come as no surprise that many Latinos work in low-paying and low-status jobs as semiskilled workers and unskilled laborers. Mexican Americans make up the majority of migrant workers in the country. Cuban men belong to the only Latino minority with occupations similar to those of the white Anglo majority (Moore and Pachon, 1985). The numbers of Latino-owned homes and businesses are increasing rapidly, but they still fall far behind the national averages.

How do Latinos stand politically? Politically, Latinos are becoming a force in shaping American politics. As of 2000, there were no Latino U.S. senators, but seventeen seats in the U.S. House of Representatives were held by Latinos. Of these members of Congress, thirteen were Mexican Americans, three were of Cuban descent, and one was of Puerto Rican ancestry. Issues of education and immigration, as well as income and the quality of life, promise to keep Latinos politically active.

> No one can make you feel inferior without your consent.
>
> **Eleanor Roosevelt**
> **American humanitarian**

Native Americans

Today, Native Americans number just over two million. About five hundred separate tribes and bands have been identified in the United States. This great diversity is generally unrecognized because of stereotyped images of Native Americans based on old Hollywood films and paperback adventures of the Old West. In fact, however, tribal groups such as the Navajo and Sioux are as different from one another as Anglo Americans are from Italians or Brazilians.

Using the Illustration

Ask students what the photo suggests about the relatively low level of education for many Latinos. They should realize that the economic necessity of having children work as migrant laborers means they don't have the opportunity to attend school, improve their level of education, or raise their standard of living.

Integrating the Teacher Resources

Look for the Chapter 9 Increasing Your Reading Comprehension worksheet and the Guided Reading worksheet in the Unit 3 Mastering Basic Concepts **booklet in your Teacher's Resource Box. Both will strengthen student reading comprehension skills.**

Learning Styles

Visual Have students use their artistic skills to create their own family trees. Tell students to ask their parents and other relatives about their ethnic and racial heritages. They should search through any old records or family papers available to get birth and death dates. As they trace their family trees they should note how many different racial or ethnic groups have contributed to their culture and heritage. You may want to display some of the more diverse histories or some of those that can be traced back for several generations. Ask students to discuss how they felt while completing the exercise and what new knowledge about themselves or their families they gained that increases their appreciation of their background. **L1**

Teaching Strategy

To help students understand some of the institutionalized discrimination against Native Americans, ask students if they ever played "cowboys and Indians" when they were growing up. If so, which group did they want to belong to? Most students will probably say they wanted to be the cowboys since the cowboys always "won" and the Indians usually "lost."

More About . . . Tribalism

Tribalism involves returning to the norms and values of traditional Native American societies. An excellent source for this topic is Vine Gloria Jr's "This Country Was a Lot Better Off When the Indians Were Running It", originally printed in the *New York Times Magazine,* March 3, 1970.

Controversy and Debate

Casinos and Gambling
Gaming on Indian reservations is a controversial topic that has spawned a number of statewide initiatives. It is a complex issue and one that is worthy of outside research by interested students. Some URLs that provide various perspectives are listed below. They address both federal and state concerns.

http://www.ngisc.gov/research/nagaming.html

http://indy4.fdl.cc.mn.us/~isk/games/abaurrea/assign5.htm

http://alabamafamily.org/98gti/gambling/gam04.htm

Some Native American tribes are becoming more economically independent through the gaming industry. Not everyone agrees that this will result in long-term gains.

What is the current situation of Native Americans? Native Americans, perhaps more than any other minority, are suffering today from the effects of hundreds of years of discrimination. Abject poverty remains a major fact of life among Native Americans, especially on reservations. Just over one-fourth of the Native American population live below the poverty line. Fewer Native Americans graduate from high school than any other major minority group.

Native Americans have the lowest annual income of any minority group in the United States ($21,619). Only 20 percent of all employed Native American men and women hold professional, managerial, or administrative positions. One-third are in blue-collar jobs (craftworkers, supervisors, machine operators, and nonfarm laborers). In 2000, there were no Native American members of the U.S. House or Senate (U.S. Bureau of the Census, 2000d).

Are conditions on reservations better or worse? About one-fourth of Native Americans live on reservations. For these Native Americans, the situation is considerably worse than for those living off the reservations. Fully 50 percent of those on reservations live below the poverty level, compared with over 25 percent of the total Native American population. Reservation dwellers earn only $16,000 per year on average. The rate of college education for Native Americans living on reservations is only about half that for those living off reservations—5 percent versus 9.3 percent (U.S. Bureau of the Census, 1993e, 1993i).

A recent development on reservations is the introduction of casino-type gaming establishments. Native American gaming both on and off reservations has grown unexpectedly into an enormous, rapidly expanding industry. In 1999, over 184 tribes were operating more than 300 gaming facilities. Gaming revenues had exceeded $5 billion. Tribes had received almost $2 billion of this amount. Over half the tribal revenues, however, had gone to only ten of the tribes. Given the poor social and economic conditions on reservations, it is not surprising that the gaming industry has been embraced by many Native Americans as a source of money. The long-term effects, however, are yet to be seen.

Asian Americans

More than 10 million Asians live in the United States, comprising 4 percent of the total population. Like Latinos, Asians come from many different national and ethnic backgrounds. The largest groups are from China, the Phillipines, Japan, India, Korea, and Vietnam.

If a success story can be told for any minority group in America, those groups are Chinese and Japanese Americans. Even for them, however, the road has not been smooth.

Paired Learning Activity

A fun activity that illustrates the rich multicultural backgrounds of many famous Americans is called Celebrity Name Changers. Have students find the real names of some celebrities. For example, Martin Sheen's birth name was Ramon Estevez; Cher is really Cherilyn Sarkisian; Woody Allen is Allen Konigsberg; and Cary Grant was born Archibald Leach. Discuss with students the various reasons people have for changing their names. Do they need to have Anglicized names to be recognized or is it just easier to have names that can be easily pronounced or remembered? Are some occupations or career paths more tolerant of ethnic names than others? There is a web site you may want to tell students about that lists the real names of celebrities in many fields, but mostly media and entertainment. The URL is **http://www.iit.edu/ ~jfiga/BI/GUIDES/medi.html** L1

How have Chinese Americans fared over the years? Attracted at first by the California gold rush, Chinese immigrants arrived in large numbers during the 1850s. They worked as agricultural laborers, on railroad crews, and in low-paying industrial jobs. When hard times hit in the 1870s, unemployed European Americans began to compete for jobs that the Chinese had held. Race riots erupted, and the children of Chinese immigrants were barred from attending schools in San Francisco. Chinese Americans were driven into large urban ghettos known as Chinatowns, where they are still concentrated today. Pressure by congressmen from California led to the Chinese Exclusion Act of 1882, which virtually ended Chinese immigration to the United States for nearly a hundred years.

Although Chinese Americans, in many ways, remain isolated from American life, their situation began to improve after 1940. American-born Chinese college graduates began to enter professional occupations, and Chinese American scholars and scientists began to make publicly recognized contributions to science and the arts. Most Americans today recognize Chinese Americans' willingness to work hard, their dedication to education, and their contributions to American society.

What has been the history of Japanese Americans in the United States? Early diplomatic relations between the United States and Japan were warm and cordial. But beginning in 1885, large numbers of Japanese men immigrated to the West Coast of the United States. Their arrival coincided with the attempt described above to exclude Chinese immigrants. The Japanese suffered prejudice and discrimination during these early years. Nevertheless, they moved from being laborers in certain industries (railroads, canning, logging, mining, meat packing) to being successful farmers.

When the Japanese began to compete with white farmers, however, anti-Japanese legislation was passed. The California Alien Land Bill of 1913, for example, permitted Japanese to lease farmland for a maximum of three years; it did not allow land they owned to be inherited by their families. In 1924, the U.S. Congress halted all Japanese immigration, and the 126,000 Japanese already in the United States became targets for still more prejudice, discrimination, stereotyping, and scapegoating.

In 1942, Japan attacked Pearl Harbor Naval Base in Hawaii, an act that brought the United States into World War II. Wartime hysteria generated a fear of a possible Japanese invasion that led President Franklin Roosevelt to issue Executive Order 9066. This emergency law moved more than 110,000 Japanese people into internment camps away from the West Coast. Historians later agreed that the Japanese Americans had posed no security threat during World War II. (Immigrants from Germany and Italy were not relocated, even though their countries were also at war with the United States.) Eventually, in 1987, the Supreme Court ruled that the internment of Japanese Americans was "based upon racism rather than military necessity."

Over 100,000 Japanese residents in America were sent to internment camps during World War II. Many lost homes and businesses as a result.

Teaching Strategy

A good source for teaching about traditional Chinese values is the culture's very rich storehouse of folk tales, poetry, and literature. Students would find books by Amy Tan very appealing.

Tell students that although the text emphasizes the successful upward mobility of the Chinese Americans, there is still a large underclass of Chinese Americans who live in poverty in urban Chinatowns in California, New York, Hawaii, Illinois, Texas, and other states. Fully one-third of all Chinese Americans were born in the United States.

Points to Stress

In spite of the fact that Japanese American income is more than 30 percent above the national average, it is not quite as good as it sounds. Most Japanese Americans live in states with the highest costs of living (e.g. California and Hawaii). Also, many Japanese Americans have more family members working than white families. These facts mean that the Japanese Americans have a net personal income smaller than that of whites.

Teaching Strategy

Many children of Japanese American families who were sent to internment camps are alive today. If possible, invite an internee to speak to the class about race relations and the war hysteria of the 1940s. How have things changed during the years since then?

Focus on Research

Survey Research: The Legacy of Racism

According to many scholars, African Americans today suffer more from low economic class than from racism. In a well-known study of the early 1990s, one sociologist, Joe Feagin, challenged this line of argument. Feagin set up a study that looked at African Americans' access to public accommodations, including restaurants, hotels, and motels.

Feagin interviewed middle-class African Americans in several cities. He wished to study African Americans in the middle class because they would have the economic resources needed to take advantage of public accommodations. His research was guided by several questions:

Do middle-class African Americans still experience racism in public accommodations?

If so, how is it manifested?

What means do middle-class African Americans use to handle discrimination?

What are the effects of discrimination on its victims?

Feagin conducted 37 in-depth interviews. Those interviewed were drawn from a larger group of 135 middle-class African Americans in several large cities.

The interviewees were representative of the larger sample based on such characteristics as occupation, age, income, education, sex, and location. The initial participants in the study were identified as middle class by city-based consultants. Names of additional participants were suggested by the first people interviewed. (This is known as "snowball" sampling.) Middle class was defined as "those holding a white-collar job (including those in professional, managerial, and clerical jobs), college students preparing for white-collar jobs, and owners of successful businesses."

Middle-class African Americans, Feagin concluded, still experience discrimination based on race. Several types of discrimination were reported by the respondents, including avoidance, verbal attack, physical abuse, and subtle slights. Rejection and poor service were the most common forms of discrimination, however.

Focus on Research

Students might want to research recent examples of discrimination. In the 1990s a popular restaurant chain settled a lawsuit brought about when it was discovered that several of its restaurants had refused to seat African Americans (or rendered very poor service). Managers in many of those restaurants excused their discriminatory actions by saying that it would be easier to deal with criticism from "headquarters" for breaking the law than to displease local patrons. Ask students what responsibility they think corporations should shoulder for the actions of their employees in these matters.

Reinforcing Vocabulary

This article refers to the concept of paranoia. If students have had psychology, they will probably recognize this term. As used here, however, the term means a tendency on the part of an individual or group toward excessive or irrational suspiciousness and distrustfulness of others, especially from the dominant class.

Cooperative Learning Activity

To help students relate to the concept presented in this feature about "black paranoia," have them work in groups to identify similar strains of paranoia in other groups. For example, women might get "paranoid" when males try to open doors for them or carry bags for them because it represents an attempt to "take care of them" or that males view them as weak or ineffective. Obviously, this is a perception and not a reality, but it does affect behavior. Another example might be teens who feel like they are followed when they enter a nice department store. (Sometimes, in fact, this is not paranoia, but reality.)
L1

According to Feagin, the most tragic cost of this continuing discrimination is the ongoing physical and psychological drain felt by the victims. Isolated discriminatory acts may appear insignificant to whites, but years of being the target of discriminatory actions have a cumulative effect. Many African Americans report having developed a "second eye" to analyze interracial situations. As one respondent said:

> *I think that it causes you to have to look at things from two different perspectives. You have to decide whether things that are done or slights that are made are made because you are black or they are made because the person is just rude, or unconcerned and uncaring. So it's kind of a situation where you're always kind of looking to see with a second eye or a second antenna just what's going on* (Feagin, 1991:115).

Feagin concluded that what may appear to American whites as "black paranoia," then, is actually a developed sensitivity to continuous discriminatory encounters. Despite decades of legal protection, Feagin says, African Americans have not attained the full promise of the American dream. Although middle-class African Americans work hard for their success, it is too often overshadowed by the legacy of past racist actions.

Because of decades of racism and discrimination, this obviously successful African American couple may still have trouble getting a cab driver to stop for them.

Working with the Research

1. Do you agree that disadvantages related to economic class are currently more harmful to African Americans than racism and discrimination? Why or why not?
2. Do you believe that Feagin adequately tested his hypothesis? Explain your conclusion.
3. Which of the three major theoretical perspectives best fits Feagin's research study? Defend your choice.

Answers to Working with the Research

1. Student answers will vary, probably according to their own economic and social class.
2. Students should point out that Feagin attempted to spread his research over a large geographic area (several cities) and backed it up with 37 in-depth interviews, which is a considerable amount of work and research.
3. Answers will vary.

Integrating the Teacher Resources

A lesson plan for a student research project related to the content of this chapter can be found in Doing Sociology: Focus on Research, available in your Teacher's Resource Box.

Working With the Data

Figure 9.7 Students should be able to see quite clearly the direct (positive) correlation between educational levels and income.

Open-Response Question

Ask students why they think some white ethnic groups such as the Irish or the Italians have been more successful than other minorities in acculturating or assimilating. *(Students should realize that besides the issue of physical similarities to the mainstream culture, the Irish and Italians were both successful at organizing and using the franchise in various times and places to consolidate their power. Remind students that it is not raw numbers but how vocal or organized a group is that determines its influence.)*

Integrating the Teacher Resources

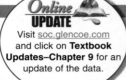

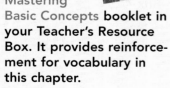

Look for the Chapter 9 Vocabulary Activity worksheet in the Unit 3 Mastering Basic Concepts **booklet in your Teacher's Resource Box. It provides reinforcement for vocabulary in this chapter.**

Figure 9.7 Socioeconomic Characteristics of Minorities

This figure presents some important social and economic characteristics of the majority and larger minorities in the U.S. Can you make sociological generalizations about income level and education based on these data?

	Whites	African Americans	Latinos	Native Americans	Asian Americans
Percent of Families in Poverty	7.7%	23.6%	22.8%	25.9%	10.7%
Median Income	$44,366	$27,910	$30,735	$21,619	$51,205
Percent with High School Diploma	84.3%	77.0%	56.1%	66%	84.7%
Percent with College Degree	25.9%	15.4%	10.9%	9.4%	42.4%

Source: U.S. Bureau of the Census, 2000.

Online UPDATE
Visit soc.glencoe.com and click on **Textbook Updates–Chapter 9** for an update of the data.

Japanese Americans have not had to deal with the centuries of prejudice and discrimination endured by African Americans and Native Americans. Nevertheless, they have overcome great hardship and have become one of the most successful racial minorities in the United States (Zwiegenhaft and Domhoff, 1998).

Why have so many Asian Americans been successful? In large part, Asian Americans have been successful because they have used the educational system for upward mobility. This is reflected in the academic achievement of school-aged Asian Americans, whose average SAT scores are 45 points higher than the general high school population. Furthermore, over 42 percent of Asian Americans have completed four years of college, compared with about 26 percent of whites and 11 percent of Latinos (U.S. Bureau of the Census, 2000c).

White Ethnics

White ethnics are the descendants of immigrants from Eastern and Southern European nations, particularly Italy and Poland. They also include Greek, Irish, and Slavic peoples. The majority are blue-collar workers living in small communities surrounding large cities in the eastern half of the United States.

During the 1960s, white ethnics gained the undeserved reputation of being conservative, racist, pro-war "hardhats." In fact, surveys conducted during the 1960s showed white ethnics to be more against the Vietnam War than white Anglo-Saxon Protestants. Catholic blue-collar workers were found to be more liberal than either Protestant blue-collar workers or the country as a whole. They were more likely to favor a guaranteed annual wage, more

Demonstration

To show students that white ethnics have also experienced prejudice throughout history until they were assimilated, show them the Bogardus scale of the 1930s.

Sociologist Emory Bogardus wanted to study *social distancing*—the degree to which people would feel comfortable with immigrants (white ethnics) in this country. His scale had people evaluate several immigrant groups based on the following criteria: Would you be willing to have group members

(a) excluded from the country?
(b) allowed only as visitors to your country?
(c) gain citizenship in this country?

likely to vote for an African American presidential candidate, and more concerned about the environment. Finally, white ethnics tended to be more sympathetic to government help for the poor and more in favor of integration.

White ethnics have not traditionally been the victims of occupational or income discrimination. Despite their relative success, many white ethnics have in recent years become very conscious of their cultural and national origins. There is, in fact, a white ethnic "roots" movement. The new trend toward white ethnic identity began with the black power movement of the 1960s. Just as many African Americans decided that they wanted to preserve their cultural and racial identities, many white ethnics now believe that "white ethnicity is beautiful." Many think that the price of completely abandoning one's cultural and national roots is simply too high.

Lillian Rubin (1994) links the continuing accent on white ethnicity to the rising demands of ethnic minorities. White ethnics, she believes, are attempting to establish a public identity that enables them to take a seat at the "multicultural table."

Why do many of these descendants of European immigrants wish to be identified as a minority group?

Section 4 Assessment

1. How are general discrimination and institutionalized discrimination different?
2. In what ways have white ethnics influenced American culture?
3. What does the level of Latino participation at the top of the American political structure suggest about the relationship between cultural group membership and political power in the United States?
4. Does the economic situation of Native Americans today help or hurt the economy?

Critical Thinking

5. **Drawing Conclusions** Do you think that affirmative action has affected American culture positively or negatively? Explain.

"Choose your friends by their character and your socks by their color. Choosing your socks by their character makes no sense, and choosing your friends by their color is unthinkable."

Anonymous

Pulling It All Together

Remind students that the purpose of this section is not to rate which minority has received the "best" or the "worst" treatment, but to understand how equality of opportunity and achievement on a societal level is affected by a person's race and ethnicity.

Answers to Section 4 Learning Check

1. Discrimination is the unequal, and often unfair, treatment of other groups (often minorities). Institutionalized discrimination is a type of discrimination resulting from unfair practices that are part of the structure of society and that have grown out of traditional, accepted behaviors.
2. Answers will vary but should draw on specific material contained in the chapter.
3. The low level of Latino participation at the top of the political structure indicates that cultural membership can influence access to political power as much as racial membership.
4. Answers will vary but should draw on specific material contained in the chapter.

Critical Thinking

5. Answers will vary.

(d) work with you in your job?
(e) live on the same street as you?
(f) gain membership in a club?
(g) become your personal friends?
(h) marry into your group?

Bogardus's results showed that many people wanted minimum contact with first generation white ethnics. The study also showed that within a generation most of the immigrants had fully assimilated into the mainstream of American society.

See **http://www.cybergeo.presse.fr/essoct/texte/socdis.htm** for more detailed information on Bogardus and the scale for determining social distance.

ANSWERS CHAPTER 9 ASSESSMENT

Reviewing Vocabulary

1.	d	**10.**	f
2.	g	**11.**	n
3.	b	**12.**	k
4.	a	**13.**	m
5.	h	**14.**	j
6.	l	**15.**	p
7.	c	**16.**	o
8.	i	**17.**	r
9.	e	**18.**	q

Reviewing the Facts

1. A minority
2. Distinctive physical or cultural characteristic; possess a common sense of identity; labeled as a minority class.
3. Anglo-conformity; cultural pluralism; accommodation
4. Assimilation
5. Prejudice is learned behavior OR prejudice is taught
6. Institutionalized discrimination
7. Conflict Theory
8. Japanese American
9. The majority of white ethnics are blue-collar workers. They have affected business by pushing politically for a guaranteed annual wage and for environmental protection from industry.
10. Eastern and Southern Europe

CHAPTER 9 ASSESSMENT

Summary

Section 1: Minority, Race, and Ethnicity

Main Idea: Sociologists have specific definitions particular to their field of study for minority, race, and ethnicity. Ethnic minorities have historically been subjected to prejudice and discrimination.

Section 2: Racial and Ethnic Relations

Main Idea: Patterns of racial and ethnic relations take two forms: assimilation and conflict. Patterns of assimilation include Anglo-conformity, melting pot, cultural pluralism, and accommodation. Conflict patterns include genocide, population transfer, and subjugation.

Section 3: Theories of Prejudice and Discrimination

Main Idea: Prejudice involves attitudes, while discrimination is about behavior. Prejudice usually leads to discrimination. Conversely, in some instances, discrimination creates prejudiced attitudes through stereotyping. Each of the three major perspectives looks at different aspects of prejudice.

Section 4: Minority Groups in the United States

Main Idea: Discrimination in the United States has caused some ethnic, and racial groups to lag behind the white majority in jobs, income, and education. Progress is being made, but gains remain fragile. African American, Latino, Asian American, Native American, and white ethnics are the largest minority groups in this country.

SOCIOLOGY Online

Self-Check Quiz
Visit the *Sociology and You* Web site at soc.glencoe.com and click on **Chapter 9—Self-Check Quizzes** to prepare for the chapter test.

Reviewing Vocabulary

Complete each sentence, using each term once.

a. minority
b. stereotype
c. hate crime
d. self-fulfilling prophecy
e. race
f. institutionalized discrimination
g. ethnic minority
h. underclass
i. subjugation
j. assimilation
k. de jure segregation
l. de facto segregation
m. prejudice
n. discrimination
o. cultural pluralism
p. racism
q. genocide
r. hidden unemployment

1. An expectation that leads to behavior that causes the expectation to become a reality is called ______________.
2. ______________ is a group identified by cultural, or religious, or national characteristics.
3. A set of ideas based on distortion, exaggeration, and oversimplification is called ______________.
4. ______________ is a group of people with physical or cultural characteristics different from the dominant group.
5. People living in poverty and either continuously unemployed or underemployed are known as ______________.
6. The denial of equal access based on law is called ______________.
7. A criminal act that is motivated by prejudice is called ______________.
8. ______________ is a minority group that is denied equal access to benefits of society.
9. People who share certain inherited physical characteristics are known as ______________.
10. ______________ are unfair practices that are part of the structure of a society.
11. Treating people differently because of their ethnicity, race, religion, or culture is called ______________.

12. ______________ is the denial of equal access based on everyday practice.
13. ______________ is best described as negative attitudes toward some minority and its individual members.
14. ______________ is the blending or fusing of minority groups into the dominant society.
15. Extreme prejudice is called ______________.
16. ______________ is assimilation that maintains element of ethnic roots.
17. ______________ is unemployment that includes people who are not counted in traditional work categories.
18. The systematic effort to destroy a population is known as ______________.

Reviewing the Facts

1. What is the name given to people who have some distinctive characteristic, are dominated by the majority, and are denied equal treatment?
2. What is a feature that is characteristic of a minority group?
3. Name the three patterns of assimilation.
4. What is the name of the process that occurred throughout American history when waves of immigrants came to this country and eventually became full members of the dominant class?
5. What does the lyric of the following song suggest about prejudice? "You've got to be taught to hate and fear, it's got to be drummed in your dear little ear."
6. How would sociologists explain the fact that on average, African Americans earn $64 for every $100 earned by whites?
7. What sociological perspective focuses on the majority's subjugation of minorities as a weapon of power and domination?
8. Examine Figure 9.7 on page 300. Which racial minority has come the closest to achieving mainstream white status?
9. How have white ethnics affected business in American society?
10. From what part of the world did the ancestors of white ethnics emigrate?

Thinking Critically

1. **Making Inferences** Several years ago, a high school principal canceled his school's senior prom when it was brought to his attention that perhaps a dozen students were planning to bring dates from other races. A reaction this extreme is rare, but strong cultural norms about interracial dating do exist. These norms vary by class and region. Recent studies have shown that over half of all teens in the United States have dated someone of another race, but interracial marriages are not common. Why do you think people might be willing to date but not marry outside their race?
2. **Applying Concepts** Recently, the students and administration at a largely Latino high school wanted to change the name of the school to honor a deceased Hispanic community leader. When the school had been built, the neighborhood had been primarily Anglo. Many of the old graduates protested the name change, and the original name was kept. Can you use what you have learned in this chapter about the relationship between cultural group membership and political power to explain why the decision was made to keep the school's old name?
3. **Drawing Conclusions** A recent documentary examined a suburb in the Midwest where the racial balance had gradually changed from mostly white to mostly African American. Even though statistics proved that school scores had not dropped and that the quality of government services remained the same, the perception was that property values had declined. What do you think was responsible for this perception? What can be done to avoid this type of thinking?
4. **Applying Concepts** Many businesses, colleges, and schools have banned "hate speech" and "fighting words" that express views based on bigotry or racism. Some people believe that this ban is the same as censorship and that it vio-

ANSWERS
Chapter 9 Assessment

Thinking Critically

1. Students will realize that the social norms for dating are not as rigid as the norms for marriage. The offspring of interracial relationships struggle with identity issues and the couple might have to deal with relatives not receptive to this union. Even though interracial relationships have increased, they still represent a very small percentage of all marriages.
2. Some students will suggest that the school tradition, keeping the old name, is the best way to go. Others will say that the politically correct thing to do is to change the name to reflect the current diversity of the neighborhood and honor a cultural hero. Students should be willing to analyze the reasons for their resistance to change or their willingness to accept change.
3. White flight is really about the difference between perception and reality. Students should be able to suggest many stereotypes and misconceptions that would lead to a perception of declining values and standards when the facts do not support the claim.

ANSWERS CHAPTER 9 ASSESSMENT

4. Answers will vary on how students see this issue, it might be helpful to have students imagine what it would feel like if they became the target of hate speech.
5. and **6.** These problems present a classic example of institutionalized discrimination as a race metaphor. If Tony is running with ankle weights, he would have to have superior skills to overcome that obstacle. A policy would need to be enacted to guarantee that Tony could get a fair chance. Issues of affirmative action and reverse discrimination exist here. Compensating Tony is like affirmative action, trying to level the playing field for minorities, but Ayesha might feel that this is actually reverse discrimination. Students will have lots of opinions on this, see if they can agree on a solution that would be fair for all.
7. Answers will vary.
8. Answers will vary.
9. Two ovals = unequal educational opportunity, unfair hiring. Oval below=low-level jobs
10. Answers will vary.

CHAPTER 9 ASSESSMENT

lates First Amendment rights to freedom of speech. Others say that the right to free speech ends when speech causes psychological or emotional harm, or when society may be endangered. What is your opinion on hate speech? How would you handle an individual who was routinely offensive about your race, gender, or nationality?

5. **Implementing Solutions** Read the following scenario, and then answer the questions that follow based on your best instincts and reasoning: Two people are in a twenty-mile race. The winner will receive a prize of $100,000. Two of the competitors—Lynn and Tony—are very good runners, and both are in good physical condition. At the beginning of the race Tony is told to put a set of ten-pound ankle weights on each leg, but Lynn is not. In fact, Lynn does not even know about the weights. When Lynn reaches the thirteen-mile marker, Tony is two miles behind. He is not only exhausted but is also experiencing- a shortened running stride and is off-rhythm because of the weights. The judges decide to remove the ankle weights from Tony.
   - **a.** Is it fair to continue the race with each runner finishing from his or her present position, or should Tony be moved forward in the race?
   - **b.** What is fair to both parties?
   - **c.** Assume that the race cannot be restarted. How do we compensate the runner who had to carry extra weights for over half of the race?
   - **d.** Are there solutions to the problem?
   - **e.** Since the problem is difficult to solve, would it be fair simply to ignore it and conclude that things will eventually work out?
6. **Analyzing Information** Suppose there was a third competitor in the race described above. Ayesha is almost as good a runner as Tony and Lynn. Ayesha does not have to wear ankle weights, but both Tony and Lynn have high-quality professional running shoes, and Ayesha has to run in cheap "tennies." At the time the race is stopped, Ayesha has run twelve miles. If you compensate Tony by moving him forward, Ayesha is likely to feel that the race is still not fair.
   - **a.** Is there a way to make the race fair for all three runners? Remember, you cannot restart the race.
   - **b.** How is institutional discrimination similar to the race described in these questions? What are the issues in both?
7. **Evaluating Information** Explain how the experiences of various Native American tribes have been different from other racial and ethnic minority groups in the United States. Discuss whether you think allowing gaming on Indian reservations is a long-term benefit or disadvantage for Native Americans.
8. **Making Comparisons** How has the African American experience in the United States been different from that of other racial and ethnic minority groups?
9. **Understanding Cause and Effect** Use the diagram below to show the cause and effect relationship between discrimination and poverty. Incorporate the elements of unequal educational opportunity, unfair hiring practices, and low-level jobs to complete your diagram.

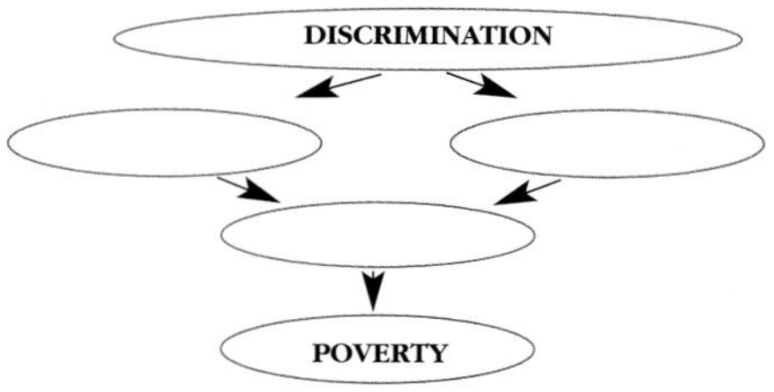

10. **Evaluating Information** Have any of the methods of role conflict resolution used by African Americans and Latinos worked?

Sociology Projects

1. Some students will have difficulty doing this activity, others will enjoy it and it might get family members involved. Students could expand on this by interviewing relatives and getting their impressions on the race and/or ethnicity of their family and how it affected them.
2. Ask students who complete this activity to bring their family albums in to share with the whole class. Students who create especially complete albums should be encouraged to volunteer to use them as teaching aids for younger classes on multicultural topics.
3. Students are going to have to listen very attentively for these remarks. They are so ingrained that most students have become desensitized to them. If several students do this assignment, it might have tremendous impact as they present together.

Sociology Projects

1. **Race and Ethnicity** Write a brief answer to each of the following questions.
   - **a.** How would you describe yourself racially or ethnically?
   - **b.** How do you think others would describe you?
   - **c.** How important is your race or ethnicity to you personally?
   - **d.** Do you believe that race or ethnicity is a factor in how your friends relate to you?
   - **e.** Is your community (neighborhood) a reflection of your race or ethnicity?
   - **f.** Do you place much importance on race or ethnicity?
   - **g.** Do you think others put a lot of importance on your race or ethnicity?
   - **h.** Is race an important issue in society, or do we make too much of it? Is ethnicity an important issue?

   After you have answered these questions, form a group with two or three of your classmates and share your responses to questions a–h. Do you believe their assessments were accurate?
2. **Ethnic and Racial Heritage** This project will give you an opportunity to create a family tree. Ask parents and other relatives about your ethnic/racial heritage, going back as far as you can. Chances are you have relatives who have old photos with dates and other pieces of information. As you trace your family tree, note when new cultures, races, or ethnicities join the family. If this has happened several times in your family, consider how it complicates assigning yourself to a specific racial and ethnic category. You might want to turn this project into an album that your whole family can enjoy and pass on.
3. **Prejudice** Prejudice is so ingrained in our culture that we may not realize how much of it goes on every day. Starting now, keep track of all the examples of stereotyping, hate speech, racial and ethnic insults, and other types of prejudice that you encounter in the course of your day. (For example, a friend might say quite seriously, "All men are insensitive.") After one week, bring your journal to class to share. Can you identify any obvious targets or patterns in the comments you recorded?
4. **Native Americans and White Ethnics** This chapter deals extensively with the effects of American culture on various racial and ethnic groups. Minorities, of course, also affect American culture. How have Native Americans and white ethnics influenced American advertising and food? Which of the two minorities has had the greatest influence on each of these two aspects of American culture? Information may be found in print, online, in documentaries, and through interviews with a Native American and a white ethnic.

Technology Activity

1. The textbook describes a stereotype as a set of ideas based on distortion, exaggeration, and oversimplification that is applied to all members of a social category. Popular media often use stereotypes to convey assumed meanings about characters and situations. The Movies Cliché List at http://www.movie cliches.com/ provides an abundant list of stereotypes used in films.
   - **a.** Select "Women" from the Cliché Topics. Name some of the stereotypes about women suggested by the list.
   - **b.** Do the same for "Men" and "Minorities."
   - **c.** Based on what you have read in the text and on these lists, do you think stereotypes are helpful in understanding social categories?

ANSWERS CHAPTER 9 ASSESSMENT

4. Answers will vary. Form student teams and ask them to collect information from various sources. Reports could be made to class.

Technology Activity

1. This would be a good activity to assign to a pair of students, especially if one of them is an ESL student. The visuals will help that student understand some of the more abstract concepts.

Enrichment Reading

This reading is really an excellent one for high school students. Written in a narrative style, it is easy for students to follow. The surprising (and discouraging) element is that it was written, not in the 1950s or 1960s, but in 1997!

Chapter 9

Enrichment Reading

The Skin Color Tax

Patricia J. Williams

Several years ago, at a moment when I was particularly tired of the unstable lifestyle that academic careers sometimes require, I surprised myself and bought a real house. Because the house was in a state other than the one where I was living at the time, I obtained my mortgage by telephone. I am a prudent little squirrel when it comes to things financial, always tucking away stores of nuts for the winter, and so I meet the **criteria** of a quite good credit risk. My loan was approved almost immediately.

A little while later, the contract came in the mail. Among the papers the bank forwarded were forms documenting **compliance** with the Fair Housing Act, which outlaws racial discrimination in the housing market. The act monitors lending practices to prevent banks from redlining—redlining being the phenomenon whereby banks circle certain neighborhoods on the map and refuse to lend in those areas. It is a practice for which the bank with which I was dealing, **unbeknownst** to me, had been cited previously—as well as since. In any event, the act tracks the race of all banking customers to prevent such discrimination. Unfortunately, and with the **creative variability of all illegality,** some banks also use the racial information disclosed on the fair housing forms to engage in precisely the discrimination the law seeks to prevent.

I should repeat that to this point my entire mortgage transaction had been conducted by telephone. I should also note that I speak a Received Standard English, regionally marked as Northeastern perhaps, but not easily identifiable as black. With my credit history, my job as a law professor and, no doubt, with my accent, I am not only middle class but apparently match the cultural stereotype of a good white person. It is thus, perhaps, that the loan officer of the bank, whom I had never met, had checked off the box on the fair housing form indicating that I *was* white.

Race shouldn't matter, I suppose, but it seemed to in this case, so I took a deep breath, crossed out "white" and sent the contract back. That will teach them to presume too much, I thought. A done deal, I assumed. But suddenly the transaction came to a screeching halt. The bank wanted more money, more points, a higher rate of interest. Suddenly I found myself facing great resistance and much more debt. To make a long story short, I threatened to sue under the act in question, the bank quickly backed down and I **procured** the loan on the original terms.

What was interesting about all this was that the reason the bank gave for its new-found **recalcitrance** was not race, heaven forbid. No, it was all about economics and increased risk: The reason they gave was that property values in that neighborhood were suddenly falling. They wanted more money to buffer themselves against the snappy winds of projected misfortune.

The bank's response was driven by demographic data that show that any time black people move into a neighborhood, whites are overwhelmingly likely to move out. In droves. In panic. In concert. Pulling every imaginable resource with them, from school funding to garbage collection to social workers who don't want to work in black neighborhoods. The imagery is awfully catchy, you had to admit: the neighborhood just tipping on over like a terrible accident, whoops! Like a pitcher, I suppose. All that fresh wholesome milk spilling out running away . . .

Integrating the Teacher Resources

To further assess student comprehension of this chapter, use Chapter Test A or B available in the Chapter and Unit Tests booklet in your Teacher's Resource Box.

leaving the dark echoing, upended urn of the inner city.

In retrospect, what has remained so fascinating to me about this experience was the way it so exemplified the problems of the new rhetoric of racism. For starters, the new rhetoric of race never mentions race. It wasn't race but risk with which the bank was so concerned.

Second, since financial risk is all about economics, my exclusion got reclassified as just a consideration of class. There's no law against class discrimination, goes the argument, because that would represent a restraint on that basic American freedom, the ability to contract or not. If schools, trains, buses, swimming pools and neighborhoods remain segregated, it's no longer a racial problem if someone who just happens to be white keeps hiking up the price for someone who accidentally and purely by the way happens to be black. Black people end up paying higher prices for the attempt to integrate, even as the integration of oneself threatens to lower the value of one's investment.

By this measure of mortgage-worthiness, the ingredient of blackness is cast not just as a social toll but as an actual tax. A fee, an extra contribution at the door, an admission charge for the high costs of handling my dangerous propensities, my inherently unsavory properties. I was not judged based on my independent attributes or financial worth; not even was I judged by statistical profiles of what my group actually does. (For in fact, anxiety-stricken, middle-class black people make grovelingly good cake-baking neighbors when not made to feel defensive by the unfortunate historical strategies of bombs, burnings or abandonment.) Rather, I was being evaluated based on what an abstraction of White Society writ large thinks we—or I—do, and that imagined "doing" was treated and thus established as a self-fulfilling prophecy. It is a dispiriting message: that some in society apparently not only devalue black people but devalue *themselves* and their homes just for having us as part of their landscape.

"I bet you'll keep your mouth shut the next time they plug you into the computer as white," laughed a friend when he heard my story. It took me aback, this postmodern pressure to "pass," even as it highlighted the intolerable logic of it all. For by "rational" economic measures, an investment in my property suggests the selling of myself.

Source: Patricia J. Williams, "Of Race and Risk," *The Nation* (December 29, 1997):10.

What Does it Mean?

compliance
agreement with; following the terms of

creative variability of all illegality
cleverness of wrongdoers to get what they want

criteria
standards on which judgments or decisions are made

procured
obtained

recalcitrance
reluctance; unwillingness

unbeknownst
not knowing; unaware

"Let's just forget for a moment that you're black."

Read and React

1. What does the author mean when she writes "All that fresh wholesome milk spilling out running away . . . leaving the dark echoing, upended urn of the innter city"?
2. What are the main issues of what the author calls the "problems of the new rhetoric of racism"?
3. Why has the author titled this article *The Skin Color Tax*?

Answers to Read and React

1. The author is alluding to the phenomenon of white flight.
2. The author contends that the problem is that the new "rhetoric of racism" does not deal directly with the issue of race, with morality or values. Rather, it deals with indirect results of actions by large groups of people. Thus, there is no one or nothing concrete to "blame" or to fault, thus it is hard to place blame or to correct.
3. The author believes that she must pay a premium to society for perceived risks because of her skin color.

Integrating the Teacher Resources

Additional primary source readings for this chapter can be found in Culture Studies: The Sociological Perspective, available in your Teacher's Resource Box. Questions for students are included.

Chapter Preview

Section 1 (pages 310–315)

All societies expect people to behave in certain ways based on their sex. Through socialization, members of a society acquire an awareness of themselves as masculine or feminine.

Section 2 (pages 316–321)

The functionalist perspective focuses on the origins of gender differences. Conflict theory looks at the reasons gender differences continue to exist. Symbolic interactionism attempts to explain the ways in which gender is acquired.

Section 3 (pages 322–329)

Women today are still subject to prejudice and discrimination. This imbalance is seen most clearly in the areas of economics, law, and politics.

Section 4 (pages 330–332)

The relatively low social standing of older people is based on ageism. Each of the theoretical perspectives has a unique slant on ageism.

Section 5 (pages 333–338)

The poverty rate for America's elderly population stands at over 10 percent. Members of racial and ethnic minorities are in the poorest ranks. Older people exert political influence through their high voting rate and their support of special interest groups.

CHAPTER 10

Inequalities of Gender and Age

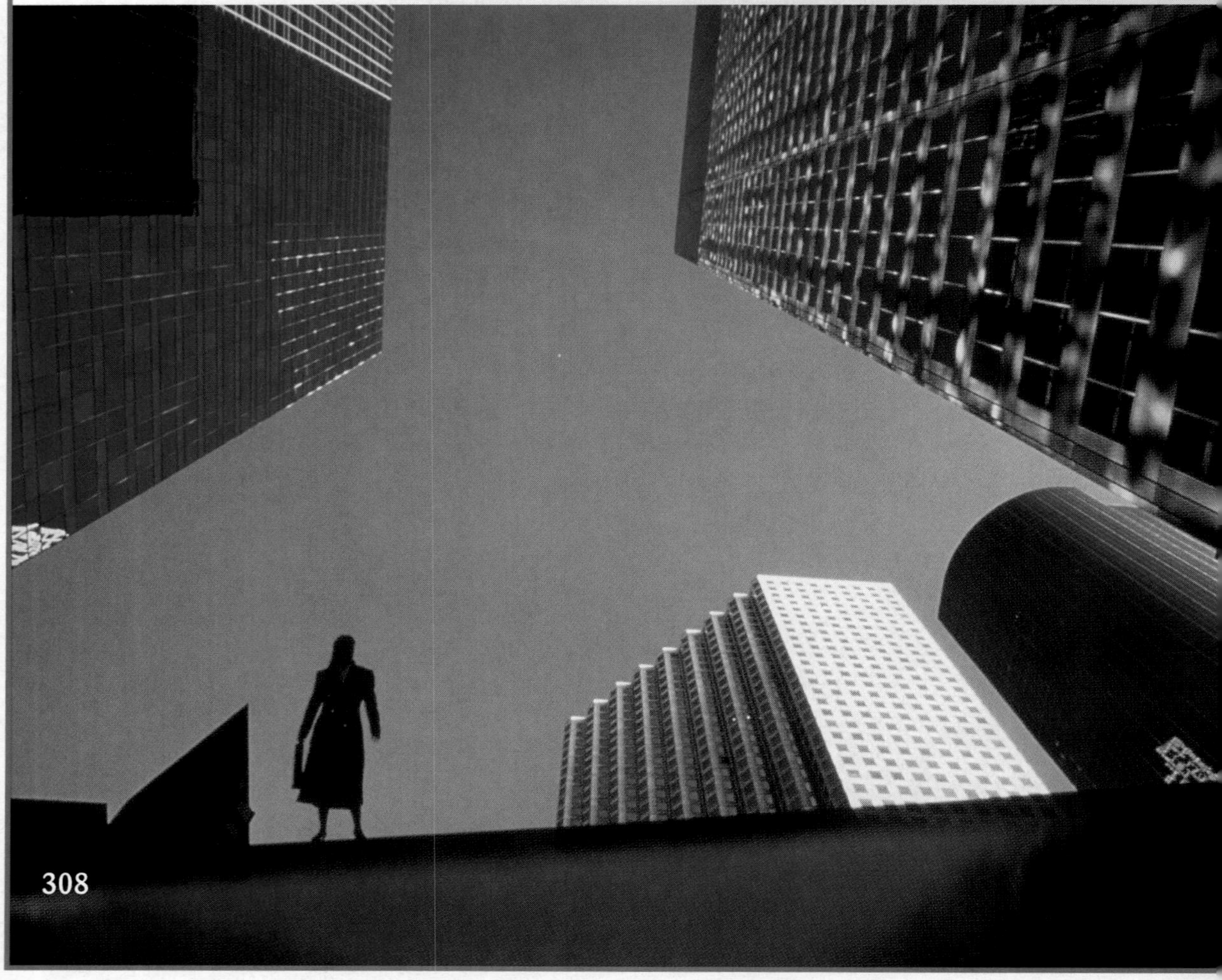

Lead-Off Activity

Deborah Tannen argues in her book, *Talking from 9 to 5,* that gender affects the way women communicate in ways that often stifle their effectiveness in the workplace. In preparation for this chapter on gender inequality, try the following "test" with your students. Ask them to write one or two paragraphs as a response to the following prompt: If you were president of the United States, what is the most important recommendation you would make to the Congress? The issue is not really important here, because after they have written you will ask them to count up the number of action/forceful verbs they used and how many directives or orders they gave. The point is to make students aware that there are socializing factors that influence women's position and success in the business world beyond their personal and individual characteristics.

Using Your Sociological Imagination

True or false? Women in the United States lead the world in efforts to achieve job equality with men.

Did you answer "true" to this statement? If so, you may be interested in the following facts. Among industrialized nations, America is surprisingly near the bottom of the list in ranking male/female income equality. Only Luxembourg and Japan have wider gaps than the United States between what men and women earn for doing the same work. Swedish women in manufacturing jobs, for example, earn about 90 percent of the wages paid men, while females in the United States earn only 72 percent of the wages paid men for the same work (U.S. Bureau of the Census, 2000a).

Throughout history, men have dominated the social, political, and economic spheres outside the home. Traditionally, women have assumed responsibility for child care and household tasks. These domestic tasks are generally undervalued in industrial societies, where a person's contributions to society are pegged to monetary rewards. Women—thought to be dependent, passive, and deferring—have usually been considered subordinate to independent, aggressive, and strong men. This division of labor based on sex has almost always led to gender inequality.

This chapter examines how various cultures view gender roles and also how America looks at its aged population.

Sections

1. **Sex and Gender Identity**
2. **Theoretical Perspectives on Gender**
3. **Gender Inequality**
4. **Ageism**
5. **Inequality in America's Elderly Population**

Learning Objectives

After reading this chapter, you will be able to

- distinguish the concepts of sex, gender, and gender identity.
- summarize the perspectives on gender taken by functionalists, conflict theorists, and symbolic interactionists.
- describe the status of women in the United States.
- compare and contrast the ways in which functionalism, conflict theory, and symbolic interactionism approach ageism.
- discuss the inequality experienced by America's elderly.

SOCIOLOGY Online

Chapter Overview
Visit the *Sociology and You* Web site at soc.glencoe.com and click on **Chapter 10—Chapter Overviews** to preview chapter information.

309

Using Your Sociological Imagination

Many students erroneously assume that since the United States leads the world in the level of material lifestyle that most of its citizens achieve that it also leads the world in other indicators, such as health, equality, and education. Students may have already heard of the "glass ceiling" metaphor in the business world to explain income inequality between the sexes. The metaphor is that while women can *see* the top jobs, they can't necessarily get into those jobs. They are blocked by "invisible" barriers related to their gender roles and gender-based obligations. Ask students if they have heard their parents talk about the glass ceiling.

Using the Illustration

Ask students what they see in the photo. After they figure out that those are buildings around the edges, they should point out the businesswoman. How can they tell she is a businesswoman? Is this a common or uncommon sight where students live? Are they comfortable with the idea of women in places of importance in business? You might get an idea about the gender bias (or lack of) in your class.

Demonstration

This is an old joke, but it is possible your students haven't yet heard it. Ask them to solve the following riddle: *A young man was in a serious accident and taken to the hospital for an emergency brain operation. The brain surgeon looked at the boy and said, "I can't operate on him. He is my son." But the surgeon was not the boy's father. Explain how this could be.* The answer, that many people don't consider, is that the physician is a female, and thus the boy's mother. Some of your students will have no problem with this, but others may still be of a class or culture that does not automatically think of women as surgeons.

As a follow-up to this activity, ask students if they know of any other riddles or puzzles that are gender-based. You might also suggest they look for jokes that are funny only because of assumptions of male or female behaviors.

L1

Using the Section Preview

Write this sentence on the board: *You inherit your sex but you learn your gender.* Discuss or debate this statement. Tell students that it is impossible to study newborn babies to determine whether gender socialization is taking place from the minute they are born. Girls and boys seem to be treated differently and the extent to which socialization is a factor can't be denied.

Teaching Strategy

There are many nursery rhymes, fairy tales, and fables that reinforce cultural and societal norms about gender. Ask students to collect and bring in examples of gender socialization. As a related activity, obtain a copy of *Once Upon a More Enlightened Time* by James Fionn Garner. This is a collection of gender-neutral fairy tales that get silly at times, but that really help students see the subtle but influential role that culture plays in socialization.

Section 1 Sex and Gender Identity

Key Terms

- sex
- biological determinism
- gender identity

Section Preview

All societies expect people to behave in certain ways based on their sex. Through socialization, members of a society acquire an awareness of themselves as masculine or feminine. Behavioral differences between men and women are culturally conditioned.

Defining Male and Female

What are little girls made of?
Sugar and spice
And everything nice
That's what little girls are made of.

What are little boys made of?
Snips and snails
And puppy dog tails
That's what little boys are made of.

As the above well-known nursery rhyme indicates, when it comes to males and females, most Americans believe that anatomy is destiny. If men and women behave differently, it is assumed to be because of their **sex**—the biological distinction between male and female. Males are assumed to be naturally more aggressive than women and to be built for providing and protecting. Thought of as being naturally more passive, females are believed to be designed for domestic work. If this popular conception were true, men

sex
classification of people as male or female based on biological characteristics

Many Americans believe that infant boys are just naturally more active than infant girls. Would you agree or not?

Cooperative Learning Activity

Gender assumptions Break the class into small groups to discuss whether the following statements are true or false. (For the sake of time, you may want each group to tackle just one of the issues.) Students should base their decisions on what they believe—they are not yet expected to have any specific data. After they make their "mini-reports" tell them what research has found out about these gender assumptions.

(1) Women talk more than men. *(Research indicates that in spite of what most people believe, just the opposite is true. In one study, men talked on the average of 10 minutes more than women about an engraving. Students might point out*

and women in all societies would behave uniformly in their unique ways because of inborn biological forces beyond their control. This way of thinking is called **biological determinism**—the belief that behavioral differences are the result of inherited physical characteristics.

biological determinism principle that behavioral differences are the result of inherited physical characteristics

The theory of biological determinism lacks scientific proof. Significant behavioral differences between men and women have not been causally linked to biological characteristics. Although biology may create some behavioral tendencies in the sexes, such tendencies are so weak that they are easily overridden by cultural and social influences (Ridley, 1996; Sapolsky, 1997).

From the moment of birth—on the basis of obvious external biological characteristics—males and females are treated differently. Few parents in American society point with pride to the muscular legs and broad shoulders of their baby girls or to the long eyelashes, rosebud mouth, and delicate curly hair of their baby boys. Rather, parents stress the characteristics and behaviors that fit the society's image of the ideal male or female, including modes of dress, ways of walking, manner of talking, play activities, and life aspirations.

Girls and boys gradually learn to behave as their parents expect. From this process comes **gender identity**—an awareness of being masculine or feminine, based on culture. Sociologist Margaret Andersen succinctly captured the difference between sex and gender.

gender identity a sense of being male or female based on learned cultural values

The terms sex and gender have particular definitions in sociological work. Sex refers to the biological identity of the person and is meant to signify the fact that one is either male or female. . . . Gender refers to the socially learned behaviors and expectations that are associated with the two sexes. Thus, whereas "maleness" and "femaleness" are biological facts, becoming a woman or becoming a man is a cultural process. Like race and class, gender is a social category that establishes, in large measure, our life chances and directs our social relations with others. Sociologists distinguish sex and gender to emphasize that gender is a cultural, not a biological, phenomenon (Andersen, 1997).

Sociologists are part of an ongoing debate concerning the reasons for gender differences. At the heart of the debate is the so-called nature versus nurture issue: Does biology or socialization play a greater role in gender differences? Today, research by sociologists and other investigators is aimed at answering these

Gender identities go way back.

Making Connections to Other Cultures

Students may be interested in comparing what the typical day would be like for a girl or boy in another country in respect to what activities they would be expected to perform based on their gender—or, what activities they would be forbidden to participate in. For example, would teenage girls in Iran be allowed to wear make-up to school? Would they even be attending school? Internet research could provide some interesting results to share with other students. Ask students to prepare a database of their findings. Additionally, they can develop questions and answers regarding any cultural patterns that may have become apparent from their research.
L2

that the study might yield different results depending upon what topic is brought up for discussion. Also, students might wonder if there is a connection between the art of talking and the art of communicating.)

(2) Women are more likely than men to touch each other. *(Research has determined that women are no more likely than men to touch other people; "touchiness" is a function of personality and modeling, not gender.)*

(3) Women use less personal space than men. *(Research does bear this finding out. Men tend to take up more space than women.)*

L1

Points to Stress

It is critical that students understand the difference between gender and sex. Remind them that sex refers to being biologically and sexually male or female; gender refers to the attributes and dispositions that cultures attribute to each sex. Explain to students that they will see that definitions of gender and gender roles vary between cultures and even within cultures when class and race are taken into consideration. Finally, for a memory aid, tell them that Barbie and GI Joe dolls are examples of gender-based toys because they reinforce cultural and societal norms and roles.

Integrating the Teacher Resources

Look for the Chapter 10 Learning Goals Outline, a reproducible student worksheet in the Unit 3 Mastering Basic Concepts **booklet in your Teacher's Resource Box. It can be used to preview or review chapter content.**

questions scientifically. Definitions of masculinity and femininity are now based on research rather than just on tradition and "common knowledge."

Biology, Culture, and Behavior

As noted earlier, there are obvious biological differences between males and females. Biological differences between the sexes include distinctive muscle-to-bone ratios and how fat is stored. The differences in reproductive organs, however, are much more important, because they result in certain facts of life. Only men can impregnate; only women are able to produce eggs, give birth, and nurse infants. Throughout life reproductive hormones influence development in both males and females.

Are male and female brains different? Recent research indicates that the brains of men and women are slightly different in structure (Gur et al., 1995). For example, men show more activity in a region of the brain thought to be tied to adaptive evolutionary responses such as fighting. Women have more activity in a newer, more highly developed region of the brain thought to be linked to emotional expression. The female brain is less specialized than the male brain. Women tend to use both sides of the brain simultaneously when performing a task. Whereas men tend to process verbal tasks on the left side of the brain, women are more likely to use both sides. Women tend to use both ears when listening and men tend to use the right ear.

Do such biological differences lead to differences in social behavior? This is precisely the

Tennessee women's basketball coach Pat Summit does not fit the popular stereotype of womanly behavior. Neither does Saturday Night Live's *"Pat" character. In fact, no one is quite sure what gender SNL Pat is, anyway.*

Survey

This activity calls for students to peruse newspapers and weekly newsmagazines for articles focusing on how gender roles are changing in our society—or in other cultures if you want to expand the scope. Students should find the articles, read them, and summarize them in a standard format. The articles might focus on changing responsibilities in the home for men, or increased opportunitites for women. They should especially be on the lookout for interesting quotes or sound bytes to lead off their summaries.
L2

question overlooked by biological determinists who, without evidence, assume that physical differences result in biologically programmed differences in social behavior. It is true that female babies are more sensitive to sound, probably because they listen with both ears rather than one. And male infants and children are more active in play—shouting, yelling, hitting—than females.

Biological determinists point to research that indicates men and women in dozens of different cultures (at varying stages of economic development) are associated with some distinctly different ways of behaving. For example, men and women differ in what they look for in romantic and sexual partners. Men value physical appearance more than women do. Women place more emphasis on social class and income. Men tend to prefer slightly younger mates, while women favor slightly older ones. In addition, males in general tend more toward physical aggressiveness in conflict situations (Buss, Malamuth, and Winstead, 1998).

The fact that such differences appear in many cultures suggest to some people that they have a biological cause. However, we don't yet know for sure to what extent these differences result from biology or culture, and the debate on this issue can be furious.

How do sociologists view behavior? The majority of sociologists argue that gender-related behavior is not primarily the result of biology. They look to culture for clues. In her classic study of three primitive New Guinean peoples, anthropologist Margaret Mead (1950) demonstrated the influence of culture and socialization on gender role behavior.

Among the Arapesh, Mead found that both males and females were conditioned to be cooperative, unaggressive, and empathetic. Both men and women in this tribe behaved in a way that is consistent with the more traditional concept of the female gender role. Among the Mundugumor, in contrast, both men and women were trained to be "masculine"—they were aggressive, ruthless, and unresponsive to the needs of others. In the

Anthropologist Margaret Mead's research on primitive cultures added greatly to our knowledge of gender and human nature.

Points to Stress

You may want to discuss with students how traditional gender role socialization affects health. Over a life time, women enjoy better health than men. In the United States, female life expectancy is about ten years longer than for males. As a result of traditional gender socialization, men learn to be more aggressive. Higher rates of suicide, accidents, and violence are thought to be a result. Men are also taught to be more competitive and more secretive with their inner feelings. Men are encouraged to engage in activities detrimental to their health such as excessive smoking and drinking of alcohol. Sociologists contend that the traditional conception of masculinity mirrors what doctors call "coronary-prone behavior" and psychologists label "Type-A personality." Movement from traditional gender socialization will affect this difference.

On-Demand Writing

At the point where the text discusses raising children in a relatively gender-free environment, you may want to skip ahead to the Enrichment Reading on page 342. The story is about a young child named "X" who is raised so that no one knows "its" gender. It's also about the consequences for the society around this child. It is humorous and obviously a satire, but an excellent jumping off point for discussion.

You may want to introduce this reading by asking the class: *What would you say if you saw a couple with a newborn baby and asked them what it was (boy or girl) and they said they didn't know?*

Follow up by having students write a paragraph explaining their responses to the story.

L2

Net Worthy

An interesting web site for exploring female courtship strategies can be found at **http://world.topchoice.com/~psyche/love/strategy.html** Another site for pointing out differences between male and female approaches to love and romance is in the Love Test at **http://www.apa.org/releases/bliss.html** (As always, it is wise to preview web sites for age appropriateness, as these sites are subject to change.)

Pulling it All Together

This section emphasized the interplay between biology and socialization according to gender and how both needs are interrelated in the socialization of male and female behaviors.

Answers to Section 1 Assessment

1. Sex refers to the fact that one is either male or female; gender refers to the socially learned behaviors and expectations that are associated with the two sexes.
2. Gender traits are acquired through a person's culture.
3. Students should be able to defend either a "true" or a "false" answer to this question. Some behaviors are biologically based (true), but they can be influenced by culture (and so the student might answer false.)

Critical Thinking

4. Answers will vary.

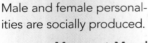

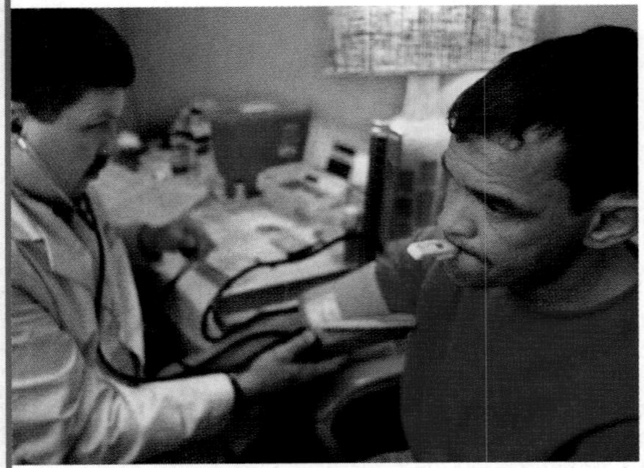

Males have proven that they can also function successfully in careers that require a high degree of nurturing and communication skills.

Tchambuli tribe, the gender roles were the opposite of those found in Western society. Women were dominant, impersonal, and aggressive, and men were dependent and submissive.

On the basis of this evidence, Mead concluded that human nature is sufficiently flexible to rule out biological determination of gender roles. Cross-cultural research since Mead's landmark work has clearly supported her findings: gender roles are not fixed at birth (Janssen-Jurreit, 1982; Montagu, 1998).

Case studies have also been examined on infants whose parents intentionally treated their children as if they belonged to the opposite sex. Apparently, individuals can fairly easily be socialized into the gender of the opposite sex. What's more, after a few years, these children resist switching back. In general, research on gender identity indicates that biological tendencies can be greatly influenced by culture and society (Schwartz, 1987; Shapiro, 1990; Ridley, 1996; Sapolsky, 1997).

What can we conclude from studies about male and female behaviors? In general, researchers investigating behavioral differences between the sexes have not been able to prove that any particular behavior has a biological cause. One researcher's findings tend to contradict another's.

Any conclusions we reach should also take into account several difficulties with the research. Many studies seek to find differences but ignore the overriding similarities between males and females. To make matters worse, researchers often fail to note the variation that exists *within* each sex. Some men, for example, tend to be submissive and noncompetitive, and some women are aggressive and competitive.

While biological characteristics exist, they can be modified through social influences. In other words, men and women can learn to be submissive or aggressive by mirroring the behaviors of influential role models, such as parents or siblings. Also, this is a good time to remind ourselves that human behavior is the result of multiple causes.

> "Male and female personalities are socially produced."
>
> Margaret Mead
> American anthropologist

Section 1 Assessment

1. How is gender different from sex?
2. How are gender traits acquired?
3. Researchers investigating behavioral differences between the sexes have now proven that several significant behaviors have a biological cause. *T* or *F*?

Critical Thinking

4. **Summarizing Information** Suppose that, after your graduation, one of your teachers invites you back to speak to the class on the biological determinism versus socialization debate as it relates to gender. How would you summarize the effects that scientific research on gender has had on males and females of your generation?

Demonstration

This is a fun "trick" activity that some students may get caught in. Ask students to commit to whether they think men or women are the stronger sex. After they have decided to go with the men, tell them you are willing to bet that women are stronger and you will prove it. Choose the huskiest boy and the weakest girl in the classroom to be the guinea pigs in this demonstration. Put a straight back chair next to a wall (with the seat parallel, so that the back is perpendicular to the wall) and have the two volunteers (one at a time) stand in front of the chair. Instruct them to

Another Time: Manly Hearted Women

In the northern [Native American] Plains cultures, certain women adopted elements of male social behavior, acting aggressive and domineering. The Blackfoot called them *ninauposkitzipxe,* which means literally "the manly hearted women." Women ordinarily were passive and docile, but manly hearted women were aggressive and outspoken in public affairs. At the same time they were wives and mothers and were involved in female tasks.

Manly hearted women were invariably wealthy, due in large part to their own industry. They could tan more buffalo robes and produce better quality and greater amounts of quill and beadwork than other women. Many were also medicine women, which not only enhanced their status but also brought them additional wealth. Their wealth was a key factor in their relations with men, because among the Blackfoot wealth and generosity were more highly regarded than bravery and war deeds in determining social status.

Because of their wealth and industry, manly hearted women were major economic assets to their husbands, and thus desirable wives. These same characteristics also made them independent. Within the family a manly hearted woman had an equal say, if not the dominant voice. As a Blackfoot once commented . . . , "It's easy to spot a manly hearted woman; the husband simply has nothing to say." Not only did they retain control of their own wealth, but they frequently controlled the property of their husbands as well. Because they were economically more self-sufficient than other women, many manly hearted women chose to divorce their husbands and support their children by their own industry.

Their public behavior also distinguished them. Their wealth made it possible for them always to dress in the finest clothes. Whereas other women modestly covered themselves with shawls and blankets, manly hearted women usually did not.

The Blackfoot Indians thought manly hearted women made good wives.

Whereas most women were retiring and quiet in public discussions, manly hearted women joined in and even argued with others, "just as though they were men." Whereas other women were shy at dances, manly hearted women aggressively chose their own partners. They were known for their sharp and cutting remarks, and it was said that a manly hearted woman would "take no lip" from either a man or another woman.

Source: Excerpted from James Peoples and Garrick Bailey, *Humanity* (Belmont, CA: Wadsworth, 2000), pp. 164–165.

Thinking It Over

How would you use this manly hearted women story to argue that gender identity of American women is not biologically determined?

Another Time

Obviously you will want to discuss socialization and its impact on gender, but there are also studies on babies born with tendencies towards masculinity although they are anatomically female. These cases are rare but do exist. These individuals enjoy doing masculine tasks like chopping wood but they are females. The research on these individuals suggests that they received a "bath" of the male hormone at a critical stage in fetal development which explains their masculine behavior despite their feminine physiology.

Answer to Thinking it Over

Students will immediately have examples of females that act manly. They will also have examples of males that act feminine. They might want to research the genetic studies on gender development as mentioned above or discuss the stigma attached to being labeled "feminine" or "masculine." What price do those individuals pay for not fulfilling their expected gender role?

lean over and rest their foreheads against the wall. Then they should reach down, grab the chair by the seat and the back and lift it—and then (AFTER THE CHAIR IS IN THEIR HANDS) ask them to straighten up. If done correctly, the girl will be able to stand straight, but the boy will be too "weak." The trick, of course, is that the male's center of gravity is the chest, whereas the female has her center of gravity in her hips. The male cannot overcome his own gravity to straighten up.
L1

Using the Section Preview

Ask students who come from two-parent families with both parents working to indicate whether their father or mother does more work around the home. Sociologist Arlie Hochschild's classic work, *Second Shift,* discusses the division of labor in two parent families. (Students will be introduced to this theory in Chapter 11 when they read about dual-income families.) Hochschild's research finds that even though the feminist movement created an awareness of the uneven distribution of domestic work among men and women, these disparities still exist in two-parent families. Women complain of working 9 to 5 and 5 to 9. Students might want to discuss if this exists in their home. This is an example of the conflict perspective—genders in competition.

Integrating the Teacher Resources

For Spanish-speaking students, you may wish to use the reproducible worksheets available in the Spanish Supplements booklet in your Teacher's Resource Box. In addition to providing Spanish translations of selected Mastering Basic concepts worksheets, the booklet contains English and Spanish summaries of the chapter's key points.

Section 2 Theoretical Perspectives on Gender

Key Term

- **gender socialization**

Section Preview

The functionalist perspective focuses on the origins of gender differences. Conflict theory looks at the reasons gender differences continue to exist. Symbolic interactionism attempts to explain the ways in which gender is acquired.

Functionalism and Gender

Functionalists argue that any pattern of behavior that does not benefit society will become unimportant. According to functionalism, the division of responsibilities between males and females survived because it benefited human living. Early humans found that the division of labor based on sex was efficient. In part because of their size and muscular strength, men hunted and protected. In addition, men were assigned these dangerous tasks because they were more expendable than women. One male was enough to ensure that the group's chances of surviving through reproduction; one woman was not. Thus, it hurt the group's chances of survival less to lose a man.

Today, functionalists recognize that the traditional division of labor has created problems, or dysfunctions, for modern society. These dysfunctions are examined later, in the discussion on gender inequality.

This family is structured along traditional gender roles. How would the functionalist interpret this arrangement?

Conflict Theory and Gender

According to conflict theory, it is to the advantage of men to prevent women from gaining access to political, economic, and social resources. If men can prevent women from developing their potential, they can maintain

On-Demand Writing

Students get very excited and interested when the topic of gender arises. Many of their questions and concerns, however, are the subject or focus of psychology rather than sociology. Ask students to think for a few minutes about what differences a pyschologist and a sociologist might take in their approach toward gender studies. Ask them to write a few paragraphs on this topic and suggest topics of study that would reflect this difference. For example, on the topic of education, a sociologist might look at whether all-girl schools show a significantly higher percentage of graduates that enter traditionally masculine fields of study, such as engineering or aviation. A psychologist might examine why a teacher responds in a particular way to a female student.
L2

the status quo. By keeping the traditional division of labor intact, men can preserve the privileges they enjoy.

Perhaps the most recent example of maintaining the gender status quo was found in Afghanistan, when the ruling Taliban militia practiced "gender apartheid." This gender war trapped women in a way of life unknown elsewhere in the modern world (O'Dwyer, 1999). The Taliban prohibited girls from attending school and banned women from all work outside the home. Women who left home without the protection of a male relative were punished, and the windows of houses were painted black to prevent anyone from catching a glimpse of the women. In public, women remained mute; even the soles of their shoes were soft to prevent wearers from making noise and drawing attention to themselves.

Women are moving into traditional male roles in business in greater numbers. Not everyone appears to be ready for this.

Conflict theorists see traditional gender roles as outdated. Although these conventional roles may have been appropriate in hunting and gathering, horticultural, and agricultural societies, they are inappropriate for the industrial and postindustrial era.

Male physical strength may have been important when hunting was the major means of subsistence, but work in modern society does not place men at an advantage over women in that regard. In addition, demographic characteristics make women today more available for work outside the home. Women are marrying later, are having fewer children, are younger when their last child leaves home, are remaining single in greater numbers, and are increasingly choosing to be single parents. (See Chapter 11 for more information on women and the family.) According to conflict theorists, women who prefer careers in fields formerly reserved for men have every right to make that choice, whether or not it is "functional" for society.

Symbolic Interactionism and Gender

Symbolic interactionists focus on how boys and girls learn to act the way they are "supposed to act." This process is called **gender socialization.** Gender is acquired in large part from interaction with parents, teachers, and peers. In addition, gender concepts are taught through the mass media. Indeed, the effect of the media is very powerful.

gender socialization
the social process of learning how to act as a boy or girl

How do parents contribute to gender socialization? Parents are vitally important in gender socialization because they transfer values and attitudes regarding how boys and girls should behave. The learning of gender begins at birth and is well established by the time the child is two

Teaching Strategy

To explore student attitudes, ask them to discuss their perspectives on gender roles in American society. They could be encouraged to think about gender roles in the past, present, and future. The discussion could be open to everyone from the beginning or you might use a panel or debate format to encourage class participation.
L1

Demonstration

If possible, arrange to get a copy of Sandra Bem's study of gender attributes (known as the BEM scale.) This questionnaire asks students to rate more than sixty different attributes on a scale from 1 to 7. An evaluation sheet allows them to convert these raw scores to a summary of gender characteristics. Besides being fun and informative, the exercise should help students understand that there is a very wide range of behaviors and overlapping of attitudes within either gender.
L1

World View

Ask students if, in their community, fewer women than men are employed in the labor force. Why do they think this is the case?

Answers to Interpreting the Map

1. Students should point out that in underdeveloped countries it is necessary for everyone to work just to survive. In developed countries the reasons are usually less related to survival and more related to desire for material goods.
2. Answers will vary.

Controversy and Debate

This text does not discuss ambiguities of sex and gender in the sociological context. The author bases his discussions on two separate and distinct biological sexes. Sociology has recognized, however, that the question of sex or the issue of gender is not always that clear cut. Hermaphrodites are generally the result of a hormone imbalance created before birth. Their biological sex is indeterminate or ambiguous. A transsexual is an individual with a genetic identity of one sex and a gender identity of another. While some cultures have individuals known as berdaches, hijras, or xaniths—usually male—who assume a female identity—Western culture does not accept this "third" or neutral gender. These individuals are referred to as transvestites.

World View

Women in the Workplace

In most countries of the world, fewer women than men are employed in the labor force. In addition, the higher-paying jobs and better opportunities mostly still go to men. This map shows the percentage of women in various national labor forces.

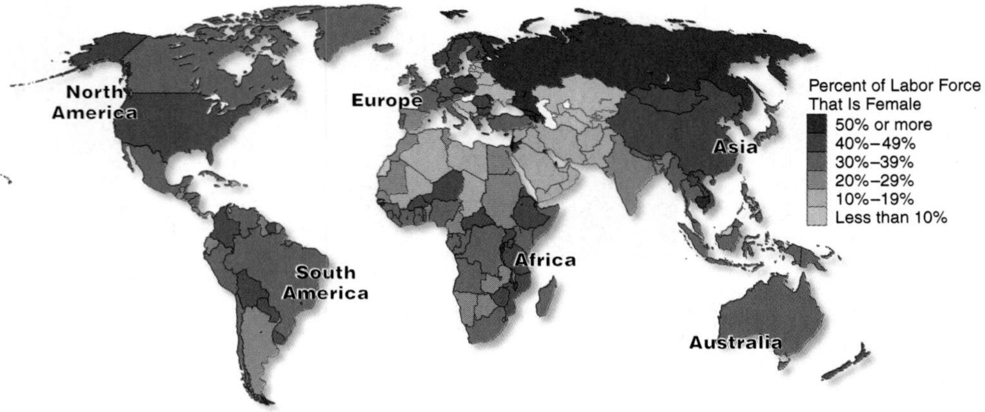

Interpreting the Map

1. The countries with the highest percentage of women in the workplace include both highly developed countries such as the United States, Germany, and France and relatively undeveloped countries such as Mongolia, Tanzania, and Ethiopia. Can you think of some reasons for this?
2. Create a graph representing any other patterns you may find in this map.

Adapted from *The State of the World Atlas,* 5th ed.

and a half years old (Davies, 1990). Immediately after birth, friends and relatives give gifts "appropriate" to the child's sex, such as blue or pink blankets, baseball playsuits or frilly dresses, and trucks or dolls. (In fact, when boys do play with dolls, they are called *action figures* to distinguish the boys' toys from "girl" toys.) Studies of infant care have found that girls are cuddled more, talked to more, and handled more gently than are boys. Parents expect boys to be more assertive than girls are, and they discourage them from clinging.

Gender is also taught and reinforced in the assignment of family chores. In an investigation of almost seven hundred children between the ages of two and seventeen, Lynn White and David Brinkerhoff (1981) found that boys were often given "masculine" jobs, such as cutting grass and shoveling snow. Girls were more often assigned "feminine" chores, such as washing dishes and cleaning up the house.

Demonstration

Gender roles Write the following terms on the board or make up a worksheet for this activity: achiever, aggressive, analytical, caring, confident, dynamic, deferential, devious, intuitive, loving, manipulative, nurturing, organized, passive, planner, powerful, sensitive, strong, relationship-oriented, rule-oriented. (If students don't know the meaning of the words, don't explain them at this point. Advise them to continue doing the best they can.) On the first list, have students mark an M for male or F for female depending on whether they think a particular characteristic or word is defined by society as a masculine or feminine trait. Once they have done that, ask them to do the same thing, M or F, but this time, if they think that same word is essential for leader-

In what ways do schools reinforce gender socialization? Although the most critical period of gender socialization occurs during early childhood, gender socialization occurs through the schools as well (Martin, 1998). Observation of preschool teachers reveals that many teachers encourage different behaviors from boys and girls. This pattern continues in the elementary school years.

Myra and David Sadker, in an extensive study of fourth-, sixth-, and eighth-grade students, found boys to be more assertive in class. Boys were eight times more likely than girls to call out answers, whereas girls sat patiently with their hands raised. The researchers linked this classroom behavior to the differential treatment given boys and girls by teachers. Teachers were more likely to accept the answers given by boys who called out answers. Girls who called out in class were given such messages as, "In this class we don't shout out answers; we raise our hands." According to Sadker and Sadker, the message is subtle and powerful: "Boys should be academically assertive and grab teacher attention; girls should act like ladies and keep quiet" (Sadker and Sadker, 1995).

Other areas in junior high school and high school, where gender socialization is concentrated, include clothing styles, school elections, social functions, and after-school activities.

In their book *Failing at Fairness,* the Sadkers examined sexism from elementary school through college. They concluded that, through differential treatment, America's schools often shortchange females. Academically, girls typically outperform boys in the early years of school. Through the transmission of gender role values, well-intentioned teachers often dampen female competitiveness. Girls, the study concludes, are subtly but systematically taught to be passive, to dislike math and science, and to defer to boys. Females tend to carry these attitudes into adult life and into the working world.

SOCIOLOGY Online

Student Web Activity Visit the *Sociology and You* Web site at soc.glencoe.com and click on **Chapter 10—Student Web Activities** for an activity on gender socialization in schools.

Figure 10.1 Focus on Theoretical Perspectives

Gender Inequality. Each of the major theoretical perspectives can focus on gender inequality in its own unique way. Explain why the examples given fit each theoretical perspective. How would each of the other theories approach the same social arrangement differently?

Theoretical Perspective	Social Arrangement	Example
Functionalism	Gender-based division of labor	Women are expected to perform household tasks for the benefit of society.
Conflict Theory	Patriarchy (male domination)	Women are denied high status occupations for the benefit of men.
Symbolic Interactionism	Favoring males over females in the classroom	Few females believe they can become scientists.

More About . . . All Girls Schools

For students interested in learning about gender issues in schools, the American Association of University Women has devoted much literature to the subject. Students can go to their web site for further information. Also, the AAUW sponsored a classic work on girls in schools called, *School Girls* by Peggy Orenstein.

Working with the Data

Figure 10.1 The functionalist perspective would say that if the division of labor suited the social arrangement, maintained order and stability, it would be necessary. The conflict perspective would say that men use their power to subjugate women and maintain their own power. In the symbolic interactionist perspective, the behavior of the teachers reinforces male behavior at a price to the females. A conflict theorist would say that confining women to the household is due to competition for limited resources, jobs and only serves men. A functionalist would say that if the society functions better as a result of patriarchy, then that is good for society.

ship in an organization in business or government. Tell them they should not change any of the answers from the first round.

Have students raise their hands for each characteristic that they deemed masculine. Then once you have gone through the list, do the same thing for the characteristics best suited for leadership. What should happen is that characteristics deemed masculine will probably be correlated with those deemed as necessary for leadership. Ask students if they believe effective leadership exists because it is also consistent with usually masculine attributes. This question should stimulate a lively discussion. **L1**

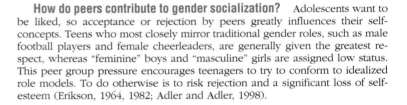

These active girls do not fit the stereotypical image of male football player/female cheerleader.

How do peers contribute to gender socialization? Adolescents want to be liked, so acceptance or rejection by peers greatly influences their self-concepts. Teens who most closely mirror traditional gender roles, such as male football players and female cheerleaders, are generally given the greatest respect, whereas "feminine" boys and "masculine" girls are assigned low status. This peer group pressure encourages teenagers to try to conform to idealized role models. To do otherwise is to risk rejection and a significant loss of self-esteem (Erikson, 1964, 1982; Adler and Adler, 1998).

> "Women who seek to be equal to men lack ambition."
>
> **automobile bumper sticker**

Section 2 Assessment

1. Why do functionalists believe that gender differences have survived?
2. How do symbolic interactionists explain gender roles?
3. How do teachers and peers influence the development of gender concepts?

Critical Thinking

4. **Analyzing Information** Of the major factors influencing gender identity, which do you think has had the most effect on your development? Explain.

Pulling it All Together

The three sociological perspectives emphasize different views of gender.
The functionalists look at the origins of gender differences, the conflict perspective considers why these differences exist and the symbolic interactionist perspective attempts to understand how gender is acquired.

Answers to Section 2 Assessment

1. Functionalists believe that gender differences have survived because they have benefited human living. (However, today functionalists realize that traditional division of labor has created dysfunctions in society.)
2. Symbolic interactionists believe that boys and girls learn ways of behaving (acquiring gender concept or gender socialization) through the influence of and interaction with parents, teachers, peers, and mass media.
3. Teachers influence the development of gender concepts through differential treatment of boys and girls. Teachers often dampen female competitiveness, and girls are subtly but systematically taught to be passive, to dislike math and science, and to defer to boys.

Critical Thinking

4. Answers will vary, however students will probably note that peers influence gender concepts by their acceptance or rejection of each other.

Survey

To look at the role that gender socialization plays, have students visit a video arcade and make notes on the following:

a. Are the characters mainly male or female?
b. What roles do they assume in the game?
c. What stereotyped roles do these characters assume?
d. How are males portrayed? How are the females portrayed?
e. Who tends to be the hero? Males or females?
f. What impact does this have on youth? Is it possible that we are so used to seeing it, that we fail to see its impact?

Visit some other stores at the mall and look for additional examples of gender socialization.
L2

Sociology Today

Gender-Based Hierarchy

In the not-too-distant past, most doctors were men, who worked closely on a daily basis with female nurses and receptionists who were clearly subordinate to them. This pattern has not disappeared despite the influx of women into the ranks of physicians. In many occupational settings today, most of the executives, supervisors, or higher-level professionals are men, assisted by female secretaries, clerks, aides, or lower-level managers. . . .

When women enter a workplace they frequently find a male hierarchy already established. Whether a woman's entry creates tensions for herself or others in the workplace presumably depends on the level of the job she takes and the source of any authority inherent in the job. She may come in at a subordinate level as a clerk or receptionist. But if she comes in at the same level as male coworkers, she will be faced with the unaccustomed process of jockeying for position among them, and competing with them for the attention and approval of the people higher up in the hierarchy. If she comes in as a manager or supervisor who has male subordinates, she must learn how to deal with people who may want her job, or who may find it difficult to adjust to being supervised by a woman. Some men believe so strongly in male superiority that they resist women's advancement up the workplace hierarchy. Such men sometimes say quite explicitly that it would be "an insult to their intelligence" to be supervised by a woman. . . . And there are fairly widespread male beliefs concerning the "natural" (male-dominant) relation between the sexes. In adulthood there is a strong stereotype associating power with masculinity . . . just as there was in childhood, so that women in supervisory positions generate ambivalent reactions in men: are they to treat this woman as a powerful person or a feminine person? If she is seen as feminine, then a man with traditional attitudes might feel it is appropriate to be protective and chivalrous, or at least courteous, while at the same time failing to take her seriously where work-related matters are concerned; clearly, he would expect to be the person who "takes charge" when they interact. Can he forget that a female supervisor is female, and adapt himself to a situation where she is the one who takes charge? It is much easier for men—and perhaps for many women too—to slip into a traditional male boss/female secretary or male doctor/female nurse kind of work relationship in which the "appropriate" power relationships between the sexes are maintained in the workplace hierarchy. Such traditional attitudes may be weakening, but they are still prevalent enough to impede the promotion of women in many situations.

Excerpted from Eleanor E. Maccoby, *The Two Sexes: Growing Up Apart, Coming Together.* Cambridge, MA: Harvard University Press, 1998, pp. 247–248.

Doing Sociology

Talk to several men and women with work experience. Ask them a few open-ended questions that you make up to test Maccoby's contention. In your verbal or written report, be specific about similarities or differences in male and female answers.

On-Demand Writing

Ask students if they agree that traditional gender roles are changing, or whether they believe that peer groups still favor "idealized role models." Ask them to examine their own situations to see if they feel any pressure from their friends to conform to certain standards. For instance, do the girls always seem to be discussing dieting and losing weight? Do the boys spend way too much time bolstering their reputations as ladies' men or "rough & ready" guys? Have students write a few paragraphs that express their views.
L2

Sociology Today

This article reflects attitudes deeply ingrained in our culture. Have students examine such cultural attitudes about men and women as why some men don't want to have female bosses.

An interesting "sidelight" of gender and peer pressure involves the fact that sociological studies have discovered that it is more "acceptable" for girls to assume boys' roles than the reverse. Being a "tomboy" does not seem to be as norm-violating as being a "wuss." Ask students to hypothesize why they think this is so.

Answer to Doing Sociology

Advise students that they need to be careful with the questions that they ask. Some questions might be "Do you have any female or male supervisors? Does it matter to you if your supervisor is male or female? Do you prefer a male or female supervisor? Why? Would you like to see more male or female supervisors? Students might want to ask questions related to other professions such as, "Would you like to see a female president? Could a female be a commanding general of the U.S. Army?"

Section 3 Gender Inequality

Key Terms

- sexism
- occupational sex segregation

Section Preview

Although great progress has been made, women today are still subject to prejudice and discrimination. This imbalance of power is seen most clearly in the areas of economics, law, and politics.

sexism
a set of beliefs, attitudes, norms, and values used to justify sexual inequality

Women as a Minority Group

Most scientists consider biological determinism to be a moral threat because historically it has been used to rationalize the treatment of some people as inferior. This view, in short, has led to racism and *sexism*. **Sexism** is defined as a set of beliefs, attitudes, norms, and values used to justify gender inequality. Just as minorities suffer from the effects of racism, women are hurt by sexism. Sexist ideology—the belief that men are naturally superior to women—has been used and is still being used to justify men's leadership and power positions in the economic, social, and political spheres of society.

Isn't sex discrimination disappearing? The answer is yes and no. Some segments of American society now have more positive attitudes about women. And a few women now hold key positions traditionally reserved for men. In 1999, for example, Carleton Fiorina became the first female CEO (chief executive officer) of one of the thirty companies that make up the Dow Jones Industrial Average. In that same year, Eileen Collins became the first female NASA shuttle commander.

Still, a careful examination reveals many gaps in social rights, privileges, and rewards for women in the United States (Valian, 1998). These gaps, although they have closed somewhat in recent years, are reflected in the continuing inequality experienced by American women (Bianchi and Spain, 1996; Riley, 1997).

Hewlett-Packard president and CEO Carleton Fiorina has successfully battled sexism in her career.

Occupational and Economic Inequality

By far the most important labor development in the United States over the last thirty years has been the dramatic increase in the number and proportion of women in the workforce. In 1999, 65 percent of women worked outside the home compared with 77 percent of men. That same year, women represented just under 50 percent of the U.S. labor force. (See Figure 10.2 on the next page.)

Using the Section Preview

Share with students the fact that the areas where women have made the most gains are in education, health care, and human service jobs. Ask students why they think the pursuit of gender equality has been more successful in these areas and why they think women have not been as successful in achieving job equality in the areas of economics, law, and politics.

Teaching Strategy

Have students create a hypothesis about gender discrimination in sports at your school. Do they think that boys' sports are more valued? If so, have them conduct a survey, referring to chapter 2 for the correct methodology. They should create a study and then see what other research corroborates their findings.
L3

Integrating the Teachers Resources

Look for the Chapter 10 Vocabulary Activity worksheet in the Unit 3 Mastering Basic Concepts booklet in your Teacher's Resource Box. It provides reinforcement for vocabulary in this chapter.

Observation

Ask students to work in pairs to reconnoiter a neighborhood toy store to see the balance of gender specific and gender neutral toys. Have students walk down one aisle (avoiding the dolls and trucks aisles) and identify toys by whether the packaging is designed to appeal to girls, boys, or both. Have them put their results in a visual report form and share it with the rest of the class.
L2

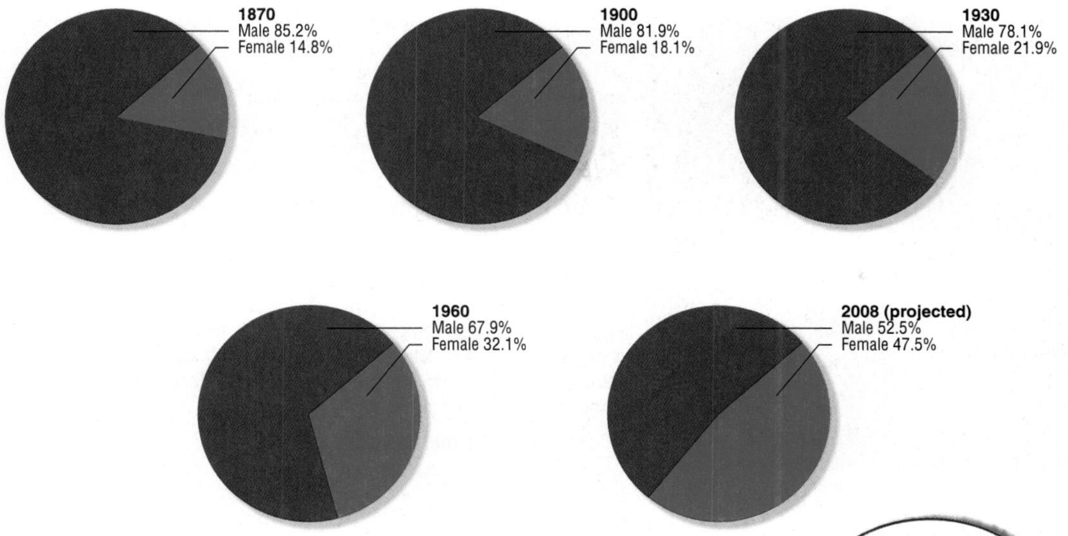

Figure 10.2 Composition of the U.S. Labor Force, by Sex: 1870–2006. *As this figure demonstrates, the male-female composition of the U.S. labor force has steadily moved toward parity. The female percentage of the labor force has moved from less than 15 percent in 1870 to just under 50 percent today. What do you think is the most important social consequence of this change?*

Source: U.S. Bureau of Labor Statistics, 2001.

Online UPDATE
Visit soc.glencoe.com and click on **Textbook Updates–Chapter 10** for an update of the data.

The greatest change in patterns of work involves married women with children under six years of age. The proportion of women in this group who work outside the home rocketed from 19 percent in 1960 to 37 percent in 1975 to 64.6 percent in 2000 (U.S. Bureau of Labor Statistics, 2001). (A discussion of working women's effects on the family appears in Chapter 11.)

What kinds of jobs are women doing? Although women are participating in the labor force at increasing levels, they are concentrated in lower-status occupations. This is known as **occupational sex segregation.** Only 11 percent of engineer positions are held by women, and about 29 percent of attorney jobs. By contrast, women occupy nearly all of the "pink-collar" jobs—secretaries, clerks, stenographers—whose purpose is to support those higher up the occupational ladder (U.S. Bureau of the Census, 2000d). Moreover, when women are in high-status occupational groups, they are concentrated in lower-prestige, lower-paid jobs. Female lawyers in firms seldom occupy the higher-level administrative positions. Even within female-dominated occupations, such as public school administration, a disproportionate share of higher positions are filled by men.

occupational sex segregation the concentration of women in lower-status positions

Do women earn less than men? As you read in the Using Your Sociological Imagination feature at the beginning of the chapter, there is a

Working with the Data

Figure 10.2 Students will most likely refer to the great effect that working women have had on family and home activities. Ask students if they think the proportion of females in the labor force will continue to increase, or do they think it will level off.

You might also want to discuss how modern scientific research has changed work-related norms among women. Students should recognize that recent scientific research has failed to establish any biological basis for gender-based norms. As a result, norms differentiating between male and female are weakening.

Teaching Strategy

At this point you might ask students to complete Project # 1 in the Chapter Review on page 340. This activity will allow students to see how a subtle form of sexism permeates our society, in this case through the medium of magazines. Have students turn their collection of pictures into a booklet and display them in the class. It has tremendous impact when all the projects are gathered together.
L2

Survey

To provide an opportunity for students to internalize some of the concepts in this chapter regarding gender inequalities, as well as to practice some of the mathematical research skills needed by sociologists, ask them to conduct a survey. Work with students to develop survey questions regarding gender, economics, and employment, then have each student collect a specified number of responses. You can structure the survey to be answered by females only, or by both men and women. Questions may include items such as "Do you work outside the home?" or "Who makes more money in your home – the male or the female?" To conclude, you may want to have students work in small groups to tabulate the results of their survey and then compare the findings from the different groups.
L2

wide discrepancy between the earnings of American women and men. In 1999, women who worked full-time earned only seventy-two cents for every dollar earned by men. To put it another way, women now work about seven days to earn as much as men earn in five days. The good news is that this salary gap has decreased since 1980, when women were earning 60 percent as much as men. (See Figure 10.3 below.)

Are all occupations affected? In virtually every occupational category, men's earning power outstrips that of women. The earnings gap persists, regardless of educational attainment. Women in the same professional occupations as men earn less than their male counterparts, as illustrated in Figure 10.4 on the opposite page. This is true even for women who have pursued careers on a full-time basis for all of their adult lives. Furthermore, males in female-dominated occupations typically earn more than women.

How do American women fare globally? As noted in the Using Your Sociological Imagination feature opening this chapter, women in the United States do not fare very well economically compared with women in other developed countries. Here, of course, we are talking about relative earning power, or what women earn compared to men—not absolute dollar amounts. Although women in the United States are not at the bottom of the equality list, they are closer to the bottom than the top. In dramatic contrast is Australia, where women earn more than men! (See Figure 10.5.)

These Japanese women are almost certainly not earning as much as men in equivalent positions.

Online UPDATE
Visit soc.glencoe.com and click on **Textbook Updates–Chapter 10** for an update of the data.

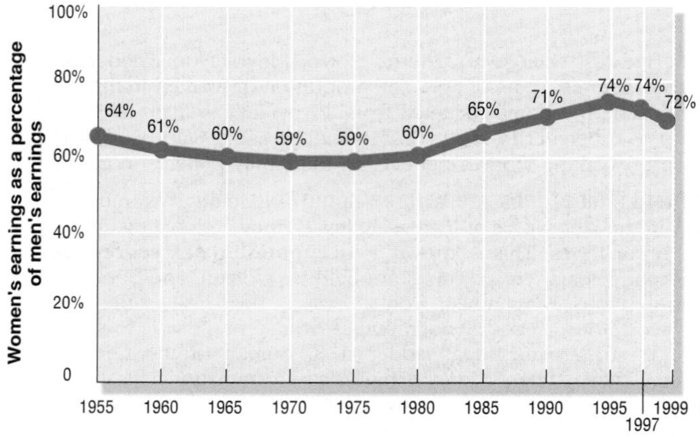

Figure 10.3 What Women Earn Compared to Men. *This figure traces the ratio of women's to men's earnings since 1955. Discuss two important conclusions you can make from these data. Use material in the text to help.*

Source: U.S. Department of Labor, Bureau of Labor Statistics, 2001.

Controversy and Debate

Sometimes you hear it said that women want it both ways—-they want to work and they want to have families. Society today is very "conflicted" about the responsibilities of women toward careers and families. Women get many mixed messages. To see what the students think about this issue, make this statement in a casual but sincere manner: "Well it's no wonder that women don't earn as much money. How could they when they are continually taking time off to have children?" Let students react to this statement and for those that seem particularly concerned, suggest they do some research to analyze how pregnancy affects earnings for women. Recommend that they look at countries with relatively permissive policies for paternity leaves for men, such as the Scandanavian countries. Have students report back to the class with what they have uncovered.

Working with the Data

Figure 10.3 Students might wonder about the drop in women's wages from 1965 to 1980. Ask students to suggest reasons this might have occurred. *(Possible answers include a recession or high unemployment—both situations would make the labor market for women less favorable.)*

Interdisciplinary Activity

Multicultural Studies Assign students (individually or in groups) the task of describing the cultural attitudes towards women in other cultures. This activity will help students understand how one's socialization contributes to one's understanding of their gender role.

(Be sure students look at a variety of countries, developed and undeveloped.) As an extension activity, ask students to discuss how American companies with overseas employees should structure their organizations

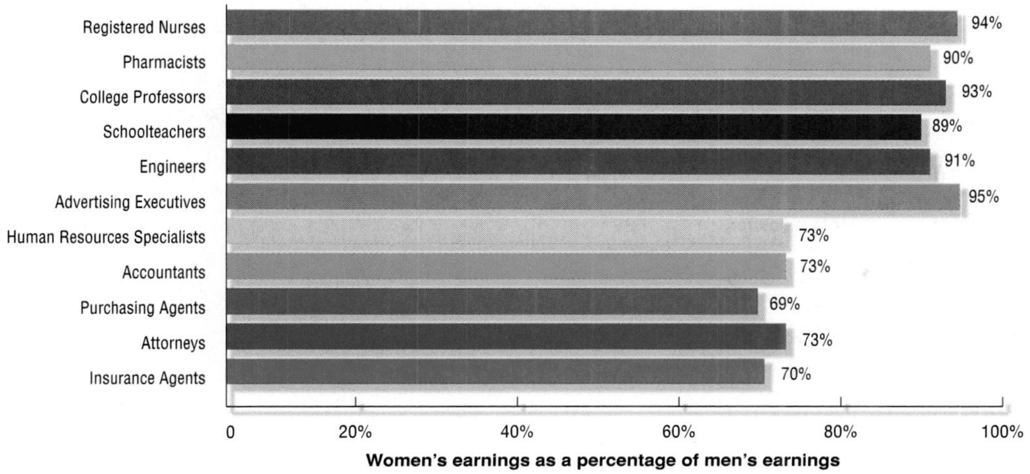

Figure 10.4 Female-to-Male Earnings: 2000. *On average, women in the U.S. earn about 72 cents for every dollar a man earns. In what way do the data in this figure support the contention that gender inequality is real?*

Source: "The 21st Annual Salary Survey," *Working Woman* (August, 2000).

Legal and Political Inequality

Supporters of women's rights point to laws that show a bias against women. National, state, and local legal codes, they claim, reflect a sexual bias that results in important differences between the levels of political power of women and men.

What are some biases in law? An example that women's groups point to is the U.S. Supreme Court decision that refused to grant women the legal guarantee of health insurance benefits for pregnancy-related medical costs. This was despite the fact that medical coverage for conditions unique to men—such as prostate problems and vasectomies—was routinely provided.

Some states have traditionally refused women the right to keep their own surnames after marriage. Other states have had *protective legislation* restricting women's rights. Such protective legislation limited the number of hours women could work. It also limited the conditions under which they could work, with actions such as barring women from toxic areas because of potential birth defects in their children. It even limited the kinds of work they could do by regulating such matters as the amount of weight a woman could be permitted to lift (thirty pounds). Supporters of these laws viewed them as

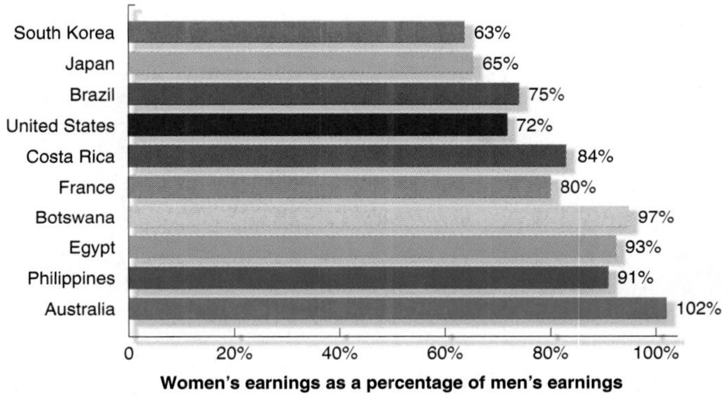

Figure 10.5 Women's Wages Compared with Men's Wages in Selected Countries. *This figure compares what men and women earn in various foreign countries. The data only considers the wages of nonagricultural workers. What does the score of 102 percent for Australia mean?*

Source: International Labour Organization, *Yearbook of Labour Statistics*, 2000.

Working with the Data

Figure 10.4 Students should conclude that the professions where women and men come the closest to equal pay are those that have traditionally been open to women the longest. In the traditional male occupations, wage inequity is more pronounced.

Working with the Data

Figure 10.5 Students should understand that the rank, or score, of 102 percent for Australia means that women actually earn more than men by 2 percent. See if students can suggest any reason why this may be so. *(Because of the "rough and ready" conditions in Australia and its unique history of settlement, women were forced to take a more active role in the economy. As such, the nation has a history of strong gender equality and women have suffered less from economic discrimination.)*

to reflect the host national culture and still serve the interests of the business. Should they, in fact, take the culture into consideration if it violates basic American norms (or legal requirements) such as equality in the workplace? If you don't have time to do this now, you may want to use this activity when students are studying Chapter 9 about political and economic issues.
L2

Working with the Data

Figure 10.6 The area of politics is still male dominated. Women got off to a very late start in elective politics because the vote was withheld from them for many years. However, women appear to be participating in elective politics at an increasing rate. The number of female U.S. senators increased from two to nine over the 1990s.

The text states that the number of women holding public office in the United States is among the lowest in the Western world. Ask students why they think this is true? Do they have suggestions for changing this, or are things OK the way they are now?

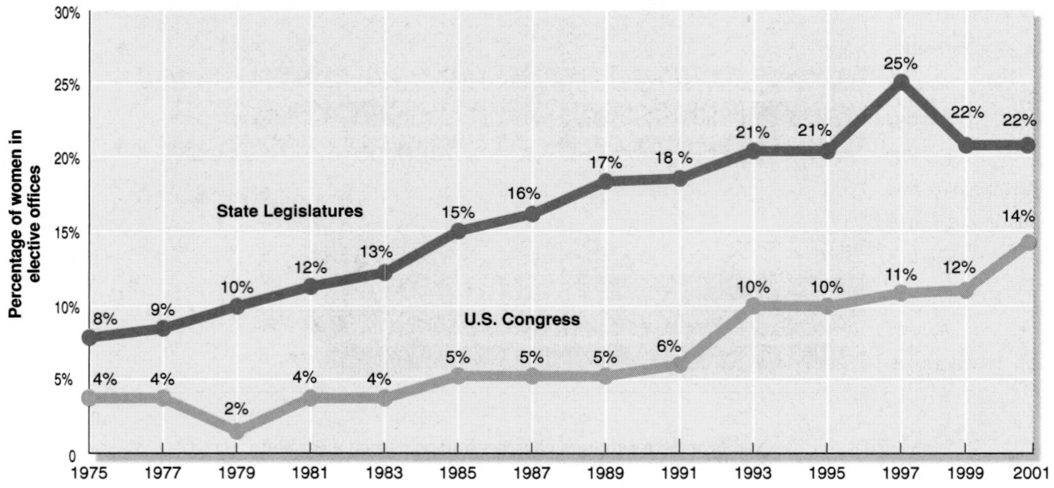

Figure 10.6 Percentages of Women in Elective Offices. *This graph shows the degree of female success in elective politics from 1975 to today. Explain why the figures are still so low.*

Source: Center for the American Woman and Politics, National Information Bank on Women in Public Office, Eagleton Institute of Politics, Rutgers University.

safeguards against abuse and exploitation of women. However, the end result was that women were denied certain jobs, many of which are better paid than more traditional occupations for women.

Passage of Title VII of the Civil Rights Act of 1964 nullified such laws but their practice still lingers. Moreover, the Family and Medical Leave Act (1993), which requires that employees be given up to twelve weeks without pay for childbirth, adoption, personal illness, or caring for a family member with a serious illness, still negatively affects women. Because women are more likely to take maternity leave than men are to take paternity leave, this legislation gives employers another reason to give hiring preference to men.

> "This woman's place is in the House—the House of Representatives."
>
> Bella Abzug
> U.S. representative

There are differences by gender in criminal law as well. Certain crimes are typically associated with one gender or the other. For example, laws against prostitution are generally enforced against only the female prostitutes, while their male customers go free.

How do American women stand politically? Women appear to be participating in elective politics at an increasing rate. (See Figure 10.6 above.) Recently, the numbers of female governors, lieutenant governors, attorneys general, and mayors have been growing. Some increases have occurred at the national level as well. In 1988, Geraldine Ferraro became the first female vice-presidential candidate in the history of the United States; Madeleine Albright was named the first female secretary of state in 1996; Elizabeth Dole campaigned for her party's nomination for president before the election of 2000.

Still, although women constitute more than half the population, they hold a relatively small proportion of important political positions. (See Figure 10.7.)

Careers in Sociology

Students might be interested in learning about entry-level careers in helping to balance the inequalities of gender and age.

- **Eligibility workers** screen prospective beneficiaries of government programs to determine eligibility for the program's services.
- **Lobbying researchers** identify information that can be used to support the positions and the efforts of lobbyists. This work involves library research, attendance at conferences and committee meetings, and writing of reports. Employers include special and public interest groups and professional lobbyists.
- **Social work assistants** help to furnish counseling and referral services to individuals and families. They handle intake, maintain files, interact with referral agencies, and document cases. Government

Figure 10.7 Women in National, State, and Local Political Positions, 1999

This table contains the number and percentage of women today in selected political positions. Describe the types of political offices in which women have been the most successful.

Position	Number of Women	Percentage Female
Federal legislative branch		
U.S. representative	60	14%
U.S. senator	13	13
House leadership post	5	1
Senate leadership post	5	5
Federal judicial branch		
Supreme Court justice	2	22
U.S. Court of Appeals, chief judge	1	8
U.S. District Court judge	7	8
Federal executive branch		
Cabinet member	3	21
Executive agency head	2	22
Principal advisor, office of the president	4	36
State executive branch		
Governor	5	10
Lt. governor	17	34
Attorney general	8	16
Secretary of state	13	26
State treasurer	11	22
State legislative branch		
State representative	1,267	23
State senator	396	20
Local executive branch		
Mayors of 100 largest cities	12	12
Mayors of cities over 30,000	202	21
All mayors and municipal council members in cities over 10,000	4,513	21

Source: Center for the American Woman and Politics, Rutgers University, "Fact Sheet," 2001.

Online UPDATE
Visit soc.glencoe.com and click on **Textbook Updates–Chapter 10** for an update of the data.

agencies, hospitals, and social workers in private practice hire assistants.

- **Sociological research assistants** do analysis, study policy issues, prepare reports, and coordinate interdisciplinary studies. They may work for "think tanks," universities, or public research agencies.
- **Survey assistants** help design survey interviews and questionnaires, interview subjects, manage interviewers, collect and analyze data, and document and present findings. Government agencies and private surveying and market research organizations hire survey assistants.

Students can link to **http://www.careermag.com/diversity/saludos1.html** for more ideas.

Working with the Data

Figure 10.7 The pattern that should emerge is that women have been more successful on the local levels as opposed to the state and federal levels. Is this because women don't get hired into ranking positions (glass ceiling) thus they are not qualified by experience for key appointments or positions when they become available? Do students think that women don't have the same aspirations as men? With the emphasis that men put on power, would it make sense that women would aspire to powerful positions?

Teaching Strategy

Ask students to work in groups to present short role-plays or skits about how working, social, or political conditions have changed for women over the last 200 years. Any good history textbook will provide basic information about such topics as the impact of protective legislation on women, working hours, occupational trends, etc. Fears around the turn of the century surrounded lengthening the workday and the adverse effects that would have on women who might bear children. Have students research these laws and how they affected American attitudes about the role that women should play in society.
L2

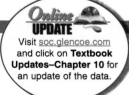

Pulling it All Together

The prejudice and discrimination that still plague women are exemplified in sexism, occupational, economic and political inequality, due in part to attitudes that have remained throughout history.

Answers to Section 3 Assessment

1. Sexism is defined as a set of beliefs, attitudes, norms, and values used to justify gender inequality.
2. Answers may include some of the following examples cited in the text: the U.S. Supreme Court refused to grant women the legal guarantee of health insurance benefits for pregnancy-related medical costs; some states refuse women the right to keep their own surnames after marriage; some states have *protective legislation* restricting women's rights (regarding working hours and conditions), which may deny them certain jobs; some laws are only enforced against one gender (laws against prostitution are generally only enforced against women).

Critical Thinking

3. Answers will vary, but should be supported with reasons and examples, where possible.

Women are more likely than men to take extended leaves of absence for such things as maternity leave. How does this affect their lifetime earnings?

Women occupied only 13.8 percent of the seats in the U.S. House of Representatives in 2001. And although the number of female U.S. senators increased from two to thirteen over the 1990s, women still represented just 13 percent of the Senate in 2001 (Center for the American Woman and Politics, 2001). Women in Congress have seldom risen to positions of power. Only ten females chair House or Senate standing committees.

The record for women in appointed offices is also poor. Although there have been recent increases in the number of appointments, the total is extremely small. When President Jimmy Carter appointed two women to his cabinet in 1977, it was the first time two women had sat on the Cabinet at one time. President Bill Clinton, almost twenty years later, appointed three women to Cabinet posts. Still, the total number of women who have ever served as Cabinet officers is very small. President Ronald Reagan appointed the first woman Supreme Court justice, Sandra Day O'Connor, in 1981; and President Clinton elevated Ruth Bader Ginsburg to the high court in 1993. Only a small percentage of federal judges are women.

The number of women holding public office in the United States is among the lowest in the Western world. With some notable exceptions, Western European nations have much greater female political participation. In the Scandinavian countries, for example, up to 20 percent of members of parliament are women.

Sociologists Richard Zwiegenhaft and William Domhoff (1998) do point out that women are now part of the power elite. The power elite is no longer the exclusively male group it used to be. Still, women are seriously underrepresented, and most of those women who do join the power elite come from upper-class backgrounds.

> "If women want any rights more than they's got, why don't they just take them, and not be talking about it."
>
> Sojourner Truth
> American abolitionist

Section 3 Assessment

1. Define *sexism*.
2. Give several examples of legal bias against women.

Critical Thinking

3. **Evaluating Information** Do you support or oppose affirmative action programs for women in the workplace? Give reasons for your answer.

Paired Learning Activity

Although women are showing up more frequently in the power elite, many women in these "exalted" positions are very hesitant to speak out. One reporter described the problems she had interviewing women for an article about women and the Fortune 500. While they were very candid off the record, very few were willing to be identified (or attributed). Have students work in pairs to discuss why they think women who are talented enough to reach the highest executive positions should be reluctant to speak out. *(The reporter believed the women's reluctance to be identified was consistent with their sense that being a woman or minority board member brought extra attention, and required extra diligence on their part "to preserve privacy and to be viewed as models of appropriate behavior by their colleagues on boards and by others in general.")*
L1

Tech Trends

Men, Women, and the Internet

Although women are still subject to discrimination in some technical careers, such as computer programming and information systems analysis, they are finding more and better opportunities in Internet business fields than in any other area of business. Women have founded and become chief executive officer (CEO) of many high-tech companies, including Marimba, Oxygen Media, iVillage, DoubleClick, Women.com, togglethis, and The Mining Company. Kim Polese, CEO of Marimba, was featured on more business magazine covers in 1998 than Bill Gates, founder and CEO of Microsoft.

These unanticipated opportunities for women are due to several factors. First, whereas most American industries developed when women were expected to stay at home, the system that would become the Internet was started only about thirty years ago. The Internet itself did not become really popular until the mid-1990s. By that time, women had already entered the workforce in large numbers and had begun to occupy mid- and upper-level management positions.

Second, women are able to profit from the tremendous demand for experienced marketing managers created by the Internet. Because women are responsible for some 85 percent of purchasing decisions in non-Internet businesses, they have the experience to move into marketing management positions. Internet companies have turned to these women to fill important positions.

The Internet is helping to open up greater gender equality in the workplace.

Third, the Internet has created an astronomical demand for skilled high-tech workers. American high-tech firms are desperate for workers, and they are turning to women as an underutilized resource.

Of course, not all women entering Internet businesses escape sexism. This trend, nonetheless, is a step toward greater workplace equality. Because the Internet has rapidly become such a large part of the U.S. economy, and because it will only continue to grow, the information age holds considerable promise for gender equality.

Analyzing the Trends

Choose one of the three major theoretical perspectives, and analyze the rise of women in Internet businesses. Use information from this chapter to support your analysis. Predict whether or not the rise of women in Internet businesses will lead to improved gender equality in other workplace arenas.

Tech Trends

Ask students to react to this statement: *The Internet has cracked the glass ceiling for women.* This feature gives several reasons why that might be true.

Answer to Analyzing the Trends

Student answers will vary, but should follow the general line: functionalism looks at how the Internet supports existing social structures; conflict theory emphasizes the accessibility to economic opportunities the Internet allows to women; and a symbolic interactionism looks at how the anonymity of the Internet might help women break out of gender stereotypes.

Integrating the Teacher Resources

Look for Ethics, Values, and Technology: Real-Life Issues in Society, available in your Teacher's Resource Box. The booklet provides primary source readings dealing with real-life controversies. Student worksheets are included.

Cooperative Learning Activity

To look ahead to the next section, you may want students to spend 20 minutes on this activity. Have students work in cooperative groups to develop an appreciation for some of the societal problems of aging. Ask students to first brainstorm problems encountered by the elderly. Then have them go back over their list and divide these problems into anticipated problems of ageism and unanticipated problems. For example, people can't predict when their eyes will begin to fail them or when they will need to quit driving, but they can anticipate that these things will happen or could happen. If students include some of the issues they learn about in these groups on the survey questionnaire in a later activity (see page 330), it will help them understand the perspective of ageism.
L2

Using the Section Preview

This is a fun activity to jump-start student interest in this section. It is called Inherent Value. Hold up a $20.00 bill (or any smaller denomination). Ask students, Who would like this $20.00 bill? Hands should go up immediately. Tell the class that you will give the $20.00 bill to one of them, but first, you want to do something. Crumple up the bill. Now ask, who still wants it? Hands will still go up. Say, now what if I do this? Drop it, step on it, grind it into the floor with your shoe. Pick it up, all dirty and crumpled. Now who still wants it? Hands will still go up. Tell the class that they have just learned a valuable lesson. No matter what was done to the money, they still wanted it because its value did not decrease by the wear-and-tear it had received.

Then ask them to imagine that in their lives they had been crumpled, stepped on, dropped and ground into the floor. Tell them that although they have not lost their inherent worth or value, society seems to have declared that they are not worth the same as they were when they were younger. Tell them they will look at why U.S. society appears to devalue the elderly. (Note: Several activities and features in Chapter 16 on population are relevant to the topics covered here. See especially the Enrichment reading on pages 564–565.)

Section 4 Ageism

Key Terms

- age stratification
- ageism

Section Preview

The relatively low social standing of older people is based on ageism. Each of the theoretical perspectives has a unique slant on ageism. Stereotypes are often used to justify prejudice and discrimination, which can harm the self-concepts of older people.

age stratification
the unequal distribution of scarce resources based on age

ageism
a set of beliefs, attitudes, norms, and values used to justify age-based prejudice and discrimination

Defining Ageism

Chronological age is another basis for social ranking. For this reason, sociologists are interested in **age stratification**—when the unequal distribution of scarce resources (power, wealth, prestige) in a society is based on age. Like inequality based on race, ethnicity, or gender, age stratification must be socially justified. The rationale for aged-based inequality comes in the form of **ageism**—a set of beliefs, attitudes, norms, and values used to justify prejudice and discrimination against a particular age group. Although age can be an advantage or disadvantage for any group, sociologists are especially interested in inequality among older people. As the median age of the U.S. population grows older, this form of ageism affects more and more people.

Functionalism and Ageism

According to functionalists, elderly people in a given society are treated according to the role the aged play in that society. In many societies, ageism is not an issue. In fact, elderly people in many cultures are treated with great respect and honor. (See the Focus on Research on page 334.)

In agricultural societies, elderly males usually play important roles, such as the role of priest or elder. Donald Cowgill and Lowell Holmes give examples of societies in which the elderly are highly valued.

> *In all of the African societies, growing old is equated with rising status and increased respect. Among the Igbo, the older person is assumed to be wise: this not only brings him respect, since he is consulted for his wisdom, it also provides him with a valued role in his society. The Bantu elder is "the Father of His People" and revered as such. In Samoa, too, old age is "the best time of life" and older persons are accorded great respect. Likewise, in Thailand, older persons are honored and deferred to and Adams reports respect and affection for older people in rural Mexico (Cowgill and Holmes, 1972).*

Survey

Students can conduct a mini-field research project by taking advantage of resources right in their own community. Have students identify a nursing home, senior citizen center, or other public or private location where elderly people might congregate and could be interviewed. Students should then devise a set of open-ended questions (see Chapter 2) that ask elderly people to consider how the work world has changed since they were new to the job market. (Or, you may advise students to narrow the field of questions to a range they are comfortable handling.) Some questions might include: Does your job still exist in the same form today? What would you do today if you were entering the job market? How did you cope with retirement? and so forth. Students can work together to tabulate their answers and present this information for Chapter 13 when they look at the economic institution.

L2

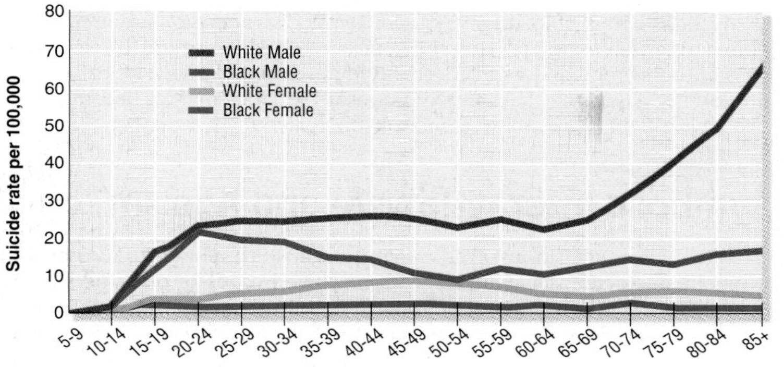

Figure 10.8 U.S. Suicide Rates by Age, Gender, and Racial Group, 1997. *This figure charts U.S. suicide rates by age, gender, and racial category. Why do you think suicide rates climb for males at about age 65? Use material from the textbook in your answer.*

Source: National Institute of Mental Health, September, 1999.

Online UPDATE Visit soc.glencoe.com and click on **Textbook Updates–Chapter 10** for an update of the data.

In early colonial America, no stigma was attached to age. In fact, to be elderly brought respect along with the opportunity to fill the most prestigious positions in the community. It was believed that God looked with favor on those who reached old age. The longer one lived, the more likely he or she was to have been chosen to go to heaven. The Bible linked age with living a moral life: "Keep my commandments, for length of days and long life shall they add unto thee." During the 1600s and 1700s, Americans even tried to appear older than they actually were. Men and women wore clothing that made them appear older and covered their hair with powdered wigs. During the 1700s, people often inflated their age when reporting to census takers.

Attitudes about aging changed greatly as industrialization changed the nature of work. In a technical society, an adult's value lessens when he or she no longer contributes fully to the common good. Thus, aging tends to lead to lower status. Because modern societies change rapidly, younger workers are more likely to possess the current skills needed in the workplace. As individuals get older, their skills are more likely to be out of date in the workplace. Thus, they lack the "wisdom" that is most highly valued.

This loss of status with older age might help explain the increase in the suicide rate for men beginning at about retirement age. (See Figure 10.8.) Men may have greater difficulty in older age than women because they have been socialized in a culture that encourages men to identify strongly with work while they are younger, but denies them a sense of value after retirement.

> "When a man retires and time is no longer a matter of urgent importance, his colleagues generally present him with a watch."
>
> **R. C. Sherriff**
> **American humorist**

Conflict Theory and Ageism

Competition over scarce resources lies at the heart of ageism for the conflict perspective. Elderly people compete with other age groups for economic resources, power, and prestige. In preindustrial societies, older people often get a fair share of the scarce resources. This is because work in preindustrial society is labor intensive, and all available hands must be utilized. Also, the elderly are sources of valuable knowledge about practices and history.

Industrial society, in contrast, usually has more workers than it needs. In addition, industrial societies save scarce resources by replacing high-priced older workers with less costly younger ones. Forced retirement is one way the more powerful age groups remove elderly competitors.

Working With the Data

Figure 10.8 Students should respond to the caption question showing some realization that age 65 is retirement for many males. Those who have centered their lives around their jobs may get depressed when faced with the loss of prestige, income, and status.

Points to Stress

The concept of aging leading to a loss of self-esteem and status in Western nations is a key one—and a fairly recent development from the historical perspective. If they don't quite accept this, ask them to think of fairy tales, fables, and legends that involve wise and respected "old" men and women, especially in the Native American, African, and Hispanic traditions.

Careers in Sociology

Another career that grows out of a sociology degree is the field of gerontology, agencies and people who specialize in services for the aged. They advise elderly people and family members about choices in housing, transportation, and long-term care. They also coordinate and monitor services. A gerontological counselor provides services to elderly persons who face changing lifestyles because of poor health problems, and helps families cope with these changes. Social workers with backgrounds in gerontology are finding work in the growing numbers of assisted living and senior living communities. The aged population is increasing rapidly, creating greater demand for health related and other social services. Students can connect to the Gerontological Society of America for more information at **http://www.geron.org**

Pulling It All Together

Take the three sociological perspectives of aging and have students identify all three with an example of each. Why are social attitudes about the elderly so negative? Have students try to create some positive ways that American society could make greater use of the elderly.

Answers to Section 4 Assessment

1. Sexism and ageism both result from stereotypes that are used to justify inequality. Each is a set of beliefs, attitudes, norms, and values used to justify prejudice and discrimination—against a particular sex in the first instance, and against a particular age group in the second.

2. a. C
b. S
c. F
d. F/students might argue C, as well
e. S
f. C

Critical Thinking

3. Answers will vary, but most people would probably agree that ageism does exist and is a problem in American society. Students should expand on their opinions.

According to conflict theory, prejudice and discrimination are used by the dominant group as weapons in the control of minority groups. If older people can be stereotyped as intellectually dull, closed-minded, inflexible, and unproductive, forcing their retirement from the labor market becomes relatively easy. This leaves more jobs available for younger workers.

Many elderly people are realizing that learning computer skills will help them keep in touch with friends, keep updated on financial and health issues, and allow them to find part-time work, if desired.

Symbolic Interactionism and Ageism

Like racism, ageism involves creating negative stereotypes. According to symbolic interactionists, children learn negative images of older people just as they learn other aspects of culture. Through the process of socialization, stereotypes of elderly people are often firmly implanted into a child's view of the world. Negative images of older people have been observed in children as young as three years old (Hillier and Barrow, 1999).

What are some stereotypes of the elderly? By definition, stereotypes are inaccurate, because they do not apply to all members of a group. Stereotypes of older people are no exception, as much research has shown. Most elderly people are not senile, forgetful, or "daft." Old age is not a sexless period for the majority of those over sixty-five. There are few age differences on job-related factors. Most elderly people are able to learn new things and adapt to change (Atchley, 1999).

In summary, there is enough evidence to challenge the truth of popular stereotypes of elderly people. Of course, some older people do fit one or more of these stereotypes (as some young people fit societal stereotypes), and many individuals are likely to fit one or more of them as they reach age seventy. This fact, however, does not justify applying the stereotypes to all older people at any age or for mindlessly applying them to individuals in their fifties and sixties.

Section 4 Assessment

1. How are sexism and ageism "two sides of the same coin"?
2. Below are several statements about older people. Identify each statement with one major theoretical perspective: functionalism (F), conflict theory (C), or symbolic interactionism (S).
   - **a.** Ageism results in part from an oversupply of labor.
   - **b.** Young people are uncomfortable around older people.
   - **c.** The stigma attached to aging promotes a low self-concept among older people.
   - **d.** Ageism is associated with industrialization.
   - **e.** Older people are stereotyped.
   - **f.** Ageism exists in part because older workers are inefficient.

Critical Thinking

3. **Evaluating Information** Do you think ageism is a problem in American society? Support your case with information.

Using Problem-Solving Skills

Examining stereotypes Ask students if they think elderly people drive generally worse or better than teenagers. Most likely, they will offer anecdotes from their personal experiences about how slow or unaware most older drivers are. Remind them that using their sociological imagination means looking at things from a broader perspective and being aware that things are not always what they seem. Challenge them to research statistics on driving and see how many fatalities are the result of elderly people driving slow. Sources of information include the library, the Internet or local insurance companies. They may also want to contact a local police department and see if they have records related to the age of drivers and accidents.
L2

Section 5

Inequality In America's Elderly Population

Key Term

- interest group

Elderly People as a Minority Group

Because early research tended to study older people in institutions, studies focused on people with diminished mental and physical capacities. This perspective coincided with the American public's negative view of elderly people. Sociologists believe that the best way to expose this blaming of older people for their situation is to view them as a minority (Hillier and Barrow, 1999).

Racial, ethnic, and religious groups have long been considered as minorities. As you have seen, women have recently been recognized as a minority group. Not until recently have researchers viewed older people as a distinct segment of society subject to the same discrimination and stereotyping as other minority groups.

Economics of the Elderly

The economic situation among America's older people has improved since 1960, but as a group older Americans are far from being well off. Several factors make it hard to determine exactly how elderly people compare economically with other groups, however. For one thing, the way poverty among older people is measured distorts the real picture.

Why is poverty measured differently for older people? Despite the fact that elderly people spend proportionately more on health care and housing than younger people, the federal government assumes that older people require less money to live. If the standard used for younger age categories were applied to elderly people, their poverty rate would increase from 9.7 percent to 15 percent. Poverty rates also fail to take into account the older people who are officially considered to be "near poor." These people make up just over 6 percent of the elderly population. Counting these at-risk elderly people, about 16 percent of those over age sixty-five is poor (U.S. Bureau of the Census, 2000b).

Nor do official statistics include the "hidden poor" among the elderly population. These older people live either in institutions or with relatives because they cannot afford to live independently. Inclusion of these people would substantially raise the poverty rate for elderly Americans.

Unfortunately, life is not this comfortable for a large segment of America's elderly population.

Section Preview

The poverty rate for America's elderly population stands at 9.7 percent. Members of racial and ethnic minorities are in the poorest ranks. The political process offers the major source of power for elderly Americans. Older people exert political influence through their high voting rate and their support of special interest groups.

Using the Section Preview

If you have Internet access in the classroom, ask students to visit the census bureau web site mentioned in Chapter 2, (**www.census.gov**) and look at poverty rates and voting rates by age of population. Have them share their findings with the class. If you don't have access in class, you might want to download some of these statistics and create overhead transparencies to share with the class.

Reteaching

To be sure students understand how the high incomes of a relatively small group of elderly people can skew the average income for all aged, you may want to direct students back to page 47 to review the concepts of mean, median, and mode.

Encouraging Citizenship Activity

Ask students to make a one-to-one contact with an elderly person (advise the student not to approach them on that basis!) who has lived through and has personal knowledge of a historical event, such as the Vietnam War or civil rights marches. The student should interview the senior, using their best listening and interviewing skills, to get a sense of what was going on with "everyday people,"—one of the aims of the new historians in writing social history. One student may find a senior he or she thinks is interesting enough to come and address the whole class. This is a good service project both because it sends students out to the community to make connections between what they learn in school and real life, and it also takes advantage of latent resources in the senior population.
L1

Focus on Research

Case Study: A Town without Pity

In the mountains of Western Ireland lies the old agricultural town of Ballybran. Power in this town traditionally lay in the hands of the "old ones," particularly the senior males. Here, sociologist Nancy Scheper-Hughes spent a year doing fieldwork, studying the effects of modernization on the society. She identifies the basic demographic shift that has led to the death of the rural Irish gerontocracy [rule by elders], describes the negative consequences of this change for the elderly, and discusses several areas in which the loss of social standing among the elderly is reflected.

Scheper-Hughes found that with modernization and with dependence on imported food came a lessening of respect for the skills and knowledge of the old farmers.

Underlying this picture, of course, is the devaluating of the agricultural way of life among these people. At an earlier time, the patriarchal father delayed retirement and sparked intense competition among his sons for rights to the family lands. Now heir selection is determined more by the process of elimination than the choice of the father—"the last one to escape (usually the youngest son) gets stuck by default with an unproductive farm and saddled with a life of celibacy and greatly resented service to the 'old people'" (Scheper-Hughes, 1983:134).

The result of all this for the aged parents is fairly clear: They no longer have the economic power base they once used to control the younger generation and to maintain their superior status in the family and community. Because young people prefer to be "liberated" from the land, the "old ones" control little that the youth want. The awe and respect for the elderly that once characterized the community has, in many cases, been replaced by not only pity but also contempt. The demise of the traditional family farming–based culture leaves the elderly father, in Scheper-Hughes's words, a "broken figure." Toleration from his adult children is the most he can expect, open ridicule the worst. With the erosion of their economic power, the elderly have also lost their cherished role as preservers of the ancient Celtic traditions—the myths, stories, songs, prayers, and proverbs. In fact, the young tend to reject these traditions. Worse, the majority of high school students resent having to study the Irish language, a "dead" language that they believe will be of no use to them in the commercial and professional world outside the rural community.

Focus on Research

This research can be generalized to help students discuss what uses a society finds for its aging population. Have students brainstorm what roles the elderly might serve that would benefit all of us. Encourage students to think beyond the role of volunteers. Although this role is an important one, it also plays into a stereotype.

More About . . . Disengagement and Activity

One aspect of aging you may want to discuss with students (if your schedule allows) involves disengagement theory. Disengagement occurs when people reduce their level of social involvement. Advocates of *disengagement* theory contend that such withdrawal is natural to the aging process. According to *activity* theory, older people have the same psychological and social needs as they did in middle age. Barring ill health or disability, activity theory attributes a desire among the aging to remain socially involved. *Differential disengagement* theory has been developed in answer to these two opposing perspectives. Some research backs this latter theory, which contends that older people withdraw from social activities but remain involved in others. Factors such as health, finances, and opportunities affect the degree of disengagement.

On-Demand Writing

Anthropologist Colin Turnbull lived for two years among an African tribe called the Ik (pronounced EEK). During his stay, he witnessed some very disturbing behavior. He relates the following story: An old blind woman had taken a bad fall. She was nearly dead from hunger and thirst, and Turnbull gave her food and water and asked if she wanted to be taken to a shelter in another village. She refused, saying that she was looking for her son. Turnbull knew the son and suggested that he would not want to see her. She agreed, but knew she was dying and wanted to be near her son in her

Ageism has had many negative effects on these older people. Without a meaningful work identity, the once-proud leaders have no sense of place in the community. Alcoholism, diminished self-esteem, and depression are widely seen among those over age fifty. Many are single, widows or widowers, without family or friends to take care of them. Scheper-Hughes writes, "The Irish village of the west coast today embodies a broken culture; a state of affairs most detrimental to the aged who are unable to flee or accept new values, and who, consequently, are left to contemplate the wreckage" (Scheper-Hughes, 1983:145).

As "progress" comes to both city and country, many of the local elderly population find their skills are not needed and that they have no role to play in the life of the community.

Working with the Research

1. Which research methods are best suited to a study like this? Explain.
2. Which theoretical perspective do you think contributes most to how we can understand what happened in this village?

Answers to Working with the Research

1. Students should say that an observational study or surveys would work best here. Researchers would use the surveys to ask specific questions that could be generalized for all the inhabitants and observation to get a feel for what is happening.
2. The conflict perspective because the elderly compete for limited resources. It is actually functional for the old ones to be out of the mainstream as it serves the interest of the community not to have them working. From a symbolic interactionist perspective, negative stereotypes would be created.

Integrating the Teacher Resources

A lesson plan for a student research project related to the content of this chapter can be found in Doing Sociology: Focus on Research, available in your Teacher's Resource Box.

last days. She asked Turnbull to give her some extra food to use as a bribe to buy her way inside her son's house. She found her son, and he took the food, but he did not let her into his house. She died a short time later in the dirt outside his door.

Ask students to write their reactions to this story. Are there similarities to the case study in the Focus on Research feature on this page? Ask students to picture themselves in a similar situation. What would they do? How would they deal with it? Do they think this type of behavior is possible in the United States? Why or why not? **L2**

Figure 10.9 Poverty Rates Among Americans Aged 65 and Over: 1960–1999. *This figure documents the changing poverty rate among Americans aged 65 and over since 1960. Explain why it would be misleading to cite the current poverty rate as evidence that America's aged population is economically well off.*

Source: U.S. Census Bureau, 1966–2000.

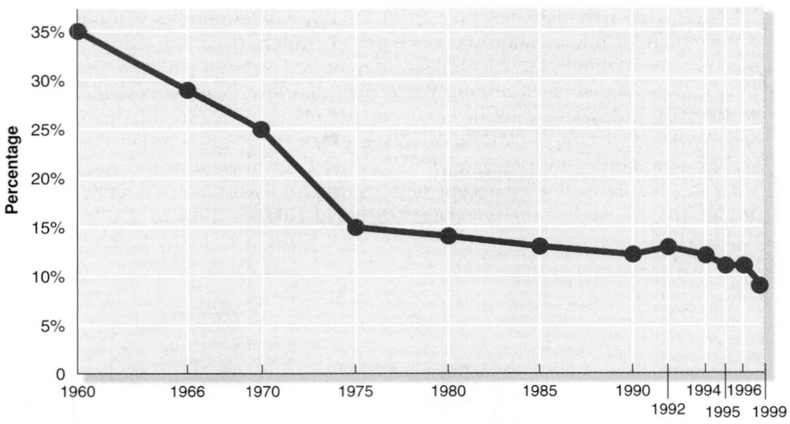

The income gap among elderly people also distorts the economic picture. Some older people have moderate to high incomes based on dividends from assets, cash savings, and private retirement programs. Most elderly Americans, however, do not have sources of income beyond Social Security benefits. The existence of a small percentage of high-income older people gives the false impression that most older people are economically well off. Figure 10.9 shows the poverty rate for elderly people since 1960.

This elderly man is part of America's "hidden poor." What does that mean?

What other factors affect elderly Americans? Older people who are members of racial or ethnic minority groups are generally in worse condition than older white Americans. The poverty rate among older African Americans is three times that for whites. For older Latinos, the poverty rate is more than two and one-half times that of non-Latino white Americans. Problems that racial and ethnic minorities face because of discrimination become magnified in old age.

Elderly women constitute one of the poorest segments of American society. Women over age sixty-five are twice as likely to live in poverty than their male counterparts (U.S. Bureau of the Census, 1996b). Elderly women most likely to be poor are single women who either have never married or are divorced, separated, or widowed. This is not surprising, because the roots of poverty among older women lie in their work-related experiences. Because older women were discouraged or blocked from better jobs throughout their work lives, they are unable to support themselves in their later years (Sidel, 1996).

Overall, what is the economic position of older people in the United States? In summary, then, elderly people are economically better off than they were four decades ago. Despite this improvement, large segments of Americans over sixty-five years of age live either in poverty or near poverty. This is especially true for elderly members of racial and ethnic minorities and for elderly women.

Working with the Data

Figure 10.9 You may want to check student understanding of the author's contention that the decreasing poverty rate for elderly people is misleading because of (1) the skewed incomes of very wealthy people and (2) false assumptions about lower costs of living for elderly folks.

Open-Response Question

Ask students to hypothesize about why voter turnout increases with age. If they need some prompting, tell the students that your hypothesis about why the elderly are most likely to vote is based on their experiences with key events in history. Many of them experienced the Great Depression, World War II, the Korean War, fear of Communism, the Vietnam War, etc. Since they have seen so many threats to democracy, they feel it imperative to exercise their right to vote, which validates that they are free. Now, tell your students that you also think that's why people today don't vote. We have become secure and don't fear that those rights will be taken away. Students might want to interview people of different generations to corroborate this hypothesis.

On-Demand Writing

Ask students to write a few paragraphs in response to the following prompt: *Whatever problems racial and ethnic minorities face because of discrimination become magnified in old age.* Ask volunteers to share their mini-essays with the class. **L2**

Percentage of Population Aged Sixty-five and Over

The *graying of America* refers to the growing elderly population. Improved medical care, better nutrition, and healthier lifestyles have all contributed to longer life expectancies in the United States. This map shows the percentage of the population that is aged sixty-five years old and over in each state.

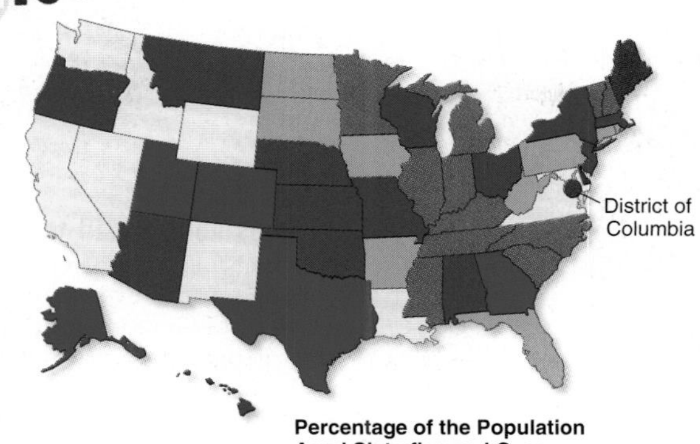

Source: *The World Almanac of the U.S.A.*, Allan Carpenter and Carl Provorse, Mahwah, NJ: World Almanac Books, 2001.

Percentage of the Population Aged Sixty-five and Over
- More than 14%
- 13%
- 12%
- 11%
- Less than 11%

Interpreting the Map

1. Describe the distribution pattern of elderly people across the United States. Create a chart representing the distribution pattern.
2. Where is your state in this distribution?
3. Research the voting rate for elderly people in your state. Is it higher or lower than the national average?

Source: U.S. Bureau of the Census, 2000.

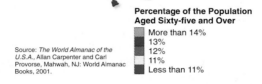

By now, students should be very familiar with the concept that the population in the United States is getting older because of the baby boomers. If not, review this concept using a population pyramid such as those found on page 545 in Chapter 16.

Answers to Interpreting the Map

1. With a few exceptions, the Western part of the U.S. is younger. The northeast is older. A line of states from the top of the midwest to the mid-south is in the middle. Ask students to pose questions about the demographic patterns shown on the charts they create.
2. Answering this question is a student exercise.
3. Student answers will vary.

Political Power and the Elderly

Given the limited economic resources of older people, it is clear that any power they hold is gained through the political process. Especially important are the voting booth and political interest groups.

What is the voting turnout among elderly Americans? Voting turnout in the United States increases with age. Since the mid-1980s, Americans aged sixty-five and over have been the most active voters in presidential and congressional elections. In 1996, for example, 67 percent of this group voted in the presidential election, compared with just over 30 percent of eighteen- to twenty-four-year-olds and just over 49 percent of twenty-five- to forty-four-year-olds (U.S. Bureau of the Census, 1997a).

Learning Styles

Musical/Interpersonal To help students dispel stereotypes regarding elderly people and to help them better understand the position of seniors, ask them to accept a challenge. Have students choose a song or piece of music that especially appeals to them, and then list the reasons why they like it. Then have students select someone they know who is age 65 or older. Ask the students to share their favorite musical selection with the person, and to invite the person to share in return. Direct the students to discuss the piece of music with the person, concentrating on the things about the music that each appreciates. To conclude the activity, discuss in class what the students found out or discovered about the older person. Was the experience easy or difficult for them? Awful? Enjoyable? Do they think they might spend more time in the future with that person? Why or why not?

L1

Working with the Data

Figure 10.10 Two statements that students might deduce from the table are that white males are underrepresented in the poverty category and that more women are in the poverty category than men. The social category of people most likely to be poor are African American women.

Pulling It All Together

In this section, students looked at issues that confront the elderly from poverty to their political power and interest groups to protect that power. The Baby-boomers will have profound effects on the elderly population in the next 20–30 years.

Answers to Section 5 Assessment

1. c.
2. The diversity of older Americans makes unity a harder goal to achieve. This, in turn, weakens their political clout. One effective way to overcome this lack of unity would be for older Americans to join special interest groups

Critical Thinking

3. Answers will vary.

Figure 10.10 Selected Socioeconomic Characteristics of Elderly Americans. *From this figure, some comparative statements can be made about the economic situation of elderly Americans. What are two important statements that can be supported by these data?*

Source: U.S. Bureau of the Census, 2000.

	Whites	African Americans	Latinos	Women	Men
Median Income	$14,774	$9,766	$8,780	$10,943	$19,079
Percent in Poverty	7.6%	22.7%	20.4%	21.7%	16.3%

Does voting lead to political power? Most analysts believe that the potential political power of elderly Americans as a group is not fully realized because of the diversity of the older population. Because older people cut across many important divisions in American society—social class, ethnicity, race, geographic area, religion—they do not speak with a unified political voice. In fact, they do not vote as a bloc on any political question, even on issues related directly to their interests. This lack of unity weakens their political clout. As the population of the United States ages, however, and the number of elderly voters increases, it is possible that "gray power" may become a significant political force.

interest group
a group organized to influence political decision making

What is the role of interest groups? **Interest groups** are organized to influence political decision making. Millions of Americans belong to interest groups that target ageism, such as the American Association for Retired Persons (AARP) and the Gray Panthers. These groups have been effective in protecting programs that benefit older Americans, such as Medicare and Social Security.

> "The older I get, the more I distrust the familiar doctrine that age brings wisdom."
>
> **H. L. Mencken**
> **American critic**

Section 5 Assessment

1. Of the following, which is an accurate statement?
   a. Since 1960, the economic situation for elderly people in the United States has deteriorated.
   b. The poverty rate for Americans over age sixty-five is lower than the official count indicates.
   c. Problems of older Americans who are members of racial or ethnic minorities are generally more severe than problems of elderly whites.
   d. Older Americans are politically vulnerable.
2. What can older Americans do to increase their impact on government policy and legislation?

Critical Thinking

3. **Drawing Conclusions** Create mini-profiles of five elderly people you know. Identify them by racial, ethnic, gender, and occupational group. Interview each of them briefly about their main concerns regarding aging in America. What conclusions can you draw from these interviews?

CHAPTER 10 ASSESSMENT

Summary

Section 1: Sex and Gender Identity

Main Idea: All societies expect people to behave in certain ways based on their sex. Through socialization, members of a society acquire an awareness of themselves as masculine or feminine.

Section 2: Theoretical Perspectives on Gender

Main Idea: The functionalist perspective focuses on the origins of gender differences. Conflict theory looks at the reasons gender differences continue to exist. Symbolic interactionism attempts to explain the ways in which gender is acquired.

Section 3: Gender Inequality

Main Idea: Although great progress has been made, women today are still subject to prejudice and discrimination. This imbalance of power is seen most clearly in the areas of economics, law, and politics.

Section 4: Ageism

Main Idea: The relatively low social standing of older people is based on ageism. Each of the theoretical perspectives has a unique slant on ageism.

Section 5: Inequality In America's Elderly Population

Main Idea: The poverty rate for America's elderly population stands at over 10 percent. Members of racial and ethnic minorities are in the poorest ranks. The political process offers the major source of power for elderly Americans. Older people exert political influence through their high voting rate and their support of special interest groups.

SOCIOLOGY Online

Self-Check Quiz
Visit the *Sociology and You* Web site at soc.glencoe.com and click on **Chapter 10—Self-Check Quizzes** to prepare for the chapter test.

Reviewing Vocabulary

Complete each sentence using each term once.

a. gender identity
b. sex
c. gender socialization
d. sexism
e. occupational sex segregation
f. ageism
g. biological determinism
h. age stratification
i. interest group

1. An organization that attempts to influence political decision making is called ____________.
2. ____________ is the unequal distribution of scarce resources based on age.
3. The classification of people as male or female based on biological characteristics is called ____________.
4. ____________ is the concentration of one gender in certain occupations.
5. ____________ is a set of beliefs, attitudes, norms, and values used to justify sexual inequality.
6. The belief that behavioral differences are due to inherited physical characteristics is called ____________.
7. ____________ is a set of beliefs, attitudes, norms, and values used to justify age-based prejudice and discrimination.
8. ____________ is an awareness of being masculine or feminine.
9. The social process of learning how to act as a boy or girl is called ____________.

Reviewing the Facts

1. According to the functionalist perspective what was the main result of the division of labor?
2. Which sociological perspective emphasizes the effects of parents, teachers, and peers on gender socialization?

ANSWERS CHAPTER 10 ASSESSMENT

Reviewing Vocabulary

1. i
2. h
3. b
4. e
5. d
6. g
7. f
8. a
9. c

Reviewing the Facts

1. To ensure the survival of the species.
2. Symbolic interactionist perspective
3. Answers will vary: availability of more jobs; increase in divorce rate makes it necessary for more women to work outside of the home; increase in single-parent households.
4. Answers will vary: women are concentrated in low-status jobs; occupational sex segregation (women placed in lower-status occupations); disproportional share of higher positions are filled by men.
5. The "near poor" (those who spend the greater portion of their income on healthcare and housing); the hidden poor (those who live in institutions or with relatives because they cannot afford to live independently).
6. Through the political process: exercising their voting rights; participating in and supporting interest groups focusing on protecting the rights of the elderly.

Thinking Critically

1. From this discussion students should realize that the effect of biology can't be ignored but socialization is probably more important in understanding gender-role differences based on sex.
2. There are many values or attitudes affected by the lessening importance of physical strength in most occupations. One point students might put forth is that developing a muscular frame is a function of recreation or leisure, as opposed to necessity.
3. This scenario usually provokes a great debate, with the females (surprisingly enough!)

Chapter 10 Assessment

3. How would you explain the increase in women's participation in the labor force?
4. Give one reason why the gap between men's and women's salaries persists.
5. What segment of the poor population is often not included in the statistics on elderly poor people?
6. According to the text, what is the best way that the elderly can effect social change on their own behalf?

Thinking Critically

1. **Analyzing Information** A common phrase in sociology is "you inherit your sex and learn your gender." What do you think this phrase means?
2. **Applying Concepts** Physical strength is not as important for males today as it was in past times. The nature of work has changed so that not as many jobs require stamina or physical strength. What impact do you think this devaluing of muscle strength has on society? List five attitudes or values that could be affected.
3. **Evaluating Information** Certain jobs, such as firefighting, still require great physical strength and stamina. Often, these positions have minimum requirements to ensure that employees can fulfill all the necessary duties. Because of biology, men generally find it easier to meet many of these physical requirements. Some cities have responded by lowering the standards for women to ensure that women are represented in these vocations. Other cities have refused and have been subjected to discrimination lawsuits. What are some arguments for and against the policy of lowering standards to ensure representation of women in certain jobs? Are there situations in which you would allow different standards? Are there situations in which you would not? Discuss your views.
4. **Making Inferences** Some schools have experimented with girls-only classes. Research seems to suggest that this situation helps to increase self-esteem in young girls. Do you think your schoolwork would improve if you attended a girls-only or boys-only school? Do you think there are differences in the way that girls and boys learn?
5. **Drawing Conclusions** U.S. society has definite expectations about female and male roles. What are the gender norms concerning personal appearance? Do these norms work against women? Do they work against males?
6. **Categorizing Information** Elderly people remain a forgotten population in our society. We place them in nursing homes, or we complain that they drive too slowly. How might our society take advantage of the natural skills, knowledge, and wisdom of older people? Suggest three ways in which your community could benefit from programs and activities aimed at utilizing these strengths. Use the diagram below to summarize your suggestions.

STRENGTHS OF THE ELDERLY	PROGRAM/ACTIVITY THAT UTILIZES STRENGTH

7. **Making Inferences** The text discusses some of the stereotypes associated with older people. Using recent research on these stereotypes, do you think the norms underlying ageism will diminish? Check your thoughts against the opinions of a few elderly people.

Sociology Projects

1. **Advertising and the Image of Women** Search old magazines and newspapers to create a scrapbook of how marketers can use gender negatively (to encourage stereotypes, for example) or positively (to create new images).

   Gather several magazines with lots of advertising that you have permission to cut up. (Waiting rooms in doctors' and dentists' offices and car repair shops are good sources—just be sure to ask permission!) Carefully cut out twenty ads that feature women. Paste each ad to a sheet of paper. Then label each ad accord-

340

ANSWERS Chapter 10 Assessment

frequently asserting that they should have to do the same amount of push-ups as boys. Students might also suggest that these jobs should involve a large amount of teamwork, which would minimize the importance of individual variations in strength. Or, they might stress that life-and-death situations override the importance of equity in these vocations.

4. Again, this is a great question for stimulating class debate. The research says, however, that learning styles between boys and girls are at the heart of this issue of how well they learn and in what settings. Girls work better in cooperative settings away from the competitive nature of male interactions.
5. Most students will agree that, in spite of gains made by liberation groups, girls are generally more looks-conscious, in part because their peers are judging them (looking glass-self) and because they want to appear attractive. Boys go through phases of being concerned with their looks, but focus more on overall physique than on looks or fashion.
6. Student answers will vary. Example for chart:

   Strength: reading and math skills

   Program: tutoring in the primary grades at the local school.
7. Answers will vary. Students, however, should include specific research findings related to norms and underlying ageism for both their own opinions and the opinions of some older people. Students need to show whether recent research findings are affecting these norms.

Sociology Projects

1. A version of this activity was presented earlier in the teacher's edition. It really allows students to see how the media creates images that are so ingrained in us, that we fail to see what it is doing until we put it together in a booklet. Have students share their booklets with the class and display some of them around the room.

ing to one of the negative or positive criteria listed below. Feel free to make up your own categories if needed.

a. reinforces a female stereotype
b. uses sex appeal to sell a product
c. encourages a women to be beautiful
d. idealizes youthful appearance
e. reinforces gender roles of children
f. generally offensive, degrading, or insulting
g. shows a woman in a leadership role
h. shows a woman in a nontraditional role
i. shows a minority woman in a professional capacity

When you have completed your "scrapbook," analyze the ads for negative and positive uses of gender marketing. Write a brief paragraph summarizing your findings.

2. Gender This activity is a thought problem and requires a great deal of imagination. What would your day be like if you awoke one morning and suddenly found that you had changed gender? As you go about your day, think of everything that would be different if you were a member of the opposite sex. Write down several things that stand out as you go through the day. For example, if you are on a sports team, would you be likely to be on that team if you changed gender? Would you be playing a different sport?

3. Lifestyles for the Elderly Create a poster or other visual aid that depicts how life has changed for elderly people during the twentieth century. You may want to talk to grandparents or others about what life was like for older people in the past. How do you think longevity and health factors have changed lifestyle for older people?

4. Create a Skit Instead of a visual aid as suggested in the previous activity, interview an elderly person and create a skit based upon his or her remarks. Some of the questions you may want to ask include

a. What do you consider to be the joys or rewards of aging?
b. What are some of the problems or disadvantages?
c. How were you affected by your retirement? Was it a positive or negative experience?
d. What is your view of teenagers today?

5. Observation Observe people of all ages in a variety of settings, such as restaurants, malls, and offices. Do their clothing and actions fit age-appropriate norms of our culture? What exceptions do you note?

6. The Elderly and Advertising Analyze television commercials for the way older people are portrayed. How frequently are older people represented in advertising material? What types of products do they normally market? Is a pattern or stereotype being perpetuated by the television advertising community?

Technology Activity

1. The Center for the American Woman and Politics is a useful web site to find facts about women elected to public office in the United States. Go to its web site at http://www.rci.rutgers.edu/~cawp/. Select "State by State Fact Sheets" and then click on your state in the map that appears.

a. How many women are currently serving in your state's legislature?
b. Where does your state rank in comparison to other states?
c. When was a woman first elected to a statewide office or to the U.S. Congress?
d. Now click on "Facts Main Page" and select "Findings at a Glance" under the Publications heading. On page 4 of this document, find the three issues where gender differences in priorities were the greatest. What were they?
e. On page 7, were women more or less likely to conduct legislative business in the public view?
f. Based on your review of the "Findings at a Glance" do you think women make effective elected officials?

ANSWERS Chapter 10 Assessment

2. If students take the time to write this thoughtfully, they can hopefully appreciate how changing one's gender would completely transform their life. You might have members of the opposite gender evaluate how realistic the stories are.

3. If you have pictures of the elderly when they were young and they are willing to let you share them with the class, you can see evidence of the aging process and social changes that occur.

4. Two-minute skits are usually effective and allow students to say what they need. The other students often enjoy seeing how their classmates approached this activity.

5. Ask students what they learned from this activity. Can they make any hypothesis about the importance of appearance to the elderly?

6. This could be a challenging activity as students will have to look closely to find a number of older actors in "meaty" roles. Although some shows are specifically about the elderly like Golden Girls, most have only an occasional elderly actor. Students might want to analyze the roles that the elderly play on TV. Are these the result of cultural attitudes on the elderly?

Technology Activity

1. Answers will vary according to state location.

Integrating the Teacher Resources

Look for the Alternative Assessments booklet in your Teacher's Resource Box for essay tests and performance assessment activities based on this chapter.

Enrichment Reading

Students will love this story of a non-gendered child. Allow them to discuss the article and gender variation among males and females. There is a test called the BEM scale that assesses attributes associated with males and females based on a rating scale of 1-7. Students might be interested in taking this test. When students have completed the test, some will be surprised at their results. Tell students that this scale shows how much gender variation exists individually.

Integrating the Teacher Resources

Additional primary source readings for this chapter can be found in Culture Studies: The Sociological Perspective, available in your Teacher's Resource Box. Questions for students are included.

Chapter 10

Enrichment Reading

The Story of Baby X

by Lois Gould

"Once upon a time, a baby named X was born. This baby was named X so that nobody could tell whether it was a boy or a girl." So begins a children's story by Lois Gould about gender stereotypes.

X was given to Mr. and Ms. Jones, a couple carefully screened from thousands of applicants, as an experiment. The Joneses were to follow only one rule: X was not to be socialized as masculine or feminine, but was to learn everything a child could. Assisted by a heavy *Official Instruction Manual,* the Joneses promised to follow this rule as closely as possible. They agreed to take equal turns feeding and caring for X, to spend as much time bouncing as cuddling the baby, and to praise X for being strong just as often as for being sweet. But trouble began almost right away when the Joneses' friends and relatives asked whether X was a boy or a girl.

> When the Joneses smiled and said "It's an X!" nobody knew what to say. They couldn't say, "Look at her cute little dimples." And they couldn't say "Look at his husky little biceps!' And they couldn't even say just plain "kitchy-coo." In fact, they all thought that the Joneses were playing some kind of rude joke.

The Joneses were, of course, being quite serious, but all the same, other people became irritated and embarrassed:

> "People will think there's something wrong with it!" some of them whispered. "There *is* something wrong with it!" others whispered back.

And what did baby X think about all the fuss? It simply finished its bottle with a loud and satisfied burp.

Finding toys for X was another problem. The first trip to the toy store brought this immediate question from the store clerk: "Well, now, is it a boy or a girl?" In the storekeeper's mind, footballs and fire engine sets were for boys and dolls and housekeeping sets were for girls. But the Joneses knew that they had to be sure baby X had *all* kinds of toys to play with, including:

> a boy doll that made pee-pee and cried "Pa-Pa." And a girl doll that talked. They also bought a storybook about a brave princess who rescued a handsome prince from his ivory tower, and another one about a sister and brother who grew up to be a baseball star and a ballet star, and you had to guess which was which.

But the biggest problem came when X was old enough to begin school, where the children were treated according to their sex. Boys and girls lined up separately, played games separately, and, of course, used different bathrooms. The other children had never met an X before, and just *had* to know what its sex really was. But the Joneses had raised X very carefully so that there was no easy answer:

> You couldn't tell what X was by studying its clothes; overalls don't button right-to-left, like girl's clothes, or left-to-right, like boy's clothes. And you couldn't tell whether X had a girl's short haircut or a boy's long haircut. And it was very hard to tell by the games X liked to play. Either X

played ball very well for a girl, or else X played house very well for a boy.

The other children found X a very strange playmate: one day it would ask boys to weave some baskets in the arts and crafts room, and the next day it would ask some girls to go shoot baskets in the gym. But X tried very hard to be friendly to everyone and to do well in school. And X did *very* well in school, winning spelling bees, athletic events and coming in second in a baking contest (even X's aren't perfect). As other children noticed what a good time X was having in school, they began to wonder if maybe X wasn't having twice as much fun as they were!

From then on, some really funny things began to happen. Susie who sat next to X in class, suddenly refused to wear pink dresses to school any more. She insisted on wearing red-and-white checked overalls—just like X's. Overalls, she told her parents, were much better for climbing monkey bars. Then Jim, the class football nut, started wheeling his little sister's doll carriage around the football field. He'd put on his entire football uniform, except for the helmet. Then he'd put the helmet *in* the carriage, lovingly tucked under an old set of shoulder pads. Then he'd start jogging around the field. He told his family that X did the same thing, so it must be okay. After all, X was now the team's star quarterback.

But this kind of behavior in the children horrified their parents. And when Peggy started using Joe's hockey skates while Joe enjoyed using Peggy's needlepoint kit, matters went from bad to worse. X was to blame for all this! So the Parents' Association at school demanded that X be identified as a boy or a girl and be forced to act accordingly. A psychiatrist was asked to conduct a full examination and report back to the parents. If, as most suspected, X was found to be a very confused child, it should be expelled from school altogether.

The teachers were puzzled by this; after all, X was one of their very best students. But the school—as well as the Joneses—finally agreed to let X be examined.

The next day the psychiatrist arrived at the school and began a long examination of X while everyone waited anxiously outside. When the psychiatrist finally emerged from the examination room, the results were not what most people expected. "In my opinion," the psychiatrist told them, "young X here is just about the *least* mixed up child I've ever examined!" The doctor explained that by the time the X's sex really mattered, everyone would know what it was.

This of course, made the Joneses very happy, and delighted the scientists who had begun the experiment in the first place. And later that day, X's friends (dressed in red-and-white checked overalls) came over to X's house to play. They found X in the backyard playing with a new tiny baby.

"How do you like our new baby?" X asked the other children proudly.

"It's got cute dimples," said Jim.

"It's got husky biceps, too," said Susie.

"What kind of baby is it?" asked Joe and Peggy.

X frowned at them. Can't you tell?" Then X broke into a big mischievous grin. "It's a Y!"

Source: Adapted from Lois Gould, "X: A Fabulous Child's Story," *Ms.*, Vol. 1 (December, 1972):74–76, 105–106.

Read and React

1. What was your first reaction to this story?
2. Summarize the underlying hypothesis in the Baby X story.
3. Could a scientific experiment be constructed to test this hypothesis? If so, describe it. If not, explain why.
4. Discuss the ethical implications of such an experiment if one were conducted.

Answers to Read and React

1. Letting students just share their first reactions will probably result in some eye-opening discussion that exposes many gender stereotypes.
2. The hypothesis might be something like this: If children are not labeled specifically by gender at birth and allowed to continue to grow without a gender designation, then they are likely to be treated on the basis of their very specific personalities and talents rather than their sex.
3. Probably not likely unless in a laboratory setting. Socialization is everywhere and it would not be realistic to think that a child could avoid all the gender socialization messages.
4. Using a human subject (see Chapter 2, Ethics in Research) would violate the American Sociological Association's code of ethics. The potential harm that could be caused to the child X would outweigh the benefits of any research.

UNIT 4

NOTES to the Teacher

A social institution is defined as "a cluster of social structures that collectively meet one or more of the basic needs of a society." Institutions to be discussed in this book include family, education, politics, economy, religion, and sport. While each institution is organized differently, changes in quite different ways, and is responsible for different functions or needs of society, they are also interdependent.

From the functionalist point of view, the family is the institution in most danger since its functions have changed most dramatically. The economic and educational functions performed in the family prior to the industrial revolution have been usurped and some would say that its only remaining function is that of socio-emotional support. That the family has taken on more diverse forms in recent years is evidence that the functions are indeed changing, forcing a like change in its structure.

There is some controversy about how prevalent the nuclear family form has been in western society but it is clear that a plurality of family forms now exist. These different forms have created pressure on the legal system to support both the dissolution and formation of families: the enforcement of child support orders and the call to legalize same-sex marriages.

Of major concern to most state and city governments is the fact that half of the child support awards in the United States go completely unpaid, with another quarter of those awards receiving partial payment. This problem is a major contributor to the problem of the feminization of poverty (discussed in Chapter 8) since women are usually given custody of children, are the potential recipients of child support payments, earn less on average, and incur child care expenses when working. When these custodial mothers have trouble supporting themselves due to child care problems, balancing work and family needs, and low wages, the state and local governments become responsible for short-term or long-term assistance.

The political campaign to legalize same-sex marriages highlights the desire for the legitimacy of marriage and family by a group of people who have been barred

UNIT 4

SOCIAL INSTITUTIONS

Enrichment Readings

from participating in such a legal relationship due to the gender of their partners. Gays and lesbians have become increasingly visible in society and are increasingly mobilized and vocal about how their rights as citizens are denied due to their sexual orientation. While the public debate about this topic is by no means decided, it is important to notice that the right to marriage is societally and historically defined. Discussions of how marriage is dying because of high divorce rates must be countered by attending to the counter trend of those who wish to be married, but cannot legally do so.

The interdependence of institutions are also illustrated in the theories of Karl Marx who felt strongly that the economy was the base of society, the most important feature upon which all other institutions are built. Thus, in a society with a capitalist economy, the political and religious systems (among others) serve the needs of the capitalists and represent their interests. This is most evident in the discussion in Chapter 12 of the "hidden curriculum" that teaches conformity so as to create a population of good workers who follow the orders of their supervisors. Max Weber also spoke about the interdependence of the economy and religious systems in his study of capitalism and Protestantism. He found that the two systems have an elective affinity for one another: they each require people to work hard, one for salvation, the other to fuel the economy.

While religion and science both address the problem of how to make sense of the world, they are not always mutually exclusive. When one recognizes that science gives us tools to understand the empirical world and how human beings behave in it, you can also recognize that religion gives us information about how the nonmaterial or spiritual world may work. Alternatively, one may see that a social scientific understanding of the world can help explain how human beings behave and what the results of their interactions (social structures) may be, no matter if some other entity is responsible for putting us here. The Pope, in his apologies about past sins of the Catholic Church acknowledges the sociological impact of his church: that human beings run religious organizations, interpret the sacred texts, and have a major role in socializing people and in exercising power in society, and they are not infallible.

UNIT 4 Social Institutions

Chapters	Pacing Chart
11 THE FAMILY 1. Family and Marriage Across Cultures 2. Theoretical Perspectives and the Family 3. Family and Marriage in the United States 4. Changes in Marriage and Family	**Pages 348-350, 352, 357-361, 363-370.** Includes basic definitions of family, chart summarizing family structures; functions of the family and sources of conflict are examined; marriage and divorce; family violence; changes in family relationships and emerging family patterns. *This plan omits discussions of family structure, marriage arrangements, and cultural influences on mate selection.*
12 EDUCATION 1. Development and Structure of Education 2. Functionalist Perspective 3. Conflict Perspective 4. Symbolic Interactionism	**Pages 388-389, 396-400, 403-407.** The bureaucratic nature of formal education, manifest and latent functions of schools;and general issues of inequality in education. *This plan omits democratic reforms in the classrooms and alternatives to the public school system; meritocracy and schools; and socialization and sexism in public education.*
13 POLITICAL AND ECONOMIC INSTITUTIONS 1. Power and Authority 2. Political Power in American Society 3. Economic Systems 4. The Modern Corporation 5. Work in the Modern Economy	**Pages 424-427, 433-439, 446-456.** Includes definitions of power and authority; voting trends and patterns, the role of interest groups, nature of the modern corporation, changing nature of work, and economic globalization. *Does not include types of political systems or the text discussions of capitalism, socialism, and mixed economic systems.*
14 RELIGION 1. Religion and Sociology 2. Theoretical Perspectives 3. Religious Organization and Religiosity 4. Religion in the United States	**Pages 464-473, 479-480, 485-488.** Discussions of the sociological basis for studying religion; looks at religiosity and fundamentalism, and religion and class. *Does not include the distinctions between types of religious organizations, the development of religion in the United States, and U.S. secularization.*
15 SPORT 1. The Nature of Sport 2. Theoretical Perspectives and Sport 3. Social Issues in Sport	You may choose to skip the study of this secondary institution, although students find it relevant and interesting.

Key to Ability Levels

Activities in the teacher's material have been coded for varying learning styles and abilities.

L1 **BASIC** activities for all students

L2 **AVERAGE** activities for average to above-average students

L3 **CHALLENGING** activities for above-average students

ELL **ENGLISH LANGUAGE LEARNER** activities

Teacher Resource Manager

Teacher Classroom Resources

Unit 4 Mastering Basic Concepts
- Learning Goals Outlines
- Graphic Organizers
- Vocabulary ActivitiesInterpreting Data
- Increasing Your Reading Comprehension
- Guided Readings
- Student Journal Prompts
- Vocabulary and Chapter Review Quizzes

Spanish Supplements
- Learning Goals Outlines
- Bilingual Chapter Summaries
- Vocabulary and Chapter Review Quizzes

Chapter & Unit Tests w/ Final Exam and Answer Key
- Chapters 11–15 Tests A and B
- Unit 4 Test

Alternative Assessments
- Performance Assessments
- Portfolio Assessments
- Chapter Essay Tests

Culture Studies: The Sociological Perspective
- Readings 19–25

Including:
- Reading 23: Simple Gifts

Doing Sociology: Focus on Research
- Research Projects 10–13

Ethics, Values, and Technology: Real-Life Issues in Society
- Readings 17–23

Including:
- Reading 20: Making the Grade Harder

Transparency Binder

Chapter 11
- 30–37

Including:
- 33: Race & Latino Origin of Children
- 36: Child Abuse

Chapter 12
- 38–43

Including:
- 40: Comparing the Length of the School Year
- 42: High School and Bachelor's Degree Completion Rates for Selected Asian & Pacific Groups

Chapter 13
- 44–50

Including:
- 47: Profile of the American Voter

Chapter 14
- 51: Church-going vs. Never Attends

Multimedia

TeacherWorks™
All-In-One Planner and Resource Center

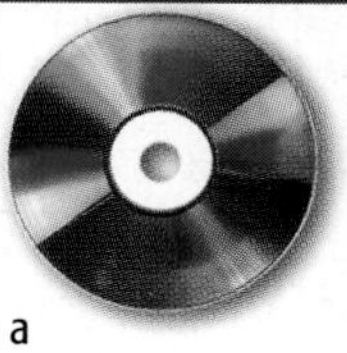

- **Interactive Teacher Edition** Access your Teacher Wraparound Edition and your classroom resources with a few easy clicks.
- **Interactive Lesson Planner** Planning has never been easier! Organize your week, month, semester, or year with all the lesson helps you need to make teaching creative, timely, and relevant.

Interactive Student Edition CD-ROM

This CD-ROM contains the complete Student Edition with, simple navigation and search functions and links to Web activities and resources.

ExamView® Pro Testmaker CD-ROM

Easy-to-use software includes an extensive question bank and allows you to create fully customized tests that can be administered in print or online.

Vocabulary PuzzleMaker CD-ROM

This software lets you create crossword puzzles, word search puzzles, and jumbo puzzles using chapter vocabulary.

Presentations for the Classroom on CD-ROM

This PowerPoint presentation provides a step-by-step outline and supporting visuals for classroom lectures.

SOCIOLOGY Online

Use our Web site for additional resources. All essential content is covered in the Student Edition.

You and your students can visit soc.glencoe.com, the Web site companion to *Sociology and You.* The student text directs students to the Web site for **Chapter Overviews, Student Web Activities, Self-Check Quizzes,** and **Textbook Updates**.

Answers are provided for you in the **Web Activity Lesson Plan**.

Chapter Preview

Section 1 (pages 348–356)

In all societies, the family has been the most important institution. It produces new generations, socializes the young, provides care and affection, regulates sexual behavior, transmits social status, and provides economic support.

Section 2 (pages 357–362)

The family is the very core of human social life. It is not surprising that each of the major perspectives focuses on the family. Functionalism emphasizes the benefits of the family for society. The conflict perspective looks at why males dominate in the family structure. Symbolic interactionism studies how the family socializes children and promotes the development of self-concept.

Section 3 (pages 363–370)

Modern marriages are based primarily on love, but there are many reasons for marrying—and as many reasons given for divorce. Although the American family provides social and emotional support, violence in this setting is not uncommon. Child abuse and spousal abuse are serious problems in too many American families.

Section 4 (pages 371–380)

Many new patterns of marriage and family living have emerged in the United States. In spite of these new arrangements, the traditional nuclear family is not going to be replaced on a broad scale.

CHAPTER 11

The Family

Lead-Off Activity

Ask students to write down the characteristics they look for in choosing a potential mate. Answers will probably include details about looks, personality, values, and the like. Tell students that they have just described their ideal mate. Have them compare the characteristics of their ideal mate to their own characteristics. Explain that the sociological reality is that a person will likely choose a mate that has characteristics similar to his or her own. He or she will most likely be of similar age, religion, race and/or ethnicity, educational background, and socio-economic status; from the same geographic location; and possess similar values. Statistically speaking, a person is much more likely to marry a person like him- or herself than an "ideal" person with a different background and dissimilar characteristics.
L1

USING Your Sociological Imagination

Test your knowledge about the American family by identifying the following statements as true or false.

1. About half of the couples in the United States who marry will divorce.
2. A new family structure develops after divorce.
3. High school sweethearts who marry have a less than 10 percent chance of being together twenty years later.
4. In more than half of all marriages, both the husband and wife work outside the home.
5. The divorce rate has been steadily climbing since 1960.

If you thought the first four questions were true and the last question was false, then you probably have a good sense of what is happening with marriage and families in the United States. It is true that the divorce rate is higher in the United States than in many other industrialized nations. However, recent data on divorce provide some grounds for optimism. Although the divorce rate rose dramatically from 1960 to 1985, the last fifteen years have actually seen a decline in the rate of divorce.

The next five chapters in this unit will look at family, education, economics, politics, religion, and sports. Sociologists refer to each of these as a *social institution*—a system of statuses, roles, norms and social structures that are organized to satisfy some particular basic needs of society. Chapter 11 focuses on the most important of these institutions—the family.

Sections

Learning Objectives

After reading this chapter, you will be able to

- describe types of family structure and norms for marriage arrangements.
- compare and contrast views of the family proposed by the three major perspectives.
- outline the extent and cause of divorce in America.
- give an overview of family violence in the United States.
- discuss the future of the family in the United States.

SOCIOLOGY Online

Chapter Overview
Visit the *Sociology and You* Web site at soc.glencoe.com and click on **Chapter 11—Chapter Overviews** to preview chapter information.

USING Your Sociological Imagination

Emphasize to students that the changes in the American family mentioned in this feature are fairly recent occurrences. Ask students what these changes say about American society. Bring up the possibility that the institution of marriage in the United States is being shaped by sociological forces, including changes in the nature of work, and laws that make divorce easier to obtain. Ask students if they agree that the nature of marriage is changing as a result of these sociological forces. Or, is society adapting to accommodate the changing state of the institution of marriage? Are these changes necessarily bad?

Using the Section Preview

The family is the primary vehicle of socialization of young children. Until children attend school, most, if not all, of their socialization occurs within the family. School provides the first opportunity for youngsters to test their social skills with other children. Children from dysfunctional homes are often first made aware of the observable differences between themselves and others when attending school.

Open-Response Question

Ask students to take a sheet of paper and write a brief answer to this prompt. *If an alien from another planet landed in your backyard and asked you to describe the basic social unit (the family) how would you do this?* Then ask volunteers to read their answers. How do they compare?

Section 1 Family and Marriage Across Cultures

Key Terms

- family
- marriage
- nuclear family
- extended family
- patrilineal
- matrilineal
- bilateral
- patriarchy
- matriarchy
- equalitarian
- patrilocal
- matrilocal
- neolocal
- monogamy
- polygamy
- polygyny
- polyandry
- exogamy
- incest taboo
- endogamy
- homogamy
- heterogamy

Section Preview

In all societies, the family has been the most important of all social institutions. It produces new generations, socializes the young, provides care and affection, regulates sexual behavior, transmits social status, and provides economic support.

Defining the Family

If asked to identify a family, most of us would say we know one when we see one. We are surrounded by families wherever we go, and most of us live in family settings. However, families come in all shapes and sizes, and defining the term *family* is sometimes difficult. Legally, the word *family* is used to describe many relationships: parents and children; people related by blood, marriage, or adoption; a group of people living together in a single household, sharing living space and housekeeping. Since the word *family*

If asked to describe this image, the first thought of most people would be that of a happy family.

Cooperative Learning Activity

Assign students to groups, then ask each group to imagine a society without families. What would that society be like? How would the basic needs of people be met? How would children be cared for? How would training and values be instilled? Who would fulfill the children's needs for love and affection? Have each group answer these questions by designing an imaginary society. Would students like to live there? Have groups share their societies with the rest of the class. In what ways are they similar? How do they differ? How well do they meet the needs of growing children? What type of adults would be produced by each society? Students who are interested in this proposition might read Aldous Huxley's *Brave New World,* a satire that includes family-free society.
L2

does not have a precise meaning, many laws define the term when they use it. For example, zoning laws that set aside certain areas for single-family homes define family one way. Laws involving insurance, social security, or inheritance may define family in other ways. For sociologists, however, **family** is defined as a group of people related by marriage, blood, or adoption. While the concept of family may appear simple on the surface, the family is a complex social unit with many facets. Of all the social institutions, the family has the greatest impact on individual behavior.

The family we are born into, or the family of birth, is called the *family of orientation*. It provides children with a name, an identity, and a heritage. In other words, it gives the child an ascribed status in the community. The family of orientation "orients" (or directs) children to their neighborhood, community, and society and locates them in the world.

The *family of procreation* is established upon marriage. **Marriage** is a legal union between a man and a woman based on mutual rights and obligations. (Marriages between two persons of the same sex have been ruled legally invalid by U.S. courts.) The marriage ceremony signifies that it is legal (officially sanctioned) for a couple to have offspring and to give the children a family name. The family of procreation becomes the family of orientation for the children created from the marriage.

family
a group of people related by marriage, blood, or adoption

marriage
a legal union based on mutual rights and obligations

nuclear family
family structure composed of one or both parents and children

extended family
two or more adult generations of the same family whose members share economic resources and a common household

Two Basic Types of Families

There are two basic types of families. The **nuclear family**, the smallest group of individuals that can be called a family, is composed of a parent or parents and any children. The **extended family** consists of two or more adult generations of the same family whose members share economic resources and live in the same household. Extended families may also contain close relatives, such as grandparents, children, grandchildren, aunts, uncles, and cousins.

Why would sociologists not call these relatives an extended family?

> "The family is the essential presence—the thing that never leaves you, even if you have to leave it."
>
> **Bill Buford**
> writer

Making Connections to Other Cultures

Have students pick a country that interests them and research the typical family structure of that country. They should answer the following questions: Is the typical family structure the same throughout the country? Do different cultures within a single country have different family structures? How are families in other countries different from American families? Have students share their findings with the class.
L2

Integrating the Teacher Resources

Look for the Chapter 11 Learning Goals Outline, a reproducible student worksheet in the Unit 4 Mastering Basic Concepts booklet in your Teacher's Resource Box. It can be used to preview or review chapter content.

Interdisciplinary Activity

History Have students, working individually or in groups, research families in different historical times and cultures. (Societies to study might include Sparta, Rome, French nobility of the Middle Ages, sixteenth century Scotland, and so on.) Students should consider formation of the family (how many generations were included?), values instilled, functions of the various family members, and so on. Have the students or groups of students share their knowledge, and discuss as a class what they have learned about families in these various time periods. In what society would students have preferred to live? Why? In which would they least have liked to live? Why?
L2

Making Connections to Other Cultures

Use thick yarn or string to have students create a grid on the bulletin board. On the vertical axis of the grid, have them list the countries about which they are to be responsible for getting family information. On the horizontal axis create a series of columns that identify the information to be gathered and posted. Such items might include: family structure, marriage ceremonies, marriage form, mate selection process, divorce, roles of males, roles of females, roles of children, or other family characteristics that they would be interested in learning more about. Have teams of students research and post, in an eye-catching manner, information about the marriage practices in the specific cultures.

Once the bulletin board has been completed and discussed, have each student prepare a similar grid of what he or she would include about families in the United States. Have them compare their efforts.

L1

How did family structures develop? As discussed in Chapter 5, the development of agriculture and industry shaped society. These developments also shaped family structure.

In the earliest societies, hunting and gathering were the primary family activities. Small bands of nuclear families followed herds of animals and changing seasons, moving around constantly, never staying long in any one place.

When humans domesticated animals to help with tilling the soil and cultivating crops (about nine thousand years ago), they no longer needed to be mobile to maintain a food supply. Families began to farm, settle down, and establish roots. Large families were needed to plow and harvest. The growth of family farms encouraged the development of the extended family. Agriculture became the basis of the economy, and the extended family was essential for successful farming.

As societies moved from agricultural economies to industrialized ones, the extended family was slowly replaced by the nuclear family. Large families were no longer needed to work on the farm. Industrial and postindustrial economies favor the nuclear family that has fewer mouths to feed and that is easier to move (Goode, 1970; Nydeggar, 1985).

Patterns of Family Structure

patrilineal
descent and inheritance is passed through the male line

matrilineal
descent and inheritance is passed through the female line

bilateral
descent and inheritance are passed equally through both parents

patriarchy
the pattern in which the oldest man living in the household has authority over the rest of the family members

matriarchy
the pattern in which the oldest woman living in the household has authority over all other family members

Whether nuclear or extended, families behave in similar ways across cultures. These patterns of behavior relate to inheritance, authority, and place of residence.

Who inherits? Determining who becomes head of the family—for purpose of descent—and who owns the family property—for inheritance—are extremely important to families. Three arrangements are used.

- In a **patrilineal** arrangement, descent and inheritance are passed from the father to his male descendants. The people of Iran and Iraq, and the Tikopia in the western Pacific live in patrilineal societies.
- In a **matrilineal** arrangement, descent and inheritance are transmitted from the mother to her female descendants. Some Native American tribes, such as the Pueblo peoples of the Southwest, are matrilineal.
- In some societies, descent and inheritance are **bilateral**—they are passed equally through both parents. Thus both the father's and mother's relatives are accepted equally as part of the kinship structure. Most families in the United States today are bilateral.

Who is in authority? Similar patterns govern authority in a family.

- In a **patriarchy,** the oldest man living in the household has authority over the rest of the family members. We see this in many countries around the world, such as Iraq and China. In its purest form, the father is the absolute ruler.
- In a **matriarchy,** the oldest woman living in the household holds the authority. So rare is matriarchal control that controversy exists over whether any society has ever had a genuinely matriarchal family structure.

Learning Styles

Visual Obtain a map of your state, a map of the United States, and either a globe or a map of the world. Have students identify the locations of their extended family members, including grandparents, siblings living away from home, cousins, uncles and aunts. Most likely, few students have the majority of their extended family living nearby. This geographic distance can result in less regular personal contact with relatives. Ask students how they remain "connected" with their extended families. How many use the Internet to keep their families connected?
L1, ELL

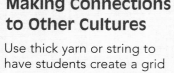

- With **equalitarian** control, authority is split evenly between husband and wife. Many families in the Scandinavian countries and in the United States follow the equalitarian model.

equalitarian
family structure in which authority is evenly shared between the husband and wife

Where do couples live? Where newly married couples set up their households also varies from culture to culture.

- The **patrilocal** pattern, such as in premodern China, calls for living with or near the husband's parents.
- Residing with or near the wife's parents is expected under a **matrilocal** pattern. The Nayar caste of Kerala in southern India is an illustration of this type of arrangement.
- In the **neolocal** pattern (if finances allow) married couples establish residences of their own. This is the Euro-American model. Extended families, of course, have different norms.

patrilocal
refers to the pattern in which married couples live with or near the husbands' parents

matrilocal
refers to the pattern in which married couples live with or near the wives' parents

neolocal
refers to the pattern in which newly married couples set up their own households

Marriage Arrangements

Mention a wedding and Americans commonly think of a bride walking down the aisle in a long white gown. She and the groom make vows that involve some form of loving, honoring, and (until recently, in some cases) obeying. In other cultures, the wedding ceremony looks very different. This is part of the ceremony among the Reindeer Tungus of Siberia:

> *After the groom's gifts have been presented, the bride's dowry is loaded onto the reindeer and carried to the groom's lodge. There, the rest of the ceremony takes place. The bride takes the wife's place—that is, at the right side of the entrance of the lodge—and members of both families sit around in a circle. The groom enters and follows the bride around the circle, greeting each guest, while the guests, in their turn, kiss the bride on the mouth and hands. Finally, the go-betweens spit three times on the bride's hands, and the couple is formally "husband and wife." More feasting and revelry bring the day to a close (Ember and Ember, 1999:310–311).*

monogamy
a marriage consisting of one man and one woman

Whatever form it takes, the marriage ceremony is an important ritual announcing that a man and woman have become husband and wife, that a new family has been formed, and that any children born to the couple can legitimately inherit the family name and property.

What forms do marriage take? **Monogamy**—the marriage of one man to one woman—is the most widely practiced form of marriage in the world today. In fact, it is the only form of marriage that is legally

Although wedding ceremonies may vary, the basic social structures of marriage are common to all societies.

Teaching Strategy

A fun way to illustrate for students the extensive cost and effort involved in planning a wedding is to have them plan their own hypothetical wedding. Have students begin by deciding upon occupations for themselves and their spouse. Next, have students research the starting salaries of those jobs and decide upon a budget for the wedding based upon their income. You might want to have the class brainstorm the different items and services involved: churches, reception halls, clothing for the bride, groom, and wedding party, etc. Have students contact churches, tuxedo shops, food caterers, etc. for price information. If students plan to obtain financial assistance from their parents, have them discuss with their parents how much involvement each party will have in planning the wedding. (This could spark some interesting discussions if parents and students find out that they have different ideas about aspects of the wedding!) Students might be surprised at the cost and amount of planning required to arrange a wedding.
L2

Learning Styles

Linguistic/Spatial This chapter's vocabulary can be confusing because many of the terms have similar roots. To give students an opportunity to practice some of the terms in a way that may help to give them a more applied meaning, divide the students into groups. Assign each group to create a graphic display of their own devising (two- or three-dimensional) that visually explains the meaning of the following terms: Group 1—patterns of behavior relating to inheritance (patrilineal, matrilineal, and bilateral); Group 2—patterns of behavior relating to authority (patriarchy, matriarchy, and equalitarian); and Group 3—patterns of behavior relating to place of residence (neolocal, patrilocal, and matrilocal). Conclude with a class discussion of the terms and a real-world example of each.
L2

More About . . . Polygyny

In some cultures where polygyny is practiced, having more than one wife is regarded as symbol of a man's high social status. Have students research cultures that practice or have practiced polygyny and answer the following questions: What are some cultures that attach social ranking to having more than one spouse? Are there any societal rules that govern who may take more than one wife? Are there limits as to how many wives a man may take?

Points to Stress

Remind students of the different types of societies discussed in Chapter 5. For example, the industrial and post-industrial revolutions led to the prevalence of the nuclear family unit by changing the roles of men and women both in the workplace and at home. These social transformations changed family structure, but the importance of the family and its role in society has not changed. Family is still the most important social institution.

Working with the Data

Figure 11.1 You might want to discuss with students how you want them to interpret the phrase "general nature" of the family. What should be included in their description?

polygamy
the marriage of a male or female to more than one person at a time

polygyny
the marriage of one man to two or more women at the same time

polyandry
the marriage of one woman to two or more men at the same time

acceptable in the United States and in most Western societies. Some often-married people practice *serial* monogamy—having several husbands or wives, but being married to only one at a time.

In contrast to monogamy, **polygamy** involves the marriage of a male or female to more than one person at a time. It takes two forms: polygyny and polyandry.

Polygyny is the marriage of one man to two or more women at the same time. An obvious example of polygyny is found in the Old Testament. King Solomon is reported to have had seven hundred wives and three hundred concubines. Although common in earlier societies, polygyny is not practiced widely in any society today. (However, in 1999, the president of the Muslim Russian republic of Ingushetia signed a decree legalizing the practice of polygyny. Democratic activists challenged the ruling.)

Polyandry—the marriage of one woman to two or more men at the same time—is an even rarer form of marriage. It is known to have been common in only two societies: in Tibet and among the Todas of India (Queen et al., 1985). Where polyandry has existed, it usually has consisted of several brothers sharing a wife.

You have been introduced to a lot of new terms that relate to family structure and marriage arrangements. Figure 11.1 illustrates several of the characteristics of these family and marriage forms to help you understand and remember them.

Figure 11.1 Families/Marriages

This chart summarizes possible variations in family and marriage forms. Describe the general nature of the American family using terms from this table.

Nuclear Family Composition	parents and children
Extended Family Composition	parents, children, and other relatives
Inheritance	patrilineal (inherit through the father) or matrilineal (inherit through the mother) or bilateral (inherit through both)
Authority	patriarchal (father rules the family) or matriarchal (mother rules the family) or equalitarian (parents share authority)
Residence	patrilocal (couple lives with or near husband's parents) or matrilocal (couple lives with or near wife's parents) or neolocal (couple lives apart from both parents)
Marriage Composition	polygyny (one husband, many wives) or polyandry (one wife, many husbands) or monogamy (one husband, one wife)

Paired Learning Activity

Have students work in pairs and use library resources to learn more about family patterns in other countries. They should investigate marriage customs, family roles, use of power and authority, and child-rearing practices. Have students write a summary of their findings and report to the class. Discuss these questions with the class: How are family patterns in different cultures affected by such things as religion, economic factors, government, etc.? Why is polygyny more common than polyandry? Why are patriarchal societies more common than matriarchal societies? Why do you think families in Western societies are more egalitarian than families in other parts of the world?
L2

World View

Types of Marriages

Monogamy—the marriage of one man and one woman—is the only legal form of marriage in all industrial and postindustrial societies. It is also the only form of marriage allowed by law in the Western Hemisphere. However, in many African and southern Asian nations, where Islam is the predominant religion, polygyny—the marriage of one man to two or more women at the same time—is legal. This map shows the countries where monogamy and polygyny are legal forms of marriage.

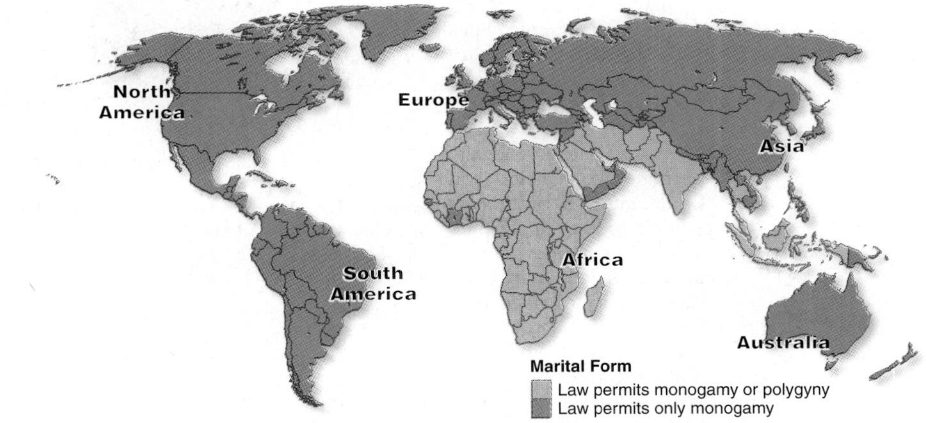

Interpreting the Map

1. Suggest one or more reasons for the widespread presence of polygyny in Africa, Southwest Asia (the Middle East), India, and Southeast Asia.
2. Why do you think the caption explains that the map shows only the countries where polygyny and monogamy are legal forms of marriage?

Choosing a Mate

Suppose you came home from school one afternoon and your parents asked you to come into the living room to meet your future husband or wife. You might wonder if you had somehow been beamed to another planet. Similarly, you will probably never enroll in a college course entitled "Negotiating Dowries with Prospective In-laws," this being a skill not much in demand today. If, however, you assume that you have complete freedom of choice in the selection of a marriage partner, you are mistaken. All cultures and societies, including the United States, have norms and laws about who may marry whom.

On-Demand Writing

Choosing when to begin and whom to date is not a process done in isolation. The decision of a teen couple to date affects both of their families and the community as a whole. Conversely, the family and community have some effect on the couple's dating processes. Ask students to write answers to the following questions: 1) When should parents begin discussing values related to the dating process? Why? 2) What personal values are important to consider in relation to dating? 3) What role does the community play in dating? 4) Does the community have a responsibility to provide dating activity options? If so, what types of options should be available?

L2

World View

The text states that monogamy is the only legal form of marriage in the Western Hemisphere. Be sure students understand the implied assumption that the word "known" is inserted before legal. Also, they may claim that Mormonism, or the Church of the Latter-Day Saints, allows plural marriages. Today, Latter-Day Saints can presently be married to only one woman at a time. However, during the nineteenth-century, LDS men were allowed to marry more than one wife under certain conditions. You might ask students to recall the characteristics of a preindustrial society. Why would these types of societies be likely to allow polygyny to be a part of their culture? *(One possible answer is that more wives produce more children to help with the farming, herding, etc.)*

Answers to Interpreting the Map

1. One reason students should mention is that Islam is the predominant religion in many of those countries. They are also agricultural societies dependent upon human labor to grow food.
2. There may be forms of marriage practiced in areas that are not legalized by the country's government.

Teaching Strategy

Remind students of the differences between nationality, ethnicity, and race. Ask students what their nationality is and what their parents' nationality is. Then ask them what their ethnicity is and what their parents' ethnicity is. The nationalities and ethnicities may or may not be different. Few students will say that they are solely of one ethnicity, although there may be some students who are solely of a particular race. As endogamy becomes rarer and rarer, fewer and fewer people are descended from only one nationality, ethnicity, or race.

Working with the Data

Figure 11.2 Ask students to generalize about the data in this figure. They should reply that mixed race marriages are becoming more acceptable in our culture and because of this, we will probably continue to see an increase in mixed race marriages.

Reteaching

Write the terms age, religion, geographic location, values, race/ethnicity, educational background and socioeconomic status on the board. Drawing from the Lead-Off activity on page 346, tell students that a tendency towards homogamy is the sociological reality. Have students ask their parents if they exhibit similarities in the above-mentioned characteristics, and report the findings back to the class.

exogamy
the practice of marrying outside one's group

incest taboo
a norm forbidding marriage between close relatives

Exogamy refers to mate-selection norms requiring individuals to marry someone outside their kind or group. (*Exo* is a prefix meaning "outside".) The most important norms relating to exogamy are called **incest taboos,** which forbid marriage between certain kinds of relatives. In the traditional Chinese culture, for example, two people with identical family names could not marry unless their family lines were known to have diverged at least five generations previously (Queen et al., 1985). In the United States, you are not legally permitted to marry a son or daughter, a brother or sister, a mother or a father, a niece or nephew, or an aunt or uncle. In twenty-nine states, marriage to a first cousin is prohibited. Furthermore, it is illegal to marry a former mother-in-law or father-in-law. Incest is almost universally prohibited, although exceptions were common among the royalty of ancient Europe, Hawaii, Egypt, and Peru. Even in these instances, most members of the royal families chose partners to whom they were not related by blood.

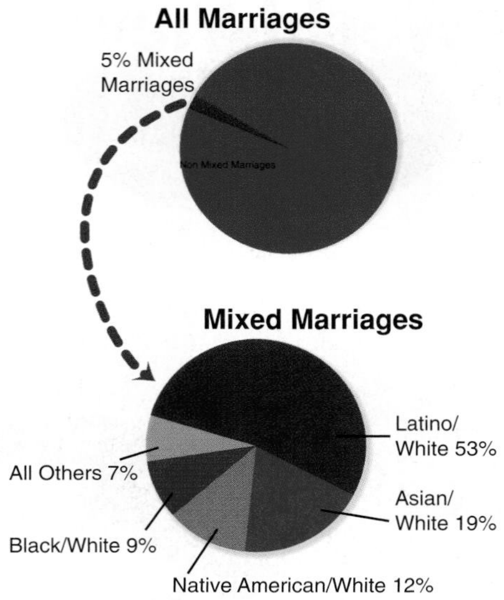

Figure 11.2 Mixed Marriages and Intergroup Married Couples in the United States.
Although only 5 percent of marriages in the U.S. are mixed, the number has quadrupled since 1980.

Source: American Demographics, Population Reference Bureau, 1998; Miliken Institute, 2001.

endogamy
marriage within one's own group as required by social norms

Endogamy involves mate-selection norms that require individuals to marry within their own kind. (*Endo* is a prefix that means "inside.") In the United States, for example, norms have required that marriage partners be of the same race. These norms are not as strong as they once were. Although they represent only five percent of all marriages in the United States, mixed marriages have quadrupled since 1980. Figure 11.2 shows the racial and ethnic breakdown of intergroup marriages today. Also, class lines are crossed with greater frequency because more Americans of all social classes are attending college together. Finally, norms separating age groups have weakened.

homogamy
the tendency to marry someone similar to oneself

Norms encouraging (rather than requiring) marriage within a group usually exist. And people are most likely to know and prefer to marry others like themselves. For these reasons, people tend to marry those with social characteristics similar to their own. This tendency, the result of the rather free exercise of personal choice, is known as **homogamy.**

For example, in spite of what fairy tales and movies often tell us, it is rare for the son or daughter of a multimillionaire to marry someone from a lower

Cooperative Learning Activity

Although many countries are becoming more Westernized in their dating and marriage practices, traditions remain in many cultures.

In contemporary Japan for example, where half of the marriages are self-arranged, many couples still prefer a marriage in which they are matched. The go-betweens, usually a husband and wife referred to as a *nakado,* act together as mediators to introduce a couple, assist in negotiating arrangements between the two families, run the wedding and reception, and counsel the married couple if problems arise in their relationship.

Even couples who marry for love in Japan have an honorary go-between. The go-between arranges a meeting, known as a *miai,* between a man and a woman who have similar social status, education, and hobbies. The go-between usually initiates the relationship by sending a letter from class. Furthermore, most marriages in the United States occur between individuals who are about the same age. Most people who are marrying for the first time marry someone who also has not been married before. Divorced people tend to marry others who have been previously married. Finally, people tend to choose marriage partners from their own communities or neighborhoods.

Although it is still the exception in the United States, **heterogamy** is rising. In heterogamous marriages, partners are dissimilar in some important characteristics. More American marriages, for instance, are crossing traditional barriers of age, race, social class, and ethnicity. This trend results from several factors. America has become more racially and ethnically integrated, so that people have an opportunity to mix more freely. The television and film industries help foster heterogamy by the sympathetic portrayal of couples and families from different racial and social backgrounds. In addition, class lines are crossed with greater frequency, and norms separating age groups have weakened.

Are these two individuals in a homogenous or heterogamous relationship? Explain.

> Success in marriage is not so much finding the right person as it is being the right person.
>
> **Anonymous**

heterogamy
marriage between people with differing social characteristics

Section 1 Assessment

1. What is the difference between a nuclear and an extended family? Which type represents your household?
2. Why are nuclear families more common in industrial societies?
3. What is another term for the family of birth?
4. Indicate whether exogamy (Ex), endogamy (En), or homogamy (H) is reflected in each of the following situations.
   - **a.** Catholics are supposed to marry Catholics.
   - **b.** A father is not permitted to marry his daughter.
   - **c.** Members of the same social class marry.
   - **d.** A brother and sister are legally prohibited from marrying.
   - **e.** People tend to marry others of the same age.
   - **f.** Rich people marry other wealthy people.

Critical Thinking

5. **Synthesizing Information** Write a paragraph based on personal knowledge or experience that supports or refutes the idea that homogamy dominates American society.

Answers to Section 1 Assessment

1. A nuclear family is the smallest group of individuals that can be called a family—parent(s) and any children; an extended family consists of two or more adult generations of the same family whose members share economic resources and live in the same household.
2. Nuclear families are more common in industrial societies because there are fewer mouths to feed and relocating is easier.
3. Another term is family of orientation.
4. a. H
   b. Ex
   c. H
   d. Ex
   e. En
   f. H

(This question should encourage discussion as students defend their answers. The amount of censure/criticism from society should enter into choices. For example, how important is it now for a Catholic to marry a Catholic (personal choice—homogamy, or required—endogamy)? How much criticism would be involved in a marriage involving a large age difference? Would it make a difference if this marriage was between an older man/younger woman as opposed to a younger man/older woman?)

Critical Thinking

5. Answers will vary.

the man to the woman. The two families often hire detectives to check the backgrounds and interview people who know the man and the woman.

Customs in India are similar to those in Japan, but also include the stipulation that the woman's educational level be no higher than the man's. Matchmakers sometimes consult horoscopes when arranging marriages in India. The groom's representative often exchanges gifts with the bride's family, thus adding to the obligation of the relationship.

After sharing this information with students, have them work in groups to discuss the following questions. 1) How would matchmaking practices work in our country? How would they affect the lives of teenagers? 2) Do you think matchmaking would result in more stable families? Why or why not?
L2

Another Time

This is certainly not the kind of wedding that most Americans would envision. But elements of the Hopi wedding appear in weddings in Maintown, U.S.A. Ask students to pick out similar social patterns, such as the involvement of the families, and the importance of being able to show you can support a family.

Answers to Thinking It Over

1. Students' answers will vary but should show an understanding of the fact that the new bride has been told her "place" in the household pecking order. It also "proves" the worthiness of the bride to join the new family.
2. Traditions such as the Hopi wedding customs provide cultures with social stability.

Another Time: Courtship and Marriage Among the Hopi

Courtship and marriage customs among the Hopi Indians of the southwestern United States are quite different from those of the dominant U.S. culture.

Once the decision to marry is made by the young couple, the boy goes in the evening after supper to the girl's house and there states his intentions to her parents. If he is acceptable, he is told to go home and tell his parents about it. The girl then grinds cornmeal or makes bread, and carries it to the house of her prospective groom. At this time the mother of the boy may refuse the bread or meal, in which case the match is usually broken off. If, however, the food is accepted, it is given by the mother to her brothers and to her husband's clansmen, and the wedding plans go forward.

After this event the girl returns home to grind more meal with the help of her kinswomen, while the boy fetches water and chops wood for his mother. In the evening after these chores are completed, the bride dresses in her manta beads and her wedding blanket. Accompanied by the boy, who carries the meal she has ground, she walks barefoot to his house. There she presents the meal to her prospective mother-in-law and settles down for a temporary three-day stay before the wedding. During this period the young couple may see each other, but they [do not become intimate].

At some time during the three-day period the groom's house is visited, or "attacked," by his paternal aunts, who break in on the bride and shower her with [abusive language] and often with mud. They accuse her of laziness, inefficiency, and stupidity. The boy's mother and her clanswomen protect the girl and insist that the accusations are unfounded. In spite of appearances all this is carried off in a good-humored way, and finally the aunts leave, having stolen the wood their nephew had brought his mother. The wood is used to bake piki, which is given to the mother, and thus all damages are paid for.

On the morning of the fourth day the marriage is consummated. On this occasion the girl's relatives wash the boy's hair and bathe him, while the boy's relatives do the same for the girl. The couple may now sleep together as man and wife, but they remain at the boy's mother's house until the girl's wedding garments are complete. These garments are woven by the groom, his male relatives, and any men in the village who wish to participate.

Source: Stuart A. Queen and Robert W. Habenstein, *The Family in Various Cultures,* 4th ed. (Philadelphia: Lippincott, 1974, pp. 54–55, 56–58. Copyright 1952, © 1961, 1967, 1974 by J.B. Lippincott Company.) Reprinted by permission of Harper & Row, Publishers.

Contemporary Hopi Indians play traditional roles during a formal ceremony.

Thinking It Over

1. What do you think the staged "fight" with the groom's aunts signifies?
2. What are some of the advantages Hopi society gains by following these wedding customs?

Careers in Sociology

Provide students with the following information about social work.

Social work is a profession for those with a strong desire to help people, to make things better, and to make a difference. Social workers help people function the best way they can in their environment, deal with their relationships with others, and solve personal and family problems.

Through direct counseling, social workers help clients identify concerns, consider solutions, and find resources. Social workers consult and counsel clients and arrange for services. They may refer clients to specialists such as debt counseling, childcare or elder care, public assistance, or alcohol or drug rehabilitation. They follow through to assure that services are helpful and that

Section 2 Theoretical Perspectives and the Family

Key Term

- socioemotional maintenance

Functionalism

For the functionalists, the family plays many roles, including socializing the young, providing social and emotional support, managing reproduction, regulating sexual activity, transmitting social status, and serving as an economic center. Let's look more closely at each of these functions.

How does the family socialize children? In addition to caring for an infant's physical needs, parents begin the vital process of teaching the child what he or she must learn to learn to participate in society. During the first year, the infant begins to mimic words and, later, sentences. During the second and third years, parents begin to teach the child values and norms of behavior. By being role models and through training and education, the family continues the process of socialization in each new stage of development.

What do functionalists believe about the roles associated with this father and daughter?

What is the socioemotional function of the family? Another major function of the family is **socioemotional maintenance.** Generally, the family is the one place in society where an individual is unconditionally accepted and loved. Family members accept one another as they are; every member is special and unique. Without this care and affection, children will not develop normally. (See Chapter 4, pages 111–112 on children raised in isolation.) They may have low self-esteem, fear rejection, feel insecure, and eventually find it difficult to adjust to marriage or to express affection to their own children. Even individuals who are well integrated into society require support when adjusting to changing norms and in developing and continuing healthy relationships. Here again, the family can provide socioemotional maintenance.

Section Preview

The family is the very core of human social life. It is not surprising that each of the major perspectives focuses on the family. Functionalism emphasizes the benefits of the family for society. The conflict perspective looks at the reasons males dominate in the family structure. Symbolic interactionism studies the way the family socializes children and promotes the development of self-concept.

socioemotional maintenance provision of acceptance and support

Using the Section Preview

Students tend to be interested in the study of family because they are able to relate to it. Other social institutions are more abstract and further removed from a student's world. Have students perform the family ranking exercise listed on page 382 (#1 under Projects and Activities). Most students are acutely aware of the strengths and limitations of their family. Knowledge and understanding of their current family can help students foresee what they may want when they are ready to start a family of their own.

Reinforcing Vocabulary

The root *socio* (if students haven't sussed it out for themselves) refers to society. It originally came from the Latin word Socius, meaning companion or partner. Related words based on the same root include associate, sequel, sociable, and even suit.
ELL

clients make proper use of the services offered. Social workers may review eligibility requirements, help fill out forms and applications, visit clients on a regular basis, and provide support during crises.

Social workers practice in: Child welfare or family services, child or adult protective services, mental health, health care, schools, criminal justice, occupational, social work administrators, planners, and policy-makers.

There is a growing need for social workers. For information about career opportunities in social work, contact: National Association of Social Workers: **http://www.naswdc.org/**

Working with the Data

Figure 11.3 You might want to have your students take this survey and see how close your class comes to the national averages. Students might want to analyze the survey by the individual aspects and dimensions involved. What reasons might explain high and low scores?

It might be interesting for students to take the survey home for their parents to take, basing their answers on how they believe they rate. Then they should compare their own answers with those of their parents to see what kind of discrepancies, if any, exist. You might want to average the parents' answers for the entire class. Who was closer to the students' answers, moms or dads? Why do students think this might be the case?

Integrating the Teacher Resources

Look for the Chapter 11 Analyzing and Interpreting Data worksheet in the Unit 4 Mastering Basic Concepts booklet in your Teacher's Resource Box for skill-building exercises based on the graphs, charts, and maps in this chapter.

Figure 11.3 American Youths Grade Their Parents

In a national survey, Americans in the seventh through the twelfth grades were asked to "grade" their mothers and fathers. The results are shown below. The left-hand column lists various aspects of child rearing, and the remaining columns indicate the percentage of students who assigned each grade. For example, on the dimension "Raising me with good values," 69 percent gave their fathers an A, 17 percent a B, and so forth.

Grading Dad

Aspect of Child Rearing	**Assigned Grade** A	B	C	D	F
Raising me with good values	69%	17%	8%	4%	2%
Appreciating me for who I am	58	21	11	8	2
Encouraging me to enjoy learning	58	24	12	4	2
Making me feel important and loved	57	22	13	6	2
Being able to go to important events	55	22	13	5	5
Being there for me when I am sick	52	20	16	8	4
Spending time talking with me	43	24	19	10	4
Establishing traditions with me	41	26	15	11	7
Being involved in school life	38	24	19	12	7
Being someone to go to when upset	38	22	15	12	13
Controlling his temper	31	27	20	10	12
Knowing what goes on with me	31	30	17	12	10

Grading Mom

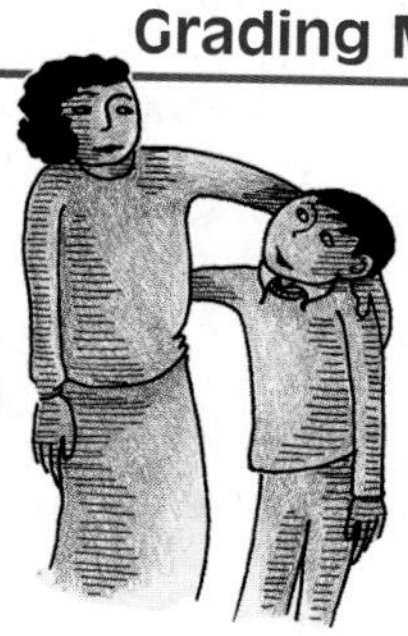

Aspect of Child Rearing	**Assigned Grade** A	B	C	D	F
Being there for me when I am sick	81%	11%	5%	2%	1%
Raising me with good values	74	15	6	3	2
Making me feel important and loved	64	20	10	5	1
Being able to go to important events	64	20	10	3	3
Appreciating me for who I am	63	18	8	6	5
Encouraging me to enjoy learning	59	23	12	3	3
Being involved in school life	46	25	13	10	6
Being someone to go to when upset	46	22	13	8	9
Spending time talking with me	43	33	14	6	4
Establishing traditions with me	38	29	17	10	6
Knowing what goes on with me	35	31	15	10	9
Controlling her temper	29	28	19	12	11

1. Based on this data, what conclusions would you draw about the closeness of families in America?
2. Select the three aspects of child rearing you think are most important, and compare the grade you would give your parent or parents on these aspects with the grades in this national sample.

Source: Ellen Galinsky, *Ask the Children* (New York: William Morrow & Co., Inc., 1999).

Demonstration

This powerful demonstration illustrates how intertwined (and dangerous in some cases) relationships can become when sexual activity is not regulated. You'll need one index card for each student in the class, and red yarn. Write an M (monogamous) on one index card, write an A (abstinent) on two index cards, and write HIV+ on yet another index card. Leave all the other index cards blank. Shuffle the cards together, and hand a card to each student. The students with the M and A cards should remain at their desks, while all the other students should walk around the room, gathering three signatures from various classmates. Emphasize that students must get signatures from a variety of students, not just their friends. When students are done gath-

What important functions are being fulfilled by this family?

What is the reproductive function of the family? Society cannot survive without new members. The family provides an orderly means for producing new members, generation after generation. So important is this function that for many cultures and religions, it is the primary purpose for sexual relations. In many societies in developing nations the failure of a wife to bear children can lead to divorce. Residents of places such as the Punjab region of North India, for example, view children as an economic necessity. The significance of having children is also seen in the hundreds of rituals, customs, and traditions that are associated with pregnancy and birth in virtually all cultures around the world. (Later in the chapter, we look at the rise of marriages without children in the United States.)

How does the family regulate sexual activity? In no known society are people given total sexual freedom. Even in sexually permissive societies, such as the Hopi Indians, there are rules about mating and marrying. Norms regarding sexual activities vary from place to place. Families in a few cultures, such as in the Trobriand Islands, encourage premarital sex. Other societies, like those in Iran and Afghanistan, go to great lengths to prevent any contact between nonrelated single males and females. The United States has traditionally fallen somewhere between these two extremes. In the ideal culture in the United States, adolescents would abstain from sexual activity. In real culture, however, the abundance of sexual references directed at teens by the advertising and entertainment industries make abstinence very difficult and even seem undesirable. Clearly, we are sending a mixed message to young people today. One of the consequences of this cultural confusion is the increase in teenage pregnancies and the number of teenagers having abortions. But whatever the norms, it is almost always up to the family to enforce them.

How does the family transmit social status? Families provide economic resources that open and close occupational doors. The sons and daughters of high-income professionals, for example, are more likely to attend college and graduate school than are the children of blue-collar workers. Consequently, the children of professionals are more likely as adults to enter professional occupations. The family also passes on values that affect social status. The children of professionals, for example, tend to feel a greater need to pursue a college degree than their counterparts from blue-collar families. In these and many other ways, the family affects the placement of children in the stratification structure.

What is the economic function of the family? At one time, families were self-sufficient economic units whose members all contributed to the production of needed goods. Every family member would join in such tasks as growing food, making cloth, and taking care of livestock. The modern American family is a unit of consumption rather than production. Adult members—increasingly including working mothers—are employed outside the home and pool their resources to buy what they need. But the end result is the same. The family provides what is needed to survive.

> Home is the place where, when you have to go there, they have to take you in.
>
> **Robert Frost**
> **American poet**

Controversy and Debate

An ethical debate in our time centers around the number of children families should have. As students will see in Chapter 16, population continues to increase over time as infant mortality rates decrease and life expectancy increases due to technological improvements in health care. Have students debate these questions: How many children should a couple have? How many is enough? How many is too many? Should governments dictate policies regarding the number of children a couple should have? Students might want to consider and debate the impact of such policies in China.

ering signatures, give three pieces of red yarn to each student who had a card signed. Call the student with the HIV+ card to the front of the room. Have the students who signed that card come to the front of the room, and create a human chain using their pieces of red yarn as links. Continue the process, creating a chain beginning with the person with the HIV+ card, to include all the students who signed cards. You will see that with the exception of the students with the M card and the A cards, all the students have put themselves at risk for contracting the AIDS virus. This demonstration should spark an interesting discussion.
L1

Teaching Strategy

Some students may need no help, but others may find it hard to envision the difficulty of raising a family on a limited income. This is a common source of conflict in many families. Have them create a family budget using the poverty line threshold for a family of four ($17,050 in 2000). You can find current poverty threshold lines by visiting the Institute for Poverty Research website at **www.ssc.wisc.edu/irp/** Have students look in the newspaper classified ads to find housing costs in your area. Students will also need to estimate expenses for utilities, food, clothing, transportation, etc. Students will probably grossly over or underestimate the amount of money needed to survive. Ask students what some consequences are for families for whom survival is a day-to-day struggle.
L2

Points to Stress

The best way to explain the symbolic interactionist perspective is to inform students that the family is at the same time the most public and the most private of all social institutions. Because of its inherent private nature, it also has the ability to be the most violent of institutions, since violence may occur without intervention. Some sociologists believe that the culture of violence begins at home and that if families were less violent, much of the violence we see in society would diminish. Ask students to react to those statements.

Feminist Betty Friedan is the godmother of the American women's movement. Many conflict theorists study her writings.

Conflict Theory

Conflict theorists focus on the way family members compete and cooperate. Most family structure throughout history has been patriarchal and patrilineal. Women have historically and traditionally been considered the property of men, and the control of family members and property has typically passed through male bloodlines. This male dominance has been considered "natural" and "legitimate." Thus, most family systems have had built-in gender inequality.

How does conflict theory explain gender relationships in the family? According to conflict theorists, males are dominant and in control; females have traditionally been expected to be submissive helpers. In the traditional division of labor, males work outside the home for finances to support the family. Women remain at home to prepare meals, keep house, and care for the children. Women are unpaid laborers who make it possible for men to earn wages. With men having control over the money, the wives and mothers are kept in a dependent and powerless role. According to the conflict perspective, families in the past, then, have fostered social inequality.

How do the ideas of feminist writers fit with conflict theory? Writers and activists who organize on behalf of women's rights and interests have come to be called feminists. Many feminists today view the family from the conflict perspective. They believe that family structure is the source of the inequality between men and women in society. They point out that men have had control over women since before private property and capitalism existed. Women's contributions in the home (mother and homemaker) are not paid and are therefore undervalued in a capitalist society. Attempts by women to gain more power within the family structure can result in conflict.

Symbolic Interactionism

According to symbolic interactionism, a key to understanding behavior within the family lies in the interactions among family members and the meanings that members assign to these interactions.

How does the family help develop a person's self-concept? Socialization begins within the family. As family members share meanings and feelings, children develop self-concepts and learn to put themselves mentally in the place of others. Interactions with adults help children acquire human personality and social characteristics. Children develop further as they meet others outside the home.

According to symbolic interactionists, relationships within the family are constantly changing. A newly married couple will spend many months (perhaps years) testing their new relationship. As time passes, the initial relationship changes, along with some aspects of the partners' personalities, including self-concepts. These changes occur as the partners struggle with such problem issues as chores and responsibilities, personality clashes, and in-laws.

Using Decision-Making Skills

This activity is most suitable for mature classrooms in that it deals with some sensitive, if realistic, social problems.

Read the following scenario to students. Having lived in this city all of your life, you know people well and feel they are especially friendly to anyone and everyone. Age, health, race, gender, education, ethnicity, and family status have never mattered. Recently your aunt divorced her husband due to his lengthy sentence given for a crime against humanity. That's all your parents will tell you about this situation. Because your aunt is undergoing chemotherapy for an illness no one will discuss, you learn that your cousin will be coming to stay with you for at least half of the school year. You and your cousin are one year apart; that's good because you will be able to introduce him to your friends and even double date together. As you prepare to share your bedroom and tell your

With the arrival of children comes a new set of adjustments. Parental views may differ on child-rearing practices, number of children desired, and education for the children. The situation is made even more complex by the new member of the family, who must also become part of the interaction patterns.

> Children have more need of models than of critics.
>
> Carolyn Coats
> author for young adults

Section 2 Assessment

1. Match the following examples with the major theoretical perspectives: functionalism (F), conflict theory (C), symbolic interactionism (SI)
   - **a.** fathers "giving away" brides
   - **b.** having children
   - **c.** development of self-concept
   - **d.** newly married partners adjusting to each other
   - **e.** child abuse
   - **f.** social class being passed from one generation to another

Critical Thinking

2. **Finding the Main Idea** Select a memorable family experience (such as the Thanksgiving holiday) and interpret it from the viewpoint of one of the three major perspectives.

Figure 11.4 Focus on Theoretical Perspectives

Perspectives on the Family. Both functionalism and conflict theory are concerned with the ways social norms affect the nature of the family. Symbolic interactionism tends to examine the relationship of the self to the family. How might functionalism and conflict theory focus on the self?

Theory	Topic	Example
Functionalism	Sex norms 	Children are taught that sexual activity should be reserved for married couples.
Conflict Theory	Male dominance	Husbands use their economic power to control the ways money is spent. 
Symbolic Interactionism	Developing self-esteem	A child abused by her parents learns to dislike herself. 

Pulling It All Together

This section emphasized the functionalist, conflict, and interactionist perspectives of the family. Each of these perspectives considers the family as a private as well as public institution.

Answers to Section 2 Assessment

1. a. F
   b. F
   c. SI
   d. SI
   e. C
   f. F

Critical Thinking

2. Answers will vary.

Integrating the Teacher Resources

Look for the Chapter 11 Increasing Your Reading Comprehension worksheet and the Guided Reading worksheet in the Unit 4 Mastering Basic Concepts booklet in your Teacher's Resource Box. Both will strengthen student reading comprehension skills.

friends that he's coming within the week, the doorbell rings. You are upstairs, so your mother answers the door. You can hear people talking in hushed tones, and occasionally words such as "AIDS, risky business, welfare, trashy people, divorce, communicable disease, and dirt bags" dart past your ears. You hear the door slam as Mom's sobs echo throughout the house. Dad is enraged when he comes home from work and hears what happened.

Using the decision-making process, determine what you will do in an attempt to remedy this series of questionable events and save face for your family. Based on this scenario, ask students to discuss in groups where they believe the responsibility of the family is the greatest—to the larger society as a whole, or to protect the individual family members. Would students feel the same if the story involved turning in a drug addict or an escaped felon?
L2

Sociology Today

You might have students turn in their rankings of the items listed on the survey. The answers should be turned in anonymously with only the gender of the participant indicated on the paper. Compile the results of the survey by gender and discuss with the class. On what items were males and females similar in their answers? On what items were they very different? Are there noticeable gender differences for a significant number of the items? What do students think this means?

Answer to Doing Sociology

Answers will vary

Integrating the Teacher Resources

For review or enrichment, use the Student Journal Prompts for this chapter, available in the Unit 4 Mastering Basic Concepts booklet in your Teacher's Resource Box.

Sociology Today: Looking for Mr. or Ms. Right

This activity will give you some ideas for evaluating whether a current boyfriend or girlfriend is a good candidate for a successful long-term relationship.

From the list on the right, (and on a separate sheet of paper), list the ten most important qualities to you. (Number 1 as the most important, number 2 the next most important, and so forth.) Then fold your paper in half. In the right-hand column, either have your partner fill out the questionnaire or rank the characteristics yourself according to how you think your partner would.

I am looking for a partner who . . .

	Partner	Self	
1.	____	____	is honest and truthful.
2.	____	____	is fun to be with.
3.	____	____	is of the same educational background.
4.	____	____	will take care of me.
5.	____	____	wants to have children.
6.	____	____	communicates well with me.
7.	____	____	will share household jobs and tasks.
8.	____	____	is a good friend with whom I can talk.
9.	____	____	is of the same religious background.
10.	____	____	makes decisions.
11.	____	____	earns good money.
12.	____	____	is physically attractive.
13.	____	____	is in love with me and I with him/her.
14.	____	____	encourages me to be my own person.
15.	____	____	has interests like mine in making money and having fun.
16.	____	____	makes me feel important.
17.	____	____	is faithful.
18.	____	____	shares mutual interests in home, children, romantic love, and religion.
19.	____	____	has had a happy childhood with happily married parents.
20.	____	____	is emotionally mature.
21.	____	____	is prepared to support a family.
22.	____	____	is interested in waiting to marry until age twenty-two or older.
23.	____	____	wants a six-month to two-year engagement period.

Evaluating Your Responses. Which of the items listed on the right do you think are the most important in predicting marital success? According to research, the last seven items (17–23) are the most important. High compatibility between you and your partner on these seven characteristics would probably increase your chances of marital success. A low degree of matching does not, of course, ensure an unhappy marriage or a divorce, but it does suggest areas that may cause problems in the future.

Adapted from the Department of Human Development and Family Studies, Colorado State University.

Doing Sociology

Do you think that the qualities listed in the questionnaire are relevant to you in choosing a wife or a husband? Why or why not? Are there characteristics more important to you and your friends? Explain.

Paired Learning Activity

Students might want to research the issue of teenagers as breadwinners for the family. Before they begin their research, ask students the reason why most teens work. Do most teens work to help support their families, or do teens work just to earn spending money? They might want to look at how the role of teenage workers has changed throughout history. Another interesting angle students can investigate is how and why companies gear marketing strategies to target teenage consumers. What kinds of products does the media try to sell to teenage audiences? Have students work in pairs to find answers to these questions. **L1**

Section 3

Family and Marriage in the United States

Key Terms

- divorce rate
- marriage rate

The Nature of the American Family

The United States is a large, diverse society. Describing the "typical" family might be impossible. There are, however, more similarities than differences among American families. As the various ethnic groups blend into life in the United States, their families tend to follow the American pattern described below.

- Families are nuclear (a household contains only a set of parents and their children).
- Families are bilateral (they trace lineage and pass inheritance equally through both parents).
- Families are democratic (partners share decision making equally).
- Families are neolocal (each family lives apart from other families).
- Families are monogamous (each includes only one husband and one wife at a time).

Section Preview

Modern marriages are based primarily on love, but there are many reasons for marrying—and as many reasons for divorce. Although the American family provides social and emotional support, violence in this setting is not uncommon. Child abuse and spousal abuse are serious problems in too many American families.

Romantic Love and Marriage

To Americans, it's like the old song—"Love and marriage go together like a horse and carriage." In a recent poll of the American public, 83 percent of both men and women rated "being in love" as the most vital reason to marry.

The relationship between love and marriage is not always viewed in this way. Among the British feudal aristocracy, romantic love was a game of pursuit played outside of marriage. Marriage was not thought to be compatible with deeply romantic feelings. In ancient Japan, love was considered a barrier to the arrangement of marriages by parents. Among Hindus in India today, parents or other relatives

In the United States today, the norm is for love to precede the marriage vows. Not all societies share this norm.

Using the Section Preview

This section is full of topics that are of high interest to students. You might want to allow students to prepare research papers or projects based on the various subjects in this unit.

Ask students how many of them think they will marry within five years? Ten years? Never? Surveys show that more and more people are putting marriage off or staying single and never marrying. (They should also know that many young people who are convinced they will never marry change their minds when they meet a certain person, when their careers are more established, or when conditions and events change.)

More About . . . Age at Marriage

The average age at marriage for females is twenty-five, while the average age for males is twenty-seven. These ages are substantially higher than they were just one generation ago. Ask students what factors have contributed to the rise in the average age at which people marry. What other implications might this have for society?

Encouraging Citizenship Activity

As a class, "adopt" a family—or several families—in need of some assistance, perhaps a single parent family that is in economic distress. To find a family, ask students for suggestions or contact social services or a church for referrals. Referring agencies may be able to help you ascertain what the family needs. Students may be able to provide support by baby-sitting, tutoring, providing transportation, or preparing healthy meals. Stress to students that in providing assistance they treat family members with respect. After the class has done this for a designated period of time, say two or three months, have students write up the results of the project. Ask students what they learned from the experience.
L1

Working with the Data

Figure 11.5 Answers to the caption questions include:

(a) Although there was a slight increase in the marriage rate when World War II began, by far the greatest rise was from 1945–1948 when the soldiers returned to the States and settled down to marry and raise families.

(b) The marriage rate spiked immediately after the war as soldiers returned home to resume their lives. The marriage rate then began to decline as more Americans attended college (GI Bill) and more women entered the labor force.

(c) The divorce rate may have peaked in the 1980s because many baby boomers (who are more accepting of divorce) were able to leave unhappy marriages. Couples began having fewer children which made it easier for women to leave husbands.

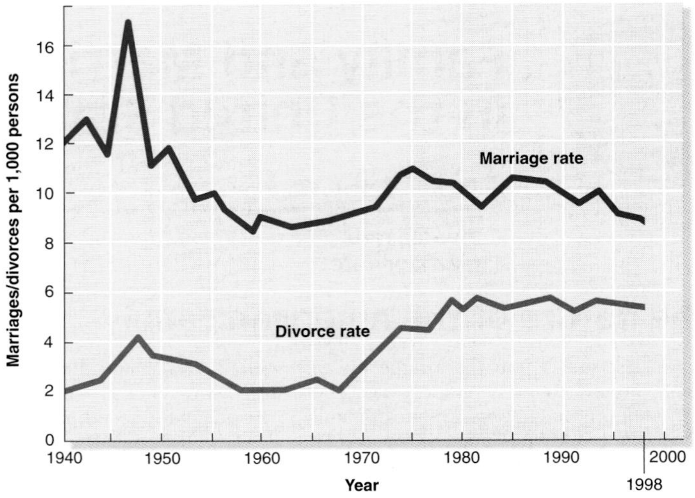

Figure 11.5 Divorce and Marriage Rates: 1940–1998. *Can you apply what you learned in history to interpret this chart? (a) What happened in the mid-1940s that caused the dramatic rise in marriage rates during this period? (b) Why do you think the marriage rate dropped so low in the 1950s? (c) What are some possible reasons that the divorce rate peaked in 1980?*

Source: National Vital Statistics Reports 47, 1999.

are expected to find suitable mates for the young. Criteria for mate selection include caste, wealth, family reputation, and appearance. Love is not absent in Hindu marriages, but love follows marriage rather than the other way around (Cox, 1999).

While romantic love is almost always stated as a condition for marriage in modern societies, it is seldom the only condition. People marry for many reasons, and romantic love may be only one of many reasons. A person may marry to enter a powerful family or to advance a career. One of the strongest motivations for marriage is conformity. Parents expect their children to marry after a certain age and worry about them—perhaps even pressure them—if their children remain single very long. Peers are another source of pressure. Since well over 90 percent of all adults in the United States do marry, conformity must certainly be a motivating factor.

Americans typically believe that a marriage that is not based on romantic love cannot last. It is more accurate to say that a marriage based only on romantic love is almost sure to fail. While love may be a good start, it is only the beginning. For a marriage to last, a couple must build a relationship that goes beyond romantic love (Crosby, 1985).

marriage rate the number of marriages per year for every one thousand members of a population

The **marriage rate**—the number of marriages per year for every thousand members of the population—has fluctuated, in the United States, since 1940. As shown in Figure 11.5, the marriage rate peaked at over 16.0 immediately following World War II. Since then, the marriage rate, with ups and downs, has been cut in half.

Divorce

divorce rate the number of divorces per year for every one thousand members of the population

The **divorce rate** is the number of divorces per year for every one thousand members of the population. Except for a peak and decline after World War II, the divorce rate in the United States increased slowly between 1860 and the early 1960s. A dramatic increase occurred over the next twenty years, when

Survey

Sociologist Mary Riege Laner has done extensive research on real vs. ideal perceptions of marriage in her college classes. She found that most students have idealized views of what marriage will be. Her research has also examined how people who have been married have a different perception of what marriage really is. Have students brainstorm why young people have an idealized view of marriage, what agents of socialization create this perception, and how it differs from the reality of marriage. Might this explain why divorce rates are near 50%? To carry this a step further, see if you can recreate Laner's findings. Have the class create an informal survey about marriage expectations. After students take the survey, have them give the same survey to their parents, and compare the results. How do these responses compare to Mary Riege Laner's?
L2

Snapshot of America

Marriage Rates

As noted in the text, the U.S. marriage rate overall has declined dramatically since 1940. Variation in the marriage rate among individual states is interesting. The lowest marriage rate occurs in New Jersey. Nevada has far and away the highest marriage rate.

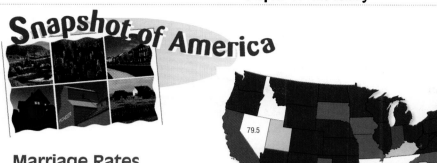

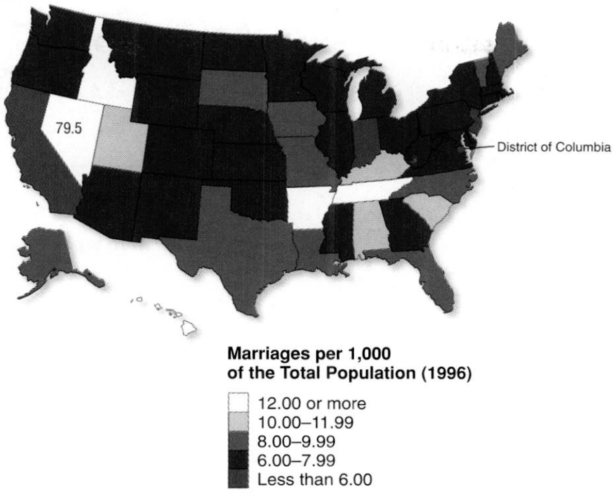

Interpreting the Map

1. Create a chart comparing the marriage rate in your state with other states, keeping in mind that the national average is just over 8.0. Pose a question for your classmates to answer describing their reaction to your state's position in the marriage rate ranking.
2. Would you expect the divorce rates of states to be correlated with their marriage rates? Make a prediction before looking up the divorce rates for comparison. Report your findings to the class.

Source: PRIMEDIA Reference Inc., 1998.

the divorce rate more than doubled (from 2.2 percent in 1960 to 5.3 percent in 1981). Since then, the rate has leveled off. In fact, it has declined slightly since 1985. (See Figure 11.5 on page 364.)

What are the causes of divorce? Both personal and societal factors influence why people divorce. At the individual level, these factors include:

- the age of the people when they married. The later the age upon marriage, the lower the chance of divorce.
- how many years the partners have been married. The longer the marriage, the lower the chance of divorce.
- the nature and quality of the relationship. The more respect and flexibility exists between the partners, the lower the chance of divorce.

Sociologists are most concerned with how larger forces in society affect marriages. There are four main factors. First, the divorce rate rises during economic prosperity and goes down when times are hard. This is probably

Snapshot of America

Ask students why they think the marriage rate in New Jersey is so low. Why is the marriage rate to high in Nevada?

Answers to Interpreting the Map

1. Student answers will vary.
2. Student answers will vary.

Reteaching

A common myth about fathers and divorce is that many men turn into "deadbeat dads," who fail to provide child support, and soon after become "no-show" dads, who fail to perform visitation with their children. Research suggests that since many states now garnish wages immediately after a court's divorce decree is in place, it is not easy for fathers to avoid paying child support. Research has shown that the main reason some men do not pay child support is because they are unemployed. In addition, some men who are labeled as no-show fathers live more than 100 miles from their children, making regular visitation difficult. Ask students why this myth is perpetuated against divorced fathers, and what the social implications are for fathers who are stigmatized as "deadbeats" or "no-shows."

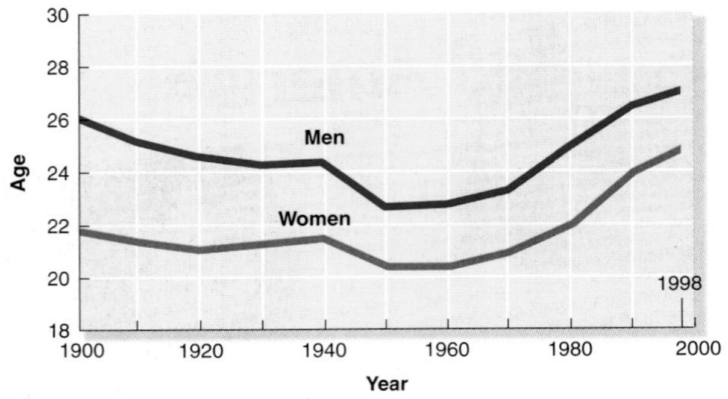

Figure 11.6 Median Age at First Marriage. *This figure shows changes in the median age at first marriage in the U.S. since 1900. The marrying age for both men and women has been on the increase since the 1960s. How might this trend affect the future divorce rate?*

Source: U.S. Bureau of the Census, March 1998.

> No matter how many communes anybody invents, the family always creeps back.
>
> **Margaret Mead**
> **anthropologist**

because people are more likely to make changes and take chances when they are not worried about basic survival.

Second, the rise in the divorce rate after 1960 followed the growing up of the baby-boom generation. Baby boomers did not attach a stigma to divorce the way earlier generations did and so were more likely to leave unhappy marriages than to stay.

Third, the increasing financial independence of women means they are more willing to end bad marriages. They are not as dependent (especially if there are no children) upon the husband's willingness to support an ex.

Fourth, American values and attitudes about marriage and divorce are changing. Society is much more forgiving of divorce and remarriage. Women, especially, are no longer "punished," as they were in the past, for leaving a marriage.

What does the future for marriage look like? For several reasons, there is a good chance that the recent decline in the U.S. divorce rate may continue:

- The average age at first marriage in the United States is increasing. (See Figure 11.6.) We know that the later people marry, the less likely they are to divorce. (Mature individuals have more realistic expectations about their mates and have fewer economic and career problems.) This trend is likely to continue well into the twenty-first century.
- The average age of the population of the United States is increasing as baby boomers grow older. This exceptionally large generation set records for divorce in the late 1960s and 1970s. Baby boomers now range in age from the mid thirties to the early fifties, which removes them from the age bracket that produces the highest divorce rates.
- American couples are having fewer children, and the children are spaced farther apart. This reduces pressure on marriages.

Working with the Data

Figure 11.6 Students might reasonably think that with individuals waiting longer before marriage the divorce rate will decrease. It will be years before data is available to prove or disprove hypotheses.

Controversy and Debate

Sometimes sociologists help rectify unfair social policy with their research. However, in the following case, extremely biased research led to detrimental misconceptions and policies regarding custody and child support issues. In 1985, sociologist Lenore Weitzman researched the economic hardships faced by women after divorce, and reported that women tended to suffer greater economic hardship following divorce than men did. In response to Weitzman's research, one state passed 14 laws to ensure that women would not be economically strapped. Recent research has uncovered that Weitzman's research was questionable. In *Divorced Dads: Shattering the Myths,* psychologist Sanford Braver found that the economic gap between men and women after divorce is not nearly as large as Weitzman contended. In fact, divorced fathers whose wages are garnished by court decree for child support payments suffer severe economic hardship. This is particularly true of fathers who remain involved in their children's lives following divorce.

Cooperative Learning Activity

Write the following italicized statements on the board and ask students to meet in a group to decide whether each of the statements is true or false. They should record their answers and the reasons for their answers on paper. Then come together as a class to share their responses. (The answers are provided after the statements.)

(1) *Wife battering is a predominantly lower class phenomenon.* False. Women in families on lower incomes are more likely to come to the notice of helping agencies because wealthy women hide their injuries. Research indicates that there are no socioeconomic barriers to domestic violence.

(2) *Wife battering occurs more often in some ethnic groups than others.* False. Spouse abuse can manifest itself in any society where there is an unequal power imbalance between men and women, regardless of ethnicity.

(3) *Alcohol is the main cause of domestic*

Tragically, violence has been a pattern of some family relationships throughout history.

Family Violence

Americans have traditionally denied the existence of widespread violence in the family setting. Violent behavior has in the past mistakenly been associated mostly with lower-class families. Part of the reason for this attitude was the fact that the first research in this area used law enforcement and public medical records. Because the police and hospitals dealt mostly with the lower classes (middle and upper classes had lawyers and private doctors), the statistics were skewed toward the lower class. We are learning that domestic violence occurs at all class levels.

Is violence in the family common? Although the family provides a safe and warm emotional haven, it can in some cases be a hostile environment. Family violence, or domestic violence, affects all members of the family—children, spouses, and older people. Celebrated trials during the 1990s brought increased public attention to the issue of domestic violence. For more than a year, media focus was centered on the trial of football superstar O. J. Simpson, accused of the murder of his former wife Nicole Brown Simpson and Ronald Goldman. Evidence presented during the trial indicated that Simpson had abused her when they were married. In another high-profile case, the wealthy Menendez brothers were convicted of the murder of their parents. (Trial evidence indicated that the brothers had been abused as children.)

According to a national survey, almost one-quarter of adults in the United States report having been physically abused as children. In most cases, physical violence involves a slap, a shove, or a severe spanking. However, kicking, biting, punching, beating, and threatening with a weapon are part of abusive violence as well. Furthermore, according to estimates, one of every four girls and one in ten boys are victims of sexual aggression, either within the home

Controversy and Debate

A noted psychologist has written extensively about the need for requiring parenting licenses for people who want to have children. (*Licensing Parents: Can We Prevent Child Abuse and Neglect?* Jack C. Westman,1994, Insight Books.) Westman's book offers solutions to the problems of child abuse and neglect, and also outlines a plan to implement parent licensing. Have students research this topic, and report back to the class. This controversial topic should provoke great discussion.

Integrating the Teacher Resources

For Spanish-speaking students, you may wish to use the reproducible worksheets available in the Spanish Supplements booklet in your Teacher's Resource Box. In addition to providing Spanish translations of selected Mastering Basic Concepts worksheets, the booklet contains English and Spanish summaries of the chapter's key points.

violence. False. Alcohol may trigger, but is not the major cause of domestic violence. 'Being under the influence' at the time of the assault may provide the perpetrator with what he feels to be an excuse for his behavior, however.

(4) *Women who are battered must be crazy or neurotic.* False. Studies have shown that women in violent relationships are no more psychiatrically or psychologically disturbed than other women. What we may label as 'crazy' or 'disturbed' behaviour are often tactics adopted by battered women in an attempt to survive in a very difficult, intolerable and possibly life-threatening situation.

(5) *Once a battered woman, always a battered woman.* False. Most women who have successfully managed to escape a violent relationship alive are very careful to choose a different type of relationship the next time.

L1

Country	Reported Abuse
	Industrialized Countries
Canada	**29%** of ever-married/common law–partnered women report being physically assaulted by a current or former partner since the age of sixteen.
New Zealand	**20%** of women report being hit or physically abused by a male partner.
Switzerland	**20%** of women report being physically assaulted.
United Kingdom	**25%** of women had been punched or slapped by a partner or ex-partner in their lifetimes.
United States	**28%** of women report at least one episode of physical violence from their partner.
	Asia and the Pacific
Korea	**38%** of wives report being physically abused by their spouses in the last year.
Thailand	**20%** of husbands acknowledge physically abusing their wives at least once in their marriage.
	Middle East
Egypt	**35%** of women report being beaten by their husbands at some point in their marriage.
Israel	**32%** of women report at least one episode of physical abuse by their partners during the last twelve months; 30% report sexual coercion by their husbands in the last year.
	Africa
Kenya	**42%** of women report ever being beaten by a partner; of those, 58% report that they were beaten often or sometimes.
Uganda	**41%** of women report being beaten or physically harmed by a partner; 41% of men report beating their partners.
	Latin America and the Caribbean
Chile	**26%** report at least one episode of violence by a partner, 11% report at least one episode of severe violence, and 15% of women report at least one episode of less severe violence.
Columbia	**19%** of women have been physically assaulted by their partners in their lifetimes.
Mexico	**30%** report at least one episode of physical violence by a partner; 13% report physical violence within the last year.

Figure 11.7 Events of Domestic Violence against Women in Selected Countries. *Levels of domestic violence against women clearly vary from country to country.*

Source: World Health Organization, 1997.

or outside (Heller, Kempe, and Krugman, 1999; Pryor, 1999). Reported child sexual abuse in the United States has skyrocketed in recent years. Between 1976 and 1997, the number of reported child abuse cases rose from 662,000 to over 3 million. Statistics collected nationally indicate that 47 out of every 1,000 children are reported annually as victims of child maltreatment (Wang and Daro, 1998). Child sexual abuse goes beyond physical contact. Some children are forced into pornography or are made to view pornography in the presence of the abuser. What's worse, the abuser is usually someone the child trusts—a parent, friend of the family, child care giver, brother.

At least four million women are battered by their husbands annually, probably many more. Over four thousand women each year are beaten to death. The extent of physical abuse is underestimated in part because three-fourths of spousal violence occurs during separation or after divorce, and most research is conducted among married couples.

Is abuse always directed against women? Husband abuse is frequently overlooked in studies of physical abuse. Although marriages in the United States are generally male dominated, it seems there is equality in the

Working with the Data

Figure 11.7 Students should research factors or variables that might explain why certain countries have high or low rates of domestic violence. Are there cultural factors such as the low status of women in some societies, stigma of reporting domestic violence cases, etc. that might contribute to higher rates of domestic violence against women?

Integrating the Transparencies

Numerous transparencies related to this chapter are provided in the *Sociology and You* Transparency Binder.

Cooperative Learning Activity

Is the family a *private* or *public* institution? Are families able to live private lives, unaffected by public opinion; or, does the public sector have the right to impose certain standards on family life? Ask your students to debate the issue of community involvement in child abuse and neglect. Have students discuss the following topics in groups.

1. *Family as a public institution.* The community has a responsibility and right to step inside the family to insure the safety and well-being of children.
2. *Family as a private institution.* The family has a responsibility and right to raise children according to their own values.

After groups have come to a consensus on each topic, have a representative from each group share with the rest of the class what their group decided. Try to come to a consensus with the entire class on both topics. **L2** use of physical violence. One set of researchers found that almost one-third of the husbands in their survey had acted violently against their wives and that wives were almost as likely to have used physical violence against their husbands. Other studies also show that husbands and wives assault each other at about the same rate. Much of the violence committed by women, however, involves self-protection or retaliation, and as a category, females are not as violent as males (Gelles, 1997).

Is abuse always physical? Family violence is not limited to physical abuse. Verbal and psychological abuse are also a part of many families. Psychologists report that the feelings of self-hate and worthlessness that are often the effects of abuse can be as damaging as physical wounds. And more than nine million children in the United States suffer from neglect, a condition of being ignored rather than abused.

What is the most common form of family violence? Probably the most frequent and most tolerated violence in the family occurs between children. This *sibling violence* appears to be prevalent and on the rise. Abuse among siblings may be based on rivalry, jealousy, disagreements over personal possessions, or incest. Although it declines somewhat as children get older, it does not disappear.

Little is known about abuse of elderly people, because less research has been done in this area. Abuse of older people usually takes the form of physical violence, psychological mistreatment, economic manipulation, or neglect. Estimates of elder abuse range from 500,000 to 2.5 million cases annually (Gelles, 1997). Some observers fear that abuse of older people will increase as baby boomers age and the population grows older.

Abuse directed against the elderly in nursing homes has been a recent concern of social activists.

"All happy families resemble each other; each unhappy family is unhappy in its own way."

Count Leo Tolstoy
Russian writer

Section 3 Assessment

1. Choose the word from each pair that best describes the typical American family.
   - **a.** nuclear or extended
   - **b.** patrilineal or bilateral
   - **c.** neolocal or matrilocal
   - **d.** polygynous or monogamous
2. Identify three factors discussed in the text that are associated with divorce.

Critical Thinking

3. **Making Predictions** What is your prediction for the divorce trend in the United States in 2050? Use information in this section to support your answer.

Pulling it All Together

Although marriage is based on the notion of romantic love, there are many other reasons for marrying. There are also many reasons for divorce. The existence of family violence against spouses, siblings and extended family members suggests that the family is either a reflection of society or catalyst for social problems.

Answers to Section 3 Assessment

1. a. nuclear
   b. bilateral
   c. democratic
   d. neolocal
   e. monogamous
2. Three factors associated with divorce are: age (the higher the age, the lower the chance of divorce); the number of years the partners have been married (the longer the marriage, the lower the chance of divorce); and nature and quality of the relationship (respect and flexibility are needed for a successful marriage).

Critical Thinking

3. Answers will vary. Students should defend their answers.

Demonstration

As you begin a discussion of domestic violence with the class, have two students (whom you have secretly prompted ahead of time) beat on their desks about every 30 seconds to represent occurrences of acts of domestic violence and child abuse. This should have quite an impact upon the students once they realize what the sounds represent.
L1

Tech Trends

Technology and the Family

According to many experts, the influence of technology is just as far-reaching in the home as in the office. Activities in the home are changing dramatically because of recent technological innovations.

Because more American families are living farther from relatives, more are using the Internet to stay in touch with each other. Birth announcements, reunion plans, gift registries for weddings, and funeral arrangements are now being shared with families and friends on-line (Bulkeley, 1997). Although somewhat impersonal, these social connections may reduce social isolation and friction in families.

Many, however, see a darker side to new technology for the family. For example, one critic offers this concern: "If we wish to raise our children as androids who respond to Internet packets rather than parental guidance, I can't think of a better way to do that than to put computer networks in homes" (Wingfield, 1998:R23).

Another critic believes that high-tech home equipment like cable television, the Internet, and video games increasingly rules the lives of American families. Children who spend a great deal of time alone with these technological wonders, are deprived of frequent and intense social contact with other children, their parents, and other adults in the neighborhood. Consequently, the current generation of children could very well be the first to grow up with highly deficient social skills. Offering indirect support for this conclusion is the fact that almost three-fourths of Americans say they do not know their neighbors. The number of Americans who admit they have spent no time with the people living next to them has doubled in the last twenty years (Quintanilla, 1996).

The computer, to an even greater degree than the television, is being credited with isolating family members.

Technology can also separate, socially, those family members who use the new technology from those who do not. For example, some couples who depend on web pages to inform their relatives of family news have found that some family members cannot share in this information. Older members of the family who do not have access to the Internet often feel cut off from the rest of the family (Bulkeley, 1997).

Analyzing the Trends

A dark picture of the Internet has been presented in this feature. Think of some positive consequences of this technology for the family. Discuss two of them.

Tech Trends

Students might want to peruse newspapers for articles that examine the impact of the Internet on social relations. Can they find evidence that substantiates the author's contention that the Internet deprives people of basic social skills?

Answer to Analyzing the Trends

It should not be hard for students to think of positive uses of the Internet. The Internet can bring families together as they search for web sites, play games on line or communicate via email. Many employees even email their relatives regularly from the workplace. Though employers might frown on this practice, it has connected families who used to rely on communication via telephone and letters.

Integrating the Teacher Resources

Look for Ethics, Values, and Technology: Real-Life Issues in Society, available in your Teacher's Resource Box. The booklet provides primary source readings dealing with real-life controversies. Student worksheets are included.

Careers in Sociology

Use the following information to explain to students the difference between social work and counseling.

Through direct counseling or referral to other services, social workers help people solve a range of personal problems. Counselors help people evaluate interests, abilities, and disabilities, and deal with personal, social, academic, and career problems. Counselors assist with personal, family, educational, mental health, and career decisions and problems. Their duties depend on who they serve and the settings in which they work.

- Rehabilitation counselors help people deal with the personal, social, and vocational effects of disabilities.

Section 4

Changes in Marriage and Family

Key Terms

- blended family
- adolescents
- dual-employed marriages
- cohabitation
- boomerang kids

Blended Families

The relatively high divorce rate in the United States has created the **blended family**—a family formed when at least one of the partners in a marriage has been married before and has a child or children from the previous marriage. This type of family can become extremely complicated (Ganong and Coleman, 1994; Barnes, 1998). Here's an example: A former husband (with two children in the custody of their biological mother) marries a new wife with two children in her custody. They have two children of their own. The former wife also remarries a man with two children, one in his custody and one in the custody of his former wife. That former wife has remarried and has had a child with her second husband, who has custody of one child from his previous marriage. The former husband's parents are divorced, and both have remarried. Thus, when he remarries, his children have two complete sets of grandparents on his side, plus one set on the mother's side, plus perhaps more on the stepfather's side (Cox, 1999).

Blended families create a new type of extended family, a family that is not based strictly on blood relationships. As the example above shows, it is possible for a child in a blended family to have eight grandparents. Of

Section Preview

Many new patterns of marriage and family living have emerged in the United States. They include blended families, single-parent families, child-free families, cohabitation, same-sex domestic partners, and families with boomerang children. In spite of these new arrangements, the traditional nuclear family is not going to be replaced on any broad scale.

blended family
a family formed when at least one of the partners in a marriage has been married before and has a child or children from a previous marriage

Americans knew the "Brady Bunch" family long before the term blended families became common.

Using the Section Preview

The stability of a social institution lies in its ability to withstand and adapt to social change. The durability of the American system is often credited to the adaptability and flexibility of the Constitution. Ask students before reading to suggest ways the family has changed.

Teaching Strategy

Television shows are full of examples of the different types of families mentioned in this section. Have students pay attention to how families are portrayed on their favorite television programs. Have them ascertain what types of families they see and judge how realistic these portrayals of American families are. Do these television shows address some of the familial problems they have been studying in this course (domestic violence, changes in family structure, etc.)?
L1

- Employment, or vocational, counselors help individuals make career decisions.
- Mental health counselors emphasize prevention and work with individuals and groups to promote optimum mental health.
- Other counseling specialties include marriage and family, multicultural, or gerontological counseling.

For general information about counseling, as well as information on school, college, mental health, rehabilitation, multicultural, career, marriage and family, and gerontological counseling, contact American Counseling Association at:
http://www.counseling.org

course, not all blended families are this complicated. But about 40 percent of households in the United States contain biologically unrelated individuals.

Many blended families are successful, especially if they make adjustments during the first few years. Children from previous marriages, however, are one factor in the higher divorce rates among second marriages (Baca Zinn and Eitzen, 1998).

What major problems face blended families? Sociologists point to three major problems facing blended families—a lack of money, stepchildren's dislike of the new spouse, and uncertainty about roles played by stepparents.

- **Money difficulties.** Financial demands from both the former and present families generally result in lower incomes in stepfamilies. Remarried husbands are often legally obligated to support children from their previous marriages. Second wives may resent losing the income spent on children from a previous marriage.
- **Stepchildren's antagonism.** Hoping for a reunion of their original parents, stepchildren may try to derail the new marriage. Even five years after divorce, about a third of stepchildren continue to strongly disapprove of their original parents' divorce. This is especially true for teenagers, who can be very critical of their stepparents' values and personalities.
- **Unclear roles.** The roles of stepparents are often vague and ambiguous. A stepchild often doesn't consider a parent's new spouse as a "real" father or mother. It is also not clear to stepparents or stepchildren how much power the new spouse really has. Issues involving control and discipline reflect power struggles within the family, especially with teenagers involved.

SOCIOLOGY Online

Student Web Activity
Visit the *Sociology and You* Web site at soc.glencoe.com and click on **Chapter 11—Student Web Activities** for an activity on blended families.

Single-Parent Families

Over one out of four American families is a single-parent family. By far the greatest proportion of these households are headed by women (almost 76 percent). Only 10 percent of children living with one parent are in a male-headed household.

Why do women head the vast majority of single-parent households? Although courts today are more sensitive to the fathers' claims, women in all social classes are still more likely to win custody of their children in cases of separation and divorce. Unwed mothers or women

A debate exists over the appropriateness of celebrities choosing to be single mothers.

Teaching Strategy

Several years ago, former Vice President Dan Quayle caused a commotion among the American public when he suggested that the television show *Murphy Brown* was immoral. The fictitious star of the show had conceived a child out of wedlock with no intention of marrying the father. More recently, pop star Madonna did a similar thing, and more and more unmarried women seem to be following suit. Have students debate whether these women have acted immorally or whether social norms have changed, with marriage no longer being a prerequisite for having children. (Students will probably not know this, of course, but you could tell them about the huge scandal that broke in Hollywood when Ingrid Bergman's love affair with the Italian director Roberto Rossellini led her first husband to divorce her. The resulting social disapproval forced her to quit Hollywood and return to Europe. It was many years before she was "allowed" to return.)
L1

On-Demand Writing

Divorce and becoming part of a blended family strongly affect almost all children touched by these circumstances. These effects may last into adulthood and significantly reduce self-esteem.

It should be stressed that divorce is never the children's fault. Children cannot do anything to prevent it. Even though children are not responsible for divorce, many people (and our legal system) believe that children's rights are of paramount concern during divorce proceedings.

Ask your students to consider what rights should be given to children before, during, and following legal divorce. The following list may prove useful to get them started on their composition.

abandoned by their husbands and/or the fathers of their children make up a large part of poor single-parent households. Finally, poor women marry (or remarry) at a very low rate.

Though significantly fewer, there is an increasing number of well-educated, professional women who head single-parent households. With the stigma of unwed motherhood declining, more affluent unmarried women are *choosing* to have children and to care for them alone. These women have the economic resources to support an independent family. Finally, well-educated women are adopting higher standards for selecting husbands (Seligmann, 1999).

What are the effects of single-parent families on children? Approximately 30 percent of America's children (defined as people under the age of eighteen) live in households with one parent. African American and Latino children are more likely than white children to live with only their mothers because of high divorce and out-of-wedlock birth rates, and lower rates of marriage and remarriage (U.S. Bureau of the Census, 1998a). Figure 11.8 shows how the number of never-married and single parents increased among African Americans and Latinos from 1983 to 1994. In general, the chances are increasing that American children will live at least part of their youth in a fatherless home.

Adolescents (persons from the ages of twelve to seventeen) who live with one parent or with a stepparent have much higher rates of deviant behavior, including delinquency, drug and alcohol abuse, and teenage pregnancy, than adolescents living with both natural parents (Dornbush et al., 1985; Popenoe, 1999). A national sample of twelve- to seventeen-year-olds indicates that arrests, school discipline, truancy, running away, and smoking occur more often in single-parent and stepparent families, regardless of income, race, or ethnic background.

adolescents
youths from the ages of twelve to seventeen

These figures do not point to a lack of concern in single parents as much as they show the built-in problems of single parenting. Single working parents must struggle to provide their children with the time, attention, and guidance that two parents can give. Because the single mother typically makes little money, she has added financial problems. Finding good child care and adequate housing in a suitable neighborhood is often very difficult.

Online UPDATE
Visit soc.glencoe.com and click on **Textbook Updates–Chapter 11** for an update of the data.

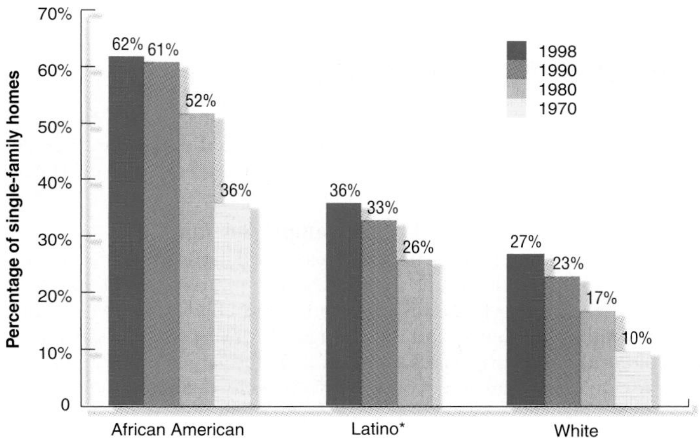

Figure 11.8 Percentage of Single-Parent Families: 1970–1998. *This graph compares the percentage of African American, Latino, and white families that have never married or have one parent. What generalization can you make from this data?*

*Note: Latino data not available for 1970.

Source: U.S. Bureau of the Census, 1998.

Controversy and Debate

As students read about single-parent families, they will encounter statistics that show that children from single-parent families seem to have more behavioral and financial difficulties than children from dual-parent families. Some students will object to this claim, while others will express agreement. Allow students to look at the positive and negative aspects of single- vs. dual-parent families. They might want to discuss this in groups based on their own family situations.

Working with the Data

Figure 11.8 One trend that students should mention is that the number of single-parent families for all groups is on the increase. There is a higher percentage of Latino single-parent families than white single-parent families. There is a higher percentage of African American single-parent families than both Latino and white single-parent families. Students also might mention that since the early 1980s, more than half of all African American families are single-parent families.

1. Children should have the right to answers to their questions about divorce.
2. Children should be spared form hearing negative comments from one parent about the other.
3. Children should have the right to see their non-custodial parent and grandparents.
4. Children should have the right to be children and not be expected to take on adult roles following divorce.
5. Children should have the right . . .

L1

Points to Stress

Tell students that you recently found the following headlines in the news: "Number of Childless Couples on the Rise," and "Fewer Women Having Children." Then ask them what they think is contributing to this decrease. Allow students to discuss this issue for a few minutes. Most will probably accept the headlines as fact. Then point out that if they look in their textbooks, they will see that although 19% of American women who have ever been married do not have children, this is only a 4% increase since 1970. While this change is statistically significant due to the large numbers involved, emphasize that students still need to look critically at information they read in newspapers or magazines. Some will trumpet sensational or inaccurate headlines in order to sell copies. Students should not interpret such headlines as proof that our civilization is in danger of extinction.

Childless Marriages

About one-fifth of couples today remain childless. In this an upward or downward trend?

In the past, married women without children were seen as failing to fulfill their "duty" as wives. In fact, in many religions, the inability to have children is still one of the few allowed reasons for divorcing a woman. Historically, married childless women were pitied and looked down upon, and single women rarely achieved respectability outside the role of "spinster aunt."

Why are some married women now choosing not to have children? Around 19 percent of American women who have ever been married do not have children in 2000, compared with about 15 percent in 1970 (U.S. Bureau of the Census, 2000d). It is unclear if this upward trend will continue. Today, the reasons married women give for choosing not to have children are varied. Social stigmas against childless married women are disappearing. It is no longer automatically accepted that having children is the primary reason for marriage. Some women have elected to pursue personal or career goals instead. Other people, both men and women, have basic moral issues about raising children in what they consider to be an immoral world. Sometimes, having children is put off so long that it becomes hard for couples to make the adjustment to raising a family. Finally, it is important to remember that not all couples without children have chosen to be that way. Physical or psychological problems keep some couples from having children.

Are marriages happier with or without children? The answer to this question generally depends upon the couple's decision about having children. Among childless couples who want children, marital happiness is generally lower than for married couples with children. However, research shows that couples who by choice have no children appear to be happier and more satisfied with their marriages and lives than couples with children (Cox, 1999).

Dual-Employed Marriages

dual-employed marriages marriages in which both spouses work outside the home

In families where both parents are working outside the home, special strains are put on the marriage. Women in these **dual-employed marriages** are apparently expected to handle most of the household and child-care responsibilities in addition to their full-time jobs.

What are drawbacks to the dual-employed family? Because they must combine employment with child care and household tasks, married working women work about fifteen hours more a week than men. Sociologist Arlie Hochschild calls this home- and child-based work "the second shift." Although men spend an average of four to six hours per week in household and child-care duties, women bear the larger burden.

In addition to this greater workload, women in dual-employed marriages must cope with role conflict. They are torn between the time requirements of

Cooperative Learning Activity

Divide the class into groups of four or five and provide a family conflict for each group to resolve. The conflicts might have to do with performance of chores, curfew, dating, allowance, family time versus time with friends, and so on. Have each group work together to resolve the situation. Then have groups share their conflict and resolution to the rest of the class. Discuss the conflicts and resolutions.
L1

their jobs and their desire to spend more time with their children and husbands. Feelings of guilt may arise from not being able to meet all expectations of wife, mother, and breadwinner.

Men in dual-employed marriages are generally unwilling to assume household responsibilities equal to those of their wives. Even so, they feel the negative effects of role conflict and excessive demands on their time. In addition, having an employed wife, particularly if she earns more, may not fit with men's images of themselves as providers.

Is there a positive side to dual employment? Dual employment offers advantages as well as disadvantages. On balance, the effects of employment on the psychological well-being of women have been beneficial (Moen, 1992; Crosby, 1993; Cox, 1999). Working outside the home provides a wider set of social relationships and greater feelings of control, independence, and self-esteem. Employment also appears to provide a social and emotional cushion for women when their children leave home. Compared with women who do not work outside the home, employed women tend to have more outlets for self-expression (Adelmann et al., 1989; Wolfe, 1998). If a mother prefers working outside the home, other family members often benefit from her employment. With two incomes, there is more money to spend for purchases that raise the standard of living. Sons and daughters of working mothers also benefit in noneconomic ways. Daughters of working mothers are more likely to see themselves as working adults, as capable of being economically independent, and as benefiting from further education. Sons are more likely to choose wives with similar attitudes toward education and employment.

A functionalist might suggest that this mother's economic function is clashing with her socioemotional function.

For men, benefits of a dual-employed marriage include freedom from the responsibility of being the sole provider, increased opportunity for job changes, and opportunities to continue education. Men with employed wives can share the triumphs and defeats of the day with someone who is in the same situation. If their wives are happier working outside the home, husbands enjoy a better marital relationship. Those husbands who take advantage of the opportunity can form a closer relationship with their children by being more active parents (Booth and Crouter, 1998).

Cohabitation

Cohabitation—living with someone in a marriagelike arrangement without the legal obligations and responsibilities of formal marriage—has been a widely discussed alternative to traditional monogamy for some time. In fact, the number of American adults cohabiting increased from about one-half million to over seven million between 1970 and 2000. According to a nationwide

cohabitation
a marriagelike living arrangement without the legal obligations and responsibilities of formal marriage

More About . . . Cohabitation

Cohabitation has lost some of the social approbation it used to carry. This is another example of how society is constantly redefining its social norms. What was perceived as sinful twenty years ago is now seen as acceptable by some. Research shows, however, that cohabitation before marriage does not necessarily improve marriage success rates. As explained in the text, couples that lived together before marriage are more likely to divorce than couples who did not cohabitate.

Learning Styles

Bodily-kinesthetic/Interpersonal/Linguistic To help students better understand families different from their own, have them do some roleplay. Give each group the following topics/situations: back-to-school night, parent/teacher conference, friend having an all-night party, drugs found in room, and wanting to borrow the car. Ask each group to represent one of the following family patterns: traditional nuclear family, blended family, single-parent family, dual-employed marriage (with children), cohabitation of heterosexual couple. Give each group time to discuss situations and assign and practice roles. Then, as time allows, ask each group to act out what might happen as you discuss each of the topics/situations outlined above. Finish by comparing and contrasting how each of the different family types deal with the topics/situations.
L2

Focus on Research

Survey Research: Spanking and Antisocial Behavior

Like many children in the United States, you probably experienced spanking and other legal forms of physical corporal punishment from your parents. In the mid-1980s, research revealed that over 90 percent of parents used corporal punishment on young children, and more than half continued its use during the early teen years. Although high, this rate of corporal punishment was less than in the 1950s (99 percent) and the mid-1970s (97 percent). The rate has declined further since 1985, but nearly all American children still experience some form of corporal punishment.

The use of corporal punishment to correct or control the behavior of children is widely accepted in American culture. "Spare the rod and spoil the child" is a warning deep in our national consciousness. However, Strauss and his colleagues (1997) present evidence contradicting the notion that corporal punishment improves children's behavior.

These researchers used data from interviews with a sample of over eight-hundred mothers of children aged six to nine years in a national study. (This was a longitudinal study, one that follows respondents over a period of time.) This study compared parents' use of corporal punishment with antisocial behavior in children. The study defined corporal punishment as "the use of physical force with the intention of causing a child to experience pain, but not injury, for the purpose of correction or control of the child's behavior" (Strauss, Sugarman, and Giles-Sims, 1997:761). Slapping a child's hand or buttocks and squeezing a child's arm are examples. A measure of antisocial behavior was based on the mothers' reports of their children's behavior: "cheats or tells lies," "bullies or is cruel or mean to others," "does not feel sorry after misbehaving," "breaks things deliberately," "is disobedient at school," and "has trouble getting along with teachers."

Since this was a longitudinal study, information on the frequency of parents' use of corporal punishment was collected *before* reports on subsequent antisocial behavior. Contrary to common expectations, Strauss found that the higher the use of corporal punishment, the higher the level of antisocial behavior two years later.

At the end of their report, the authors move from being strictly social scientists to making a practical child-rearing recommendation.

Survey

The American Psychological Association has noted that physical punishment in children can cause habitual violence in those children. They indicate that using physical punishment to stop undesirable behavior creates such feelings as hatred, fear, anger, and resentment in the children. The parents, too, suffer from the physical punishment with feelings of confusion.

Several alternatives to physical punishment are suggested by psychologists. Behavior modification is most often suggested. It can take several forms such as, giving rewards (stickers, privileges, hugs,

Focus on Research

Answers to Working with the Research

Students will love to debate this topic. There are numerous articles on corporal punishment available in libraries or on the Internet. Have students read about spanking and other forms of corporal punishment then hold a debate about its pros and cons. Ask students to defend their arguments by citing examples and evidence from their research.

Integrating the Teacher Resources

A lesson plan for a student research project related to the content of this chapter can be found in Doing Sociology: Focus on Research, available in your Teacher's Resource Box.

Strauss and his colleagues suggest that the reduction or elimination of corporal punishment could lower antisocial behavior in children. In addition, given research indicating a relationship between antisocial behavior in childhood and violence and other crime in adulthood, society at large could benefit from abandoning the use of corporal punishment in child rearing. They state it this way:

> *Thus, because almost all American children experience [corporal punishment] varying degrees, our findings suggest that almost all American children could benefit from a reduction or elimination of [corporal punishment]. Moreover, considering research showing that [antisocial behavior] in childhood is associated with violence and other crime as an adult, society as whole, not just children, could benefit from ending the system of violent child-rearing that goes under the euphemism of spanking (Strauss, Sugarman, and Giles-Sims, 1997).*

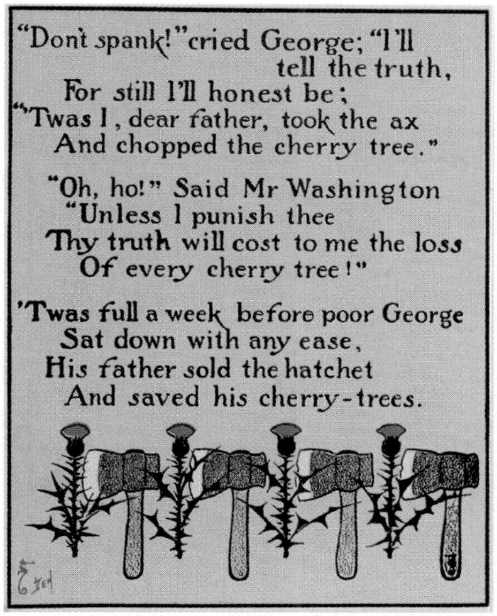

Spanking as a corrective for bad behavior was a norm in the past, as evidenced by this popular 1899 woodcut.

Working with the Research

1. Does a link between childhood corporal punishment and antisocial behavior surprise you? Explain.
2. Suppose that you are on a panel reporting on child rearing to the President of the United States. Using the Strauss study as a model, describe the study you would conduct on a possible relationship between childhood corporal punishment and adult crime.
3. How do you anticipate these children will discipline their children later in life?
4. Describe what you think would be more effective means of discipline.
5. Do you think that social science evidence such as this has affected teacher disciplining behavior in schools? Will it? Should it? Explain.

Answers to Working With the Research

1. Strauss found that among children, the higher the use of corporal punishment, the higher the level of antisocial behavior two years later.
2. A longitudinal study would need to be conducted with interviews and surveys that track reports of childhood corporal punishment and adult crime. The panel might want to look at the severity of the corporal punishment and the length of time (amount of years) that it went on.
3. If students have studied psychology, they might point to Alfred Bandura's social learning theory. Children who witnessed violence directed at others were more likely to model that behavior themselves.
4. Answers will vary. Allow students to choose sides and debate this topic. The discussion will illustrate to students how much variation exists among parenting styles.
5. Answers will vary, but students should refer to Strauss' findings in making their points.

verbal praise) for positive behavior. Negative behavior is dealt with through revocation of privileges, time outs, and so on.

Have students conduct a survey of their schoolmates. In the survey, students should ask what forms of physical punishment or behavior modification schoolmates think they will use when they have a child to rear. (The survey should be anonymous, of course.) If closed-ended, the survey should list physical punishments (within reason) and several types of behavior modification. Students should work together to analyze results.
L2

More About . . . Lasting Marriages

Noted professor John Gottman has written *Why Marriages Succeed and Fail: and How You Can Make Them Last.* (1994) Simon and Schuster, Inc. He can predict with incredible accuracy the likelihood of a successful marriage. On his weekend retreats with couples, Gottman gives couples several simple tasks to perform together. By ascertaining the level of cooperation between the two people, he has been able to predict with 95% accuracy whether or not the marriage will endure.

More About . . . Happy Marriages

Many marriage counselors believe that happy marriages are characterized by five qualities: power, closeness, intimacy, commitment and autonomy. In successful marriages, the "power" role is shared; partners take turns making decisions based on the situation. You might want to share this characteristic with students and ask them if they know couples who fit this criteria.

Open-Response Questions

Ask students why they think Vermont is the first state in the country to legalize same-sex civil unions. Wouldn't they have expected a more politically liberal state, such as California, to be first to pass such a law?

survey, over one-fourth of adults in the United States have cohabited (U.S. Bureau of the Census, 1998a).

Cohabitation has risen among people of all ages and marital statuses, particularly among the young and the divorced. By 2000, about 53 percent of all unmarried-couple households were maintained by someone under thirty-five years of age and about forty-one percent involved at least one child under age fifteen.

Is cohabitation a workable alternative to marriage? Research reports on cohabitation are not encouraging. Only about 25 percent of cohabitating couples stay together more than four years, reflecting a lower level of certainty about commitment than is true in married couples. This lack of commitment is probably an important reason for the lower satisfaction among cohabiting couples than among married couples (Nock, 1995). Another factor is the higher rate of abuse among cohabiting women than among married, divorced, or separated women.

Cohabitation has not fulfilled the promise of providing good experience for future marriage (Cox, 1999). Cohabitation does not appear to improve the quality of later marriage. Couples who cohabited have shown lower marital adjustment than couples who had not lived together. Finally, premarital cohabitation is associated with a higher risk of divorce (Brown and Booth, 1996).

Same-Sex Domestic Partners

Because of the social stigma that surrounds homosexuality, it is impossible to know precisely what proportion of the American population is homosexual. The Institute of Sex Research, founded by Alfred Kinsey, estimates that homosexuals constitute about 10 percent of the U.S. population (13 percent of the males, 5 percent of the females). Although estimating the number of cohabiting same-sex couples is difficult, the number is known to be increasing, both on college campuses and in the general public. It may have been in recognition of that increase that Vermont passed a bill in April of 2000 recognizing "civil unions" for same-sex partners. Same-sex couples united in civil unions would qualify for the same state benefits as married couples (and be held to the same burdens upon breakup). Same-sex unions are certain to remain a controversial issue confronting U.S. culture for many years to come.

While marriage is still a thriving institution, more people today are embracing the single life.

Single Life

An increasing number of Americans are choosing to remain single rather than to marry. More than 26 million Americans over the age of fifteen now live alone, an increase of nearly 150 percent since 1970. Although many of these people will eventually marry, an increasing percentage will remain single all their lives (U.S. Bureau of the Census, 2000d).

Why are more Americans choosing to live alone? Remaining single has always been a choice that has carried a stigma in the United States. Historically, society frowned on men and women who did not marry. It was seen as a form of deviance. England started taxing bachelors at the end of the seventeenth century and Missouri followed suit in 1820. The stigma attached to remaining single has faded over the past two decades, however. More single Americans are choosing to remain unmarried, pursuing careers or raising children from a former marriage.

On-Demand Writing

Couples in the Scandinavian countries (Sweden, Norway, Denmark, and Iceland) have taken cohabitation further than what we typically think of cohabitation in the United States. For years now, couples have cohabited before, during, and after children have become a part of the relationship. And they feel free to change relationships at any time. Often, children don't know the status of their parents, whether or not they are married.

Opponents to the rejection of the marriage institution state that statistics have shown that parents who are not married are two to three times more likely to separate. They also say that people have become too

Will the current trend toward remaining single continue? It is too early to predict whether the increase in singlehood will lead to a decline in marriage at all ages. Although singlehood is an increasingly popular alternative to traditional marriage, people are not necessarily rejecting marriage. The implication is that many young adults wish to expand the period of "freedom" after leaving home and are unwilling to rush into the responsibilities of early marriage and parenthood.

> A majority of colonial Americans probably spent some time in a stepfamily.
>
> Stephanie Coontz
> social historian

Boomerang Kids

The boomerang is a weapon that, when thrown, returns in a wide arc to its point of origin. The term **boomerang kids** is being applied to young adults who either leave home and return or stay at home and live with parents. American adults aged eighteen to thirty-four have a much higher probability of living in their parents' home than Americans of the same age thirty years ago. More than one-fourth of adults eighteen to thirty-four years old now live with their parents (U.S. Bureau of the Census, 1996a).

boomerang kids
adult children who return to the home of origin or who continue to live with parents

Why are more adult children returning home? Increasing numbers of adult children are living with their parents for several reasons. Because young adults are marrying later, more stay at home longer. In addition, more are continuing their education and find living at home the best solution to the problem of supporting themselves and paying school expenses. Many young adults return home even after completing their education because the high cost of living outstrips their earning capacity. Also, since parents tend to give their children a home after a failed marriage, the high divorce rate is increasing the proportion of young adults living at home.

What are some consequences of the boomerang effect? Costs associated with education, day-to-day living, and perhaps even a grandchild or two can create financial strain for older parents whose adult children live with them. Many parents complain that their adult children do not share in expenses or help around the house. The children's presence robs their parents of privacy and may prevent them from developing relationships with spouses and friends. It is not surprising that higher marital dissatisfaction among middle-aged parents is associated with adult children living at home.

Adult children who find themselves in this situation suffer as well. Adult children who have returned home have normally been forced by circumstances to do so. They are likely to be having difficulties balancing school and work, making their way economically, forming a family, or surviving the aftermath of a divorce. They know the burden they represent. In addition, returning home usually means giving up some freedom.

In spite of these problems, most families appear to adjust well to the return of older children (Mitchell and Gee, 1996). This is especially true when the returning older child is able to help with expenses and household duties.

"Can't I just stay here with you and Mom? I don't like what I've seen of the real world."

The thoughts of a boomerang kid. Mom and Dad are not buying it, are they?

Working with the Quote

You might have students do some historical research to find information to corroborate the statement made in the quote. Do students think this is true? Why or why not? What would have led to this during colonial times? *(high death rates)*

Addressing Current Social Issues

Students might want to look at how prevalent this phenomenon of "boomerang kids" is in the general population. Do they have older siblings who have moved back in with their parents after leaving home for a while? What do they think could account for the increase in adult children returning to their parents' homes? What implications could this have for society?

Teaching Strategy

To provide closure for the main ideas in this chapter, you may want to ask students to complete the learning objectives on text page 347.

selfish and don't work hard enough to keep relationships together. It's too easy to walk away and begin a new relationship.

After sharing this information with students, have them write a short essay in which they state their feelings about the effect of cohabitation on society. Is this something they would like to see become part of the American culture? Why or why not? Ask for volunteers to share their essays with the rest of the class. This activity might lead into a class debate, if you have the time. As always, the trick to this kind of a debate in sociology is to keep the students focused on the social, rather than the personal or individual, impact.
L2

Pulling it All Together

Patterns of marriage and family have changed throughout history, but the basic structure of the social institution known as the American family remains unchanged.

Answers to Section 4 Assessment

1. While a nuclear family is defined as simply parents and children, the blended family is a more complex version caused by the high rate of divorce. It may include children from previous marriages, stepparents, and additional sets of grandparents.
2. The percentage of African-American and Latino single-parent families is increasing more rapidly than the number of white single-parent families. The economic status of African-Americans and Latinos is lower than that of whites overall. Women of all races are often trapped in lower status and lower-paying jobs while trying to support children (women are more likely to receive custody after divorce). Poor women marry or remarry at a very low rate, which makes for more minority single-parent families.
3. Answers will vary.
4. Yes. An increasing percentage of single Americans will remain single all their lives.

Critical Thinking

5. Answers will vary.

Looking Forward

Belief that the family will continue is found even in the most futuristic views.

In early 2000, Darva Conger and Rick Rockwell were big news. This couple, who had never met before, married as part of a television contest called "Who Wants to Marry a Millionaire?" Most Americans shook their heads, wondering if this event marked the final stages of deterioration of the family. While this was truly a bizarre media event, thankfully, it is not representative of the state of the American family.

What is the future of the American family? If the frequency of marriage and remarriage is any indication, the nuclear family is not disappearing. Over 90 percent of men and women in the United States marry sometime during their lives. We have seen that many Americans have been experimenting with alternative living arrangements. Nevertheless, among Americans the nuclear family remains the most popular choice (U.S. Bureau of the Census, 2000d). Contrary to a long-standing fear, many Americans are not avoiding marriage permanently. They are simply postponing it or sampling it more often.

The American family is changing, however. So-called traditional households—those with a husband–wage earner, wife–homemaker, and two children—today account for less than one-fourth of all American households, compared with over 60 percent in 1950. This proportion is not expected to grow. Continued increases are expected for other family lifestyles, such as the dual-employed family and the single-parent family. The question, then, is not whether the family will survive. The question is what forms will the family take.

Whatever else happens, the trend toward more working parents is likely to continue. This trend promises increased strain for parents, children, and society. We have already discussed problems for parents associated with balancing work and home responsibilities. A reduction in close and continuous parental care for children during their early developmental years is another important consequence. Also, as more parents work, parental supervision of children and teenagers declines (*Starting Points,* 1994; Poponoe, 1996; Poponoe, Elshtain, and Blankenhorn, 1996).

Section 4 Assessment

1. How does a blended family differ from a nuclear family?
2. Which group is increasing more rapidly: the number of white single-parent families or the number of African American and Latino single-parent families? What reasons are offered for this?
3. Is your family a dual-employed family? How do the cultural values of your parents affect their economic behavior?
4. Is it true that Americans today are married for a smaller proportion of their lives than were Americans of previous generations?

Critical Thinking

5. **Making Predictions** Some people believe that in the future the nuclear family will be a reality for only a minority of Americans. Do you agree or disagree? Explain.

CHAPTER 11 ASSESSMENT

Summary

Section 1: Family and Marriage Across Cultures

Main Idea: In all societies, the family has been the most important of all social institutions. It produces new generations, socializes the young, provides care and affection, regulates sexual behavior, transmits social status, and provides economic support.

Section 2: Theoretical Perspectives and the Family

Main Idea: The family is the very core of human social life. It is not surprising that each of the major perspectives focuses on the family. Functionalism emphasizes the benefits of the family for society. The conflict perspective looks at the reasons males dominate in the family structure. Symbolic interactionism studies the way the family socializes children and promotes the development of self-concept.

Section 3: Family and Marriage in the United States

Main Idea: Modern marriages are based primarily on love, but there are many reasons for marrying—and as many reasons for divorce. Although the American family provides social and emotional support, violence in this setting is not uncommon. Child abuse and spousal abuse are serious problems in too many American families.

Section 4: Changes in Marriage and Family

Main Idea: Many new patterns of marriage and family living have emerged in the United States. They include blended families, single-parent families, child-free families, cohabitation, same -sex domestic partners, and families with boomerang children. In spite of these new arrangements, the traditional nuclear family is not going to be replaced on any broad scale.

SOCIOLOGY Online

Self-Check Quiz
Visit the *Sociology and You* Web site at soc.glencoe.com and click on **Chapter 11—Self-Check Quizzes** to prepare for the chapter test.

Reviewing Vocabulary

Complete each sentence using each term once.

a. monogamy
b. polyandry
c. polygyny
d. exogamy
e. endogamy
f. homogamy
g. patrilineal
h. blended family
i. dual-employed marriage
j. boomerang kids

1. ______________ is a family formed with children from a previous marriage.
2. The marriage of one woman to two or more men at the same time is called ______________.
3. The marriage of one man to two or more women at the same time is called ______________.
4. ______________ are young adults who live with their parents.
5. A marriage in which both partners work for pay is called ______________.
6. ______________ is the marriage within one's own group as required by social norms.
7. The marriage of one man to one woman is called ______________.
8. The tendency to marry someone similar to oneself is called ______________.
9. ______________ is the practice of marrying outside of one's group.
10. ______________ is the arrangement in which descent is traced through the father.

Reviewing the Facts

1. Sociologist define three types of family structures. List and describe those structures.
2. In addition to providing a warm and loving atmosphere that fulfills social and emotional needs, what are the other vital functions of the family?

ANSWERS CHAPTER 11 ASSESSMENT

Reviewing Vocabulary

1. h
2. b
3. c
4. j
5. i
6. e
7. a
8. f
9. d
10. g

Reviewing the Facts

1. Family of birth—the family that we are born into; Family of orientation—family that directs or orients children to their neighborhood, community and society, and locates them in the world; Family of procreation—family that is established upon marriage.
2. Regulation of sexual activity; socialization of children.
3. The family has historically maintained male dominance over females.
4. Monogamy is the most widely practiced form in the world today.
5. Men, women and children from all classes are the victims of family violence.

Thinking Critically

1. Traditional roles about masculinity and femininity still are a significant factor in who carries the heaviest load of housework. Students might extend this question by asking men and women of different ethnicities about the importance and need for sharing domestic housework.
2. If current trends continue, families might spend less and less time together. With parents and children having increasingly busy schedules, it seems that families will have to make conscious choices to reserve time to spend together.
3. Gottman's research, mentioned earlier in the chapter (see page 378 of the teacher's edition), is concerned with how well couples interact when given several tasks to perform together. Gottman looks at how the power relationship is played out, and the

ANSWERS CHAPTER 11 ASSESSMENT

degree to which one partner can compromise in the task. It is ethical because Gottman obtains a signed waiver from the couple agreeing to do this.

4. You might want students to look for media examples of idealized versions of marriage. Television, movies, and magazines might promote the myth that newly married couples can expect to live "happily ever after." Ask students to find realistic representations of marriage in the media. Have them report back to the class on what they find.
5. Functionalism—emphasizes benefit of family for society. Conflict Theory—looks at the reasons males dominate the family structure. Symbolic Interactionism—studies the way the family socializes children and promotes development of self-concept.

CHAPTER 11 ASSESSMENT

3. How would conflict theorists describe the family?
4. What is the most widely practiced form of marriage around the world today?
5. Who are the victims of family violence?

Thinking Critically

1. **Analyzing Information** According to Hochschild's *second shift* explanation, gender equity in the home does not exist. Why do men, on average, still do less housework than women? Do attitudes about masculinity have anything to do with this? Do women naturally feel inclined to do the housework, given their role as nurturers and caretakers? How might gender stereotypes contribute to inequality in the household?
2. **Making Inferences** One of the characteristics of families is that family members spend time together. As people grow busier and busier, however, spending time together becomes more difficult. Predict the future: twenty years down the road, what do you think will be a typical amount of family time? Do you believe family time will disappear, or do you think family members will always make time for each other, no matter what? Explain your views.
3. **Making Inferences** A prominent sociologist who studies marital relationships says that he can predict with 95 percent accuracy whether a newly married couple will fail or succeed in their marriage. He has newlyweds attend a retreat and perform a series of tasks, videotaping each couple's interactions as they work on projects together. At the end of the weekend, he tells the couples what he observed and what it could mean for the future of their marriages. Remember, his accuracy rating is 95 percent.
   - **a.** What do you think he looks for while he watches couples' interactions?
   - **b.** Do you believe his approach is ethical?
   - **c.** If you had the opportunity as a newlywed, would you attend this retreat? Why or why not?
4. **Analyzing Information** Research on never-married individuals shows that they believe their marriages will be ideal. However, research on married couples suggests that their expectations of marital bliss don't last very long. Why do you think people have expectations of marriage that do not seem to reflect what marriage is really like? Areas to explore might include portrayals of marriage in movies and on TV.
5. **Summarizing Information** Use a chart like the one below to summarize the view of the family as proposed by the three theoretical perspectives.

Sociological Perspective	View of the Family
Functionalism	
Conflict Theory	
Symbolic Interactionism	

Sociology Projects

1. **Family Characteristics** On a piece of paper, rate your family members based on the following characteristics. Use a scale of 1 to 5, with 1 being the lowest (weakest) and 5 being the highest (strongest).
   - spending time together
   - expressing appreciation for each other
   - dealing with conflict
   - communicating with one another
   - spiritual wellness
   - commitment and follow-through

   You can total your scores and divide by 6 to come up with a mean value for your family. After completing the activity, you may want to discuss your results with family members to see if they agree with your evaluation or share your perspectives. Are there other characteristics that are more important to your family than the ones on this list?

Sociology Projects

1. This rating scale of families was devised by a sociologist 25 years ago. Tell students that they do not have to share their results with others unless they are comfortable doing so. Most students will likely not be surprised by the results of the rating scale; teens are very aware of the strengths and weaknesses of their family. You might want to use this activity to open a general discussion of families and what makes them strong.
2. As an alternative, some groups are now trying to prevent divorces by having newlyweds look at the potential areas that might cause conflict in their relationship, and to address these issues early in the marriage. Have students discuss other methods that might help a couple avoid divorce.
3. Students could turn this into a fairly lengthy research project looking at an entire class or segment of the school population. Remember that your sample might not be representative of the general population. Students might want to speculate as to why the numbers turn out the way they do. Refer to Chapter 2 for a look at research methods.

2. **Divorce** The text listed several reasons why couples divorce. Working with a classmate, brainstorm several additional factors contributing to divorce (for example, no-fault divorce laws in some states). Give at least one reason why each of these factors has caused an increase in divorce over time. After you have come up with a list of at least five factors, discuss with your partner what would happen if the factors were eliminated (for example, if conditions allowing divorce were made stricter). Do you think these changes would improve society? Why or why not? Be prepared to present your findings to the class and to argue your position.
3. **Research Project** Divide a sheet of paper into three columns, labeled A, B, and C. In column A, write the number of children in your immediate family. In column B, write the number of children in your father's immediate family (include siblings that are no longer living). In column C, write the number of children in your mother's immediate family. One student should collect all the papers and tabulate the results. Has the number of children in the families represented in your class decreased since your parents' generation? Prepare a graph of the similarities or differences.
4. **The Second Shift** To see whether the second-shift explanation applies to your family, conduct the following experiment over the course of one week. Write down the number of hours you see your mother (or stepmother) doing housework each day. Then write down the number of hours your father (or stepfather) spends working in or around the house. In class, compile the numbers logged by all your classmates. Is the second-shift explanation valid for your class? (If you are living in a single-parent family, keep track of the number of hours of housework performed by that parent, but not by any children in the household.)

Technology Activity

1. Using your school or local library and the Internet, research family violence over the last 30 years—1970 to 1980; 1980 to 1990; 1990 to Present. Create a graph to show statistically the frequency of reported incidents of violence. In your own words, using correct grammar, spelling, punctuation, and terms learned in this chapter, write an essay that summarizes your graph. In the essay, consider reasons or changes in society that you believe influence the frequency of reported incidents of family violence. Consider the impact, if any, of hotlines and Public Service Announcements regarding family violence. Determine whether the information that you have found on reported incidents is correct and complete. Support your decision with at least two reasons.

ANSWERS
Chapter 11 Assessment

Integrating the Teacher Resources

To further assess student comprehension of this chapter, use Chapter Test A or B available in the Chapter and Unit Tests booklet in your Teacher's Resource Box.

4. This could turn into a neat little research project. Tell students that they might want to conduct their observations without their parents and other family members knowing about it. Sometimes discretion in research gets the best results. Have students share their findings with the rest of the class.

Technology Activity

1. Answers will vary. The key here is reported incidents. Many incidents go unreported so the data is incomplete or inaccurate. Social class, norms, and socioemotional factors may contribute to the under reporting. PSA's and hotlines have an impact because they offer support and practical alternatives.

Chapter 11

Enrichment Reading

Life Without Father

by David Popenoe

"Fathers should be neither seen nor heard," Oscar Wilde once wrote. "That is the only proper basis for family life." With each passing year, American society has increasingly become an immense social testing ground for this proposition. Unfortunately for Wilde's reputation as a social analyst, to say nothing about the health of our society, the results have proved highly unsupportive. American fathers are today more removed from family life than ever before in our history. And according to a growing body of evidence, this **massive erosion of fatherhood** contributes mightily to many of the major social problems of our time. . . .

The print pages and airwaves have been filled with discussions of fatherhood in recent decades. Yet most discussions have focused on just one issue—how to get fathers to share their traditional breadwinner role and take up a new (for them) child-care-provider role. The call from younger women has been loud and clear: We need a new conception of fatherhood, a "new father," one who will help equally in the home just as women now strive to help equally in the workplace; one who will share the **"second shift"** with his mate.

The father's role—what society expects of fathers—has indeed changed enormously in recent years. Fathers are expected to be more engaged with their children and involved with housework—if not nearly as much as most women would like, certainly far more than the past generation of fathers would have thought possible.

This role change has been highly positive in most respects. But with all the concentration on "role equality" in the home, the larger and more **ominous** trend of modern fatherhood has been mostly overlooked. We have been through many social revolutions in the past three decades—sex, women's liberation, divorce—but none more significant for society than the startling emergence of the absent father, a kind of **pathological counterpart** to the new father.

While the new father has been emerging gradually for most of this century, it is only in the past thirty years that we have witnessed the enormous increase in absent fathers. In times past, many children were left fatherless through his premature death. Today, the fathers are still alive and out there somewhere; the problem is that they seldom see much, if anything, of their children.

The main reason for contemporary father absence is the dramatic decline of marriage. . . . What this means, in human terms, is that about half of today's children will spend at least a portion of their growing-up years living apart from their fathers.

As a society, we can respond to this new fatherlessness in several ways. We can, as more and more of us seem to be doing, simply declare fathers to be unnecessary, superfluous. This is the response of "single parents by choice." It is the response of those who say that if daddies and mommies are expected to do precisely the same things in the home, why do we need both? It is the response of those who declare that unwed motherhood is a woman's right, or that single-parent families are every bit as good as two-parent families, or that divorce is generally beneficial for children.

In my view, these responses represent a human tragedy—for children, for women, for men, and for our society as a whole. . . . Fathering is different from mothering; involved fathers are **indispensable** for the good of children and soci-

Enrichment Reading

The title of this article, *Life Without Father,* is a play on words. It is taken from the play *Life with Father* which opened on Broadway in 1939, which was itself based primarily on Clarence Day, Jr.'s, autobiographical books, *God and My Father, Life with Father, and Life with Mother.*

Clarence Day, Jr., was literally on his deathbed while writing these books, and, after their publication and moderate success, he almost sold the movie rights to Paramount, but changed his mind when he learned the studio intended them as vehicles for W. C. Fields. Day did not live to see the production of the play, *Life with Father.* After major actors and actress had declined to play the leading roles, author Howard Lindsay and his wife, actress Dorothy Stickney, undertook them. The play finally opened, the critics raved, and it was an immediate hit. The Lindsays continued as Mother and Father for the next five years.

You may want to read parts of the original book to the students and compare the roles that society assigned to fathers at that time.

ety; and our growing [trend in] national fatherlessness is a disaster in the making. . . .

No one predicted this trend, few researchers or government agencies have monitored it, and it is not widely discussed, even today. But its importance to society is second to none. Father absence is a major force lying behind many of the attention-grabbing issues that dominate the news: crime and delinquency; premature sexuality and out-of-wedlock teen births; deteriorating educational achievement; depression, substance abuse, and alienation among teenagers; and the growing number of women and children in poverty. These issues all point to a **profound deterioration** in the well-being of children. Some experts have suggested, in fact, that the current generation of children and youth is the first in our nation's history to be less well-off—psychologically, socially, economically, and morally—than their parents were at the same age. Or as Senator Daniel Patrick Moynihan has observed, "the United States . . . may be the first society in history in which children are distinctly worse off than adults."

Along with the growing father absence, our cultural view of fatherhood is changing. Few people have doubts about the fundamental importance of mothers. But fathers? More and more the question is being raised, are fathers really necessary? Many would answer no, or maybe not. And to the degree that fathers are still thought necessary, fatherhood is said by many to be merely a social role, as if men had no inherent biological predisposition whatsoever to acknowledge and to invest in their own offspring. If merely a social role, then perhaps anyone is capable of playing it. . . .

The decline of fatherhood and of marriage cuts at the heart of the kind of environment considered ideal for childrearing. Such an environment, according to a substantial body of knowledge, consists of an enduring two-parent family that engages regularly in activities together, has many of its own routines and traditions, and provides a great deal of quality contact with their parents' world of work. In addition, there is little concern on the part of children that their parents will break up. Finally, each of these ingredients comes together in the development of a rich family subculture that has lasting meaning and strongly **promulgates** such family values as responsibility, cooperation, and sharing. . . .

What the decline of fatherhood and marriage in America really means, then, is that slowly, insidiously, and relentlessly our society has been moving in an ominous direction—toward the devaluation of children. There has been an alarming weakening of the fundamental assumption, long at the center of our culture, that children are to be loved and valued at the highest level of priority. Nothing could be more serious for our children or our future.

Source: Excerpted from David Popenoe, *Life Without Father* (New York: The Free Press, 1996), pp. 1–2, 14.

What Does it Mean?

indispensable
absolutely necessary

massive erosion of fatherhood
great numbers of fathers not present in the home

ominous
dangerous; darkly threatening

pathological counterpart
diseased opposite

profound deterioration
very great decline

promulgates
teaches

second shift
work to be done at home

Read and React

1. Briefly state the main point of Popenoe's reading. Is he correct? Is he too pessimistic? Explain.
2. Explain why Popenoe thinks that Oscar Wilde's statement that "fathers should be neither seen nor heard" is wrong. Do you think Wilde was wrong? Why or why not?
3. Discuss the reasons Popenoe gives for the decline of the father's presence in the contemporary American family.
4. According to Popenoe, nothing could be more serious for children than the trend he sees toward "life without father." Why do you agree or disagree?

Answers to Read and React

1. Students may interpret the tone of this article differently, but it is very definitely a serious evaluation with not a lot of hope for the future, unless conditions change. Popenoe's main thesis could be summed up in the statement he makes on the top of page 385 ". . . our growing [trend in] national fatherlessness is a disaster in the making."
2. Students should realize that Oscar Wilde was being ironic in his comment about fathers. Also, the Victorian concept of the overbearing, interfering, authoritarian father figure is quite different from the norms of today.
3. The main reason that Popenoe suggests for the "absent father" is the decline of marriage among the last two generations. More children are spending a longer portion of their childhood in single-parent homes, and the majority of single-parent households are headed by women.
4. Student answers will vary.

Chapter Preview

Section 1 (pages 388–395)
Schools have become more and more bureaucratic. Advocates of open classrooms and cooperative learning contend that bureaucratically run schools fail to take into account the emotional and creative needs of individual children.

Section 2 (pages 396–399)
Functionalists see the emergence of the educational institution as a response to society's needs. The manifest functions of education include the transmission of culture, creation of a common identity, selection and screening of talent, and promotion of personal growth and development. Schools also serve latent functions.

Section 3 (pages 400–408)
In theory, America is a meritocracy in which social status is achieved. Proponents of the conflict perspective identify flaws in this model by pointing to inequality in our schools. Methods and programs aimed at promoting educational equality have been developed.

Section 4 (pages 409–415)
Symbolic interactionists emphasize the socialization that occurs in schools. Through the hidden curriculum, children are taught values, norms, beliefs, and attitudes. Much of this socialization helps young people make the transition from home to the larger society.

CHAPTER 12

Education

386

Lead-Off Activity

Tell students that they will be tested on the material in this chapter within the next few days. However, tell them that before you give them a test for their grade, they'll be allowed to create their own tests that the class will use to prepare for your exam. Have students work in groups to write their tests. Stress that they must include the basic concepts and theories stated in the chapter. Most students will inevitably create a standard test, but see if any try to create a nontraditional test. Once their tests are finished, have each group administer their test to the entire class. You might want to see how the scores compare between the various tests and discuss which test was most reliable

USING Your Sociological Imagination

Columnist Ann Landers published this letter from a teacher about the hidden realities of teaching in America.

Let me see if I have this right. . . . I am also to instill a sense of pride in their ethnicity, modify disruptive behavior and observe them for signs of abuse.

I am to fight the war on drugs and sexually transmitted diseases, check their backpacks for guns and knives, and raise their self-esteem. I am to teach them patriotism, good citizenship, sportsmanship and fair play . . . I am to . . . maintain a safe environment, write letters of recommendation for student employment and scholarships, encourage respect for the cultural diversity of others, always making sure I give the girls in my class 50% of my attention.

I am required to work . . . toward additional certification and a master's degree, to sponsor the cheerleaders or the sophomore class (my choice); and after school, I am to attend committee and faculty meetings. . . .

I am to be a paragon of virtue, such that my presence will awe my students into being obedient and respectful of authority. I am to do all of this with just a piece of chalk, a bulletin board and a few books (some of which I may have to purchase myself). And for doing this, I am to be paid a starting salary that, in some states, qualifies my family for food stamps.

Is that all?

(Excerpted from "A Lesson on the Realities of Teaching," *The Los Angeles Times*, January 28, 2000).

Sections

1. **Development and Structure of Education**
2. **Functionalist Perspective**
3. **Conflict Perspective**
4. **Symbolic Interactionism**

Learning Objectives

After reading this chapter, you will be able to

- discuss schools as bureaucracies.
- outline the basic functions of education.
- evaluate the merit-based nature of public education.
- describe the ways in which schools socialize students.
- discuss educational inequality.

SOCIOLOGY Online

Chapter Overview
Visit the *Sociology and You* Web site at soc.glencoe.com and click on **Chapter 12—Chapter Overviews** to preview chapter information.

USING Your Sociological Imagination

Ask students to compare the current role of the teacher as described in this feature, with the role of teachers twenty to thirty years ago. To provide this perspective, ask a retired teacher to come to class and tell students how things have changed over the last two decades. What has happened sociologically to cause teachers' roles to have changed so dramatically?

and valid. After being tested on the same concepts several times, students should become very familiar with the chapter material, and score very well on the "real" test that you administer. In addition, have students discuss the problems involved in the use of standardized testing. What are some alternatives? Tell students that standardized tests such as the ACT and SAT are used so frequently that it would take a major overhaul of the educational system to create tests that allow people to be assessed differently and more creatively. What implications might this have for students? **L2**

Using the Section Preview

To help students understand how bureaucracy relates to education, remind them of the concepts of formal organizations (see Chapter 6, pages 190–196 and 200–201), and have them revisit Chapter 1, page 20, "The McDonaldization of Higher Education." If students haven't already done so, have them apply the McDonaldization concepts of efficiency, calculability, predictability, use of technology, irrationality and the iron cage, and look for examples of the rationalization of the bureaucratic structure at your school.

Using the Illustration

Have students compare the classrooms pictured in the photos. How have computers changed education in the last several years? How do students think computers will change education in the future?

Integrating the Teacher Resources

Look for the Chapter 12 Learning Goals Outline, a reproducible student worksheet in the Unit 4 Mastering Basic Concepts **booklet in your Teacher's Resource Box. It can be used to preview or review chapter content.**

Section 1 Development and Structure of Education

Key Terms

- formal schooling
- open classroom
- cooperative learning
- integrative curriculum
- voucher system
- charter schools
- magnet schools
- for-profit schools

Section Preview

Schools are becoming more bureaucratic. Advocates of open classrooms and cooperative learning contend that bureaucratically run schools fail to take into account the emotional and creative needs of individual children.

Bureaucracy in Education

School administration in the early 1900s was based on a factory model of education. Educators believed that children could be and should be educated in much the same way as cars were mass produced.

> *Schooling came to be seen as work or the preparation for work; schools were pictured as factories, educators as industrial managers, and students as the raw materials to be inducted into the production process. The ideology of school management was recast in the mold of the business corporation, and the character of education was shaped after the image of industrial production (Cohen and Lazerson, 1972:47).*

Although teachers and administrators work hard today to personalize the time you spend in school, public education in this country remains very much an impersonal bureaucratic process. Schools today are still based on specialization, rules and procedures, and impersonality.

The 1954 classroom on the left clearly reflects the traditional mass production approach to education. Recently, as seen in the photo at the right, there has been more of an attempt to personalize education.

Paired Learning Activity

According to teachers, "no computers in the classroom" is the number one reason they do not use digital content. The shortage of equipment does not allow them to integrate technology into their curriculum. Those teachers who do have access to computers, say they just don't have enough time and incentive to use the digital content over the traditional content they have available.

Have students work in pairs to talk with teachers in your school. They should ask the teachers how they use computers in their teaching. The answers will vary from, "Not at all," from the teachers who don't have access to computers to "All the time," from teachers who have access to computer labs and have one or more computers in their classrooms depending on how your school views and implements technology.
L1

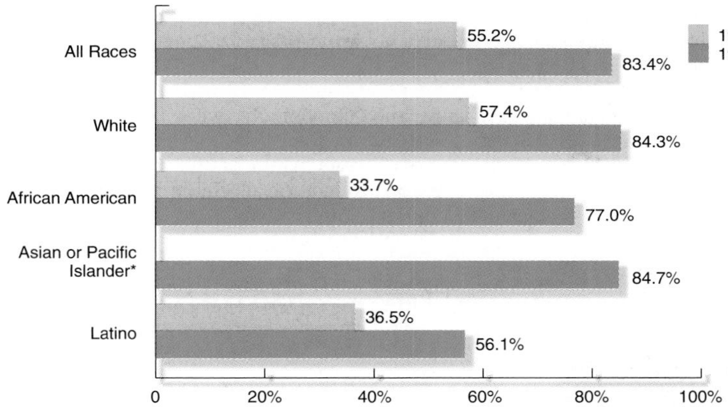

Figure 12.1 High School Graduates by Race (1970 and 1999). *Displayed in this figure are the percentages, by racial and ethnic category, of persons 25 years old and older who have completed high school. Note that the proportion of high school graduates in each group has increased sharply between 1970 and 1999. As a result, each of these groups is placing more pressure on public schools to accommodate their members.*

*Note: No data available for Asian or Pacific Islander for 1970.
Source: U.S. Bureau of the Census, 2000.

Why should schools be standardized? For administrators, there are many advantages to following a bureaucratic model. For instance, in the discussion of formal organizations in Chapter 6, you read that one of the characteristics of a bureaucracy is the tendency to specialize. Professional educators are specialists—administrators, classroom teachers, librarians, curriculum specialists who decide on courses and content, and so forth.

In the bureaucratic model, education can be accomplished most efficiently for large numbers of students when they are at similar stages in their ability and development. (There were, in fact, just over 53 million students in the public school system in 2000. Figure 12.1 shows the increasing percentage of young people from all races and ethnic groups who are completing high school.) In this way, a teacher can develop one lesson plan for a number of students. Age-based classrooms, in which all students receive the same instruction, reflect the impersonal, bureaucratic nature of schools.

Efficiency, the ultimate goal of a bureaucracy, is also increased when teachers teach the same, or at least similar, content. Materials can be approved and purchased in bulk, and testing can be standardized. This practice also allows students to transfer from one school to another and continue studying approximately the same things. Rules and procedures exist to ensure that all of this happens.

Schools are also part of a much larger bureaucratic system. This system begins with the federal government and progresses layer by layer through state and local governments. (See page 191 in Chapter 6 for an organizational chart of a public school district.)

> “Bureaucracy is a challenge to be confronted with a righteous attitude, a tolerance for stupidity, and a bulldozer when necessary.”
>
> **Anonymous**

Working with the Data

Figure 12.1 Ask students why they think African Americans made such an increase in number of graduates from 1970 to 1998. Why did Latinos not make as much of an increase? What might be done to increase the number of Latino graduates?

Integrating the Teacher Resources

Look for the Chapter 12 Analyzing and Interpreting Data worksheet in the Unit 4 Mastering Basic Concepts **booklet in your Teacher's Resource Box for skill-building exercises based on the graphs, charts, and maps in this chapter.**

Survey

Have students survey teachers in the school about their teaching styles. (Students might want to refer back to Chapter 2, Methods of Research for information on constructing a survey.) Help students come up with a list of different teaching styles (such as open-classroom format, cooperative learning, etc.), then have the students poll teachers about the different format(s) they use. Students might also ask open-ended questions to have teachers describe the teaching styles they use. Students should inform the teachers they survey that their names will be kept confidential. After the class has conducted the survey, compile the results and have students analyze the use of the different teaching styles in the school.

Controversy and Debate

Remind students that the educational system in the United States was established around an agricultural work force. Having three months off during the summer allowed students to help with the planting and harvesting of crops. However, times have changed. Most students no longer have the need to help with the family farm.

Have students design an educational system that will meet the needs of an informational society such as we live in now. What changes would they make to the school year? Would length of classes change? Would the design of schools change? How about instructional methods? Subjects offered? Use of technology? Ask for volunteers to share their new designs with the rest of the class.

What do critics of the bureaucratic model say? Critics claim that the old factory, or bureaucratic, model is not appropriate for schooling. Children, they point out, are not inorganic materials to be processed on an assembly line. Children are human beings who come into school with previous knowledge and who interact socially and emotionally with other students. According to critics of **formal schooling,** education that is provided and regulated by society, the school's bureaucratic nature is unable to respond to the expressive, creative, and emotional needs of all children. These critics prefer several less rigid, more democratic alternatives.

formal schooling
education that is provided and regulated by society

Democratic Reforms in the Classroom

Working cooperatively in groups is one of the more democratic school reforms of the twentieth century.

Since colonial times, providing citizens with a good education has been an important value in the United States. The Puritans in Massachusetts in 1647 required towns with more than fifty families to hire a schoolmaster. The Land Ordinance of 1785 required that some of the monies from the sale of public land be used to build schools. The first public schools were quite authoritarian, with firm rules and sharp lines drawn between students and teacher.

The American progressive education movement of the 1920s and 1930s was a reaction to the strict Victorian authoritarianism of early nineteenth-century schools. Educational philosopher John Dewey (1859–1952) led the progressive education movement, which emphasized knowledge related to work and to individual student interests. The progressive movement, with its child-centered focus, almost disappeared in the 1950s but reappeared in the 1960s as the humanistic movement. The humanistic movement supported the elimination of restrictive rules and codes and the involvement of students in the educational process. The aim of the humanistic movement was to create a more democratic, student-focused learning environment (Ballantine, 1993). It has proven to be an influential forerunner of classroom reform. Three ways to express the humanistic educational impulse are the *open classroom, cooperative learning,* and the *integrative curriculum.*

What is the open classroom? The **open classroom** is a nonbureaucratic approach to education based on democratic relationships, flexibility, and noncompetitiveness. Here educators avoid the sharp authoritarian line traditionally drawn between teachers and students. The open classroom drops the idea that all children of a given age should follow a standardized curriculum. On the belief that competition is not a good motivator for children, the open classroom abandons the use of graded report cards based on comparison of student performance.

open classroom
a nonbureaucratic approach to education based on democracy, flexibility, and noncompetitiveness

The open classroom, introduced in the 1960s, has resurfaced in the 1990s. Cooperative learning and the integrative curriculum are two important extensions of the open-classroom approach.

Integrating the Teacher Resources

To reinforce key ideas, use the Chapter 12 Graphic Organizer, a reproducible student worksheet in the Unit 4 Mastering Basic Concepts booklet in your Teacher's Resource Box.

Encouraging Citizenship Activity

Help students plan and start a tutoring group for fellow students who are struggling academically.

Before you begin, there are several things students will need to do to prepare to give quality service. The first thing they should do is to assess their own academic strengths and weaknesses. (It would probably not be a good idea to tutor someone in math if they are failing it.) The next thing students need to do is study the subjects they do feel qualified to help others with. Then, it would be a good idea for them to do an inventory of teaching styles that have been helpful to themselves (as well as teaching techniques that were counterproductive). Finally, they should learn as much as they can about learning styles, so that

What is cooperative learning? **Cooperative learning** takes place in a nonbureaucratic classroom structure in which students study in groups, with teachers as guides rather than as the controlling agents (the "guide on the side" versus the "sage on the stage" approach). According to the cooperative learning method, students learn more if they are actively involved with others in the classroom (Sizer, 1996). The traditional teacher-centered approach rewards students for being passive recipients of information and requires them to compete with others for grades and teacher recognition. Cooperative learning, with its accent on teamwork rather than individual performance, is designed to encourage students to concentrate more on the process of getting results than how their answers compare to those of other students. Cooperation replaces competition. Students typically work in small groups on specific tasks. Credit for completion of a task is given only if all group members do their parts.

cooperative learning
instructional method that relies on cooperation among students

Using this approach successfully requires some expertise on the part of the teacher and can initially discourage students who are motivated by letter grades based on individual work. Nevertheless, some benefits of the cooperative learning approach have been documented (Children's Defense Fund, 1991). For example,

- uncooperativeness and stress among students is reduced.
- academic performance increases.
- students have more positive attitudes toward school.
- racial and ethnic antagonism decreases.
- self-esteem increases.

What is the integrative curriculum? As you have seen, the curriculum is predetermined for students in the traditional classroom. In the **integrative curriculum,** however, the curriculum is created by students and teachers working together. Since students are asked to participate in curriculum design and content, the integrative curriculum is democratic in nature. Giving students such power obviously deviates from the traditional subject-centered curriculum. Students and teachers become collaborators (Barr, 1995).

integrative curriculum
an approach to education based on student-teacher collaboration

Subject matter is selected and organized around certain real-world themes or concepts. An example is a sixth-grade unit of study on water quality in Washington State.

In an integrative curriculum, students apply teachings from many disciplines at the same time. Students shown here are on a field trip to explore mineral production in a local community.

More About . . . Cooperative Learning

The government's *SCANS Report for America 2000* identified skills and qualities that are generally considered necessary for a worker or employee to be effective. Possessing interpersonal skills is one of the workplace competencies named in the report. Interpersonal skills are defined as being able to work on teams, teach others, serve customers, lead, negotiate, and work well with people from culturally diverse backgrounds.

Cooperative learning attempts to teach students these interpersonal skills in the classroom so they will be able to implement them in the workplace. Cooperative learning is not, however, a new concept. It has been around since humans realized that they could accomplish more and with better results if they worked cooperatively. In the first century, Quintilian suggested that students would benefit by learning from each other. The concept of students teaching and learning from each other came to the United States in the early 1800s. Since that time, there have been periods when cooperative learning had strong advocates and periods when it did not.

they can recognize a learning pattern when they see one and accommodate their own teaching style to it. Finally, stress the importance of continuity and follow-through. Students should not begin the project if they are not committed to it.

Once you have covered the groundwork, help them set up a tutoring station and find a reasonable time to tutor (after school? during lunch? during tutorial periods if your school has them?). Students should make themselves available to help other students for a minimum of 20 hours. You might have them work one-on-one, or you might have them work with groups of students.
L3

Another Time

You might want students who are foreign born to relate their own stories about education both here and abroad. Also, ask students why some people take their education for granted. Is it because they see education as a birthright and not a privilege?

Again, if students use the McDonaldization concepts mentioned earlier in the chapter, they can assess the degree to which schools are becoming bureaucratized.

Answers to Thinking it Over

1.–2. Answers will vary.

Another Time: Understanding Freedom and Education in America

One hundred years ago, Russian immigrant Marie Antin wrote about her first days at school in the United States. Reading about her reactions might make Americans more appreciative of the public school system they often criticize.

Education was free. That subject my father had written about repeatedly, as comprising his chief hope for us children, the essence of American opportunity, the treasure that no thief could touch, not even misfortune or poverty. It was the one thing that he was able to promise us when he sent for us; surer, safer, than bread or shelter.

In the past, schools played an important role in transmitting American culture to many immigrant children. Are schools today still carrying on that function?

On our second day I was thrilled with the realization of what this freedom of education meant. A little girl from across the alley came and offered to conduct us to school. My father was out, but we five between us had a few words of English by this time. We knew the word school. We understood. This child, who had never seen us till yesterday, who could not pronounce our names, who was not much better dressed than we, was able to offer us the freedom of the schools of Boston! No application made, no question asked, no examinations, rulings, exclusions; no machinations, no fees. The doors stood open for every one of us. The smallest child could show us the way.

This incident impressed me more than anything I had heard in advance of the freedom of education in America. It was a concrete proof—almost the thing itself. One had to experience it to understand it.

Source: Excerpted from Marie Antin, *The Promised Land* (New York, 1912).

Thinking It Over

1. Describe your thoughts and feelings about your school experiences as you think about Antin's perspective.
2. Do you agree with the author that education is the chief hope for children? Explain.

The unit became a part of an actual water quality project that originated in the Great Lakes region of the United States but now spans the globe. Lessons were organized around the actual work of determining water quality in Puget Sound. These lessons culminated in students' reporting to community groups about the quality of the water. In this way learning was relevant to a real-world problem that the students contributed to solving (Simmons and El-Hindi, 1998:33).

Instruction in this unit emphasized hands-on experience and utilized the multiple intelligences of various students. The latter idea recognizes that not all students in a classroom learn in identical ways. Students bring to any unit of study a variety of learning styles, interests, and abilities. Different units of study will engage students in varying ways.

Points to Stress

Introduce the multiple intelligences to your students by listing them on the board: artistic, musical, verbal-linguistic, spatial, interpersonal, intrapersonal, naturalistic, math/science, and kinesthetic. The multiple intelligencies call into question the current American educational process, which is geared towards math/science and verbal/linguistic intelligences. Ask students how schools might restructure themselves to address the other intelligences.

Paired Learning Activity

The Japanese have a highly bureaucratic structure of education, which seems to foster high educational standards. Japanese students consistently score among the highest in the world on aptitude tests. This might suggest that highly bureaucratic institutions can provide great benefit to their users. Have students work in pairs to research the bureaucratic structure of Japanese educational institutions, and compare and contrast them with educational institutions in the United States.

Another point to stress: If colleges and universities are at the forefront of American education, they serve to dictate the standardized tests for college admission. In addition, college professors often work with state committees to create new editions of standardized tests. If this is the case, ask students why they think university faculty doesn't make more of an effort to work with high school teachers in their content areas. **L2**

Back-to-Basics Movement

In the 1990s, the "back-to-basics" movement emerged alongside cooperative learning and the integrative curriculum. Worried by low scores on achievement tests, supporters of this movement pushed for a return to a traditional curriculum ("reading, writing, and arithmetic") based on more bureaucratic methods.

What started the back-to-basics movement? In 1983, America received an educational wake-up call. The National Commission on Excellence in Education issued a report dramatically entitled *A Nation at Risk*. Catching the attention of politicians and the general public, it warned of a "rising tide of mediocrity" in America's schools. Because of deficiencies in its educational system, the report claimed, America was at risk of being overtaken by some of its world economic competitors (Gardner, 1983).

Unlike the recommendations of the progressive and humanistic reform movements, most of the solutions offered by the commission were bureaucratic in nature. The report urged a return to more teaching of basic skills such as reading and mathematics. High school graduation requirements should be strengthened to include four years of English, three years of mathematics, three years of science, three years of social studies, and a half year of computer science. School days, the school year, or both should be lengthened. Standardized achievement tests should be administered as students move from one level of schooling to another. High school students should be given significantly more homework. Discipline should be tightened through the development and enforcement of codes for student conduct.

voucher system
system in which public school funds may be used to support public, private, or religious schools

Alternatives to the Public School System

The debate over the most effective classroom methods continues. Meanwhile, educators and politicians are looking beyond the classroom to how schools are organized, funded, and administered. A new debate has arisen over school choice. The school choice movement promotes the idea that the best way to improve schools is by using the free enterprise model and creating some competition for the public school system. Supporters of school choice believe that parents and students should be able to select the school that best fits their needs and provides the greatest educational benefit. Methods used to accomplish this goal include the *voucher system, charter schools, magnet,* and *for-profit* schools.

What is a voucher system? People in favor of a **voucher system** say that the government should make the money spent per child on public education available to families to use for public, private, or religious schools. Families who chose a public school would pay nothing, just as in the current system. Parents who chose a religious or other private school would receive a government voucher to be used to pay a portion of the tuition equal to the amount the government spends per child in the public school system. Any additional tuition would be paid by the parents. A voucher plan in Cleveland, for example, provides publicly funded scholarships of just

This charter school in Harlem is one alternative to the public school system.

More About . . . American Education

In the late 1950s, the American public questioned the effectiveness of the nation's educational system when the Soviet Union launched *Sputnik,* the first satellite to orbit the earth. Americans were so concerned about losing the space race to the Soviets that Congress appropriated money for math and science education. Current critics claim that the American educational system is again in decline. Have students list some problems that might indicate that American education is in trouble, such as the rise in school violence, poor standardized test scores, etc. Ask students to consider whether current policies of educational reform are reactionary or whether there is legitimate cause for concern. You may want to have students debate this issue.

Cooperative Learning Activity

School vouchers, school choice, charter schools, magnet schools, and for-profit schools are some of the most hotly debated topics in education today. Have groups of students research one of these areas. Groups might want to take a pro or con stance on the issues, or they may want to provide an overview of both sides of a particular issue. If you have groups with pro and con stances, you might have a class discussion or debate on the issues.
L2

Pulling it All Together

In this unit, the bureaucratic structure of education was discussed. In addition, democratic educational reforms were examined. A "back-to-basics" movement caught on in the 1980s as fears heightened that the American educational system was failing. On the heels of that, public schools have faced growing competition from the school voucher system, charter schools, magnet schools, and for-profit schools. Despite all these changes, the institution of education remains solid.

Answers to Section 1 Assessment

1. Three ways in which U.S. schools follow the bureaucratic model are: specialization—professional educators are specialists, such as administrators, classroom teachers, curriculum specialists, librarians, etc.; impersonality—age-based classroom policy in which all students receive the same instruction; rules and procedures—teachers teach the same or similar material so materials can be approved and purchased in bulk, testing can be standardized, students can transfer and continue studying the same things.

(continued on page 395)

over $2,000 annually to almost four thousand city children. Most parents have chosen to spend the money at private schools rather than keep their children in public schools. The basic idea is that public schools would have to compete for the students and thus would improve their services. If parents were not happy with a school, they would have the freedom to remove their children and place them elsewhere.

Public reaction to the voucher approach has been mixed. So far, public vouchers affect only about one-tenth of 1 percent of American school children. Large-scale public programs exist in only two cities—Cleveland and Milwaukee. In 1999, Florida initiated the first statewide public voucher program. African American and Latino parents tend to prefer a voucher system because it provides some financial help to remove their children from public schools that they believe have let their children down. Because most whites seem to be satisfied with the public schools, they have not embraced the voucher system in large numbers (Thomas and Clemetson, 1999).

> "Education makes people easy to lead, but difficult to drive; easy to govern, but impossible to enslave."
>
> **Lord Brougham**
> **Scottish statesman**

Courts have generally treated voucher systems as unconstitutional because they may contradict the principle of separation of church and state. On the other hand, a 1998 U.S. Supreme Court ruling validated a Wisconsin law allowing state money to go to low-income students for either private or parochial education schools. Whereas the U.S. Supreme Court has not ruled directly on the constitutionality of school vouchers, some state and federal judges have. Vouchers have been declared unconstitutional by lower court judges in Florida, Ohio, and Vermont. Since these cases are under appeal, one or more will likely reach the Supreme Court soon (Perry and McGraw, 1999).

Up to now the evidence on the effectiveness of the voucher system is inconsistent. Although compared to public schools, some voucher programs have improved student test scores, other programs have produced no improvement (Toch and Cohen, 1998).

Critics fear that if this system were implemented, inner-city schools would suffer even more, since few inner-city parents could afford to make up the difference between the amount of the voucher and the cost of the highest-quality private schools. They also fear that national and local commitment to public education would decline, leaving the public school system in worse shape than it is now. Furthermore, the need to regulate private and religious schools would increase bureaucracy.

What are charter schools and magnet schools? **Charter schools** are publicly funded schools operated like private schools by public school teachers and administrators. Freed of answering to local school boards, charter schools have the latitude to shape their own curriculum and to use non-traditional or traditional teaching methods .

> **charter schools**
> public schools that are operated like private schools by public school teachers and administrators

The Mosaica Academy, which opened in 1998 in Pennsylvania, is deliberately not organized along public school lines. The school day is nearly two hours longer than at public school and the school year is twenty days longer. This school created its own curriculum with the goal of immersing students in the development of civilizations over 4,000 years (Symonds, 2000). By 2002, there will be some 3,000 charter schools across the United States. The success of these schools is directly tied to the commitment and talent of the teachers and the principals, and to the support of parents.

> **magnet schools**
> public schools that focus on particular disciplines or areas, such as fine arts or science

Magnet schools are public schools that attempt to achieve high standards by specializing in a certain area. One school may emphasize the

Learning Styles

Linguistic/Interpersonal/Logical-mathematical The 1983 report by the National Committee on Excellence in Education was basically a report card for the public school system. Conduct a survey to give students an opportunity to give a report card to your school, as well as an opportunity to practice research/math skills. After discussing Section 1, students can begin collecting data by interviewing people at your school, including students, teachers, administrators, support staff, and parents. Students should performing arts while another might stress science. Magnet schools are designed to enhance school quality and to promote desegregation. They have become a significant factor in improving urban education.

Calvin expects to reap the rewards of education, but has a problem with the effort of getting educated.

What is the nature of for-profit schools? Some reformers do not believe local or federal government is capable of improving the educational system. Government, they say, is too wasteful and ineffective. Why not look to business and market forces to solve the problems facing schools today? **For-profit schools** would be supported by government funds but run by private companies. By borrowing from modern business practices, the argument goes, these schools could be efficient, productive, and cost effective. Marketplace forces would ensure that the best schools will survive.

for-profit schools
schools run by private companies on government funds

The most comprehensive for-profit organization is Edison, which launched a $40-million, three-year campaign in 1992 to develop its program. Edison schools feature challenging curriculums, along with a schedule that has children in school almost a third longer than the average public school. Beginning in the third grade, students are equipped with a computer and modem to take home, in order to access Edison's intranet system (Symonds, 2000).

Critics of this approach are bothered by the idea of mixing profit and public service. What would happen to the students when their needs were weighed against the profit margin? Would for-profit schools skimp on equipment, services, and training? Another problem involves oversight. That is, with a for-profit system, voters would lose the power to influence officials and educational policy.

Section 1 Assessment

1. State three ways in which schools in the United States follow the bureaucratic model.
2. Identify three specific types of reform in public education.

Critical Thinking

3. **Analyzing Information** Explain why such reforms as open classrooms and integrative learning are characterized as more democratic than the traditional or bureaucratic approach.
4. **Summarizing Information** First briefly summarize the ideas about school choice presented in this section. Then evaluate them. Do you favor one approach over another? Give reasons for your choice.

2. Three types of reform in public education are: open classroom—a nonbureaucratic approach based on democratic relationships, flexibility, and noncompetitiveness that drops the idea of a standardized curriculum for a given age; extensions of the open classroom are: cooperative learning—a nonbureaucratic structure where students study in groups with teachers as guides instead of controlling agents; and integrative curriculum—curriculum is created by students and teachers working together; students participate in curriculum design and content, which is a more democratic approach.

Critical Thinking

3. Open classrooms and integrative learning are characterized as more democratic because they eliminate some of the rules and regulations of the traditional approach and allow for more student choice and involvement.

4. Students should expand upon the different methods available to accomplish the goal of selecting the school which best fits needs and provides the greatest benefits. If one approach is favored, reasons should be given.

keep track of which category each person fits into. Include questions regarding how your school is doing in areas of manifest and latent functions. When data has been gathered, ask students to tabulate the results of their survey, comparing the findings from the different groups. Be sure to discuss areas of agreement and disagreement between the categories of those surveyed. Ask students to brainstorm ways your school could improve in areas that consistently received "low grades." **L2**

Using the Section Preview

Use this opportunity to have students think about how the functions of education are used to transmit society's values. Have students refer back to Chapter 3, page 90, then brainstorm examples of things students learn in school that reflect these values. For example, such things as teaching citizenship are part of the democratic ideal. Point out to students that we could expect that other societies educate with the same purpose in mind, using education to transmit their cultural values.

Reteaching

An easy way to get students to understand the difference between manifest and latent functions is to have them apply these concepts to education. Ask students, "Why do you go to school?" *(Likely answers would include: to learn, to socialize, and to prepare for the job market.)* As a class, discuss these answers and have students distinguish between the manifest and latent function of education. Socialization is a latent function of education. Learning and preparing for the job market are manifest or intended functions of education. As you continue this exercise, students will soon easily grasp the concepts.

Section 2 Functionalist Perspective

Key Terms

- manifest function
- latent function
- tracking

Section Preview

Functionalists see the emergence of the educational institution as a response to society's needs. The manifest functions of education include transmission of culture, creation of a common identity, selection and screening of talent, and promotion of personal growth and development. Schools also serve latent functions.

manifest function
an action that produces an intended and recognized result

latent function
an action that produces an unintended and unrecognized result

Manifest Functions of Education

According to the functionalists, social institutions develop because they meet one or more of society's basic needs. Functionalists distinguish between a **manifest function,** which is an intended and recognized result, and a **latent function,** which is an unintended and unrecognized result. (Refer to page 26 to review the meanings of these terms.) The educational institution performs several vital manifest functions in modern society. Schools teach obvious academic skills such as reading, writing, and mathematics. They also transmit culture, create a common identity for members of society, select and screen talent, and promote personal growth and development. Let's look more closely at each of these functions.

How do schools transmit culture? Schools transmit culture by instilling in students the basic values, norms, beliefs, and attitudes of the society. The value of competition, for example, is taught through emphasis on grades, sports, and school spirit. Teaching the culture is absolutely essential if a society is to survive from one generation to the next.

Is the teacher lecturing to these students fulfilling a manifest or latent function?

Careers in Sociology

Ask students the following question; then discuss the answers provided. How can you tell if teaching is the right career for you?

College faculty should have inquiring, analytical minds, and a strong desire to learn and share that knowledge. They must be able to communicate clearly and logically. They should be able to establish rapport with students and provide models for them of the principles of academic integrity and intellectual honesty. They must be self-motivated and able to work though they receive little direct supervision.

In addition to being knowledgeable in their subject, the ability to communicate, inspire trust and confidence, and motivate students, as well as understand educational and emotional needs, is essential for

World View

Illiteracy Rates

One of the functions of education is to promote literacy—the key to continued learning, problem solving, and information analysis. This map shows rates of illiteracy among persons fifteen years of age and older in various countries of the world. Because of cultural norms and discrimination, more women than men are illiterate.

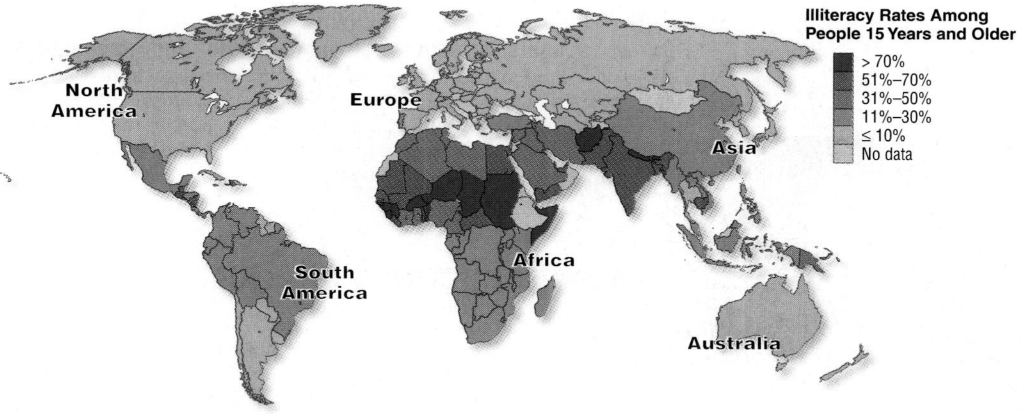

Interpreting the Map

1. Do you see a pattern in the rates of illiteracy? Explain.
2. How does the United States measure up?

Adapted from *The State of the World Atlas,* 5th ed.

How do schools help create a common identity? Although television is now a strong competitor, the educational system remains the major force in creating a common identity among a diverse population. Learning an official language, sharing in national history and patriotic themes, and being exposed to similar informational materials promote a shared identity. The result is a society with homogeneous values, norms, beliefs, and attitudes. Schools in the United States contribute to this process. By attending local schools, newly arrived immigrant children, without the ability to speak and write English, soon learn to participate in the American way of life.

The current debate in the United States over bilingual education touches on the role that schools play in creating a common identity. People who emphasize recognizing and honoring cultural diversity usually support teaching in the student's own language, at least for some period of time. Opponents of bilingual education argue that bilingual education hinders the development of a common American identity and has not been proven to help students

"Education has in America's whole history been the major hope for improving the individual and society."

Gunnar Myrdal
Swedish economist

World View

Ask students why they think some cultures do not allow women to be educated. Do they think it is because a woman's primary purpose is to give birth and raise children. Is this old-fashioned thinking? Are women, given the chance, capable of more? You might conduct a class debate on this issue. It will be interesting to notice if lines are drawn according to gender.

Answers to Interpreting the Map

1. Students should note that illiteracy is highest in the poorest countries (no surprise here). Reasons might include: children are needed to help work the farm or help in other ways; education may not be available in the poorer areas; the people may not belong to the dominant ethnic group; and there may be a different language used for the test.
2. Answers will vary but should indicate that the U. S. is among those nations with the lowest illiteracy rates.

kindergarten, elementary, secondary school, and adult basic education teachers. Teachers must be able to recognize and respond to individual differences, and employ teaching methods that will result in higher achievement. They should be organized, dependable, patient, and creative. Teachers must also be able to work cooperatively and communicate effectively with other teaching staff, support staff, parents, and other members of the community.

For information on national teacher certification, contact: National Board for Professional Teaching Standards, **http://www.nbpts.org**

succeed academically. Conservative political efforts have led twenty-three states to adopt English as their official language. The creation of a similar law for the nation is being discussed in Congress.

How do schools select and screen students? For over fifty years, scores on intelligence and achievement tests have been used for grouping children in school. The stated purpose of testing is to identify an individual's talents and aptitudes. Test scores have also been used for **tracking**—placing students in curricula consistent with expectations for the students' eventual occupations. (Tracking is discussed further in Section 3 when we look at inequalities in education.) Counselors use test scores and early performance records to predict careers for which individuals may be best suited.

tracking
placement of students in programs according to academic ability levels

How do schools promote personal growth and development? Schools expose students to a wide variety of perspectives and experiences that encourage them to develop creativity, verbal skills, artistic expression, intellectual accomplishment, and cultural tolerance. In this way, education provides an environment in which individuals can improve the quality of their lives. In addition, schools attempt to prepare students for the world of work.

Do you consider the opportunity to flirt a positive or negative latent function of schools?

Latent Functions of Education

The educational institution has latent functions as well. Some are positive; others are not. Educators do not usually think of schools as day-care facilities for dual-employed couples or single parents. Nor do parents vote for additional school taxes so that their sons and daughters can find dates or marriage partners. Also, schools are not consciously designed to prevent delinquency by holding juveniles indoors during the daytime. Nor are schools intended as training grounds for athletes. Nonetheless, all of these activities are latent functions of the school system.

Each of the latent functions just mentioned is considered a positive contribution to society. But some consequences are negative, or dysfunctional. Tracking, for example, can perpetuate an unequal social-class structure from generation to generation. In addition, evidence suggests that tracking is harmful to those placed on "slower" tracks (Hurn, 1993).

Section 2 Assessment

1. List the essential functions of education described in the text.
2. What is the difference between a manifest and a latent function in education?
3. What type of function do schools perform when they keep children for their working parents?

Critical Thinking

4. **Making Comparisons** What do you think is the most significant latent function schools perform? Consider the advantages and disadvantages.

Pulling it All Together

The sociological perspective of functionalism studies the manifest functions of education: cultural transmission, creation of a cultural identity, selection and screening of talent, and promotion of personal growth and development. The educational institution has latent functions as well: schools are sometimes considered day care facilities, as training grounds for athletic talent and schools sometimes foster the perpetuation of social-class differences.

Answers to Section 2 Assessment

1. Functions of education include teaching basic academic skills such as reading, writing and mathematics; transmitting culture; creating a common identity for members of society; selecting and screening talent; and promoting personal growth and development.
2. A manifest function is an intended and recognized result, and a latent function is an unintended and unrecognized result.
3. This is a latent function of education.

Critical Thinking

4. Answers will vary, but students may consider some of the latent functions listed in the text—daycare, matchmaking possibilities, delinquency prevention, athlete training—and should give positive and negative aspects of the one they consider most significant.

On-Demand Writing

A growing debate in education is the use of Advanced Placement (AP) courses as criteria for college admissions. Some universities are now denying admission to students who have taken no AP courses in high school. Some students who take AP courses feel that this is fair, since AP classes are more rigorous than non-AP classes. Other students who don't take AP classes might not have the time to handle the additional work of AP classes due to other commitments such as an after-school job or athletics. Or, the schools may not offer the advanced courses. However, these students

Sociology Today

Educating Yourself for the Future

By the time you graduate from high school, the competition for well-paying entry-level jobs will be stiffer than ever before. Here are some tips to keep you in demand—whether you are college bound or going directly into the job market.

Career counselors urge job seekers to think in terms of *lifelong learning*. Never think of your education as coming to an end. The excerpt below is as true today as it was a generation ago.

> *For education the lesson is clear: its prime objective must be to increase the individual's "cope-ability"—the speed and economy with which he can adapt to continual change. . . . It is not even enough for him to understand the present, for the here-and-now environment will soon vanish. Johnny must learn to anticipate the directions and rate of change. He must, to put it technically, learn to make repeated, probabilistic, increasingly long-range assumptions about the future (Toffler, 1970:403).*

Preparation for the future involves attempting to predict the future demand for particular occupations. The *Occupational Outlook Handbook* and the *Occupational Outlook Handbook for College Graduates* can be very helpful in this regard. Each year in these volumes, the U.S. Department of Labor publishes detailed predictions for specific occupations.

Educating yourself for the future also means being prepared to enter an occupation for which you have no specific training. You must remain willing to retrain and to enter an entirely new occupation—for example, to move from bank teller to computer programmer.

In spite of the fact that you will probably change occupations over the course of your work life, you should try to determine your true job preference before you spend a great deal of time learning a job that turns out not to be the one you want. Over half of all young people entering a chosen field quit their jobs within one year. This fact has led some observers to argue that few young people really understand the nature of the work for which they are preparing. How do you find out what jobs you would really enjoy? Volunteering time in a specific work situation can help. For example, hospitals usually have volunteer programs in which medical practitioners can be observed. If you think you would like to be a physician, nurse, or other health-care worker, get involved in one of these programs. You will not only help others but will help yourself, as well.

Finally, educating yourself for the future includes preparing for leisure choices. Careers have become so specialized that they satisfy only a small part of people's interests. Many high schools, colleges, and universities sponsor noncredit courses and seminars on such topics as personal development, photography, fine arts, and alternative lifestyles. These courses permit you to either pursue long-standing interests or develop new ones.

Doing Sociology

Make an informal survey of as many working adults as possible. Ask them what additional training, if any, they have undergone since taking their first jobs. Then ask them what plans they have for future training. Summarize your results, and bring the report to class to share.

argue, even without AP classes on their transcripts, they are as worthy candidates for admission as the AP students. Ask students what their views are on this issue. Do they think policies like these perpetuate social inequality? Students might want to look at the policies at colleges and universities in your area. Have students write a short essay expressing their views. Then have volunteers share their views with the rest of the class. You might have a class debate on this issue.

L2

Sociology Today

A recent book, The Ambitious Generation: America's Teenagers, Motivated but Directionless by Barbara Schneider and David Stevenson (1999, Yale University Press) examines student preparation for careers. The authors overwhelmingly found that if students began devising their career plans early, in their freshmen year of high school, they were more likely to be successful and fulfill those goals. Students who were indecisive and wavering between job possibilities were more likely later to settle for jobs they had not necessarily intended to be in. The authors suggest that students, counselors, and parents work together to help teens plan for and achieve their career goals.

Answer to Doing Sociology

If every student in class interviews five working adults, you could have a nice little study of working adults in your community. Be sure that students interview adults in various professions. Many professions encourage professional growth. Have students find out how many adults have had extensive computer training. Many of these adults did not have any computer skills when they left high school.

Using the Section Preview

Jonathan Kozol's book *Savage Inequalities,* provides what is perhaps the best illustration of the conflict perspective and the discrepancies that exist in America's schools. The video based on Kozol's book, *Children in America's Schools* is available through Insight Media. This 90-minute video captures the differences between a wealthy school district and other, poorer school districts where the buildings are literally falling apart. Both the book and the video show compelling examples of inequality in education. You may want to use excerpts from the book and video in class.

Integrating the Teacher Resources

For Spanish-speaking students, you may wish to use the reproducible worksheets available in the Spanish Supplements booklet in your Teacher's Resource Box. In addition to providing Spanish translations of selected Mastering Basic Concepts worksheets, the booklet contains English and Spanish summaries of the chapter's key points.

Section 3 Conflict Perspective

Key Terms

- meritocracy
- competition
- educational equality
- cognitive ability
- cultural bias
- school desegregation
- multicultural education
- compensatory education

Section Preview

In theory, America is a meritocracy in which social status is achieved. Proponents of the conflict perspective identify flaws in this model by pointing to inequality in our schools. Methods and programs aimed at promoting educational equality have been developed.

meritocracy
a society in which social status is based on ability and achievement

competition
system in which rewards are based on relative performance

Meritocracy

Conflict theorists attempt to show that popular conceptions about the relationship between schools and society are not entirely accurate. Schools and society often touch each other in complicated and unobvious ways.

In a **meritocracy,** social status is based on ability and achievement rather than social-class background or parental status. In theory, all individuals in a meritocracy have an equal chance to develop their abilities for the benefit of themselves and their society. A meritocracy, then, gives everyone an equal chance to succeed. It is free of barriers that prevent individuals from developing their talents.

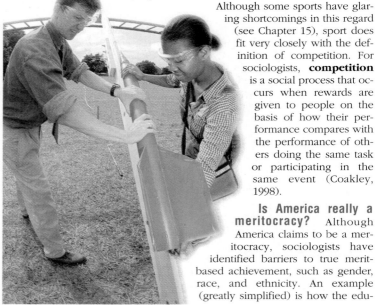

Participating in academic contests, such as building rockets, is one way teachers can find those students who merit special recognition.

Meritocracy is based on competition. For this reason, sport is seen as the ultimate meritocracy. Although some sports have glaring shortcomings in this regard (see Chapter 15), sport does fit very closely with the definition of competition. For sociologists, **competition** is a social process that occurs when rewards are given to people on the basis of how their performance compares with the performance of others doing the same task or participating in the same event (Coakley, 1998).

Is America really a meritocracy? Although America claims to be a meritocracy, sociologists have identified barriers to true merit-based achievement, such as gender, race, and ethnicity. An example (greatly simplified) is how the edu-

Using Conflict Resolution Skills

Read the following to students:

Bob Hentzen, a songwriter and activist for children and the elderly in poverty, wrote the following lyrics describing inequality in education in Central America:

"By candlelight I learned to study,
up to grade six, first in my class.
That's the end for a Mayan child,
seems as though our mind stops there."

Imagine that a new national law was passed prohibiting students in the United States from attending school past age 10. At age 11 all children must attend a vocational training program for two years; a transfer into the workforce in an indentured capacity would end after 5 years or the cation system favors the wealthy. Schools in wealthy neighborhoods are significantly better than schools in economically disadvantaged areas. It follows, then, that students attending wealthier schools get a better education than students attending poorer schools. Furthermore, students attending poorer schools do not learn the values, manners, language, and dress of people in more affluent schools. Because the majority of students in poorer schools are members of racial and ethnic minorities, they find themselves at a disadvantage when applying for higher-level jobs that lead to higher incomes. (See Figure 12.2.)

How do minorities perform on college entrance exams? There are related barriers to achievement faced by racial and ethnic minorities. An important one of these is lower performance on college entrance examinations. African Americans, Latinos, and Native Americans have lower average scores on the Scholastic Assessment Test (SAT) than whites. (See Figure 12.3 on page 402.) Sociologists attribute this fact, in part, to the differences in school quality noted above. And both school quality and SAT performance are related to social class. Children from upper-class and upper-middle-class families attend more affluent schools. These children also have higher SAT scores. Social class clearly affects SAT performance.

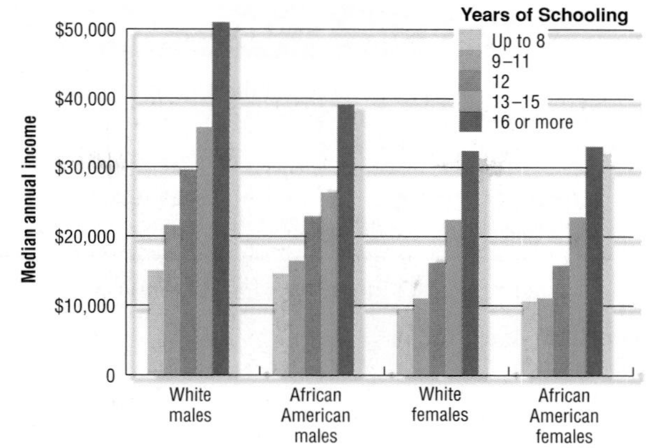

Figure 12.2 Median Annual Income by Gender, Race, and Education. *Clearly, this graph documents the income advantage that white males in the U.S. have over white females and African Americans of both sexes. Explain how this data challenges the existence of a true meritocracy.*

Source: U.S. Bureau of the Census, 2000.

Online UPDATE
Visit soc.glencoe.com and click on **Textbook Updates–Chapter 12** for an update of the data.

Social class is a strong predictor of success on the SATs. How is race related to social class?

Working with the Data

Figure 12.2 By definition, a meritocracy gives everyone an equal chance to succeed. It is obvious from this table, however, that gender and race play a part in the success (or lack of success) of the American worker.

More About . . . College Entrance Exams

A table of ACT (American College Test) scores is included with Discussion Question 4 on page 417 in this chapter (National Education Statistics, 1999). Ask students what correlation they see between family income and student test scores. What might explain why students with higher family incomes also had higher scores? Point out that 15 percent of respondents did not answer the question about family income, and that these respondents had a composite score of 20.8. What conclusions might students draw from this information? For the latest statistics on family income and ACT scores, you can visit the ACT, Inc. web site at: **http://www.act.org/news/data/99/t9.html**. This web site is updated every summer after test scores are compiled.

teenager turned eighteen. There would be no summer or winter vacations during that time and daily attendance is mandatory.

At age eighteen the teenager's competency would be evaluated to determine if he or she will remain in the workforce or be allowed the opportunity to attend college to work toward a professional field certification such as doctor, lawyer, teacher, pilot, business owner, or song and movie producer.

Write a persuasive letter to the president of the United States stating your opinion about this issue, and offer suggestions, if any, for improvement. Be sure to elaborate and cite specific examples.

L3

Working with the Data

Figure 12.3 Students might say that SAT scores should not be the only criteria on which to judge student performance. Since these tests reflect only certain intelligencies, other factors need to be considered. Some colleges still provide opportunities for students based on the student's willingness to succeed, not just academic performance.

Reteaching

To illustrate the earning power of higher education, write the following on the board: High school diploma = $23,317. Undergraduate college degree = $40,753. Professional degrees = $71,868. These are the median annual incomes of workers at each of these educational levels. Suppose that a person's working "lifetime" is 20 years. Ask students to calculate the differences in income between these levels over a working lifetime (both in dollars and percentages). Students should be able to see from this that education is a worthwhile investment. For more information on the relationship between education and income, visit the Bureau of Labor Statistics website at **www.bls.gov/opub/ted/1998/Oct/wk3/art05.htm** Ask students to consider the conflict theorist perspective: If earnings over a lifetime are a reflection of educational level, what happens when some people are presented with greater educational opportunities than others?

Figure 12.3 SAT SCORES BY RACE AND ETHNICITY

An examination of this table reveals the gap in average SAT scores for whites and Asian Americans versus African Americans, Latinos, and Native Americans. Interpret these data as a conflict theorist would in the context of the U.S. as a meritocracy.

Racial/Ethnic Category	SAT Verbal Mean Scores	SAT Math Mean Scores	Totals
Native American or Alaskan Native	482	481	963
Asian, Asian American, or Pacific Islander	499	565	1064
African American	434	426	860
Latino Background			
Mexican or Mexican American	453	460	913
Puerto Rican	456	451	907
Latin American, South American, Central American, or Other Latino	461	467	928
White (excluding Latino origin)	528	530	1058

Source: The College Board, 2001.

Why are SAT scores considered vital to a meritocratic American society?

How do SAT scores influence economic achievement? The SAT, created in 1926, was originally used to identify talented youth, regardless of social class background, so they could attend elite colleges and universities (Lemann, 1991). Ironically, as we have just seen, social class is a major factor in SAT performance. Consequently, social class (through SAT performance) still influences who will attend the institutions that are the gateway to America's higher social classes.

Don't the rewards tied to high SAT scores mean that America is a meritocracy? On the surface it does seem that merit is being rewarded in the system just outlined. After all, it is those who do better academically who enjoy higher levels of success.

There are two problems with this conclusion. The first is the advantage some people have because their parents' social class creates an unlevel playing field. Talent in the lower social classes often does not get recognized and developed. Second is the assumption that SAT performance measures academic ability and the likelihood of success in both college and life. For example, African American students who attend the most prestigious schools—including those students with lower SAT scores (below 1000) complete college at a

Learning Styles

Linguistic/Bodily-Kinesthetic Policy makers and educators are exploring ways to promote educational equality. Two methods being used are school desegregation and compensatory education. Divide the class into two groups to stage an informal debate. Assign one group to be pro and the other con regarding the benefits of the two methods listed above. Allow students time to research the assigned topics. You may want to divide the class into groups of four, two pro and two con, to do the actual higher rate than black students attending less rigorous institutions. They are also more likely to go on to graduate or professional schools (Bowen and Bok, 2000). Apparently these students are succeeding because they attended better schools, even if they don't have high SAT scores.

At the least, these findings raise doubts about the ability of the SAT to achieve a level playing field. Recognizing this, an official at the Educational Testing Service (ETS)—developer and marketer of the SAT—announced in 1999 that ETS was creating a "strivers" score. The idea was to adjust a student's SAT score to factor in social class as well as racial and ethnic characteristics thought to place him or her at a competitive disadvantage. Any student whose original score exceeded by 200 points the score predicted for their social class, racial, or ethnic category would be considered a "striver." The strivers score would be made available to colleges and universities to use, if they desired, in their admissions decisions (Glazer, 1999; Wildavsky, 1999). The proposal was quickly withdrawn after a firestorm of criticism from both privileged and disadvantaged sources.

> It is no longer correct to regard higher education solely as a privilege. It is a basic right in today's world.
>
> **Norman Cousins**
> **American essayist**

Equality and Inequality in Education

The situation for those disadvantaged by social class, racial, and ethnic background is actually even more complicated. As already implied, it is tied to the larger issue of educational equality and inequality. **Educational equality** exists when schooling produces the same results, in terms of achievement and attitudes, for lower-class and minority children as it does for less disadvantaged children. Results, not resources, are the test of educational equality (Coleman et al., 1966).

educational equality
condition in which schooling produces the same results for lower-class and minority children as it does for other children

Do schools provide educational equality? Research has shown that even the best teachers often evaluate students on the basis of their social class and their racial and ethnic characteristics. This tendency to judge students on nonacademic criteria is especially apparent in the practice of tracking. Researchers report that social class and race heavily influence student placement in college preparatory, vocational, or basic tracks regardless of their intelligence or past academic achievement (Oakes and Lipton, 1996; Taylor et al., 1997). Once students are placed, their grades and test scores are

Would you expect to find educational equality in these two schools?

Making Connections to Other Cultures

In Kenya, a UNICEF survey found that 80 percent of pre-school children suffer from worm infestations, and more than 50 percent from anemia. Health problems such as these can severely retard children's growth and intellectual development. However, studies have also found that improvements in basic nutrition and health surveillance can prevent these defects. Countries such as Kenya are mobilizing to train teachers to recognize health-related learning problems. Ask students if they are aware of any health-related learning problems in American schools.

Integrating the Teacher Resources

Look for the Chapter 12 Increasing Your Reading Comprehension worksheet and the Guided Reading worksheet in the Unit 4 Mastering Basic Concepts booklet in your Teacher's Resource Box. Both will strengthen student reading comprehension skills.

debate in order to allow more students to present their cases. When the debates are finished, take a vote. Do students feel that school segregation and compensatory education promote educational equality? What ideas do students have that might work even better? You may want to give extra credit to students who are willing to attend a school board meeting to present their ideas for improving education at your school.
L3

Discuss with students where the dollars for education go. Most of the money never makes it to the classroom; it is spent on salaries for administrators and support staff, building and vehicle maintenance, and so on.

Answers to Interpreting the Map

1. Answers will vary.
2. One obvious pattern students should mention is that the northeastern states seem to spend more money per student than most other states.
3. Answers will vary.

Points to Stress

The book *The Bell Curve* (mentioned on page 405) attempted to explain that differences in educational attainment were a result of inherited intellectual ability. Most of the sociological community has refuted this claim. Stress to students that who we are is largely the combination of both genetics and the environment. People are not products of nature *versus* nurture but of nature *and* nurture.

School Expenditures

Everyone has heard "You get what you pay for." Because of this idea, many people use the amount of money spent on public schools as a measure of the quality of education. The accompanying map shows that some states spend more than twice as much per student as other states.

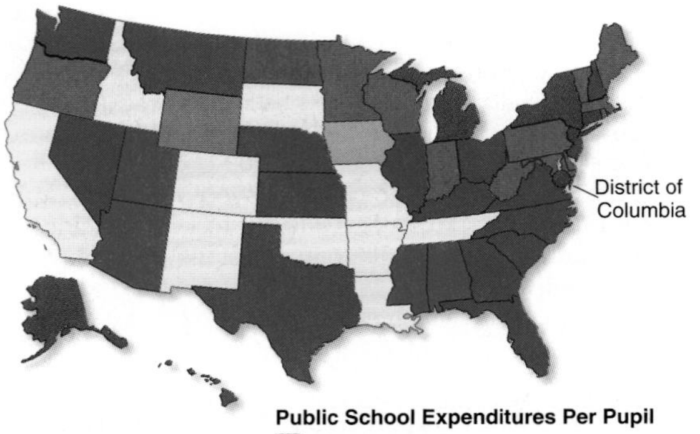

Interpreting the Map

1. How does your state compare with other states in school expenditures?
2. Do you see a regional pattern in public school funding? Explain.
3. What other factors might you want to know to determine if the amount of money spent affected the quality of education delivered?

Source: U.S. Bureau of the Census, 2000.

influenced more by the track they are on than by their current performance. Regardless of earlier school performance or intelligence, the academic performance of college-bound students increases, whereas the performance of those on a noncollege track decreases. In other words, schools are not successfully providing educational equality for their students.

Cognitive Ability

cognitive ability capacity for thinking abstractly

The technical term for intelligence is **cognitive ability**—the capacity for thinking abstractly. Dating back to the turn of the twentieth century, there has been a tradition in schools to attempt to measure cognitive ability.

Because cognitive ability testing is an important element in sorting and tracking students, it contributes to educational inequality. Whenever cognitive ability tests are discussed, the question of inherited intelligence always arises.

Interdisciplinary Activity

History When South Africa first desegregated the Potgietersrus Primary School in 1996, sixteen black children were transferred to the school. On their first day, tension was so high that they had to be protected by a police cordon of 100 officers, armored vehicles, and dogs. Although some white students and parents supported the desegregation, the majority of white students refused to go to the school. Twenty of the 700 white students chose to remain at home to protest.

The desegregation of the Primary School helped to set an important national prece-

Is intelligence inherited? In the past, some people assumed that individual and group differences in measured intellectual ability were due to genetic differences. This assumption, of course, underlies Social Darwinism. (See pages 15–16 for a brief explanation of these assumptions.)

A few researchers still take this viewpoint. More than thirty years ago Arthur Jensen (1969), an educational psychologist, contended that the lower average intelligence score among African American children may be due to heredity. A recent book by Richard Herrnstein and Charles Murray (1996), entitled *The Bell Curve,* is also in the tradition of linking intelligence to heredity. According to these authors, humans inherit 60 to 70 percent of their intelligence level. Herrnstein and Murray further contend that the fact of inherited intelligence makes largely futile the efforts to help the disadvantaged through programs such as Head Start and affirmative action.

What are arguments against the inherited intelligence theory? Most social scientists oppose the genetic explanation of intelligence differences between races because it fails to consider the effects of the social, psychological, and economic environment on intelligence. Even those social scientists who believe that genetics plays an important role in intelligence criticize both the interpretations of the evidence and the public policy conclusions contained in *The Bell Curve.* They point to the body of research that runs counter to Herrnstein's and Murray's thesis. More specifically, they see intelligence not as an issue of nature *versus* nurture but as a matter of genetics *and* environment (Morganthau, 1994; Wright, 1996). We know, for example, that city dwellers usually score higher on intelligence tests than do people in rural areas, that higher-status African Americans score higher than lower-status African Americans, and that middle-class African American children score about as high as middle-class white children. We also have discovered that as people get older, they usually score higher on intelligence tests. These findings, and others like them, have led researchers to conclude that environmental factors affected test performance at least as much as genetic factors (Samuda, 1975; Schiff and Lewontin, 1987; Jencks and Phillips, 1998). One of these environmental factors is a *cultural bias* in the measurement of cognitive ability.

Do you think heredity or environment will have a greater effect on these boys' intelligence?

What are culturally biased intelligence tests? Robert Williams (1974) is one of the many earlier social scientists who argued that intelligence tests have a **cultural bias,** that they unfairly measure the cognitive abilities of people in some social categories. Specifically, intelligence tests are said to be culturally biased because they are designed for middle-class children. The results measure learning and environment as much as they measure intellectual ability. Consider this intelligence test item cited by Daniel Levine and Rayna Levine:

cultural bias
the unfair measurement of the cognitive abilities of people in some social categories

A symphony is to a composer as a book is to what?

a. paper
b. a musician
c. a sculptor
d. a man
e. an author

According to critics, higher-income children find this question easier to answer correctly than lower-income children because they are more likely to have been exposed to information about classical music. The same charge was made by critics of a recent SAT question that used a Bentley (a luxury-model

Reteaching

Have each student devise an analogy like the one in the text. Then have them trade analogies with another student. Are they able to solve the analogies correctly? Do students disagree as to the correct answer? Have students examine the possibility that others might not draw the same connections as they do in these analogies. Could this be a result of cultural factors or language barriers? For example, in one study, students were given the following analogy: a person is to a chair as a cup is to a ________, a) saucer b) table c) plant d) spoon. The correct answer is a) saucer, since a cup rests in a saucer as a person rests in a chair. However, some students taking the test were unfamiliar with the word saucer, since they didn't use saucers to rest their cups in at home. These students chose table as the correct answer, with the rationale that a cup can rest on a table. Ask students to try to write new analogies that are free of cultural bias. They will probably find it quite difficult.

dent which eventually led to the removal of the old apartheid education system.

Ask the students in the class to discuss what effect the desegregation might have had on the academic performance of the sixteen black children attending the Potgietersrus Primary School, and what additional pressures they might have faced from teachers and peers. (For example, might they have encountered pressure to perform as well as or better than their peers, and might they have encountered discrimination from the teaching staff?) **L2**

Open-Response Questions

If your school does not have weighted grades (where extra grade points are attached to AP or Honors classes, for example) propose to the class that as of next week the grading scale will change to give a higher grade point value to classes that are considered harder. All of the history classes and some math and science classes will use a 4.5 scale (where an A is worth 4.5 grade points, a B is worth 3.5 grade points, etc). Sociology will still be on the 4.0 scale. Ask students if the weighted grading system would impact their course selection. Some students would probably elect to take classes using the higher GPA scale, particularly if they need high GPAs to get into competitive colleges or universities. Have the class openly debate the merits of this system. If your school already uses it, what benefits does it have and why do some students and teachers oppose it?

Pulling it All Together

This section dealt with the conflict perspective of education. Conflict theorists would argue that ascribed status and social class set the tone for education in America, and lead to educational inequality. Culturally biased college entrance exams and cognitive ability tests and school segregation are manifestations of this phenomenon.

automobile) as its illustration. Several studies have indicated that because most intelligence tests assume fluency in English, minorities cannot do as well on intelligence tests. Some researchers have suggested that many urban African American students are superior to their white classmates on several dimensions of verbal capacity, but this ability is not recognized, because intelligence tests do not measure those specific areas (Gould, 1981; Goleman, 1988; Hurn, 1993).

Some researchers have shown that the testing situation itself affects performance. Low-income and minority students, for example, score higher on intelligence tests when tested by adult members of their own race or income group. Apparently children can feel threatened when tested in a strange environment by someone dissimilar to them. Middle-class children are frequently eager to take the tests because they have been taught the importance both of test results and of academic competitiveness. Because low-income children do not recognize the importance of tests and have not been taught to be academically competitive, they ignore some of the questions or look for something more interesting to do. Other researchers report that nutrition seems to play a role in test performance. Low-income children with poor diets may do less than their best when they are hungry or when they lack particular types of food over long periods of time.

school desegregation the achievement of a racial balance in the classroom

Promoting Educational Equality

Although it is difficult to completely overcome the barriers of economic and social class, policy makers and educators are exploring ways to promote educational equality. Two methods are *school desegregation* and *compensatory education*.

The governor of Nebraska is part of a program to educate school students on the culture of minority groups in their state.

Does desegregation always promote equality? In this discussion, **school desegregation** refers to the achievement of a racial balance in the classroom. Desegregated classrooms can have either positive or negative effects on the academic achievement of minority children. Mere physical desegregation without adequate support may actually harm both white and African American children. However, desegregated classrooms with an atmosphere of respect and acceptance improve academic performance (Orfield et al., 1992).

Minority students who attend desegregated public schools get better jobs and earn higher incomes than minority students who attend segregated schools. The formal education they receive is only part of the reason. Middle-class students become models for the behavior, dress, and language often required by employers in the middle-class hiring world.

Interdisciplinary Activity

History You might want students to examine the *Brown vs. Board of Education* decision of May 17, 1954. NAACP lawyer Thurgood Marshall argued that racially segregated schools may have been intended to be "separate but equal," but were, in fact, inherently unequal. Sociologists testified that the schools attended by black students lacked the resources to provide an education equal to what white students received. Students might want to research this famous Supreme Court decision that reversed the *Plessy vs. Ferguson* verdict and attempted to desegregate American sections from schools. For a follow up, have them read sections from Kozol's *Savage Inequalities.*
L3

In addition, exposure to people of different backgrounds can lead to better racial and ethnic relations (Hawley and Smylie, 1988). On this evidence rests the promise of **multicultural education**—an educational curriculum that accents the viewpoints, experiences, and contributions of minorities (women as well as ethnic and racial minorities).

multicultural education an educational curriculum that emphasizes differences among gender, ethnic, and racial categories

What is the purpose of multicultural education? Among minorities, school attendance and academic performance appear to increase with multicultural education. Multicultural education attempts to dispel stereotypes and to make the traditions of minorities valuable assets for the broader culture (McLaren, 1997; Ladson-Billings, 1998).

Multicultural education has its critics, however. According to some opponents, encouraging people to think of themselves as culturally separate and unique divides rather than unites American society. Some critics point to instances in which multicultural programs, such as African American studies programs, actually promote feelings of racial separation in schools.

Does compensatory education work? The term **compensatory education** refers to specific curricular programs designed to overcome deficiency. Special compensatory programs provided during early childhood, it appears, can improve the school achievement of disadvantaged children (Zigler and Styfco, 1993; Campbell and Ramey, 1994).

compensatory education specific curricular programs designed to overcome a deficiency

The best-known attempt at compensatory education is Head Start. This federally supported program prepares disadvantaged preschoolers for public school. Its goal is to provide disadvantaged children an equal opportunity to develop their potential. Follow-up studies report positive long-term results. Low-income youngsters between the ages of nine and nineteen who had been in preschool compensatory programs performed better in school. They had higher achievement test scores and were more motivated academically than low-income youths who had not been in compensatory education programs (Bruner, 1982; Etzioni, 1982). Later research also supports the benefits of Head Start (Mills, 1998). For example, compared to their peers, a group of children who scored lower on intelligence tests when they entered a Head Start program later had better school attendance, completed high school at a higher rate, and entered the workforce in greater proportion.

Section 3 Assessment

1. Do you think the United States is a meritocracy, as stated in the text?
2. What is meant by the term *educational equality?*
3. What role conflicts does multicultural education pose for teachers?

Critical Thinking

4. **Finding the Main Idea** Students from higher social classes are more likely to go to college than students from the lower classes. How does this fit with the idea of meritocracy?
5. **Evaluating Information** If schools fail to provide educational quality, what do you think will be the consequences in terms of role conflict?

"Education is what survives when what has been learned has been forgotten."

B.F. Skinner
American psychologist

Answers to Section 3 Assessment

1. According to the text, although America claims to be a meritocracy, gender, race, and ethnicity present barriers to true merit-based achievement.
2. Educational inequality occurs when schooling does not produce the same results, in terms of achievement and attitudes, for lower-class and minority children as it does for less disadvantaged children.
3. Emphasizing multicultural education can work against the traditional teachers' role of reducing racial separation in schools.

Critical Thinking

4. Students should note the discrepancy: A meritocracy would have us believe that ability and achievement are the only criteria for success and that all students have an equal chance to succeed.
5. Answers will vary.

Role Play

Have students work together in groups to prepare role plays that depict multicultural education they have experienced. Students should think back to all of the classes they have had, and consider how the teacher implemented multiculturalism into the classroom. After groups have had a chance to present their role plays, conduct a class discussion on multicultural education. Do students enjoy it? Does it add to their educational experience? If so, in what way? If not, why not? Ask students to describe multicultural activities they would like to see implemented in their classes.
L2

Tech Trends

As many teachers are aware, the computer is changing the face of education. Teachers whose students sit at a computer become facilitators, directing their students where to go to look for information. Students' wishes that teachers not lecture may soon become reality.

Answers to Analyzing the Trends

1. Students might say that teachers will become monitors, showing students how to use the technology. Students might want to think about how long it will take for this change to occur throughout all schools in the country. Since some schools are still lagging behind in computer use, it seems realistic that these other changes are still far off in the future.
2. Conflict theorists would naturally see that the social inequality of spending on education would widen the gap between social classes. Schools that could afford this technology would give their students advantages that other schools could not. Society would become more stratified.
3. In theory, we would not need schools. Teachers would become facilitators to assist students with technology, which could mean that we would still need schools.

Tech Trends

School's Out . . . Forever?

In a recent book, *The Age of Spiritual Machines,* author Ray Kurzweil makes forecasts concerning life in the twenty-first century. He claims that, by the end of the century, computers will be the most intelligent "beings" on the planet. Specific predictions on education in 2009 include the following scenarios.

The majority of reading is done on displays, although the "installed base" of paper documents is still formidable. The generation of paper documents is dwindling, however, as the books and other papers of largely twentieth-century vintage are being rapidly scanned and stored. Documents circa 2009 routinely include embedded moving images and sounds.

Students of all ages typically have a computer of their own, which is a thin tabletlike device weighing under a pound with a very high resolution display suitable for reading. Students interact with their computers primarily by voice and by pointing with a device that looks like a pencil. Keyboards still exist, but most textual language is created by speaking. Learning materials are accessed through wireless communication.

Preschool and elementary school children routinely read at their intellectual level using print-to-speech reading software until their reading skill level catches up. These print-to-speech reading systems display the full image of documents, and can read the print aloud while highlighting what is being read. Synthetic voices sound fully human. Although some educators expressed concern in the early '00 years that students would rely unduly on reading software, such systems have been readily accepted by children and their parents. Studies have shown that students improve their reading skills by being exposed to synchronized visual and auditory presentations of text.

Learning at a distance (for example, lectures and seminars in which the participants are geographically scattered) is commonplace. This also helps to relieve congested campuses and cut back on the burning of gasoline in city limits.

Technology is changing the face of education in this country. Some futurists predict that distance learning technology may eventually replace the traditional school building.

Analyzing the Trends

1. If Kurzweil's predictions came true, how would education's role in the socialization of students change?
2. If Kurzweil's predictions came true, would social stratification play a more or less important role in education than it does now? Use information from the chapter to support your answer.
3. If the predictions in the article came to pass, would we still need schools? Why or why not?

Demonstration

Evidence that education is changing can be seen in the number of people receiving degrees on-line and using alternative methods of taking classes. Teleconferencing is one such technique—students watch a professor teach on a television screen and then communicate questions and concerns using audio devices. If you have the equipment available, set up a teleconference class for students to watch. If you don't have the capabilities of setting up a teleconference class in your classroom or at your school,

Section 4

Symbolic Interactionism

Key Terms

- hidden curriculum
- self-fulfilling prophecy

The Hidden Curriculum

Symbolic interactionists are very interested in how schools transmit culture through the socialization process. Besides teachers and textbooks, which we will discuss later, the most important agent of this socialization process is the *hidden curriculum*. Modern society places considerable emphasis on the verbal, mathematical, and writing skills an adult needs to obtain a job, read a newspaper, balance a checkbook, and compute income taxes. However, schools teach much more than these basic academic skills. They also transmit to children a variety of values, norms, beliefs, and attitudes.

Fire drills teach safety procedures, but they also reinforce the importance of obedience and cooperation, part of the school system's hidden agenda.

What is the hidden curriculum? The **hidden curriculum** is the nonacademic agenda that teaches children norms and values such as discipline, order, cooperativeness, and conformity. These citizenship skills are thought to be necessary for success in modern bureaucratic society, whether one becomes a doctor, a college president, a computer programmer, or an assembly-line worker. Over the years, schools, for example, socialize children for the transition from their closely knit, cooperative families to the loosely knit, competitive adult occupational world. The school provides systematic practice for children to operate independently in the pursuit of personal and academic achievement. The values of conformity and achievement are emphasized through individual testing and grading. Because teachers evaluate young people as students, not as relatives, friends, or equals, students participate in a model for future secondary relationships—employer-employee; salesperson-customer; lawyer-client.

Section Preview

Symbolic interactionists emphasize the socialization that occurs in schools. Through the hidden curriculum, children are taught values, norms, beliefs, and attitudes. Much of this socialization helps young people make the transition from home to the larger society.

hidden curriculum the nonacademic agenda that teaches discipline, order, cooperativeness, and conformity

Using the Section Preview

To help students understand the power of social interactions between teacher and student, have them conduct an informal research project. Tell students to discreetly observe (remember, all research has a degree of deception in it) several teachers interacting with students. Ask students to observe things such as how often the teacher calls on boys, and how often he or she calls on girls. Does the teacher seem to only call on certain students? Does he or she only ask harder questions of the "smart kids"? Students need to try to be objective in their observations. They should also refrain from identifying by name the teachers they study. You may want to have students consult other research on this topic. A good source is the American Association of University Women (AAUW), an organization that has done extensive research on the fairness of treatment between girls and boys in the classroom.

check with your local college. If they have the necessary technology, ask if you can bring your class to watch a teleconference class.

After students have experienced a teleconference class, ask if they think these trends will continue and what this might mean for teachers. Would they enjoy "going to school" this way? Why or why not? What would be the advantages? the disadvantages?
L2

Controversy and Debate

Ask students to bring their history textbooks to class (or borrow some from a colleague). Divide the class into groups and have each group take a chapter from the text. Have students scrutinize their chapters for instances where the text seems to be objective in its reporting of historical events. They should also look for instances where it appears that the book is presenting only the American point of view. You might want to ask a history teacher to come in and see if student's perceptions were accurate.

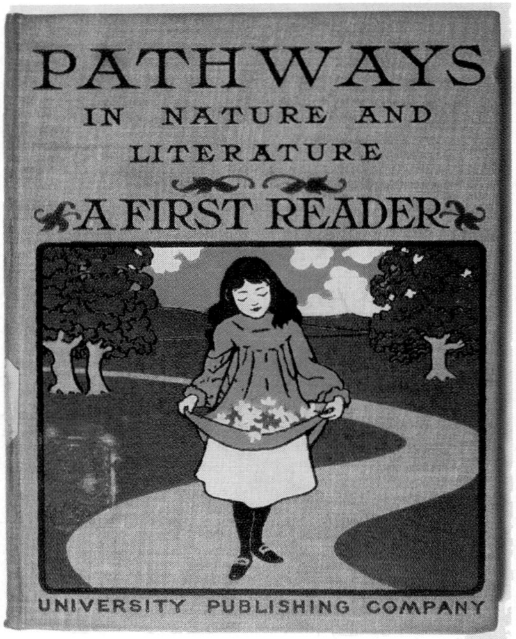

What, in addition to academic content, do textbooks teach students?

Textbooks

A critical part of the hidden curriculum is the development of patriotism and a sense of civic duty in future adults. For this reason, courses such as history and government generally present a view of history that favors the nation. Accounts of the American Revolution, for example, are not the same in British and American textbooks. Because few societies are willing to admit to their imperfections, schools tend to resist teaching critical accounts of history. For example, for many years U.S. history textbooks failed to portray the U.S. government's harsh treatment of Native American peoples.

Textbooks convey values and beliefs as much by what they omit as by what they include. While today's textbooks present a more balanced picture, surveys of primary school textbooks written before the 1980s found they almost always presented men in challenging and aggressive activities while portraying women as homemakers, mothers, nurses, and secretaries. Women were not only placed in traditional roles but also appeared far less frequently in the books than men did. When women did appear, they were not initiators of action, but played passive roles. Minority groups were rarely present in textbooks, and when they were it was often in a negative context.

Similarly, textbooks tended to portray all students as living in "little white houses with white picket fences." That image may have been part of the worldview of middle-class Americans, but parents of low-income or inner-city children complained that such pictures of middle-class life harmed their children. Poor children who compared their homes with middle-class homes felt out of place (Trimble, 1988; Gibson and Ogbu, 1991).

Today, active parent groups, minority special interest groups, and state boards of education work with textbook publishers to ensure that a more balanced picture of society is presented to students. Problems arise, however, when conflicts occur over whose view of society is the most accurate.

Teachers and Socialization

Classroom teachers have a unique and important role in socializing children. Teachers are usually a child's first authority figures outside the family, and children spend a lot of time in school. In addition, most parents urge their children to obey teachers, in part because their children's futures are affected by school performance

How do teachers affect students' performance? All teachers set academic tasks for their students, but teachers affect children unintentionally as well. In a classic 1989 study, Robert Rosenthal and Lenore Jacobson explored the **self-fulfilling prophecy**—a prediction that results in behavior that makes the prediction come true. In their study, elementary school teachers were given a list of children in their classrooms who, according to the researchers, were soon to blossom intellectually. Actually, these children were

self-fulfilling prophecy
a prediction that results in behavior that makes the prediction come true

Demonstration

To demonstrate the power of teachers' self-fulfilling prophecies, write a series of ten numbers between 120 and 140 on the board, then relate the following story to your students. On the first day of class, a teacher was given a list of her students. Next to each student's name was a number such as the ones on the board. The teacher saw these numbers and was tremendously excited to begin the school year. In fact, she went out and bought extra materials. At the end of the school year, her students had shown incredible progress. When the principal came up to the teacher and con-

Figure 12.4 Focus on Theoretical Perspectives

Investigating education. This table illustrates differences in the ways the major theoretical perspectives investigate education as a social institution. It is, of course, possible for a theoretical perspective to study education using one of the concepts associated in this table with another perspective. Explain, for example, how conflict theory would interpret the hidden curriculum and tracking.

Theoretical Perspective	Concept	Example
Functionalism	Tracking	 Schools shape the occupational future of children by placing them in educational programs based on test scores and early school performance.
Conflict Theory	Meritocracy	Students attending better schools have an occupational advantage over students from poorer schools. 
Symbolic Interactionism	Hidden curriculum	 Schools teach children the values of conformity and achievement.

picked at random from the school roster and were no different from other children in the school. At the end of the year, this randomly selected group of children significantly improved their scores on intelligence tests, while their classmates as a group did not. According to Rosenthal and Jacobson, the teachers expected the "late bloomers" to spurt academically. Consequently, the teachers treated these students as if they were special. This behavior on the part of the teachers encouraged the students to become higher academic achievers. (See Focus on Research on page 298. Also see Chapter 9, page 288, for a more general discussion of the self-fulfilling prophecy.)

Another early study by sociologist Eleanor Leacock (1969) found the self-fulfilling prophecy at work in a study of second and fifth graders in black and white low- and middle-income schools. And both studies demonstrate that self-fulfilling prophecies can transmit negative self-impressions as well as positive ones.

Do teachers foster sexism? As described in Chapter 10, children are taught to adopt the "appropriate" gender identity in school (Martin, 1998). Following a long line of earlier researchers, Myra Sadker and David Sadker (1995) have contended that America's teachers are often unfair to girls because they treat girls differently than boys based on assumptions and stereotypes of what is appropriate behavior. Well-meaning teachers unconsciously transmit sexist expectations of how male and female students should behave.

SOCIOLOGY Online

Student Web Activity
Visit the *Sociology and You* Web site at soc.glencoe.com and click on **Chapter 12—Student Web Activities** for an activity on sexism in schools.

Working with the Data

Figure 12.4 Conflict theory would say that the hidden curriculum attempts to guarantee that everyone has mainstream American values or that everyone becomes a good citizen. Tracking would guarantee that the privileged would maintain their social standing and the less fortunate would keep their current place in society.

Integrating the Teacher Resources

Look for Ethics, Values, and Technology: Real-Life Issues in Society, available in your Teacher's Resource Box. The booklet provides primary source readings dealing with real-life controversies. Student worksheets are included.

gratulated her, the teacher thanked the principal for giving her so many students with high IQs. The principal asked her "What do you mean?" "Well," the teacher replied, "on the first day of class, you gave me a list of student names with their IQs." "Those weren't IQ numbers; they were locker numbers!" the principal responded. Ask students to provide examples of teachers' self-fulfilling prophecies that they know of or have experienced firsthand. Do they think the self-fulfilling prophecy applies to certain groups of students at your school, such as AP students?
L2

Answers to Interpreting the Map

1. The correlation seems to be that the more states spend per student on education, the fewer dropouts the states have.
2. Students should note that those states with high percentages of the population living below the poverty level also have high rates of dropouts.

High School Dropouts

For many jobs, a high school diploma is a minimum requirement. People who do not complete high school earn only about three-fourths as much as high school graduates. This map shows the percentage of teenagers (aged sixteen to nineteen) in each state who are high school dropouts.

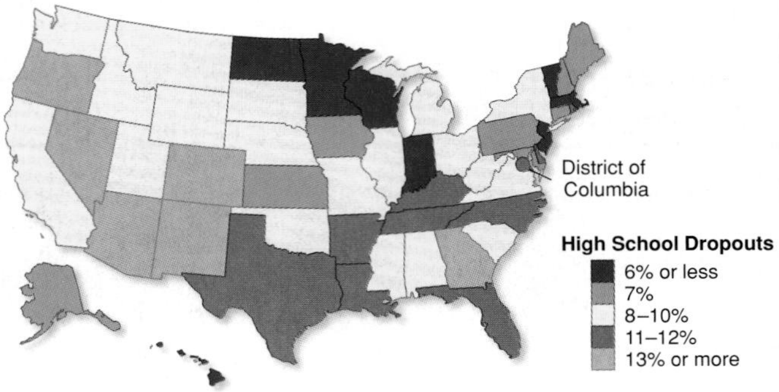

Source: *2001 Kids Count Data Sheet.* (Washington, DC: Population Reference Bureau, 2001).

Interpreting the Map

1. Compare this map with the Snapshot on page 404. Do you see a relationship between the money spent per student and the percentage of high school dropouts?
2. Compare this map with the Snapshot on page 261. Do you see any relationship between the percentage of high school dropouts and the percentage of the population living below the poverty line?

Source: *2001 Kids Count Data Sheet* (Washington, DC: Population Reference Bureau, 2001).

Girls, for example, learn to talk softly, to avoid certain subjects (especially math and science), to defer to the alleged intellectual superiority of boys, and to emphasize appearance over intelligence. As a result, in a coeducational setting boys are

- ❖ five times more likely to receive the most attention from teachers.
- ❖ three times more likely to be praised.
- ❖ eight times more likely to call out in class.
- ❖ three times more talkative in class.
- ❖ twice as likely to demand help or attention.
- ❖ twice as likely to be called on in class.

The conclusions seem to be incontrovertible: in general boys talk more, move more, have their hands up more, do more, argue more, get more of the teachers' attention than do girls in a coeducational setting (Sadker and Sadker, 1995).

On-Demand Writing

Women attempting to gain an education in Iran are subjected to many pressures to conform. These pressures can be subtle or overt. Subtle pressures include behavioral expectations that are transmitted by teachers and textbooks. All women depicted in Iranian textbooks are shown wearing the traditional "hijab" or veil, a practice which is intended to promote the perception of women as traditional mothers and household wives. Women are discouraged from attending law school because they are deemed "too emotional" to be able to practice law effectively. There are also many formal restrictions placed on women's education: for example, women are not eligible

But, what about all the progress that has been made? Contrary to the expectation of some, such inequalities are not gone from the educational scene. Writers who paint a rosier picture have so far failed to produce convincing evidence to support it (Deak, 1998).

There is objective evidence that girls are guided in school toward traditional female jobs and away from high-paying, powerful, and prestigious jobs in science, technology, and engineering (Millicent, 1992). True, significantly more high school girls want to go into engineering today than in the past. But five times more men than women receive bachelor's degrees in engineering.

What evidence has been presented about the advantages of single-gender schools?

These gender-based discrepancies cannot be explained by ability differences. Girls perform almost as well as boys on math and science tests (O'Sullivan, Reese, and Mazzeo, 1997). Girls score higher than boys at reading and writing at all grade levels and are more likely to attend college (Greenwald et al., 1999). Moreover, females fare better in single-gender schools and single-gender classes in coeducational schools.

> *Girls in these situations, in general, get better grades, report that they learn more and are more positive about the learning situation, have higher self-esteem, and more often move on to advanced courses than do girls in regular coeducational situations (Deak, 1998:19–20).*

"Education is the transmission of civilization."

Will and Ariel Durant
authors/philosophers

Section 4 Assessment

1. Cite an example from your earlier schooling that you believe presented a viewpoint of history that was incomplete or slanted toward one perspective.

Critical Thinking

2. **Making Generalizations** Besides parents and teachers, what authority figures do young children meet?
3. **Applying Concepts** Describe a time when you were the subject of a self-fulfilling prophecy.
4. **Applying Concepts** Provide examples from your own experience to support or contradict the existence of the hidden curriculum.

Pulling it All Together

This section dealt with the interactionist perspective. It examined education's hidden curriculum, textbooks as cultural transmitters, and student/teacher interactions based on gender and self-fulfilling prophecies.

Answers to Section 4 Assessment

1. Answers will vary. One example would be the manner in which older textbooks depicted racial and sexual stereotypes.

Critical Thinking

2. Answers will vary.
3. Answers will vary.
4. Answers will vary as students use their own particular experiences to answer this question.

Teaching Strategy

To provide closure for the main ideas in this chapter, you may want to ask students to complete the learning objectives on text page 387.

for government scholarships to study abroad unless they are married and accompanied by their husbands.

Ask students how they would feel if all the females in their textbooks were depicted wearing floor-length skirts or carrying babies. How would such representations influence their behavior? Ask the students to skim through their textbook and describe the way that women are depicted. Are certain types of women shown more frequently than others? For example, are any of the women shown wearing provocative clothing, or in aggressive postures?
L1

Focus on Research

Case Study: Pygmalion in the Classroom

Are your beliefs strong enough to affect your feelings or behavior? You have probably experienced how your feelings and behavior change upon receiving new information. A feeling of well-being usually follows learning that you did better on an important math exam than you thought you could. You may even be encouraged enough to study math more enthusiastically in the future. If your own perceptions can affect your feelings and behavior, is it possible that someone else's beliefs about you can also influence your feelings and behavior? The idea that this can happen is called the *self-fulfilling prophecy*. As noted earlier, two social scientists, Robert Rosenthal and Lenore Jacobson (1989), studied the self-fulfilling prophecy in a school setting.

For their case study, these researchers chose Oak School, a public elementary school located in a predominantly lower-class community. They hypothesized that children whose teacher expected their IQ scores to increase would in fact increase their scores more than comparable children whose teacher expected no IQ gains.

Students who are treated as if they are expected to perform at high levels often do.

At the beginning of the study, a test was given to all of the Oak School students. Although it was falsely advertised as a predictor of academic "blooming" or "spurting," it was actually a non-verbal intelligence test. Rosenthal and Jacobson subsequently identified for the teachers 20 percent of the children who allegedly were ready for a dramatic increase in intellectual growth. In fact, the researchers had selected the names of these students by using a table of random numbers. The difference in potential for academic growth between the children said to

Focus on Research

Social psychologist Elliot Aronson's solution to this problem is to create "jigsaw puzzle classrooms." Since students naturally want to work with their friends, Aronson proposes that teachers allow students to work in groups. Each group works on a specific task, which culminates in a class project. When a group has completed its task, the students in that group disperse to share their information with another group. This guarantees that all students will interact with other students and that all transmit and learn the same information.

Integrating the Teacher Resources

A lesson plan for a student research project related to the content of this chapter can be found in Doing Sociology: Focus on Research, available in your Teacher's Resource Box.

Careers in Sociology

Ask students, "What's 'special' about special education?" Then, share these answers with them.

Special education teachers work with children and youths with a variety of disabilities or other special instructional needs, including the gifted and talented. Most special education teachers instruct students at the elementary, middle, and secondary school level, although some teachers work with infants and toddlers.

Special education teachers are legally required to help develop an Individualized Education Program (IEP) for each special education student. The IEP sets personalized goals for each student and is tailored to a student's individual learning style and ability. This program includes a transition be on the verge of "blooming" and the rest of the students existed only in the minds of the teachers.

Intellectual growth was measured by the difference between a child's IQ score at the end of the previous school year and that same child's IQ score eight months after the next school year began. As Rosenthal and Jacobson expected, the children in the "blooming" group gained more IQ points than the other children (a 12-point gain versus an 8-point gain). The IQ gain of the children in the "blooming" group over the other students was the most pronounced among first and second graders. First graders in the "blooming" group gained over 27 IQ points, compared with 12 points in the remainder of the class. Among second graders, the advantage was 16.5 IQ points to 7.

Low teacher expectations do not necessarily prevent good students from doing well in school. And high teacher expectations cannot spur poor learners to the highest levels of achievement; however, high teacher expectations can be a powerful motivator for low performers who are capable of doing much better (Madon, Jussim, and Eccles, 1997). This occurs because teachers with high expectations for students treat them in special ways—they tend to smile and look at them more often, set higher goals for them, praise them more frequently, coach them in their studies, and give them more time to study (Rendon and Hope, 1996).

Operation of the self-fulfilling prophecy has been confirmed by other researchers in many other social settings (Myers, 1999). Research subjects behave as they think researchers expect, and a client's progress in therapy is influenced by the therapist's expectation. People who are expected by others to be hostile will exhibit more hostile behavior.

Working with the Research

1. How do you think the self-fulfilling prophecy works? That is, how are expectations transmitted from one person to another, and how do these expectations produce behavior?
2. What are the implications of the self-fulfilling prophecy for students? For teachers?
3. Explain why the self-fulfilling prophecy supports the labeling process discussed on pages 214–217 in Chapter 7.

Answers to Working with the Research

1. The teacher holds the belief that a student is or is not smart and treats that student accordingly. Students also come to classify other students as smart or not. Students and teachers then react and conduct their behavior to meet the expectation or lack of expectation.
2. Students who have low expectations placed on them will not exert much effort. On the other hand, students will work harder to meet higher expectations. The teacher will work harder to help the high-achieving student, and will work less with a low-achiever.
3. If students are labeled as smart or dumb, they will either try hard to live down that label or they will come to believe the label. If the student believes the label, it has become a self-fulfilling prophecy.

Integrating the Teacher Resources

Look for the Alternative Assessments booklet in your Teacher's Resource Box for essay tests and performance assessment activities based on this chapter.

plan outlining specific steps to prepare students for middle school or high school, or in the case of older students, a job or postsecondary study. Teachers review the IEP with the student's parents, school administrators, and often the student's general education teacher. Teachers work closely with parents to inform them of their child's progress and suggest techniques to promote learning at home.

For more information, contact the National Clearinghouse for Professions in Special Education, Council for Exceptional Children, **http://www.special-ed-careers.org**

Answers Chapter 12 Assessment

Reviewing Vocabulary

1. h
2. b
3. f
4. e
5. c
6. d
7. g
8. a

Reviewing the Facts

1. Self-fulfilling prophecy
2. A manifest function of education is an intended and recognized result of education; a latent function of education is an unintended and unrecognized result of education. Examples: Manifest (academic skills; the transmitting of culture; the creation of a common societal identity; nurture talent; promote personal growth and development, etc.) Latent (day-care facility for dual-employed or single parents; place where students find dates and/or marriage partners; training ground for athletes, etc.)
3. Teachers; textbooks; the hidden curriculum
4. The hidden curriculum is the non-academic agenda that teaches discipline, order, a sense of cooperation, and conformity. It fosters citizenship skills that are believed to be necessary for success in a modern bureaucratic society.
5. Compensatory education refers to specific curricular programs designed to overcome deficiency. An example of compensatory education would be Head Start.
6. Charter schools are publicly funded schools operated like private schools. Magnet schools are public schools that attempt to achieve high standards by specializing in a certain area.

Thinking Critically

1. In cooperative learning, students share thoughts and ideas and learn from one another. Students might also be exposed to and begin to consider other individual perspectives. Since most work situations require this type of interaction, cooperative learning mirrors real-life situations.
2. One benefit of competition is that it creates a situation where the "best and

Chapter 12 Assessment

Summary

Section 1: Development and Structure of Education

Main Idea: Schools are becoming more bureaucratic. Advocates of open classrooms and cooperative learning contend that bureaucratically run schools fail to take into account the emotional and creative needs of individual children.

Section 2: Functionalist Perspective

Main Idea: Functionalists see the emergence of the educational institution as a response to society's needs. The manifest functions of education include transmission of culture, creation of a common identity, selection and screening of talent, and promotion of personal growth and development. Schools also serve latent functions.

Section 3: Conflict Perspective

Main Idea: In theory, America is a meritocracy in which social status is achieved. Proponents of the conflict perspective identify flaws in this model by pointing to inequality in our schools. Methods and programs aimed at promoting educational equality have been developed.

Section 4: Symbolic Interactionism

Main Idea: Symbolic interactionists emphasize the socialization that occurs in schools. Through the hidden curriculum, children are taught values, norms, beliefs, and attitudes. Much of this socialization helps young people make the transition from home to a larger society.

SOCIOLOGY Online

Self-Check Quiz
Visit the *Sociology and You* Web site at soc.glencoe.com and click on **Chapter 12—Self-Check Quizzes** to prepare for the chapter test.

Reviewing Vocabulary

Complete each sentence using each term once.

a. open-classroom model
b. cooperative learning
c. tracking
d. meritocracy
e. educational equality
f. multiculturalism
g. hidden curriculum
h. self-fulfilling prophecy

1. ______________ is a prediction that results in behavior that makes the prediction come true.
2. A nonbureaucratic classroom structure in which students study in groups is called ______________.
3. An educational curriculum that accents the viewpoints, experiences, and contributions of minorities is called ______________.
4. ______________ is equality defined in terms of the effects or results of schooling.
5. Placing students in curricula consistent with expectations for their eventual occupations is called ______________.
6. ______________ is social status based on achievement rather than social class or parental class.
7. ______________ includes discipline, order, cooperation, and conformity.
8. ______________ did away with the sharp authoritarian line between teacher and students.

Reviewing the Facts

1. A student is told by teachers that he will not amount to anything. He then begins to fail subjects he has normally passed. What term would sociologists use to describe this occurrence?
2. Explain the difference between a manifest function of education and a latent function of education. Give three examples of each function.

FUNCTION	EXAMPLE 1	EXAMPLE 2	EXAMPLE 3
Manifest			
Latent			

416

3. What are the three agents that assist schools to transmit culture through the socialization process?
4. What is the hidden curriculum and what purpose does it serve?
5. What is compensatory education? Give an example.
6. What is the difference between a charter school and a magnet school?

Thinking Critically

1. **Drawing Conclusions** Most real-world work situations involve a high degree of cooperation. Still, much of our educational system remains competitive. ACT and SAT tests are not taken cooperatively, for example. As you read in the chapter, cooperative learning has been offered as an alternative to individual learning. Based on your experience with cooperative learning, do you agree that it is a better way of learning? Why or why not?
2. **Analyzing Information** Do you think that our society benefits more from competitive situations or cooperative situations? Can both approaches be beneficial to society? In what instances might one approach be preferred to the other?
3. **Applying Concepts** On pages 20–21 in Chapter 1, you read about the McDonaldization of higher education. Using the concepts of efficiency, calculability, predictability, and technology, discuss how high schools are becoming McDonaldized.
4. **Making Inferences** The following is a list of student scores on the ACT test and family income. What might explain why students with higher family incomes also have higher ACT scores? Could intervening variables exist? How might an understanding of poverty explain the discrepancy in scores related to income?
5. **Drawing Conclusions** In the table in question 4, notice that 15 percent of the respondents did not answer the question about family income.

Family Income	ACT Score	Percent of Respondents
Less than $18,000	18.4	9%
$18,000–$24,000	19.2	7%
$24,000–$30,000	19.9	7%
$30,000–$36,000	20.5	7%
$36,000–$42,000	20.8	8%
$42,000–$50,000	21.2	9%
$50,000–$60,000	21.6	10%
$60,000–$80,000	22.1	13%
$80,000–$100,000	22.7	7%
Over $100,000	23.4	8%
No data provided	—	15%

These respondents had a composite score of 20.8. What conclusions might you draw about family income and ACT scores based on the "no response" group?

6. **Analyzing Information** A recent study of high school advanced placement (AP) courses revealed that students who had taken numerous AP courses, in some cases fourteen or fifteen, were admitted to the elite universities of that state. Other students who had also taken AP courses, but had taken significantly fewer of them, were denied entrance to those schools. Does this finding support or weaken the claim that the United States is a meritocracy? Explain.
7. **Understanding Cause and Effect** An elementary school teacher was given a list of her students on the first day of class. Next to each student's name was a number. One was 132, another was 141, and so forth. The teacher saw these numbers and was tremendously excited to begin the school year. In fact, she went out and bought extra materials. At the end of the school year, her students had shown incredible progress. When the principal came up to the teacher and congratulated her, the teacher thanked the principal for giving her so many students with high IQs. The principal said, "What do you mean?" "Well," the teacher replied, "on the first day of class, you gave me that list of student names with their IQs." "Those weren't IQ numbers; they were locker numbers!" The principal responded. Whether

brightest" are successful, ensuring that society is run and served by the most qualified people. On the other hand, cooperative situations foster creativity and innovation, since a wide array of perspectives can be presented and considered. Both approaches can be beneficial.

3. Have students revisit Chapters 1 and 5 pages 4 and 138, to refresh their recollection of this concept. Having them evaluate their school will give them insights into the bureaucratic process, such as why it is necessary, and what its pitfalls are.
4. If you didn't do this activity with students when it appeared in this Teacher's Edition on page 401, have them look at it now. Student responses may include the following: families with higher incomes can spend money for their children to take practice ACT tests; wealthier schools might offer numerous courses that more adequately prepare students for the exam, teachers might gear learning more to the test. Ask students how poverty, on the assumption that it hampers learning, might explain the test scores. They may mention lack of resources, poorer quality of teachers, etc.
5. Students should say that the "No response" group chose not to answer the income level question or didn't have the information available to them. Did those students overlook the question, thus putting them in the no response category?
6. Students will usually react to this question based on their own situation. Students who take AP or other advanced classes will feel they deserve to be accepted to elite universities because of their hard work. Students who were denied admittance might feel that they were judged on unfair criteria, with a good GPA and extracurricular activities no longer being sufficient. If students argue from a functionalist perspective, this is justified. If they argue from a conflict perspective, this policy will just perpetuate more inequalities.

ANSWERS CHAPTER 12 ASSESSMENT

7. This classic story shows students how teachers are influenced by the perceptions they have of their students. Students will probably enjoy investigating the extent to which this happens in your school.
8. This debate is raging in several states. Lawsuits will arise for years to come as parents sue the state when their children fail the tests, and thus are not allowed to graduate. You might want the class to develop an exit exam that they think would be reliable, valid, and able to be passed by all qualified students.

Sociology Projects

1–2. Projects 1 and 2 can be done simultaneously. You might want to have students do this to see how the system works at a level they may have never seen or even contemplated before. If students attend an actual meeting, they could create the mock school board and argue the issues that were addressed by the board.
3. Several teachers who have tried this activity reported that it helped to break down stereotypes that students had about students from other schools.
4. Students can get really creative with this project. Some will do full scale models of an ideal school. See if you can have your students' projects put on display in the school library or some other display area.
5. If students are serious about this project, they can submit their proposals to a teacher and an administrator for review. If students take the time to research other schools, they will see examples of things other schools do that might also work at your school. They might also see that your school's policies work better than those of other schools!
6. Tell students that they need to use deception here to do good research. Tipping off the teacher will bias how the teacher acts and will invalidate the research. Tell students that observing a few teachers is interesting, but not necessarily reliable research. Another set of teachers might yield completely different results.
7. Building on what students did for Project 4, they can envision how the

CHAPTER 12 ASSESSMENT

this story is true or not, it is a good example of the self-fulfilling prophecy (or the Pygmalion effect). What might have happened if the numbers next to the students' names had been 94 or 97? Do you think that teachers in your school do the same thing this teacher did?

8. **Analyzing Information** To ensure that all students have a minimum standard of knowledge before leaving school, several states now require high school seniors to pass a comprehensive exam. Passing the test would give employers and colleges some assurance that a certain standard of achievement was met. Some parents are challenging the exam, claiming that students with passing grades could fail to get into a good college if they failed the exam. Others contend that students who have failed to pass classes could pass the exam and get credit. They argue that many students are unmotivated learners but could pass such an exam. From a societal viewpoint, what position would you take? Would you favor the examination? Could you propose a compromise solution that would satisfy both sides?

Sociology Projects

1. **School Board Meetings** Attend a school board meeting in your community. Obtain a copy of the agenda from the board of education several days before the meeting. Choose one controversial or proposed issue to research. After the meeting, approach one of the board members to interview on this issue and find out his or her position. Report back to your class about the issue, giving an objective view from various perspectives. (As an alternative, you might want to visit a PTO or PTA meeting and find out how parents and teachers view one particular issue.)
2. **Mock School Board Meeting** Organize a mock school board meeting at your school. First, attend a regular school board meeting to become familiar with the procedures. (Many communities broadcast school board meetings on local cable channels.) Select an issue that is of interest to you or that will affect your high school. Work with classmates to fill these roles: school board president (to act as a neutral moderator), several school board members, several community members, and several students (to function as observers and take notes on what they see and hear). It would be a good idea for students to spend some time researching the chosen issue. Each school board member will be allowed a few minutes for opening remarks. Community members must be allowed to express their views, and then a vote should be taken on the issue.
3. **School Issues** Contact a student or students from another high school in your area. (These might be students you have met through church, sports, or other activities.) Compare how your schools function. Look at such issues as discipline and detention, attendance policy, making up work, extra credit, and support for extracurricular activities. Identify two areas in which your schools differ. Discuss these differences with a counselor, your principal, or an assistant principal to see if you can explain why the policy differences exist. (Are the differences a result of the bureaucracy, or do they have physical or geographical causes? Does anyone really know why things are done in a particular way?) Offer explanations for the differences, and arrange to present your findings to the class.
4. **The Ideal School of the Future** You are an architect who has been hired by your school district to design the ideal school of the future. Money is no object, and property owners who pay taxes have stated that they will spare no expense to keep the project going. Your task is to create a draft of the floor plan for the building, outside space, ball fields, bathrooms, cafeteria, and so forth. Identify the purpose of all the rooms (classrooms, labs, resource areas, exercise rooms, saunas, and so on). Submit your plan to your class (which will act as the community). Be prepared to redo the plan based on class members' recommendations. Remember, you are working for them.

5. **School Handbooks** Form a committee with some of your classmates to reevaluate your student handbook. If your school prints such a handbook, look at it and make recommendations for change. If your school does not have a handbook, formulate one. In either case, consider such issues as the following: description of the school day, length of class periods, attendance policies, discipline policies, requirements for graduation, required courses for specific subjects (the guidance office should have this information), extracurricular activities, student rights, and map of the building. If your school's handbook is missing any of these, make a recommendation that it be added. Research other schools to see what their policies are. Ask your teacher if your committee can present its findings to a school administrator.
6. **Observing Classrooms** This mock experiment will you give some experience in recording data and formulating a conclusion. You should conduct the experiment for at least five days. As you sit in your classes throughout the day, discreetly keep track of what happens when students raise their hands. Can you determine a pattern for who is called upon? Do the teachers tend to call on boys more than girls? On noisy students more than quiet ones? On conservative dressers more than radical dressers? Summarize your findings. Remember to remain objective and to respect individuals' privacy at all times. (Don't feel bad if you can't seem to identify a pattern—it just means your teacher is sensitive to his or her students. This is still good research.)
7. **Schools in 2020** Design a school that will function in the year 2020, taking into account predicted advances in technology and presumed changes in social relationships and social roles.
8. **School Culture** Do a study of your school culture, including norms, roles, statuses, groups and subcultures. Include information about where people gather, common symbols and traditions, educational rites of passage, etc.
9. **Stakeholders** Stakeholders are people who have a vested interest in a process, or who are directly affected by a process. Identify the stakeholders of American education: the students, parents, colleges, technical schools, the military, employers, etc. What are their competing perceptions of the functions of education?

Technology Activity

1. The Center for Education Reform maintains a web site devoted to information about charter schools. Visit this site at http://www.edreform.com/charter_schools/. Select "Reform FAQS" and then click on "Charter Schools" that is colored blue.
   a. What are the three principles that govern charter schools?
   b. Be prepared to discuss the advantages and disadvantages of charter schools.
   c. Based on your review of this web site, do you feel that the Center for Education Reform presents an unbiased picture of charter schools?
   d. Now use your favorite search engine and see if there are any charter schools in your area with web sites. If there are, visit the site and find out about them. Do any of them sound attractive to you?

419

ANSWERS Chapter 12 Assessment

school of the future might look. What changes will have to be made? Will desks or computer centers be the norm? Have students consider these factors based on chapter material.

8. Students can refer back to previous chapters that discuss norms, groups, rites of passage, etc. This will probably amount to a qualitative study, since it may be difficult to generate any quantitative data. Students might also want to interview several students to get their opinions on some of these behaviors.

9. Students will see school as a necessary evil; some will actually say they enjoy school. Parents want their children to reap the benefits of a good education. Institutions of higher learning benefit from the preparation that students receive from high schools. Employers need students to have "job ready" skills, so companies might want to influence school curriculum and skill development. Sometimes the aims of each of these groups are in conflict. Functionally, any institution that perpetuates the existing social order benefits society. Education provides this benefit by preparing its members to work in society.

Technology Activity

1. a. accountability, choice, autonomy
b. Advantages: Charters provide opportunity for better child-centered education, and the chance for communities to create the greatest range of educational choices for their children. Operators have the opportunity and the incentive to create schools that provide new and better services to students. And charters, bound only by the high standards they have set for themselves, inspire the rest of the system to work harder and be more responsive to the needs of the children. Disadvantages include: underfunding.
c. Answers will vary.
d. Answers will vary.

Enrichment Reading

This article is excerpted from the book, *Savage Inequalities,* which is considered the classic work on school inequalities. If students read the book, they might find examples from your own state, as Kozol visited numerous schools from all parts of the country. Students might want to read one chapter and write a report based on that information.

Integrating the Teacher Resources

Additional primary source readings for this chapter can be found in Culture Studies: The Sociological Perspective, available in your Teacher's Resource Box. Questions for students are included.

Chapter 12

Enrichment Reading

Savage Inequalities

by Jonathan Kozol

Jonathan Kozol is sociology's best known and most consistent advocate of educational reform. Kozol (1992) sees the roots of educational inequality in social inequality: Poor neighborhoods have poor schools. In the passage below, Kozol describes East St. Louis High School, an African American school located in "the most distressed small city in America." There are few jobs, no regular trash collection, and little protection from the pollution spewed from two chemical plants.

East St. Louis, says the chairman of the state board [of education], "is simply the worst possible place I can imagine to have a child brought up. . . . The community is in desperate circumstances." Sports and music, he observes, are, for many children here, "the only avenues of success." Sadly enough, no matter how it ratifies the stereotype, this is the truth; and there is a **poignant** aspect to the fact that, even with class size soaring and one quarter of the system's teachers being given their dismissal, the state board of education demonstrates its genuine but **skewed** compassion by attempting to leave sports and music untouched by the overall **austerity.**

Even sports facilities, however, are degrading by comparison with those found and expected at most high schools in America. The football field at East St. Louis High is missing almost everything—including goalposts. There are a couple of metal pipes—no crossbar, just the pipes. Bob Shannon, the football coach, who has to use his personal funds to purchase footballs and has had to cut and rake the football field himself, has dreams of having goalposts someday. He'd also like to let his students have new uniforms. The ones they wear are nine years old and held together somehow by a patchwork of repairs. Keeping them clean is a problem, too. The school cannot afford a washing machine. The uniforms are carted to a corner laundromat with fifteen dollars' worth of quarters. . . .

In the wing of the school that holds vocational classes, a damp, unpleasant odor fills the halls. The school has a machine shop, which cannot be used for lack of staff, and a woodworking shop. The only shop that's occupied this morning is the auto-body class. A man with long blond hair and wearing a white sweat suit swings a paddle to get children in their chairs. "What we need the most is new equipment," he reports. "I have equipment for alignment, for example, but we don't have money to install it. We also need a better form of **egress.** We bring the cars in through two other classes." Computerized equipment used in most repair shops, he reports, is far beyond the high school's budget. It looks like a very old gas station in an isolated rural town. . . .

The science labs at East St. Louis High are 30 to 50 years outdated. John McMillan, a soft-spoken man, teaches physics at the school. He shows me his lab. The six lab stations in the room have empty holes where pipes were once attached. "It would be great if we had water," says McMillan. . . .

In a seventh grade social studies class, the only book that bears some relevance to black concerns—its title is *The American Negro*—bears a publication date of 1967. The teacher invites me to ask the class some questions. Uncertain where to start, I ask the students what they've learned about the civil rights campaigns of recent decades.

A 14-year-old girl with short black curly hair says this: "Every year in February we are told to read the same old speech of Martin Luther King. We read it every year. 'I have a dream. . . .' It does begin to seem—what is the word?" She hesitates and then she finds the word: **"perfunctory."**

I ask her what she means.

"We have a school in East St. Louis named for Dr. King," she says. "The school is full of sewer water and the doors are locked with chains. Every student in that school is black. It's like a terrible joke on history."

It startles me to hear her words, but I am startled even more to think how seldom any press reporter has observed the irony of naming segregated schools for Martin Luther King. Children reach the heart of these hypocrisies much quicker than the grown-ups and the experts do.

Source: Excerpted from Jonathan Kozol, *Savage Inequalities* (New York: Harper Collins, 1992), p. 35.

What Does it Mean?

austerity
hardship; severity

egress
act of coming out; exiting

perfunctory
routine; without enthusiasm

poignant
deeply affecting; touching

skewed
slanted; distorted

Jonathan Kozol, a long-time social activist, is author of seven award-winning books which focus on the plight of the disadvantaged children of our nation. Savage Inequalities: Children in America's Schools, *shows the disparities in America's public school system.*

Read and React

1. What does Kozol mean by "educational inequality"? Do you agree or disagree with his view? Why?
2. Does Kozol believe there is a link between economic resources and educational inequality? Explain. Discuss why you agree or disagree.
3. If Kozol were going to speak to your local school board, what would you like to say to him regarding educational inequality?
4. Is educational inequality a problem in your school? In other schools in your community? Elaborate.
5. Imagine yourself in the school Kozol describes. How would it affect your education, view of life, and future?

Answers to Read and React

1. Kozol relates educational inequality to social inequality. Some students will disagree because they don't see the relationship between poverty and school performance. Other students will talk of the injustice that this creates.
2. Kozol believes that discrepancies in educational funding due to poverty tax bases explain in part the inequalities of schools. Depressed areas simply don't provide enough funding to support their schools.
3. Student answers to this question will probably be similar to their responses to question 1.
4. Students are acutely aware of this. If they have ever visited other schools, they know that some schools have more resources than others. Students might want to research how much money their school district spends per year on each student.
5. Answers will vary. If you can obtain a copy of the video *Children in America's Schools,* students can see firsthand the differences between a wealthy and an impoverished school district.

Chapter Preview

Section 1 (pages 424–432)

Political systems can be based on three types of authority: charismatic, traditional, and rational-legal. Democratic, totalitarian, and authoritarian are types of political systems. In democracies, power lies with elected officials. Totalitarian systems have absolute rulers who control all aspects of political and social life. Authoritarian rulers possess absolute control but often permit some personal freedoms.

Section 2 (pages 433–439)

The two major models of political power are elitism and pluralism. Advocates of the conflict perspective believe American society is controlled by elites. Pluralists, whose view is associated with functionalism, depict power as widely distributed among interest groups.

Section 3 (pages 440–445)

Capitalist economics are based on private property and the pursuit of profit. In socialist economies, the means of production are owned collectively. Government has an active role in planning and controlling the economy.

Section 4 (pages 446–449)

Corporations affect domestic political decision making and influence the political and economic institutions of countries around the world.

Section 5 (pages 450–456)

Workers today face a changing job structure. More corporations are downsizing and replacing full-time employees with consultants or temporary workers.

CHAPTER 13

Political and Economic Institutions

422

Lead-Off Activity

Power and authority are utilized by government agencies. The policies adopted by these institutions can be examined using the concepts of Max Weber and Robert Merton. Ask students to draw four boxes on a piece of paper and to give each box one of the following labels: functional, dysfunctional, manifest, and latent. Provide a list of some key political issues such as the death penalty, drunk driving laws, and the legalization of marijuana. Ask students to pick one of the issues and then fill in each box with attributes

USING Your Sociological Imagination

Not so long ago, Americans looked at workers in Japan with "half-horrified awe." Rumors of workers slaving away ten hours a day, six days a week, made the rounds of corporate America. "You're so lucky to be working here," crowed U.S. bosses. "If you worked in Japan, you wouldn't be taking long lunches or two-week vacations. You'd sleep at the office and see your family on Sunday."

Management theorists likened the relationship between Japanese workers and supervisors to that of the family. A new management style based on the Japanese model was proposed. Where Type X was a worker needing close supervision and Type Y was a creative, self-directed worker, the new Type Z was an individual whose culture was focused entirely on work.

Today the reality is that Americans put in more hours than workers in any other industrialized country, including Japan. Between 1977 and 1997, the average work week among salaried American workers lengthened from forty-three to forty-seven hours. In that same period, the number of workers putting in more than fifty hours per week went from 24 percent to 37 percent. In fact, Americans work an equivalent of eight weeks longer every year than Western Europeans. Given these figures, it is even more surprising that over 80 percent of people at work say they are satisfied with their jobs. Where, why, and how Americans work are just some of the issues examined in this chapter on political and economic institutions in the United States.

Sections

1. **Power and Authority**
2. **Political Power in American Society**
3. **Economic Systems**
4. **The Modern Corporation**
5. **Work in the Modern Economy**

Learning Objectives

After reading this chapter, you will be able to

- distinguish among power, coercion, and authority.
- identify three forms of authority.
- discuss differences among democracy, totalitarianism, and authoritarianism.
- explain how voting is an exercise of power.
- list characteristics of capitalism and socialism.
- describe America's changing workforce.
- discuss the consequences of corporate downsizing.

SOCIOLOGY Online

Chapter Overview
Visit the *Sociology and You* Web site at soc.glencoe.com and click on **Chapter 13—Chapter Overviews** to preview chapter information.

USING Your Sociological Imagination

A seminal work on this topic is Janet B. Schor's *The Overworked American: The Unexpected Decline of Leisure Time*. Some Americans complain of not having enough leisure time for themselves. At the same time, others claim that they don't know what to do with themselves if they are not working. Have students debate the decline of leisure time and what role social factors might play in this phenomenon.

of the different perspectives. For example, the functional perspective of the death penalty would be that it guarantees that the worst criminals will be put to death. The dysfunctional perspective would claim that the death penalty targets minorities. Its manifest function is that society would be better off without these criminals, and a latent function would be that prisoners live off of taxpayers for many years before execution.
L2

Using the Section Preview

Have your students imagine the following scenario. Your sociology class is on a cruise in the South Sea, when a violent storm causes the ship to sink. About 200 of the 600 passengers escape the sinking ship by lifeboat. (Fortunately, the entire class survives.) The lifeboats, which are carrying some medicine, food, and water, make it to a remote island. The food supply will last only a short time, and while some foods like oranges and pineapples grow on the island, they are not in abundance. There is no means of communication available to summon help. In addition, the sinking ship did not send a distress message, so there is no guarantee that anyone will know the survivors are missing for quite some time. Have students work in groups to devise a political system to control the situation. They must devise a plan for rationing the food, and decide upon the following: a) who will lead; b) how rules will be made; c) who will enforce the rules; d) who will work; e) who will supervise, etc.

Integrating the Teacher Resources

Look for the Chapter 13 Learning Goals Outline, a reproducible student worksheet in the Unit 4 Mastering Basic Concepts booklet in your Teacher's Resource Box. It can be used to preview or review chapter content.

Section 1 Power and Authority

Key Terms

- **economic institution**
- **political institution**
- **power**
- **coercion**
- **authority**
- **charismatic authority**
- **traditional authority**
- **rational-legal authority**
- **representative democracy**
- **totalitarianism**
- **authoritarianism**

Section Preview

Authority is the sanctioned use of power. Political systems can be based on three types of authority: charismatic, traditional, and rational-legal. Democratic, totalitarian, and authoritarian are types of political systems. In democracies, power lies with elected officials. Totalitarian political systems have absolute rulers who control all aspects of political and social life. Authoritarian rulers possess absolute control but often permit some personal freedoms.

economic institution institution that determines how goods and services are produced and distributed

political institution institution that determines how power is obtained and exercised

Definitions of Power and Authority

In 1997, the powerful Teamsters Union went on strike against United Parcel Service (UPS) to protest the company's cost-cutting policy of eliminating permanent positions and replacing them with part-time or temporary positions. When UPS asked President Clinton to intervene in the dispute (on the grounds that the company provided an essential national service), it demonstrated the close connection between business and government in modern American society.

The set of functions that concern the production and distribution of goods and services for a society is called the **economic institution.** Because economic decisions affect how valuable resources are shared between organizations and the general public, conflicts inevitably arise. The responsibility for handling these conflicts is the institution through which power is obtained and exercised—the **political institution.** These two institutions are so closely interrelated that it is very hard to think of them as

These prison inmates are subject to the power of the political institution that convicted them.

Demonstration

To help students better understand the meaning of the word *coercion,* demonstrate "control through force" in your classroom. (Of course, you don't want students to know this is what you're doing.) Demand that students do things that are not normally required. For example, you might insist that students sit up straight at their desks. Or, have them recopy their homework until it's perfect. Any unusual request that you can insist on will do. Be sure to debrief students after you've finished. They separate. For a beginning study of sociology, however, we can think of economics as the distribution of resources and politics as the exercise of power. This chapter will look first at how politics affects group behaviors and then at the economic scene.

What is power? As stated in Chapter 1, Max Weber profoundly influenced sociological theory. You read about him again in Chapter 6, which examined formal organizations and bureaucracies. Weber's contribution to political sociology deals with his identification of different forms of power and authority. Weber defined **power** as the ability to control the behavior of others, even against their will. Power takes various forms. Some people, for example, wield great power through their personal appeal or magnetism. John F. Kennedy, Martin Luther King, Jr., and César Chávez were able to influence others through the force of their charismatic personalities.

power
the ability to control the behavior of others

Weber recognized another form of power that he called **coercion.** Coercion is the use of physical force or threats to exert control. A blackmailer might extort money from a politician. A government might take, without compensation, the property of one of its citizens. In such cases, the victims do not believe this use of power is right. In fact, they normally are resentful and want to fight back. Weber recognized that a political system based on coercive power is inherently unstable; that is, the abuses of the system itself cause people to rise against it.

coercion
control through force

What is authority? Weber also believed that a political institution must rest on a stable form of power if it is to function and survive. This more stable form of power is **authority.** Authority is power accepted as legitimate by those subject to it. For example, students take exams and accept the results they receive because they believe their teachers have the right (authority) to determine grades. Most citizens pay taxes because they believe their government has the right (authority) to collect money from them.

authority
power accepted as legitimate by those subject to it

More About . . . César Chávez

César Chávez (1927–1993) emerged as a national leader for farm workers and a hero to many Hispanics. Quiet and humble, he nonetheless effected changes that helped thousands. He consistently advocated nonviolent methods for achieving his aims. He, like his role model Mahatma Gandhi, often fasted for long periods to bring attention to a particular issue.

Integrating the Teacher Resources

To reinforce key ideas, use the Chapter 13 Graphic Organizer, a reproducible student worksheet available in the Unit 4 Mastering Basic Concepts booklet in your Teacher's Resource Box.

need to know that your behavior was part of a demonstration and that you haven't totally "lost it."

Ask students how it felt to be controlled by force (coercion). What were the major frustrations? Ask students if they have ever been in a situation where their behavior was controlled by force. (Be sensitive to students who might not want to answer this question. You may have some who have experienced some form of physical abuse.) **L1**

Teaching Strategy

The following passage is paraphrased from Max Weber's book *On Charisma and Institution Building.* Weber stated that the charismatic leader demands obedience and a following by virtue of his mission. His success determines whether he finds them. Using Martin Luther King Jr. as the example, have students identify characteristics of King based on Weber's contention that his followers would find him. In 1956, King was a young minister just out of divinity school and new to Montgomery, Alabama. He was chosen to lead the Montgomery Improvement Association because he was the least visible of the local ministers. He had not yet established a reputation, but was able to step onto the stage of history.

César Chávez, John F. Kennedy, and Martin Luther King, Jr. were charismatic leaders. What does charismatic mean?

Forms of Authority

Weber identified three forms of authority—*charismatic, traditional,* and *rational-legal.* People who live under governments based on these forms recognize authority figures as holders of legitimate power.

charismatic authority authority that arises from the personality of an individual

What is charismatic authority? **Charismatic authority** arises from a leader's personal characteristics. Charismatic leaders lead through the power or strength of their personalities or the feelings of trust they inspire in a large number of people. In addition to Kennedy, King, and Chávez, Nelson Mandela and Fidel Castro have strong personalities that make them highly charismatic leaders.

For modern nation-states, however, charismatic authority alone is too unstable to provide a permanent basis of power. It is linked to an individual and is therefore difficult to transfer to another. When charismatic leaders die, the source of power is removed. Adolf Hitler, himself a charismatic leader, made an attempt at the end of World War II to name his successor. But as historian John Toland has noted

Integrating the Teacher Resources

Look for the Chapter 13 Increasing Your Reading Comprehension worksheet and the Guided Reading worksheet in the Unit 4 Mastering Basic Concepts booklet in your Teacher's Resource Box. Both will strengthen student reading comprehension skills.

Learning Styles

Linguistic/Bodily-kinesthetic Like all organizations, high schools are based on some form of rational-legal authority. Divide students into three groups and ask them to research types of political systems: democratic, totalitarian, and authoritarian. Then ask each group to choose an issue that is current at your school, or in your community. Examples might include dress codes, evening curfews, and gang relations. Have

Hitler's death brought an abrupt, absolute end to National Socialism. Without its only true leader, it burst like a bubble. . . . What had appeared to be the most powerful and fearsome political force of the twentieth century vanished overnight. No other leader's death since Napoleon had so completely obliterated a regime (Toland, 1976:892).

So even governments controlled by charismatic leaders must eventually come to rely on other types of authority. The two alternatives to charismatic authority identified by Weber are traditional authority and rational-legal authority.

What is traditional authority? In the past, most states relied on **traditional authority,** in which the legitimacy of a leader is rooted in custom. Early kings often claimed to rule by the will of God, or divine right. The peaceful transfer of power was possible because only a few individuals, such as offspring or other close relatives, were eligible to become the next ruler. The kings in eighteenth-century Europe, for example, counted on the custom of loyalty to provide a stable political foundation. Tradition provided more stability than charismatic authority could have provided.

traditional authority
forms of authority in which the legitimacy of a leader is rooted in custom

rational-legal authority
form of authority in which the power of government officials is based on the offices they hold

What is rational-legal authority? Most modern governments are based on a system of **rational-legal authority.** In this type of government, power resides in the offices rather than in the officials. Those who hold government offices are expected to operate on the basis of specific rules and procedures that define and limit their rights and responsibilities. Power is assumed only when the individual occupies the office. Many leaders in religious organizations, such as priests, rabbis, archbishops, or mullahs, also fall under this category of authority.

Since rational-legal authority is invested in positions rather than in individuals, persons lose their authority when they leave their formal positions of power. When a new president is elected, for example, the outgoing president becomes a private citizen again and gives up the privileges of the office. Furthermore, leaders are expected to stay within the boundaries of their legal authority. Even presidents (Richard Nixon, for example) can lose their power if their abuse of power is made public. Thus, legal authority also limits the power of government officials.

King Jigme Singye Wangchuck rules Bhutan through the exercise of traditional authority.

Types of Political Systems

As societies have evolved through the centuries, so have different forms of political systems (Nolan and Lenski, 1999). In hunting and gathering societies, there was very little formal government. Political leaders were typically chosen on the basis of exceptional physical prowess or personal charisma. Formal governmental structures emerged with the development of agricultural economies and the rise of city-states. As societies became more diversified with the development of commerce, industry, and technology, government began to take the form of the national political state. Examples of strong nation-states include France, Spain, and England between the years 1200 and 1500. Gradually, traditional authority was replaced by rational-legal authority. Contemporary nation-states can be classified into three basic types: *democratic, totalitarian,* and *authoritarian.*

Teaching Strategy

Ask interested students to research the divine right of kings. When and where was this theory of government first proclaimed? What is the history of opposition to this idea? Ask students to share their research with the rest of the class.
L3

More About . . . Traditional Authority

Tell students that Bhutan has one of the last absolute monarchies in the world. Despite the recent rapid progress in education, health, sanitation and communication, Bhutan remains a monarchy with no written constitution or bill of rights and where serious human rights violations have been reported.

Her Majesty, the Queen of England is the United Kingdom's Head of State. She carries out significant constitutional functions, presides at ceremonial occasions, visits local communities, and is Britain's representative to the world.

The power and duties of the British monarchy have changed dramatically over the years. Students might want to research the history of the British monarchy. Or, if they would like more information about the monarchy today, they can visit the official web site of the British monarchy at **http://www.royal.gov.uk/index.htm**

each group create a skit to illustrate how that issue would be handled by the people in different types of authority roles: a charismatic leader, a traditional authoritarian, and a rational-legal leader. Conclude each role-play with a discussion of how students feel the issues would be handled in each of the political systems, and then how students would like to see the issues handled.
L2

Points to Stress

Rational-legal authority is based on a smooth transfer of power. Have students analyze how the office of the presidency of the United States is passed from one president to the next. Point out that the presidential election is held in November, while the inauguration isn't held until Jan. 20th of the following year. This "lame duck period" allows for the successful transfer of power. The outgoing and in-coming presidents usually meet between November and January to brief the new president. The point to stress is that our society can change leaders without causing any upheaval, an indication that American democracy functions very smoothly.

Democracy

representative democracy
a system of government that uses elected officials to fulfill majority wishes

Democracy in its pure form, as practiced by the ancient Greeks, involves all citizens in self-government. This type of direct democracy is similar to that practiced in New England town meetings, where the citizens debated and voted directly on various issues. More familiar to us today is **representative democracy,** in which elected officials are responsible for fulfilling the wishes of the majority of citizens.

What assumptions are made in a representative democracy? Representative democracy operates under two assumptions. The first is that realistically, not everyone in modern society can be actively involved in all political decision making. Thus, although citizens are expected to vote, most citizens are not expected to be deeply involved in politics. Second, political candidates who fail to satisfy the wishes of the majority are not expected to win reelections.

> "Power tends to corrupt, and absolute power corrupts absolutely."
>
> Lord Acton
> English historian

With the major two-party system of the United States, we have a "winner take all" form of representative democracy. Here, the party with the most votes wins the election. In other countries, as in Europe where third-party systems are common, political parties participate in the government to the extent that they win representation in general elections. For example, one party might win 40 percent of the vote and control 40 percent of the legislature. Three other parties might take 20 percent each and control a combined 60 percent of the legislature. This proportional representation system seems to be more democratic as it tends to encourage compromises and cooperation in forming governments. Governments formed under this system can be fragile, however, and shifting political alliances may be able to force new elections after short periods of time.

Germany's parliamentary system is a representative democracy.

Integrating the Teacher Resources

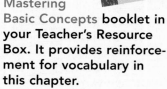

Look for the Chapter 13 Vocabulary Activity worksheet in the Unit 4 Mastering Basic Concepts booklet in your Teacher's Resource Box. It provides reinforcement for vocabulary in this chapter.

Cooperative Learning Activity

If your students question the importance of direct and indirect democracy, tell them to meet in small groups and analyze how they would live under both. Have the groups write their responses to the following questions: What examples of direct democracy within your school or local government can you cite? How do the direct democracies function? How effective are they? What examples of representative democracy can you cite within your school or local government? How are the representatives selected? To whom are they responsible? How effective do the students or citizens consider their representatives?
L2

World View

Political Freedom

Democracy is unevenly distributed worldwide. The accompanying map classifies countries according to three degrees of political freedom: free, partly free, and not free.

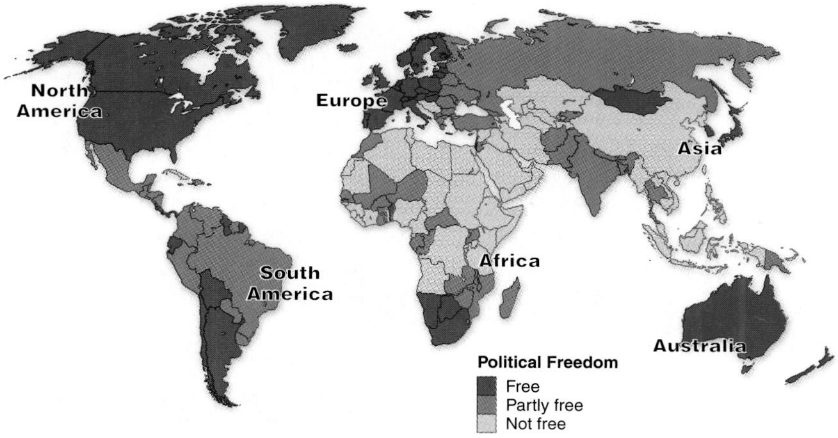

Interpreting the Map

1. Do you see any pattern in the degree of political freedom around the world?
2. Predict how political freedom around the world will change in the next fifty years. Explain your predictions.

Source: Freedom House, Washington, D.C., 1998.

Is democracy spreading? The collapse of Soviet communism and the end of the Cold War have created opportunities for more societies to adopt democratic forms of government. Still, there is little evidence that democratic societies are on the rise (Karatnycky, 1995; Vanhanen, 1997). Nearly 80 percent of the world's people live in countries classified as "partly free" or "not free." (See World View above.) "Free" political systems are primarily associated with advanced economic development and are found mainly in a few nations: the nations of Western Europe, Canada, Australia, the United States, some Latin American countries, Japan, and a few African nations.

World View

Ask students to explain what is meant by the terms *free, partly free,* and *not free.* Which degree of freedom is most prevalent in the world today? Which is least prevalent? Why do students think this is so?

Answers to Interpreting the Map

1. Students may not see a pattern in the degree of political freedom. However, you might want to point out that the countries with advanced economic development tend to have the highest degree of freedom.
2. Answers will vary. However, students might point out that as more countries become industrialized and the economic development of the countries increases, the degree of political freedom will probably tend to increase also. Despite such novels as *Brave New World,* it is not common to find a high degree of technology linking a low degree of personal freedom.

On-Demand Writing

Have students write a paragraph explaining why countries with advanced economic development have a higher degree of freedom than countries with a lesser degree of economic development. If possible, students should cite specific countries as examples. Ask volunteers to share their essays with the rest of the class. For discussion, have the class determine how many *different* reasons students gave in answer to the question.
L2

Working with the Data

Figure 13.1 To help students better understand the concepts of pure democracy, representative democracy, authoritarianism, and totalitarianism use the figure as a review. Go over each type of political institution and have students describe it and give an example that is not mentioned in the figure. They should also include questions and answers about the countries listed and the type of political system practiced. You might also ask students to use their word processing program to transfer the information to a database.

Working with the Quote

Ask students to read the quote by Josef de Maistre. Do students understand what he is saying? Do they agree with what he is saying? Have the students who agree stand on one side of the classroom. Have the students who disagree stand on the other side of the classroom. Those who are undecided should stand in the middle. Allow students on the agree and disagree sides to give reasons for their feelings. If their arguments persuade someone to their way of thinking, the person whose mind has been changed can move to the appropriate side of the room. Take a count of the agree, disagree, and undecided students before beginning. Take another count at the end of the activity. Which side is favored? Is this a surprise to students?

Figure 13.1 The Political Continuum. *Political institutions offer varying degrees of freedom for their members.*

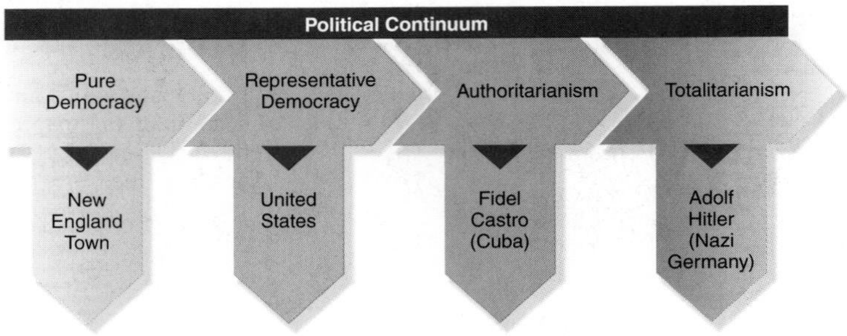

Totalitarianism

totalitarianism
a political system in which a ruler with absolute power attempts to control all aspects of a society

Totalitarianism lies at the opposite end of the political spectrum from democracy. In this type of political system, a ruler with absolute power attempts to control all aspects of a society. Characteristics of totalitarian states include

- a single political party, typically controlled by one person.
- a well-coordinated campaign of terror.
- total control of all means of communication.
- a monopoly over military resources.
- a planned economy directed by a state bureaucracy.

Examples of totalitarian states include Iraq under Saddam Hussein, the former Soviet Union, and Nazi Germany.

> Every nation has the government it deserves.
>
> **Josef de Maistre**
> **French diplomat**

Hitler's National Socialist (Nazi) government, which came to power in Germany in the early 1930s, offers a good example of the way a totalitarian system works. Despite presenting a false image of democracy to the world, Hitler and the National Socialist Party held all the power. Hitler's absolute control was strengthened by the Gestapo secret police and SS troops, who terrorized both Hitler's political enemies and private citizens. With few exceptions, all news media were either seized by the party or eliminated. Hitler dominated the armed forces, often devising his own military plans over the opposition of his generals. Nazi Germany's four-year economic plans included strategies for budgets, production, organization of factories, and forced labor.

Why can we classify Adolf Hitler as a totalitarian leader?

Role Play

Assign students to groups. Each group will develop and act out role plays that demonstrate how totalitarianism works. In the role plays students should illustrate the different aspects of totalitarianism listed above as well as control of the hearts and minds of the people, and active involvement of the people in the achievement of the goals of the regime no matter what the cost to the people. Students should show how totalitarian states attempt to accomplish these things through use of mass pro-

What category of leader does Cuban President Fidel Castro represent?

Authoritarianism

For sociologists, authoritarianism is a middle category between democracy and totalitarianism, although it is closer to totalitarianism than to democracy. **Authoritarianism** refers to a political system controlled by elected or nonelected rulers who usually permit some degree of individual freedom but do not allow popular participation in government. Countless governments have leaned toward totalitarianism but have fallen short of all its defining characteristics. These governments are classified as authoritarian. Examples include certain monarchies (the dynasties of the shahs of Iran), and military seizures of power (Fidel Castro's takeover of Cuba).

authoritarianism
a political system controlled by elected or nonelected rulers who usually permit some degree of individual freedom

Section 1 Assessment

1. What is the difference between authority and coercion?
2. Which type of authority places the strongest limits on government officials?
3. Explain how direct democracy differs from representative democracy.
4. Briefly describe the three major types of political systems.

Critical Thinking

5. **Sequencing Information** Like all organizations, high schools are based on some form of authority. Explain, with examples, which form or forms of authority you believe are applicable to high schools.
6. **Synthesizing Information** In which form of government would you expect to find charismatic authority? Traditional authority? Rational-legal authority?

paganda and high-tech media. Have a class discussion after each role play to determine which aspects of totalitarianism were portrayed and to what effect.

You might want to discuss with students how the period following World War I opened the door to extremist political parties throughout the world. What occurred during this time period to allow such parties to come to power? **L1**

Answers to Section 1 Assessment

1. Coercion is a form of power that is thought to be wrong by its victims. Authority is the more stable form of power, and is accepted as legitimate by those subject to it.
2. The type of authority with the strongest limits on officials is rational-legal authority—power resides in the offices rather than in the officials.
3. Direct democracy is democracy in its pure form; it involves all citizens in self-government. In representative democracy, elected officials are responsible for fulfilling the wishes of the majority of citizens.
4. *Democracy:* in most cases, representative democracy—elected officials are responsible for fulfilling the wishes of the majority of citizens; *totalitarianism:* a ruler with absolute power attempts to control all aspects of a society; *authoritarianism:* a political system controlled by nonelected rulers who usually permit some degree of individual freedom but do not allow popular participation in government.

Critical Thinking

5. Answers will vary.
6. Answers will vary and should stimulate discussion.

Another Place: China's One-Child Policy

How much control a government has over daily life varies greatly from one political system to another. The excerpt below describes one way in which a strict, authoritarian government exerts control.

China's communist government adopted the one-child policy in 1979 in response to the staggering doubling of the country's population during Mao Zedong's rule. Mao, who died in 1976, was convinced that the country's masses were a strategic asset and vigorously encouraged the Chinese to produce even-larger families.

China's family-planning officials wield awesome powers, enforcing the policy through a combination of incentives and deterrents. For those who comply, there are job promotions and small cash awards. For those who resist, they suffer stiff fines and loss of job and status within the country's tightly knit and heavily regulated communities. The State Family Planning Commission is the government ministry entrusted with the tough task of curbing the growth of the world's most populous country, where 28 children are born every minute. It employs about 200,000 full-time officials and uses more than a million volunteers to check the fertility of hundreds of millions of Chinese women.

When a couple wants to have a child—even their first, allotted one—they must apply to the family-planning office in their township or workplace, literally lining up to procreate. "If a woman gets pregnant without permission, she and her husband will get fined, even if it's their first," . . . "it is fair to fine her, because she creates a burden on the whole society by jumping her place in line."

The official Shanghai Legal Daily last year reported on a family-planning committee in central Sichuan province that ordered the flogging of the husbands of 10 pregnant women who refused to have abortions. According to the newspaper, the family-planning workers marched the husbands one by one into an empty room, ordered them to strip and lie on the floor and then beat them with a stick, once for every day their wives were pregnant.

Source: Excerpted from Daniela Deane, "The Little Emperors," *Los Angeles Times Magazine* (July 26, 1992): 138, 140. © Daniela Deane.

Thinking It Over

What types of propaganda might the Chinese government use to enforce its one-child policy? Use material in the description above to bolster your answer.

China's authoritarian government gave it the power needed to institute strict population controls.

Careers in Sociology

Ask students the following question. After they have had a chance to give their own answers, share the answers below with them. Can I combine interests in politics and sociology in a career?

Definitely. For example, political scientists study the origin, development, and operation of political systems and public policy. They conduct research on subjects such as relations between the United States and other countries, institutions and political life of nations, politics of small towns or a major metropolis, or the decisions of the U.S. Supreme Court. They analyze the structure and operation of governments as well as various political entities. Depending on the

Another Place

Although this topic will be revisited in Chapter 16, you may want to ask students if the United States, whose population will double over the next 100 years, should consider legislating the number of children that families can have. Students will be eager to debate this issue. Would using the tactics employed by the Chinese government be beneficial?

Answer to Thinking It Over

Answers will vary. Students should use concepts outlined in the text.

Integrating the Teacher Resources

For Spanish-speaking students, you may wish to use the reproducible worksheets available in the Spanish Supplements booklet in your Teacher's Resource Box.

Section 2

Political Power in American Society

Key Terms

- political socialization
- pluralism
- elitism
- interest group
- power elite

Influence of the Vote

Like all other democracies today, the United States emphasizes political participation through voting. Voting is an important source of power for citizens. It enables us to remove incompetent, corrupt, or insensitive officials from office. It also allows us to influence issues at the local, state, and national levels.

How much real choice do voters have? In practice, the amount of real choice exercised through voting is limited. The range of candidates from which to choose is restricted because of the power of political parties. Usually, only a candidate endorsed by a major political party has a chance of winning a state or national office. To get party support, a candidate must appeal to the widest possible number of voters. As a result, candidates often resemble each other more than they differ. In addition, the cost of running a political campaign today limits the choice of candidates to those who have party backing or are independently wealthy. George W. Bush, for example, announced in August of 2000 that he had spent nearly $150 million for his presidential campaign.

Section Preview

The two major models of political power are elitism and pluralism. Advocates of the conflict perspective believe American society is controlled by elites. Pluralists, whose view is associated with functionalism, depict power as widely distributed among interest groups. Voting does not seem to be an effective means for nonelites to influence political decisions in the U.S.

John McCain, Alan Keyes, and George W. Bush all campaigned for the 2000 Republican Party presidential nomination. How many African Americans have you seen run for President of the United States? What does this tell you about the relationship between racial membership and political power in the United States?

Using the Section Preview

Have students examine their personal lives to determine how the agents of political socialization (family, education, mass media, economic status, occupation, age and gender) have shaped their political beliefs. Students might also want to interview their parents to ask what their political views are and how they have formulated them.

Using the Illustration

Students may or may not be able to name Alan Keyes or Jesse Jackson from previous elections. In any event, the exceedingly small number of African American presidential candidates illustrates the strong relationship between racial membership and political power. Membership in minority racial groups clearly blocks Americans from greater access to political power.

topic, a political scientist might conduct a public opinion survey, analyze election results, analyze public documents, or interview public officials.

Another example–political campaign workers assist in planning, fund raising, research, writing issue statements, canvassing, and assessing voter attitudes. They work for candidates or interest groups during political election campaigns. These entry-level jobs frequently lead to permanent positions with political organizations or officeholders.

For more information, contact the American Political Science Association at **http://www.apsanet.org/**

Net Worthy

Here are several political-oriented web sites that students might find interesting and fun. The site **www.govote.com** features a 20 question quiz about political issues that matches you with your presidential soul mate and maps your political personality. Another site, **www.issues2000.org**, shows recent quotes by political candidates on 23 major issues. A third website, **www.vote-smart.com**, allows students to look at candidates from alternative groups such as the Green, Grassroots, and Anti-Hypocrisy parties.

Political socialization helps to determine what political battles we choose to fight.

On what do we base our votes? Most attitudes and beliefs that are expressed as political opinions are gained through a learning process called **political socialization.** This process can be formal, as in government class, or informal. The informal process interests sociologists because it involves such factors as the family, the media, economic status, and educational level. Studies have shown that most political socialization is informal.

political socialization informal and formal processes by which a person develops political opinions

A brief summary of the major agents of political socialization follows.

- *The family.* Children learn political attitudes the same way they learn values and norms, by listening to everyday conversations and by watching the actions of other family members. The influence of the family is strong. In one study, more high school students could identify their parents' political party affiliation than any other of their parents' attitudes or beliefs.
- *Education.* The level of education a person has influences his or her political knowledge and participation. For example, more highly educated men and women tend to show more knowledge about politics and policy. They also tend to vote and participate more often in politics.
- *Mass media.* Television is the leading source of political and public affairs information for most people. Television and other mass media can determine what issues, events, and personalities are in the public eye. By publicizing some issues and ignoring others, and by giving some stories high priority and others low priority, the media decide the relative importance of issues. The mass media obviously play an important role in shaping public opinion, but the extent of that role is unclear. Studies indicate that the media have the greatest effect on people who have not yet formed opinions.

SOCIOLOGY Online

Student Web Activity Visit the *Sociology and You* Web site at soc.glencoe.com and click on **Chapter 13—Student Web Activities** for an activity on political socialization.

Encouraging Citizenship Activity

Have students do the following: Get involved with government at the local level. Ask them to go to several town meetings to find out what the issues are that face your community. Isolate one issue that you think is important. Research the issue thoroughly. Find out what kinds of political agendas are in play concerning the issue. Make note of how personalities get entangled in the issue. Be sure to find out who will profit, and who will lose financially by a resolution in either direction. Once they have analyzed the issue, and learned all they can about it, encourage them to volunteer to help the

❖ *Economic status and occupation.* Economic status clearly influences political views. Poor people are more likely to favor government-assistance programs than wealthy people, for example. Similarly, where you work affects how you vote. Corporate managers are more likely to favor tax shelters and aid to businesses than hourly workers in factories.

❖ *Age and gender.* Young adults tend to be more progressive than older persons on such issues as racial and gender equality. Women tend to be more liberal than men on such issues as abortion rights, women's rights, health care, and government-supported child care.

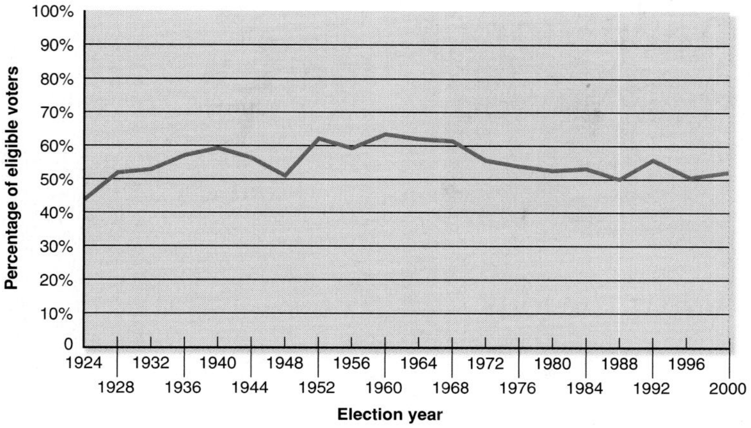

Figure 13.2 Voter Participation in Presidential Elections: 1924–2000 *Is there any correlation between the confidence level and the voter participation rate? Explain.*

Source: *The Almanac of American Politics 2002* (Washington, DC: National Journal, 2002).

How fully do Americans take advantage of the right to vote? In 2000, 51 percent of eligible U.S. voters exercised their right (see Figure 13.2). Less than a fourth of the American people voted for George W. Bush, a proportion comparable to the 20 percent who elected President Reagan in 1980 (Lewis, 2000). In fact, the United States has one of the the lowest voter turnout rate in the industrialized world (Federal Election Commission, 2001).

The American public's interest in voting is very low, partly because of a relatively low level of confidence in political leaders. Another reason for lower voter turnout is that political parties are no longer as instrumental in getting voters to the polls as they once were. In general, minorities, the lower class and the working class tend to vote in smaller proportions than whites and the middle and upper classes. Members of minorities, people with little education, and people with smaller incomes are less likely to vote in both congressional and presidential elections.

Two Models of Political Power

In a democratic society, two major models of political power are evident—*pluralism* and *elitism*. According to **pluralism,** political decisions are the result of bargaining and compromise among special interest groups. No one group holds the majority of power. Rather, power is widely distributed throughout a society or community. In contrast, according to **elitism,** a community or society is controlled from the top by a few individuals or organizations. Power is concentrated in the hands of an elite group whose members have common interests and backgrounds. The masses are very weak politically.

pluralism
system in which political decisions are made as a result of bargaining and compromise among special interest groups

elitism
system in which a community or society is controlled from the top by a few individuals or organizations

council members who share their feelings about the best way to solve the issue. They might wind up addressing envelopes, or handing out flyers, or answering phones. They might also consider addressing the council from the point of view of a young adult and the impact the issue might have on the future. Finally, they can serve the community by spreading the word about the issue. Let students know that it is satisfying to get personally involved in politics. **L3**

Working with the Data

Figure 13.2 Ask students if they think there is a correlation between the confidence level and the voter participation rate. *(It appears that as confidence level goes down, voter participation also declines. However, in 1992 when public confidence was down, there was an increase in voter participation.)*

Points to Stress

Many people from the working and lower classes feel that the political system doesn't adequately serve their needs. Thus, there is a high level of voter apathy among this social class. Political influence is largely dictated by availability of resources, meaning that one typically needs money to enter the political arena. Based on this premise, the political system is geared for those who have money, and who can exert their power economically as well as politically.

Integrating the Transparencies

A "Profile of the American Voter" transparency and other transparencies related to the content of this chapter are provided in the *Sociology and You* Transparency Binder.

Snapshot of America

Ask students if they believe the voter turnout rates are acceptable. Then ask them what reasons might account for some of these low rates. *(Answers include the inability to vote on a particular day; residency and registration requirements; a sense that it won't make a difference; being turned off by political campaigns; long ballots; lack of interest; satisfaction with the status quo; and indecision.)*

Answers to Interpreting the Map

1. The regions with the lowest voter turnout include the South, Southwest, and the Western states, including California.
2. Low voter turnout in the above states could be a result of high minority populations, the groups most likely to feel alienation from the political system. These are the individuals that might not be registered, who cannot meet residency requirements, who lack the language, and who are not vested into the system.
3. Answers will vary. Students ideas for increasing voter turnout can be very creative and would be worth sharing as a class.

Snapshot of America

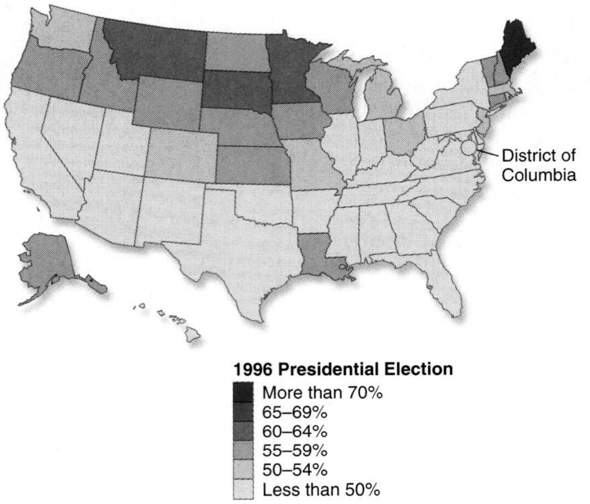

Voter Turnout

It is commonly said that the voter holds the power in American politics. What often goes unsaid is that to exercise this power, the voter must actually vote. This map shows the voter turnout, as a percentage of the eligible voting population, in each state for the 1996 presidential election. (Official data for the 2000 presidential election is not available until 2004.)

Interpreting the Map

1. Do you see any patterns in the voting rates? Describe them.
2. Identify some reasons for the distribution of rates.
3. What should be done to increase voter turnout rates?

Source: Federal Election Commission, http//www.fec.gov. January 2000.

Functionalists think that pluralism based on the existence of diverse *interest groups* best describes the distribution of power in America. While recognizing competition among interest groups, functionalists contend that it is based on an underlying consensus regarding the goals of the entire society. Elitism is based on the conflict perspective. This theory of power distribution assumes that the elites are constantly working to maintain their hold on society's major institutions. In so doing, elites force others to help them reach their own goals. These two models are illustrated in Figure 13.3.

Functionalist Perspective: Pluralism

According to pluralists, major political decisions in the United States are not made by an elite few. As an example, they point to the beneficiaries of the 2001 tax-cut bill. Tax breaks came not only to the wealthy, such as Microsoft's Bill Gates, but also to groups with more modest resources, such as churches and mental health care facilities.

Interdisciplinary Activity

Political Science Help students consider the differences between political parties and interest groups. Can students suggest some interest groups that might attract members of both major political parties? How do you imagine active party members function within that interest group?

If students are unsure of the importance of interest groups, have them locate a copy of the current *Encyclopedia of Associations* to find organizations that are relevant to student interests. Tell students to list five

Figure 13.3 Focus on Theoretical Perspectives

Characteristics of Two Models of Political Power. This table illustrates the way the functionalist and conflict perspectives view political power. Several key features of the political system are compared. Which theory do you think best describes power in the U.S.? Explain.

Characteristics	FUNCTIONALIST PERSPECTIVE (Pluralist Model)	CONFLICT PERSPECTIVE (Power Elite Model)
Who exercises power?	Bargaining and compromising interest groups	National political, economic, and military leaders
What is the source of power?	Resources of interest groups	Leadership positions in major institutions
Where is power located?	Spread widely among interest groups	Concentrated in hands of elites
How much influence do nonelites have?	Nonelites have considerable influence on public policy	Nonelites have very little influence on public policy
What is the basis for public policy decisions?	Goals and values are shared by the general public	Preferences of the elites

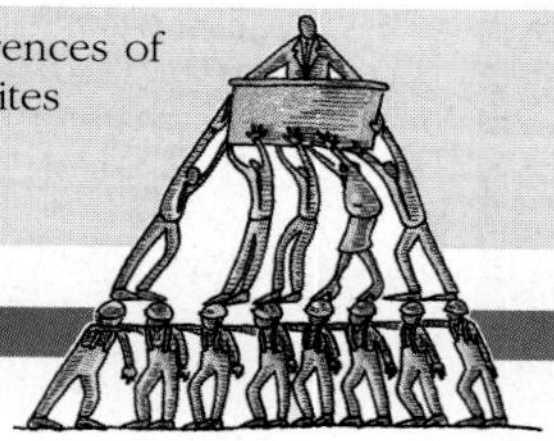

An **interest group** is a group organized to influence political decision making. Group members share one or more goals. The goals may be specific to the group's own members—as in the case of the National Rifle Association—or may involve a larger segment of society—as in the case of ecology-oriented groups such as the Sierra Club—Figure 13.4 on page 438 lists several current interest groups, sizes, and issues.

interest group
a group organized to influence political decision making

Pluralists contend that decisions are made as a result of competition among special interest groups, each of which has its own stake in the issues. In addition to reaching their own ends, interest groups try to protect themselves from opposing interest groups. Responsibility falls to government leaders to balance the public welfare with the desires of various special interests.

Interest groups are not new to American politics. In the nineteenth century they were active in extending women's rights and promoting the abolition of slavery. The twentieth century saw such active interest groups as the Women's Christian Temperance Union and early labor unions. The 1960s, with controversies surrounding civil rights, the Vietnam War, the environment, the women's movement, and corporate power, strengthened many interest groups and led to the creation of a number of new ones (Clemens, 1997).

Working with the Data

Figure 13.3 Students who answer that the functionalist perspective dominates will tend to be those who see the process as democratic, with all citizens having a say in how the government is run. Those that take the conflict perspective will say that a few powerful people run the government and the general public has little say.

Teaching Strategy

Ask students to identify high school and youth oriented interest groups. Students Against Drunk Driving is an example. Have students identify the key issues for these interest groups and the impact that they have on initiating change.
L2

interest groups that represent their political, social, or economic interests. Then have the students research one group and report their findings to their classmates. Tell the class that their reports should answer the following questions: In what way does this group represent your interests? How does this group promote its ideas? Do you think this group is effective? Why or why not?
L2

Working with the Data

Figure 13.4 Students' responses to whether they believe interest groups promote or hinder democracy will vary. However, if they believe interest groups promote democracy they should cite the functionalist perspective, which sees power as being spread among bargaining and compromising interest groups. If students believe interest groups hinder democracy, they should cite the conflict perspective, which sees power as being in the hands of political, economic, and military leaders.

Teaching Strategy

Ask some students to research the Women's Temperance Movement. Why were they so influential in bringing about the passage of the Volsted Act (Prohibition) of 1919? Have them try to relate this to contemporary interest groups with similar agendas. L2

Types of Interest Groups

	Organization	Membership	Objectives
ECONOMIC GROUPS	**Business**		
	U.S. Chamber of Commerce	200,000 medium and small businesses	Lobby for businesses
	National Association of Home Builders	200,000 members	Work for a friendly regulatory environment for the housing industry
	Agricultural		
	National Farmers Union	300,000 farm and ranch families	Represent family farms
	American Farm Bureau Federation	3 million members	Lobby for agribusiness and owners of large farms
	Professional		
	American Medical Association (AMA)	271,000 members	Oppose government involvement in medical practices
	American Bar Association (ABA)	360,000 members	Protect rights of U.S. citizens
	Labor		
	AFL–CIO	Over 100 affiliated unions (14 million members)	Protect members from unfair labor practices
	United Mine Workers	130,000 members	Advance the goals of mine workers
NON-ECONOMIC GROUPS	**Public Interest**		
	League of Women Voters (LWV)	1,100 local leagues; 130,000 members and supporters	Simplify voter registration
	Common Cause	265,000 members	Advocate political reform
	Public Citizen	100,000 members	Focus on consumer issues
	Single-Issue		
	Sierra Club	550,000 members	Protect scenic areas
	National Audubon Society	550,000 members	Restore natural ecosystems
	Greenpeace USA	2,100,000 members	Protect the environment
	Ideological		
	Americans for Democratic Action (ADA)	65,000 members	Support liberal social, economic, and foreign policies
	Christian Coalition	2,000,000 members	Promote Christian values
	National Organization of Women (NOW)	250,000 members	Protect the rights of women

Figure 13.4 Types of Interest Groups. *The United States government is influenced by a wide variety of interest groups. This figure provides some examples of the most important types. Do you believe that the influence of all these interest groups promotes or hinders democracy? Explain your answers, using conflict theory or functionalism.*

Using Problem-Solving Skills

Read the following to students.

One privilege of living in a democratic country is the choice of whether or not to participate in the political process through voting. Voting, then, offers citizens a voice about a variety of situations such as the removal of corrupt officials, incompetent legislators, enactment of new laws devised to increase safety and security to school students, tax incentives, humanitarian assistance, or educational reforms, to name just a few.

In the past, the U.S. government decided against involvement in the tribal warfare be-

New interest groups are born all the time. The environmental lobby is a good example. There were relatively few environmental interest groups before the passage of major environmental legislation (such as the Clean Water Act) in the 1960s. The success of this legislation spawned additional groups, now numbering three times the original total. This added clout produced additional environmental legislation—for example, the 1990 Clean Air Act Amendments—that subsequently led to the creation of other interest groups (Schmidt, Shelly, and Bardes, 1999).

Conflict Perspective: The Power Elite

Sociologist C. Wright Mills was a leading proponent of the elitist perspective. In the 1950s, he claimed that the United States no longer had separate economic, political, and military leaders. Rather, the key people in each area overlapped to form a unified group that he labeled the **power elite.**

power elite
a unified group of military, corporate, and government leaders

According to Mills, members of the power elite share common interests and similar social and economic backgrounds. Elites are educated in select boarding schools, military academies, and Ivy League schools; belong to the Episcopalian and Presbyterian churches; and come from upper-class families. Members of the power elite have known each other for a long time, have mutual acquaintances of long standing, share many values and attitudes, and intermarry. All this makes it easier for them to coordinate their actions to obtain what they want.

Section 2 Assessment

1. What are the major agents of political socialization?
2. How do elitists differ from pluralists in explaining the relationship between racial membership and political power in the U.S.?
3. According to C. Wright Mills, which of the following is NOT part of the power elite?
   a. military organizations
   b. educational leaders
   c. large corporations
   d. executive branch of the government

Critical Thinking

4. **Analyzing Information** On page 435, the author writes: "Members of minorities, people with little education, and people with smaller incomes are less likely to vote in both congressional and presidential elections." Do you think that pluralists or elitists are more likely to use advertising to change the political attitudes of individuals in these social categories? Explain.
5. **Drawing Conclusions** Is America a pluralist society, or is it controlled by a power elite? Support your conclusion with information from this text and other classes.

"The ballot is stronger than the bullet."

Abraham Lincoln
U. S. president

Answers to Section 2 Assessment

1. The major agents of informal political socialization are the family, education, mass media, economic status and occupations, and age and gender.
2. In pluralism, political decisions are the result of bargaining and compromise among special interest groups. No one group holds the majority of power. Rather, power is widely distributed throughout a society or community. In elitism, a community or society is controlled from the top by a few individuals or organizations. Power is concentrated in the hands of an elite group whose members have common interests and backgrounds.
3. d

Critical Thinking

4. Since pluralists believe that political decision making is formed through interest groups, they would be more likely to use propaganda to encourage people in these social categories to become politically engaged. Elitists, who contend that political decisions are made by an elect few, would see no need to influence the political attitudes of people in these social categories because their input does not count.
5. Answers will vary and should be supported with information from the text and other classes.

tween the Hutu and Tutsi tribes. Over 100,000 Hutu's died. However, our military peacekeepers became involved in Kosovo and took a stand against ethnic cleansing.

Now have students use the problem-solving process to determine the force and focus of political power in America. Is the emphasis on economic or political innuendo rather than humanitarianism? Have them draft and organize a petition to be sent to the United States Congress either supporting or opposing our intervention policies.
L3

Using the Section Preview

Emphasize that the functionalist perspective would view capitalism as a means of maintaining the order and stability of society. A conflict theorist would cite Marx, stating that the capitalists exploit the workers for their own economic gain. Refer back to Chapter 1 to review Marx's beliefs on capitalism. Be sure that students can draw parallels between the bourgeoisie and proletariat and the middle and working classes of American society.

Section 3

Economic Systems

Key Terms

- capitalism
- monopolies
- oligopolies
- socialism

Section Preview

Capitalist economies are based on private property and the pursuit of profit, and government, in theory, plays a minor role in regulating industry. In socialist economies, the means of production are owned collectively, and government has an active role in planning and controlling the economy.

capitalism
an economic system based on private ownership of property and the pursuit of profit

monopolies
companies that have control over the production or distribution of a product or service

oligopolies
combinations of companies that control the production or distribution of a product or service

Capitalism

Economic systems, as suggested earlier, involve the production and distribution of goods and services. **Capitalism** is an economic system founded on two basic premises: the sanctity of private property and the right of individuals to profit from their labors.

Capitalists believe that individuals, not government, deserve to own and to control land, factories, raw materials, and the tools of production. They argue that private ownership benefits society. Capitalists also believe in unrestricted competition with minimum government interference.

How is capitalism thought to benefit society? According to Adam Smith, an eighteenth-century Scottish social philosopher and founder of economics, a combination of the private ownership of property and the pursuit of profit brings advantages to society. Because of competition, Smith stated, individual capitalists will always be motivated to provide the goods and services desired by the public at prices the public is willing and able to pay. Capitalists who produce inferior goods or who charge too much will soon be out of business because the public will turn to their competitors. The public, Smith reasoned, will benefit through economic competition. Not only will the public receive high-quality goods and services at reasonable prices, but also capitalists will always be searching for new products and new technologies to reduce their costs. As a result, capitalist societies will use resources efficiently.

Actually, no pure capitalist economy exists in the world. In practice, there are important deviations from Smith's ideal model. One of these deviations involves the tendency to form *monopolies* and *oligopolies*.

What are monopolies and oligopolies? When capitalist organizations experience success, they tend to grow until they become giants within their particular industries. In this way, capitalism fosters the rise of **monopolies,** companies that control a particular market, and **oligopolies,** combinations of companies working together to control a market. New organizations find it difficult to enter these markets, where they have little hope of competing on an equal basis. Thus, competition is stifled.

Among other problems, the creation of monopolies and oligopolies permits price fixing. Consumers must choose between buying at the "going price" set by the sellers or not buying at all.

A recent example of monopolistic practices in the U.S. economy involves the Microsoft Corporation. Microsoft manufactures, among other products, the Windows operating system—by far the most popular operating system for

Integrating the Teacher Resources

Look for the Alternative Assessments booklet in your Teacher's Resource Box for essay tests and performance assessment activities based on this chapter.

Paired Learning Activity

Reread with students the third paragraph on this page (beginning with "How is capitalism thought to benefit society?"). Ask students if capitalism is a good thing. Can it ever be a bad thing? What happens to companies that can't compete with larger competitors? Is this always fair? Discuss with students how many small "mom and pop" stores and businesses are being hurt or even put out of business by larger chain stores because the chains can sell items at a lower cost to the consumer. Ask again if this is fair. Why do students feel the way they do? It is always most important to get the best deal for your dollar? Have students work together in pairs to write a paper that answers the opening question, "How is capitalism thought to benefit society?" Also have them explain how capitalism can hurt society. Ask for volunteers to share their papers.
L2

personal computers. Computer manufacturers typically include Windows on the machines they sell. In the 1990s, Microsoft began to insist that manufacturers include its Internet browser, Explorer, on their computers as well. The manufacturers were also instructed not to install another browser in addition to Explorer. If they refused, Microsoft would withhold their license to sell Windows on the machines. Because Microsoft had so much power over computer manufacturers, other makers of Internet browsers, such as Netscape, were essentially excluded from the market (Chandbasekaran, 1999). Eventually, the federal government took Microsoft to court, where it was ruled that Microsoft did indeed engage in monopolistic practices. Not surprisingly, the corporation had some success in its 2001 appeal of this decision.

The enormous success of Bill Gates and Microsoft led to a federal investigation of the software giant's business practices.

The Role of Government in Capitalism

Adam Smith is often misinterpreted as saying that government should have a strictly hands-off approach where the economy is concerned. While Smith strongly opposed overregulation by government, he reserved a place for some regulation. Because one of the legitimate roles of government was to protect its citizens from injustice, Smith knew that the state might have to "step in" to prevent abuses by businesses. In fact, the U.S. government has always been involved in the workings of the economy.

How does the government contribute to the U.S. economy? The Constitution expressly provided a role for the national government in the promotion of a sound economy. Government functions include the regulation of

The Federal Aviation Authority (FAA) conducts jetliner crash tests as part of the federal government's authority over private business. In what way might cultural values promote such government involvement?

Using the Illustration

Answers to the caption question will vary but should provoke discussion and reflect differences in the role of government in capitalist and socialist societies.

Interdisciplinary Activity

History At certain times in U.S. history, the federal government has played a key role in directing the economy. Have students look in a history book for information about the role of government during the Great Depression and about Franklin Delano Roosevelt's New Deal programs. Some students might also want to research social issues related to the Great Depression to see how the economic institution affected all avenues of life. Some areas to examine might be juvenile delinquency, divorce, crime, poverty, etc. **L2**

Working with the Data

Figure 13.5 Adam Smith would probably think that the government is too involved in the U.S. economy. Ask students if they would agree. Go over each item in the chart with students and ask how things would be different if the government was not involved. Do students think things would be better or worse? Why?

More About . . . Socialism

In the first half of the nineteenth century, the pitiful conditions found in the slums, mines, and factories created by the Industrial Revolution gave rise to the movement known as socialism. Early socialism was largely the product of intellectuals who believed in the equality of all people and who wanted to replace competition with cooperation in industry. To later socialists, especially the followers of Karl Marx, such ideas were merely impractical dreams. The later socialists, in contempt of the earlier theorists, labeled them utopian socialists.

Figure 13.5 Examples of Government and Regulatory Assistance

The government is extensively involved in the U.S. economy. What would Adam Smith say about this?

Public utilities are often owned and operated by state or local governments.
The agricultural industry feels the influence of government through price controls and embargoes on exports to other countries.
Antitrust legislation exists to control the growth of corporations.
The federal government is heavily involved in the defense industry.
Business could not survive without publicly financed roadways, airports, and waterways.
Publicly funded public schools, colleges, and universities supply business with a skilled workforce and provide basic research for product development.
The U.S. military protects American international business interests.
Government supports business through tax breaks.
Legislation requires labor and business to obey labor laws.

commerce, development of a strong currency, creation of uniform standards for commerce, and the provision of a stable system of credit. In 1789, Congress supported our shipping industry through a tariff on goods imported by foreign ships. Since this initial move into the economy, the federal government has continued to help business, labor, and agriculture. For example, the federal government aids private industry through loan guarantees—as in the 1980s government guarantee (up to $1.5 billion) to bail out the Chrysler Corporation. Also, U.S. labor is strengthened by the government through regulations on such matters as minimum wages, maximum working hours, health and safety conditions, and unemployment support. Then there are the small farmers and agribusinesses that receive financial assistance amounting to billions of dollars each year (Patterson, 1999). See Figure 13.5 for additional examples of government economic and regulatory assistance.

socialism
an economic system founded on the belief that the means of production should be controlled by the people as a whole

Socialism

Socialism is an economic system founded on the belief that the means of production should be controlled by the people as a whole. The state, as the people's representative, should own and control property. Under a socialist system, government directs and controls the economy. The state is expected to ensure all members of society a share in the monetary benefits.

Interdisciplinary Activity

History Marxist thought dominated the world scene for most of the twentieth century. (Remind students that Karl Marx developed the theory of public ownership of the means of production.) Communism, the antithesis of capitalism, would form the basis for much of the hysteria that drove United States foreign policy during the Cold War. (You might explain to students that communism is one form of Marxist socialism.) Communism contributed an ideological edge to the existing military threat of the

How is socialism thought to benefit society? Socialist theory points to important benefits for workers. Workers under capitalism receive wages below the value their labor produces and have little control over their work. In theory, workers under socialism should profit because both the state and the workplace exist for their benefit. As a result, workers should be able to exert significant control over both their work organizations and the policy directions of the society as a whole.

Does socialism work this perfectly? Cases of pure socialism are as rare as cases of pure capitalism. Strict socialist systems have not been successful in eliminating income inequalities nor have they been able to develop overall economic plans that guarantee sustained economic growth. In the socialistic economy of the former Soviet Union, for example, some agricultural and professional work was performed privately by individuals who worked for a profit. Significant portions of housing were privately owned as well. Managers received salaries that were considerably higher than those received by workers, and managers were eligible for bonuses such as automobiles and housing. Private enterprise existed in Poland under Russian communist rule. Service businesses, such as restaurants and hotels, had a significant degree of private ownership. Hotels, in fact, were typically built and managed by multinational chains. Because Poles could travel abroad, they formed business relationships, learned about capitalist methods, imported goods to fill demand, and brought back hard currency. They then used the hard currency earned abroad to create private businesses (Schnitzer, 2000).

"Socialism works, but nowhere as efficiently as in the beehive and the anthill."

Laurence Peter
U. S. business writer

Sweden has a socialist government. What types of market relationships would you expect to find there?

Working with the Quote

Ask students to explain what they think the quote means. Do they think Peter is being supportive or critical of socialism? How is socialism exhibited in the beehive and ant hill? Who controls the means of production in a beehive? Who controls it in an ant hill?

Share this quote by Robert L. Heilbroner (*Reflections: The Triumph of Capitalism,* in the *New Yorker*, January 23, 1989) with students. "Less than seventy-five years after it officially began, the contest between capitalism and socialism is over: capitalism has won." Ask students if they agree with the quote. Why or why not?

Integrating the Teacher Resources

For review or enrichment, use the Student Journal Prompts for this chapter, available in the Unit 4 Mastering Basic Concepts booklet in your Teacher's Resource Box.

Soviet Union after World War II. After the Revolution of 1917, the United States experienced no less than two "Red Scares," when constitutional freedoms were revoked to protect the country from the "evils" of communism. Most Americans understood the fear, but had little understanding of what communism actually was.

If you have the opportunity, you might ask one of your school's history teachers to talk with your class about socialism and communism in the history of the world.
L1

As this Shanghai Kentucky Fried Chicken restaurant reflects, elements of capitalism are being introduced into China.

Mixed Economic Systems

Most nations fall between the extremes of capitalism and socialism and include elements of both economic systems. Countries in Western Europe, for example, have developed capitalist economic systems in which both public and private ownership play important roles. In these nations, highly strategic industries (banks, transportation, communications, and some others) are owned and operated by the state. Other industries are privately owned but are more closely regulated than in the United States (Harris, 1997; Ollman, 1998).

As the former Soviet Union lost control over its republics and Eastern Europe, many of these formerly socialist countries began to move toward capitalism. Czechoslovakia, in several ways, has shifted from public to private ownership of businesses. Private property nationalized after the Russians took over in 1948 has been returned to the original owners or their heirs. These assets moved from the public to the private sector are valued at about $5 billion. Many small shops and businesses have been sold in public auctions. In 1992, Czechoslovakia sold over 1,000 of its bigger state enterprises to its citizens. During 1992–93 as it broke into the Czech Republic and Slovakia, 25 percent of the nations' assets were privatized. In Hungary, state-owned enterprises have been allowed to become privately owned companies. Over one million Hungarians have been given the right to buy land, businesses, buildings, or other property taken over by the Russians in 1949. Nearly all of the state-owned small businesses are now in the hands of private owners. Agricultural cooperatives have also been privatized (Schnitzer, 2000).

In 1991, Cuba's communist party allowed some degree of capitalism by permitting plumbers, carpenters, and other tradespeople to work for profit. China has been incorporating moderate free market reforms into its economy since the late 1970s (Muldavin, 1999).

Section 3 Assessment

1. Government policies are usually based on cultural values. Can you identify important differences in the cultural values underlying governmental policies that promote either capitalism or socialism?
2. How successful has socialism been as an economic system? Defend your answer.
3. What is meant by a mixed economic system?

Critical Thinking

4. **Making Comparisons** Briefly compare and contrast the advantages of capitalism and socialism.

Pulling it All Together

Economic systems such as capitalism, socialism, and mixed economic systems were the focus of this section.

Answers to Section 3 Assessment

1. Underlying government policies promoting capitalism are private property rights and the right to profit from one's own efforts. Government policies in a socialistic economic system reflect cultural values such as public ownership of property, worker control of the economy, and widespread sharing of economic benefits.
2. Socialism has not been successful as an economic system. It has failed to eliminate economic inequalities and has not developed overall economic plans that guarantee sustained growth.
3. A mixed economic system is one that includes elements of more than one economic system, i.e., socialism where some private ownership (capitalism) is allowed.

Critical Thinking

4. Answers will vary.

Survey

Over the past few years, the Internet has come to play a big part in the world in which we live. As mentioned in "Tech Trends," the Internet is a great tool for dispensing information. But is the information always accurate? How can we know? How much faith does the public put into the information dispensed on the Internet?

Help your students develop a survey to solicit answers to some of these questions from their peers, parents, and others. The survey should have a question about age (it will be interesting to note if there are differences in answers according to age). Other

Tech Trends

Cybernews and Democracy

Reporting the news has been part of the United States since its founding. Indeed, freedom of the press is one of the basic guarantees of the Bill of Rights. During the twentieth century, television displaced newspapers as the primary source of news for most Americans. Now, the Internet is promising to make much greater changes in the way news is gathered and delivered.

Central to the changes is the fact that today anyone with access to the Internet is free to "report" the news. Internet journalist Matt Drudge says that now, "any citizen can be a reporter" (Trigaboff, 1998:55). Drudge portrays the Internet as a democratizing institution eliminating differences between reporters and readers.

Many journalists, however, worry about the negative effects of instant reporting via the Internet. Sources for stories often go unchecked as reporters sacrifice accuracy for speed. Reporters on the Internet generally do not have editors reviewing their stories, in-house attorneys worrying about lawsuits, or publishers making judgment calls about the appropriateness of news stories. Joseph C. Goulden, director of media analysis for Accuracy in Media, a nonprofit, grassroots citizens watchdog of the news media, describes the reporting style on the Internet as "Ready, fire, aim" (Rust and Danitz, 1998:23).

In the United States, one of the justifications for the freedom of the press is its role in delivering accurate information to voters. If Internet reporting represents a trend toward greater inaccuracy, this traditional contribution of a free press to American democracy could be weakened. What if voters grew to distrust even more the information they received and thus became increasingly cynical about the political process?

At this time no one can be sure what the future holds for Internet journalism. One thing, though, is certain: Internet journalism will have a profound impact on the way news is reported (Kinsley, 1998).

Matt Drudge became the symbol of Internet news reporting in the late 1990s. Is Internet journalism good or bad for democracy?

Analyzing the Trends

There is no question that the Internet will affect how democracy is practiced in the U.S. Discuss some ways in which the federal government currently uses the Internet to affect group behavior.

Tech Trends

You might want to focus on the question posed in the article: What if voters grew to distrust even more the information they received and thus became increasingly cynical about the political process? Students might want to think of options. Should campaigns be focused around ethical considerations that prevent back stabbing and name calling and focus strictly on the issues?

Answer to Analyzing the Trends

Answers will vary. This is an excellent opportunity to have students (perhaps in groups) go online to find specific examples.

Integrating the Teacher Resources

Look for Ethics, Values, and Technology: Real-Life Issues in Society, available in your Teacher's Resource Box. The booklet provides primary source readings dealing with real-life controversies. Student worksheets are included.

questions might include: Do you use the Internet to research information? On a scale of 1 to 10, with 1 being not very trustworthy and 10 being very trustworthy, how would you rate the information you find on the Internet? An open-ended question you might ask is how can they tell if the information is accurate.

Have the class analyze the results. What trends, if any, do they see? Do the answers differ according to age? Why do students think this is the case? What conclusions might they draw from this limited survey? **L2**

Using the Section Preview

Students will be interested in looking at Forbes magazine's list of the top 100 companies in America. This information can be accessed from the Forbes website: **www.forbes.com**. Students might want to look at the nature of business conducted by these top corporations. They should see if one industry dominates the list, and compare this to what industries used to dominate the economy in previous years. They might also want to pick one company on the list and research it.

More About . . . the Power Elite

A recent book, *Diversity in the Power Elite,* examines the extent to which the power elite has diversified in gender and race. Although women and minorities have made inroads in the power elite, research found that women and blacks that sit on corporate boards usually sit on the boards of several different organizations. This is consistent with the text's explanation of interlocking webs among powerful corporations. However, it also indicates that women and minorities have made fewer gains than might appear initially, since only a handful of women and minorities are in these power positions.

Section 4 The Modern Corporation

Key Terms

- corporation
- interlocking directorates
- conglomerates
- multinationals

Section Preview

Corporations, especially those with multinational connections, have grown very powerful. Corporate managers affect domestic political decision making and influence the political and economic institutions of countries around the world.

corporation
an organization owned by shareholders, who have limited liability and limited control

The Nature of Corporations

Sociologists study corporations because of their great importance in modern economic systems. U.S. corporations, for example, not only dominate the American economic system but also influence the economies of nations around the world. Corporations represent massive concentrations of wealth. And because of their economic muscle, corporations such as Microsoft, IBM, and General Electric command the attention of government decision makers. As a result, government policies regarding such matters as consumer safety, tax laws, and relationships with other nations usually reflect corporate influence.

What are corporations, anyway? A **corporation** is an organization owned by shareholders. These shareholders have *limited liability* and *limited control.* Limited liability means they cannot be held financially responsible for actions of the corporation. For example, shareholders are not expected to pay debts the corporation owes. At the same time, they do not have a direct voice in the day-to-day operations of the firm. Shareholders are formally entitled to vote regularly for members of the board of directors. But in practice candidates are routinely approved as recommended by the existing board. The real control of a corporation rests with the board of directors and management.

Corporate Influence

Top corporate officials have tremendous influence on government decisions. This is true for several reasons. Because of their personal wealth and organizational connections, corporate officials are able to reward or punish elected government officials through investment decisions. For example, suppose a town depends on a single large corporation for jobs and other economic advantages. Corporate officials are deciding whether to increase their operation in this town or move some of the facilities to another town, which would endanger local jobs. Town officials are likely to do what they can to make corporate officials happy so that new investment will be made locally.

This agricultural worker is paid by a large corporation rather than a small business/farmer. Which employer would be more secure?

Cooperative Learning Activity

Many of the richest people in the world also make significant contributions to charities and foundations. Have students work in groups to research Andrew Carnegie, William D. Rockefeller, and more recent examples such as Bill Gates and Donald Trump. Ask students to report back to the class on the numerous charitable organization and foundations that benefit from their wealth.
L1

In what other ways do corporations wield power? Such political clout by large corporations is multiplied through **interlocking directorates.** A directorate is another name for the board of directors. Directorates interlock when the heads of corporations sit on one another's boards. Although by law competing corporations may not have interlocking directorates, such directorates are legal for noncompeting corporations. For example, various members of the General Motors board of directors also sit on the boards of many other corporations, including Eastman Kodak, Bristol-Myers, Squibb, and Merck and Company. It is not difficult to imagine the political power created by a web of interlocks among already powerful corporations.

interlocking directorates
directorates that result when heads of corporations sit on one another's boards

The political power of corporations is also enhanced through **conglomerates**—networks of unrelated businesses operating under a single corporate umbrella. RJR Nabisco, Inc., for example, holds companies in such different areas as tobacco, pet foods, candy, cigarettes, food products, bubble gum, research, and technology. A listing of the company's North American subsidiaries covers nearly an entire page in *Who Owns Whom* (1998).

conglomerates
networks of unrelated businesses operating under one corporate umbrella

multinationals
firms based in highly industrialized societies with operating facilities throughout the world

Multinational Corporations

The political influence of corporations is not confined to their countries of origin. The world is increasingly being influenced by **multinationals**—firms based in highly industrialized societies with operating facilities throughout the world. Improvements in communication and transportation technology have allowed these companies to exert wide control over their global operations.

How powerful are multinational corporations? Suppose we combined all the political and economic units in the world and then chose the hundred largest units. Of these hundred units, fifty-one would be multinational corporations rather than countries. Several corporations based in the United States—ExxonMobil, IBM, General Motors, Ford Motor Company, AT&T, Wal-Mart Stores, and General Electric—have sales volumes exceeding the annual economic output of some industrialized nations. Figure 13.6 compares some multinational corporations with selected nations.

Wal-Mart Stores, Inc. $119.3 Billion	vs.	Greece $119.1 Billion
Volkswagen AG $65.3 Billion	vs.	New Zealand $65 Billion
IBM International Business Machines Corp. $78.5 Billion	vs.	Egypt $75.5 Billion
Mitsubishi Corporation $128.9 Billion	vs.	South Africa $129.1 Billion
Sony Corporation $55 Billion	vs.	Czech Republic $54.9 Billion
General Electric Company $90.8 Billion	vs.	Israel $92 Billion

Figure 13.6 Total Revenue of Multinational Corporations versus National Gross Domestic Products. *This table compares the revenue of selected multinational corporations to the gross domestic product (value of all goods produced and consumed domestically) of some countries. Were you surprised by any of the information?*
Source: "Multinational Corporations," *Foreign Policy,* 113 (Winter, 1998–99).

What are the effects of multinational corporations? Defenders of multinationals argue that the corporations provide developing countries with technology, capital, foreign markets, and products that would otherwise be unavailable to them. Critics claim that multinationals actually harm the economies of the foreign nations in which they locate by exploiting natural resources, disrupting local economies, introducing inappropriate technologies and products, and increasing the

Making Connections to Other Cultures

Have students brainstorm, or provide for them, a list of well-known corporate names in categories such as cars, clothing, foods, beverages, electronics, and restaurant chains. Assign teams of students the task of searching the Internet for specific companies in each category. They should bring back to class for show and tell at least: 1) a printout of the parent company's home page, 2) a list of, or map showing, the countries that the company is active in, and 3) one printout related to the company that they just felt was interesting.

After students have shown and told what they found out about the companies, post the results of their efforts and have them write about: 1) what new knowledge they learned from the activity, and 2) what questions that new knowledge raises about political and economic institutions.
L2

Working with the Data

Figure 13.6 There are a number of individual companies that have a total revenue greater than the gross domestic product of many countries.

Survey

Have students compose lists of large chain stores in your area such as Barnes and Noble, Home Depot, Wal-Mart, etc. Ask students if they know of any smaller, family-owned operations in your area being driven out of business by these large chains. Discuss what this means in terms of the American Dream and the future. Students might want to survey or interview small business owners for their reactions to these changes in society.
L2

Sociology Today

Historical reasons for laws in regard to employee rights might make for some interesting research projects. For example, protectionism laws at the turn of the century reduced the number of hours that women could work so that they would be better suited for motherhood. These same laws today would be viewed as Anti-Constitutional and discriminatory. Students might want to research such laws and their social implications.

Answers to Doing Sociology

1. Answers will vary.
2. This could make for interesting discussion. Students might want to share their parents' answers with the class. Ask students if they think the kind of job a person has influences the amount of employee rights. Are higher-status, better-paying jobs necessarily guaranteeing more employee rights?

Sociology Today: Employee Rights

The Supreme Court of the United States has historically granted employers a great deal of power over their employees. In 1878, a New York company posted a list of rules that told employees, among other things, "On the Sabbath, everyone is expected to be in the Lord's House" and "All employees are expected to be in bed by 10:00 P.M." At the turn of the nineteenth century, Henry Ford's automobile workers were carefully watched by management for signs of bad character. Many Ford Motor Company employees lost their jobs for smoking, drinking, or criticizing the firm.

Even today, some employee rights are curtailed at work. The Constitution, for example, protects free speech for all citizens. Employees, however, can be prevented from printing and distributing a critical newsletter to customers of their companies. Of recent concern is the right of employers to track workers' movements on the Internet and to read personal e-mails.

Today, a growing employee rights movement is pushing for greater political and legal protection on the job. Here is a partial list of the rights that many workers feel should be theirs today.

- the right to a job
- the right to protection from arbitrary or sudden termination
- the right to privacy of possessions and person in the workplace, including freedom from arbitrary searches, use of polygraphs, surreptitious surveillance, and intrusive psychological or medical testing
- the right to a clean, healthy, and safe environment on the job, including freedom from undue stress, sexual harassment, cigarette smoke, and exposure to toxic substances
- the right to be informed of records and information kept and to have access to personnel files
- the right to freedom of action, association, and lifestyle when off duty
- the right to freedom of conscience and to inform government or media about illegal or socially harmful corporate actions
- the right to due process for grievances against the employer

Many of these rights already exist; others need to be discussed with employers. There is one thing most employees and employers agree on, however. If employees take a balanced approach to pursuing their rights on the job, both individuals and organizations will benefit.

Doing Sociology

1. Some observers believe that violations of employee rights contradict the rational-legal basis of organizational authority. Do you agree? Why or why not?
2. Discuss the above list of workers' rights with your parents or other adults who work outside the home. Ask them if they know whether or not these rights exist in their workplaces. Are there any rights not on the list that they believe should be added?

Careers in Sociology

See if students can answer this question: What are some of the sociological careers dealing with political and economic institutions?

After they've offered some answers, share these answers with them.

- **Foreign service officers** work in foreign service posts to represent and administer United States embassies and foreign service programs.
- **Intelligence officers** research and analyze a diversity of geopolitical issues on behalf of the government. They are employed by intelligence services such as the Federal Bureau of Investigation (F.B.I.), the Central Intelligence Agency (C.I.A.), the National Security Agency, and military intelligence agencies.
- **Legislative aides** perform research, writing and liaison functions for a state or

Some multinationals are so successful that their products are widely (and illegally) copied. Here, a "faked" Nike athletic shoe is readied for sale in Shanghai, China.

> The modern corporation is a political institution; its purpose is the creation of legitimate power in the industrial hemisphere.
>
> **Peter Drucker**
> **management author**

amount of income inequality. Multinationals, these critics note, rely on inexpensive labor or abundant raw materials in developing nations while returning their profits to corporate headquarters and shareholders in rich nations. Multinationals' domination of their industries has made it difficult for the economically developing nations to establish new companies that can compete with the multinationals. As a result, multinationals may slow rather than promote economic development in these nations.

Section 4 Assessment

1. Discuss limited liability and limited control in relation to the modern corporation.
2. Describe the influence of the corporation in the world today. Identify some of the benefits and negative consequences for society.

Critical Thinking

3. **Drawing Conclusions** Would you rather work for a large, multinational corporation or for yourself as an independent businessperson? Explain your choice.

Answers to Section 4 Assessment

1. Shareholders (owners of a corporation) have limited liability, which means they cannot be held financially responsible for actions of the corporation—they are not expected to pay a corporation's debts—but with this limited liability, shareholders have limited control. This means they do not have a direct voice in the day-to-day operations of the firm and, though they are formally entitled to vote for members of the board of directors, usually candidates are approved as recommended by the existing board. Therefore, real control rests with the board of directors and management.
2. Because of their economic muscle, large corporations command the attention of, and are therefore able to influence, government decision makers. Government policies, including relationships with other countries, reflect corporate influence. Answers will vary concerning benefits and negative consequences for society.

Critical Thinking

3. Answers will vary.

U.S. senator or congressional representative or a municipal officeholder. Positions are typically secured through direct contact with an officeholder.

- **Lobbying organizers** distribute materials and disseminate information about a particular issue or organization, recruit volunteers, solicit funds, and organize such efforts as rallies, letter-writing campaigns, and voter registration drives.

Employers include special and public interest groups and professional lobbyists.

For information on how to get an entry-level job, check out **http://www.college-grad.com/**

Using the Section Preview

Over one quarter of the jobs in the United Sates pay less than a living wage of $8 an hour. Several companies are trying to rectify this. Students might want to visit the web site **www.responsiblewealth.org** for insights into the problem and for the names of companies that are attempting to offer employees a decent living wage.

Teaching Strategy

If you have students who work, ask them to tell the class about their worst work experiences. Responses will likely include complaints about monotony, lack of responsibility, problems with peers, attitude of the boss, and poor pay. Marx identified four dimensions to worker alienation: 1) the product of labor; 2) the process of labor; 3) others; and 4) the self. Have students relate these concepts to the examples they provided.
L2

Section 5 Work in the Modern Economy

Key Terms

- primary sector
- secondary sector
- tertiary sector
- occupations
- core tier
- peripheral tier
- downsizing
- contingent employment

Section Preview

Workers today face a changing job structure. More corporations are downsizing and replacing full-time employees with consultants or temporary workers. Evidence indicates that this trend is having some negative consequences.

primary sector
that part of the economy producing goods from the natural environment

secondary sector
that part of the economy engaged in manufacturing goods

tertiary sector
that part of the economy providing services

The Changing Nature of Work

To understand work in modern society you need to be familiar with the three basic economic sectors. They are *primary, secondary,* and *tertiary.*

How do the economic sectors differ? The **primary sector** of an economy depends on the natural environment to produce economic goods. The types of jobs in this sector vary widely—farmer, miner, fisherman, timber worker, rancher. In the **secondary sector,** manufactured products are made from raw materials. Occupations in this sector include factory workers of all types, from those who produce computers to those who turn out Pokémon cards. Those in the secondary sector are popularly known as blue-collar workers. Employees in the **tertiary sector** provide services. If today you went to school, filled your car with gas, stopped by the bank, and visited your doctor, you spent most of your time and someone's money in the tertiary (service) sector. Other service industries include insurance, real estate, retail sales, and entertainment. More and more people in these industries are white-collar workers.

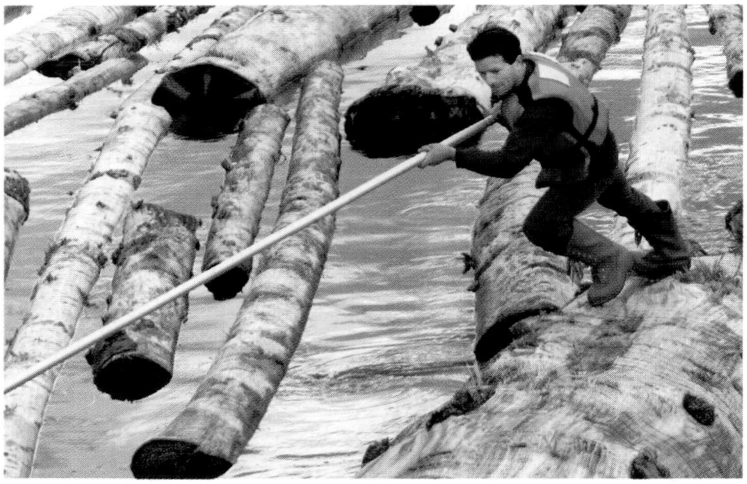

To which sector of the economy does this California logger belong?

Survey

It might be interesting for students to interview some people who have been part of the work force for a number of years. They should be able to tell students about changes they have seen in the types of jobs available and the skills and education required for those jobs.

Help students develop questions similar to the following:

- How many years have you been part of the workforce?
- Have you ever been forced to change jobs? If yes, why?

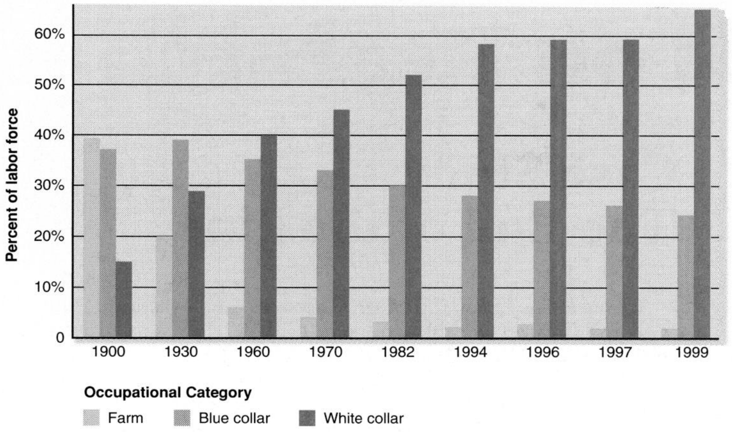

Figure 13.7 Changes in Labor Force by Occupational Category. *This figure tracks changes in the U.S. labor force from 1900 to 1999. Which labor division is growing the fastest?*

Source: U.S. Department of Labor, Bureau of Labor Statistics, 1999.

How have the three sectors changed historically? Obviously, the primary sector dominated the preindustrial economy. At that stage of economic development, physical goods were made by hand. This balance began to change with the mechanization of farming in the agricultural economy. Mechanical inventions (cotton gin, plow, tractor), along with the application of new scientific methods (seed production, fertilization, and crop rotation), drastically increased production. During the 1800s, the average farmer could feed five workers or so. Today, the figure is eighty. At the same time production increased, labor demands decreased. Primary sector workers have declined from almost 40 percent of the labor pool in 1900 to about 2 percent today.

With other technological advancements in industry (power looms, motors of all types, electrical power) came the shift of agricultural workers from farms to factories, ushering in the secondary sector. As Figure 13.7 indicates, the percentage of the U.S. labor force engaged in blue-collar jobs reached almost 40 percent in 1900.

Just as in agriculture, technological developments permitted greater production with fewer workers. Since World War II, the fastest-growing occupations in the secondary sector have been white-collar—managers, professionals, sales workers, clerical workers. In 1956, white-collar workers for the first time accounted for a larger proportion of the U.S. labor force than blue-collar workers. In manufacturing industries, the number of white-collar workers is now three times the number of blue-collar workers.

Technological progress did not stop with the secondary sector. As relative growth in the proportion of workers in goods-producing jobs was decreasing, the demand for labor in the tertiary section was increasing. Fueled by computer technology, the United States economy moved from a manufacturing base to a knowledge, or information, base. The current demand is for people who can manage information and deliver services. Today, the proportion of white-collar workers in the U.S. is about 70 percent, up from just below 30 percent in 1930. (See Figure 13.7.)

Blue-collar workers, such as the longshore workers pictured here, may be an endangered species.

Working with the Data

Figure 13.7 Since World War II, the fastest growing occupations in the secondary sector have been white collar. For the first time, in 1956, white-collar workers accounted for a larger proportion of the U.S. labor force than blue-collar workers.

Open-Response Question

If you refer students back to Chapter 5, you can relate historical events with their impact on the working world. For example, each social transformation altered the nature of work. The preindustrial age kept workers at home; the industrial age forced people to relocate to where jobs could be found; and the post-industrial age has led to a dramatic increase in the number of dual earner households. Have students relate these social forces to the lives of people living in those times.

- What changes have you seen in the work force (i.e., fewer of certain types of jobs, jobs becoming more technical, etc.)?
- Have you had to develop new skills to stay competitive in your field?
- Have you had to return for further education or training to stay competitive in your field?
- What changes do you see in the future for your field?

Have students work together to analyze the data they collect. See what conclusions they can draw from the information.
L1

Focus on Research

This is the classic example of the shift from the industrial to the postindustrial age. Have students refer back to Chapter 5. As the economy shifted from over a century of manufacturing as the principal source of production to a service sector economy, towns that had relied largely on manufacturing for jobs were devastated. This occurred most noticeably in the Northeast and the Midwest. If students live in this area, have them look for examples of how towns and cities in their areas were affected. If you live in a town or city that has witnessed an economic boom, what factors have contributed to it?

Focus on Research

Case Study: The End of the Line

Because she grew up near Chrysler's auto plant in Kenosha, Wisconsin, researcher Kathryn Marie Dudley had a special interest in studying the cultural fallout from the plant's closing in 1988. Dudley's research is a case study of a large plant in a one-industry community experiencing relocations, downsizings, and job eliminations. She offers Kenosha as a typical example of the effect of changing work patterns on midsize towns. As indicated in the excerpt below, the plant changes over the past few decades are seen as part of the shift from an industrial to a postindustrial society:

> *What was once a fundamental segment of the American economic structure—heavy industry and durable goods manufacturing—has now become a marginal part of the national portfolio. As this sector of the economy gives way to the new "knowledge industries," workers in this sector are being superseded as well. In America's new image of itself as a postindustrial society, individuals still employed in basic manufacturing industries look like global benchwarmers in the competitive markets of the modern world (Dudley, 1994:161).*

When the auto plant was finally shut down, Dudley did in-depth follow-up interviews with autoworkers and with a wide variety of professionals in the Kenosha area. Interview questions were open-ended to give informants freedom to roam where their thoughts and feelings took them. Dudley's only restriction was that the interviews be geared to the cultural meaning of what was happening to the community because of its declining employment base.

For Dudley, the demolition of the auto plant was a metaphor for the dismantling of the way of life created since the early 1950s among U.S. blue-collar workers in core manufacturing industries. These increasingly displaced blue-collar workers, contends Dudley, find themselves caught between two interpretations of success in America. On the one hand, middle-class professionals justify their place in society by reference to their educational credentials and "thinking" jobs. Blue-collar workers, on the other hand, legitimize their place in society on the basis of the high market value society has traditionally placed on their hard labor. One ex-auto worker, whom Dudley calls Al Tirpak, captured the idea beautifully:

Observation

Ask students to make a list of careers they are seriously thinking of pursuing. (They may need to consult relatives to complete this assignment.) In this list they can include careers their peers are considering pursuing. Now they should make a list of jobs their parents and others in their parents' age group have held. Finally, they should list jobs their grandparents and their contemporaries held. When finished, they

We're worth fifteen dollars an hour because we're producing a product that can be sold on the market that'll produce that fifteen dollars an hour. . . . I don't know if you want to [base a person's value] strictly on education. You can send someone to school for twelve years and they can still be doing something that's socially undesirable and not very worthwhile for society. I don't know if they should get paid *just* because they had an education. In my mind, yuppie means *young unproductive parasite*. We're gonna have an awful lot of yuppies here in Kenosha that say they are doing something worthwhile when, really, they aren't (Dudley, 1994:169).

Due to the massive loss of high-paying factory jobs, Dudley contends that the blue-collar vision of success is coming to "the end of the line." These workers have lost their cultural niche to a postindustrial world where work is based on education and the application of knowledge.

Dudley documents the blue-collar workers' view of this new reality. From her extensive interviews, she constructs a portrait of their struggle to preserve their cultural traditions in a world in which the type of employment on which these traditions were built is decreasing. The penalty for not creating new cultural supports for a sense of social worth, Dudley concludes, will be life in a state of confusion with a sense of failure.

The shift from an industrial to a postindustrial economy will necessarily result in plant shutdowns and layoffs.

Working with the Research

1. What is the focus of Dudley's research?
2. What does Dudley's conclusion mean for blue-collar workers in terms of their way of life?
3. Do you think Dudley's research methods are strong enough to support her conclusion?
4. Do you believe that Dudley can be objective in this study of her hometown? Explain your answer.

should have three fairly distinct lists.

As students look at the lists, they should try to determine what industries the jobs are in. Do the industries change according to which list they are working with? For example, are the jobs students and their peers have listed in the same or different industries as the jobs listed by parents? Grandparents? Do students see a trend occurring? If so, to what do they attribute the trend?
L2

Answers to Working with the Research

1. Dudley wanted to study the effects of the changing work patterns of a typical mid-sized town.
2. They were trying to preserve the cultural traditions of the blue-collar community in a world that is eliminating the type of employment upon which these traditions were built.
3. Dudley used open-ended questions to allow for a free flow of thoughts and feelings of her interviewees. She emphasized the cultural meaning of the community's loss of its employment base.
4. Answers will vary, but there is no reason to believe that she could not be objective. Knowing some of the interviewees might have helped her obtain more in-depth answers.

Integrating the Teacher Resources

A lesson plan for a student research project related to the content of this chapter can be found in Doing Sociology: Focus on Research, available in your Teacher's Resource Box.

Open-Response Questions

To help students understand how Weber's Protestant work ethic is ingrained in our culture, have students answer the following questions: a) What would you rather be doing right now, other than sitting in class? b) Why are you in class rather than doing what you want to do? c) Why don't you skip class? d) Why do you want to get good grades? e) Why do you want to get a good salary? f) Why do you want the things you want? g) How would you feel if you didn't get the job and salary you want?

Most students will answer these questions so that the responses all build on one other, which is the point. The work ethic is so much a part of their socialization that most students never question why they do what they do. The institutions are structured so that few alternatives exist.

Teaching Strategy

To provide closure for the main ideas in this chapter, you may want to ask students to complete the learning objectives on text page 423.

To what tier of America's occupational structure do these California aircraft workers belong?

occupations
categories of jobs that involve similar activities at different work locations

core tier
an occupational structure composed of large firms dominating their industries

peripheral tier
an occupational structure composed of smaller, less profitable firms

Occupational Structure

Occupations are categories of jobs that involve similar activities at different work locations. For example, teacher, dental assistant, film producer, and electrician are all occupations because each position requires similar training and involves some standard operations. The United States Department of Labor has identified over 500 occupations with more than 21,000 various specialties within the broader occupation categories.

What is the shape of the U.S. occupational structure? A two-tier occupational structure has developed in the U.S. One tier—the **core**—includes jobs with large firms holding dominant positions within their industries. Computer technology, pharmaceutical, and aerospace firms are prime examples. About 35 percent of U.S. workers are in the core. The other level—the **peripheral tier**—is composed of jobs in smaller firms that either are competing for business left over from core firms or are engaged in less profitable industries such as agriculture, textiles, and small-scale retail trade. Most U.S. workers—around 65 percent—are employed in the peripheral tier.

What is the nature of core and peripheral jobs? Historically, jobs in the core paid more, offered better benefits, and provided longer-term employment. This is not surprising since the firms involved are large and highly profitable. Peripheral jobs are characterized by low pay, little or no benefits, and short-term employment. These features follow from the weaker competitive position and the smaller size of the employing firms.

How are the core and peripheral tiers changing? The industries that have supplied most of the core jobs in the U.S. have been scaling back during the last 20 years, laying off experienced workers and not hiring new ones. As early as 1983, for example, a steel mill in Hibbing, Minnesota, that once employed 4,400 people had a payroll of only 650 ("Left Out," 1983). Since 1983, the Weirton Steele Company continued to cut its production capacity by another 30 percent and has laid off more than half of its workforce (Riederer, 1999). In fact, more than 43 million jobs have been eliminated in the United States since 1979. Over 570,000 job cuts were announced in the United States in 1998, more than half of which occurred in manufacturing plants (McNamee and Muller, 1998; Riederer, 1999). Of course, as these top-tier jobs have been disappearing, peripheral jobs have become a larger share of the total jobs.

The good economic news, fueled by microchip technology, is that the U.S. economy continues its healthy growth and unemployment remains low. The bad economic news is that the new jobs are not as good as the manufacturing jobs they are replacing. The newer industries provide few jobs suited to the skills and backgrounds of laid-off manufacturing workers. Moreover, most jobs in high-tech industries pay minimal wages and offer few chances for promotion. Responsible positions with high pay are held by a very small proportion of high-tech employees.

Learning Styles

Linguistic/Logical-mathematical/Spatial/Intra-personal To assist students in better understanding work in modern society, ask students to conduct a survey and then create a graphic representation of the results. Surveys can be structured to include questions regarding which economic sectors people work in and which tier (the core or peripheral) is more represented by people known to your students. Be sure to discuss ethics before making decisions on survey questions. Have each student collect

Thus, reemployment of laid-off workers is a significant problem. While the overwhelming majority of the over five million U.S. workers laid off between 1979 and 1992 had held full-time jobs, only half reported taking new full-time jobs. Another third were either unemployed or were no longer in the labor force. The rest were working part-time, running their own businesses, or occupied as unpaid family workers (Uchitelle and Kleinfield, 1996).

What difference does this make to U.S. workers? As has probably already crossed your mind, this trend makes a huge difference. The U.S. economy has been losing higher-paying jobs and gaining lower-paying jobs. This helps explain why, since the 1970s, the majority of workers have been losing economic ground. While thirty years ago one American worker alone could support a family, the dual-employed married couple has become the norm today.

This process, known as *downwaging,* is expected to continue in the twenty-first century. Of the ten job categories projected to grow between 1994 and 2005, five pay below the poverty level. Only two of the top ten shrinking job categories fall below the poverty threshold (U.S. Bureau of the Census, 2000d). Many sociologists believe that the job loss and downwaging trends threaten the American dream. (Newman, 1993; Barlett and Steel, 1996).

downsizing
the process by which companies reduce their workforces

Downsizing and Contingent Employment

contingent employment
the hiring of part-time, short-term workers

Clearly, the occupational structure in the United States has changed dramatically over the last few decades. *Downsizing* and *contingent employment,* two strategies used by top management, reduce employment in core industries. A discussion of these related practices will help explain why the U.S. occupational structure is changing.

Downsizing is the process by which companies reduce the size of their full-time workforces. **Contingent employment** involves hiring people on a part-time or short-term basis. Although corporate downsizing had been going on since the late 1970s, it accelerated during the 1980s and 1990s. Since 1985, an estimated four million people have lost their jobs to downsizing alone. This trend is expected to continue (Sloan, 1996; Belton, 1999).

Corporate downsizing is associated with lower pay.

Why are downsizing and contingent employment taking place on such a large scale? Part of the motivation for downsizing is based on top management's belief that their companies employ a surplus of people and that, thanks to computers and other labor-saving technology, work can be done by fewer employees without reductions in efficiency and effectiveness. Top management also points to lower profits caused by increasing foreign competition. And it is true that about 20 percent of all U.S. workers are directly exposed to foreign competition (McNamee and Muller, 1998). Companies have responded to increased foreign competition by moving

Reteaching

The American Dream promotes the belief that everyone can be successful, and is an essential part of our culture. As mentioned in the chapter, downsizing threatens the ideal of the American Dream. Have students refer back to Chapter 8 to revisit the Horatio Alger myth—that everyone can go from rags to riches. Some sociologists are concerned that the gap between the "haves" and the "have nots" will continue to increase. Ask students to consider the implications of this phenomenon.

Integrating the Teacher Resources

For review, use the Chapter 13 Vocabulary Quiz and Chapter Quiz available in the Unit 4 Mastering Basic Concepts **booklet in your Teacher's Resource Box.**

a specified number of responses. To conclude, you may want to have students work in small groups to tabulate the results of their survey and then create a graphic representation of their findings. Be sure to compare and contrast the results from the different groups. What type of occupations seem to be the most prevalent? What type of occupations do students want to have? What can they do now to prepare themselves to get the jobs they want?
L2

Pulling it All Together

The structure of work is changing. Corporate downsizing is replacing full-time workers with part-time or temporary workers, and evidence suggests that this trend might have negative consequences.

Answers to Section 5 Assessment

1. In agriculture and industry, technological advances have led to inceased productivity resulting in more white-collar occupations: managers, sales workers, and clerical workers.

 As the proportion of workers (blue-collar) in goods-producing jobs was decreasing, the demand for labor in the services (tertiary) sector was increasing. Also, the computer industry changes the economy from a manufacturing base to a knowledge, or information, base. Therefore there is presently a high demand for people who can deliver services and manage information.

2. An immediate advantage of downsizing is that companies are able to cut costs. Long-term drawbacks are that this practice is creating further opposition between those controlling the capital (the employers) and those who do not (the workers). Workers' trust in their employers is eroding, and therefore so is their loyalty.

Critical Thinking

3. Answers will vary.

Figure 13.8 Evidence of Declining Trust In Management. *According to this graph, employee trust in management declined between 1995 and 1997. Are any of these factors affecting trust more important to you than others?*

Source: *Towers Perrin Workplace Index* (Boston, MA), 1998.

1995	1997
In general, workplace policies are administered fairly.	59%	56%
The company fills jobs with the most-qualified candidates.	55%	49%
In general, promotions are fair.	51%	45%
Overall, the company considers my interests.	50%	41%
Top performers receive more pay.	48%	44%

0 10% 20% 30% 40% 50% 60% 70% 80% 90% 100%
Percent Agreeing

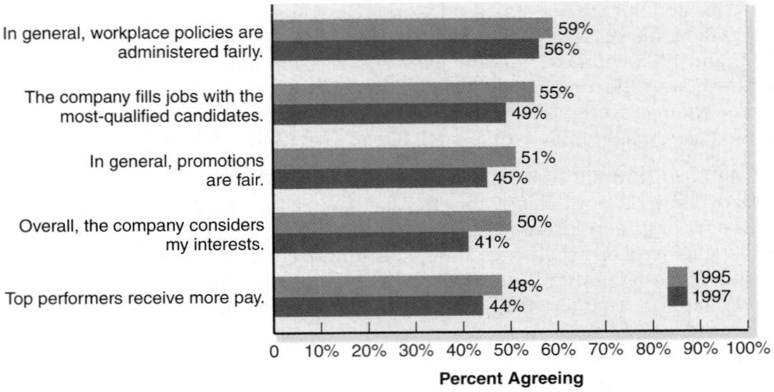

operations overseas and by replacing full-time employees with part-time workers hired to do a limited amount of work for a specified time period.

Contingent employment is a cost-cutting device. Unlike full-time employees, contingent workers receive lower pay and are not entitled to expensive benefits such as vacation time, health insurance, and retirement benefits.

Does downsizing and contingent employment have a downside? According to Robert Reich, former secretary of the U.S. Department of Labor, downsizing and contingent employment will create greater polarization between those who control capital and those who do not. Some critics believe the "disposable" workforce is the most important trend in business today. They contend that it is fundamentally changing the relationship between Americans and their employers.

A survey of 2,500 employees across the United States confirms that employees' attitudes toward their employers are changing. Although employees express high job satisfaction, their trust in management appears to be eroding. Workers seem to be losing some faith in management's commitment to them. (See Figure 13.8.)

Trust and loyalty are difficult to maintain when employees do not believe company policies treat them fairly. As time passes, additional research will help to focus attention on the full effects of corporate downsizing and contingent employment.

This unhappy worker has been caught in a corporate downsizing. What negative effects is this experience likely to have on him?

Section 5 Assessment

1. Why have white-collar jobs increased faster than jobs in other sectors of the workforce since the 1930s?
2. What are some immediate benefits of downsizing? Some long-term drawbacks?

Critical Thinking

3. **Drawing Conclusions** Would you like to spend your work life as a contingent employee? Why or why not?

Demonstration

Employment determines the status of a person in their family and, often, in their community. Employment provides the income and in many ways, it structures the life of the employee. So, the unemployment that results from downsizing can be devastating to the individual, the family, and in some cases, the entire community.

Ask someone you know who is or has been unemployed at some time to speak to your class. Make sure they will be comfortable with questions the students might ask. Have students prepare questions in advance for the speaker to answer. Students should focus on the effect the unemployment had on the person and their family.

L1

CHAPTER 13 ASSESSMENT

Summary

Section 1: Power and Authority

Main Idea: Authority is the sanctioned use of power. Political systems can be based on three types of authority: charismatic, traditional, and rational-legal. Democratic, totalitarian, and authoritarian are types of political systems.

Section 2: Political Power in American Society

Main Idea: The two major models of political power are elitism and pluralism. Advocates of the conflict perspective believe American society is controlled by elites. Pluralists, whose view is associated with functionalism, depict power as widely distributed among interest groups. Voting does not seem to be an effective means for nonelites to influence political decisions in the U.S.

Section 3: Economic Systems

Main Idea: Capitalist economies are based on private property and the pursuit of profit, and government, in theory, plays a minor role in regulating industry. In socialist economies, the means of production are owned collectively, and government has an active role in planning and controlling the economy.

Section 4: The Modern Corporation

Main Idea: Corporations, especially those with multinational connections, have grown very powerful. Corporate managers affect domestic political decision making and influence the political and economic institutions of countries around the world.

Section 5: Work in the Modern Economy

Main Idea: Workers today face a changing job structure. More corporations are downsizing and replacing full-time employees with consultants or temporary workers. Evidence indicates that this trend is having some negative consequences.

SOCIOLOGY Online

Self-Check Quiz
Visit the *Sociology and You* Web site at soc.glencoe.com and click on **Chapter 13—Self-Check Quizzes** to prepare for the chapter test.

Reviewing Vocabulary

Complete each sentence using each term once.

a. charismatic authority
b. monopoly
c. downsizing
d. traditional authority
e. power elite
f. pluralism
g. elitism
h. primary sector
i. interest group
j. corporation
k. rational-legal authority
l. power

1. The ability to control the behavior of others is called ______.
2. ______ is the authority that arises from the personality of an individual.
3. The form of authority in which the power of government officials is based on their offices is called ______.
4. ______ is the form of authority in which the legitimacy of a lead is rooted in custom.
5. A group organized to influence political decision making is called ______.
6. ______ is a system in which a community or society is controlled from the top by a few individuals or organizations.
7. The process in which political decisions are made as a result of competition and compromise among special interest groups is called ______.
8. A coalition of top military, corporate, and government leaders is called the ______.
9. ______ is an organization owned by shareholders who have limited liability and limited control.
10. The reduction of a corporation's workforce is called ______.
11. A company that has control over the production or distribution of a product or service is called a ______.
12. Economic activities such as farming, fishing, or mining are known as the ______.

ANSWERS CHAPTER 13 ASSESSMENT

Reviewing Vocabulary

1. l
2. a
3. k
4. d
5. i
6. g
7. f
8. e
9. j
10. c
11. b
12. h

Reviewing the Facts

1. The ability to control the behavior of others even against their will.
2. The controlling of communities or societies from the top by a few individuals or organizations.
3. Military Leaders; Government Leaders; Corporate Leaders
4. The system founded on the belief that the means of production should be owned collectively by the people and that government should play an active role in planning and controlling the economy.
5. mixed economy
6. Downsizing is the process by which companies reduce their workforce. In general, the disadvantages of extensive downsizing may be greater than the advantages.

Thinking Critically

1. If students remember points emphasized in Chapter 7, they will recall that obedience is a key component to the success of charismatic leaders like Hitler and Koresh. They demanded and needed complete obedience from their followers. Contrast these examples against the leadership of charismatic leaders like Martin Luther King, Jr. and Mahatma Gandhi who earned respect and admiration from their followers. An enlightened citizenship is one solu-

CHAPTER 13 ASSESSMENT

Reviewing the Facts

1. How did Max Weber define power?
2. What is elitism? Give an example.
3. According to C. Wright Mills, who controls the power in the United States? Use the diagram below to illustrate your answer.

CONTROL OF POWER IN THE UNITED STATES ACCORDING TO C. WRIGHT MILLS

__________ __________ __________

POWER

4. What is socialism? Give an example.
5. The economic system of most nations most closely follows which system?
6. What is downsizing? In general, what can be said about the relationship between the disadvantages of downsizing and the advantages of downsizing?

Thinking Critically

1. **Making Inferences** Charismatic leaders such as Adolf Hitler and Branch Davidian cult leader David Koresh show us that the ability to exert control over people has little to do with issues of right and wrong. Why do people embrace men like Hitler or Koresh? What kind of training or education is essential in a democracy to counter the effects of dangerous yet charismatic leaders?
2. **Drawing Conclusions** The topic of enforced population control (see Another Place, page 432) is an intriguing one for many Americans. On average, families in the United States in 2000 have two children. Does government ever have a right to legislate how many children couples are allowed to have? Should Americans be encouraged to have only two children for social reasons? Should income and educational levels be factors in how large families should be? Under what circumstances, if any, would government have a legitimate say in the size of families?
3. **Analyzing Information** The National Rifle Association (NRA) is one of the most powerful special interest groups in the country. Its membership is close to three million (slightly more than 1 percent of the U.S. population). Yet many people in the organization report that only a handful of the members are active and vocal. Why does the NRA get so much attention when only a small minority of its members express their opinions? How have these members influenced politicians?
4. **Analyzing Information** According to conflict theorists, members of the power elite control many aspects of not only politics but society at large. A recent book tried to examine the diversity of the power elite—that is, how many women and minorities are in its membership. Discuss the extent to which you think women and minorities are represented in the power elite.
5. **Evaluating Information** Many individuals in the history of the United States have exerted control over the political process because of their personal wealth. Examples include Andrew Carnegie, John D. Rockefeller, and—more recently—Microsoft founder Bill Gates. Capitalism encourages the accumulation of wealth. Do you think the government should put limits on how much wealth any one individual or organization can control? Why or why not?
6. **Evaluating Information** There is growing concern about the accuracy of the news reports that we receive daily, particularly from the Internet. Inaccuracies and sensationalized stories are becoming more and more common. What could this do to the credibility of news reporting? What does this say about the current state of American society?

ANSWERS CHAPTER 13 ASSESSMENT

tion. Citizens who are aware of the limits of power and understand the Constitution are more likely to make informed choices.

2. You might want to let students debate the ethical aspects of this issue. As you will see in Chapter 16, population growth is a global concern. Students might want to argue that people have an obligation to regulate child birth based on economic liability—it simply is not economically beneficial in today's world to have many children, as it was at other times in history.
3. Again, this discussion question could turn into a debate as students research the pros and cons of gun control. Some will then be able to ascertain the extent to which politicians are influenced by the NRA, and also by other interest groups that oppose guns.
4. One way to examine diversity in the power elite is to obtain a Forbes magazine or visit the website: **www.forbes.com** and look at the lists of the wealthiest people in the US. Of the top 100, how many on the list are women or minorities? There will be very few. Of course, this does not mean that women and minorities don't hold key positions in corporations. However, they might not be the ones owning or running the corporations.
5. Students could research the topic of "Robber Barons" or "Captains of Industry," as they have been called in history. What problems did Carnegie and Rockefeller encounter in amassing their wealth? How are they similar to modern tycoons like Gates and Michael Dell?
6. The best way for students to assess the reliability of news reporting is to look at several sources and check for the consistency of the reporting. If stories corroborate, it would suggest that the reporting is reliable. When students find inconsistencies, have them report on why that might be.

Sociology Projects

1. **Political Influence** As an extension of question #5 above, instead of putting limits on how much wealth any one individual or organization could accumulate, consider the options that the government might use to limit the political influence of wealthy individuals and organizations. Using proper spelling, punctuation and grammar, write a brief essay listing and describing those options.
2. **Employee Rights** Review the list of employee rights in the Sociology Today feature on page 448. If you have a job, try to find out which of these rights your current employer recognizes. You might want to ask your manager if your company has a brochure that lists employee rights. If you don't have a job, discuss this activity with a friend who is working.
3. **Political Cartoons** Look in the newspaper or weekly newsmagazines for a political cartoon. Analyze the cartoon, and write a brief summary of the message you think the cartoonist is trying to get across. Does the cartoon have a political agenda? Does it reflect the viewpoint of a special interest group or a specific branch of government? Be sure to discuss the symbolism used by the artist in the cartoon. Be prepared to present your cartoon to the class for further discussion.
4. **Government at the Local Level** Visit or call your local city hall to find out the schedule for city council or school board meetings. Arrange to attend the next meeting. Review the agenda for the meeting, and record what happens at the meeting. Identify all the other social institutions that were affected by the decisions made at the meeting the night you attended. (In many towns, local city council or board meetings are televised on cable channels. Check with the city or your local cable carrier to see if this is the case for your location.)
5. **Political Beliefs** On a sheet of paper, write down your own political party affiliation and your parents' political party affiliations. Next, write down your views on some key issues that you feel strongly about, such as immigration or minority rights. Write down your parents' views on these topics. Do you and your parents share the same political beliefs? You might also want to try comparing your views with a friend's. Are your views and your friend's views similar? If so, do you think that this might explain why you are friends? Do you think that people tend to associate more with those who share similar political beliefs?

Technology Activities

1. One of the topics of debate about corporations in America is whether they have any responsibilities beyond making a profit for their shareholders. Some people say that corporations have a "social responsibility" to make their communities better places. Two companies that act on their social responsibilities are Ben & Jerry's and The Body Shop. Go to their web sites at http://www. benjerry.com/ and http://www. thebodyshop.ca/.
   a. Find their mission statements and read them. What do these companies believe about social responsibility?
   b. What specific actions do they take to make their communities better places?
2. Using your school or local library and the Internet, research and rank the 20 largest corporations in the United States according to their net worth. Also, research and rank the ten wealthiest individuals in the United States according to their net worth. Do you see any correlation or affiliation between the wealthy individuals and the powerful corporations (e.g., membership in one of the corporations, member on the directorate of one or more of the corporations, etc.)? Create a database to record your research. Summarize your research in a paragraph using proper spelling and grammar construction.

ANSWERS Chapter 13 Assessment

Sociology Projects

1. Answers will vary. The objective is to arrive at the idea of limits on contributions to political parties to limit the influence of the wealthy.
2. Ask working students how well they know their rights as workers. Are they versed on sexual harassment policies, worker's compensation, etc.?
3. You might want to consult a colleague in the social studies department for ideas for this activity. Many social studies teachers have good ideas about teaching students about political cartoons. Some teachers let students create their own political cartoons, for example.
4. Students will probably learn a lot from attending or viewing one of these meetings by gaining exposure to the decision-making process. Some school boards allow students on the board. If your school district does not currently do so, inquire if students might be considered for such a position.
5. Ask students if they think that political views are formulated through socialization. Do their parents impress their values and ideologies upon them?

Technology Activities

1. Ben and Jerry's mission statement says they are committed "To operate the Company in a way that actively recognizes the central role that business plays in the structure of society by initiating innovative ways to improve the quality of life of a broad community - local, national, and international."

   The Body Shop mission statement says "We dedicate our business to the pursuit of social and environmental change."
2. Answers will vary.

Enrichment Reading

Students might not attach a stigma to fast-food jobs, since those who have them are working and contributing to society. Point out that most teens working in fast-food jobs will not be working there in 5 years. Often, these are starter jobs that allow young people to develop a resume to take to other more prestigious jobs.

Chapter 13

Enrichment Reading

No Shame in My Game

by Katherine S. Newman

Katherine Newman has created a rich portrait of minimum-wage workers employed in four fast-food restaurants in central Harlem. These are the "working poor"—they hold jobs and pay taxes, but they do not earn enough money to buy the basic necessities of life. In the passage below, Newman argues that the working poor share the same basic values as the rest of American society. The shame referred to in the reading lies in society's view that employment in fast-food jobs is somehow degrading.

Swallowing ridicule would be a hardship for almost anyone in this culture, but it is particularly hard on minority youth in the inner city. They have already logged four or five years' worth of interracial and cross-class friction by the time they get behind a [Burger Barn] cash register. More likely than not, they have also learned from peers that self-respecting people don't allow themselves to be "dissed" without striking back. Yet this is precisely what they must do if they are going to survive in the workplace.

This is one of the main reasons why these [fast-food] jobs carry such a powerful stigma in American popular culture: they fly in the face of a national attraction to autonomy, independence, and the individual's "right" to respond in kind when dignity is threatened. In ghetto communities, this stigma is even more powerful because—ironically—it is in these **enclaves** that this mainstream value of independence is most vigorously elaborated and **embellished.** Film characters, rap stars, and local idols base their claim to notoriety on standing above the crowd, going their own way, being free of the ties that bind ordinary mortals. There are white parallels, to be sure, but this is a powerful **genre of icons** in the black community, not because it is a disconnected subculture but because it is an intensified version of a perfectly recognizable American middle-class and working-class fixation.

It is therefore noteworthy that thousands upon thousands of minority teens, young adults, and even middle-aged adults line up for jobs that will subject them, at least potentially, to a kind of character assassination. They do so not because they start the job-seeking process with a different set of values, one that can withstand society's contempt for fast-food workers. They take these jobs because in so many inner-city communities, there is nothing better in the offing. In general, they have already tried to get better jobs and have failed, landing at the door of Burger Barn as a last resort. . . .

The stigma also stems from the low social status of the people who hold these jobs: minorities, teenagers, immigrants who often speak halting English, those with little education, and (increasingly in affluent communities afflicted with labor shortages) the elderly. To the extent that the prestige of a job refracts the social characteristic of its average **incumbents,** fast-food jobs are hobbled by the perception that people with better choices would never purposely opt for a "McJob." . . . There is no quicker way to indicate that a person is barely deserving of notice than to point out he

Integrating the Teacher Resources

Additional primary source readings for this chapter can be found in Culture Studies: The Sociological Perspective, available in your Teacher's Resource Box. Questions for students are included.

or she holds a "chump change" job at Kentucky Fried Chicken or Burger King. . . .

Ghetto youth are particularly sensitive to the status degradation entailed in stigmatized employment. As Elijah Anderson . . . and others have pointed out, a high premium is placed on independence, autonomy, and respect among minority youth in inner-city communities—particularly by young men. No small amount of mayhem is committed every year in the name of injured pride. Hence jobs that routinely demand **displays of deference** force those who hold them to violate "macho" behavior codes that are central to the definition of teen culture. There are, therefore, considerable social risks involved in seeking a fast-food job in the first place, one that the employees and job-seekers are keenly aware of from the very beginning of their search for employment.

It is hard to know the extent to which this stigma discourages young people in places like central Harlem from knocking on the door of a fast-food restaurant. It is clear that the other choices aren't much better and that necessity drives thousands, if not millions, of teens and older job-seekers to ignore the stigma or learn to live with it. But no one enters the central Harlem job market without having to face this **gauntlet.**

Source: Excerpted from Katherine S. Newman, *No Shame in My Game,* New York: Alfred A. Knopf, 1999, pp. 93, 95.

What Does it Mean?

display of deference
acting in a humble or compliant way

embellish
to add to; to make more attractive

enclave
a territory or cultural unit within a foreign territory

gauntlet
ordeal or challenge

genre of icons
category or type of symbols

incumbent
occupant, job holder

Read and React

1. Who are the "working poor"? Give some examples of the types of jobs the working poor would hold.
2. According to Newman, the working poor share the same values as the rest of American society. Discuss the evidence she gives for this. Is she convincing?
3. Why did Newman select *No Shame in My Game* for her book title?
4. Do you think a stigma is attached to being a fast-food worker? Explain.
5. What do you think Newman means by "status degradation" in the context of her research?

Answers to Read and React

1. Examples might include maids, doormen, parking attendants, etc. These jobs provide little opportunity for advancement and are at the low end of the economic scale.
2. These teens are actively seeking work, which suggests that they possess the value that work is important.
3. The teens depicted in this book realize that by working they shed the stereotype of the poor. Instead of shame, they feel a sense of pride that they are "in the game," working.
4. Answers will vary, depending on the student's perception of the job.
5. These teens are degraded by their peers and degraded by society for working in low paying jobs. Newman points out that despite stereotypes, these poor people do work, even though their status has been degraded from both sides.

Chapter Preview

Section 1 (pages 464–466)

Religion is concerned with sacred things. Durkheim concluded that every religion separates the sacred from the profane. Sociologists face some unique problems studying religion. They do not evaluate the validity of various religions but look at those aspects of religion that can be measured and observed in society.

Section 2 (pages 467–474)

Religion has several functions. It legitimates the structure of society, promotes social unity, and provides a sense of meaning and belonging. Marx argued that religion is used to justify and maintain the group in power. Weber believed that religion could promote social change. He connected the Protestant ethic and the rise of capitalism.

Section 3 (pages 475–480)

The major forms of religious organization are churches, denominations, sects and cults. Religiosity—the ways people express their religious interests and convictions—can be analyzed in terms of five dimensions: belief, ritual, intellect, experience, and consequences.

Section 4 (pages 481–488)

Through the process of secularization, the sacred and the profane are intermixed. There has been a revival of religious fundamentalism in the United States. The major religious faiths can be analyzed by major social characteristics.

CHAPTER 14

Religion

Lead-Off Activity

Before students begin studying the chapter, have them complete this activity. On paper, have them answer the following questions: a) How do you define religion? b) What does religion mean to you? c) Do you believe in the supernatural? d) If you do believe in the supernatural, how do you imagine it to be?

Allow students to discuss their answers for a short period. If your class is like most others, spirits and tempers might begin to rise. At this point break off the discussion and

Using Your Sociological Imagination

More than thirty years after the Beatles' last recording session, the group's tapes and CDs are still being sold by the millions. But there was a moment—at the height of the Beatles' popularity—when radio stations around the United States banned their music and teenagers stomped on their records.

The angry reaction was the result of a comment made by John Lennon in a 1966 London interview:

> *Christianity will go. It will vanish and shrink. I needn't argue with that; I'm right and I will be proved right. We're more popular than Jesus now; I don't know which will go first—rock 'n 'roll or Christianity.*

When the remark was printed in the United States, the resulting uproar caught many by surprise. Lennon's statement was quoted out of context. If the entire interview had been printed, the response might have been less extreme. Nevertheless, efforts to explain the remark failed, and Lennon was forced to apologize for saying something he hadn't really intended to say. Contrary to popular belief, it appeared that many young Americans took their religion seriously.

Today, many people fear that religious influence in the United States is declining. Evidence, however, reveals that America—compared with other industrialized nations—remains fairly religious. This chapter views religion within the context of sociology, defines religion as an institution, and explores the ways people express their religious beliefs.

Sections

1. **Religion and Sociology**
2. **Theoretical Perspectives**
3. **Religious Organization and Religiosity**
4. **Religion in the United States**

Learning Objectives

After reading this chapter, you will be able to

- explain the sociological meaning of religion.
- describe the different views of religion as seen by the major theoretical perspectives.
- distinguish the basic types of religious organization.
- discuss the meaning and nature of religiosity.
- define secularization and describe its relationship to religiosity in the United States.
- discuss religious fundamentalism in the United States from the sociological perspective.

SOCIOLOGY Online

Chapter Overview
Visit the *Sociology and You* Web site at soc.glencoe.com and click on **Chapter 14—Chapter Overviews** to preview chapter information.

Using Your Sociological Imagination

Students will love to discuss the extent of religious influence in the United States and in their own lives. Studies show that teens are the least religious of all age groups but many students in your class will probably disagree. As adolescents struggle for self-identity, they often search for new heroes. Ask students who their heroes are. Do they consider their heroes godlike?

have them begin to examine the chapter to see how sociologists view religion. What do they find about the way sociologists study religion? Is the study objective or subjective? Stress that each individual is free to define religion as they choose, but there are general characteristics that hold true for all religions, and it is these characteristics that will be studied in this chapter. (This activity is the same as #3 in the chapter end projects and activities.) **L1**

Using the Section Preview

Religion is socially constructed. That is, humans create religions and assign religious meaning to objects. For example, Native Americans worship animals and nature as sacred, just as others might worship a crucifix or a statue of Buddha. Once people give meaning to objects, the profane becomes the sacred. However, what is sacred to one person might not have the same meaning to another. Durkheim called these "meaningless" objects totems—hence, the name of the Native American "totem poles."

More About . . . Studying Religion

Students will probably want to know how sociologists study religion. Several models have been suggested. Joachim Wach, in *Sociology of Religion* believed that religious expression occurred in three dimensions—the theoretical, which represents the strength of one's doctrinal adherence; the cultic, which involves the depth of an individual's devotional practice and worship; and the sociological, which reflects the extent of an individual's fellowship activities. Another model is provided by late theories of studying religiosity using intrinsic and extrinsic dimensions. Organizational religiosity deals with church attendance. Non-organizational religiosity consists of prayer or TV viewing. Subjective religiosity deals with the personal meaning that one attributes to religion.

Section 1 Religion and Sociology

Key Terms

- religion
- sacred
- profane

Section Preview

Religion is concerned with sacred things. Durkheim concluded that every religion separates the sacred from the profane. Sociologists studying religion face some unique problems. They do not judge the validity of various religions but rather look at those aspects of religion that can be measured and observed in society.

religion
a unified system of beliefs and practices concerned with sacred things

sacred
holy; set apart and given a special meaning that goes beyond, or transcends, immediate existence

profane
nonsacred

The Sociological Meaning of Religion

A **religion** is a unified system of beliefs and practices concerned with sacred things. This definition comes from Emile Durkheim, whose work was based on studies of the Australian aborigines in the late nineteenth century. According to Durkheim, every society distinguishes between the **sacred**—things and ideas that are set apart and given a special meaning that goes beyond, or transcends, immediate existence—and the **profane,** or nonsacred aspects of life. Profane in this context does not mean unholy. It simply means commonplace and not involving the supernatural. Another word for profane is *secular.*

Sacred things take on a public character that makes them appear important in themselves; profane things do not. The particular things considered sacred vary from culture to culture. For example, Bolivian tin miners attach sacred meaning to figures of the devil and to figures of bulls. Because Americans do not share these religious beliefs, these cultural items are part of their nonsacred, or profane, world. Moreover, some nonreligious aspects of culture can assume a sacred character. Here, two sociologists illustrate the difference between the sacred and the profane:

> *When Babe Ruth was a living idol to baseball fans, the bat he used to slug his home runs was definitely a profane object. It was Ruth's personal instrument and had little social value in itself. Today, however, one of Ruth's bats is enshrined in*

Buddhas, like this one in a Korean temple, are sacred objects in the Far East and Southeast Asia, and wherever Buddhists live. What makes an object sacred?

Demonstration

The Babe Ruth bat analogy on this page, helps students think of profane objects that have taken on sacred meaning. To illustrate how this occurs, use two sticks, one shorter than the other, to make a crucifix. (You might use an American flag or an eagle instead.) Show students the crucifix and ask them what it is. Most will identify it as a cross or crucifix. Deny that it's a cross and tell the class that you've simply put together two sticks, and that you might hang your tomatoes from it, or you might use it as a sword, etc. Ask students how and when these two sticks went from being profane objects to sacred objects. Most likely, they will refer to Christianity and the story of Christ's crucifixion. Stress that through this religious belief, human beings attached sacred meaning to the formerly profane cross. Until people assign meaning to an object, it carries no sacred meaning.

the Baseball Hall of Fame. It is no longer used by anyone. It stands, rather, as an object which in itself represents the values, sentiments, power, and beliefs of all members of the baseball community. What was formerly a profane object is now in the process of gaining some of the qualities of a sacred object (Cuzzort and King, 1976:27).

Babe Ruth's bat illustrates two particulars about the sociological study of religion. First, a profane object can become sacred, and vice versa. Second, sociologists can deal with religion without becoming involved in theological issues. By focusing on the cultural and social aspects of religion, sociologists avoid questions about the ultimate validity of any particular religion. This point is so important that it needs more explanation.

Is this Ford Mustang convertible a sacred or secular object? Why?

The Sociological Study of Religion

The sociological study of religion involves looking at a set of meanings attached to a world beyond human observation. Because this nonphysical world cannot be directly observed, this task is particularly difficult. Sociologists have to ask themselves hard questions: How can we find evidence for something that can't be seen? How can we remain objective about such a value-laden subject, especially when we have our own beliefs? Is science really the proper tool to evaluate religion?

Obviously, sociologists cannot study the unobservable. Consequently, they avoid the strictly spiritual side of religion and focus on social aspects of religion that can be measured and observed. Sociologists, then, are not in the business of determining which religions people ought to follow. Sociologists keep their own faith personal while investigating the *social* dimensions of religion. Like people in any other occupation, sociologists themselves follow a variety of religions.

Sociologists study the social aspects of religion. One such aspect is the charitable work done by members of different religious organizations.

Section 1 Assessment

1. How does the sociological definition of religion differ from how you previously thought of religion?
2. How do sociologists manage to study religion if they can't see the spiritual world?

Critical Thinking

3. **Evaluating Information** Do you think religion can be studied scientifically? Using the material just presented, make an argument for or against this practice.

Pulling it All Together

In this section, religion is described as being concerned with sacred things. Sociologists do not attempt to judge the validity of religion. Instead, they examine those social aspects of religion that can be measured and observed.

Answers to Section 1 Assessment

1. Answers will vary, but one difference is that sociologists avoid questions about the ultimate validity of any particular religion and instead teach that what is "sacred" and what is "profane/secular" vary from culture to culture. A person practicing a certain religion is involved with the issues, beliefs, and practices (and has a set definition of what is sacred and what is profane) concerning that religion.
2. Sociologists are unable to study the unobservable (spiritual) world. Therefore, they avoid the strictly spiritual side of religion and focus on cultural and social aspects of religion that can be measured and observed.

Critical Thinking

3. Answers will vary and should be supported.

Demonstration

To help students understand how sociologists can objectively study religion, ask them several hypothetical questions. For example, if someone belongs to a cult, is he or she more likely to be mentally unstable? If African Americans attend church more frequently than whites, are they likely to be more religious? Note that sociologists can measure and study these behaviors centered around religion without becoming involved in theological issues. Emphasize that religion is based on values, while science is based on observation. You might ask students what they would want to study about religion from a sociological standpoint. Have them create some hypotheses. These hypotheses could become research projects. (You may want to check with your school district administrators first, if you are thinking of allowing students to conduct research on religiosity.)

Another Place

Religion at War

As part of studying the effects of religion on society, sociologists note that throughout history, religion has both promoted social stability and led to social conflict. In this excerpt from the article *Religion at War*, the conflict aspect is highlighted.

In virtually every one of the world's 480 major wars since 1700, each side has imagined itself to be exclusively on the side of God, Gött, Allah, Dieu or other names for the deity.

Religion is often so closely linked with ethnic or national identity as to be seen as inseparable from them. Thus a struggle for expressions of ethnic or national identity is experienced as a religious war. This is so of the current unrest in the Punjab, created by Sikh demands for a separate Sikh state.

Religion evokes powerful emotions and commitments. It is capable of producing believers whose faith moves them to acts of great self-sacrifice and charity. At the same time it can produce believers who feel that their faith calls them to struggle violently in what they believe to be a just cause. One example is the Hindi/Muslim tension in India focused on Ayodhya. Here, a mosque built in the 15th century was destroyed in 1992 by militant Hindus because it is believed to have been built over the birthplace of the Hindu god Rama. While the majority of Hindis and Muslims have lived together peacefully for generations, extremists on both sides are capable of arousing violence through use of powerful religious symbols.

In many faiths, the issue of whether warfare is permissible has given rise to various theories of the just war. Such theories seek to define whether believers can ever engage in the use of violence. The usual conclusion is that violence—including warfare—is only acceptable in pursuit of a greater good. The problem, however, is who defines the greater good?

Source: Joanne O'Brien and Martin Palmer, *The State of Religion Atlas*. New York: Simon & Schuster, 1993, p. 117. Reprinted by permission.

Thinking It Over

Does functionalism or conflict theory best explain the link between strong religious conviction and war? Why?

Activists of a Hindu religious sect demand the right to build a temple on the site of a demolished mosque. Why are wars and conflicts often rooted in religious beliefs and values?

Another Place

Have students research religious wars in history. Ask them to cite the social factors that contributed to the war or were the result of the war, such as ideology or migrations. How might the causes of these wars been averted?

Answer to Thinking it Over

Students may answer the functionalist approach provides the most thorough explanation of religious conflict. They would say that the war was justified to maintain the order and stability of the system, to preserve the existing religious order. If they say it is conflictual, they would see the conflict over groups competing over values or limited resources or powerful people trying to exert control over some segment of the population.

Integrating the Teacher Resources

Look for the Chapter 14 Learning Goals Outline, a reproducible student worksheet in the Unit 4 Mastering Basic Concepts booklet in your Teacher's Resource Box. It can be used to preview or review chapter content.

Careers in Sociology

Ask students the following question: Can I be a sociologist and maintain my personal religious beliefs? After they have shared their ideas, read this answer to them.

The answer is, yes. An example of a career that combines sociology and religion is that of minister. Protestant ministers lead congregations in worship services and administer the various rites of the church. In many denominations, ministers follow a traditional order of worship; in others, they adapt the services to the needs of youth and other groups within the congregation. In addition to these duties, ministers officiate at weddings, funerals, and other occasions.

Ministers who serve small congregations usually work personally with parishioners.

Section 2 Theoretical Perspectives

Key Terms

- legitimate
- spirit of capitalism
- Protestant ethic

Functionalism and Religion

Religion exists in some form in virtually all societies. (See Figure 14.1 on page 468 and World View on page 469 for a global distribution of major religions.) The earliest evidence of religion and religious customs and taboos has been traced as far back as 50,000 B.C. Humans had by then already begun to bury their dead, a practice based on the belief in existence after death. Evidence of religious practices appears in many ancient cultures. In Rome, there were specific gods for objects and events—a god of trees, a god of money, a goddess of fever. While the early Hebrews believed that pigs were unclean animals whose pollution would spread to all who touched or tasted them, the tribes of New Guinea considered pigs holy creatures worthy of ancestral sacrifice (Harris, 1974).

Emile Durkheim, the first sociologist to examine religion scientifically, wondered why it is that all societies

Section Preview

Religion has several functions. It legitimates the structure of society, promotes social unity, and provides a sense of meaning and belonging. Marx argued that religion is used to justify and maintain the group in power. Weber believed that religion could promote social change. He connected the Protestant ethic and the rise of capitalism.

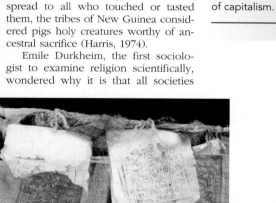

We know that religion is an important part of almost all societies because of the religious symbols most have left behind.

Those who serve large congregations may share specific aspects of the ministry with one or more associates or assistants, such as a minister of education or a minister of music.

Employment alternatives include working in youth counseling, family relations, and social welfare organizations; teaching in religious educational institutions; or serving as chaplains in the Armed Forces, hospitals, universities, and correctional institutions.

For information on sociology and religion, try **http://hirr.hartsem.edu/resources/default.htm**.

Using the Section Preview

Durkheim began the sociological study of religion by examining the function religion performs for society. Today, sociologists realize that religion meets individuals' needs by providing a sense of meaning and belonging, helping them make sense of the world.

Teaching Strategy

Ask students to discuss the following questions: Who goes to church? What types of people go to church? If students answer mostly older people and families, they would be correct. Studies have shown (Stolzenberg, Blair-Loy and Waite, 1995) that church attendance is correlated with people who fit conventional norms. That is, families with young children are the most likely to attend church. The elderly also score high on religiosity scales. Teens and people who don't fit conventional norms such as divorcees and gays/lesbians are least likely to attend church. It seems that churches become reflections of societal expectations of behavior.

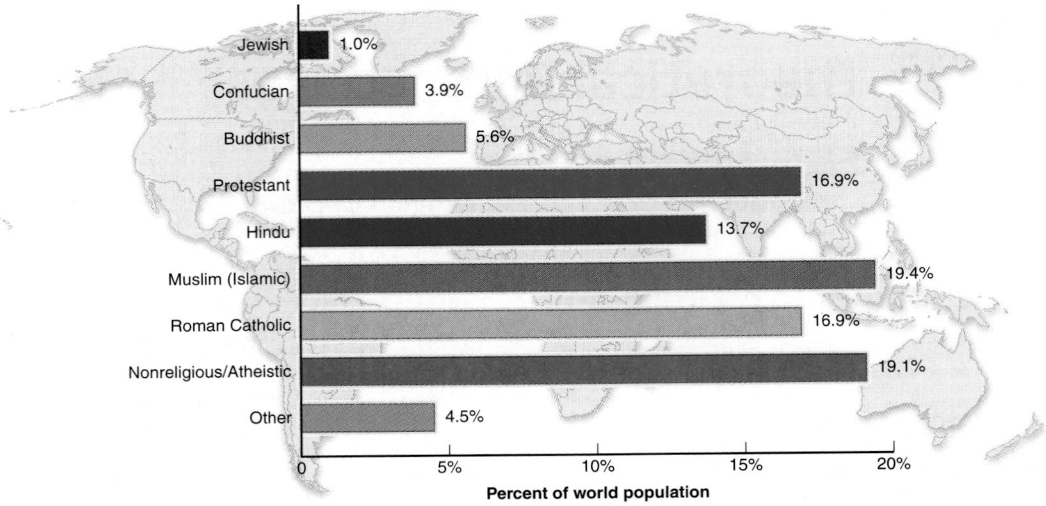

Figure 14.1 Division of World Population by Religions. *This graph compares the number of all religious believers belonging to a particular religion to the total estimated world population.*

have some form of religion. In one of his books, *The Elementary Forms of Religious Life* (1915), Durkheim offered an explanation rooted in the function religion performs for society. The essential function of religion, he believed, was to provide through sacred symbols a mirror for members of society to see themselves. Through religious rituals, people worship their societies and thereby remind themselves of their shared past and future existence.

Following Durkheim's lead, sociologists have identified the following social functions of religion.

legitimate
to justify or give official approval to

- *Religion gives formal approval to existing social arrangements.* Religious doctrine and scripture **legitimate** the status quo. Religion, then, justifies or gives authority to social norms and customs. A society's religion explains why the society is—and should be—the way it is. It tells us why some people have power and others do not, why some are rich and others poor, why some are common and others elite. Many social customs and rituals are based on religion. According to Durkheim, legitimation is the central function of religion.
- *Religion encourages a sense of unity.* Religion, according to Durkheim, is the glue that holds society together. Without religion, society would be chaotic. As Cuzzort and King have stated (1976), Durkheim "provided the greatest justification for religious doctrine ever formulated by a social scientist when he claimed that all societies must have religious commitments. Without religious dedication there is no social order."

  In some cases, though, religion causes societies to fragment, even to the point of civil war. Religion divides Catholics and Protestants in Northern Ireland. Thus, while it is accurate to say that religion is usually a source of social unity, it can also divide a society. (See Another Place, page 466.)
- *Religion provides a sense of understanding.* Religion not only explains the nature of social life and encourages social unity, it also provides

Working with the Data

Figure 14.1 Make sure students note that the X-axis on this graph only goes up to 20 percent, so that they have the right perspective on the bars. Also, ask them what religion seems to have the largest proportion of the world's population. They may answer Islam. Then point out that Roman Catholicism and Protestantism are shown as distinct religions. What happens if the figures for these two churches are combined? *(Christianity then becomes the religion with the largest percentage of followers.)*

Making Connections to Other Cultures

Islam is the dominant religion throughout a large portion of the world. Muslims perform specific duties throughout the day that serve as reminders of their religious beliefs. Five times a day (at dawn, at noon, in midafternoon, at dusk, and after dark) Muslims pray facing in the direction of Mecca. Muslims give alms to fellow citizens as a symbol of their faith, and abstain from eating pork or drinking alcohol. These daily acts of faith act, as Emile Durkheim wrote, as a mirror in which members of society see themselves reflected, and they also act as a common bond, which unites the different members of the community.

On-Demand Writing

Since identity formation takes place during adolescence, teens are likely to either disengage from religion or to internalize it as part of their identity at this point in their lives (Glover, 1996). Teens aged 14–17 had significantly lower rates of religiosity than older groups. In another study, (Donahue and Benson, 1995) 54 percent of 6th graders reported attending church once a week, compared to only 34 percent of 12th graders. Various reasons have been given to explain this decrease in religiosity in teens. It was suggested that 6th graders would be more strongly influenced to attend church by parental wishes and peer pressure, which may not be the case for

World View

Religions of the World

This map displays the worldwide distribution of all religions. Emile Durkheim showed that suicide rates vary according to group characteristics. One of these characteristics was religious background. For example, Durkheim showed that the suicide rate is lower among Catholics than among Protestants.

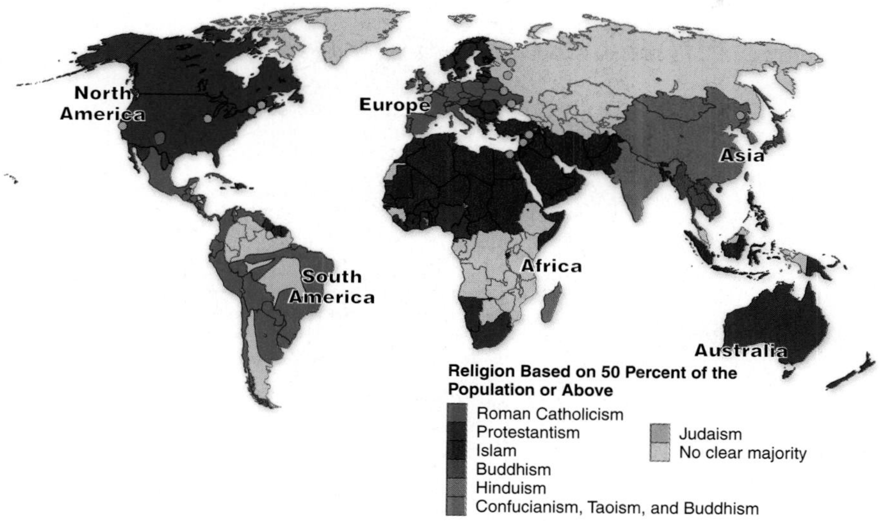

Interpreting the Map

1. Based on the information shown in this map, identify two countries where you would expect to find lower rates of suicide than in England.
2. What information on the map did you use in your analysis?

Adapted from *World Atlas,* 19th ed., Rand McNally.

individuals meaning beyond day-to-day life. People mark important events in life—birth, sexual maturity, marriage, death—with religious ceremonies and explain such events in religious terms. Religion gives believers a sense of their place in the cosmos and gives eternal significance to a short and uncertain earthly existence.

❖ *Religion promotes a sense of belonging.* Religious organizations provide opportunities for people to share important ideas, ways of life, and ethnic or racial backgrounds. Religion supplies a kind of group identity. People usually join religious organizations freely and feel a

World View

Durkheim wrote *Suicide* over 100 years ago (1897). Ask students if they think suicide rates based on one's religion would still be a valid measurement today. Are Catholics less likely to commit suicide than Protestants? Answering these questions would make an interesting research project.

Answers to Interpreting the Map

1. Answers will vary, should include two of the following: Mexico, any of the Central American countries, Portugal, Spain, France, Italy, Germany, Poland, etc.
2. Answers will vary.

Teaching Strategy

Ask students how religion might be dysfunctional. Answers may include: religion legitimizes inequalities, prevents social change, might stifle new thoughts and ideas, and might cause wars or other conflicts. Have students look for real life examples of the dysfunctions that religion can cause.
L2

12th graders. Another variable was the idea of "religious capital." Children socialized with religion as an important part of their lives tend to build up religious capital. This religious capital is stored, so even if children leave religion during adolescence, they are likely to eventually return to it. Again, the extent to which these individuals reflect conventional norms is also a factor in their religiosity.

Ask students to write their opinions on whether teens are more or less religious than other demographic groups. They should include what they know of their friends' feelings also. Ask volunteers to share their views with the rest of the class.
L1

Working with the Data

Figure 14.2 As a change of pace, ask students to identify how the major religions are similar, rather than different. Similarities include: all except Buddhism and Confucianism believe in some form of God or gods, most have a founder, all are hundreds of years old. Differences include: geographic location of religions, specific beliefs regarding God or a supreme being, founders, etc.

More About . . . Marx

Karl Marx once called religion "the opiate of the masses, the soul of a soulless society." From a conflict perspective, Marx viewed religion as suiting those in power. They would use religion to exploit those less fortunate. Ask students if they think Marx was correct.

Integrating the Teacher Resources

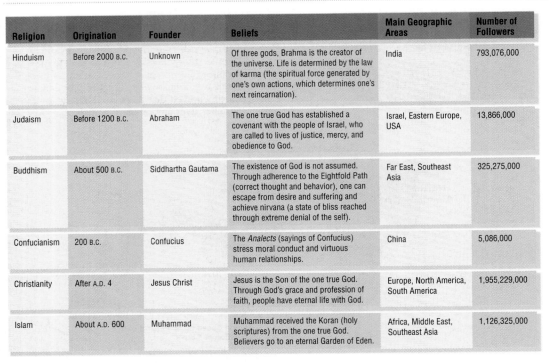

To reinforce key ideas, use the Chapter 14 Graphic Organizer, a reproducible student worksheet available in the Unit 4 Mastering Basic Concepts **booklet in your Teacher's Resource Box.**

Religion	Origination	Founder	Beliefs	Main Geographic Areas	Number of Followers
Hinduism	Before 2000 B.C.	Unknown	Of three gods, Brahma is the creator of the universe. Life is determined by the law of karma (the spiritual force generated by one's own actions, which determines one's next reincarnation).	India	793,076,000
Judaism	Before 1200 B.C.	Abraham	The one true God has established a covenant with the people of Israel, who are called to lives of justice, mercy, and obedience to God.	Israel, Eastern Europe, USA	13,866,000
Buddhism	About 500 B.C.	Siddhartha Gautama	The existence of God is not assumed. Through adherence to the Eightfold Path (correct thought and behavior), one can escape from desire and suffering and achieve nirvana (a state of bliss reached through extreme denial of the self).	Far East, Southeast Asia	325,275,000
Confucianism	200 B.C.	Confucius	The *Analects* (sayings of Confucius) stress moral conduct and virtuous human relationships.	China	5,086,000
Christianity	After A.D. 4	Jesus Christ	Jesus is the Son of the one true God. Through God's grace and profession of faith, people have eternal life with God.	Europe, North America, South America	1,955,229,000
Islam	About A.D. 600	Muhammad	Muhammad received the Koran (holy scriptures) from the one true God. Believers go to an eternal Garden of Eden.	Africa, Middle East, Southeast Asia	1,126,325,000

Figure 14.2 Major World Religions. *This figure summarizes characteristics and beliefs of the major world religions being widely practiced today.*

degree of influence within these organizations. For many people in modern society, membership in a religious organization provides a sense of community. This feeling of belonging helps to counteract depersonalization, powerlessness, and rootlessness.

> Religions are many and diverse, but reason and goodness are one.
>
> **Elbert Hubbard**
> **American writer**

Conflict Theory and Religion

Conflict theory focuses on how religion works to either inhibit or encourge social change. Two early and important sociologists who looked at religion from these perspectives were Karl Marx and Max Weber.

Why did Marx call religion the "opiate of the masses"? Marx believed that once people have created a unified system of sacred beliefs and practices, they act as if it were something beyond their control. They become "alienated" from the religious system they have set up. People have the power to change (or, better yet, in Marx's mind, to abandon) the religion they have created. They don't do so, however, because they see it as a binding force to which they must conform. Religion, Marx wrote, is used by the ruling class to justify its economic, political, and social advantages over the oppressed. Those in power justify poverty, degradation, and misery as God's will. To eliminate inequalities and injustices is to tamper with God's plan. Religion, then, gives people a sense that all is the way it should be.

On-Demand Writing

Marx believed that religion is frequently used by the ruling classes to justify social inequalities.

In India, society is divided into a rigid hierarchy that is maintained generation after generation, and which allows little mobility out of the position to which a person is born. These divisions were originally established over 3,000 years ago by Aryan priests, and later became incorporated into Hindu law. The four original castes were the Brahmans, a priestly class; the Kshatriyas, a warrior class; the Vaisyas, who were a farmer and merchant class; and finally, the Sudras, who were a class of servants and laborers. Far below these castes were those people who were considered to have no caste at all. These were, for many years,

World View

Gender Inequality in Religion

Women have been fighting for equal rights in all aspects of society—religion as well as government and business. In some religions women have equal status within their orders. Other religions see feminism as a "Western" issue and irrelevant to their faiths. This map shows how major denominations in each country view the status of women.

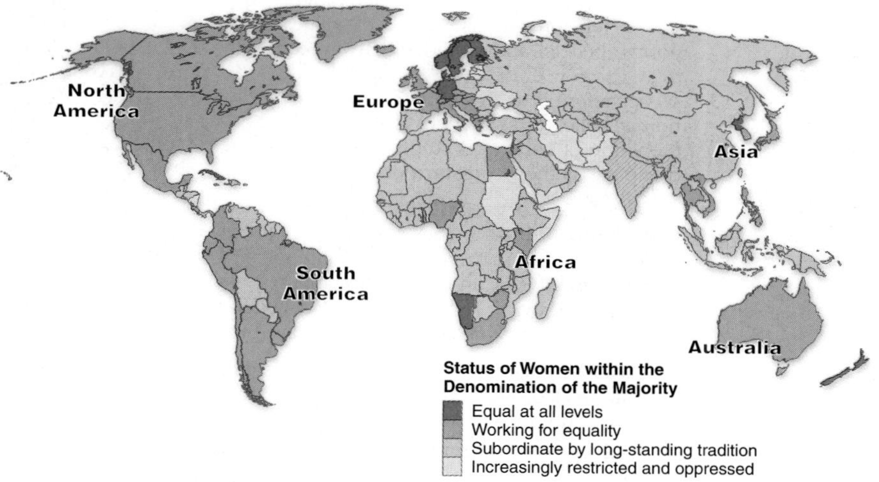

Interpreting the Map

1. Do you see any patterns of inequality in women's rights in religion? Explain.
2. Where in the world would a woman be most likely to head an entire religious organization? Support your answer. Do some research to see if this has occurred. If it has not, explain why.
3. How does the United States compare with the Scandinavian countries in terms of gender equality? Why do you think this difference exists?
4. How would you explain the mixed status of women in India?

Adapted from *The State of the Religion Atlas*. New York: Touchstone.

How did Weber link Protestantism and capitalism? Whereas Marx believed that religion works against social change, Max Weber suggested that religion sometimes encourages social change. He pointed to the relationship between Protestantism and the rise of capitalism. Weber wondered why capitalism emerged in northwestern Europe and America and not in other parts of the world. A possible answer lay in what he termed the *spirit of capitalism*

World View

Ask students why they think that in the United States, one of the more progressive countries in the world, women are still working for equality in religion.

Answers to Interpreting the Map

1. The more industrialized nations seem to have greater equality or are working for equality of women's rights in religion.
2. A woman would be most likely to head an entire religious organization in Norway, Sweden, Finland, Germany, Namibia, Cuba, or New Zealand. Students' answers to the research will vary.
3. The Scandinavian countries have gender equality; the U.S. is working toward it. Students answers will vary.
4. India has a mixed religious base of Moslems and Hindus. These faiths have different levels of gender equality.

known as "Untouchables." The Untouchables were actually the aboriginal inhabitants of India. These outcasts from society suffered tremendous hardships and injustices, which persist to this day, despite the efforts of social reformers such as Mohandas Gandhi. The caste system has been perpetuated by the Hindu ideas of *samsara* (reincarnation) and karma (quality of action): an example of the use of religion to justify social inequalities.

Ask your students to write down their feelings about this issue and share their ideas with the rest of the class.
L1

More About . . . Calvinism

Another doctrine of Calvinism was that of predestination, the belief that one's eternal salvation or damnation was predetermined by God. There was nothing that could be done to change one's ultimate outcome, although there was no way to be absolutely sure of salvation. Calvinists lived their lives as if they were predestined to be saved. Engaging in any impious behavior would surely guarantee that one would not be saved.

Open-Response Question

Ask students if they think the work ethic in the United States is disappearing or changing. If they say yes, ask them what they think are the causes or reasons for this. Students might answer that the Protestant work ethic is the dominant ethic of the white middle class. Many cultures do not have the same work ethic, which is not to say that they are lazy, but rather that profit and reinvestment are not given the same priority or societal value.

Open-Response Question

Ask students to use the symbolic interactionist approach to explain how religion might be viewed differently by men and by women. Can students use the functionalist approach to explain how religious language reinforces male and female roles?

spirit of capitalism the obligation to reinvest money in business rather than to spend it

Protestant ethic a set of values, norms, beliefs, and attitudes stressing hard work, thrift, and self-discipline

and the *Protestant ethic*. With capitalism, work became a moral obligation rather than a mere necessity. If businesses were to grow, money (capital) had to be put back into the business rather than spent. Investment for the future was more important than immediate consumption. All of this Weber called the **spirit of capitalism.**

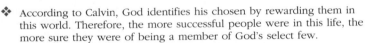

The theology of sixteenth-century theologian John Calvin formed the basis for the Protestant ethic.

Most major religions did not define hard work as an obligation or demand the reinvestment of capital for further profits (rather than for immediate enjoyment). But some Protestant sects did. Here, then, was a religion with a cluster of values, norms, beliefs, and attitudes that favored the emergence of modern capitalism. Weber referred to this cluster of values, norms, beliefs, and attitudes that stressed the virtue of hard work, thrift, and self-discipline as the **Protestant ethic.**

What is the nature of the Protestant ethic? The Protestant ethic is often associated with John Calvin (1509–1564), an early Protestant theologian. Calvin's followers were known as Calvinists. Calvinist beliefs illustrate several features of the Protestant ethic.

- According to Calvin, God identifies his chosen by rewarding them in this world. Therefore, the more successful people were in this life, the more sure they were of being a member of God's select few.
- Consumption beyond necessity was considered sinful; those who engaged in self-pleasure were agents of the devil.
- Calvinists believed there was an underlying purpose of life: glorification of God on earth through one's occupational calling. Because everyone's material rewards were actually God's, and the purpose of life was to glorify God, profits should be multiplied (through reinvestment) rather than used in the pursuit of personal pleasures.

Symbolic Interactionism and Religion

Sociologist Peter Berger (1990) captured the relationship between religion and symbolic interactionism in his book, *The Sacred Canopy*. In this book, Berger explored the idea that humans create from their religious traditions, a canopy, or cover, of symbolic meanings, to "lay" over the secular world. These otherworldly symbolic meanings are used to guide everyday social interaction. Religious beliefs, rituals, and ideas tell people the difference between the sacred and the profane and provide stability and security in a changing and uncertain existence.

Symbolic interactionism, for example, helps us understand the expression "there are no atheists in foxholes." Insecurity and uncertainty, of course, are at a peak in the life-and-death situation of war, and the desire to regain

Demonstration

Here is a demonstration to illustrate how symbolic interactionism interprets sacredness. Tell students that as of today, the "high five" is a sacred symbol that is only to be used as a sign of reverence. Reward students for correct answers, high test scores, etc. by honoring them with high fives. Soon students will see that the symbolic interaction of the high five has meaning because the class has given it meaning. What would happen if students started applying that meaning when people outside of class gave them a high five? Others wouldn't understand the significance of the gesture. What reactions might this evoke?

Figure 14.3 Focus on Theoretical Perspectives

Religion. This table shows that in examining religion the three major perspectives focus on different aspects. Discuss the conclusion of any one of the theories in light of your experience with the institution of religion.

Theoretical Perspective	Focus	Conclusion
Functionalist 	Look at contributions of religion to society.	Religion legitimates social arrangements. It promotes social unity. It provides a sense of understanding. It encourages a sense of belonging.
Conflict Theory	Elites use religion to manipulate the masses.	Religion is used by the most powerful to justify their economic, political, and social advantages. 
Symbolic Interactionism 	People create symbolic meanings from their religious beliefs, rituals, and ideas.	People use their socially created symbolic meanings to guide everyday social interactions.

security and certainty is a natural human response. Religious meanings, especially those related to an afterlife, can offer some relief. Japanese kamikaze pilots in World War II and Middle Eastern terrorists infuse their sometimes suicidal behavior with ultimate meaning by focusing on their reward beyond life. Less dramatically, people enduring troubled marriages can be strengthened by their commitment to uphold their holy vows of matrimony spoken in a place of worship.

Each of the three major theoretical perspectives aids in the sociological study of religion. Figure 14.3 shows the unique light each perspective sheds.

> "You have not converted a man because you have silenced him."
>
> **John, Viscount Morley**
> **English statesman**

Section 2 Assessment

1. How did Karl Marx view religion?
2. What was Weber's contribution to the sociological study of religion?
3. What did Berger mean by the phrase "the sacred canopy"?

Critical Thinking

4. **Analyzing Information** Does the Protestant ethic still exist in America today? Use Weber's analysis to justify your position.

Cooperative Learning Activity

Divide the class into groups to discuss the expression "there are no atheists in foxholes." They should also discuss the Japanese kamikaze pilots and terrorists. What are students' thoughts on these topics? Do they believe a "foxhole conversion" is legitimate? Why or why not? What do they think about sacrificing one's life for a religious cause? Why would a society encourage the norm? How would society benefit from a loss of its members? **L1**

Working with the Data

Figure 14.3 Answers will vary, and will depend on each student's personal views. A person taking the functional perspective will see how religion has contributed to society. Conflict theorists see how religion is full of conflict, and symbolic interactionists will see how religious symbols guide social interactions. For example, a student wearing a crucifix on his or her neck makes a statement to others.

Answers to Section 2 Assessment

1. Marx believed that religion is used by the ruling class to justify its control and advantages over the oppressed.
2. Weber believed the Protestant ethic encouraged the spirit of capitalism. This ethic considered hard work to be a moral obligation, and encouraged reinvestment of capital for further profits (instead of using it for immediate gratification).
3. Berger believed that people created a canopy, or cover, of symbolic meanings from their religious traditions to "lay" over the secular world to guide everyday social interaction.

Critical Thinking

4. Answers will vary and should be supported.

Tech Trends

Is Cloning Humans Ethical?

Aldous Huxley's 1932 novel *Brave New World* described a society in which babies were created in test tubes. Another novel—*The Boys from Brazil*, written by Ira Levin and published in 1972—features a story about German Nazis cloning Adolf Hitler. Both of these books play on our fears about the effects and ethics of human cloning (a nonsexual creation of a genetically identical copy). Although no human has yet been cloned, the reproduction of a sheep called Dolly in February 1997, along with several subsequent clonings of mice, sheep, and pigs, have made the question much more pertinent today than it was a few years ago.

Even though the technology is not yet available to clone humans, companies and scientists are already beginning to offer their services to interested individuals. Dr. Richard Seed, an American physicist, announced in 1998 that he plans to clone humans, using himself as the first subject. He also plans to open a for-profit clinic to assist childless couples in cloning themselves. A company called Valiant Venture, Ltd., has been formed to offer cloning services to humans—for as "little" as $200,000. Valiant Venture, Ltd., is owned by the Raelian Movement, an international cult whose members claim that life on earth was created in laboratories by extraterrestrials.

More traditional religious groups have expressed serious concerns about cloning. According to the general argument of Judaism and Christianity, human cloning allows the sacred process of generating life to enter the profane realm. A group of scientists sponsored by the Church of Scotland reached the following conclusions.

- If humans are cloned, people will be placing themselves in a position only God has occupied.
- The basic dignity and uniqueness of each individual will be violated.
- Political power could influence the creation of clones.
- Cloning will be limited to those who can afford it.

On the other hand, might it not be beneficial to clone Bill Gates, Mother Theresa, or Michael Jordan? What about the potential contributions from a new Christiaan Barnard, the South African physician who did the first heart transplant in 1967? Human cloning is just the latest in a long line of medical technologies that affect the length and quality of life. Society will have to decide if cloning is so different from other scientific advances that it should be legally prohibited.

Analyzing the Trends

What role, if any, should religion play in the debate over human cloning? Include some information from this chapter to support your answer.

Tech Trends

Interested students can find information about anti-cloning movements on the web by searching on the key words *Movement Against the Cloning of Humans*, or on *Jeremy Rifkin*. Rifkin, an antibiotechnology activist, is the leading opponent of human cloning. Proponents of cloning say that it could help research for the prevention of Parkinson's disease and Alzheimer's. Have students debate the pros and cons of this topic.

Answers to Analyzing the Trends

Hopefully, students will be able to approach this question from the sociological perspective. That is, what is the effect of cloning on society? Realistically, this issue pits religion versus science and secularism versus fundamentalism. If students debate the topic, be sure the secular and religious points of view are equally represented.

Integrating the Teacher Resources

Look for Ethics, Values, and Technology: Real-Life Issues in Society, available in your Teacher's Resource Box. The booklet provides primary source readings dealing with real-life controversies. Student worksheets are included.

On-Demand Writing

In January 2000, the first clone of a clone (a 96-pound calf) was born in Japan. The first rhesus monkey was cloned in Oregon, and Geron Corporation received a patent from the British government that covered cloned human embryos.

Researchers are interested in cloning for hundreds of reasons from animal research to improving agricultural products to fighting diseases in humans. But the concern about the ethics is also growing daily, led by antibiotechnology activist Jeremy Rifkin. Rifkin is opposed to any patenting of human gene technology on the grounds that "human life cannot be intellectual property." On the other side, cloning offers hope to make advances in fighting diseases that had previously been "untouchable," such as Parkinson's and Alzheimer's.

Explain to students that the vision of mad scientists creating giant "baby farms" in petrie dishes is not realistic. Most cloning

Using the Section Preview

Have students work in groups to research different religions or religious denominations. Have them answer the following: What is the religion's origin? What are the fundamental beliefs, religious rites, and worship rules? Who are the leaders? How many members are there? Who is the deity? What is the religion's holy book? Students might want to create posters or PowerPoint presentations to share their research with the class.

Section 3 Religious Organization and Religiosity

Key Terms

- church
- denomination
- sect
- cult
- religiosity

Section Preview

The major forms of religious organization are churches, denominations, sects, and cults. Religiosity—the ways people express their religious interests and convictions—can be analyzed in terms of five dimensions: belief, ritual, intellect, experience, and consequences.

Religious Organization

In Western societies, most people practice religion through some organizational structure. For this reason, the nature of religious organization is an important component of the sociological study of religion. Early scholars identified four basic types of religious organization: *church, denomination, sect,* and *cult.*

How do sociologists distinguish among the basic types of religious organization? To sociologists, a **church** is a life-encompassing religious organization to which all members of a society belong. This type of religious organization exists when religion and the state are closely intertwined. In Elizabethan England, for example, Archbishop Richard Hooker of the Church of England wrote that "there is not any man of the Church of England but the same man is also a member of the commonwealth; nor any man a member of the commonwealth which is not also of the Church of England." As you can see, the sociological definition of *church* is different from the one commonly used in American society. When Americans talk about "churches," they are actually referring to denominations.

A **denomination** is one of several religious organizations that most members of a society accept as legitimate. Because denominations are not tied to the state, membership in them is voluntary, and competition among them for

church
a life-encompassing religious organization to which all members of a society belong

denomination
one of several religious organizations that most members of a society accept as legitimate

The Amish are a religious sect. How does a sect differ from a church, denomination, or cult?

Integrating the Teacher Resources

Look for the Chapter 14 Vocabulary Activity worksheet in the Unit 4 Mastering Basic Concepts booklet in your Teacher's Resource Box. It provides reinforcement for vocabulary in this chapter.

projects involve the prodding of immature (embryonic) cells to grow into one particular kind of more than 200 types of specialized cells such as blood, liver, or brain cells. Access to these specialized cells enables scientists to conduct many more experiments and procedures to help discover the causes of disease. For example, scientists hope to eventually be able to create healthy brain cells from the patient's own genetic material. Researchers are also looking for ways to use cells other than those from embryos, such as skin or kidney. It is the use of embryonic cells which many people find controversial.

Cloning watchdogs are worried not just about the abuse of cloning, but how the benefits of this research will be distributed. Will only the wealthy be able to afford the new hearts and lungs that might be cloned? Have your students write their views of this controversial topic.
L2

Sociology Today

Understanding the Danger of Cults

In late November 1978, news began to arrive in the United States that a semireligious, socialistic colony in Guyana, South America, headed by the Reverend Jim Jones—founder of the California-based People's Temple—had been the scene of a shocking suicide-murder rite in which some nine hundred people died from cyanide poisoning. Many Americans wondered how people could have become involved in something like that.

Some dismissed the participants as ignorant or mentally unbalanced. But as more news came out, it became known that many of the members were fairly well-educated young people and that Jones was trusted and respected by some members of the California political establishment. We also learned that such events, although rare, have occurred before.

Why are people willing to join extremist religious groups? Sociology can help us understand the motivations.

- *Most converts to extremist religious groups seek friendship, companionship, acceptance, warmth, and recognition.* These groups can provide a supportive community that helps overcome past loneliness and isolation. They can provide emotional ties that converts have not found at home, school, church, or work. Many groups even adopt kinship terms to give recruits new identities to separate them from their former lives.
- *Most extremist religious groups emphasize immediate experience and emotional gratification.* Converts "feel" religion rather than merely think about it. Whether by meditation, speaking in tongues, or singing hymns, followers have frequent and intense emotional experiences they have not found elsewhere.
- *Extremist religious groups emphasize security through strict authority.* Under a firm authority structure and a clear, simple set of beliefs and rules, converts have something in which they can believe. Converts think they can exchange

The Reverend Jim Jones was the leader of a religious colony in Guyana, South America, where some nine hundred people were involved in a suicide-murder rite.

Sociology Today

The importance of understanding the danger of some cults should be made clear to students. The actions of several cults, such as Heaven's Gate, the Branch Davidians, and the group headed by Jim Jones have resulted in the deaths of their members.

More recently in Uganda, more than 900 members of the Movement for the Restoration of the Ten Commandments of God cult were murdered/committed suicide. Ask students if they think people research cults and other groups before joining. If not, why don't they?

Open-Response Question

Ask students to theorize about what kind of personality traits are most common among cult leaders. What types of personalities do they think would most likely respond to the leader's personality?

Encouraging Citizenship Activity

This activity will help students increase their ability to tolerate opinions they may not agree with—a necessary skill in a multicultural democracy. Ask students to learn what religions are represented in school. Help them organize and implement a panel discussion of the various religions represented. (Make sure that they have permission to hold the discussion and that they hold it after school hours, as a voluntary panel, not as something required.)

Have students in the discussion explain their religion, its beliefs, and practices. Try to find similarities between the various religions. The objective of such a discussion should be increasing understanding, tolerance, learning, and ultimately, unity. **L1** uncertainty, doubt, and confusion for trust and assurance through absolute obedience.

- *Extremist religious groups claim to offer authenticity and naturalness in an "artificial" world.* By emphasizing such things as natural foods, communal living apart from civilization, and a uniform dress code, these groups attempt to show they are not part of the flawed outside world.

Religious movements may not actually be able to meet their followers' needs any better than the outside world. Many of these religious groups lead to disillusionment, frustration, and bitterness when members realize that they cannot completely escape the outside world, which is full of uncertainty, confusion, fuzzy choices, and shades of gray. Moreover, many of these religious groups have joined the consumer society they profess to deplore, attractively packaging and selling themselves to the public. Not only may the new religious groups not solve the problems people in modern society must face, many are as inauthentic as they accuse society of being.

Some key questions exist to evaluate the authenticity of any religious group's claims. For purposes of self-protection, these questions should be answered carefully before committing to an extremist religious group.

Friends and family mourn the loss of loved ones who died in Jim Jones's People's Temple mass suicide.

- Does it require that you cut yourself off from family and friends?
- Does it consider drugs to be a major vehicle for true religious experiences?
- Is corporal punishment or intensive, hours-long psychological conditioning a part of its program?
- Does it claim to have special knowledge that can be revealed only to insiders?

If the answer to any *one* of these questions is yes, you stand a chance of getting "hooked." If the answers to *several* of these questions are positive, the chances of getting hooked increase dramatically.

Doing Sociology

1. Do you agree or disagree with the reasons given for why people join extremist religious groups? Discuss each reason and explain why you agree or disagree.
2. Can you think of other reasons why people may be attracted to such groups? Show that any reason you identify does not fit into one of the four reasons stated.
3. If you had a friend considering membership in an extremist religious group, how would you use the information in this Sociology Today to discourage him or her?

Answers to Doing Sociology

1. Answers will vary.
2. One answer is that teens tend to be attracted to alternatives. Teens might see such a group as "cool" and helpful for defining their identity.
3. After students have shared their suggestions, you might want to arrange for a school psychologist or other expert to address this issue further.

Integrating the Teacher Resources

Look for Chapter 14 Analyzing and Interpreting Data worksheet in the Unit 4 Mastering Basic Concepts booklet in your Teacher's Resource Box for skill-building exercises based on the graphs, charts, and maps in this chapter.

On-Demand Writing

Have students do some Internet research to find the stories of people who were former (reclaimed) members of extremist religious groups. They should try to get answers to such questions as: What attracted the person to the group? Why did they stay? Why did they decide to leave? What was life like as part of the group?

If you can locate a former cult member, you might invite him or her to talk with your class. Have students prepare questions to ask the speaker ahead of time.

L1

members is socially acceptable. Being one religious organization among many, a denomination generally accepts the values and norms of the secular society and the state, although it may at times oppose them. As mentioned, most American "churches"—Methodist, Episcopalian, Presbyterian, Baptist, Roman Catholic, and Reform Jew, for example—are actually denominations.

sect
a religious organization that arises out of a desire to reform an existing religious organization

A **sect** is a religious organization formed when members of an existing religious organization break away in an attempt to reform the "parent" group. Generally, sect members believe that some valuable beliefs or traditions have been lost by the parent organization, and they form their own group to save these features. Thus, they see themselves not as establishing a new religious faith but as redeeming an existing one. The withdrawal of a sect from the parent group is usually psychological, but some sects go farther and form communal groups apart from the larger society. The Separatists, or Pilgrims, who landed at Plymouth in 1620, wished to reform the Church of England from which they had separated. Another example is the Amish, a sect formed in 1693 when a Swiss bishop named Jacob Amman broke from the Mennonite church in Europe (Kraybill and Olshan, 1994). Less extreme sects in the United States today include the Seventh-Day Adventists, the Quakers, and the Assemblies of God.

cult
a religious organization whose characteristics are not drawn from existing religious traditions within a society

Unlike a sect, a **cult** is a religious organization whose characteristics are not drawn from existing religious traditions within a society. Whether imported from outside the society or created within the society, cults bring something new to the larger religious environment. We often think of cults as engaging in extreme behavior. The world has been shocked twice in recent years. In 1997, reports came of the ritualistic suicides of thirty-nine members of the Heaven's Gate cult in California (Thomas, 1997). Dwarfing this incident was the mass killing of ap-

In 1997, thirty-nine members of the Heaven's Gate cult in California committed ritualistic suicide. Most cults are not this dangerous, however.

SOCIOLOGY Online

Student Web Activity
Visit the *Sociology and You* Web site at soc.glencoe.com and click on **Chapter 14—Student Web Activities** for an activity on religious organizations.

Open-Response Question

Ask students why denominations are most likely to develop and thrive in a pluralistic society.

Teaching Strategy

Have students research various cults such as Heaven's Gate, the Branch Davidians, or the Jonestown cult. Have students look for the similar characteristics that define cults such as the need for a charismatic leader (see Chapter 13) and members' need to belong. Have students identify the distinctions between these cults as well.
L2

Integrating the Teacher Resources

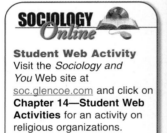

Look for the Chapter 14 Increasing Your Reading Comprehension worksheet and the Guided Reading worksheet in the Unit 4 Mastering Basic Concepts booklet in your Teacher's Resource Box. Both will strengthen student reading comprehension skills.

Cooperative Learning Activity

Santeria is a religion with roots in West Africa, in what is now Nigeria and Benin. Yoruba citizens who were taken to Cuba as slaves developed the religion, blending the worship of African deities (or *orishas*) with Roman Catholic beliefs. Santeria rites are led by a priest or a priestess, and frequently involve animal sacrifice. Reincarnation is also a core belief of this hybrid religion.

Have your students work in groups to discuss how they would classify Santeria: as a church, denomination, sect or cult. Encourage students to discuss what aspects of the religion might help to classify it: for

Calvin and Hobbes are engaged in a conversation about religiosity. Their beliefs are clashing.

proximately 1,000 members of the Ugandan cult called the Movement for the Restoration of the Ten Commandments of God ("Cult Killings Exceed Jonestown Toll," 2000). Cults do not usually appear in such an extreme and bizarre form, however. More conventional examples of cults are the Unification Church, the Divine Light Mission, and the Church of Scientology (Clark, 1993).

Religiosity

Sociologists Charles Glock and Rodney Stark are two sociologists who have studied religion and society. Their work has focused on **religiosity**—the types of religious attitudes and behavior people display in their everyday lives.

religiosity
ways in which people express their religious interests and convictions

How do people display religiosity? Glock and Stark identify five dimensions of religiosity: belief, ritual, an intellectual dimension, experience, and consequences (Glock, 1965; Stark, 1968).

- *Belief* refers to what a person considers to be true. People may, for example, believe that Jesus is the son of God or that there is no God but Allah.
- A *ritual* is a religious practice that the members of a religion are expected to perform. A ritual may be private, such as personal prayer, or public, such as attending mass.
- The *intellectual dimension* of religiosity may involve knowledge of holy or sacred scripture or an interest in such religious aspects of human existence as evil, suffering, and death. Religious persons are expected to be knowledgeable about their faith.

The display of religious affiliation varies widely. Golfer Tiger Woods wears a Buddha image, and a Jewish boy reads from the Torah at his Bar Mitzvah.

Reteaching

It is important that students understand the difference between *religion* and *religiosity.* Reinforce the text explanation by telling them that religiosity relates to observable behavior. Religiosity is an indicator that a person is "religious" but since there is no way to know what is in a person's heart, it is impossible to connect religiosity directly to religiousness. You might tell students that the gap between religiousness and religiosity is called hypocrisy.
ELL

Points to Stress

Although most rituals are religious in origin, many other areas have ritual behaviors associated with them. Sports figures and entertainers often go through procedures that border on rituals to ensure a positive outcome. Ask students if they have rituals they follow in their secular lives.

example, is it practiced by all the members of the society? Is it an attempt to reform a "parent" religion? Explain that the reason the Yoruba slaves incorporated Catholic beliefs into the religion was because they were prohibited from practicing African forms of worship. Does that mean that it should not be considered an offshoot of Christianity? Ask for volunteers to share their group's answers with the rest of the class.
L2

Snapshot of America

Religious Believers

Religion is common to all societies. Although the majority of Americans are Christian, many other faiths are represented in the United States. This map shows the percentage of the population of each state who identify themselves as members of a faith or religion.

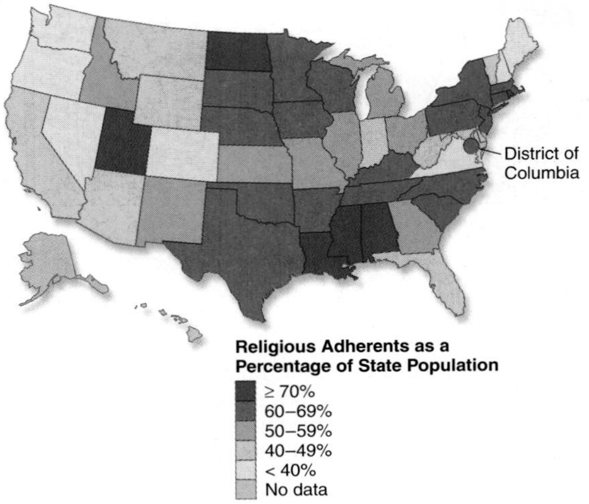

Interpreting the Map

1. Create a database comparing the number of religious believers in your state with other states in your region.
2. What do you think this map says about the state of religion in the U.S.? Explain.

Adapted from *The State of the U.S.A. Atlas*. New York: Touchstone.

- *Experience* encompasses certain feelings attached to religious expression. This dimension is the hardest to measure. For example, a religious believer may feel "close" to the deity when praying.
- *Consequences* are the decisions and commitments people make as a result of religious beliefs, rituals, knowledge, or experiences. Consequences may be social, such as opposing or supporting capital punishment, or personal, as when practicing sexual abstinence before marriage or telling the truth regardless of the cost.

Section 3 Assessment

1. In your own words, describe the difference between a cult and a sect.
2. Give one example of each of the five dimensions of religiosity, using examples not given in the text.

Critical Thinking

3. **Summarizing Information** Of the dimensions of religiosity discussed in the text, which do you think is most important to denominations today? Give reasons for your answer.

Snapshot of America

Answers to Interpreting the Map

1. Answers will vary. In addition to creating a database, have students write questions and answers about the number of religious believers in their state versus other states in their region.
2. It appears that, overall, more than 50 percent of Americans profess some kind of religious beliefs. Students may think this is a good sign, or they may see it more negatively. They should support their answers.

Answers to Section 3 Assessment

1. A sect is a religious organization formed when members of an existing religious organization break away in an attempt to reform the "parent" group. A religious cult's characteristics are not drawn from existing religious traditions. Instead of attempting to reform existing traditions, a cult introduces new ideas.
2. Students should think up their own examples for belief, ritual, intellectual dimension, experience, and consequences.

Critical Thinking

3. Answers will vary.

Section 4

Religion in the United States

Key Terms

- **secularization**
- **fundamentalism**

The Development of Religion in America

The search for religious freedom was only one of many reasons Puritan colonists came to America—but it was an important one. From the outset, the Puritans viewed themselves as a religious example for the world to follow and admire. Sociologist Robert Bellah has described the American religious connection this way:

> *In the beginning, and to some extent ever since, Americans have interpreted their history as having religious meaning. They saw themselves as being a "people" in the classical and biblical sense of the word. They hoped they were a people of God (Bellah et al. 1991:2).*

Section Preview

Through the process of secularization, the sacred and the profane tend to become intermixed. There has been a revival of religious fundamentalism in the United States. Religious faiths can be analyzed by major social characteristics such as class, and political tendencies.

The U.S. guarantees religious freedom. Pictured clockwise from the bottom left are a Hindu priest in Ohio, an Islamic prayer group in Maine, a Baptist congregation in Alabama, and a Jewish Chanukah celebration in Maryland.

Using the Section Preview

The separation of church and state is the foundation for freedom of religion in this country. Students might want to research the origins of religious thinking in this country by examining the writings of Thomas Jefferson, John Locke, and others whose philosophies were incorporated into the Bill of Rights. Have students report back to the class with their findings.

Integrating the Teacher Resources

For review or enrichment, use the Student Journal Prompts for this chapter, available in the Unit 4 Mastering Basic Concepts booklet in your Teacher's Resource Box.

Demonstration

To examine how religion might influence students' choice of friends, ask them to write their own religious affiliation on a piece of paper. Then have them write down the names of five friends and their religious backgrounds. Now have students consider the following questions: Did your friendships develop because of your religious affiliation? Have your friendships ever been tested because of your religious differences? How important is religion to you personally and in your friendships?
L1

The framers of the U.S. Constitution seldom raised arguments against religious faith. They were, however, sharply critical of any entanglement between religion and the state. Indeed, the ideas of separation of church and state and freedom of religious expression are cornerstones of American life. Despite this tradition, people in the United States have experienced incidents of religious persecution, including some directed at immigrant groups.

Religion has always been of great importance in American life; but historically, it has played a more active part in some periods than in others. There have been several "Awakenings" in U.S. history when religious principles have guided the development of culture and society. The 1830s, for example, saw new life come to many religious reform movements, including those against slavery and drinking alcohol. Later, the Protestant-led temperance movement resulted in the outlawing of alcohol for a short period during the 1920s.

Secularization in the United States

secularization
process through which the sacred loses influence over society

Countering the growth of religion in U.S. history is **secularization.** Through this process, the sacred loses influence over society, or aspects of the sacred enter into the secular (profane) world of everyday life. For example, formal education originally was a function of religion. Most early teachers and professors were clerics and church members. Over time in the United States, this function was taken over by the state, although many church-sponsored schools still exist.

Is secularization destroying religion in the United States? Evidence is mixed concerning the relative importance of religion in the United States today. On the one hand, some findings indicate a decline in the importance of religion. The percentage of Americans claiming that religion is very important in their lives fell from 75 percent in 1952 to 57 percent in 2001. (See Figure 14.4.) Scores on the Princeton Religion Index, made up of eight leading indicators, have also declined since the 1940s. In 1957, 14 percent of the public indicated that they believed religion was losing influence on American life. In 2001, 55 percent of the public saw a loss of influence (Gallup, 2001).

On the other hand, some recent research has found Americans today to still be highly committed to religion. Whether measured by the number of churches per capita, the proportion of regular churchgoers, or financial support of the churches, sociologist Theodore Caplow observed a trend toward greater involvement in religious affairs (Caplow, 1998).

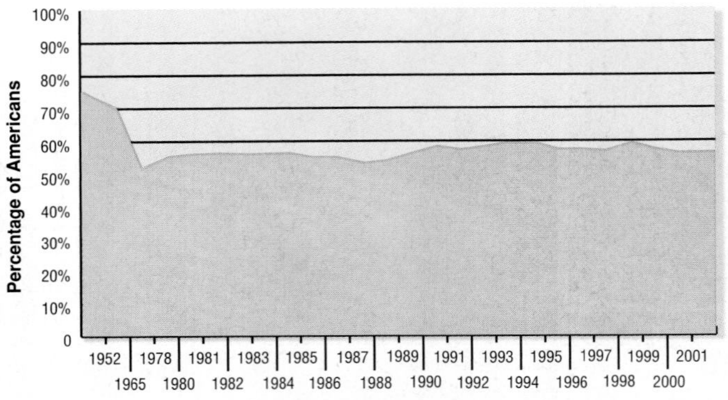

Figure 14.4 Percentage of Americans Saying Religion Is Very Important in Their Lives: 1952–2001. *This figure tracks changes in the percentage of Americans who say that religion is very important in their lives. Why do you think the percentage was so high in the early 1950s? What prediction do you make for the next ten years?*

Source: The Gallup Organization, Gallup polls on religion.

Reteaching

Students who are not familiar with the period of history called the Great Awakening or the Second Awakening should pick up a high school history book and refresh their memories. This period was an interesting and exciting time in our history and many social reforms grew out of these movements.

Working with the Data

Figure 14.4 The 1950s was a period characterized by great conformity. Many people went to church because they worried about how it would look to the neighbors if they weren't seen in church. Also, the country had just come through World War II and people were mindful of how fragile life and society could be.

Survey

To personalize your students' understanding of the sociology of religion in this country, ask them to conduct a survey. The questions they ask should parallel the information concerning religious preferences and religion, class, and politics. For example: "Do you believe in God or a universal spirit?" "Do you believe in life after death?" "Do you believe in heaven?" "Do you believe in hell?" "Do you believe in angels?" "Are you affiliated with any religious denomination, and if so, which one?" "Do you attend a church or synagogue in a typical week?" "What is your political affiliation?" When students have completed tabulation of their results, have them compare their results with those presented in Section 4. Do the results match? Why or why not?
L2

Figure 14.5 Global Comparisons in Religiosity

This table compares the level of religiosity among selected industrialized countries. Which finding do you think is the most important? Which finding is the most surprising to you? Explain in both cases.

Consider Selves Religious Persons		Attend Church at Least Weekly		Average Ratings of Importance of God*	
Italy	83%	Ireland	82%	United States	8.2
United States	81	United States	43	Ireland	8.0
Ireland	64	Spain	41	Northern Ireland	7.5
Spain	63	Italy	36	Italy	6.9
Great Britain	58	West Germany	21	Spain	6.4
West Germany	58	Czechoslovakia	17	Finland	6.2
Hungary	56	Ethnic Lithuanians	15	Belgium	5.9
France	51	Non-ethnic Lithuanians	12	Great Britain	5.7
Non-ethnic Lithuanians	50	Great Britain	14	West Germany	5.7
Czechoslovaks	49	Hungary	13	Norway	5.4
Scandinavia	46	France	12	Netherlands	5.3
Ethnic Lithuanians	45	Scandinavia	5	Hungary	4.8
				France	4.7
				Denmark	4.4

"10" is of highest importance.

Source: *Religion in America*, (Princeton, NJ: Princeton Religion Research Center).

In fact, as suggested in the Sociological Imagination opening this chapter, America still appears to be a religious nation when compared with other industrialized countries (see Figure 14.5). Only 8 percent of the American population is without a religious preference. About 88 percent identify themselves as Protestants, Catholics, Jews, or Mormons. There are now over three hundred recognized denominations and sects and thousands of independent congregations in the United States (Linder, 2000). About seven in ten Americans belong to some church, and over half of these claim to be active in their congregations. Four Americans in ten claim they have attended a church or synagogue in a typical week. (In England, for example, the average weekly church attendance is 14 percent.) Furthermore, although the proportion of Americans belonging to a church or synagogue has declined slightly from a high of 76 percent in 1947 to 69 percent in 1995, church attendance has changed very little over the years. Since 1939, weekly church or synagogue attendance in the United States has remained relatively stable—from 41 percent to 43 percent in 1995.

Americans also tend to support traditional religious beliefs. Ninety-six percent of the American population believe in God or a universal spirit, 65 percent believe in life after death, 90 percent believe in heaven, and 73 percent believe

Working with the Data

Figure 14.5 Students will naturally be interested to see that we rank ourselves highly in considering religious persons and in the importance of God in one's life. However, our church attendance, although high in comparison to other countries, does not appear to be a strong value. Students should discuss these variables and come up with several hypotheses about apparent contradictions or anomalies.

More About . . . Church Attendance

One study (Hardaway, 1993) found that even though people may report going to church regularly, actual observed attendance at church is not consistent with their reports. In this study, 33 percent of the Protestants surveyed reported attending church but the researcher observed that only 20 percent actually attended. Of the 51 percent of Catholics who reported attending church, only 28 percent were observed in attendance. This suggests that, in reality, people go to church much less often than they claim. Emphasize to students that claims about church attendance may be the most unreliable indicator of religiosity.

Focus on Research

If students visit the census bureau web site: **www.census.gov** they can find statistics on religion in the U.S. They might want to look at the size of the various groups that are most likely to view the electronic church, to ascertain the extent to which this medium might be utilized religiously.

Answers to Working with the Research

1. Those with less than a high school education, lower income groups, females, people over thirty-five years of age, blue-collar workers, retired persons, homemakers, regular churchgoers, and fundamentalists.
2. Students will probably disagree on this. Research suggests that this population is small but social changes can quickly cause anxiety. If it could figure out how to provide the sense of belonging that a physical church does, the electronic church might some day replace the traditional church.

Integrating the Teacher Resources

A lesson plan for a student research project related to the content of this chapter can be found in Doing Sociology: Focus on Research, available in your Teacher's Resource Box.

Focus on Research

Survey Research: The Electronic Church

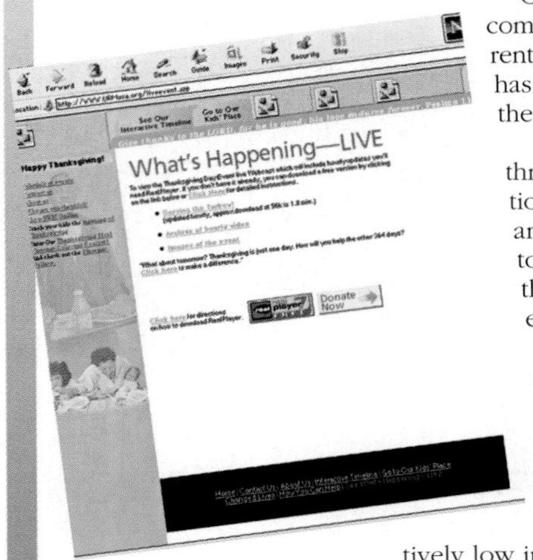

Along with the more "traditional" forms of radio and television, the Internet also offers remote religious services.

Old-time religious evangelists traveled from community to community and preached to the faithful in tents, open fields, or rented meeting halls. Modern-day communications technology has changed all that. To a great extent, radio, television, and the Internet are replacing the traditional meeting places.

Although the "electronic church" (church attendance through telecommunications) has attracted considerable attention, disagreement exists as to the actual size of its audience and the extent of its impact. Many television evangelists claim to have very large audiences, but most rating services estimate the total religious television audience to be of a rather modest size, approximately ten to thirteen million viewers.

William Stacey and Anson Shupe (1982) have advanced sociological understanding of the electronic church by examining the characteristics of its viewers. They surveyed residents of the Dallas–Fort Worth metropolitan area. This area is often referred to as the "buckle" of the southern Bible Belt.

Stacey and Shupe found regular viewers to have relatively low incomes and less than a high school education. Viewers also tended to be female, to be over thirty-five years of age, and to have large families. Blue-collar workers were more likely than white-collar workers to watch, but retired persons and homemakers were more likely to be viewers than people with jobs.

People who attended church regularly tended to watch, an important finding because it contradicted the claim that the electronic church was depriving local churches of members. Fundamentalists were more likely than reformed or moderate believers to tune in. The electronic church preaches to the converted who are already predisposed, or self-selected, to seek out its messages.

Working with the Research

1. According to Stacey and Shupe's research, what demographic groups are most likely to watch religious programming?
2. Would you predict that the electronic church will have greater social impact in the future? Why or why not?

Paired Learning Activity

Ask students to work with a partner to research the different churches in your community. (You may wish to assign one church to each pair.) Which churches consider themselves to be fundamentalist? Which do not? Students should write letters or make phone calls to get the information. Ask students to talk to the pastor or minister to find out if the church officially supports (with contributions or labor) any political or in hell. Seventy-two percent believe in the existence of angels (Gallup, 1996).

Religious Preferences

What are the religious preferences in the U.S.? Although there are over three hundred denominations and sects in the United States, Americans are largely Protestant (58 percent) and belong to a few major denominations—Baptist (20 percent), Methodist (10 percent), Lutheran (6 percent), Presbyterian (4 percent), and Episcopalian (4 percent). Fourteen percent prefer various other Protestant denominations. Catholics constitute a relatively large proportion of the American population (25 percent) and Jews a relatively small proportion (2 percent). As noted earlier, only 8 percent of Americans have no religious preference (Gallup, 1996). Figure 14.6 lists religious organizations in the United States with memberships above 300,000.

Religious Organizations in the U.S.	Number of Members
Roman Catholic Church	60,280,454
Southern Baptist Convention	15,663,296
United Methodist Church	8,538,662
Jewish	6,840,000
Lutheran Church in America	5,190,489
Muslim	5,000,000
Presbyterian Church (U.S.A.)	3,669,489
Episcopal Church	2,536,550
Assembly of God	2,387,982
United Church of Christ	1,472,213
Jehovah's Witnesses	966,243
Christian Church (Disciples of Christ)	929,725
Seventh-Day Adventist	790,731
Church of the Nazarene	601,900
Salvation Army	453,150
Wisconsin Evangelical Lutheran Synod	412,478
Reformed Church in America	306,312

Figure 14.6 Membership in Selected Religious Organizations in the United States. *On the basis of these data, how would you describe the religious composition of the U.S.?*

Sources: Gale Research and composite sources, 1995–1997.

Fundamentalism in America

Any careful observer of religion in the United States over the last twenty years or so will note the rise of religious *fundamentalism* in the country, especially among Protestant denominations. **Fundamentalism** is based on the desire to resist secularization and to adhere closely to traditional religious beliefs, rituals, and doctrines. It is, of course, inaccurate to limit fundamentalism to Protestants alone. Fundamentalism is found in all religions, including the Roman Catholic, Jewish, and Muslim faiths. This discussion, however, will focus on Protestant fundamentalism.

fundamentalism
the resistance of secularization and the rigid adherence to traditional religious beliefs, rituals, and doctrines

It is not surprising that most fundamentalists are politically conservative, given that the roots of contemporary religious fundamentalism are in the latter part of the nineteenth century. Two issues disturbed the early fundamentalists. First, fundamentalists were concerned about the spread of secularism. Science was challenging the Bible as a source of truth and Marxism was portraying religion as an opiate for the masses, Darwinism was challenging the biblical interpretation of creation, and religion was generally losing its traditionally strong influence on all social institutions. Second, fundamentalists rejected the movement away from emphasis on the traditional message of Christianity toward an emphasis on social service (Johnstone, 1996).

Since the late 1960s, the largest American Protestant denominations—Methodists, Lutherans, Presbyterians, Episcopalians—have either been declining in membership or fighting to hold their own. In contrast, contemporary

Working with the Data

Figure 14.6 Students should see that the largest single religious group, by far, in the United States is the Roman Catholic Church. Remind students that some religions, such as Catholicism, have many members who are "nominally" active, that is, they belong to the organization because of birth (ascribed status). Other groups have memberships that are very active, so that absolute numbers alone do not necessarily indicate the level of power or influence they can wield. There are many issues to consider when evaluating an organization's influence and strength.

Addressing Current Social Issues

Ask students which racial/gender group they think is most religious. Are women more religious than men? What age group is most religious? According to the General Social Survey, African Americans are overwhelmingly the most religious ethnic group in the United States. Female church attendance was 59 percent, compared to 46 percent for males. Of those 65 years and older, 74 percent reported attending church regularly. African Americans, females, and the elderly scored higher than their counterparts on all other measures of religiosity.

social special interest groups. In other words, is there a social or political agenda attached to this church? If so, are members expected to follow the officially sanctioned policies or does the church allow dissenters? Remind students to state their questions in objective, non-offensive terms and to be respectful of all opinions. **L2**

Working with the Data

Figure 14.7 Student answers will vary, but they should note that it is likely that the trend will continue, based on information presented in the text.

More About . . . Religion and Politics

From the beginning of the Republic, America has struggled to reconcile religion and political democracy. Since Thomas Jefferson wrote about the Creator in the Declaration of Independence, the nation has been guided (at least in part) by a sense of divine mission. But when you get down to specific details, history offers little evidence of "a direct interplay between faith and presidential leadership." Four of the presidents were sons of preachers: Chester A. Arthur, Grover Cleveland, Woodrow Wilson, and Herbert Hoover. Only Wilson, however, had training in a seminary. Jimmy Carter was the most "manifestly pious" of the modern presidents, but did not succeed in getting elected to a second term in office. It appears that the separation of church and state is taken very seriously by White House aspirants.

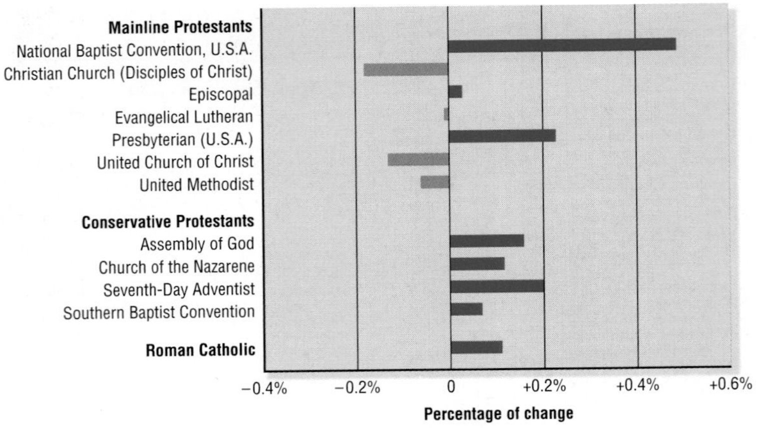

Figure 14.7 American Church Membership Trends: 1990–1999. *Do you believe that this pattern will continue in the twenty-first century? Explain your conclusion using text materials.*

Source: *Yearbook of American and Canadian Churches, 1999.*

fundamentalist denominations have been growing. Fundamentalists exist in all Protestant organizations, but they are predominantly found in such religious bodies as the Mormons, the Assemblies of God, the Seventh-Day Adventists, the Baptists, and the Jehovah's Witnesses. (See Figure 14.7.)

What is the nature of fundamentalism today? The theological agenda of today's fundamentalists is very close to that of their forebears in the nineteenth century.

Fundamentalists believe in the literal truth of the Scriptures, or in taking the Bible at "face value." Protestant fundamentalism involves being "born again" through acceptance of Jesus Christ as the Son of God who was sent to redeem mankind through his sacrifice. Fundamentalist doctrine includes belief in the responsibility of all believers to give witness for God, the presence of Satan as an active force for evil, and the destruction of the world prior to the Messiah's return to establish His kingdom on earth.

Are all fundamentalists alike? Religious organizations that share in much of the fundamentalist theology have some unique beliefs and practices of their own. An example is neo-Pentacostalism—or the *charismatic movement,* as it is sometimes called—which has occurred for the most part within traditional religious organizations, particularly the Roman Catholic and Episcopal churches. Those involved in this movement often speak of receiving "the baptism of the Holy Spirit." But central to most neo-Pentecostal groups is the experience of "speaking in tongues," which believers claim is a direct gift of the Holy Spirit (Cox, 1992, 1996; Hunt, Hamilton, and Walter, 1998).

Why is fundamentalism so strong today? Several reasons for the growth of fundamentalism have been proposed.

- Many Americans feel their world is out of control. The social order of the 1950s was shattered by a string of traumatic events beginning with the civil rights movement and progressing through campus violence, political assassinations, the Vietnam War, and Watergate. Increases in substance abuse, illegitimate births, divorce, and crime are taken as signs of moral decline. Fundamental religion, with its absolute answers and promise of eternal life, provides a strong anchor in a confusing, bewildering world.

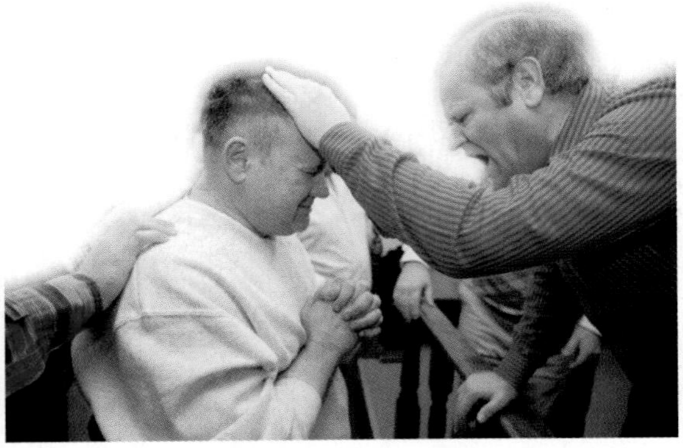

This charismatic minister in Atlanta is engaged in faith healing.

Using Decision-Making Skills

Separate the class into groups of 4 to 5 students each. Each group will assume the role of student, teacher, parent, or assistant principal. Groups will then determine a positive or negative response to the following scenario and submit a written response to be read to the class. Each group will make a recommendation. After each group shares, the class must agree on the appropriate action to take. Consensus, compromise, and negotiation are important skills to address.

Scenario:
Members of the Youth for Christ and the Fellowship of Christian Athletes have requested permission to hold lunch time prayer meetings as well as to continue meeting before school on Wednesdays at the flagpole.

- Fundamentalist churches, by emphasizing warmth, love, and caring, provide solace to people who are witnessing and experiencing the weakening of family and community ties. Mainline churches tend to be more formal and impersonal.
- Fundamentalist churches offer what they consider a more purely sacred environment, in contrast to mainline denominations that fundamentalists see as accommodating to secular society.
- The electronic church, in its role as part of the mass media, has been an important contributing factor in the growth of religious fundamentalism. (See Focus on Research on page 484.)

Religion, Class, and Politics

Religious affiliation is related to social class. There are marked differences in social class (as measured by education and income) among the various religions in the United States. Generally speaking, Presbyterians, Episcopalians, and Jews are at the top of the stratification structure. Below them are Lutherans, Catholics, and Methodists, followed by Baptists. Because these are average figures, there are, of course, many individual exceptions to these rankings.

Differences in religiosity exist between the upper and lower classes as well. Religion is important at both ends of the stratification structure, but the upper and lower classes express their beliefs in different ways. The upper classes display their religiosity through church membership, church attendance, and observance of ritual, whereas people in the lower classes more often pray privately and have emotional religious experiences.

Political affiliation, too, is related to religion. Followers of the Jewish faith are particularly aligned with the Democratic Party, followed in strength of support by Catholics and Protestants. This is predictable, because Protestants generally are more politically conservative than Catholics or Jews, and the Democratic Party is generally not associated with political conservatism in the United States today. Of the major Protestant denominations, the greatest support for the Republican Party is found among Episcopalians and Presbyterians. This is hardly surprising, because the upper classes are more likely to be identified with the Republican Party.

There are some contradictions in this general pattern. Despite their affiliation with the more conservative Republican Party, Episcopalians and Presbyterians are less conservative than Baptists, who are the strongest supporters of the Democratic Party of all Protestant denominations, especially in the South.

Religion, Science, and Society

Both science and religion examine humanity's relationship to the world, but they examine it in very different ways. Religion involves matters beyond human observation, while science is all about observation. These fields of study are not mutually exclusive. Many scientists are religious individuals, while many professional clergy appreciate and support the intellectual achievements of the field of science.

Sometimes, however, these two institutions can appear to be in conflict. Depending on the values and norms of the culture, society may favor religious

More About . . . Religion and Science

The Scopes Monkey Trial of 1925 is a famous example of the clash between religion and science. In 1925, John Scopes, a young biology teacher, was arrested for teaching the theory of evolution to his high school class. At the time, it was against the law in the state of Tennessee to teach anything other than creationism. The two lawyers in the case, Clarence Darrow and William Jennings Bryan, both legends in their own right, argued the case, which garnered much media attention. (It also happened to be one of the first trials covered by radio). Scopes was ultimately found guilty and forced to pay a $100.00 fine, but the state of Tennessee never enforced the law again, due to the widespread media attention it received. The movie *Inherit the Wind* is based on this trial, and should be available in most video stores.

Your principal has tasked you with serving on a committee made up of eight students (two from each grade level), two teachers, two parents, and two assistant principals. Your committee has been directed to reach a group consensus: whether to allow religious freedom to these groups or restrict their activities on campus. You ponder their constitutional rights of free speech and expression, and you remember a comment that Richard W. Riley, the Secretary of Education, recently stated on the news: "Public schools can neither foster religion nor preclude it."

Will you allow religious freedom, or restrict their activities? Explain your reasons for your decision.

L1

Pulling it All Together

There are several social characteristics that can be utilized to understand religious faith, such as social class and political affiliation. Over time, the sacred and profane have become intermixed in secularization. A movement called fundamentalism, which is based on the desire to resist secularization, has gained in popularity recently.

Answers to Section 4 Assessment

1. Through secularization, the sacred loses influence over society, or aspects of the sacred enter into the secular (profane) world of everyday life. It is important to explore this process because secularization counters the growth of religion, which has always been of great importance in American life.
2. Generally, Protestants are more politically conservative than Catholics and Jews, and therefore lean more towards the Republican Party (the greatest support is found among Episcopalians and Presbyterians). Catholics and Jews are more inclined toward the liberal perspective of the Democratic Party.

Critical Thinking

3. Answers will vary.

Religion and science sometimes come into heated conflict. One famous case was the 1925 "Monkey Trial" of John Thomas Scopes in Tennessee.

or scientific explanations. In the United States, following the principle of separation of state and church, it has been common to keep religion apart from government-sponsored institutions. Scientific explanations for natural phenomena, when commonly accepted, have been taught in the schools, leaving religious groups free to teach other interpretations within their organizations.

Strict fundamentalists do not believe that scientific theories such as the theory of evolution and the Big Bang theory of creation should be presented in public schools as facts, while Bible-based explanations such as creationism are not even discussed. In 1999, fundamentalists used their influence in the Kansas Board of Education to remove any questions about evolution from the state high school exit examination. Until repealed in 2001, Kansas teachers were no longer required to teach the theory of evolution.

Today, many people are questioning whether "pure science" can remain independent of cultural or social norms, as some scientists believe. Scientific discoveries and processes, such as cloning and gene therapy, are moving into ever more ethically debatable areas. The result appears obvious: the interface between science and religion is sure to increase. Society, in particular government, will need to learn how to deal constructively with apparent contradictions in these two areas.

> "Science without religion is lame, religion without science is blind."
>
> **Albert Einstein**
> **Nobel Laureate physicist**

Section 4 Assessment

1. What is secularization and why is it an important process to explore?
2. Describe the relationship between religion and political allegiance in the U.S.

Critical Thinking

3. **Analyzing Information** Analyze how progress in scientific research will affect religious beliefs and practices over the next twenty-five years.

Learning Styles

Linguistic/Bodily-kinesthetic Both science and religion examine humanity's relationship to the world, but they examine it in very different ways. After reading and discussing Religion, Science, and Society, ask students to role-play what they think might have transpired in 1999 when fundamentalists used their influence in the Kansas Board of Education to remove questions about evolution from the state high school examination. You may either ask students to do additional research about the experience, or to purely speculate after reading the information in the text. Conclude with a discussion of the fact that scientific discoveries and processes are moving into ever more ethically debatable areas, with the result that the interface between science and religion will increase. How can society learn to deal constructively with apparent contradictions in these two areas?
L3

CHAPTER 14 ASSESSMENT

ANSWERS CHAPTER 14 ASSESSMENT

Summary

Section 1: Religion and Sociology

Main Idea: Religion is concerned with sacred things. Sociologists studying religion face some unique problems. They do not judge the validity of various religions but rather look at those aspects of religion that can be measured and observed in society.

Section 2: Theoretical Perspectives

Main Idea: Religion has several functions. It legitimates the structure of society, promotes social unity, and provides a sense of meaning and belonging. Marx argued that religion is used to justify and maintain the group in power. Weber believed that religion could promote social change. He connected the Protestant ethic and the rise of capitalism.

Section 3: Religious Organization and Religiosity

Main Idea: The major forms of religious organization are churches, denominations, sects, and cults. Religiosity—the ways people express their religious interests and convictions—can be analyzed in terms of five dimensions: belief, ritual, intellect, experience, and consequences.

Section 4: Religion in the United States

Main Idea: Through the process of secularization, the sacred and the profane tend to become intermixed. Religious faiths can be analyzed by major social characteristics such as class, and political tendencies.

SOCIOLOGY Online

Self-Check Quiz
Visit the *Sociology and You* Web site at soc.glencoe.com and click on **Chapter 14—Self-Check Quizzes** to prepare for the chapter test.

Reviewing Vocabulary

Complete each sentence using each term once.

a. religion
b. sacred
c. profane
d. legitimate
e. spirit of capitalism
f. Protestant ethic
g. church
h. denomination
i. sect
j. cult
k. religiosity
l. secularization
m. fundamentalism

1. ____________ is the word used to describe things and ideas that are set apart and given a special meaning.
2. A religious movement based on the desire to adhere closely to traditional beliefs, rituals, and doctrines is called ____________.
3. The ____________ are the nonsacred aspects of life.
4. ____________, is the name given to a cluster of values, norms, beliefs, and attitudes that favored the growth of capitalism.
5. ____________ means to justify or give official approval to.
6. A religious organization arising out of a desire to reform another religious organization is called ____________.
7. ____________ is the obligation to reinvest money rather than spending it.
8. ____________ is the name given to a life-encompassing religious organization to which all members of a society belong.
9. A unified system of beliefs and practices concerned with sacred things is called ____________.
10. The ways in which people express their religious interests and convictions is called ____________.
11. A ____________ is a religious organization whose characteristics are not drawn from existing religious tradition within a society.
12. The process through which the sacred loses influence over society is known as ____________.

Integrating the Teacher Resources

For review, use the Chapter 14 Vocabulary Quiz and Chapter Quiz available in the Unit 4 Mastering Basic Concepts booklet in your Teacher's Resource Box.

Reviewing Vocabulary

1. b
2. m
3. c
4. f
5. d
6. i
7. e
8. g
9. a
10. k
11. j
12. l
13. h

Reviewing the Facts

1. Class and political tendencies.
2. There is no significant increase or decrease since 1970.
3. Order will vary: Church Attendance + Church Membership + Observance of Rituals = Religiosity
4. A cult.
5. Emile Durkeim

ANSWERS CHAPTER 14 ASSESSMENT

Thinking Critically

1. The cross can mean whatever someone wants it to mean. It is only because society has assigned it religious meaning that people immediately identify its symbolism. If someone had never before seen a crucifix, it is likely that it would have no meaning to them.
2. Many students will say that sermons are boring and long. Ask students what they would want to hear about if they could decide on the subject matter of sermons. Invite students to write "sermons" on topics of their choosing.
3. Christmas seems to be the most prominent example of how our society integrates materialism with the religious meaning of holidays. Students might want to discuss examples of how their families avoid materialism in their religious celebrations.
4. Sociologists study the social dimensions of religion, but not the theological. They can use sophisticated statistical measures to determine if variables like church attendance affect religiosity.
5. Answers will vary.
6. African American history has been heavily influenced by religion. Historians attribute this to slavery—churches became sanctuary from the oppression that existed. As the Civil Rights movement gained momentum, African Americans unified through churches. Religion has proven to be a source of strength and power in this minority community.
7. Reasons for teenagers' lack of interest in religion and church attendance can include an inability to relate to church doctrine, greater interest in other activities (athletics, work, etc.), and rebellion against parents and other authority figures.

Sociology Projects

1. See page 462 (Lead-Off Activity) in the Teacher's Edition for questions students should consider when researching religions.
2. A good choice for this activity is football. Some people view and treat football like a religion. For example, it

CHAPTER 14 ASSESSMENT

13. A ______________ is one of several religious organizations that most members of a society accept as legitimate.

Reviewing the Facts

1. Religious faiths can be analyzed by two major social characteristics. What are those characteristics?
2. Based on Figure 14.4 on page 482, have the percentage of Americans who claim that religion is very important in their lives, decreased over time, increased over time, or showed no significant change.
3. How does the upper social class define its religiosity? Use the diagram below to record your answer.

RELIGIOSITY AS DEFINED BY THE UPPER CLASS

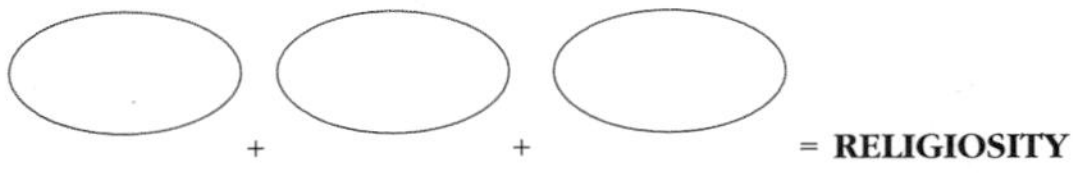

4. In 1978, the Reverend Jim Jones led hundreds of people who belonged to his group in a mass suicide-murder. What term is used to describe Jones's religious organization?
5. Which sociologist published *The Elementary Forms of Religious Life* in 1915 and spoke of the functions of religion?

Thinking Critically

1. **Making Inferences** The crucifix is a widely known symbol even to non-Christians. How do the various meanings attached to this symbol relate to an understanding of Durkheim's concept of the sacred and profane? Could the crucifix easily represent other things if it was not for its relationship to Christ? Explain your answer.
2. **Drawing Conclusions** Current research says that religion often reflects conventional (traditional) norms. Accordingly, religious clergy tend to address their messages to the more traditional segments of society. Sermons, for example, are aimed at the typical married family arrangement (mother, father, two children). What effect, if any, do you think this could have on general attendance at gatherings?
3. **Analyzing Information** The United States has one of the highest standards of living in the world. It also has one of the most materialistic cultures and societies. Do you think this says anything about the religiosity of Americans?
4. **Making Inferences** Ninety-six percent of all Americans say they believe in God. Nevertheless, defining who is or is not religious is very difficult. Some people don't go to church yet claim to be religious, while others go to church but don't seem to be religious, for example. What dilemmas do all these issues present for sociologists who want to study religiosity? What variables could help to explain what religiosity is? Why do you think sociologists should research this issue at all?
5. **Analyzing Information** Do you think that economic decisions are influenced by religiously-based motivations? Elaborate.
6. **Evaluating Information** Based on scales developed by sociologists, African Americans rate higher in religiosity than other racial or ethnic groups. Men like Martin Luther King, Jr., and Ralph Abernathy and women like Aretha Franklin have attributed their success to the role religion played in their lives. What events in this country's history might have contributed to the role that religion plays in the African American community?
7. **Applying Concepts** Many people appear to be less interested in religion during their teenage years. This might be seen in falling church attendance for this age group. Using your sociological imagination, suggest some reasons for this apparent lack of interest. Consider developmental (age) and social factors. Depending on your answers, what suggestions might you make to religious organizations looking for ideas on how to keep teenagers involved and active?

Sociology Projects

1. **Researching Religions** Choose a religion, denomination, sect, or cult to research. You can learn about the group by talking with some of its members. You can also find excellent material in libraries and on the Internet. (Be sure to consider the source of all information gathered from the Internet. Check it for bias, accuracy, and "hidden agendas.") In your research, focus on the following aspects of the group: its origin; fundamental beliefs, important rituals or ceremonies; internal social changes that occurred over time; and membership demographics (social class, ethnicity, and so forth). You may want to work with a classmate. Based on your research, prepare a report with visual aids that can be given orally. (You may want to use a computer presentation package such as PowerPoint.)
2. **Sacred and Profane** The chapter discusses the concepts of *sacred* and *profane*. Any object by itself is profane; people give it sacred meaning. Working with two of your classmates, select an object (profane), and create a skit in which you show how the profane object might become a sacred object.
3. **Defining and Analyzing Religion** This exercise will help you understand the difficulty social scientists have when it comes to defining and analyzing religion. Take out a piece of paper and answer the following questions:
   - **a.** How do you define religion?
   - **b.** What does it mean to you?
   - **c.** Do you believe in the supernatural?
   - **d.** If you do believe in the supernatural, how do you imagine it to be?

   After everyone in class has completed these questions, turn to your neighbor and compare your answers with his or her answers. Note the similarities and differences. Share your answers with as many of your classmates as possible.
4. **Charitable Organizations** Contact a religious organization in your neighborhood, and arrange to take part in some community service activity in which this organization is involved. Pay close attention to the various ways in which these groups conduct charitable work. Report to the class on the effectiveness of your service—both for the recipient and for yourself. Then consider how your community would be affected if the group stopped providing this service. Would some political or non-governmental organization continue it?
5. **Attitudes on Religion** Design a survey that would allow you to conduct an "unofficial" study of student attitudes toward religion. (You may want to refer back to the section on survey methods in Chapter 2.) Remember that your questions are directed at social practices and not at what or why individuals specifically believe. Some topics you may want to ask about include attendance at religious services, prayer, and belief in an afterlife. Information about respondents' ethnic and religious backgrounds would prove useful as well. Compare your survey with the surveys created by your classmates. Work with four or five students to combine your questions into the best survey possible, and ask twenty students to complete the survey for your group. Report your findings to the class. Do these results reflect the community you live in? Do you think that teens are more or less outwardly religious than adults?

Technology Activity

1. Using your school or local library and the Internet, research information on the clergy during the middle ages. Based on your research and the material you read in this chapter, how would you classify their religious organization? Some of the characteristics of the clergy might be regarded as a cult. Explain why the clergy in the middle ages were not a cult. Using proper grammar, sentence structure, spelling, and punctuation, write a paragraph defending your conclusion.

ANSWERS CHAPTER 14 ASSESSMENT

causes them to congregate regularly on Sundays (in front of the television or at football games). You might have students use this scenario and design a skit likening a football game to a church service. Be sure to be sensitive to students who might not see the humor in this activity.

3. This is the Lead-Off Activity for this chapter. If you didn't have students answer these questions at the beginning of the chapter, have them do so now.
4. Many churches engage in volunteer work in the community. If students are already members of a religious organization, they might want to investigate why it performs the kinds of charity work it does.
5. If students address the five dimensions of religiosity, they should be able to construct a good survey of attitudes on religion. Check with an administrator before conducting this survey, however. Some might find the subject matter too personal.

Technology Activity

1. Basically there are elements that are the same as those found in cults (e.g., uniform dress; separated from family). However, the clergy was part of a religious organization that had characteristics that were drawn from existing religious traditions within the society. A cult is not drawn from such existing societal traditions.

Enrichment Reading

The concept of the sacred cow might be a difficult one for students to take seriously, given the vast consumption of beef products in this country. Inform students that this is a great example of cultural relativism—understanding a culture based on its standards, and not our own. You can draw parallels between Indians and their sacred cow to Native Americans and the buffalo. Native Americans consider the buffalo sacred, and essential for survival. The slaughter of the buffalo brought about demise of the Plains Indians. Both cultures attached sacred meaning to the animals that were a necessity for their way of life.

Integrating the Teacher Resources

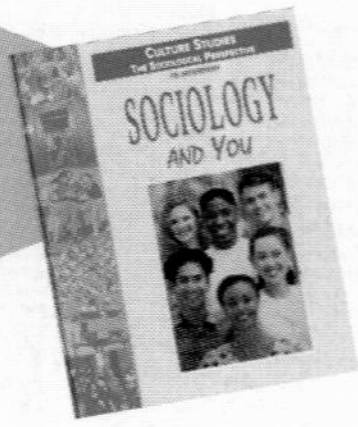

Additional primary source readings for this chapter can be found in Culture Studies: The Sociological Perspective, **available in your Teacher's Resource Box. Questions for students are included.**

Chapter 14

Enrichment Reading

India's Sacred Cow

by Marvin Harris

People often take their own religion for granted, overlooking its connections with the rest of society. We are better able to see the link between religious beliefs and culture when we examine an unfamiliar setting. Marvin Harris's analysis of the place of the cow in Hinduism provides such a backdrop.

News photographs that came out of India during the famine of the late 1960s showed starving people stretching out bony hands to beg for food while sacred cattle strolled behind undisturbed. The Hindu, it seems, would rather starve to death than eat his cow or even deprive it of food. The cattle appear to browse unhindered through urban markets eating an orange here, a mango there, competing with people for meager supplies of food.

By Western standards, spiritual values seem more important to Indians than life itself. Specialists in food habits . . . consider Hinduism an irrational **ideology** that compels people to overlook abundant, nutritious foods for scarcer, less healthful foods.

Cow worship . . . carries over into politics. In 1966 a crowd of 120,000 people, led by holy men, demonstrated in front of the Indian House of Parliament in support of the All-Party Cow Protection Campaign Committee. In Nepal, the only **contemporary** Hindu kingdom, cow slaughter is severely punished. As one story goes, the car driven by an official of a United States agency struck and killed a cow. In order to avoid the international incident that would have occurred when the official was arrested for murder, the Nepalese magistrate concluded that the cow had committed suicide. . . .

The easy explanation for India's devotion to the cow, the one most Westerners and Indians would offer, is that cow worship is an integral part of Hinduism. Religion is somehow good for the soul, even it if sometimes fails the body. Religion orders the cosmos and explains our place in the universe. Religious beliefs, many would claim, have existed for thousands of years and have a life of their own. They are not understandable in scientific terms.

But all this ignores history. There is more to be said for cow worship than is immediately apparent. The earliest Vedas, the Hindu sacred texts from the second millennium B.C., do not prohibit the slaughter of cattle. Instead, they ordain it as part of sacrificial rites. The early Hindus did not avoid the flesh of cows and bulls; they ate it at ceremonial feasts presided over by Brahman priests. Cow worship is a relatively recent development in India; it evolved as the Hindu religion developed and changed.

This evolution is recorded in royal **edicts** and religious texts written during the last 3,000 years of Indian history. The Vedas from the first millennium B.C. contain contradictory passages, some referring to ritual slaughter and others to a strict taboo on beef consumption. . . . [M]any of the sacred-cow passages were incorporated into the texts by priests of a later period.

By 200 A.D. the status of Indian cattle had undergone a spiritual transformation. The Brahman priesthood **exhorted** the population to **venerate** the cow and forbade them to abuse it or to feed on it. Religious feasts involving the ritual slaughter and consumption of livestock were eliminated and meat eating was restricted to the nobility.

Anthropologist Marvin Harris contends that science and culture can explain the reason cows are sacred to Hindus. How does he attempt to support his claim?

What Does it Mean?

ascertain
determine

contemporary
modern, current

edict
official proclamation or law

exhorted
strongly urged

ideology
a systematic body of thought about human culture or society

politically expedient
based on practical or advantageous reasons

venerate
worship or revere

By 1000 A.D., all Hindus were forbidden to eat beef. Ahimsa, the Hindu belief in the unity of all life, was the spiritual justification for this restriction. But it is difficult to **ascertain** exactly when this change occurred. An important event that helped to shape the modern complex was the Islamic invasion, which took place in the eighth century A.D. Hindus may have found it **politically expedient** to set themselves off from the invaders, who were beefeaters, by emphasizing the need to prevent the slaughter of their sacred animals. Thereafter, the cow taboo assumed its modern form and began to function much as it does today.

Source: Excerpted from James M. Henslin, *Down to Earth Sociology: Introductory Readings,* 10th ed., The Free Press, 1999.

Read and React

1. Summarize your understanding (prior to reading this article) of the Hindu religious belief about cows. Has your opinion changed after reading it? Why or why not?
2. How do non-Hindu people's reactions to the sacred cow relate to ethnocentrism and cultural relativism? Explain in each case, drawing on material in the reading.

Answer to Read and React

1. Answers will vary. Some students will find the Hindu belief difficult to understand.
2. Ethnocentrists view things from their own cultural perspective. Cultural relativists view things according to the standards of other cultures. Ethnocentrists would likely not understand how a culture would choose preservation of cows over feeding a starving population. The cultural relativist would see the symbolic value of the animal to the culture.

Integrating the Teacher Resources

For Spanish-speaking students, you may wish to use the reproducible worksheets available in the Spanish Supplements booklet in your Teacher's Resource Box. In addition to providing Spanish translations of selected Mastering Basic Concepts worksheets, the booklet contains English and Spanish summaries of the chapter's key points.

Chapter Preview

Section 1 (pages 496–502)

As a social institution, sport fulfills some important societal needs. One of these is helping individuals identify with other members of society. Sport subcultures have developed around both team and individual sports. For this reason, sport is a reflection of society.

Section 2 (pages 503–511)

Functionalists see sport positively, as a means for socializing young people, promoting social integration, providing a release for tensions, and developing sound character. Conflict theorists believe that organized sports can be harmful to character development. Symbolic interactionists focus on the self-concepts and relationships developed through sport activities.

Section 3 (pages 512–519)

Sport contributes to upward mobility among collegiate athletes, but the opportunities are too few. Minorities still face discrimination in sport. Women in sport suffer from gender-based stereotypes. Although this situation is slowly improving, intercollegiate female athletes do not receive treatment equal to males.

Chapter 15

Sport

Please see the correlation to the American Sociology Association standards located in the front of this text.

Lead-Off Activity

Recent research on sports images in the media (Vise, 1999) has found that that major sports magazines use an overwhelmingly large proportion of pictures of male athletes compared to female athletes. Have students work in groups to examine magazines like *Sports Illustrated* and *ESPN: The Magazine* and concentrate on the pictures of the athletes depicted. If possible, groups should look at one year's worth of issues, with the exception of any swimsuit editions. (You might ask students why these magazines have swimsuit editions in the first place.) Before they begin, have students form hypotheses as to how frequently women and minorities are presented in these magazines and why this is so. Have students compare the number of times males and females are featured on the covers, then have them compare the portrayals of men and women

USING Your Sociological Imagination

I haven't been the same since. I love it. All of a sudden I find I'm stronger than anyone else in the place—all the girls and practically all of the guys. . . . The boys respected me right away, and that's important. They all act like they're so tough, then you go in and lift more than they can. They can't ignore that there's a girl over in the corner doing more than them, and they hang their heads.

As this young female power lifter tells us, playing sport can positively affect the self-image of females, as well as improve gender relations. The desire to achieve such benefits was part of the motivation for the passage of Title IX of the Educational Amendment Act passed by the U.S. Congress in 1972. Title IX makes gender discrimination illegal in any educational institution receiving federal funds. Thanks to Title IX an increasing number of females have joined school athletic teams. Critics of Title IX fear that shifting funds from men's sports places an unfair strain on the most popular athletic programs, but defenders of Title IX do not believe that men's programs must suffer for women to gain opportunities (Nixon and Frey, 1996).

Some sociologists refer to social institutions such as sport, health, and entertainment as *secondary institutions.* These institutions are less pervasive than the family, education, politics, economics, or religion, but they also occur in every society. This chapter will look at how sport contributes to the functioning and nature of society in the United States.

Sections

1. **The Nature of Sport**
2. **Theoretical Perspectives and Sport**
3. **Social Issues in Sport**

Learning Objectives

After reading this chapter, you will be able to

- justify sport as an American institution.
- compare and contrast sport in America from a functionalist, conflict, and symbolic interactionist perspective.
- understand the relationship between American sport and social mobility.
- cite evidence of sexism and racism in American sport.

SOCIOLOGY Online

Chapter Overview
Visit the *Sociology and You* Web site at soc.glencoe.com and click on **Chapter 15—Chapter Overviews** to preview chapter information.

USING Your Sociological Imagination

Many universities are being faced with making changes to their athletic programs to comply with Title IX. Students might want to research programs at local universities to find out how Title IX has affected the schools. Have students relate gender inequity to sport.

Many of your students may actually be too young to remember a time when high school sports was a boys' domain. Fortunately for female athletes, schools are becoming increasingly responsive to pressures from women's groups to support female athletic programs.

Using the Illustration

Sport is a major part of many students' school life. With some students, in fact, it may be the prime motivator for attending school! Other students who do not participate in team or individual sports, may not be able to really understand the importance of sport in the American culture. Take a quick survey of the room to find out how many students believe that the quality of their education (or at least the time spent in school) would be seriously affected if all sports programs were cancelled or moved off campus.

throughout the magazines. In addition to recording the number of images, they should also look at how each subject is presented: action vs. non-action shots, black and white photos vs. color, head shot vs. full body shot; in uniform vs. not in uniform, etc. Ask students to also note the representation of white, black, Hispanic, and Asian athletes. How does the research match up with the students' hypotheses? Some students might want to research the target audience of these magazines and consider the following questions: 1) Do the images in the magazines reflect the demographics of the target audiences? 2) Does it appear that the publisher might be using these images to attract a certain types of audiences? 3) Considering the demographics of the target audiences, do the images appear to promote racial stereotypes?
L1

Using the Section Preview

Have students answer the question, "What do sports mean to me?" Sports have greater meaning to some than to others, so some students may be reluctant to answer the question. Stress that some students don't participate in mainstream sports but still consider themselves athletic. Ask students to share their viewpoints.

Using the Illustration

Students are provided with a sociological definition of sport on this page. The most important difference is that sport involves a set of rules that determine group behavior. Some activities, such as skiing, may be a sport or a game depending upon the circumstances. Competitive skiing, as in the Olympics, is a sport. Cross-country skiing as a family activity is more like a game. Discuss what makes a game different to ensure they understand what sport means to sociologists.

Integrating the Teacher Resources

Look for the Chapter 15 Learning Goals Outline, a reproducible student worksheet in the Unit 4 Mastering Basic Concepts booklet in your Teacher's Resource Box. It can be used to preview or review chapter content.

Section 1 The Nature of Sport

Key Terms

- sport
- sport subculture

Section Preview

As a social institution, sport fulfills some important societal needs. One of these is helping individuals identify with other members of society. Sport subcultures have developed around both team and individual sports. For this reason, sport is a reflection of society.

sport
a set of competitive activities in which winners and losers are determined by physical performance within a set of established rules

A Definition of Sport

For most people, sport consists of certain leisure activities, exercise, and spectator events. It is actually more complex than that. Sociologists define **sport** as a set of competitive activities in which winners and losers are determined by physical performance within a set of established rules. While sport is an important aspect of recreation, many forms of recreation do not involve sport. Sport sociologist Jay J. Coakley (1998) sees a spontaneous race between two skiers as more of a contest than a sport. Although a contest between skiers involves physical activity and competition, it does not involve definite rules or standardized conditions.

Sport as a Social Institution

Institutions fulfill certain basic needs and reflect the most important aspects of a society. The five most commonly recognized social institutions have been examined in preceding chapters: family, education, government, economic systems, and religion. Although these social institutions take different forms in different societies, they appear in every society because they fulfill needs common to all societies.

What is the difference between a sport and a game?

Learning Styles

Bodily-kinesthetic/Spatial The definition of sport used by sociologists is more confining than the definition in common usage. Sociologists define sport as a set of competitive activities in which winners and losers are determined by physical performance within a set of established rules. Ask students to work in pairs to create a new sport. Their sport must conform to the definition used by sociologists. When they are satisfied that they have met all the requirements, ask students to prepare a graphic to explain their new sport to the class. Allow time for presentations to be made. To conclude, you may want to allow the class to vote on the sport that they would like to actually try. If possible, go outside and play! (In reality, many of the activities your students devise will probably fall under the category of games, but the virtue of this activity is in the process, not the end result.) **L1**

Sport teaches basic values and aids in socialization.

Because societies have additional needs, there are additional social institutions. Sport is one of these. Sport teaches some of the basic values of society. It also promotes attachment to society. For example, a society requires that its members identify with it. Members must feel that belonging to the society is an important part of who they are. Sport aids in this identification of self with society.

Chariot racing in ancient Rome is a clear illustration of this social identification. Athletes would risk their lives in this dangerous sport in part to reflect their self-identification as Romans.

> *The individual, even when free, did not belong to himself; he was strictly subordinated to the city. His life, his death, were only episodes in the history of the group. To confront death was not an act of exceptional heroism; it was the normal way of proving oneself a Roman (Auguet, 1972:198).*

Sport, Culture and Society

Sport plays a central role in American society in part because it reflects the culture's emphasis on achievement.

> *People who visit the United States from other countries are often amazed at the extent to which competition [in sport] is used to distribute rewards and evaluate the work of human beings (Coakley, 1998:82).*

Open-Response Questions

Ask students if they have ever participated in non-school related sports, for example Little League, community basketball, etc. Ask what kind of experience they had. Was it a positive experience, or negative? What made them feel the way they do? What did they learn from the experience (something other than sports skills)? Is this an experience they would recommend to others? Why or why not?

As you ask questions, develop a grid on the board. Down the left side of the grid, list the different types of sports in which students have participated. Across the top, list the types of experiences they had, positive or negative. You might want to keep track of the answers by gender, also. See what conclusions students can draw from the information presented.

More About . . . Spectators

There is research that discusses the cathartic effect that sport has on spectators. Cheering, yelling, booing, and catcalling while watching a ballgame, for example, allows people to release pent-up aggressions. In addition, the spectator is allowed to release negative feelings and stress in an appropriate setting. This positive consequence of sport is part of the functionalist perspective.

Open-Response Questions

Ask students if they believe that Americans in general overvalue winning. Are we too competitive as a culture? Is the maxim "It's not whether you win or lose, but how you play the game" really a social norm? Or is this an example of ideal versus real culture? (Refer students back to Chapter 3 for a discussion of real and ideal culture.)

Integrating the Teacher Resources

To reinforce key ideas, use the Chapter 15 Graphic Organizer, a reproducible student worksheet available in the Unit 4 Mastering Basic Concepts booklet in your Teacher's Resource Box.

The prevailing American view of sport is the one expressed by the late Vince Lombardi, coach of the Green Bay Packers of the National Football League during the 1960s: "Winning is not everything. It is the only thing." For the most part, sport continues to be dominated by achievement-oriented values.

Sport reflects society, so it is not surprising that males dominate the sports world just as they do many other aspects of American society. Females are second to men overall in power, income, and job opportunities in sports just as they are in business, education, medicine, and law (Eitzen, 1999).

Some progress toward equality is being made, however, especially on the college level. The Virginia Tech and Louisiana Tech women's basketball teams, for example, are currently drawing more fans than the men's teams. Women are making inroads in professional tennis and golf, and a women's professional basketball league has been formed. The place of women in athletics was given a healthy boost when Mia Hamm and her teammates captured the 1999 World Cup in soccer. But equality of opportunity for women in sports is a distant goal, not one that is just around the corner.

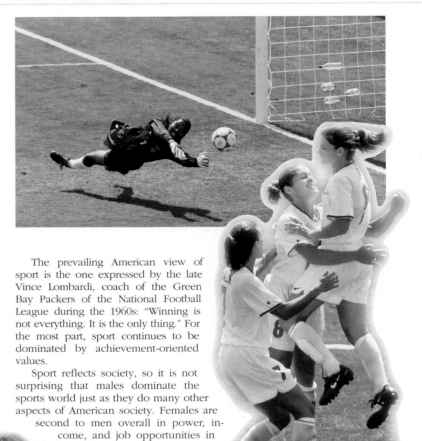

As women's place in American society changes, their place in sport also changes. Until only a few years ago, Virginia Tech basketball standout Amy Wetzel and World Cup soccer star Mia Hamm could only dream of a sport spotlight.

Demonstration

Ask students if they can name the last five Heisman trophy winners, the last five World Series winners, or the last five schools that won your conference championships in football, basketball, etc. Students will probably have difficulty naming any, let alone the last five. You may encounter a few students who don't know what the Heisman trophy is. Now ask students to name five influential teachers, five good friends, or five people they enjoy spending time with. Stress to students that, as much as our society emphasizes sport, our memory of it is fleeting. Have students discuss why this is. (Sport is not as important to the general society because it does not impact us directly. It is also one reason why sociologists refer to sport as a secondary institution.)

L1

Another Time

Racing in Rome

The chariot races of the Roman Empire, made famous in America by the movie *Ben Hur*, involved considerable skill and courage. Charioteers delivered the violence required to please the crowd.

At the end of a race, the charioteers drove abreast, wheel against wheel, for the whole length of the track, whipping their horses madly to gain the half-length which might assure their victory. At this point skill turned into pure violence; each charioteer was no longer content merely to hamper his adversary but took the risk of overturning him by driving his chariot against him in order to break its axle, or of destroying him by whipping his horses into the rear of his chariot. To ward off his maneuver the charioteer so threatened no longer leaned forward but literally "hung on the necks of his horses." He had no need to turn round to see what was happening. He could already feel the breath of his pursuers and the rhythmic shock of their hooves shaking the back of his chariot. A few seconds later, if he had not succeeded in gaining a little ground, there would no longer be either rival, chariot or team, but only an amorphous mass littering the middle of the track.

It was the most spectacular and most popular of all the events of the circus; so much that charioteers did their utmost to involve their rivals in this maneuver in front of the imperial box. For a Roman it summed up all the poetry of the circus; with a sharp, dry crack the fragile box carrying a man was reduced to powder at full speed; the overheated axle collapsed and splinters flew in all directions; the horses crashed into the sand head over heels in a clutter of straps or, seized with panic, broke away from the harness which held them. Before the final catastrophe, the charioteer had to draw the dagger at his waist and cut the reins which, wound about him, bound him to his team; if he succeeded in doing this he had a chance of emerging from the wreck merely bruised, his body full of splinters. But sometimes he was pitched out head first by the violence of the impact. Then he had no time for this simple act and, if the horses did not fall, was dragged across the circus. As he wore nothing but a tunic held by a set of straps across the chest, his only protection was a leather helmet, insufficient to save his life in such circumstances. But the aggressor did not always emerge unscathed; at the moment of impact his horses reared up and came down again with their forefeet between the spokes of the wheel of the damaged chariot which was turning in the air; they crashed down, their bones broken, whinnying with pain, and the charioteer, halted in full career, ran the same risks as his rival.

Source: Roland Auguet, *Cruelty and Civilization: The Roman Games* (London: George Allen and Unwin Ltd., 1972), pp. 131–132. Reprinted by permission.

Thinking It Over

Some athletes today engage in "extreme sports" such as sky surfing, street luge, and snowboarding. The criteria for an extreme sport is that it is nonmotorized; has a sanctioning body; is deemed as extreme or unusual; and requires learned skills, conditioning, and practice. Do you think chariot racing of ancient Rome is similar to the extreme sports of today? Why or why not?

Another Time

Students will want to discuss how "civilized" our society has become. It is hard to imagine that any society would sanction such a violent sporting event. Today, the more violent sports like football require athletes to wear substantial protection. Despite this, people still get badly hurt.

Answer to Thinking it Over

Students will have varying opinions on how violent these sports are in comparison to the chariot races of ancient Rome. Some students might want to report back to the class on the safety precautions involved in each of these extreme sports.

Integrating the Teacher Resources

Look for the Chapter 15 Vocabulary Activity worksheet in the Unit 4 Mastering Basic Concepts booklet in your Teacher's Resources Box. It provides reinforcement for vocabulary in this chapter.

Observation

If you have the opportunity, show the movie *Ben Hur* to your students. It is a lengthy movie, so if time is an issue, show only the famous chariot race. After the viewing, ask students for their reactions. Was the scene too violent? Do they think it was realistic? How does the violence in the movie compare to actual violence in sports today? Is there any comparison?

You might also show portions of the Mad Max *Thunderdome* movie that show the actual Thunderdome "game." Do students think spectators in our society will ever degenerate to the levels of those in the movie? Or, are we already there? Have students defend their answers with examples.

Teaching Strategy

Find articles in local newspapers about recent incidents of violence in sports. Share them with the class, then have students decide in groups if perpetrator of sport violence should face the same consequences as someone who commits a street crime. Should a sport's governing body alone decide punishment? If not, how and by whom should punishments be decided?
L2

Addressing Current Social Issues

What happens when winning becomes the most important goal? In November of 1999, an Illinois high school hockey player got into a ruckus with a player on another team and smacked the rival player on the back with a hockey stick. The blow sent the player careening into the boards where his spinal cord was severed, leaving the young man paralyzed. The player who struck the blow was charged with aggravated battery and could spend five years in juvenile detention.

Lawyers for the defendant insist that the blow occurred as part of a game that was still in progress and was an unfortunate accident.The state's district attorney argued that the player wasn't merely attempting to play hockey but intending to hurt his opponent.

Ask your class what they would decide if they were on the jury. Should the young man be held responsible for his actions while on the ice?

Sport Subcultures

sport subculture
a group with distinct roles, values, norms, and beliefs that is organized around a sport activity

The relationship between sport, society, and culture can also be seen in *sport subcultures*. A **sport subculture** is a group within the larger context of sport that has some of its own distinct roles, values, norms. These subcultures are organized around a sport activity and beliefs vary widely. Sociologist Michael Smith (1979) wanted to know if violence among hockey players is due to involvement in a "subculture of violence." In this kind of subculture, violence is the expected response to a perceived challenge or insult—a jostle, a glance, a derogatory remark. Following this norm is essential in acquiring and maintaining honor, especially when challenges are associated with masculinity.

Smith found that hockey players favor violence more than nonplayers. Because of the expectations of coaches and teammates, many hockey players act violently during games. In fact, players criticize teammates who aren't violent. As one National Hockey League player put it:

> *I don't think that there's anything wrong with guys getting excited in a game and squaring off and throwing a few punches. That's just part of the game. It always has been. And you know if you tried to eliminate it, you wouldn't have hockey any more. You look at hockey from the time it was begun, guys gets excited and just fight, and it's always been like that (Eitzen, 1996:165).*

According to sport sociologists, violence in a sport like hockey persists because it is part of a subculture. Do you think some sport subcultures encourage violence?

Kent Pearson (1981) researched subcultures involving water-related sports in Australia and New Zealand. He found major cultural differences between surfboard riders and surf lifesavers. Surfboard riders avoid formal organizations, work with loose and flexible definitions of the territory in which their sport will occur, place a heavy emphasis on physical prowess and individualism, and generally oppose the larger society. In contrast, surf lifesaving clubs are highly organized entities that stage competitions involving swimming, boating, and lifesaving. The territory for such competitions is precisely defined, and formal rules are employed.

Even in nonteam sports, subcultures emerge. Thoroughbred jockeys have developed a subculture with a strong emphasis on displaying dignity, maintaining integrity, and remaining cool. The ideal within the subculture of jockeys is a fiery animal with a cool rider.

> *The cool jockey can wait patiently with a horse in a pocket and get through on the inside, risking the possibility that there will be no opening. Coolness is waiting far back in the pack, risking the possibility that his horse will not "get up" in time. Coolness is sparing the whip on a front-running horse when another animal has pressed into the lead, risking the possibility that once his horse is passed he will not get started again. All these activities are taken by observers as instances of a jockey's character. In short, moral character is coolness in risky situations (Scott, 1981:146–147).*

Using Decision-Making Skills

You may want to provide students with the following steps to complete this decision-making activity.

1. Identify the problem
2. Gather information; research
3. Make a list of options, both pro and con
4. Choose a solution
5. Implement the solution
6. Validate the solution by giving specific reasons for making this decision.

Then read students this decision-making scenario:

Jared confides in you that he desperately wants to win the powerlifting competition for his weight class. Lately you've noticed that he is bulking up nicely; he's lifting more weight than ever before. However, he

What values are at the center of the unique jockey subculture?

Jockeys take such chances partly because their subculture requires it. Jockeys who fail to display gallantry, integrity, and coolness—qualities expected of them by horse owners, trainers, and other jockeys—do not receive their choice of horses and therefore win few races. Failing to take risks leads to lost opportunities.

Section 1 Assessment

1. Do you agree that in order for an activity to be a sport, it should include a defined set of rules? Why or why not?
2. Which of the following is *not* an example of sport?
   - **a.** a baseball game between two major league teams
   - **b.** a baseball game between two minor league teams
   - **c.** a spontaneous race between two cyclists
   - **d.** a swim meet involving amateur athletes

Critical Thinking

3. **Analyzing Information** Think about sports in your school. How is the cultural value of achievement reflected in the behavior of athletes, peers, teachers, and parents? Give some specific examples.

> "There are several differences between a football game and a revolution. For one thing, a football game usually lasts longer and the participants wear uniforms. Also, there are more injuries at a football game."
>
> **Alfred Hitchcock**
> **director and producer**

Pulling it All Together

Sport serves important social needs, such as providing self-identification with others in society. Sport also creates subcultures around team and individual sports, thus mirroring society at large.

Answers to Section 1 Assessment

1. A set of established rules is part of the sociologist's definition of sport. However, many people see a more generalized view of sport as consisting of leisure activities, exercise, and spectator events. Students should clarify their opinions and discuss them with others having the opposite viewpoint.
2. C.

Critical Thinking

3. Sport reflects our culture's emphasis on achievement, therefore playing a central role in American society.

seems to be extremely tense lately, which might be due to his failing grade in precalculus. You warned him not to enroll, but he wouldn't listen. You also notice that Jared's face is acne-ridden now, and his skin has taken on a yellow pallor. You suspect he is taking steroids, and as his best friend, you are concerned.

Have students decide what to do and determine the best, most justifiable option.

Then ask them to write letters to Jared explaining their decision. Have students read their letters to the class. How do they relate Jared's situation to what they've read in Section 1?

L2

Tech Trends

The author of this feature believes that the institution of sport can be viewed as a mirror of society. Ask students if they agree with this assessment.

Answers to Analyzing the Trends

1. Answers will vary. Based on the article, students might say that sport is rife with conflict, that groups competing with each other reflect the conflict in the larger society. A functionalist might say that despite some dysfunctions, sport still maintains a high degree of order and stability in the best interests of society.
2. Some students love the World Wrestling Federation (WWF). Others are appalled by it. This answer is subjective. If students think wrestling is barbaric, they are likely to relate it closely to the chariot races.

Tech Trends

Mass Media and Sports

Sport fulfills two functions. It teaches some of the basic values of society, and it promotes attachment to society. During televised sports events, the National Collegiate Athletic Association (NCAA) and the National Football League (NFL) regularly show student athletes and professional sports stars working with children and disadvantaged persons, behavior reflecting both of these functions.

How do we square this positive picture of sport with the "dark" side of sport that is continuously fed the public by the mass media? Much of the media coverage of modern sports now focuses on the bad, tough-guy image of athletes, coaches, and owners. Not only is "winning the only thing," as Vince Lombardi, legendary coach of the Green Bay Packers, said. Now, the winners are expected to have an attitude.

Dennis Rodman, a forward in the National Basketball Association (NBA), gained fame from media coverage of his cross-dressing and physical assaults. Roberto Alomar achieved negative recognition when he spat on an umpire during the 1997 baseball season.

Some critics fear that the mass media and entertainment promoters are ruining the integrity of sport in America.

And these are the "respectable" sports! The newer sports on the mass-media horizon—Gladiator Sports, Roller Derby, Wrestle Mania—are going much farther. Look at the names of events that the World Wrestling Federation (WWF) has recently sponsored: "Road Rage Tour" and "War Zone." Its biggest television draws include individuals with stage names such as "Vic Venom," "Road Dog Jesse James," "Bret 'The Hit Man' Hart," and "The Undertaker." Women have also achieved star status in WWF wrestling. Chyna, "the ninth wonder of the world" and Jacqueline, two-time WWF Women's Champion, draw as many fans as the men.

So, does mass-media sports coverage reflect basic social values and promote societal identification? Where is the coverage of teamwork, sportsmanship, and character development? Do we simply celebrate with the media the message of unrivaled competition and winning at any cost? At times, it appears the latter is the case, especially when everyday behavior seems to mirror the negative presentation of sport.

If you want to witness such behavior on a daily basis, attend most any children's athletic contest. Be sure to watch players, parents, and coaches. In fact, when registering their children for a team, parents across America are now being required to pledge themselves to a code of good behavior.

Analyzing the Trends

1. Based on how they are presented in the media would you analyze sports in America from the (dys)functionalist or the conflict perspective function? What perspective do you believe is reflected in the media presentation of sports?
2. "Fake" wrestling is growing in popularity since it began being marketed as sports entertainment. In what ways is the role WWF wrestling plays in society similar to and different from the Roman chariot races?

Integrating the Teacher Resources

Look for Ethics, Values, and Technology: Real-Life Issues in Society, **available in your Teacher's Resource Box.**

Learning Styles

Linguistic/Interpersonal/Logical-mathematical Stanley Eitzen is a sport sociologist who wrote, "American sport embodies American values—striving for excellence, winning, individual and team competition, and materialism. Parents want their children to participate in sport because participation teaches them the basic values of American society and builds character." Ask students to design a survey to test the validity of this quote. Work with the class so that all students are using identical

Section 2 Theoretical Perspectives and Sport

Culture and Sport

Sport is a major social activity through which culture is created and reinforced. As noted earlier, sociologists recognize this important aspect of sport.

> *American sport embodies American values—striving for excellence, winning, individual and team competition, and materialism. Parents want their children to participate in sport because participation teaches them the basic values of American society and builds character (Eitzen, 1999:3).*

Although sociologists agree that sport mirrors society, and that the relationship is complex, they disagree over the social implications of sport. Sport sociologist Stanley Eitzen has written a book on the paradoxes, or contradictions, of sport in America. (See Figure 15.1 on page 504.) Functionalists, who tend to concentrate on the benefits of sport, are represented in Eitzen's book. So are conflict theorists, who see a social downside to sport. Symbolic interactionists focus on personal meanings derived from sport.

Sport has long been an important basis for stratification in high schools.

Section Preview

Functionalists see sport positively, as a means for socializing young people, promoting social integration, providing a release for tensions, and developing sound character. Conflict theorists believe that organized sports can be harmful to character development. Symbolic interactionists focus on the self-concepts and relationships developed through sport activities.

Using the Section Preview

Have students give specific examples, taken from their own experiences, of the four functions of sport. For example, if they are fans of a particular sports team, do they share a sense of community or identity with other fans of that team?

Using the Illustration

Ask students what to "play like girls" used to mean. In what other sports are women gaining social acceptance and national recognition?

Integrating the Teacher Resources

Look for the Chapter 15 Increasing Your Reading Comprehension worksheet and the Guided Reading worksheet in the Unit 4 Mastering Basic Concepts booklet in your Teacher's Resource Box. Both will strengthen student reading comprehension skills.

survey questions. Remind students to consider ethics as they debate and vote to finalize questions to be used. (Questions should be both open- and closed-ended.) Assign students to survey a specific quantity of people who are parents. You may want to include gender and race information in the survey. When students have completed tabulation of their results, have them compare their results with Eitzen's quote. Do the results match? Why or why not?
L2

Working with the Data

Figure 15.1 Students should have no difficulty in seeing the paradoxes in sport in America (assuming, of course, they understand the meaning of the word *paradox*. A paradox is a statement or situation that contradicts itself; that seems both true and false at the same time.)

Controversy and Debate

Numerous recent articles have discussed the declining attendance at high school sporting events. Twenty years ago, packed houses at school sport events were the norm. Now, however, many schools no longer fill stadiums or gymnasiums for sporting events. Allow students to research this topic, determining what factors have contributed to this decline. If your school is one where students avidly attend sporting events, contrast your school with a school that has low event attendance.

Figure 15.1 Sport Paradoxes

Stanley Eitzen, a highly respected sport sociologist, argues that sport is inherently contradictory (Eitzen, 1999). Here are a few of the paradoxes Eitzen identifies. Do you agree with Eitzen that these paradoxes exist?

Social Integration

- Sport can unite different social classes and racial/ethnic groups
  but
- sport can heighten barriers that separate groups.

Fair Play

- Sport promotes fair play by teaching the importance of following the rules
  but
- sport's emphasis on winning tempts people to cheat.

Physical Fitness

- Sport promotes muscle strength, weight control, endurance, and coordination
  but
- sport can lead to the use of steroids and other drugs, excessive weight loss or gain, and injuries.

Academics

- Sport contributes to higher education through scholarships and fund raising
  but
- sport takes money away from academics and emphasizes athletic performance over learning and graduation.

Social Mobility

- Sport allows athletes who might otherwise not attend college to obtain an education
  but
- only a few can achieve the promise of fame and wealth in the professional ranks.

Source: D. Stanley Eitzen, *Fair and Foul* (Lanham, MD: Rowman & Littlefield Publishers, Inc. 1999), pp. 4–7.

Functionalism

How do functionalists view the role of sport in society? Functionalists think sport is important primarily because it helps society work more smoothly. It does this by performing the following functions (Eitzen and Sage, 1997).

- *Sport teaches basic beliefs, norms, and values.* Sport readies us for adult roles. Games, for instance, prepare participating athletes for work in organizations. Young people who are exposed to competitive sport become more achievement motivated than those who are not. And the earlier the exposure occurs, the higher the orientation towards achievement. This is important because achievement-motivation is essential to productivity in the modern economy.
- *Sport promotes a sense of social identification.* A team binds people to their community and nation. Clevelanders are united in their love of the Browns, Indians, and Cavaliers. Around midcentury, the United States at times seemed to be divided into Dodger and Yankee fans. The Atlanta Braves are trying to be "America's team." Higher social integration results.

Careers in Sociology

Ask students if they think sociology and sports can be combined in a career. After students have answered, tell them the following: Increased interest in sports medicine, exercise physiology, physical fitness, and conditioning is opening up these careers. People in these professions are doing research on how the human body reacts during exercise, what helps people improve cardiovascular condition, and what role nutrients play in physical fitness. While some do research, others specialize in sports medicine, and still others work in fitness centers. Coaches and instructors instruct, inform, and encourage participants. Other workers with similar duties include athletic directors and trainers, dietitians and nutritionists, physical therapists, recreational therapists, school teachers, and umpires.

Cleveland Browns fans identified so strongly with their city's football team that the city brought suit to keep the team name and colors from leaving town.

- *Sport offers a safe release of aggressive feelings generated by the frustrations, anxieties, and strains of modern life.* It is socially acceptable to yell and scream for an athletic team. Similar behavior directed at a teacher, principal, parent, or employer can have negative consequences.
- *Sport encourages the development of character.* Coaches, school officials, and parents often draw a parallel between sport and "life." "When the going gets tough, the tough get going" is a sentiment expressed in most locker rooms. The hard work, discipline, and self-sacrifice demanded by team sports become part of an athlete's value system.

What are the social dysfunctions of sport? Functionalists have identified some drawbacks to sport. Because sport reflects society, it draws on achievement-oriented values that can be intensified to an extreme degree (Koln, 1992). When achievement and winning come to be seen as the primary goals of sport, any method of winning—including violence and cheating—may be encouraged.

We need not look far to see examples of violence in sport. Coaches and fans expect athletes to place their physical well-being on the line. Players in many sports are expected to resort to violence. In high school football, aggressive behavior is defended as preparation for "real-life" competition. Pressures are intensified at the professional level, where many sports have developed the informal role of *enforcer*—a team member whose major responsibility is to intimidate, provoke, and even injure opponents (Coakley, 1998). Edmonton Oilers hockey player Marty McSorley used his hockey stick to deliver a vicious blindside slash to the head of opposing player Donald

> You give 100 percent in the first half of the game, and if that isn't enough in the second half you give what's left.
>
> **Yogi Berra**
> **baseball coach**

Teaching Strategy

Sport is not the only activity that employs the concept of an "enforcer." In fact, the term is often used instead of bouncer to describe the job of peacekeeper in a bar or nightclub. Ask students to suggest other activities that use the role of enforcer.

More About . . . the Student-Athlete

Sociologists Peter and Patricia Adler's article, "The Gloried Self," poignantly depicts the conflict perspective of the student-athlete. Media creates glorified images of athletes, who begin to believe they are above the normal consequences of society. Since the athlete's role is to bring glory to their team and school, wins and successes serve to further elevate their status. To read more about this, see Adler, Patricia and Adler, Peter: "The Gloried Self: The Aggrandizement and the Constriction of Self," (*Sociology: Exploring the Architecture of Everyday Life*. 3rd edition. David Newman. Pine Forge Press.)

Other careers that can combine sociology and sports are sports announcers in radio and television, physical training instructors, amusement and recreation services workers, and professional athletes.

For more information, check out these links:

American Council on Exercise, **http://www.acefitness.org**
National High School Athletic Coaches Association, **http://www.hscoaches.org**
American and National Therapeutic Recreation Associations, **http://www.atra-tr.org**, and **http://www.nrpa.org/branches/ntrs.htm**.

World View

You might have students research any Olympics that have occurred since the 1998 Winter Olympic Games.

Answers to Interpreting the Map

1. Answers will vary. Students should understand that some countries put more emphasis on the Olympics than others do. Some countries have more economic resources to spend on athletes training for the Olympics.
2. By the 1940s, the Olympics had become a forum in which athletes from radically different political environments were expected to compete as equals. Democrats, Communists, and even Nazis have participated in the Games as rivals and fellow athletes. On rare occasions, the Olympics have been used to express international outrage: as when countries accused of human rights violations have been forbidden to participate. Because the Olympic Games are based on a concept of international cooperation, the exclusion of a country is viewed as a particularly significant form of sanction.

World View

Olympic Success

Sport also plays an important role in today's global society. For some time, the winning of Olympic medals has been a source of regional and global prestige. This map shows the number of medals earned by each country in the 2000 Summer Olympic Games.

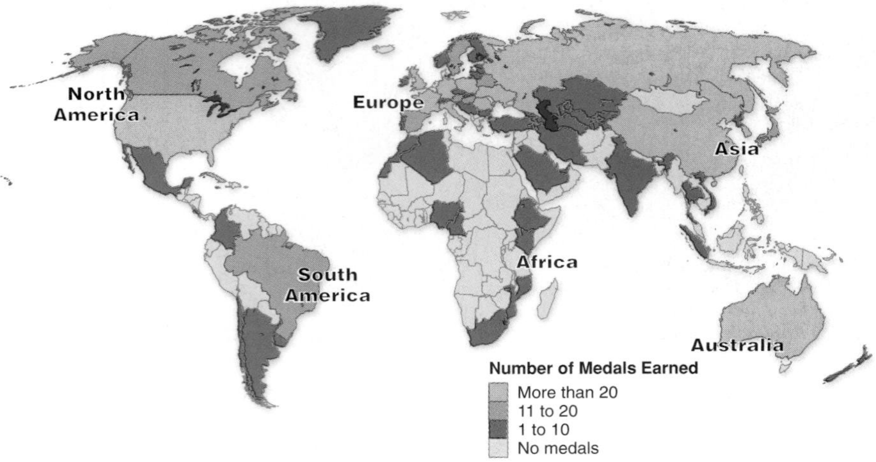

Interpreting the Map

1. Why do you think there is such wide variation in the number of Olympic medals earned?
2. Do the Olympics illustrate a connection between sport and politics? Explain.

Source: Orbital Decisions, http://www.orbital.co.za/text/sydney2000/medals.htm.

Brashear in February of 2000. The attack was the culmination of a game marked by injuries and was the result of the long-standing rivalry between two "top enforcers."

Cheating may not be as easy as violent behavior to identify, but is often present, nonetheless. Cheating was no doubt involved when American Olympic skater Nancy Kerrigan was struck on the right leg with a metal rod by an assailant later linked to her competitor, Tonya Harding. In 2000, the Atlanta Braves were penalized for signing a player before his sixteenth birthday. They had followed the precedent of the Los Angeles Dodgers in 1999. Cheating can even extend beyond players, as when a Utah state committee used illegal inducements to attract the 2000 Winter Olympics.

Encouraging Citizenship Activity

Urge students to volunteer their services as coaches for children involved in Special Olympics. Students don't really need to be athletically proficient to coach, but do need to have some kind of appreciation for the sport and genuine interest in children.

Before your students start, you might wish to bring in a school coach to talk with the class about the best ways to coach in a positive manner. Also, encourage students to get some information about the children they will be working with.

Students may wish to get the athletic department, and their athlete friends involved with Special Olympics.

Conflict Theory

Some sociologists have raised disturbing questions about the effects of sport on society. These questions are best understood through the conflict perspective. Conflict theorists are interested in who has the power and how elites use power to satisfy their own interests. To conflict theorists, sport is a social institution in which the most powerful oppress, manipulate, coerce, and exploit others. Conflict theorists highlight the ways in which sport mirrors the unequal distribution of power and money in society. They also emphasize the role of sport in maintaining inequality (Leonard, 1998).

While functionalists see sport as contributing to the unification of society, conflict theorists do not. While people from all major segments of a community or society may join in cheering for the same team, their union is only temporary.

> *When the game is over, the enthusiasm dies, the solidarity runs short, and disharmony in other relations reasserts itself. Much as one hour a week cannot answer to the religious impulse, one game a week cannot answer to the solidarity needs of a racist, sexist, or elitist society (Young, 1986).*

Basic social class divisions, in other words, will continue to exist and to affect social relationships in a community even if the local team has just won the World Series or the Super Bowl.

The contribution sport makes in forming good character is also questioned by conflict theorists. Among college athletes, studies have shown that the degree of sportsmanship apparently declines as athletes become more involved in the sports system. As sociologist Stanley Eitzen (1993a) notes, nonscholarship athletes display greater sportsmanship than those with athletic scholarships, and those who have not earned letters exhibit more sportsmanship than letter winners.

Conflict theorists can point to any number of past and present scandals in both the college and professional ranks. Americans are constantly reading in the sports section of the daily newspaper about athletes, from high school to the professional level, who are taking drugs, cheating in school, or accepting illegitimate cash "gifts." One university after another is being investigated and penalized by the National Collegiate Athletic Association. Coaches as well as players are involved in misconduct.

> *Athletes may use performance-enhancing drugs such as steroids and amphetamines to achieve a "competitive edge." . . . Big-time college coaches in their zeal to win have been found guilty of exploiting athletes, falsifying transcripts, providing illegal payments, hiring surrogate test takers, paying athletes for nonexistent summer jobs, and illegally using government Pell grants and work study monies for athletes. So much, I would argue, for the myth that "sport builds character" (Eitzen, 1996:189).*

In some cultures, sport is so important lives may depend on it. In 1994, Colombian soccer player Andres Escobar was gunned down, apparently for scoring against his own team in the World Cup soccer match against the U.S. (Colombia lost, 2–1.)

Reinforcing Vocabulary

Ask students to define the word *sportsmanship. (Conduct that includes fairness, graciousness in winning or losing, and respect for one's opponent)* See if any of your students comment on the built-in gender bias of the term. Ask them to suggest another term that has a similar meaning—it will not be easy. Obviously, "unsportspersonlike" is too awkward.

After airing the language issue, ask students to describe sportsmanship. (Do they know it when they see it?) What is sportsmanship *not* (unsportsmanlike conduct)? Can they describe incidents of unsportsmanlike conduct? Which is easier to find in a game: unsportsmanlike conduct, or sportsmanlike conduct? Which is more fun to watch? (How does the answer to this relate to how much unsportsmanlike conduct we see during games?) Does this kind of behavior carry over into real life?
ELL

Observation

Assign students to watch at least one sporting event on television; it can be any kind. Have each write the type of event they watch and keep track of how many sportsmanlike and unsportsmanlike incidents occur during the competition. Have students share their data with the class. Help them analyze the data by type of sport. Are some sports more conducive to sportsmanlike conduct? Are some more conducive to unsportsmanlike conduct? What makes the difference?
L1

Working with the Data

Figure 15.2 (See page 509.) Answers will vary. An example of the functionalist perspective is greater social integration that results from a community rallying around a team that is representing them in the state championships. An example of the conflict theory perspective is that people who don't support a popular area sports team might be scorned. An example of a symbolic interactionist view might be that students who participate in sports experience greater self-esteem than those who don't participate.

Teaching Strategy

Symbolic interactionists would also be interested in the behavior patterns displayed by the parents of Little League baseball players. In fact, quite often the parental behavior has even greater societal impact. Young players pick up cues about the importance of winning from the adults, often in spite of everything the coaches do to ensure the ideal norms are conveyed, rather than the real culture. Ask students to discuss whether they have seen these effects first hand, and if so, how they felt about it.
L1

Symbolic Interactionism

Symbolic interactionism also contributes to our understanding of sport as a social institution. This theoretical perspective concentrates on personal meanings, social relationships, and self-identity processes. Symbolic interactionists are concerned with the symbols of sports. The meanings and interpretations of these symbols are important because they affect the self-concepts, as well as the relationships, of those involved.

The social context of Little League baseball illustrates this perspective. For three years, Gary Alan Fine (1987) studied American adolescent suburban males who played Little League baseball. He discovered and documented a variety of ways in which the boys assigned meanings to their team activities. In addition, he described how these meanings and interpretations influenced the boys' social interactions and affected their self-definitions.

What were these meanings? Much of the activity of coaches and parents centered on teaching the rules of the game and teaching values, such as team play, hard work, fair play, competition, and winning. But these ten- to twelve-year-old boys formed their own interpretations of these messages. The boys misinterpreted the adult values of hard work, competition, and so forth as the "masculine" values of dominance, "toughness," and risky behavior.

How were social interaction and self-concepts affected? In the first place, the boys' behavior convinced coaches and parents that the youngsters understood and accepted their values. For example, the aggressive behavior that the boys considered as evidence of their masculinity was seen by the coaches and parents as evidence of "hustle," dedication to competition, and the desire to win. The boys were praised for this behavior, which encouraged them to continue it. "Weaker" peers, younger children, and girls in general frequently experienced the disdain of these Little Leaguers. This disrespect often led to a loss of self-esteem for children who suffered the brunt of the Little Leaguers' scorn.

This young boy might be misinterpreting what his coach is trying to teach him about sportsmanship.

Survey

Have students develop a survey to give to 10–12 year old boys who play sports. The survey should have the boys list the sports they play and then rank the following traits from 1 to 9 with, 1 being the most important and 9 being the least important when they are playing their sport. The traits are: playing by the rules, toughness, team play, hard work, fair play, dominance, competition, winning, risky behavior.

Students should analyze the results to see how closely they follow the information given in the student text. Are the rankings different for boys who play different sports? To what do students attribute this?
L2

Figure 15.2 Focus on Theoretical Perspectives

Social Effects of Sport. This table illustrates how each theoretical perspective might study an issue involving sport. For each assumption, provide a specific example from your own experience or from a team you follow.

Theoretical Perspective	Concept	Assumption
Functionalism	Social integration	Athletic teams promote togetherness and belonging in a community.
Conflict Theory	Social conflict	Deep social conflict exists within a community and persists despite widespread attachment to athletic teams.
Symbolic Interactionism	Social concept	Participation in a team sport may promote or harm self-esteem depending upon factors such as emphasis on winning and fair play.

What are some limitations of each perspective? The functionalist perspective makes important points regarding the positive and negative role of sport in society. Its critics, however, contend that many sports have become so closely tied to elite interests that they contribute more to private profit than to the general well-being of society. To investigate this point, the conflict perspective concentrates on some major concerns of sport, such as racism and sexism (discussed in the next section). On the other hand, conflict theorists tend to overlook the positive contributions of sport to society. They are accused of placing too much emphasis on the extent to which sport is manipulated and controlled by the elite. Their critics also claim that conflict theorists underestimate the character-building benefit of team sports. Symbolic interactionism contributes greatly to understanding the socialization process in sport. But, because it concentrates on social interaction, it fails to include the broader social and cultural context. For example, symbolic interactionism does not address the functions of sport in society or explore sport within the context of power and social inequality.

> "[Knute] Rockne wanted nothing but "bad losers." Good losers get into the habit of losing."
>
> George E. Allen
> American raconteur

Section 2 Assessment

1. What is the relationship between sport and achievement-oriented values?
2. Name three roles that sport plays in society, according to functionalists.
3. Summarize in one sentence the overall attitude of the conflict perspective toward sport.

Critical Thinking

4. **Finding the Main Idea** Has your self-concept or that of a friend been affected by sports? Explain the effects from the symbolic interactionist viewpoint.

Pulling it All Together

Consideration was given to the understanding of the three sociological perspectives in sports. While each perspective can be useful in our interpretation of this institution, none are without limitations.

Answers to Section 2 Assessment

1. According to functionalists, young people who engage in competitive sports become more achievement motivated than those who are not.
2. Students should list three of the following:
   - Sport teaches basic beliefs, norms, and values.
   - Sport promotes a sense of social identification.
   - Sport offers a safe release of aggressive feelings generated by the frustrations, anxieties, and strains of modern life.
   - Sport encourages the development of character.
3. The conflict perspective towards sport is that it is a social institution in which the most powerful oppress, manipulate, coerce, and exploit others (money in society, and helping to maintain inequality).

Critical Thinking

4. Answers will vary based on experiences.

On-Demand Writing

Read the following to students and then have them write their reactions to it. Ask for volunteers to read their responses to the rest of the class.

The functionalist perspective makes important points regarding the positive and negative roles of sport in society. Its critics, however, contend that many sports have become so closely tied to elite interests that they contribute more to private profit than to the general well-being of society. **L2**

Focus on Research

This article paints a disturbing picture of the culture surrounding middle-school sports. Ask students what factors might contribute to this kind of behavior. Are the coaches exploiting the developmental fears of adolescent boys? Are the boys trying to prove something to other boys? Have students create hypotheses concerning the factors contributing to this phenomenon.

Focus on Research

Case Study: Tough Guys, Wimps, and Weenies

"When are you gonna learn when it's necessary to use unnecessary roughness?"

Remember Donna Eder's study of middle-school stratification? (See pages 66–67.) She also researched the nature of middle-school sports. Using the framework of symbolic interactionism, Eder assumes that the social world of teenagers is constructed through interaction with others. Thus, everyday exchanges—insults, greetings, gossip—give teenagers a sense of their social world.

Middle-school coaches accented the value of toughness. In the world of athletics, having a "mean" attitude is masculine, and being nice is effeminate. Wrestlers, for example, were told to make opponents "suffer." Football coaches did not tolerate fighting off the field, but as a means to handle conflict among athletes, these same coaches encouraged physical force on the field.

> *I said that I had heard that Coach Paulson wasn't pleased with the way the team played. Walter and Carl both agreed. Walter* [the team manager] *said that the team didn't hit like they should have and that made the coach mad. Carl said, "Yeah, but I really socked that guy. Man, I threw him down on the concrete. Did you hear Coach James yelling, "Way to go, Orville"? (Eder, 1995:62)*

Evidence of weakness was greeted by derogatory names like "wuss," "wimp," and "girl." Ritual insults promoted stereotypically masculine behavior, particularly among higher-status boys. Stories of physical force in sports were repeated with pride. Even soccer players bragged about kicking opponents in the shins or throwing a ball into an opponent's face.

The most forcefully combative boys were the most respected. Although the coaches tried to curb physical violence outside of games and matches, many players considered fighting an appropriate way to handle all peer conflicts.

> *[The] importance of being tough extended to behavior off the playing field as well as on it. Boys were continually challenged to develop more aspects of toughness, including the ability to deny pain and suppress feelings as well as respond combatively to verbal and physical attacks. Boys who rejected these messages were*

Cooperative Learning Activity

Although conflict theorists question whether sporting events are capable of promoting social integration, the positive aspects of sport *are* being used across the world to create a sense of peace and community.

One example of this phenomenon is the European Peace Run. The Peace Run is held every two years, when thousands of volunteers commit to carrying a lighted torch across the whole of Europe. In 1999, the run began in Portugal and ended in London, England. The torch was passed from hand to hand until it had been carried *sometimes subject to ridicule by girls as well as boys, showing the difficulty boys faced when trying to escape the pressures of being masculine within this school setting (Eder, 1995: 72).*

Insult exchanges could be won by getting another boy to become angry. By losing his cool, the other boy lost his image of toughness. Some boys would insult another boy just to look good to others. An example is provided by one of the researcher's notes on Hank, the highest-status boy in the seventh grade who had a reputation for verbal assault.

Future sociologists may study the effect that team sports plays on women's aggression.

Hank does seem to enjoy conflict or competition on a one-on-one basis. A couple of times today he left the table just to go down and abuse some kid at the end of the table, calling him a pud, a squirt, or a wimp. Then he would come back and tell the group how the guy had done nothing when he had said this. Hank would get a big smile on his face and was really pleased (Eder, 1995: 73–74).

Insults and counter-insults delivered several messages. First, boys learned not to care about the feelings of others. Second, insulting, or even humiliating, their peers was a socially approved means of achieving or displaying higher status. Third, boys who humiliated low-status peers were rewarded with social recognition. This was true even if the target of ridicule was handicapped or overweight.

Working with the Research

1. Do you think this study describes sports at your school? Explain.
2. Do female athletes treat each other differently from the way boys treat each other? Explain.

Answers to Working with the Research

1. Answers will vary. You might want to open this topic up for discussion, but ask students not to mention the names of coaches or others involved.
2. Answers will vary. Have students share their perceptions of how the genders relate to one another in sports.

Integrating the Teacher Resources

A lesson plan for a student research project related to the content of this chapter can be found in Doing Sociology: Focus on Research, available in your Teacher's Resource Box.

across every country in Europe and the former Soviet Union, serving as a visible symbol of the volunteers' commitment to peace. Peace Runs are held across the globe, and many other organizations use walks and marathons to raise awareness.

Discuss the significance of such events, asking why it is that marathons and walkathons have been used so successfully to promote awareness and social concern. Do the students agree with the conflict theorists who argue that such events have no lasting impact on social integration? **L1**

Using the Section Preview

The movie *Hoop Dreams,* available on video through PBS, (**www.pbs.org/ktcal/hoopdreams/**) chronicles the lives of two young men trying to fulfill their dreams of making it in professional basketball. A teaching resource guide is available to accompany the video. The video is also useful for helping students understand social class and the struggles of two families in Chicago.

Using the Illustration

Ask students for their reactions to the cartoon. Is there an element of truth to the bumper stickers? *(More than an element, probably.)* To what do students attribute this appreciation of athletics over academics?

Section 3 Social Issues in Sport

Key Term

- stacking

Section Preview

Sport contributes to upward mobility among collegiate athletes, but the opportunities are too few. Minorities still face discrimination in sport. Women in sport suffer from gender-based stereotypes. Intercollegiate female athletes do not receive treatment equal to the treatment received by males, although this situation is slowly improving.

Sport and Social Mobility

The autobiographies of star athletes often point to sport as their way out of poverty. One educator once predicted that "football would enable a whole generation of young men in the coal fields of Pennsylvania to turn their backs on the mines that employed their fathers" (Rudolph, 1962:378). Many athletes do use sport as a means out of their equivalent "coal fields," and many minority members work their way out of poverty through sport. It is also true that the average salaries of professionals are very high (Leonard, 1998). Even so, let's examine this alleged relationship between sport and social mobility.

Does sport really promote social mobility? Participating in sport increases the likelihood of improving a person's place in the stratification structure. Whatever sport they play, college athletes tend to be better educated, earn more money, and have higher occupational prestige than their fathers. This is the very definition of upward social mobility. And in these terms, college athletes as a whole are more successful than college students who do not participate in sports (Leonard, 1998). Although this finding is meaningful, it has not settled the debate regarding how much sport promotes upward mobility for minorities.

Sports have long been an important basis for stratification in high schools.

Survey

Have students answer the following questions:

a) African Americans jump higher than whites. (agree or disagree)
b) If yes, this is due to biological differences. (agree or disagree)
c) Canadians are superior hockey players because __________.(fill in the blank)
d) The overwhelming majority of golfers are white because _________. (fill in the blank)

Before you have students discuss their answers, read them the current research on this topic.

The classic debate of nature vs. nurture is pertinent here. Although the nature perspective would argue that black athletic superiority is due to physical strength, the nurture argument contends that the relative socioeconomic status of blacks creates this pattern. Sports that require limited equipment are offered at the most economically

Does sport promote upward mobility for minorities? Some people argue that sport is a social class escalator for minorities. They point to Michael Jordan, Deion Sanders, Sammy Sosa among others. A different viewpoint argues that the emphasis on sport is harmful because it diverts attention away from learning the academic and business-related skills necessary for success in mainstream American society. Because of the lure of high salaries and prestige, many aspiring minority athletes fail to develop alternative career plans. Minority members who spend their youth sharpening their athletic skills at the expense of their general education will very likely be casualties of an unrealizable dream of wealth and glory (Lapchick and Matthews, 1999).

Some convincing evidence supports those who see sport as a barrier to upward mobility for minorities. Figure 15.3 shows that there are over one million high school football players. Just under 60,000 of these players become college football players. And 1,600 of these college players become professional players. Thus, the probability that a high school football player will make it to the pros is less than two-tenths of one percent. Similarly, a high school baseball player has a 0.2 percent chance of becoming a major leaguer. The odds are even worse for a high school basketball player, who has a 0.1 percent probability of making it to the National Basketball Association. Moreover, those who become professional athletes have short careers on the average: one to seven years for baseball players, four to six years for basketball players, and four and one-half years for football players.

Of course, this does not mean minority athletes should not enjoy the benefits of a collegiate sport. To be sure, some athletes have received good college educations who may otherwise not have had the chance. It does argue, however, that no high school athlete—minority or white, for that matter—should rely solely on sport as a ticket up the stratification structure.

The phenomenal success of Michael Jordon is frequently used to prove that sport is a path of upward mobility for minorities. Is Jordon a typical example?

Figure 15.3 High School Athletes' Chances of Advancing to the Pros. *This table shows the slim chance that high school athletes have to play a professional sport. Does this surprise you?*

Sources: National Federation of State High School Associations, 1999–2000.

	Number of Players in High School	Percentage Advancing from High School to College	Number of Players in College	Percentage Advancing from College to Professional Level	Number of Players at Professional Level	Percentage Advancing from High School to Professional Level
MALES						
Football	1,002,734	6%	57,593	3%	1,643	0.16%
Basketball	541,130	3%	15,874	2%	348	0.06%
Baseball	451,701	6%	25,938	3%	750	0.17%
Ice hockey	27,245	13%	3,647	18%	648	2.38%
Total	2,022,811	5%	103,052	3%	3,389	0.17%
FEMALES						
Basketball	451,600	3%	14,445	1%	132	0.03%
Golf	49,690	6%	3,108	2%	52	0.10%
Tennis	159,740	5%	8,314	2%	150	0.09%
Total	661,030	4%	25,867	1%	334	0.05%
Grand Total	**2,683,841**	**5%**	**128,919**	**3%**	**3,723**	**0.14%**

Points to Stress

While it is important that students understand the realities involved in planning on a career in sports, students should not misinterpret the author to assume that he is saying students should not strive to reach their dreams. They should just know the odds. Even if students don't make it to the professional level, there are many important ways they can use the skills obtained through playing high school sports. Ask students to suggest some of these ways.

Working with the Data

Figure 15.3 Students will probably be surprised by the very low percentage of athletes who actually make it to the professional level. Ask which sport offers the best chance for athletes to make it to the professional level? (ice hockey) Does this sport offer equal opportunities for all? (No. Statistically, whites from northern climates have the best chances of making it here.)

underprivileged schools. Sports that require lessons and use expensive equipment (horseback riding, for example) are usually dominated by whites. Geographic considerations also exist. Hockey is most often played in cold weather climates, and even though minorities do live in those areas, hockey is an expensive sport and seems to be the domain of white athletes. For a detailed explanation of this argument see: Gnida, John. 1995. "Teaching Nature vs. Nurture: The Case of African-American Athletic Success" *Teaching Sociology,* 23(4), 389–395.

L1

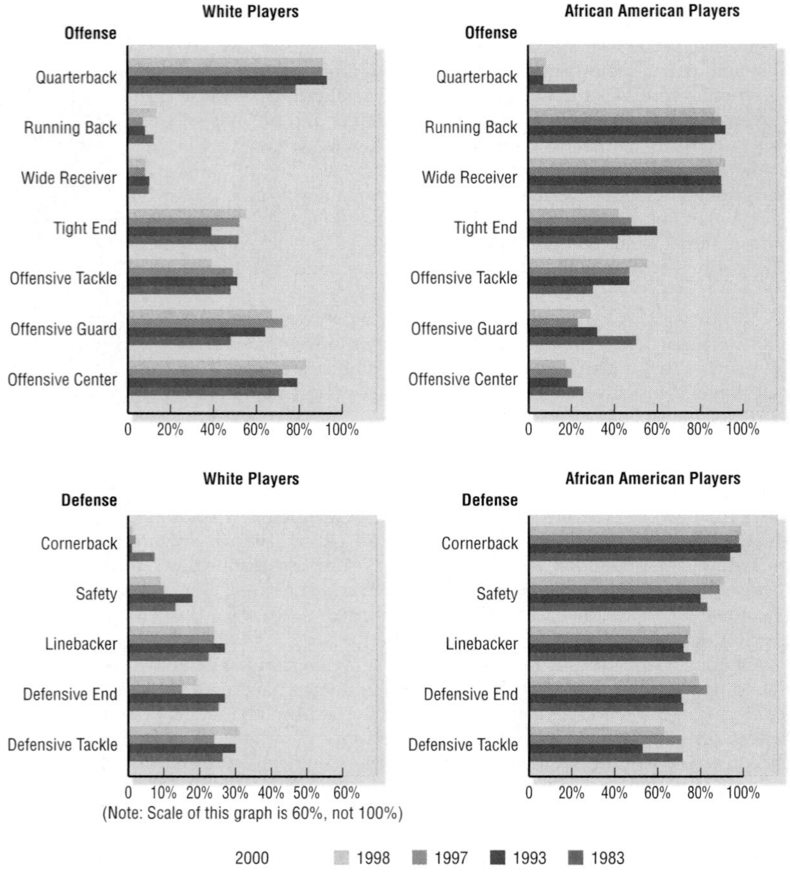

Figure 15.4 National Football League Positions, by Race. *Do you think that these data support the presence of stacking in the NFL?*

Source: Northeastern University, Center for the Study of Sport in Society, 2001.

Sport and Racism

stacking
assignment of players to less central positions on the basis of race or ethnicity

One sign of systematic discrimination shows up in what is called *stacking*. In **stacking,** players are assigned to less central positions on the basis of race or ethnicity. "Central" positions are those that involve leadership and decision-making responsibilities and thus offer a greater likelihood of influencing the outcome of the game. Historically, minorities have more often been assigned to positions requiring relatively little interaction and coordination with other players. In football, for example, African American quarterbacks are rare, while the proportions of African Americans in many defensive and other less central positions are high. (See Figure 15.4.)

Working with the Data

Figure 15.4 The data certainly make it look like stacking is an issue. For example, the number of white quarterbacks (a central position of leadership) is many times greater than the number of African American quarterbacks. The situation for minorities does appear to be improving, but at this point the changes are not significant.

Reinforcing Vocabulary

To help students understand the concept of stacking, have them give examples from a number of different sports: basketball, baseball, football, ice hockey, etc. You may also ask them to apply the concept to areas outside sport, such as politics and education. Can they identify a case of "stacking" in politics?

Observation

Ask students to watch several sports programs, paying attention to how sports announcers portray the white and minority athletes. Students will need to stay as objective as possible. Do the students notice announcers describing white and minority athletes differently? Are white athletes attributed with certain qualities not associated with minority athletes? Are minority athletes only described one certain way? **L1**

Such discrimination has important economic consequences, because the positions occupied by most African Americans have high injury rates that cut careers short. Both salaries and pension benefits are reduced as a result.

Is there salary fairness in professional sports? Discrimination in salary at the professional level exists. African Americans in the major professional sports are, on the average, paid as much as or more than their white counterparts. It is only when level of performance is controlled that discrimination appears—African Americans have lower average salaries than whites for the same level of performance. In other words, African Americans must perform better than whites to avoid pay discrimination (Eitzen and Sage, 1997).

What other areas of discrimination have been found? Minority former athletes profit much less than their white colleagues from personal appearances and commercial endorsements. They also lose out in sports-related careers when their playing days are over. While 78 percent of players in the National Basketball Association (NBA) are black, only about 16 percent of radio and television NBA sports announcers are African American, and only 3 percent of the announcers are Latino.

At the professional level, there are few minorities represented in the power structure—head coaches, general managers, owners, executives, commissioners. In 1989, Bill White became the first African American to head a major professional sports league. As of 2001, only one major sport franchise in the U.S. was owned by minorities. And no minorities in either the NFL or Major League Baseball were board chairs, presidents, or CEOs. In 2000, Michael Jordan did become president of basketball operations for the NBA's Washington Wizards. His five-year deal could eventually give him a 20 percent ownership share in the team. There were only three African American head coaches in professional football in 2001, six African American baseball managers, and one Latino baseball manager. Only 31 percent of NBA head coaches were members of minorities in 2001.

SOCIOLOGY Online

Student Web Activity
Visit the *Sociology and You* Web site at soc.glencoe.com and click on **Chapter 15—Student Web Activities** for an activity on sport and sexism.

Minorities are well represented as players in major U.S. sports. However, after their playing days are over, minorities are underrepresented in positions of power within their sport.

Teaching Strategy

Ask students if the absence of African Americans in the head positions of sports organizations surprises them. Why or why not? Ask if they think this is true in areas other than sports, such as corporations? What does this reflect about our society? Do students think this will change in the near future? Why or why not?
L1

Integrating the Teacher Resources

For review, use the Chapter 15 Vocabulary Quiz and Chapter Quiz in the Unit 4 Mastering Basic Concepts booklet in your Teacher's Resource Box.

Encouraging Citizenship Activity

An organization called Hit Racism for Six is dedicated to eliminating racism in cricket teams across Britain. It was established in 1995, after a nationally distributed magazine ran an article arguing that black people should not be allowed to play for England. Since then, Hit Racism for Six has worked to end racism in the sport by organizing public meetings, issuing pamphlets and newsletters, and lobbying.

Ask each student to locate a local organization that is working in some way to end discrimination in sports. Ask them to report to the class on the types of activities and services these organizations offer. You might ask one or two students to obtain a copy of the anti-discrimination policies used by the various teams at your school. Use the students' research to compile a listing of the organizations, and post it as a resource.
L1

Snapshot of America

Ask students why they think the viewing audience for baseball has changed from young working-class white males to older, more affluent white males.

Answers to Interpreting the Map

1. The southern and southeastern regions of the country are lower than other areas of the country in terms of baseball viewership.
2. Student answers will vary. One explanation could be that the South geographically has fewer large cities than the North, Midwest, or West coast. Large cities are needed to support a successful sports franchise. Today, Atlanta is the home of a popular baseball team as is Florida (the Marlins), but these are relatively new teams.
3. Student answers will vary.

Points to Stress

The media coverage of the United States women's soccer team during the 1999 World Cup tournament was unparalleled in women's sports history. However, the incident that occurred at the end of the championship match, where U.S. team member Brandi Chastain removed her shirt, captured a good amount of that media coverage. Ask students why they think this is. Could it be construed as a subtle indication of stereotyping by the media?

Snapshot of America

Who Are the Biggest Baseball Fans?

Baseball fans used to be young working-class white males. Today's fans are older and more affluent but still predominantly white and male. The relative lack of African American fans might be traced to baseball's traditional racist policies on the field and in the front office.

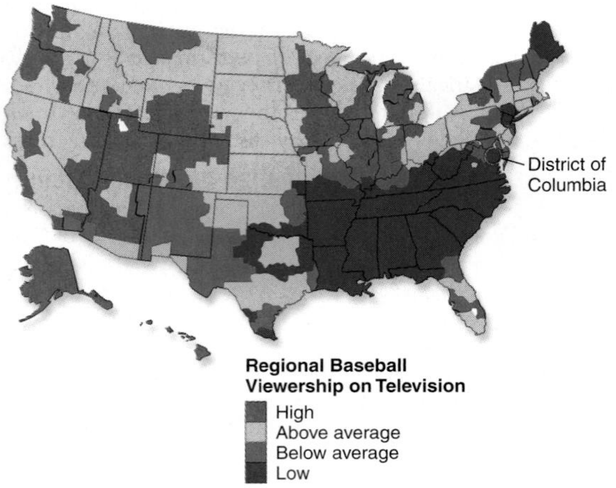

Interpreting the Map

1. Do you see any regional patterns in the rates of baseball viewership? Describe.
2. How do you explain these patterns?
3. As a baseball fan, are you similar to or different from the general pattern in your state? Why?

Adapted from *Latitudes and Attitudes: An Atlas of American Tastes, Trends, Politics, and Passions.* Boston: Little, Brown.

Sexism in Sport

Racial and ethnic minorities have not been the only victims of prejudice and discrimination in sport. Women have experienced sexism in athletics. The cultural roots of sexism date back at least as far as the ancient Greeks. Greek gods were depicted as athletic, strong, powerful, competitive, rational, physical, and intellectual. Many Greek goddesses were passive, beautiful, physically weak, supportive, unathletic, and sexually attractive. (The few active, strong goddesses were usually not attractive to nor attracted by men. To Greek males, women who were physically or intellectually superior to them were unfeminine.) These gender definitions have survived in large part for the past 2,500 years. Their influence is felt in sport just as it is in other aspects of social life.

Survey

Have students develop a survey using the following statements. Since 1991:

- Female participation in sports is changing.
- Female participation in team sports has increased most in soccer and basketball.
- Female participation has increased in fitness activities such as exercising with equipment, running and jogging, and working out at athletic clubs.
- Female participation in in-line skating has increased significantly.
- Female participation has increased in

Although sexism in sports has been decreasing, women athletes continue to suffer from inequalities.

What are some of the consequences of sexism? Stereotypes have traditionally discouraged females from playing sports. For centuries, the idea that playing sports makes females more masculine has been widespread. To be an athlete, females were told, is to be unfeminine. This stigma discouraged many females from participating in athletics and tyrannized many of those who did. Another barrier was the old, discredited argument that sports harm a woman's health, particularly her ability to have children.

Sexism has denied females equal access to organized sports. At the local level, resistance to female participation in sports continues to exist. It was not until the mid-1970s that, under legal threat, the national Little League organization ended its males-only policy. Only when the 1972 Educational Amendment Act (Title IX) was passed were public high schools and colleges required to offer females equal access to sports. Originally, Title IX was interpreted as providing equal opportunity in "all" sport programs of institutions receiving federal funds. Ambiguities in Title IX have led to many legal suits. Important issues remain unresolved. Currently, the courts favor matching the ratio of males and females in a school's athletic programs to their proportionate numbers in the student body of that school (Blum, 1993).

Why has the percentage of women coaching women's programs declined? Women are still denied equal access to the power structure of sport (Lapchick and Matthews, 2001). What's more, although Title IX increased equality for female athletes, it led to a decrease in the number of coaching and administrative positions held by women. In the early 1970s, women's intercollegiate teams were headed almost entirely by women. As of 2000, more than half of the NCAA women's teams were coached by men. (See Figure 15.5 on page 518.) Less than 20 percent of all women's programs were headed by a female administrator, and females held

Making Connections to Other Cultures

Women athletes are breaking gender stereotypes in Japan by excelling in professional wrestling, where female wrestling is already a respected sport.

One outstanding woman athlete, Kyoko Hamaguchi, comes from a long line of male wrestlers, and is actively supported by her father and family. When, at the age of thirteen, she competed in a prestigious Tokyo bodybuilding contest, she was the event's youngest competitor ever. She is currently the world female wrestling champion.

Women's wrestling is likely to be introduced as an official event at the 2004 Olympic Games in Athens.

You can connect sport to culture by asking students to compare Japanese female wrestling, with its dignity and high social approval, with American female wrestlers such as Chyna and Jacqueline and others who appear at World Wrestling Federation events.

L1

Teaching Strategy

To provide closure for the main ideas in this chapter, you may want to ask students to complete the learning objectives on text page 495.

outdoor sports such as backpacking, canoeing, kayaking, and rafting.

Students should survey people in your community. The survey should be designed for agree/disagree answers. The survey should also ask for responses about the public in general and about people you know personally. Have students compile the results. Do they find that people in your community are aware of the changes in the numbers of women participating in individual and team sports?

L1

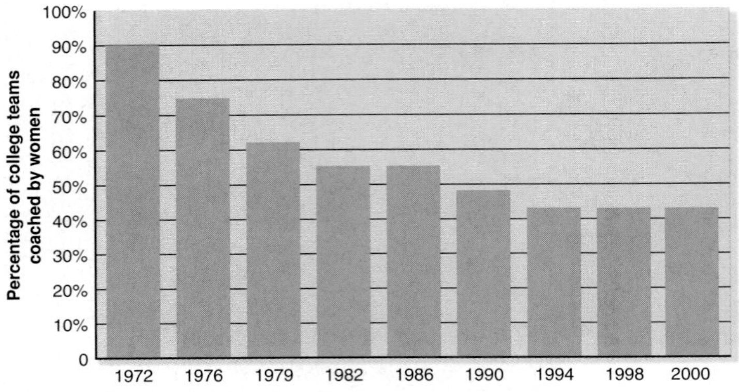

Figure 15.5 Percentage of College Women's Athletic Teams Coached by Women. *What is most interesting to you about these data?*

Source: Center for the Study of Sport in Society, 2001.

only one-third of all administrative jobs in women's programs (Acosta and Carpenter, 1997).

Ironically, Title IX may be one reason for this decline. As the money and prestige associated with women's programs have increased, men have found these coaching jobs much more attractive. And conflict theorists believe that men, who are overwhelmingly in charge of athletic programs and who have the power to make hiring decisions, are more likely to choose men as coaches (Nixon and Frey, 1996).

Are women represented at the national level? Currently, professional sports for women include a Women's National Basketball Association (WNBA), a volleyball league, a golf tour, and a tennis circuit. As we have already seen, few women athletes make it to the professional ranks. Even those women who become professionals earn significantly less than their male counterparts (Levin, 1996). Golf, for example, is one of the few professional sports offering significant opportunities for women. Still, the leading money winner on the men's tour typically earns more than twice as much as the leading money winner on the women's tour. This disparity is reflected in the total prize money for the Professional Golfers' Association (PGA) and the Ladies Professional Golf Association (LPGA) tours—men $132 million; women $36 million.

There are some positive, if small, signs of change. In addition to her Nike commercial, U.S. soccer star Mia Hamm has a lucrative deal with Gatorade. Chamique Holdsclaw, an extremely talented female professional basketball player for the Washington Mystics, obtained an unheard-of (for women athletes) five-year contract with Nike, plus her own signature Holdsclaw shoe (Hammel and Mulrine, 1999).

> "You don't save a pitcher for tomorrow. Tomorrow it may rain."
>
> **Leo Durocher**
> **baseball coach**

Section 3 Assessment

1. What advice would you give to a young man or woman planning to become a professional athlete? Use the information in this chapter in your response.
2. How did the Educational Amendment Act of 1972 (Title IX) affect women's sport programs?

Critical Thinking

3. **Analyzing Information** "American females experience more prejudice and discrimination in sport than males." Explain why you agree or disagree with this statement.

Pulling it All Together

This section explored the inequalities that exist in sports. Racial and gender discrimination still exist in sport. Women are not afforded the same treatment as their male counterparts.

Answers to Section 3 Assessment

1. Answers should emphasize that even though college athletes as a whole tend to become more successful than college students who do not participate in athletics, the statistical odds of making a successful living as a professional athlete are very low. Therefore, athletes should develop alternate career plans and should not neglect learning the academic and business-related skills that are necessary for success in mainstream society. If students wish to elaborate, they could add that minorities in professional sports often suffer from discrimination (for example, higher injury rates due to "stacking," lower salaries, fewer commercial endorsements, and fewer opportunities in the sports power structure). Also, sexism in organized sports continues to put women at a disadvantage.
2. The 1972 Educational Amendment Act (Title IX) required public high schools and colleges to offer females equal access to sports.

Critical Thinking

3. Answers will vary.

Careers in Sociology

Ask students to consider how they would answer the following question: Can I use what I'm learning in sociology in a fun job now that will lead to a career later?

After they have had a chance to answer, share with them the following information. The recreation field has a large number of part-time, seasonal, and volunteer jobs. These jobs include summer camp counselors, lifeguards, craft specialists, and after-school and weekend recreation program leaders. The vast majority of workers serve as activity leaders at local day-camp programs, or in youth organizations, camps, nursing homes, hospitals, senior centers, YMCAs, and other settings. Some serve on local park and recreation boards and commissions. Volunteer experience, part-time

Sociology Today

How to Avoid Bigotry in Sport

Sports sociologist J. Coakley supports the concerns of many Native Americans on the issue of team names. He wrote the following article, about this issue.

Most of us are not very concerned about the use of Native American names by many athletic teams. But to Native Americans, war whoops and tomahawk chopping portray negative stereotypes.

Using stereotypes to characterize Native Americans in the U.S. is so common that most people don't even realize they are doing it. This has occurred for so long that the stereotypes are now widely accepted as valid depictions of native peoples. When these stereotypes are used as a basis for team names, mascots, and logos, sports become a way of perpetuating an ideology that exploits, trivializes, and demeans the history and cultural heritage of Native Americans.

If teachers, administrators, and students in U.S. schools had a deep knowledge of the rich and diverse cultures of Native Americans and realized the discrimination native peoples currently face, they would not use names such as Indians, Redskins, Chiefs, Braves, Savages, Tribe, and Redmen for their teams; they would not allow Anglo students to entertain fans by dressing up as caricatures of Native Americans, and they would not allow fans to mimic Native American chants or act out demeaning stereotypes of war-whooping, tomahawk-chopping Native Americans.

Schools should not use any Native American name or symbol in connection with sport teams unless they do the following:

1. Sponsor a special curriculum to inform students of the history, cultural heritage, and current living conditions of the native group after which their sport teams are named. Unless 70 percent of the students can pass annual tests on this information, schools should drop the names they say are used to "honor" native people.
2. Publish two press releases per year in which information about the heritage and current circumstances of the native peoples honored by their team names is described and analyzed; publish similar materials annually in school newspapers and yearbooks.
3. Once per year, during homecoming or a major sport event, sponsor a special ceremony designed by and for native peoples in the local area, with the purpose of informing students and parents about the people they say they honor with their team names.

Source: Jay J. Coakley, *Sport in Society*. 6th ed. Boston: Irwin McGraw-Hill, 1998, pp. 272–273.

Doing Sociology

Is there a sport symbol in your community, or state, that might be offensive to Native Americans? Has the existence of this offensive symbol hurt your community or state economically? Could it in the future? Should it? Explain.

work during school, or a summer job can lead to a full-time career as a recreation worker.

Persons planning recreation careers should be outgoing, good at motivating people, and sensitive to the needs of others. Good health and physical fitness are typically required, while activity planning calls for creativity and resourcefulness.

Individuals contemplating careers in recreation at the supervisory or administrative level should develop managerial skills.

More information is available from the National Recreation and Park Association, **http://www.nrpa.org** and the National Employee Services and Recreation Association, **http://www.nesra.org**.

Sociology Today

This article should spark a lot of debate in class. If your school uses a Native American mascot, have the class conduct a survey to see if students would support changing it.

Answer to Doing Sociology

Have students research a school in your area that has or had a Native American mascot to find out how the issue was handled. Some schools have threatened not to play schools with these mascots unless the mascots are changed. Ask students if they think this is an effective way to handle the situation.

Integrating the Teacher Resources

To further assess student comprehension of this chapter, use Chapter Test A or B and the Unit 4 Test, which are available in the Chapter and Unit Tests booklet in your Teacher's Resource Box.

ANSWERS CHAPTER 15 ASSESSMENT

Reviewing Vocabulary

1. i
2. f
3. g
4. h
5. d
6. c
7. e
8. a
9. b
10. j

Reviewing the Facts

1. Because it is compatible with the American values of competition and achievement.
2. Answers will vary and may include: to promote a sense of social identity; to promote social integration; to provide relief of tensions; to develop good character.
3. Conflict theorists view sport as being controlled by an elite group; views organized sports as being harmful to character development.

CHAPTER 15 ASSESSMENT

Summary

Section 1: The Nature of Sport

Main Idea: As a social institution, sport fulfills some important societal needs. One of these is helping individuals identify with others members of society. Sport subcultures have developed around both team and individual sports. For this reason, sport is a reflection of society.

Section 2: Theoretical Perspectives and Sport

Main Idea: Functionalists see sport positively, as a means for socializing young people, promoting social integration, providing a releaser for tensions, and developing sound character. Conflict theorists believe that organized sports can be harmful to character development. Symbolic interactionists focus on the self-concepts and relationships developed through sport activities.

Section 3: Social Issues in Sport

Main Idea: Sport contributes to upward mobility among collegiate athletes, but the opportunities are too few. Minorities still face discrimination in sport. Women in sport suffer from gender-based stereotypes. Intercollegiate female athletes do not receive treatment equal to the treatment received by males, although this situation is slowly improving.

SOCIOLOGY Online

Self-Check Quiz
Visit the *Sociology and You* Web site at soc.glencoe.com and click on **Chapter 15—Self-Check Quizzes** to prepare for the chapter test.

Reviewing Vocabulary

Complete each sentence using each term once.

a. sport
b. Title IX
c. sports subculture
d. functionalist perspective on sport
e. conflict perspective on sport
f. symbolic interactionist perspective on sport
g. social mobility in sport
h. stacking
i. salary equity
j. sexism in sport

1. The assumption that all athletes are paid based on level of performance is known as ________.
2. The perspective that is most concerned with the relationships of those involved is called ________.
3. Using sport to improve a position in the stratification structure is known as ________.
4. ________ is the assigning of less central positions to minorities.
5. ________ is the perspective that emphasizes the positive contributions of sport to society.
6. A set of norms that surround a particular sport is called ________.
7. ________ is the perspective that sees sport as an institution in which the most powerful oppress, manipulate, coerce, and exploit others.
8. ________ is a set of competitive activities in which winners and losers are determined by physical performance within a set of established rules.
9. ________ was established with the intent of increasing opportunity for female athletes in school settings.
10. The defining of sport as a masculine activity is known as ________.

4.

Perspective	Summary
Functionalist	Sees sport as important primarily because it helps society work more smoothly.
Conflict Theorist	Sees sport negatively. Believes sport is a social institution in which the most powerful oppress, coerce, manipulate and exploit others. Sport mirrors the unequal distribution of power, money and wealth in society.
Symbolic Interactionist	Sees sport as being positive or negative depending on the experience of the participant in the sport interaction. Sees the meanings and interpretation of symbols of sport as being very important. Believes that the symbols of sport affect the self-concept and relationships of participants in sport.

5. Sports contribute positively toward upward social mobility but is not a real determinant of upward social mobility because of the limited number of opportunities.

Reviewing the Facts

1. Why does sport play an important role in American society?
2. According to the functionalists, what is one purpose of sport?
3. What is the conflict theorists view of sport as an institution?
4. Outline and summarize sport from the three sociological perspectives. Create a diagram similar to the one below to record your answer.

PERSPECTIVE	SUMMARY
Functionalist	
Conflict Theorist	
Symbolic Interactionist	

5. Identify the relationship between sport and social mobility.

Thinking Critically

1. **Drawing Conclusions** High school athletes with superior skills are often given extraordinary help in meeting college entrance requirements, including coaching for achievement and aptitude tests. Many students feel this is unfair to those who have higher grades but aren't accepted. Others justify the practice. They point out that athletics bring in lots of money for colleges. They also say that athletes have skills as rare as high intelligence and so deserve their sports scholarships every bit as much as others deserve academic scholarships. Do you think it is fair for athletes to be given help meeting college entrance requirements?
2. **Analyzing Information** The use of mascots is at the center of a current debate in sports. Some schools have made efforts to change their school nicknames and mascots so as not to offend various groups that might have been negatively portrayed by these mascots and nicknames. Do you think that schools and teams have an obligation to take such actions? Or should teams be allowed to retain their traditional nicknames and mascots?
3. **Making Generalizations** Typically, the rewards associated with a particular skill or occupation tell us how much society values that skill or occupation. Sports superstars are rewarded very highly. Relatively few "superstars" in the field of teaching or medicine make salaries comparable to those of successful professional athletes. Do you believe this indicates that U.S. society doesn't value education and health care as highly as sports? What other factors might influence compensation and salary?
4. **Making Inferences** Nearly 80 percent of the players in the National Basketball Association are African American, while over 90 percent of the members of the National Hockey League are white. Baseball and football are more evenly mixed. How would you explain the lack of African Americans in hockey and their apparent overrepresentation in basketball? (See also Activity 3 on the following page.)
5. **Evaluating Information** In the National Basketball Association draft, the best players go to the teams that completed the previous season with the worst records. Why do you think the NBA uses this approach instead of allowing the best players to go to the teams with the most prestige, status, and monetary resources?
6. **Applying Concepts** Here's a thought experiment to try. Using your answer to number 5 above, see if you can apply your reasoning to the institution of the family. Imagine that NBA teams are like families in various social classes and that each generation is like a season of professional basketball. Wouldn't it be fair to ask the winning families (those at the top of the social class ladder) not to pass on their advantages to their offspring? In other words, for the competition to be fair, wealthier families should not be allowed to go to the best schools but instead should be sent to the schools with the fewest resources. The logic used here is that the best and most talented succeed anywhere. What is the fallacy in this argument?

ANSWERS CHAPTER 15 ASSESSMENT

Thinking Critically

1. Answers will vary. Some students will feel that it is not fair for athletes to receive extra help while non-athletes have to attain good grades for college admission without assistance. Others will feel that college sports provide social and individual benefits and that justifies helping athletes. This topic should spark an interesting debate.
2. Students will have varying opinions. Some will feel that the mascots don't reflect attitudes about various groups. Others will feel that political correctness necessitates a higher degree of sensitivity. Students might want to discuss schools in your area that have had to deal with this issue.
3. Ask students how social structure creates these inequalities that exist between prestige and income. Have students refer back to Chapter 8 on job prestige and income.
4. Research on this topic is covered on pages 512–513 (bottom panel) of the teacher edition. The sociologist looked at geographic factors related to sports, as well as the amount of money required to participate in specific sports.
5. In theory, the draft is designed to eventually create parity among teams. Each team is given the chance to improve itself annually. In reality, however, there are many factors that prevent this from happening. Free agency has watered down the effectiveness of the NBA draft, as players can switch teams more freely than in years past. Some teams are able to improve without utilizing the draft. Some teams that annually get high draft picks are no better after several years of getting quality picks.
6. Students will likely claim that the idea is ridiculous. Ask them if it is fair that those who have the most are rewarded with more. Have students think of ways that income and wealth could be used based on the idea of the NBA draft.

ANSWERS CHAPTER 15 ASSESSMENT

7. Durkheim believed that the crowd could compel people to do things not necessarily possible at other times. This is the logic of the home court advantage—the crowd serves as the "6th man," spurring the team on. Research on this topic suggests that athletes' adrenaline flow increases with crowd intensity, and that adrenaline can be a stressor when the crowd is hostile.
8. a) economist
   b) psychologist
   c) sociologist
   d) sociologist
   e) sociologist
   f) sociologist/political scientist

Sociology Projects

1. Students can really run with this project. Some might want to follow a team's batting averages or homerun totals on a daily basis, for example. Students could analyze how team statistics don't always tell the story but statistics also don't lie.
2. This is an opportunity for students to perform some qualitative research. Do students' findings correlate? Ask students if they think their sample is representative. Can their information be generalized? Students might want to further explore the home court advantage by consulting this article: Eldon E. Synder and Dean Purdy. "The Home Court Advantage in Collegiate Basketball." *Sociology of Sport Journal* (1985) # 2, 352–356. Although the article is older, the information is as relevant as when the study was conducted. Students might also want see if more current resources are available.
3. Students can contact coaches, players, and parents to find out costs for each sport. This activity is related to the thesis presented earlier that the cost of a sport is correlated to who plays the sport. For example, hockey requires rink time. In cold weather cities, the ponds and lakes provide free rink time.
4. If students work in groups, they can quickly cover all the teams of one professional sport, concentrating on the managers, coaches, and upper management personnel. This information might be available from the particular

CHAPTER 15 ASSESSMENT

7. **Drawing Conclusions** In referring to the way a crowd of people can motivate a team of players, Emile Durkheim once said, "There are occasions when this strengthening and vivifying action of society is especially apparent. In the midst of an assembly animated by a common passion, we become susceptible of acts and sentiments of which we are incapable when reduced to our own forces." Do you believe that a home court or home field advantage really exists? Do players rise to the occasion when cheered on by the home crowd? Are there ever times when athletes might play better when not at home?
8. **Evaluating Information** Pretend that you are attending a professional tennis match with an economist, a political scientist, a psychologist, and a sociologist. Link each of the questions below to the discipline most likely to give a complete answer.
   a. How did the hot dogs get to be five dollars?
   b. Why do some athletes fall apart after a bad call?
   c. What is the socioeconomic status of the players?
   d. Does tennis reflect mainstream values?
   e. How did Americans lose their dominance in this sport?
   f. Why does it seem that all tennis courts are located in wealthy neighborhoods?

Sociology Projects

1. **Sports and Statistics** The sports section is a great place to examine how statistics are used. For one week follow a team in any sport that is currently in season. Track several team and individual statistics. Do dramatic changes occur in the statistics, or are the changes insignificant? Can you offer any reason for the change or lack of change? Compare your team's statistics with those of a classmate's team. Analyze the validity of the statistics. Do they accurately tell the story, or can statistics deceive us?
2. **The Home Court Advantage** Interview athletes who participate in several of your school's sports. Ask the following questions.
   a. What are the advantages of playing at home?
   b. What are the disadvantages of playing on the road?
   c. What factors contribute to home court advantage?
   d. What factors hinder better performances on the road?
   e. Do you ever prefer to play at home?
   f. Compare your notes with those of your classmates to see if there is consensus.
3. **The Cost of Sports** Research suggests that participation in sports reflects geographic location and economic conditions. For instance, basketball is an urban game that does not require a lot of money to play. All one needs is a ball and a place to shoot. Conduct research on other major sports—football, baseball, hockey, skiing, tennis, and golf. Try to determine where and by whom these sports tend to be played. How much does it cost an individual who is not professional to play these sports? Share your results with the class.
4. **Minorities in Coaching and Management** The text discusses underrepresentation of minorities in coaching and management positions. To find out whether this pattern still holds, conduct a quick survey of your own. (If your teacher allows, you may want to work in groups.) Concentrating on professional sports, what are the names of coaches and managers from all the teams in a national league. Use the Internet to find answers to these questions. (Most professional sports leagues include at least twenty-five teams.) Identify as many of the coaches and managers as possible by race and ethnicity. What is the proportion of minority coaches and managers in your sample?
5. **Sports Apparel** One way to see the impact of sports on U.S. society is to walk the halls of any American high school. (You may rather observe people at a mall or shopping center if your school does not allow clothes with commercial

logos.) To get an idea how many people at your school wear clothes that represent sports teams or sports activities, sit in one place for fifteen minutes and simply count the number of students and teachers wearing sports clothing. Are many students wearing clothing representing their own high school teams? Or do most favor logos from local college or professional teams? Do you think wearing team clothes fosters a sense of identification with the team?

6. **Sports in Film** Numerous movie videos deal with sports themes. Select a video, and write a report on it using concepts discussed in the chapter. For example, the film *Jerry McGuire* touches on player salaries and issues of race, among other themes. Present your report to the class.
7. **Sports as a Social Institution** Imagine that you are a visitor from a planet where the institution of sport does not exist. The objective of your visit to Earth is to observe social interactions in sport in order to determine whether sport is an institution that should be established on your planet.

   As a "visitor" you attend a game of basketball, football, volleyball and baseball. What conclusions would you make regarding the social interactions of those involved in the game? Consider and list any perceived negative or positive interactions. Analyze those interactions as either being constructive or destructive to the development of desirable social interactions on your planet.

   Write a one-page essay that summarizes your findings and supports your decision to recommend or to not recommend that sport be established as an institution on your planet.

Technology Activity

1. Using your favorite search engine, do a search for "sociology of sport."
   - **a.** How many web page matches did your search find? What does that indicate to you about the importance of this subject?
   - **b.** Go to the electronic journal *Sociology of Sport On-Line* (sosol) at http://www.brunel.ac.uk/depts/sps/sosol/index.htm. Review the table of contents of the most recent issue. What types of topics are covered by the authors?
   - **c.** Click on Overview. Where is this journal published? Why was it started?

league's website. The NFL website is **www.nfl.com**

5. Students are conducting a quantitative study of sports apparel. Remind students to include shoes in their study. It will be interesting to note the number of people who are wearing the colors of local sports teams. Students might want to interview other students about why they wear such clothing.
6. You might suggest movies such as *Jerry McGuire, Hoop Dreams,* or *Hoosiers.* If students choose another video, review it for appropriateness before students begin this project. Allow students to show a five minute clip of the video to the class when they present their reports.
7. Answers will vary. Positive notions of competition and achievement should surface along with social identity and the development of self-concept and good character. Negative notions of coercion, manipulation, inequity of power and the development of poor self-concept and undesirable characteristics like cheating or winning at all costs may also surface. (Depending on whether the student recommends or does not recommend sport as an institution to be established on the planet.)

Technology Activity

1. a. The search engine may not find many matches.
   b. Answers will vary.
   c. The journal is published at Brunel University in England. "The purpose of the journal is to provide an international electronic forum for the stimulation and dissemination of research concepts and theory relating to the sociological examination of sport, physical education and coaching."

Enrichment Reading

Have students refer back to Chapter 10 on gender and examine the changes that have occurred that have altered our perceptions of women in sports. Suggest that students interview some adults who can relate how society viewed women and sports twenty years ago.

Ask students if they understand the article's reference (in column 2 on page 524) to Babe Didrikson. If not, tell them that Mildred Ella Zaharis, néle Didrikson was one of the most famous female athletes of her day. She was born in 1914 in Port Arthur, Texas, and died September 27, 1956 in Galveston. She was a remarkable performer in basketball and in track and field and later a leading golfer.

Integrating the Teacher Resources

Additional primary source readings for this chapter can be found in Culture Studies: The Sociological Perspective, **available in your Teacher's Resource Box. Questions for students are included.**

Chapter 15

Enrichment Reading

We Don't Like Football, Do We?

by D. Stanley Eitzen

If you grew up female in America, you heard this: *Sports are unfeminine*. And this: *Girls who play sports are tomboys*. You got this message: *Real women don't spend their free time sliding feet-first into home plate or smacking their fists into soft leather gloves*.

So you didn't play or you did play and either way you didn't quite fit. You didn't fit in your body—didn't learn to live there, breathe there, feel dynamic and capable. Or maybe you fell madly, passionately in love with sports but didn't quite fit in society, never saw yourself—basketball player, cyclist, golfer—reflected in movies, billboards, magazines.

Or you took a middle ground, shying away at first but then later sprinting toward aerobics and weight lifting and in-line skating, **relishing** your increasing endurance and grace and strength. Even then, though, you sensed that something was wrong: all the ads and articles seemed to focus on weight loss and beauty. While those may have inspired you to get fit in the first place, there are more important things, you now know, than how you looked. No one seemed to be talking about pride, pleasure, power, possibility.

If you grew up male in America, you heard this: Boys who *don't* play sports are sissies or . . . [homosexuals]. And this: Don't throw like a girl. You got this message: Sports are a male initiation rite, as fundamental and natural as shaving and deep voices—a **prerequisite,** somehow, to becoming an American man. So you played football or soccer or baseball and felt competent, strong, and bonded with your male buddies. Or you didn't play and risked ridicule.

Whether we were inspired by Babe Ruth or Babe Didrikson or neither, and whether we played kickball with our brothers or sisters or both, all of us, female and male, learned to associate sports prowess and sports privilege with masculinity. Even if the best athlete in the neighborhood was a girl, we learned from newspapers, television, and from our own parents' prejudices that batting, catching, throwing, and jumping are not neutral, human activities, but somehow more naturally a male domain. **Insidiously** our culture's reverence for men's professional sports and its silence about women's athletic accomplishments shaped, defined, and limited how we felt about ourselves as women and men.

. . . You may have noticed that boys are no longer the only ones shooting baskets in public parks. One girl often joins the boys now, her hair dark with sweat, her body alert as a squirrel's. Maybe they don't pass her the ball. Maybe she grabs it anyway, squeezes mightily through the barricade of bodies, leaps skyward, feet flying.

Or she teams with other girls. Gyms fill these days with the rowdy sounds of women hard at play: basketballs seized by calloused hands, sneakers squealing like shocked mice. The players' high, urgent voices resonate, too—"Here!" "Go!"—and right then nothing exists for them except the ball, the shifting constellation of women, the chance to be fluid, smooth, alive.

This West Virginia high school student is a starter on her school's only varsity basketball team.

What Does it Mean?

insidiously
developing in a stealthy and harmful manner so gradually as to become established before being apparent

prerequisite
required as a prior condition to something

relishing
being pleased with or gratified by

What does this mean? What does it mean that everywhere, women are running, shooting baskets, getting sweaty and exhausted and euphoric? What changes when a woman becomes an athlete?

Everything.

On playing fields and in gyms across America, women are engaged in a contest with higher stakes than trophies or ribbons or even prize money. Through women's play, and through their huddles behind the scenes, they are deciding who American women will be. Not just what games they will play, but what role they will play in this still-young nation. Not only what their bodies will look like, but what their bodies can do.

Adapted from Mariah Burton Nelson. "We Don't Like Football, Do We?" in D. Stanley Eitzen, *Sport in Contemporary Society: An Anthology,* 5th ed., St. Martin's Press, Inc., 1996, pp. 25–26.

Read and React

1. State briefly the main point of this article.
2. What do you think is the author's viewpoint on the relationship between gender and sport? Do you agree with him?
3. Do you believe that attitudes in the United States regarding female participation in sport is changing? Explain.
4. From which theoretical perspective is the author writing? Use examples to illustrate that perspective.

Answers to Read and React

1. The main point of this article is that men and women often use sport to help define who and what they are. With the acceptance of women into the field of sport and the realization that not all males have to play sports, individuals are freeing themselves from some gender-based stereotypes.
2. The author seems to takes the position that gender is not the important consideration. It is not that men play better, it is that women are out there experiencing the same things men experience.
3. Evidence of changing attitudes can be seen in the media coverage of the women's U.S. soccer team during the World Cup. The media can no longer relegate women's sports to the back pages of newspapers. Women's sports are capable of arousing as much national pride as men's sports.
4. Students might argue that the author is writing from the symbolic interactionist perspective, concerned about how women view themselves (and men as well.) The functional perspective would view participation of women in sports as maintaining the order and stability of society. It could be viewed from the conflict perspective if one looks at the inequality that still exists, or at the barriers that are hampering equality in sports programs.

NOTES to the Teacher

Social change takes place due to many factors including demographic shifts, urbanization, and collective behavior.

Fertility, mortality, and migration are the primary concepts that demographers use when describing populations and developing projections of future population growth and composition. Students often appreciate these factors of people being born, dying, and moving in and out of geographic areas as obvious and relatively simple to calculate. What students often find problematic are the projections of future growth or decline. For example, knowing that populations grow exponentially indicates that the world population is steadily increasing and in tracking the numbers, demographers warn us often about overpopulation. That we reached a world population of six billion a few months earlier in 1999 than they had projected was cause for much concern in the demographic community. Seemingly opposed to this is the discussion of a declining rate of increase and achieving zero population growth. The key to explaining this apparent paradox is an opportunity to highlight the differences between using raw numbers or simple frequencies and using statistical rates. One may emphasize how the rate of population increase may decline compared to past rates, but the population does increase in number since the rate is still above zero.

Urbanization is closely related to population dynamics because of the third factor, migration. One of the primary reasons we have large cities that are continuing to grow is because of the movement of populations in and out of various nations and regions. In the search for work and a decent standard of living, people migrate from place to place either within a particular nation or between nations. Developing countries are also prone to a phenomenon in which one or a very few cities become "primate cities," extremely large urban environments that serve as primary conduits for industrial activities for the whole country. Mexico City is one excellent example as it is the largest urban city in a nation that is primarily agricultural or rural; corporations have located their headquarters there and businesses that support those corporations (e.g., financial and real estate services) proliferate.

The behavior of people in groups of vary-

UNIT 5

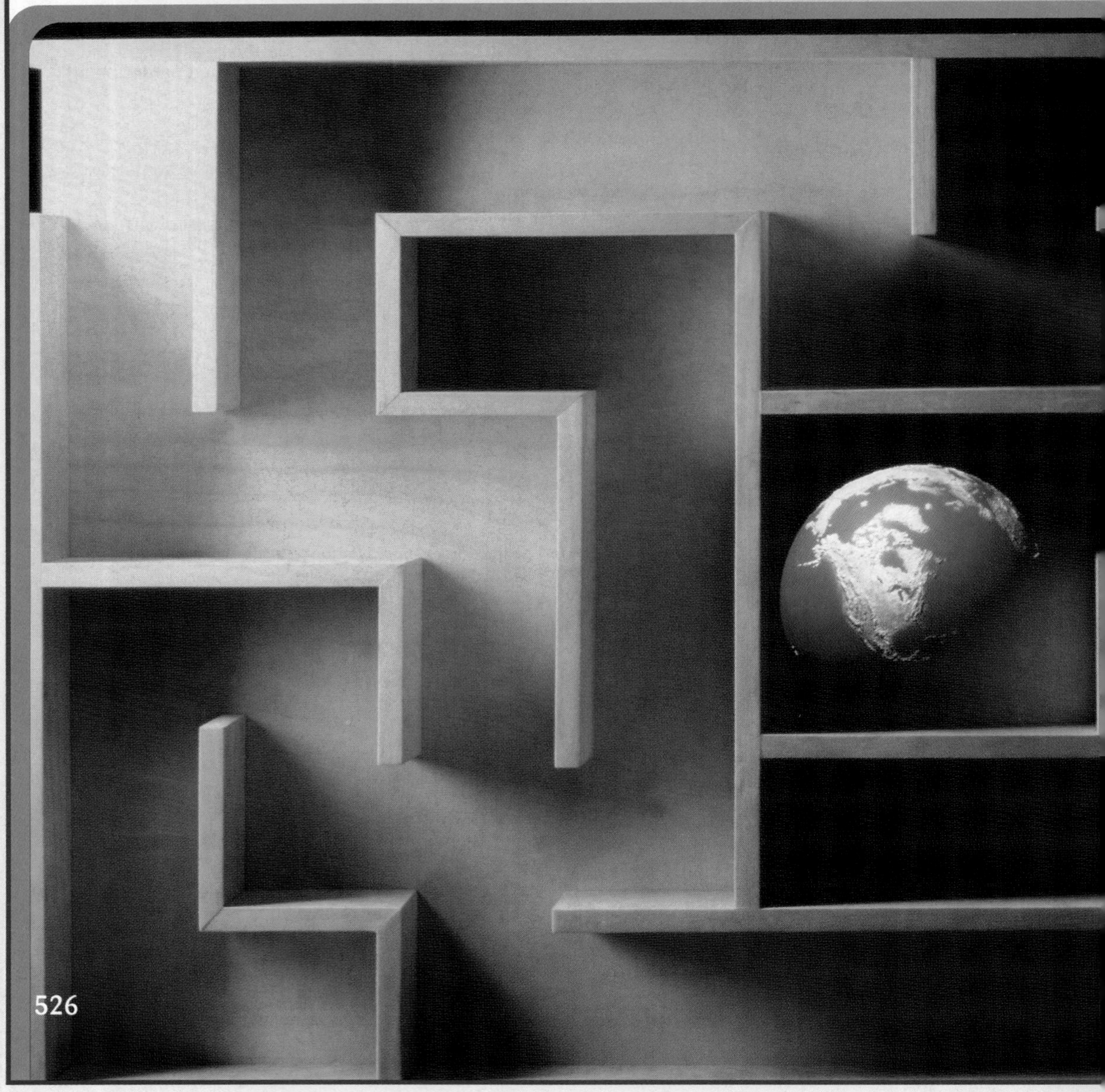

526

SOCIAL CHANGE

Chapter 16

Population and Urbanization

Chapter 17

Collective Behavior and Social Change

Enrichment Readings

Chapter 16 – David Stipp "Life Expectancy: Surprising Demographic Trends" page 564

Chapter 17 – Report: Falling Through the Net page 600

527

ing size and the outcomes of their interactions exert pressures on society for change. The processes of discovery, invention, and diffusion are implicated in these behaviors and are also related to the contribution of technology in social change, which are, in turn, evidence of the increasing rationalization mentioned in previous chapters.

The contribution of technology to our lives is a rational one. Life becomes more standardized, more predictable because of the increasing uses of technology in all areas of life. We use technology not only to produce more goods more efficiently, but also to bring order to our lives. Ritzer's *McDonaldization of Society* mentioned in Chapter 6 highlights the rationalization of food production and consumption. Ask your students why we use the term *fast food.* You not only get your food quickly, but you consume it as quickly. Compare the total time involved for dining in a finer restaurant with picking up dinner through a drive-through window. Despite any sophistication we might assume due to our use of rational processes and our "advanced" state of society, we are still subject to the "irrational" effects of hearsay and superstition. The movies *Urban Legends* and *Gossip* highlight the dramatic effect of such behaviors.

When people in a given society act in accordance with a trend or supposed information (e.g., rumors, fads, fashions, hysteria, panic), specific pressures are exerted on the marketplace to respond by providing the appropriate goods or services. The Y2K rumors escalated into jobs for computer programmers and in retail establishments as people prepared for a supposed black-out by purchasing new computers, software, food, and emergency equipment. Our reliance on technology to provide for the material concerns of life indeed makes us increasingly dependent upon such technology.

Change instituted through the revolution, reformation, or redemption of social movements is not always easy nor quick but it is a sign of the power of people to alter their societies for the better.

Chapters

Pacing Chart*

16 POPULATION AND URBANIZATION

1. The Dynamics of Demography
2. World Population
3. The Urban Transition
4. Urban Ecology

Pages 530-533, 538-539, 541-546, 548-554. Covers birth and death rates; doubling time and exponential growth; government plans for population control; population pyramids; and urbanization and suburbanization.

This accelerated plan excludes the study of migration, the demographic transition, and theories of city growth.

17 SOCIAL CHANGE AND COLLECTIVE BEHAVIOR

1. Social Change
2. Theoretical Perspectives on Social Change
3. Collective Behavior
4. Social Movements

All sections of this text introduce or reinforce important sociological concepts that are of special interest to students of this age and developmental level.

Lesson Planning

You will find detailed daily lesson plans for both traditional class scheduling and block scheduling in your Teacher's Resource Box.

***Note: While the authors of *Sociology and You* do not recommend skipping chapters or sections of the textbook, they are teachers like yourselves and know you must sometimes make scheduling compromises. If your schedule demands that you move more quickly through this book, you may want to focus on the pages listed above.**

Key to Ability Levels

Activities in the teacher's material have been coded for varying learning styles and abilities.

L1 BASIC activities for all students

L2 AVERAGE activities for average to above-average students

L3 CHALLENGING activities for above-average students

ELL ENGLISH LANGUAGE LEARNER activities

Teacher Resource Manager

Teacher Classroom Resources

Unit 5 Mastering Basic Concepts
- Learning Goals Outlines
- Graphic Organizers
- Vocabulary Activities
- Analyzing and Interpreting Data
- Increasing Your Comprehension
- Guided Readings
- Student Journal Prompts
- Vocabulary and Chapter Review Quizzes

Spanish Supplements
- Learning Goals Outlines
- Bilingual Chapter Summaries
- Vocabulary and Chapter Review Quizzes

Chapter & Unit Tests w/ Final Exam and Answer Key
- Chapter 16 Tests A and B
- Chapter 17 Tests A and B
- Unit 5 Test
- Final Exam

Alternative Assessments
- Performance Assessments
- Portfolio Assessments
- Chapter Essay Tests

Culture Studies: The Sociological Perspective
- Reading 26: The Street Children of Ulan Bator
- Reading 27: Ancient Rome
- Reading 28: The Great Famine
- Reading 29: Salem Witch Trials
- Reading 30: Tiananmen Square

Doing Sociology: Focus on Research
- Research Project 14: Where Do We Grow From Here?
- Research Project 15: You've Got Mail!

Ethics, Values, and Technology: Real-Life Issues in Society
- Reading 24: Medical Ethics: Do You Want to Live a Hundred Years?
- Reading 25: The Right to Die: Euthanasia

Transparency Binder

Chapter 16
- 52: World Future Population Map

Multimedia

TeacherWorks™
All-In-One Planner and Resource Center
- **Interactive Teacher Edition** Access your Teacher Wraparound Edition and your classroom resources with a few easy clicks.
- **Interactive Lesson Planner** Planning has never been easier! Organize your week, month, semester, or year with all the lesson helps you need to make teaching creative, timely, and relevant.

Interactive Student Edition CD-ROM
This CD-ROM contains the complete Student Edition with, simple navigation and search functions and links to Web activities and resources.

ExamView® Pro Testmaker CD-ROM
Easy-to-use software includes an extensive question bank and allows you to create fully customized tests that can be administered in print or online.

Vocabulary PuzzleMaker CD-ROM
This software lets you create crossword puzzles, word search puzzles, and jumbo puzzles using chapter vocabulary.

Presentations for the Classroom on CD-ROM
This PowerPoint presentation provides a step-by-step outline and supporting visuals for classroom lectures.

SOCIOLOGY Online

Use our Web site for additional resources. All essential content is covered in the Student Edition.

You and your students can visit soc.glencoe.com, the Web site companion to *Sociology and You.* The student text directs students to the Web site for **Chapter Overviews, Student Web Activities, Self-Check Quizzes,** and **Textbook Updates**.

Answers are provided for you in the **Web Activity Lesson Plan**.

Chapter Preview

Section 1 (pages 530–535)

Demography is the scientific study of population. Population data are very important today, in part because of their use by government and industry. Demographers use three population processes to account for population change: fertility, mortality, and migration.

Section 2 (pages 536–547)

The theory of Thomas Malthus predicted that population size would ultimately outstrip the food supply, resulting in mass starvation and death. Another theory, demographic transition, looks at economic development to predict population patterns.

Section 3 (pages 548–555)

With the Industrial Revolution came a major increase in the rate of urbanization. The development of factories was an especially important influence on the location of cities.

Section 4 (pages 556–560)

Urban ecologists have developed four major theories of growth: concentric zone theory, sector theory, multiple nuclei theory, and peripheral theory. Combining insights from all four theories is useful to our understanding of urban ecology.

Please see the correlation to the American Sociology Association standards located in the front of this text.

CHAPTER 16

Population and Urbanization

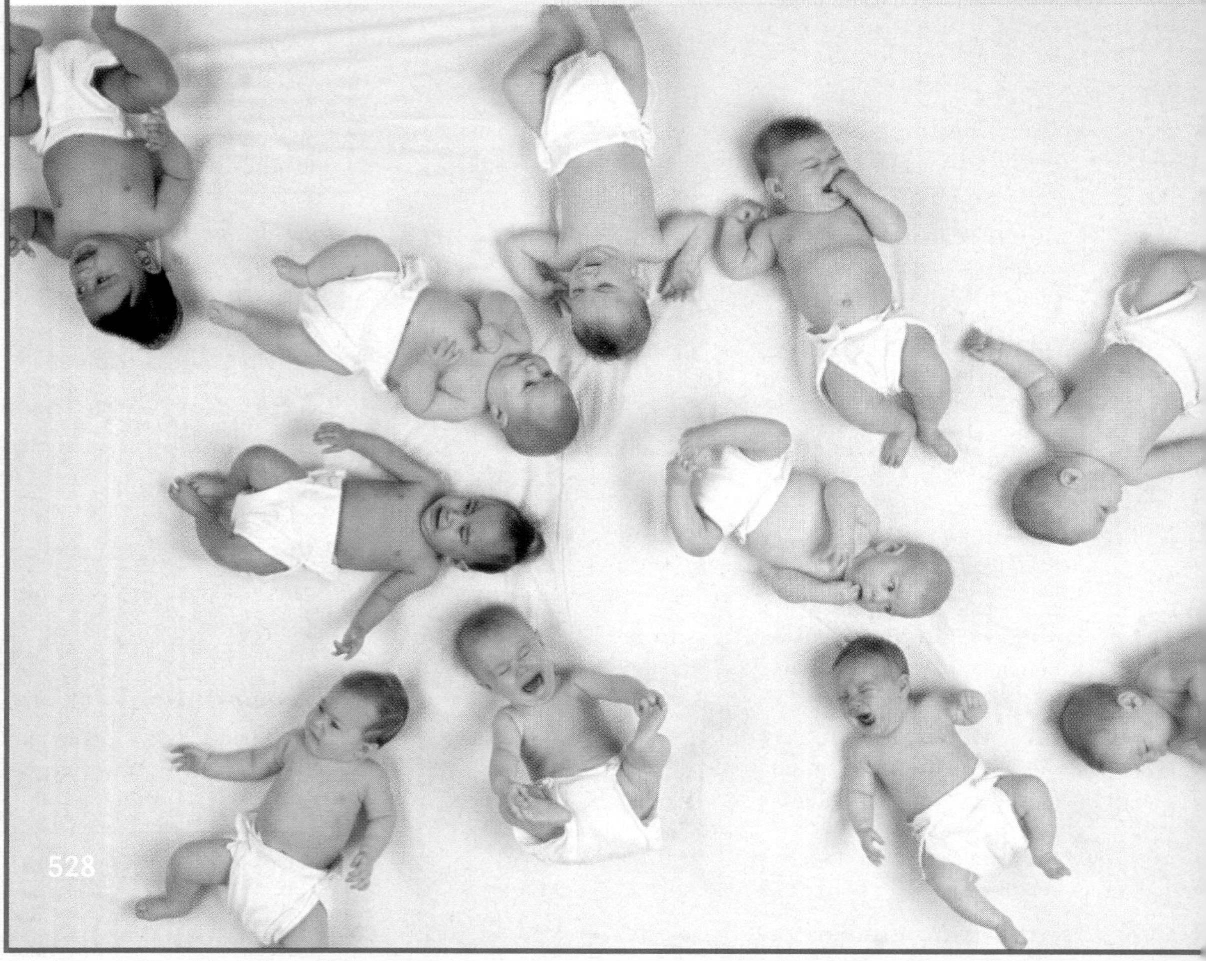

Lead-Off Activity

To begin this chapter's study of population, ask each student to select any two countries in the world to focus on. You might want to make sure that students choose so that countries aren't duplicated. Have students pick two indicators or variables to research about their countries, such as doubling time, infant mortality rate, life expectancy, crude death rate, live birth rate or the gross national product per capita. When they have completed their research, have students form hypotheses (refer to Chapter 2;

USING Your Sociological Imagination

Suppose you read the following story in your local newspaper.

On October 12, 1999, the United Nations officially declared that the world's population had reached six billion. United Nations Secretary-General Kofi Annan was visiting Sarajevo, Bosnia, when the historic milestone was reached. To symbolize the event, he chose a baby boy born in a local clinic at two minutes after midnight to be named "Baby Six Billion."

How big is six billion? If you counted a hundred numbers every minute for eight hours a day, five days a week, it would take you five hundred years to reach six billion!

According to Zero Population Growth (ZPG), the world's population is currently growing at a rate of 86 million people per year. If asked about the reason for this rapid world population growth, what would you say? Like most people, you would probably refer to the high birth rate in developing countries. You could point out that every year, 94 million infants are born—equal to the population of Mexico—or that every time you watch a half-hour TV program, 4,860 infants are born.

This explanation, however, is only half of the story. It leaves out the other side of the equation—the death rate. The population in these countries is growing rapidly because their birth rates remain high while their death rates have dropped sharply, thanks to modern medicine, improved sanitation, and better hygiene. In this chapter, we look at demography and discuss why this issue is important to sociologists.

Sections

Learning Objectives

After reading this chapter, you will be able to

- identify the three population processes.
- relate the ideas of Thomas Malthus to population changes.
- predict world population trends.
- trace the development of preindustrial and modern cities.
- compare and contrast four theories of city growth.

SOCIOLOGY Online

Chapter Overview
Visit the *Sociology and You* Web site at soc.glencoe.com and click on **Chapter 16—Chapter Overviews** to preview chapter information.

USING Your Sociological Imagination

Students may not be impressed with the numbers in this feature because six billion is virtually impossible to conceptualize. It is also hard for students to relate to overpopulation because most of the growth is in the developing countries and not in the industrialized world, so they don't see it. One area where they might be able to conceptualize crowding is on the freeways, if they live in a large urban area. They must hear their parents complain about the ever-increasing number of cars on the road. Ask students if they believe that there is a limit to the number of people that the world can support. If they do believe this, is the world population near that point?

also Activity #1 on page 562) about why the statistics for that particular variable are so, and present their findings to the class. You can find information on the variables mentioned above online at **www.prb.org**. You can also use a World Population Data Sheet, which is available for purchase from Population Reference Bureau, 1875 Connecticut Ave. NW, Suite 520. Washington, DC 20009-5728. Phone: (202) 483-1100 Fax: (202) 328-3937 E-mail: popref@prb.org
L2

Using the Section Preview

Ask student to explain why they think population data is important to the government and industry. Why would this sort of data be needed? *(This data is used to help determine federal social and fiscal policy for grants and funding; businesses use the data for determining market and sales strategies.)*

Teaching Strategy

Share this with your students—it could be a real eye-opener for picturing what the world "looks like." If we whittled the global village down to 100 people, while maintaining the current demographic proportions, it would consist of fifty-one females and forty-nine males. Seventy would be non-white, seventy would be non-Christian, and fifty percent of the world' s wealth would be in the hands of six people. All six would be from the United States. Eighty inhabitants would live in substandard housing, seventy would be unable to read, fifty would suffer from malnutrition, and only one would have a college education. No one person would own a computer.

Section 1 The Dynamics of Demography

Key Terms

- population
- demography
- fertility
- fecundity
- crude birth rate
- fertility rate
- total fertility rate
- mortality
- life span
- life expectancy
- crude death rate
- infant mortality rate
- migration
- gross migration rate
- net migration rate

Section Preview

Demography is the scientific study of population. The collection of population data is very important today, in part because of its use by government and industry. Demographers consider three population processes when looking at population change: fertility, mortality, and migration.

The Changing Population

Social structures reflect the ability of the land to support people.

Sociologists study population because it affects social structure, especially in crowded areas. They look for patterns that will help them understand and predict how groups of people will behave. For example, they might examine the relationship between population growth and politics. We know that historically the growth of minorities in the United States has benefited Democrats more than Republicans (Tilgrove, 1999). But the situation today is different with respect to Latinos. Now the largest minority in the United States, Latinos are not firmly aligned with either political party. Regardless of political affiliation, the growth of minority populations affects how congressional districts are drawn and is one reason why census taking can be a controversial topic. Or sociologists might study trends in population shifts, such as the aging baby boomers, to help plan for hospitals and long-term nursing facilities.

population
a group of people living in a particular place at a specified time

demography
the scientific study of population

How do sociologists define population? A **population** is a group of people living in a particular place at a specified time. The scientific study of population is called **demography** (*demo* is a Greek word that means "people"). To study population, demographers look at many factors, including the number of people (size); how and where they are located (distribution); what groups make up the population (composition); and the ages represented in the population (age structure). Demographers also analyze three processes: birth *(fertility)*, death *(mortality)*, and movement from one place to another *(migration)*. Major changes in populations come from one or all of these three processes. In the following sections, we look at the factors and processes that affect populations.

Demonstration

Ask everyone in the class to write a list of two or three ways that they plan to support themselves after retirement. Then ask them to rate their level of concern about retirement on a scale of 1 to 10, with 1 indicating no concern, and 10 indicating a very high level of concern. They should write the number at the end of their paragraph. When they are finished, survey the class by running through the scale and asking for a show of hands.

Next, inform students that the number of senior citizens living in the United States is expected to *double* by the year 2030. This means that by the time your students retire, Social Security may not be available as a

How might fertility drugs affect the crude birth rate?

Fertility

Fertility measures the actual number of children born to a woman or to a population of women. **Fecundity** is the potential number of children that could be born if every woman reproduced as often as biology allowed. Obviously, fertility rates are much lower than fecundity rates. The highest realistic fecundity rate you could expect from a society would be about fifteen births per woman. The record fertility rate for a group probably is held by the Hutterites, who migrated a century ago from Switzerland to North and South Dakota and Canada. Hutterite women in the 1930s were giving birth to an average of more than twelve children each (Westoff and Westoff, 1971). The Hutterites give us a good estimate of fecundity, because they are the best example of *natural fertility*—the number of children born to women in the absence of conscious birth control (Weeks, 1999).

fertility
a measure of the number of children born to a woman or a population of women

fecundity
the maximum rate at which women can physically produce children

How is fertility measured? The **crude birth rate** is the annual number of live births per one thousand members of a population. The crude birth rate varies considerably from one country to another. The crude birth rate for the United States is fifteen per one thousand. Niger, in West Africa, experiences a very high crude birth rate of fifty-three per one thousand; and Germany, a very low rate of nine per one thousand.

crude birth rate
the annual number of live births per one thousand members of a population

To calculate the crude birth rate, divide the annual number of live births by the total population and multiply that number by 1,000.

$$\text{Crude Birth Rate} = \frac{\text{Number of Live Births}}{\text{Total Population}} \times 1{,}000$$

The term *crude* in this case means rough, or approximate. The crude birth rate is approximate because it is based on the entire population rather than just women of child-bearing age. It also ignores the age structure of the population. Both sex and age affect the number of live births in any given year. Consequently, in addition to the crude birth rate, demographers use the **fertility rate**—the annual number of live births per one thousand women

fertility rate
the annual number of live births per one thousand women aged fifteen to forty-four

More About . . . the Hutterites

Tell students that this close-knit religious community in South Dakota all descended from sixty-four founders. They have often been studied because of the relative purity of the mixing within the group, rather than with outsiders.

Teaching Strategy

To show students how demographic information is used, have them imagine that they are marketers studying teenagers as a target demographic group. Ask them to brainstorm the kinds of products teenagers would buy. Answers will typically include clothes, CDs, computer games, shoes, etc. From that list, have students think about other related industries that are affected by teenagers' purchasing power, and create a web of how they are related. For example, CDs, concert tickets, and home video sales and rentals are similar items that teens frequently buy.
L1

means of support. The working to retired ratio will drop from 4.1 to 2.3. (See page 546.) This will put an enormous strain on the country's resources, and many seniors may have to rely more heavily on their own savings for support.

In light of this information, ask students to again rank their level of concern on a scale of 1–10. How many of them are more concerned about retirement than before?

Reassure students by letting them know that demographic research has allowed policy makers and individuals to begin planning for this shift over thirty years in advance.
L1

Ask students if they agree that teens are not given as much respect as other demographic groups. Does the media play a part in this? How are teens portrayed on television? What news stories about teens do we usually hear about? Do teens, as a whole, act in a way deserving of the respect of society?

Answers to Interpreting the Map

1. The eastern states and Florida have the smallest concentrations of young people. A high concentration of retired people live in Florida.
2. From this map, it appears that the population of the United States is aging. Census information and population pyramids (see page 545) would help students further describe the age structure of the United States population.

Percentage of Population Under 18

Many high school students feel that as members of society they are not given enough respect by society. One reason could be that there are too few people in this age bracket to influence policy makers. This map shows the percentage of each state's population aged eighteen years of age.

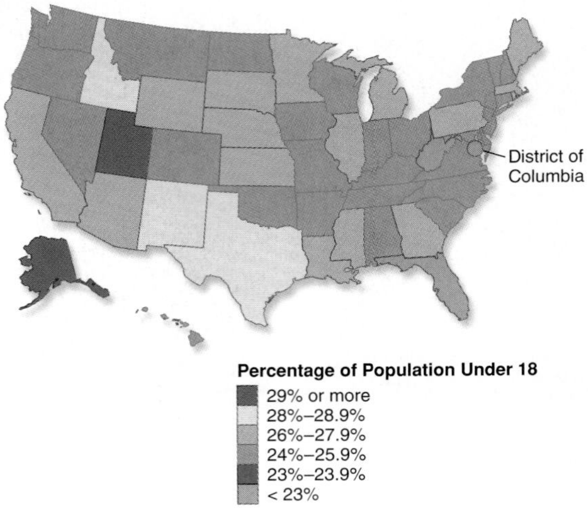

Interpreting the Map

1. Which states have the smallest concentrations of young people? Can you explain why?
2. From this map, can you make any generalization about the American population? What additional information would help you to further describe the age structure of the U.S. population? Get that information for your state.

Source: U.S. Bureau of the Census, 2001.

total fertility rate
average number of children born to a woman during her lifetime

aged fifteen to forty-four. The rate that is easiest to use is the **total fertility rate,** or the average number of children born to a woman during her lifetime. Currently, total fertility rates in the world range from 5.2 in Africa to 1.4 in Europe.

What other factors influence birth rate? The birth rate of a population is influenced by both health and social factors. For example, widespread disease (especially rubella, or German measles) causes the birth rate to decline because many pregnancies end in miscarriages. Social factors affecting the birth rate include the average age at marriage, the level of economic development, the availability and use of contraceptives and abortion, the number of women in the labor force, the educational status of women, and social attitudes toward reproduction.

The U.S. birth rate in recent years has shown a steady decline. More couples today consider two children—or even one child—a desirable number. Work patterns have affected the birth rate as well. More American women today are postponing having children until their late twenties and early thirties. As a result, women are having fewer children.

Integrating the Teacher Resources

Look for the Chapter 16 Learning Goals Outline, a reproducible student worksheet in the Unit 5 Mastering Basic Concepts booklet in your Teacher's Resource Box. It can be used to preview or review chapter content.

Survey

Personalizing the information in this chapter will help students better understand why sociologists study population and urbanization. Either as an in-class activity, or as an assignment, conduct a mini census. Ask each student to answer the following questions: "How many people are in your family?" "What are their ages?" "Who in your family is employed?" "What type of jobs do they do?" "How long has your family lived in the home you live in now?" "If your family has lived somewhere else within

Mortality

Mortality refers to death. To analyze patterns of mortality within a population, sociologists look at *life span* and *life expectancy*. **Life span** is the most advanced age to which humans can survive. We know for sure of a Japanese man who lived nearly 121 years, but few people even approach this age. **Life expectancy** is the average number of years that persons in a given population born at a particular time can expect to live. World life expectancy is sixty-seven years (*World Population Data Sheet,* 2001).

mortality
deaths within a population

life span
the most advanced age to which humans can survive

life expectancy
the average number of years that persons in a given population born at a particular time can expect to live

How is mortality measured? The **crude death rate** is figured by dividing the annual number of deaths by the total population and multiplying by 1,000. Like the crude birth rate, the crude death rate varies widely throughout the world. The worldwide average crude death rate is nine per one thousand persons. Looking at specific regions of the world, the death rate varies from a low of six per thousand in Latin America to a high of fourteen per thousand in Africa and Hungary. The death rate in the United States is about nine per thousand (*World Population Data Sheet,* 2001).

crude death rate
the annual number of deaths per thousand members of a population

Demographers are also interested in the variations in death rates for specific groups. They have devised *age-specific death rates* to measure the number of deaths per thousand persons in a specific age group, such as fifteen- to nineteen-year-olds or sixty- to sixty-four-year-olds. This allows them to compare the risk of death to members of different groups. Although death eventually comes to everyone, the rate at which it occurs depends on many factors, including age, sex, race, occupation, social class, standard of living, and health care.

The **infant mortality rate**—the number of deaths among infants under one year of age per one thousand live births—is considered a good indicator of the health status of any group. This is because infants are the first to suffer

infant mortality rate
the annual number of deaths among infants under one year of age per one thousand live births

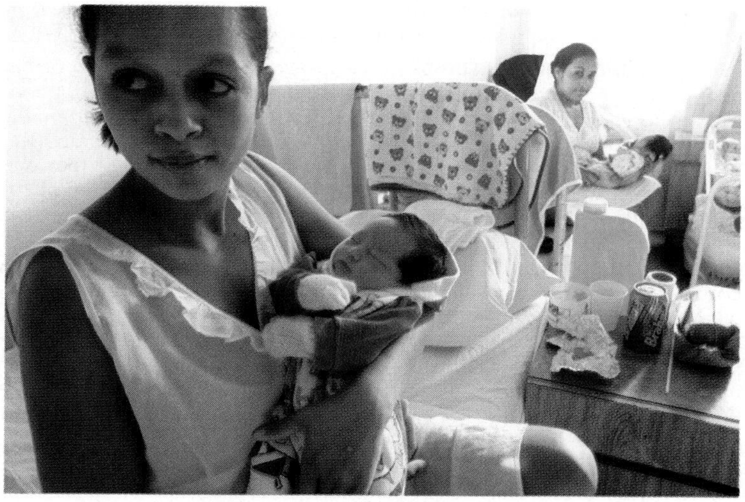

This Brazilian mother attends a local clinic to get health care for her infant.

Controversy and Debate

Students love to discuss the reasons why women in the United States outlive men. Have them list some stereotypical reasons why they think this is so. (One example is "men work harder than women do, and have shorter lives because of it.") Then have students research the reasons why these perceptions aren't true, and what some of the real reasons are behind women's longer life expectancy.

A web search under a good search engine, such as Google using the key words "reasons why women live longer than men" brings up a number of informative URLs. Students can practice their Internet source evaluation skills with this topic.

the past ten years, where did they live?" Either ask students to tabulate the results of the in-class census, or assign them to take a mini-census of a prescribed number of people. Discuss the results and ask students to compare their results with the information given in the text. Discuss with students the issue of privacy. If people agree to participate in the census, students should guarantee their anonymity.
L1

Working with the Data

Figure 16.1 The birth rate began to climb due to an increase in the food supply, but the death rate began to fall thanks to improved hygiene and medical advances.

Teaching Strategy

Have students research major migrations that have taken place in United States history, such as the Dust Bowl migrations to California in the 1930s or Native American migrations just prior to the turn of the last century. Have students report on the social factors that resulted in these migrations and how they changed the population and culture of the areas migrated to.
L1

Pulling it All Together

Demography is the study of population and provides useful information for government and industry. Demographers use three processes to account for population change, fertility, mortality and migration.

Integrating the Teacher Resources

To reinforce key ideas, use the Chapter 16 Graphic Organizer, a reproducible worksheet available in the Unit 5 Mastering Basic Concepts **booklet in your Teacher's Resource Box.**

Figure 16.1 World Population Growth. *This figure shows estimated world population growth to 2150. What factors do you think led to the sharp rise in population around 1850?*

Source: Washington, DC: Population Reference Bureau.

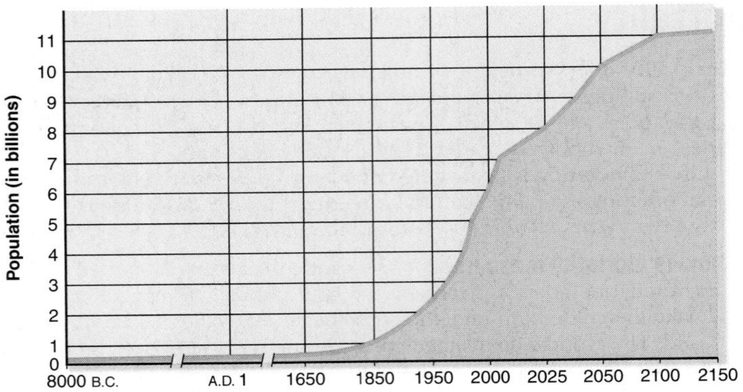

from a lack of good medical care and sanitation. Infants in developing countries are almost eight times more likely to die before their first birthday than infants in the developed nations. Working together, the birth rates, fertility rates, and mortality rates determine the world population growth. (See Figure 16.1.)

Migration

migration
the movement of people from one geographic area to another

Migration refers to the movement of people from one geographic area to another. Migration can occur within a country or between countries. An example of migration from country to country is the resettlement of Asian refugees from Vietnam and Cambodia in countries around the world. Many of the refugees who settle in the United States in one particular city or region later move to another region, thus becoming internal migrants. Anyone who moves from one part of the country to another—say, from New York to Arizona—is engaging in internal migration.

gross migration rate
the number of persons per year per one thousand members of a population who enter or leave a geographic area

net migration rate
the annual increase or decrease per one thousand members of a population resulting from migration into and out of the population

How is migration measured? The **gross migration rate** into or out of an area is the number of persons per one thousand members of a population who enter or leave a geographic area in a given year. *Net migration* is the difference between the number of people entering and leaving an area. Thus, the **net migration rate** is the annual increase or decrease per one thousand members of a population resulting from movement into and out of the population. In 1999, for example, the United States had a net migration rate of about 3.0 per one thousand population. That is, 3.0 more persons per one thousand population entered the country than left the country. It is also possible of course, to have a negative net migration rate showing more people overall left an area than entered it.

When the U.S. Census Bureau reports migration rates, it refers only to the number of legal immigrants. Many people violate immigration laws to enter the United States. In the 1970s, the issue of illegal immigration—primarily from Latin American and Caribbean countries—became a major concern and continues to be controversial today. There are no precise statistics on either the illegal immigration rate or the total number of illegal aliens living in the United States. Estimates of the current number of illegal aliens range from three million to six million persons.

Observation

To help students gain a better understanding of why so many people migrate to the United States, you might assign the following research project.

Ask students to talk with someone who has migrated to the United States from another country. (It doesn't matter which country they have come from.) During the conversation, students should ask the following questions (and any others you feel are important).

- What country are you from?
- When did you arrive in the United States?

Another Place

The Graying of Japan

Birth rates and death rates have important social and cultural consequences. In Japan, elders have traditionally been held in high esteem. This tradition is threatened by a combination of two factors: People are generally living longer, and there are fewer young people to support the elders' existence. As they lose respect, many older Japanese now pray in their temples for a quick death.

The population of Japan is aging faster than any on earth, a result of declining birth and death rates. The situation of the elderly of Japan is like the proverbial glass of water that is either half full or half empty, depending on whether the positive or negative aspects of their lives are emphasized. In some ways, elderly Japanese are better off than the elderly of the other developed countries. They hold the position of "honorable elders," a reflection of the Confucian precept of duty owed to parents. Japan even has a national holiday, "Respect for the Aged Day," September 15th, when most offices and factories are closed. Furthermore, a relatively high proportion of elderly Japanese live with their adult children, which is often cited as evidence of the reverence this country pays to the aged.

However, it can also be argued that elderly Japanese are not really so well off and that the "ecstasy years" of old age are losing their rosy glow—if they truly ever had one. Among the more sensational evidence cited are the supposedly high rate of suicide among elderly Japanese and the existence of temples where the elderly go to pray for a quick death. Also, in recent years, the number of activities for or honoring the elderly on their special day have been few and far between. For most Japanese, September 15th is just another holiday.

The particularly rapid pace of aging in Japan and the potential consequences have captured the attention of policymakers and officials. [A major government report] listed population aging along with internationalization and maturation of the economy as the three major challenges for twenty-first-century Japan. Japanese prime ministers have regularly referred to aging as they have set the policy agenda, recognizing that population aging affects many aspects of the society and the economy.

Source: Linda G. Martin, "The Graying of Japan," *Population Bulletin* (Washington, DC).

Thinking It Over

Are the effects of the graying of Japan best explained by functionalism, conflict theory, or symbolic interactionism? Defend your choice.

Section 1 Assessment

1. What three major processes affect the way populations change?
2. How might data about age-specific death rates or population shifts be of use?
3. Why is the infant mortality rate a key statistic for health workers?

Critical Thinking

4. **Drawing Conclusions** Why is demography increasingly important? Think of a way in which the federal government could use some specific piece of demographic data. State how this information would help the government make a policy decision.

"You have to enjoy getting older."

Clint Eastwood
actor and director

Answer to Thinking it Over

1. The functionalist point of view would look for order and stability to result from this situation. However, if the problems of elder suicide and economic burden persist, it will be conflict driven. The symbolic interactionist perspective would be interested in the social interactions.

Answers to Section 1 Assessment

1. The three processes are fertility, death, and migration.
2. Insurance companies, especially those that provide medical and life insurance, are very interested in age-specific death rates.
3. Infants are the first to suffer from a lack of good medical care and sanitation.

Critical Thinking

4. Answers will vary. An example would be a population shift like aging baby boomers and how it will affect Medicare and Social Security, and the need for hospitals and long-term care facilities.

- Did your family come with you (or you with them), or did you come alone? Why did you come alone?
- Why did you decide to leave your country?
- Why did you decide to come to the United States?
- Have things worked out for you the way you had hoped? Why or why not?

Have students compile their results and see what conclusions they come to.

If you have the opportunity, you might invite someone who has migrated to the United States to speak to the class.

L1

Using the Section Preview

This activity is great for showing students how inequitably population and per capita income are distributed throughout the world. Bring in 100 Hershey's Kisses, and use signs to designate different areas of the room to represent North America, Europe, Asia, Africa, Latin America, and Oceania. Randomly assign students to continents based on the following population ratios: 5 percent of the class should go to North America, 13 percent to Europe, 59 percent to Asia, 14 percent to Africa, 8 percent to Latin America, and 1 percent to Oceania (Australia, New Zealand and island nations). Have the students stand under the appropriate sign. (For example, out of a class of 30, 2 students would go to the sign marked North America, 4 to Europe, 18 to Asia, 4 to Africa, 2 to Latin America, and 0 to Oceania.)

Now distribute the candy in the following manner: 43 pieces to North America, 26 to Europe, 3 to Asia, 1 to Africa, 4 to Latin America, and 23 to Oceania. This should make the point that developed areas have a per capita income greatly in excess of developing countries. Be sure to stress that North America, with only 5 percent of the world's population, consumes nearly half of the world's resources.

Section 2 World Population

Key Terms

- census
- doubling time
- exponential growth
- demographic transition theory
- zero population growth
- population momentum
- replacement level
- population control
- family planning
- population pyramid
- dependency ratio

Section Preview

Thomas Malthus (1798) predicted that population size would ultimately outstrip the food supply, resulting in mass starvation and death. The demographic transition theory looks at economic development to predict population patterns. While the rate of world population growth is slowing, the world's population will continue to increase for many years. Population control has become a concern of many governments worried about providing for their future citizens.

census
regularly occurring count of a particular population

The Problem of Population Growth

No organization has actually ever counted all the people in the world. World population figures are a composite of best estimates and national **census** figures where available. While many countries count and categorize people living in those countries, the quality of census data varies a great deal and can be very unreliable. Nevertheless, world population growth patterns can be identified.

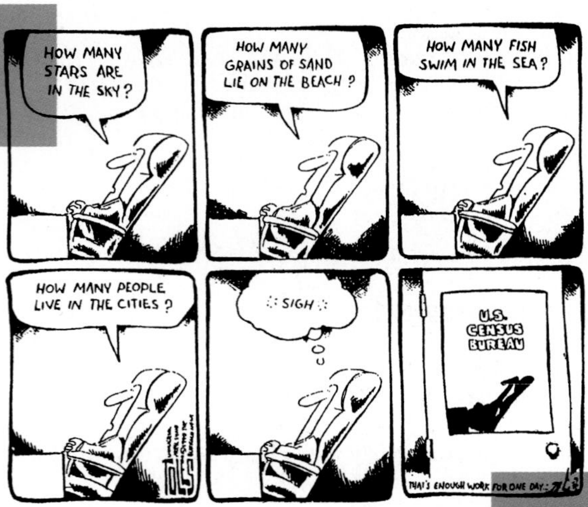

If the counting of the population is a problem in developed societies, imagine the difficulty with obtaining accurate counts in developing societies.

Demonstration

Use the following slightly chaotic but effective activity to illustrate psychological problems related to population density. (This will also reinforce Chapter 3 lessons about how cultures adapt to physical pressures on society.) Have the whole class stand up and squeeze into one corner of the room. Barricade them in using desks. (Because this might make people feel claustrophobic, first make sure that none of your students will react adversely to the demonstration). Pass to each student a pen

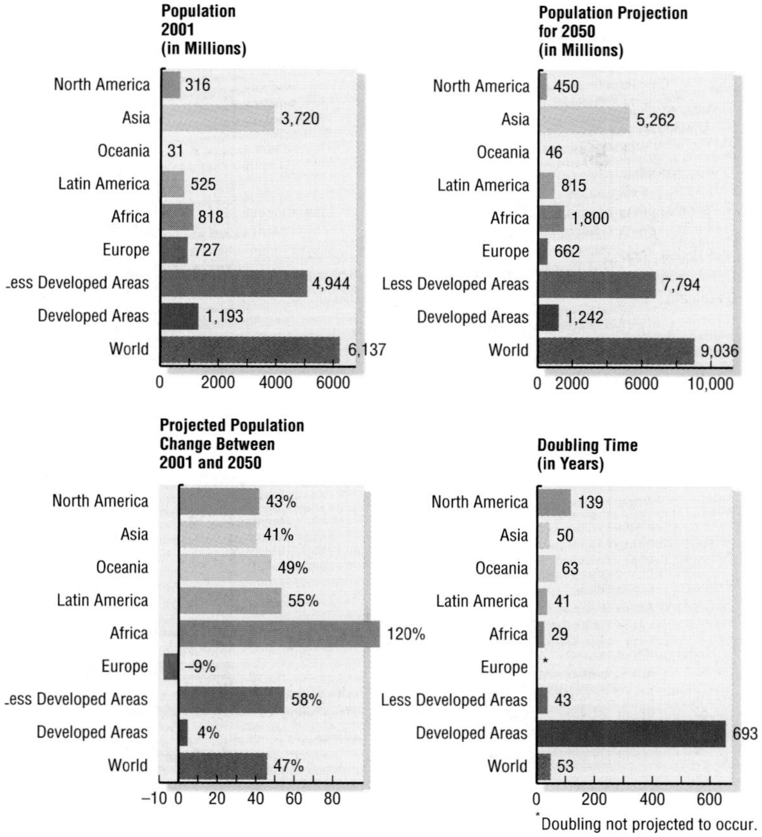

Figure 16.2 Population Projections by Regions of the World. *This graph displays population projections, by regions of the world, from 2001 to 2050. Note the dramatic difference in population doubling time between less developed areas and developed areas.*

Source: Adapted from *World Population Data Sheet, 2001.*

Online UPDATE
Visit soc.glencoe.com and click on **Textbook Updates–Chapter 16** for an update of the data.

Rapid world population growth is a relatively recent phenomenon. In fact, your grandparents have seen more population growth during their lifetimes than occurred during the preceding four million years. An estimated 250 million people were on the earth in A.D. 1. (Refer back to Figure 16.1 on page 534.) It was not until 1650 that the world's population doubled, to half a billion. The second doubling occurred in 1850, bringing the world population to one billion. By 1930, only eighty years later, another doubling had taken place. Only forty-five years after that, in 1976, a fourth doubling raised the world's population to four billion. At the current growth rate, the world's population is expected to double again in about fifty years and will approach eight billion persons by the year 2025. As you can see, the number of years between each doubling of the population—called, for obvious reasons, the **doubling time**—is getting shorter and shorter (*World Population Data Sheet,* 1999). Figure 16.2 breaks down world population projections by region. Figure 16.3 on the next page looks at key demographic statistics by world regions.

doubling time
number of years needed to double the base population size

Working with the Data

Figure 16.2 Draw students' attention to the bottom graph on the right (Doubling Time). Ask students why the doubling time in less developed areas is so much less than it is in developed areas. Make sure they note that Europe is not expected to double. Why do they think this is the case? Have them look at the graph on the bottom left. Note that Europe's population is expected to drop between 2001 and 2050. To what would students attribute this drop?

Teaching Strategy

The text states that students' "grandparents have seen more population growth during their lifetimes than occurred during the preceding four million years." Have students interview their grandparents (or other elderly people) and ask what they have noticed about the change in population in their lifetimes. How can they tell the population has increased? What has changed? Ask students to share their grandparents' answers with the class.
L1

and copy of an article to read, and tell them that they must outline the article, but they can't spread out or otherwise move. One student will likely emerge as the leader and devise a method for accomplishing this task. Most will be frustrated by it, particularly as time goes on. Still others will yell and want to get out. Let them go back to their seats after a reasonable amount of time, and have them relate this experience to urban crowding. Have them consider how difficult it would be to function if we were also expected to perform under these crowded conditions.
L1

Working with the Data

Figure 16.3 There will always be a correlation between birth rates and fertility rates because fertility rates are derived from birth rates (while fecundity is not). Similarly, death rates will rise or fall with infant mortality rates, but are not as directly tied, since the death rates include all demographic groups, not just infants.

Teaching Strategy

Ask students to imagine playing eighteen holes of miniature golf, with a monetary prize going to the winner of each hole. On the first hole, the winner gets 10 cents. The winner of the second hole gets 20 cents; the winner of the third hole gets 40 cents. The prize money for each hole doubles in value, so the winner of the fourth hole will get 80 cents. Have students calculate the prize for the eighteenth hole. (The answer is $13,107.20.) This should vividly show students how exponential growth has a runaway effect.

Integrating the Teacher Resources

Look for the Chapter 16 Vocabulary Activity worksheet in the Unit 5 Mastering Basic Concepts booklet in your Teacher's Resource Box. It provides reinforcement for vocabulary in this chapter.

Figure 16.3 World Birth Rates, Death Rates, and Infant Mortality Rates. *Would you always expect to see a correlation between crude birth rates and total fertility rates for a country? Between crude death rates and infant morality rates?*

Source: Washington, DC: Population Reference Bureau, 2001.

Online UPDATE Visit soc.glencoe.com and click on **Textbook Updates–Chapter 16** for an update of the data.

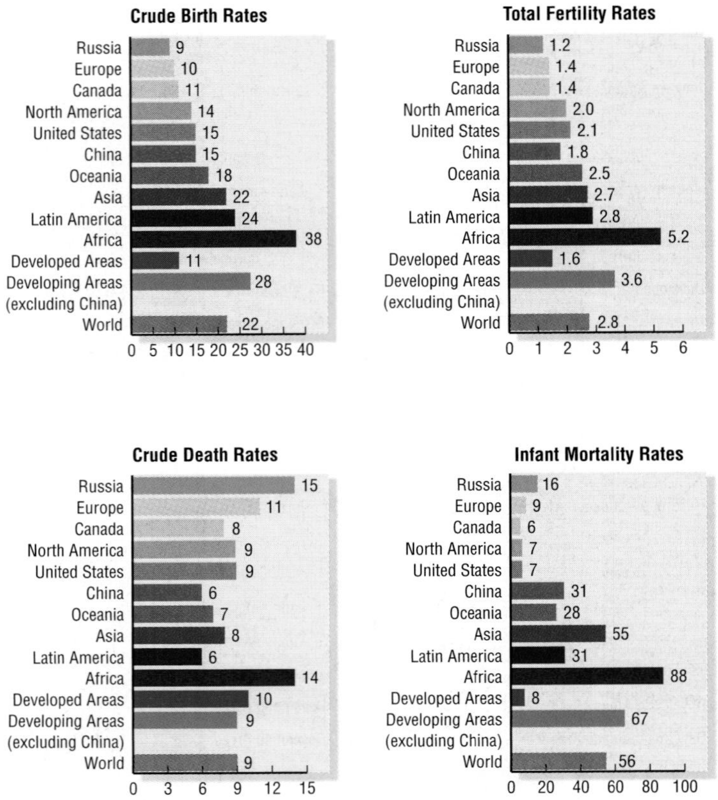

exponential growth growth in which the amount of increase is added to the base figure each time period

Why is the world's population growing so fast? The population has increased so dramatically in part because of the way population increases. We are accustomed to thinking in terms of *linear growth,* whereby amounts increase arithmetically (as in the progression 1, 2, 3, 4, 5 . . .). Population, however, does not grow linearly. It follows the principle of **exponential growth,** and increases geometrically (as in the progression 2, 4, 8, 16, 32). With exponential growth, the *amount* of increase is greater each time period even though the *rate* of increase remains the same. This is because each increase is added to the base amount and becomes part of the calculation for the next rise.

A classic example of exponential growth follows: The story tells of a clever minister who presented a beautiful chess set to his king. In return, he asked only that the king give one grain of rice for the first square on the chessboard; two grains, or double the amount, for the second square; four (doubling again) for the third; and so forth. The king, not being mathematically minded, agreed and ordered the rice brought forth. The eighth square required 128 grains, and the twelfth took more than a pound of rice. Long before reaching

Demonstration

Tell all the students to take out a piece of notebook paper. Ask them to fold the paper in half, then fold it in half again. Tell them to keep folding the paper in half and to keep track of the number of folds they make. The first 4 or 5 folds are easy, but the 6th and 7th folds are very difficult to do. Bring the strongest boy and girl up to the front of the class and tell them that they must keep folding the paper in half, using all the strength they have. (They'll have to stop after the 6th or 7th fold.) Tell students the sixty-fourth square, the king's coffers were depleted. Even today, the world's richest king could not produce enough rice to fill the final square. It would require more than 200 billion tons, or the equivalent of the world's current total production of rice for the next 653 years.

If a population is growing at 1 percent per year, it takes seventy years to double. For example, suppose the population of a city was 50,000 in 1800. At a growth rate of 1 percent, that population would grow to 100,000 in 1870. By 1940 it would reach 200,000; by 2010, 400,000. Recalling the chessboard example, you can see that even a 1 percent growth rate can have serious consequences. The number of people added each year becomes part of the total population, which then increases by another 1 percent in the following year.

Malthus and Population Growth

Concern about population is not new. In 1798, Thomas Robert Malthus, an English minister and economist, published *An Essay on the Principle of Population*. In his essay, Malthus described relationships between population growth and economic development. Here are the key concepts in his theory.

English minister and economist Thomas Malthus wrote about the ability of the food supply to keep up with population growth.

- Population, if left unchecked, will exceed the food supply. This is because population increases exponentially, while the food supply does not.
- Checks on population can be *positive* or *preventive*. Positive factors are events or conditions that increase mortality. They include famine, disease, and war. Preventive factors decrease fertility and include sexual abstinence and marrying at a later age. (Remember that at the time Malthus wrote there was no reliable birth control. For this conservative minister, sexual abstinence was the only acceptable way to reduce the number of births.)
- For the poor, any improvement in income is eaten up in additional births. This leads to lower per-person food consumption, lower standards of living, and eventually death.
- The wealthy and well educated already exercise preventive checks.

How did Malthus apply his theory to population control? Malthus believed that positive checks on population growth could be avoided through education of the poor. With education, he wrote, the poor would raise their standard of living and choose to have smaller families. That part of Malthus's theory is not generally known, however, because he is most remembered for his dire predictions that overpopulation would result in famine and poverty.

The Demographic Transition

Although wrong in some of his key assumptions, Malthus had a lasting impact on population study. His is not the only theory, however. Developed

Controversy and Debate

As stated in the text, Malthus suggested that there are positive (famine, disease, war) and preventive (later marriages and sexual abstinence) measures to control population growth. His ideas influenced the work of Charles Darwin. Ask students to explain how Malthus' ideas might have influenced Darwin's ideas about natural selection.

Integrating the Teacher Resources

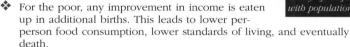

For Spanish-speaking students, you may wish to use the reproducible worksheets available in the Spanish Supplements booklet in your Teacher's Resource Box. In addition to providing Spanish translations of selected Mastering Basic Concepts worksheets, the booklet contains English and Spanish summaries of the chapter's key points.

that each fold of the paper represents a geometric progression, similar to doubling time. Each effort to fold the paper required more strength (in this scenario, strength represents resources). As Malthus predicted, when the resources are in short supply, the population's doubling time becomes a problem. Students will quickly grasp this concept.
L1

Working with the Data

Figure 16.4 Ask students to place the world regions in their current demographic stage. Europe—Stage 4, Canada—Stage 4, North America—Stage 4, United States—Stage 4, China— Stage 3, Oceania—Stage 3, Asia—Stage , Latin America—Stage 3, Africa—Stage 2,

Net Worthy

Here is a list of web sites that students can use to do research on various countries and related variables: All contain links to other related sites.

United Nations homepage:
www.un.org

Yahoo!GeoCities:
www.geocities.com

Europa:
www.europa.eu.int

The CIA World Factbook 1999:
www.odci.gov/cia/publications/factbook/

The World Health Organization:
www.who.org

Integrating the Transparencies

A Future Population World Map transparency is provided in the *Sociology and You* Transparency Binder.

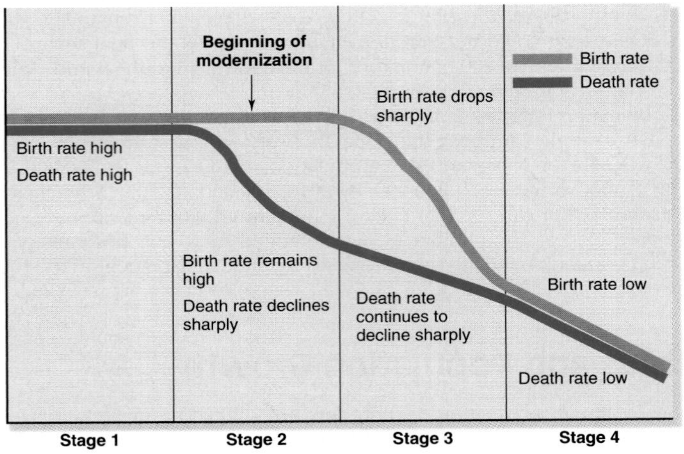

Figure 16.4 Stages of the Demographic Transition. *This figure illustrates the demographic transition. Stage 1 begins with small population growth due to a balance between birth rates and death rates (both at high levels). In Stage 2, population grows dramatically because the death rate decreases so much faster than the birth rate. Population growth begins to slow in Stage 3, when the birth rate belatedly drops sharply. Stage 4 is again a condition of smaller population growth because birth rates and death rates come into balance (both at low levels).*

demographic transition theory theory that population growth is a function of the level of economic development in a country

nations have followed a pattern of population growth different from that predicted by Malthus's theory. The **demographic transition theory** looks at the stages of economic development in a country to make predictions about population growth. This theory takes into consideration two things Malthus did not predict—agricultural productivity and reliable methods of birth control. Demographic transition theory describes four stages of population growth. (See Figure 16.4 shown above.)

- Stage 1. Both the birth rate and the death rate are high. Population growth is slow. No countries are at this stage today.
- Stage 2. The birth rate remains high, but the death rate drops sharply because of modernizing factors such as sanitation, increased food production, and medical advances. The rate of population growth is very high. Most sub-Saharan African countries are presently at this stage.
- Stage 3. The birth rate declines sharply, but because the death rate continues to go down, population growth is still rapid. Many Latin American countries are currently at this stage.
- Stage 4. Both the birth rate and the death rate are low, and the population grows slowly if at all. Anglo America, Europe, and Japan are at this stage today.

Future World Population Growth

World population growth has reached a turning point. After more than two hundred years of increase, the annual population growth rate is declining. The current growth rate is 1.3 percent, compared with the peak of 2.04 percent in the late 1960s. Moreover, the rate is projected to drop to zero by the year 2100.

But as we have seen, despite the reduction in the annual growth rate and birth rate, the world's population will continue to increase. Nearly seven billion people are expected to inhabit the globe by 2010. Throughout the first

Using Conflict Resolution Skills

Use this persuasion/negotiation/compromise/debate with students.

Format:

1. identify the problem
2. develop a hypothesis
3. prepare data to validate hypothesis
4. debate issue
5. reach consensus

After separating the class into two groups (one for voluntary control and the other for involuntary control), students should prepare information and plan a debate. At the end of the debate, a consensus must be reached by both sides, or both sides lose.

half of the twenty-first century, the annual growth rate is expected to decline until world population stabilizes at about eleven billion people. (See Figure 16.5.) At this point, the world will have reached **zero population growth**—when deaths are balanced by births so that the population does not increase (*World Population Data Sheet,* 2001).

Contrary to popular belief, limiting the average family size to two children does not immediately produce zero population growth. There is a time lag of sixty to seventy years because of the high proportion of young women of childbearing age in the world's population. Even if each of these women had only two children, the world population would grow.

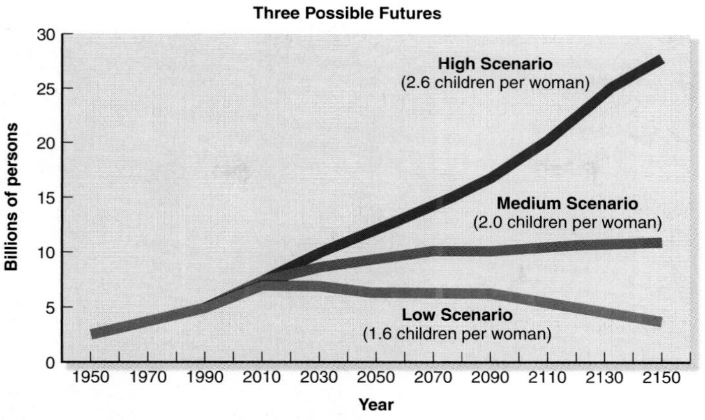

Figure 16.5 Long-Range Projections of World Population: 2000–2150. *The United Nations' estimate of future growth is based on three different assumptions. The high scenario would push world population growth to over 27 billion. The medium scenario would result in a world population of about 11 billion. The low scenario would leave the world population at about 4 billion.*

Source: Population Reference Bureau, Washington, DC, 2001.

The time lag is what demographers call **population momentum.** The growth of the world's population, like a huge boulder rolling down a mountain, cannot be stopped immediately. But the sooner the momentum of current population growth is halted, the better. The sooner the world fertility rate reaches the **replacement level** (the rate at which people replace themselves without adding to the population) the sooner zero population growth will be reached. The ultimate size of the world's population, when it does stop growing, depends greatly on the timing of reaching replacement level. To state it another way, for each decade it takes to reach replacement level, the world's population will increase by 15 percent.

zero population growth
situation in which deaths are balanced by births so that the population does not increase

population momentum
inability to stop population growth immediately because of previous high rate of growth

replacement level
birth rate at which a couple replaces itself without adding to the population

population control
attempts by government to control birth rates

Population Control

As discussed earlier, death rates in both developing and developed nations have already dropped dramatically. Any significant progress in curbing world population growth must concentrate on lowering birth rates. **Population control** refers to the conscious attempt to regulate population size through national birth control programs.

Is government-sponsored population control new? Historically, most societies were more concerned with increasing the population than with overpopulation. Many births were needed to offset the high death rates from disease and poor hygiene. With surplus populations, aggressive nations were able to maintain larger armies. Agricultural societies needed large numbers of people to work the land. Aging parents wanted to be more secure in old age. High birth rates were also encouraged in countries with religious laws against birth control.

Working with the Data

Figure 16.5 This graph illustrates the concept of how quickly geometric increases in population show results. The remarkable increase in population that results from a birth rate only 0.6 of a percent higher should help students understand that when dealing with large numbers, it doesn't take a big percentage to make a difference.

Teaching Strategy

Create three signs, "Strongly Agree," "Agree," and "Unsure," and put them up in different areas of the classroom. Then present this statement to the students: "World population growth must be stopped and Congress must legislate it. Couples should have no more than one child." Have students go to the sign that reflects how they feel. Have each of these groups discuss their point of view and develop a position paper defending it. When the papers are complete have the three groups debate the moral implications of such legislation.
L2

Scenario:
Assuming that Thomas Robert Malthus' predictions could come true, our globe won't be able to feed the population if preventative measures aren't taken. By 2010, demographers have predicted the world population will reach 7 billion, eventually reaching about 11 billion people before reaching zero population growth.

Debate what can be done to curb population growth. Would voluntary or involuntary birth control to retard population growth be a viable solution? What societal issues are involved with enforcing involuntary population control programs?
L2

Points to Stress

The desired family size tends to decrease as nations complete the transition from agricultural to industrial societies. As people move away from farming and into the cities, where they depend on industry and technology, the average number of children per family decreases. Ask the students why they think this is. *(In agricultural cultures, children are needed to increase the family's productivity by helping in the house and in the fields. A large number of children leads to a larger production of crops and therefore income. In industrial societies, children generally do not contribute to the family income, and must be fully supported. Therefore, couples must have fewer children if they wish to increase their financial stability.)*

European countries, such as Germany, have been very successful in controlling population growth through family planning.

Since the middle of the twentieth century, however, more (but certainly not all) governments have come to view high birth rates as a threat to their national well being. By 1990, most countries had in place formal programs to reduce birth rates. Government policies for population control range from voluntary to compulsory.

family planning the voluntary use of population control methods

What is voluntary population control? The voluntary use of population control methods is generally known as **family planning.** Governments that support family planning provide information and services that help couples have only the number of children they want. Voluntary government policies range from indirect means such as family planning education to direct means such as distributing birth control materials at health clinics.

Even when effective, however, family planning programs merely enable families to achieve their *desired* family size. Unfortunately for effective population control, the desired family size in many nations is quite high. The average preferred family size (number of children) in African nations is 7.1; in Middle-Eastern nations, 5.1; in Latin American nations, 4.3; and in Asian Pacific nations, 4.0. In European countries, the average preferred family size ranges from 2.1 to 2.8.

How successful is voluntary population control? Family planning has succeeded in Taiwan, where the birth rate had fallen below replacement level by 2000. Taiwan's family planning efforts were launched under very favorable conditions. When the Japanese withdrew from Taiwan after World War II, they left behind a labor force trained for industrial work. Consequently, the Taiwanese were able to use this advantage to build an expanding economy. With economic development came a decline in both birth and death rates. In short, the Taiwanese went through the demographic transition fairly rapidly.

India was a different story. Family planning there got off to a very slow start, and the country has been unable to reduce the rate of population growth through voluntary means. Family planning efforts failed because government officials and family planners did not take the broader social context

Integrating the Teacher Resources

Look for the Alternative Assessments booklet in your Teacher's Resource Box for essay tests and performance assessment activities based on this chapter.

Cooperative Learning Activity

Assign students to groups for this activity. Have groups discuss the following:

The one-child policy in China has resulted in an increase in the rate of female infanticide. There are many reasons including those that follow. In such places as South America and South Asia (and many places in between), women often lead lives where discrimination is institutionalized. In some particularly repressive societies female children are given less food than male children, are not allowed to participate in education, into account. For one thing, India did not have Taiwan's advantage of relatively rapid economic development. In addition, the Indian officials and planners did not make enough efforts to overcome cultural and religious opposition to birth control. Nor did they find enough ways to effectively communicate birth control information and technology. Finally, the national birth control program was left in the hands of individual state governments to implement.

Efforts to control population began to succeed in India only after the government turned to a sterilization program in 1976. Although the government did not use the force of law, a system of *disincentives* had the effect of compulsion. Those who could not produce official proof of a sterilization were denied such things as business permits, gun licenses, and ration cards for the purchase of basic goods (Weeks, 1999).

India's population control programs have been only moderately successful at best.

Have compulsory population control methods ever been used successfully? Both China and Singapore have forced population control policies that seem to achieve their goals. China has been successful in reducing its total fertility rate from 7.5 in 1963 to 1.8 in 2001 through a system of rewards and punishments that includes a "one-child" policy. One-child families receive a larger retirement pension and enjoy preference in housing, school admission for their children, and employment. Families with more than one child are subject to an escalating tax on each child, and they get no financial aid from the government for the medical and educational costs of their extra children.

The island city-state of Singapore began formally discouraging large families in 1969. The government passed laws that penalized parents with large families (Weeks, 1999). These measures included

- denial of a paid eight-week maternity leave.
- loss of an income tax allowance.
- diminished access to public housing.
- increased maternity costs for each additional child.
- a lower likelihood of children's entering good schools.

China's population control efforts have been very effective. This poster of a mother and baby was designed to promote small families.

and often are refused necessary medical care. Ask groups to discuss the connection between gender (sex) and power in these countries. Ask students to share any conclusion they come to with the rest of the class. **L1**

Reinforcing Vocabulary

Students who are LEP or ESL should have little trouble with the term *disincentives* if they break it up. Ask students to identify the root word (incite = to stimulate). An incentive, then, is something that acts as a stimulant, or encouragement. The negative prefix *dis* means the opposite, or not, or to take away. Putting it all together, the word means something that discourages an action.
ELL

More About . . . Population Control

Although China's compulsory population control methods have been viewed as a success, they have had tragic consequences for the female population. The rate of female infanticide increased dramatically after China put its "one-child" policy into place. Because female children are viewed as a burden in Chinese society, families that are allowed to have only one child may choose to kill their female babies in hopes of having a son. The practice of female infanticide was widespread before compulsory population control; since the policies were instituted, some estimates have placed the number of female infanticides in China as high 10,000 per year.

These policies worked so well that the total fertility rate in Singapore dropped from 4.5 children per woman to 1.4 between 1966 and 1985. In fact, the government became worried about the reduction in population size and, in 1987, reversed some of its earlier policies. The government of Singapore now supports three or more children for people able to afford them (Yap, 1995). Despite this effort, Singapore's total birth rate of 1.6 is still below replacement level.

Does one child make a difference? The importance of limiting family size, even by one child, can be illustrated by population projections for the United States. Even though the United States is unlikely to increase to a three-child average in the future, the hypothetical American case can help us understand the importance of population control. Figure 16.6 contrasts the projected population of the United States in the year 2070 for an average family size of two children and an average family size of three children. When small decreases in the death rate and net migration at the present level are assumed, an average two-child family size would result in a population of 300 million in 2015. Taking the hypothetical average family size of three children, the U.S. population would grow to 400 million by 2015. As time passed, the difference of only one extra child per family would assume added significance. By 2070, the two-child family would produce a population of 350 million, but the three-child family would push the population close to one billion! To say it another way, with an average family of two children, the U.S. population would not quite double itself between 1970 and 2070. But should the three-child family have been the average, the population would have doubled itself twice during this same period.

The consequences of limiting population in developing regions becomes clearer when the effect of even one child added to the average number of children in a family is recognized. Moreover, the addition of one child per family has a greater effect as the population base gets larger; not only is one extra person added, but theoretically that one person will be involved with the reproduction of yet another three, and on it goes. The largest populations are found in developing countries, which also have the largest average number of children per family.

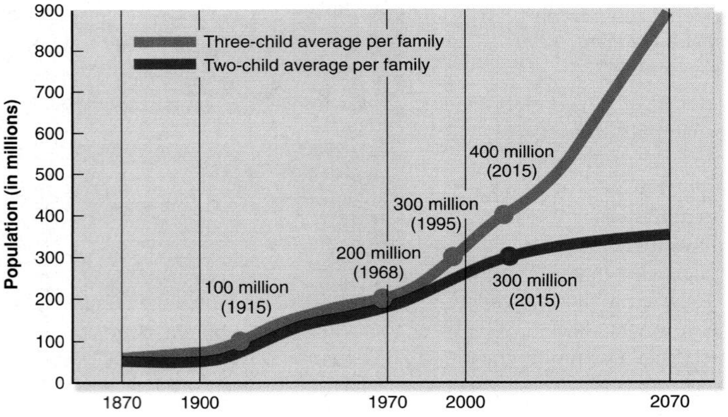

Figure 16.6 Projected Populations of the United States. *This graph illustrates the importance of reaching the population replacement level (two children per family). Are you surprised at the difference in U.S. population growth caused by an average of three children per family versus two children?*

Working with the Data

Figure 16.6 Students will likely be surprised at the difference one child per family can make. The principle of exponential growth explains that the amount of increase is greater even though the rate of increase remains the same. This is because each increase is added to the base amount and becomes part of the calculation for the next rise. (See page 538 for a review of exponential growth.)

Integrating the Teacher Resources

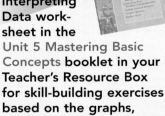

Look for the Chapter 16 Analyzing and Interpreting Data worksheet in the Unit 5 Mastering Basic Concepts **booklet in your Teacher's Resource Box for skill-building exercises based on the graphs, charts, and maps in this chapter.**

On-Demand Writing

As people in the United States have begun to live longer, there has developed what is sometimes called "the sandwich generation." (Ask students if they are familiar with this term.) The sandwich generation refers to the middle aged of our society who still have children dependent on them and now find that their parents are also dependent on them. The generation in the middle feels "sandwiched" in between the dependents. In many cases, families end up with three generations living under one roof. In the past, this was quite common in our culture. But, in recent years, the tradition of having multiple generations under one roof has nearly disappeared.

Population Pyramids

Population pyramids allow you to see at a glance the age and sex composition of a population. Age and sex are key indexes to fertility and mortality rates, which in turn are used to project school and housing needs, health resources, and other key social services. Population pyramids illustrate the *dependency ratio* that results from different rates of population growth. The **dependency ratio** is the ratio of persons in the dependent ages (under fifteen and over sixty-four) to those in the "economically active" ages (fifteen to sixty-four). The two aspects of the dependency ratio are *youth dependency* and *old-age dependency*. Developing nations have much higher youth dependency than developed nations. Developed nations have significantly higher old-age dependency. Figure 16.7 displays typical age-sex pyramids for developed and developing nations.

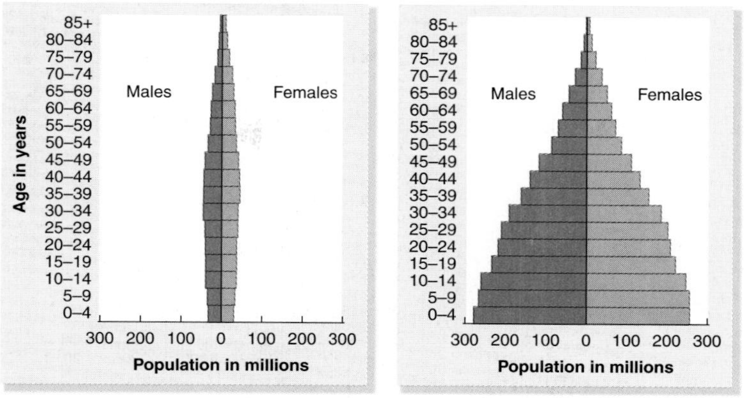

Figure 16.7 Age-Sex Pyramids in Developed and Less Developed Countries. *This figure shows general population patterns by age and sex in developed and developing countries. Using the dependency ratio, explain why children in developed countries are economically better off than those in the developing nations.*

Source: United Nations Population Division.

Why is the dependency ratio important? For developing countries such as Mexico, a high youth dependency means that national income must be diverted from economic development to provide food, housing, and education for its large young population. In developed countries such as the United States, rising old-age dependency creates a different set of problems. With a larger

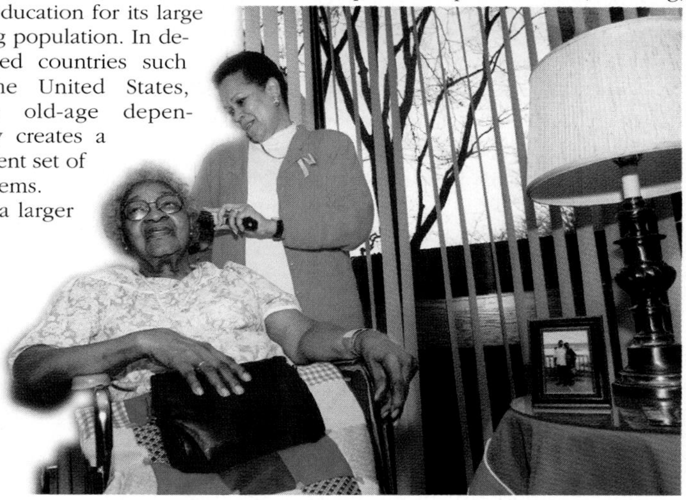

America's aging population is raising the dependency ratio. Why should that concern you?

population pyramid
a graphic representative of the age and sex composition of a population

dependency ratio
the ratio of dependent persons to economically active persons

Working with the Data

Figure 16.7 In less developed nations the dependency ratio is much greater than in developed countries. This is caused by the larger number of dependent persons (mostly children) than economically active persons. In developed countries (especially those below the replacement level) the economically active segment of the population is larger than the dependent segment of the population. With more people contributing to the economy, and fewer being dependent, the children in developed countries get a larger share of the resources than the children in less developed countries. (This, of course, does not guarantee that the available resources are equally distributed among all children.)

Teaching Strategy

If your students are doing the Lead-Off Activity on page 528 of this chapter, have them research their country's population pyramids. Ask them to consider what impact population pyramids have on gross national product per capita.
L3

Ask students if their own families, or any families they know, have three generations living in the same house. What are the special compromises that need to made in this situation? What are the benefits? How has it affected each generation? Ask students to write their feelings about the "sandwich generation" syndrome. If they don't have personal information to draw from, have them write about how they think they would feel. What kinds of things could be done to make things easier for each generation? Ask volunteers to share their work with the rest of the class.
L2

Answers to Section 2 Assessment

1. Linear growth occurs when amounts increase arithmetically (1, 2, 3, 4). In exponential growth, the *amount* of increase is greater each time period (2, 4, 8, 16, 32) even though the *rate* of increase remains the same (because each increase is added to the base amount and becomes part of the calculation for the next rise).
2. Positive checks on population are factors that increase mortality, such as famine, disease, and war.
3. The demographic transition theory looks at the economic development of a country to make predictions about population growth. Western (developed) nations have reliable birth control methods with higher agricultural productivity, and better sanitation and medical advances than underdeveloped nations. This means lower birth rates and lower death rates.
4. c (eleven billion)

Critical Thinking

5. Answers will vary. Students may also want to discuss how the dependency ratio will be affected when zero population growth is achieved, and how this will impact on developed and developing countries.

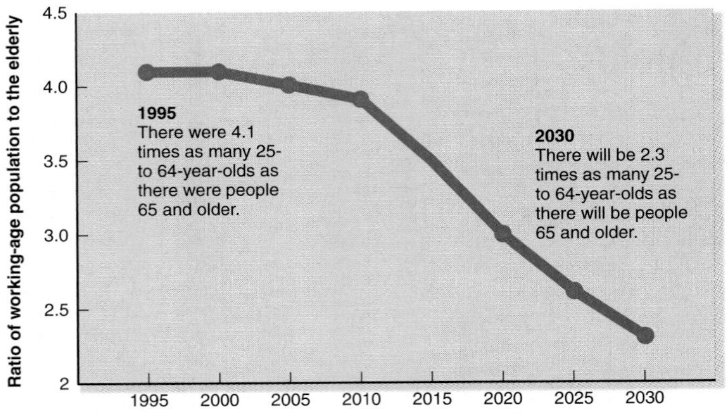

Figure 16.8 Ratio of Working-Age Population to the Elderly in the U.S. 25-to-64-Year-Olds vs 65 and Older. *This graph illustrates the rising old-age dependency occurring in the U.S.*

Source: Reference Bureau, Washington, D.C.

older population, there are fewer young people in the labor force to support the growing number of older people. For example, in the United States in 1995 there were just over four times as many 25-year-olds as 64-year-olds. By 2030, there will be only 2.3 times as many. (See Figure 16.8.) This shift will increase the burden on the young to pay for Social Security and Medicare. Other problems will include the need for increasing health care services and institutional arrangements for the long-term care of elderly people.

> "Mankind owes to the child the best it has to give."
>
> UN declaration

Section 2 Assessment

1. Briefly explain the difference between exponential and linear growth.
2. What are positive checks?
3. How does the demographic transition theory reflect the development of Western nations?
4. Which of the following figures is the world's population most likely to reach before it stops growing?
   - **a.** four billion
   - **b.** eight billion
   - **c.** eleven billion
   - **d.** twenty-five billion

Critical Thinking

5. **Evaluating Information** Given the exponential rate at which population grows, discuss the effect of zero population growth on the size of the world's population in 2020.

Learning Styles

Artistic/Verbal As the population of the United States continues to age, the need for more and better facilities and activities for seniors is becoming more critical. Have students survey your community to determine the type of care, facilities, and activities available specifically for senior citizens. Undoubtedly there are rest homes or convalescent facilities for those who are unable to care for themselves. But, are there senior centers where independent seniors can go for fun and fellowship? Are there senior day-care centers where families can leave seniors who cannot take care of themselves

Sociology Today: Demography for Businesses

Businesses have discovered that they can grow bigger by targeting smaller groups of consumers. These groups, called generations, or cohorts, are defined by important life experiences. Events occurring when people first become economic adults (usually between ages 17 and 21) affect their lifelong attitudes and values. These attitudes and values are unlikely to change as a person ages. So the kind of music that is popular during these formative years often remains the preferred type of music for life. Similarly, early lifetime experiences influence preferences in many other product and service categories.

Studies of the U.S. population have identified seven distinct groups described in the table below. Which cohort are you? Your parents?

Cohort	Description	Born	Popular Music Styles
The Depression cohort	The G.I. generation	1912–1921	Big band
The World War II cohort	The Depression generation	1922–1927	Swing
The Postwar cohort	The silent generation	1928–1945	Frank Sinatra/Rat Pack
The Boomers I cohort	The Woodstock generation	1946–1954	Rock and roll
The Boomers II cohort	The zoomer generation	1955–1965	Rock and roll, disco
The generation X cohort	The baby-buster generation	1966–1976	Grunge, rap, country western
The Boomlet cohort	The echo-boom generation	1977–	Retro-swing, Latin

Doing Sociology

Have short interviews with members of at least two of the demographic business cohorts profiled above. Identify a number of differences in preferences for products between the members of different cohorts.

Source: Berkowitz, Kerin, Hartley, and Rudelius, *Marketing,* 5th ed. Chicago: Irwin, 1997.

The products in this mall store have been selected by taking into account the buying preferences of teenagers.

Sociology Today

You might want to have students look at how tastes in music have a ripple effect on our culture. What other industries are affected by consumers' tastes in music? For example, people who like Big Band music go to dance halls, while people who like rock and roll go to concerts. Each affects different aspects of culture.

Answer to Doing Sociology

It should be really interesting to see what students get from these interviews. Have them look for distinct preferences in music among members of the same generation. Some baby boomers will have listened to the San Francisco sound (Grateful Dead, Jefferson Airplane), while others will be big Beatles or Elton John fans. Ask interviewees why they listen to what they listen to. Were they influenced by parents, peers, etc.?

during the day while the family is at work and school? Are there groups that offer legal and medical advice for senior citizens?

Have students design an oral presentation, make a poster, or compile a pamphlet of the information they find. They may want to make copies and distribute the pamphlet to fellow students to share with family members. Ask students if they think your community is doing all it can and should be doing to aid senior citizens. **L2**

Using the Section Preview

Play a little game with students called free association. Tell them you are going to say a word and they should respond with the first word that comes to mind. Write these words on the board and use them for a discussion to introduce this section. The words are "city" and "suburb."

Teaching Strategy

For a great resource on the changes brought about to cities by the shift from an industrial to post-industrial economy, read *City Building in America* by Anthony Orum, Westview Press, 1995. Orum examined several cities to show how the shift away from manufacturing industries adversely affected cities largely dependent on these jobs. He also contrasted these cities with those that emphasize service sector jobs or post-industrial jobs. Orum gives considerable attention to his hometown of Milwaukee, Wisconsin.

Section 3

The Urban Transition

Key Terms

- **city**
- **urbanization**
- **overurbanization**
- **suburbanization**
- **central-city dilemma**
- **gentrification**
- **edge city**

Section Preview

The first preindustrial cities developed in fertile areas where surplus food could be grown. With the Industrial Revolution came a major increase in the rate of urbanization. The development of factories was an especially important influence on the location of cities. Urbanization in developed and developing nations has occurred at different speeds. The United States is now primarily a suburban nation.

city
dense and permanent concentration of people living in a specific area and working primarily in nonagricultural jobs

urbanization
process by which an increasingly larger portion of the world's population lives in cities

Defining a City

When does a village become a city? In Denmark and Sweden, an area with 200 inhabitants officially qualifies as a city. Populous Japan uses a much higher number—30,000. The cutoff point used by the U.S. Census Bureau to define a city is a population of 2,500. This number was set at a time when urbanization had just begun and population concentrations were small. It is obviously low for modern times.

A city is more than just a reasonably large number of people, however. Cities are also long-lasting. The periodic Woodstock rock festivals gather a large number of people in one place, but only for short periods of time. Clearly, large gatherings alone do not make a city. Cities also have a centralized economic focus. That is, they provide people with a chance to work in commerce, industry, or service. In summary, a **city** is a dense and permanent concentration of people living in a limited geographic area who earn their living primarily through nonagricultural activities.

Crowded inner cities and sprawling suburbs appear in all American cities.

Urbanization

The world has been greatly changed by **urbanization**—the process by which an increasingly larger portion of the world's population lives in or very near to cities. Urbanization has been so common that it is now taken for granted in many parts of the world. Today, almost as many people live in urban areas as in rural areas. This is a fairly recent development in human history.

Role Play

The following exercise will help to demonstrate that rapid urbanization has sociopsychological as well as socioeconomic consequences.

Hand out the following set of instructions on a piece of paper to all but three members of the class:

"Get up and walk around the room as though you were walking on a busy street in New York City. You should walk quickly and not make eye contact with anyone. Do not respond to greetings from strangers. You are in a hurry, and strangers could be dangerous."

Distribute the following instructions to only three member of the class:

What were early cities like? The first cities appeared about five or six thousand years ago and were quite small by modern standards. One of the world's first major cities was Ur, located at the point where the Tigris and Euphrates Rivers meet (in modern-day Iraq). At its peak, Ur held only about 24,000 people. Later, during the time of the Roman Empire, it is unlikely that many cities had populations larger than 33,000. The population of Rome itself was probably under 350,000.

In addition to their small size, the cities of ancient and medieval periods contained only a small portion of the world's population. As recently as 1800, less than 3 percent of the world's population lived in cities of 20,000 or more. By contrast, today, 46 percent of the world's population live in urban areas. In North America, 75 percent of the population live in cities (*World Population Data Sheet,* 2001). How did cities develop so quickly and why have cities replaced rural living for most people?

Preindustrial Cities

The first urban settlements were located in Mesopotamia and were established around 3500 B.C. This was after people learned how to cultivate plants and domesticate animals, a period known as the *agricultural revolution*. The Mesopotamian region is among the world's most fertile areas and the farmers in the area were able to provide enough extra, or surplus, food to feed people in the cities. A surplus food supply is necessary for urbanization to occur.

Who lived in preindustrial cities? Besides available food, people needed other reasons to gather in cities. Cities tended to attract four basic types of people: elites, functionaries, craftspeople, and the poor and destitute. For elites, the city provided a setting for consolidating political, military, or religious power. The functionaries were the political or religious officials who carried out the plans of the elites. Their lives were undoubtedly easier than those of the peasant-farmers in the countryside. Craftspeople, still lower in the stratification structure, came to the city to work and sell their products to the elites and functionaries. The poor came hoping to find work but were seldom able to improve their condition.

Do preindustrial cities still exist today? Africa, Asia, and Latin America are only partly industrialized. For this reason, many of their cities still have some preindustrial characteristics. This is particularly true in capital cities because they are a magnet to the rural poor seeking a better life. Rural migrants are attracted to these cities because there are limited opportunities for making a living in the rural areas and the city promises a better life. Unfortunately, most of those who migrate to the cities are disappointed, because the expected employment opportunities do not exist. The migrants end up living in terrible slums.

In Calcutta, India, for example, 12 million people are crowded into a city whose last major sewer line was built in 1896. Epidemics are frequent, and disease is commonplace. Calcutta's housing supply, waterworks, electrical system, and other facilities are not sufficient to cope with the city's rapid growth.

Calcutta, India, remains essentially a preindustrial city.

Reteaching

Have students use the text to make visual aids (charts and posters) that highlight the major differences between preindustrial and modern cities. They should also identify elements that appear in both types of cities. For example, both cities needed a commercial center—whether it be an open-air market or Wall Street.

"You come from a small town and are trying to find a particular address. Walk around and ask two or three people if they know where South Street is. Be sure to smile politely and extend your hand in a friendly manner."

Give the students two or three minutes to follow these instructions, then have them sit down. Ask the "small towners" how it felt to be ignored by the city people. Ask the city people how it felt to have to ignore an apparently friendly person. Given this experience, what do they think the psychological consequences of rapid urbanization might be? (Or, you may want to save this activity for introducing the concept or urbanism, which arises in Chapter 17.)

L1

World View

The United States is one of those countries in the 60 percent–79 percent range of urban population as a proportion of the total population. Do students find this surprising? Do they see it as a problem? Why or why not?

Answers to Interpreting the Map

1. These countries never developed the rural, agricultural economy typical of the more fertile soils of the U.S. and Western Europe. In the cities of developing countries, people have moved from the countryside to the city because expanding rural populations cannot be supported by the existing subsistence economy and they hope to find work in the cities. However, the supply of labor from the countryside is greater than the demand for labor in the cities. A high rate of urban unemployment has resulted.
2. Increased urbanization will likely lead to more cases of overurbanization in the future. The cities will be unable to supply adequate jobs and housing for its inhabitants.

World View

Urban Population as a Proportion of Total Population

As discussed in the text, the Industrial Revolution encouraged the rapid growth of cities. The map below shows that many countries now have urban populations that comprise 60 percent or more of their total populations.

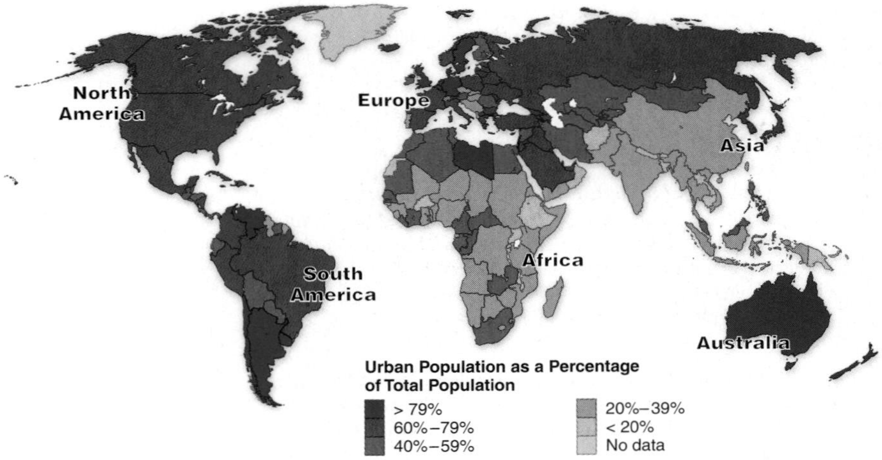

Interpreting the Map

1. The map shows that countries such as England, Germany, and Sweden have urban populations that make up over 80 percent of their total populations. This can be explained by the effects of the Industrial Revolution, since these countries' economies are highly developed. However, other countries, such as Venezuela, Argentina, and Libya, which are not highly developed, also have urban populations that comprise over 80 percent of their totals. Can you think of reasons why this is so? Explain.
2. What effects will increased urbanization have on countries and the world?

Adapted from *The State of the World Atlas*, 5th ed.

The Rise of the Modern City

Beginning in the 1700s, the Industrial Revolution created major changes in transportation, agriculture, commerce, and industry. Technological developments led to better agricultural productivity and more efficient transportation systems. Farm workers were free to leave rural areas and move into cities. More important, however, was the spread of factories.

Encouraging Citizenship Activity

Share the following activity with students: You have studied urbanization and by now you know how inner cities are often abandoned to crime and filth. You probably can't do much about crime, but you can do something about filth. You can clean it up. (Students may not need to go into inner cities. Many more suburban areas have regions of urban blight that could use some help.)

Look for an organization that sponsors beautification of city blocks. Volunteer to pick up the trash, or do whatever is needed. Recycle the empty bottles. Sweep the sidewalks. After you have done that, start spiffing things up. Repair fences, fill in broken

Figure 16.9 Focus on Theoretical Perspectives

Urban Society. This table illustrates how functionalism and conflict theory might approach the study of urban society. Symbolic interactionism was not included. Why do you think it was excluded? Can you suggest a research topic in either population or urbanization for which symbolic interactionism would be appropriate?

Theoretical Perspective	Concept	Sample Research Topic
Functionalism	Urbanization	Study of the relationship between population density and the suicide rate
Conflict Theory	Overurbanization	Investigation of the relationship between the distribution of scarce resources and social class

Factories were not established to encourage the growth of cities, but they had that effect. Factory owners tended to build in the same area to share raw materials and to take advantage of natural features such as water power and river transport. Machinery and equipment makers located their plants next to the factories they would be supplying. All these businesses in turn attracted retailers, innkeepers, entertainers, and a wide range of people offering services to city dwellers. The more services offered, the more people were attracted, maintaining the cycle of urban growth. The industrial world was becoming an urbanized world.

World Urbanization

Urbanization is a worldwide movement. From 1800 to the mid-1980s, the number of urban dwellers increased one hundred times, while the population increased only about fivefold. Over 2.8 billion people—nearly 46 percent of the world's population—now live in urban areas. In developed countries, 75 percent of the population lives in urban areas compared to 40 percent in developing countries. (See Figure 16.10 on page 553.)

What are the patterns for urbanization? Developed and developing countries have distinct patterns of urbanization. Most of the urban growth in developing countries before the turn of the century occurred through colonial expansion. Western countries, which had been involved in colonial expansion since the late fifteenth century, held half the world under colonial rule by the latter part of the nineteenth century. It has been only since World War II that many of these colonial countries have become independent nations (Bardo and Hartman, 1982).

Working with the Data

Figure 16.9 The symbolic interactionist perspective would be interested in the social interactions that comprise urban life. It is more likely that people know what others do rather than who they are. For example, people may not know their neighbors personally, but can recognize them on sight. The impersonality of urban life is contrasted by individuals having smaller, tighter social networks. Chicago school sociologists Louis Wirth and Robert Park devoted much time to studying urban interactions. Students might want to visit the Dead Sociologist's website (mentioned in Chapter 1) to research some major sociologists' perspectives on urban life.

Integrating the Teacher Resources

Look for the Chapter 16 Increasing Your Reading Comprehension worksheet and the Guided Reading worksheet in the Unit 5 Mastering Basic Concepts booklet in your Teacher's Resource Box. Both will strengthen student reading comprehension skills.

cement, paint street numbers on the curb, fix broken street lights. Prop up broken mailboxes. If you can, plant some flowers or trees. If at all possible find an agency or organizationt that works with the people who live in the disadvantaged areas. Remember though, it is their home; don't try to impose your sense of aesthetics on the residents. Work with the volunteer group officials to find out what local residents want done. **L1**

Reinforcing Vocabulary

A number of terms are used to describe economically disadvantaged countries. These include "developing countries" and "less developed countries." Until very recently, the countries were known collectively as the "Third World." Extremely poor countries were called the "Fourth World." The reason for these changes lies in a fundamental shift in our approach to economic development. For the first time, economists and policy makers are placing an emphasis on culture, and trying to avoid terms which compare "developed" and "developing" countries. Sociologists and economists now feel uncomfortable using terms that imply a "better" or "worse" relationship. There was a time when developing nations were commonly called "underdeveloped;" a way of thinking that has its roots in colonial expansion. Within a few years, most people will probably abandon the terms "developing" and "developed" in favor of an even more neutral phraseology, which divides nations into "North" and "South." Another term students might be hearing in their government or economics classes is "economics retransition". The term has been popular since the fall of the former U.S.S.R.

Since gaining independence, these former colonies have been experiencing rapid urbanization and industrialization. In fact, urbanization in these areas is now proceeding nine times faster than it did in the West during its urban expansion period. The rate of urbanization for major industrial nations in the West was 15 percent each decade throughout the nineteenth century. In the 1960s, the rate of urbanization in major developing countries was 20 percent per decade (Light, 1983).

What are some other differences in the pattern of world urbanization? In the first place, industrialization in developing countries, unlike the Western experience, has not kept pace with urbanization. Cities of North America and Europe had jobs for all migrants from rural areas. In the cities of developing nations, the supply of labor from the countryside is greater than the demand for labor in the cities. A high rate of urban unemployment is the obvious result. The term **overurbanization** has been created to describe a situation in which a city is unable to supply adequate jobs and housing for its inhabitants.

overurbanization
situation in which a city cannot supply adequate jobs and housing for its inhabitants

Another difference between urbanization in developed and developing countries is the number and size of cities. When grouped by size, cities in developed countries form a pyramid: a few large cities at the top, many medium-sized cities in the middle, and a large base of small cities. In the developing world, in contrast, many countries have one tremendously big city that dwarfs a large number of villages. Calcutta, India, and Mexico City are examples. Of the world's ten largest cities, only two—Shanghai and Calcutta—were in developing countries in 1950. By 2000, as you can see in Figure 16.10 on the opposite page, seven of the top ten largest urban areas were in developing countries. By the end of the twenty-first century, it is predicted that there will be twenty-one "megacities" with populations of ten million or more. Eighteen of these will be in developing countries, including the most impoverished societies in the world.

Los Angeles drivers spend about 82 hours a year, two full weeks of work, waiting in traffic. Does this mean that Los Angeles is overurbanized?

What are "push" and "pull" factors? In explaining why people in developing countries move to large cities with inadequate jobs and housing, urban sociologists point to the operation of "push" and "pull" factors. People are pushed out of their villages because expanding rural populations cannot be supported by the existing agricultural economy. They are forced to migrate elsewhere, and cities are at least an alternative. Poor people are also attracted to cities in the belief there are opportunities for better education, employment, social welfare support, and good medical care. Unfortunately, they are likely to be disappointed.

Suburbanization in the United States

Unlike cities in the developing world, cities in the United States have recently been losing population, not gaining. Since 1950, the proportion of the population living in suburbs has more than doubled. **Suburbanization** occurs when central cities lose population to the surrounding areas. The United States is now predominantly suburban.

suburbanization
loss of population of a city to surrounding areas

What makes suburbanization possible? Suburbanization has become an important trend partly because of technological developments. Improvements in communication (such as telephones, radios, and television and later computers, fax machines, and the Internet) have allowed people to live away

Careers in Sociology

Ask students if they know what career best utilizes the sociology of population and urbanization.

After students have offered answers, share the following information with them. Urban and regional planners and their assistants are population and urbanization sociologists. They develop long- and short-term land use plans to provide for growth and revitalization of urban, suburban, and rural communities, while helping local officials make decisions concerning social, economic, and environmental problems. Under the supervision of a city or regional planner, assistants conduct research into the economic, environmental, and social consequences of development in order to support strategies for appropriate growth from the central city without losing touch with what is going on there. Developments in transportation (especially trains, highways, automobiles, and trucks) have made it possible both for people to commute to work and for many businesses to leave the central city for suburban locations.

Technology is not the only cause of suburbanization. Both cultural and economic pressures have encouraged the development of suburbs. Partly because of America's frontier heritage, American culture has always had a bias against urban living. Some Americans prefer urban life, but most report that they would rather live in a rural setting. Even those who choose to live in the city believe they are giving up some advantages. Suburbs, with their low-density housing, have allowed many people to escape the problems of urban living without leaving the urban areas completely. Suburbs are attractive because of decreased crowding and traffic congestion, lower taxes, better schools, less crime, and reduced pollution.

The scarcity and high cost of land in the central city also encourages suburbanization. Developers of new housing, retail, and industrial projects often find suburban locations far less expensive than those near the central city. Finally, government policy has often increased the impact of economic forces. Federal Housing Administration regulations, for example, have favored the financing of new houses (which can be built most cheaply in suburban locations) rather than the refurbishing of older houses in central cities. Among other things, this has led to the *central-city dilemma*.

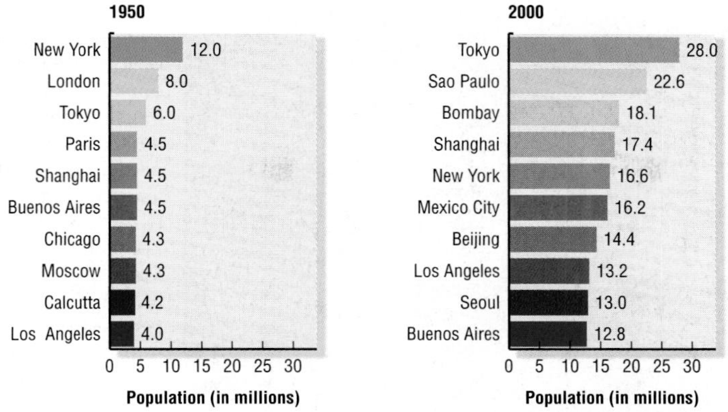

Figure 16.10 World's Largest Urban Areas: 1950, 2000. *This figure compares the world's largest urban areas in 1950 and 2000. What is the most surprising aspect of these data to you?*

Source: Population Division of the UN Secretariat Estimate.

What is the central-city dilemma? When suburbanization first became noticeable in the 1930s, only the upper and middle classes could afford to leave the central city. Not until the 1950s did the white working class follow them. Despite federal legislation prohibiting housing discrimination, the suburbs remained largely white until the 1970s. Since then, central-city minorities have moved to the suburbs in greater numbers. Still, the percentage of African Americans living in central cities has declined only slightly since 1970 (Farley, 1997; Palen, 1997).

The problem is not merely that minorities remain trapped in inner cities. Businesses have followed the more affluent people to the suburbs where they can find lower tax rates, less expensive land, less congestion, and their customers who have already left the city. Accompanying the exodus of the middle class, manufacturers, and retailers is the shrinking of the central-city tax base. As a result, the central city has become increasingly populated by the poor, the unskilled, and the uneducated. This has created the **central-city dilemma**—the concentration of a large population in need of public services (schools, transportation, health care) without the tax base to provide them.

Can the central-city dilemma be solved? Some countertrends exist. There are city governments now requiring certain public employees to live in

SOCIOLOGY Online

Student Web Activity
Visit the *Sociology and You* Web site at soc.glencoe.com and click on **Chapter 16—Student Web Activities** for an activity on suburbanization.

central-city dilemma concentration of people in need of public services without tax base–generated money to provide for them

Working with the Data

Figure 16.10 Student answers will vary. However, they will likely point out the tremendous growth evidenced in the figure. For example, the population of Tokyo more than doubled twice in 50 years. The population of Los Angeles more than tripled, and so on. Students may also point out that the largest cities 50 years ago were in developed countries. Now, 50 years later, many of the largest cities are in less developed countries. And as the text states, by 2100, 18 of 21 megacities will be in impoverished nations.

More About . . . Suburbanization

A classic work on the changes suburbanization caused in the American landscape is Kenneth T. Jackson's *Crabgrass Frontier,* Oxford University Press, 1985. Despite its copyright date, this book is not dated. Some of Jackson's predictions can be challenged, but the basic reasons Jackson wrote about in 1985 that spawned suburban growth remain true today.

and renovation of rural, suburban, or urban areas.

Planners promote the best use of a community's land and resources for residential, commercial, institutional, and recreational purposes. Planners may be involved in various other activities, including decisions on alternative public transportation system plans, resource development, and protection of ecologically sensitive regions.

For information, contact the American Planning Association, **http://www.planning.org**.

For information about careers in demography, contact the Population Association of America, **http://www.popassoc.org**.

Pulling it All Together

This section dealt with the changes urbanization has caused throughout history. It covered the growth of suburbs due to social and governmental policies. New trends such as gentrification were also examined.

Answers to Section 3 Assessment

1. Urbanization is the process by which an increasingly larger portion of the world's population lives in or very near to cities.
2. Two conditions for the development of modern cities were technological developments (which led to better agricultural productivity and more efficient transportation systems) and the spread of factories (which attracted machinery and equipment makers and eventually retailers, innkeepers, and entertainers, etc.).
3. Preindustrial cities still exist in Africa, Asia, and Latin America.
4. Migration to the suburbs is called *suburbanization*.

Critical Thinking

5. Answers will vary, but students should point out that preindustrial cities will continue to exist as long as there are developing (only partly industrialized) countries.

This view of Dallas was taken from the rooftop pool area of an old garment factory converted into luxury apartments.

gentrification
the development of low-income areas by middle-class homebuyers, landlords, and professional developers

edge city
a suburban unit specializing in a particular economic activity

> Our national flower is the concrete cloverleaf.
>
> Lewis Mumford
> U.S. novelist

the city. Some parts of inner cities are being restored through **gentrification**—the development of low-income areas by middle-class home buyers, landlords, and professional developers. Finally, there is a fairly significant movement of whites back to the central city. This movement is particularly evident among baby boomers who are remaining single or establishing childless or two-income families. Because these people are not as heavily involved in child rearing, they prefer central-city living more than the previous generation did (Palen, 1997). The importance of these countertrends for easing the central-city dilemma remains to be seen. They certainly have not been sufficiently important to stop the emergence of *edge cities*.

What are edge cities? As stated, increasing numbers of businesses and jobs have followed people to the suburbs. In fact, "suburban downtowns" are changing the face of urban America. An **edge city** is a smaller, more focused, version of an urban downtown. It is a suburban unit that specializes in a particular economic activity (Garreau, 1991). Employment in one edge city may focus on computer technology; employment in another, on financial services or health care. A specialized edge city, of course, will have many other types of economic activities as well, such as industrial tracts, office parks, distribution and warehousing clusters, and home offices of national corporations. Edge cities are actually little cities in themselves with a full range of services, including schools, retail sales, restaurants, malls, recreational complexes, medical facilities, and hotels and motels.

Edge cities do not have legal and physical boundaries separating them from the larger urban area in which they are located. This has not prevented names from being attached to several of them. Tyson's Corner is located in northern Virginia near Washington, D.C., Los Colinas is close to the Dallas-Fort Worth airport, and King of Prussia is northwest of Philadelphia. Some edge cities bear the names of highways, such as Route 128 outside of Boston.

Section 3 Assessment

1. Give a brief definition of *urbanization*.
2. What are two conditions necessary for the development of modern cities?
3. Where are preindustrial cities located today?
4. What term do sociologists use to describe mass migration to the suburbs?

Critical Thinking

5. **Analyzing Information** Do you think preindustrial cities can continue to exist? Why or why not?

On-Demand Writing

Gentrification has been an important force in improving inner- and edge-cities. The movement of upwardly-mobile individuals into many traditionally poor areas has caused a growth in the economy of those areas. For example, old apartment buildings are being renovated and new housing is being constructed. Old businesses are replaced by trendier and wealthier establishments. However, as a result of these changes, many low-income families can no longer afford to live in that area. Many family-owned businesses are driven out by competitors. The poorer individuals who

Tech Trends

Virtual Communities

Some people find life in the big city so impersonal that they feel no sense of belonging to a community. Recently organizers in several locations have been trying to use the Internet to rebuild community relationships through electronic networks. These *dedicated*—specialized—virtual communities use communications technology to link people who live in the same area, city, or neighborhood.

Organizers of community networks share the goals of local participation, community building, and democracy. As with the New England colonies' town meetings, the ideal of the new community networks is to include everyone. Supporters of the new technology claim that electronic communications will allow people to reestablish more personal relationships.

As with all projects involving technology, though, the problem of "electronic stratification" arises. Because of the costs involved, access to technological advances is not equally distributed throughout the community. Low-income individuals and families cannot afford computers or Internet access, and public agencies are not ready to supply sufficient funding. Furthermore, as computers become more sophisticated, people who are not already computer literate (especially lower-income people) will have an increasingly difficult time catching up. The technologically poor will become technologically poorer.

iVillage.com is a Web site offering a virtual community for women.

The Boulder (Colorado) Community Network (BCN), established in the mid-1990s, experienced many of these problems. The founders of BCN trained many different Boulder groups to use community networks. They found that acceptance varied widely among the groups. For example, residents at a local senior citizens' home became avid users of the community computers placed in their facility. In contrast, a group of low-income single parents virtually ignored the existence of the computers and the Internet, even after extensive training (Virnoche, 1998).

If community networks do become firmly established, critics warn, the "human factor" will still be lacking. When people meet through the Internet, they have no social clues, such as body language and facial expressions, with which to learn about their new acquaintances. No matter how much you learn about another person on-line, critics say, you have not met someone for real until you meet in person (Herbert, 1999).

Analyzing the Trends

What do you think will be the most significant effects of virtual communities on social roles?

depended on the neighborhood are forced to move out as the area is claimed, or "colonized," by its new occupants. The ethnic or historical character of the neighborhood is often irretrievably lost in this process.

Ask the class to write a brief statement supporting or criticizing gentrification. Ask volunteers to read their statements to the class. Do they feel that economic advancement justifies the "colonization" of these neighborhoods? Does gentrification really benefit the occupants of poor neighborhoods?
L2

Tech Trends

Ask students if they would or already do participate in a virtual community such as that described here. Do they know any friends or relatives who participate?

Answer to Analyzing the Trends

1. Answers will vary. Ask students to consider if, in the future, the frequency of face-to-face interactions will decrease. Could human interactions be replaced solely by interactions via computer?

Integrating the Teacher Resources

Look for *Ethics, Values, and Technology: Real-Life Issues in Society*, available in your Teacher's Resource Box. The booklet provides primary source readings dealing with real-life controversies. Student worksheets are included.

Using the Section Preview

To preview and illustrate the concepts covered in this section, obtain a map of a large city in your area and create transparencies of it, applying the concentric zone, sector, and multiple nuclei models to explain the growth of the city. Ask an urban sociologist to come in and explain how that particular city developed according to the theories of urban growth. Consider taking your class on a walking tour of the downtown area. Some historical societies offer these walking tours.

Open-Response Question

Although these theories of city growth stress factors such as business, immigration, and transportation, the government also plays an important role in the growth of our cities. In fact, entire government agencies are devoted to urban development and city planning. The most important of these is HUD—the Department of Housing and Urban Development.

Ask your students to brainstorm to come up with a list of ways that government can influence the growth of a city. If they have trouble getting started, offer the following suggestions: public transportation, location of schools, sanitation, water supply, zoning, roads and freeways, taxes, etc.

Section 4

Urban Ecology

Key Terms

- **urban ecology**
- **concentric zone theory**
- **sector theory**
- **multiple nuclei theory**
- **peripheral theory**

Section Preview

Urban ecologists have developed four major theories of city growth: concentric zone theory, sector theory, multiple nuclei theory, and peripheral theory. Combining insights from all four theories is useful to our understanding of how humans relate to city environments.

The Nature of Urban Ecology

Although every city is unique, patterns have been found in the way humans interact with the cities they inhabit. **Urban ecology** is the study of the relationships between humans and their city environments.

In the 1920s and 1930s, sociologists at the University of Chicago studied the effects of the city environment on city residents. They asked such questions as why there are differences between areas of a city, how do different areas affect one another, and what processes change an area. To answer these and other questions, the University of Chicago sociologists developed theories of urban ecology, including theories of city growth (Flanagan, 1993; Kleniewski, 1997; Micklin and Poston, 1998).

urban ecology
the study of the relationships between humans and city environments

Theories of City Growth

Sociologists focus on four major theories of city growth. *Concentric zone theory* describes urban growth in terms of circular areas that grow from the central city outward. *Sector theory* emphasizes the importance of transportation routes in the process of urban growth. *Multiple nuclei theory* focuses on specific geographic or historical influences. *Peripheral theory* emphasizes the growth of suburbs around the central city. The four approaches lead to quite different images of urban space. (See Figure 16.11 on the facing page.) No city exactly fits any of these images, however. Indeed, the theories tell us more when considered together than they tell us separately. To understand why this is so, we must first examine each theory.

What is concentric zone theory? Ernest Burgess (1925), like other early sociologists at the University of Chicago, was interested in the causes and consequences of Chicago's growth. His work led to the **concentric zone theory,** which describes city growth in terms of distinctive zones—zones that develop from the central city outward in a circular pattern. Many northern cities that experienced a great deal of immigration and rapid growth developed this way.

concentric zone theory
theory that describes urban growth in terms of circular areas that grow from the central city outward

As illustrated in Figure 16.11, the innermost circle is the *central business district,* the heart of the city. This district contains major government and private office buildings, banks, retail and wholesale stores, and entertainment and cultural facilities. Because land values in the central city are high, space is at a premium. The central business district contains a large proportion of a city's important businesses partly because the less important

Learning Styles

Spatial/Linguistic To assist students in gaining not just an understanding, but an appreciation of the scientific study of population (demographics), give them an opportunity to be a city planner/developer. After reading and discussing sections 3 and 4, ask students to use the information they have learned to design what they feel would be the ideal city. Ask them to create some type of graphic representation (such

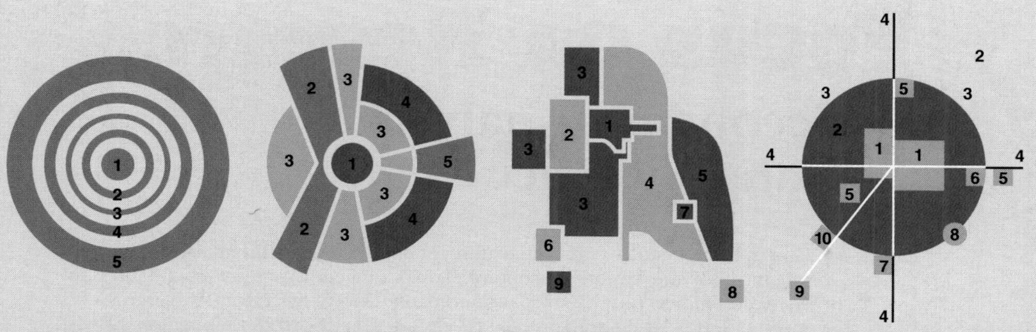

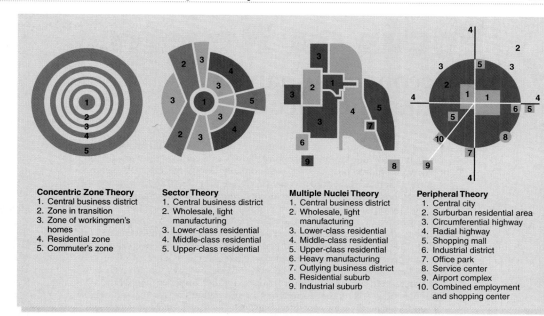

Figure 16.11 Theories of City Growth. *This figure diagrams the four major theories of city growth. Discuss one important contribution each theory makes to our understanding of urban growth.*

Source: Adapted from Chauncy D. Harris, *Urban Geography,* 1997.

ones are unable to compete for the expensive space in the central business district.

The central business district strongly influences other parts of a city. Its influence is especially clear in the zone immediately surrounding it. Burgess called this the *zone in transition* because it is in the process of change. As new businesses and activities enter the central business district, the district expands by invading the next zone. This area may have been a residential area inhabited by middle- or upper-class families, who left because of the invasion of business activities. Most of the property in this zone is bought by those with little interest in the area. Rather than investing money in building maintenance, landowners simply extract rent from the property or sell it at a profit after the area has become more commercialized. Until the zone in transition is completely absorbed into the central business district (which may never occur), it is used for slum housing, warehouses, and marginal businesses that are unable to compete economically for space in the central business district itself. In short, the invasion of business activities creates deterioration for the zone in transition.

Surrounding the zone in transition are three zones devoted primarily to housing. The *zone of workingmen's homes* contains modest but stable neighborhoods populated largely by blue-collar workers. In the northern United States, the zone of workingmen's homes is often inhabited by second-generation immigrants who have had enough financial success to leave the deteriorating zone in transition. Next comes a *residential zone* containing mostly middle-class and upper-middle-class neighborhoods. Single-family dwellings dominate this zone, which is inhabited by managers, professionals, white-collar workers, and some well-paid factory workers. On the outskirts of

"The planner's problem is to find a way of creating, within the urban environment, the sense of belonging."

Leo Marx
philosopher and culturist

Making Connections to Other Cultures

This excerpt will help students connect to Americans of the nineteenth century.

Before identifying the author of this quote, read the selection and ask students to guess when it was written.

"A man walks his tedious miles through the same interminable street every day, elbowing his way through a buzzing multitude of men, yet never seeing a familiar face... Every man seems to feel that he has got the duties of two lifetimes to accomplish in one, and so he rushes, rushes, rushes, and never has time to be companionable—never has any time at his disposal to fool away on matters which do not involve dollars and duty and business."

In 1867, Mark Twain made these observations on the effects of city life.

as a model or thematic map) that can be presented along with an oral report to the class. Students should make sure that their city meets all the requirements of the definition of "city" as well as including the means necessary to meet the needs of the inhabitants. (Refer to the information in sections 3 and 4.) Note: You may or may not want to allow students to "plan" preindustrial as well as modern cities.

Focus on Research

Secondary Analysis: Gang Violence

Gangs have been a constant feature of the American urban landscape during most of the twentieth century. James Hagedorn's research (1998), however, led him to propose that postindustrial society has changed patterns of gang violence. Hagedorn's conclusions are based on a combination of three methods: a review of the research of others, secondary analysis of data collected by other researchers, and original data gathered himself.

Gangs (mostly male) in the industrial period were tied to specific neighborhoods and new immigrant groups. Gang violence primarily centered on "turf" battles among neighborhood peer groups. Pride in violence came from defending territory. Violence provided excitement and a sense of place in a group. Nevertheless, these working- and lower-class boys would eventually move on to hold decent jobs, have families, and live in better neighborhoods.

Gangs today still tend to form around racial and ethnic groups and neighborhoods. Currently, gangs tend to be African American, Latino, or Asian, just as earlier gangs were formed mostly by European immigrants, such as those from Ireland, Italy, or Eastern Europe. According to Hagedorn, however, postindustrial gangs are different in important ways. First, gang violence has significantly increased. Second, gang-related homicides have risen dramatically. Gang violence, he notes, skyrocketed at the same time American corporations were moving well-paying jobs away from the central city. As legitimate work disappeared in inner cities, gangs turned from their earlier territorial emphasis to participation in the illegitimate drug market. The common outlook of gang members today is expressed by this gang member:

> *I got out of high school and I didn't have a diploma, wasn't no jobs, wasn't no source of income, no nothing. That's basically the easy way for a . . . young man to be—selling some dope—you can get yourself some money real quick, you really don't have nothing to worry about, nothing but the feds. You know everybody in your neighborhood. Yeah, that's pretty safe just as long as you don't start smoking it yourself (Hagedorn, 1998:390).*

Significantly, this gang member was not a teenager. While a minority of gang members remain committed to the drug economy, most seek "legit" jobs as they approach their thirties.

Working with the Research

1. Explain why urban gangs tend to form around minority groups.
2. Relate Hagedorn's findings on urban gang violence, to Merton's strain theory, discussed in Chapter 7.

Focus on Research

There has been so much written about gangs that a literature search on this topic could be overwhelming to students at the high school level. This summary of James Hagedorn's research places gangs in the sociological context of postindustrial society.

Depending upon the location of your school, your students may or may not have firsthand experience with gang violence. You might consider inviting a representative of the legal or court systems in to talk about gang activity in your area.

Answers to Working with the Research

1. Merton's strain theory (from Chapter 7) would classify gangs as "rebellionist". The social structure has deprived them of opportunities, creating an anomic situation. Gangs look for alternative means to accomplish the cultural goals, which include non-sanctioned methods like crime.
2. Students should remember that the strain theory stated that when socially approved methods of obtaining goals do not work, people find other ways. Gang members in urban setting belong to the innovation category (using illegal means to achieve) or to rebellion (replacing existing norms with a different—and deviant—set).

Cooperative Learning Activity

Divide the students into four groups and assign a theory of city growth to each. Ask each group to design a fictitious town using the theory that they have been assigned. Their design should include a map of the town based on the models provided in the text, and a brief written history that would explain the town's development. The written history should include information on the town's ethnic make-up, its major source the city, often outside the official city limits, is the *commuter's zone,* which contains upper-class and upper-middle-class suburbs.

What is sector theory? Not everyone agreed with Burgess's theory of how cities grow. The sociologist Homer Hoyt (1939) offered another model—**sector theory.** Hoyt's work indicated that growth patterns do not necessarily spread out in rings from the central business district. Instead, growth is more strongly affected by major transportation routes.

sector theory
theory that emphasizes the importance of transportation routes in the process of urban growth

As Figure 16.11 shows, sectors tend to be pie-shaped, with wedges radiating from the central business district to the city's outskirts. Each sector is organized around a major transportation route. Once a given type of activity is organized around a transportation route, its nature tends to be set. Thus, some sectors will be predominantly industrial, others will contain stores and professional offices, others will be "neon strips" with motels and fast-food restaurants, and still others will be residential sectors, each with its own social class and ethnic composition.

As in concentric zone theory, cities are generally circular in shape. But because of the importance of transportation routes extending from the central business district, the boundaries of many cities form a starlike pattern, rather than a uniformly circular shape. The exact shape of a city, however, is not a major issue in sector theory. Emphasis here is on how patterns of growth are organized around transportation routes. Cities that follow this pattern include Seattle, Richmond, and San Francisco.

What is multiple nuclei theory? Many cities have areas that cannot be explained by either concentric zone or sector theory. Chauncy Harris and Edward Ullman (1945) suggested that cities do not always follow a pattern dependent on a central district. The **multiple nuclei theory** states that a city may have several separate centers, some devoted to manufacturing, some to retail trade, some to residential use, and so on. These specialized centers can develop because of the availability of automobiles and highways. They reflect such factors as geography, history, and tradition. The city of Boston fits this model.

multiple nuclei theory
theory that focuses on specific geographic or historical influences on urban growth

What is peripheral theory? The three theories of urban growth just discussed were originally developed more than fifty years ago. Despite their age, the insights of each theory still help us to understand how cities have expanded from the center outward. This is especially the case for older cities such as Chicago and San Francisco. Many cities today, however, no longer have a central city core to which other parts of the metropolitan area are oriented all of the time.

peripheral theory
theory that emphasizes the growth of suburbs around the central city

Dependence on shipping, railroads, and heavy manufacturing has been replaced by more flexible means of transportation, such as cars and trucks. And large urban areas are now encircled by highways. New technologies (fax machines, cell phones, computers, the Internet) are also loosening the ties of most parts of the city to the central city core. As a result, many cities are now oriented *away* from the older urban core.

As noted earlier, many Americans have moved from the city to the suburbs. They have done so in part because many businesses—offices, factories, schools, retail stores, restaurants, health centers—are also in the suburbs. To describe changes in urban areas today, urban geographer Chauncy Harris (1997) has formulated the **peripheral theory.** The dominant feature of this model is the growth of suburbs (and edge cities) around

Explain which theory of urban growth best accounts for this suburban office building.

Teaching Strategy

Have students decide which theory of city growth best describe the city in which you live or a nearby large city. Does your city fall into the concentric zone theory? Does it have circular areas that grow or have grown from the central city outward? Does sector theory fit your city? Does city growth follow transportation routes? Does your city fit the multiple nuclei theory? Are there several separate centers around which growth has occurred? Or, does peripheral theory better fit your city? Does your city have suburbs that have grown up around and away from the central part of the city?

It might be interesting to have someone from your city's planning department speak to your class about the planned future growth of your city. Students might ask the speaker which of the theories of city growth best fits your city. **L2**

of industry, whether or not the town has a large immigrant population or a large central business district. Is there a major transportation route? Each group will need to explore their assigned theory of growth to find the answers to these questions. Encourage the students to be as creative and as specific as possible. When their research is finished, they should present their cities to the class.

Pulling it All Together

Urban ecology is the study of relationships between people and their urban environments. Patterns of migration emerge as cities grow. Several theories such as concentric zone theory, sector theory, multiple nuclei theory, and peripheral theory are given to explain these migration patterns.

Answers to Section 4 Assessment

1. Answers will vary.
2. Major transportation routes, around which patterns of growth are organized, constitute the driving force behind the sector theory.
3. The multiple nuclei theory allows for unique factors affecting each city's land use and does not predict a particular pattern of land use for all cities. It states that a city may have several specialized centers (i.e., for manufacturing, retail trade, residential use).

Critical Thinking

4. Answers will vary.
5. Students should reread the bulleted list of important factors of each theory and use their own perspectives to answer the question. Additionally, ask students to write questions and answers about the theories.

> Men come together in cities in order to live. They remain together in order to live the good life.
>
> Aristotle
> Greek philospher

and away from the central cities. (See Figure 16.11.) Peripheral theory brings urban growth research up to date.

Which of these theories of city growth is correct? As suggested earlier, no single theory covers the dynamics of city growth for all cities. But each theory emphasizes the importance of certain factors that cannot be overlooked by anyone interested in city growth.

- Concentric zone theory emphasizes the fact that growth in any one area of a city is largely influenced by politics and economics. According to this theory, the distribution of space is heavily influenced by those with the money to buy the land they want for the purposes they have in mind.
- Sector theorists have also contributed to an understanding of urban growth. As they have noted, transportation routes have a strong influence on cities. Decisions about the placement of railroad lines had important effects on the growth of cities in the nineteenth and early twentieth centuries. Highways and major streets have an even larger impact now.
- Although multiple nuclei theory is vague in its predictions, the types of geographic and historical factors it emphasizes are also important for understanding any specific city.
- Peripheral theory has brought urban growth research up to date by emphasizing the development of suburbs around the central city.

Section 4 Assessment

1. Provide a brief description of each of the following zones.
   - **a.** central business district
   - **b.** commuters' zone
   - **c.** residential zone
   - **d.** zone in transition
   - **e.** zone of workingmen's homes
2. What is the driving force behind the sector theory?
3. Why is the multiple nuclei theory considered more flexible than the concentric zone theory or the sector theory?

Critical Thinking

4. **Summarizing Information** Summarize the evolution of cities, focusing on the differences between life in preindustrial cities and life in industrial and suburban cities.
5. **Applying Concepts** Discuss the major contributions the four theories of city growth have made to our understanding of city growth.

On-Demand Writing

The newest theory of city growth is focused on the development of the suburbs. Recently, this phenomenon has come to be known as "urban sprawl." It has been argued by many critics that the suburbs have contributed to the destruction of the sense of community that marks older neighborhoods. According to these critics, residents of the suburbs have no ties to their communities, and the communities themselves lack individuality. They contend that the suburbs are a "vacuum" best symbolized by strip malls and a "drive-through culture."

Central to this debate is an argument known as the "superstore wars." Superstores such as Wal-Mart and Home

CHAPTER 16 ASSESSMENT

Summary

Section 1: The Dynamics of Demography

Main Idea: Demography is the scientific study of population. The collection of population data is very important today, in part because of its use by government and industry. Demographers consider three population processes when looking at population change: fertility, mortality, and migration.

Section 2: World Population

Main Idea: Thomas Malthus (1798) predicted that population size would ultimately outstrip the food supply, resulting in mass starvation and death. The demographic transition theory looks at economic development to predict population patterns. While the rate of world population growth is slowing, the world's population will continue to increase for many years.

Section 3: The Urban Transition

Main Idea: The first preindustrial cities developed in fertile areas where surplus food could be growth. With the Industrial Revolution came a major increase in the rate of urbanization. The development of factories was an especially important influence on the location of cities. Urbanization in developed and developing nations has occurred at different speeds. The United States is now primarily a suburban nation.

Section 4: Urban Ecology

Main Idea: Urban ecologists have developed four major theories of city growth: concentric zone theory, sector theory, multiple nuclei theory, and peripheral theory.

SOCIOLOGY Online

Self-Check Quiz
Visit the *Sociology and You* Web site at soc.glencoe.com and click on **Chapter 16—Self-Check Quizzes** to prepare for the chapter test.

Reviewing Vocabulary

Complete each sentence using each term once.

a. demography
b. fertility
c. fecundity
d. crude birth rate
e. fertility rate
f. mortality
g. crude death rate
h. infant mortality rate
i. migration
j. doubling time
k. replacement level
l. urban ecology

1. ____________ is the number of children born to a woman or a population of women.
2. The annual number of live births per one thousand women aged fifteen to forty-four is called ____________.
3. ____________ refers to the deaths within a population.
4. The annual number of deaths per one thousand members of a population is called ____________.
5. ____________ is the annual number of deaths among infants under the age of one per one thousand live births.
6. The number of years needed to double the base population is known as the ____________.
7. ____________ is the birth rate at which a couple replaces itself without adding to the population.
8. The scientific study of population is called ____________.
9. The study of relationships between humans and their city environments is called ____________.
10. ____________ is the movement of people from one geographic area to another.
11. The annual number of live births per one thousand members of a population is called ____________.
12. ____________ is the maximum rate at which women can physically produce children.

561

Depot will enter a quiet suburb, offering a wide selection of items at considerably lower prices than local businesses can afford. Before long, the local businesses are forced to close their doors, despite the length of time they have been in the community, and despite the superior, personalized customer service they offer. The result is an increasingly homogenized suburban culture.

Ask your students to write a brief opinion piece stating whether or not they are in favor of superstores moving into neighborhoods. Are better goods and prices worth the loss of community?
L2

ANSWERS CHAPTER 16 ASSESSMENT

Reviewing Vocabulary

1. b	**5.** h	**9.** l
2. e	**6.** j	**10.** i
3. f	**7.** k	**11.** d
4. g	**8.** a	**12.** c

Reviewing the Facts

1. Students should list and describe fertility, mortality, and migration.
2. Suburbanization is the loss of population from the central city to the surrounding areas; the trend of the central cities to lose their populations to the outer areas surrounding the central cities.
3. Education of the poor. Universal education.
4. Population momentum is the inability to stop population growth *immediately* because of the previous high rate of growth (i.e., because it is already in motion).
5. Zero population is the point at which there is a balance between the number of deaths and the number of births. Replacement level is the rate at which people replace themselves

ANSWERS CHAPTER 16 ASSESSMENT

without adding to the population. When the replacement level is actually reached it will be equal to zero population.

6. Students should list and explain concentric zone theory, sector theory, multiple nuclei theory, and peripheral theory.

Thinking Critically

1. Some students will see immigration as a problem, but should also realize it is less ethnicity and race, and more social class that is a predictor of family size and thus population growth.
2. Transplants, pharmaceutical products, in-vitro fertilization, etc. are contributing to the increase in population through longer life spans and more births, as the death rate is being lowered by medical advances.
3. Answers will vary.
4. Distribution of resources is key. As areas experience natural disasters, food will have to be supplied there. Famine can be averted if coordination efforts exist to move food from areas of surplus to where it is needed.
5. Research has shown that higher levels of education are correlated to smaller family size. Student opinions about how effectively education can balance cultural and societal norms will differ.
6. Durkheim would have concluded that social cohesion (see Chapter 2) would decrease the likelihood of suicide. Vice versa, the lack of social integration in urban areas would create an anomic situation, increasing the risk of suicide.
7. By definition, a municipality is required to provide certain services in order for a community of 2500 to qualify as a city. Students might want to determine what those services entail.

Sociology Projects

1. This project is the also the Lead-Off activity for this chapter. If students have not already done this activity, have them do so now. Provide them with the web sites mentioned in the Networthy feature on page 540.

CHAPTER 16 ASSESSMENT

Reviewing the Facts

1. Identify and describe the three population processes. Use a diagram similar to the one below to record your answers.

Process	Description
1.	
2.	
3.	

2. What is suburbanization?
3. What was Thomas Malthus' solution for overpopulation?
4. In your own words, explain population momentum.
5. What is the difference between replacement level and zero population growth?
6. List and explain the four major theories of city growth.

Thinking Critically

1. **Making Generalizations** The United States is actually nearing zero population growth—except for the influx of immigrants. Recall from your history or government classes as many of the benefits and disadvantages of open immigration as you can and discuss them in class. Do you think immigration should be a factor in considering methods of controlling population? Why or why not?
2. **Drawing Conclusions** Sometime in October 1999, the world population reached six billion. As you read in the chapter, the population is expected to reach seven billion by 2010. How are technological improvements contributing to this rapid growth?
3. **Analyzing Information** Technology has been credited with increasing population growth. In what ways might it be employed to slow down the rate of population growth?
4. **Making Inferences** One of the great debates concerning population growth is whether there is enough food to supply the world. Some argue that, each year, tons of food supplies sit in bins waiting to be used but are wasted because there is no way to get the supplies where they are needed. Others argue that we can raise agricultural productivity no higher and will soon be unable to feed the world. What factors affect the availability of food in developing nations? In industrial and postindustrial societies?
5. **Drawing Conclusions** Universal education, according to Thomas Malthus, could be the great equalizer in raising the quality of life for all human beings. As a budding sociologist, would you agree with Malthus that education is the only real solution to current world problems? Would universal education really level the playing field for all? Explain your views.
6. **Making Inferences** Emile Durkheim was concerned about the changes brought on by the Industrial Revolution. He studied suicide rates and found them to be higher in urban areas. What factors might contribute to higher suicide rates in urban areas that would not be factors in rural areas? Do you think Durkheim's findings hold today, or is the likelihood of suicide just as great in rural and suburban areas?
7. **Applying Concepts** By U.S. Census Bureau definition, a population of 2,500 qualifies a community to be called a city. What are some factors that clearly distinguish communities of 2,500 from places such as Los Angeles and New York? Do you consider your community to be a city in the modern sense? Why or why not?

Sociology Projects

1. **Doubling Time** Choose a country and find its doubling time. Then, using the library or multimedia sources, identify reasons for that country's doubling time. Consider some of the variables mentioned in the text, such as infant mortality rate, wars, and epidemics. Be prepared to give a brief oral report to the class on your findings.

2. **The Effects of Doubling Time** Review the analogy of the chessboard given on page 538 of the text. Now, get a calculator and draw a chessboard with sixty-four squares. Starting with one "person" on the first square, start doubling the number of people for each square. At what point do the numbers become unmanageable? How does this little demonstration illustrate the effects of doubling time?
3. **Demographic Transition** Pick another country. Of the four stages of demographic transition described on pages 539–540, which one best reflects the country you chose? What are the factors that caused you to place the country at this stage?
4. **Theories of Urban Growth** Obtain a map of a large city in your area. (If you live in a fairly large city, use a map of it.) By looking at the map, can you determine if patterns of growth in this city proceeded according to one of the theories of urban growth described in the chapter? If so, take a marker and illustrate the patterns on the map. You might also talk with people in the city who have some knowledge of how the city changed over time, such as the local historical society, city clerks, or a local sociologist. Try to find out what growth pattern the city followed.
5. **Social Institutions** By definition, all communities have the following social institutions: family, education, science/technology, politics, religion, sports, and economy. Locate a map of your community (city hall is a good source for these maps). With two or three classmates, pick a part of town for the focus of your project. In the part of town you chose, take a photograph of at least one example of each type of institution. For the family, for instance, you might take a picture of a house. Look to see how many of the institutions are in your chosen neighborhood, and then bring back some item or souvenir from each of the institutions, if possible. For example, if you select a restaurant (economic institution) you might bring back a menu. *Be sure to ask permission for everything you take.* Present your photos and souvenirs to the class on a poster board.
6. **World Population Growth** Talk with some older people in your family or neighborhood about how the growing world population has affected them. Ask them to identify some changes that have taken place since 1960 (when the world population was only three billion). Write down their comments in the form of a script, as if you were interviewing them for a magazine article.
7. **Urban Planning** Choose three classmates to join you as members of the Urban Planning Board of Betterville, USA. As members of the Urban Planning Board, it is your task to jointly design the city for redevelopment. Examine the four major theories of city growth. Determine which theory or combination of theories you would use to design Betterville. Create a visual representation of your city design (e.g., blueprint, chart, artist rendering, etc.). Write a one-page essay explaining the theory or combination of theories that you chose and the rationale for your choice.

Technology Activity

1. William Julius Wilson, a sociologist at Harvard University, has done extensive research on what the text calls the central-city dilemma. The Public Broadcasting System (PBS) sponsored an on-line forum with Dr. Wilson, called "A Look at the Truly Disadvantaged." Go to this web site at http://www.pbs.org/newshour/forum/november96/wilson_11-29.html and select "Why is inner city education so poor?"
   - **a.** What is to blame for the poor results often obtained in inner city schools, according to Dr. Wilson?
   - **b.** Now select "How can inner cities be reconnected to the rest of American society?" What are Dr. Wilson's recommendations for solving the central-city dilemma?
   - **c.** Read some of the "Viewer comments." Do you agree or disagree with any of the comments shown there? What do you think could be done to solve the problems in inner cities?

563

2. Some of your math whizzes may appreciate the challenge presented by this classic problem.
3. Answers will depend completely on the countries students choose.
4. Here students will be considering the concentric zone theory, sector theory or multiple nuclei theory. They will need to know a little about the history of the city they are analyzing.
5. Students usually have fun creating photo essays. This activity gives them the opportunity to see the institutions that comprise a neighborhood. They might consider making this into a video presentation also.
6. These interviews can take on several forms. Some might cover how neighborhoods have changed; others will focus on the growth of communities and how some current neighborhoods didn't exist 30 years ago.
7. Answers will vary. Designs should incorporate one of the major theories of city growth. Visuals should reflect placement of banks, other businesses, residential areas, transportation networks, etc.

Technology Activity

1. At the time of printing, answers to this question were as follows:
   - a. The problem is related to the way in which public education is organized in the United States. The quality of local public schools is in large measure related to the resources of local governments.
   - b. The best way would be through proposals that achieve the objective of city-suburban cooperation. These range from proposals to create metropolitan governments, to proposals for metropolitan tax base sharing (currently in effect in Minneapolis/St. Paul) and collaborative metropolitan planning.
   - c. Student answers will vary.

Enrichment Reading

Discuss with students the following questions regarding the elderly.

1. Does "development" continue after age 60 or is this final period of life marked only by "decline"? Give some examples.
2. What does your community do to promote full and active lives for the elderly?
3. What jobs are available for the elderly?
4. Have elderly relatives, neighbors, or friends had a positive impact on your life? How?
5. What are the advantages and disadvantages of mandatory retirement?
6. What can you do to make a difference in the life of the elderly?

Integrating the Teacher Resources

Additional primary source readings for this chapter can be found in Culture Studies: The Sociological Perspective**, available in your Teacher's Resource Box. Questions for students are included.**

Chapter 16

Enrichment Reading

Life Expectancy: Surprising Demographic Trends

by David Stipp

Baby boomers have ushered in most every major trend over the past 50 years. But it was their grandparents who initiated the most radical demographic change of the past half-century—a dramatic decline in death rates at older ages. In fact, about the time boomers were rambunctiously burning draft cards, their elders quietly began **nullifying actuarial tables.** By 1990 there were more than 1.5 million Americans age 85 and over who wouldn't have been alive if death rates had stayed at the 1960 level.

Extrapolating this trend, demographer James Vaupel has made a bold prediction: Half of the girls and a third of the boys recently born in the developed world will live to be 100. Vaupel similarly expects millions of former flower children to defy federal population forecasts and make good on their old chant, "Hell no, we won't go!"—he has projected there could be nearly 37 million boomers age 85 and over by 2050, more than twice the government's best guess. That would mean a much higher proportion of senior citizens nationwide than Florida has today. . . .

Vaupel [is] no shallow visionary. A few years ago many of his colleagues scoffed when he challenged a grim **canon** about aging. It holds that death rates rise exponentially with age in adult animals, including humans—the older you are, the theory goes, the more likely you are to die. Aided by other researchers, he marshaled data on everything from Swedish women to Medflies to show it ain't so; for good measure, he threw in supporting data on the death rates of old cars. The team demonstrated that mortality can plateau and, strangely, even drop among the very old—as if the Fates were nodding off after a long wait.

Vaupel sees this "mortality deceleration" as a subplot of a grand mystery that has preoccupied demographers for over a decade: Why have the elderly been living longer than their forebears since about 1970? Some of the causes are obvious, such as the **averting** of millions of fatal heart attacks by blood-pressure drugs widely used since the 1960s. But many experts on aging feel that such well-known factors can't explain the trend's surprising speed and breadth. . . .

Casting about for explanations, some demographers theorize that deep, little-understood changes are afoot that will help sustain the trend for decades. Vaupel has stuck his neck out farther than most by proposing that the aging process may actually slow down in very old people, an idea based on his mortality-deceleration work. That particular idea remains highly controversial. But Vaupel's **bullish** view that longevity gains will continue apace is widely shared. Indeed, many demographers are now more bullish than the Social Security Administration, which projects that the decline in old-age death rates will slow to a crawl early in the next century.

The bulls' predictions raise a burning issue: If we receive a gift of extra years, will it turn out to be a **Pandora's box** filled with hobbling diseases? For most of this century death rates and the prevalence of chronic diseases among the elderly have dropped in tandem. But "we're balanced on a razor's edge," says Eric Stallard, a demography professor at Duke University. If medical advances make mortality fall faster than disease, we'll wind up spending costly extra years in nursing homes. Or worse: "We may face the gruesome prospect of poor, disabled, homeless older Americans living out the end of their lives on city streets and in parks," warns Edward L. Schneider, dean of gerontology at the University of South Carolina.

Source: Adapted from David Stipp, "Hell No, We Won't Go," *Fortune,* July 19, 1999: 102, 104.

This active older couple is enjoying the increasing longevity in modern society. What are some of the most important consequences of this trend?

What Does it Mean?

averting
turning aside; avoiding

bullish
optimistic; encouraging

canon
an accepted principle or rule

extrapolating
projecting known data into an area not known or experienced

nullifying actuarial tables
reversing current population trends

Pandora's box
source of many troubles (based on a Greek myth about a box of evils released by a curious woman who had been instructed not to open the box)

Read and React

1. What is the surprising demographic trend referred to in the title of this article?
2. What has happened to the death rates in the United States since 1960?
3. What is meant by the term *mortality deceleration?*
4. What are some positive and negative effects an aging population would have on the social structure of this country?

Answers to Read and React

1. The death rate among Americans age 85 and older is declining.
2. Death rates in the United States have declined since 1960.
3. Vaupel says that mortality can plateau and even drop among the very old, something he calls mortality deceleration.
4. Student answers will vary. They might note that an increase in the elderly population, will lower the dependency ratio of workers for elders. There may not be enough money in Social Security to take care of the elders so more may live in poverty, etc.

Chapter Preview

Section 1 (pages 568–577)

Social change refers to new behaviors that have long-term and relatively important consequences. Discovery, invention, and diffusion are the major social processes through which social change occurs. Important sources of social change are technology, population, the natural environment, revolution, and war.

Section 2 (pages 578–580)

The functionalist and conflict perspectives view social change in very different ways. The functionalist perspective depicts societies as relatively stable. Following a major change, these integrated systems seek a new equilibrium. According to the conflict perspective, societies are unstable systems that are constantly undergoing change.

Section 3 (pages 581–590)

Collective behavior describes how people behave when they are united by a single short-term goal. Rumors, facts, fashions, mass-hysteria, and panics are examples of collective behaviors. Crowds gather and behave in different ways depending on the stimuli and conditions present. Contagion theory and emergent norm theory describe crowd behavior.

Section 4 (pages 591–596)

Social movements are more permanent and more organized than other types of collectivities. Theories to explain how social movements develop include value-added theory and resource mobilization theory.

CHAPTER 17

Social Change and Collective Behavior

Lead-Off Activity

To help students become familiar with the meaning of social change, have them do the following activity.

Ask students to talk with someone they know who is from an earlier generation, such as their grandparents or parents (grandparents would be best). Students should ask the person the following questions:

What was life like when you were a teenager? Specifically, what were each of the following like?

- School
- Family life
- Career plans
- Leisure activities
- The area in which you live

USING Your Sociological Imagination

When you see photos or films showing the Plains Indians of the Old West—Sioux, Crow, and so forth—what do you think about the culture of those Native Americans? If you're like most of us, you may assume that it had remained unchanged for many centuries—that these people dressed and acted in exactly the same way as their ancestors.

We often assume that nonindustrial societies such as these stand still over time. Actually, though, sociology teaches us that change comes to all societies. Whether by borrowing from other cultures, discovering new ways of doing things, or creating inventions that ripple through society, all peoples experience social change.

Let's return to the example of the Plains Indians. You may picture these tribes as fierce, buffalo-hunting warriors. Perhaps images of Sitting Bull and Crazy Horse astride fast horses attacking Custer come to mind, leading you to think that their ancestors for centuries had also ridden horses. In fact, horses were a relatively recent introduction to Plains Indian culture in the 1800s. The Spanish brought modern horses to North America, and not until the late 1600s and early 1700s were horses available in large numbers to the Plains Indians. Early Native American tribes on the Plains had been nomads living more off wild food plants than buffalo. This chapter will examine different ways change affects society.

Sections

1. **Social Change**
2. **Theoretical Perspectives on Social Change**
3. **Collective Behavior**
4. **Social Movements**

Learning Objectives

After reading this chapter, you will be able to

- illustrate the three social processes that contribute to social change.
- discuss how technology, population, natural environment, revolution, and war cause cultures to change.
- describe social change as viewed by the functionalist and conflict perspectives.
- discuss rumors, fads, and fashions.
- compare and contrast theories of crowd behavior.
- compare and contrast theories of social movements.

SOCIOLOGY Online

Chapter Overview
Visit the *Sociology and You* Web site at soc.glencoe.com and click on **Chapter 17—Chapter Overviews** to preview chapter information.

USING Your Sociological Imagination

To help students understand the concept of diffusion, have them brainstorm and list elements of other cultures that have crept into American culture. For instance, many people today identify with the Native Americans' concept of stewardship of the earth and the Japanese idea of Feng Shui. (Feng Shui devotees believe that physical placement of objects affect spirituality and composure. This practice is becoming popular in some areas of the country.) What elements of other cultures that have diffused into our own can students describe?

After students have gathered answers to the questions, they should compare the answers to their own experiences. Ask them to answer these questions.

- How is your life different from the person you talked with?
- How is it similar?
- Do these differences reflect social change? In what way?
- What caused the changes? Changes in social institutions? Technology? The environment?

Have students discuss their answers as a class.
L1

Using the Section Preview

Have students create a time line based on the 365-day calendar of history discussed on this page. You might want to have students work in small groups, or you can have the entire class work on one time line. Display the completed time lines in your classroom.

Points to Stress

Social change sometimes brings about unforseen or "mixed bag" effects. Although society attempts to make changes for the better, sometimes unforeseen negative results of these changes can come back to haunt us. For example, in the 1950s a drug called Thalidomide was widely prescribed to ease the suffering of pregnant women. Thalidomide proved to cause numerous severe birth defects. Today, anti-psychotic drugs improve daily psychological functioning for thousands of people, but can produce adverse side effects. In yet another example, affirmative action has created great educational and career opportunities for minorities and women. However, it has also resulted in a growing stigma against women and minorities in schools and the workplace, who may be perceived as less qualified than others. Have students consider other social policies that seem to have these boomerang or mixed bag effects.

Section 1

Social Change

Key Terms

- social change
- social processes
- discovery
- invention
- diffusion
- technology
- revolution
- war

Section Preview

Social change refers to new behaviors that have long-term and relatively important consequences. Discovery, invention, and diffusion are the major social processes through which social change occurs. Important agents of social change are technology, population, the natural environment, revolution, and war.

social change
new societal behaviors with important long-term consequences

Defining Social Change

Change is one of the most constant features of American society. This is so true that it is almost a cliché. In fact, all societies change—some rapidly, others more slowly. For sociologists, **social change** occurs when many members of the society adopt new behaviors. The behaviors must have long-term and important consequences.

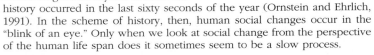

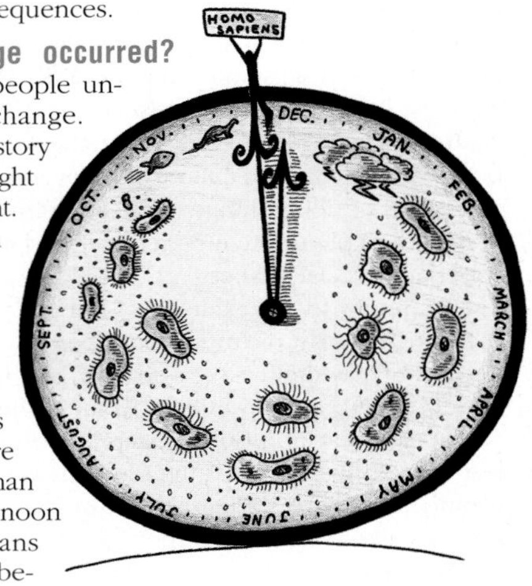

How fast has social change occurred? Scientists use an analogy to help people understand the pace of social change. Imagine for a moment the entire history of Earth as a 365-day period. Midnight of January 1 is the starting point. Today's date is December 31. Each Earth "day" represents about twelve million years. The first form of life, a simple bacterium, appeared in February. More complex life, such as fish, appeared about November 20. On December 10, the dinosaurs appeared; by Christmas they were extinct. The first recognizable human beings did not appear until the afternoon of December 31. Modern humans *(homo sapiens)* emerged shortly before midnight that day. All of recorded history occurred in the last sixty seconds of the year (Ornstein and Ehrlich, 1991). In the scheme of history, then, human social changes occur in the "blink of an eye." Only when we look at social change from the perspective of the human life span does it sometimes seem to be a slow process.

Can social change be predicted? It is difficult to predict how a society will change. This is partly because the course of change in a society depends on the nature of the existing culture. For example, two societies that adopt a democratic form of government may develop in very different ways. Both Britain and the United States are democracies. But their histories prior to becoming democracies were different, since Britain had a royal tradition. As a result, democratic government took different forms in these two nations.

Learning Styles

Linguistic/Spatial There are many vocabulary terms and concepts to learn in this information-rich chapter. With students working alone or with a partner, give them time to choose (or you may want to assign) one particular term or concept. Ask students to prepare a graphic illustration of some type to present the concept to the class. Presentations can be two- or three-dimensional, electronic, or paper-based, etc. To review the content of the chapter, allow class time for presentations. Extra credit could be given for students who incorporate some form of sociological research (e.g. a survey) into their presentation. This activity can be adapted to serve as a review for the final exam for the class.
L1

Figure 17.1 Key Assumptions in Predicting Social Change in America

The most accurate predictor of trends in American society has been the Frenchman Alexis de Tocqueville. Tocqueville's *Democracy in America,* which was published in the 1830s, displayed an amazing grasp of American society. Tocqueville's success has been attributed to several key assumptions he made. Do you think that any of these assumptions are less important today in predicting social change than the others?

1. **Major social institutions would continue to exist.** Unlike many of his contemporaries—and many of ours—Tocqueville did not expect the family, religion, or the state to disappear or to be greatly changed.
2. **Human nature would remain the same.** Tocqueville did not expect men and women to become much better or worse or different from what history had shown them to be.
3. **Equality and the trend toward centralized government would continue.**
4. **The availability of material resources (such as land, minerals, and rich soils) limits and directs social change.**
5. **Change is affected by the past, but history does not strictly dictate the future.**
6. **There are no social forces aside from human actions.** Historical events are not foreordained by factors beyond human control.

Adapted from Theodore Caplow, *American Social Trends* (New York: Harcourt Brace Jovanovich, 1991), p. 216.

In addition, change does not merely "happen" to people. People in a society can consciously decide for themselves how change will occur. They can, for example, deliberately avoid a predicted state of affairs (Caplow, 1991).

These facts should not discourage people from attempting to understand changes in society. Alexis de Tocqueville was a Frenchman who published a remarkably penetrating study of American society after a tour in the early 1830s. The accuracy of his predictions was based upon sound assumptions he made about American society. Figure 17.1 discusses these basic premises.

> The past is a foreign country. They do things differently there.
>
> **L.P. Hartley**
> **short story author**

Why do some societies change faster than others? Understanding why some societies change faster than others is another difficult task. Sociologists have identified several important social processes that influence the pace of social change. In addition, several specific factors play important roles. We turn first to the social processes and then to the specific agents, or factors, that affect rates of change.

Social Processes

A process is a series of steps that lead gradually to a result. As you get closer to graduation from high school, you may decide to continue your formal education. You will then begin a process of applying for acceptance to various colleges. If you follow all the steps in the necessary order and meet the colleges' criteria for entrance, the end result of your application process will be an acceptance letter.

Working with the Data

Figure 17.1 Answers will vary. (1) Social institutions tend to maintain the status quo. (2) Students may debate whether or not human nature has changed—it would be hard to prove that it had, especially in the short time since Tocqueville wrote. (3) More social equality exists than ever before. (4) Resources are in abundant supply but there is the concern that eventually these resources will be depleted. (5) Humans have tremendous ability to dictate their future and are not necessarily caught in patterns of the past. (6) Human agency also exists, which is the ability of one individual to have profound influence on society. This last point will probably elicit the most student comment.

Survey

On the popular television show *Ally McBeal,* many of the scenes take place in a company unisex bathroom. This example brings up an opportunity to discuss the idea of whether equality of opportunity means sameness and conformity or whether it means not letting biology dictate social and economic destiny. Are unisex bathrooms really a part of equality of opportunity? Have students conduct a survey about the possibilities of creating unisex bathrooms in public buildings. Where might it be appropriate? Where would it be inappropriate? Ask students if they feel unisex bathrooms take social change too far. Might there be practical reasons for unisex bathrooms that would justify their creation? **L1**

Rapid social change means that generations do not share certain knowledge. Besides "snail-mail," what are some other products or technologies that might become obsolete?

Cultures and societies experience **social processes** that result in significant changes. Three important social processes are *discovery, invention,* and *diffusion.*

How does discovery promote social change? In the **discovery** process, something is either learned or reinterpreted. When early ocean explorers did not fall off the end of the world, they changed what all but a few people believed about the shape of the earth. With this geographical knowledge came new patterns of migration, commerce, and colonization. Salt, another early discovery, was first used to flavor food. Because it was so highly valued, it also came to be used as money in Africa and as a religious offering among early Greeks and Romans. Fire was used at first by prehistoric peoples for warmth and cooking. Later, people discovered that fire could be used to clear fields, to create ash for fertilizer, and to melt ores to combine into new metals.

social processes
series of steps leading to change on a societal level

discovery
process by which something is learned or reinterpreted

invention
the creation of something new from previously existing items or processes

diffusion
process by which one culture or society borrows from another culture or society

What is the role of invention in social change? **Invention** is the creation of something new from items or processes that already exist. Examples of physical inventions come easily to mind. Consider the airplane. It was not so much the materials Orville and Wilbur Wright used—most of the parts were available—but the way the brothers combined these materials that enabled them to make their successful flight at Kitty Hawk.

The pace of social change through invention is closely tied to how complex the society or culture already is. The greater the number of existing items, or elements, the more ways they can be combined into inventions. Thus, the more complex and varied a society, the more rapidly it will change. This helps to explain why people reached the moon less than seventy years after the Wright brothers' first flight, even though scientists believe that several million years had passed between the appearance of the human species and the invention of the airplane. NASA was able to reach the moon relatively quickly because the United States had become advanced in such areas as physics, aerodynamics, and the manufacturing of specialized materials.

How important is diffusion in social change? When one group borrows something from another group—norms, values, foods, styles of architecture—change occurs through the process of **diffusion.** The extent and rate of diffusion depend on the degree of social contact. The more contact a group has with another group, the more likely it is that objects or ideas will be exchanged. In other words, social contact has the same effect on diffusion that complexity has on invention.

Borrowing may involve entire societies. The American colonists learned methods of growing cotton that were first developed in India. Potatoes from South America were transplanted across the Atlantic to become Ireland's most important food crop. Diffusion may also take place between groups within the same society. African American musicians were the creators of a jazz subculture that spread throughout white America (and into other countries as well).

Using the Illustration

Ask students if they think there is a generation gap here, or if Dad is just not up on the latest inventions. What inventions do students use that their parents might not use?

More About . . . the Internet

The first Internet exchanges began in 1969 under the authority of the U.S. Department of Defense. It was known as ARPAnet, a worldwide network of computers linking university scientists, military, and computer experts. ARPAnet was seen as a Cold War mechanism to defend the United States against the threat of communism. Eventually the system linked universities, government facilities, and corporations around the world, all of whom shared the costs and technical work of running the system.

Integrating the Teacher Resources

Look for the Chapter 17 Learning Goals Outline, a reproducible student worksheet in the Unit 5 Mastering Basic Concepts **booklet in your Teacher's Resource Box. It can be used to preview or review chapter content.**

Survey

This activity is similar to the Lead-Off Activity on page 566, however, it focuses more specifically on technology.

For this activity, students should interview at least two people; one person in their parents' generation, and one person in their grandparents' generation. (If it's possible for students to interview someone in their eighties or nineties, the answers will be even more dramatic.) Students should ask the interviewees to list the technological changes they have seen within their life-

By which social process did this image of Elvis reach Jerusalem, Israel?

Before it is widely accepted, a borrowed element must harmonize with the group culture. In spite of the fact that unisex fashion is popular in America today, wearing a Scottish kilt on the job could get a construction worker laughed off the top of a skyscraper. Wearing kilts still clashes with the American definition of manhood. If skirts are ever to become as acceptable for American men as pants are for women, either their form will have to be modified or the cultural concept of masculinity will have to change.

Diffusion may involve using only part of a borrowed characteristic or trait. The Japanese, for example, accept capitalism but resist the American form of democratic government, style of conducting business, and family structure. Diffusion almost always involves picking and choosing.

In modern society, most aspects of culture are borrowed rather than created. The processes of discovery and invention are important, but usually far more elements enter a society through cultural diffusion.

Technology

Besides the three processes for social change, sociologists have identified some major forces that lead to change. **Technology** includes knowledge and hardware (tools) that are used to achieve practical goals. The appearance of new technology is generally a sign that social change will soon follow (MacKenzie and Wajcman, 1998).

technology
knowledge and tools used to achieve practical goals

How important is technology to social change? Technology is a prime promoter of social change. *Time* magazine's selection of Albert Einstein as the man of the century reflected the magazine's conclusion that the twentieth century will be remembered most for its advances in science and technology (Golden, 1999).

The creation of the silicon chip, which led to the computer revolution, has brought about technological change at an astounding rate. It took more than a century for telephones to spread to 94 percent of the homes

Using the Illustration

Elvis is one of the most widely diffused U.S. cultural icons of the 20th century. Ask students to suggest others. *(the Coca-cola trademark; the Statue of Liberty.)*

Teaching Strategy

To show students how they take technology for granted, have them perform the following activity. Sit in a car for 10 minutes with the engine shut off. Don't listen to the radio or operate anything else. Observe what you think and feel. Secondly, find an area free of traffic (such as an empty parking lot) and drive the car for 10 minutes, but go no faster than 10 miles an hour. Again, observe what you think and feel. Lastly, turn off all electrical or electronic appliances in your house and sit for 10 minutes, observing what goes on inside you and outside you. Write your reactions down and share with the class the following day. Address this question: are we so used to technology that performing without it or in limited capacity causes cognitive dissonance?
L1

times. They may need to prompt the interviewees by asking for specific changes such as:

- Transportation
- Communication
- Entertainment
- Kitchen and household appliances
- Health care

Students should also ask interviewees how they think these technological changes changed society. Did the changes make society better? Why or why not?
L1

Controversy and Debate

Have students discuss what the costs will be of supporting the baby boomer generation as they reach old age. Remind them that many of their teachers fall into this category. Have students research the dilemmas that all societies face when a large segment of its population becomes economically dependent.

Teaching Strategy

If your schedule allows, you may want to tell students about the role of technology in modernization according to the conflict perspective.

According to modernization theory, technological change has brought much of the world from a state of generalized poverty to high productivity and levels of living. Therefore, the answer to global poverty is the promotion of technological change in poor countries. World-systems theory is not so optimistic. Advocates contend that the world is divided into "core" nations (highly skilled labor force, high standard of living) and "peripheral" nations (low skill levels, low standard of living). Peripheral nations are said to be economically retarded in part because of their domination and exploitation by core nations. Consequently, perpetuation of the gap between core and peripheral nations is ensured.

in the United States. In contrast, in less than five years the Internet had reached over 25 percent of Americans. (See page 29 for a comparison of the number of years it took for various technologies to be adopted in U.S. households.)

The changes that resulted from the use of computers are almost impossible to list. In 1999, social historian Francis Fukuyama described a workplace undergoing a transformation. The effects of these changes, he claims, will be as great as those of the Industrial Revolution. Telecommunications technology, for example, will allow many to work from their homes, but it will result in far less human interaction (McGinn and Raymond, 1997–98). In the field of medicine, computer technology has radically changed many surgical techniques. Microsurgeries and radio wave therapy are examples (Cowley and Underwood, 1997–98). Drivers in Germany can get real-time computer-generated information on traffic problems on the autobahn by using cell phones or electronic consoles in their cars.

These college students at a campus cyber café seem very comfortable with the fast pace of technological change in American society.

Population

Changing demographics are another important factor for creating social change. A classic example is the huge increase in the birth of babies following the return of American soldiers at the end of World War II (the so-called baby boom). Americans born between 1946 and 1964 caused the expansion of child healthcare facilities and created the need for more teachers and schools in the 1950s and 1960s. On the other hand, the generation following baby boomers now in their thirties and in the labor market are experiencing increased competition for jobs and fewer opportunities to move up the career ladder. As the baby boomers retire, problems of health care and Social Security loom large. Longer working hours, retraining programs, and reeducation for older people will probably become political issues for future elections. As America's population continues to age, more attention is being paid to our senior citizens. Already, there are more extended-care homes, an increase in geriatric emphasis in medicine, and more television advertising and programming targeting the aging elderly population.

In 1986, the Chernobyl nuclear plant in Ukraine had a meltdown. This event added to opposition in the U.S. to using nuclear power as an energy source.

The Natural Environment

Interaction with the natural environment has, from the earliest times, also transformed American life. The vast territory west of the thirteen colonies permitted the nation to expand, ultimately to the Pacific Ocean. This western movement helped shape our cultural identity and values. It also caused untold changes, most tragically the destruction of many Native American cultures.

The environment continued to shape historical events, especially when natural disasters occurred. The Great Depression of the 1930s was due in part to a long drought that hit the Midwestern plains states. Overplanting and plowing had upset the fragile ecosystem and turned the prairies into a giant "dust bowl."

Learning Styles

Bodily-kinesthetic/Interpersonal Ask students to imagine with you that a device has been discovered that allows for unlimited travel by humans. This device will allow users to become time travelers, going into the past or into the future. Divide students into groups. Assign each group to select (or you assign) a time and place to which they would like to travel. Each group should outline a rough sketch of what they believe will happen when the traveler arrives. Allow each group to present their skit. Discuss the ramifications of time travel. What kind of difference might it make to the society that

Another Time

The Horse Among the Plains Indians

Diffusion is one of the social processes that creates social change. The society of the Plains Indians in the west central United States was altered drastically by the European introduction of the horse—an example of diffusion.

In the nineteenth century, horses were the primary means of transportation and as such were an integral part of Plains Indian culture. The modern horse, however, was not native to the Americas, but was first brought by the Spanish. It was not until the late 1600s and early 1700s that horses in any numbers became available to the tribes of the Great Plains. . . .

The horse truly revolutionized life among the Plains tribes. The horse drastically altered the economic base and changed the lifestyle of these peoples. On horseback a hunter armed with bow and arrow could find and kill enough bison within a few months to feed his family for the year. Not only could he kill larger numbers of game animals, but he could pack the meat onto horses and readily transport it vast distances. Horses also allowed for the transporting of increased quantities of material goods. Teepees increased in size, and clothing and other material items became increasingly abundant and elaborate in decoration. For the first time these widely scattered groups could gather together in large camps, sometimes numbering in the thousands, for at least a portion of the year. In short, the horse quickly elevated the Plains tribes to relative prosperity.

The horse also sharply altered the relationship between these peoples and the neighboring farming tribes. The once relatively inoffensive nomads were now transformed into aggressive, predatory raiders. The Plains tribes were now capable of quickly assembling large parties of horse-mounted warriors who could raid the sedentary farming villages with impunity. The military balance of power had shifted.

In the decades immediately after the acquisition of the horse, the original Plains tribes flourished. Attacks on the neighboring farming peoples had a devastating effect, and many villages were abandoned. It was not long, however, before many cultivators saw both the economic and the military advantages derived from being horse-mounted nomadic bison hunters. The Cheyenne and some of the Dakota abandoned the life of settled farmers and moved westward to the plains to become nomadic, teepee-dwelling, bison hunters themselves. As they moved onto the plains, they came to challenge directly the original Plains tribes for dominance over critical hunting resources, which intensified warfare. As a result, warfare and the warrior tradition became an integral part of Plains Indian values, social organization, and behavior.

Source: Adapted from James Peoples and Garrick Bailey, *Humanity,* 5th ed. Belmont, CA: Wadsworth, 2000, p. 284.

Thinking It Over

1. List at least five major changes that resulted from the introduction of the horse to the culture of the Plains Indians.
2. Identify an item that has been introduced to your culture from another place. (This item could be food, clothing, an invention, or even an idea.) What effect has it had on your life?

is visited? What if the time traveler couldn't reverse the trip? Would they like to be a time traveler, going along to a new time and/or place? Would it make a difference if two or more people could travel together? If time allows, you might want to show a video of time travel such as one of the *Back to the Future* videos. A more serious (!) look at time travel and social change is the classic by H. G. Welles, *The Time Machine.* Another age appropriate but more contemporary look at time travel is Michael Crichton's *Timeline.*
L2

Another Time

Be sure to mention that some time later other factors also seriously altered the Plains Indians' lifestyle. These factors included the availability of guns, introduction of diseases that did not exist prior to contact with whites, and decline of the buffalo as a resource. All this marked the beginning of the end of a way of life for the Plains Indians.

Answers to Thinking it Over

1. The horse gave the hunter greater mobility. He had the ability to easily transport his kill. The entire village gained mobility, which became important in shifting military power among tribes. Native-Americans began to unify, since the horse allowed travel across the Plains. Horses also allowed them to assemble into larger armies to fight off invaders.
2. Answers will vary.

World View

Ask students why they think Finland has the same ratio of Internet connections as the United States. Then, you might ask student how many people they know who are not connected to the Internet—the answer to this will probably reflect the socioeconomic levels of the school's neighborhoods.

Answers to Interpreting the Map

1. The pattern is related to the industrialization and level of development of the countries. Basically, the more industrialized a country is, the more Internet connections it has. This is pretty predictable, given the reliance of the Internet on telephone connections and technology infrastructures.
2. Student answers will vary, however, they should be aware that social change will likely take place faster in countries with more Internet connections. Remind them that authoritarian governments (see Chapter 13) like China are very concerned about regulating Internet commerce and content.

World View

Internet Connections

As this map shows, the number of people connected to the Internet varies widely from country to country. As of the late 1990s, nearly 60 percent of Internet connections were on the North American continent. This map shows the number of computers connected to the Internet per 100,000 people.

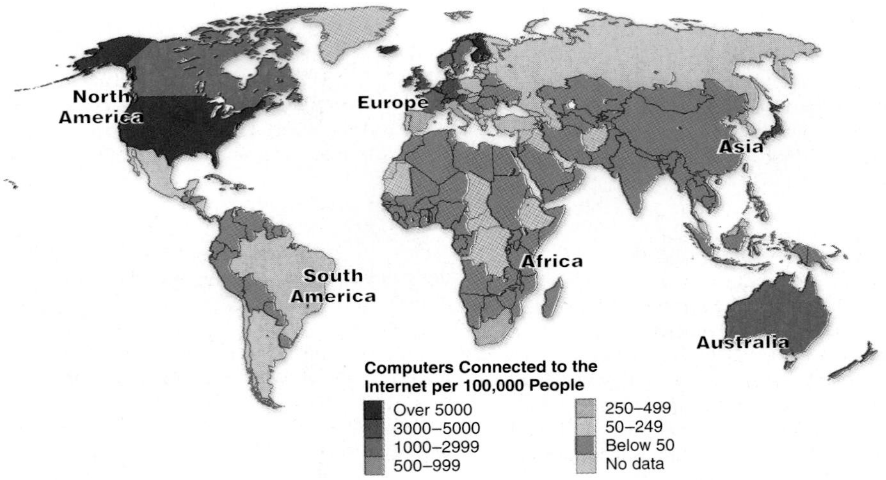

Interpreting the Map

1. Do you see a pattern in the number of connections to the Internet? Explain.
2. What implications might this distribution have for future social change?

Adapted from *Atlas of the Future*. New York: Macmillan, 1998.

In the early 1970s, OPEC (an organization of oil-producing nations) launched an embargo, refusing to sell its oil to other countries. Because of the natural short supply of oil without the contribution of the oil-rich Mideastern countries, oil products became scarce and expensive, contributing to economic inflation in the United States in the 1970s and early 1980s. As a result, Americans began driving smaller, more fuel-efficient automobiles.

Revolution and War

revolution
sudden and complete overthrow of a social or political order

Revolution and war are related factors that lead to social change. A **revolution** involves the sudden and complete overthrow of an existing social or political order. A revolution is often, but not always, accompanied by vio-

Paired Learning Activity

Have pairs of students research the history of the automobile. You might assign pairs to look at a specific decade in the development of the car. Students should look for changes in the design and cost of the car. What was occurring in society at the time to affect the changes? Using the example given in the text, during the oil embargo of the early 1970s, car manufacturers made smaller, more fuel-efficient automobiles. What happened to automobiles during the 1950s and the 1990s when the economy was healthy? (Expansive designs and huge cars in the 50s; in the 90s sport utility vehi-

lence. Most revolutionaries expect that the revolution will bring about fundamental changes. Marx, for example, expected workers' revolutions to eliminate class-based inequality and therefore to have a profound effect on the social and economic structures of the societies in which they occurred.

Are revolutions normally followed by radical changes? According to Charles Tilly, a revolution results in the replacement of one set of power holders by another (Tilly, 1978, 1997). In the view of another respected sociologist, a post-revolutionary society is eventually replaced by a society that looks much like the original one (Brinton, 1990). Radical changes are rarely permanent because people tend to revert to more familiar customs and behaviors. They do so in part because continuity with the past provides security and a blueprint for behavior.

Wars often bring about social change because culturally dissimilar societies, such as the U.S. and Kuwait, come into increased contact.

What sorts of changes do follow revolutions? In most cases, the new social order created by a successful revolution is likely to be a compromise between the new and the old. Consider the example of China, the site of a communist revolution in the 1940s. The revolution has not resulted in the wholesale changes promised by its leaders. One of the revolutionary reforms, for example, promised liberation from sexism. The situation for Chinese women has improved, but sexual equality is a far-distant dream in that country ("Closing the Gap," 1995).

How does war promote social change? **War** is organized, armed conflict that occurs within a society or between nations. Sociologist Robert Nisbet (1989) described how war brings about social change through diffusion discovery, and invention. Social change is created through diffusion because wars break down barriers between societies, bringing people from different societies together. This association leads to the adoption of new ways of thinking, feeling, and behaving.

war
organized, armed conflict that occurs within a society or between nations

Wars also promote invention and discovery. For example, during World War I (1914–1918), the pressure of war enabled the U.S. government to promote and finance the development of such technologies as the airplane, automobile, nylon, and radio. Each contributed to a cultural revolution after the war. And America's culture, both during and after World War I, was imported by societies all over the world.

> "Every generation revolts against its fathers and makes friends with its grandfathers."
>
> **Lewis Mumford**
> **American author**

Section 1 Assessment

1. Briefly describe three important processes for social change.
2. Provide one example each (not given in the text) of how population and interaction with the natural environment have caused social change.
3. Explain how war can be both a positive and a negative force for social change.

Critical Thinking

4. **Drawing Conclusions** Identify a major social change that has occurred in your lifetime. What do you think are the major sources of this change—discovery, diffusion, or invention? Be careful to relate the manner of change to the *nature* of the change itself.

Answers to Section 1 Assessment

1. The three important processes for social change are discovery, invention, and diffusion.
2. Students could discuss the growing minority populations (especially Latinos) and how they change a city—for example, Little Havana in Miami.
3. War can cause diffusion—barriers are broken down and people from different societies are brought together leading to new ways of thinking, feeling, and behaving; aspects of one society are borrowed by another. Also, invention and discovery are positive forces for social change. (The U.S. government promoted and financed development of such technologies as airplanes, automobiles, nylon, and radio during World War I).
   War is seen as a negative force for social change when it does nothing to alleviate—or even furthers—oppression by not upholding human rights, or when it merely replaces one ineffective government with another. Loss of life and property are usually consequences of war.

Critical Thinking

4. Answers will vary.

cles became the rage and continued to get bigger and bigger.) Ask pairs to share their information with the rest of the class. You might have them combine all of the information into a time line of the history of the automobile to post on the wall of the classroom. Students with artistic abilities could illustrate the changes made to the automobile. Be sure to indicate on the time line what was occurring that caused, or at least affected, the changes.
L2

Focus on Research

Have students return to Chapter 8, Social Stratification, for validation of Katherine Newman's thesis. What proof exists that society is becoming more stratified, making attaining the American dream more and more unrealistic?

Have students talk with their parents and/or grandparents about the American Dream. Do they believe it still exists? Is it still attainable? Do they believe they have achieved it? Why or why not?

Integrating the Teacher Resources

A lesson plan for a student research project related to the content of this chapter can be found in Doing Sociology: Focus on Research, available in your Teacher's Resource Box.

Focus on Research

Case Study: Is the American Dream Dying?

Americans have long expected to achieve a higher standard of living than their parents. Instead, according to Katherine Newman (1994), social and economic change are placing the American Dream in jeopardy. The downscaling of jobs and pay that occurred during the 1980s and 1990s has replaced earlier optimism with anger, doubt, and fear.

Newman spent two years conducting personal interviews with 150 Americans living in "Pleasanton," a suburban community representative of much of America. Pleasanton is a mix of skilled blue-collar workers and white-collar professionals from a variety of ethnic and religious origins. Her respondents were schoolteachers, guidance counselors, and sixty families whose children were then grown.

The residents of Pleasanton believed that the promise of America had taken an unexpected wrong turn, and they were trying to make sense of it. Newman attempted to understand the residents' view of this downward mobility. The stresses associated with changing economic conditions, she believed, would bring cultural expectations, disappointments, and conflicts close enough to the surface for a trained social scientist to see. As the study progressed, she did, in fact, see conflict between parents and grown children, disagreements along lines of race and ethnicity, and unhappy marriages. The following statement reveals a baby boomer's shattered confidence in the American Dream.

> *I'll never have what my parents had. I can't even dream of that. I'm living a lifestyle that's way lower than it was when I was growing up and it's depressing. You know it's a rude awakening when you're out in the world on your own. . . . I took what was given to me and tried to use it the best way I could. Even if you are a hard worker and you never skipped a beat, you followed all the rules, did everything they told you you were supposed to do, it's still horrendous. They lied to me. You don't get where you were supposed to wind up. At the end of the road it isn't there. I worked all those years and then I didn't get to candy land. The prize wasn't there . . . (Newman, 1994:3).*

After a detailed and often personal exploration of what Newman calls the "withering American Dream," she turns to the larger social and political implications for society. She explores the transition from a society of upward mobility based on effort and merit to a society in which social classes of birth increasingly dictate future social and economic positions.

On-Demand Writing

Be sure that students understand what is meant by the "American Dream." This concept means that each person should have, with hard work, the right to expect to succeed and to better themselves or move to a higher position in life. In the past, those who worked hard could achieve the American Dream. Often, people were limited only by their own ambition. Today, however, many people believe that the American Dream is not as attainable as it once was. As indicated in the Focus on Research, despite hard work and sustained effort, many people aren't able to achieve even what their parents have achieved. To some, the American Dream is symbolized

According to Newman, the soul of America is at stake. She raises these questions: Will Americans turn to exclusive self-interest, or will they care for others as well as themselves? Will suburbanites turn a blind eye to the rapidly deteriorating inner cities? Will the generational, racial, and ethnic groups turn inward, or will they attempt to bridge the divides that threaten to separate them further?

A partial answer to these questions is reflected in public opinion about federal, state, and local tax revenues. If the residents of Pleasanton are any guide, Americans do not wish to invest in the common good. Public schools, colleges, universities, and inner cities, for example, are receiving a rapidly declining share of public economic support. In conclusion, Newman states:

> *This does not augur well for the soul of the country in the twenty-first century. Every great nation draws its strength from a social contract, an unspoken agreement to provide for one another, to reach across the narrow self-interests of generations, ethnic groups, races, classes, and genders toward some vision of the common good. Taxes and budgets—the mundane preoccupations of city hall—express this commitment, or lack of it, in the bluntest fashion. Through these mechanistic devices, we are forced to confront some of the most searching philosophical questions that face any country: What do we owe one another as members of a society? Can we sustain a collective sense of purpose in the face of the declining fortunes that are tearing us apart, leaving those who are able to scramble for advantage and those who are not to suffer out of sight? (Newman, 1994:221)*

A former G.E. worker stands in front of signs lamenting the move of a plant from North Carolina to Mexico. This thirty-year veteran of the closing plant would agree that the American dream is dying.

Working with the Research

1. Think about your past experiences at home and in other social institutions (such as schools and churches). What is your conception of the American dream, based on these experiences? Critically analyze the ways in which society shaped your conception.
2. Newman's research was done in the early 1990s. Do you believe that she is right about the fate of the American dream? Explain.
3. If the American dream is withering, many social changes are in store. Describe the major changes you foresee.
4. Suppose Katherine Newman had decided to place her study in the context of sociological theory. Write a conclusion to her book from the theoretical perspective—functionalist, or conflict—that you think is most appropriate.

Answers to Working with the Research

1. Schools teach us that hard work will help us realize our dreams educationally and career wise. We believe that if we live a good life, good things will happen to us. Parents want all the best for their children. All this is part of the American dream.
2. This article examines the post industrial era and its effects on a suburban community of blue collar workers obviously impacted by the changes that have occurred by the shift away from manufacturing.
3. There will be a need for retraining of workers. It will no longer be possible to succeed in the job market with just a high school diploma. Technical skills, computer skills, and more specialized skill sets will be required.
4. The conflict theorist would view these changes in Marxian terms. The worker is exploited for the sake of the capitalist class. The functionalist would say that even though this will cause disequilibrium, a return to order and stability will eventually occur.

by winning the lottery or appearing on "Who Wants To Be a Millionaire?"

Have students write an essay that expresses their feelings on the concept of the American Dream. What does it mean to them? Do they believe it is still attainable by most people or just a few? Why?

If students would like to read further on the American Dream, you might suggest the following books:

- Robert H. Ropers. *Persistent Poverty: The American Dream Turned Nightmare.* New York: Insight Books, 1991.
- Katherine S. Newman. *Declining Fortunes: The Withering of the American Dream.* New York: Basic Books, 1993.

L2

Using the Section Preview

The story of the Little Rock Nine, the nine African American students that first integrated Central High School in Little Rock, Arkansas in 1957, might be interesting to study from the three sociological perspectives. Have students research this topic, and look for examples that show how each perspective could have analyzed particular events. Several historians believe that schools are social laboratories—that much societal change occurs in schools. Ask students to explain how that might be.

Teaching Strategy

Ask your students to talk about what they feel is necessary for society to be in a state of equilibrium. Encourage them to discuss both physical indicators of stability, such as the availability of food, and social indicators of stability, such as the existence of a police force, or the practice of marriage. Then ask them what sort of things might be considered an indication of temporary instability. Indicators of instability could include natural disasters, such as earthquakes, or societal crises, such as a stock market collapse or a riot.

Section 2 Theoretical Perspectives on Social Change

Key Terms

- equilibrium
- urbanism

Section Preview

The functionalist and conflict perspectives view social change in very different ways. The functionalist perspective depicts societies as relatively stable. Following a major change, these integrated systems seek a new equilibrium. According to the conflict perspective, societies are unstable systems that are constantly undergoing change. Symbolic interactionism identifies decreasing shared values as a source of social instability.

The Functionalist Perspective

Because functionalism emphasizes social stability and continuity, it may seem contradictory to refer to a functionalist theory of social change. There are, however, two functionalist theories of social change—proposed by William Ogburn and Talcott Parsons—that are especially interesting. Both of these theories are based on the concept of *equilibrium*.

Close your eyes and imagine a tightrope walker inching his way across a deep chasm on a narrow rope. If you have an active imagination, you will picture him continually shifting his body and using a pole to counterbalance the effects of the wind as well as the effects of his own motions. The tightrope walker is concerned with maintaining equilibrium. When used by sociologists, **equilibrium** describes a society's tendency to react to changes by making small adjustments to keep itself in a state of functioning and balance.

A society in change, then, moves from stability to temporary instability and back to stability. Sociologists refer to this as a dynamic, or moving, equilibrium. For example, in 1972, a broken dam led to the destruction of the community of Buffalo Creek, West Virginia. The physical destruction of the community was accompanied by death and the loss of the old way of life. Despite the ensuing chaos, residents of the community slowly pulled their lives together again. Although things were not the same as before, a new equilibrium was built out of the physical, social, and human wreckage (Erikson, 1976).

equilibrium
a state of functioning and balance, maintained by a society's tendency to make small adjustments to change

Social equilibrium was shaken for a while, after an earthquake caused the collapse of this Los Angeles area freeway.

On-Demand Writing

The decrease in shared meanings and perceptions has had a profound impact on learning. Scholars have realized that the "universal" perspective often excluded the views of many different groups, particularly those of minorities and women. Until recently, historical texts, for example, have focused on political and military spheres which excluded women. Women's work was not perceived to be vital to society's wellbeing. Therefore, we have almost no record of how women lived.

Scholars are now very careful to avoid these biases. Historians, academics, writers, psychiatrists, and sociologists must recognize and contend with the fact that they are

Figure 17.2 Focus on Theoretical Perspectives

Social Change. This table provides one example each of how the functionalist, conflict, and symbolic interactionist perspectives view social change. Describe how a functionalist would look at an interest group and how a conflict theorist would view equilibrium.

Theoretical Perspective	Concept	Example
Functionalism	Equilibrium	Continuity in the nature of the presidency despite scandals in the Nixon and Clinton administrations
Conflict Theory	Interest group	Enactment of civil rights laws in the 1960s as a result of the struggle over racial equality
Symbolic Interactionism	Urbanism	The smaller proportion of social interaction in a large city compared to a small town is based on a decrease in the number of shared meanings

The 1960s saw the norms of sexual behavior change radically. After skyrocketing, for example, teenage pregnancy is declining. Although Americans do not follow the norms of the 1950s, a retreat from extremes is occurring as new norms of sexual behavior are being established.

The Conflict Perspective

According to the conflict perspective, social change is the result of struggles among groups for scarce resources. Social change is created as these conflicts are resolved. Many of the basic assumptions of the conflict perspective emerge from the writings of Karl Marx about social class conflicts (see page 16). Marx wrote that "without conflict, no progress: this is the law which civilization has followed to the present day."

Sociologists such as Ralf Dahrendorf have adapted many of Marx's ideas. Dahrendorf believes that the resources at stake are more than economic. The quest for power is the source of social change in his view. Whereas Marx saw conflict between two opposing social classes, Dahrendorf sees conflict among groups at all levels of society. Social change thus comes from a multitude of competing interest groups. These groups can be political, economic, religious, racial, ethnic, or gender based. Society changes as power relationships among interest groups change.

History seems to favor Dahrendorf's viewpoint over Marx's. Class conflict has not occurred in any capitalist society; social classes have not been polarized

> "The single greatest power in the world today is the power to change."
>
> **Karl Deutsch**
> **Harvard professor**

Working with the Data

Figure 17.2 A functionalist would see an interest group as necessary to maintain the stability of a society. As long as society was not harmed by that interest, it would be functional. The conflict theorist would view equilibrium as resulting from conflict. Conflict would be necessary to upset the existing arrangement and create a new state of equilibrium.

More About . . . Conflict Perspective

The *Opposing Viewpoints* series published by Greenhaven Press is an excellent resource for looking at social issues that relate to the conflict perspective. For more information, contact: Greenhaven Press, Inc. P.O. Box 289009 San Diego, CA 92128-9009 Phone: 800-231-5163 or email info@greenhaven.com

writing from a particular moral, social, racial, and gender perspective. They are striving to recognize their biases and avoid assumptions that may be true for them, but not for other people.

Write the following phrases on the chalkboard: Age, member of a democracy, Westerner. Then ask students to list two or three biases that may accompany these characteristics.

Finally, ask your students to write a brief composition explaining whether or not they believe that a "universal" perspective is possible now, and whether it will be possible in the future.

L2

Pulling it All Together

The functionalist perspective views societies as relatively stable. According to the conflict perspective societies are unstable and undergo constant change. Symbolic interactionists ascertain the extent to which people share meanings. As these shared interpretations of the world decrease, social ties weaken and social interaction becomes more impersonal.

Answers to Section 2 Assessment

1. Answers will vary. Students need to make adjustments to maintain equilibrium in school, for example, and with friends and parents.
2. Marx's theories were based on class conflict as opposed to Dahrendorf's belief that there are competing groups at all levels of society. Dahrendorf believes the quest for power is the source of social change.
3. Answers will vary. The strongest case can be made for the conflict perspective because it depicts social change as a consequence of struggles between groups.

Critical Thinking

4. Students should support their opinions by discussing whether or not it's true that social change can result from making adjustments in an effort to maintain stability and balance (functionalism), as well as from conflict among competing groups for power (i.e., society changes as the power structure changes) (conflict theory).

into major warring factions. Rather, capitalist societies are composed of countless competing groups. In America, racial groups struggle over the issue of equal economic opportunity, environmentalists and industrialists argue about environmental protection and economic development, and so on, with many other groups at odds with opposing groups over their own special issues.

Symbolic Interactionism

Human beings, according to symbolic interactionism, interact with others on the basis of commonly shared symbols. The nature and frequency of social interaction are affected by the extent to which people share meanings. As shared interpretations of the world decrease, social ties weaken and social interaction becomes more impersonal.

The relationship between shared meanings and the nature of social interaction can be illustrated within the context of the change from an agricultural economy to an industrial one. Accompanying this shift is the emergence of urbanization and its distinctive way of life. This distinctive way of life is known as **urbanism.**

urbanism
the distinctive way of life shared by the people living in a city

What is the way of life associated with urbanism? According to German sociologist Ferdinard Tönnies (1957), social interaction prior to the Industrial Revolution was based on shared tradition. In rural settings, daily life revolved around family, common norms and values, and an interest in the welfare of all community members. Tönnies thought that urbanization creates a very different way of life. In urban society, he wrote, social interaction is impersonal and fragmented because most people with whom one interacts are strangers who share little common tradition.

Sociologists have both agreed and disagreed with Tönnies ever since he introduced this view of urbanism in 1887. According to Tönnies's critics, the way of life in urban society is much more varied than he described it (Gans, 1968). While some urbanites may have hardly any shared meanings on which to base social interaction with others (poor people, elderly people), many others share meanings on which they interact (members of ethnic neighborhoods, members of artistic subcultures).

We need not worry about the outcome of this ongoing debate. It has been the subject of research for sociologists for a long time. What matters here is that this research is guided by ideas of symbolic interactionism.

SOCIOLOGY Online

Student Web Activity
Visit the *Sociology and You* Web site at soc.glencoe.com and click on **Chapter 17—Student Web Activities** for an activity on urbanism.

Assessment—Section 2

1. Describe an area of your life that would benefit from having more equilibrium. How might you achieve this?
2. How did Dahrendorf's interpretation differ from Marx's theory of social change?
3. What theory of social change best explains the enactment of civil rights laws in the 1960s?

Critical Thinking

4. **Finding the Main Idea** Are functionalism and conflict theory compatible as explanations for social change? Clearly distinguish the two perspectives in formulating your answer.

Demonstration

To illustrate how there can be more than one solution to a single problem, present the following situation to the class. You have nine pearls, of which eight are real and one is fake. All the real ones are the same weight. The fake pearl weighs less than the real ones. How many times must you use a balance scale to weed out the fake one? Have students work on this in groups and present their solutions to the class. This demonstrates the flexibility of social problem solving—that there can be more than one solution to a given problem, that some solutions are better than others; but what is also important is that the whole group accepts the problem as one worthy of solving and also agrees to support the solution.

Section 3

Collective Behavior

Key Terms

- collective behavior
- collectivity
- dispersed collectivity
- rumor
- urban legend
- fad
- fashion
- mass hysteria
- panic
- crowd
- mob
- riot
- contagion theory
- emergent norm theory
- convergence theory

Defining Collective Behavior

Collective behavior refers to the spontaneous behavior of people who are responding to similar stimuli. Let's look more closely at some of the terms in this definition. First, what is meant by *collective?* When sociologists use this term, they are referring to a large number of people who do not normally interact and who do not necessarily share clearly defined norms. Sociologists call such a gathering of people a **collectivity.** Stimuli are outside events or persons that cause a response. Putting it all together, collective behavior involves spontaneous social interaction in which loosely connected participants influence one another's behavior.

The study of collective behavior poses a large problem. Sociologists are used to studying structured, not unplanned, behavior. How are researchers going to investigate a social phenomenon that occurs spontaneously? In spite

Section Preview

Collective behavior describes how people behave when they are united by a single short-term goal. Rumors, fads, fashions, mass-hysteria, and panics are examples of collective behaviors. Crowds gather and behave in different ways depending on the stimuli and conditions present. Contagion theory and emergent norm theory describe crowd behavior.

collective behavior
the spontaneous behavior of a group of people responding to similar stimuli

collectivity
collection of people who do not normally interact and who do not share clearly defined norms

Some twenty people were badly injured following a 1947 panic in Nice, France. Sociologists see some structure even in such spontaneous social behavior.

Role Play

To ensure that students understand the concept of collective behavior, divide the class into groups and have each group develop a role play that demonstrates collective behavior. After each group has presented its role play, ask the following questions: Was there a group involved in the behavior? Was the action spontaneous? (Obviously, the action won't be spontaneous, but it should give the impression of being unplanned.) What was the stimuli people responded to?
L1

Using the Section Preview

Ask your students if any of them have ever witnessed a mosh pit at a concert, or participated in moshing. If students have witnessed it, ask them what they think the rules of moshing are. (Are there rules or norms, or is the norm "no rules"?) How does moshing sometimes result in conflict? What are the shared meanings derived from moshing? As students answer these questions, tell them that they have applied the three sociological perspectives to examine this form of collective behavior.

Using the Illustration

If students ask why the people in this picture are panicking, you can tell them the crowd was fleeing in advance of French colonial troops. The troops had been brought in to stop a communist-supported general strike. Students should note the people on the sidewalk at the top of the photo falling over each other in their haste to escape. One soldier has seized a demonstrator with a bicycle.

Teaching Strategy

It might be fun to have your class start a fad and see if it catches on at the school. Before you begin, you might want to notify the principal or an administrator. Be sure the fad is something safe and non-intrusive. For instance, students could wear one pant leg rolled up, and different colored socks on each foot. (The "cooler" the fad, however, the more likelihood that it will spread. Teens are very reluctant to draw attention to themselves unless others are also engaging in the behavior.) Have the class engage in their fad for several days, to see if it catches on. Ask students why they think some fads catch on and others don't. Do fads have to be generated by the media or stores or can small groups start them?

Teaching Strategy

Ask students to search old magazines, the Internet, and other media for images of old fashions, including both men's and women's fashions. Start a collection of these pictures and display them around the room, grouping them by decades or eras. Ask students to analyze changes in fashion. Have any of these fashions made comebacks?
L1

dispersed collectivity
collectivity made up of people who are not physically connected but who follow common rules or respond to common stimuli

of collective behavior. In the more structured forms, such as crowds and social movements, people are in physical contact. We will look at these interactions in the following sections. In a **dispersed collectivity** people are widely scattered. Nevertheless, they are in some way following common rules or responding to common stimuli. Behavior among members of dispersed collectivities is not highly individualized:

> *When people are scattered about, they can communicate with one another in small clusters of people; all of the members of a public need not hear or see what every other member is saying or doing. And they can communicate in a variety of ways—by telephone, letter, Fax machine, computer linkup, as well as through second-, or third-, or fourth-hand talk in a gossip or rumor network* (Goode, 1992:255).

Swing dancing (shown here in 1950s style) has become popular again.

Rumors, Legends, Fads, and Fashions

People will typically respond to certain information in similar ways, even when physically separated. *Rumors, fads,* and *fashions* are collective behaviors characteristic of dispersed collectivities.

What is a rumor? A **rumor** is a widely circulating story of questionable truth. Rumors are usually spread by people about events or other people that are of great interest to themselves. The mass media exploit the public's fascination with rumors. Entertainment magazines devote themselves exclusively to rock idols and movie stars; tabloid newspapers are loaded with suggestive guesswork, half-truths, and innuendos; even mainstream news publications offer accounts of the rich, famous, and offbeat. As these examples suggest, rumors and gossip are closely related.

You probably heard many rumors about what would happen when the clock struck midnight on the last day of 1999. According to these rumors, power grids would fail, elevators would stop working, and the stock market would crash as the year 2000 began. According to another rumor, a fast-food restaurant chain was increasing the protein content of its hamburgers by adding ground worms. Then there was the warning about combining a soft drink and a popular candy—a combination that would supposedly cause the stomach to explode. None of these rumors proved true; but they were spread and believed, in part, because they touched on people's insecurities, uncertainties, and anxieties.

rumor
a widely circulating piece of information that is not verified as being true or false

How are urban legends started? Related to rumors are what Jan Harold Brunvand calls *urban legends* (Brunvand, 1989). **Urban legends** are moralistic tales passed along by people who swear the stories happened to someone they know or to an acquaintance of a friend or family member. Instead of fairy tales that take place in the far-distant past, urban legends take place in shopping malls, on city subways, and in schools. The tales often focus on current concerns and fears, such as AIDS and inner-city gangs. A typical story tells about a man who wakes up in a hotel room missing a kidney. Another describes alligators roaming the sewer systems of big cities. As cautionary tales, urban legends warn us against engaging in risky behaviors

urban legend
a moralistic tale which focuses on current concerns and fears of the city or suburb dweller

Encouraging Citizenship Activity

Give students the following assignment to increase their understanding of rumors and how they work.

Working with your English and drama departments, write, produce, direct, and perform in a play about the damage that can be caused by spreading gossip and rumors. Use the information you have learned in this chapter, but make the play dramatic, rather than preachy or didactic. If possible, include scenes about rumors on the Internet. Make the play directly relevant to your school, but also internationalize it if you can.

Consult with the English departments about how plays are structured, and what elements must be evident to make good drama. Let the English department help you with writing dialogue and stage directions.

Enlist the help of the drama department in learning how to build workable sets, how to block scenes and how to act convincingly.

Perform the play for the school.
L3

by pointing out what has supposedly happened to others who did what we might be tempted to try. Like rumors, urban legends permit us to play out some of our hidden fears and guilt feelings by being shocked and horrified at others' misfortune.

Are fads long lasting? A **fad** is an unusual behavior pattern that spreads rapidly, is embraced zealously, and then disappears after a short time. The widespread popularity of a fad rests largely on its novelty. Students in the early 1970s introduced the "streaking" fad—running naked across college grounds or through occupied classrooms. More recent fads include body piercing, tatoos, retro-swing dancing, and snowboarding.

What are fashions? Fads are adopted by a particular group; fashions are much more widespread. A **fashion** is a behavior pattern that is widely approved but is expected to change periodically. In the United States today, the "in" fashions for clothing are introduced seasonally and usually involve changes in such features as skirt length and lapel width. High school students wishing to be fashionable wear the labels of Tommy Hilfiger, FUBU, Abercrombie & Fitch, Gap, and Nike.

Fashion changes show up most often in items that involve personal appearance such as clothing, jewelry, and hairstyles; but automobile design, home decorating, architecture, and politics are also subject to fashion. Slang is a language-based fashion. Slang terms go in and out of favor very quickly (Lofland, 1993). *Cool, the cat's pajamas, groovy, tubular, neat, tough, fine, awesome, rad, bad, phat,* and *sick* are all slang terms of approval that were popular among young people of various decades.

fad
an unusual behavior pattern that spreads rapidly and disappears quickly

fashion
a widely accepted behavior pattern that changes periodically

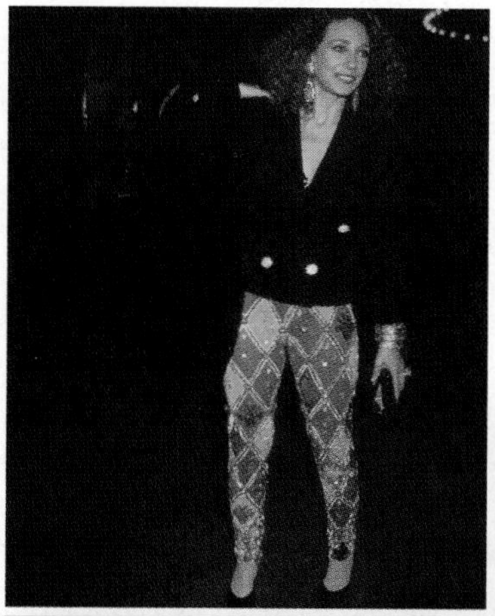

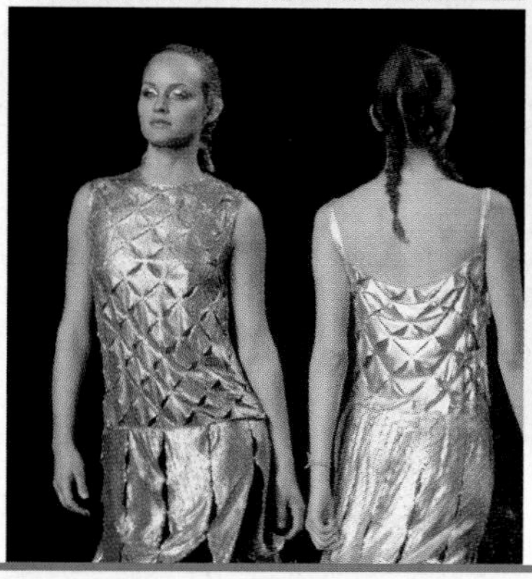

Fashion in dress is constantly changing. Can you identify each of these styles with a decade between 1960–2000?

Teaching Strategy

Feminists often point to the way folklore and tradition perpetuate inequality. A favorite example is the story of Little Red Riding Hood. (For more on this topic you may want to consult the classic text by Bruno Bettelheim, *Uses of Enchantment: The Meaning and Importance of Fairy Tales.* New York: Random House, 1976.)

Little Red Riding Hood was a young woman who strayed off the path and found herself in danger of being eaten by a "big, bad wolf." This story, told to children all over the world, strikes a chord because it plays on two very real fears. It is a story about both the dangers of women's sexual autonomy, and of the pitfalls that women face when they venture out alone. It also teaches children to be wary of strangers, and warns them of the severe consequences of disobedience.

Divide the students into groups of four or five, and tell them to choose a fairytale or an urban legend. Ask them to analyze the story, pointing out the hidden moral assumptions and fears that makes the story compelling or frightening. What lesson is the story trying to teach? Each group should make a presentation to the class, beginning with a retelling of the legend, and ending with a discussion of its meaning.

L1

Sociology Today

Answers to Doing Sociology

1. Answers will vary. It is important, however, that students describe the event they choose in terms of all four characteristics of a disaster.
2. Answers will vary. The most obvious answer is functionalism because all post-attack behavior was aimed at restoring order. Students may also focus on the motivation behind the act from a conflict perspective. Or, students may emphasize the social interaction that occurred following the plane crashes.

Integrating the Teacher Resources

Look for the Chapter 17 Analyzing and Interpreting Data worksheet in the Unit 5 Mastering Basic Concepts **booklet in your Teacher's Resource Box for skill-building exercises based on the graphs, charts, and maps in this chapter.**

Sociology Today

Terrorist Attacks and Disaster Myths

You fail a test, lose a boyfriend, have a minor auto accident, suffer defeat by an archrival's basketball team. You might well describe each of these occasions as a "disaster." For sociologists, however, the term disaster is limited to events with the following characteristics:

- Extensive damage to property
- Great loss of human life
- Massive disruption to everyday living
- Unpredictability and suddenness of a short-term event

Researchers typically divide disasters into "natural disasters" such as floods, earthquakes, hurricanes and "technological accidents" such as airline crashes, nuclear plant meltdowns, and ship sinkings. But how can we classify the September 11, 2001 attacks on the World Trade Center in New York City and the Pentagon in Washington D.C.? It was neither natural nor an accident. But, it had all the characteristics of a disaster. In fact, terrorism is introducing a new type of disaster: one that involves technology; one that is intentional; and one that is caused by humans.

The World Trade Center and Pentagon attacks obviously met the criteria of a disaster. Less obviously, they also exposed as false many popular beliefs about human behavior in disasters. Let's consider four such myths within the context of this national tragedy.

- **Victims of disasters panic.** Contrary to this myth, disaster victims do not generally panic. While some individuals in disasters may panic and while mass panics may follow disasters, the prevailing response is one of general composure and problem-solving behavior. Some inside the

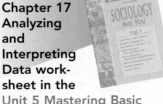

Firefighters raising the flag at the World Trade Center rescue site.

Mass Hysteria and Panics

Mass hysteria exists when collective anxiety is created by acceptance of one or more false beliefs. Orson Welles's famous "Men from Mars" radio broadcast in 1938, though based entirely on H. G. Wells's novel *The War of the Worlds,* caused nationwide hysteria. About one million listeners became frightened or disturbed and thousands of Americans hit the road to avoid the invading Martians. Telephone lines were jammed as people shared rumors, anxieties, fears, and escape plans (Houseman, 1948; Cantril, 1982; Barron, 1988).

A classic example of mass hysteria was the response to imagined witches in seventeenth-century Salem, Massachusetts (refer to Doing Research in Chapter 7, "Deviance and Social Control"). Twenty-two people labeled witches died—twenty by execution—before the false testimony of several young girls began to be questioned. The mass hysteria dissipated only after the false beliefs were discredited. There has been some hysteria in the United States regarding AIDS. A 1987 Gallup poll showed that a substantial propor-

Using Problem-Solving Skills

Separate students into groups of three or four. One student acts as recorder while others problem solve what should be done to remedy this situation. One reader from each group will share what the group has written. The class, as a whole, must choose the best solution by a majority vote on a secret ballot.

Scenario: At least once a month your school holds a practice fire or tornado drill for student protection and quick response. Most students feel comfortable knowing the plan and routine for these drills. However, today, while your teacher is out of the room escorting a student to the health clinic, the warning bell sounds; instead of the three beeps, there are five. No one knows what to do; this is the first time there have been five beeps.

Students in your class realize that the weather is warm and sunny, so there is little probability of a tornado. No one smells

World Trade Center did response with incapacitating emotion. One secretary in shock, for example, had to be carried out by a fellow worker. Some people jumped from the towers. But the disaster failed to set off a widespread panic. Many who heeded the first building-wide instructions died after calmly remaining in their offices. And many of the survivors remained as interested observers, forcing police to broadcast an urgent plea for them to hurry away for their own safety.

- **Disaster victims respond as isolated individuals.** Typically, we picture disaster victims as individuals trying to save only themselves. Actually, according to research, people immediately engage in group efforts to help others. People in the World Trade Center with cell phones offered them to other victims desperate to call family or friends. Scores of New York police and over 300 firefighters died while working together to rescue trapped victims.
- **Disaster victims leave the scene as soon as possible.** Contrary to this myth, the majority of victims remain near the disaster site. Rather than fleeing, most victims of the World Trade Center disaster remained to help others, to witness the fire and rescue efforts, or to think about returning to their offices. In addition, large numbers of volunteers and off-site emergency personnel actually rushed *to* the scene. So many New Yorkers offered to donate blood that many were turned away. Bellevue Hospital at one point had five doctors for each emergency ward patient. Four firefighters who were playing golf on Staten Island saw the first plane hit the north tower. Three of those four lost their lives in rescue efforts, and they were just a few of the hundreds of firefighters who died after *entering* the disaster site. To help rescuers searching for survivors under the rubble, ironworkers, many of whom had built the World Trade Center, labored together in 12-hour volunteer shifts clearing away twisted steel.
- **Crime is prevalent during disasters.** Rather than increasing, crime actually decreases after a disaster. While some isolated instances of criminal behavior occur, the crime rate in a disaster falls. After the World Trade Center disaster, some looting in surrounding buildings was reported, and a Picasso drawing valued at $320,000 was stolen from a Madison Avenue art gallery. More importantly, the overall crime rate in New York City declined 34 percent in the week following the disaster. According to the NYPD, arrests were down 64 percent compared to the same seven days the previous years.

Doing Sociology

1. Think of some event you formerly considered a disaster. Explain why it was not a disaster from a sociological viewpoint.
2. Do you think that the behavior following the terrorist attack on the World Trade Center is best explained by functionalism, conflict theory, or symbolic interactionism? Explain your choice.

tion of Americans held false beliefs regarding the spread of AIDS—30 percent believed insect bites could spread the disease, 26 percent related the spread to food handling or preparation, 26 percent thought AIDS could be transmitted via drinking glasses, 25 percent saw a risk in being coughed or sneezed upon, and 18 percent believed that AIDS could be contracted from toilet seats (Gallup, 1988). These mistaken ideas persisted on a widespread basis despite the medical community's conclusion that AIDS is spread through sexual contact, by sharing hypodermic needles, and by transfusion of infected blood. By the late 1990s, knowledge, tolerance, compassion, and understanding of AIDS had increased enough that the frequency of these rumors dropped off.

mass hysteria
collective anxiety created by the acceptance of one or more false beliefs

What is the difference between mass hysteria and a panic? A **panic** occurs when people react to a real threat in fearful, anxious, and often self-damaging ways. Panics usually occur in response to such unexpected events as fires, invasions, and ship sinkings. Over 150 people, for example, died in the Kentucky Beverly Hills Supper Club in 1977 when a panic reaction to a

panic
reaction to a real threat in fearful, anxious, and often self-damaging ways

Making Connections to Other Cultures

Crowds were a vital part of many Greek festivities and legends. Spectatorship was a form of civic duty. The main theatrical events of the year were free and mandatory for all citizens. It was believed that watching an actor die a heroic death would inspire an audience to bravery. Therefore, the transformation that took place when a crowd shifted from conventional to expressive, and even to acting, was a subject of fascination to the ancient Greeks. (Of course they did not use those terms!) They had great faith in the power of the group dynamic.

One of the most impressive of the Greek legends involves the Maenads. These were women who became frenzied with wine. They would rush in a group across the hillsides, tearing into pieces any animals they came across and devouring its raw flesh. They were said to dismember young men. This inversion of women's role is an illustration of the Greek's belief in the power of the mob.

smoke or sees anything burning as they look down the hall and out the windows. A rumor begins circulating through your class that it's a bomb. You heard someone whisper "cafeteria, today, bad" in the hallway en route to class. Now you begin to worry.

One student in the back row starts to sob; another gets up and paces the room while another student wants to leave the classroom and make a phone call. The rest of the class waits for someone to do something … anything. Trying to dispel any rumors and worrying about panic, you try to take charge of the situation and calm fellow students. What will you do and say to maintain control in your sociology classroom? **L1** fire caused a jamming of the escape routes. Interestingly enough, people often do not panic after natural disasters such as earthquakes and floods. Although panics may occur at the outset, major natural catastrophes usually lead to highly structured behavior (Erikson, 1976; Dynes and Tierney, 1994).

Crowds

crowd
a temporary collection of people who share an immediate common interest

A **crowd** is a temporary collection of people who share an immediate common interest. The temporary residents of a large campground, each occupied with his or her own activities, would not be considered a crowd. Sociologists would call this kind of gathering an *aggregate*. But if some stimulus, such as the landing of a hot-air balloon or the sudden appearance of a bear, drew the campers together, the aggregate would become a crowd.

People in a crowd often have no predefined ideas about the way they should behave. They do, however, share the urgent feeling that something either is about to happen or should be made to happen.

Are there different types of crowds? Sociologist Herbert Blumer (1969a) has distinguished four basic types of crowds.

1. A *casual crowd* is the least organized, least emotional, and most temporary type of crowd. Although the people in a casual crowd share some point of interest, it is minor and fades quickly. Members of a casual crowd may gather with others to observe the aftermath of an accident, to watch someone threatening to jump from a building, or to listen to a street rap group.
2. A *conventional crowd* has a specific purpose and follows accepted norms for appropriate behavior. People watching a film, taking a chartered flight to a university ball game, or observing a tennis match are in conventional crowds. As in casual crowds, there is little interaction among members of conventional crowds.
3. *Expressive crowds* have no significant or long-term purpose beyond unleashing emotion. Their members are collectively caught up in a dominating, all-encompassing mood of the moment. Free expression of emotion—yelling, crying, laughing, jumping—is the main characteristic of this type of crowd. Hysterical fans at a rock concert, the multitude gathered at Times Square on New Year's Eve, and the some 250,000 Americans at the Woodstock music festival in 1999 are all examples of expressive crowds.
4. Finally, a crowd that takes some action toward a target is an *acting crowd*. This type of crowd concentrates intensely on some objective and engages in aggressive behavior to achieve it. Protestors at the 1999 World Trade Organization (WTO) meeting in Seattle were an acting crowd. Although the protests involved many groups with various objectives, they all shared the goal of placing "people before profits" (Klee, 1999). A conventional crowd may become an acting crowd, as when European soccer fans abandon the guidelines for spectators in order to attack the officials. Similarly, an expressive crowd may become an acting one, as in the case of celebrating Super Bowl fans who wind up overturning cars and destroying property. Mobs are acting crowds, as are crowds engaging in riots.

Each of these photos can be associated with a type of crowd. Which photo shows an acting crowd?

Reteaching

Have students observe crowds in different settings such as malls, concerts, cafeterias, etc. They should try to find examples of each of the different types of crowds (casual crowd, conventional crowd, expressive crowd, acting crowd). Tell students to look for similarities and differences between the various crowds as outlined in the text and to report to the class on their observations.

Integrating the Teacher Resources

Look for the Chapter 17 Increasing Your Reading Comprehension worksheet and the Guided Reading worksheet in the Unit 5 Mastering Basic Concepts booklet in your Teacher's Resource Box. Both will strengthen reading comprehension skills.

On-Demand Writing

Have you ever watched a wonderful movie at a theater and then rented the movie several months later, only to discover that it wasn't as good as you remembered? Often, your positive first impression was influenced by the environment in which you saw the film. Being among a crowd of spectators can make a comedy funnier, and a scary movie more terrifying. It can provide a sense of unity and belonging to hear a whole roomful of strangers laugh or gasp at the same moment.

Being part of a crowd can also be frightening. A group that seems out of control, or a group that seems to expect a certain kind of behavior, can be terrifying.

What are mobs and riots? A **mob** is an emotionally stimulated, disorderly crowd that is ready to use destructiveness and violence to achieve a purpose. A mob knows what it wants to do and considers all other things distractions. In fact, individuals who are tempted to deviate from the mob's purpose are pressured to conform. Concentration on the main event is maintained by strong leadership.

Mobs have a long and violent history. Many students are familiar with the scenes of mob actions described by Charles Dickens in the classic story *A Tale of Two Cities*. The formation of mobs is not limited to revolutions, however. During the mid-1700s, American colonists mobbed tax collectors as well as other political officials appointed by the British. During the Civil War, more than one thousand people were killed or injured as armed mobs protested against the Union Army's draft. Mobs in the American South have acted as judges, juries, and executioners in the lynching of African Americans (as well as some whites) since the end of the nineteenth century.

Some acting crowds, although engaged in deliberate destructiveness and violence, do not have the mob's sense of common purpose. These episodes of crowd destructiveness and violence are called **riots**. Riots involve a much wider range of activities than mob action. Whereas a mob surges to burn a particular building, to lynch an individual, or to throw bombs at a government official's car, rioters often direct their violence and destructiveness at targets simply because they are convenient. People who participate in riots typically lack power and engage in destructive behavior as a way to express their frustrations. A riot, usually triggered by a single event, is best understood within the context of long-standing tensions.

Ghetto riots tore through many large American cities during the summer of 1967. The riots occurred against a background of massive unemployment, uncaring slum landlords, poverty, discrimination, and charges of police brutality. In 1990, thousands of angry citizens stormed the secret police headquarters in East Berlin. Although no one was killed or injured, the protest aroused widespread fear that the country was about to drop into anarchy (Bierman, 1990). In 1992 police officers charged in the beating of Rodney King in Los Angeles were acquitted by a jury. In the aftermath of the acquittals, Los Angeles experienced America's deadliest riots in twenty-five years. Two days of rioting left the City of Angels with at least 53 dead, 2,300 injured, over 16,000 arrested, and an estimated $800 million in damage from looting and burning (Duke and Escobar, 1992; Mathews, 1992).

mob
emotional crowd ready to use violence for a specific purpose

riot
episode of largely random destruction and violence carried out by a crowd

Riots occurred in 1992 in Los Angeles after the acquittals of four white officers accused of the beating of African American motorist Rodney King. This looter took advantage of the riot to add to her wardrobe.

Theories of Crowd Behavior

Theories have been developed to explain crowd behavior. The three most important are *contagion theory, emergent norm theory* and *convergence theory*.

What is contagion theory? *Contagion* often refers to the spread of disease from person to person. Accordingly, **contagion theory** focuses on the spread of emotion in a crowd. As emotional intensity in the crowd increases, people temporarily lose their individuality to the "will" of the crowd. This makes it possible for a charismatic or manipulative leader to direct crowd behavior, at least initially.

Contagion theory has its roots in the classic 1895 work of Gustave Le Bon (originally published in 1895). Le Bon was a French aristocrat who disdained

contagion theory
theory stating that members of crowds stimulate each other to higher and higher levels of emotion and irrational behavior

Reinforcing Vocabulary

This section on crowd behavior introduces three terms that some students may be meeting for the first time: *contagion, emergent,* and *convergence*. The mental image of an out of control contagious disease wreaking havoc on an unsuspecting population is probably a good mnemonic for recalling contagion theory.

Tell students that *emerge* means to come out of, or to come into view. In this theory, norms come into view as the crowd develops.

If you give students a mental image of cars *converging* on the freeway from different on-ramps, it may help them remember convergent theory. The cars are all going the same place and meeting others who are like minded.
ELL

Teaching Strategy

Have students consider researching famous riots in history for examples of mob behavior. Students might want to concentrate on the moment that became the catalyst for the riot breaking out. Have them analyze what could have been done to avert the riot. Some examples are provided in the text.
L2

The line between a casual crowd and a mob can be disturbingly thin. Super Bowl fans who overturn cars begin by celebrating, and a group fight on the street often begins with a couple of good-natured slaps on the back. This potential for group action is part of the excitement of being part of a crowd.

Ask your students to describe an occasion when they acted as part of a crowd. Was it frightening? How and why did the presence of the crowd enhance or detract from the event?
L2

More About . . . Emergent Norm Theory

Sociologist Steven E. Clayman (1993) studied audience participation in an attempt to determine how the individuals in the group decide what is going on and how norms are involved in the behavior of the group. In studying the members of an audience listening to a speech, Clayman found that individuals will applaud immediately and independently at the end of the speech. However, if they disliked the speech and felt it should be booed rather than applauded, they would wait to coordinate their booing with others. They were unwilling to boo alone. Ask students why they think audience members are unwilling to boo alone. Would they boo alone? Why or why not?

Riot police officers look at a fire set by fans during a 1996 soccer game in Athens. How does contagion theory describe the behavior that led to the fire?

crowds made up of the masses. People in crowds, Le Bon thought, were reduced to a nearly subhuman level.

> *By the mere fact that he forms part of an organized crowd, a man descends several rungs in the ladder of civilization. Isolated, he may be a cultivated individual; in a crowd, he is a barbarian—that is, a creature acting by instinct. He possesses the spontaneity, the violence, the ferocity, and also the enthusiasm and heroism of primitive beings* (Le Bon, 1960:32).

Herbert Blumer (1969a) has offered another version of contagion theory. Blumer avoids Le Bon's elitist bias but still implies that crowds are irrational and out of control. For Blumer, the basic process in crowds is a "circular reaction"—people mutually stimulating one another. This process includes three stages. In *milling,* the first stage, people move around in an aimless and random fashion, much like excited herds of cattle or sheep. Through milling, people become increasingly aware of and sensitive to one another; they enter something akin to a hypnotic trance. All of this prepares the crowd to act in a concerted and spontaneous way.

The second stage, *collective excitement,* is a more intense form of milling. At this stage, crowd members become impulsive, unstable, and highly responsive to the actions and suggestions of others. Individuals begin to lose their personal identities and take on the identity of the crowd.

The last stage, *social contagion,* is an extension of the other stages. Behavior in this stage involves rigid, unthinking, and nonrational transmission of mood, impulse, or behavior. We see such behavior, for example, when fans at soccer games in Europe launch attacks on referees that disrupt games and leave people injured or even killed. Taking a less extreme case, people at auctions can find themselves buying objects of little or no value to them because they have become caught up in the excitement of bidding.

emergent norm theory
theory stating that norms develop to guide crowd behavior

What is emergent norm theory? Sociologists today realize that much crowd behavior, even in mobs, is actually very rational (McPhail, 1991). **Emergent norm theory** stresses the similarity between daily social behavior and crowd behavior. In both situations, norms guide behavior (Turner, 1964; Turner and Killian, 1987). So even within crowds, rules develop. These rules are *emergent* norms because the crowd participants are not aware of the rules until they find themselves in a particular situation. The norms develop on the spot as crowd participants pick up cues for expected behavior.

Contagion theory proposes a collective mind that motivates members of the crowd to act. According to emergent norm theory, people in a crowd are present for a variety of reasons. Hence, they do not all behave in the same way. Conformity may be active (some people in a riot may take home as many watches and rings as they can carry) or passive (others may simply not interfere with the looters, although they take nothing for themselves). In Nazi Germany, for instance, some people destroyed the stores of Jewish merchants, while others watched silently.

convergence theory
theory that states that crowds are formed by people who deliberately congregate with like-minded others

What is convergence theory? Both the contagion and emergent norm theories of crowd behavior assume that individuals are merely responding to those around them. It may be a more emotional response (as in contagion theory) or a more rational response (as in emergent norm theory). In other words, the independent variable in crowd behavior is the crowd itself. In contrast, in **convergence theory** crowds are formed by people who deliberately

Integrating the Teacher Resources

For review or enrichment, use the Student Journal Prompts for this chapter, available in the Unit 5 Mastering Basic Concepts booklet in your Teacher's Resource Box.

Cooperative Learning Activity

Contagion theory is not very complimentary of human nature. Le Bon called members of a crowd barbarians. The milling stage likens people to herds of sheep or cattle. In the last stage, social contagion, crowd members become unthinking and nonrational. Le Bon said that in a crowd people will do things they would never do when acting alone.

Divide the class into groups to discuss contagion theory. Begin by asking students if they have ever seen television coverage of a riot. (If you can obtain news footage of a riot, it would be useful to show it to the

Police made mass arrests in 1992 when anti-abortion activists attempted to blockade a Milwaukee abortion clinic. How does this behavior relate to convergence theory?

congregate with others who they know to be like-minded. According to convergence theory, the independent variable in crowd behavior is the desire of people with a common interest to come together.

There have been many instances of crowds gathering in front of clinics to discourage abortions. This behavior, say convergence theorists, does not simply occur because people happened to be at the same place and are influenced by others. Such a crowd is motivated to form because of shared values, beliefs, and attitudes (Berk, 1974).

Section 3 Assessment

1. How is a dispersed collectivity different from other types of collectivities?
2. Some observers at a lynching do not participate but do not attempt to stop the lynching. Which of the following theories of crowd behavior best explains this?
   - **a.** contagion theory
   - **b.** crowd decision theory
   - **c.** emergent norm theory
   - **d.** convergence theory

Critical Thinking

3. **Making Generalizations** Rumors may or may not be true. Do you think most rumors turn out to be false? Why or why not?
4. **Applying Concepts** Identify a current rumor, fad, or fashion. Explain why it is part of a dispersed collectivity.
5. **Applying Concepts** Think of a crowd you have been part of, and identify it as one of the four types of crowds described in the text. Provide examples of behavior within the crowd (yours or someone else's) that illustrate why it was that particular type.

> "The Mob has many Heads, but no Brains."
>
> **Thomas Fuller**
> **English minister**

Pulling it All Together

Collective behaviors such as rumors, fads, fashions, mass hysteria and panics are examples of unified behavior. Contagion theory and emergent norm theory describe crowd behavior when certain stimuli and conditions are present.

Answers to Section 3 Assessment

1. Unlike other collectives that involve spontaneous social interaction where people are in physical contact and influenced by others' behavior, a dispersed collectivity involves people who may be widely scattered, but are nevertheless following common rules or responding to common stimuli. Members may communicate in small clusters and therefore may not hear or see what every other member is seeing or hearing (examples are rumors, legends, fads, and fashions).

2. c (emergent norm theory)

Critical Thinking

3. Answers will vary; students may want to support their opinions with examples.

4. Answers will vary.

5. Answers will vary.

class. Or, portions of the movie *Woodstock* might be appropriate.) Ask students to describe to the members of their group what the riot was like. Were the people barbarians? Did they mill around like cattle or sheep? Did they do things that they likely would not have done had they been alone? Why do students think people behave this way? Do they think the people are really acting irrationally, or do they know what they are doing? Have groups share their insights with the rest of the class.
L2

Tech Trends

Ask students about rumors that have started or been passed around by email. One recent rumor stated that people shouldn't flash their high beams at a car that was driving at night with no headlights. Anyone who did would be attacked as part of a gang initiation rite. Students might want to share rumors they have encountered on the Internet.

Answer to Analyzing the Trends

As mentioned in Chapter 2, one way to determine if information is credible is to analyze the web site. Or, they can find out if the source of the information is reputable. This may not always be possible, so if students have doubts about the legitimacy of information, they should probably not consider it true until it can be verified. Consult pages 47 and 48 in Chapter 2 for additional suggestions.

Integrating the Teacher Resources

Look for Ethics, Values, and Technology: Real-Life Issues in Society, **avail-able in your Teacher's Resource Box. The book-let provides primary source readings dealing with real-life controver-sies. Student worksheets are included.**

Tech Trends
Rumors at Warp Speed

Even before e-mail and the Internet, rumors spread like wildfire. Now, with instantaneous and multiple communications, there is virtually no limit to how fast a rumor can travel. A recent example demonstrates how quickly rumors can spread through the Internet.

The "gangsta" rapper Tupac Shakur was shot four times while riding in a car on the Las Vegas strip. A week after his death, a rumor surfaced that he was still alive. This rumor became so widespread on the Internet that the television show *Nightline* reported it. *Nightline* gave no credence to the story, but it found the rumor itself worth reporting. The rumor is still believed by many of Shakur's fans.

The Internet has rumors, gossip, and conspiracy theories to satisfy almost any taste. *Conspiracy Nation,* a magazine devoted to conspiracy theories, has a web site that describes dozens of rumors about plots. A recent offering, for example, explored efforts by the "new world order" to clone human beings. Other articles have examined a variety of theories on political assassinations and suicides (Rust and Danitz, 1998). E-mail chain letters spread rumors ranging from impending doom caused by various computer viruses to tales of free vacations and cash prizes (Branscum, 1999). Clearly, the Internet can accelerate and magnify the effects of such rumors.

And the effects of rumors can be serious. A recent Internet rumor erroneously charged a reputable on-line information publisher with selling its customers' credit and medical histories. Another rumor, originated by Internet tabloid journalist Matt Drudge, charged a key Clinton White House aide with wife abuse. These types of rumors can have serious effects on a person's reputation or the financial stability of a company.

Such damage can now occur overnight, be long lasting, and even become irreversible. "Now the Internet is taking hearsay global at light speed, shaking up the media and blurring fact and fiction like never before" (Rust and Danitz, 1998: 22).

The rapper Tupac Shakur was widely rumored to still be alive a week after he was shot to death on the Las Vegas strip. This rumor was spread on the Internet.

Analyzing the Trends

How much credibility do you give to information from an Internet source? What criteria do you think should be used to evaluate the validity of information?

Using Decision-Making Skills

The Tech Trends article should remind us that while the information we receive on the Internet is convenient, it may not always be accurate. (See pages 47 and 48 for a complete skills-based activity on evaluating web sites.) Students may again need reminding that just because something is posted on the Internet, doesn't mean it is true. Find a few Internet sites for students to evaluate

using their knowledge of decision-making skills and the following criteria. Using their findings, students should decide whether the web site is a good source of information.

1. Is the information accurate? Are there spelling errors? Are the graphs and tables easy to read? Is a source given for the information?

Section 4

Social Movements

Key Terms

- social movement
- revolutionary movement
- reformative movement
- redemptive movement
- alternative movement
- value-added theory
- resource mobilization theory

The Nature of Social Movements

The **social movement** is the most highly structured, rational, and enduring form of collective behavior. Several defining elements characterize social movements.

- a large number of people
- a common goal to promote or prevent social change
- structured organization with commonly recognized leaders
- activity sustained over a relatively long time period

Examples of past and present social movements include the American Revolution, abolitionism, the suffragette movement, the pro-life and pro-choice movements, and the environmental movement.

Most social movements are started to stimulate change. As the definition indicates, however, a social movement may instead oppose change. Conservative political and fundamentalist religious organizations for example, are engaged in a concerted effort to oppose abortion (Tax, 1999). The National Rifle Association has focused its resources and membership on blocking certain gun control legislation (Walsh and Suro, 1999).

"Listen–just take one of our brochures and see what we're all about . . . In the meantime, you may wish to ask yourself, 'Am I a happy cow?'"

A very human need to belong is a prime motivator for joining social movements. What other motivations might be responsible for causing a person to join a social movement?

Section Preview

Social movements are more permanent and more organized than other types of collectivities. Theories to explain how social movements develop include value-added theory and resource mobilization theory.

social movement
movement whose goal is to promote or prevent social change; the most structured and rational form of collective behavior

Using the Section Preview

Students will probably be familiar with the Civil Rights Movement and the Student Movements of the 1960s. You might want to have them dissect these movements sociologically, using the two theoretical perspectives—value-added theory and resource mobilization theory. Other possible topics are the abortion movement, and recent protests against Nike and other shoe manufacturers.

Teaching Strategy

Using the definition in the text, ask students to determine which of the following would be considered a social movement: feminism, a political lobby, the Black Panthers, mass hysteria, Christianity.

2. Who sponsors the web site? Is it a reputable organization? Is it an organization that has goals and purposes you agree with?
3. Is the information up to date? When was the web page last updated? (If there is no date on the page, it's impossible to tell how current the information is.)
4. Is the information presented as fact or opinion? Does the author present his or her opinion as fact? Are there advertisers sponsoring the page? If so, how does that effect the content of the page?
5. What audience is the web page written for? Does it target students, scholars, etc.? How will that affect the information presented?

Ask students to share their information with the rest of the class.
L2

Working with the Data

Figure 17.3 Have students work independently to list more examples of each of the behaviors listed in the figure. Then have the class work together to combine their lists, deleting any duplicate answers. Which collective behaviors have the most examples? Which have the fewest? Why do students think this is the case?

Reinforcing Vocabulary

Ask students to define the term *revolution*. They will either suggest the scientific meaning of a complete orbit of a celestial body, or they may offer the political definition of a complete and sudden change. Ask students to try to figure out what connects these two meanings. (They may suggest that after a revolution, like the heavenly body, the people are often right back where they started.)

Ask students if there is a difference between a revolutionary movement and a revolution. If there is a difference, what is it?

Figure 17.3 Major Forms of Collective Behavior

Behavior	Definition	Example
Rumor	A widely circulating piece of information that is not verified as being true or false	Continuously repeated prediction that airplanes would crash on a massive scale on January 1, 2000
Urban legend	A moralistic tale which focuses on current concerns and fears of the city or suburban dweller	Fierce alligators in New York City's sewer system
Fad	An unusual behavior pattern that spreads rapidly and disappears quickly (although it may reappear)	Body piercing
Fashion	A widely accepted behavior pattern that changes periodically	Nike shoes
Crowd	A temporary collection of people who share an immediate interest	New Year's celebrants at Times Square in New York City
Mob	An emotional crowd ready to use violence for a specific purpose	Lynch mob
Riot	An episode of largely random destruction and violence carried out by a crowd	Destructive behavior following the acquittal of police officers who were filmed using extreme force against Rodney King
Social movement	Movement whose goal is to promote or prevent social change	Civil Rights movement

Primary Types of Social Movements

Despite commonalities, various social movements have unique characteristics. It is difficult to compare the civil rights movement with the environmental movement. This has led sociologists to study differences between social movements. David Aberle (1991) has identified four basic types of social movements.

revolutionary movement a social movement that attempts to change the total structure of society

❖ A **revolutionary movement** attempts to change a society totally. The American Revolution was one of the most successful revolutionary movements in history. Another example is the revolutionary movement

Interdisciplinary Activity

History During the 18th century in France, printing presses became available to members of the general population. There was a widespread awareness of the social injustices of the time, and the combination of the two facts led to a literary and philosophical movement known as the Enlightenment. The Enlightenment promoted a generalized belief in the need for social reform. Towards the end of the eighteenth century, the situation was worsened by a food shortage and by a widespread fear of invasion and banditry. Finally, open revolt took place when a group of young cafe-goers encouraged a crowd to storm one of the city's prisons. Social order could not be re-established, led by Mao Zedong in China. As a result of Mao's revolutionary movement, a communist government was instituted.

Demonstrators, with banners in hand, ride a truck in route to Tiananmen Square to protest for democracy and human rights in Beijing, China in 1989. Explain the type of social movement this demonstration best illustrates.

- A **reformative movement** aims to effect more limited changes in a society. The Women's Christian Temperance Union (an antialcohol organization founded in 1874) and the antiwar movement of the 1960s illustrate this type of social movement.
- A **redemptive movement** focuses on changing people completely. The religious cult of David Koresh (the Branch Davidians) was a redemptive movement.
- An **alternative movement** seeks only limited changes in people. Zero Population Growth, an organization that celebrated its thirtieth anniversary in 1998, illustrates such a movement. It attempts to persuade people to limit the size of their families. It does not advocate sweeping lifestyle changes, however; nor does it advocate legal penalties for large families.

reformative movement
a social movement that attempts to make limited changes in society

redemptive movement
a social movement which seeks to change people completely

alternative movement
a social movement that focuses on bringing about limited changes in people

Theories of Social Movements

Because of the highly structured nature of social movements, sociologists have been able to analyze this form of collective behavior. Two major theories of social movements have evolved. One is *value-added theory,* and the other is *resource mobilization theory.*

What is value-added theory? Before discussing value-added theory, we need to understand the concept of adding value. In the value-added process, each step in the creation of a product contributes, or adds value, to the final entity. Neil Smelser, the sociologist who originated the value-added theory of social movements, gives an example involving automobile production.

> *An example of [the value-added process] is the conversion of iron ore into finished automobiles by a number of stages of processing. Relevant stages would be mining, smelting, tempering, shaping, and combining the steel with other parts, painting, delivering to retailer, and selling. Each stage "adds its value" to the final cost of the finished product. The key element in this example is that the earlier stages must combine according to a certain pattern before the next stage can contribute its particular value to the finished product, an automobile. Painting, in order to be effective as a "determinant" in shaping the product, has to "wait" for the completion of the earlier processes. Every stage in the value-added process, therefore, is a necessary condition for the appropriate and effective condition of value in the next stage (Smelser, 1971:13–14).*

Smelser used this process as a model to understand social movements. The **value-added theory** identifies six conditions that must exist in order for social movements to occur.

value-added theory
theory holding that certain conditions must exist for social movements to occur

Controversy and Debate

We live in a country whose Constitution was written by a revolutionary government. It is predicated on the idea that citizens have the right to choose their form of government. However, there are some limits on the ways that citizens can work for change. It is a crime to advocate the violent overthrow of the government. Flag-burning and criticism, however, are legal and therefore viable forms of protest.

Encourage students to discuss their views on flag-burning. Would a law against flag-burning be a form of social control? When do social controls become oppressive?

Teaching Strategy

Revolutionary movements have often looked outside national lines and to foreign governments for support. When the movement is based in the lower classes, or when it is unpopular, such tactics can be necessary in order to raise funds. Would the U.S. government be justified in funding a revolution in a foreign country? When has this happened in history?

because the National Guard joined in the revolt.

These are the events that led up to the French Revolution. Each sentence is an example of one of the six conditions of the value-added theory. If any of these events had not happened, the French Revolution could not have taken place.

Ask your students to work in groups of five or six to construct a narrative, or a description, of a social movement that satisfies each of the six conditions. Their example may be made up or drawn from history.
L2

Working with the Data

Figure 17.4 If possible, bring in speakers to talk with the class about the structural strains listed in the figure. Or, a history teacher from your school might be persuaded to talk with your class. Students should have questions prepared to ask the speakers. Information should include: Why was this topic important? What was happening at the time to make this a timely issue? Were there any prominent leaders? Were these issues of interest to political leaders or to activists? How many grass roots organizations grew out of these movements?

If you can't bring in speakers, have the students talk with their parents or grandparents (or other adults) and ask them the questions listed above. Ask students what they learned from the people they talked with? What did they learn about structural strains?

1960s	1970s	1980s	1990s	2000s
Hot Topics Vietnam War Civil Rights	**Hot Topics** Clean Air and Water Female Empowerment	**Hot Topics** International Human Rights Endangered Species Sexual Harassment	**Hot Topics** Gay Rights Sweatshop Labor Medical Use of Marijuana	**Hot Topics** Globalization Corporate Dominance Immigration

Figure 17.4 Hot Buttons for College Activists. *According to Robert Merton, protest movements are reactions on structural strains of burning importance. College activists have been moved to action by different structural strains since the 1960s.*

Source: **U.** *The National College Magazine* (February, 2000).

1. *Structural conduciveness.* The environment must be social-movement friendly. The college student demonstrations in the 1960s and 1970s occurred because of the war in Vietnam, yes, but also because most college campuses had convenient sites for rallies and protest meetings.
2. *Structural strains.* A second condition promoting the emergence of a social movement is the presence of conflicts, ambiguities, and discrepancies within a society. Without some form of strain, there is no stimulus for change. A key discrepancy in the antiwar movement case was the government's continued stance that there was no war (no legal war had been declared), despite the vast resources being devoted to battle and the obvious combat casualties. (Figure 17.4 identifies major structural strains that have mobilized college students since the 1960s.)
3. *Generalized beliefs.* Generalized beliefs include a general recognition that there is a problem and agreement that something should be done to fix it. Two shared beliefs were crucial to the antiwar movement. One was the belief that the Johnson and Nixon administrations were not telling the truth about the war. Another was that the Vietnam War was so morally wrong that it had to be stopped.
4. *Precipitating factors.* One or more significant events must occur to galvanize people into action. On April 30, 1970, President Nixon ordered the invasion of the neutral country of Cambodia. This event was a show of force to the North Vietnamese government with which the United States government was negotiating to end the war.
5. *Mobilization of participants for action.* Once the first four conditions exist, the only remaining step is to get the people moving. Massive demonstrations were part of the political furor the Cambodian invasion provoked. More than 100,000 opponents of the Vietnam War marched on Washington, D.C. Hundreds of colleges were forced to close as a result of strikes by 1.5 million students.

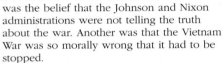

This famous photograph of the tragic antiwar demonstrations at Kent State University in 1970 captured the attention of the nation.

Careers in Sociology

Ask student if they think careers in sociology will be feasible when they're ready to work full time. After students have had a chance to answer, share the following information with them.

The future looks bright for sociology. People are beginning to realize that we have to try to understand and solve problems in the United States and around the world–problems that affect individuals and problems that affect societies. Some of the best employment prospects may be in policy research and administration, in clinical and applied sociological practice, as well as in the traditional areas of teaching and basic research.

Snapshot of America

Women in the Workplace

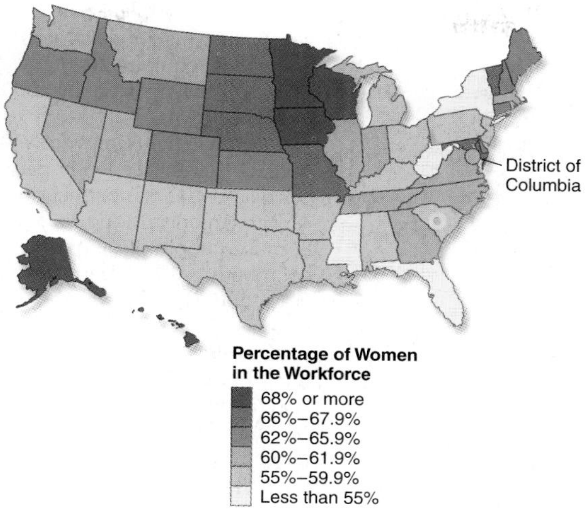

The number of women in the U.S. workplace is related to social change and social movements. The U.S. female workforce shot up during World War II. Once the soldiers returned home, however, a large percentage of those working women quit work to raise families. Owing in part to the women's movement, the U.S. has seen a peacetime resurgence of women entering the workforce. This map shows the percentage of women in each state who are active in the labor force.

Interpreting the Map

1. Relate strain theory, the women's movement, and increased female labor force participation.
2. How does your state compare with other states in terms of female employment? Describe.

Adapted from *The World Almanac of the U.S.A.* 1998.

6. Social control. The sixth determinant of a social movement is ineffective *social control*. Actions of the media, police, courts, community leaders, and political officials can lead to the success or failure of a social movement. If the right kind of force is applied, a potential social movement may be prevented, even though the first five determinants are present. Efforts to control the situation may block the social movement, minimize its effects, or make matters worse. Efforts to control the antiwar movement, for example, were actually counterproductive. During the student antiwar protests following the Cambodian invasion, the Ohio National Guard, mobilized by the governor of Ohio, killed four students and wounded twenty-two others on the Kent State University campus. Two African American students were killed during an antiwar protest at Jackson State University in Mississippi. Such heavy-handedness on the part of politicians and law enforcement officials only stimulated further protest that hastened the ending of the war.

Snapshot of America

Ask students to do a quick mental survey of the adult women they know. What percentage of them are a part of the workforce? How does this percentage compare to the percentage of women in the workforce in your state?

Answers to Interpreting the Map

1. Strain theory states that deviance is more likely to occur when a gap exists between cultural goals and the ability to achieve these goals by legitimate means. In the United States an important goal is success and the material possessions that go with it. Often, in order for families to achieve the success and material possessions they desire, more income is needed. The women's movement made it easier for women to achieve higher status jobs in the workforce. This has enabled families to achieve the additional income needed to reach their goals of success and material possessions.
2. Answers will vary.

There are increasing opportunities in the careers serving a post-industrial economy. Sociologists have the ability to take in the big picture, the ability to bring multiple sources of information and data to bear on a problem, the ability to take the role of the other, and the ability to communicate to different audiences.

These factors combine for an optimistic employment picture for sociology students. For job-hunting information, check out these links: **http://www.wilpaterson.edu/wpcpages/sch-hmss/sociology/career.htm** and **http://osiris.colorado.edu/POLSCI/RES/job.html.**

Pulling it All Together

Social movements are the most organized and permanent of all forms of collective behavior. Two theories exist to explain how social movements develop. They are value-added theory and the resource mobilization theory.

Answers to Section 4 Assessment

1. A social movement is the most highly structured, rational, and enduring form of collective behavior. The defining characteristics are:
   - a large number of people
   - a common goal to promote or prevent social change
   - activity sustained over a relatively long time period.
2. d (Women's Christian Temperance Union)
3. As in the value-added theory, Smelser's theory of social movements is that each step (stage) is a necessary condition and must be successful (add value) in order for the next step to be successful.
4. The resource mobilization theory of social movements is a focus on the process through which members of a social movement secure and use the resources needed to advance their cause (human skills and material goods).

Critical Thinking

5. Answers will vary.

resource mobilization theory theory of social movements that focuses on the use of resources to achieve goals

What is resource mobilization theory? **Resource mobilization theory** focuses on the process through which members of a social movement secure and use the resources needed to advance their cause. Resources include human skills such as leadership, organizational ability, and labor power, as well as material goods such as money, property, and equipment (Cress and Snow, 1996; McCarthy and Wolfson, 1996).

The civil rights movement of the 1960s succeeded in part because of the commitment of African Americans and in part because people of other races contributed the money, energy, and skills necessary to stage repeated protests. In contrast, the gay movement in the United States has experienced difficulty partly because of a relative shortage of money, foot soldiers, and affluent supporters.

Muslim worshippers donate money to aid relief effort for Turkey, which was devastated by a tremendous earthquake in 1999. Relate this behavior to resource mobilization theory.

> One hundred and eighty-one years ago, our forefathers started a revolution that still goes on.
>
> **Dwight D. Eisenhower**
> **U.S. president**

Section 4 Assessment

1. How would a sociologist define the term *social movement?*
2. Which of the following is an example of a reformative social movement?
   a. the French Revolution
   b. Zero Population Growth
   c. the Branch Davidians
   d. Women's Christian Temperance Union
3. How is Smelser's theory of social movements an example of the value-added process?
4. Briefly explain the resource mobilization theory of social movements.

Critical Thinking

5. **Synthesizing Information** If you wished to mount a social movement to change some U.S. policy (i.e., air pollution limits), which theory of social change would most likely guide your strategy? Explain why you would select a particular theory and how it would guide your approach.

Survey

Many students complain of feeling powerless to change anything in their school environment. Have students consider creating a school-wide survey that elicits social change. Ask the administration to agree to distribute this survey annually to obtain student feedback on a variety of issues.

CHAPTER 17 ASSESSMENT

Summary

Section 1: Social Change

Main Idea: Social change refers to new behaviors that have long-term and relatively important consequences. Discovery, invention, and diffusion are the major social processes through which social change occurs. Important agents of social change are technology, population, the natural environment, revolution, and war.

Section 2: Theoretical Perspectives on Social Change

Main Idea: The functionalist perspective depicts societies as relatively stable. Following a major change, these integrated systems seek a new equilibrium. According to the conflict perspective, societies are unstable systems that are constantly undergoing change. Symbolic interactionism identifies decreasing shared values as a source of social instability.

Section 3: Collective Behavior

Main Idea: Collective behavior describes how people behave when they are united by a single short-term goal. Rumors, fads, fashions, mass hysteria, and panics are examples of collective behaviors. Contagion theory and emergent norm theory describe crowd behavior.

Section 4: Social Movements

Main Idea: Social movements are more permanent and more organized than other types of collectives. Theories to explain how social movements develop include value-added theory and resource mobilization theory.

SOCIOLOGY Online

Self-Check Quiz
Visit the *Sociology and You* Web site at soc.glencoe.com and click on **Chapter 17—Self-Check Quizzes** to prepare for the chapter test.

Reviewing Vocabulary

Complete each sentence using each term once.

a. social movement
b. contagion theory
c. rumor
d. revolution
e. fashions
f. fads
g. crowd
h. collective behavior
i. emergent norm theory
j. social change
k. technology

1. New societal behaviors with long-term and relatively important consequences are called ______________.
2. ______________ is the knowledge and hardware used to achieve practical goals.
3. ______________ is a type of social movement that may involve the violent toppling of a political regime.
4. The spontaneous and unstructured social behavior of people who are responding to similar stimuli is known as ______________.
5. ______________ is a widely circulating story of questionable truth.
6. The unusual behavior patterns that spread rapidly, are embraced zealously, and then disappear in a short time are called ______________.
7. ______________ are behavior patterns that are widely approved but expected to change periodically.
8. A temporary collection of people who share a common interest are known as a ______________.
9. ______________ emphasizes the irrationality of crowds, created when members stimulate one another to higher and higher levels of emotional intensity.
10. ______________ stresses the similarity between daily social behavior and crowd behavior.
11. The form of collective behavior that has the most structure is called ______________.

597

ANSWERS CHAPTER 17 ASSESSMENT

Reviewing Vocabulary

1. j
2. k
3. d
4. h
5. c
6. f
7. e
8. g
9. b
10. i
11. a

Reviewing the Facts

1. Discovery, Invention, Diffusion
2. Students should list and describe contagion theory, emergent norm theory, and convergence theory.
3. Technology, Population, Natural Environment, Revolution, War
4. The value-added theory of social movements holds that certain conditions must exist in order for social movements to occur; each step in the process contributes to the final outcome.
5. Revolutionary Movement—attempts to make limited changes in society; Redemptive Movement—seeks to change people completely; Alternative Movement—focuses on bringing about limited change in people.
6. Focuses on the use of resources to achieve goals. Resources could be money, special skills, or material goods.

Thinking Critically

1. This example represents resistance to social change. As long as we say, "That's the way its always been," we have no need to change. There is comfort in consistency and predictability. The question not answered in the anecdote is whether the children are content with their grandfather's answer or whether they agitate for change.
2. Some students might think that a unisex bathroom is depicted for shock value. Answers will vary as students debate

ANSWERS CHAPTER 17 ASSESSMENT

whether television mirrors changes in society or sets the trends.

3. This phenomenon used to be called yellow journalism—sensationalizing news stories to increase circulation and readership.
4. Answers will vary. It appears that body piercing is becoming a fashion and not just a fad. Social acceptance causes these things to change. Currently, people's perceptions of body piercing is changing. It is still not accepted widely, however in areas outside large cities.

Integrating the Teacher Resources

To further assess student comprehension of this chapter, use Chapter Test A or B and the Unit 5 Test, available in the Chapter and Unit Tests booklet in your Teacher's Resource Box.

CHAPTER 17 ASSESSMENT

Reviewing the Facts

1. Use a diagram similar to the one below to show the cause and effect relationship between the three major social processes and social change.

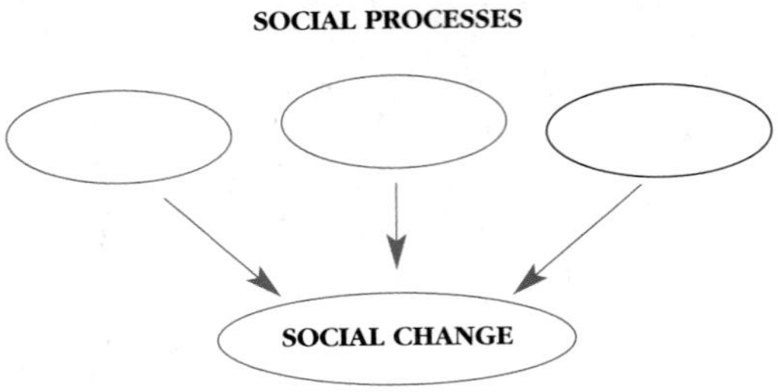

2. Identify and describe the three theories of crowd behavior.
3. What are the five important agents of social change?
4. In your own words explain the value-added theory of social movements.
5. List and describe the four primary types of social movements.
6. Explain the resource mobilization theory of social movements.

Thinking Critically

1. **Applying Concepts** Once upon a time, a family decided to grow orange trees. After several years of hard work and struggle, the first oranges appeared on the trees. Every year after that, when the oranges appeared, the father would say, "Everyone is entitled to choose one orange from the crop." The business thrived and expanded. The children were puzzled that even when the orange grove had grown to include over a thousand trees, they were allowed only one orange a year. Finally, when the children were grown and had children of their own, one of the grandchildren said, "Grandpa, every year we produce hundreds of thousands of oranges, and every year you tell us that we can have only one orange. Why is that?" Grandpa replied, "Because that's the way it's always been." In what way is this story a metaphor for society?
2. **Analyzing Information** Television shows often mirror changes taking place in some segments of society. Sometimes, these changes have not yet reached the mainstream culture. (One popular program centers many of its scenes in a unisex workplace bathroom.) What role do you think television has in changing society? Do you think its influence is more positive or negative?
3. **Evaluating Information** In this country, it is common to read about rumors circulated by the media, especially tabloid newspapers and television news magazine programs. How justified are newspapers and news reporters in publicizing unverified information? Should viewers be responsible for evaluating the information themselves? Should the news sources be penalized for not investigating or verifying rumors? What are the consequences for society if news sources are not reliable?
4. **Drawing Conclusions** Twenty years ago, body piercing (other than for earrings) was considered deviant behavior. Today, it is fast becoming a social norm in many classes and social categories. Do you think that body piercing is a fad or a fashion? What factors might cause a behavior that is not desirable in one generation to become accepted just one generation later?

Sociology Projects

1. **Technology** Over the next few days, look for new technologies that have initiated social changes within the last five years. For example, Web TV is a fairly new technological invention. Make a list of such items, including things that you have heard are coming but have not yet been released. For each item write down what earlier development made the new item possible. For example, high-definition TV was a result of knowledge gained from aerospace

Sociology Projects

1. Point out to students that even though new inventions are created daily, cultural lag (see Chapter 3) always exists. The culture always lags behind technology, partly due to the fact that it would be virtually impossible to buy and replace things every time new technology comes out. One of the most startling technological flops was the 8-track cassette player. It seemed to become obsolete as soon as it came out.
2. Students will have fun depicting the fads that have surfaced during their lifetimes, as well as during their parents' and grandparents' lifetimes. If some parents and grandparents still have some old fad memorabilia, like an old hula hoop, have students bring them in for show and tell.
3. This activity was previously mentioned on page 582 (Teaching Strategy). If you don't want to make this a class project,

satellite projects. Share your findings with classmates. You will probably be amazed at how extensive your list is. Post it in the classroom, and add to it as you hear about more changes.

2. **Fads** Look through old and new magazines for examples of fads that have appeared since you were born. (Examples might include retro platform shoes and Beanie Babies.) Create a collage illustrating those fads. Are some of the fads still around? Have they been replaced by similar fads? Ask your parents or grandparents what some fads were when they were teenagers. Find pictures, or ask them if they can provide you with examples. Make a poster or arrange the pictures in a booklet format that explains some of the unusual fads.
3. **Crowd Behavior** As an experiment in crowd behavior, try to start a new fad or fashion in your school. For example, get everyone in your group or class to agree to start wearing necklaces with metal washers on them or unmatched socks. If several of you do this, you might be able to convince others that a new fad has begun. If the fad does not catch on, list reasons why you think your peers were resistant to change in this case.
4. **Rumors** Search the library magazine catalog or Internet for rumors concerning a public figure. Identify the source and evaluate its credibility. Or, research a lawsuit filed by a public figure over the publication of a false story.
5. **Fads and Fashions** Working in groups, collect some old high school yearbooks from parents and relatives. Comb through them looking for examples of fads and fashions from different decades. Present your findings to the whole class.
6. **Rumors and the Media** As an extension to "Thinking Critically," question number 3, consider and list the options that a news reporter has when he or she receives unverified stories to report. Suggest possible consequences associated with each option.

Technology Activity

1. Jan Harold Brunvand coined the term *urban legend* to describe a type of rumor that is long lasting and widely believed. This term is commonly used now, and if you search the Internet, you will find many sites devoted to this subject.
   a. Select a few of the web sites (two good ones are at http://www.urbanlegends.com/ and http://www.snopes.com/) and review them. Be prepared to share one or two of them with your class.
   b. What common elements do these urban legends have? Do your observations correspond with those of Urbanlegends.com?
   c. What role do you think the Internet plays in spreading these urban legends?

have individual students see if they can start a fad by enlisting the support of friends. The results should make for some interesting discussion.

4. The Clinton scandal involving Monica Lewinsky is a recent case students can examine. How much of what was written or said in the media about Monica Lewinsky consisted of rumors? How much was true? Have students use this or a similar story and ascertain the degree of truth in the reporting. One way to do this is to have students see how many times the stories are corroborated by other sources.
5. Your school library should have copies of older yearbooks. If your school librarian is reluctant to lend out the old yearbooks, have him or her bring them to your class to show. Have students compare hairstyles, clothing, expressions, news events, etc.
6. Answers will vary. Options: Report story without verifying sources or delay story until information is verified.

ANSWERS CHAPTER 17 ASSESSMENT

Consequences: May receive pressure from network to report the story, so position or job may be at stake. If unverified story proves to be untrue, legal action could be taken against the news station and reporter's position or job may be lost.

Technology Activity

1. a–b. Student answers will vary depending on the web sites they visit.
   c. Students will probably realize that the Internet allows for much faster and easier spreading of urban legends.

Integrating the Teacher Resources

Look for the Alternative Assessments booklet in your Teacher's Resource Box for essay tests and performance assessment activities based on this chapter.

Enrichment Reading

Have students return to Chapter 8, Social Stratification and Chapter 12, Education, for more information on how stratification and educational opportunity might correlate with Internet use.

Chapter 17

Enrichment Reading

Falling Through the Net

Computer technology is changing the face of American society. Access to personal computers and the Internet is even affecting the nature of social stratification. Digital technology has become such an important tool for economic success that it threatens to create a new divide between haves and have-nots.

Information tools, such as the personal computer and the Internet, are increasingly critical to economic success and personal advancement. *"Falling Through the Net: Defining the Digital Divide"* finds that more Americans than ever have access to telephones, computers, and the Internet. At the same time, however, . . . there is still a significant "digital **divide**" separating American information "haves" and "have nots." Indeed, in many instances, the digital divide has *widened*. . . .

The good news is that Americans are more connected than ever before. Access to computers and the Internet has soared for people in all demographic groups and geographic locations. At the end of 1998, over 40 percent of American households owned computers, and one-quarter of all households had Internet access. Additionally, those who were less likely to have telephones (chiefly, young and minority households in rural areas) are now more likely to have phones at home.

Accompanying this good news, however, is the persistence of the digital divide between the information rich (such as Whites, Asians/Pacific Islanders, those with higher incomes, those more educated, and dual-parent households) and the information poor (such as those who are younger, those with lower incomes and education levels, certain minorities, and those in rural areas or central cities). The 1998 data reveal significant **disparities,** including the following:

- Households with incomes of $75,000 and higher are more than *twenty times* more likely to have access to the Internet than those at the lowest income levels, and more than *nine times* as likely to have a computer at home.
- Whites are more likely to have access to the Internet from home than Blacks or Hispanics have from *any* location.
- Black and Hispanic households are approximately *one-third* as likely to have home Internet access as households of Asian/Pacific Islander descent, and roughly *two-fifths* as likely as White households.
- Regardless of income level, Americans living in rural areas are lagging behind in Internet access. Indeed, at the lowest income levels, those in urban areas are more than twice as likely to have Internet access than those earning the same income in rural areas.

For many groups, the digital divide has *widened* as the information "haves" outpace the "have nots" in gaining access to electronic resources. The following gaps with regard to home Internet access are representative:

- The gaps between White and Hispanic households, and between White and Black households, are now more than six percentage points larger than they were in 1994.

Integrating the Teacher Resources

Additional primary source readings for this chapter can be found in Culture Studies: The Sociological Perspective**, available in your Teacher's Resource Box. Questions for students are included.**

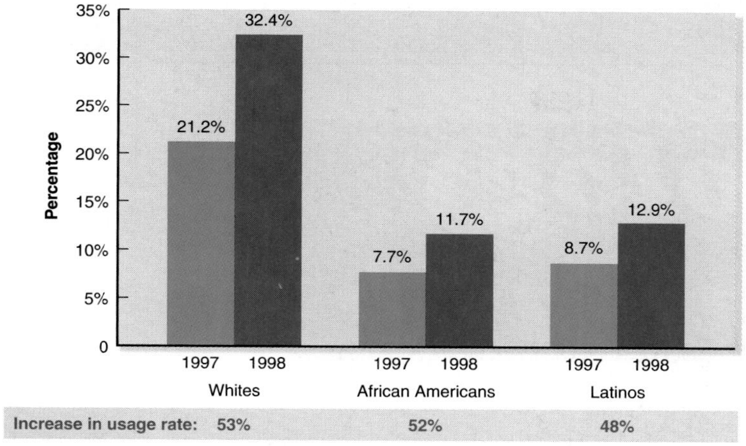

Figure 17.5 Minorities and the Internet. *This figure reveals the digital divide in the United States between whites, African Americans, and Latinos. What do you think are the most important consequences of this divide?*

Source: "Report Finds Net Users Increasingly White, Well Off," *Washington Post,* July 9, 1999, p. A20.

What Does it Mean?

divide
as a noun, something that separates two areas; a point or line of division

disparities
marked differences in quality or character (usually where you would not expect them)

irrespective
regardless; without relation to

❖ The digital divides based on education and income level have also increased in the last year alone. Between 1997 and 1998, the divide between those at the highest and lowest education levels increased 25 percent, and the divide between those at the highest and lowest income levels grew 29 percent.

Nevertheless, the news is not all bleak. For Americans with incomes of $75,000 and higher, the divide between Whites and Blacks has actually narrowed considerably in the last year. This finding suggests that the most affluent American families, **irrespective** of race, are connecting to the Net.

Source: "Falling Through the Net: Defining the Digital Divide," a Report on the Telecommunications and Information Technology Gap in America (Washington, DC: National Telecommunications and Information Administration, U.S. Department of Commerce, July 1999)

Read and React

1. What is the main idea of this report on Internet access?
2. What does the term *information rich* (in the third paragraph) mean?
3. Who is more likely to have Internet access, whites or Asian/Pacific Islanders? How can you tell?
4. Why do you think urban Americans are more than twice as likely to have Internet access as rural Americans with the same income level?
5. In what category has the gap between African Americans and whites significantly narrowed? What explanation would you offer for this?
6. What is the net effect of this trend? How serious a problem is it?

Answers to Read and React

1. A digital divide is being created by the use of the Internet. Information has the ability to create a culture of digital "haves and have nots."
2. Our society is information rich because of our technological ability to access information.
3. More white households have access to the Internet than Asian/Pacific Islander households do.
4. Answers will vary. Students might suggest that the faster pace of life or the need to "keep up with the Joneses" is more common in urban settings.
5. The gap between whites and African Americans is the smallest at higher income levels, where income exceeds $75,000 per year.
6. The net effect could be that Internet access will become the norm for the transmission of information and those without will be greatly hampered.

Sociology DataBank

CONTENTS

SOCIOLOGY Online

Visit the *Sociology and You* Web site at soc.glencoe.com and click on **Textbook Updates–Databank** for an update of the data.

The Family

For sociologists, a *family* is a group of people related by marriage, blood, or adoption.

Percent of Children Living in Working Poor Families

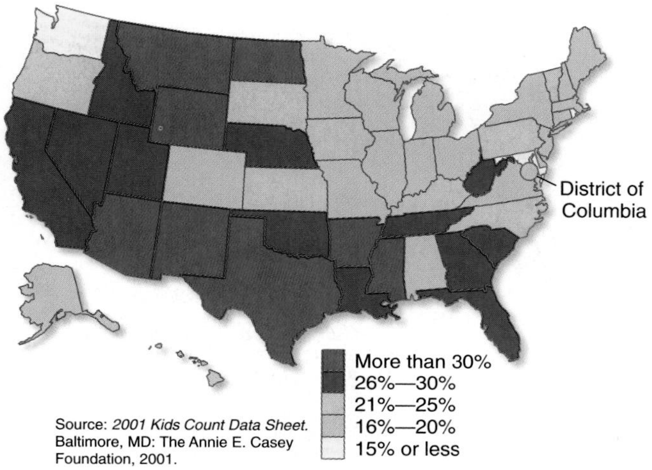

Source: *2001 Kids Count Data Sheet.* Baltimore, MD: The Annie E. Casey Foundation, 2001.

Americans Who Identified With More Than One Race, 2000

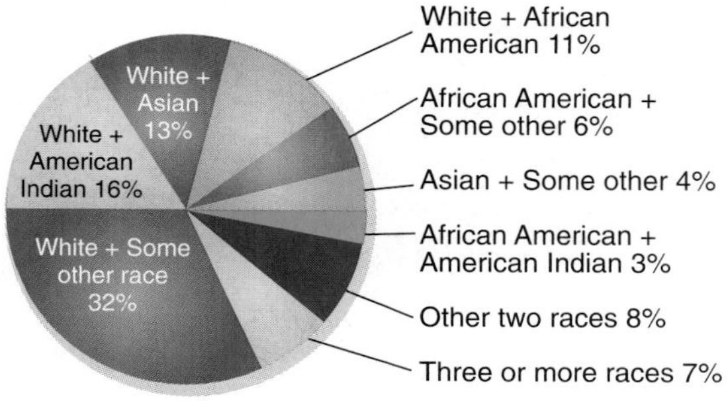

Total multiracial Americans = 6,826,228

Source: First Glimpses From the 2000 U.S. Census Population Bulletin Vol. 56, No. 2 June 2001.

Child Abuse and Neglect Cases 1990 to 1998, by Type

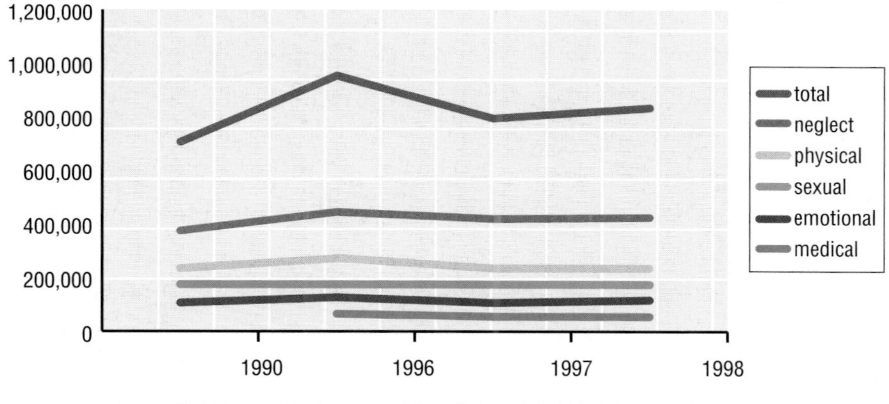

Source: U.S. Bureau of the Census. *Statistical Abstract of the United States 2000.* Washington DC: U.S. Government Printing Office.

EDUCATION

Education is the social institution responsible for the transmission of knowledge to its members. This includes academic knowledge, vocational skills, and a society's beliefs, norms, and values.

How Educated Are Young Workers?

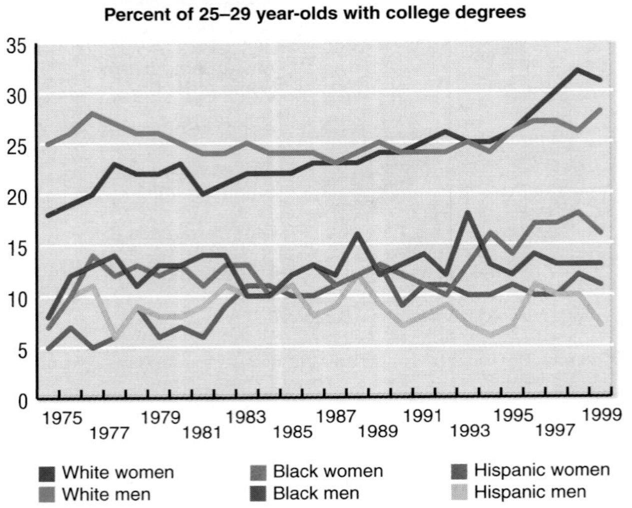

Source: *2000 United States Population Data Sheet.* Washington, DC: Population Reference Bureau, 2000.

Percent of Postsecondary Graduates by Sex, 1960 to 2000.

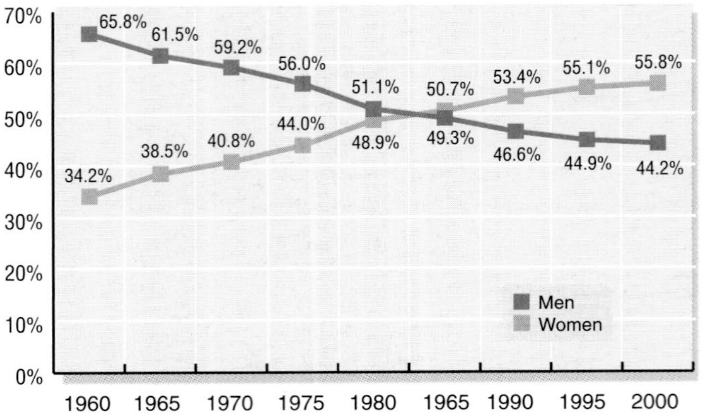

Source: *Digest of Educational Statistics.* Washington DC: U.S. National Center for Education Statistics, 2001. Http://www.nces.gov.

Education Spending

Median Household Income by State (3-year average 1996–1998)

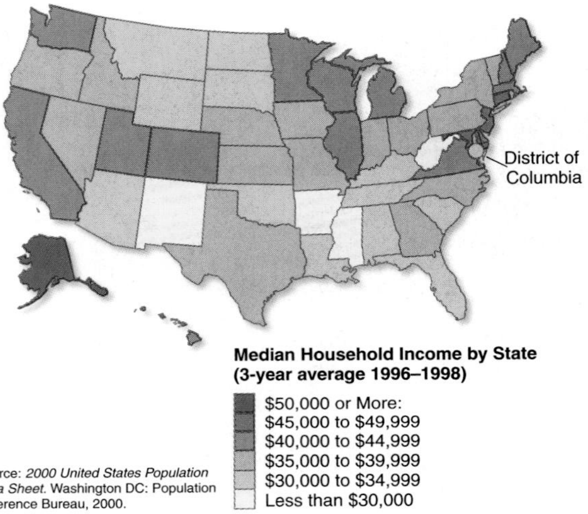

Source: *2000 United States Population Data Sheet.* Washington DC: Population Reference Bureau, 2000.

School Expenditures

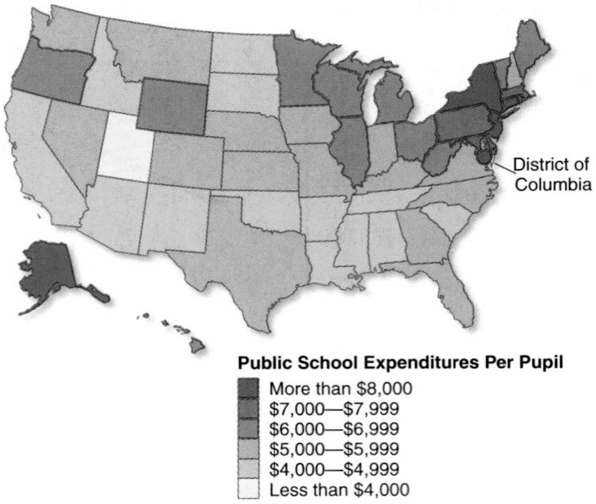

Educational Attainment of the Population by Age Group (1999)

At Least Upper Secondary Education

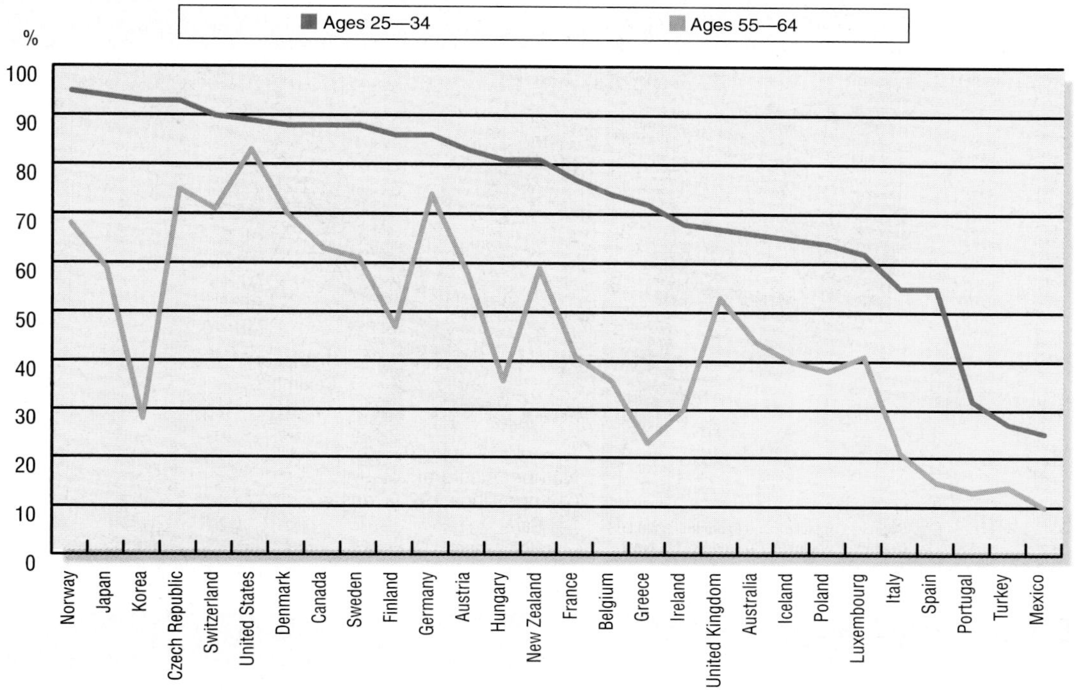

At Least Tertiary Education

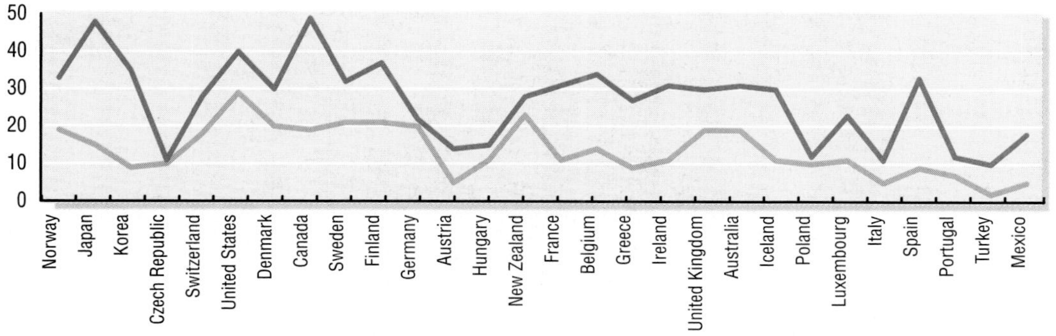

Source: Education at a Glance 2001. Paris: Organization for Education Cooperation and Development.

The Political Institution

The *political institution* is the body through which power is obtained and exercised to maintain order and handle conflict in the society.

Electoral Votes by State, 2000

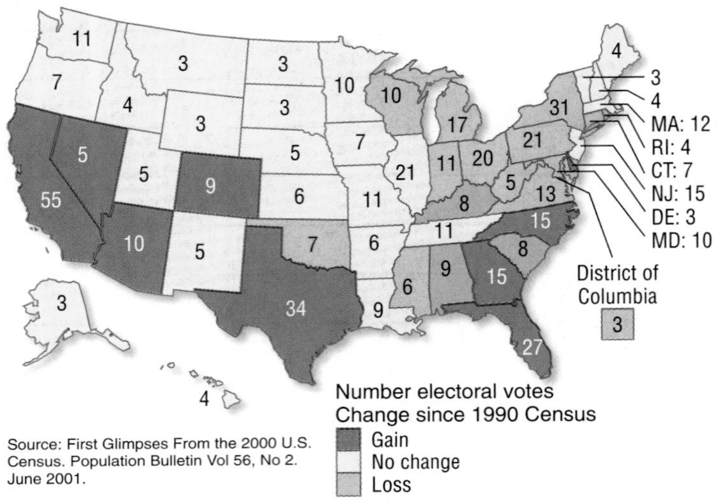

Source: First Glimpses From the 2000 U.S. Census. Population Bulletin Vol 56, No 2. June 2001.

U.S. House Delegations

(As determined by the 2000 elections)

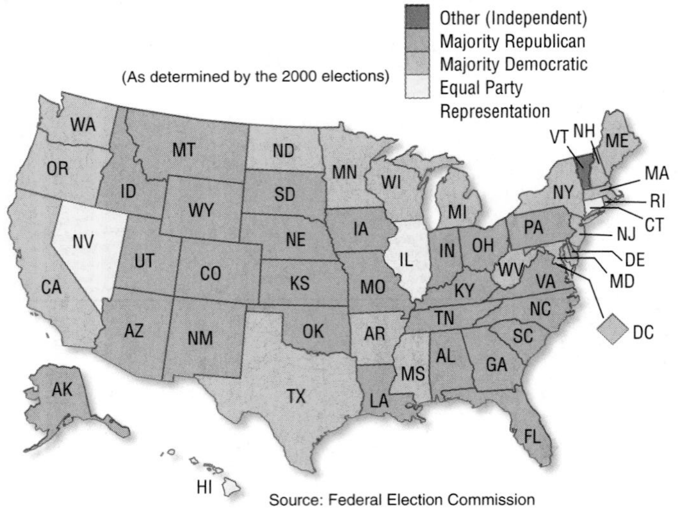

Source: Federal Election Commission

Political Action Committee (PAC) Count—1977 to Present

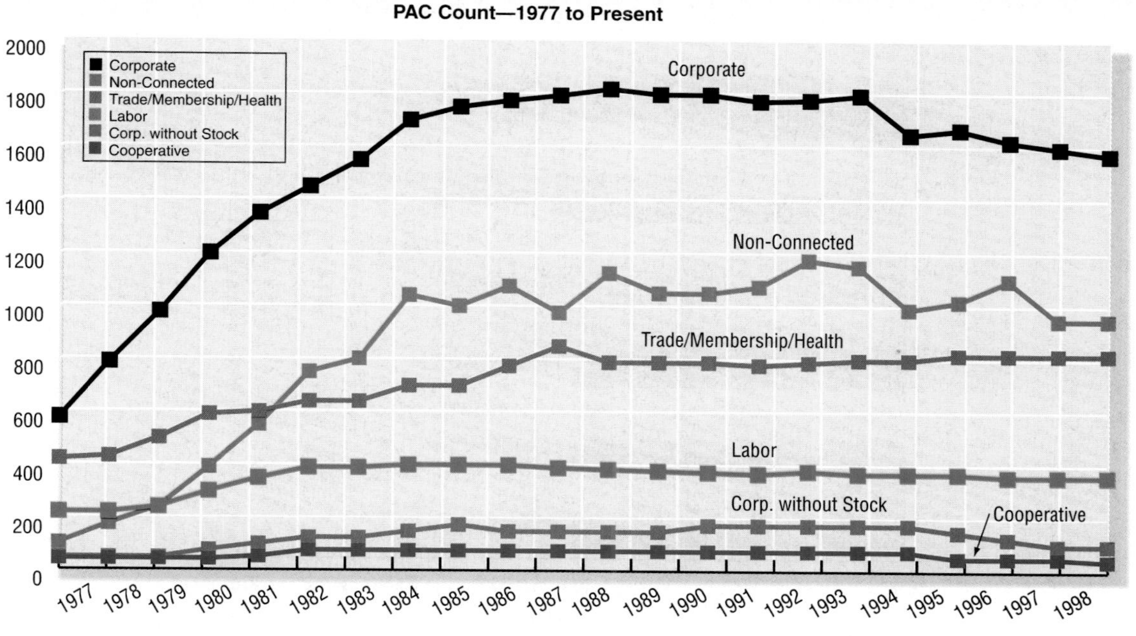

Source: Federal Election Commission.

Overall Campaign Spending at the Federal Level (in millions of dollars)

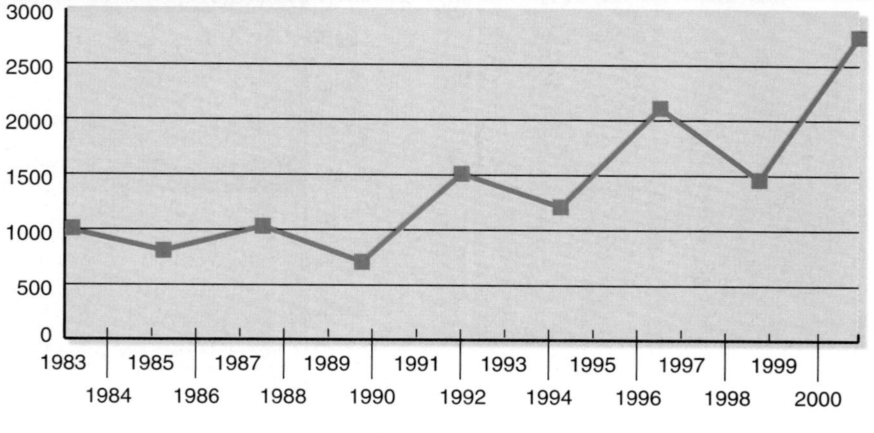

Source: Federal Election Commission Reports.

Reported Voting by Age Group—Presidential Elections, 1976–1996

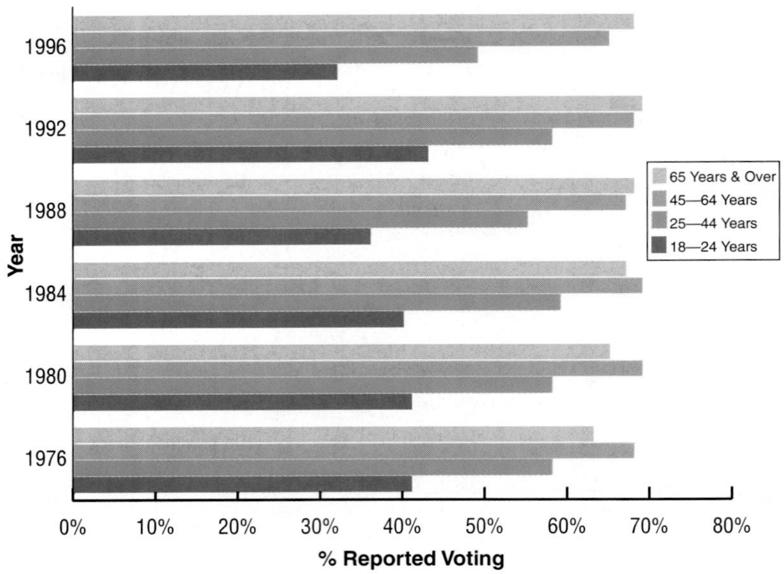

Source: Federal Election Commission

Most Recent Voter Turnouts in National Elections

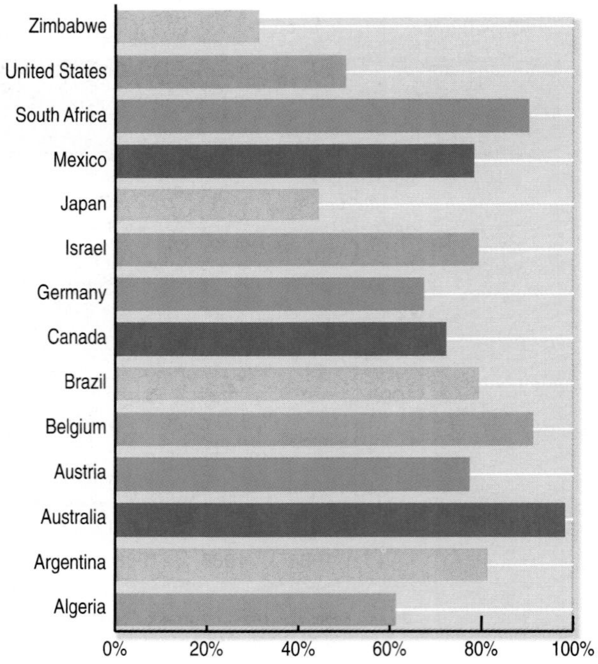

Source: Federal Election Commission

THE ECONOMY

The *economy* is the social institution that regulates the production and distribution of goods and services for a society.

What Jobs Do Women Have?

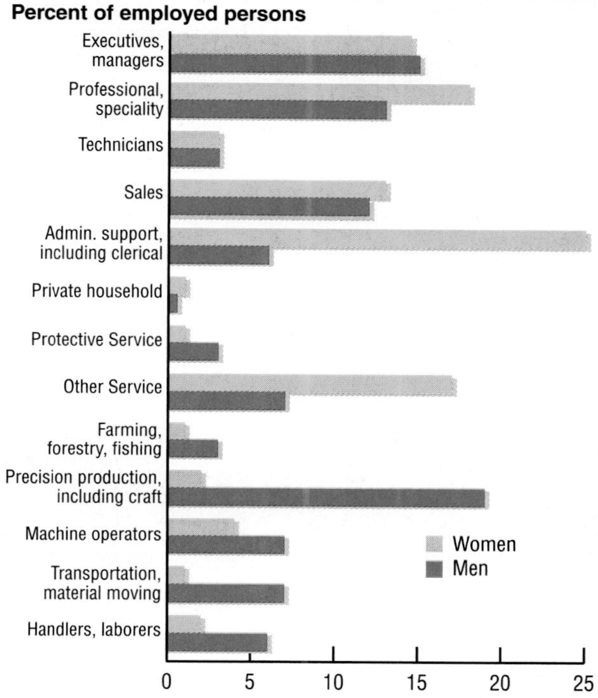

Source: *2000 United States Population Data Sheet.* Washington, DC: Population Reference Bureau, 2000.

Who's Entering and Staying in the Labor Force?

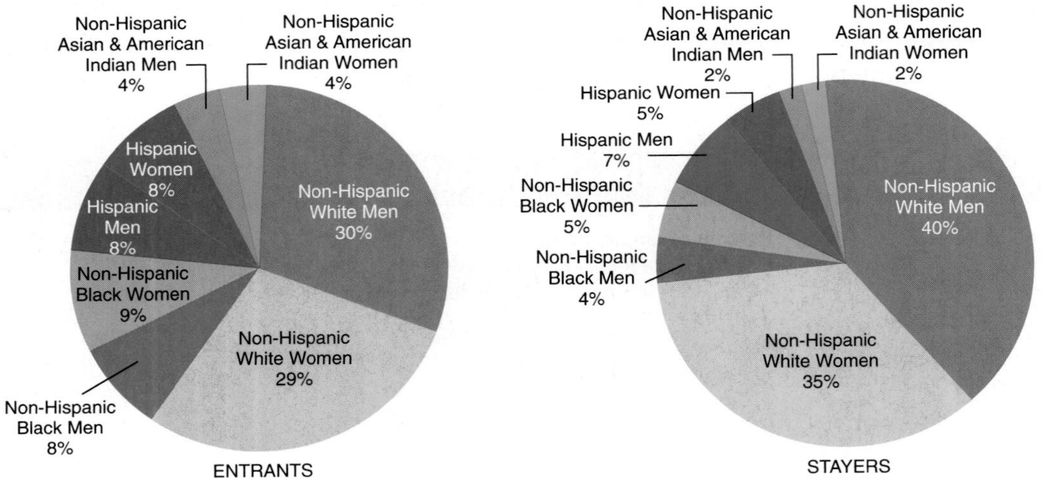

Source: *2000 United States Population Data Sheet.* Washington, DC: Population Reference Bureau, 2000.

Median Net Worth of Households by Monthly Household Income Quintile Groups: 1993 and 1995

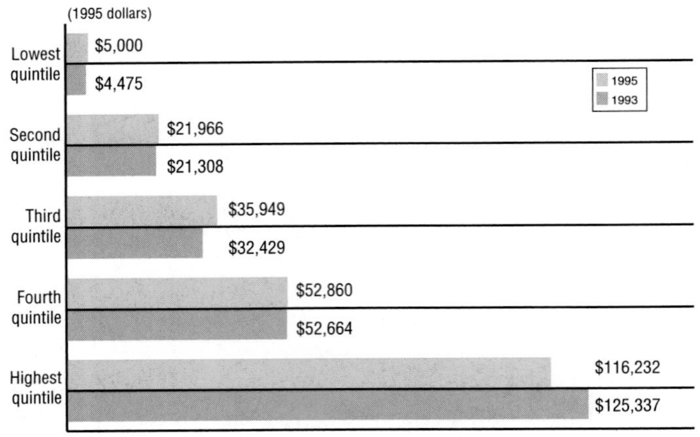

Source: U.S. Bureau of the Census. *"Household Net Worth and Asset Ownership."* Washington, DC: U.S. Government Printing Office, 2000.

Gross National Income in Purchasing Power Parity Per Capita for Selected Countries, 1999

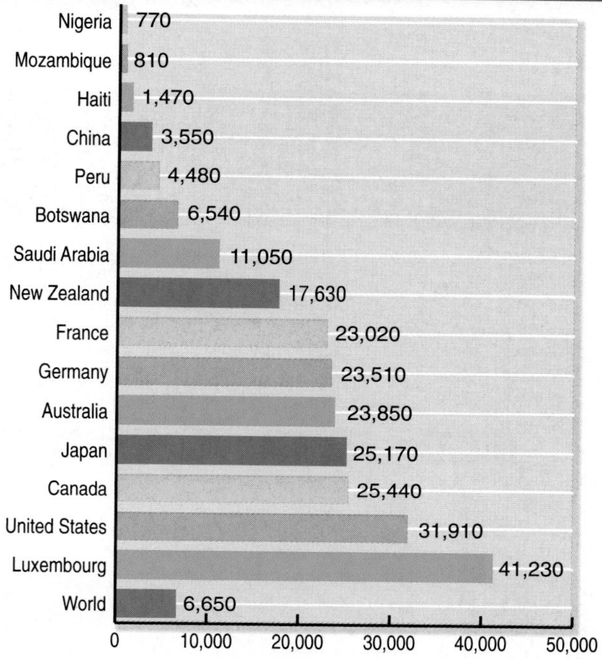

Source: *2001 World Population Data Sheet.* Washington DC: Population Reference Bureau, 2001.

Percent of Workers Who Are Self-Employed (3-year average 1997–1999)

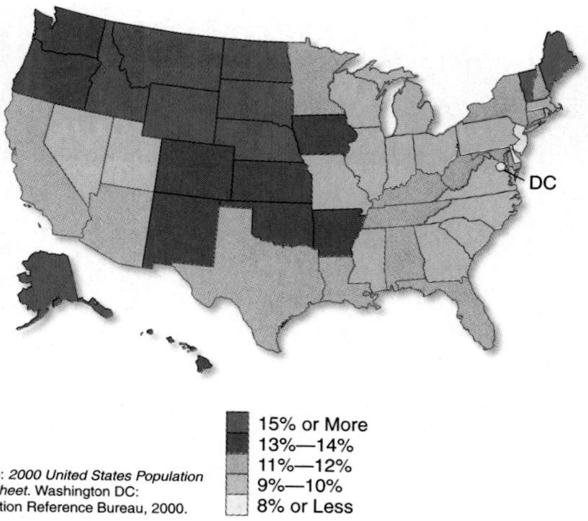

Source: *2000 United States Population Data Sheet.* Washington DC: Population Reference Bureau, 2000.

RELIGION

Religion is a unified system of beliefs and practices concerned with sacred things.

Percent of Americans Who Think Religion Is Increasing or Losing Its Influence

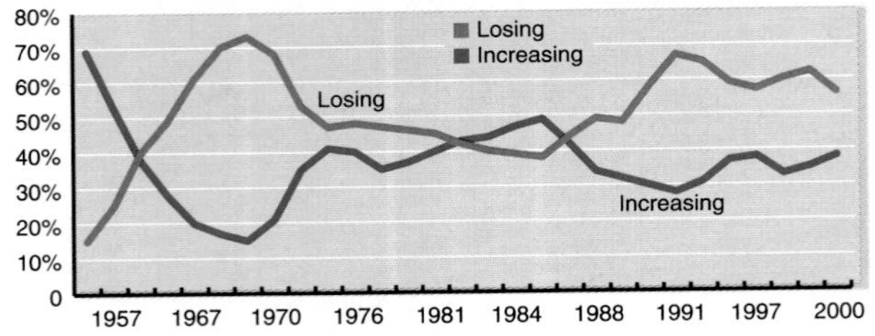

Source: The Gallup Organization

U.S. Per Capita Income/ Per Member Giving as a Percent of Income

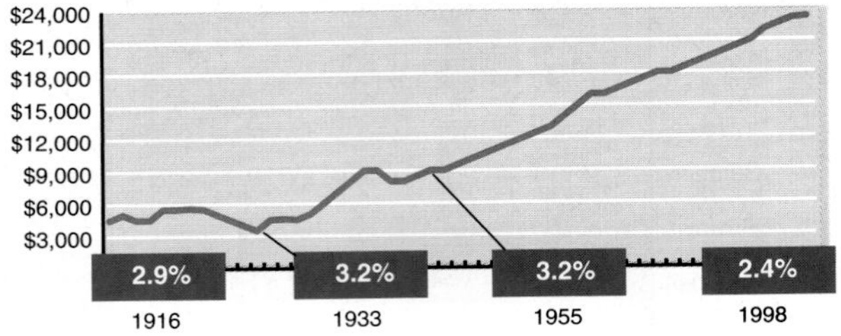

Percent of Americans Who Believe that Religion Can Answer All of Today's Problems or Is Old-Fashioned

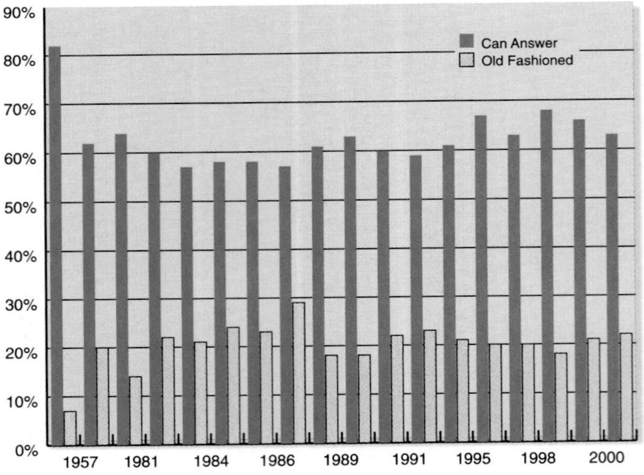

Source: The Gallup Organization.

Giving as a Percent of Income and Membership as a Percent of U.S. Population, 1968–1998

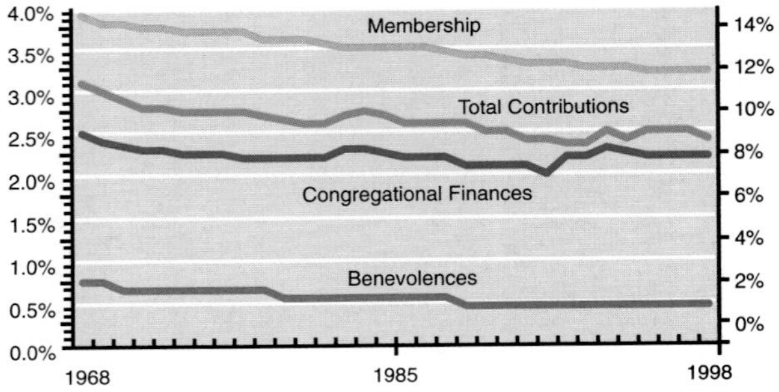

SPORT

Sport is a set of competitive activities in which winners and losers are determined by physical performance within a set of established rules.

Participation in High School and NCAA Sponsored Sports, 1982 to 2000

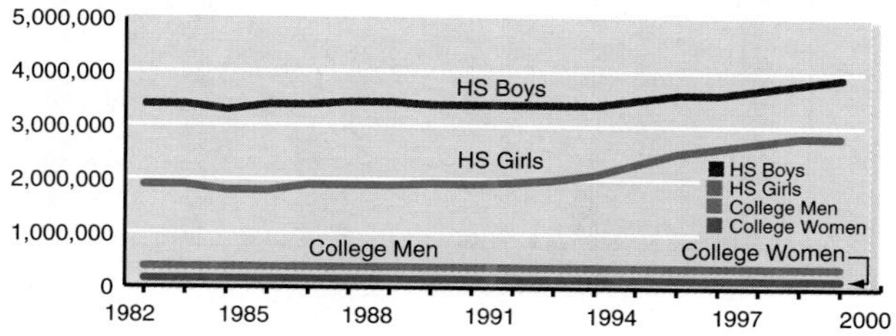

Sources: National Federation of State High School Associations and the National Collegiate Athletic Association.

Interest in Professional Sports Based on Attendance At Professional Sporting Events: United States by Demographics

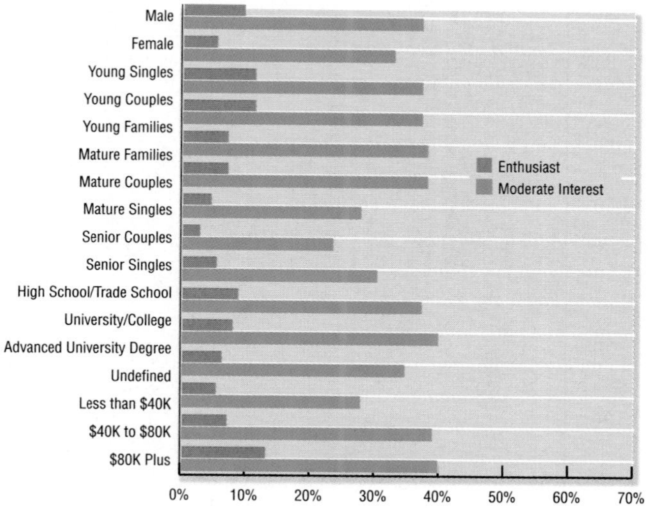

Source: Lang, David. *"Interest in Professional Sports (As a Spectator) Profile Report."* April 2001.

Racial Composition of Players in Men's Professional Leagues and the WNBA

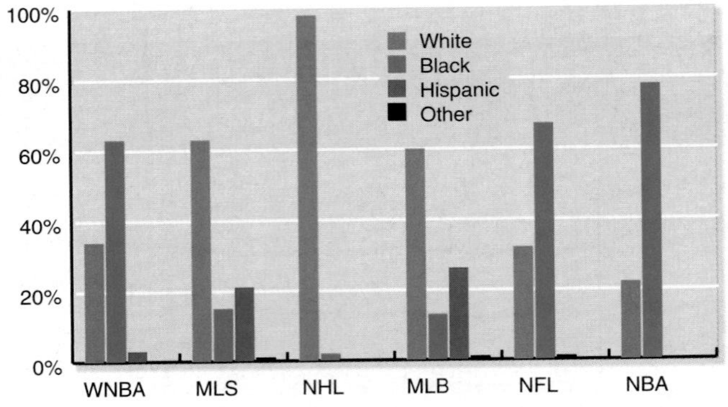

Source: Lapchick, Richard E., and Kevin J. Matthews (2001). *"2001 Racial and Gender Report Card."* Boston: Northeastern University s Center for the Study of Sport in Society.

Percent Increase in Applications to Colleges and Universities in the Three Years Following a National Championship

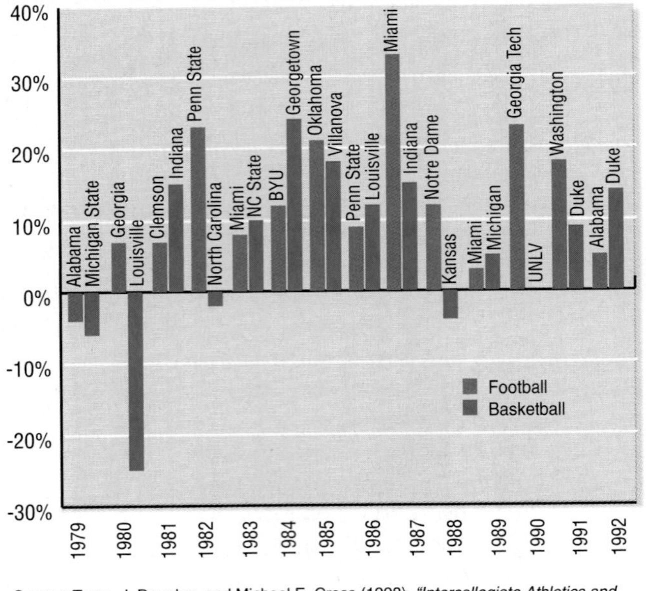

Source: Toma, J. Douglas, and Michael E. Cross (1998). *"Intercollegiate Athletics and Student College Choice: Exploring the Impact of Championship Seasons on Undergraduate Applications."* Research in Higher Education 39, 633—661.

American Sociological Association's Code of Ethics

The American Sociological Association's (ASA's) Code of Ethics sets forth the principles and ethical standards that underlie sociologists' professional responsibilities and conduct. These principles and standards should be used as guidelines when examining everyday professional activities. They constitute normative statements for sociologists and provide guidance on issues that sociologists may encounter in their professional work.

The Preamble and General Principles of the Code are aspirational goals to guide sociologists toward the highest ideals of sociology. Although the Preamble and General Principles are not enforceable rules, they should be considered by sociologists in arriving at an ethical course of action and may be considered by ethics bodies in interpreting the Ethical Standards.

The Ethical Standards set forth enforceable rules of conduct by sociologists. Most of the Ethical Standards are written broadly in order to apply to sociologists in varied roles, and the application of an Ethical Standard may vary depending on the context. The Ethical Standards are not exhaustive. Any conduct that is not specifically addressed by this Code of Ethics is not necessarily ethical or unethical.

Preamble

This Code of Ethics articulates a common set of values upon which sociologists build their professional and scientific work. The Code is intended to provide both the general principles and the rules to cover professional situations encountered by sociologists. It has as its primary goal the welfare and protection of the individuals and groups with whom sociologists work. It is the individual responsibility of each sociologist to aspire to the highest possible standards of conduct in research, teaching, practice, and service.

The development of a dynamic set of ethical standards for a sociologist's work-related conduct requires a personal commitment to a lifelong effort to act ethically; to encourage ethical behavior by students, supervisors, supervisees, employers, employees, and colleagues; and to consult with others as needed concerning ethical problems. Each sociologist supplements, but does not violate, the values and rules specified in the Code of Ethics based on guidance drawn from personal values, culture, and experience.

General Principles

The following General Principles are aspirational and serve as a guide for sociologists in determining ethical courses of action in various contexts. They exemplify the highest ideals of professional conduct.

Principle A: Professional Competence Sociologists strive to maintain the highest levels of competence in their work; they recognize the limitations of their expertise; and they undertake only those tasks for which they are qualified by education, training, or experience. They recognize the need for ongoing education in order to remain professionally competent; and they utilize the appropriate scientific, professional, technical, and administrative resources needed to ensure competence in their professional activities. They consult with other professionals when necessary for the benefit of their students, research participants, and clients.

Principle B: Integrity Sociologists are honest, fair, and respectful of others in their professional activities—in research, teaching, practice, and service. Sociologists do not knowingly act in ways that jeopardize either their own or others' professional welfare. Sociologists conduct their affairs in ways that inspire trust and confidence; they do not knowingly make statements that are false, misleading, or deceptive.

Principle C: Professional and Scientific Responsibility Sociologists adhere to the highest scientific and professional standards and accept responsibility for their work. Sociologists understand that they form a community and show respect for other sociologists even when they disagree on theoretical, methodological, or personal approaches to professional activities. Sociologists value the public trust in sociology and are concerned about their ethical behavior and that of other sociologists that might compromise that trust. While endeavoring always to be collegial, sociologists must never let the desire to be collegial outweigh their shared responsibility for ethical behavior. When appropriate, they consult with colleagues in order to prevent or avoid unethical conduct.

Principle D: Respect for People's Rights, Dignity, and Diversity Sociologists respect the rights, dignity, and worth of all people. They strive to eliminate bias in their professional activities, and they do not tolerate any forms of discrimination based on age; gender; race; ethnicity; national origin; religion; sexual orientation; disability; health conditions; or marital, domestic, or parental status. They are sensitive to cultural, individual, and role differences in serving, teaching, and studying groups of people with distinctive characteristics. In all of their work-related activities, sociologists acknowledge the rights of others to hold values, attitudes, and opinions that differ from their own.

Principle E: Social Responsibility Sociologists are aware of their professional and scientific responsibility to the communities and societies in which they live and work. They apply and make public their knowledge in order to contribute to the public good. When undertaking research, they strive to advance the science of sociology and to serve the public good.

Ethical Standards

The complete text of the Ethical Standards can be found at the ASA web site. Excerpts from this code are reproduced here.

1. Professional and Scientific Standards: Sociologists adhere to the highest possible technical standards that are reasonable and responsible in their research, teaching, practice, and service activities.
2. Competence: Sociologists conduct research, teach, practice, and provide service only within the boundaries of their competence, based on their education, training, supervised experience, or appropriate professional experience.
3. Representation and Misuse of Expertise: Because sociologists' scientific and professional judgments and actions may affect the lives of others, they are alert to and guard against personal, financial, social, organizational, or political factors that might lead to misuse of their knowledge, expertise, or influence.
4. Delegation and Supervision: Sociologists provide proper training and supervision to their students, supervisees, or employees and take reasonable steps to see that such persons perform services responsibly, competently, and ethically.
5. Nondiscrimination: Sociologists do not engage in discrimination in their work based on age; gender; race; ethnicity; national origin; religion; sexual orientation; disability; health conditions; marital; domestic, or parental status; or any other applicable basis proscribed by law.
6. Non-exploitation: Whether for personal, economic, or professional advantage, sociologists do not exploit persons over whom they have direct or indirect supervisory, evaluative, or other authority such as students, supervisees, employees, or research participants.
7. Harassment: Sociologists do not engage in harassment of any person, including students, supervisees, employees, or research participants. Harassment consists of a single intense and severe act or of multiple persistent or pervasive acts which are demeaning, abusive, offensive, or create a hostile professional or workplace environment. Sexual harassment may include sexual solicitation, physical advance, or verbal or non-verbal conduct that is sexual in nature. Racial harassment may include unnecessary, exaggerated, or unwarranted attention or attack, whether verbal or non-verbal, because of a person's race or ethnicity.

8. Employment Decisions: Sociologists have an obligation to adhere to the highest ethical standards when participating in employment-related decisions, when seeking employment, or when planning to resign from a position.

9. Conflicts of Interest: Sociologists maintain the highest degree of integrity in their professional work and avoid conflicts of interest and the appearance of conflict. Conflicts of interest arise when sociologists' personal or financial interests prevent them from performing their professional work in an unbiased manner.

10. Public Communication: Sociologists adhere to the highest professional standards in public communications about their professional services, credentials and expertise, work products, or publications, whether these communications are from themselves or from others.

10.02 In working with the press, radio, television, or other communications media or in advertising in the media, sociologists are cognizant of potential conflicts of interest or appearances of such conflicts (e.g., they do not provide compensation to employees of the media), and they adhere to the highest standards of professional honesty (e.g., they acknowledge paid advertising).

11. Confidentiality: Sociologists have an obligation to ensure that confidential information is protected. They do so to ensure the integrity of research and the open communication with research participants and to protect sensitive information obtained in research, teaching, practice, and service. When gathering confidential information, sociologists should take into account the long-term uses of the information, including its potential placement in public archives or the examination of the information by other researchers or practitioners.

11.02 Sociologists may confront unanticipated circumstances where they become aware of information that is clearly health- or life-threatening to research participants, students, employees, clients, or others. In these cases, sociologists balance the importance of guarantees of confidentiality with other principles in this Code of Ethics, standards of conduct, and applicable law.

Confidentiality is not required with respect to observations in public places, activities conducted in public, or other settings where no rules of privacy are provided by law or custom. Similarly, confidentiality is not required in the case of information available from public records.

11.06 Sociologists do not disclose in their writings, lectures, or other public media confidential, personally identifiable information concerning their research participants, students, individual or organizational clients, or other recipients of their services which is obtained during the course of their work, unless consent from individuals or their legal representatives has been obtained.

When confidential information is used in scientific and professional presentations, sociologists disguise the identity of research participants, students, individual or organizational clients, or other recipients of their services.

12. Informed Consent: Informed consent is a basic ethical tenet of scientific research on human populations. Sociologists do not involve a human being as a subject in research without the informed consent of the subject or the subject's legally authorized representative, except as otherwise specified in this Code. Sociologists recognize the possibility of undue influence or subtle pressures on subjects that may derive from researchers' expertise or authority, and they take this into account in designing informed consent procedures.

12.04 In undertaking research with children, sociologists obtain the consent of children to participate, to the extent that they are capable of providing such consent, except under circumstances where consent may not be required.

12.05 Sociologists never deceive research participants about significant aspects of the research that would affect their willingness to participate, such as physical risks, discomfort, or unpleasant emotional experiences.

12.06 Sociologists obtain informed consent from research participants, students, employees, clients, or others prior to videotaping, filming, or recording them in any form, unless these activities involve simply naturalistic observations in public places and it is not anticipated that the recording will be used in a manner that could cause personal identification or harm.

13. Research Planning, Implementation, and Dissemination: Sociologists have an obligation to promote the integrity of research and to ensure that they comply with the ethical tenets of science in the planning, implementation, and dissemination of research. They do so in order to advance knowledge, to minimize the possibility that results will be misleading, and to protect the rights of research participants.

13.01 Planning and Implementation: In planning and implementing research, sociologists minimize the possibility that results will be misleading.

Sociologists take steps to implement protections for the rights and welfare of research participants and other persons affected by the research.

In their research, sociologists do not encourage activities or themselves behave in ways that are health- or life-threatening to research participants or others.

In planning and implementing research, sociologists consult those with expertise concerning any special population under investigation or likely to be affected.

13.04 Reporting on Research: Sociologists do not fabricate data or falsify results in their publications or presentations.

In presenting their work, sociologists report their findings fully and do not omit relevant data. They report results whether they support or contradict the expected outcomes.

Sociologists report sources of financial support in their written papers and note any special relations to any sponsor. In special circumstances, sociologists may withhold the names of specific sponsors if they provide an adequate and full description of the nature and interest of the sponsor.

14. Plagiarism: In publications, presentations, teaching, practice, and service, sociologists explicitly identify, credit, and reference the author when they take data or material verbatim from another person's written work, whether it is published, unpublished, or electronically available.

15. Authorship Credit: Sociologists take responsibility and credit, including authorship credit, only for work they have actually performed or to which they have contributed.

Sociologists ensure that principal authorship and other publication credits are based on the relative scientific or professional contributions of the individuals involved, regardless of their status. In claiming or determining the ordering of authorship, sociologists seek to reflect accurately the contributions of main participants in the research and writing process.

A student is usually listed as principal author on any multiple-authored publication that substantially derives from the student's dissertation or thesis.

20. Adherence to the Code of Ethics: Sociologists have an obligation to confront, address, and attempt to resolve ethical issues according to this Code of Ethics.

20.01 Familiarity with the Code of Ethics: Sociologists have an obligation to be familiar with this Code of Ethics, other applicable ethics codes, and their application to sociologists' work. Lack of awareness or misunderstanding of an ethical standard is not, in itself, a defense to a charge of unethical conduct.

20.02 Confronting Ethical Issues: When sociologists are uncertain whether a particular situation or course of action would violate the Code of Ethics, they consult with other sociologists knowledgeable about ethical issues, with ASA's Committee on Professional Ethics, or with other organization entities such as institutional review boards.

When sociologists take actions or are confronted with choices where there is a conflict between ethical standards enunciated in the Code of Ethics and laws or legal requirements, they make known their commitment to the Code and take steps to resolve the conflict in a responsible manner by consulting with colleagues, professional organizations, or the ASA's Committee on Professional Ethics.

20.03 Fair Treatment of Parties in Ethical Disputes: Sociologists do not discriminate against a person on the basis of his or her having made an ethical complaint.

Sociologists do not discriminate against a person based on his or her having been the subject of an ethical complaint. This does not preclude taking action based upon the outcome of an ethical complaint.

20.04 Reporting Ethical Violations of Others: When sociologists have substantial reason to believe that there may have been an ethical violation by another sociologist, they attempt to resolve the issue by bringing it to the attention of that individual if an informal resolution appears appropriate or possible, or they seek advice about whether or how to proceed based on this belief, assuming that such activity does not violate any confidentiality rights. Such action might include referral to ASA's Committee on Professional Ethics.

20.05 Cooperating with Ethics Committees: Sociologists cooperate in ethics investigations, proceedings, and resulting requirements of the American Sociological Association. In doing so, they make reasonable efforts to resolve any issues of confidentiality. Failure to cooperate may be an ethics violation.

20.06 Improper Complaints: Sociologists do not file or encourage the filing of ethics complaints that are frivolous and are intended to harm the alleged violator rather than to protect the integrity of the discipline and the public.

Honoring America

For Americans, the flag has always had a special meaning.
It is a symbol of our nation's freedom and democracy.

Flag Etiquette

Over the years, Americans have developed rules and customs concerning the use and display of the flag. One of the most important things every American should remember is to treat the flag with respect.

- The flag should be raised and lowered by hand and displayed only from sunrise to sunset. On special occasions, the flag may be displayed at night, but it should be illuminated.
- The flag may be displayed on all days, weather permitting, particularly on national and state holidays and on historic and special occasions.
- No flag may be flown above the American flag or to the right of it at the same height.
- The flag should never touch the ground or floor beneath it.
- The flag may be flown at half-staff by order of the president, usually to mourn the death of a public official.
- The flag may be flown upside down only to signal distress.
- When the flag becomes old and tattered, it should be destroyed by burning. According to an approved custom, the Union (stars on blue field) is first cut from the flag; then the two pieces, which no longer form a flag, are burned.

★ ★ ★ ★ ★ ★ ★ ★

The Star-Spangled Banner

O! say can you see, by the dawn's early light,
What so proudly we hail'd at the twilight's last gleaming,
Whose broad stripes and bright stars through the perilous fight,
O'er the ramparts we watched, were so gallantly streaming?
And the Rockets' red glare, the Bombs bursting in air,
Gave proof through the night that our Flag was still there;
O! say, does that star-spangled banner yet wave
O'er the Land of the free and the home of the brave!

The Pledge of Allegiance

I pledge allegiance to the Flag of the United States of America and to the Republic for which it stands, one Nation under God, indivisible, with liberty and justice for all.

Glossary

A

absolute poverty the absence of enough money to secure life's necessities

achieved status a position that is earned or chosen

actuarial tables statistics of life expectancies; used as basis for life insurance costs

age stratification the unequal distribution of scarce resources based on age

ageism a set of beliefs, attitudes, norms, and values used to justify age-based prejudice and discrimination

agricultural society a society that uses plows and draft animals in growing food

alternative movement a social movement that focuses on bringing about limited changes in people

anomie a social condition in which norms are weak, conflicting, or absent

anticipatory socialization the voluntary process of preparing to accept new norms, values, attitudes, and behaviors

ascribed status a position that is neither earned nor chosen but assigned

assimilation the blending or fusing of minority groups into the dominant society

authoritarianism a political system controlled by nonelected rulers who usually permit some degree of individual freedom

authority the legitimate or socially approved use of power

averting turning aside; prevention

B

beliefs ideas about the nature of reality

bilateral family arrangement where descent and inheritance are passed equally through both parents

biological determinism principle that behavioral differences are the result of inherited physical characteristics

bourgeoisie class owning the means for producing wealth

bullish optimistic; hopeful

bureaucracy a formal organization based on rationality and efficiency

C

canon an accepted principle or rule

capitalism an economic system based on private ownership of property and the pursuit of profit

capitalist person who owns or controls the means for producing wealth

case study intensive study of a single group, incident, or community

caste system a stratification structure that does not allow for social mobility

causation the belief that events occur in predictable ways and that one event leads to another

census regularly occurring count of a particular population

central-city dilemma concentration of people in need of public services without tax base–generated money to provide for them

charismatic authority authority that arises from the personality of an individual

charter schools public schools that are operated like private schools by public school teachers and administrators

church a life-encompassing religious organization to which all members of a society belong

city dense and permanent concentration of people living in a specific area and working primarily in non-agricultural jobs

class conflict the ongoing struggle between the bourgeoisie (owners) and the proletariat (working) classes

class consciousness identification with the goals and interests of a social class

closed-ended questions questions a person must answer by choosing from a limited, predetermined set of responses

coercion interaction in which individuals or groups are forced to behave in a particular way

cognitive ability capacity for thinking abstractly

collective behavior the spontaneous behavior of a group of people responding to similar stimuli

collectivity collection of people who do not normally interact and who do not share clearly defined norms

compensatory education specific curricular programs designed to overcome a deficiency

competition system in which rewards are based on relative performance

concentric zone theory theory that describes urban growth in terms of circular areas that grow from the central city outward

conflict interaction aimed at defeating an opponent

conflict perspective approach emphasizing the role of conflict, competition, and constraint within a society

conformity behavior that matches group expectations

conglomerates networks of unrelated businesses operating under one corporate umbrella

contagion theory theory stating that members of a crowd stimulate each other to higher and higher levels of emotion and irrational behavior

contingent employment the hiring of part-time, short-term workers
control theory theory that compliance with social norms requires strong bonds between individuals and society
convergence theory theory that states that crowds are formed by people who deliberately congregate with like-minded others
cooperation interaction in which individuals or groups combine their efforts to reach a goal
cooperative learning instructional method that relies on cooperation among students
core tier an occupational structure composed of large firms dominating their industries
corporation an organization owned by shareholders, who have limited liability and limited control
correlation a measure of the relationship between two variables
counterculture a subculture deliberately and consciously opposed to certain central beliefs or attitudes of the dominant culture
crime acts committed in violation of the law
criminal justice system system comprising institutions and processes responsible for enforcing criminal statutes
crowd a temporary collection of people who share an immediate common interest
crude birthrate the annual number of live births per one thousand members of a population
crude death rate the annual number of deaths per one thousand members of a population
cult a religious organization whose characteristics are not drawn from existing religious traditions within a society
cultural bias the unfair measurement of the cognitive abilities of people in some social categories
cultural particulars the ways in which a culture expresses universal traits
cultural pluralism desire of a group to maintain some sense of identity separate from the dominant group
cultural universals general cultural traits that exist in all cultures
culture knowledge, values, customs, and physical objects that are shared by members of a society

D

de facto segregation denial of equal access based on everyday practice
de jure segregation denial of equal access based on the law
demographic transition theory theory that population growth is a function of the level of economic development in a country
demography the scientific study of population
denomination one of several religious organizations that most members of a society accept as legitimate
dependency ratio the ratio of dependent persons to economically active persons
dependent variable a characteristic that reflects a change
desocialization the process of giving up old norms, values, attitudes, and behaviors
deterrence discouraging criminal acts by threatening punishment
deviance behavior that departs from societal or group norms
deviant a person who breaks significant societal or group norms
differential association theory theory that individuals learn deviance in proportion to the number of deviant acts to which they are exposed
diffusion process by which one culture or society borrows from another culture or society
discovery process by which something is learned or reinterpreted
discrimination treating people differently based on ethnicity, race, religion, or culture
dispersed collectivity collectivity made up of people who are not physically connected but who follow common rules or respond to common stimuli
doubling time number of years needed to double the base population size
downsizing the process by which companies reduce their work forces
dramaturgy approach that depicts human interaction as theatrical performances
drive impulse to reduce discomfort
dysfunction negative consequence of an aspect of society

E

economic institution institution that determines how goods and services are produced and distributed
edge city a suburban unit specializing in a particular economic activity
educational equality condition in which schooling produces the same results for lower-class and minority children as it does for other children
elitism system in which a community or society is controlled from the top by a few individuals or organizations
emergent norm theory theory stating that norms develop to guide crowd behavior
endogamy marriage within one's own group as required by social norms
equalitarian family structure where authority is evenly shared between the husband and wife

equilibrium a society's tendency to react to changes by making adjustments to keep itself in a state of functioning and balance
ethnic minority group identified by cultural, religious, or national characteristics
ethnocentrism judging others in terms of one's own cultural standards
exogamy the practice of marrying outside one's group
exponential growth growth in which the amount of increase is added to the base figure each time period
extended family two or more adult generations of the same family whose members share economic resources and a common household
extrapolating predicting based on past experiences

F
fad an unusual behavior pattern that spreads rapidly and disappears quickly
false consciousness adoption of the ideas of the dominant class by the less powerful class
family a group of people related by marriage, blood, or adoption
family planning the voluntary use of population control methods
fashion a widely accepted behavior pattern that changes periodically
fecundity the maximum rate at which women can physically produce children
feminization of poverty a trend in U.S. society in which women and children make up an increasing proportion of the poor
fertility a measure of the number of children born to a woman or a population of women
fertility rate the annual number of live births per one thousand women aged fifteen to forty-four
field research research that takes place in a natural (nonlaboratory) setting
folkways norms that lack moral significance
for-profit schools schools run by private companies on government funds
formal organization a group deliberately created to achieve one or more long-term goals
formal sanctions sanctions imposed by persons given special authority
formal schooling education that is provided and regulated by society
fundamentalism the desire to resist secularization and to adhere closely to traditional religious beliefs, rituals, and doctrines

G
game stage Mead's third stage in the development of role taking; children anticipate the actions of others based on social rules
Gemeinschaft "community"; preindustrial society based on tradition, kinship, and close social ties
gender identity a sense of being male or female based on learned cultural values
gender socialization the social process of learning how to act as a boy or girl
generalized other integrated conception of the norms, values, and beliefs of one's community or society
genocide the systematic effort to destroy an entire population
gentrification the development of low-income areas by middle-class homebuyers, landlords, and professional developers
Gesellschaft "society"; industrial society characterized by weak family ties, competition, and impersonal social relationships
gross migration rate the number of persons per year per one thousand members of a population who enter or leave a geographic area
group at least two people who have one or more goals in common and share common ways of thinking and behaving
groupthink when thinking in a group is self-deceptive, based on conformity to group beliefs, and created by group pressure to conform

H
hate crime a criminal act motivated by prejudice
hidden curriculum the informal and unofficial aspects of culture that children are taught in school, such as conformity or cooperation
hidden unemployment unemployment that includes people not counted in the traditional unemployment categories
horizontal mobility a change in occupation within the same social class
horticultural society a society that survives primarily through the growing of plants
hunting and gathering society a society that survives by hunting animals and gathering edible foods
hypothesis of linguistic relativity theory stating that our idea of reality depends largely upon language
hypothesis testable statement of relationships among variables

I
"I" the part of the self that accounts for unlearned, spontaneous acts
ideal culture cultural guidelines that group members claim to accept
imitation stage Mead's first stage in the development of role taking; children begin to imitate behaviors without understanding why
in-group exclusive group demanding intense loyalty

incarceration a method of protecting society from criminals by keeping them in prisons
incest taboo a norm forbidding marriage between certain kinds of relatives
income amount of money received by an individual or group over a specific time period
independent variable a characteristic that causes something to occur
industrial society a society that depends on science and technology to produce its basic goods and services
infant mortality rate the annual number of deaths among infants under one year of age per one thousand live births
informal organization groups within a formal organization in which personal relationships are guided by norms, rituals, and sentiments that are not part of the formal organization
informal sanctions rewards or punishments that can be applied by most members of a group
instincts innate (unlearned) patterns of behavior
institutionalized discrimination unfair practices that grow out of common behaviors and attitudes and that are a part of the structure of a society
integrative curriculum an approach to education based on student-teacher collaboration
interest group a group organized to influence political decision making
intergenerational mobility a change in status or class from one generation to the next
interlocking directorates directorates that result when heads of corporations sit on one another's boards
intervening variable a variable that changes the relationship between an independent and a dependent variable
interview a survey method in which a trained researcher asks questions and records the answers
invention the creation of something new from previously existing items or processes
iron law of oligarchy theory that power increasingly becomes concentrated in the hands of a few members of any organization

L

labeling theory theory that society creates deviance by identifying particular members as deviant
latent function an action that produces an unintended and unrecognized result
law a norm that is formally defined and enforced by officials
legitimate justify or give official approval to
life expectancy the average number of years that persons in a given population born at a particular time can expect to live
life span the most advanced age to which humans can survive
looking-glass self an image of yourself based on what you believe others think of you

M

magnet schools public schools that focus on particular disciplines or areas, such as fine arts or science
manifest function an action that produces an intended and recognized result
marriage a legal union based on mutual rights and obligations
mass media means of communication designed to reach the general population
master status a position that strongly affects most other aspects of a person's life
material culture the concrete, tangible objects of a culture
matriarchy the pattern in which the oldest woman living in the household has authority over all other family members
matrilineal family arrangement where descent and inheritance is passed through the female line
matrilocal the pattern in which married couples live with or near the wives' parents
"me" the part of the self formed through socialization
mechanical solidarity social dependency based on a widespread consensus of values and beliefs, enforced conformity, and dependence on tradition and family
mechanization the process of replacing animal and human power with machine power
meritocracy a society in which social status is based on ability and achievement
migration the movement of people from one geographic area to another
minority a group of people with physical or cultural traits different from those of the dominant group in the society
mob emotional crowd ready to use violence for a specific purpose
monogamy a marriage consisting of one man and one woman at a time
monopolies companies that have control over the production or distribution of a product or service
mores norms that have moral dimensions and that should be followed by members of the society
mortality deaths within a population
multicultural education an educational curriculum that emphasizes differences among gender, ethnic, and racial categories
multinationals firms based in highly industrialized societies with operating facilities throughout the world

multiple causation the belief that an event occurs as a result of several factors working in combination
multiple nuclei theory theory that focuses on specific geographic or historical influences on urban growth

N
negative deviance involves behavior that underconforms to accepted norms
neolocal the pattern in which newly married couples set up their own households
net migration rate the annual increase or decrease per one thousand members of a population resulting from migration into and out of the population
nonmaterial culture ideas, knowledge, and beliefs that influence people's behavior
norms rules defining appropriate and inappropriate behavior
nuclear family family structure composed of one or both parents and children
nullifying causing to have no value or force; negating

O
obligations behaviors that individuals are expected to perform toward others
occupational sex segregation the concentration of women in lower-status positions
occupations categories of jobs that involve similar activities at different work locations
oligopolies combinations of companies that control the production or distribution of a product or service
open class system a system in which social class is based on merit and individual effort; movement is allowed between classes
open classroom a nonbureaucratic approach to education based on democracy, flexibility, and noncompetitiveness
open-ended questions questions a person is to answer in his or her own words
organic solidarity social interdependency based on a high degree of specialization in roles
out-group group targeted by an in-group for opposition, antagonism, or competition
overurbanization when a city cannot supply adequate jobs and housing for its inhabitants

P
Pandora's box a source of trouble
participant observation a case study where the researcher becomes a member of the group being studied
pastoral societies societies where food is obtained primarily by raising and taking care of animals
patriarchy the pattern in which the oldest man living in the household has authority over the rest of the family members
patrilineal family arrangement where descent and inheritance is passed through the male line
patrilocal the pattern in which married couples live with or near the husbands' parents
peer group set of individuals of roughly the same age and interests
peripheral theory theory that emphasizes the growth of suburbs around the central city
peripheral tier an occupational structure composed of smaller, less profitable firms
perspective a particular point of view
play stage Mead's second stage in the development of role taking; children act in ways they imagine other people would
pluralism system in which political decisions are made as a result of bargaining and compromise among special interest groups
political institution institution that determines how power is obtained and exercised
political socialization informal and formal processes by which a person develops political opinions
polyandry the marriage of one woman to two or more men at the same time
polygamy the marriage of a male or female to more than one person at a time
population a group of people living in a particular place at a specified time or a group of people with certain specified characteristics
population control attempts by government to control birth rates
population momentum inability to stop population growth immediately because of previous high rate of growth
population pyramid a graphic representative of the age and gender composition of a population
positive deviance involves behavior that overconforms to social expectations
positivism the belief that knowledge should be derived from scientific observation
postindustrial society a society in which the economic emphasis is on providing services and information
power the ability to control the behavior of others
power elite a unified group of military, corporate, and government leaders
prejudice widely held negative attitudes toward a group (minority or majority) and its individual members
prestige recognition, respect, and admiration attached to social positions
primary deviance deviance involving occasional breaking of norms that is not a part of a person's lifestyle or self-concept
primary group people who are emotionally close, know one another well, and seek one another's company

primary relationships interactions that are intimate, personal, caring, and fulfilling
primary sector that part of the economy producing goods from the natural environment
profane nonsacred aspects of life
proletariat class that labors without owning the means of production; those who labor for the bourgeoisie
Protestant ethic a set of values, norms, beliefs, and attitudes stressing hard work, thrift, and self-discipline

Q

qualitative variable a characteristic that is defined by its presence or absence in a category
quantitative variable a characteristic that can be measured numerically
questionnaire a written set of questions to be answered by a research participant

R

race people sharing certain inherited physical characteristics that are considered important within a society
racism an extreme form of prejudice that assumes superiority of one group over others
rational-legal authority form of authority in which the power of government officials is based on the offices they hold
rationalization the mind-set emphasizing knowledge, reason, and planning
real culture actual behavior patterns of members of a group
recidivism a repetition of or return to criminal behavior
redemptive movement a social movement which seeks to change people completely
reference group group used for self-evaluation and the formation of attitudes, values, beliefs, and norms
reflex automatic reaction to physical stimulus
reformative movement a social movement that attempts to make limited changes in society
rehabilitation process of changing or reforming a criminal through socialization
relative poverty a measure of poverty based on the economic disparity between those at the bottom of a society and the rest of the society
religion a unified system of beliefs and practices concerned with sacred things
religiosity ways in which people express their religious interests and convictions
replacement level birthrate at which a couple replaces itself without adding to the population
representative democracy a system of government that uses elected officials to fulfill majority wishes
representative sample a sample that accurately reflects the characteristics of the population as a whole
resocialization the process of adopting new norms, values, attitudes, and behaviors
resource mobilization theory theory of social movements that focuses on the use of resources to achieve goals
retribution punishment intended to make criminals pay compensation for their acts
revolution sudden and complete overthrow of a social or political order
revolutionary movement a social movement that attempts to change the total structure of society
rights behaviors that individuals can expect from others
riot episode of largely random destruction and violence carried out by a crowd
role conflict condition in which the performance of a role in one status interferes with the performance of a role in another status
role expected behavior associated with a particular status
role performance the actual behavior of an individual in a role
role strain condition in which the roles of a single status are inconsistent or conflicting
role taking assuming the viewpoint of another person and using that viewpoint to shape the self-concept
rumor a widely circulating piece of information that is not verified as being true or false

S

sacred things and ideas that are set apart and given a special meaning that goes beyond, or transcends, immediate existence
sample a group of people that represents a larger population
sanctions rewards and punishments used to encourage people to follow norms
school desegregation the achievement of a racial balance in the classroom
scientific method the recognition and formulation of a problem, the collection of data through observation and experiment, and the formulation and testing of hypotheses
secondary analysis using precollected information for data collection and research purposes
secondary deviance deviance in which an individual's life and identity are organized around breaking society's norms

secondary group people who share only part of their lives while focusing on a goal or task
secondary relationships impersonal interactions involving limited parts of personalities
secondary sector that part of the economy engaged in manufacturing goods
sect a religious organization that arises out of a desire to reform an existing religious organization
sector theory theory that emphasizes the importance of transportation routes in the process of urban growth
secularization process through which the sacred loses influence over society
self-concept an image of yourself as having an identity separate from other people
self-fulfilling prophecy an expectation that leads to behavior that causes the expectation to become reality
sex classification of people as male or female based on biological characteristics
sexism a set of beliefs, attitudes, norms, and values used to justify sexual inequality
significant others those people whose reactions are most important to your self-concept
social aggregate people temporarily in the same place at the same time
social category a group of people who share a social characteristic
social change new societal behaviors with important long-term consequences
social class segment of society whose members hold similar amounts of resources and share values, norms, and an identifiable lifestyle
social control ways to encourage conformity to society's norms
social dynamics the study of social change
social exchange a voluntary action performed in the expectation of getting a reward in return
social interaction the process of influencing each other as people relate
social mobility the movement of individuals or groups between social classes
social movement movement whose goal is to promote or prevent social change; the most structured and rational form of collective behavior
social network a web of social relationships that joins a person to other people and groups
social processes series of steps leading to change on a societal level
social sanctions rewards or punishments that encourage conformity to social norms
social solidarity the degree to which a society is unified
social statics the study of social stability and order
social stratification ranking of people or groups according to their unequal access to scarce resources
social structure the patterned interaction of people in social relationships
socialism an economic system founded on the belief that the means of production should be controlled by the people as a whole
socialization the process of learning to participate in a group
society a specific territory inhabited by people who share a common culture
sociobiology the study of the biological basis of human behavior
sociological imagination the ability to see the link between society and self
sociological perspective a view that looks at the behavior of groups, not individuals
sociology the scientific study of social structure (human social behavior)
spirit of capitalism the obligation to reinvest money in business rather than to spend it
sport a set of competitive activities in which winners and losers are determined by physical performance within a set of established rules
sport subculture a group with distinct roles, values, norms, and beliefs that is organized around a sport activity
spurious correlation a relationship between two variables that is actually caused by a third factor
stacking assignment of players to less central positions on the basis of race or ethnicity
status a position a person occupies within a social structure
status set all of the statuses that a person occupies at any particular time
stereotype a distorted, exaggerated, or oversimplified image applied to a category of people
stigma an undesirable trait or label that is used to characterize an individual
strain theory theory that deviance is more likely to occur when a gap exists between cultural goals and the ability to achieve these goals by legitimate means
subculture a group that is part of the dominant culture but that differs from it in some important respects
subjugation process by which a minority group is denied equal access to the benefits of a society
suburbanization loss of population of a city to surrounding areas
survey research method in which people respond to questions
symbol anything that stands for something else and has an agreed-upon meaning attached to it

symbolic interactionism approach that focuses on the interactions among people based on mutually understood symbols

T

taboo a rule of behavior, the violation of which calls for strong punishment

technology knowledge and tools used to achieve practical goals

tertiary sector that part of the economy providing services

theoretical perspective a set of assumptions accepted as true

total fertility rate average number of children born to a woman during her lifetime

total institutions places in which people are separated from the rest of society and controlled by officials in charge

totalitarianism a political system in which a ruler with absolute power attempts to control all aspects of a society

tracking placement of students in programs according to academic ability levels

traditional authority forms of authority in which the legitimacy of a leader is rooted in custom

U

underclass people typically unemployed who came from families that have been poor for generations

urban ecology the study of the relationships between humans and city environments

urban legend a moralistic tale which the teller swears happened to someone he or she knows

urbanism the idea that urbanization involves a distinctive way of life

urbanization the shifting of population from farms and villages to large cities

V

value-added theory theory holding that certain conditions must exist for social movements to occur

values broad ideas about what is good or desirable shared by people in a society

variable a characteristic that is subject to change

verstehen understanding social behavior by putting yourself in the place of others

vertical mobility a change upward or downward in occupational status or social class

victim discounting process of reducing the seriousness of the crimes that injure people of lower status

voucher system system in which public school funds may be used to support public, private, or religious schools

W

war organized, armed conflict that occurs within a society or between nations

wealth total economic resources held by a person or group

white-collar crime job-related crimes committed by high-status people

working poor people employed in low-skill jobs with the lowest pay who do not earn enough to rise out of poverty

Z

zero population growth situation in which deaths are balanced by births so that the population does not increase

Glosario

A

absolute poverty—pobreza absoluta falta de dinero suficiente para cubrir las necesidades de la vida
achieved status—estado logrado posición que se gana o elige
actuarial tables—cuadros actuariales estadísticas de expectativas de vida, usadas como bases para los costos de los seguros de vida
age stratification—estratificación por edad distribución desigual de recursos escasos basada en la edad
ageism—discriminación por edad conjunto de creencias, actitudes, normas y valores usados para justificar la discriminación y prejuicios basados en la edad
agricultural society—sociedad agrícola una sociedad que usa el arado y animales de tiro para cultivar los alimentos
alternative movement—movimiento alternativo movimiento social que se enfoca hacia el logro de obtener cambios limitados en las personas
anomie—desmandado condición social en la cual las normas son débiles, conflictivas o ausentes
anticipatory socialization—socialización anticipadora el proceso voluntario de prepararse para aceptar nuevas normas, valores, actitudes y comportamientos
ascribed status—estado adscrito posición que no es ganada ni elegida sino asignada
assimilation—asimilación la mezcla o fusión de grupos minoritarios con la sociedad dominante
authoritarianism—autoritarismo sistema político controlado por mandatarios no elegidos quienes generalmente permiten algún grado de libertad individual
authority—autoridad poder aceptado como legítimo o aprobado socialmente por aquellos sometidos a él
averting—evitando dejado a un lado, prevención

B

beliefs—creencias ideas sobre la naturaleza de la realidad
bilateral family arrangements—arreglos familiares bilaterales cuando la descendencia y la herencia se transmite a través de ambos padres
biological determinism—determinismo biológico principio que sostiene que las diferencias en comportamiento son el resultado de características físicas heredadas
bourgeoisie—burguesía clase que posee los medios para producir riquezas
bullish—alcista optimista, esperanzado
bureaucracy—burocracia organización formal basada en la racionalidad y eficiencia

C

canon—canon principio o regla aceptado
capitalism—capitalismo sistema económico basado en la posesión privada de la propiedad y la persecución del lucro
capitalist person—persona capitalista persona que posee o controla los medios para producir riquezas
case study—estudio de caso estudio intensivo sobre un grupo, incidente o comunidad
caste system—sistema de castas estratificación de estructura que no permite la movilidad social
causation—causalidad creencia que los sucesos ocurren de manera predecible y que un hecho lleva a otro
census—censo cuenta periódica de una población en particular
central-city dilemma—dilema de ciudad principal concentración de personas en necesidad servicios públicos sin contar con los medios producidos por los impuestos para proporcionarlos
charismatic authority—autoridad carismática autoridad que emana de la personalidad de un individuo
charter schools—escuelas diferenciadas escuelas públicas que operan como escuelas privadas pero con profesores y administradores del Estado
church—iglesia organización religiosa que abarca un sistema de vida a la cual pertenecen todos los miembros de una sociedad
city—ciudad área específica donde habita una densidad y concentración permanente de personas que mantienen empleos primariamente no agrícolas
class conflict—conflicto de clases lucha permanente entre la clase burguesa (propietarios) y la proletaria (trabajadores)
class consciousness—conciencia de clase identificación con las metas e intereses de una clase social
closed-ended questions—preguntas limitadas preguntas que una persona debe contestar eligiendo entre una variedad limitada y predeterminada de respuestas
coercion—coerción interacción en la cual individuos o grupos están forzados a actuar de una manera determinada
cognitive ability—habilidad cognoscitiva capacidad de pensar en forma abstracta
collective behaviour—conducta colectiva el comportamiento espontáneo de un grupo de personas que responden a estímulos similares

collectivity—colectividad conjunto de personas que normalmente no interactúan y que no comparten normas claramente definidas

compensatory education—educación compensatoria programas específicos de educación diseñados para superar una deficiencia

competition—competencia sistemas en los cuales las recompensas están basadas en desempeños relativos

concentric zone theory—teoría de zona concéntrica teoría que describe el crecimiento urbanístico en términos de áreas circulares que crecen desde la ciudad principal a la periferia

conflict—conflicto interacción dirigida hacia la derrota de un oponente

conflict perspective—perspectiva de conflicto enfoque que enfatiza el papel que juega el conflicto, la competencia y la restricción dentro de una sociedad

conformity—conformidad conducta acorde a las expectativas de grupo

conglomerates—conglomerados redes de firmas no relacionadas que operan bajo la protección de una corporación

contagion theory—teoría de contagio teoría que sostiene que los miembros de una multitud se estimulan mutuamente para alcanzar niveles cada vez más altos de emoción y conducta irracional

contingent employment—empleo contingente la contratación de empleados a medio tiempo por períodos cortos

control theory—teoría de control teoría que sostiene que la adhesión a las normas sociales requiere de fuertes lazos entre los individuos y la sociedad

convergence theory—teoría de convergencia teoría que sostiene que las multitudes están formadas de personas que deliberadamente se juntan con otras que piensan lo mismo

cooperation—cooperación interacción mediante la cual individuos o grupos combinan sus esfuerzos para alcanzar un objetivo

cooperative learning—aprendizaje cooperativo método de instrucción que se basa en la cooperación entre estudiantes

core tier—primera línea estructura ocupacional compuesta de grandes firmas que dominan a sus industrias

corporation—corporación organización que es propiedad de los accionistas quienes tienen responsabilidad y control limitado

correlation—correlación medida de la relación entre dos variables

counterculture—anticultura subcultura que deliberada y conscientemente se opone a ciertas creencias y actitudes esenciales de la cultura dominante

crime—crímenes actos cometidos en violación de la ley

criminal justice system—sistema de justicia criminal sistema que comprende las instituciones y procesos responsables de hacer cumplir los estatutos criminales

crowd—multitud número temporal de personas que comparten un interés común inmediato

crude birthrate—tasa bruta de nacimientos número anual de nacimientos con vida por cada mil miembros de una población

crude death rate—tasa bruta de fallecimientos número anual de defunciones por cada mil miembros de una población

cult—culto organización religiosa cuyas características no se originan de las tradiciones religiosas existentes en una sociedad

cultural bias—prejuicio cultural la medición injusta de las habilidades cognoscitivas de las personas pertenecientes a ciertas categorías sociales

cultural knowledge—conocimiento cultural valores, costumbres y objetos físicos que son compartidos por los miembros de una sociedad

cultural particulars—peculiaridades culturales la forma en que una cultura expresa características universales

cultural pluralism—pluralismo cultural deseo de un grupo de mantener algún sentido de identidad distinto al del grupo dominante

cultural universals—manifestaciones culturales universales características culturales generales que existen en todas las culturas

D

de facto segregation—segregación de facto negación a igualdad de acceso basado en la práctica

de jure segretation—segregación legal negación a igualdad de acceso basado en la ley

demographic transition theory—teoría de transición demográfica teoría que sostiene que el aumento de la población es una función relacionada al nivel del desarrollo económico de un país

demography—demografía el estudio científico de la población

denomination—creencia una de varias organizaciones religiosas que la mayoría de los miembros de una sociedad aceptan como legítima

dependency ratio—porcentaje de dependientes la relación de personas dependientes de alguien con respecto a las económicamente avtivas

dependent variable—variable dependiente característica que refleja un cambio

desocialization—desocialización el proceso de renunciar a antiguas normas, valores, actitudes y conductas

deterrence—disuasión disuadir de cometer actos criminales amenazando con el castigo
deviance—desviación conducta que se aleja de normas sociales o de grupos sociales
deviant—desviado persona que quiebra normas importantes de la sociedad o de grupos sociales
differential association theory—teoría diferencial de asociación teoría que sostiene que la proporción de individuos que se convierten en desviados guarda relación con el número de desviaciones a las que han estado sometidos
diffusion—difusión proceso por el cual una cultura o sociedad toma prestado de otra cultura o sociedad
discovery—descubrimiento proceso mediante el cual algo es aprendido o vuelto a interpretar
discrimination—discriminación trato diferente a las personas basado en la etnia, raza, religión o cultura
dispersed collectivity—colectividad dispersa colectividad formada por personas que no están conectadas físicamente pero que siguen reglas comunes o responden a estímulos comunes
doubling time—momento de duplicación número de años necesarios para duplicar el tamaño de la población base
downsizing—reducirse el proceso mediante el cual las empresas reducen su fuerza laboral
dramaturgy—dramaturgia enfoque que describe las interacciones humanas como representaciones teatrales
drive—empuje impulso para reducir el malestar
dysfunction—disfunción consecuencia negativa de un aspecto de la sociedad

E

economic institutions—instituciones de economía instituciones que determinan como se deben producir y distribuir los bienes y servicios
edge city—ciudad satélite unidad suburbana que se especializa en una actividad económica determinada
educational equality—igualdad educacional condición en la cual la enseñanza produce los mismos resultados en los niños de clases sociales más bajas o pertenecientes a las minorías que en el resto de los niños
elitism—elitismo sistema en el cual una comunidad o sociedad está controlada desde arriba por unos pocos individuos u organizaciones
emergent norm theory—teoría de normas emergentes teoría que sostiene que las normas se desarrollan para guiar la conducta de las multitudes
endogamy—endogamia matrimonio dentro de su grupo social, como lo exigen las normas sociales
equalitarian family structure—estructura familiar igualitaria es en la que la autoridad está distribuida en forma pareja entre el marido y la esposa
equilibrium—equilibrio la tendencia de una sociedad de reaccionar a los cambios haciendo ajustes para mantenerse en un estado balanceado de funcionamiento
ethnic minority—minoría étnica grupo identificado por características culturales, religiosas o nacionales
ethnocentrism—etnocentrismo juzgar a los demás en términos de sus propios estándares culturales
exogamy—exogamia práctica de casarse con alguien de fuera de su grupo social
exponential growth—crecimiento exponencial crecimiento en el cual la cantidad de aumento es agregada a la cifra base en cada período de tiempo
extended family—prolongación familiar dos o más generaciones adultas de la misma familia cuyos miembros comparten los recursos económicos en una vivienda común
extrapolating—extrapolación predicciones basadas en experiencias pasadas

F

fad—furor forma de comportamiento inusual que se extiende rápidamente y desaparece rápido
false consciousness—falsa conciencia adopción de ideas de la clase dominante por la clase menos poderosa
family—familia grupo de personas relacionadas por matrimonio, sangre, o adopción
family planning—planificación familiar el uso voluntario de métodos de control de la población
fashion—moda patrón de comportamiento generalmente aceptado que cambia periódicamente
fecundity—fecundidad la tasa máxima en la cual las mujeres pueden físicamente producir niños
feminization of poverty—feminización de la pobreza tendencia de la sociedad estadounidense en la cual las mujeres y los niños representan una proporción en el aumento de la pobreza
fertility—fertilidad medición de los hijos nacidos a una mujer o a una población de mujeres
fertility rate—tasa de fertilidad el número anual de nacimientos vivos por mil mujeres entre las edades de quince a cuarenta y dos
field research—investigación en terreno investigación que tiene lugar en ambientes naturales (no de laboratorio)
folkways—costumbres populares normas que no tienen significado moral
formal organization—organización formal grupo creado específicamente para lograr una o más metas a largo plazo
formal sanctions—sanciones formales sanciones impuestas por personas a quienes se les ha dado autoridad especial

formal schooling—educación formal educación proporcionada y regulada por la sociedad
for-profit schools—colegios gananciales colegios administrados por compañías privadas con fondos del gobierno
fundamentalism—fundamentalismo deseo de resistir a la secularización y adherir estrictamente a creencias religiosas tradicionales, rituales y doctrinas

G
game stage—etapa de juego la tercera etapa de Mead en el desarrollo de adoptar roles, los niños anticipan las acciones de terceros basados en las leyes sociales
Gemeinschaft "community"—comunidad de "clan" sociedad preindustrial basada en la tradición, parentesco y estrechos vínculos sociales
gender identity—identidad de género sentido de ser hombre o mujer basado en valores culturales aprendidos
gender socialization—socialización del género el proceso social de aprender la forma de actuar de un niño o niña
generalized—generalización otra forma integrada de concepción de las normas, valores y creencias de la propia comunidad o sociedad
genocide—genocidio esfuerzo sistemático de destruir una población completa
gentrification—incorporación de áreas populares el desarrollo de áreas de bajos ingresos por compradores de casas de la clase media, rentistas o corredores profesionales de propiedades
Gesellschaft "society"—sociedad de firmas sociedad industrial carente de lazos familiares y caracterizada por la competencia y relaciones sociales impersonales
gross migration rate—tasa bruta de migración el número de personas por cada mil miembros de una población que entra o sale de un área geográfica
group—grupo al menos dos personas que tienen uno o más objetivos en común y que comparten formas de pensar o de comportarse
groupthink—pensamiento de grupo cuando el pensamiento en grupo es engañoso pues está basado en la conformidad a las creencias del grupo creada bajo la presión ejercida por el mismo grupo para concordar

H
hate crime—crimen de odio acto criminal provocado por el prejuicio
hidden curriculum—curriculum oculto los aspectos culturales informales y extraoficiales que se les enseña a los niños en el colegio tales como la cooperación y conformidad
hidden unemployment—desempleo oculto desempleo que incluye a personas que no forman parte de las categorías tradicionales de desempleo
horizontal mobility—movilidad horizontal cambios en la ocupación dentro de una misma clase social
horticultural society—sociedad hortícola sociedad que sobrevive primariamente a través del cultivo de plantas
hunting and gathering society—sociedad de caza y recolección sociedad que sobrevive por medio de la caza y recolección de alimentos
hypothesis of linguistic relativety—hipótesis de relatividad lingüística teoría que sostiene que nuestra idea de la realidad depende en gran medida del lenguaje
hypothesis testable—hipótesis verificable enunciación de las relaciones entre variables

I
"I"—él Yo parte de la personalidad responsable de los actos espontáneos no aprendidos
ideal culture—cultura ideal pautas culturales que los miembros del grupo dicen aceptar
imitation stage—etapa de imitación la primera etapa de Mead en el desarrollo de toma de roles: los niños empiezan a imitar conductas sin saber por qué
incarceration—encarcelamiento método de protección a la sociedad de los criminales manteniéndolos en prisiones
incest taboo—tabú de incesto norma que prohibe el matrimonio entre cierto nivel de parentesco
income—ingreso cantidad de dinero recibido por un individuo o grupo en un período específico de tiempo
independent variable—variable independiente característica que hace que algo ocurra
industrial society—sociedad industrial sociedad que depende de la ciencia y la tecnología para producir sus bienes y servicios básicos
infant mortality rate—tasa de mortalidad infantil el número anual de muertes de niños menores de un año por cada mil nacimientos vivos
informal organizations—organizaciones informales grupos dentro de organizaciones formales en los cuales las relaciones personales están guiados por normas, rituales y sentimientos que no forman parte de las organizaciones formales
informal sanctions—sanciones informales recompensas o castigos que pueden ser aplicados por la mayoría de los miembros de un grupo
in-group—grupo exclusivo grupo exclusivo que exige lealtad incondicional
instincts—instintos cánones innatos (no aprendidos) de conducta
institutionalized discrimination—discriminación institucionalizada prácticas injustas que emanan de conductas y actitudes comunes y que forman parte de la estructura de una sociedad

interest group—grupo de interés grupo organizado para influir las decisiones políticas
intergenerational mobility—movilidad intergeneracional cambio en el estado o clase de una generación a la otra
intergrative curriculum—programa integrante un enfoque educativo basado en la colaboración profesor-alumno
interlocking directorates—directorios entrelazados los directorios que resultan cuando las cabezas de algunas corporaciones forman parte de los directorios de otras
intervening variable—variable interviniente variable que cambia la relación entre una variable independiente y una dependiente
interview—entrevista método de encuesta en el cual un investigador entrenado formula preguntas y registra las respuestas
invention—invención creación de algo nuevo de ítems o procesos que existían previamente
iron law of oligarchy—ley del hierro de la oligarquía teoría que sostiene que el poder se concentra cada vez más en las manos de unos pocos miembros de cualquier organización

L
labeling theory—teoría de etiquetado teoría que sostiene que la sociedad crea la desviación identificando a ciertos miembros como desviados
latent function—acción latente que produce un resultado no deseado y no admitido
law—ley norma formalmente definida e impuesta por funcionarios públicos
legitimate—legitimar justificar o dar aprobación oficial a algo o alguien
life expectancy—expectativa de vida el número promedio de años de esperanza de vida de personas de una población determinada, nacidas en un tiempo determinado
life span—período de vida la edad más avanzada que pueden alcanzar los seres humanos
looking-glass self—espejo de sí mismo imagen que uno tiene de sí mismo basado en lo que cree que los otros piensan de él

M
magnet schools—escuelas imán escuelas públicas enfocadas hacia disciplinas o áreas específicas, como ser las bellas artes o la ciencia
manifest function—función declarada acción que produce un efecto deseado y admitido
marriage—matrimonio unión legal basada en derechos y obligaciones mutuas
mass media—medios de comunicación—conjunto de medios de comunicación diseñados para llegar a la población en general
master status—condición dominante estado social que afecta fuertemente la mayoría de los otros aspectos de la vida de una persona
material culture—cultura material los objetos concretos y tangibles de una cultura
matriarchy—matriarcado forma de organización en la cual la mujer de más edad que vive en una casa tiene autoridad sobre todos los otros miembros de la familia
matrilineal—por línea materna arreglo familiar según el cual la descendencia y la herencia se transmiten por línea materna
matrilocal—cerca de la madre modelo en el cual las parejas casadas viven cerca o con los padres de la esposa
"me"—"Yo" la parte de uno mismo formada a través de la socialización
mechanical solidarity—solidaridad mecánica dependencia social basada en un consenso muy divulgado de valores y creencias, conformidad impuesta y dependencia de la tradición y la familia
mechanization—mecanización el proceso de reemplazar la potencia humana y animal por potencia mecánica
meritocracy—meritocracia sociedad en la cual el estado social está basado en la habilidad y logros
migration—migración el movimiento de personas de un área geográfica a otro
minority—minoría grupo de personas con peculiaridades físicas o culturales diferentes de las del grupo dominante de la sociedad
mob—masas multitud emocional lista a ejercer la violencia para un propósito específico
monogamy—monogamia matrimonio consistente de un solo hombre y mujer por vez
monopolies—monopolios compañías que tienen el control de la producción o distribución de un producto o servicio
mores—mases normas que tienen dimensiones morales y que los miembros de una sociedad debería cumplir
mortality—mortalidad muertes dentro de una población
multicultural education—educación multicultural un programa de estudios que enfatiza las diferencias existentes entre los géneros, las etnias y las categorías raciales
multinational firms—firmas multinacionales basadas en sociedades altamente industrializadas con instalaciones operativas en todo el mundo

multiple causation—causalidad múltiple la creencia que un suceso ocurre como resultado de varios factores operando en combinación

multiple nuclei theory—teoría de núcleos múltiples teoría que se enfoca en influencias específicas geográficas o históricas sobre el crecimiento urbano

N

negative deviance—desviación negativa involucra una actitud inconformista hacia las normas aceptadas

neolocal—nuevos hogares la forma en que los recién casados establecen sus propios hogares

net migration rate—tasa neta de migración el incremento o disminución anual por cada mil integrantes de una población resultante de población migrante que entra o sale

nonmaterial culture—cultura no material ideas, conocimientos y creencias que influencian la conducta de las personas

norms—normas reglas que definen un comportamiento adecuado e inadecuado

nuclear family—núcleo familiar estructura familiar compuesta de uno o los dos padres y sus hijos

nullifying—anulación causando que no tenga valor ni fuerza: negando

O

obligations—obligaciones conducta que se espera que tengan los individuos

occupational sex segregación—segregación ocupacional por sexo a concentración de mujeres en posiciones de menor importancia

occupations—ocupaciones categorías de trabajos que involucran actividades similares en diferentes ubicaciones de trabajo

oligopolies—oligopolios combinación de compañías que controlan la producción o distribución de un producto o servicios

open-class system—sistema social abierto sistema en el cual las clases sociales están basadas en el mérito y el esfuerzo individual; el movimiento entre clases sociales está permitido

open-classroom—educación abierta un enfoque no burocrático de la educación basado en la democracia, la flexibilidad y carente de competencia

open-ended questions—preguntas libres preguntas que una persona debe responder en sus propias palabras

organic solidarity—solidaridad de cuerpo interdependencia social basada en un alto grado de especialización en los diferentes roles

out-group—grupo externo grupo dirigido por un grupo exclusivo para fines de oposición, antagonismo o competencia

overurbanization—sobreurbanización cuando una ciudad no es capaz de proporcionar trabajos y habitación adecuados a sus habitantes

P

Pandora's box—la caja de Pandora fuente de conflictos

participant observation—observación del participante en un estudio de caso, cuando el investigador se convierte en miembro del grupo estudiado

pastoral societies—sociedades pastorales sociedades en las cuales se obtiene el alimento de la crianza y cuidado de los animales

patriarchy—patriarcado modelo en el cual el hombre de más edad que habite en una casa tiene autoridad sobre el resto de los miembros de la familia

patrilineal—por línea paterna arreglos familiares mediante el cual la descendencia y la herencia se transmiten por la línea paterna

patrilocal—cerca del padre modelo en el cual las parejas casadas viven con o cerca de los padres del esposo

peer group—grupo de pares grupo de individuos de aproximadamente la misma edad e intereses

peripheral theory—teoría periférica teoría que enfatiza el crecimiento de los suburbios alrededor de una ciudad principal

peripheral tier—línea periférica estructura ocupacional compuesta por firmas más pequeñas con menores ganancias

perspective—perspectiva un punto de vista particular

play stage—etapa de juego segunda etapa de Mead en el desarrollo de la toma de roles, los niños actúan de la forma en que se imaginan actuarían otras personas

pluralism—pluralismo sistema en el cual las decisiones políticas se toman como resultado de negociaciones y compromisos entre grupos de intereses determinados

political institutions—instituciones políticas instituciones que determinan como se obtiene y se ejerce el poder

political socialization—socialización política procesos formales e informales mediante los cuales una persona desarrolla sus opiniones políticas

polyandry—poliándrico el matrimonio de una mujer a uno o dos hombres al mismo tiempo

polygamy—poligamia el matrimonio de un hombre o mujer a más de una persona al mismo tiempo

polygyny—poligenia el matrimonio de un hombre a dos o más mujeres al mismo tiempo

population—población grupo de personas que viven en un lugar específico en un tiempo determinado ó grupo de personas con ciertas características específicas

population control—control de la población intentos del gobierno de controlar la tasa de nacimientos
population momentum—ímpetu de poblamiento incapacidad de detener de inmediato el crecimiento de la población debido a una previa alta taza de crecimiento
population pyramid—pirámide de la población gráfico representativo de la composición de una población por edad y sexo
positive deviance—desviación positiva involucra un comportamiento que se conforma excesivamente a las expectativas de la sociedad
positivism—positivismo creencia que el conocimiento debe derivar de la observación científica
postindustrial society—sociedad post-industrial sociedad en la cual el énfasis está puesto en proporcionar servicios e información
power—poder habilidad para controlar el comportamiento de otros
power elite—elite de poder grupo unificado de líderes del gobierno, militares y de la industria
prejudice—prejuicio actitudes negativas muy difundidas hacia un grupo (mayoritario o minoritario) y sus miembros individuales
prestige—prestigio reconocimiento, respeto y admiración ligados a posiciones sociales
primary deviance—desviación primaria desviación que comprende un rompimiento ocasional de las normas y no forma parte del estilo de vida o autoconcepto de la persona
primary group—grupo primario grupo de personas unidas por lazos emocionales, con relaciones íntimas, personales, y satisfactorias
primary relationships—relaciones primarias interacciones íntimas, personales, afectuosas y satisfactorias
primary sector—sector primario la parte de la economía que produce bienes procedentes del medio ambiente natural
profane—profano los aspectos no sagrados de la vida
proletariat—proletariado clase social que trabaja sin poseer los medios de producción; aquéllos que trabajan para la burguesía
Protestant ethic—ética protestante conjunto de valores, normas, creencias y actitudes que enfatizan el trabajo duro, la frugalidad y la autodisciplina

Q

qualitative variable—variable cualitativa característica que se define por su presencia o ausencia en una categoría
quantitative variable—variable cuantitativa característica que se puede medir numéricamente
questionnaire—cuestionario conjunto de preguntas escritas que deben ser respondidas por un participante de una investigación

R

race—raza personas que comparten ciertas características físicas heredadas que son consideradas importantes dentro de una sociedad
racism—racismo forma extrema de prejuicio que asume superioridad de un grupo sobre otros
rationalization—racionalización estado de la mente que enfatiza el conocimiento, la razón y la planificación
rational-legal authority—autoridad racional legal forma de autoridad en la cual el poder de los funcionarios de gobierno está basado en el cargo que ocupan
real culture—cultura real pautas efectivas de comportamiento de los miembros de un grupo
recidivism—reincidencia repetición o vuelta a una conducta criminal
redemptive movement—movimiento redentor movimiento social que busca el cambio completo de las personas
reference group—grupo de referencia grupo utilizado como autoevaluación y desarrollo de actitudes, valores, creencias, y normas
reflex—reflejo reacción automática a estímulos físicos
reformative movement—movimiento reformista movimiento social que intenta efectuar cambios limitados en la sociedad
rehabilitation—rehabilitación proceso para cambiar o reformar a un criminal por medio de la socialización
relative poverty—pobreza relativa sistema para medir la pobreza basado en la desigualdad económica existente entre aquéllos que se encuentran en el extremo inferior de la escala social y el resto de la sociedad
religion—religión sistema unificado de creencias y prácticas relativas a cosas sagradas
religiosity—religiosidad formas en que las personas expresan sus intereses y convicciones religiosas
replacement level—nivel de reemplazo tasa de nacimientos en la cual la pareja se reemplaza a sí misma sin aumentar la población
representative democracy—democracia representativa sistema de gobierno que usa a funcionarios elegidos para satisfacer los deseos de la mayoría
representative sample—muestra representativa muestra que refleja con exactitud las características de la población tomada en su totalidad
resocialization—resocialización el proceso de adoptar nuevas normas, valores, actitudes, y conductas

resource mobilization—movilización de recursos teoría de movimiento social que se centra en el uso de los recursos para lograr metas
retribution—punición castigo que tiene como objetivo que los criminales paguen compensación por sus actos
revolution—revolución derrocamiento repentino y total de un orden político o social
revolutionary movement—movimiento revolucionario movimiento social que intenta cambiar la estructura total de la sociedad
rights—derechos conductas que los individuos pueden esperar de otros
riot—disturbio episodio de violencia y destrucción aleatoria llevada a cabo por una multitud
role—rol la conducta esperada asociada a un estado social determinado
role conflict—conflicto de roles condición en la cual la ejecución del rol de un estado social interfiere con la ejecución del rol de otro estado social
role performance—desempeño de un rol la conducta real de un individuo en un rol
role strain—tensión de rol condición en la cual los roles de un solo estado social son inconsistentes o conflictivos
role taking—tomar un rol asumir el punto de vista de otra persona y usar ese punto de vista para moldear el concepto de sí mismo
rumor—rumor trozo de información de gran difusión que no ha sido verificada como verdadera o falsa

S

sacred—sagrado objetos e ideas que se ponen aparte y a las cuales se les da un significado especial que va más allá o trasciende la existencia inmediata
sample—muestra grupo de personas que representan una población mayor
sanctions—sanciones recompensas o castigos usados para estimular a las personas que sigan las normas
school desegregation—integración escolar el logro del equilibrio racial en una sala de clases
scientific method—método científico el reconocimiento y formulación de un problema, la recolección de datos a través de la información y la experiencia y la formulación y comprobación de hipótesis
secondary analysis—análisis secundario la utilización de información prerrecolectada para propósitos de recolección de datos e investigación
secondary deviance—desviación secundaria desviación en la cual la vida e identidad de un individuo están organizadas en torno al rompimiento de las normas sociales
secondary group—grupo secundario personas que comparten sólo parte de sus vidas mientras se centran en una meta o labor
secondary relationships—relaciones secundarias interacciones impersonales que involucran porciones limitadas de las personalidades
secondary sectors—sectores secundarios aquella parte de la economía que se ocupa de los bienes manufacturados
sect—secta organización religiosa que proviene de un deseo de reformar una organización religiosa ya existente
sector theory—teoría de sector teoría que enfatiza la importancia de las rutas de transporte en el proceso de crecimiento urbano
secularization—secularización el proceso a través del cual lo sagrado pierde influencia sobre la sociedad
self-concept—autoconcepto imagen de sí mismo como teniendo una identidad separada de la de otras personas
self-fulfilling prophecy—profecía autocumplida predicción que tiene como resultado una conducta que hace que lo esperado se convierta en realidad
sex—sexo clasificación de las personas en masculino o femenino basada en características biológicas
sexism—sexismo conjunto de creencias, actitudes, normas y valores usados para justificar la desigualdad de los sexos
significant others—personas importantes aquéllas personas cuyas reacciones son las más importantes para su autoconcepto
social aggregate—agregado social agrupaciones de personas al mismo tiempo en el mismo lugar
social categories—categorías sociales grupos de personas que comparten una característica social
social change—cambio social nuevas conductas sociales con consecuencias importantes en el largo plazo
social class—clase social segmento de la sociedad cuyos miembros poseen cantidades similares de recursos y comparten valores, normas y un estilo de vida identificable
social control—control social formas para estimular la conformidad a las normas sociales
social dynamics—dinámica social el estudio del cambio social
social exchange—intercambio social acción voluntaria llevada a cabo con la esperanza de obtener una recompensa a cambio
social interaction—interacción social el proceso de influenciar a otras personas mientras las personas se relacionan entre sí

social mobility—movilidad social el movimiento de individuos o personas entre clases sociales
social movement—movimiento social movimiento cuyo objetivo es promover o prevenir los cambios sociales; la forma mejor estructurada y racional de conducta colectiva
social network—red social red de relaciones sociales que unen una persona a otras personas y grupos
social processes—procesos sociales serie de pasos que llevan a un cambio en el nivel social
social sanctions—sanciones sociales premios o castigos que incentivan la conformidad con las normas sociales
social solidarity—solidaridad social el grado en que una sociedad está unida
social statics—estática social el estudio de la estabilidad y orden social
social stratification—estratificación social la clasificación de personas o grupos de acuerdo a su acceso desigual a los recursos escasos
social structure—estructura social las interacciones moldeadas de las personas en las relaciones sociales
socialism—socialismo sistema económico basado en la creencia que los medios de producción deben ser controlados por las personas como un todo
socialization—socialización el proceso de aprendizaje a participar en un grupo
society—sociedad territorio específico habitado por personas que comparten una cultura en común
sociobiology—sociobiología el estudio de la base biológica del comportamiento humano
sociological imagination—imaginación sociológica habilidad para ver el vínculo entre la sociedad y uno mismo
sociological perspective—perspectiva sociológica punto de vista que mira el comportamiento de grupos, no de individuos
sociology—sociología el estudio científico de la estructura social (conducta social humana)
spirit of capitalism—espíritu del capitalismo la obligación de reinvertir el dinero en negocios en vez de gastarlo
sport—deporte conjunto de actividades competitivas en las cuales los ganadores y los perdedores se determinan por el desempeño físico, bajo un conjunto de reglas establecidas
sport subculture—subcultura deportiva grupo que desempeña roles determinados, valores y creencias organizadas alrededor de una actividad deportiva
spurious correlation—correlación espuria relación entre dos variables que es realmente ocasionada por un tercer factor
stacking—relegación designación de jugadores a posiciones menos importantes sobre una base de raza o etnicidad
status—estado posición que ocupa una persona dentro de la estructura social
status set—conjunto de estados todas las posiciones que ocupa una persona en un tiempo específico
stereotype—estereotipo imagen distorsionada, exagerada o demasiado simplificada aplicada a una categoría de personas
stigma—estigma rasgo o calificación no deseada que se usa para caracterizar a un individuo
strain theory—teoría de tensión teoría que sostiene que las desviaciones ocurren cuando existe un espacio entre las metas culturales y la habilidad para lograr esas metas por medios legítimos
subculture—subcultura grupo que forma parte de la cultura dominante pero que difiere de ella en algunos aspectos importantes
subjugation—subyugación proceso por medio del cual se le niega a un grupo minoritario el acceso a los beneficios de una sociedad
suburbanization—suburbanización pérdida de población de una ciudad a las áreas circundantes
survey research—investigación por encuesta método en el cual las personas responden a preguntas
symbol—símbolo cualquier cosa que representa otra cosa y que tiene un significado acordado
symbolic interactionism—interacción simbólica enfoque que se centra en las interacciones entre las personas basadas en símbolos que ambas entienden

T

taboo—tabú regla de conducta cuya violación exige de un castigo severo
technology—tecnología conocimiento y herramientas utilizados par lograr metas prácticas
tertiary sector—sector terciario la parte de la economía que proporciona servicios
theoretical perspective—perspectiva teórica conjunto de suposiciones que se aceptan como verdaderas
total fertility rate—tasa de fertilidad total promedio de niños que tiene una mujer durante su vida
total institutions—instituciones absolutas lugares en que las personas son separadas del resto de la sociedad y controladas por los funcionarios a cargo
totalitarianism—totalitarismo sistema político en el cual un gobernante con poderes absolutos trata de controlar todos los aspectos de una sociedad

tracking—clasificación colocación de los alumnos en programas acordes a sus niveles de habilidad académica

traditional authority—autoridad tradicional formas de autoridad en las cuales la legitimidad de un líder tiene sus raíces en la costumbre

U

underclass—clase inferior personas típicamente desempleadas que provienen de familias que han sido pobres por generaciones

urban ecology—ecología urbans el estudio de las relaciones entre los seres humanos y el medio ambiente de las ciudades

urban legend—leyenda urbana una historia moralista que el narrador jura que le pasó a alguien que él o ella conocen

urbanism—urbanismo la idea que la urbanización involucra un estilo particular de vida

urbanization—urbanización proceso por medio del cual una porción más grande de la población mundial vive en las ciudades

V

value added theory—teoría de valor agregado teoría que sostiene que ciertas condiciones deben estar dadas para que los movimientos sociales ocurran

values—valores idea amplia sobre lo que es bueno o deseable compartida por muchos integrantes de una sociedad

variable—variable característica sujeta a cambios

verstehen—empatía la comprensión de la conducta humana poniéndose uno mismo en el lugar de otros

vertical mobility—movilidad vertical cambio hacia arriba o hacia abajo del estado ocupacional o clase social

victim discounting—clasificación de víctimas procedimiento mediante el cual se reduce la gravedad de los crímenes que dañan a personas de estratos bajos

voucher system—sistema de comprobantes sistema en el cual los fondos de las escuelas fiscales pueden utilizarse para subsidiar a escuelas públicas, privadas, o religiosas

W

war—guerra conflicto armado organizado que ocurre dentro de una sociedad o entre naciones

wealth—riqueza el total de los recursos económicos que posee una persona o grupo

white-collar crime—crimen de ejecutivos crímenes relacionados al trabajo cometido por personas de condición alta

working poor—trabajadores pobres personas empleadas en trabajos que requieren de un grado elemental de habilidad con los sueldos más bajos y que no ganan lo suficiente para salir de la pobreza

Z

zero population growth—crecimiento cero de la población situación en la cual las muertes están equilibradas con los nacimientos de modo que no crece la población

References

A

Acosta, R. Vivian, and Linda Jean Carpenter. "Women in Intercollegiate Sport: A Longitudinal Study—Nineteen Year Update, 1987–1996." Department of Physical Education, Brooklyn College, 1997.

Adelmann, P. K., T. C. Antonucci, S. E. Crohan, and L. M. Coleman (1989). "Empty Nest, Cohort, and Employment in the Well-Being of Midlife Women." *Sex Roles*, 173–189.

Adler, Emily Stier, and Roger Clark (1999). *How It's Done: An Invitation to Social Research*. Belmont, CA: Wadsworth Publishing Company.

Adler, Patricia A., and Peter Adler (1998). *Peer Power*. New Brunswick: Rutgers University Press.

Allport, Gordon (1958). *The Nature of Prejudice*. Garden City, NY: Doubleday.

American Sociological Association (1995). "Careers in Sociology." Washington, DC.

Andersen, Margaret L. (1997). *Thinking About Women*. 4th ed. Boston: Allyn and Bacon.

Asch, Solomon E. (November 1955). "Opinions and Social Pressure." *Scientific American 193*, 31–35.

Atchley, Robert C. (1999). *Social Forces and Aging*. 9th ed. Belmont, CA: Wadsworth.

Auguet, Roland (1972). *Cruelty and Civilization*. London: George Allen and Unwin, Ltd.

____. (1972). *Crueldad y Civilización: Los Juegos Romanos*. Barcelona: Aymá.

B

Baca Zinn, Maxine, and D. Stanley Eitzen (1998). "Economic Restructuring and Systems Inequality." In Margaret L. Andersen and Patricia Hill. (eds.), *Race, Class, and Gender: An Anthology*. 3rd ed. Belmont, CA: Wadsworth Publishing Co., pp. 233–237.

Bai, Matt, and Andrew Murr (January 25, 1999). "Go for the Greed." *Newsweek*.

Ballantine, Jeanne H. (1993). *The Sociology of Education*. 3rd ed. Englewood Cliffs, NJ: Prentice Hall.

Bardo, John W., and John J. Hartman (1982). *Urban Sociology*. Itasca, IL: Peacock.

Barlett, Donald L., and James B. Steele (1996). *America: Who Stole the Dream?* Kansas City, KA: Andrews and McMeel.

Barner, Robert (1996). "The New Millennium Workplace: Seven Changes that Will Challenge Managers—and Workers." *The Futurist 30*, 14–19.

Barnes, et al. (1998). *Growing Up in Stepfamilies*. New York: Oxford University Press.

Barr, C. (1995). "Pushing the Envelope: What Curriculum Integration Can Be." In E. Brazee and J. Capelluti. (eds.), *Dissolving Boundaries: Toward an Integrative Curriculum*. Columbus, OH: National Middle School Association.

Barron, James (September 16, 1988). "Fondly Recalling a Martian Invasion." *New York Times*, B1, B3.

Barry, Norman P. (1999). *Welfare*. 2nd ed. Minneapolis: University of Minnesota Press.

Beaton, Rod (February 25–27, 2000). "Braves Penalized for Illegal Signing." *USA Today* :1A.

Becker, Howard S. (1991). *Outsiders*. New York: Free Press.

Begley, Sharon (November 1, 1993). "Not Just a Pretty Face." *Newsweek*, 63–67.

____. (February 28, 2000). "Getting Inside a Teen Brain." *Newsweek*, 58–59.

Bell, Daniel (1999). *The Coming of Post-Industrial Society*. New York: Basic Books.

Bellah, Robert N., et al. (1991). *The Good Society*. New York: Knopf.

Belton, Beth (March 2, 1999). "Fear Forces Employees to Take Initiative." *USA Today*.

Benokraitis, Nijole V. (1999). *Subtle Sexism*. Thousand Oaks, CA: Sage.

____. (1998). *Marriages and Family*. Englewood Cliffs, NJ: Prentice Hall.

Berger, Peter L. (1990). *The Sacred Canopy: Elements of a Sociological Theory of Religion*. New York: Doubleday & Co.

Berk, Richard A. (1974). *Collective Behavior*. Dubuque, IA: William C. Brown.

Bianchi, Suzanne M. (June 1990). "America's Children: Mixed Prospects." *Population Bulletin 45*, 3–41.

Bierman, John (January 29, 1990). "Frustration and Fury." *Maclean's, 29*.

Blum, Debra E. (August 11, 1993). "Men Turn to Federal Anti-Bias Laws to Protect Teams from the Chopping Block." *Chronicle of Higher Education*, A33–A34.

Blumer, Herbert. "Collective Behavior." In Alfred M. Lee (ed.), *Principles of Sociology*. 3rd ed. New York: Barnes & Noble, 1969a, pp. 65–121.

____. (1969b). *Symbolic Interactionism.* Englewood Cliffs, NJ: Prentice Hall.

Booth, Alan, and Ann C. Crouter. (eds.). (1998). *Men in Families: When Do They Get Involved? What Difference Does It Make?* Mahwah, NJ: Lawrence Erlbaum Associates.

Bowen, William G., and Derek Bok (2000). *The Shape of the River: Long-Term Consequences of Considering Race in College and University Admissions.* Princeton, NJ: Princeton University Press.

Brajuha, Mario, and Lyle Hallowell (January 1986). "Legal Intrusion and the Politics of Fieldwork: The Impact of the Brajuha Case." *Urban Life 14*, 454–478.

Branscum, Deborah (March 1, 1999). "Go On, Break the Chain." *Newsweek, 58.*

Brinton, Crane (1990). *The Anatomy of Revolution.* New York: Knopf.

Brodie, Mollyann (1995). *The Four Americas: Government and Social Policy Through the Eyes of America's Multi-Racial and Multi-Ethnic Society.* A report of the Washington Post/Kaiser Family Foundation/Harvard Survey Project. Menlo Park, CA: Kaiser Family Foundation.

Brown, Susan L., and Alan Booth (August 1996). "Cohabitation versus Marriage: A Comparison of Relationship Quality." *Journal of Marriage and the Family 58*, 668–678.

Bruner, Jerome (January 1982). "Schooling Children in a Nasty Climate." *Psychology Today*, 57–63.

Brunvand, Jan Harold (1989). *Curses! Broiled Again!* New York: Norton.

Bulkeley, William M. (June 16, 1997). "Family Portrait: Web Pages Allow Families to Keep in Touch." *The Wall Street Journal,* R24.

Burgess, Ernest W. (1925). "The Growth of the City." In Robert E. Park, Ernest W. Burgess, and Robert D. McKenzie (eds.), *The City.* Chicago: University of Chicago Press, pp. 47–62.

Buss, David M., Neil M. Malamuth, and Barbara A. Winstead (1998). "Sex, Power, Conflict: Evolutionary and Feminist Perspectives." *Contemporary Psychology 43.*

C

Campbell, Frances A., and Craig T. Ramey (1994). "Effects of Early Intervention on Intellectual and Academic Achievement: A Follow-Up Study of Children from Low-Income Families." *Child Development 65*, 684–698.

Cantril, Hadley (1982). *The Invasion from Mars.* Princeton, NJ: Princeton University Press.

Caplow, Theodore (1991). *American Social Trends.* New York: Harcourt Brace Jovanovich.

____. (February 1998). "The Case of the Phantom Episcopalians." *American Sociological Review 63,* 137–145

Casbergue, Renee M., and Judith Kieff (Spring 1998). "Marbles Anyone? Traditional Games in the Classroom." *Childhood Education*, 143–147.

Casler, Lawrence (1965). "The Effects of Extra Tactile Stimulation on a Group of Institutionalized Infants." *Genetic Psychology Monographs 71*, 137–175.

Center for the American Woman and Politics. "Fact Sheet." April 1999.

Chagnon, Napoleon A. (1997). *Yanomamö.* 5th ed. Fort Worth: Harcourt Brace College Publishers.

Chamberlain, Gary (October 4, 1999). "Metal Wars." *Design News 115.*

Chambliss, William J. (November/December 1973). "The Saints and the Roughnecks." *Society, 11*, 24–31.

Chang, Iris (1998). *The Rape of Nanking: The Forgotten Holocaust of World War II.* New York: Viking Penguin.

Chandbasekaran, Rajiv (June 25, 1999). "Microsoft Trial Ends After 8 Months," *The Washington Post*, A1, A20.

Children's Defense Fund (1991). *The State of America's Children—1991.* Washington, DC: Children's Defense Fund.

Clark, Charles S. (May 7, 1993). "Cults in America." *C Q Researcher,* 3, 385–408.

"Closing the Gap." (September 2, 1995) *The Economist* 74.

Coakley, Jay J. (ed.). (1998). *Sport in Society.* 6th ed. Boston: Irwin/McGraw-Hill.

Cohen, David, and Marvin Lazerson (March/April 1972). "Education and the Corporate Order." *Socialist Revolution 2*, 47–72.

Coleman, James S., et al. (1966). *Equality of Educational Opportunity.* Washington, DC: U.S. Government Printing Office.

Coleman, James W. (September 1987). "Toward an Integrated Theory of White-Collar Crime." *American Journal of Sociology 93*, 406–439.

Cooley, Charles Horton (1902). *Human Nature and the Social Order.* New York: Scribner's.

Cox, Frank D. (1999). *Human Intimacy: Marriage, the Family, and Its Meaning.* Belmont, CA: Wadsworth Publishing Company.

Cox, Harvey (1977). *Turning East: The Promise and Peril of the New Orientalism.* New York: Simon and Schuster.

____. (1992). *Religion in the Secular City.* New York: Simon & Schuster.

____. (1996). *Fire from Heaven*. London: Cassell.

____. (1996). *Fire from Heaven: The Rise of Pentecostal Spirituality and the Reshaping of Religion in the Twenty-First Century*. Reading, MA: Addison Wesley Longman, Inc.

Cowgill, Donald O., and Lowell D. Holmes (eds.). (1972). *Aging and Modernization*. New York: Appleton-Century-Crofts.

Cowley, Geoffrey, and Anne Underwood (Winter, 1997–98). "Surgeon, Drop that Scalpel." *Newsweek* 77–78.

Crain, Robert L. (January 1970). "School Integration and Occupational Achievement of Negroes." *American Journal of Sociology 75,* 593–606.

Crain, Robert L., and Carol S. Weisman (1972). *Discrimination, Personality and Achievements*. New York: Seminar Press.

Cress, Daniel M., and David A. Snow (December 1996). "Mobilization at the Margins: Resources, Benefactors, and the Viability of Homeless Social Movement Organizations." *American Sociological Review 61,* 1089–1109.

Crewdson, John (March 13, 1994). "Fraud in Breast Cancer Study." *Chicago Tribune 1*.

Crosby, F. E. (1993). *Juggling*. New York: Free Press.

Crosby, John F. (1985). *Reply to Myth: Perspectives on Intimacy*. New York: Wiley.

Cuzzort, R. P., and E. W. King (1976). *Humanity and Modern Social Thought*. 2nd ed. Hinsdale, IL: Dryden Press.

D

Darder, Antonia, and Rodolfo D. Torres (1997). *The Latino Reader*. Malden, MA: Blackwell.

Davies, Bronwyn (1990). *Frogs and Snails and Feminist Tales*. New York: Pandora Press.

Deak, JoAnn (1998). *How Girls Thrive*. Washington, DC: National Association of Independent Schools.

Degler, Carl N. (1991). *In Search of Human Nature*. New York: Oxford University Press.

DeYoung, Alan J. (1989). *Economics and American Education*. White Plains, NY: Longman.

DiIulio, John J., Jr., and Anne Morrison Piehl (Fall 1991). "Does Prison Pay?: The Stormy National Debate Over the Cost-Effectiveness of Imprisonment." *The Brookings Review* 28–35.

Doreian, Patrick, and Frans N. Stokman (1997). *Evolution of Social Networks*. Amsterdam: Gordon & Breach Publishers.

Dornbush, Sanford M., et al. (1985). "Single Parents, Extended Households, and the Control of Adolescents." *Child Development 56,* 326–341.

Dudley, Kathryn Marie (1997). *The End of the Line: Lost Jobs, New Lives in Postindustrial America*. Chicago: The University of Chicago Press.

Dudley, William (ed.) (1999). *Media Violence*. San Diego, CA: Greenhaven Press.

Duke, Lynne, and Gabriel Escobar (May 10, 1992). "A Looting Binge Born of Necessity, Opportunity." *Washington Post* Al, A23.

Durkheim, Emile (1964a). *The Division of Labor in Society*. New York: Free Press.

____. *Suicide*. Translated by John A. Spaulding and George Simpson (1964b). Edited by George Simpson. New York: Free Press.

____. *The Elementary Forms of the Religious Life* (1995). New York: Free Press.

Dynes, Russell R., and Kathleen J. Tierney (eds.) (1994). *Disasters, Collective Behavior, and Social Organization*. Newark: University of Delaware Press.

E

Eccles, Jacquelynne, et al. (February, 1993). "Development During Adolescence: The Impact of Stage-Environment Fit on Young Adolescents' Experiences in Schools and in Families." *American Psychologist 48,* 90–101.

Eder, Donna (1995). *School Talk*. New Brunswick, NJ: Rutgers University Press.

Eitzen, D. Stanley (1993). *Sport in Contemporary Society: An Anthology*. 4th ed. New York: St. Martin's Press.

____. "The Dark Side of Competition." In D. Stanley Eitzen (ed.) (1996), *Sport in Contemporary Society*. 5th ed. New York: St. Martin's Press, pp. 185–192.

____. *Fair and Foul: Beyond the Myths and Paradoxes of Sport*. Lanham, MA: Rowman & Littlefield Publishers, 1999.

Eitzen, D. Stanley, and George H. Sage (1997). *Sociology of North American Sport*. 6th ed. Boston: WCB McGraw-Hill.

El Nasser, Haya (June 25, 1996). "Judges Say 'Scarlet Letter' Angle Works." *USA Today* 1A–2A.

Elikann, Peter T. (1996). *The Tough-On-Crime Myth: Real Solutions to Cut Crime*. New York: Plenum.

Elkin, Frederick, and Gerald Handel (1991). *The Child and Society*. 5th ed. New York: McGraw-Hill.

Ember, Carol R., and Melvin Ember (1999). *Anthropology*. 9th ed. Upper Saddle River, NJ: Prentice Hall.

Erikson, Erik H. (1964). *Childhood and Society*. 2nd ed. New York: Norton.

____. (1982). *The Life Cycle Completed*. New York: Norton.

Erikson, Kai. *Sociological Visions*. Blue Ridge Summit, PA: Rowman & Littlefield Publishers, 1997.

Erikson, Kai T. (1976). *Everything in Its Path*. New York: Simon & Schuster.

Espiritu, Yen Le (1996). *Asian American Men and Women*. Thousand Oaks, CA: Sage.

Etzioni, Amitai (October 1982). "Education for Mutuality and Civility." *Futurist 16,* 4–7.

Evans, Jean. *Three Men*. New York: Knopf, 1954.

F

Farley, Reynolds (1996). *The New American Reality: Who We Are, How We Got There, Where We Are Going*. New York: Russell Sage Foundation.

Fausto-Sterling, Anne (1987). *Myths of Gender*. New York: Basic Books.

Feagin, Joe R. (February 1991). "The Continuing Significance of Race: Antiblack Discrimination in Public Places." *American Sociological Review 56,* 101–115.

Fedarko, Kevin (December 6, 1993). "Bodies of Evidence." *Time 70.*

Federal Election Commission. (2001) "International Voter Turnout." http://www.fec.gov/.

Fine, Gary Alan (1987). *With the Boys: Little League Baseball and Preadolescent Culture*. Chicago: University of Chicago Press.

____. (1996). *The Culture of Restaurant Work*. Berkeley and Los Angeles: University of California Press.

Fischer, David Hackett (1977). *Growing Old in America*. New York: Oxford University Press.

Fishman, Mark, and Gray Cavender. (eds.) (1998). *Entertaining Crime*. Hawthorne, NY: Aldine de Gruyter.

Flanagan, William G. (1993). *Contemporary Urban Sociology*. New York: Cambridge University Press.

Fukuyama, Francis (May 1999a). "The Great Disruption: Human Nature and the Reconstitution of Social Order." *Atlantic Monthly 283*, 55–80.

G

Galloway, Joseph L. (March 3, 1999). "In the Heart of Darkness." *U.S. News & World Report*.

Gallup, George H., Jr. (2001). *The Gallup Poll*. http://www.gallup.com/poll/.

Gallup, George H., Jr. (1988). *The Gallup Poll*. Wilmington, DE: Scholarly Resources.

____. (1994a). *The Gallup Poll, Public Opinion 1993*. Wilmington, DE: Scholarly Resources.

____. (1996). *Religion in America 1996*. Princeton, NJ: The Princeton Religion Research Center.

Game, Ann, and Andrew W. Metcalfe (1996). *Passionate Sociology*. Thousand Oaks, CA: Sage.

Gamst, Glenn, and Charles M. Otten (Summer 1992). "Job Satisfaction in High Technology and Traditional Industry: Is There a Difference?" *The Psychological Record* 413–425.

Ganong, Lawrence, and Marilyn Coleman (1994). *Remarried Family Relationships*. Thousand Oaks, CA: Sage.

Gans, Herbert J. (1968). *People and Plans*. New York: Basic Books.

____. (July/August 1971). "The Uses of Poverty: The Poor Pay All." *Social Policy* 2, 20–24.

Gardner, David Pierpont (1983). *A Nation at Risk: The Imperative for Educational Reform*. Report of the National Commission on Excellence in Education. Washington, DC: U.S. Government Printing Office.

Garreau, J. (1991). *Edge City: Life on the New Frontier*. New York: Doubleday.

Gegax, T. Trent, and Matt Bai (May 10, 1999). "Searching for Answers." *Newsweek* 30–34.

Gelles, Richard J. (1997). *Intimate Violence in Families*. 3rd ed. Thousand Oaks, CA: Sage.

George, Yolanda S., Shirley M. Malcolm, and Laura Jeffers (May 1993). "Computer Equity for the Future." *Communications of the ACM 36,* 78–81.

Gerstel, Naomi, and Harriet Engel Gross (1995). "Gender and Families in the United States: The Reality of Economic Dependence." In Jo Freeman (ed.), *Women: A Feminist Perspective*. 5th ed. Mountain View, CA: Mayfield, pp. 92–127.

Gerth, H. H., and C. Wright Mills (eds.) (1958). *From Max Weber*. New York: Oxford University Press.

Gibbons, Tom (February 24, 1985). "Justice Not Equal for Poor Here." *Chicago Sun-Times* 1, 18.

Gibson, Margaret A., and John V. Ogbu (1991). *Minority Status and Schooling*. New York: Garland Publishing.

Giddens, Anthony (1987). *Social Theory and Modern Sociology*. Stanford, CA: Stanford University Press.

____. (1997). *Introduction to Sociology*. 2nd ed. New York: Norton.

Gilbert, Dennis (1998). *The American Class Structure*. 5th ed. Belmont, CA: Wadsworth Publishing Company.

Glazer, Nathan (1999). "The End of Meritocracy." *The New Republic*.

Glick, P., and S. L. Lin (February 1986). "More Young Adults Are Living with Their Parents: Who Are They?" *Journal of Marriage and the Family,* 107–112.

Goffman, Erving (1961a). *Encounters*. Indianapolis: Bobbs-Merrill.

____. (1963). *Stigma*. Englewood Cliffs, NJ: Prentice- Hall.

____. (1974). *The Presentation of Self in Everyday Life*. New York: Overlook Press.

____. (1979). *Gender Advertisements*. New York: Harper & Row.

____. (February 1983). "The Interaction Order." *American Sociological Review 48,* 1–17.

Golden, Frederic (December 31, 1999). "Albert Einstein: Person of the Century." *Time*, 62–65.

Goleman, D. (April 10, 1988). "An Emerging Theory on Blacks' IQ Scores." *New York Times Education Supplement,* 22–24.

Goode, Erich (1992). *Collective Behavior*. Fort Worth, TX: Sanders College Publishing.

Goode, William J. (1970). *World Revolution and Family Patterns*. New York: Free Press.

Gould, Stephen Jay (1981). *The Mismeasurement of Man*. New York: Norton.

Greenwald, Elissa A., Hilary R. Persky, Jay R. Campbell, and John Mazzeo (1999). *NAEP 1998 Writing: Report Card for the Nation and the States*. Washington, DC: National Center for Education Statistics.

Griffin, John Howard (1961). *Black Like Me*. Boston: Houghton Mifflin.

Gur, R. C., et al. (January 27, 1995). "Sex Differences in Regional Cerebral Glucose Metabolism During a Resting State." *Science 267,* 528–531.

H

Hagan, Frank E. (1994a). *Introduction to Criminology*. 3rd ed. Chicago: Nelson-Hall Publishers.

Hagan, John (1994b). *Crime and Disrepute*. Thousand, Oaks, CA: Pine Forge Press.

Hagedorn, John M. (1998). "Gang Violence in the Postindustrial Era." In Michael Tonry and Mark H. Moore (eds.), *Youth Violence*. Chicago: The University of Chicago Press, pp. 365–419.

Hammel, Sara, and Anna Mulrine (July 12, 1999). "They Get More than Just Game." *U.S. News and World Report*.

Handel, Gerald (ed.). (June 1990). "Revising Socialization Theory." *American Sociological Review 55,* 463–466.

Harlow, Harry F. (1967). "The Young Monkeys." *Psychology Today 5*, 40–47.

Harlow, Harry F., and Margaret Harlow (November 1962). "Social Deprivation in Monkeys." *Scientific American 207,* 137–146.

Harlow, Harry F., and Robert R. Zimmerman (August 1959). "Affectional Responses in the Infant Monkey." *Science 21,* 421–432.

Harris, Chauncy D. (1997). "'The Nature of Cities' and Urban Geography in the Last Half Century." *Urban Geography*, 15–35.

Harris, Judith Rich (1998). *The Nurture Assumption: Why Children Turn Out the Way They Do?* New York: Free Press.

Harris, Marvin (1974). *Cows, Pigs, Wars, and Witches*. New York: Random House.

Hawking, Stephen W. (1998). *A Brief History of Time*. New York: Bantam Books.

Hawley, W. D. (1985). "Achieving Quality Integrated Education—With or Without Federal Help." In F. Schultz (ed.). *Annual Editions: Education 85/86*. Guilford, CT: Dushkin Publishing, pp. 142–145.

Hawley, W. D., and M. A. Smylie (1988). "The Contribution of School Desegregation to Academic Achievement and Racial Integration." In P. A. Katz and D. A. Taylor (eds.), *Eliminating Racism*. New York: Plenum Press, pp. 281–297.

Heller, Mary Edna, Ruth S. Kempe, and Richard D. Krugman (1999). (eds.). *The Battered Child*. 5th ed. Chicago: University of Chicago Press.

Herbert, Wray (March 22, 1999). "Getting Close, But Not Too Close." *U.S. News Online*. http://www.usnews.com.

Herrnstein, Richard J., and Charles Murray (1996). *The Bell Curve: Intelligence and Class Structure in American Life*. New York: Free Press.

Hillier, Susan, and Georgia M. Barrow (1999). *Aging, the Individual, and Society*. 7th ed. Belmont, CA: Wadsworth Publishing Company.

Hilts, Philip (1997). "Smoke Screen." In Jerome H. Sknolnick and Elliott Currie (eds.), *Crisis in American Institutions*. New York: Longman, pp. 29–38.

Hirschi, Travis (1972). *Causes of Delinquency*. Berkeley: University of California Press.

Hochschild, Arlie R. (1997). *The Time Bind: When Work Becomes Home and Home Becomes Work*. New York: Henry Holt.

Hoebel, E. Adamson (1983). *The Law of Primitive Man*. New York: Atheneum.

Hoecker-Drysdale, Susan (1994). *Harriet Martineau*. Oxford: Berg Publishers.

Hoffman, Karen E. (November 9, 1998). "Internet as Gender-Equalizer?" *Internet World*.

Holt, John (1967). *How Children Fail*. New York: Dell.

Houseman, John (December 1948). "The Men from Mars." *Harper's Magazine 197,* 74–82.

Hoyt, Homer (1939). *The Structure and Growth of Residential Neighborhoods in American Cities.* Washington, DC: Federal Housing Authority.

Hunt, Stephen, Malcolm Hamilton, and Tony Walter. (eds.) (1998). *Charismatic Christianity: Sociological Perspectives.* New York: St. Martin's Press.

Hurley, Jennifer A. (ed.) (1998). *Racism.* San Diego, CA: Greenhaven Press.

Hurn, Christopher J. (1993). *The Limits and Possibilities of Schooling.* 3rd ed. Boston: Allyn and Bacon.

I

Ikeda, Keiko (1998). *A Room Full of Mirrors.* Stanford, CA: Stanford University Press.

J

Jacoby, Sanford M. (1997). *Modern Manors: Welfare Capitalism Since the New Deal.* Princeton, NJ: Princeton University Press.

Janssen-Jurreit, Marie Louise (1982). *Sexism.* New York: Farrar Strauss Giroux.

Jencks, Christopher, and Meredith Phillips (September-October 1998). "America's Next Achievement Test: Closing the Black-White Test Score Gap." *The American Prospect 40,* 44–53.

Jensen, Arthur (Winter 1969). "How Much Can We Boost IQ and Scholastic Achievement?" *Harvard Educational Review 39,* 1–123.

Johnson, David W., and Frank P. Johnson (1994). *Joining Together.* 5th ed. Boston: Allyn and Bacon.

Johnstone, Ronald L. (1996). *Religion in Society.* 5th ed. Upper Saddle River, NJ: Prentice Hall.

Jones, James M. (1993). *Bad Blood* (expanded ed.). New York: Free Press.

K

Karatnycky, Adrian (January/February 1995). "Democracies on the Rise, Democracies at Risk." *Freedom Review 26*, 5–10.

Katz, James E., and Philip Aspden (December 1997). "A Nation of Strangers?" *Communications of the ACM* 81–87.

Kelly, Delos H. (ed.) (1996). *Deviant Behavior.* 5th ed. New York: St. Martin's Press.

Kephart, William M., and William Zellner (1998). *Extraordinary Groups.* 6th ed. New York: St. Martin's Press.

Kids Count Data Sheet (2001). Baltimore, MD: The Annie E. Casey Foundation, 2001.

Kilson, Martin L. (1998). "The State of African-America Politics." In Lee A. Daniels (ed.), *The State of Black America 1998.* New York: National Urban League, pp. 247–270.

Kinsley, Michael (February 2, 1998). "In Defense of Matt Drudge." *Time* 41.

Kitano, Harry H. (1993). *Japanese Americans.* New York: Chelsea House.

Klee, Kenneth (December 13, 1999). "The Siege of Seattle." *Newsweek* 30–39.

Kleniewski, Nancy (1997). *Cities, Change, and Conflict.* Belmont, CA: Wadsworth.

Kohn, Alfie (1992). *No Contest: The Case Against Competition.* Revised edition. Boston: Houghton Mifflin Company.

Konner, Melvin (July-August, 1999). "Darwin's Truth, Jefferson's Vision." *The American Prospect* 30–38.

Kraybill, Donald B., and Marc A. Olshan (eds.) (1994). *The Amish Struggle with Modernity.* Hanover, NH: University Press of New England.

Kuhn, Thomas S. (1996). *The Structure of Scientific Revolutions.* 3rd ed. Chicago: University of Chicago Press.

L

Ladson-Billings, Gloria (1998). "From Soweto to the South Bronx: African Americans and Colonial Education in the United States." In Carlos Alberto Torres and Theodore R. Mitchell (eds.), *Sociology of Education.* Albany, NY: State University of New York Press, pp. 247–264.

Lamanna, Marianne, and Agnes Riedmann (1997). *Marriages and Families: Making Choices and Facing Change.* 6th ed. Belmont, CA: Wadsworth.

Lampert, Leslie (May 1993). "Fat Like Me." *Ladies Home Journal,* 154ff.

Landry, Bart (1988). *The New Black Middle Class.* Berkeley: University of California Press.

Lanier, Mark M., and Stuart Henry (1997). *Essential Criminology.* Boulder, CO: Westview Press.

Lapchick, Richard E., and Kevin J. Matthews (1999). *1998 Racial and Gender Report Card.* Center for the Study of Sport in Society: Northeastern University.

Lapchick, Richard E., and Kevin J. Matthews (2001). *2001 Racial & Gender Report Card.* Center for Study of Sport in Society: Northeastern University.

Laub, John H., and Janet L. Lauritsen (1998). "The Interdependence of School Violence with Neighborhood and Family Conditions." In Delbert S. Elliott, Beatrix A. Hamburg, and Kirk R. Williams (eds.), *Violence in*

American Schools. New York: Cambridge University Press, pp. 127–155.

Lawrence, Frederick M. (1999). *Punishing Hate; Bias Crimes Under American Law*. Cambridge, MA: Harvard University Press.

Le Bon, Gustave (1960). *The Crowd*. New York: Viking.

Leacock, Eleanor Burke (1969). *Teaching and Learning in City Schools*. New York: Basic Books.

"Left Out." (March 21, 1983). *Newsweek* 26–35.

"Lego: Fighting the Video Monsters." (January 30, 1999). *The Economist 57*.

Lemann, Nicholas (1991). *The Promised Land*. New York: Knopf.

Lemert, Charles, and Ann Branaman. (eds.) (1997). *The Goffman Reader*. Malden, MA: Blackwell Publishers.

Lemert, Edwin M. (1972). *Human Deviance, Social Problems, and Social Control*. 2nd ed. Englewood Cliffs, NJ: Prentice Hall.

Leonard, Wilbert Marcellus, II. (1998). *A Sociological Perspective of Sport*. Boston: Allyn & Bacon.

Lester, David (1998). *The Death Penalty*. 2nd ed. Springfield, IL: Charles C Thomas.

Levin, Jack, and Jack McDevitt (1993). *Hate Crimes: The Rising Tide of Bigotry and Bloodshed*. New York: Plenum.

Levin, Susanna (1996). "The Spoils of Victory: Who Gets Big Money from Sponsors, and Why." In D. Stanley Eitzen (ed.), *Sport in Contemporary Society*. 5th ed. New York: St. Martin's Press, pp. 367–372.

Levine, Daniel U., and Rayna F. Levine (1996). *Society and Education*. 9th ed. Boston: Allyn and Bacon.

Levine, Rhonda (1998). *Social Class and Stratification*. Blue Ridge Summit, PA: Rowman & Littlefield.

Liebow, Elliot (1967). *Talley's Corner*. Boston: Little, Brown.

Light, Ivan (1983). *Cities in World Perspective*. New York: Macmillan.

Linden, Eugene (March 22, 1993a). "Can Animals Think?" *Time* 55–61.

Linder, Eileen W. (ed.) (2000). *Yearbook of American and Canadian Churches*. Nashville, TN: Abingdon Press.

Little, Suzanne (February 1975). "Sex Roles in Faraway Places." *Ms.*, 77ff.

Lofland, John (1993). *Polite Protesters*. Syracuse, NY: Syracuse University Press.

Longmire, Dennis R. (1996). "American Attitudes Among the Ultimate Weapon: Capital Punishment." In Timothy J. Flanagan and Dennis Longmire (eds.), *Americans View Crime and Justice*. Thousand Oaks, CA: Sage, pp. 93–108.

Lopreato, Joseph (1990). "From Social Evolutionism to Biocultural Evolutionism." *Sociological Forum 5*, 187–212.

Loprest, Pamela (1999). *Families Who Left Welfare: Who Are They and How Are They Doing?* Washington, DC: The Urban Institute.

Ludwig, Jack. "Gallup Social Audit On Black/White Relations In The U.S." (July 11, 2001). http://www. gallup.com.

M

Maccoby, Eleanor E. (1997). *The Two Sexes: Growing Up Apart, Coming Together*. Cambridge, MA: Belknap Press of Harvard University Press.

MacKenzie, Donald A., and Judy Wajcman (eds.) (1999). *The Social Shaping of Technology*. 2nd ed. Bristol, PA: Taylor & Francis, Inc.

Madon, S., L. Jussim, and J. Eccles (1997). "In Search of the Powerful Self-Fulfilling Prophecy." *Journal of Personality and Social Psychology 72*, 791–809.

Malthus, Thomas (1798). *An Essay on the Principle of Population*. London: Reeves and Turner.

Marriott, M. (August 11, 1991). "Afrocentrism: Balancing or Skewing History?" *New York Times* 1, 18.

Martin, Karin A. (August 1998). "Becoming a Gendered Body: Practices of Preschools." *American Sociological Review Association 63*, 494–511.

Martinez, Valerie J., R. Kenneth Godwin, Frank R. Kemerer, and Laura Perna (September 1995). "The Consequences of School Choice: Who Leaves and Who Stays in the Inner City." *Social Science Quarterly 76*, 485–501.

Mason, Philip (1970). *Patterns of Dominance*. New York: Oxford University Press.

Mathews, Tom (May 11, 1992). "The Siege of L.A." *Newsweek* 30–38.

Mauer, Marc. "The Crisis of the Young African American Male and the Criminal Justice System." http://www. sentencing project.org/, 1999.

McCarthy, John D., and Mark Wolfson (December 1996). "Resource Mobilization by Local Social Movement Organizations: Agency, Strategy, and Organization in the Movement Against Drinking and Driving." *American Sociological Review 61*, 1070–1088.

McGinn, Daniel, and Joan Raymond (Winter 1997–98). "Workers of the World, Get Online." *Newsweek* 32–33.

McLaren, Peter (1997). "Multiculturalism and the Postmodern Critique: Toward a Pedagogy of Resistance and Transformation." In A. H. Halsey, et al. (eds.), *Education*. New York: Oxford University Press, pp. 520–540.

McNamee, Mike, and Joann Muller (December 21, 1998). "A Tale of Two Job Markets." *Business Week 3609,* 38.

McPhail, Clark (1991). *Myth of the Madding Crowd.* Hawthorne, NY: Aldine de Gruyter.

Mead, George Herbert (1934). *Mind, Self and Society.* Chicago: University of Chicago Press.

Mead, Margaret (1950). *Sex and Temperament in Three Primitive Societies.* New York: Mentor Books.

Menaghan, E. G., and T. L. Parcel (1991). "Parental Employment and Family Life: Research in the 1980's." In A. Booth (ed.), *Contemporary Families.* Minneapolis: National Council on Family Relations, pp. 361–380.

Merton, Robert K. (1968). *Social Theory and Social Structure* (enlarged ed.). New York: Free Press.

____. (1996). *On Social Structure and Science.* Chicago: University of Chicago Press.

Michels, Robert (1949). *Political Parties.* New York: Free Press.

Micklin, Michael and Dudley L. Poston, Jr. (ed.) (1998). *Continuities in Sociological Human Ecology.* New York: Plenum Press.

Milgram, Stanley (1963). "Behavioral Study of Obedience." *Journal of Abnormal and Social Psychology 67,* 371–378.

____. (1964). "Group Pressure and Action Against a Person." *Journal of Abnormal and Social Psychology 6,* 137–143.

____. (1965). "Some Conditions of Obedience and Disobedience to Authority." *Human Relations 18,* 57–76.

____. (1974). *Obedience to Authority.* New York: Harper & Row.

Miller, Greg, and Stuart Silverstein (February 5, 2000). "Even Corporate Perks Join the Dot.com Revolution. *The Los Angeles Times* A1.

Millicent, Lawton (February 12, 1992). "Schools' 'Glass Ceiling' Imperils Girls, Study Says." *Education Week* 17.

Mills, C. Wright (1959). *The Sociological Imagination.* New York: Oxford University Press.

Mills, Kay. *Something Better for My Children: The History and People of Head Start.* New York: NAL/Dutton, 1998.

Mitchell, B., and E. Gee (October 1996). "Boomerang Kids and Midlife Parental Marital Satisfaction." *Family Relations* 442–448.

Moen, Phyllis (1992). *Women's Two Roles.* New York: Auburn House.

Montagu, Ashley (1998). *The Natural Superiority of Women.* 5th ed. Thousand Oaks, CA: Altamira Press.

Moore, Joan, and Harry Pachon (1985). *Hispanics in the United States.* Englewood Cliffs, NJ: Prentice Hall.

Moorhead, Gregory, Richard Ference, and Chris P. Neck (1991). "Group Decision Fiascoes Continue: Space Shuttle Challenger and a Revised Groupthink Framework." *Human Relations 44,* 539–550.

Moorhead, Gregory, Christopher P. Neck, and Mindy S. West (February/March, 1998). "The Tendency toward Defective Decision Making within Self-Managing Teams: The Relevance of Groupthink for the 21st Century." *Organizational Behavior and Human Decision Processes* 327–351.

Morganthau, Tom (October 24, 1994). "IQ: Is It Destiny?" *Newsweek* 53–55.

Morris, Norval, and Michael Tonry (1990). *Between Prison and Probation.* New York: Oxford University Press.

Muldavin, Joshua (June 3, 1999). "Commentary: Market Reforms Breed Discontent." *Los Angeles Times* B9.

Murdock, George P. (1945). "The Common Denominator of Cultures." In Ralph Linton (ed.), *The Science of Man in the World Crisis.* New York: Columbia University Press, pp. 123–142.

Myers, David G. (1999). *Social Psychology.* 6th ed. Boston: McGraw-Hill College.

N

Nanda, Serena, and Richard L. Warms (1998). *Cultural Anthropology.* 6th ed. Belmont, CA: Wadsworth.

"National Television Violence Study: Executive Summary." Studio City, CA: Mediascope, Inc., 1998.

Newborne, Burt. (2001). "Reclaiming Democracy." *The American Prospect* (March 12–26):18–24.

Newman, Katherine S. (1993). *Declining Fortunes.* New York: Basic Books.

____. (1999). *Falling from Grace.* Updated edition. Berkeley, CA: University of California Press.

Nie, Norman H., and Lutz Erbring (February 17, 2000). "Internet and Society: A Preliminary Report." Stanford Institute for the Quantitative Study of Society.

Niebuhr, H. Richard (1968). *The Social Sources of Denominationalism.* New York: World.

Nisbet, Robert A. (1989). *The Present Age.* New York: Harper & Row.

Nixon, Howard L. II, and James H. Frey (1996). *A Sociology of Sport.* Belmont, CA: Wadsworth Publishing Co.

Nock, Steven L. (January 1995). "A Comparison of Marriages and Cohabiting Relationships." *Journal of Family Issues 16,* 53–76.

Nolan, Patrick, and Gerhard E. Lenski (1999). *Human Societies*. 8th ed. New York: McGraw Hill College.

Novak, Michael (1996). *The Unmeltable Ethnics*. 2nd ed. New Brunswick: Transaction.

Nydeggar, Corinne N. (1985). "Family Ties of the Aged in Cross-Cultural Perspective." In Beth B. Hess and Elizabeth W. Markson (eds.), *Growing Old in America*. New Brunswick, NJ: Transaction Press.

O

Oakes, Jeannie, and Martin Lipton. In Laura I. Rendon and Richard O. Hope (eds.) (1996). *Educating a New Majority: Transforming America's Educational System for Diversity*. San Francisco: Jossey-Bass Publishers, pp. 168–200.

O'Brien, Joanne, and Martin Palmer (1993). *The State of Religion Atlas*. New York: Touchstone.

O'Dwyer, Thomas (October 27, 1999). "The Taliban's Gender Apartheid." *The Jerusalem Post* 6.

Office of Management and Budget. "A Citizen's Guide to the Federal Budget." *Budget of the United States Government Fiscal Year 2000*, 1999. http://www.access.gpo.gov/usbudget/fy2000/guide02.html.

Ollman, Bertel (1998). *Market Socialism*. New York: Routledge.

Olzak, Susan, and Joane Nagel (eds.) (1986). *Competitive Ethnic Relations*. San Diego, CA: Academic Press.

Orfield, Gary A., et al. (1992). "Status of School Desegregation: The Next Generation." Report to the National School Board Association. Alexandria, VA: National School Board Association.

Ornstein, Robert, and Paul Ehrlich (1991). *New World New Mind*. London: Paladin.

O'Sullivan, Christine Y., Clyde M. Reese, and John Mazzeo (1997). *NAEP 1996 Science Report Card for the Nation and the States*. Washington, DC: National Center for Educational Statistics.

P

Palen, John J. (1997). *The Urban World*. 5th ed. New York: McGraw-Hill.

Passell, Peter (November 9, 1994). "'Bell Curve' Critics Say Early I.Q. Isn't Destiny." *New York Times* B10.

Patterson, James T. (1986). *America's Struggle Against Poverty: 1900–1985*. Cambridge, MA: Harvard University Press.

Patterson, Thomas E. (1999). *The American Democracy*. 4th ed. Boston: McGraw-Hill.

Pearson, Kent. "Subcultures and Sport." In John W. Loy, Jr., Gerald S. Kenyon, and Barry D. McPherson (eds.) (1981). *Sport, Culture, and Society*. 2nd ed. Philadelphia: Lee & Febiger, pp. 131–145.

Pearson, Patricia, and Michael Finley (1997). *When She Was Bad: Violent Women and the Myth of Innocence*. New York: Viking Penguin.

Peoples, James, and Garrick Bailey (2000). *Humanity: An Introduction to Cultural Anthropology*. 5th ed. Belmont, CA: Wadsworth.

Perry, Joellen, and Dan McGraw (September 6, 1999). "In Cleveland, It's a Back-to-School Daze." *U.S. News & World Review*.

Pfeffer, Jeffrey (1997). *New Directions for Organization Theory*. New York: Oxford University Press.

Phu, Vu Duy (December 14, 1998). "Vietnam—Anticipating IT." *Vietnam Economic News*.

Plog, Fred, and Daniel G. Bates. (1990). *Cultural Anthropology*. 3rd ed. New York: McGraw-Hill.

Pollard, Kelvin (1999). "U.S. Diversity is More than Black and White." Washington, DC: Population Reference Bureau.

Pontell, Henry N. (1984). *A Capacity to Punish*. Bloomington: Indiana University Press.

Popenoe, David (1999). *Life Without Father*. Cambridge, MA: Harvard University Press.

Popenoe, David, Jean Bethke Elshtain, and David Blankenhorn (1996). *Promises to Keep: Decline and Renewal of Marriage in America*. Lantham, MD: Rowman and Littlefield Publishers.

Pryor, Douglas W. (1999). *Unspeakable Acts: Why Men Sexually Abuse Children*. New York: New York University Press.

Q

Queen, Stuart A., Robert W. Habenstein, and Jill S. Quadagno (1985). *The Family in Various Cultures*. 5th ed. New York: Harper & Row.

Quintanilla, Michael (May 20, 1996). "Turning Off to Save the Family." *Los Angeles Times* E1–E2.

R

Redhead, Steve (1997). *Subcultures to Clubcultures*. Malden, MA: Blackwell.

Rendon, Laura J., and Richard O. Hope. (eds.) (1996). *Educating a New Majority*. San Francisco: Jossey-Bass Publishers.

Rennison, Callie Maroe (1999). "Criminal Victimization 1998, Changes 1997–98 with Trends 1993–98." U.S. Department of Justice, Bureau of Justice Statistics, Office of Justice Programs.

Reskin, Barbara (1993). "Sex Segregation in the Workplace." *Annual Review of Sociology 19*, 241–270.

Richmond, P. (January 19, 1986). "Weighing the Odds." *Colorado Springs Gazette Telegraph,* F1–F4.

Ridley, Matt (1996). *The Origins of Virtue.* New York: Viking.

Riederer, Richard K. (March 1999). "Battered by the World Financial Crisis." *33 Metal Producing 37,* 42–45.

Riley, Nancy E. (1997). *Gender, Power, and Population Change.* Washington, DC: Population Reference Bureau.

Ritzer, George (1996). *McDonaldization of Society.* Revised edition. Thousand Oaks, CA: Pine Forge Press.

____. (1998). *The McDonaldization Thesis: Explorations and Extensions.* Newbury Park, CA: Sage Publications.

Rochon, Thomas R. (1998). *Culture Moves: Ideas, Activism, and Changing Values.* Princeton, NJ: Princeton University Press.

Roethlisberger, F. J., and William J. Dickson (1964). *Management and the Worker.* New York: Wiley.

Rosenthal, Robert, and Lenore Jacobson (1989). *Pygmalion and the Classroom.* New York: Irvington Publishers.

Rosenzweig, Jane (July-August 1999). "Can TV Improve Us?" *The American Prospect 45,* 58–63.

Rosin, Hanna, and John F. Harris (August 3, 1999). "Welfare Reform is on a Roll." *The Washington Post* A1, A6.

Rubin, Lillian B. (1994). *Families on the Faultline.* New York: HarperCollins.

Rudolph, Frederick (1962). *The American College and University.* New York: Random House.

Rust, Michael, and Tiffany Danitz (March 9, 1998). "New Medium Fuels Ancient Passion." *Insight on the News* 22–23.

S

Sadker, Myra, and David Sadker (1995). *Failing at Fairness.* New York: Simon & Schuster.

Samuda, Ronald (1975). *The Psychological Testing of American Minorities.* New York: Dodd, Mead.

Samuelson, Paul A., and William D. Nordhaus (1995). *Microeconomics.* 15th ed. New York: McGraw-Hill.

Sandberg, Jared (July 19, 1999). "Spinning a Web of Hate." *Newsweek* 28–29.

Sapir, Edward (1929). "The Status of Linguistics as a Science." *Language 5,* 207–214.

Sapolsky, Robert (October 1997). "A Gene for Nothing." *Discover* 40–46.

Sarat, Austin. (ed.) (1998). *The Killing State: Capital Punishment in Law, Politics, and Culture.* New York: Oxford University Press.

Schaeffer, Richard T. (1993). *Racial and Ethnic Groups.* 6th ed. New York: Longman.

Schaeffer, Robert K. (1997). *Understanding Globalization.* Lanham, MD: Rowman & Littlefield Publishers.

Scheper-Hughes, Nancy (1983). "Deposed Kings: The Demise of the Rural Irish Gerontocracy." In Jay Sokolorsky (ed.), *Growing Old in Different Societies.* Belmont, CA: Wadsworth, pp. 130–146.

Schiff, Michel, and Richard Lewontin (1987). *Education and Class.* New York: Oxford University Press.

Schmidt, Steffen W., Mack C. Shelley, and Barbara A. Bardes (1999). *American Government and Politics Today.* Belmont, CA: Wadsworth.

Schnitzer, Martin C. (2000). *Comparative Economic Systems.* 7th ed. Cincinnati, OH: South-Western College Publishing.

Schrag, Peter (1977). "The Forgotten American." In John Walton and Donald E. Carns (eds.), *Cities in Change.* 2nd ed. Boston: Allyn and Bacon, pp. 129–137.

Schwartz, Barry (1987). *The Battle for Human Nature.* New York: Norton.

Scott, Martin B. (1981). "The Man on the Horse." In John W. Loy, Jr., Gerald S. Kenyon, and Barry D. McPherson (eds.), *Sport, Culture, and Society.* 2nd ed. Philadelphia: Lee & Febiger, pp. 146–156.

Seligmann, Jean (July 26, 1999). "Husbands No, Babies, Yes." *Newsweek* 53.

Sellin, Thorsten (1991). *The Penalty of Death.* Beverly Hills, CA: Sage.

Shapiro, Isaac, and Robert Greenstein (1999). *The Widening Income Gulf.* Washington, DC: Center on Budget and Policy Priorities.

Shapiro, Laura (May 28, 1990). "Guns and Dolls." *Newsweek* 54–65.

Shattuck, John (August 14, 1997). "Ending Africa's Tragedy." *The Christian Science Publishing Society,* 19.

Sidel, Ruth (1996). *Keeping Women and Children Last.* New York: Penguin Putnam, Inc.

Simmel, Georg (1964). *Conflict and the Web of Group Affiliation.* Translated by Kurt H. Wolff. New York: Free Press.

Simmons, J. L. (1969). *Deviants.* Berkeley, CA: Glendessary Press.

Simmons, Sally Lynn, and Amelia E. El-Hindi (November 1998). "Six Transformations for Thinking about Integrative Curriculum." *Middle School Journal 30,* 32–36.

Singh, Sarban (September 16, 1998). "Shift in Focus." *Malaysian Business* 54.

Sizer, Theodore (1996). *Horace's Hope: What Works for the American High School.* Boston: Houghton Mifflin.

Skolnick, Jerome H. (July-August 1998). "The Color of Law." *The American Prospect 39,* 90–95.

Sloan, Allan (February 26, 1996). "The Hit Men." *Newsweek* 44–48.

Smelser, Neil J. (1971). *Theory of Collective Behavior.* New York: Free Press.

____. (1976). *The Sociology of Economic Life.* 2nd ed. Englewood Cliffs, NJ: Prentice Hall.

Smith, Michael D. (December 1979). "Hockey Violence: A Test of the Violent Subculture Hypothesis." *Social Problems 27,* 235–247.

Snipp, C. Matthew (1992). "Sociological Perspectives on American Indians." *Annual Review of Sociology 18,* 351–371.

____. (November 1996). "A Demographic Comeback for American Indians?" *Population Today 24,* 4–5.

Snyder, Howard N., and Melissa Sickmund (1999). *Juvenile Offenders and Victims: A National Report.* Rockville, MD: Juvenile Justice Clearinghouse.

Spitze, G. (1991). "Women's Employment and Family Relations: A Review." In A. Booth (ed.), *Contemporary Families.* Minneapolis: National Council on Family Relations, pp. 381–404.

Spitzer, Steven (1980). "Toward a Marxian Theory of Deviance." In Delos H. Kelly (ed.), *Criminal Behavior.* New York: St. Martin's Press, pp. 175–191.

Spohn, Cassia C. (Winter 1995). "Courts, Sentences, and Prisons." *Daedalus 124,* 119–143.

Stacey, William, and Anson Shupe (December 1982). "Correlates of Support for the Electronic Church." *Journal for the Scientific Study of Religion 21,* 291–303.

Starr, Mark (February 7, 1994b). "She Can Skate, But She Can't Hide." *Newsweek 21.*

Starting Points April, 1994. The Report of the Carnegie Task Force on Meeting the Needs of Young Children. Carnegie Corporation of New York.

The State of America's Children: A Report From the Children's Defense Fund. Boston: Beacon Press, 1998.

Stavans, Ilan (1996). *The Hispanic Condition.* New York: Harper Collins.

Stefancic, Jean, and Richard Delgardo (eds.) (1998). *The Latinola Condition.* New York: New York University Press.

Stockard, Jean, and Miriam M. Johnson (1992). *Sex and Gender in Society.* 2nd ed. Englewood Cliffs, NJ: Prentice-Hall.

Stoll, Cliff (1995). *Silicon Snake Oil.* New York: Doubleday.

Strasburger, Victor C. (1995). *Adolescents and the Media: Medical and Psychological Impact.* Newbury Park, CA: Sage.

Straus, Murray A., David B. Sugarman, and Jean Giles-Sims (August 1997). "Spanking by Parents and Subsequent Antisocial Behavior of the Child." *Archives of Pediatrics and Adolescent Medicine,* 761–767.

Street-Level. http://streetlevel.iit.edu. 1999.

Sumner, William Graham (1906). *Folkways.* Boston: Ginn.

Sutherland, Edwin H. (1940). "White-Collar Criminality." *American Sociological Review 5,* 1–12.

____. (1983). *White-Collar Crime.* New Haven, CT: Yale University Press.

Swinton, David H. (1989). "Economic Status of Blacks." In *The State of Black America 1989.* New York: National Urban League, pp. 129–152.

Symonds, William C. (February 7, 2000). "For-Profit-Schools." *Business Week* 64ff.

T

Tax, Meredith (May 17, 1999). "World Culture War." *The Nation.*

Taylor, Shelley E., Letitia Ann Peplau, and David O. Sears (1997). *Social Psychology.* 9th ed. Englewood Cliffs: Prentice-Hall.

Tellegen, Auke, D. T. Lykken, T. J. Bouchard, Jr., and M. McGue (August 1993). "Heritability of Interests: A Twin Study." *Journal of Applied Psychology* 649–661.

Thomas, Evan (April 7, 1997). "The Next Level." *Newsweek* 28–36.

Thomas, Evan, and Lynette Clemetson (November 22, 1999). "A New War Over Vouchers." *Newsweek* 46.

Thornton, Russell (1984). "Cherokee Population Losses During the Trail of Tears: A New Perspective and a New Estimate." *Ethnohistory 31*, 289–300.

Tilly, Charles (1978). *From Mobilization to Revolution.* Reading, MA: Addison-Wesley.

____. *Social Processes* (1997). Lantham, MD: Rowan and Littlefield, 1997.

Tilove, Jonathan (May-June 1999). "The New Map of American Politics." *The American Prospect.*

To Establish Justice, To Insure Domester Tranquility: A Thirty Year Update of the National Commission on the Causes and Prevention of Violence. Washington, DC: The Milton S. Eisenhower Foundation.

Toch, Thomas, and Warren Cohen (November 23, 1998). "Public Education: A Monopoly No Longer." *U.S. News & World Report* 25.

Toland, John. *Adolph Hitler* (1976). Garden City, NY: Doubleday.

Tönnies, Ferdinand (1957). *Community and Society*. Translated and edited by Charles P. Loomis. East Lansing: Michigan State University Press.

Trigaboff, Dan (June 8, 1998). "Drudge Begrudged." *Broadcasting & Cable* 55.

Trimble, J. E. (1988). "Stereotypical Images, American Indians, and Prejudice." In P. A. Katz and D. A. Taylor (eds.), *Eliminating Racism*. New York: Plenum Press, pp. 181–202.

Troeltsch, Ernst (1931). *The Social Teachings of the Christian Churches*. New York: Macmillan.

Turner, Jonathan H., Leonard Beeghley, and Charles H. Powers (1989). *The Emergence of Sociological Theory*. 2nd ed. Chicago: Dorsey Press.

Turner, Ralph H. (1964). "Collective Behavior." In Robert E. L. Faris (ed.), *Handbook of Modern Sociology*. Chicago: Rand McNally, pp. 382–425.

Turner, Ralph H., and Lewis M. Killian (1987). *Collective Behavior*. 3rd ed. Englewood Cliffs, NJ: Prentice Hall.

U

Uchitelle, Louis, and N. R. Kleinfield (1996). "The Price of Jobs Lost." In *The New York Times* Special Report *The Downsizing of America*. New York: Random House.

U.S. Bureau of the Census. (2000c). "Educational Attainment, by Race, and Hispanic Origin." Current Population Reports. http://www.census.gov/population/www/socdemo/education.html.

U.S. Bureau of the Census. "Educational Attainment—Total Money Earnings in 1999 of Persons 18 Years Old and Over, by Age, Race, Hispanic Origin, Sex, and Work Experience in 1999." Washington, DC: U.S. Government Printing Office, 2000e.

U.S. Bureau of the Census (2000a). "Money Income in the United States: 1999." Current Population Reports, P60–209. Washington, DC: U.S. Government Printing Office.

U.S. Bureau of the Census. *Money Income of Households, Families, and Persons in the United States: 1992*. Current Population Reports. Series P-60. No. 184. Washington, DC: U.S. Government Printing Office, 1993a.

U.S. Bureau of the Census. (2000b). "Poverty in the United States, 1999." Current Population Reports, Series P60–210. Washington, DC: U.S. Government Printing Office.

____. (1993e). *1990 Census of Population, Social and Economic Characteristics, American Indian and Alaska Native Areas*. Section 1 of 2. CP-2–1A. Washington, DC: U.S. Government Printing Office.

U.S. Bureau of the Census. (2000d). *Statistical Abstract of the United States: 2000*. Washington, DC: U.S. Government Printing Office.

____. (1993i). *School Enrollment, Social and Economic Characteristics of Students: October 1992*. Current Population Reports. Series P-20. No. 474. Washington, DC: U.S. Government Printing Office.

____. (1996a). *Statistical Abstract of the United States: 1996*. Washington, DC: U.S. Government Printing Office.

____. (1996b). *Poverty in the United States: 1995*. Current Population Reports. Series P-60. No. 194. Washington, DC: U.S. Government Printing Office.

____. (1998a). *Statistical Abstract of the United States: 1998*. Washington, DC: U.S. Government Printing Office.

____. (1998c). Current Population Reports Series, P23–194, *Population Profile of the United States: 1997*. Washington, DC: U.S. Government Printing Office.

____. (1999a). "Poverty 1997—Poverty Estimates by Selected Characteristics." *Current Population Survey, March, 1998*. http://www.census.gov/hhes/poverty/poverty97/pv97est1.html.

____. (1999b). "Income 1997—Table B." *Current Population Survey, March, 1998*. http://www.census.gov/hhes/income/income97/in97dis.html.

____. (1999e). "Asset Ownership of Households: 1993—Table F." http://www.census.gov/hhes/www/wealth/wlth93f.html.

____. (1999f) "Resident Population Estimates of the United States by Sex, Race, and Hispanic Origin: April 1, 1990 to April 1, 1999." *Population Estimates Program*. http://www.census.gov/population/estimates/nation/intfile3-1.txt.

____. (1993). U.S. Department of Labor, Bureau of Labor Statistics. *Employment in Perspective: Women in the Labor Force*. No. 865. Washington, DC: U.S. Government Printing Office.

____. (1997a). *Employment in Perspective: Women in the Labor Force*. Report 860. Washington, DC: U.S. Government Printing Office.

____. (1997b). *Employment and Earnings*. Washington, DC: U.S. Government Printing Office.

V

Valian, Virginia (1998). *Why So Slow? The Advancement of Women*. Cambridge, MA: MIT Press.

Vanhanen, Tatu (1997). *Prospects of Democracy.* London: Routledge.

Virnoche, Mary E. (1998). "The Seamless Web and Communications Equity: The Shaping of a Community Network." *Science, Technology, & Human Values, 23,* 199–220.

W

Walsh, Edward, and Roberto Suro (June 19, 1999). "NRA Achieves Its Goal: Nothing." *The Washington Post,* A1, A6.

Wallechinsky, David, and Irving Wallace (1981). *The People's Almanac #3.* New York: Bantam.

Wang, C. T., and D. Daro (1998). *Current Trends in Child Abuse Reporting and Fatalities: The Results of the 1997 Annual Fifty State Survey.* Chicago, IL: Prevent Child Abuse America.

Weeks, John R. (1999). *Population.* 6th ed. Belmont, CA: Wadsworth.

Weingart, Peter, et al. (eds.) (1997). *Human by Nature: Between Biology and the Social Sciences.* Mahwah, NJ: Lawrence Erlbaum Associates.

Westoff, Leslie Aldridge, and Charles F. Westoff (1971). *From Now to Zero.* Boston: Little, Brown.

White, Lynn, and David B. Brinkerhoff (September 1981). "The Sexual Division of Labor: Evidence from Childhood." *Social Forces 60,* 170–181.

Who Owns Whom 1998/1999 (1998). High Wycombe, UK: Dun and Bradstreet Ltd.

Whorf, Benjamin Lee (1956). *Language, Thought and Reality.* Edited by John B. Carroll. Cambridge, MA: MIT Press.

Whyte, William Foote (1993). *Street Corner Society.* 4th ed. Chicago: University of Chicago Press.

Wiesel, Elie (April 12, 1999). "The Question of Genocide." *Newsweek.*

Wildavsky, Ben (September 13, 1999). "Grading on a Curve: A New Controversy Erupts Over Race, Class, and SAT Scores." *U.S. News & World Report.*

Williams, Robin M., Jr. (1970). *American Society.* 3rd ed. New York: Knopf.

Wilson, Craig (February 25–27, 2000). "Why People Will Do Almost Anything to Get on TV." *USA Today* 1A, 2A.

Wilson, William Julius (1984). "The Urban Underclass." In Leslie W. Dunbar (ed.), *Minority Report.* New York: Pantheon, pp. 75–117.

____. (1997). *When Work Disappears: The World of the New Urban Poor.* New York: Knopf.

Wingfield, Nick (June 15, 1998). "Family Planning: The Computer Server Promises to do to the Home What It Has Already Done for Business." *The Wall Street Journal* R18, R23.

Wirth, Louis (1945). "The Problem of Minority Groups." In Ralph Linton (ed.), *The Science of Man in the World Crisis.* New York: Columbia University Press, pp. 347–372.

Wolfe, Alan (1998). *One Nation, After All.* New York: Viking.

World Population Data Sheet. Washington, DC: Population Reference Bureau, 1999.

World Without Work. In Robert Staples (ed.) (1999), *The Black Family.* Belmont, CA: Wadsworth Publishing Company, pp. 291–311.

World Population Data Sheet. (2001). Washington, D.C.: Population Reference Bureau.

Wright, Kevin N. (1987). *The Great American Crime Myth.* New York: Praeger.

Wright, Robert (1996). *The Moral Animal.* New York: Pantheon Books.

Y

Yamagata, Hisashi, et al. (November 1997). "Sex Segregation and Glass Ceilings: A Comparative Statics Model of Women's Career Opportunities in the Federal Government Over a Quarter Century." *American Journal of Sociology 103,* 566–632.

Yap, M. T. (1995). "Singapore's 'Three or More' Policy: The First Five Years." *Asia-Pacific Population Journal 10,* 39–52.

Yorke, Liselle. (2000). "Joint Center Releases 1999 National Court of Black Elected Officials." Washington, DC: Joint Center for Political and Economic Studies.

Young, T. R. (January 1986). "The Sociology of Sport: Structural Marxist and Cultural Marxist Approaches." *Sociological Perspectives 29,* 3–28.

Z

Zamble, Edward, and Vernon L. Quinsey (1997). *The Criminal Recidivism Process.* New York: Cambridge University Press.

Zborowski, Mark (1952). "Cultural Components in Response to Pain." *Journal of Social Issues 8,* 16–30.

____. (1969). *People in Pain.* San Francisco: Jossey-Bass.

Zellner, William W. (1999). *Countercultures: A Sociological Analysis.* 2nd ed. New York: St. Martin's Press.

Zigler, Edward, and Sally J. Styfco (eds.) (1993). *Head Start and Beyond*. New Haven, CT: Yale University Press.

Zimbardo, Philip G., S. M. Anderson, and L. G. Kabat (June 26, 1981). "Induced Hearing Deficit Generates Experimental Paranoia." *Science,* 1529–1531.

Zweigenhaft, Richard L., and G. William Domhoff (1998). *Diversity in the Power Elite*. New Haven: Yale University Press.

Index

Q

R

T

U

Credits

Photo Credits

CHAPTER 1 **2** The Stock Market, Jon Feingersh **4** The Stock Market, Tom & Dee Ann McCarthy **6** Index Stock Photo, Andrea Booher **7**(1) Index Stock Photo, Omni Photo Communications, Inc. **7**(2) Index Stock Photo, Palmer Brilliant **7**(3) Index Stock photo, Frank Pedrick **7**(4) ©AFP/Corbis **8** Index Stock Photo, SW Production **10** ©Francis G. Mayer/Corbis **11** Index Stock Photo, SW Production **14** North Wind Picture Archives **15**(top) ©Corbis **15**(bottom) Brown Brothers **16** ©Archivo Iconografico, S.A./Corbis **17**(top) ©Bettmann/Corbis **17**(bottom) Brown Brothers **19**(left) ©Bettmann/Corbis **19**(right) ©Bettmann/Corbis **20** Index Stock Photo, Jeff Greenberg **21**(left) ©Bettmann/Corbis **21**(right) ©Bettmann/Corbis **25**(top) Index Stock Photo, Black Box **25**(bottom) Index Stock Photo **26** Tony Stone Images, Ben Edwards **31** Index Stock Photo, Jeffrey Blackman

CHAPTER 2 **36** ©PhotoDisc **38** ©Don Milici **40** Index Stock Photo, Grantpix **43** Associated Press, Christopher Pfuhl **44** Associated Press, Jean Whiteside **47** Associated Press, Elise Amendola **50** ©AFP/Corbis, Wayne Scarberry **54** ©Archivo Iconografico, S.A./Corbis **59** Tony Stone Images, Andy Sacks **60** Associated Press, Tom Uhlman **62** Tony Stone Images, Jed & Kaoru Share **66** Index Stock Photo, SW Production

CHAPTER 3 **68** Index Stock Photo, Omni Photo Communications, Inc. **70** (top left) Associated Press, Enric Marti **70**(top right) Associated Press, Lynne Sladky **70**(bottom left) Associated Press, David Longstreath **70**(middle right) Associated Press, Katsumi Kasahara **70**(bottom right) Associated Press **72** ©Kevin Fleming/Corbis **73** ©Michael Pole/Corbis **74** Index Stock Photo **75** ©Digital Art/Corbis **76** ©Joel W. Rogers/Corbis **76**(top) Index Stock Photo **77**(bottom) ©Werner Forman/Corbis **79** Index Stock Photo **81** Index Stock Photo **83**(left) ©Digital Stock **83**(right) ©Digital Stock **84**(top left) Associated Press, Eric Risberg **84**(bottom left) Associated Press, Gail Oskin **84**(right) Associated Press, Ruth Fremson **87** ©Digital Stock **89** Associated Press, Patrick D. Pagnano **90**(top) Index Stock Photo **90**(bottom) Index Stock Photo **92** Index Stock Photo **94** Index Stock Photo, Daniel Fort **95** Associated Press, Denis Farrell **96** Index Stock Photo **97** ©James Marshall/Corbis **98** Index Stock Photo **100** Associated Press, Frank Boxler **105** Index Stock Photov **106** ©Michael S. Yamashita/Corbis

CHAPTER 4 **108** The Stock Market **110** ©Hulton-Deutsch Collection/Corbis **111** Associated Press, B. K. Bangash **112** The Stock Market, Chuck Savage **113** Index Stock Photo, Ewing Galloway **115** Index Stock Photo, Omni Photo Communications, Inc. **118** Index Stock Photo **119** The Stock Market, Mug Shots **120** ©Hulton-Deutsch Collection/Corbis **121**(left) Index Stock Photo, SW Production **121**(right) The Stock Market, George Shelley **123**(top) Tony Stone Images, Lori Adamski Peek **123**(bottom) ©Nik Wheeler/Corbis **124** Index Stock Photo, SW Production **126** The Stock Market, David Brooks **127** Index Stock Photo, SW Production **128** Associated Press, Brett Coomer **132** Index Stock Photo, Phil Cantor **136** Associated Press, Mark Van Manen

CHAPTER 5 **138** ©Adam Woolfitt/Corbis **140** Tony Stone Images, Karan Kapoor **141** Index Stock Photo, Powerstock-ZEFA **143** ©PhotoDisc **144** ©News Service, Stanford University **147** Index Stock Photo, SW Production **151** Index Stock Photo, SW Production **152** Tony Stone Images, Tony May **154** Tony Stone Images, Paul Chesley **156** Tony Stone Images, Nick Gunderson **157** ©Archivo Iconografico, S.A./Corbis **158** Associated Press, Dario Lopez-Mills **159** ©Bettmann/Corbis **160** ©Charles O-Rear/Corbis **162** Associated Press, Peter Morgan **164** Associated Press, Charles Bennett

CHAPTER 6 **170** Index Stock Photo, Bill Romerhaus **172**(left) Tony Stone Images, Don Smetzer **172**(right) Index Stock Photo, Patricia Barry Levy **173** Index Stock Photo, Stewart Cohen **175** Tony Stone Images, Jon Riley **176** Associated Press, Greg Baker **177**(left) Tony Stone Images, Robert E. Daemmrich **177**(right) ©PhotoDisc **178** ©Corbis Images **181** Associated Press, Jane Hwang **182** Darko Bandic/AP Wide World Photos **183** Index Stock Photo, Len Rubenstein **184**(top) Associated Press, Damian Dovarganes **184**(bottom) ©Bettmann/Corbis **187** Index Stock Photo, Chip Henderson **189** From the film "Obedience," copyrighted in 1965 by Stanley Milgram and distributed by The Pennsylvania State University, Media Sales **190**(top) Associated Press, Tsugufumi Matsumoto **190**(bottom) Tony Stone Images, Bruce Ayres **195** Index Stock Photo, SW Production **201** Associated Press, Vincent Yu

CHAPTER 7 **202** Associated Press, Tom Zubak **203**(top) Associated Press, Ed Wray **203**(bottom) Associated Press, Shane Harvey **207** Index Stock Photo, SW Production **208** ©Corbis **209** Associated Press **210** Associated Press, Kathy Willens **212** Index Stock Photo, SW Production **213** Associated Press, Lacy Atkins **215** Associated Press, William Plowman **216** ©Bettmann/Corbis **217** ©Bettmann/Corbis **218** Associated Press, Cheryl A. Miller **219**(left) Associated Press, Pat Sullivan **219**(right) Associated Press, Gregory Rice **221** Associated Press, Ron Edmonds **224** Associated Press, Frank Anderson **228** Index Stock Photo, Mauritius **229**(top) Associated Press, Paul Sakuma **229**(bottom) Associated Press, Dan Krauss **231** Index Stock Photo, John Boykin

CHAPTER 8 **238** Associated Press, H. Rumph, Jr. **240**(top) Index Stock Photo, Ted Wilcox **240**(bottom) Associated Press, Dale Fulkerson **242** Associated Press **246**(top) Associated Press, Brian Bohannon **246**(bottom left) Associated Press, Chris Pizzello **246**(bottom right) Associated Press, Kevork Djansezian **248** Index Stock

Photo, Steven Begleiter **249** ©Arte & Immagini SRL/Corbis **250**(left) The Stock Market, John Maher **250**(right) The Stock Market, Nancy Ney **251**(top) Associated Press, Bob Mooney **251**(bottom) Index Stock Photo, Craig Wikowski **253** Index Stock Photo, SW Production **255**(top) Associated Press, Richard Drew **255**(bottom) Tony Stone Images, Frank Siteman **257** Associated Press, Eric Draper **258** Associated Press **259**(left) Associated Press, David Longstreath **259**(right) Associated Press, Mike Derer **262** Associated Press, Lou Krasky **264**(top) Index Stock Photo, Benelux Press **264**(bottom) Associated Press, Don Ryan **265** The Stock Market, Lester Lefkowitz **266** Index Stock Photo, Steve Starr **267** Associated Press, Stevan Morgain **268** Index Stock Photo, Ami Katz

CHAPTER 9 **274** Associated Press, Charles Tasnadi **276** The Stock Market, Mug Shots **277** The Stock Market, George Disario **282** Woolaroc Museum, Bartlesville, OK **284**(top) ©Bill Aron, PhotoEdit **284**(bottom) Associated Press, Leslie E. Kossoff **285** Associated Press, Dan Loh **286** Index Stock Photo, Gary Conner **289** Associated Press, William Thomas Cain **290** Associated Press, Dave Martin **292** Associated Press, Bebeto Matthews **293** Associated Press, Joe Marquette **295** Associated Press, Eric Draper **296** Associated Press, Wilfredo Lee **297** ©Corbis **299** Index Stock Photo, Phil Cantor **301** Associated Press, Stephen Morton

CHAPTER 10 **308** The Stock Market, Dale O'Dell **310**(left) ©Jennie Woodcock, Reflections Photolibrary/Corbis **310**(right) ©Hannah Gal/Corbis **312**(left) Associated Press, Amy Sancetta **312**(right) ©Buena Vista Television/Shooting Star **313** Associated Press/American Museum of Natural History **314** Associated Press, Daniel Hulshizer **315** ©Corbis **316** Index Stock Photo, Mitch Diamond **317** Index Stock Photo, Zephyr Pictures **320** Associated Press, Wilfredo Lee **322** Associated Press, Ben Margot **324** Associated Press, Shizuo Kambayashi **328** Index Stock Photo, ZEFA-Motions Emotions **329** Associated Press, Charles Rex Arbogast **330** ©PhotoDisc **332** Associated Press The Republic, Joe Harpring **333** Index Stock Photo, Omni Photo Communications, Inc. **335**(left) Associated Press, Ruth Fremson **335**(right) Associated Press, Audrey Woods **336** Index Stock Photo, Allen Russell

CHAPTER 11 **344** The Stock Market, Alan Schein **346** ©PhotoDisc **348** The Stock Market, Jose Luis Pelaez, Inc. **349** Associated Press, Tanya Breen **351** Associated Press **355** Werner Bokelberg/Getty **356** Index Stock Photo, Phil Lauro **357** Index Stock Photo, Kindra Clineff **359** Index Stock Photo, Myrleen Cate **360** Associated Press, Anat Givon **363** The Stock Market, Jose Luis Pelaez, Inc. **367** ©Christel Gerstenberg/Corbis **369** Associated Press, Mark Foley **370** Index Stock Photo, Bonnie Kamin **371** ©Bettmann/Corbis **372** AFP/Corbis **374** Index Stock Photo, Benelux Press **377** ©Corbis **378** ©Digital Stock **380** Associated Press/Fox Broadcasting Company

CHAPTER 12 **386** The Stock Market, Jose L. Pelaez **388**(left) Associated Press **388**(right) Tony Stone Images, Walter Hodges **390** The Stock Market, Mug Shots **391** Associated Press, Tim Hynds **392** ©Corbis **393** Associated Press, Lynsey Addario **395** Tony Stone Images, Bob Daemmrich **396** The Stock Market, Tom & DeeAnn McCarthy **400** Associated Press, Joe Richard **401** Associated Press, Mary Ann Chastain **403**(left) Index Stock Photo, Jim Scourietis **403**(right) Associated Press, Pablo Martinez Monsivais **405** Index Stock Photo, Frank Siteman **406** Associated Press, Laurie DeWitt **408** Associated Press/Herald-Leader, Dana Johnson **409** Associated Press/Clarksburg Exponent, Steven Wayne Rotsch **410** ©Richard T. Nowitz/Corbis **413** Associated Press, Nick Ut **414** Tony Stone Images, Alan Levenson **421** Associated Press

CHAPTER 13 **422** Associated Press, Jon Kieckhefer **424** Associated Press, Daniel Portnoy **425** Index Stock Photo, Table Mesa Prod. **426**(top right) Associated Press **426**(left) Associated Press, Alan Greth **426**(bottom right) Associated Press **427** Associated Press, Sherwin Crasto **428** Associated Press, Michael Jung Pool **430** Associated Press **431** Associated Press, Jose Goitia **432** Associated Press, Greg Baker **433** Associated Press, Eric Draper **434**(left) Associated Press, Itsu Inouye **434**(top right) Associated Press, Maribeth Brown **434**(bottom right) Associated Press, Julia Malakie **441**(top) Associated Press, Jeff Christensen **441**(bottom) Associated Press, Chris Polk **443** Index Stock Photo, Tina Buckman **444** Associated Press, Eugene Hoshiko **445** Associated Press, Michael Caulfield **446** Associated Press/The Cincinnati Enquirer **449** Associated Press **450** Associated Press, Susan Ragan **451** Associated Press, Roger Werth **453** Associated Press, Gary Tramontina **454** Associated Press, John Hayes **456** Associated Press, Gail Oskin **461** ©Mark Richards, PhotoEdit

CHAPTER 14 **462** Index Stock Photo: Omni Photo Communications, Inc.; Color Point Studio; Dennis Curran; Eunice Harris **464** Index Stock Photo, Craig Brown **465**(top) Index Stock Photo, Image Port **465**(bottom) Associated Press, Rose Palmisano **466** ©AFP/Corbis **467**(top) Associated Press, Charles Becker **467**(bottom left) Index Stock Photo, Kadir Kir **467**(bottom right) Index Stock Photo, Daniel Bailey **472** ©Archivo Iconografico, S.A./Corbis **474** The Stock Market, Sanford/Agliolo **475** Index Stock Photo, Michael Long **476** ©Bettmann/Corbis **477** ©Ted Streshinsky/Corbis **478** Associated Press/Internet **479**(left) Associated Press, Charles Dharapak **479**(right) Tony Stone Images, Bil Aron **481**(top left) Associated Press, Joan Seidel **481**(top right) Associated Press, Dave Martin **481**(bottom left) Associated Press, Julie Vennitti **481**(bottom right) Index Stock Photo, Dave Bartruff **484** Associated Press/Union Rescue Mission Web **486** Associated Press, John Bazemore **488** Associated Press **493** Associated Press, John Moore

CHAPTER 15 **494** Index Stock Photo, Bill Bachmann **496**(top) ©Digital Stock **496**(bottom) Index Stock Photo, ZEFA-Taste of Europe **497**(top) Associated Press, Paul Vathis **497**(bottom) Associated Press, Patricia McDonnell **498**(top) Associated Press, Eric Risberg **498**(middle)

Associated Press, Eric Risberg **498**(bottom) Associated Press, Chris Gardner **499** Associated Press **500** Associated Press/Vancouver Province, Gerry Kahrmann **501** ©Digital Stock **502** Associated Press, Stuart T. Wagner **503** Associated Press, Mark Duncan **507** Associated Press, Doug Pizac **508** ©Anne Griffith Betz/Corbis **511** The Stock Market, Mug Shots **513** Associated Press, Robin Nowacki **515** Associated Press, Orlin Wagner **517**(top left) Associated Press, Denise L. Oles **517**(top right) Associated Press, Mark Lennihan **517**(bottom) Duomo/CORBIS **519** Associated Press, Paul Sakuma **525** Associated Press, Rhonda Simpson

CHAPTER 16 **526** The Stock Market, George B. Diebold **528** The Stock Market, Jon Feingersh **530** Associated Press, Greg Baker **531** Associated Press, Susan Plageman **533** Associated Press, Dado Galdieri **539** ©Bettmann/Corbis **542** The Stock Market, Bob Krist **543**(top) Associated Press, John McConnico **543**(bottom) ©Owen Franken/Corbis **545** Associated Press, Elizabeth Ellis **547** The Stock Market, Chuck Savage **548**(top) Index Stock Photo, Chris Minerva **548**(bottom) Index Stock Photo, Phil Lauro **549** Index Stock Photo, Powerstock-ZEFA **552** Associated Press, Nick Ut **554** Associated Press, Eli Grothe **559** Index Stock Photo, John Connell **565** Index Stock Photo, Mark Gibson

CHAPTER 17 **566** Associated Press, Dave Martin **571** Index Stock Photo, Dave Bartruff **572**(top) Index Stock Photo, Stewart Cohen **572**(bottom) Associated Press, Volodymyr Repik **573** ©Robert Holmes/Corbis **575** Associated Press, Lauren Rebours **577** Associated Press, Nell Redmond **578** Associated Press, Doglas C. Pizac **581** ©Bettmann/Corbis **582** ©Hulton-Deutsch Collection/Corbis **583**(top right) ©Bettmann/Corbis **583**(bottom right) ©Bettmann/Corbis **583**(middle) Frank Capri/SAGA/Archive Photos **583**(top left) Darlene Hammond/Archive Photos **583**(bottom left) Associated Press, Mark Lennihan **584** Thomas E. Franklin/Bergen Record/Saba/Corbis **586**(top) Index Stock Photo, Omni Photo Communications, Inc. **586**(middle) Associated Press, Dave Duprey **586**(bottom) Associated Press, Eric Draper **587** Associated Press, Bob Galbraith **588** Associated Press, Paris Saris **589** Associated Press, Mark Hertzberg **590** Associated Press, Eric Draper **593** ©Kevin R. Morris/Corbis **594** John Filo/Archive Photos **596** Associated Press, Jill Connelly

Handbook Credits

HB-1 Bob Daemmrich Stock Boston **HB-2** Michael Newman/ PhotoEdit **HB-3** David Young-Wolf/PhotoEdit **HB-5** Reuters NewMedia Inc./Corbis **HB-8** Jeffrey W. Myers/CORBIS **HB-9** Steve Chenn/CORBIS **HB-15** Pascal Quittemelle/Stock Boston **HB-16** David Young Wolf/Stone

Cartoon Credits

18 © 1991, Mike Marland, (Reprinted with permission.) **30** *Tank McNamara*, © 1996, Universal Press Syndicate, Millar/Hinds. (Reprinted with permission.) **39** *Doonesbury*, © 1980, Universal Press Syndicate, G. B. Trudeau. (Reprinted with permission.) **53** © Sidney Harris, *The Chronicle of Higher Education*. (Reprinted with permission.) **88** *The Far Side*, © 1994 FarWorks, Inc. (Reprinted with permission.) All rights reserved. **91** *Calvin and Hobbes*, © 1990 Watterson. Reprinted with permission of Universal Press Syndicate. All rights reserved. **122** © 1993, Chronicle Features, Gail Machlis. (Reprinted with permission.) **131** *Cathy*, © Cathy Guisewhite, Universal Press Syndicate. (Reprinted with permission.) **142** © 1991, *The New Yorker Magazine, Inc.*, Francino. (Reprinted with permission.) **146** © 1998, *The New Yorker Magazine, Inc.*, C. Barsotti. (Reprinted with permission.) **153** *The Far Side*, © *The Far Side Gallery 5*, Gary Larson. (Reprinted with permission.) **185** © *The New Yorker Magazine*, Inc., Henry Martin. (Reprinted with permission.) **192** *Calvin and Hobbes*, © Bill Watterson, *Scientific Progress Goes Boink*, page 39. (Reprinted with permission.) **215** Tank McNamara, © Universal Press Syndicate, Millar/Hinds. (Reprinted with permission.) **244** © 1992, *The New Yorker Magazine, Inc.*, W. Miller. (Reprinted with permission.) **251** *Funky Winkerbean* by Tom Batiuk. © by and permission of News America Syndicate. **262** © Creator's Syndicate, Jeff Shesol. (Reprinted with permission.) **307** © 1996 *The New Yorker Collection*, Mick Stevens. (Reprinted with permission.) **311** © 1995, *The New Yorker Collection*, Donald Reilly. (Reprinted with permission.) **375** © Chronicle Features, Gail Machlis. (Reprinted with permission.) **379** ©1989, *The New Yorker Collection*, Henry Martin. (Reprinted with permission.) **395** *Calvin and Hobbes*, © Bill Watterson, *The Calvin and Hobbes Tenth Anniversary Book*. (Reprinted with permission.) **402** © 1998, *The New Yorker Collection*, Roz Chast. (Reprinted with permission.) **455** © Toles, *The Buffalo News*. (Reprinted with permission.) **479** *Calvin and Hobbes*, © Bill Watterson, *The Calvin and Hobbes Tenth Anniversary Book*. (Reprinted with permission.) **503** © 1999, *The Green Bay Press Gazette*, Joe Heller. (Reprinted with permission.) **510** Sidelines, © 1999, *The Green Bay Press Gazette*, Joe Heller. (Reprinted with permission.) **512** © 1991, Millar/Hinds, Universal Press Syndicate. (Reprinted with permission.) **536** © Toles, 1990, *The Buffalo News*. (Reprinted with permission.) **570** © King Features Syndicate, Jim Bergman. (Reprinted with permission.) **591** *The Far Side*, © Universal Press Syndicate, Gary Larson. (Reprinted with permission.) **HB-7** *Calvin and Hobbes* © 1995, Watterson. Reprinted with permission of Universal Press Syndicate. All rights reserved.